ALL GLORY TO ŚRĪ GURU AND GAURĀṄGA

ŚRĪMAD BHĀGAVATAM

of

KṚṢṆA-DVAIPĀYANA VYĀSA

नैवोद्विजे पर दुरत्ययवैतरण्या-
स्त्वद्वीर्यगायनमहामृतमग्नचित्तः ।
शोचे ततो विमुखचेतस इन्द्रियार्थ-
मायासुखाय भरमुद्वहतो विमूढान् ॥४३॥

naivodvije para duratyaya-vaitaraṇyās
tvad-vīrya-gāyana-mahāmṛta-magna-cittaḥ
śoce tato vimukha-cetasa indriyārtha-
māyā-sukhāya bharam udvahato vimūḍhān

(p. 551)

BOOKS by
His Divine Grace
A. C. Bhaktivedanta Swami Prabhupāda

Bhagavad-gītā As It Is
Śrīmad-Bhāgavatam, cantos 1–10 (12 vols.)
Śrī Caitanya-caritāmṛta (17 vols.)
Teachings of Lord Caitanya
The Nectar of Devotion
The Nectar of Instruction
Śrī Īśopaniṣad
Easy Journey to Other Planets
Kṛṣṇa Consciousness: The Topmost Yoga System
Kṛṣṇa, The Supreme Personality of Godhead (3 vols.)
Perfect Questions, Perfect Answers
Teachings of Lord Kapila, the Son of Devahūti
Transcendental Teachings of Prahlāda Mahārāja
Dialectic Spiritualism—A Vedic View of Western Philosophy
Teachings of Queen Kuntī
Kṛṣṇa, the Reservoir of Pleasure
The Science of Self-Realization
The Path of Perfection
Search for Liberation
Life Comes from Life
The Perfection of Yoga
Beyond Birth and Death
On the Way to Kṛṣṇa
Geetār-gan (Bengali)
Vairāgya-vidyā (Bengali)
Buddhi-yoga (Bengali)
Bhakti-ratna-bolī (Bengali)
Rāja-vidyā: The King of Knowledge
Elevation to Kṛṣṇa Consciousness
Kṛṣṇa Consciousness: The Matchless Gift
Back to Godhead magazine (founder)

A complete catalog is available upon request.

Bhaktivedanta Book Trust
3764 Watseka Avenue
Los Angeles, California 90034

Bhaktivedanta Book Trust
P.O. Box 262
Botany
N. S. W. 2019, Australia

ŚRĪMAD BHĀGAVATAM

Seventh Canto
"The Science of God"

With the Original Sanskrit Text,
Its Roman Transliteration, Synonyms,
Translation and Elaborate Purports

by

His Divine Grace
A.C. Bhaktivedanta Swami Prabhupāda
Founder-*Ācārya* of the International Society for Krishna Consciousness

THE BHAKTIVEDANTA BOOK TRUST
Los Angeles · London · Stockholm · Bombay · Sydney

Readers interested in the subject matter of this book are invited by the International Society for Krishna Consciousness to correspond with its Secretary at either of the following addresses:

International Society for Krishna Consciousness
P. O. Box 262
Botany
N. S. W. 2019
Australia

International Society for Krishna Consciousness
3764 Watseka Avenue
Los Angeles, California 90034

First Printing, 1987: 5,000 copies

Printed in Singapore

Library of Congress Cataloging in Publication Data (Revised)

Purāṇas. Bhāgavatapurāṇa. English and Sanskrit.
Śrīmad-Bhāgavatam.

In English and Sanskrit.
Translation of: Bhāgavatapurāṇa
Includes index.
Contents: Canto 1. Creation (1 v)— Canto 2. The cosmic manifestation (1 v)— Canto 3. The status quo (2 v)— Canto 4. The creation of the fourth order (2 v)— Canto 5. The creative impetus (1 v)— Canto 6. Prescribed duties for mankind (1 v)— Canto 7. The science of God (1 v)— Canto 8. Withdrawal of the cosmic creations (1 v)— Canto 9. Liberation (1 v)— Canto 10. The summum bonum (4 v)— Canto 11. General history (2 v)— Canto 12. The age of deterioration (1 v)

Cantos 10 (v 2-4), 11 and 12 by Hridayananda Goswami Ācāryadeva, completing the great work of His Divine Grace A. C. Bhaktivedanta Swami Prabhupāda; Sanskrit editing by Gopīparāṇadhana dāsa Adhikārī.

1. Purāṇas. Bhāgavatapurāṇa—Criticism, interpretation, etc. I. Bhaktivedanta Swami, A. C., 1896-1977. II. Title.
BL1140.4.B432E5 1987 294.5'925 87-25585
ISBN 0-89213-258-2 (v. 9)

Table of Contents

Appendixes

Preface

We must know the present need of human society. And what is that need? Human society is no longer bounded by geographical limits to particular countries or communities. Human society is broader than in the Middle Ages, and the world tendency is toward one state or one human society. The ideals of spiritual communism, according to *Śrīmad-Bhāgavatam*, are based more or less on the oneness of the entire human society, nay, of the entire energy of living beings. The need is felt by great thinkers to make this a successful ideology. *Śrīmad-Bhāgavatam* will fill this need in human society. It begins, therefore, with an aphorism of Vedānta philosophy, *janmādy asya yataḥ*, to establish the ideal of a common cause.

Human society, at the present moment, is not in the darkness of oblivion. It has made rapid progress in the fields of material comforts, education and economic development throughout the entire world. But there is a pinprick somewhere in the social body at large, and therefore there are large-scale quarrels, even over less important issues. There is need of a clue as to how humanity can become one in peace, friendship and prosperity with a common cause. *Śrīmad-Bhāgavatam* will fill this need, for it is a cultural presentation for the respiritualization of the entire human society.

Śrīmad-Bhāgavatam should be introduced also in the schools and colleges, for it is recommended by the great student-devotee Prahlāda Mahārāja in order to change the demoniac face of society.

kaumāra ācaret prājño
dharmān bhāgavatān iha
durlabhaṁ mānuṣaṁ janma
tad apy adhruvam artha-dam
(*Bhāg*. 7.6.1)

Disparity in human society is due to lack of principles in a godless civilization. There is God, or the Almighty One, from whom everything emanates, by whom everything is maintained and in whom everything is merged to rest. Material science has tried to find the ultimate source of creation very insufficiently, but it is a fact that there is one ultimate source of everything that be. This ultimate source is explained rationally and authoritatively in the beautiful *Bhāgavatam,* or *Śrīmad-Bhāgavatam.*

Śrīmad-Bhāgavatam is the transcendental science not only for knowing the ultimate source of everything but also for knowing our relation with Him and our duty toward perfection of the human society on the basis of this perfect knowledge. It is powerful reading matter in the Sanskrit language, and it is now rendered into English elaborately so that simply by a careful reading one will know God perfectly well, so much so that the reader will be sufficiently educated to defend himself from the onslaught of atheists. Over and above this, the reader will be able to convert others to accepting God as a concrete principle.

Śrīmad-Bhāgavatam begins with the definition of the ultimate source. It is a bona fide commentary on the *Vedānta-sūtra* by the same author, Śrīla Vyāsadeva, and gradually it develops into nine cantos up to the highest state of God realization. The only qualification one needs to study this great book of transcendental knowledge is to proceed step by step cautiously and not jump forward haphazardly as with an ordinary book. It should be gone through chapter by chapter, one after another. The reading matter is so arranged with the original Sanskrit text, its English transliteration, synonyms, translation and purports so that one is sure to become a God-realized soul at the end of finishing the first nine cantos.

The Tenth Canto is distinct from the first nine cantos because it deals directly with the transcendental activities of the Personality of Godhead, Śrī Kṛṣṇa. One will be unable to capture the effects of the Tenth Canto without going through the first nine cantos. The book is complete in twelve cantos, each independent, but it is good for all to read them in small installments one after another.

I must admit my frailties in presenting *Śrīmad-Bhāgavatam,* but still I am hopeful of its good reception by the thinkers and leaders of society on the strength of the following statement of *Śrīmad-Bhāgavatam* (1.5.11):

tad-vāg-visargo janatāgha-viplavo
yasmin prati-ślokam abaddhavaty api

nāmāny anantasya yaśo 'ṅkitāni yac
chṛṇvanti gāyanti gṛṇanti sādhavaḥ

"On the other hand, that literature which is full of descriptions of the transcendental glories of the name, fame, form and pastimes of the unlimited Supreme Lord is a transcendental creation meant for bringing about a revolution in the impious life of a misdirected civilization. Such transcendental literature, even though irregularly composed, is heard, sung and accepted by purified men who are thoroughly honest."

Oṁ tat sat

A. C. Bhaktivedanta Swami

Introduction

"This *Bhāgavata Purāṇa* is as brilliant as the sun, and it has arisen just after the departure of Lord Kṛṣṇa to His own abode, accompanied by religion, knowledge, etc. Persons who have lost their vision due to the dense darkness of ignorance in the age of Kali shall get light from this *Purāṇa*." (*Śrīmad-Bhāgavatam* 1.3.43)

The timeless wisdom of India is expressed in the *Vedas,* ancient Sanskrit texts that touch upon all fields of human knowledge. Originally preserved through oral tradition, the *Vedas* were first put into writing five thousand years ago by Śrīla Vyāsadeva, the "literary incarnation of God." After compiling the *Vedas,* Vyāsadeva set forth their essence in the aphorisms known as *Vedānta-sūtras. Śrīmad-Bhāgavatam* (*Bhāgavata Purāṇa*) is Vyāsadeva's commentary on his own *Vedānta-sūtras.* It was written in the maturity of his spiritual life under the direction of Nārada Muni, his spiritual master. Referred to as "the ripened fruit of the tree of Vedic literature," *Śrīmad-Bhāgavatam* is the most complete and authoritative exposition of Vedic knowledge.

After compiling the *Bhāgavatam,* Vyāsa imparted the synopsis of it to his son, the sage Śukadeva Gosvāmī. Śukadeva Gosvāmī subsequently recited the entire *Bhāgavatam* to Mahārāja Parīkṣit in an assembly of learned saints on the bank of the Ganges at Hastināpura (now Delhi). Mahārāja Parīkṣit was the emperor of the world and was a great *rājarṣi* (saintly king). Having received a warning that he would die within a week, he renounced his entire kingdom and retired to the bank of the Ganges to fast until death and receive spiritual enlightenment. The *Bhāgavatam* begins with Emperor Parīkṣit's sober inquiry to Śukadeva Gosvāmī: "You are the spiritual master of great saints and devotees. I am therefore begging you to show the way of perfection for all persons, and especially for one who is about to die. Please let me know what a man should hear, chant, remember and worship, and also what he should not do. Please explain all this to me."

Śukadeva Gosvāmī's answer to this question, and numerous other questions posed by Mahārāja Parīkṣit, concerning everything from the nature of the self to the origin of the universe, held the assembled sages in rapt attention continuously for the seven days leading up to the king's death. The sage Sūta Gosvāmī, who was present in that assembly when Śukadeva Gosvāmī first recited *Śrīmad-Bhāgavatam,* later repeated the *Bhāgavatam* before a gathering of sages in the forest of Naimiṣāraṇya. Those sages, concerned about the spiritual welfare of the people in general, had gathered to perform a long, continuous chain of sacrifices to counteract the degrading influence of the incipient age of Kali. In response to the sages' request that he speak the essence of Vedic wisdom, Sūta Gosvāmī repeated from memory the entire eighteen thousand verses of *Śrīmad-Bhāgavatam,* as spoken by Śukadeva Gosvāmī to Mahārāja Parīkṣit.

The reader of *Śrīmad-Bhāgavatam* hears Sūta Gosvāmī relate the questions of Mahārāja Parīkṣit and the answers of Śukadeva Gosvāmī. Also, Sūta Gosvāmī sometimes responds directly to questions put by Śaunaka Ṛṣi, the spokesman for the sages gathered at Naimiṣāraṇya. One therefore simultaneously hears two dialogues: one between Mahārāja Parīkṣit and Śukadeva Gosvāmī on the bank of the Ganges, and another at Naimiṣāraṇya between Sūta Gosvāmī and the sages at Naimiṣāraṇya forest, headed by Śaunaka Ṛṣi. Furthermore, while instructing King Parīkṣit, Śukadeva Gosvāmī often relates historical episodes and gives accounts of lengthy philosophical discussions between such great souls as Nārada Muni and Vasudeva. With this understanding of the history of the *Bhāgavatam,* the reader will easily be able to follow its intermingling of dialogues and events from various sources. Since philosophical wisdom, not chronological order, is most important in the text, one need only be attentive to the subject matter of *Śrīmad-Bhāgavatam* to appreciate fully its profound message.

The translators of this edition compare the *Bhāgavatam* to sugar candy—wherever you taste it, you will find it equally sweet and relishable. Therefore, to taste the sweetness of the *Bhāgavatam,* one may begin by reading any of its volumes. After such an introductory taste, however, the serious reader is best advised to go back to the First Canto and then proceed through the *Bhāgavatam,* canto after canto, in its natural order.

This edition of the *Bhāgavatam* is the first complete English translation of this important text with an elaborate commentary, and it is the first widely available to the English-speaking public. The first twelve volumes (Canto One through Canto Ten, Part One) are the product of the scholarly and devotional effort of His Divine Grace A. C. Bhaktivedanta Swami Prabhupāda, the founder-*ācārya* of the International

Society for Krishna Consciousness and the world's most distinguished teacher of Indian religious and philosophical thought. His consummate Sanskrit scholarship and intimate familiarity with Vedic culture and thought as well as the modern way of life combine to reveal to the West a magnificent exposition of this important classic. After the departure of Śrīla Prabhupāda from this world in 1977, his monumental work of translating and annotating *Śrīmad-Bhāgavatam* has been continued by his disciples Hridayananda dāsa Goswami and Gopīparāṇadhana dāsa.

Readers will find this work of value for many reasons. For those interested in the classical roots of Indian civilization, it serves as a vast reservoir of detailed information on virtually every one of its aspects. For students of comparative philosophy and religion, the *Bhāgavatam* offers a penetrating view into the meaning of India's profound spiritual heritage. To sociologists and anthropologists, the *Bhāgavatam* reveals the practical workings of a peaceful and scientifically organized Vedic culture, whose institutions were integrated on the basis of a highly developed spiritual world view. Students of literature will discover the *Bhāgavatam* to be a masterpiece of majestic poetry. For students of psychology, the text provides important perspectives on the nature of consciousness, human behavior and the philosophical study of identity. Finally, to those seeking spiritual insight, the *Bhāgavatam* offers simple and practical guidance for attainment of the highest self-knowledge and realization of the Absolute Truth. The entire multivolume text, presented by the Bhaktivedanta Book Trust, promises to occupy a significant place in the intellectual, cultural and spiritual life of modern man for a long time to come.

—The Publishers

CHAPTER ONE

The Supreme Lord Is Equal to Everyone

In this chapter, in response to a question by Mahārāja Parīkṣit, Śukadeva Gosvāmī gives his conclusions concerning how the Supreme Personality of Godhead, although the Supersoul, friend and protector of everyone, killed the Daityas, the demons, for the sake of Indra, the King of heaven. In his statements, he totally refutes the arguments of people in general who accuse the Supreme Lord of partiality. Śukadeva Gosvāmī proves that because the body of the conditioned soul is infected by the three qualities of nature, dualities arise such as enmity and friendship, attachment and detachment. For the Supreme Personality of Godhead, however, there are no such dualities. Even eternal time cannot control the activities of the Lord. Eternal time is created by the Lord, and it acts under His control. The Supreme Personality of Godhead, therefore, is always transcendental to the influence of the modes of nature, *māyā*, the Lord's external energy, which acts in creation and annihilation. Thus all the demons killed by the Supreme Lord attain salvation immediately.

The second question raised by Parīkṣit Mahārāja concerns how Śiśupāla, although inimical toward Kṛṣṇa from his very childhood and always blaspheming Kṛṣṇa, attained salvation in oneness when Kṛṣṇa killed him. Śukadeva Gosvāmī explains that because of their offenses at the feet of devotees, two attendants of the Lord in Vaikuṇṭha named Jaya and Vijaya became Hiraṇyakaśipu and Hiraṇyākṣa in Satya-yuga, Rāvaṇa and Kumbhakarṇa in the next *yuga*, Tretā-yuga, and Śiśupāla and Dantavakra at the end of Dvāpara-yuga. Because of their fruitive acts, Jaya and Vijaya agreed to become the Lord's enemies, and when killed in that mentality, they attained salvation in oneness. Thus even if one thinks of the Supreme Personality of Godhead in envy, he attains salvation. What then is to be said of devotees who always engage in the Lord's service with love and faith?

TEXT 1

श्रीराजोवाच
समः प्रियः सुहृद्ब्रह्मन् भूतानां भगवान् स्वयम् ।
इन्द्रस्यार्थे कथं दैत्यानवधीद्विषमो यथा ॥ १ ॥

śrī-rājovāca
samaḥ priyaḥ suhṛd brahman
bhūtānāṁ bhagavān svayam
indrasyārthe kathaṁ daityān
avadhīd viṣamo yathā

śrī-rājā uvāca—Mahārāja Parīkṣit said; *samaḥ*—equal; *priyaḥ*—beloved; *suhṛt*—friend; *brahman*—O *brāhmaṇa* (Śukadeva); *bhūtānām*—toward all living entities; *bhagavān*—the Supreme Lord, Viṣṇu; *svayam*—Himself; *indrasya*—of Indra; *arthe*—for the benefit; *katham*—how; *daityān*—the demons; *avadhīt*—killed; *viṣamaḥ*—partial; *yathā*—as if.

TRANSLATION

King Parīkṣit inquired: My dear brāhmaṇa, the Supreme Personality of Godhead, Viṣṇu, being everyone's well-wisher, is equal and extremely dear to everyone. How, then, did He become partial like a common man for the sake of Indra and thus kill Indra's enemies? How can a person equal to everyone be partial to some and inimical toward others?

PURPORT

In *Bhagavad-gītā* (9.29) the Lord says, *samo 'haṁ sarva-bhūteṣu na me dveṣyo 'sti na priyaḥ:* "I am equal to everyone. No one is dear to Me, nor is anyone My enemy." In the previous canto, however, it has been observed that the Lord sided with Indra by killing the demons on his account (*hata-putrā ditiḥ śakra-pārṣṇi-grāhena viṣṇunā*). Therefore, the Lord was clearly partial to Indra, although He is the Supersoul in everyone's heart. The soul is extremely dear to everyone, and similarly the

Supersoul is also dear to everyone. Thus there cannot be any faulty action on the part of the Supersoul. The Lord is always kind to all living entities, irrespective of form and situation, yet He took the side of Indra just like an ordinary friend. This was the subject of Parīkṣit Mahārāja's inquiry. As a devotee of Lord Kṛṣṇa, he knew very well that Kṛṣṇa cannot be partial to anyone, but when he saw that Kṛṣṇa acted as the enemy of the demons, he was somewhat doubtful. Therefore he posed this question to Śukadeva Gosvāmī for a clear answer.

A devotee cannot accept that Lord Viṣṇu has material qualifications. Mahārāja Parīkṣit knew perfectly well that Lord Viṣṇu, being transcendental, has nothing to do with material qualities, but to confirm his conviction he wanted to hear from the authority Śukadeva Gosvāmī. Śrīla Viśvanātha Cakravartī Ṭhākura says, *samasya kathaṁ vaiṣamyam:* since the Lord is equally disposed toward everyone, how can He be partial? *Priyasya katham asureṣu prīty-abhāvaḥ.* The Lord, being the Supersoul, is extremely dear to everyone. Why, then, should the Lord display unsympathetic behavior toward the *asuras?* How is this impartial? *Suhṛdaś ca kathaṁ teṣv asauhārdam.* Since the Lord says that He is *suhṛdaṁ sarva-bhūtānām*, the well-wisher of all living entities, how could He act with partiality by killing demons? These questions arose in the heart of Parīkṣit Mahārāja, and therefore he inquired from Śukadeva Gosvāmī.

TEXT 2

न ह्यस्यार्थः सुरगणैः साक्षान्निःश्रेयसात्मनः ।
नैवासुरेभ्यो विद्वेषो नोद्वेगश्चागुणस्य हि ॥ २ ॥

na hy asyārthaḥ sura-gaṇaiḥ
sākṣān niḥśreyasātmanaḥ
naivāsurebhyo vidveṣo
nodvegaś cāguṇasya hi

na—not; *hi*—certainly; *asya*—His; *arthaḥ*—benefit, interest; *sura-gaṇaiḥ*—with the demigods; *sākṣāt*—personally; *niḥśreyasa*—of the highest bliss; *ātmanaḥ*—whose nature; *na*—not; *eva*—certainly; *asurebhyaḥ*—for the demons; *vidveṣaḥ*—envy; *na*—not; *udvegaḥ*—

fear; *ca*—and; *aguṇasya*—who possesses no material qualities; *hi*—certainly.

TRANSLATION

Lord Viṣṇu Himself, the Supreme Personality of Godhead, is the reservoir of all pleasure. Therefore, what benefit would He derive from siding with the demigods? What interest would He fulfill in this way? Since the Lord is transcendental, why should He fear the asuras, and how could He be envious of them?

PURPORT

We should always remember the distinction between spiritual and material. That which is material is infected by material qualities, but these qualities cannot touch that which is spiritual, or transcendental. Kṛṣṇa is absolute, whether He is in the material world or spiritual world. When we see partiality in Kṛṣṇa, this vision is due to His external energy. Otherwise how could His enemies attain salvation after being killed by Him? Everyone who deals with the Supreme Personality of Godhead gradually acquires the qualities of the Lord. The more one advances in spiritual consciousness, the less he is affected by the duality of material qualities. The Supreme Lord, therefore, must certainly be freed from these qualities. His enmity and friendship are external features presented by the material energy. He is always transcendental. He is absolute, whether He kills or bestows His favor.

Envy and friendship arise in one who is imperfect. We fear our enemies because in the material world we are always in need of help. The Lord, however, does not need anyone's help, for He is *ātmārāma.* The Lord says in *Bhagavad-gītā* (9.26):

patraṁ puṣpaṁ phalaṁ toyaṁ
yo me bhaktyā prayacchati
tad ahaṁ bhakty-upahṛtam
aśnāmi prayatātmanaḥ

"If a devotee offers Me with devotion a little leaf, a flower, fruit or water, I shall accept it." Why does the Lord say this? Is He dependent on the offering of the devotee? He is not actually dependent, but He likes to be dependent upon His devotee. This is His mercy. Similarly, He does not fear the *asuras.* Thus there is no question of partiality in the Supreme Personality of Godhead.

TEXT 3

इति नः सुमहाभाग नारायणगुणान् प्रति ।
संशयः सुमहाञ्जातस्तद्भवांश्छेत्तुमर्हति ॥ ३ ॥

iti naḥ sumahā-bhāga
nārāyaṇa-guṇān prati
saṁśayaḥ sumahāñ jātas
tad bhavāṁś chettum arhati

iti—thus; *naḥ*—our; *su-mahā-bhāga*—O glorious one; *nārāyaṇa-guṇān*—the qualities of Nārāyaṇa; *prati*—toward; *saṁśayaḥ*—doubt; *su-mahān*—very great; *jātaḥ*—born; *tat*—that; *bhavān*—Your Lordship; *chettum arhati*—please dispel.

TRANSLATION

O greatly fortunate and learned brāhmaṇa, whether Nārāyaṇa is partial or impartial has become a subject of great doubt. Kindly dispel my doubt with positive evidence that Nārāyaṇa is always neutral and equal to everyone.

PURPORT

Since Lord Nārāyaṇa is absolute, His transcendental qualities are described as one. Thus His punishments and His offerings of favor are both of the same value. Essentially, His inimical actions are not displays of enmity toward His so-called enemies, but in the material field one thinks that Kṛṣṇa is favorable to devotees and unfavorable to nondevotees. When Kṛṣṇa finally instructs in *Bhagavad-gītā, sarva-dharmān parityajya mām ekaṁ śaraṇaṁ vraja,* this is meant not only for Arjuna but for every living entity within this universe.

TEXTS 4–5

श्रीऋषिरुवाच
साधु पृष्टं महाराज हरेश्चरितमद्भुतम् ।
यद् भागवतमाहात्म्यं भगवद्भक्तिवर्धनम् ॥ ४ ॥
गीयते परमं पुण्यमृषिभिर्नारदादिभिः ।
नत्वा कृष्णाय मुनये कथयिष्ये हरेः कथाम् ॥ ५ ॥

śrī-ṛṣir uvāca
sādhu pṛṣṭaṁ mahārāja
hareś caritam adbhutam
yad bhāgavata-māhātmyaṁ
bhagavad-bhakti-vardhanam

gīyate paramaṁ puṇyam
ṛṣibhir nāradādibhiḥ
natvā kṛṣṇāya munaye
kathayiṣye hareḥ kathām

śrī-ṛṣiḥ uvāca—the sage Śrī Śukadeva Gosvāmī said; *sādhu*—excellent; *pṛṣṭam*—inquiry; *mahā-rāja*—O great King; *hareḥ*—of the Supreme Lord, Hari; *caritam*—activities; *adbhutam*—wonderful; *yat*—from which; *bhāgavata*—of the Lord's devotee (Prahlāda); *māhātmyam*—the glories; *bhagavat-bhakti*—devotion to the Lord; *vardhanam*—increasing; *gīyate*—is sung; *paramam*—foremost; *puṇyam*—pious; *ṛṣibhiḥ*—by the sages; *nārada-ādibhiḥ*—headed by Śrī Nārada Muni; *natvā*—after offering obeisances; *kṛṣṇāya*—to Kṛṣṇa Dvaipāyana Vyāsa; *munaye*—the great sage; *kathayiṣye*—I shall narrate; *hareḥ*—of Hari; *kathām*—the topics.

TRANSLATION

The great sage Śukadeva Gosvāmī said: My dear King, you have put before me an excellent question. Discourses concerning the activities of the Lord, in which the glories of His devotees are also found, are extremely pleasing to devotees. Such wonderful topics

always counteract the miseries of the materialistic way of life. Therefore great sages like Nārada always speak upon Śrīmad-Bhāgavatam because it gives one the facility to hear and chant about the wonderful activities of the Lord. Let me offer my respectful obeisances unto Śrīla Vyāsadeva and then begin describing topics concerning the activities of Lord Hari.

PURPORT

In this verse Śukadeva Gosvāmī offers his respectful obeisances *kṛṣṇāya munaye*, which means to Kṛṣṇa Dvaipāyana Vyāsa. One must first offer one's respectful obeisances to one's spiritual master. Śukadeva Gosvāmī's spiritual master is his father, Vyāsadeva, and therefore he first offers his respectful obeisances to Kṛṣṇa Dvaipāyana Vyāsa and then begins describing topics of Lord Hari.

Whenever there is an opportunity to hear about the transcendental activities of the Lord, we must take it. Śrī Caitanya Mahāprabhu recommends, *kīrtanīyaḥ sadā hariḥ:* one should always engage in *kṛṣṇa-kathā* by chanting and talking about Kṛṣṇa and hearing about Him. That is the only occupation of a Kṛṣṇa conscious person.

TEXT 6

निर्गुणोऽपि ह्यजोऽव्यक्तो भगवान् प्रकृतेः परः ।
स्वमायागुणमाविश्य बाध्यबाधकतां गतः ॥ ६ ॥

nirguṇo 'pi hy ajo 'vyakto
bhagavān prakṛteḥ paraḥ
sva-māyā-guṇam āviśya
bādhya-bādhakatāṁ gataḥ

nirguṇaḥ—without material qualities; *api*—although; *hi*—certainly; *ajaḥ*—unborn; *avyaktaḥ*—unmanifest; *bhagavān*—the Supreme Lord; *prakṛteḥ*—to material nature; *paraḥ*—transcendental; *sva-māyā*—of His own energy; *guṇam*—material qualities; *āviśya*—entering; *bādhya*—obligation; *bādhakatām*—the condition of being obliged; *gataḥ*—accepts.

TRANSLATION

The Supreme Personality of Godhead, Viṣṇu, is always transcendental to material qualities, and therefore He is called nirguṇa, or without qualities. Because He is unborn, He does not have a material body to be subjected to attachment and hatred. Although the Lord is always above material existence, through His spiritual potency He appeared and acted like an ordinary human being, accepting duties and obligations, apparently like a conditioned soul.

PURPORT

So-called attachment, detachment and obligations pertain to the material nature, which is an emanation from the Supreme Personality of Godhead, but whenever the Lord descends and acts in this material world, He does so in His spiritual position. Although His activities materially appear different, spiritually they are absolute and nondifferent. Thus it is an imposition upon the Supreme Lord to say that He is envious of anyone or friendly to anyone.

In *Bhagavad-gītā* (9.11) the Lord clearly says, *avajānanti māṁ mūḍhā mānuṣīṁ tanum āśritam:* "Fools deride Me when I descend in a human form." Kṛṣṇa appears on this earth or within this universe without any change in His spiritual body or spiritual qualities. Indeed, He is never influenced by the material qualities. He is always free from such qualities, but He appears to act under material influence. This understanding is *āropita,* or an imposition. Therefore Kṛṣṇa says, *janma karma ca me divyam:* whatever He does, being always transcendental, has nothing to do with material qualities. *Evaṁ yo vetti tattvataḥ:* only devotees can understand the truth of how He acts. The fact is that Kṛṣṇa is never partial to anyone. He is always equal to everyone, but because of imperfect vision, influenced by material qualities, one imposes material qualities upon Kṛṣṇa, and when one does so he becomes a *mūḍha,* a fool. When one can properly understand the truth, one becomes devoted and *nirguṇa,* free from material qualities. Simply by understanding the activities of Kṛṣṇa one can become transcendental, and as soon as one is transcendental he is fit to be transferred to the transcendental world. *Tyaktvā dehaṁ punar janma naiti mām eti so 'rjuna:* one who understands the activities of the Lord in truth is transferred to the spiritual world after he gives up his material body.

TEXT 7

सत्त्वं रजस्तम इति प्रकृतेर्नात्मनो गुणाः ।
न तेषां युगपद्राजन् ह्रास उल्लास एव वा ॥ ७ ॥

sattvaṁ rajas tama iti
prakṛter nātmano guṇāḥ
na teṣāṁ yugapad rājan
hrāsa ullāsa eva vā

sattvam—the mode of goodness; *rajaḥ*—the mode of passion; *tamaḥ*—the mode of ignorance; *iti*—thus; *prakṛteḥ*—of material nature; *na*—not; *ātmanaḥ*—of the spirit soul; *guṇāḥ*—qualities; *na*—not; *teṣām*—of them; *yugapat*—simultaneously; *rājan*—O King; *hrāsaḥ*—diminution; *ullāsaḥ*—prominence; *eva*—certainly; *vā*—or.

TRANSLATION

My dear King Parīkṣit, the material qualities—sattva-guṇa, rajo-guṇa and tamo-guṇa—all belong to the material world and do not even touch the Supreme Personality of Godhead. These three guṇas cannot act by increasing or decreasing simultaneously.

PURPORT

The original position of the Supreme Personality of Godhead is one of equality. There is no question of His being influenced by *sattva-guṇa*, *rājo-guṇa* or *tamo-guṇa*, for these material qualities cannot touch the Supreme Lord. The Lord is therefore called the supreme *īśvara. Īśvaraḥ paramaḥ kṛṣṇaḥ:* He is the supreme controller. He controls the material qualities (*daivī hy eṣā guṇamayī mama māyā*). *Mayādhyakṣeṇa prakṛtiḥ sūyate:* material nature (*prakṛti*) works under His order. How, then, can He be under the qualities of *prakṛti*? Kṛṣṇa is never influenced by the material qualities. Therefore there is no question of partiality in the Supreme Personality of Godhead.

TEXT 8

जयकाले तु सत्त्वस्य देवर्षीन् रजसोऽसुरान् ।
तमसो यक्षरक्षांसि तत्कालानुगुणोऽभजत् ॥ ८ ॥

jaya-kāle tu sattvasya
devarṣīn rajaso 'surān
tamaso yakṣa-rakṣāṁsi
tat-kālānuguṇo 'bhajat

jaya-kāle—in the time of prominence; *tu*—indeed; *sattvasya*—of goodness; *deva*—the demigods; *ṛṣīn*—and the sages; *rajasaḥ*—of passion; *asurān*—the demons; *tamasaḥ*—of ignorance; *yakṣa-rakṣāṁsi*—the Yakṣas and Rākṣasas; *tat-kāla-anuguṇaḥ*—according to the particular time; *abhajat*—fostered.

TRANSLATION

When the quality of goodness is prominent, the sages and demigods flourish with the help of that quality, with which they are infused and surcharged by the Supreme Lord. Similarly, when the mode of passion is prominent the demons flourish, and when ignorance is prominent the Yakṣas and Rākṣasas flourish. The Supreme Personality of Godhead is present in everyone's heart, fostering the reactions of sattva-guṇa, rajo-guṇa and tamo-guṇa.

PURPORT

The Supreme Personality of Godhead is not partial to anyone. The conditioned soul is under the influence of the various modes of material nature, and behind material nature is the Supreme Personality of Godhead; but one's victory and loss under the influence of *sattva-guṇa, rajo-guṇa* and *tamo-guṇa* are reactions of these modes, not of the Supreme Lord's partiality. Śrīla Jīva Gosvāmī, in the *Bhāgavata-sandarbha*, has clearly said:

sattvādayo na santīśe
yatra ca prākṛtā guṇāḥ
sa śuddhaḥ sarva-śuddhebhyaḥ
pumān ādyaḥ prasīdatu

hlādinī sandhinī samvit
tvayy ekā sarva-saṁsthitau
hlāda-tāpa-karī miśrā
tvayi no guṇa-varjite

According to this statement of the *Bhāgavata-sandarbha*, the Supreme Lord, being always transcendental to the material qualities, is never affected by the influence of these qualities. This same characteristic is also present in the living being, but because he is conditioned by material nature, even the pleasure potency of the Lord is manifested in the conditioned soul as troublesome. In the material world the pleasure enjoyed by the conditioned soul is followed by many painful conditions. For instance, we have seen that in the two great wars, which were conducted by the *rajo-guṇa* and *tamo-guṇa*, both parties were actually ruined. The German people declared war against the English to ruin them, but the result was that both parties were ruined. Although the Allies were apparently victorious, at least on paper, actually neither of them were victorious. Therefore it should be concluded that the Supreme Personality of Godhead is not partial to anyone. Everyone works under the influence of various modes of material nature, and when the various modes are prominent, the demigods or demons appear victorious under the influence of these modes.

Everyone enjoys the fruits of his qualitative activities. This is also confirmed in *Bhagavad-gītā* (14.11–13):

sarva-dvāreṣu dehe 'smin
prakāśa upajāyate
jñānaṁ yadā tadā vidyād
vivṛddhaṁ sattvam ity uta

lobhaḥ pravṛttir ārambhaḥ
karmaṇām aśamaḥ spṛhā
rajasy etāni jāyante
vivṛddhe bharatarṣabha

aprakāśo 'pravṛttiś ca
pramādo moha eva ca

tamasy etāni jāyante
vivṛddhe kuru-nandana

"The manifestations of the modes of goodness can be experienced when all the gates of the body are illumined by knowledge.

"O chief of the Bhāratas, when there is an increase in the mode of passion, the symptoms of great attachment, uncontrollable desire, hankering, and intense endeavor develop.

"O son of Kuru, when there is an increase in the mode of ignorance, madness, illusion, inertia and darkness are manifested."

The Supreme Personality of Godhead, who is present in everyone's heart, simply gives the results of the increase in the various qualities, but He is impartial. He supervises victory and loss, but He does not take part in them.

The various modes of material nature do not work all at once. The interactions of these modes are exactly like seasonal changes. Sometimes there is an increment of *rajo-guṇa*, sometimes of *tamo-guṇa* and sometimes *sattva-guṇa*. Generally the demigods are surcharged with *sattva-guṇa*, and therefore when the demons and the demigods fight, the demigods are victorious because of the prominence of their *sattva-guṇa* qualities. However, this is not the partiality of the Supreme Lord.

TEXT 9

ज्योतिरादिरिवाभाति सङ्घातान्न विविच्यते ।
विदन्त्यात्मानमात्मस्थं मथित्वा कवयोऽन्ततः॥९॥

jyotir-ādir ivābhāti
saṅghātān na vivicyate
vidanty ātmānam ātma-sthaṁ
mathitvā kavayo 'ntataḥ

jyotiḥ—fire; *ādiḥ*—and other elements; *iva*—just as; *ābhāti*—appear; *saṅghātāt*—from the bodies of demigods and others; *na*—not; *vivicyate*—are distinguished; *vidanti*—perceive; *ātmānam*—the Supersoul; *ātma-stham*—situated in the heart; *mathitvā*—by discerning; *kavayaḥ*—expert thinkers; *antataḥ*—within.

His Divine Grace
A. C. Bhaktivedanta Swami Prabhupāda
Founder-Ācārya of the International Society for Krishna Consciousness

PLATE ONE: When Jaya and Vijaya, the gatekeepers of Vaikuṇṭha, forbade the four sage sons of Brahmā to enter, the sages cursed them to take birth as demons in the material world. (*pp. 49-51*)

PLATE TWO: Hiraṇyakaśipu's severe austerities caused fire to come from his head, and this fire and its smoke spread throughout the sky, encompassing the upper and lower planets and burning them. (*pp. 132-33*)

PLATE THREE: When Brahmā sprinkled transcendental water upon Hiraṇyakaśipu's body, which had been eaten away by insects, the demon arose, endowed with limbs stronger than thunderbolts. (*pp. 149–50*)

PLATE FOUR: Shouting "Chop him up! Pierce him!" Hiraṇyakaśipu's henchmen began striking Prahlāda, who sat silently, meditating on the Supreme Lord. (*p. 279*)

PLATE FIVE: The servants of Hiraṇyakaśipu tried to kill Prahlāda by hurling him from the top of a hill, but, as always, the Supreme Lord protected him from any harm. (*p. 282*)

PLATE SIX: As Indra was arresting Prahlāda's mother, Nārada Muni appeared and said, "O Indra, this woman is sinless. You must immediately release her." (*p. 341*)

PLATE SEVEN: When his demoniac teachers were absent, Prahlāda taught his classmates the science of Kṛṣṇa consciousness, beginning with chanting the holy names. The boys readily accepted his instructions and rejected that of their teachers. (*p. 413*)

PLATE EIGHT: Lord Nṛsiṁhadeva captured Hiraṇyakaśipu and placed him on His lap. Then, in the doorway of the assembly hall, the Lord very easily tore the demon to pieces with His nails. (*p. 443*)

PLATE NINE: Hiraṇyakaśipu's soldiers came by the thousands to battle Lord Nṛsiṁhadeva, but the Lord killed all of them merely with the tips of His nails. (*p. 445*)

PLATE TEN: By the touch of Lord Nṛsiṁhadeva's hand on his head, Prahlāda was completely freed of all material contaminations and desires, and he began to offer prayers. (*p. 483*)

PLATE ELEVEN: After Lord Śiva had killed the demons with a barrage of fiery arrows, Maya Dānava brought them back to life by dropping them into a nectar-filled well he had created. (*pp. 632-34*)

PLATE TWELVE: Fully equipped by Lord Kṛṣṇa with all military paraphernalia, Lord Śiva joined his arrows to his bow and then set fire to all three residences of the demons. (*pp. 638–39*)

PLATE THIRTEEN: Nārada Muni, the supreme spiritual master of human society, instructed King Yudhiṣṭhira on ideal behavior, social organization and family life. (*p. 649*)

PLATE FOURTEEN: Situated in everyone's heart, the Supreme Lord is directing the wanderings of all living entities, who are seated as on a machine made of the material energy. (*p. 807*)

PLATE FIFTEEN: The progenitors of the universe cursed Upabarhaṇa with these words: "Because you have committed an offense, may you immediately become a lowborn *śūdra*, devoid of beauty!" (*p. 906*)

TRANSLATION

The all-pervading Personality of Godhead exists within the heart of every living being, and an expert thinker can perceive how He is present there to a large or small extent. Just as one can understand the supply of fire in wood, the water in a waterpot, or the sky within a pot, one can understand whether a living entity is a demon or a demigod by understanding that living entity's devotional performances. A thoughtful man can understand how much a person is favored by the Supreme Lord by seeing his actions.

PURPORT

In *Bhagavad-gītā* (10.41) the Lord says:

yad yad vibhūtimat sattvaṁ
śrīmad ūrjitam eva vā
tat tad evāvagaccha tvaṁ
mama tejo-'ṁśa-sambhavam

"Know that all beautiful, glorious and mighty creations spring from but a spark of My splendor." We have the practical experience of seeing that one person is able to do very wonderful things whereas another cannot do those same things and cannot even do things that require only a little common sense. Therefore, how much a devotee has been favored by the Supreme Personality of Godhead can be tested by the activities the devotee has performed. In *Bhagavad-gītā* (10.10) the Lord also says:

teṣāṁ satata-yuktānāṁ
bhajatāṁ prīti-pūrvakam
dadāmi buddhi-yogaṁ taṁ
yena mām upayānti te

"To those who are constantly devoted and who worship Me with love, I give the understanding by which they can come to Me." This is very practical. A teacher instructs the student if the student is capable of taking more and more instructions. Otherwise, in spite of being instructed by the teacher, the student cannot make strides in his understanding.

This has nothing to do with partiality. When Kṛṣṇa says *teṣāṁ satata-yuktānāṁ bhajatāṁ prīti-pūrvakam/ dadāmi buddhi-yogaṁ tam,* this indicates that Kṛṣṇa is prepared to give *bhakti-yoga* to everyone, but one must be capable of receiving it. That is the secret. Thus when a person exhibits wonderful devotional activities, a thoughtful man understands that Kṛṣṇa has been more favorable to this devotee.

This is not difficult to understand, but envious persons do not accept that Kṛṣṇa has bestowed His favor upon a particular devotee in accordance with his advanced position. Such foolish persons become envious and try to minimize an advanced devotee's activities. That is not Vaiṣṇavism. A Vaiṣṇava should appreciate the service rendered to the Lord by other Vaiṣṇavas. Therefore a Vaiṣṇava is described in *Śrīmad-Bhāgavatam* as *nirmatsara.* Vaiṣṇavas are never envious of other Vaiṣṇavas or of anyone else, and therefore they are called *nirmatsarāṇāṁ satām.*

As *Bhagavad-gītā* informs us, one can understand how one is saturated with *sattva-guṇa, rajo-guṇa* or *tamo-guṇa.* In the examples given herewith, fire represents the mode of goodness. One can understand the constitution of a container for wood, petrol or other inflammable substances by the quantity of the fire. Similarly, water represents *rajo-guṇa,* the mode of passion. A small skin and the vast Atlantic Ocean both contain water, and by seeing the quantity of water in a container one can understand the size of the container. The sky represents the mode of ignorance. The sky is present in a small earthen pot and also in outer space. Thus by proper judgment one can see who is a *devatā,* or demigod, and who is an *asura,* Yakṣa or Rākṣasa according to the quantities of *sattva-guṇa, rajo-guṇa* and *tamo-guṇa.* One cannot judge whether a person is a *devatā,* an *asura* or a Rākṣasa by seeing him, but a sane man can understand this by the activities such a person performs. A general description is given in the *Padma Purāṇa: viṣṇu-bhaktaḥ smṛto daiva āsuras tad-viparyayaḥ.* A devotee of Lord Viṣṇu is a demigod, whereas an *asura* or Yakṣa is just the opposite. An *asura* is not a devotee of Lord Viṣṇu; instead, for his sense gratification he is a devotee of the demigods, *bhūtas, pretas* and so on. Thus one can judge who is a *devatā,* who is a Rākṣasa and who is an *asura* by how they conduct their activities.

The word *ātmānam* in this verse means *paramātmānam.* The

Paramātmā, or Supersoul, is situated in the core of everyone's heart (*antataḥ*). This is confirmed in *Bhagavad-gītā* (18.61). *Īśvaraḥ sarva-bhūtānāṁ hṛd-deśe 'rjuna tiṣṭhati.* The *īśvara*, the Supreme Personality of Godhead, being situated in everyone's heart, gives directions to everyone in terms of one's capabilities in taking the instructions. The instructions of *Bhagavad-gītā* are open to everyone, but some people understand them properly, whereas others understand them so improperly that they cannot even believe in the existence of Kṛṣṇa, although reading Kṛṣṇa's book. Although the *Gītā* says *śrī-bhagavān uvāca*, indicating that Kṛṣṇa spoke, they cannot understand Kṛṣṇa. This is due to their misfortune or incapability, which is caused by *rajo-guṇa* and *tamo-guṇa*, the modes of passion and ignorance. It is because of these modes that they cannot even understand Kṛṣṇa, whereas an advanced devotee like Arjuna understands Him and glorifies Him, saying, *paraṁ brahma paraṁ dhāma pavitraṁ paramaṁ bhavān:* "You are the Supreme Brahman, the supreme abode and purifier." Kṛṣṇa is open to everyone, but one needs the capability to understand Him.

By external features one cannot understand who is favored by Kṛṣṇa and who is not. According to one's attitude, Kṛṣṇa becomes one's direct adviser, or Kṛṣṇa becomes unknown. This is not Kṛṣṇa's partiality; it is His response to one's ability to understand Him. According to one's receptiveness—whether one be a *devatā*, *asura*, Yakṣa or Rākṣasa—Kṛṣṇa's quality is proportionately exhibited. This proportionate exhibition of Kṛṣṇa's power is misunderstood by less intelligent men to be Kṛṣṇa's partiality, but actually it is no such thing. Kṛṣṇa is equal to everyone, and according to one's ability to receive the favor of Kṛṣṇa, one advances in Kṛṣṇa consciousness. Śrīla Viśvanātha Cakravartī Ṭhākura gives a practical example in this connection. In the sky there are many luminaries. At night, even in darkness, the moon is extremely brilliant and can be directly perceived. The sun is also extremely brilliant. When covered by clouds, however, these luminaries are not distinctly visible. Similarly, the more one advances in *sattva-guṇa*, the more his brilliance is exhibited by devotional service, but the more one is covered by *rajo-guṇa* and *tamo-guṇa*, the less visible his brilliance, for he is covered by these qualities. The visibility of one's qualities does not depend on the partiality of the Supreme Personality of Godhead; it is due to various coverings in different proportions. Thus one can understand how far he has advanced in terms of *sattva-guṇa* and how much he is covered by *rajo-guṇa* and *tamo-guṇa.*

TEXT 10

यदा सिसृक्षुः पुर आत्मनः परो
रजः सृजत्येष पृथक स्वमायया ।
सत्त्वं विचित्रासु रिरंसुरीश्वरः
शयिष्यमाणस्तम ईरयत्यसौ ॥१०॥

yadā sisṛkṣuḥ pura ātmanaḥ paro
rajaḥ sṛjaty eṣa pṛthak sva-māyayā
sattvaṁ vicitrāsu riraṁsur īśvaraḥ
śayiṣyamāṇas tama īrayaty asau

yadā—when; *sisṛkṣuḥ*—desiring to create; *puraḥ*—material bodies; *ātmanaḥ*—for the living entities; *paraḥ*—the Supreme Personality of Godhead; *rajaḥ*—the mode of passion; *sṛjati*—manifests; *eṣaḥ*—He; *pṛthak*—separately, predominantly; *sva-māyayā*—by His own creative energy; *sattvam*—the mode of goodness; *vicitrāsu*—in various types of bodies; *riraṁsuḥ*—desiring to act; *īśvaraḥ*—the Personality of Godhead; *śayiṣyamāṇaḥ*—being about to conclude; *tamaḥ*—the mode of ignorance; *īrayati*—causes to rise; *asau*—that Supreme.

TRANSLATION

When the Supreme Personality of Godhead creates different types of bodies, offering a particular body to each living entity according to his character and fruitive actions, the Lord revives all the qualities of material nature—sattva-guṇa, rajo-guṇa and tamo-guṇa. Then, as the Supersoul, He enters each body and influences the qualities of creation, maintenance and annihilation, using sattva-guṇa for maintenance, rajo-guṇa for creation and tamo-guṇa for annihilation.

PURPORT

Although material nature is conducted by the three qualities—*sattva-guṇa, rajo-guṇa* and *tamo-guṇa*—nature is not independent. As the Lord says in *Bhagavad-gītā* (9.10):

mayādhyakṣeṇa prakṛtiḥ
sūyate sa-carācaram
hetunānena kaunteya
jagad viparivartate

"This material nature is working under My direction, O son of Kuntī, and it is producing all moving and unmoving beings. By its rule this manifestation is created and annihilated again and again." The different changes in the material world take place as actions and reactions of the three *guṇas*, but above the three *guṇas* is their director, the Supreme Personality of Godhead. In the various types of bodies given to the living entities by material nature (*yantrārūḍhāni māyayā*), either *sattva-guṇa, rajo-guṇa* or *tamo-guṇa* is prominent. The body is produced by material nature according to the direction of the Supreme Personality of Godhead. Therefore it is said here, *yadā sisṛkṣuḥ pura ātmanaḥ paraḥ,* indicating that the body is certainly created by the Lord. *Karmaṇā daiva-netreṇa:* according to the *karma* of the living entity, a body is prepared under the Supreme Lord's supervision. Whether the body is of *sattva-guṇa, rajo-guṇa* or *tamo-guṇa,* everything is done by the direction of the Supreme Lord through the agency of the external energy (*pṛthak sva-māyayā*). In this way, in different types of bodies, the Lord (*īśvara*) gives directions as Paramātmā, and again, to destroy the body, He employs the *tamo-guṇa.* This is the way the living entities receive different types of bodies.

TEXT 11

कालं चरन्तं सृजतीश आश्रयं ।
प्रधानपुम्भ्यां नरदेव सत्यकृत् ॥११॥

kālaṁ carantaṁ sṛjatīśa āśrayaṁ
pradhāna-pumbhyāṁ nara-deva satya-kṛt

kālam—time; *carantam*—moving; *sṛjati*—creates; *īśaḥ*—the Supreme Personality of Godhead; *āśrayam*—shelter; *pradhāna*—for the material energy; *pumbhyām*—and the living entity; *nara-deva*—O ruler of men; *satya*—true; *kṛt*—creator.

TRANSLATION

O great King, the Supreme Personality of Godhead, the controller of the material and spiritual energies, who is certainly the creator of the entire cosmos, creates the time factor to allow the material energy and the living entity to act within the limits of time. Thus the Supreme Personality is never under the time factor nor under the material energy.

PURPORT

One should not think that the Lord is dependent on the time factor. He actually creates the situation by which material nature acts and by which the conditioned soul is placed under material nature. Both the conditioned soul and the material nature act within the time factor, but the Lord is not subject to the actions and reactions of time, for time has been created by Him. To be more clear, Śrīla Viśvanātha Cakravartī Ṭhākura says that creation, maintenance and annihilation are all under the supreme will of the Lord.

In *Bhagavad-gītā* (4.7) the Lord says:

yadā yadā hi dharmasya
glānir bhavati bhārata
abhyutthānam adharmasya
tadātmānaṁ sṛjāmy aham

"Whenever and wherever there is a decline in religious practice, O descendant of Bharata, and a predominant rise of irreligion—at that time I descend Myself." Since Kṛṣṇa, the Supreme Personality of Godhead, is the controller of everything, when He appears He is not within the limitations of material time (*janma karma ca me divyam*). In this verse the words *kālaṁ carantaṁ sṛjatīśa āśrayam* indicate that although the Lord acts within time, whether *sattva-guṇa*, *rajo-guṇa* or *tamo-guṇa* is prominent, one should not think that the Lord is under time's control.

Time is within His control, for He creates time to act in a certain way; He is not working under the control of time. The creation of the material world is one of the Lord's pastimes. Everything is fully under His control. Since creation takes place when *rajo-guṇa* is prominent, the Lord creates the necessary time to give facilities for *rajo-guṇa*. Similarly, He also creates the necessary times for maintenance and annihilation. Thus this verse establishes that the Lord is not under the limitations of time.

As stated in the *Brahma-saṁhitā, īśvaraḥ paramaḥ kṛṣṇaḥ:* Kṛṣṇa is the supreme controller. *Sac-cid-ānanda-vigrahaḥ:* He possesses a blissful, spiritual body. *Anādiḥ:* He is not subordinate to anything. As the Lord confirms in *Bhagavad-gītā* (7.7), *mattaḥ parataraṁ nānyat kiñcid asti dhanañjaya:* "O conqueror of wealth [Arjuna], there is no truth superior to Me." Nothing can be above Kṛṣṇa, for He is the controller and creator of everything.

The Māyāvādī philosophers say that this material world is *mithyā*, false, and that one should therefore not bother about this *mithyā* creation (*brahma satyaṁ jagan mithyā*). But this is not correct. Here it is said, *satya-kṛt:* whatever is created by the Supreme Personality of Godhead, *satyaṁ param*, cannot be called *mithyā*. The cause of the creation is *satya*, true, so how can the effect of the cause be *mithyā?* The very word *satya-kṛt* is used to establish that everything created by the Lord is factual, never false. The creation may be temporary, but it is not false.

TEXT 12

य एष राजन्नपि काल ईशिता
सत्त्वं सुरानीकमिवैधयत्यतः ।
तत्प्रत्यनीकानसुरान् सुरप्रियो
रजस्तमस्कान् प्रमिणोत्युरुश्रवाः ॥१२॥

ya eṣa rājann api kāla īśitā
sattvaṁ surānīkam ivaidhayaty ataḥ
tat-pratyanīkān asurān sura-priyo
rajas-tamaskān pramiṇoty uruśravāḥ

yaḥ—which; *eṣaḥ*—this; *rājan*—O King; *api*—even; *kālaḥ*—time; *īśitā*—the Supreme Lord; *sattvam*—the mode of goodness; *sura-*

anīkam—numbers of demigods; *iva*—certainly; *edhayati*—causes to increase; *ataḥ*—hence; *tat-pratyanīkān*—inimical to them; *asurān*—the demons; *sura-priyaḥ*—being the friend of the demigods; *rajaḥ-tamaskān*—covered by passion and ignorance; *pramiṇoti*—destoys; *uru-śravāḥ*—whose glories are widespread.

TRANSLATION

O King, this time factor enhances the sattva-guṇa. Thus although the Supreme Lord is the controller, He favors the demigods, who are mostly situated in sattva-guṇa. Then the demons, who are influenced by tamo-guṇa, are annihilated. The Supreme Lord induces the time factor to act in different ways, but He is never partial. Rather, His activities are glorious, therefore He is called Uruśravā.

PURPORT

The Lord says in *Bhagavad-gītā* (9.29), *samo 'haṁ sarva-bhūteṣu na me dveṣyo 'sti na priyaḥ:* "I envy no one, nor am I partial to anyone. I am equal to all." The Supreme Personality of Godhead cannot be partial; He is always equal to everyone. Therefore when the demigods are favored and the demons killed, this is not His partiality but the influence of the time factor. A good example in this regard is that an electrician connects both a heater and a cooler to the same electrical energy. The cause of the heating and cooling is the electrician's manipulation of the electrical energy according to his desire, but factually the electrician has nothing to do with causing heat or cold, nor with the enjoyment or suffering that results.

There have been many historical incidents in which the Lord killed a demon, but the demon attained a higher position by the mercy of the Lord. Pūtanā is an example. Pūtanā's purpose was to kill Kṛṣṇa. *Aho bakī yaṁ stana-kāla-kūṭam.* She approached the house of Nanda Mahārāja with the purpose of killing Kṛṣṇa by smearing poison on her breast, yet when she was killed she attained the highest position, achieving the status of Kṛṣṇa's mother. Kṛṣṇa is so kind and impartial that because he sucked Pūtanā's breast, He immediately accepted her as His mother. This superfluous activity of killing Pūtanā did not diminish the

Lord's impartiality. He is *suhṛdaṁ sarva-bhūtānām*, the friend of everyone. Therefore partiality cannot apply to the character of the Supreme Personality of Godhead, who always maintains His position as the supreme controller. The Lord killed Pūtanā as an enemy, but because of His being the supreme controller, she attained an exalted position as His mother. Śrīla Madhva Muni therefore remarks, *kāle kāla-viṣaye 'piśitā. dehādi-kāraṇatvāt surānīkam iva sthitaṁ sattvam.* Ordinarily a murderer is hanged, and in the *Manu-saṁhitā* it is said that a king bestows mercy upon a murderer by killing him, thus saving him from various kinds of suffering. Because of his sinful activities, such a murderer is killed by the mercy of the king. Kṛṣṇa, the supreme judge, deals with matters in a similar way because He is the supreme controller. The conclusion, therefore, is that the Lord is always impartial and always very kind to all living entities.

TEXT 13

अत्रैवोदाहृतः पूर्वमितिहासः सुरर्षिणा ।
प्रीत्या महाक्रतौ राजन् पृच्छतेऽजातशत्रवे ॥१३॥

atraivodāhṛtaḥ pūrvam
itihāsaḥ surarṣiṇā
prītyā mahā-kratau rājan
pṛcchate 'jāta-śatrave

atra—in this connection; *eva*—certainly; *udāhṛtaḥ*—was recited; *pūrvam*—previously; *itihāsaḥ*—an old story; *sura-ṛṣiṇā*—by the great sage Nārada; *prītyā*—with joy; *mahā-kratau*—at the great Rājasūya sacrifice; *rājan*—O King; *pṛcchate*—to the inquiring; *ajāta-śatrave*—Mahārāja Yudhiṣṭhira, who had no enemy.

TRANSLATION

Formerly, O King, when Mahārāja Yudhiṣṭhira was performing the Rājasūya sacrifice, the great sage Nārada, responding to his inquiry, recited historical facts showing how the Supreme Personality of Godhead is always impartial, even when killing demons. In this regard he gave a vivid example.

PURPORT

This relates to how the Lord exhibited His impartiality even when killing Śiśupāla in the arena of the Rājasūya *yajña* performed by Mahārāja Yudhiṣṭhira.

TEXTS 14–15

दृष्ट्वा महाद्भुतं राजा राजसूये महाक्रतौ ।
वासुदेवे भगवति सायुज्यं चेदिभूभुजः ॥१४॥
तत्रासीनं सुरऋषिं राजा पाण्डुसुतः क्रतौ ।
पप्रच्छ विस्मितमना मुनीनां शृण्वतामिदम् ॥१५॥

dṛṣṭvā mahādbhutaṁ rājā
rājasūye mahā-kratau
vāsudeve bhagavati
sāyujyaṁ cedibhū-bhujaḥ

tatrāsīnaṁ sura-ṛṣiṁ
rājā pāṇḍu-sutaḥ kratau
papraccha vismita-manā
munīnāṁ śṛṇvatām idam

dṛṣṭvā—after seeing; *mahā-adbhutam*—greatly wonderful; *rājā*—the King; *rājasūye*—called Rājasūya; *mahā-kratau*—at the great sacrifice; *vāsudeve*—into Vāsudeva; *bhagavati*—the Personality of Godhead; *sāyujyam*—merging; *cedibhū-bhujaḥ*—of Śiśupāla, the King of Cedi; *tatra*—there; *āsīnam*—seated; *sura-ṛṣim*—Nārada Muni; *rājā*—the King; *pāṇḍu-sutaḥ*—Yudhiṣṭhira, the son of Pāṇḍu; *kratau*—at the sacrifice; *papraccha*—asked; *vismita-manāḥ*—being struck with wonder; *munīnām*—in the presence of the sages; *śṛṇvatām*—listening; *idam*—this.

TRANSLATION

O King, at the Rājasūya sacrifice, Mahārāja Yudhiṣṭhira, the son of Mahārāja Pāṇḍu, personally saw Śiśupāla merge into the body of the Supreme Lord, Kṛṣṇa. Therefore, struck with wonder, he inquired about the reason for this from the great sage Nārada, who

was seated there. While he inquired, all the sages present also heard him ask his question.

TEXT 16

श्रीयुधिष्ठिर उवाच
अहो अत्यद्भुतं ह्येतद्दुर्लभैकान्तिनामपि ।
वासुदेवे परे तत्त्वे प्राप्तिश्चैद्यस्य विद्विषः ॥१६॥

śrī-yudhiṣṭhira uvāca
aho aty-adbhutaṁ hy etad
durlabhaikāntinām api
vāsudeve pare tattve
prāptiś caidyasya vidviṣaḥ

śrī-yudhiṣṭhiraḥ uvāca—Mahārāja Yudhiṣṭhira said; *aho*—oh; *ati-adbhutam*—very wonderful; *hi*—certainly; *etat*—this; *durlabha*—difficult to attain; *ekāntinām*—for the transcendentalists; *api*—even; *vāsudeve*—in Vāsudeva; *pare*—the supreme; *tattve*—Absolute Truth; *prāptiḥ*—the attainment; *caidyasya*—of Śiśupāla; *vidviṣaḥ*—envious.

TRANSLATION

Mahārāja Yudhiṣṭhira inquired: It is very wonderful that the demon Śiśupāla merged into the body of the Supreme Personality of Godhead even though extremely envious. This sāyujya-mukti is impossible to attain even for great transcendentalists. How then did the enemy of the Lord attain it?

PURPORT

There are two classes of transcendentalists—the *jñānīs* and the *bhaktas.* The *bhaktas* do not aspire to merge into the existence of the Lord, but the *jñānīs* do. Śiśupāla, however, was neither a *jñānī* nor a *bhakta,* yet simply by envy of the Lord he attained an exalted position by merging into the Lord's body. Certainly this was astonishing, and therefore Mahārāja Yudhiṣṭhira inquired about the cause for the Lord's mysterious mercy to Śiśupāla.

TEXT 17

एतद्वेदितुमिच्छामः सर्व एव वयं मुने ।
भगवन्निन्दया वेनो द्विजैस्तमसि पातितः ॥१७॥

etad veditum icchāmaḥ
sarva eva vayaṁ mune
bhagavan-nindayā veno
dvijais tamasi pātitaḥ

etat—this; *veditum*—to know; *icchāmaḥ*—desire; *sarve*—all; *eva*—certainly; *vayam*—we; *mune*—O great sage; *bhagavat-nindayā*—because of blaspheming the Lord; *venaḥ*—Vena, the father of Pṛthu Mahārāja; *dvijaiḥ*—by the *brāhmaṇas; tamasi*—into hell; *pātitaḥ*—was thrown.

TRANSLATION

O great sage, we are all eager to know the cause for this mercy of the Lord. I have heard that formerly a king named Vena blasphemed the Supreme Personality of Godhead and that all the brāhmaṇas consequently obliged him to go to hell. Śiśupāla should also have been sent to hell. How then did he merge into the Lord's existence?

TEXT 18

दमघोषसुतः पाप आरभ्य कलभाषणात् ।
सम्प्रत्यमर्षी गोविन्दे दन्तवक्रश्च दुर्मतिः ॥१८॥

damaghoṣa-sutaḥ pāpa
ārabhya kala-bhāṣaṇāt
sampraty amarṣī govinde
dantavakraś ca durmatiḥ

damaghoṣa-sutaḥ—Śiśupāla, the son of Damaghoṣa; *pāpaḥ*—sinful; *ārabhya*—beginning; *kala-bhāṣaṇāt*—from the unclear speech of a child; *samprati*—even until now; *amarṣī*—envious; *govinde*—toward

Śrī Kṛṣṇa; *dantavakraḥ*—Dantavakra; *ca*—also; *durmatiḥ*—evil-minded.

TRANSLATION

From the very beginning of his childhood, when he could not even speak properly, Śiśupāla, the most sinful son of Damaghoṣa, began blaspheming the Lord, and he continued to be envious of Śrī Kṛṣṇa until death. Similarly, his brother Dantavakra continued the same habits.

TEXT 19

शपतोरसकृद्विष्णुं यद्ब्रह्म परमव्ययम् ।
श्वित्रो न जातो जिह्वायां नान्धं विविशतुस्तमः ॥१९॥

śapator asakṛd viṣṇuṁ
yad brahma param avyayam
śvitro na jāto jihvāyāṁ
nāndhaṁ viviśatus tamaḥ

śapatoḥ—of both Śiśupāla and Dantavakra, who were blaspheming; *asakṛt*—repeatedly; *viṣṇum*—Lord Kṛṣṇa; *yat*—which; *brahma param*—the Supreme Brahman; *avyayam*—without diminution; *śvitraḥ*—white leprosy; *na*—not; *jātaḥ*—appeared; *jihvāyām*—on the tongue; *na*—not; *andham*—dark; *viviśatuḥ*—they did enter; *tamaḥ*—hell.

TRANSLATION

Although these two men—Śiśupāla and Dantavakra—repeatedly blasphemed the Supreme Personality of Godhead, Lord Viṣṇu [Kṛṣṇa], the Supreme Brahman, they were quite healthy. Indeed, their tongues were not attacked by white leprosy, nor did they enter the darkest region of hellish life. We are certainly most surprised by this.

PURPORT

Kṛṣṇa is described by Arjuna in *Bhagavad-gītā* (10.12) as follows: *paraṁ brahma paraṁ dhāma pavitraṁ paramaṁ bhavān.* "You are the

Supreme Brahman, the supreme abode and purifier." Herein this is confirmed. *Viṣṇuṁ yad brahma param avyayam.* The Supreme Viṣṇu is Kṛṣṇa. Kṛṣṇa is the cause of Viṣṇu, not vice versa. Similarly, Brahman is not the cause of Kṛṣṇa; Kṛṣṇa is the cause of Brahman. Therefore Kṛṣṇa is the Parabrahman (*yad brahma param avyayam*).

TEXT 20

कथं तस्मिन् भगवति दुरवग्राह्यधामनि ।
पश्यतां सर्वलोकानां लयमीयतुरञ्जसा ॥२०॥

kathaṁ tasmin bhagavati
duravagrāhya-dhāmani
paśyatāṁ sarva-lokānāṁ
layam īyatur añjasā

katham—how; *tasmin*—that; *bhagavati*—in the Supreme Personality of Godhead; *duravagrāhya*—difficult to attain; *dhāmani*—whose nature; *paśyatām*—looked on; *sarva-lokānām*—while all the people; *layam īyatuḥ*—became absorbed; *añjasā*—easily.

TRANSLATION

How was it possible for Śiśupāla and Dantavakra, in the presence of many exalted persons, to enter very easily into the body of Kṛṣṇa, whose nature is difficult to attain?

PURPORT

Śiśupāla and Dantavakra were formerly Jaya and Vijaya, the doorkeepers of Vaikuṇṭha. Merging into the body of Kṛṣṇa was not their final destination. For some time they remained merged, and later they received the liberations of *sārūpya* and *sālokya*, living on the same planet as the Lord in the same bodily form. The *śāstras* give evidence that if one blasphemes the Supreme Lord, his punishment is to remain in hellish life for many millions of years more than one suffers by killing many *brāhmaṇas.* Śiśupāla, however, instead of entering hellish life, immediately and very easily received *sāyujya-mukti.* That such a privilege had been offered to Śiśupāla was not merely a story. Everyone saw it happen; there was no scarcity of evidence. How did it happen? Mahārāja Yudhiṣṭhira was very much surprised.

TEXT 21

एतद् भ्राम्यति मे बुद्धिर्दीपार्चिरिव वायुना ।
ब्रूह्येतदद्भुततमं भगवान्ह्यत्र कारणम् ॥२१॥

etad bhrāmyati me buddhir
dīpārcir iva vāyunā
brūhy etad adbhutatamaṁ
bhagavān hy atra kāraṇam

etat—concerning this; *bhrāmyati*—is flickering; *me*—my; *buddhiḥ*—intelligence; *dīpa-arciḥ*—the flame of a candle; *iva*—like; *vāyunā*—by the wind; *brūhi*—please tell; *etat*—this; *adbhutatamam*—most wonderful; *bhagavān*—possessing all knowledge; *hi*—indeed; *atra*—here; *kāraṇam*—the cause.

TRANSLATION

This matter is undoubtedly very wonderful. Indeed, my intelligence has become disturbed, just as the flame of a candle is disturbed by a blowing wind. O Nārada Muni, you know everything. Kindly let me know the cause of this wonderful event.

PURPORT

The *śāstras* enjoin, *tad-vijñānārthaṁ sa gurum evābhigacchet:* when one is perplexed by the difficult problems of life, to solve them one must approach a *guru* like Nārada or his representative in the disciplic succession. Mahārāja Yudhiṣṭhira therefore requested Nārada to explain the cause for such a wonderful event.

TEXT 22

श्रीबादरायणिरुवाच
राज्ञस्तद्वच आकर्ण्य नारदो भगवानृषिः ।
तुष्टः प्राह तमाभाष्य शृण्वत्यास्तत्सदः कथाः ॥२२॥

śrī-bādarāyaṇir uvāca
rājñas tad vaca ākarṇya
nārado bhagavān ṛṣiḥ
tuṣṭaḥ prāha tam ābhāṣya
śṛṇvatyās tat-sadaḥ kathāḥ

śrī-bādarāyaṇiḥ uvāca—Śrī Śukadeva Gosvāmī said; *rājñaḥ*—of the King (Yudhiṣṭhira); *tat*—those; *vacaḥ*—words; *ākarṇya*—after hearing; *nāradaḥ*—Nārada Muni; *bhagavān*—powerful; *ṛṣiḥ*—sage; *tuṣṭaḥ*—being satisfied; *prāha*—spoke; *tam*—him; *ābhāṣya*—after addressing; *śṛṇvatyāḥ tat-sadaḥ*—in the presence of the assembly members; *kathāḥ*—the topics.

TRANSLATION

Śrī Śukadeva Gosvāmī said: After hearing the request of Mahārāja Yudhiṣṭhira, Nārada Muni, the most powerful spiritual master, who knew everything, was very pleased. Thus he replied in the presence of everyone taking part in the yajña.

TEXT 23

श्रीनारद उवाच
निन्दनस्तवसत्कारन्यक्कारार्थं कलेवरम् ।
प्रधानपरयो राजन्नविवेकेन कल्पितम् ॥२३॥

śrī-nārada uvāca
nindana-stava-satkāra-
nyakkārārthaṁ kalevaram
pradhāna-parayo rājann
avivekena kalpitam

śrī-nāradaḥ uvāca—Śrī Nārada Muni said; *nindana*—blasphemy; *stava*—praise; *satkāra*—honor; *nyakkāra*—dishonor; *artham*—for the purpose of; *kalevaram*—body; *pradhāna-parayoḥ*—of nature and the Supreme Personality of Godhead; *rājan*—O King; *avivekena*—without discrimination; *kalpitam*—created.

TRANSLATION

The great sage Śrī Nāradajī said: O King, blasphemy and praise, chastisement and respect, are experienced because of ignorance. The body of the conditioned soul is planned by the Lord for suffering in the material world through the agency of the external energy.

PURPORT

In *Bhagavad-gītā* (18.61) it is said:

īśvaraḥ sarva-bhūtānāṁ
hṛd-deśe 'rjuna tiṣṭhati
bhrāmayan sarva-bhūtāni
yantrārūḍhāni māyayā

"The Supreme Lord is situated in everyone's heart, O Arjuna, and is directing the wanderings of all living entities, who are seated as on a machine, made of material energy." A material body is manufactured by the external energy according to the direction of the Supreme Personality of Godhead. The conditioned soul, being seated on this machine, wanders throughout the universe, and because of his bodily conception of life he only suffers. Actually the suffering of being blasphemed and the enjoyment of being praised, the acceptance of a good welcome or of chastisement by harsh words, are felt in the material conception of life; but since the body of the Supreme Personality of Godhead is not material but *sac-cid-ānanda-vigraha,* He is unaffected by insults or greetings, blasphemy or prayers. Being always unaffected and complete, He does not feel extra pleasure when offered nice prayers by the devotee, although the devotee benefits by offering prayers to the Lord. Indeed, the Lord is very kind to His so-called enemy because one who always thinks of the Personality of Godhead as an enemy also benefits, although he thinks of the Lord adversely. If a conditioned soul, thinking of the Lord as an enemy or a friend, somehow or other becomes attached to the Lord, he receives great benefit.

TEXT 24

हिंसा तदभिमानेन दण्डपारुष्ययोर्यथा ।
वैषम्यमिह भूतानां ममाहमिति पार्थिव ॥२४॥

hiṁsā tad-abhimānena
daṇḍa-pāruṣyayor yathā
vaiṣamyam iha bhūtānāṁ
mamāham iti pārthiva

hiṁsā—suffering; *tat*—of this; *abhimānena*—by the false conception; *daṇḍa-pāruṣyayoḥ*—when there is punishment and chastisement; *yathā*—just as; *vaiṣamyam*—misconception; *iha*—here (in this body); *bhūtānām*—of the living entities; *mama-aham*—mine and I; *iti*—thus; *pārthiva*—O lord of the earth.

TRANSLATION

My dear King, the conditioned soul, being in the bodily conception of life, considers his body to be his self and considers everything in relationship with the body to be his. Because he has this wrong conception of life, he is subjected to dualities like praise and chastisement.

PURPORT

Only when a conditioned soul accepts the body as himself does he feel the effects of chastisement or praise. Then he determines one person to be his enemy and another his friend and wants to chastise the enemy and welcome the friend. This creation of friends and enemies is a result of one's bodily conception of life.

TEXT 25

यन्निबद्धोऽभिमानोऽयं तद्वधात्प्राणिनां वधः ।
तथा न यस्य कैवल्यादभिमानोऽखिलात्मनः ।
परस्य दमकर्तुर्हि हिंसा केनास्य कल्प्यते ॥२५॥

yan-nibaddho 'bhimāno 'yaṁ
tad-vadhāt prāṇināṁ vadhaḥ
tathā na yasya kaivalyād
abhimāno 'khilātmanaḥ
parasya dama-kartur hi
hiṁsā kenāsya kalpyate

yat—in which; *nibaddhaḥ*—bound; *abhimānaḥ*—false conception; *ayam*—this; *tat*—of that (body); *vadhāt*—from the annihilation; *prāṇinām*—of the living beings; *vadhaḥ*—annihilation; *tathā*—similarly; *na*—not; *yasya*—of whom; *kaivalyāt*—because of being absolute, one without a second; *abhimānaḥ*—false conception; *akhila-ātmanaḥ*—of the Supersoul of all living entities; *parasya*—the Supreme Personality of Godhead; *dama-kartuḥ*—the supreme controller; *hi*—certainly; *hiṁsā*—harm; *kena*—how; *asya*—His; *kalpyate*—is performed.

TRANSLATION

Because of the bodily conception of life, the conditioned soul thinks that when the body is annihilated the living being is annihilated. Lord Viṣṇu, the Supreme Personality of Godhead, is the supreme controller, the Supersoul of all living entities. Because He has no material body, He has no false conception of "I and mine." It is therefore incorrect to think that He feels pleasure or pain when blasphemed or offered prayers. This is impossible for Him. Thus He has no enemy and no friend. When He chastises the demons it is for their good, and when He accepts the prayers of the devotees it is for their good. He is affected neither by prayers nor by blasphemy.

PURPORT

Because of being covered by material bodies, the conditioned souls, including even greatly learned scholars and falsely educated professors, all think that as soon as the body is finished, everything is finished. This is due to their bodily conception of life. Kṛṣṇa has no such bodily conception, nor is His body different from His self. Therefore, since Kṛṣṇa has no material conception of life, how can He be affected by material prayers and accusations? Kṛṣṇa's body is described herewith as *kaivalya,* nondifferent from Himself. Since everyone has a material bodily conception of life, if Kṛṣṇa had such a conception what would be the difference between Kṛṣṇa and the conditioned soul? Kṛṣṇa's instructions in *Bhagavad-gītā* are accepted as final because He does not possess a material body. As soon as one has a material body he has four deficiencies, but since Kṛṣṇa does not possess a material body, He has no deficiencies. He is always spiritually conscious and blissful. *Īśvaraḥ paramaḥ kṛṣṇaḥ sac-cid-ānanda-vigrahaḥ:* His form is eternal, blissful knowledge. *Sac-cid-ānanda-vigrahaḥ, ānanda-cinmaya-rasa* and *kaivalya* are the same.

Kṛṣṇa can expand Himself as Paramātmā in the core of everyone's heart. In *Bhagavad-gītā* (13.3) this is confirmed. *Kṣetrajñaṁ cāpi māṁ viddhi sarva-kṣetreṣu bhārata:* the Lord is the Paramātmā—the *ātmā* or Superself of all individual souls. Therefore it must naturally be concluded that He has no defective bodily conceptions. Although situated in everyone's body, He has no bodily conception of life. He is always free from such conceptions, and thus He cannot be affected by anything in relation to the material body of the *jīva.*

Kṛṣṇa says in *Bhagavad-gītā* (16.19):

tān ahaṁ dviṣataḥ krūrān
saṁsāreṣu narādhamān
kṣipāmy ajasram aśubhān
āsurīṣv eva yoniṣu

"Those who are envious and mischievous, who are the lowest among men, are cast by Me into the ocean of material existence, into various demoniac species of life." Whenever the Lord punishes persons like demons, however, such punishment is meant for the good of the conditioned soul. The conditioned soul, being envious of the Supreme Personality of Godhead, may accuse Him, saying, "Kṛṣṇa is bad, Kṛṣṇa is a thief" and so on, but Kṛṣṇa, being kind to all living entities, does not consider such accusations. Instead, He takes account of the conditioned soul's chanting of "Kṛṣṇa, Kṛṣṇa" so many times. He sometimes punishes such demons for one life by putting them in a lower species, but then, when they have stopped accusing Him, they are liberated in the next life because of chanting Kṛṣṇa's name constantly. Blaspheming the Supreme Lord or His devotee is not at all good for the conditioned soul, but Kṛṣṇa, being very kind, punishes the conditioned soul in one life for such sinful activities and then takes him back home, back to Godhead. The vivid example for this is Vṛtrāsura, who was formerly Citraketu Mahārāja, a great devotee. Because he derided Lord Śiva, the foremost of all devotees, he had to accept the body of a demon called Vṛtra, but then he was taken back to Godhead. Thus when Kṛṣṇa punishes a demon or conditioned soul, He stops that soul's habit of blaspheming Him, and when the soul becomes completely pure, the Lord takes him back to Godhead.

TEXT 26

तस्माद्वैरानुबन्धेन निर्वैरेण भयेन वा ।
स्नेहात्कामेन वा युञ्ज्यात् कथञ्चिन्नेक्षते पृथक् ॥२६॥

tasmād vairānubandhena
nirvaireṇa bhayena vā
snehāt kāmena vā yuñjyāt
kathañcin nekṣate pṛthak

tasmāt—therefore; *vaira-anubandhena*—by constant enmity; *nirvaireṇa*—by devotion; *bhayena*—by fear; *vā*—or; *snehāt*—from affection; *kāmena*—by lusty desires; *vā*—or; *yuñjyāt*—one should concentrate; *kathañcit*—somehow or other; *na*—not; *īkṣate*—sees; *pṛthak*—something else.

TRANSLATION

Therefore by enmity or by devotional service, by fear, by affection or by lusty desire—by all of these or any one of them—if a conditioned soul somehow or other concentrates his mind upon the Lord, the result is the same, for the Lord, because of His blissful position, is never affected by enmity or friendship.

PURPORT

From this verse one should not conclude that because Kṛṣṇa is unaffected by favorable prayers or unfavorable blasphemy one should therefore blaspheme the Supreme Lord. This is not the regulative principle. *Bhakti-yoga* means *ānukūlyena kṛṣṇānuśīlanam:* one should serve Kṛṣṇa very favorably. This is the real injunction. Here it is said that although an enemy thinks of Kṛṣṇa unfavorably, the Lord is unaffected by such antidevotional service. Thus He offers His benedictions even to Śiśupāla and similarly inimical conditioned souls. This does not mean, however, that one should be inimical toward the Lord. The stress is given to the favorable execution of devotional service, not purposeful blasphemy of the Lord. It is said:

nindāṁ bhagavataḥ śṛṇvaṁs
tat-parasya janasya vā
tato nāpaiti yaḥ so 'pi
yāty adhaḥ sukṛtāc cyutaḥ

One who hears blasphemy of the Supreme Personality of Godhead or His devotees should immediately take action or should leave. Otherwise he will be put into hellish life perpetually. There are many such injunctions. Therefore as a regulative principle one should not be unfavorable toward the Lord but always favorably inclined toward Him.

Śiśupāla's achievement of oneness with the Supreme Lord was different because Jaya and Vijaya, from the very beginning of their material existence, were ordained to treat the Supreme Lord as an enemy for three lives and then return home, back to Godhead. Jaya and Vijaya inwardly knew that Kṛṣṇa is the Supreme Personality of Godhead, but they purposely became His enemies to be delivered from material life. From the very beginning of their lives they thought of Lord Kṛṣṇa as an enemy, and even though blaspheming Lord Kṛṣṇa, they chanted the holy name of Kṛṣṇa constantly along with their inimical thoughts. Thus they were purified because of chanting the holy name of Kṛṣṇa. It is to be understood that even a blasphemer can be freed from sinful activities by chanting the holy name of the Lord. Certainly, therefore, freedom is assured for a devotee who is always favorable to the service of the Lord. This will be clear from the following verse. By rapt attention fixed upon Kṛṣṇa, one is purified, and thus one is delivered from material life.

Śrīla Viśvanātha Cakravartī Ṭhākura has very nicely explained the word *bhayena,* which means "by fear." When the *gopīs* went to Kṛṣṇa in the dead of night, they certainly feared chastisement by their relatives—their husbands, brothers and fathers—but nonetheless, not caring for their relatives, they went to Kṛṣṇa. There was certainly fear, but this fear could not check their devotional service to Kṛṣṇa.

One should not mistakenly think that Lord Kṛṣṇa must be worshiped by an inimical attitude like that of Śiśupāla. The injunction is *ānukūlyasya grahaṇaṁ prātikūlyasya varjanam:* one should give up unfavorable activities and accept only favorable conditions in devotional service. Generally, if one blasphemes the Supreme Personality of Godhead he is punished. As the Lord says in *Bhagavad-gītā* (16.19):

tān ahaṁ dviṣataḥ krūrān
saṁsāreṣu narādhamān
kṣipāmy ajasram aśubhān
āsurīṣv eva yoniṣu

There are many such injunctions. One should not try to worship Kṛṣṇa unfavorably; otherwise he must be punished, at least for one life, to be purified. As one should not try to be killed by embracing an enemy, a tiger or a snake, one should not blaspheme the Supreme Personality of Godhead and become His enemy in order to be put into hellish life.

The purpose of this verse is to emphasize that even the enemy of the Lord can be delivered, not to speak of His friend. Śrīla Madhvācārya also says in many ways that one should not blaspheme Lord Viṣṇu through one's mind, words or actions, for a blasphemer will go to hellish life along with his forefathers.

karmaṇā manasā vācā
yo dviṣyād viṣṇum avyayam
majjanti pitaras tasya
narake śāśvatīḥ samāḥ

In *Bhagavad-gītā* (16.19–20) the Lord says:

tān ahaṁ dviṣataḥ krūrān
saṁsāreṣu narādhamān
kṣipāmy ajasram aśubhān
āsurīṣv eva yoniṣu

āsurīṁ yonim āpannā
mūḍhā janmani janmani
mām aprāpyaiva kaunteya
tato yānty adhamāṁ gatim

"Those who are envious and mischievous, who are the lowest among men, are cast by Me into the ocean of material existence, into various demoniac species of life. Attaining repeated birth amongst the species of demoniac life, such persons can never approach Me. Gradually they sink down to the most abominable type of existence." One who blasphemes the Lord is put into a family of *asuras*, in which there is every chance of forgetting the service of the Lord. Lord Kṛṣṇa further states in *Bhagavad-gītā* (9.11–12):

avajānanti māṁ mūḍhā
mānuṣīṁ tanum āśritam
paraṁ bhāvam ajānanto
mama bhūta-maheśvaram

Mūḍhas, rascals, blaspheme the Supreme Lord because He appears exactly like a human being. They do not know the unlimited opulence of the Supreme Personality of Godhead.

moghāśā mogha-karmāṇo
mogha-jñānā vicetasaḥ
rākṣasīm āsurīṁ caiva
prakṛtiṁ mohinīṁ śritāḥ

Anything done by those who have taken the attitude of enemies will be baffled (*moghāśāḥ*). If these enemies try to be liberated or to merge into the existence of Brahman, if they desire to be elevated to the higher planetary systems as *karmīs*, or even if they desire to return home, back to Godhead, they will certainly be baffled.

As for Hiraṇyakaśipu, although he was extremely inimical toward the Supreme Personality of Godhead, he always thought of his son, who was a great devotee. Therefore by the grace of his son, Prahlāda Mahārāja, Hiraṇyakaśipu was also delivered by the Supreme Personality of Godhead.

hiraṇyakaśipuś cāpi
bhagavan-nindayā tamaḥ
vivakṣur atyagāt sūnoḥ
prahlādasyānubhāvataḥ

The conclusion is that one should not give up pure devotional service. For one's own benefit, one should not imitate Hiraṇyakaśipu or Śiśupāla. This is not the way to achieve success.

TEXT 27

यथा वैरानुबन्धेन मर्त्यस्तन्मयतामियात् ।
न तथा भक्तियोगेन इति मे निश्चिता मतिः ॥२७॥

yathā vairānubandhena
martyas tan-mayatām iyāt
na tathā bhakti-yogena
iti me niścitā matiḥ

yathā—as; *vaira-anubandhena*—by constant enmity; *martyaḥ*—a person; *tat-mayatām*—absorption in Him; *iyāt*—may attain; *na*—not; *tathā*—in a like manner; *bhakti-yogena*—by devotional service; *iti*—thus; *me*—my; *niścitā*—definite; *matiḥ*—opinion.

TRANSLATION

Nārada Muni continued: By devotional service one cannot achieve such intense absorption in thought of the Supreme Personality of Godhead as one can through enmity toward Him. That is my opinion.

PURPORT

Śrīmān Nārada Muni, the topmost pure devotee, praises Kṛṣṇa's enemies like Śiśupāla because their minds are always completely absorbed in Kṛṣṇa. Indeed, he thinks himself deficient in the inspiration of being feelingly absorbed in Kṛṣṇa consciousness. This does not mean, however, that the enemies of Kṛṣṇa are more elevated than Kṛṣṇa's pure devotees. In the *Caitanya-caritāmṛta* (*Ādi* 5.205) Kṛṣṇadāsa Kavirāja Gosvāmī also thinks of himself in such a humble way:

jagāi mādhāi haite muñi se pāpiṣṭha
purīṣera kīṭa haite muñi se laghiṣṭha

"I am a worse sinner than Jagāi and Mādhāi and am even lower than the worms in the stool." A pure devotee always thinks himself more deficient than everyone else. If a devotee approaches Śrīmatī Rādhārāṇī to offer some service to Kṛṣṇa, even Śrīmatī Rādhārāṇī thinks that the devotee is greater than She. Thus Nārada Muni says that according to his opinion the enemies of Kṛṣṇa are better situated because they are fully absorbed in thoughts of Kṛṣṇa in terms of killing Him, just as a very lusty man always thinks of women and their association.

The essential point in this connection is that one should be fully absorbed in thoughts of Kṛṣṇa, twenty-four hours a day. There are many devotees in *rāga-mārga*, which is exhibited in Vṛndāvana. Whether in *dāsya-rasa, sakhya-rasa, vātsalya-rasa* or *mādhurya-rasa*, all the devotees of Kṛṣṇa are always overwhelmed by thoughts of Kṛṣṇa. When Kṛṣṇa is away from Vṛndāvana tending the cows in the forest, the *gopīs*, in the *mādhurya-rasa*, are always absorbed in thoughts of how Kṛṣṇa walks in the forest. The soles of His feet are so soft that the *gopīs* would not dare keep His lotus feet on their soft breasts. Indeed, they consider their breasts a very hard place for the lotus feet of Kṛṣṇa, yet those lotus feet wander in the forest, which is full of thorny plants. The *gopīs* are absorbed in such thoughts at home, although Kṛṣṇa is away from them. Similarly, when Kṛṣṇa plays with His young friends, mother Yaśodā is very much disturbed by thoughts that Kṛṣṇa, because of always playing and not taking His food properly, must be getting weak. These are examples of the exalted ecstasy felt in Kṛṣṇa's service as manifested in Vṛndāvana. This service is indirectly praised by Nārada Muni in this verse. Especially for the conditioned soul, Nārada Muni recommends that one somehow or other be absorbed in thoughts of Kṛṣṇa, for that will save one from all the dangers of material existence. Full absorption in thought of Kṛṣṇa is the highest platform of *bhakti-yoga*.

TEXTS 28–29

कीटः पेशस्कृता रुद्धः कुड्यायां तमनुस्मरन् ।
संरम्भभययोगेन विन्दते तत्स्वरूपताम् ॥२८॥
एवं कृष्णे भगवति मायामनुज ईश्वरे ।
वैरेण पूतपाप्मानस्तमापुरनुचिन्तया ॥२९॥

kīṭaḥ peśaskṛtā ruddhaḥ
kuḍyāyāṁ tam anusmaran
saṁrambha-bhaya-yogena
vindate tat-svarūpatām

evaṁ kṛṣṇe bhagavati
māyā-manuja īśvare
vaireṇa pūta-pāpmānas
tam āpur anucintayā

kīṭaḥ—the grassworm; *peśaskṛtā*—by a bee; *ruddhaḥ*—confined; *kuḍyāyām*—in a hole in a wall; *tam*—that (bee); *anusmaran*—thinking of; *saṁrambha-bhaya-yogena*—through intense fear and enmity; *vindate*—attains; *tat*—of that bee; *sva-rūpatām*—the same form; *evam*—thus; *kṛṣṇe*—in Kṛṣṇa; *bhagavati*—the Personality of Godhead; *māyā-manuje*—who appeared by His own energy in His eternal humanlike form; *īśvare*—the Supreme; *vaireṇa*—by enmity; *pūta-pāpmānaḥ*—those purified of sins; *tam*—Him; *āpuḥ*—attained; *anucintayā*—by thinking of.

TRANSLATION

A grassworm confined in a hole of a wall by a bee always thinks of the bee in fear and enmity and later becomes a bee simply because of such remembrance. Similarly, if the conditioned souls somehow or other think of Kṛṣṇa, who is sac-cid-ānanda-vigraha, they will become free from their sins. Whether thinking of Him as their worshipable Lord or an enemy, because of constantly thinking of Him they will regain their spiritual bodies.

PURPORT

In *Bhagavad-gītā* (4.10) the Lord says:

vīta-rāga-bhaya-krodhā
man-mayā mām upāśritāḥ
bahavo jñāna-tapasā
pūtā mad-bhāvam āgatāḥ

"Being freed from attachment, fear and anger, being fully absorbed in Me and taking refuge in Me, many, many persons in the past became purified by knowledge of Me—and thus they all attained transcendental love for Me." There are two ways of constantly thinking of Kṛṣṇa—as a devotee and as an enemy. A devotee, of course, by his knowledge and *tapasya*, becomes free from fear and anger and becomes a pure devotee. Similarly, an enemy, although thinking of Kṛṣṇa inimically, thinks of Him constantly and also becomes purified. This is confirmed elsewhere in *Bhagavad-gītā* (9.30), where the Lord says:

api cet sudurācāro
bhajate mām ananya-bhāk
sādhur eva sa mantavyaḥ
samyag vyavasito hi saḥ

"Even if one commits the most abominable actions, if he engages in devotional service he is to be considered saintly because he is properly situated." A devotee undoubtedly worships the Lord with rapt attention. Similarly, if an enemy (*sudurācāraḥ*) always thinks of Kṛṣṇa, he also becomes a purified devotee. The example given here concerns the grassworm that becomes beelike because of constantly thinking of the bee that forces it to enter a hole. By always thinking of the bee in fear, the grassworm starts to become a bee. This is a practical example. Lord Kṛṣṇa appears within this material world for two purposes—*paritrāṇāya sādhūnāṁ vināśāya ca duṣkṛtām:* to protect the devotees and annihilate the demons. The *sādhus* and devotees certainly think of the Lord always, but *duṣkṛtīs*, the demons like Kaṁsa and Śiśupāla, also think of Kṛṣṇa in terms of killing Him. By thinking of Kṛṣṇa, both the demons and devotees attain liberation from the clutches of material *māyā.*

This verse uses the word *māyā-manuje.* When Kṛṣṇa, the Supreme Personality of Godhead, appears in His original spiritual potency (*sambhavāmy ātma-māyayā*), He is not forced to accept a form made by material nature. Therefore the Lord is addressed as *īśvara*, the controller of *māyā.* He is not controlled by *māyā.* When a demon continuously thinks of Kṛṣṇa because of enmity toward Him, he is certainly freed from the sinful reactions of his life. To think of Kṛṣṇa in any way, in terms of His name, form, qualities, paraphernalia or anything pertaining to Him, is beneficial for everyone. *Śṛṇvatāṁ sva-kathāḥ kṛṣṇaḥ puṇya-śravaṇa-kīrtanaḥ.* Thinking of Kṛṣṇa, hearing the holy name of Kṛṣṇa or hearing the pastimes of Kṛṣṇa will make one pure, and then he will become a devotee. Our Kṛṣṇa consciousness movement is therefore trying to introduce the system of somehow or other letting everyone hear the holy name of Kṛṣṇa and take Kṛṣṇa's *prasāda*. Thus one will gradually become a devotee, and his life will be successful.

TEXT 30

कामाद् द्वेषाद्भयात्स्नेहाद्यथा भक्त्येश्वरे मनः ।
आवेश्य तदघं हित्वा बहवस्तद्गतिं गताः ॥३०॥

kāmād dveṣād bhayāt snehād
yathā bhaktyeśvare manaḥ
āveśya tad-aghaṁ hitvā
bahavas tad-gatiṁ gatāḥ

kāmāt—from lust; *dveṣāt*—from hatred; *bhayāt*—from fear; *snehāt*—from affection; *yathā*—as well as; *bhaktyā*—by devotion; *īśvare*—in the Supreme; *manaḥ*—the mind; *āveśya*—absorbing; *tat*—of that; *agham*—sin; *hitvā*—giving up; *bahavaḥ*—many; *tat*—of that; *gatim*—path of liberation; *gatāḥ*—attained.

TRANSLATION

Many, many persons have attained liberation simply by thinking of Kṛṣṇa with great attention and giving up sinful activities. This great attention may be due to lusty desires, inimical feelings, fear, affection or devotional service. I shall now explain how one receives Kṛṣṇa's mercy simply by concentrating one's mind upon Him.

PURPORT

As stated in *Śrīmad-Bhāgavatam* (10.33.39):

vikrīḍitaṁ vraja-vadhūbhir idaṁ ca viṣṇoḥ
śraddhānvito 'nuśṛṇuyād atha varṇayed yaḥ
bhaktiṁ parāṁ bhagavati pratilabhya kāmaṁ
hṛd-rogam āśv apahinoty acireṇa dhīraḥ

If a bona fide listener hears of Kṛṣṇa's pastimes with the *gopīs*, which seem to be lusty affairs, the lusty desires in his heart, which constitute the heart disease of the conditioned soul, will be vanquished, and he will become a most exalted devotee of the Lord. If one who hears of the *gopīs'* lusty behavior with Kṛṣṇa becomes free from lusty desires, certainly the *gopīs* who approached Kṛṣṇa became free from all such desires. Similarly, Śiśupāla and others who were very much envious of Kṛṣṇa and who constantly thought of Kṛṣṇa became free from envy. Nanda Mahārāja and mother Yaśodā were fully absorbed in Kṛṣṇa consciousness because of affection. When the mind is somehow or other fully absorbed in Kṛṣṇa, the material part is very soon vanquished, and the spiritual part—attraction to Kṛṣṇa—becomes manifest. This indirectly confirms that if one thinks of Kṛṣṇa enviously, simply because of thinking of Kṛṣṇa he becomes free from all sinful reactions and thus becomes a pure devotee. Examples of this are given in the following verse.

TEXT 31

गोप्यः कामाद्भयात्कंसो द्वेषाच्चैद्यादयो नृपाः ।
सम्बन्धाद् वृष्णयः स्नेहाद्यूयं भक्त्या वयं विभो ॥३१॥

gopyaḥ kāmād bhayāt kaṁso
dveṣāc caidyādayo nṛpāḥ
sambandhād vṛṣṇayaḥ snehād
yūyaṁ bhaktyā vayaṁ vibho

gopyaḥ—the *gopīs; kāmāt*—out of lusty desires; *bhayāt*—out of fear; *kaṁsaḥ*—King Kaṁsa; *dveṣāt*—out of envy; *caidya-ādayaḥ*—Śiśupāla and others; *nṛpāḥ*—kings; *sambandhāt*—out of kinship; *vṛṣṇayaḥ*—the Vṛṣṇis or the Yādavas; *snehāt*—out of affection; *yūyam*—you (the Pāṇḍavas); *bhaktyā*—by devotional service; *vayam*—we; *vibho*—O great King.

TRANSLATION

My dear King Yudhiṣṭhira, the gopīs by their lusty desires, Kaṁsa by his fear, Śiśupāla and other kings by envy, the Yadus by their familial relationship with Kṛṣṇa, you Pāṇḍavas by your great affection for Kṛṣṇa, and we, the general devotees, by our devotional service, have obtained the mercy of Kṛṣṇa.

PURPORT

Different persons achieve different types of *mukti—sāyujya, sālokya, sārūpya, sāmīpya* and *sārṣṭi*—according to their own intense desire, which is called *bhāva.* Thus it is described here that the *gopīs*, by their lusty desires, which were based upon their intense love for Kṛṣṇa, became the most beloved devotees of the Lord. Although the *gopīs* at Vṛndāvana expressed their lusty desires in relationship with a paramour (*parakīya-rasa*), they actually had no lusty desires. This is significant of spiritual advancement. Their desires appeared lusty, but actually they were not the lusty desires of the material world. *Caitanya-caritāmṛta* compares the desires of the spiritual and material world to gold and iron. Both gold and iron are metal, but there is a vast difference in their value. The lusty desires of the *gopīs* for Kṛṣṇa are compared to gold, and material lusty desires are compared to iron.

Kaṁsa and other enemies of Kṛṣṇa merged into the existence of Brahman, but why should Kṛṣṇa's friends and devotees have the same position? Kṛṣṇa's devotees attain the association of the Lord as His constant companions, either in Vṛndāvana or in the Vaikuṇṭha planets. Similarly, although Nārada Muni wanders in the three worlds, he has exalted devotion for Nārāyaṇa (*aiśvaryamān*). The Vṛṣṇis and Yadus and the father and mother of Kṛṣṇa in Vṛndāvana all have familial relationships with Kṛṣṇa; Kṛṣṇa's foster father and mother in Vṛndāvana, however, are more exalted than Vasudeva and Devakī.

TEXT 32

कतमोऽपि न वेनः स्यात्पञ्चानां पुरुषं प्रति ।
तस्मात् केनाप्युपायेन मनः कृष्णे निवेशयेत् ॥३२॥

katamo 'pi na venaḥ syāt
pañcānāṁ puruṣaṁ prati
tasmāt kenāpy upāyena
manaḥ kṛṣṇe niveśayet

katamaḥ api—anyone; *na*—not; *venaḥ*—the atheistic King Vena; *syāt*—would adopt; *pañcānām*—of the five (previously mentioned); *puruṣam*—the Supreme Personality of Godhead; *prati*—in regard to;

tasmāt—therefore; *kenāpi*—by any; *upāyena*—means; *manaḥ*—the mind; *kṛṣṇe*—in Kṛṣṇa; *niveśayet*—one should fix.

TRANSLATION

Somehow or other, one must consider the form of Kṛṣṇa very seriously. Then, by one of the five different processes mentioned above, one can return home, back to Godhead. Atheists like King Vena, however, being unable to think of Kṛṣṇa's form in any of these five ways, cannot attain salvation. Therefore, one must somehow think of Kṛṣṇa, whether in a friendly way or inimically.

PURPORT

Impersonalists and atheists always try to circumvent the form of Kṛṣṇa. Great politicians and philosophers of the modern age even try to banish Kṛṣṇa from *Bhagavad-gītā.* Consequently, for them there is no salvation. But Kṛṣṇa's enemies think, "Here is Kṛṣṇa, my enemy. I have to kill Him." They think of Kṛṣṇa in His actual form, and thus they attain salvation. Devotees, therefore, who constantly think of Kṛṣṇa's form, are certainly liberated. The only business of the Māyāvādī atheists is to make Kṛṣṇa formless, and consequently, because of this severe offense at the lotus feet of Kṛṣṇa, they cannot expect salvation. Śrīla Viśvanātha Cakravartī Ṭhākura says in this connection: *tena śiśupālādi-bhinnaḥ pratikūla-bhāvaṁ didhīṣur yena iva narakaṁ yātīti bhāvaḥ.* Except for Śiśupāla, those who go against the regulative principles cannot attain salvation and are surely destined for hellish life. The regulative principle is that one must always think of Kṛṣṇa, whether as a friend or enemy.

TEXT 33

मातृष्वस्रेयो वश्चैद्यो दन्तवक्रश्च पाण्डव ।
पार्षदप्रवरौ विष्णोर्विप्रशापात्पदच्युतौ ॥३३॥

mātṛ-ṣvasreyo vaś caidyo
dantavakraś ca pāṇḍava
pārṣada-pravarau viṣṇor
vipra-śāpāt pada-cyutau

mātṛ-svasreyaḥ—the son of the mother's sister (Śiśupāla); *vaḥ*—your; *caidyaḥ*—King Śiśupāla; *dantavakraḥ*—Dantavakra; *ca*—and; *pāṇḍava*—O Pāṇḍava; *parṣada-pravarau*—two exalted attendants; *viṣṇoḥ*—of Viṣṇu; *vipra*—by *brāhmaṇas; śāpāt*—because of a curse; *pada*—from their position in Vaikuṇṭha; *cyutau*—fallen.

TRANSLATION

Nārada Muni continued: O best of the Pāṇḍavas, your two cousins Śiśupāla and Dantavakra, the sons of your maternal aunt, were formerly associates of Lord Viṣṇu, but because they were cursed by brāhmaṇas, they fell from Vaikuṇṭha to this material world.

PURPORT

Śiśupāla and Dantavakra were not ordinary demons, but were formerly personal associates of Lord Viṣṇu. They apparently fell to this material world, but actually they came to assist the Supreme Personality of Godhead by nourishing His pastimes within this world.

TEXT 34

श्रीयुधिष्ठिर उवाच
कीदृशः कस्य वा शापो हरिदासाभिमर्शनः ।
अश्रद्धेय इवाभाति हरेरेकान्तिनां भवः ॥३४॥

śrī-yudhiṣṭhira uvāca
kīdṛśaḥ kasya vā śāpo
hari-dāsābhimarśanaḥ
aśraddheya ivābhāti
harer ekāntināṁ bhavaḥ

śrī-yudhiṣṭhiraḥ uvāca—Mahārāja Yudhiṣṭhira said; *kīdṛśaḥ*—what kind of; *kasya*—whose; *vā*—or; *śāpaḥ*—curse; *hari-dāsa*—the servant of Hari; *abhimarśanaḥ*—overcoming; *aśraddheyaḥ*—incredible; *iva*—as if; *ābhāti*—appears; *hareḥ*—of Hari; *ekāntinām*—of those exclusively devoted as exalted attendants; *bhavaḥ*—birth.

TRANSLATION

Mahārāja Yudhiṣṭhira inquired: What kind of great curse could affect even liberated viṣṇu-bhaktas, and what sort of person could curse even the Lord's associates? For unflinching devotees of the Lord to fall again to this material world is impossible. I cannot believe this.

PURPORT

In *Bhagavad-gītā* (8.16) the Lord clearly states, *mām upetya tu kaunteya punar janma na vidyate:* one who is purified of material contamination and returns home, back to Godhead, does not return to this material world. Elsewhere in *Bhagavad-gītā* (4.9) Kṛṣṇa says:

janma karma ca me divyam
evaṁ yo vetti tattvataḥ
tyaktvā dehaṁ punar janma
naiti mām eti so 'rjuna

"One who knows the transcendental nature of My appearance and activities does not, upon leaving the body, take his birth again in this material world, but attains My eternal abode, O Arjuna." Mahārāja Yudhiṣṭhira, therefore, was surprised that a pure devotee could return to this material world. This is certainly a very important question.

TEXT 35

देहेन्द्रियासुहीनानां वैकुण्ठपुरवासिनाम् ।
देहसम्बन्धसम्बद्धमेतदाख्यातुमर्हसि ॥३५॥

dehendriyāsu-hīnānāṁ
vaikuṇṭha-pura-vāsinām
deha-sambandha-sambaddham
etad ākhyātum arhasi

deha—of a material body; *indriya*—material senses; *asu*—life breath; *hīnānām*—of those devoid; *vaikuṇṭha-pura*—of Vaikuṇṭha; *vāsinām*—of the residents; *deha-sambandha*—in a material body; *sambaddham*—bondage; *etat*—this; *ākhyātum arhasi*—please describe.

TRANSLATION

The bodies of the inhabitants of Vaikuṇṭha are completely spiritual, having nothing to do with the material body, senses or life air. Therefore, kindly explain how associates of the Personality of Godhead were cursed to descend in material bodies like ordinary persons.

PURPORT

This very significant question would be difficult for an ordinary person to answer, but Nārada Muni, being an authority, could answer it. Therefore Mahārāja Yudhiṣṭhira inquired from him, saying, *etad ākhyātum arhasi:* "only you can explain the reason." From authoritative sources it can be discerned that associates of Lord Viṣṇu who descend from Vaikuṇṭha do not actually fall. They come with the purpose of fulfilling the desire of the Lord, and their descent to this material world is comparable to that of the Lord. The Lord comes to this material world through the agency of His internal potency, and similarly, when a devotee or associate of the Lord descends to this material world, he does so through the action of the spiritual energy. Any pastime conducted by the Supreme Personality of Godhead is an arrangement by *yogamāyā,* not *mahāmāyā.* Therefore it is to be understood that when Jaya and Vijaya descended to this material world, they came because there was something to be done for the Supreme Personality of Godhead. Otherwise it is a fact that no one falls from Vaikuṇṭha.

Of course, a living entity who desires *sāyujya-mukti* remains in Kṛṣṇa's Brahman effulgence, which is dependent on Kṛṣṇa's body (*brahmaṇo hi pratiṣṭhāham*). Such an impersonalist who takes shelter of the Brahman effulgence must surely fall down. This is stated in the *śāstra* (*Bhāg.* 10.2.32):

ye 'nye 'ravindākṣa vimukta-māninas
tvayy asta-bhāvād aviśuddha-buddhayaḥ
āruhya kṛcchreṇa paraṁ padaṁ tataḥ
patanty adho 'nādṛta-yuṣmad-aṅghrayaḥ

"O Lord, the intelligence of those who think themselves liberated but who have no devotion is impure. Even though they rise to the highest point of liberation by dint of severe penances and austerities, they are sure to fall down again into material existence, for they do not take shelter at Your lotus feet." The impersonalists cannot reach the Vaikuṇṭha planets to become associates of the Lord, and therefore, according to their desires, Kṛṣṇa gives them *sāyujya-mukti.* However, since *sāyujya-mukti* is partial *mukti,* they must fall again to this material world. When it is said that the individual soul falls from Brahmaloka, this applies to the impersonalist.

From authoritative sources it is learned that Jaya and Vijaya were sent to this material world to fulfill the Lord's desire to fight. The Lord also sometimes wants to fight, but who can fight with the Lord but a very confidential devotee of the Lord? Jaya and Vijaya descended to this world to fulfill the Lord's desire. Therefore in each of their three births—first as Hiraṇyākṣa and Hiraṇyakaśipu, second as Rāvaṇa and Kumbhakarṇa, and third as Śiśupāla and Dantavakra—the Lord personally killed them. In other words, these associates of the Lord, Jaya and Vijaya, descended to the material world to serve the Lord by fulfilling His desire to fight. Otherwise, as Mahārāja Yudhiṣṭhira says, *aśraddheya ivābhāti:* the statement that a servant of the Lord could fall from Vaikuṇṭha seems unbelievable. How Jaya and Vijaya came to this material world is explained by Nārada Muni as follows.

TEXT 36

श्रीनारद उवाच
एकदा ब्रह्मणः पुत्रा विष्णुलोकं यदृच्छया ।
सनन्दनादयो जग्मुश्चरन्तो भुवनत्रयम् ॥३६॥

śrī-nārada uvāca
ekadā brahmaṇaḥ putrā
viṣṇu-lokaṁ yadṛcchayā
sanandanādayo jagmuś
caranto bhuvana-trayam

śrī-nāradaḥ uvāca—Śrī Nārada Muni said; *ekadā*—once upon a time; *brahmaṇaḥ*—of Lord Brahmā; *putrāḥ*—the sons; *viṣṇu*—of Lord Viṣṇu; *lokam*—the planet; *yadṛcchayā*—by chance; *sanandana-*

ādayaḥ—Sanandana and the others; *jagmuḥ*—went; *carantaḥ*—traveling about; *bhuvana-trayam*—the three worlds.

TRANSLATION

The great saint Nārada said: Once upon a time when the four sons of Lord Brahmā named Sanaka, Sanandana, Sanātana and Sanat-kumāra were wandering throughout the three worlds, they came by chance to Viṣṇuloka.

TEXT 37

पञ्चषड्ढायनार्भाभाः पूर्वेषामपि पूर्वजाः ।
दिग्वाससःशिशून् मत्वा द्वाःस्थौ तान् प्रत्यषेधताम् ॥ ३७॥

pañca-ṣaḍḍhāyanārbhābhāḥ
pūrveṣām api pūrvajāḥ
dig-vāsasaḥ śiśūn matvā
dvāḥ-sthau tān pratyaṣedhatām

pañca-ṣaṭ-dhā—five or six years; *āyana*—approaching; *arbha-ābhāḥ*—like boys; *pūrveṣām*—the ancients of the universe (Marīci and the rest); *api*—even though; *pūrva-jāḥ*—born before; *dik-vāsasaḥ*—being naked; *śiśūn*—children; *matvā*—thinking; *dvāḥ-sthau*—the two gate guards, Jaya and Vijaya; *tān*—them; *pratyaṣedhatām*—forbade.

TRANSLATION

Although these four great sages were older than Brahmā's other sons like Marīci, they appeared like small naked children only five or six years old. When Jaya and Vijaya saw them trying to enter Vaikuṇṭhaloka, these two gatekeepers, thinking them ordinary children, forbade them to enter.

PURPORT

In this regard, Śrīla Madhvācārya says in his *Tantra-sāra:*

dvāḥ-sthāv ity anenādhikāra-sthatvam uktam

adhikāra-sthitāś caiva
vimuktāś ca dvidhā janāḥ
viṣṇu-loka-sthitās teṣāṁ
vara-śāpādi-yoginaḥ

adhikāra-sthitāṁ muktiṁ
niyataṁ prāpnuvanti ca
vimukty-anantaraṁ teṣāṁ
vara-śāpādayo nanu

dehendriyāsu-yuktaś ca
pūrvaṁ paścān na tair yutāḥ
apy abhimānibhis teṣāṁ
devaiḥ svātmottamair yutāḥ

The purport is that the personal associates of Lord Viṣṇu in Vaikuṇṭhaloka are always liberated souls. Even if sometimes cursed or blessed, they are always liberated and never contaminated by the material modes of nature. Before their liberation to Vaikuṇṭhaloka they possessed material bodies, but once they come to Vaikuṇṭha they no longer have them. Therefore even if the associates of Lord Viṣṇu sometimes descend as if cursed, they are always liberated.

TEXT 38

अशपन् कुपिता एवं युवां वासं न चार्हथः ।
रजस्तमोभ्यां रहिते पादमूले मधुद्विषः ।
पापिष्ठामासुरीं योनिं बालिशौ यातमाश्वतः ॥३८॥

aśapan kupitā evaṁ
yuvāṁ vāsaṁ na cārhathaḥ
rajas-tamobhyāṁ rahite
pāda-mūle madhudviṣaḥ
pāpiṣṭhām āsurīṁ yoniṁ
bāliśau yātam āśv ataḥ

aśapan—cursed; *kupitāḥ*—being full of anger; *evam*—thus; *yuvām*—you two; *vāsam*—residence; *na*—not; *ca*—and; *arhathaḥ*—deserve; *rajaḥ-tamobhyām*—from passion and ignorance; *rahite*—free; *pāda-mūle*—at the lotus feet; *madhu-dviṣaḥ*—of Viṣṇu, the slayer of the Madhu demon; *pāpiṣṭhām*—most sinful; *āsurīm*—demoniac; *yonim*—to a womb; *bāliśau*—O you two fools; *yātam*—go; *āśu*—quickly hereafter; *ataḥ*—therefore.

TRANSLATION

Thus checked by the doorkeepers Jaya and Vijaya, Sanandana and the other great sages very angrily cursed them. "You two foolish doorkeepers," they said. "Being agitated by the material qualities of passion and ignorance, you are unfit to live at the shelter of Madhudviṣa's lotus feet, which are free from such modes. It would be better for you to go immediately to the material world and take your birth in a family of most sinful asuras."

TEXT 39

एवं शप्तौ स्वभवनात् पतन्तौ तौ कृपालुभिः ।
प्रोक्तौ पुनर्जन्मभिर्वां त्रिभिर्लोकाय कल्पताम् ॥३९॥

evaṁ śaptau sva-bhavanāt
patantau tau kṛpālubhiḥ
proktau punar janmabhir vāṁ
tribhir lokāya kalpatām

evam—thus; *śaptau*—being cursed; *sva-bhavanāt*—from their abode, Vaikuṇṭha; *patantau*—falling down; *tau*—those two (Jaya and Vijaya); *kṛpālubhiḥ*—by the merciful sages (Sanandana, etc.); *proktau*—addressed; *punaḥ*—again; *janmabhiḥ*—with births; *vām*—your; *tribhiḥ*—three; *lokāya*—for the position; *kalpatām*—let it be possible.

TRANSLATION

While Jaya and Vijaya, thus cursed by the sages, were falling to the material world, they were addressed as follows by the same

sages, who were very kind to them. "O doorkeepers, after three births you will be able to return to your positions in Vaikuṇṭha, for then the duration of the curse will have ended."

TEXT 40

जज्ञाते तौ दितेः पुत्रौ दैत्यदानववन्दितौ ।
हिरण्यकशिपुर्ज्येष्ठो हिरण्याक्षोऽनुजस्ततः ॥४०॥

jajñāte tau diteḥ putrau
daitya-dānava-vanditau
hiraṇyakaśipur jyeṣṭho
hiraṇyākṣo 'nujas tataḥ

jajñāte—were born; *tau*—the two; *diteḥ*—of Diti; *putrau*—the sons; *daitya-dānava*—by all the demons; *vanditau*—being worshiped; *hiraṇyakaśipuḥ*—Hiraṇyakaśipu; *jyeṣṭhaḥ*—the elder; *hiraṇyākṣaḥ*—Hiraṇyākṣa; *anujaḥ*—the younger; *tataḥ*—thereafter.

TRANSLATION

These two associates of the Lord—Jaya and Vijaya—later descended to the material world, taking birth as the two sons of Diti, Hiraṇyakaśipu being the elder and Hiraṇyākṣa the younger. They were very much respected by the Daityas and Dānavas [demoniac species].

TEXT 41

हतो हिरण्यकशिपुर्हरिणा सिंहरूपिणा ।
हिरण्याक्षो धरोद्धारे बिभ्रता शौकरं वपुः ॥४१॥

hato hiraṇyakaśipur
hariṇā siṁha-rūpiṇā
hiraṇyākṣo dharoddhāre
bibhratā śaukaraṁ vapuḥ

hataḥ—killed; *hiraṇyakaśipuḥ*—Hiraṇyakaśipu; *hariṇā*—by Hari, Viṣṇu; *siṁha-rūpiṇā*—in the form of a lion (Lord Narasiṁha);

hiraṇyākṣaḥ—Hiraṇyākṣa; *dharā-uddhāre*—to lift the earth; *bibhratā*—assuming; *śaukaram*—the boarlike; *vapuḥ*—form.

TRANSLATION

Appearing as Nṛsiṁhadeva, the Supreme Personality of Godhead, Śrī Hari, killed Hiraṇyakaśipu. When the Lord delivered the planet earth, which had fallen in the Garbhodaka Ocean, Hiraṇyākṣa tried to hinder Him, and then the Lord, as Varāha, killed Hiraṇyākṣa.

TEXT 42

हिरण्यकशिपुः पुत्रं प्रह्लादं केशवप्रियम् ।
जिघांसुरकरोन्नाना यातना मृत्युहेतवे ॥४२॥

hiraṇyakaśipuḥ putraṁ
prahlādaṁ keśava-priyam
jighāṁsur akaron nānā
yātanā mṛtyu-hetave

hiraṇyakaśipuḥ—Hiraṇyakaśipu; *putram*—son; *prahlādam*—Prahlāda Mahārāja; *keśava-priyam*—the beloved devotee of Keśava; *jighāṁsuḥ*—desirous of killing; *akarot*—enacted; *nānā*—various; *yātanāḥ*—tortures; *mṛtyu*—death; *hetave*—to cause.

TRANSLATION

Desiring to kill his son Prahlāda, who was a great devotee of Lord Viṣṇu, Hiraṇyakaśipu tortured him in many ways.

TEXT 43

तं सर्वभूतात्मभूतं प्रशान्तं समदर्शनम् ।
भगवत्तेजसा स्पृष्टं नाशक्नोद्धन्तुमुद्यमैः ॥४३॥

taṁ sarva-bhūtātma-bhūtaṁ
praśāntaṁ sama-darśanam

bhagavat-tejasā spṛṣṭaṁ
nāśaknod dhantum udyamaiḥ

tam—Him; *sarva-bhūta-ātma-bhūtam*—the soul in all entities; *praśāntam*—peaceful and without hatred, etc.; *sama-darśanam*—equal to everyone; *bhagavat-tejasā*—with the power of the Supreme Personality of Godhead; *spṛṣṭam*—protected; *na*—not; *aśaknot*—was able; *hantum*—to kill; *udyamaiḥ*—by great attempts and various weapons.

TRANSLATION

The Lord, the Supersoul of all living entities, is sober, peaceful and equal to everyone. Since the great devotee Prahlāda was protected by the Lord's potency, Hiraṇyakaśipu was unable to kill him, in spite of endeavoring to do so in various ways.

PURPORT

In this verse the word *sarva-bhūtātma-bhūtam* is very significant. *Īśvaraḥ sarva-bhūtānāṁ hṛd-deśe 'rjuna tiṣṭhati:* the Lord is equally situated in the core of everyone's heart. Thus He cannot be envious of anyone or friendly to anyone; for Him everyone is the same. Although He is sometimes seen to punish someone, this is exactly like a father's punishing his child for the child's welfare. The Supreme Lord's punishment is also a manifestation of the Lord's equality. Therefore the Lord is described as *praśāntaṁ sama-darśanam.* Although the Lord has to execute His will properly, He is equipoised in all circumstances. He is equally disposed toward everyone.

TEXT 44

ततस्तौ राक्षसौ जातौ केशिन्यां विश्रवःसुतौ ।
रावणः कुम्भकर्णश्च सर्वलोकोपतापनौ ॥४४॥

tatas tau rākṣasau jātau
keśinyāṁ viśravaḥ-sutau
rāvaṇaḥ kumbhakarṇaś ca
sarva-lokopatāpanau

tataḥ—thereafter; *tau*—the two doorkeepers (Jaya and Vijaya); *rākṣasau*—demons; *jātau*—born; *keśinyām*—in the womb of Keśinī; *viśravaḥ-sutau*—the sons of Viśravā; *rāvaṇaḥ*—Rāvaṇa; *kumbhakarṇaḥ*—Kumbhakarṇa; *ca*—and; *sarva-loka*—to all people; *upatāpanau*—giving misery.

TRANSLATION

Thereafter the same Jaya and Vijaya, the two doorkeepers of Lord Viṣṇu, took birth as Rāvaṇa and Kumbhakarṇa, begotten by Viśravā in the womb of Keśinī. They were extremely troublesome to all the people of the universe.

TEXT 45

**तत्रापि राघवो भूत्वा न्यहनच्छापमुक्तये ।
रामवीर्यं श्रोष्यसि त्वं मार्कण्डेयमुखात् प्रभो ॥४५॥**

tatrāpi rāghavo bhūtvā
nyahanac chāpa-muktaye
rāma-vīryaṁ śroṣyasi tvaṁ
mārkaṇḍeya-mukhāt prabho

tatra api—thereupon; *rāghavaḥ*—as Lord Rāmacandra; *bhūtvā*—manifesting; *nyahanat*—killed; *śāpa-muktaye*—for freedom from the curse; *rāma-vīryam*—the prowess of Lord Rāma; *śroṣyasi*—will hear; *tvam*—you; *mārkaṇḍeya-mukhāt*—from the lips of the sage Mārkaṇḍeya; *prabho*—O lord.

TRANSLATION

Nārada Muni continued: My dear King, just to relieve Jaya and Vijaya of the brāhmaṇas' curse, Lord Rāmacandra appeared in order to kill Rāvaṇa and Kumbhakarṇa. It will be better for you to hear narrations about Lord Rāmacandra's activities from Mārkaṇḍeya.

TEXT 46

तावत्र क्षत्रियौ जातौ मातृष्वस्रात्मजौ तव ।
अधुना शापनिर्मुक्तौ कृष्णचक्रहतांहसौ ॥४६॥

tāv atra kṣatriyau jātau
mātṛ-ṣvasrātmajau tava
adhunā śāpa-nirmuktau
kṛṣṇa-cakra-hatāṁhasau

tau—the two; *atra*—here, in the third birth; *kṣatriyau*—*kṣatriyas* or kings; *jātau*—born; *mātṛ-svasṛ-ātma-jau*—the sons of the mother's sister; *tava*—your; *adhunā*—now; *śāpa-nirmuktau*—freed from the curse; *kṛṣṇa-cakra*—by the disc weapon of Kṛṣṇa; *hata*—destroyed; *aṁhasau*—whose sins.

TRANSLATION

In their third birth, the same Jaya and Vijaya appeared in a family of kṣatriyas as your cousins, the sons of your aunt. Because Lord Kṛṣṇa has struck them with His disc, all their sinful reactions have been destroyed, and now they are free from the curse.

PURPORT

In their last birth, Jaya and Vijaya did not become demons or Rākṣasas. Instead they took birth in a very exalted *kṣatriya* family related to Kṛṣṇa's family. They became first cousins of Lord Kṛṣṇa and were practically on an equal footing with Him. By personally killing them with His own disc, Lord Kṛṣṇa destroyed whatever sinful reactions were left in them because of the curse of the *brāhmaṇas*. Nārada Muni explained to Mahārāja Yudhiṣṭhira that by entering Kṛṣṇa's body, Śiśupāla reentered Vaikuṇṭhaloka as the Lord's associate. Everyone had seen this incident.

TEXT 47

वैरानुबन्धतीव्रेण ध्यानेनाच्युतसात्मताम् ।
नीतौ पुनर्हरेः पार्श्वं जग्मतुर्विष्णुपार्षदौ ॥४७॥

vairānubandha-tīvreṇa
dhyānenācyuta-sātmatām
nītau punar hareḥ pārśvaṁ
jagmatur viṣṇu-pārṣadau

vaira-anubandha—bond of hatred; *tīvreṇa*—consisting of acute; *dhyānena*—by meditation; *acyuta-sātmatām*—to the effulgence of the infallible Lord; *nītau*—attained; *punaḥ*—again; *hareḥ*—of Hari; *pārśvam*—the proximity; *jagmatuḥ*—they reached; *viṣṇu-pārsadau*—the gatekeeper associates of Viṣṇu.

TRANSLATION

These two associates of Lord Viṣṇu—Jaya and Vijaya—maintained a feeling of enmity for a very long time. Because of always thinking of Kṛṣṇa in this way, they regained the shelter of the Lord, having returned home, back to Godhead.

PURPORT

Whatever their position, certainly Jaya and Vijaya always thought of Kṛṣṇa. Therefore at the end of the *mauṣala-līlā*, these two associates of the Lord returned to Kṛṣṇa. There is no difference between Kṛṣṇa's body and Nārāyaṇa's body. Therefore although they visibly entered the body of Kṛṣṇa, they actually reentered Vaikuṇṭhaloka as the doorkeepers of Lord Viṣṇu. Through Lord Kṛṣṇa's body, they returned to Vaikuṇṭha, although they seemed to have attained *sāyujya-mukti* in Kṛṣṇa's body.

TEXT 48

श्रीयुधिष्ठिर उवाच
विद्वेषो दयिते पुत्रे कथमासीन्महात्मनि ।
ब्रूहि मे भगवन्येन प्रह्लादस्याच्युतात्मता ॥४८॥

śrī-yudhiṣṭhira uvāca
vidveṣo dayite putre
katham āsīn mahātmani
brūhi me bhagavan yena
prahlādasyācyutātmatā

śrī-yudhiṣṭhiraḥ uvāca—Mahārāja Yudhiṣṭhira said; *vidveṣaḥ*—hatred; *dayite*—for his own beloved; *putre*—son; *katham*—how; *āsīt*—there was; *mahā-ātmani*—the great soul, Prahlāda; *brūhi*—please tell; *me*—unto me; *bhagavan*—O exalted sage; *yena*—by which; *prahlādasya*—of Prahlāda Mahārāja; *acyuta*—to Acyuta; *ātmatā*—great attachment.

TRANSLATION

Mahārāja Yudhiṣṭhira inquired: O my lord, Nārada Muni, why was there such enmity between Hiraṇyakaśipu and his beloved son Prahlāda Mahārāja? How did Prahlāda Mahārāja become such a great devotee of Lord Kṛṣṇa? Kindly explain this to me.

PURPORT

All the devotees of Lord Kṛṣṇa are called *acyutātmā* because they follow in the footsteps of Prahlāda Mahārāja. Acyuta refers to the infallible Lord Viṣṇu, whose heart is always infallible. Because the devotees are attached to the Infallible, they are called *acyutātmā.*

Thus end the Bhaktivedanta purports of the Seventh Canto, First Chapter, of the Śrīmad-Bhāgavatam, *entitled "The Supreme Lord Is Equal to Everyone."*

CHAPTER TWO

Hiraṇyakaśipu, King of the Demons

As described in this chapter, after the annihilation of Hiraṇyākṣa, Hiraṇyākṣa's sons and his brother Hiraṇyakaśipu were very much aggrieved. Hiraṇyakaśipu reacted very sinfully by trying to diminish the religious activities of people in general. However, he instructed his nephews about a history just to diminish their aggrievement.

When the Supreme Personality of Godhead appeared as the boar and killed Hiraṇyakaśipu's brother Hiraṇyākṣa, Hiraṇyakaśipu was very much aggrieved. In anger, he accused the Supreme Personality of Godhead of being partial to His devotees and derided the Lord's appearance as Varāha to kill his brother. He began to agitate all the demons and Rākṣasas and disturb the ritualistic ceremonies of the peaceful sages and other inhabitants of earth. For want of the performance of *yajña*, sacrifice, the demigods began wandering unseen on earth.

After finishing the ritualistic funeral ceremonies of his brother, Hiraṇyakaśipu began speaking to his nephews, quoting from the *śāstras* about the truth of life. To pacify them, he spoke as follows: "My dear nephews, for heroes to die before the enemy is glorious. According to their different fruitive activities, living entities come together within this material world and are again separated by the laws of nature. We should always know, however, that the spirit soul, which is different from the body, is eternal, inadjustable, pure, all-pervading and aware of everything. When bound by the material energy, the soul takes birth in higher or lower species of life according to varying association and in this way receives various types of bodies in which to suffer or enjoy. One's affliction by the conditions of material existence is the cause of happiness and distress; there are no other causes, and one should not be aggrieved upon seeing the superficial actions of *karma*."

Hiraṇyakaśipu then related a historical incident concerning a King Suyajña who resided in the country named Uśīnara. When the King was killed, his queens, overwhelmed with grief, received instructions, which

Hiraṇyakaśipu quoted to his nephews. Hiraṇyakaśipu related an account of a *kuliṅga* bird pierced by the arrow of a hunter while lamenting for his wife, who had also been shot by the same hunter. By narrating these stories, Hiraṇyakaśipu pacified his nephews and other relatives and relieved them of lamentation. Thus having been pacified, Diti and Ruṣābhānu, Hiraṇyakaśipu's mother and sister-in-law, engaged their minds in spiritual understanding.

TEXT 1

श्रीनारद उवाच
भ्रातर्येवं विनिहते हरिणा क्रोडमूर्तिना ।
हिरण्यकशिपू राजन् पर्यतप्यद्रुषा शुचा ॥ १ ॥

śrī-nārada uvāca
bhrātary evaṁ vinihate
hariṇā kroḍa-mūrtinā
hiraṇyakaśipū rājan
paryatapyad ruṣā śucā

śrī-nāradaḥ uvāca—Śrī Nārada Muni said; *bhrātari*—when the brother (Hiraṇyākṣa); *evam*—thus; *vinihate*—was killed; *hariṇā*—by Hari; *kroḍa-mūrtinā*—in the form of the boar, Varāha; *hiraṇya-kaśipuḥ*—Hiraṇyakaśipu; *rājan*—O King; *paryatapyat*—was afflicted; *ruṣā*—by anger; *śucā*—by grief.

TRANSLATION

Śrī Nārada Muni said: My dear King Yudhiṣṭhira, when Lord Viṣṇu, in the form of Varāha, the boar, killed Hiraṇyākṣa, Hiraṇyākṣa's brother Hiraṇyakaśipu was extremely angry and began to lament.

PURPORT

Yudhiṣṭhira had inquired from Nārada Muni why Hiraṇyakaśipu was so envious of his own son Prahlāda. Nārada Muni began narrating the story by explaining how Hiraṇyakaśipu had become a staunch enemy of Lord Viṣṇu.

TEXT 2

आह चेदं रुषा पूर्णः सन्दष्टदशनच्छदः ।
कोपोज्ज्वलद्भ्यां चक्षुर्भ्यां निरीक्षन् धूम्रमम्बरम् ॥ २ ॥

āha cedaṁ ruṣā pūrṇaḥ
sandaṣṭa-daśana-cchadaḥ
kopojjvaladbhyāṁ cakṣurbhyāṁ
nirīkṣan dhūmram ambaram

āha—said; *ca*—and; *idam*—this; *ruṣā*—with anger; *pūrṇaḥ*—full; *sandaṣṭa*—bitten; *daśana-chadaḥ*—whose lips; *kopa-ujjvaladbhyām*—blazing with anger; *cakṣurbhyām*—with eyes; *nirīkṣan*—looking over; *dhūmram*—smoky; *ambaram*—the sky.

TRANSLATION

Filled with rage and biting his lips, Hiraṇyakaśipu gazed at the sky with eyes that blazed in anger, making the whole sky smoky. Thus he began to speak.

PURPORT

As usual, the demon is envious of the Supreme Personality of Godhead and inimical toward Him. These were Hiraṇyakaśipu's external bodily features as he considered how to kill Lord Viṣṇu and devastate His kingdom, Vaikuṇṭhaloka.

TEXT 3

करालदंष्ट्रोग्रदृष्ट्या दुष्प्रेक्ष्यभ्रुकुटीमुखः ।
शूलमुद्यम्य सदसि दानवानिदमब्रवीत् ॥ ३ ॥

karāla-daṁṣṭrogra-dṛṣṭyā
duṣprekṣya-bhrukuṭī-mukhaḥ
śūlam udyamya sadasi
dānavān idam abravīt

karāla-daṁṣṭra—with terrible teeth; *ugra-dṛṣṭyā*—and fierce glance; *duṣprekṣya*—horrible to see; *bhru-kuṭī*—with frowning eyebrows; *mukhaḥ*—whose face; *śūlam*—trident; *udyamya*—raising; *sadasi*—in the assembly; *dānavān*—to the demons; *idam*—this; *abravīt*—spoke.

TRANSLATION

Exhibiting his terrible teeth, fierce glance and frowning eyebrows, terrible to see, he took up his weapon, a trident, and thus began speaking to his associates, the assembled demons.

TEXT 4–5

भो भो दानवदैतेया द्विमूर्धंस्त्र्यक्ष शम्बर ।
शतबाहो हयग्रीव नमुचे पाक इल्वल ॥ ४ ॥
विप्रचित्ते मम वचः पुलोमन् शकुनादयः ।
श्रृणुतानन्तरं सर्वे क्रियतामाशु मा चिरम् ॥ ५ ॥

bho bho dānava-daiteyā
dvimūrdhaṁs tryakṣa śambara
śatabāho hayagrīva
namuce pāka ilvala

vipracitte mama vacaḥ
puloman śakunādayaḥ
śṛṇutānantaraṁ sarve
kriyatām āśu mā ciram

bhoḥ—O; *bhoḥ*—O; *dānava-daiteyāḥ*—Dānavas and Daityas; *dvi-mūrdhan*—Dvimūrdha (two-headed); *tri-akṣa*—Tryakṣa (three-eyed); *śambara*—Śambara; *śata-bāho*—Śatabāhu (hundred-armed); *haya-grīva*—Hayagrīva (horse-headed); *namuce*—Namuci; *pāka*—Pāka; *il-vala*—Ilvala; *vipracitte*—Vipracitti; *mama*—my; *vacaḥ*—words; *pulo-man*—Puloma; *śakuna*—Śakuna; *ādayaḥ*—and others; *śṛṇuta*—just hear; *anantaram*—after that; *sarve*—all; *kriyatām*—let it be done; *āśu*—quickly; *mā*—do not; *ciram*—delay.

TRANSLATION

O Dānavas and Daityas! O Dvimūrdha, Tryakṣa, Śambara and Śatabāhu! O Hayagrīva, Namuci, Pāka and Ilvala! O Vipracitti, Puloman, Śakuna and other demons! All of you, kindly hear me attentively and then act according to my words without delay.

TEXT 6

सपत्नैर्घातितः क्षुद्रैर्भ्राता मे दयितः सुहृत् ।
पार्ष्णिग्राहेण हरिणा समेनाप्युपधावनैः ॥ ६ ॥

sapatnair ghātitaḥ kṣudrair
bhrātā me dayitaḥ suhṛt
pārṣṇi-grāheṇa hariṇā
samenāpy upadhāvanaiḥ

sapatnaiḥ—by the enemies*; *ghātitaḥ*—killed; *kṣudraiḥ*—insignificant in power; *bhrātā*—brother; *me*—my; *dayitaḥ*—very dear; *suhṛt*—well-wisher; *pārṣṇi-grāheṇa*—attacking from the rear; *hariṇā*—by the Supreme Personality of Godhead; *samena*—equal to everyone (both the demigods and demons); *api*—although; *upadhāvanaiḥ*—by the worshipers, the demigods.

TRANSLATION

My insignificant enemies the demigods have combined to kill my very dear and obedient well-wisher, my brother Hiraṇyākṣa. Although the Supreme Lord, Viṣṇu, is always equal to both of us—namely, the demigods and the demons—this time, being devoutly worshiped by the demigods, He has taken their side and helped them kill Hiraṇyākṣa.

---

*Both the demons and demigods understand the Supreme Personality of Godhead to be the supreme master, but the demigods follow the master whereas the demons defy Him. Thus the demigods and demons are compared to the two co-wives of one husband. Each wife is the *sapatnī* (co-wife) of the other, and therefore the word *sapatnaiḥ* is used here.

PURPORT

As stated in *Bhagavad-gītā* (9.29), *samo 'haṁ sarva-bhūteṣu:* the Lord is equal to all living entities. Since the demigods and demons are both living entities, how is it possible that the Lord was partial to one class of living beings and opposed to another? Actually it is not possible for the Lord to be partial. Nonetheless, since the demigods, the devotees, always strictly follow the Supreme Lord's orders, because of sincerity they are victorious over the demons, who know that the Supreme Lord is Viṣṇu but do not follow His instructions. Because of constantly remembering the Supreme Personality of Godhead, Viṣṇu, the demons generally attain *sāyujya-mukti* after death. The demon Hiraṇyakaśipu accused the Lord of being partial because the demigods worshiped Him, but in fact the Lord, like the government, is not partial at all. The government is not partial to any citizen, but if a citizen is law-abiding he receives abundant opportunities from the state laws to live peacefully and fulfill his real interests.

TEXTS 7–8

तस्य त्यक्तस्वभावस्य घृणेर्मायावनौकसः ।
भजन्तं भजमानस्य बालस्येवास्थिरात्मनः ॥ ७ ॥
मच्छूलभिन्नग्रीवस्य भूरिणा रुधिरेण वै ।
असृक्प्रियं तर्पयिष्ये भ्रातरं मे गतव्यथः ॥ ८ ॥

tasya tyakta-svabhāvasya
ghṛṇer māyā-vanaukasaḥ
bhajantaṁ bhajamānasya
bālasyevāsthirātmanaḥ

mac-chūla-bhinna-grīvasya
bhūriṇā rudhireṇa vai
asṛk-priyaṁ tarpayiṣye
bhrātaraṁ me gata-vyathaḥ

tasya—of Him (the Supreme Personality of Godhead); *tyakta-svabhāvasya*—who has given up His natural position (of being equal to everyone); *ghṛṇeḥ*—most abominable; *māyā*—under the influence of the illusory energy; *vana-okasaḥ*—behaving exactly like an animal in the jungle; *bhajantam*—unto the devotee engaged in devotional service; *bhajamānasya*—being worshiped; *bālasya*—a child; *iva*—like; *asthira-ātmanaḥ*—who is always restless and changing; *mat*—my; *śūla*—by the trident; *bhinna*—separated; *grīvasya*—whose neck; *bhūriṇā*—profuse; *rudhireṇa*—by blood; *vai*—indeed; *asṛk-priyam*—who was fond of blood; *tarpayiṣye*—I shall please; *bhrātaram*—brother; *me*—my; *gata-vyathaḥ*—becoming peaceful myself.

TRANSLATION

The Supreme Personality of Godhead has given up His natural tendency of equality toward the demons and demigods. Although He is the Supreme Person, now, influenced by māyā, He has assumed the form of a boar to please His devotees, the demigods, just as a restless child leans toward someone. I shall therefore sever Lord Viṣṇu's head from His trunk by my trident, and with the profuse blood from His body I shall please my brother Hiraṇyākṣa, who was so fond of sucking blood. Thus shall I too be peaceful.

PURPORT

The defect of the demoniac mentality is expressed in this verse very clearly. Hiraṇyakaśipu thought that Viṣṇu also becomes partial, like a child whose mind is not steady or resolute. The Lord can change His mind at any time, Hiraṇyakaśipu thought, and therefore His words and activities are like those of children. Actually, because the demons are ordinary human beings, their minds change, and being materially conditioned, they think that the Supreme Personality of Godhead is conditioned also. As the Lord says in *Bhagavad-gītā* (9.11), *avajānanti māṁ mūḍhā mānuṣīṁ tanum āśritam:* "Fools deride Me when I descend in a human form."

Demons always think that Viṣṇu can be killed. Therefore, being absorbed in thoughts of Viṣṇu's form to kill Him, at least they have the opportunity to think of Viṣṇu unfavorably. Although they are not devotees, their thinking of Viṣṇu is effective, and thus they generally attain *sāyujya-mukti.* Because the demons consider the Supreme Lord an ordinary living being, they think that they can kill Lord Viṣṇu as one might kill an ordinary person. Another fact disclosed herein is that demons are very much fond of sucking blood. Indeed, all of them are meat-eaters and bloodsuckers.

Hiraṇyakaśipu accused the Supreme Lord of having a restless mind like that of a small child who can be induced to do anything if simply offered some cakes and *lāḍḍus*. Indirectly, this indicates the true position of the Supreme Personality of Godhead, who says in *Bhagavad-gītā* (9.26):

patraṁ puṣpaṁ phalaṁ toyaṁ
yo me bhaktyā prayacchati
tad ahaṁ bhakty-upahṛtam
aśnāmi prayatātmanaḥ

"If one offers Me with love and devotion a leaf, a flower, fruit or water, I will accept it." The Lord accepts the offerings of devotees because of their transcendental love. Because they are in love with the Supreme Lord, they do not eat anything without offering it first to the Lord. The Lord does not hanker for a small leaf or flower; He has enough to eat. Indeed, He is feeding all living entities. Nonetheless, because He is very merciful and is *bhakta-vatsala*, very favorable to the devotees, He certainly eats whatever they offer Him with love and devotion. This quality should not be misjudged to be childish. The highest quality of the Supreme Lord is that He is *bhakta-vatsala;* in other words, He is always extremely pleased with His devotees. As for the word *māyā*, when used in reference to the dealings of the Supreme Personality of Godhead and His devotees, this word means "affection." The actions of the Lord to favor His devotees are not disqualifications but signs of His natural affection.

As for *rudhira*, or the blood of Lord Viṣṇu, since there is no possibility of severing Lord Viṣṇu's head from His body, there is no question of blood. But the garland that decorates Viṣṇu's body is as red as blood. When the demons achieve *sāyujya-mukti* and leave behind their sinful activities, they are blessed by Viṣṇu's garland, which is red like blood. After attaining *sāyujya-mukti*, the demons are sometimes promoted to the Vaikuṇṭha world, where they receive the reward of the Lord's garland *prasāda*.

TEXT 9

तस्मिन् कूटेऽहिते नष्टे कृत्तमूले वनस्पतौ ।
विटपा इव शुष्यन्ति विष्णुप्राणा दिवौकसः ॥ ९ ॥

tasmin kūṭe 'hite naṣṭe
kṛtta-mūle vanas-patau
viṭapā iva śuṣyanti
viṣṇu-prāṇā divaukasaḥ

tasmin—when He; *kūṭe*—the most deceitful; *ahite*—enemy; *naṣṭe*—is finished; *kṛtta-mūle*—having its roots cut off; *vanas-patau*—a tree; *viṭapāḥ*—the branches and leaves; *iva*—like; *śuṣyanti*—dry up; *viṣṇu-prāṇāḥ*—whose life is Lord Viṣṇu; *diva-okasaḥ*—the demigods.

TRANSLATION

When the root of a tree is cut and the tree falls down, its branches and twigs automatically dry up. Similarly, when I have killed this diplomatic Viṣṇu, the demigods, for whom Lord Viṣṇu is the life and soul, will lose the source of their life and wither away.

PURPORT

The difference between the demigods and the demons is here explained. The demigods always follow the instructions of the Supreme Personality of Godhead, whereas the demons simply plan to disturb or kill Him. Nevertheless, sometimes the demons very much appreciate the full dependence of the demigods upon the mercy of the Lord. This is indirect glorification of the demigods by the demons.

TEXT 10

तावद्यात भुवं यूयं ब्रह्मक्षत्रसमेधिताम् ।
सूदयध्वं तपोयज्ञस्वाध्यायव्रतदानिनः ॥१०॥

tāvad yāta bhuvaṁ yūyaṁ
brahma-kṣatra-samedhitām

sūdayadhvaṁ tapo-yajña-
svādhyāya-vrata-dāninaḥ

tāvat—as long as (I am engaged in the matter of killing Viṣṇu); *yāta*—go; *bhuvam*—to the planet earth; *yūyam*—all of you; *brahma-kṣatra*—of the *brāhmaṇas* and *kṣatriyas; samedhitām*—made prosperous by the activities (brahminical culture and Vedic government); *sūdayadhvam*—just destroy; *tapaḥ*—the performers of austerities; *yajña*—sacrifices; *svādhyāya*—study of Vedic knowledge; *vrata*—the regulative vows; *dāninaḥ*—and those giving charity.

TRANSLATION

While I am engaged in the business of killing Lord Viṣṇu, go down to the planet earth, which is flourishing due to brahminical culture and a kṣatriya government. These people engage in austerity, sacrifice, Vedic study, regulative vows, and charity. Destroy all the people thus engaged!

PURPORT

Hiraṇyakaśipu's main purpose was to disturb the demigods. He planned first to kill Lord Viṣṇu so that with Lord Viṣṇu's death the demigods would automatically weaken and die. Another of his plans was to disturb the residents of the planet earth. The peace and prosperity of the residents of earth, and all the other planets, were maintained by the *brāhmaṇas* and *kṣatriyas.* The Lord says in *Bhagavad-gītā* (4.13), *cātur-varṇyaṁ mayā sṛṣṭaṁ guṇa-karma-vibhāgaśaḥ:* "According to the three modes of material nature and the work ascribed to them, the four divisions of human society were created by Me." On all the planets there are different types of residents, but the Lord recommends, referring especially to the planet earth, which is inhabited by human beings, that society be divided into four *varṇas*—*brāhmaṇa, kṣatriya, vaiśya* and *śūdra.* Before the advent of Lord Kṛṣṇa on this earth, it is understood that the earth was managed by the *brāhmaṇas* and *kṣatriyas.* The duty of the *brāhmaṇas* is to cultivate *śamaḥ* (peacefulness), *damaḥ* (self-control), *titikṣā* (tolerance), *satyam* (truthfulness), *śaucam* (cleanliness) and *ārjavam* (simplicity), and then to advise the *kṣatriya* kings how to rule the country or planet. Following the instructions of the *brāhmaṇas*, the *kṣatriyas* should engage the populace in austerity, sacrifices, Vedic study and adherence to the rules and regulations established by Vedic principles. They should also arrange for charity to be given to the *brāhmaṇas*, *sannyāsīs* and temples. This is the godly arrangement of brahminical culture.

People are inclined to offer *yajña* because unless sacrifices are offered there will be insufficient rain (*yajñād bhavati parjanyaḥ*), which will hamper agricultural activities (*parjanyād anna-sambhavaḥ*). By introducing brahminical culture, therefore, a *kṣatriya* government should engage people in performing *yajña*, studying the *Vedas* and giving charity. Thus the people will receive their necessities for life very easily, and there will be no disturbances in society. In this regard, Lord Kṛṣṇa says in *Bhagavad-gītā* (3.12):

iṣṭān bhogān hi vo devā
dāsyante yajña-bhāvitāḥ
tair dattān apradāyaibhyo
yo bhuṅkte stena eva saḥ

"In charge of the various necessities of life, the demigods, being satisfied by the performance of *yajña* [sacrifice], supply all necessities to man. But he who enjoys these gifts, without offering them to the demigods in return, is certainly a thief."

The demigods are authorized supplying agents who act on behalf of the Supreme Personality of Godhead, Viṣṇu. Therefore, they must be satisfied by the performance of prescribed *yajñas*. In the *Vedas*, there are different kinds of *yajñas* prescribed for different kinds of demigods, but all are ultimately offered to the Supreme Personality of Godhead. For one who cannot understand what the Personality of Godhead is, sacrifice to the demigods is recommended. According to the different material qualities of the persons concerned, different types of *yajñas* are recommended in the *Vedas*. Worship of different demigods is also on the same basis—namely, according to different qualities. For example, the meat-eaters are recommended to worship the goddess Kālī, the ghastly form of material nature, and before the goddess the sacrifice of animals is recommended. But for those in the mode of goodness, the transcendental worship of Viṣṇu is recommended. Ultimately, all *yajñas* are meant for gradual promotion to the transcendental position. For ordinary men, at least five *yajñas*, known as *pañca-mahāyajña*, are necessary.

One should know, however, that all the necessities of life that human society requires are supplied by the demigod agents of the Lord. No one can manufacture anything. Consider, for example, all the eatables of human society. These eatables include grains, fruits, vegetables, milk and sugar for persons in the mode of goodness, and also eatables for the nonvegetarians, such as meats, none of which can be manufactured by men. Then again, take for example, heat, light, water and air, which are also necessities of life—none of them can be manufactured by human society. Without the Supreme Lord, there can be no profuse sunlight, moonlight, rainfall or breeze, without which no one can live. Obviously, our life is dependent on supplies from the Lord. Even for our manufacturing enterprises, we require so many raw materials like metal, sulphur, mercury, manganese and so many essentials—all of which are supplied by the agents of the Lord, with the purpose that we should make proper use of them to keep ourselves fit and healthy for the purpose of self-realization, leading to the ultimate goal of life, namely, liberation from the material struggle for existence. This aim of life is attained by performance of *yajñas*. If we forget the purpose of human life and simply take supplies from the agents of the Lord for sense gratification and become more and more entangled in material existence, which is not the purpose of creation, certainly we become thieves, and therefore we are punished by the laws of material nature. A society of thieves can never be happy, for they have no aim in life. The gross materialist thieves have no ultimate goal of life. They are simply directed to sense gratification; nor do they have knowledge of how to perform *yajñas*. Lord Caitanya, however, inaugurated the easiest performance of *yajña*, namely the *saṅkīrtana-yajña*, which can be performed by anyone in the world who accepts the principles of Kṛṣṇa consciousness.

Hiraṇyakaśipu planned to kill the inhabitants of earth so that *yajña* would stop and the demigods, being disturbed, would die automatically when Lord Viṣṇu, the *yajñeśvara*, was killed. These were the demoniac plans of Hiraṇyakaśipu, who was expert in such activities.

TEXT 11

विष्णुर्द्विजक्रियामूलो यज्ञो धर्ममयः पुमान् ।
देवर्षिपितृभूतानां धर्मस्य च परायणम् ॥११॥

viṣṇur dvija-kriyā-mūlo
yajño dharmamayaḥ pumān
devarṣi-pitṛ-bhūtānāṁ
dharmasya ca parāyaṇam

viṣṇuḥ—Lord Viṣṇu, the Supreme Personality of Godhead; *dvija*—of the *brāhmaṇas* and *kṣatriyas; kriyā-mūlaḥ*—whose root is the performance of *yajña* and the ritualistic ceremonies mentioned in the *Vedas; yajñaḥ*—personified *yajña* (Lord Viṣṇu, who is known as the *yajña-puruṣa*); *dharma-mayaḥ*—full of religious principles; *pumān*—the Supreme Person; *deva-ṛṣi*—of the demigods and great *ṛṣis* like Vyāsadeva and Nārada; *pitṛ*—of the forefathers; *bhūtānām*—and of all other living entities; *dharmasya*—of the religious principles; *ca*—also; *parāyaṇam*—the shelter.

TRANSLATION

The basic principle of brahminical culture is to satisfy Lord Viṣṇu, the personification of sacrificial and ritualistic ceremonies. Lord Viṣṇu is the personified reservoir of all religious principles, and He is the shelter of all the demigods, the great pitās, and the people in general. When the brāhmaṇas are killed, no one will exist to encourage the kṣatriyas to perform yajñas, and thus the demigods, not being appeased by yajña, will automatically die.

PURPORT

Since Viṣṇu is the central point of brahminical culture, Hiraṇyakaśipu's plan was to kill Viṣṇu, for if Viṣṇu were killed, naturally the brahminical culture would also be lost. With brahminical culture lost, *yajña* would no longer be performed, and for want of *yajña* the regular distribution of rainfall would cease (*yajñād bhavati parjanyaḥ*). Thus there would be disturbances all over the world, and naturally the demigods would be defeated. From this verse we get a clear indication of how human society is disturbed when the Vedic Āryan civilization is killed and the Vedic ritualistic ceremonies performed by the *brāhmaṇas* are stopped. *Kalau śūdra-sambhavaḥ:* because the population of the modern world consists mostly of *śūdras*, the brahminical culture is now lost and is extremely difficult to reestablish in a proper way. Therefore Lord Caitanya has recommended the chanting of the holy name of the Lord, which will revive brahminical culture very easily.

harer nāma harer nāma
harer nāmaiva kevalam
kalau nāsty eva nāsty eva
nāsty eva gatir anyathā

Because of the increment in demoniac population, people have lost brahminical culture. Nor is there a *kṣatriya* government. Instead, the government is a democracy in which any *śūdra* can be voted into taking up the governmental reigns and capture the power to rule. Because of the poisonous effects of Kali-yuga, the *śāstra* (*Bhāg.* 12.2.13) says, *dasyu-prāyeṣu rājasu:* the government will adopt the policies of *dasyus*, or plunderers. Thus there will be no instructions from the *brāhmaṇas*, and even if there are brahminical instructions, there will be no *kṣatriya* rulers who can follow them. Aside from Satya-yuga, even formerly, in the days when demons were flourishing, Hiraṇyakaśipu planned to destroy the brahminical culture and the *kṣatriya* government and thus create chaos all over the world. Although in Satya-yuga this plan was very difficult to execute, in Kali-yuga, which is full of *śūdras* and demons, the brahminical culture is lost and can be revived only by the chanting of the *mahā-mantra*. Therefore the Kṛṣṇa consciousness movement, or the Hare Kṛṣṇa movement, has been inaugurated to revive brahminical culture very easily so that people may become happy and peaceful in this life and prepare for elevation in the next. In this regard, Śrīla Madhvācārya quotes this verse from the *Brahmāṇḍa Purāṇa:*

vipra-yajñādi-mūlaṁ tu
harir ity āsuraṁ matam
harir eva hi sarvasya
mūlaṁ samyaṅ mato nṛpa

"O King, the demons think that Hari, Lord Viṣṇu, exists because of the *brāhmaṇas* and *yajña*, but factually Hari is the cause of everything including the *brāhmaṇas* and *yajña*." Therefore, through the popularizing of *hari-kīrtana*, or the *saṅkīrtana* movement, the brahminical culture and *kṣatriya* government will automatically come back, and people will be extremely happy.

TEXT 12

यत्र यत्र द्विजा गावो वेदा वर्णाश्रमक्रियाः ।
तं तं जनपदं यात सन्दीपयत वृश्चत ॥१२॥

yatra yatra dvijā gāvo
vedā varṇāśrama-kriyāḥ
taṁ taṁ janapadaṁ yāta
sandīpayata vṛścata

yatra yatra—wherever; *dvijāḥ*—the *brāhmaṇas; gāvaḥ*—the protected cows; *vedāḥ*—the Vedic culture; *varṇa-āśrama*—of the Āryan civilization of four *varṇas* and four *āśramas; kriyāḥ*—the activities; *tam tam*—that; *jana-padam*—to the city or town; *yāta*—go; *sandīpayata*—set fire; *vṛścata*—cut down (all the trees).

TRANSLATION

Immediately go wherever there is good protection for the cows and brāhmaṇas and wherever the Vedas are studied in terms of the varṇāśrama principles. Set fire to those places and cut from the roots the trees there, which are the source of life.

PURPORT

The picture of a proper human civilization is indirectly described here. In a perfect human civilization there must be a class of men fully trained as perfect *brāhmaṇas*. Similarly, there must be *kṣatriyas* to rule the country very nicely according to the injunctions of the *śāstras*, and there must be *vaiśyas* who can protect the cows. The word *gāvaḥ* indicates that cows should be given protection. Because the Vedic civilization is lost, cows are not protected, but instead indiscriminately killed in slaughterhouses. Such are the acts of demons. Therefore this is a demoniac civilization. The *varṇāśrama-dharma* mentioned here is essential for human civilization. Unless there is a *brāhmaṇa* to guide, a *kṣatriya* to rule perfectly, and a perfect *vaiśya* to produce food and protect the cows, how will people live peacefully? It is impossible.

Another point is that trees also should be given protection. During its lifetime, a tree should not be cut for industrial enterprises. In Kali-yuga, trees are indiscriminately and unnecessarily cut for industry, in particular for paper mills that manufacture a profuse quantity of paper for the publication of demoniac propaganda, nonsensical literature, huge quantities of newspapers and many other paper products. This is a sign of a demoniac civilization. The cutting of trees is prohibited unless necessary for the service of Lord Viṣṇu. *Yajñārthāt karmaṇo 'nyatra loko 'yaṁ karma-bandhanaḥ:* "Work done as a sacrifice for Lord Viṣṇu must be performed, otherwise work binds one to this material world." But if the paper mills stop producing paper, one may argue, how can our ISKCON literature be published? The answer is that the paper mills should manufacture paper only for the publication of ISKCON literature because ISKCON literature is published for the service of Lord Viṣṇu. This literature clarifies our relationship with Lord Viṣṇu, and therefore the publication of ISKCON literature is the performance of *yajña. Yajñārthāt karmaṇo 'nyatra loko 'yaṁ karma-bandhanaḥ. Yajña* must be performed, as indicated by the superior authorities. The cutting of trees simply to manufacture paper for the publication of unwanted literature is the greatest sinful act.

TEXT 13

इति ते भर्तृनिर्देशमादाय शिरसादृताः ।
तथा प्रजानां कदनं विदधुः कदनप्रियाः ॥१३॥

iti te bhartṛ-nirdeśam
ādāya śirasādṛtāḥ
tathā prajānāṁ kadanaṁ
vidadhuḥ kadana-priyāḥ

iti—thus; *te*—they; *bhartṛ*—of the master; *nirdeśam*—the direction; *ādāya*—receiving; *śirasā*—with their heads; *ādṛtāḥ*—respecting;

tathā—so also; *prajānām*—of all the citizens; *kadanam*—persecution; *vidadhuḥ*—executed; *kadana-priyāḥ*—who are expert in persecuting others.

TRANSLATION

Thus the demons, being fond of disastrous activities, took Hiraṇyakaśipu's instructions on their heads with great respect and offered him obeisances. According to his directions, they engaged in envious activities directed against all living beings.

PURPORT

The followers of demoniac principles, as described here, are thoroughly envious of the general populace. In the present day, scientific advancement exemplifies such envy. The discovery of nuclear energy has been disastrous to people in general because demons all over the world are manufacturing nuclear weapons. The word *kadana-priyāḥ* is very significant in this regard. The demoniac persons who want to kill the Vedic culture are extremely envious of the feeble citizens, and they act in such a way that ultimately their discoveries will be inauspicious for everyone (*jagato 'hitāḥ*). The Sixteenth Chapter of *Bhagavad-gītā* fully explains how the demons engage in sinful activities for the destruction of the populace.

TEXT 14

पुरग्रामव्रजोद्यानक्षेत्रारामाश्रमाकरान् ।
खेटखर्वटघोषांश्च ददहुः पत्तनानि च ॥१४॥

pura-grāma-vrajodyāna-
kṣetrārāmāśramākarān
kheṭa-kharvaṭa-ghoṣāṁś ca
dadahuḥ pattanāni ca

pura—cities and towns; *grāma*—villages; *vraja*—pasturing grounds; *udyāna*—gardens; *kṣetra*—agricultural fields; *ārāma*—natural forests; *āśrama*—hermitages of saintly persons; *ākarān*—and mines (that produce valuable metals to maintain brahminical culture); *kheṭa*—farm villages; *kharvaṭa*—mountain villages; *ghoṣān*—the little villages of cowherds; *ca*—and; *dadahuḥ*—they burned; *pattanāni*—the capitals; *ca*—also.

TRANSLATION

The demons set fire to the cities, villages, pasturing grounds, cowpens, gardens, agricultural fields and natural forests. They burned the hermitages of the saintly persons, the important mines that produced valuable metals, the residential quarters of the agriculturalists, the mountain villages, and the villages of the cow protectors, the cowherd men. They also burned the government capitals.

PURPORT

The word *udyāna* refers to places where trees are especially grown to produce fruits and flowers, which are most important for human civilization. Kṛṣṇa says in *Bhagavad-gītā* (9.26):

patraṁ puṣpaṁ phalaṁ toyaṁ
yo me bhaktyā prayacchati
tad ahaṁ bhakty-upahṛtam
aśnāmi prayatātmanaḥ

"If one offers Me with love and devotion a leaf, a flower, fruit or water, I will accept it." Fruits and flowers are very much pleasing to the Lord. If one wants to please the Supreme Personality of Godhead, he can simply offer fruits and flowers, and the Lord will be pleased to accept them. Our only duty is to please the Supreme Godhead (*saṁsiddhir hari-toṣaṇam*). Whatever we do and whatever our occupation, our main purpose should be to please the Supreme Lord. All the paraphernalia mentioned in this verse is especially meant for the satisfaction of the Lord, not the satisfaction of one's senses. The government—indeed, the entire society—should be structured in such a way that everyone can be trained to satisfy the Supreme Personality of Godhead. But unfortunately, especially in this age, *na te viduḥ svārtha-gatiṁ hi viṣṇum:* people do not know that the highest goal of human life is to please Lord Viṣṇu. On the contrary, like demons, they simply plan to kill Viṣṇu and be happy by sense gratification.

TEXT 15

केचित्खनित्रैर्बिभिदुः सेतुप्राकारगोपुरान् ।
आजीव्यांश्चिच्छिदुर्वृक्षान् केचित्परशुपाणयः ।
प्रादहञ् शरणान्येके प्रजानां ज्वलितोल्मुकैः ॥१५॥

kecit khanitrair bibhiduḥ
setu-prākāra-gopurān
ājīvyāṁś cicchidur vṛkṣān
kecit paraśu-pāṇayaḥ
prādahañ śaraṇāny eke
prajānāṁ jvalitolmukaiḥ

kecit—some of the demons; *khanitraiḥ*—with digging instruments; *bibhiduḥ*—broke to pieces; *setu*—bridges; *prākāra*—protective walls; *gopurān*—city gates; *ājīvyān*—the source of livelihood; *cicchiduḥ*—cut down; *vṛkṣān*—trees; *kecit*—some; *paraśu-pāṇayaḥ*—taking axes in hand; *prādahan*—burned down; *śaraṇāni*—the dwellings; *eke*—other demons; *prajānām*—of the citizens; *jvalita*—blazing; *ulmukaiḥ*—with firebrands.

TRANSLATION

Some of the demons took digging instruments and broke down the bridges, the protective walls and the gates [gopuras] of the cities. Some took axes and began cutting the important trees that produced mango, jackfruit and other sources of food. Some of the demons took firebrands and set fire to the residential quarters of the citizens.

PURPORT

The cutting of trees is generally prohibited. In particular, trees that produce nice fruit for the maintenance of human society should not be cut. In different countries there are different types of fruit trees. In India the mango and jackfruit trees are prominent, and in other places there are mango trees, jackfruit trees, coconut trees and berry trees. Any tree that produces nice fruit for the maintenance of the people should not be cut at all. This is a śāstric injunction.

TEXT 16

एवं विप्रकृते लोके दैत्येन्द्रानुचरैर्मुहुः ।
दिवं देवाः परित्यज्य भुवि चेरुरलक्षिताः ॥१६॥

evaṁ viprakṛte loke
daityendrānucarair muhuḥ
divaṁ devāḥ parityajya
bhuvi cerur alakṣitāḥ

evam—thus; *viprakṛte*—being disturbed; *loke*—when all the people; *daitya-indra-anucaraiḥ*—by the followers of Hiraṇyakaśipu, the King of the Daityas; *muhuḥ*—again and again; *divam*—the heavenly planets; *devāḥ*—the demigods; *parityajya*—giving up; *bhuvi*—on the planet earth; *ceruḥ*—wandered (to see the extent of the disturbances); *alakṣitāḥ*—unseen by the demons.

TRANSLATION

Thus disturbed again and again by the unnatural occurrences caused by the followers of Hiraṇyakaśipu, all the people had to cease the activities of Vedic culture. Not receiving the results of yajña, the demigods also became disturbed. They left their residential quarters in the heavenly planets and, unobserved by the demons, began wandering on the planet earth to see the disasters.

PURPORT

As stated in *Bhagavad-gītā*, the performance of *yajña* brings reciprocal good fortune for both the human beings and the demigods. When the performances of *yajña* were stopped by the disturbances of the demons, the demigods were naturally bereft of the results of *yajña* and hampered in executing their respective duties. Therefore they came down to the planet earth to see how people had become disturbed and to consider what to do.

TEXT 17

हिरण्यकशिपुर्भ्रातुः सम्परेतस्य दुःखितः ।
कृत्वा कटोदकादीनि भ्रातृपुत्रानसान्त्वयत् ॥१७॥

hiraṇyakaśipur bhrātuḥ
samparetasya duḥkhitaḥ
kṛtvā kaṭodakādīni
bhrātṛ-putrān asāntvayat

hiraṇyakaśipuḥ—Hiraṇyakaśipu; *bhrātuḥ*—of the brother; *samparetasya*—deceased; *duḥkhitaḥ*—being very much distressed; *kṛtvā*—performing; *kaṭodaka-ādīni*—ceremonies observed after a death; *bhrātṛ-putrān*—the sons of his brother; *asāntvayat*—pacified.

TRANSLATION

After performing the ritualistic observances for the death of his brother, Hiraṇyakaśipu, being extremely unhappy, tried to pacify his nephews.

TEXTS 18–19

शकुनिं शम्बरं धृष्टिं भूतसन्तापनं वृकम् ।
कालनाभं महानाभं हरिश्मश्रुमथोत्कचम् ॥१८॥
तन्मातरं रुषाभानुं दितिं च जननीं गिरा ।
श्लक्ष्णया देशकालज्ञ इदमाह जनेश्वर ॥१९॥

śakunim̐ śambaram̐ dhṛṣṭim̐
bhūtasantāpanam̐ vṛkam
kālanābham̐ mahānābham̐
hariśmaśrum athotkacam

tan-mātaram̐ ruṣābhānum̐
ditim̐ ca jananīm̐ girā
ślakṣṇayā deśa-kāla-jña
idam āha janeśvara

śakunim—Śakuni; *śambaram*—Śambara; *dhṛṣṭim*—Dhṛṣṭi; *bhūtasantāpanam*—Bhūtasantāpana; *vṛkam*—Vṛka; *kālanābham*—Kālanābha; *mahānābham*—Mahānābha; *hariśmaśrum*—Hariśmaśru; *atha*—as well as; *utkacam*—Utkaca; *tat-mātaram*—their mother; *ruṣābhānum*—Ruṣābhānu; *ditim*—Diti; *ca*—and; *jananīm*—his own mother; *girā*—by words; *ślakṣṇayā*—very sweet; *deśa-kāla-jñaḥ*—who was expert in understanding the time and situation; *idam*—this; *āha*—said; *jana-īśvara*—O King.

TRANSLATION

O King, Hiraṇyakaśipu was extremely angry, but since he was a great politician, he knew how to act according to the time and situation. With sweet words he began pacifying his nephews, whose names were Śakuni, Śambara, Dhṛṣṭi, Bhūtasantāpana, Vṛka, Kālanābha, Mahānābha, Hariśmaśru and Utkaca. He also consoled their mother, his sister-in-law, Ruṣābhānu, as well as his own mother, Diti. He spoke to them all as follows.

TEXT 20

श्रीहिरण्यकशिपुरुवाच
अम्बाम्ब हे वधूः पुत्रा वीरं मार्हथ शोचितुम् ।
रिपोरभिमुखे श्लाघ्यः शूराणां वध ईप्सितः ॥२०॥

śrī-hiraṇyakaśipur uvāca
ambāmba he vadhūḥ putrā
vīraṁ mārhatha śocitum
ripor abhimukhe ślāghyaḥ
śūrāṇāṁ vadha īpsitaḥ

śrī-hiraṇyakaśipuḥ uvāca—Hiraṇyakaśipu said; *amba amba*—my mother, my mother; *he*—O; *vadhūḥ*—my sister-in-law; *putrāḥ*—O sons of my brother; *vīram*—the hero; *mā*—not; *arhatha*—you deserve; *śocitum*—to lament about; *ripoḥ*—of the enemy; *abhimukhe*—in front; *ślāghyaḥ*—glorious; *śūrāṇām*—of those who are actually great; *vadhaḥ*—killing; *īpsitaḥ*—desired.

TRANSLATION

Hiraṇyakaśipu said: My dear mother, sister-in-law and nephews, you should not lament for the death of the great hero, for a hero's death in front of his enemy is glorious and desirable.

TEXT 21

भूतानामिह संवासः प्रपायामिव सुव्रते ।
दैवेनैकत्र नीतानामुन्नीतानां स्वकर्मभिः ॥२१॥

bhūtānām iha saṁvāsaḥ
prapāyām iva suvrate
daivenaikatra nītānām
unnītānāṁ sva-karmabhiḥ

bhūtānām—of all living entities; *iha*—in this material world; *saṁvāsaḥ*—the living together; *prapāyām*—in a place for drinking cold water; *iva*—like; *su-vrate*—O my gentle mother; *daivena*—by the superior arrangement; *ekatra*—in one place; *nītānām*—of those brought; *unnītānām*—of those led apart; *sva-karmabhiḥ*—by their own reactions.

TRANSLATION

My dear mother, in a restaurant or place for drinking cold water, many travelers are brought together, and after drinking water they continue to their respective destinations. Similarly, living entities join together in a family, and later, as a result of their own actions, they are led apart to their destinations.

PURPORT

prakṛteḥ kriyamāṇāni
guṇaiḥ karmāṇi sarvaśaḥ
ahaṅkāra-vimūḍhātmā
kartāham iti manyate

"The bewildered soul, under the influence of the three modes of material nature, thinks himself the doer of activities, which are in actuality carried out by nature." (Bg. 3.27) All living entities act exactly according to the directions of *prakṛti*, material nature, because in the material world we are fully under a higher control. All the living entities in this material world have come here only because they wanted to be equal to

Kṛṣṇa in enjoyment and have thus been sent here to be conditioned by material nature in different degrees. In the material world a so-called family is a combination of several persons in one home to fulfill the terms of their imprisonment. As criminal prisoners scatter as soon as their terms are over and they are released, all of us who have temporarily assembled as family members will continue to our respective destinations. Another example given is that family members are like straws carried together by the waves of a river. Sometimes such straws mix together in whirlpools, and later, dispersed again by the same waves, they float alone in the water.

Although Hiraṇyakaśipu was a demon, he had Vedic knowledge and understanding. Thus the advice given to his family members—his sister-in-law, mother and nephews—was quite sound. The demons are considered highly elevated in knowledge, but because they do not use their good intelligence for the service of the Lord, they are called demons. The demigods, however, act very intelligently to satisfy the Supreme Personality of Godhead. This is confirmed in *Śrīmad-Bhāgavatam* (1.2.13) as follows:

ataḥ pumbhir dvija-śreṣṭhā
varṇāśrama-vibhāgaśaḥ
svanuṣṭhitasya dharmasya
saṁsiddhir hari-toṣaṇam

"O best among the twiceborn, it is therefore concluded that the highest perfection one can achieve, by discharging his prescribed duties [*dharma*] according to caste divisions and orders of life, is to please the Lord Hari." To become a demigod or to become godly, whatever one's occupation, one must satisfy the Supreme Personality of Godhead.

TEXT 22

नित्य आत्माव्ययः शुद्धः सर्वगः सर्ववित्परः ।
धत्तेऽसावात्मनो लिङ्गं मायया विसृजन्गुणान् ॥२२॥

nitya ātmāvyayaḥ śuddhaḥ
sarvagaḥ sarva-vit paraḥ

dhatte 'sāv ātmano liṅgaṁ
māyayā visṛjan guṇān

nityaḥ—eternal; *ātmā*—spirit soul; *avyayaḥ*—inexhaustible; *śud-dhaḥ*—with no material tinge; *sarva-gaḥ*—qualified to go anywhere in the material or spiritual worlds; *sarva-vit*—full of knowledge; *paraḥ*—transcendental to material conditions; *dhatte*—accepts; *asau*—that *ātmā*, or living being; *ātmanaḥ*—of the self; *liṅgam*—a body; *māyayā*—by the material energy; *visṛjan*—creating; *guṇān*—various material qualities.

TRANSLATION

The spirit soul, the living entity, has no death, for he is eternal and inexhaustible. Being free from material contamination, he can go anywhere in the material or spiritual worlds. He is fully aware and completely different from the material body, but because of being misled by misuse of his slight independence, he is obliged to accept subtle and gross bodies created by the material energy and thus be subjected to so-called material happiness and distress. Therefore, no one should lament for the passing of the spirit soul from the body.

PURPORT

Hiraṇyakaśipu very intelligently described the position of the soul. The soul is never the body, but is always completely different from the body. Being eternal and inexhaustible, the soul has no death, but when the same pure soul desires to enjoy the material world independently, he is placed under the conditions of material nature and must therefore accept a certain type of body and suffer the pains and pleasures thereof. This is also described by Kṛṣṇa in *Bhagavad-gītā* (13.22). *Kāraṇaṁ guṇa-saṅgo 'sya sad-asad-yoni-janmasu:* the living entity is born in different families or species of life because of being infected by the modes of material nature. When conditioned by material nature, the living entity must accept a certain type of body, which is offered by nature under the direction of the Supreme Lord.

īśvaraḥ sarva-bhūtānāṁ
hṛd-deśe 'rjuna tiṣṭhati

bhrāmayan sarva-bhūtāni
yantrārūḍhāni māyayā

"The Supreme Lord is situated in everyone's heart, O Arjuna, and is directing the wanderings of all living entities, who are seated as on a machine, made of the material energy." (Bg. 18.61) The body is just like a machine, and according to the living entity's *karma*, he is offered a particular type of machine to move here and there under the control of material nature. This continues until he surrenders to the Supreme Personality of Godhead (*mām eva ye prapadyante māyām etāṁ taranti te*). Until he surrenders, the conditioned soul is carried from life to life by the arrangement of material nature.

TEXT 23

यथाम्भसा प्रचलता तरवोऽपि चला इव ।
चक्षुषा भ्राम्यमाणेन दृश्यते चलतीव भूः ॥२३॥

yathāmbhasā pracalatā
taravo 'pi calā iva
cakṣuṣā bhrāmyamāṇena
dṛśyate calatīva bhūḥ

yathā—just as; *ambhasā*—by water; *pracalatā*—moving; *taravaḥ*—the trees (on the bank of the river); *api*—also; *calāḥ*—moving; *iva*—as if; *cakṣuṣā*—by the eye; *bhrāmyamāṇena*—moving; *dṛśyate*—is seen; *calatī*—moving; *iva*—as if; *bhūḥ*—the ground.

TRANSLATION

Because of the movements of the water, the trees on the bank of a river, when reflected on the water, seem to move. Similarly, when the eyes move because of some mental derangement, the land appears to move also.

PURPORT

Sometimes, because of mental derangement, the land appears to be moving. A drunkard, for example, or a person with heart disease, sometimes feels that the land is moving. Similarly, the reflections of trees in a flowing river also appear to move. These are the actions of *māyā.* Actually the living entity does not move (*sthāṇur acalo 'yam*). The living entity does not take birth or accept death, but because of the transient subtle and gross bodies, the living entity appears to move from one place to another or be dead and gone forever. As the great Bengali Vaiṣṇava poet, Jagadānanda Paṇḍita, has said:

piśācī pāile yena mati-cchanna haya
māyā-grasta jīvera haya se bhāva udaya

According to this statement from the *Prema-vivarta,* when a living entity is conditioned by material nature, he is exactly like a person haunted by a ghost. One should therefore understand the fixed position of the spirit soul and how he is carried away by the waves of material nature to different bodies and different situations under lamentation and hankering. One achieves the success of life when he understands the constitutional position of his self and is undisturbed by the conditions created by material nature (*prakṛteḥ kriyamāṇāni guṇaiḥ karmāṇi sarvaśaḥ*).

TEXT 24

एवं गुणैर्भ्राम्यमाणे मनस्यविकलः पुमान् ।
याति तत्साम्यतां भद्रे ह्यलिङ्गो लिङ्गवानिव ॥२४॥

evaṁ guṇair bhrāmyamāṇe
manasy avikalaḥ pumān
yāti tat-sāmyatāṁ bhadre
hy aliṅgo liṅgavān iva

evam—in this way; *guṇaiḥ*—by the modes of material nature; *bhrāmyamāṇe*—when shaken; *manasi*—the mind; *avikalaḥ*—changeless; *pumān*—the living entity; *yāti*—approaches; *tat-sāmyatām*—the same condition of agitation as the mind; *bhadre*—O my gentle mother; *hi*—indeed; *aliṅgaḥ*—without a subtle or gross body; *liṅga-vān*—possessing a material body; *iva*—as if.

TRANSLATION

In the same way, O my gentle mother, when the mind is agitated by the movements of the modes of material nature, the living entity, although freed from all the different phases of the subtle and gross bodies, thinks that he has changed from one condition to another.

PURPORT

As stated in *Śrīmad-Bhāgavatam* (10.84.13):

yasyātma-buddhiḥ kuṇape tri-dhātuke
sva-dhīḥ kalatrādiṣu bhauma-ijya-dhīḥ
yat-tīrtha-buddhiḥ salile na karhicij
janeṣv abhijñeṣu sa eva go-kharaḥ

"A human being who identifies the body made of three elements as the self, who considers the by-products of the body to be his kinsmen, who considers the land of his birth worshipable, and who goes to a place of pilgrimage simply to bathe rather than to meet men of transcendental knowledge there, is to be considered like a cow or an ass." Although Hiraṇyakaśipu was a great demon, he was not as foolish as the population of the modern world. Hiraṇyakaśipu had clear knowledge of the spirit soul and the subtle and gross bodies, but now we are so degraded that everyone, including the exalted scientists, philosophers and other leaders, is under the bodily conception of life, which is condemned in the *śāstras. Sa eva go-kharaḥ:* such persons are nothing but cows and asses.

Hiraṇyakaśipu advised his family members that although the gross body of his brother Hiraṇyākṣa was dead and they were aggrieved because of this, they should not lament for the great soul of Hiraṇyākṣa, who had already attained his next destination. *Ātmā*, the spirit soul, is always unchanged (*avikalaḥ pumān*). We are spirit souls, but when carried away by mental activities (*manodharma*), we suffer from so-called material conditions of life. This generally happens to nondevotees. *Harāv abhaktasya kuto mahad-guṇāḥ:* nondevotees may possess exalted material qualities, but because they are foolish they have no good qualifications. The designations of the conditioned soul in the material world are decorations of the dead body. The conditioned soul has no information of the spirit and its exalted existence beyond the effects of the material condition.

TEXTS 25–26

एष आत्मविपर्यासो ह्यलिङ्गे लिङ्गभावना ।
एष प्रियाप्रियैर्योगो वियोगः कर्मसंसृतिः ॥२५॥
सम्भवश्च विनाशश्च शोकश्च विविधः स्मृतः ।
अविवेकश्च चिन्ता च विवेकास्मृतिरेव च ॥२६॥

eṣa ātma-viparyāso
hy aliṅge liṅga-bhāvanā
eṣa priyāpriyair yogo
viyogaḥ karma-saṁsṛtiḥ

sambhavaś ca vināśaś ca
śokaś ca vividhaḥ smṛtaḥ
avivekaś ca cintā ca
vivekāsmṛtir eva ca

esaḥ—this; *ātma-viparyāsaḥ*—bewilderment of the living being; *hi*—indeed; *aliṅge*—in that which does not possess a material body; *liṅga-bhāvanā*—accepting the material body to be the self; *eṣaḥ*—this; *priya*—with those who are very dear; *apriyaiḥ*—and with those who are not dear (enemies, those not in the family, etc.); *yogaḥ*—connection; *viyogaḥ*—separation; *karma*—the fruits of action; *saṁsṛtiḥ*—the material condition of life; *sambhavaḥ*—accepting birth; *ca*—and; *vināśaḥ*—accepting death; *ca*—and; *śokaḥ*—lamentation; *ca*—and; *vividhaḥ*—varieties; *smṛtaḥ*—mentioned in scripture; *avivekaḥ*—lack of discrimination; *ca*—and; *cintā*—anxiety; *ca*—also; *viveka*—of proper discrimination; *asmṛtiḥ*—forgetfulness; *eva*—indeed; *ca*—also.

TRANSLATION

In his bewildered state, the living entity, accepting the body and mind to be the self, considers some people to be his kinsmen and

others to be outsiders. Because of this misconception, he suffers. Indeed, the accumulation of such concocted material ideas is the cause of suffering and so-called happiness in the material world. The conditioned soul thus situated must take birth in different species and work in various types of consciousness, thus creating new bodies. This continued material life is called saṁsāra. Birth, death, lamentation, foolishness and anxiety are due to such material considerations. Thus we sometimes come to a proper understanding and sometimes fall again to a wrong conception of life.

TEXT 27

अत्राप्युदाहरन्तीममितिहासं पुरातनम् ।
यमस्य प्रेतबन्धूनां संवादं तं निबोधत ॥२७॥

atrāpy udāharantīmam
itihāsaṁ purātanam
yamasya preta-bandhūnāṁ
saṁvādaṁ taṁ nibodhata

atra—in this connection; *api*—indeed; *udāharanti*—they cite; *imam*—this; *itihāsam*—history; *purātanam*—very old; *yamasya*—of Yamarāja, the superintendent of death, who gives judgment after death; *preta-bandhūnām*—of the friends of a dead man; *saṁvādam*—discussion; *tam*—that; *nibodhata*—try to understand.

TRANSLATION

In this regard, an example is given from an old history. This involves a discourse between Yamarāja and the friends of a dead person. Please hear it attentively.

PURPORT

The words *itihāsaṁ purātanam* mean "an old history." The *Purāṇas* are not chronologically recorded, but the incidents mentioned in the *Purāṇas* are actual histories of bygone ages. *Śrīmad-Bhāgavatam* is the *Mahā-purāṇa*, the essence of all the *Purāṇas*. The Māyāvādī scholars do not accept the *Purāṇas*, but Śrīla Madhvācārya and all other authorities accept them as the authoritative histories of the world.

TEXT 28

उशीनरेष्वभूद्राजा सुयज्ञ इति विश्रुतः ।
सपत्नैर्निहतो युद्धे ज्ञातयस्तमुपासत ॥२८॥

uśīnareṣv abhūd rājā
suyajña iti viśrutaḥ
sapatnair nihato yuddhe
jñātayas tam upāsata

uśīnareṣu—in the state known as Uśīnara; *abhūt*—there was; *rājā*—a king; *suyajñaḥ*—Suyajña; *iti*—thus; *viśrutaḥ*—celebrated; *sapatnaiḥ*—by enemies; *nihataḥ*—killed; *yuddhe*—in war; *jñātayaḥ*—the kinsmen; *tam*—him; *upāsata*—sat around.

TRANSLATION

In the state known as Uśīnara there was a celebrated king named Suyajña. When the King was killed in battle by his enemies, his kinsmen sat down around the dead body and began to lament the death of their friend.

TEXTS 29–31

विशीर्णरत्नकवचं विभ्रष्टाभरणस्रजम् ।
शरनिर्भिन्नहृदयं शयानमसृगाविलम् ॥२९॥
प्रकीर्णकेशं ध्वस्ताक्षं रभसा दष्टदच्छदम् ।
रजःकुण्ठमुखाम्भोजं छिन्नायुधभुजं मृधे ॥३०॥
उशीनरेन्द्रं विधिना तथा कृतं
पतिं महिष्यः प्रसमीक्ष्य दुःखिताः ।
हताः स्म नाथेति करैरुरो भृशं
घ्नन्त्यो मुहुस्तत्पदयोरुपापतन् ॥३१॥

viśīrṇa-ratna-kavacaṁ
vibhraṣṭābharaṇa-srajam
śara-nirbhinna-hṛdayaṁ
śayānam asṛg-āvilam

prakīrṇa-keśaṁ dhvastākṣaṁ
rabhasā daṣṭa-dacchadam
rajaḥ-kuṇṭha-mukhāmbhojaṁ
chinnāyudha-bhujaṁ mṛdhe

uśīnarendraṁ vidhinā tathā kṛtaṁ
patiṁ mahiṣyaḥ prasamīkṣya duḥkhitāḥ
hatāḥ sma nātheti karair uro bhṛśaṁ
ghnantyo muhus tat-padayor upāpatan

viśīrṇa—scattered here and there; *ratna*—made of jewels; *kavacam*—protective armor; *vibhraṣṭa*—fallen off; *ābharaṇa*—ornaments; *srajam*—garlands; *śara-nirbhinna*—pierced by arrows; *hṛdayam*—the heart; *śayānam*—lying down; *asṛk-āvilam*—smeared with blood; *prakīrṇa-keśam*—his hair loosened and scattered; *dhvasta-akṣam*—his eyes obscured; *rabhasā*—with anger; *daṣṭa*—bitten; *dac-chadam*—his lips; *rajaḥ-kuṇṭha*—covered with dust; *mukha-ambho-jam*—his face, which had formerly resembled a lotus flower; *chinna*—cut off; *āyudha-bhujam*—his arms and weapons; *mṛdhe*—on the battlefield; *uśīnara-indram*—the master of the state of Uśīnara; *vidhinā*—by providence; *tathā*—thus; *kṛtam*—forced into this position; *patim*—the husband; *mahiṣyaḥ*—the queens; *prasamīkṣya*—seeing; *duḥkhitāḥ*—very much aggrieved; *hatāḥ*—killed; *sma*—certainly; *nātha*—O husband; *iti*—thus; *karaiḥ*—with the hands; *uraḥ*—the breast; *bhṛśam*—constantly; *ghnantyaḥ*—pounding; *muhuḥ*—again and again; *tat-padayoḥ*—at the feet of the King; *upāpatan*—fell down.

TRANSLATION

His golden, bejeweled armor smashed, his ornaments and garlands fallen from their places, his hair scattered and his eyes lusterless, the slain King lay on the battlefield, his entire body

smeared with blood, his heart pierced by the arrows of the enemy. When he died he had wanted to show his prowess, and thus he had bitten his lips, and his teeth remained in that position. His beautiful lotuslike face was now black and covered with dust from the battlefield. His arms, with his sword and other weapons, were cut and broken. When the queens of the King of Uśīnara saw their husband lying in that position, they began crying, "O lord, now that you have been killed, we also have been killed." Repeating these words again and again, they fell down, pounding their breasts, at the feet of the dead King.

PURPORT

As stated here, *rabhasā daṣṭa-dacchadam:* the dead King, while fighting in anger, bit his lips to show his prowess, but nonetheless he was killed by providence (*vidhinā*). This proves that we are controlled by higher authorities; our personal power or endeavor is not always supreme. We must therefore accept the position offered to us by the order of the Supreme.

TEXT 32

रुदत्य उच्चैर्दयिताङ्घ्रिपङ्कजं
सिञ्चन्त्य अस्रैः कुचकुङ्कुमारुणैः ।
विस्रस्तकेशाभरणाः शुचं नृणां
सृजन्त्य आक्रन्दनया विलेपिरे ॥३२॥

rudatya uccair dayitāṅghri-paṅkajaṁ
siñcantya asraiḥ kuca-kuṅkumāruṇaiḥ
visrasta-keśābharaṇāḥ śucaṁ nṛṇāṁ
sṛjantya ākrandanayā vilepire

rudatyaḥ—crying; *uccaiḥ*—very loudly; *dayita*—of their beloved husband; *aṅghri-paṅkajam*—the lotus feet; *siñcantyaḥ*—moistening; *asraiḥ*—with tears; *kuca-kuṅkuma-aruṇaiḥ*—which were red from the *kuṅkuma* covering their breasts; *visrasta*—scattered; *keśa*—hair; *ābharaṇāḥ*—and ornaments; *śucam*—grief; *nṛṇām*—of the people in general; *sṛjantyaḥ*—creating; *ākrandanayā*—by crying very pitiably; *vilepire*—began to lament.

TRANSLATION

As the queens loudly cried, their tears glided down their breasts, becoming reddened by kuṅkuma powder, and fell upon the lotus feet of their husband. Their hair became disarrayed, their ornaments fell, and in a way that evoked sympathy from the hearts of others, the queens began lamenting their husband's death.

TEXT 33

अहो विधात्राकरुणेन नः प्रभो
भवान् प्रणीतो दृगगोचरां दशाम् ।
उशीनराणामसि वृत्तिदः पुरा
कृतोऽधुना येन शुचां विवर्धनः ॥३३॥

aho vidhātrākaruṇena naḥ prabho
bhavān praṇīto dṛg-agocarāṁ daśām
uśīnarāṇām asi vṛttidaḥ purā
kṛto 'dhunā yena śucāṁ vivardhanaḥ

aho—alas; *vidhātrā*—by providence; *akaruṇena*—who is merciless; *naḥ*—our; *prabho*—O lord; *bhavān*—Your Lordship; *praṇītaḥ*—taken away; *dṛk*—of sight; *agocarām*—beyond the range; *daśām*—to a state; *uśīnarāṇām*—to the inhabitants of the state of Uśīnara; *asi*—you were; *vṛtti-daḥ*—giving livelihood; *purā*—formerly; *kṛtaḥ*—finished; *adhunā*—now; *yena*—by whom; *śucām*—of lamentation; *vivardhanaḥ*—increasing.

TRANSLATION

O lord, you have now been removed by cruel providence to a state beyond our sight. You had previously sustained the livelihood of the inhabitants of Uśīnara, and thus they were happy, but your condition now is the cause of their unhappiness.

TEXT 34

त्वया कृतज्ञेन वयं महीपते
कथं विना स्याम सुहृत्तमेन ते ।
तत्रानुयानं तव वीर पादयोः
शुश्रूषतीनां दिश यत्र यास्यसि ॥३४॥

tvayā kṛtajñena vayaṁ mahī-pate
kathaṁ vinā syāma suhṛttamena te
tatrānuyānaṁ tava vīra pādayoḥ
śuśrūṣatīnāṁ diśa yatra yāsyasi

tvayā—you; *kṛtajñena*—a most grateful personality; *vayam*—we; *mahī-pate*—O King; *katham*—how; *vinā*—without; *syāma*—shall exist; *suhṛt-tamena*—the best of our friends; *te*—of you; *tatra*—there; *anuyānam*—the following; *tava*—of you; *vīra*—O hero; *pādayoḥ*—of the lotus feet; *śuśrūṣatīnām*—of those engaging in the service; *diśa*—please order; *yatra*—where; *yāsyasi*—you will go.

TRANSLATION

O King, O hero, you were a very grateful husband and the most sincere friend of all of us. How shall we exist without you? O hero, wherever you are going, please direct us there so that we may follow in your footsteps and engage again in your service. Let us go along with you!

PURPORT

Formerly, a *kṣatriya* king was generally the husband of many wives, and after the death of the king, especially in the battlefield, all the queens would agree to accept *saha-māraṇa*, dying with the husband who was their life. When Pāṇḍu Mahārāja, the father of the Pāṇḍavas, died, his two wives—namely, the mother of Yudhiṣṭhira, Bhīma and Arjuna and the mother of Nakula and Sahadeva—were both ready to die in the fire with their husband. Later, after a compromise was arranged, Kuntī stayed alive to care for the little children, and the other wife, Mādrī, was allowed to die with her husband. This system of *saha-māraṇa* continued in India even until the time of British rule, but later it was discouraged, since the attitude of wives gradually changed with the advancement of Kali-yuga. Thus the system of *saha-māraṇa* has practically been abolished. Nevertheless, within the past fifty years I have seen the wife of a medical practitioner voluntarily accept death immediately when her husband died. Both the husband and wife were taken in procession in the mourning cart. Such intense love of a chaste wife for her husband is a special case.

TEXT 35

एवं विलपतीनां वै परिगृह्य मृतं पतिम् ।
अनिच्छतीनां निर्हारमर्कोऽस्तं संन्यवर्तत ॥३५॥

evaṁ vilapatīnāṁ vai
parigṛhya mṛtaṁ patim
anicchatīnāṁ nirhāram
arko 'staṁ sannyavartata

evam—thus; *vilapatīnām*—of the lamenting queens; *vai*—indeed; *parigṛhya*—taking on their laps; *mṛtam*—the dead; *patim*—husband; *anicchatīnām*—not desiring; *nirhāram*—the carrying out of the body for the funeral ceremony; *arkaḥ*—the sun; *astam*—the setting position; *sannyavartata*—passed away.

TRANSLATION

The time was appropriate for the body to be burned, but the queens, not allowing it to be taken away, continued lamenting for the dead body, which they kept on their laps. In the meantime, the sun completed its movements for setting in the west.

PURPORT

According to the Vedic system, if a person dies during the daytime it is customary for his funeral ceremony to be performed before the sun sets, regardless of whether he is burned or buried, and if he dies at night the funeral must be completed before the next sunrise. Apparently the queens continued lamenting for the dead body, the lump of matter, and would not allow it to be taken away for burning. This illustrates the strong grip of illusion among foolish persons who consider the body the self. Women are generally considered less intelligent. Because of ignorance only, the queens thought of the dead body as their husband and somehow or other thought that if the body were kept their husband would remain with them. Such a conception of the self is certainly for *go-khara*—cows and asses. We have actually seen that sometimes when a cow's calf has died the milkman cheats the cow by presenting before her the dead body of her calf. Thus the cow, who would not otherwise allow milking, licks the dead body of the calf and allows herself to be milked. This substantiates the description of the *śāstra* that a foolish man in the bodily concept of life is like a cow. Not only do foolish men and women consider the body the self, but we have even seen that the dead body of a so-called *yogī* was kept for days by his disciples, who thought that their *guru* was in *samādhi.* When decomposition began and a bad smell unfortunately began to overwhelm the yogic power, the disciples allowed the dead body of the so-called *yogī* to be burned. Thus the bodily concept of life is extremely strong among foolish persons, who are compared to cows and asses. Nowadays, great scientists are trying to freeze dead bodies so that in the future these frozen bodies may again be brought to life. The incident narrated by Hiraṇyakaśipu from history must have taken place millions of years ago because Hiraṇyakaśipu lived millions of years ago and was even then quoting from history. Thus the incident occurred before Hiraṇyakaśipu's lifetime, but the same ignorance in the bodily concept of life is still prevalent, not only among laymen but even among scientists who think they will be able to revive frozen corpses.

Apparently the queens did not want to deliver the dead body for burning because they were afraid of dying with the dead body of their husband.

TEXT 36

तत्र ह प्रेतबन्धूनामाश्रुत्य परिदेवितम् ।
आह तान् बालको भूत्वा यमः स्वयमुपागतः ॥३६॥

tatra ha preta-bandhūnām
āśrutya paridevitam

āha tān bālako bhūtvā
yamaḥ svayam upāgataḥ

tatra—there; *ha*—certainly; *preta-bandhūnām*—of the friends and relatives of the dead King; *āśrutya*—hearing; *paridevitam*—the loud lamentation (so loud that it could be heard from the planet of Yamarāja); *āha*—said; *tān*—unto them (the lamenting queens); *bālakaḥ*—a boy; *bhūtvā*—becoming; *yamaḥ*—Yamarāja, the superintendent of death; *svayam*—personally; *upāgataḥ*—after coming.

TRANSLATION

While the queens were lamenting for the dead body of the King, their loud cries were heard even from the abode of Yamarāja. Assuming the body of a boy, Yamarāja personally approached the relatives of the dead body and advised them as follows.

PURPORT

Sometimes the living entity is forced to give up his body and enter another one according to the judgment of Yamarāja. It is difficult, however, for the conditioned soul to enter another body unless the present dead body is annihilated through cremation or some other means. The living being has attachment for the present body and does not want to enter another, and thus in the interim he remains a ghost. If a living being who has already left his body has been pious, Yamarāja, just to give him relief, will give him another body. Since the living being in the body of the King had some attachment to his body, he was hovering as a ghost, and therefore Yamarāja, as a special consideration, approached the lamenting relatives to instruct them personally. Yamarāja approached them as a child because a child is not restricted but is granted admittance anywhere, even to the palace of a king. Besides this, the child was speaking philosophy. People are very much interested in hearing philosophy when it is spoken by a child.

TEXT 37

श्रीयम उवाच
अहो अमीषां वयसाधिकानां
विपश्यतां लोकविधिं विमोहः ।

यत्रागतस्तत्र गतं मनुष्यं
स्वयं सधर्मा अपि शोचन्त्यपार्थम् ॥३७॥

śrī-yama uvāca
aho amīṣāṁ vayasādhikānāṁ
vipaśyatāṁ loka-vidhiṁ vimohaḥ
yatrāgatas tatra gataṁ manuṣyaṁ
svayaṁ sadharmā api śocanty apārtham

śrī-yamaḥ uvāca—Śrī Yamarāja said; *aho*—alas; *amīṣām*—of these; *vayasā*—by age; *adhikānām*—of those advanced; *vipaśyatām*—seeing every day; *loka-vidhim*—the law of nature (that everyone dies); *vimohaḥ*—the bewilderment; *yatra*—from where; *āgataḥ*—came; *tatra*—there; *gatam*—returned; *manuṣyam*—the man; *svayam*—themselves; *sa-dharmāḥ*—similar in nature (prone to die); *api*—although; *śocanti*—they lament; *apārtham*—uselessly.

TRANSLATION

Śrī Yamarāja said: Alas, how amazing it is! These persons, who are older than me, have full experience that hundreds and thousands of living entities have taken birth and died. Thus they should understand that they also are apt to die, yet still they are bewildered. The conditioned soul comes from an unknown place and returns after death to that same unknown place. There is no exception to this rule, which is conducted by material nature. Knowing this, why do they uselessly lament?

PURPORT

The Lord says in *Bhagavad-gītā* (2.28):

avyaktādīni bhūtāni
vyakta-madhyāni bhārata
avyakta-nidhanāny eva
tatra kā paridevanā

"All created beings are unmanifest in their beginning, manifest in their interim state, and unmanifest again when they are annihilated. So what need is there for lamentation?"

Accepting that there are two classes of philosophers, one believing in the existence of the soul and the other not believing in its existence, there is no cause for lamentation in either case. Nonbelievers in the existence of the soul are called atheists by followers of Vedic wisdom. Yet even if for argument's sake we accept the atheistic theory, there is still no cause for lamentation. Apart from the separate existence of the soul, the material elements remain unmanifested before creation. From this subtle state of unmanifestation comes manifestation, just as from ether, air is generated; from air, fire is generated; from fire, water is generated; and from water, earth becomes manifested. From the earth, many varieties of manifestations take place. For example, a big skyscraper is manifested from the earth. When it is dismantled, the manifestation becomes again unmanifested and remains as atoms in the ultimate stage. The law of conservation of energy remains, but in the course of time things are manifested and unmanifested—that is the difference. Then what cause is there for lamentation, in either manifestation or unmanifestation? Somehow or other, even in the unmanifested stage, things are not lost. Both at the beginning and at the end, all elements remain unmanifested, and this does not make any real material difference.

If we accept the Vedic conclusion as stated in the *Bhagavad-gītā* (*antavanta ime dehāḥ*) that these material bodies are perishable in due course of time (*nityasyoktāḥ śarīriṇaḥ*) but that the soul is eternal, then we must remember always that the body is like a dress; therefore why lament the changing of a dress? The material body has no factual existence in relation to the eternal soul. It is something like a dream. In a dream we may think of flying in the sky or sitting on a chariot as a king, but when we wake up we can see that we are neither in the sky nor seated on the chariot. The Vedic wisdom encourages self-realization on the basis of the nonexistence of the material body. Therefore, in either case, whether one believes in the existence of the soul or one does not believe in the existence of the soul, there is no cause for lamentation for loss of the body.

In the *Mahābhārata* it is said, *adarśanād ihāyātaḥ punaś cādarśanaṁ gataḥ.* This statement could support the theory of the atheistic scientist that the child in the womb of the mother has no life but is simply a lump of matter. To follow this theory, if the lump of matter is aborted by a surgical operation, no life is killed; the body of a child is like a tumor, and if a tumor is operated upon and thrown away, no sin is involved. The same argument could be put forward in regard to the King and his queens. The body of the King was manifested from an unmanifested source, and again it became unmanifested from manifestation. Since the manifestation exists only in the middle—between the two points of unmanifestation—why should one cry for the body manifested in the interim?

TEXT 38

अहो वयं धन्यतमा यदत्र
त्यक्ताः पितृभ्यां न विचिन्तयामः ।
अभक्ष्यमाणा अबला वृकादिभिः
स रक्षिता रक्षति यो हि गर्भे ॥३८॥

aho vayaṁ dhanyatamā yad atra
tyaktāḥ pitṛbhyāṁ na vicintayāmaḥ
abhakṣyamāṇā abalā vṛkādibhiḥ
sa rakṣitā rakṣati yo hi garbhe

aho—alas; *vayam*—we; *dhanya-tamāḥ*—most fortunate; *yat*—because; *atra*—at the present moment; *tyaktāḥ*—left alone, without protection; *pitṛbhyām*—by both father and mother; *na*—not; *vicintayāmaḥ*—worry; *abhakṣyamāṇāḥ*—not being eaten; *abalāḥ*—very weak; *vṛka-ādibhiḥ*—by tigers and other ferocious animals; *saḥ*—He (the Supreme Personality of Godhead); *rakṣitā*—will protect; *rakṣati*—has protected; *yaḥ*—who; *hi*—indeed; *garbhe*—within the womb.

TRANSLATION

It is wonderful that these elderly women do not have a higher sense of life than we do. Indeed, we are most fortunate, for although we are children and have been left to struggle in material life, unprotected by father and mother, and although we are very

weak, we have not been vanquished or eaten by ferocious animals. Thus we have a firm belief that the Supreme Personality of Godhead, who has given us protection even in the womb of the mother, will protect us everywhere.

PURPORT

As stated in *Bhagavad-gītā* (18.61), *īśvaraḥ sarva-bhūtānāṁ hṛd-deśe 'rjuna tiṣṭhati:* the Lord is present in the core of everyone's heart. Thus the Lord gives protection to everyone and gives the different types of bodies the living entity wants to enjoy. Everything is done by the order of the Supreme Personality of Godhead. Therefore one should not lament the birth and death of a living being, which have been arranged by the Supreme Lord. Lord Kṛṣṇa says in *Bhagavad-gītā* (15.15), *sarvasya cāhaṁ hṛdi sanniviṣṭo mattaḥ smṛtir jñānam apohanaṁ ca:* "I am seated in everyone's heart, and from Me come remembrance, knowledge and forgetfulness." One must act according to the direction of the Lord within the heart, but because the conditioned soul wants to act independently, the Lord gives him the facility to act and experience the reactions. The Lord says, *sarva-dharmān parityajya mām ekaṁ śaraṇaṁ vraja:* "Give up all other duties and simply surrender unto Me." One who does not abide by the orders of the Supreme Personality of Godhead is given the facility to enjoy this material world. Instead of restricting him, the Lord gives the conditioned soul the opportunity to enjoy so that by mature experience, after many, many births (*bahūnāṁ janmanām ante*), he will understand that surrender to the lotus feet of Vāsudeva is the only duty of all living beings.

TEXT 39

य इच्छयेशः सृजतीदमव्ययो
य एव रक्षत्यवलुम्पते च यः ।
तस्याबलाः क्रीडनमाहुरीशितु-
श्चराचरं निग्रहसङ्ग्रहे प्रभुः ॥३९॥

ya icchayeśaḥ sṛjatīdam avyayo
ya eva rakṣaty avalumpate ca yaḥ

tasyābalāḥ krīḍanam āhur īśituś
carācaraṁ nigraha-saṅgrahe prabhuḥ

yaḥ—who; *icchayā*—by His will (without being forced by anyone); *īśaḥ*—the supreme controller; *sṛjati*—creates; *idam*—this (material world); *avyayaḥ*—remaining as He is (not having lost His own existence because of having created so many material manifestations); *yaḥ*—who; *eva*—indeed; *rakṣati*—maintains; *avalumpate*—annihilates; *ca*—also; *yaḥ*—who; *tasya*—of Him; *abalāḥ*—O poor women; *krīḍanam*—the playing; *āhuḥ*—they say; *īśituḥ*—of the Supreme Personality of Godhead; *cara-acaram*—moving and not moving; *nigraha*—in destruction; *saṅgrahe*—or in protection; *prabhuḥ*—fully able.

TRANSLATION

The boy addressed the women: O weak women! Only by the will of the Supreme Personality of Godhead, who is never diminished, is the entire world created, maintained and again annihilated. This is the verdict of the Vedic knowledge. This material creation, consisting of the moving and nonmoving, is exactly like His plaything. Being the Supreme Lord, He is completely competent to destroy and protect.

PURPORT

In this regard the queens might argue, "If our husband was protected by the Supreme Personality of Godhead when in the womb, why has he not been given protection now?" To this question the answer is, *ya icchayeśaḥ sṛjatīdam avyayo ya eva rakṣaty avalumpate ca yaḥ.* One cannot argue with the activities of the Supreme Personality of Godhead. The Lord is always free, and therefore He can protect and can also annihilate. He is not our order carrier; whatever He likes He will do. Therefore He is the Supreme Lord. The Lord does not create this material world at anyone's request, and therefore He can annihilate everything merely by His will. That is His supremacy. If one argues, "Why does He act in this way?" the answer is that He can do so because He is supreme. No one can question His activities. If one argues, "What is the purpose of this sinful creation and annihilation?" the answer is that to prove His omnipotence He can do anything, and no one can question Him. If He were answerable to us concerning why He does something and why He does not, His supremacy would be curtailed.

TEXT 40

पथि च्युतं तिष्ठति दिष्टरक्षितं
गृहे स्थितं तद्विहतं विनश्यति ।
जीवत्यनाथोऽपि तदीक्षितो वने
गृहेऽभिगुप्तोऽस्य हतो न जीवति ॥४०॥

pathi cyutaṁ tiṣṭhati diṣṭa-rakṣitaṁ
gṛhe sthitaṁ tad-vihataṁ vinaśyati
jīvaty anātho 'pi tad-īkṣito vane
gṛhe 'bhigupto 'sya hato na jīvati

pathi—on the public road; *cyutam*—some possession dropped; *tiṣṭhati*—it remains; *diṣṭa-rakṣitam*—protected by destiny; *gṛhe*—at home; *sthitam*—although situated; *tat-vihatam*—struck by the will of the Supreme; *vinaśyati*—it is lost; *jīvati*—remains alive; *anāthaḥ api*—although without a protector; *tat-īkṣitaḥ*—being protected by the Lord; *vane*—in the forest; *gṛhe*—at home; *abhiguptaḥ*—well hidden and protected; *asya*—of this one; *hataḥ*—struck; *na*—not; *jīvati*—lives.

TRANSLATION

Sometimes one loses his money on a public street, where everyone can see it, and yet his money is protected by destiny and not seen by others. Thus the man who lost it gets it back. On the other hand, if the Lord does not give protection, even money maintained very securely at home is lost. If the Supreme Lord gives one protection, even though one has no protector and is in the jungle, one remains alive, whereas a person well protected at home by relatives and others sometimes dies, no one being able to protect him.

PURPORT

These are examples of the supremacy of the Lord. Our plans to protect or annihilate do not act, but whatever He thinks of doing actually happens. The examples given in this regard are practical. Everyone has had such practical experiences, and there are also many other clear examples. For instance, Prahlāda Mahārāja said that a child is certainly dependent on his father and mother, but in spite of their presence, the child is harassed in many ways. Sometimes, in spite of a supply of good medicine and an experienced physician, a patient does not survive. Therefore, since everything is dependent on the free will of the Supreme Personality of Godhead, our only duty is to surrender unto Him and seek His protection.

TEXT 41

भूतानि तैस्तैर्निजयोनिकर्मभि-
र्भवन्ति काले न भवन्ति सर्वशः ।
न तत्र हात्मा प्रकृतावपि स्थित-
स्तस्या गुणैरन्यतमो हि बध्यते ॥४१॥

bhūtāni tais tair nija-yoni-karmabhir
bhavanti kāle na bhavanti sarvaśaḥ
na tatra hātmā prakṛtāv api sthitas
tasyā guṇair anyatamo hi badhyate

bhūtāni—all the bodies of the living entities; *taiḥ taiḥ*—their own respective; *nija-yoni*—causing their own bodies; *karmabhiḥ*—by past activities; *bhavanti*—appear; *kāle*—in due course of time; *na bhavanti*—disappear; *sarvaśaḥ*—in all respects; *na*—not; *tatra*—there; *ha*—indeed; *ātmā*—the soul; *prakṛtau*—within this material world; *api*—although; *sthitaḥ*—situated; *tasyāḥ*—of her (the material energy); *guṇaiḥ*—by different modes; *anya-tamaḥ*—most different; *hi*—indeed; *badhyate*—is bound.

TRANSLATION

Every conditioned soul receives a different type of body according to his work, and when the engagement is finished the body is finished. Although the spirit soul is situated in subtle and gross material bodies in different forms of life, he is not bound by them,

for he is always understood to be completely different from the manifested body.

PURPORT

Here it is very plainly explained that God is not responsible for the living entity's accepting different types of bodies. One has to accept a body according to the laws of nature and one's own *karma.* Therefore the Vedic injunction is that a person engaged in material activities should be given directions by which he can intelligently apply his activities to the service of the Lord to become free from the material bondage of repeated birth and death (*sva-karmaṇā tam abhyarcya siddhiṁ vindati mānavaḥ*). The Lord is always ready to give directions. Indeed, His directions are elaborately given in *Bhagavad-gītā.* If we take advantage of these directions, then in spite of our being conditioned by the laws of material nature, we shall become free to attain our original constitution (*mām eva ye prapadyante māyām etāṁ taranti te*). We should have firm faith that the Lord is supreme and that if we surrender to Him, He will take charge of us and indicate how we can get out of material life and return home, back to Godhead. Without such surrender, one is obliged to accept a certain type of body according to his *karma,* sometimes as an animal, sometimes a demigod and so on. Although the body is obtained and lost in due course of time, the spirit soul does not actually mix with the body, but is subjugated by the particular modes of nature with which he is sinfully associated. Spiritual education changes one's consciousness so that one simply carries out the orders of the Supreme Lord and becomes free from the influence of the modes of material nature.

TEXT 42

इदं शरीरं पुरुषस्य मोहजं
यथा पृथग्भौतिकमीयते गृहम् ।
यथौदकैः पार्थिवतैजसैर्जनः
कालेन जातो विकृतो विनश्यति ॥४२॥

idaṁ śarīraṁ puruṣasya mohajaṁ
yathā pṛthag bhautikam īyate gṛham

yathaudakaiḥ pārthiva-taijasair janaḥ
kālena jāto vikṛto vinaśyati

idam—this; *śarīram*—body; *puruṣasya*—of the conditioned soul; *moha-jam*—born of ignorance; *yathā*—just as; *pṛthak*—separate; *bhautikam*—material; *īyate*—is seen; *gṛham*—a house; *yathā*—just as; *udakaiḥ*—with water; *pārthiva*—with earth; *taijasaiḥ*—and with fire; *janaḥ*—the conditioned soul; *kālena*—in due course of time; *jātaḥ*—born; *vikṛtaḥ*—transformed; *vinaśyati*—is vanquished.

TRANSLATION

Just as a householder, although different from the identity of his house, thinks his house to be identical with him, so the conditioned soul, due to ignorance, accepts the body to be himself, although the body is actually different from the soul. This body is obtained through a combination of portions of earth, water and fire, and when the earth, water and fire are transformed in the course of time, the body is vanquished. The soul has nothing to do with this creation and dissolution of the body.

PURPORT

We transmigrate from one body to another in bodies that are products of our illusion, but as spirit souls we always exist separately from material, conditional life. The example given here is that a house or car is always different from its owner, but because of attachment the conditioned soul thinks it to be identical with him. A car or house is actually made of material elements; as long as the material elements combine together properly, the car or house exists, and when they are disassembled the house or the car is disassembled. The spirit soul, however, always remains as he is.

TEXT 43

यथानलो दारुषु भिन्न ईयते
यथानिलो देहगतः पृथक् स्थितः ।
यथा नभः सर्वगतं न सज्जते
तथा पुमान् सर्वगुणाश्रयः परः ॥४३॥

yathānalo dāruṣu bhinna īyate
yathānilo deha-gataḥ pṛthak sthitaḥ
yathā nabhaḥ sarva-gataṁ na sajjate
tathā pumān sarva-guṇāśrayaḥ paraḥ

yathā—just as; *analaḥ*—the fire; *dāruṣu*—in wood; *bhinnaḥ*—separate; *īyate*—is perceived; *yathā*—just as; *anilaḥ*—the air; *deha-gataḥ*—within the body; *pṛthak*—separate; *sthitaḥ*—situated; *yathā*—just as; *nabhaḥ*—the sky; *sarva-gatam*—all-pervading; *na*—not; *sajjate*—mix; *tathā*—similarly; *pumān*—the living entity; *sarva-guṇa-āśrayaḥ*—although now the shelter of the modes of material nature; *paraḥ*—transcendental to material contamination.

TRANSLATION

As fire, although situated in wood, is perceived to be different from the wood, as air, although situated within the mouth and nostrils, is perceived to be separate, and as the sky, although all-pervading, never mixes with anything, so the living entity, although now encaged within the material body, of which it is the source, is separate from it.

PURPORT

In *Bhagavad-gītā* the Supreme Personality of Godhead has explained that the material energy and spiritual energy both emanate from Him. The material energy is described as *me bhinnā prakṛtir aṣṭadhā,* the eight separated energies of the Lord. But although the eight gross and subtle material energies—namely, earth, water, fire, air, ether, mind, intelligence and false ego—are stated to be *bhinnā,* separate from the Lord, actually they are not. As fire appears separate from wood and as the air flowing through the nostrils and mouth of the body appear separate from the body, so the Paramātmā, the Supreme Personality of Godhead, appears separate from the living being but is actually separate and not separate simultaneously. This is the philosophy of *acintya-bhedābheda-tattva* propounded by Śrī Caitanya Mahāprabhu. According to the reactions of *karma,* the living being appears separate from the Supreme Personality of Godhead, but actually he is very intimately related with the

Lord. Consequently, even though we now seem neglected by the Lord, He is actually always alert to our activities. Under all circumstances, therefore, we should simply depend on the supremacy of the Supreme Personality of Godhead and thus revive our intimate relationship with Him. We must depend upon the authority and control of the Supreme Personality of Godhead.

TEXT 44

सुयज्ञो नन्वयं शेते मूढा यमनुशोचथ ।
यः श्रोता योऽनुवक्तेह स न दृश्येत कर्हिचित् ॥४४॥

suyajño nanv ayaṁ śete
mūḍhā yam anuśocatha
yaḥ śrotā yo 'nuvakteha
sa na dṛśyeta karhicit

suyajñaḥ—the king named Suyajña; *nanu*—indeed; *ayam*—this; *śete*—lies; *mūḍhāḥ*—O foolish people; *yam*—whom; *anuśocatha*—you cry for; *yaḥ*—he who; *śrotā*—the hearer; *yaḥ*—he who; *anuvaktā*—the speaker; *iha*—in this world; *saḥ*—he; *na*—not; *dṛśyeta*—is visible; *karhicit*—at any time.

TRANSLATION

Yamarāja continued: O lamenters, you are all fools! The person named Suyajña, for whom you lament, is still lying before you and has not gone anywhere. Then what is the cause for your lamentation? Previously he heard you and replied to you, but now, not finding him, you are lamenting. This is contradictory behavior, for you have never actually seen the person within the body who heard you and replied. There is no need for your lamentation, for the body you have always seen is lying here.

PURPORT

This instruction by Yamarāja in the form of a boy is understandable even for a common man. A common man who considers the body the self is certainly comparable to an animal (*yasyātma-buddhiḥ kuṇape tri-dhātuke . . . sa eva go-kharaḥ*). But even a common man can understand that after death a person is gone. Although the body is still there, a dead man's relatives lament that the person has gone away, for a common man sees the body but cannot see the soul. As described in *Bhagavad-gītā*, *dehino 'smin yathā dehe:* the soul, the proprietor of the body, is within. After death, when the breath within the nostrils has stopped, one can understand that the person within the body, who was hearing and replying, has now gone. Therefore, in effect, the common man concludes that actually the spirit soul was different from the body and has now gone away. Thus even a common man, coming to his senses, can know that the real person who was within the body and was hearing and replying was never seen. For that which was never seen, what is the need of lamentation?

TEXT 45

न श्रोता नानुवक्तायं मुख्योऽप्यत्र महानसुः ।
यस्त्विहेन्द्रियवानात्मा स चान्यः प्राणदेहयोः॥४५॥

na śrotā nānuvaktāyaṁ
mukhyo 'py atra mahān asuḥ
yas tv ihendriyavān ātmā
sa cānyaḥ prāṇa-dehayoḥ

na—not; *śrotā*—the listener; *na*—not; *anuvaktā*—the speaker; *ayam*—this; *mukhyaḥ*—chief; *api*—although; *atra*—in this body; *mahān*—the great; *asuḥ*—life air; *yaḥ*—he who; *tu*—but; *iha*—in this body; *indriya-vān*—possessing all the sense organs; *ātmā*—the soul; *saḥ*—he; *ca*—and; *anyaḥ*—different; *prāṇa-dehayoḥ*—from the life air and the material body.

TRANSLATION

In the body the most important substance is the life air, but that also is neither the listener nor the speaker. Beyond even the life air, the soul also can do nothing, for the Supersoul is actually the director, in cooperation with the individual soul. The Supersoul

conducting the activities of the body is different from the body and living force.

PURPORT

The Supreme Personality of Godhead distinctly says in *Bhagavad-gītā* (15.15), *sarvasya cāhaṁ hṛdi sanniviṣṭo mattaḥ smṛtir jñānam apohanaṁ ca:* "I am seated in everyone's heart, and from Me come remembrance, knowledge and forgetfulness." Although the *ātmā*, or soul, is present in every material body (*dehino 'smin yathā dehe*), he is not actually the chief person acting through the senses, mind and so on. The soul can merely act in cooperation with the Supersoul because it is the Supersoul who gives him directions to act or not to act (*mattaḥ smṛtir jñānam apohanaṁ ca*). One cannot act without His sanction, for the Supersoul is *upadraṣṭā* and *anumantā*, the witness and sanctioner. One who studies carefully, under the direction of a bona fide spiritual master, can understand the real knowledge that the Supreme Personality of Godhead is actually the conductor of all the activities of the individual soul, and the controller of their results as well. Although the individual soul possesses the *indriyas*, or senses, he is not actually the proprietor, for the proprietor is the Supersoul. Consequently the Supersoul is called Hṛṣīkeśa, and the individual soul is advised by the direction of the Supersoul to surrender to Him and thus be happy (*sarva-dharmān parityajya māṁ ekaṁ śaraṇaṁ vraja*). Thus he can become immortal and be transferred to the spiritual kingdom, where he will achieve the highest success of an eternal, blissful life of knowledge. In conclusion, the individual soul is different from the body, senses, living force and the airs within the body, and above him is the Supersoul, who gives the individual soul all facilities. The individual soul who renders everything to the Supersoul lives very happily within the body.

TEXT 46

भूतेन्द्रियमनोलिङ्गान् देहानुच्चावचान् विभुः।
भजत्युत्सृजति ह्यन्यस्तच्चापि स्वेन तेजसा ॥४६॥

bhūtendriya-mano-liṅgān
dehān uccāvacān vibhuḥ

bhajaty utsṛjati hy anyas
tac cāpi svena tejasā

bhūta—by the five material elements; *indriya*—the ten senses; *manaḥ*—and the mind; *liṅgān*—characterized; *dehān*—gross material bodies; *ucca-avacān*—high class and low class; *vibhuḥ*—the individual soul, which is the lord of the body and senses; *bhajati*—achieves; *utsṛjati*—gives up; *hi*—indeed; *anyaḥ*—being different; *tat*—that; *ca*—also; *api*—indeed; *svena*—by his own; *tejasā*—power of advanced knowledge.

TRANSLATION

The five material elements, the ten senses and the mind all combine to form the various parts of the gross and subtle bodies. The living entity comes in contact with his material bodies, whether high or low, and later gives them up by his personal prowess. This strength can be perceived in a living entity's personal power to possess different types of bodies.

PURPORT

The conditioned soul has knowledge, and if he wants to fully utilize the gross and subtle bodies for his real advancement in life, he can do so. It is therefore said here that by his high intelligence (*svena tejasā*), by the superior power of superior knowledge achieved from the right source—the spiritual master, or *ācārya*—he can give up his conditional life in a material body and return home, back to Godhead. However, if he wants to keep himself in the darkness of this material world, he can do so. The Lord confirms this as follows in *Bhagavad-gītā* (9.25):

yānti deva-vratā devān
pitṝn yānti pitṛ-vratāḥ
bhūtāni yānti bhūtejyā
yānti mad-yājino 'pi mām

"Those who worship the demigods will take birth among the demigods; those who worship ghosts and spirits will take birth among such beings;

those who worship ancestors go to the ancestors; and those who worship Me will live with Me."

The human form of body is valuable. One can use this body to go to the higher planetary systems, to Pitṛloka, or he can remain in this lower planetary system, but if one tries he can also return home, back to Godhead. This prowess is given by the Supreme Personality of Godhead as the Supersoul. Therefore the Lord says, *mattaḥ smṛtir jñānam apohanaṁ ca:* "From Me come remembrance, knowledge and forgetfulness." If one wants to receive real knowledge from the Supreme Personality of Godhead, one can become free from bondage to repeated acceptance of material bodies. If one takes to the devotional service of the Lord and surrenders unto Him, the Lord is prepared to give one directions by which to return home, back to Godhead, but if one foolishly wants to keep himself in darkness, he can continue in a life of material existence.

TEXT 47

यावल्लिङ्गान्वितो ह्यात्मा तावत् कर्म निबन्धनम् ।
ततो विपर्ययः क्लेशो मायायोगोऽनुवर्तते ॥४७॥

yāval liṅgānvito hy ātmā
tāvat karma-nibandhanam
tato viparyayaḥ kleśo
māyā-yogo 'nuvartate

yāvat—as long as; *liṅga-anvitaḥ*—covered by the subtle body; *hi*—indeed; *ātmā*—the soul; *tāvat*—that long; *karma*—of fruitive activities; *nibandhanam*—bondage; *tataḥ*—from that; *viparyayaḥ*—reversal (wrongly thinking the body to be the self); *kleśaḥ*—misery; *māyā-yogaḥ*—a strong relationship with the external, illusory energy; *anuvartate*—follows.

TRANSLATION

As long as the spirit soul is covered by the subtle body, consisting of the mind, intelligence and false ego, he is bound to the results of his fruitive activities. Because of this covering, the spirit

soul is connected with the material energy and must accordingly suffer material conditions and reversals, continually, life after life.

PURPORT

The living entity is bound by the subtle body, consisting of the mind, intelligence and false ego. At the time of death, therefore, the position of the mind becomes the cause for the next body. As confirmed in *Bhagavad-gītā* (8.6), *yaṁ yaṁ vāpi smaran bhāvaṁ tyajaty ante kalevaram:* at the time of death the mind sets the criteria for the spirit soul's being carried to another type of body. If a living being resists the dictation of the mind and engages the mind in the loving service of the Lord, the mind cannot degrade him. The duty of all human beings, therefore, is to keep the mind always engaged at the lotus feet of the Lord (*sa vai manaḥ kṛṣṇa-padāravindayoḥ*). When the mind is engaged at the lotus feet of Kṛṣṇa, the intelligence is purified, and then the intelligence gets inspiration from the Supersoul (*dadāmi buddhi-yogaṁ tam*). Thus the living entity makes progress toward liberation from material bondage. The individual living soul is subject to the laws of fruitive activity, but the Supersoul, Paramātmā, is not affected by the fruitive activities of the individual soul. As confirmed in the Vedic *Upaniṣad*, the Paramātmā and the *jīvātmā*, who are likened to two birds, are sitting in the body. The *jīvātmā* is enjoying or suffering by eating the fruits of the bodily activities, but the Paramātmā, who is free from such bondage, witnesses and sanctions the activities of the individual soul as the individual soul desires.

TEXT 48

वितथाभिनिवेशोऽयं यद् गुणेष्वर्थदृग्वचः ।
यथा मनोरथः स्वप्नः सर्वमैन्द्रियकं मृषा ॥४८॥

vitathābhiniveśo 'yaṁ
yad guṇeṣv artha-dṛg-vacaḥ
yathā manorathaḥ svapnaḥ
sarvam aindriyakaṁ mṛṣā

vitatha—fruitless; *abhiniveśaḥ*—the conception; *ayam*—this; *yat*—which; *guṇeṣu*—in the modes of material nature; *artha*—as a fact; *dṛk-*

vacaḥ—the seeing and talking of; *yathā*—just as; *manorathaḥ*—a mental concoction (daydream); *svapnaḥ*—a dream; *sarvam*—everything; *aindriyakam*—produced by the senses; *mṛṣā*—false.

TRANSLATION

It is fruitless to see and talk of the material modes of nature and their resultant so-called happiness and distress as if they were factual. When the mind wanders during the day and a man begins to think himself extremely important, or when he dreams at night and sees a beautiful woman enjoying with him, these are merely false dreams. Similarly, the happiness and distress caused by the material senses should be understood to be meaningless.

PURPORT

The happiness and distress derived from the activities of the material senses are not actual happiness and distress. Therefore *Bhagavad-gītā* speaks of happiness that is transcendental to the material conception of life (*sukham ātyantikaṁ yat tad buddhi-grāhyam atīndriyam*). When our senses are purified of material contamination, they become *atīndriya*, transcendental senses, and when the transcendental senses are engaged in the service of the master of the senses, Hṛṣīkeśa, one can derive real transcendental pleasure. Whatever distress or happiness we manufacture by mental concoction through the subtle mind has no reality, but is simply a mental concoction. One should therefore not imagine so-called happiness through mental concoction. Rather, the best course is to engage the mind in the service of the Lord, Hṛṣīkeśa, and thus feel real blissful life.

There is a Vedic statement *apāma-somam amṛtā abhūma apsarobhir viharāma*. With reference to such a conception, one wants to go to the heavenly planets to enjoy with the young girls there and drink *soma-rasa*. Such imaginary pleasure, however, has no value. As confirmed in *Bhagavad-gītā* (7.23), *antavat tu phalaṁ teṣāṁ tad bhavaty alpa-medhasām:* "Men of small intelligence worship the demigods, and their fruits are limited and temporary." Even if by fruitive activity or worship of the demigods one is elevated to the higher planetary systems for sense enjoyment, his situation is condemned in *Bhagavad-gītā* as *antavat*, perishable. The happiness one enjoys in this way is like the pleasure of embracing a young woman in a dream; for some time it may be pleasing, but actually the basic principle is false. The mental concoctions of happiness and distress in this material world are compared to dreams because of their falseness. All thoughts of obtaining happiness by using the material senses have a false background and therefore have no meaning.

TEXT 49

अथ नित्यमनित्यं वा नेह शोचन्ति तद्विदः ।
नान्यथा शक्यते कर्तुं स्वभावः शोचतामिति ॥४९॥

atha nityam anityaṁ vā
neha śocanti tad-vidaḥ
nānyathā śakyate kartuṁ
sva-bhāvaḥ śocatām iti

atha—therefore; *nityam*—the eternal spirit soul; *anityam*—the temporary material body; *vā*—or; *na*—not; *iha*—in this world; *śocanti*—they lament for; *tat-vidaḥ*—those who are advanced in knowledge of the body and soul; *na*—not; *anyathā*—otherwise; *śakyate*—is able; *kartum*—to do; *sva-bhāvaḥ*—the nature; *śocatām*—of those prone to lamentation; *iti*—thus.

TRANSLATION

Those who have full knowledge of self-realization, who know very well that the spirit soul is eternal whereas the body is perishable, are not overwhelmed by lamentation. But persons who lack knowledge of self-realization certainly lament. Therefore it is difficult to educate a person in illusion.

PURPORT

According to the *mīmāṁsā* philosophers, everything is eternal, *nitya*, and according to the Sāṅkhya philosophers everything is *mithyā*, or *anitya*—impermanent. Nonetheless, without real knowledge of *ātmā*, the soul, such philosophers must be bewildered and must continue to lament as *śūdras*. Śrīla Śukadeva Gosvāmī therefore said to Parīkṣit Mahārāja:

śrotavyādīni rājendra
nṛṇāṁ santi sahasraśaḥ
apaśyatām ātma-tattvaṁ
gṛheṣu gṛha-medhinām

"Those who are materially engrossed, being blind to knowledge of the ultimate truth, have many subjects for hearing in human society, O Emperor." (*Bhāg.* 2.1.2) For ordinary persons engaged in material activities there are many, many subject matters to understand because such persons do not understand self-realization. One must therefore be educated in self-realization so that under any circumstances in life he will remain steady in his vows.

TEXT 50

लुब्धको विपिने कश्चित्पक्षिणां निर्मितोऽन्तकः ।
वितत्य जालं विदधे तत्र तत्र प्रलोभयन् ॥५०॥

lubdhako vipine kaścit
pakṣiṇāṁ nirmito 'ntakaḥ
vitatya jālaṁ vidadhe
tatra tatra pralobhayan

lubdhakaḥ—hunter; *vipine*—in the forest; *kaścit*—some; *pakṣiṇām*—of birds; *nirmitaḥ*—appointed; *antakaḥ*—killer; *vitatya*—spreading; *jālam*—a net; *vidadhe*—captured; *tatra tatra*—here and there; *pralobhayan*—luring with food.

TRANSLATION

There was once a hunter who lured birds with food and captured them after spreading a net. He lived as if appointed by death personified as the killer of the birds.

PURPORT

This is another incident from the histories.

TEXT 51

कुलिङ्गमिथुनं तत्र विचरत्समदृश्यत ।
तयोः कुलिङ्गी सहसा लुब्धकेन प्रलोभिता ॥५१॥

kuliṅga-mithunaṁ tatra
vicarat samadṛśyata
tayoḥ kuliṅgī sahasā
lubdhakena pralobhitā

kuliṅga-mithunam—a pair of (male and female) birds known as *kuliṅga; tatra*—there (where the hunter was hunting); *vicarat*—wandering; *samadṛśyata*—he saw; *tayoḥ*—of the pair; *kuliṅgī*—the female bird; *sahasā*—suddenly; *lubdhakena*—by the hunter; *pralobhitā*—allured.

TRANSLATION

While wandering in the forest, the hunter saw a pair of kuliṅga birds. Of the two, the female was captivated by the hunter's lure.

TEXT 52

सासज्जत सिचस्तन्त्र्यां महिष्यः कालयन्त्रिता ।
कुलिङ्गस्तां तथापन्नां निरीक्ष्य भृशदुःखितः ।
स्नेहादकल्पः कृपणः कृपणां पर्यदेवयत् ॥५२॥

sāsajjata sicas tantryāṁ
mahiṣyaḥ kāla-yantritā
kuliṅgas tāṁ tathāpannāṁ
nirīkṣya bhṛśa-duḥkhitaḥ
snehād akalpaḥ kṛpaṇaḥ
kṛpaṇāṁ paryadevayat

sā—the female bird; *asajjata*—trapped; *sicaḥ*—of the net; *tantryām*—in the rope; *mahiṣyaḥ*—O queens; *kāla-yantritā*—being forced by time; *kuliṅgaḥ*—the male *kuliṅga* bird; *tām*—her; *tathā*—in that condition; *āpannām*—captured; *nirīkṣya*—seeing; *bhṛśa-*

duḥkhitaḥ—very unhappy; *snehāt*—out of affection; *akalpaḥ*—unable to do anything; *kṛpaṇaḥ*—the poor bird; *kṛpaṇām*—the poor wife; *paryadevayat*—began to lament for.

TRANSLATION

O queens of Suyajña, the male kuliṅga bird, seeing his wife put into the greatest danger in the grip of Providence, became very unhappy. Because of affection, the poor bird, being unable to release her, began to lament for his wife.

TEXT 53

अहो अकरुणो देवः स्त्रियाकरुणया विभुः ।
कृपणं मामनुशोचन्त्या दीनया किं करिष्यति ॥५३॥

aho akaruṇo devaḥ
striyākaruṇayā vibhuḥ
kṛpaṇaṁ mām anuśocantyā
dīnayā kiṁ kariṣyati

aho—alas; *akaruṇaḥ*—most unkind; *devaḥ*—providence; *striyā*—with my wife; *ākaruṇayā*—who is fully compassionate; *vibhuḥ*—the Supreme Lord; *kṛpaṇam*—poor; *mām*—me; *anuśocantyā*—lamenting for; *dīnayā*—poor; *kim*—what; *kariṣyati*—shall do.

TRANSLATION

Alas, how merciless is Providence! My wife, unable to be helped by anyone, is in such an awkward position and lamenting for me. What will Providence gain by taking away this poor bird? What will be the profit?

TEXT 54

कामं नयतु मां देवः किमर्धेनात्मनो हि मे ।
दीनेन जीवता दुःखमनेन विधुरायुषा ॥५४॥

kāmaṁ nayatu māṁ devaḥ
kim ardhenātmano hi me

dīnena jīvatā duḥkham
anena vidhurāyuṣā

kāmam—as He likes; *nayatu*—let Him take away; *mām*—me; *devaḥ*—the Supreme Lord; *kim*—what use; *ardhena*—with half; *ātmanaḥ*—of the body; *hi*—indeed; *me*—my; *dīnena*—poor; *jīvatā*—living; *duḥkham*—in suffering; *anena*—this; *vidhura-āyuṣā*—having a lifetime full of affliction.

TRANSLATION

If unkind Providence takes away my wife, who is half my body, why should He not take me also? What is the use of my living with half of my body, bereaved by loss of my wife? What shall I gain in this way?

TEXT 55

कथं त्वजातपक्षांस्तान् मातृहीनान् बिभर्म्यहम् ।
मन्दभाग्याः प्रतीक्षन्ते नीडे मे मातरं प्रजाः ।।५५।।

kathaṁ tv ajāta-pakṣāṁs tān
mātṛ-hīnān bibharmy aham
manda-bhāgyāḥ pratīkṣante
nīḍe me mātaraṁ prajāḥ

katham—how; *tu*—but; *ajāta-pakṣān*—who have not grown wings to fly; *tān*—them; *mātṛ-hīnān*—bereft of their mother; *bibharmi*—shall maintain; *aham*—I; *manda-bhāgyāḥ*—very unfortunate; *pratīkṣante*—they await; *nīḍe*—in the nest; *me*—my; *mātaram*—their mother; *prajāḥ*—baby birds.

TRANSLATION

The unfortunate baby birds, bereft of their mother, are waiting in the nest for her to feed them. They are still very small and have not yet grown their wings. How shall I be able to maintain them?

PURPORT

The bird is lamenting for the mother of his children because the mother naturally maintains and cares for the children. Yamarāja, however, in the guise of a small boy, has already explained that although his mother left him uncared for and wandering in the forest, the tigers and other ferocious animals had not eaten him. The real fact is that if the Supreme Personality of Godhead protects one, even though one be motherless and fatherless, one can be maintained by the good will of the Lord. Otherwise, if the Supreme Lord does not give one protection, one must suffer in spite of the presence of his father and mother. Another example is that sometimes a patient dies in spite of a good physician and good medicine. Thus without the protection of the Lord one cannot live, with or without parents.

Another point in this verse is that fathers and mothers have protective feelings for their children even in bird and beast society, not to speak of human society. Kali-yuga, however, is so degraded that a father and mother even kill their children in the womb on the plea of their scientific knowledge that within the womb the child has no life. Prestigious medical practitioners give this opinion, and therefore the father and mother of this day kill their children within the womb. How degraded human society has become! Their scientific knowledge is so advanced that they think that within the egg and the embryo there is no life. Now these so-called scientists are receiving Nobel Prizes for advancing the theory of chemical evolution. But if chemical combinations are the source of life, why don't the scientists manufacture something like an egg through chemistry and put it in an incubator so that a chicken will come out? What is their answer? With their scientific knowledge they are unable to create even an egg. Such scientists are described in *Bhagavad-gītā* as *māyayāpahṛta-jñānāḥ*, fools whose real knowledge has been taken away. They are not men of knowledge, but they pose as scientists and philosophers, although their so-called theoretical knowledge cannot produce practical results.

TEXT 56

एवं कुलिङ्गं विलपन्तमारात्
प्रियावियोगातुरमश्रुकण्ठम् ।
स एव तं शाकुनिकः शरेण
विव्याध कालप्रहितो विलीनः ॥५६॥

evaṁ kuliṅgaṁ vilapantam ārāt
priyā-viyogāturam aśru-kaṇṭham
sa eva taṁ śākunikaḥ śareṇa
vivyādha kāla-prahito vilīnaḥ

evam—thus; *kuliṅgam*—the bird; *vilapantam*—while lamenting; *ārāt*—from a distance; *priyā-viyoga*—because of the loss of his wife; *āturam*—very aggrieved; *aśru-kaṇṭham*—with tears in the eyes; *saḥ*—he (that hunter); *eva*—indeed; *tam*—him (the male bird); *śākunikaḥ*—who could kill even a vulture; *śareṇa*—by an arrow; *vivyādha*—pierced; *kāla-prahitaḥ*—being moved by time; *vilīnaḥ*—hidden.

TRANSLATION

Because of the loss of his wife, the kuliṅga bird lamented with tears in his eyes. Meanwhile, following the dictations of mature time, the hunter, who was very carefully hidden in the distance, released his arrow, which pierced the body of the kuliṅga bird and killed him.

TEXT 57

एवं यूयमपश्यन्त्य आत्मापायमबुद्धयः ।
नैनं प्राप्स्यथ शोचन्त्यः पतिं वर्षशतैरपि ॥५७॥

evaṁ yūyam apaśyantya
ātmāpāyam abuddhayaḥ
nainaṁ prāpsyatha śocantyaḥ
patiṁ varṣa-śatair api

evam—thus; *yūyam*—you; *apaśyantyaḥ*—not seeing; *ātma-apāyam*—own death; *abuddhayaḥ*—O ignorant ones; *na*—not; *enam*—him; *prāpsyatha*—you will obtain; *śocantyaḥ*—lamenting for; *patim*—your husband; *varṣa-śataiḥ*—for a hundred years; *api*—even.

TRANSLATION

Thus Yamarāja, in the guise of a small boy, told all the queens: You are all so foolish that you lament but do not see your own

death. Afflicted by a poor fund of knowledge, you do not know that even if you lament for your dead husband for hundreds of years, you will never get him back alive, and in the meantime your lives will be finished.

PURPORT

Yamarāja once asked Mahārāja Yudhiṣṭhira, "What is the most wonderful thing within this world?" Mahārāja Yudhiṣṭhira replied (*Mahābhārata, Vana-parva* 313.116):

ahany ahani bhūtāni
gacchantīha yamālayam
śeṣāḥ sthāvaram icchanti
kim āścaryam ataḥ paraṁ

Hundreds and thousands of living entities meet death at every moment, but a foolish living being nonetheless thinks himself deathless and does not prepare for death. This is the most wonderful thing in this world. Everyone has to die because everyone is fully under the control of material nature, yet everyone thinks that he is independent, that whatever he likes he can do, that he will never meet death but live forever, and so on. So-called scientists are making various plans by which living entities in the future can live forever, but while they are thus pursuing such scientific knowledge, Yamarāja, in due course of time, will take them away from their business of so-called research.

TEXT 58

श्रीहिरण्यकशिपुरुवाच
बाल एवं प्रवदति सर्वे विस्मितचेतसः ।
ज्ञातयो मेनिरे सर्वमनित्यमयथोत्थितम् ॥५८॥

śrī-hiraṇyakaśipur uvāca
bāla evaṁ pravadati
sarve vismita-cetasaḥ
jñātayo menire sarvam
anityam ayathotthitam

śrī-hiraṇyakaśipuḥ uvāca—Śrī Hiraṇyakaśipu said; *bāle*—while Yamarāja in the form of a boy; *evam*—thus; *pravadati*—was speaking very philosophically; *sarve*—all; *vismita*—struck with wonder; *cetasaḥ*—their hearts; *jñātayaḥ*—the relatives; *menire*—they thought; *sarvam*—everything material; *anityam*—temporary; *ayathā-utthitam*—arisen from temporary phenomena.

TRANSLATION

Hiraṇyakaśipu said: While Yamarāja, in the form of a small boy, was instructing all the relatives surrounding the dead body of Suyajña, everyone was struck with wonder by his philosophical words. They could understand that everything material is temporary, not continuing to exist.

PURPORT

This is confirmed in *Bhagavad-gītā* (2.18). *Antavanta ime dehā nityasyoktāḥ śarīriṇaḥ:* the body is perishable, but the soul within the body is imperishable. Therefore the duty of those advanced in knowledge in human society is to study the constitutional position of the imperishable soul and not waste the valuable time of human life in merely maintaining the body and not considering life's real responsibility. Every human being should try to understand how the spirit soul can be happy and where he can attain an eternal, blissful life of knowledge. Human beings are meant to study these subject matters, not to be absorbed in caring for the temporary body, which is sure to change. No one knows whether he will receive a human body again; there is no guarantee, for according to one's work one may get any body, from that of a demigod to that of a dog. In this regard, Śrīla Madhvācārya comments:

ahaṁ mamābhimānādi-
tva-yathottham anityakam
mahadādi yathotthaṁ ca
nityā cāpi yathotthitā

asvatantraiva prakṛtiḥ
sva-tantro nitya eva ca

yathārtha-bhūtaś ca para
eka eva janārdanaḥ

Only Janārdana, the Supreme Personality of Godhead is ever existing, but His creation, the material world, is temporary. Therefore everyone who is captivated by the material energy and absorbed in thinking "I am this body, and everything belonging to this body is mine" is in illusion. One should think only of being eternally a part of Janārdana, and one's endeavor in this material world, especially in this human form of life, should be to attain the association of Janārdana by going back home, back to Godhead.

TEXT 59

यम एतदुपाख्याय तत्रैवान्तरधीयत ।
ज्ञातयोऽहि सुयज्ञस्य चक्रुर्यत्साम्परायिकम् ॥५९॥

yama etad upākhyāya
tatraivāntaradhīyata
jñātayo hi suyajñasya
cakrur yat sāmparāyikam

yamaḥ—Yamarāja in the form of a boy; *etat*—this; *upākhyāya*—instructing; *tatra*—there; *eva*—indeed; *antaradhīyata*—disappeared; *jñātayaḥ*—the relatives; *hi*—indeed; *suyajñasya*—of King Suyajña; *cakruḥ*—performed; *yat*—which is; *sāmparāyikam*—the funeral ceremony.

TRANSLATION

After instructing all the foolish relatives of Suyajña, Yamarāja, in the form of a boy, disappeared from their vision. Then the relatives of King Suyajña performed the ritualistic funeral ceremonies.

TEXT 60

अतः शोचत मा यूयं परं चात्मानमेव वा ।
क आत्मा कः परो वात्र स्वीयः पारक्य एव वा ।
स्वपराभिनिवेशेन विनाज्ञानेन देहिनाम् ॥६०॥

ataḥ śocata mā yūyaṁ
paraṁ cātmānam eva vā
ka ātmā kaḥ paro vātra
svīyaḥ pārakya eva vā
sva-parābhiniveśena
vinājñānena dehinām

ataḥ—therefore; *śocata*—lament for; *mā*—do not; *yūyam*—all of you; *param*—another; *ca*—and; *ātmānam*—yourself; *eva*—certainly; *vā*—or; *kaḥ*—who; *ātmā*—self; *kaḥ*—who; *paraḥ*—other; *vā*—or; *atra*—in this material world; *svīyaḥ*—one's own; *pārakyaḥ*—for others; *eva*—indeed; *vā*—or; *sva-para-abhiniveśena*—consisting of absorption in the bodily concept of oneself and others; *vinā*—besides; *ajñānena*—the lack of knowledge; *dehinām*—of all the embodied living entities.

TRANSLATION

Therefore none of you should be aggrieved for the loss of the body—whether your own or those of others. Only in ignorance does one make bodily distinctions, thinking "Who am I? Who are the others? What is mine? What is for others?"

PURPORT

In this material world, the conception of self-preservation is the first law of nature. According to this conception, one should be interested in his personal safety and should then consider society, friendship, love, nationality, community and so on, which have all developed because of the bodily conception of life and a lack of knowledge of the spirit soul. This is called *ajñāna.* As long as human society is in darkness and ignorance, men will continue to make huge arrangements in the bodily conception of life. This is described by Prahlāda Mahārāja as *bharam.* In the materialistic conception, modern civilization makes enormous arrangements for huge roads, houses, mills and factories, and this is man's conception of the advancement of civilization. People do not know, however, that at any time they themselves may be kicked out of the scene and forced to accept bodies that have nothing to do with these enormous houses, palaces, roads and automobiles. Therefore when Arjuna was thinking in terms of his bodily relationships with his kinsmen, Kṛṣṇa immediately chastised him, saying, *kutas tvā kaśmalam idaṁ viṣame samupasthitam anārya-juṣṭam:* "This bodily conception of life is befitting the *anāryas*, the non-Āryans, who are not advanced in knowledge." An Āryan civilization is a civilization advanced in spiritual knowledge. Not merely by stamping oneself an Āryan does one become an Āryan. To keep oneself in the deepest darkness concerning spiritual knowledge and at the same time claim to be an Āryan is a non-Āryan position. In this connection, Śrīla Madhvācārya quotes as follows from the *Brahma-vaivarta Purāṇa:*

ka ātmā kaḥ para iti dehādy-apekṣayā

na hi dehādir ātmā syān
na ca śatrur udīritaḥ
ato daihika-vṛddhau vā
kṣaye vā kiṁ prayojanam

yas tu deha-gato jīvaḥ
sa hi nāśaṁ na gacchati
tataḥ śatru-vivṛddhau ca
sva-nāśe śocanaṁ kutaḥ

dehādi-vyatiriktau tu
jīveśau pratijānatā
ata ātma-vivṛddhis tu
vāsudeve ratiḥ sthirā
śatru-nāśas tathājñāna-
nāśo nānyaḥ kathañcana

The purport is that as long as we are in this human form of body, our duty is to understand the soul within the body. The body is not the self; we are different from the body, and therefore there is no question of friends, enemies or responsibilities in terms of the bodily conception of life. One should not be very anxious about the body's changing from childhood to boyhood, from boyhood to old age and then to apparent annihilation. Rather, one should be very seriously concerned about the soul within the body and how to release the soul from the material clutches. The living entity within the body is never annihilated; therefore one should surely know that whether one has many friends or many enemies, his friends cannot help him, and his enemies cannot do him any harm. One should know that he is a spirit soul (*ahaṁ brahmāsmi*) and that the constitutional position of the soul is unaffected by the changes of the body. In all circumstances, everyone, as a spirit soul, must be a devotee of Lord Viṣṇu and should not be concerned with bodily relationships, whether with friends or with enemies. One should know that neither we ourselves nor our enemies in the bodily conception of life are ever killed.

TEXT 61

श्रीनारद उवाच
इति दैत्यपतेर्वाक्यं दितिराकर्ण्य सस्नुषा ।
पुत्रशोकं क्षणात्त्यक्त्वा तत्त्वे चित्तमधारयत् ॥६१॥

śrī-nārada uvāca
iti daitya-pater vākyaṁ
ditir ākarṇya sasnuṣā
putra-śokaṁ kṣaṇāt tyaktvā
tattve cittam adhārayat

śrī-nāradaḥ uvāca—Śrī Nārada Muni said; *iti*—thus; *daitya-pateḥ*—of the King of the demons; *vākyam*—the speech; *ditiḥ*—Diti, the mother of Hiraṇyakaśipu and Hiraṇyākṣa; *ākarṇya*—hearing; *sa-snuṣā*—with the wife of Hiraṇyākṣa; *putra-śokam*—the great bereavement for her son, Hiraṇyākṣa; *kṣaṇāt*—immediately; *tyaktvā*—giving up; *tattve*—in the real philosophy of life; *cittam*—heart; *adhārayat*—engaged.

TRANSLATION

Śrī Nārada Muni continued: Diti, the mother of Hiraṇyakaśipu and Hiraṇyākṣa, heard the instructions of Hiraṇyakaśipu along with her daughter-in-law, Ruṣābhānu, Hiraṇyākṣa's wife. She then forgot her grief over her son's death and thus engaged her mind and attention in understanding the real philosophy of life.

PURPORT

When a relative dies one certainly becomes very much interested in philosophy, but when the funeral ceremony is over one again becomes attentive to materialism. Even Daityas, who are materialistic persons, sometimes think of philosophy when some relative meets death. The technical term for this attitude of the materialistic person is *śmaśāna-vairāgya,* or detachment in a cemetery or place of cremation. As confirmed in *Bhagavad-gītā,* four classes of men receive an understanding of spiritual life and God—*ārta* (the distressed), *jijñāsu* (the inquisitive), *arthārthī* (one who desires material gains) and *jñānī* (one who is searching for knowledge). Especially when one is very much distressed by material conditions, one becomes interested in God. Therefore Kuntīdevī said in her prayers to Kṛṣṇa that she preferred distress to a happy mood of life. In the material world, one who is happy forgets Kṛṣṇa, or God, but sometimes, if one is actually pious but in distress, he remembers Kṛṣṇa. Queen Kuntīdevī therefore preferred distress because it is an opportunity for remembering Kṛṣṇa. When Kṛṣṇa was leaving Kuntīdevī for His own country, Kuntīdevī regretfully said that she was better off in distress because Kṛṣṇa was always present, whereas now that the Pāṇḍavas were situated in their kingdom, Kṛṣṇa was going away. For a devotee, distress is an opportunity to remember the Supreme Personality of Godhead constantly.

Thus end the Bhaktivedanta purports of the Seventh Canto, Second Chapter, of the Śrīmad-Bhāgavatam, *entitled "Hiraṇyakaśipu, King of the Demons."*

CHAPTER THREE

Hiraṇyakaśipu's Plan to Become Immortal

This chapter describes how Hiraṇyakaśipu performed a severe type of austerity for material benefit, thus causing great distress throughout the universe. Even Lord Brahmā, the chief personality within this universe, became somewhat disturbed and personally went to see why Hiraṇyakaśipu was engaged in such a severe austerity.

Hiraṇyakaśipu wanted to become immortal. He wanted not to be conquered by anyone, not to be attacked by old age and disease, and not to be harassed by any opponent. Thus he wanted to become the absolute ruler of the entire universe. With this desire, he entered the valley of Mandara Mountain and began practicing a severe type of austerity and meditation. Seeing Hiraṇyakaśipu engaged in this austerity, the demigods returned to their respective homes, but while Hiraṇyakaśipu was thus engaged, a kind of fire began blazing from his head, disturbing the entire universe and its inhabitants, including the birds, beasts and demigods. When all the higher and lower planets became too hot to live on, the demigods, being disturbed, left their abodes in the higher planets and went to see Lord Brahmā, praying to him that he curtail this unnecessary heat. The demigods disclosed to Lord Brahmā Hiraṇyakaśipu's ambition to become immortal, overcoming his short duration of life, and to be the master of all the planetary systems, even Dhruvaloka.

Upon hearing about the purpose of Hiraṇyakaśipu's austere meditation, Lord Brahmā, accompanied by the great sage Bhṛgu and great personalities like Dakṣa, went to see Hiraṇyakaśipu. He then sprinkled water from his *kamaṇḍalu*, a type of waterpot, upon Hiraṇyakaśipu's head.

Hiraṇyakaśipu, the King of the Daityas, bowed down before Lord Brahmā, the creator of this universe, offering respectful obeisances again and again and offering prayers. When Lord Brahmā agreed to give him benedictions, he prayed not be killed by any living entity, not to be killed in any place, covered or uncovered, not to die in the daytime or at night, not to be killed by any weapon, on land or in the air, and not to be killed by any human being, animal, demigod or any other entity, living or nonliving. He further prayed for supremacy over the entire universe and requested the eight yogic perfections, such as *aṇimā* and *laghimā.*

TEXT 1

श्रीनारद उवाच
हिरण्यकशिपू राजन्नजेयमजरामरम् ।
आत्मानमप्रतिद्वन्द्वमेकराजं व्यधित्सत ॥ १ ॥

śrī-nārada uvāca
hiraṇyakaśipū rājann
ajeyam ajarāmaram
ātmānam apratidvandvam
eka-rājaṁ vyadhitsata

śrī-nāradaḥ uvāca—Nārada Muni said; *hiraṇyakaśipuḥ*—the demoniac king Hiraṇyakaśipu; *rājan*—O King Yudhiṣṭhira; *ajeyam*—unconquerable by any enemy; *ajara*—without old age or disease; *amaram*—immortal; *ātmānam*—himself; *apratidvandvam*—without any rival or opponent; *eka-rājam*—the one king of the universe; *vyadhitsata*—desired to become.

TRANSLATION

Nārada Muni said to Mahārāja Yudhiṣṭhira: The demoniac king Hiraṇyakaśipu wanted to be unconquerable and free from old age and dwindling of the body. He wanted to gain all the yogic perfections like aṇimā and laghimā, to be deathless, and to be the only king of the entire universe, including Brahmaloka.

PURPORT

Such are the goals of the austerities performed by demons. Hiraṇyakaśipu wanted to receive a benediction from Lord Brahmā so that in the future he would be able to conquer Lord Brahmā's abode. Similarly, another demon received a benediction from Lord Śiva but later wanted to kill Lord Śiva through that same benediction. Thus self-interested persons, by demoniac austerity, want to kill even their benedictors, whereas the Vaiṣṇava wants to remain an ever-existing servant of the Lord and never to occupy the post of the Lord. Through *sāyujya-mukti*, which is generally demanded by *asuras*, one merges into the existence of the Lord, but although one sometimes thus achieves the goal of the theory of monism, one falls down again to struggle in material existence.

TEXT 2

स तेपे मन्दरद्रोण्यां तपः परमदारुणम् ।
ऊर्ध्वबाहुर्नभोदृष्टिः पादाङ्गुष्ठाश्रितावनिः ॥ २ ॥

sa tepe mandara-droṇyāṁ
tapaḥ parama-dāruṇam
ūrdhva-bāhur nabho-dṛṣṭiḥ
pādāṅguṣṭhāśritāvaniḥ

saḥ—he (Hiraṇyakaśipu); *tepe*—performed; *mandara-droṇyām*—in a valley of Mandara Hill; *tapaḥ*—austerity; *parama*—most; *dāruṇam*—difficult; *ūrdhva*—raising; *bāhuḥ*—arms; *nabhaḥ*—toward the sky; *dṛṣṭiḥ*—his vision; *pāda-aṅguṣṭha*—with the big toes of his feet; *āśrita*—resting on; *avaniḥ*—the ground.

TRANSLATION

In the valley of Mandara Hill, Hiraṇyakaśipu began performing his austerities by standing with his toes on the ground, keeping his arms upward and looking toward the sky. This position was extremely difficult, but he accepted it as a means to attain perfection.

TEXT 3

जटादीधितिभी रेजे संवर्तार्क इवांशुभिः ।
तस्मिंस्तपस्तप्यमाने देवाः स्थानानि भेजिरे ॥ ३ ॥

jaṭā-dīdhitibhī reje
saṁvartārka ivāṁśubhiḥ
tasmiṁs tapas tapyamāne
devāḥ sthānāni bhejire

jaṭā-dīdhitibhiḥ—by the effulgence of the hair on his head; *reje*—was shining; *saṁvarta-arkaḥ*—the sun at the time of destruction; *iva*—like; *aṁśubhiḥ*—by the beams; *tasmin*—when he (Hiraṇyakaśipu); *tapaḥ*—austerities; *tapyamāne*—was engaged in; *devāḥ*—all the demigods who were wandering throughout the universe to see Hiraṇyakaśipu's demoniac activities; *sthānāni*—to their own places; *bhejire*—returned.

TRANSLATION

From the hair on Hiraṇyakaśipu's head there emanated an effulgent light as brilliant and intolerable as the rays of the sun at the time of dissolution. Seeing the performance of such austere penances, the demigods, who had been wandering throughout the planets, now returned to their respective homes.

TEXT 4

तस्य मूर्ध्नः समुद्भूतः सधूमोऽग्निस्तपोमयः ।
तीर्यगूर्ध्वमधोलोकान् प्रातपद्विष्वगीरितः ॥ ४ ॥

tasya mūrdhnaḥ samudbhūtaḥ
sadhūmo 'gnis tapomayaḥ
tīryag ūrdhvam adho lokān
prātapad viṣvag īritaḥ

tasya—his; *mūrdhnaḥ*—from the head; *samudbhūtaḥ*—generated; *sa-dhūmaḥ*—with smoke; *agniḥ*—fire; *tapaḥ-mayaḥ*—because of severe austerities; *tīryak*—sideways; *ūrdhvam*—upward; *adhaḥ*—downward; *lokān*—all the planets; *prātapat*—heated; *viṣvak*—all around; *īritaḥ*—spreading.

TRANSLATION

Because of Hiraṇyakaśipu's severe austerities, fire came from his head, and this fire and its smoke spread throughout the sky,

encompassing the upper and lower planets, which all became extremely hot.

TEXT 5

चुक्षुभुर्नद्युदन्वन्तः सद्वीपाद्रिश्चचाल भूः ।
निपेतुः सग्रहास्तारा जज्वलुश्च दिशो दश ॥ ५ ॥

cukṣubhur nady-udanvantaḥ
sadvīpādriś cacāla bhūḥ
nipetuḥ sagrahās tārā
jajvaluś ca diśo daśa

cukṣubhuḥ—became agitated; *nadī-udanvantaḥ*—the rivers and oceans; *sa-dvīpa*—with the islands; *adriḥ*—and mountains; *cacāla*—trembled; *bhūḥ*—the surface of the globe; *nipetuḥ*—fell; *sa-grahāḥ*—with the planets; *tārāḥ*—the stars; *jajvaluḥ*—blazed; *ca*—also; *diśaḥ daśa*—the ten directions.

TRANSLATION

Because of the power of his severe austerities, all the rivers and oceans were agitated, the surface of the globe, with its mountains and islands, began trembling, and the stars and planets fell. All directions were ablaze.

TEXT 6

तेन तप्ता दिवं त्यक्त्वा ब्रह्मलोकं ययुः सुराः ।
धात्रे विज्ञापयामासुर्देवदेव जगत्पते ।
दैत्येन्द्रतपसा तप्ता दिवि स्थातुं न शक्नुमः ॥ ६ ॥

tena taptā divaṁ tyaktvā
brahmalokaṁ yayuḥ surāḥ
dhātre vijñāpayām āsur
deva-deva jagat-pate
daityendra-tapasā taptā
divi sthātuṁ na śaknumaḥ

tena—by that (fire of austerity); *taptāḥ*—burned; *divam*—their residential quarters in the upper planets; *tyaktvā*—giving up; *brahma-lokam*—to the planet where Lord Brahmā lives; *yayuḥ*—went; *surāḥ*—the demigods; *dhātre*—unto the chief of this universe, Lord Brahmā; *vijñāpayām āsuḥ*—submitted; *deva-deva*—O chief of the demigods; *jagat-pate*—O master of the universe; *daitya-indra-tapasā*—by the severe austerity performed by the King of the Daityas, Hiraṇyakaśipu; *taptāḥ*—roasted; *divi*—on the heavenly planets; *sthātum*—to stay; *na*—not; *śaknumaḥ*—we are able.

TRANSLATION

Scorched and extremely disturbed because of Hiraṇyakaśipu's severe penances, all the demigods left the planets where they reside and went to the planet of Lord Brahmā, where they informed the creator as follows: O lord of the demigods, O master of the universe, because of the fire emanating from Hiraṇyakaśipu's head as a result of his severe austerities, we have become so disturbed that we could not stay in our planets but have come to you.

TEXT 7

तस्य चोपशमं भूमन् विधेहि यदि मन्यसे ।
लोका न यावन्नङ्क्ष्यन्ति बलिहारास्तवाभिभूः ॥ ७ ॥

tasya copaśamaṁ bhūman
vidhehi yadi manyase
lokā na yāvan naṅkṣyanti
bali-hārās tavābhibhūḥ

tasya—of this; *ca*—indeed; *upaśamam*—the cessation; *bhūman*—O great personality; *vidhehi*—please execute; *yadi*—if; *manyase*—you think it right; *lokāḥ*—all the inhabitants of the various planets; *na*—not; *yāvat*—as long as; *naṅkṣyanti*—will be lost; *bali-hārāḥ*—who are obedient to the worship; *tava*—of you; *abhibhūḥ*—O chief of all the universe.

TRANSLATION

O great person, chief of the universe, if you think it proper, kindly stop these disturbances, meant to destroy everything, before all your obedient subjects are annihilated.

TEXT 8

तस्यायं किल सङ्कल्पश्चरतो दुश्चरं तपः ।
श्रूयतां किं न विदितस्तवाथापि निवेदितम् ॥ ८ ॥

tasyāyaṁ kila saṅkalpaś
carato duścaraṁ tapaḥ
śrūyatāṁ kiṁ na viditas
tavāthāpi niveditam

tasya—his; *ayam*—this; *kila*—indeed; *saṅkalpaḥ*—determination; *carataḥ*—who is executing; *duścaram*—very difficult; *tapaḥ*—austerity; *śrūyatām*—let it be heard; *kim*—what; *na*—not; *viditaḥ*—known; *tava*—of you; *athāpi*—still; *niveditam*—submitted.

TRANSLATION

Hiraṇyakaśipu has undertaken a most severe type of austerity. Although his plan is not unknown to you, kindly listen as we submit his intentions.

TEXTS 9–10

सृष्ट्वा चराचरमिदं तपोयोगसमाधिना ।
अध्यास्ते सर्वधिष्ण्येभ्यः परमेष्ठी निजासनम् ॥ ९ ॥
तदहं वर्धमानेन तपोयोगसमाधिना ।
कालात्मनोश्च नित्यत्वात्साधयिष्ये तथात्मनः ॥१०॥

sṛṣṭvā carācaram idaṁ
tapo-yoga-samādhinā
adhyāste sarva-dhiṣṇyebhyaḥ
parameṣṭhī nijāsanam

tad ahaṁ vardhamānena
tapo-yoga-samādhinā
kālātmanoś ca nityatvāt
sādhayiṣye tathātmanaḥ

sṛṣṭvā—creating; *cara*—moving; *acaram*—and not moving; *idam*—this; *tapaḥ*—of austerity; *yoga*—and mystic power; *samādhinā*—by practicing the trance; *adhyāste*—is situated in; *sarva-dhiṣṇyebhyaḥ*—than all the planets, including the heavenly planets; *parameṣṭhī*—Lord Brahmā; *nija-āsanam*—his own throne; *tat*—therefore; *aham*—I; *vardhamānena*—by dint of increasing; *tapaḥ*—austerity; *yoga*—mystic powers; *samādhinā*—and trance; *kāla*—of time; *ātmanoḥ*—and of the soul; *ca*—and; *nityatvāt*—from the eternality; *sādhayiṣye*—shall achieve; *tathā*—so much; *ātmanaḥ*—for my personal self.

TRANSLATION

"The supreme person within this universe, Lord Brahmā, has gotten his exalted post by dint of severe austerities, mystic power and trance. Consequently, after creating the universe, he has become the most worshipable demigod within it. Since I am eternal and time is eternal, I shall endeavor for such austerity, mystic power and trance for many, many births, and thus I shall occupy the same post occupied by Lord Brahmā.

PURPORT

Hiraṇyakaśipu's determination was to occupy the post of Lord Brahmā, but this was impossible because Brahmā has a long duration of life. As confirmed in *Bhagavad-gītā* (8.17), *sahasra-yuga-paryantam ahar yad brahmaṇo viduḥ:* one thousand *yugas* equals one day of Brahmā. The duration of Brahmā's life is extremely great, and consequently it was impossible for Hiraṇyakaśipu to occupy that post. Nonetheless, his decision was that since the self (*ātmā*) and time are both eternal, if he could not occupy that post in one lifetime he would continue to execute austerities life after life so that sometime he would be able to do so.

TEXT 11

अन्यथेदं विधास्येऽहमयथापूर्वमोजसा ।
किमन्यैः कालनिर्धूतैः कल्पान्ते वैष्णवादिभिः ॥११॥

anyathedaṁ vidhāsye 'ham
ayathā pūrvam ojasā
kim anyaiḥ kāla-nirdhūtaiḥ
kalpānte vaiṣṇavādibhiḥ

anyathā—just the opposite; *idam*—this universe; *vidhāsye*—shall make; *aham*—I; *ayathā*—inappropriate; *pūrvam*—as it was before; *ojasā*—by dint of the power of my austerity; *kim*—what use; *anyaiḥ*—with other; *kāla-nirdhūtaiḥ*—vanquished in due course of time; *kalpa-ante*—at the end of the millennium; *vaiṣṇava-ādibhiḥ*—with planets like Dhruvaloka or Vaikuṇṭhaloka.

TRANSLATION

"By dint of my severe austerities, I shall reverse the results of pious and impious activities. I shall overturn all the established practices within this world. Even Dhruvaloka will be vanquished at the end of the millennium. Therefore, what is the use of it? I shall prefer to remain in the position of Brahmā."

PURPORT

Hiraṇyakaśipu's demoniac determination was explained to Lord Brahmā by the demigods, who informed him that Hiraṇyakaśipu wanted to overturn all the established principles. After executing severe austerities, people within this material world are promoted to the heavenly planets, but Hiraṇyakaśipu wanted them to be unhappy, suffering because of the diplomatic feelings of the demigods, even in the heavenly planets. He wanted those who were harassed in this world by material transactions to be unhappy for the same reason, even in the heavenly planets. Indeed, he wanted to introduce such harassment everywhere. One might ask how this would be possible, since the universal order has been established since time immemorial, but Hiraṇyakaśipu was proud to declare that he would be able to do everything by the power of his *tapasya*. He even wanted to make the Vaiṣṇavas' position insecure. These are some of the symptoms of asuric determination.

TEXT 12

इति शुश्रुम निर्बन्धं तपः परममास्थितः ।
विधत्स्वानन्तरं युक्तं स्वयं त्रिभुवनेश्वर ॥१२॥

iti śuśruma nirbandhaṁ
tapaḥ paramam āsthitaḥ
vidhatsvānantaraṁ yuktaṁ
svayaṁ tri-bhuvaneśvara

iti—in this way; *śuśruma*—we have heard; *nirbandham*—strong determination; *tapaḥ*—austerity; *paramam*—very severe; *āsthitaḥ*—is situated in; *vidhatsva*—please take steps; *anantaram*—as soon as possible; *yuktam*—befitting; *svayam*—yourself; *tri-bhuvana-īśvara*—O master of the three worlds.

TRANSLATION

O lord, we have heard from reliable sources that in order to obtain your post, Hiraṇyakaśipu is now engaged in severe austerity. You are the master of the three worlds. Please, without delay, take whatever steps you deem appropriate.

PURPORT

In the material world, a servant is provided for by the master but is always planning how to capture the master's post. There have been many instances of this in history. Especially in India during the Mohammedan rule, many servants, by plans and devices, took over the posts of their masters. It is learned from Caitanya literature that one big Zamindar, Subuddhi Rāya, kept a Mohammedan boy as a servant. Of course, he treated the boy as his own child, and sometimes, when the boy would steal something, the master would chastise him by striking him with a cane. There was a mark on the boy's back from this chastisement. Later, after that boy had by crooked means become Hussain Shah, Nawab of Bengal, one day his wife saw the mark on his back and inquired about it. The Nawab replied that in his childhood he had been a servant of Subuddhi Rāya, who had punished him because of some mischievous activities. Upon hearing this, the Nawab's wife immediately became agitated and requested her husband to kill Subuddhi Rāya. Nawab Hussain Shah, of course, was very grateful to Subuddhi Rāya and therefore refused to kill him, but when his wife requested him to turn Subuddhi Rāya into a Mohammedan, the Nawab agreed. Taking some water from his waterpot, he sprinkled it upon Subuddhi Rāya and declared that Subuddhi Rāya had now become a Mohammedan. The point is that this Nawab had been an ordinary menial servant of Subuddhi Rāya but was somehow or other able to occupy the supreme post of Nawab of Bengal. This is the material world. Everyone is trying to become master through various devices, although everyone is servant of his senses. Following this system, a living entity, although servant of his senses, tries to become master of the whole universe. Hiraṇyakaśipu was a typical example of this, and Brahmā was informed by the demigods of his intentions.

TEXT 13

तवासनं द्विजगवां पारमेष्ठ्यं जगत्पते ।
भवाय श्रेयसे भूत्यै क्षेमाय विजयाय च ॥१३॥

tavāsanaṁ dvija-gavāṁ
pārameṣṭhyaṁ jagat-pate
bhavāya śreyase bhūtyai
kṣemāya vijayāya ca

tava—your; *āsanam*—position on the throne; *dvija*—of the brahminical culture or the *brāhmaṇas; gavām*—of the cows; *pārameṣṭhyam*—supreme; *jagat-pate*—O master of the whole universe; *bhavāya*—for improvement; *śreyase*—for the ultimate happiness; *bhūtyai*—for increasing the opulence; *kṣemāya*—for the maintenance and good fortune; *vijayāya*—for the victory and increasing prestige; *ca*—and.

TRANSLATION

O Lord Brahmā, your position within this universe is certainly most auspicious for everyone, especially the cows and brāhmaṇas. Brahminical culture and the protection of cows can be increasingly glorified, and thus all kinds of material happiness, opulence and good fortune will automatically increase. But unfortunately, if Hiraṇyakaśipu occupies your seat, everything will be lost.

PURPORT

In this verse the words *dvija-gavāṁ pārameṣṭhyam* indicate the most exalted position of the *brāhmaṇas,* brahminical culture and the cows. In Vedic culture, the welfare of the cows and the welfare of the *brāhmaṇas* are essential. Without a proper arrangement for developing brahminical culture and protecting cows, all the affairs of administration will go to hell. Being afraid that Hiraṇyakaśipu would occupy the post of Brahmā, all the demigods were extremely disturbed. Hiraṇyakaśipu was a well-known demon, and the demigods knew that if demons and Rākṣasas were to occupy the supreme post, brahminical culture and protection of cows would come to an end. As stated in *Bhagavad-gītā* (5.29), the original proprietor of everything is Lord Kṛṣṇa (*bhoktāraṁ yajña-tapasāṁ sarva-loka-maheśvaram*). The Lord, therefore, knows particularly well how to develop the material condition of the living entities within this material world. In every universe there is one Brahmā engaged on behalf of Lord Kṛṣṇa, as confirmed in *Śrīmad-Bhāgavatam* (*tene brahma hṛdā ya ādi-kavaye*). The principal creator in each *brahmāṇḍa* is Lord Brahmā, who imparts Vedic knowledge to his disciples and sons. On every planet, the king or supreme controller must be a representative of Brahmā. Therefore, if a Rākṣasa, or demon, were situated in Brahmā's post, then the entire arrangement of the universe, especially the protection of the brahminical culture and cows, would be ruined. All the demigods anticipated this danger, and therefore they went to request Lord Brahmā to take immediate steps to thwart Hiraṇyakaśipu's plan.

In the beginning of creation, Lord Brahmā was attacked by two demons—Madhu and Kaiṭabha—but Kṛṣṇa saved him. Therefore Kṛṣṇa is addressed as *madhu-kaiṭabha-hantṛ*. Now again, Hiraṇyakaśipu was trying to replace Brahmā. The material world is so situated that even the position of Lord Brahmā, not to speak of ordinary living entities, is sometimes in danger. Nonetheless, until the time of Hiraṇyakaśipu, no one had tried to replace Lord Brahmā. Hiraṇyakaśipu, however, was such a great demon that he maintained this ambition.

The word *bhūtyai* means "for increasing opulence," and the word *śreyase* refers to ultimately returning home, back to Godhead. In spiritual advancement, one's material position improves at the same time that the path of liberation becomes clear and one is freed from material bondage. If one is situated in an opulent position in spiritual advancement, his opulence never decreases. Therefore such a spiritual benediction is called *bhūti* or *vibhūti.* Kṛṣṇa confirms this in *Bhagavad-gītā* (10.41). *Yad yad vibhūtimat sattvaṁ . . . mama tejo-'ṁśa-sambhavam:* if a devotee advances in spiritual consciousness and thus becomes materially opulent also, his position is a special gift from the Lord. Such opulence is never to be considered material. At the present, especially on this planet earth, the influence of Lord Brahmā has decreased considerably, and the representatives of Hiraṇyakaśipu—the Rākṣasas and demons—have taken charge. Therefore there is no protection of brahminical culture and cows, which are the basic prerequisites for all kinds of good fortune. This age is very dangerous because society is being managed by demons and Rākṣasas.

TEXT 14

इति विज्ञापितो देवैर्भगवानात्मभूर्नृप ।
परितो भृगुदक्षाद्यैर्ययौ दैत्येश्वराश्रमम् ॥१४॥

iti vijñāpito devair
bhagavān ātmabhūr nṛpa
parito bhṛgu-dakṣādyair
yayau daityeśvarāśramam

iti—thus; *vijñāpitaḥ*—informed; *devaiḥ*—by all the demigods; *bhagavān*—the most powerful; *ātma-bhūḥ*—Lord Brahmā, who was born from the lotus flower; *nṛpa*—O King; *paritaḥ*—being surrounded; *bhṛgu*—by Bhṛgu; *dakṣa*—Dakṣa; *ādyaiḥ*—and others; *yayau*—went;

daitya-īśvara—of Hiraṇyakaśipu, the King of the Daityas; *āśramam*—to the place of austerity.

TRANSLATION

O King, being thus informed by the demigods, the most powerful Lord Brahmā, accompanied by Bhṛgu, Dakṣa and other great sages, immediately started for the place where Hiraṇyakaśipu was performing his penances and austerities.

PURPORT

Lord Brahmā was waiting for the austerities performed by Hiraṇyakaśipu to mature so that he could go there and offer benedictions according to Hiraṇyakaśipu's desire. Now, taking the opportunity of being accompanied by all the demigods and great saintly persons, Brahmā went there to award him the benediction he desired.

TEXTS 15–16

न ददर्श प्रतिच्छन्नं वल्मीकतृणकीचकैः ।
पिपीलिकाभिराचीर्णं मेदस्त्वङ्मांसशोणितम् ॥१५॥
तपन्तं तपसा लोकान् यथाभ्रापिहितं रविम् ।
विलक्ष्य विस्मितः प्राह हसंस्तं हंसवाहनः ॥१६॥

na dadarśa praticchannaṁ
valmīka-tṛṇa-kīcakaiḥ
pipīlikābhir ācīrṇaṁ
medas-tvaṅ-māṁsa-śoṇitam

tapantaṁ tapasā lokān
yathābhrāpihitaṁ ravim
vilakṣya vismitaḥ prāha
hasaṁs taṁ haṁsa-vāhanaḥ

na—not; *dadarśa*—saw; *praticchannam*—covered; *valmīka*—by an anthill; *tṛṇa*—grass; *kīcakaiḥ*—and bamboo sticks; *pipīlikābhiḥ*—by the ants; *ācīrṇam*—eaten all around; *medaḥ*—whose fat; *tvak*—skin;

māṁsa—the flesh; *śoṇitam*—and blood; *tapantam*—heating; *tapasā*—by a severe type of penance; *lokān*—all the three worlds; *yathā*—just as; *abhra*—by clouds; *apihitam*—covered; *ravim*—the sun; *vilakṣya*—seeing; *vismitaḥ*—struck with wonder; *prāha*—said; *hasan*—smiling; *tam*—to him; *haṁsa-vāhanaḥ*—Lord Brahmā, who rides a swan airplane.

TRANSLATION

Lord Brahmā, who is carried by a swan airplane, at first could not see where Hiraṇyakaśipu was, for Hiraṇyakaśipu's body was covered by an anthill and by grass and bamboo sticks. Because Hiraṇyakaśipu had been there for a long time, the ants had devoured his skin, fat, flesh and blood. Then Lord Brahmā and the demigods spotted him, resembling a cloud-covered sun, heating all the world by his austerity. Struck with wonder, Lord Brahmā began to smile and then addressed him as follows.

PURPORT

The living entity can live merely by his own power, without the help of skin, marrow, bone, blood and so on, because it is said, *asaṅgo 'yaṁ puruṣaḥ*—the living entity has nothing to do with the material covering. Hiraṇyakaśipu performed a severe type of *tapasya,* austerity, for many long years. Indeed, it is said that he performed the *tapasya* for one hundred heavenly years. Since one day of the demigods equals six of our months, certainly this was a very long time. By nature's own way, his body had been almost consumed by earthworms, ants and other parasites, and therefore even Brahmā was at first unable to see him. Later, however, Brahmā could ascertain where Hiraṇyakaśipu was, and Brahmā was struck with wonder to see Hiraṇyakaśipu's extraordinary power to execute *tapasya.* Anyone would conclude that Hiraṇyakaśipu was dead because his body was covered in so many ways, but Lord Brahmā, the supreme living being in this universe, could understand that Hiraṇyakaśipu was alive but covered by material elements.

It is also to be noted that although Hiraṇyakaśipu performed this austerity for a long, long time, he was nonetheless known as a Daitya and Rākṣasa. It will be seen from verses to follow that even great saintly persons could not perform such a severe type of austerity. Why then was he called a Rākṣasa and Daitya? It is because whatever he did was for his own sense gratification. His son Prahlāda Mahārāja was only five years old, and so what could Prahlāda do? Yet simply by performing a little devotional service according to the instructions of Nārada Muni, Prahlāda became so dear to the Lord that the Lord came to save him, whereas Hiraṇyakaśipu, in spite of all his austerities, was killed. This is the difference between devotional service and all other methods of perfection. One who performs severe austerities for sense gratification is fearful to the entire world, whereas a devotee who performs even a slight amount of devotional service is a friend to everyone (*suhṛdaṁ sarva-bhūtānām*). Since the Lord is the well-wisher of every living entity and since a devotee assumes the qualities of the Lord, a devotee also acts for everyone's good fortune by performing devotional service. Thus although Hiraṇyakaśipu performed such a severe austerity, he remained a Daitya and a Rākṣasa, whereas Prahlāda Mahārāja, although born of the same Daitya father, became the most exalted devotee and was personally protected by the Supreme Lord. *Bhakti* is therefore called *sarvopādhi-vinirmuktam*, indicating that a devotee is freed from all material designations, and *anyābhilāṣitā-śūnyam*, situated in a transcendental position, free from all material desires.

TEXT 17

श्रीब्रह्मोवाच
उत्तिष्ठोत्तिष्ठ भद्रं ते तपःसिद्धोऽसि काश्यप ।
वरदोऽहमनुप्राप्तो व्रियतामीप्सितो वरः ॥१७॥

śrī-brahmovāca
uttiṣṭhottiṣṭha bhadraṁ te
tapaḥ-siddho 'si kāśyapa
varado 'ham anuprāpto
vriyatām īpsito varaḥ

śrī-brahmā uvāca—Lord Brahmā said; *uttiṣṭha*—please get up; *uttiṣṭha*—get up; *bhadram*—good fortune; *te*—unto you; *tapaḥ-siddhaḥ*—perfect in executing austerities; *asi*—you are; *kāśyapa*—O son of Kaśyapa; *vara-daḥ*—the giver of benediction; *aham*—I; *anuprāptaḥ*—arrived; *vriyatām*—let it be submitted; *īpsitaḥ*—desired; *varaḥ*—benediction.

TRANSLATION

Lord Brahmā said: O son of Kaśyapa Muni, please get up, please get up. All good fortune unto you. You are now perfect in the performance of your austerities, and therefore I may give you a benediction. You may now ask from me whatever you desire, and I shall try to fulfill your wish.

PURPORT

Śrīla Madhvācārya quotes from the *Skanda Purāṇa*, which says that Hiraṇyakaśipu, having become a devotee of Lord Brahmā, who is known as Hiraṇyagarbha, and having undergone a severe austerity to please him, is also known as Hiraṇyaka. Rākṣasas and demons worship various demigods, such as Lord Brahmā and Lord Śiva, just to take the post of these demigods. This we have already explained in previous verses.

TEXT 18

अद्राक्षमहमेतं ते हृत्सारं महदद्भुतम् ।
दंशभक्षितदेहस्य प्राणा ह्यस्थिषु शेरते ॥१८॥

adrākṣam aham etaṁ te
hṛt-sāraṁ mahad-adbhutam
daṁśa-bhakṣita-dehasya
prāṇā hy asthiṣu śerate

adrākṣam—have personally seen; *aham*—I; *etam*—this; *te*—your; *hṛt-sāram*—power of endurance; *mahat*—very great; *adbhutam*—wonderful; *daṁśa-bhakṣita*—eaten by worms and ants; *dehasya*—whose body; *prāṇāḥ*—the life air; *hi*—indeed; *asthiṣu*—in the bones; *śerate*—is taking shelter.

TRANSLATION

I have been very much astonished to see your endurance. In spite of being eaten and bitten by all kinds of worms and ants, you

are keeping your life air circulating within your bones. Certainly this is wonderful.

PURPORT

It appears that the soul can exist even through the bones, as shown by the personal example of Hiraṇyakaśipu. When great *yogīs* are in *samādhi*, even when their bodies are buried and their skin, marrow, blood and so on have all been eaten, if only their bones remain they can exist in a transcendental position. Very recently an archaeologist published findings indicating that Lord Christ, after being buried, was exhumed and that he then went to Kashmir. There have been many actual examples of *yogīs'* being buried in trance and exhumed alive and in good condition several hours later. A *yogī* can keep himself alive in a transcendental state even if buried not only for many days but for many years.

TEXT 19

नैतत्पूर्वर्षयश्चक्रुर्न करिष्यन्ति चापरे ।
निरम्बुर्धारयेत्प्राणान् को वै दिव्यसमाः शतम् ॥१९॥

naitat pūrvarṣayaś cakrur
na kariṣyanti cāpare
nirambur dhārayet prāṇān
ko vai divya-samāḥ śatam

na—not; *etat*—this; *pūrva-ṛṣayaḥ*—the sages before you, such as Bhṛgu; *cakruḥ*—executed; *na*—nor; *kariṣyanti*—will execute; *ca*—also; *apare*—others; *nirambuḥ*—without drinking water; *dhārayet*—can sustain; *prāṇān*—the life air; *kaḥ*—who; *vai*—indeed; *divya-samāḥ*—celestial years; *śatam*—one hundred.

TRANSLATION

Even saintly persons like Bhṛgu, born previously, could not perform such severe austerities, nor will anyone in the future be able to do so. Who within these three worlds can sustain his life without even drinking water for one hundred celestial years?

PURPORT

It appears that even if a *yogī* does not drink a drop of water, he can live for many, many years by the yogic process, though his outer body be eaten by ants and moths.

TEXT 20

व्यवसायेन तेऽनेन दुष्करेण मनस्विनाम् ।
तपोनिष्ठेन भवता जितोऽहं दितिनन्दन ॥२०॥

vyavasāyena te 'nena
duṣkareṇa manasvinām
tapo-niṣṭhena bhavatā
jito 'haṁ diti-nandana

vyavasāyena—by determination; *te*—your; *anena*—this; *duṣkareṇa*—difficult to perform; *manasvinām*—even for great sages and saintly persons; *tapaḥ-niṣṭhena*—aimed at executing austerity; *bhavatā*—by you; *jitaḥ*—conquered; *aham*—I; *diti-nandana*—O son of Diti.

TRANSLATION

My dear son of Diti, with your great determination and austerity you have done what was impossible even for great saintly persons, and thus I have certainly been conquered by you.

PURPORT

In regard to the word *jitaḥ*, Śrīla Madhva Muni gives the following quotation from the *Śabda-nirṇaya: parābhūtaṁ vaśa-sthaṁ ca jitabhid ucyate budhaiḥ.* "If one comes under someone else's control or is defeated by another, he is called *jitaḥ*." Hiraṇyakaśipu's austerity was so great and wonderful that even Lord Brahmā agreed to be conquered by him.

TEXT 21

ततस्त आशिषः सर्वा ददाम्यसुरपुङ्गव ।
मर्तस्य ते ह्यमर्तस्य दर्शनं नाफलं मम ॥२१॥

tatas ta āśiṣaḥ sarvā
dadāmy asura-puṅgava
martasya te hy amartasya
darśanaṁ nāphalaṁ mama

tataḥ—because of this; *te*—unto you; *āśiṣaḥ*—benedictions; *sarvāḥ*—all; *dadāmi*—I shall give; *asura-puṅgava*—O best of the *asuras; martasya*—of one who is destined to die; *te*—such as you; *hi*—indeed; *amartasya*—of one who does not die; *darśanam*—the audience; *na*—not; *aphalam*—without results; *mama*—my.

TRANSLATION

O best of the asuras, for this reason I am now prepared to give you all benedictions, according to your desire. I belong to the celestial world of demigods, who do not die like human beings. Therefore, although you are subject to death, your audience with me will not go in vain.

PURPORT

It appears that human beings and *asuras* are subject to death, whereas demigods are not. The demigods who reside with Lord Brahmā in Satyaloka go to Vaikuṇṭhaloka in their present bodily constructions at the time of the dissolution. Therefore although Hiraṇyakaśipu had undergone severe austerities, Lord Brahmā predicted that he had to die; he could not become immortal or even gain equal status with the demigods. The great austerities and penances he had performed for so many years could not give him protection from death. This was foretold by Lord Brahmā.

TEXT 22

श्रीनारद उवाच
इत्युक्त्वादिभवो देवो भक्षिताङ्गं पिपीलिकैः ।
कमण्डलुजलेनौक्षद्दिव्येनामोघराधसा ॥२२॥

śrī-nārada uvāca
ity uktvādi-bhavo devo
bhakṣitāṅgaṁ pipīlikaiḥ

kamaṇḍalu-jalenaukṣad
divyenāmogha-rādhasā

śrī-nāradaḥ uvāca—Śrī Nārada Muni said; *iti*—thus; *uktvā*—saying; *ādi-bhavaḥ*—Lord Brahmā, the original living creature within this universe; *devaḥ*—the principal demigod; *bhakṣita-aṅgam*—Hiraṇyakaśipu's body, which had been almost completely eaten; *pipīlikaiḥ*—by the ants; *kamandalu*—from the special waterpot in the hands of Lord Brahmā; *jalena*—by water; *aukṣat*—sprinkled; *divyena*—which was spiritual, not ordinary; *amogha*—without fail; *rādhasā*—whose power.

TRANSLATION

Śrī Nārada Muni continued: After speaking these words to Hiraṇyakaśipu, Lord Brahmā, the original being of this universe, who is extremely powerful, sprinkled transcendental, infallible, spiritual water from his kamaṇḍalu upon Hiraṇyakaśipu's body, which had been eaten away by ants and moths. Thus he enlivened Hiraṇyakaśipu.

PURPORT

Lord Brahmā is the first created being within this universe and is empowered by the Supreme Lord to create. *Tene brahma hṛdā ya ādi-kavaye:* the *ādi-deva,* or *ādi-kavi*—the first living creature—was personally taught by the Supreme Personality of Godhead through the heart. There was no one to teach him, but since the Lord is situated within Brahmā's heart, Brahmā was educated by the Lord Himself. Lord Brahmā, being especially empowered, is infallible in doing whatever he wants. This is the meaning of the word *amogha-rādhasā.* He desired to restore Hiraṇyakaśipu's original body, and therefore, by sprinkling transcendental water from his waterpot, he immediately did so.

TEXT 23

स तत्कीचकवल्मीकात् सहओजोबलान्वितः ।
सर्वावयवसम्पन्नो वज्रसंहननो युवा ।
उत्थितस्तप्तहेमाभो विभावसुरिवैधसः ॥२३॥

sa tat kīcaka-valmīkāt
saha-ojo-balānvitaḥ
sarvāvayava-sampanno
vajra-saṁhanano yuvā
utthitas tapta-hemābho
vibhāvasur ivaidhasaḥ

saḥ—Hiraṇyakaśipu; *tat*—that; *kīcaka-valmīkāt*—from the anthill and bamboo grove; *sahaḥ*—mental strength; *ojaḥ*—strength of the senses; *bala*—and sufficient bodily strength; *anvitaḥ*—endowed with; *sarva*—all; *avayava*—the limbs of the body; *sampannaḥ*—fully restored; *vajra-saṁhananaḥ*—having a body as strong as a thunderbolt; *yuvā*—young; *utthitaḥ*—arisen; *tapta-hema-ābhaḥ*—whose bodily luster became like molten gold; *vibhāvasuḥ*—fire; *iva*—like; *edhasaḥ*—from fuel wood.

TRANSLATION

As soon as he was sprinkled with the water from Lord Brahmā's waterpot, Hiraṇyakaśipu arose, endowed with a full body with limbs so strong that they could bear the striking of a thunderbolt. With physical strength and a bodily luster resembling molten gold, he emerged from the anthill a completely young man, just as fire springs from fuel wood.

PURPORT

Hiraṇyakaśipu was revitalized, so much so that his body was quite competent to tolerate the striking of thunderbolts. He was now a young man with a strong body and a very beautiful bodily luster resembling molten gold. This is the rejuvenation that took place because of his severe austerity and penance.

TEXT 24

स निरीक्ष्याम्बरे देवं हंसवाहमुपस्थितम् ।
ननाम शिरसा भूमौ तद्दर्शनमहोत्सवः ॥२४॥

sa nirīkṣyāmbare devaṁ
haṁsa-vāham upasthitam
nanāma śirasā bhūmau
tad-darśana-mahotsavaḥ

saḥ—he (Hiraṇyakaśipu); *nirīkṣya*—seeing; *ambare*—in the sky; *devam*—the supreme demigod; *haṁsa-vāham*—who rides a swan airplane; *upasthitam*—situated before him; *nanāma*—offered obeisances; *śirasā*—with his head; *bhūmau*—on the ground; *tat-darśana*—by seeing Lord Brahmā; *mahā-utsavaḥ*—very much pleased.

TRANSLATION

Seeing Lord Brahmā present before him in the sky, carried by his swan airplane, Hiraṇyakaśipu was extremely pleased. He immediately fell flat with his head on the ground and began to express his obligation to the lord.

PURPORT

Lord Kṛṣṇa says in *Bhagavad-gītā* (9.23–24):

ye 'py anya-devatā-bhaktā
yajante śraddhayānvitāḥ
te 'pi mām eva kaunteya
yajanty avidhi-pūrvakam

ahaṁ hi sarva-yajñānāṁ
bhoktā ca prabhur eva ca
na tu mām abhijānanti
tattvenātaś cyavanti te

"Whatever a man may sacrifice to other gods, O son of Kuntī, is really meant for Me alone, but it is offered without true understanding. I am the only enjoyer and the only object of sacrifice. Those who do not recognize My true transcendental nature fall down."

In effect, Kṛṣṇa says, "Persons engaged in the worship of demigods are not very intelligent, although such worship is indirectly offered to

Me." For example, when a man pours water on the leaves and branches of a tree without pouring water on the root, he does so without sufficient knowledge or without observing regulative principles. The process of watering a tree is to pour water on the root. Similarly, the process of rendering service to different parts of the body is to supply food to the stomach. The demigods are, so to speak, different officers and directors in the government of the Supreme Lord. One has to follow the laws made by the government, not by the officers or directors. Similarly, everyone is to offer his worship to the Supreme Lord only. That will automatically satisfy the different officers and directors of the Lord. The officers and directors are engaged as representatives of the government, and to offer some bribe to the officers and directors is illegal. This is stated in *Bhagavad-gītā* as *avidhi-pūrvakam.* In other words, Kṛṣṇa does not approve the unnecessary worship of the demigods.

In *Bhagavad-gītā* it is clearly stated that there are many types of *yajña* performances recommended in the Vedic literatures, but actually all of them are meant for satisfying the Supreme Lord. *Yajña* means Viṣṇu. In the Third Chapter of *Bhagavad-gītā* it is clearly stated that one should work only for satisfying Yajña, or Viṣṇu. The perfectional form of human civilization, known as *varṇāśrama-dharma*, is specifically meant for satisfying Viṣṇu. Therefore, Kṛṣṇa says, "I am the enjoyer of all sacrifices because I am the supreme master." However, less intelligent persons, without knowing this fact, worship demigods for temporary benefit. Therefore they fall down to material existence and do not achieve the desired goal of life. If, however, anyone has any material desire to be fulfilled, he had better pray for it to the Supreme Lord (although that is not pure devotion), and he will thus achieve the desired result.

Although Hiraṇyakaśipu offered his obeisances unto Lord Brahmā, he was strongly inimical toward Lord Viṣṇu. This is the symptom of an *asura. Asuras* worship the demigods as being separate from the Lord, not knowing that all the demigods are powerful because of being servants of the Lord. If the Supreme Lord were to withdraw the powers of the demigods, the demigods would no longer be able to offer benedictions to their worshipers. The difference between a devotee and a nondevotee, or *asura*, is that a devotee knows that Lord Viṣṇu is the Supreme Personality of Godhead and that everyone derives power from Him. Without worshiping the demigods for particular powers, a devotee worships Lord Viṣṇu, knowing that if he desires a particular power he can get that power while acting as Lord Viṣṇu's devotee. Therefore in the *śāstra* (*Bhāg.* 2.3.10) it is recommended:

akāmaḥ sarva-kāmo vā
mokṣa-kāma udāra-dhīḥ
tīvreṇa bhakti-yogena
yajeta puruṣaṁ param

"A person who has broader intelligence, whether he be full of material desires, free from material desires, or desiring liberation, must by all means worship the supreme whole, the Personality of Godhead." Even if a person has material desires, instead of worshiping the demigods he should pray to the Supreme Lord so that his connection with the Supreme Lord will be established and he will be saved from becoming a demon or a nondevotee. In this regard, Śrīla Madhvācārya gives the following quotation from the *Brahma-tarka:*

eka-sthānaika-kāryatvād
viṣṇoḥ prādhānyatas tathā
jīvasya tad-adhīnatvān
na bhinnādhikṛtaṁ vacaḥ

Since Viṣṇu is the Supreme, by worshiping Viṣṇu one can fulfill all one's desires. There is no need to divert one's attention to any demigod.

TEXT 25

उत्थाय प्राञ्जलिः प्रह्व ईक्षमाणो दृशा विभुम् ।
हर्षाश्रुपुलकोद्भेदो गिरा गद्गदयागृणात् ॥२५॥

utthāya prāñjaliḥ prahva
īkṣamāṇo dṛśā vibhum
harṣāśru-pulakodbhedo
girā gadgadayāgṛṇāt

utthāya—getting up; *prāñjaliḥ*—with folded hands; *prahvaḥ*—in a humble manner; *īkṣamāṇaḥ*—seeing; *dṛśā*—with his eyes; *vibhum*—the supreme person within this universe; *harṣa*—of jubilation; *aśru*—with tears; *pulaka*—with hairs standing on the body; *udbhedaḥ*—enlivened; *girā*—by words; *gadgadayā*—faltering; *agṛṇāt*—prayed.

TRANSLATION

Then, getting up from the ground and seeing Lord Brahmā before him, the head of the Daityas was overwhelmed by jubilation. With tears in his eyes, his whole body shivering, he began praying in a humble mood, with folded hands and a faltering voice, to satisfy Lord Brahmā.

TEXTS 26–27

श्रीहिरण्यकशिपुरुवाच
कल्पान्ते कालसृष्टेन योऽन्धेन तमसावृतम् ।
अभिव्यनग् जगदिदं स्वयञ्ज्योतिः स्वरोचिषा॥२६॥
आत्मना त्रिवृता चेदं सृजत्यवति लुम्पति ।
रजःसत्त्वतमोधाम्ने पराय महते नमः ॥२७॥

śrī-hiraṇyakaśipur uvāca
kalpānte kāla-sṛṣṭena
yo 'ndhena tamasāvṛtam
abhivyanag jagad idaṁ
svayañjyotiḥ sva-rociṣā

ātmanā tri-vṛtā cedaṁ
sṛjaty avati lumpati
rajaḥ-sattva-tamo-dhāmne
parāya mahate namaḥ

śrī-hiraṇyakaśipuḥ uvāca—Hiraṇyakaśipu said; *kalpa-ante*—at the end of every day of Lord Brahmā; *kāla-sṛṣṭena*—created by the time factor; *yaḥ*—he who; *andhena*—by dense darkness; *tamasā*—by ignorance; *āvṛtam*—covered; *abhivyanak*—manifested; *jagat*—cosmic manifestation; *idam*—this; *svayam-jyotiḥ*—self-effulgent; *sva-rociṣā*—by his bodily rays; *ātmanā*—by himself; *tri-vṛtā*—conducted by the three modes of material nature; *ca*—also; *idam*—this material world; *sṛjati*—creates; *avati*—maintains; *lumpati*—annihilates; *rajaḥ*—of the mode of passion; *sattva*—the mode of goodness; *tamaḥ*—and the mode of ignorance; *dhāmne*—unto the supreme lord; *parāya*—unto the supreme; *mahate*—unto the great; *namaḥ*—my respectful obeisances.

TRANSLATION

Let me offer my respectful obeisances unto the supreme lord within this universe. At the end of each day of his life, the universe is fully covered with dense darkness by the influence of time, and then again, during his next day, that self-effulgent lord, by his own effulgence, manifests, maintains and destroys the entire cosmic manifestation through the material energy, which is invested with the three modes of material nature. He, Lord Brahmā, is the shelter of those modes of nature—sattva-guṇa, rajo-guṇa and tamo-guṇa.

PURPORT

The words *abhivyanag jagad idam* refer to he who creates this cosmic manifestation. The original creator is the Supreme Personality of Godhead, Kṛṣṇa (*janmādy asya yataḥ*); Lord Brahmā is the secondary creator. When Lord Brahmā is empowered by Lord Kṛṣṇa as the engineer to create the phenomenal world, he becomes the supremely powerful feature within this universe. The total material energy is created by Kṛṣṇa, and later, taking advantage of all that has necessarily been created, Lord Brahmā engineers the entire phenomenal universe. At the end of Lord Brahmā's day, everything up to Svargaloka is inundated with water, and the next morning, when there is darkness in the universe, Brahmā again brings the phenomenal manifestation into existence. Therefore he is described here as he who manifests this universe.

Trīn guṇān vṛṇoti: Lord Brahmā takes advantage of the three modes of material nature. *Prakṛti,* material nature, is described here as *tri-vṛtā,* the source of the three material modes. Śrīla Madhvācārya comments in this connection that *tri-vṛtā* means *prakṛtyā.* Thus Lord Kṛṣṇa is the original creator, and Lord Brahmā is the original engineer.

TEXT 28

नम आद्याय बीजाय ज्ञानविज्ञानमूर्तये ।
प्राणेन्द्रियमनोबुद्धिविकारैर्व्यक्तिमीयुषे ॥२८॥

nama ādyāya bījāya
jñāna-vijñāna-mūrtaye
prāṇendriya-mano-buddhi-
vikārair vyaktim īyuṣe

namaḥ—I offer my respectful obeisances; *ādyāya*—unto the original living creature; *bījāya*—the seed of the cosmic manifestation; *jñāna*—of knowledge; *vijñāna*—and of practical application; *mūrtaye*—unto the deity or form; *prāṇa*—of the life air; *indriya*—of the senses; *manaḥ*—of the mind; *buddhi*—of the intelligence; *vikāraiḥ*—by transformations; *vyaktim*—manifestation; *īyuṣe*—who has obtained.

TRANSLATION

I offer my obeisances to the original personality within this universe, Lord Brahmā, who is cognizant and who can apply his mind and realized intelligence in creating this cosmic manifestation. It is because of his activities that everything within the universe is visible. He is therefore the cause of all manifestations.

PURPORT

The *Vedānta-sūtra* begins by declaring that the Absolute Person is the original source of all creation (*janmādy asya yataḥ*). One may ask whether Lord Brahmā is the Supreme Absolute Person. No, the Supreme Absolute Person is Kṛṣṇa. Brahmā receives his mind, intelligence, materials and everything else from Kṛṣṇa, and then he becomes the secondary creator, the engineer of this universe. In this regard we may note that the creation does not take place accidentally, because of the explosion of a chunk. Such nonsensical theories are not accepted by Vedic students. The first created living being is Brahmā, who is endowed with perfect knowledge and intelligence by the Lord. As stated in *Śrīmad-Bhāgavatam, tene brahma hṛdā ya ādi-kavaye:* although Brahmā is the first created being, he is not independent, for he receives help from the Supreme Personality of Godhead through his heart. There is no one but Brahmā at the time of creation, and therefore he receives his intelligence directly from the Lord through the heart. This has been discussed in the beginning of *Śrīmad-Bhāgavatam.*

Lord Brahmā is described in this verse as the original cause of the cosmic manifestation, and this applies to his position in the material world. There are many, many such controllers, all of whom are created by the Supreme Lord, Viṣṇu. This is illustrated by an incident described in *Caitanya-caritāmṛta.* When the Brahmā of this particular universe was invited by Kṛṣṇa to Dvārakā, he thought that he was the only Brahmā. Therefore when Kṛṣṇa inquired from His servant which Brahmā was at the door to visit, Lord Brahmā was surprised. He replied that of course Lord Brahmā, the father of the four Kumāras, was waiting at the door. Later, Lord Brahmā asked Kṛṣṇa why He had inquired which Brahmā had come. He was then informed that there are millions of other Brahmās because there are millions of universes. Kṛṣṇa then called all the Brahmās, who immediately came to visit Him. The *catur-mukha* Brahmā, the four-headed Brahmā of this universe, thought himself a very insignificant creature in the presence of so many Brahmās with so many heads. Thus although there is a Brahmā who is the engineer of each universe, Kṛṣṇa is the original source of all of them.

TEXT 29

त्वमीशिषे जगतस्तस्थुषश्च
प्राणेन मुख्येन पतिः प्रजानाम् ।
चित्तस्य चित्तैर्मनइन्द्रियाणां
पतिर्महान् भूतगुणाशयेशः ॥२९॥

tvam īśiṣe jagatas tasthuṣaś ca
prāṇena mukhyena patiḥ prajānām
cittasya cittair mana-indriyāṇāṁ
patir mahān bhūta-guṇāśayeśaḥ

tvam—you; *īśiṣe*—actually control; *jagataḥ*—of the moving being; *tasthuṣaḥ*—of the being that is dull or stationed in one place; *ca*—and; *prāṇena*—by the living force; *mukhyena*—the origin of all activities; *patiḥ*—master; *prajānām*—of all living entities; *cittasya*—of the mind; *cittaiḥ*—by the consciousness; *manaḥ*—of the mind; *indriyāṇām*—and of the two kinds of senses (acting and knowledge-gathering); *patiḥ*—the master; *mahān*—great; *bhūta*—of the material elements; *guṇa*—and the qualities of the material elements; *āśaya*—of desires; *īśaḥ*—the supreme master.

TRANSLATION

Your Lordship, being the origin of the life of this material world, is the master and controller of the living entities, both moving and stationary, and you inspire their consciousness. You maintain the mind and the acting and knowledge-acquiring senses, and therefore you are the great controller of all the material elements and their qualities, and you are the controller of all desires.

PURPORT

In this verse it is clearly indicated that the original source of everything is life. Brahmā was instructed by the supreme life, Kṛṣṇa. Kṛṣṇa is the supreme living entity (*nityo nityānāṁ cetanaś cetanānām*), and Brahmā is also a living entity, but the original source of Brahmā is Kṛṣṇa. Therefore Kṛṣṇa says in *Bhagavad-gītā* (7.7), *mattaḥ parataraṁ nānyat kiñcid asti dhanañjaya:* "O Arjuna, there is no truth superior to Me." Kṛṣṇa is the original source of Brahmā, who is the original source of this universe. Brahmā is a representative of Kṛṣṇa, and therefore all the qualities and activities of Kṛṣṇa are also present in Lord Brahmā.

TEXT 30

त्वं सप्ततन्तून् वितनोषि तन्वा
त्रय्या चतुर्होत्रकविद्यया च ।
त्वमेक आत्मात्मवतामनादि-
रनन्तपारः कविरन्तरात्मा ॥३०॥

tvaṁ sapta-tantūn vitanoṣi tanvā
trayyā catur-hotraka-vidyayā ca
tvam eka ātmātmavatām anādir
ananta-pāraḥ kavir antarātmā

tvam—you; *sapta-tantūn*—the seven kinds of Vedic ritualistic ceremonies, beginning from the *agniṣṭoma-yajña; vitanoṣi*—spread; *tanvā*—by your body; *trayyā*—the three *Vedas; catuḥ-hotraka*—of the four kinds of Vedic priests, known as *hotā, adhvaryu, brahma* and *udgātā; vidyayā*—by the necessary knowledge; *ca*—also; *tvam*—you; *ekaḥ*—one; *ātmā*—the Supersoul; *ātma-vatām*—of all living entities; *anādiḥ*—without beginning; *ananta-pāraḥ*—without end; *kaviḥ*—the supreme inspirer; *antaḥ-ātmā*—the Supersoul within the core of the heart.

TRANSLATION

My dear lord, by your form as the Vedas personified and through knowledge relating to the activities of all the yajñic brāhmaṇas, you spread the Vedic ritualistic ceremonies of the seven kinds of sacrifices, headed by agniṣṭoma. Indeed, you inspire the yajñic brāhmaṇas to perform the rituals mentioned in the three Vedas. Being the Supreme Soul, the Supersoul of all living entities, you are beginningless, endless and omniscient, beyond the limits of time and space.

PURPORT

The Vedic ritualistic ceremonies, the knowledge thereof, and the person who agrees to perform them are inspired by the Supreme Soul. As confirmed in *Bhagavad-gītā, mattaḥ smṛtir jñānam apohanaṁ ca:* from the Lord come remembrance, knowledge and forgetfulness. The Supersoul is situated in everyone's heart (*sarvasya cāhaṁ hṛdi sanniviṣṭaḥ, īśvaraḥ sarva-bhūtānāṁ hṛd-deśe 'rjuna tiṣṭhati*), and when one is advanced in Vedic knowledge, the Supersoul gives him directions. Acting as Supersoul, the Lord gives inspiration to a suitable person to perform the Vedic ritualistic ceremonies. In this connection, four classes of priests, known as *ṛtvik*, are required. They are mentioned as *hotā, adhvaryu, brahma* and *udgātā.*

TEXT 31

त्वमेव कालोऽनिमिषो जनाना-
मायुर्लवाद्यवयवैः क्षिणोषि ।
कूटस्थ आत्मा परमेष्ठ्यजो महां-
स्त्वं जीवलोकस्य च जीव आत्मा ॥३१॥

tvam eva kālo 'nimiṣo janānām
āyur lavādy-avayavaiḥ kṣiṇoṣi
kūṭa-stha ātmā parameṣṭhy ajo mahāṁs
tvaṁ jīva-lokasya ca jīva ātmā

tvam—you; *eva*—indeed; *kālaḥ*—unlimited time; *animiṣaḥ*—unblinking; *janānām*—of all living entities; *āyuḥ*—the duration of life; *lava-ādi*—consisting of seconds, moments, minutes and hours; *avayavaiḥ*—by different parts; *kṣiṇoṣi*—reduce; *kūṭa-sthaḥ*—without being affected by anything; *ātmā*—the Supersoul; *parameṣṭhī*—the Supreme Lord; *ajaḥ*—the unborn; *mahān*—the great; *tvam*—you; *jīva-lokasya*—of this material world; *ca*—also; *jīvaḥ*—the cause of life; *ātmā*—the Supersoul.

TRANSLATION

O my lord, Your Lordship is eternally awake, seeing everything that happens. As eternal time, you reduce the duration of life for all living entities through your different parts, such as moments, seconds, minutes and hours. Nonetheless, you are unchanged, resting in one place as the Supersoul, witness and Supreme Lord, the birthless, all-pervading controller who is the cause of life for all living entities.

PURPORT

In this verse the word *kūṭa-stha* is very important. Although the Supreme Personality of Godhead is situated everywhere, He is the central unchanging point. *Īśvaraḥ sarva-bhūtānāṁ hṛd-deśe 'rjuna tiṣṭhati:* the Lord is situated in full in the core of everyone's heart. As indicated in the *Upaniṣads* by the word *ekatvam*, although there are millions and millions of living entities, the Lord is situated as the Supersoul in every one of them. Nonetheless, He is one in many. As stated in the *Brahma-saṁhitā, advaitam acyutam anādim ananta-rūpam:* He has many forms, yet they are *advaita*—one and unchanging. Since the Lord is all-pervading, He is also situated in eternal time. The living entities are described as parts and parcels of the Lord because He is the life and soul of all living entities, being situated within their hearts as the *antaryāmī*, as enunciated by the philosophy of inconceivable oneness and difference (*acintya-bhedābheda*). Since the living entities are part of God, they are one in quality with the Lord, yet they are different from Him. The Supersoul, who inspires all living entities to act, is one and changeless. There are varieties of subjects, objects and activities, yet the Lord is one.

TEXT 32

त्वत्तः परं नापरमप्यनेज-
देजच्च किञ्चिद् व्यतिरिक्तमस्ति ।
विद्याः कलास्ते तनवश्च सर्वा
हिरण्यगर्भोऽसि बृहत्त्रिपृष्ठः ॥३२॥

tvattaḥ paraṁ nāparam apy anejad
ejac ca kiñcid vyatiriktam asti
vidyāḥ kalās te tanavaś ca sarvā
hiraṇyagarbho 'si bṛhat tri-pṛṣṭhaḥ

tvattaḥ—from you; *param*—higher; *na*—not; *aparam*—lower; *api*—even; *anejat*—not moving; *ejat*—moving; *ca*—and; *kiñcit*—anything; *vyatiriktam*—separate; *asti*—there is; *vidyāḥ*—knowledge; *kalāḥ*—its parts; *te*—of you; *tanavaḥ*—features of the body; *ca*—and; *sarvāḥ*—all; *hiraṇya-garbhaḥ*—the one who keeps the universe within his abdomen; *asi*—you are; *bṛhat*—greater than the greatest; *tri-pṛṣṭhaḥ*—transcendental to the three modes of material nature.

TRANSLATION

There is nothing separate from you, whether it be better or lower, stationary or moving. The knowledge derived from the

Vedic literatures like the Upaniṣads, and from all the sub-limbs of the original Vedic knowledge, form your external body. You are Hiraṇyagarbha, the reservoir of the universe, but nonetheless, being situated as the supreme controller, you are transcendental to the material world, which consists of the three modes of material nature.

PURPORT

The word *param* means "the supreme cause," and *aparam* means "the effect." The supreme cause is the Supreme Personality of Godhead, and the effect is material nature. The living entities, both moving and nonmoving, are controlled by the Vedic instructions in art and science, and therefore they are all expansions of the external energy of the Supreme Personality of Godhead, who is the center as the Supersoul. The *brahmāṇḍas*, the universes, exist during the duration of a breath of the Supreme Lord (*yasyaika-niśvasita-kālam athāvalambya jīvanti loma-vilajā jagad-aṇḍa-nāthāḥ*). Thus they are also within the womb of the Supreme Personality of Godhead, Mahā-Viṣṇu. Nothing, therefore, is separate from the Supreme Lord. This is the philosophy of *acintya-bhedābheda-tattva.*

TEXT 33

व्यक्तं विभो स्थूलमिदं शरीरं
येनेन्द्रियप्राणमनोगुणांस्त्वम् ।
भुङ्क्षे स्थितो धामनि पारमेष्ठ्ये
अव्यक्त आत्मा पुरुषः पुराणः ॥३३॥

vyaktaṁ vibho sthūlam idaṁ śarīraṁ
yenendriya-prāṇa-mano-guṇāṁs tvam
bhuṅkṣe sthito dhāmani pārameṣṭhye
avyakta ātmā puruṣaḥ purāṇaḥ

vyaktam—manifested; *vibho*—O my lord; *sthūlam*—cosmic manifestation; *idam*—this; *śarīram*—external body; *yena*—by which; *indriya*—the senses; *prāṇa*—the life air; *manaḥ*—the mind; *guṇān*—

transcendental qualities; *tvam*—you; *bhuṅkṣe*—enjoy; *sthitaḥ*—situated; *dhāmani*—in your own abode; *pārameṣṭhye*—the supreme; *avyaktaḥ*—not manifested through ordinary knowledge; *ātmā*—the soul; *puruṣaḥ*—the supreme person; *purāṇaḥ*—the oldest.

TRANSLATION

O my lord, being changelessly situated in your own abode, you expand your universal form within this cosmic manifestation, thus appearing to taste the material world. You are Brahman, the Supersoul, the oldest, the Personality of Godhead.

PURPORT

It is said that the Absolute Truth appears in three features—namely, impersonal Brahman, localized Supersoul and ultimately the Supreme Personality of Godhead, Kṛṣṇa. The cosmic manifestation is the gross material body of the Supreme Personality of Godhead, who enjoys the taste of the material mellows by expanding His parts and parcels, the living entities, who are qualitatively one with Him. The Supreme Personality of Godhead, however, is situated in the Vaikuṇṭha planets, where He enjoys the spiritual mellows. Therefore the one Absolute Truth, Bhagavān, pervades all by His material cosmic manifestation, the spiritual Brahman effulgence, and His personal existence as the Supreme Lord.

TEXT 34

अनन्ताव्यक्तरूपेण येनेदमखिलं ततम् ।
चिदचिच्छक्तियुक्ताय तस्मै भगवते नमः ॥३४॥

anantāvyakta-rūpeṇa
yenedam akhilaṁ tatam
cid-acic-chakti-yuktāya
tasmai bhagavate namaḥ

ananta-avyakta-rūpeṇa—by the unlimited, unmanifested form; *yena*—by which; *idam*—this; *akhilam*—total aggregate; *tatam*—expanded; *cit*—with spiritual; *acit*—and material; *śakti*—potency; *yuk-*

tāya—unto he who is endowed; *tasmai*—unto him; *bhagavate*—unto the Supreme Personality of Godhead; *namaḥ*—I offer my respectful obeisances.

TRANSLATION

Let me offer my respectful obeisances unto the Supreme, who in his unlimited, unmanifested form has expanded the cosmic manifestation, the form of the totality of the universe. He possesses external and internal energies and the mixed energy called the marginal potency, which consists of all the living entities.

PURPORT

The Lord is endowed with unlimited potencies (*parāsya śaktir vividhaiva śrūyate*), which are summarized as three, namely external, internal and marginal. The external potency manifests this material world, the internal potency manifests the spiritual world, and the marginal potency manifests the living entities, who are mixtures of internal and external. The living entity, being part and parcel of Parabrahman, is actually internal potency, but because of being in contact with the material energy, he is an emanation of material and spiritual energies. The Supreme Personality of Godhead is above the material energy and is engaged in spiritual pastimes. The material energy is only an external manifestation of His pastimes.

TEXT 35

यदि दास्यस्यभिमतान् वरान्मे वरदोत्तम ।
भूतेभ्यस्त्वद्विसृष्टेभ्यो मृत्युर्मा भून्मम प्रभो ॥३५॥

yadi dāsyasy abhimatān
varān me varadottama
bhūtebhyas tvad-visṛṣṭebhyo
mṛtyur mā bhūn mama prabho

yadi—if; *dāsyasi*—you will give; *abhimatān*—the desired; *varān*—benedictions; *me*—unto me; *varada-uttama*—O best of all benedictors; *bhūtebhyaḥ*—from living entities; *tvat*—by you; *visṛṣṭebhyaḥ*—who are created; *mṛtyuḥ*—death; *mā*—not; *bhūt*—let there be; *mama*—my; *prabho*—O my lord.

TRANSLATION

O my lord, O best of the givers of benediction, if you will kindly grant me the benediction I desire, please let me not meet death from any of the living entities created by you.

PURPORT

After being created from the navel of Garbhodakaśāyī Viṣṇu, Lord Brahmā, the original created living being within the universe, created many other different types of living entities to reside in this universe. Therefore, from the beginning of creation, the living entities were born of a superior living entity. Ultimately, Kṛṣṇa is the supreme living being, the father of all others. *Ahaṁ bīja-pradaḥ pitā:* He is the seed-giving father of all living entities.

Thus far, Hiraṇyakaśipu has adored Lord Brahmā as the Supreme Personality of Godhead and has expected to become immortal by the benediction of Lord Brahmā. Now, however, having come to understand that even Lord Brahmā is not immortal because at the end of the millennium Lord Brahmā will also die, Hiraṇyakaśipu is very carefully asking him for benedictions that will be almost as good as immortality. His first proposal is that he not be killed by any of the different forms of living entities created by Lord Brahmā within this material world.

TEXT 36

नान्तर्बहिर्दिवा नक्तमन्यस्मादपि चायुधैः ।
न भूमौ नाम्बरे मृत्युर्न नरैर्न मृगैरपि ॥३६॥

nāntar bahir divā naktam
anyasmād api cāyudhaiḥ
na bhūmau nāmbare mṛtyur
na narair na mṛgair api

na—not; *antaḥ*—inside (the palace or home); *bahiḥ*—outside the home; *divā*—during the daytime; *naktam*—during the night; *anyasmāt*—from any others beyond Lord Brahmā; *api*—even; *ca*—also;

ayudhaiḥ—by any weapons used within this material world; *na*—nor; *bhūmau*—on the ground; *na*—not; *ambare*—in the sky; *mṛtyuḥ*—death; *na*—not; *naraiḥ*—by any men; *na*—nor; *mṛgaiḥ*—by any animal; *api*—also.

TRANSLATION

Grant me that I not die within any residence or outside any residence, during the daytime or at night, nor on the ground or in the sky. Grant me that my death not be brought by any being other than those created by you, nor by any weapon, nor by any human being or animal.

PURPORT

Hiraṇyakaśipu was very much afraid of Viṣṇu's becoming an animal to kill him because his brother had been killed by Viṣṇu when the Lord took the shape of a boar. He was therefore very careful to guard against all kinds of animals. But even without taking the shape of an animal, Viṣṇu could kill him by hurling His Sudarśana *cakra*, which can go anywhere without the Lord's physical presence. Therefore Hiraṇyakaśipu was careful to guard against all kinds of weapons. He guarded against all kinds of time, space and countries because he was afraid of being killed by someone else in another land. There are many other planets, higher and lower, and therefore he prayed for the benediction of not being killed by any resident of any of these planets. There are three original deities—Brahmā, Viṣṇu and Maheśvara. Hiraṇyakaśipu knew that Brahmā would not kill him, but he also wanted not to be killed by Lord Viṣṇu or Lord Śiva. Consequently, he prayed for such a benediction. Thus Hiraṇyakaśipu thought himself securely protected from any kind of death caused by any living entity within this universe. He also carefully guarded against natural death, which might take place within his house or outside of the house.

TEXTS 37–38

व्यसुभिर्वासुमद्भिर्वा सुरासुरमहोरगैः ।
अप्रतिद्वन्द्वतां युद्धे ऐकपत्यं च देहिनाम् ॥३७॥
सर्वेषां लोकपालानां महिमानं यथात्मनः ।
तपोयोगप्रभावाणां यन्न रिष्यति कर्हिचित् ॥३८॥

vyasubhir vāsumadbhir vā
surāsura-mahoragaiḥ
apratidvandvatāṁ yuddhe
aika-patyaṁ ca dehinām

sarveṣāṁ loka-pālānāṁ
mahimānaṁ yathātmanaḥ
tapo-yoga-prabhāvāṇāṁ
yan na riṣyati karhicit

vyasubhiḥ—by things that have no life; *vā*—or; *asumadbhiḥ*—by entities that have life; *vā*—or; *sura*—by the demigods; *asura*—the demons; *mahā-uragaiḥ*—by the great serpents who live on the lower planets; *apratidvandvatām*—without a rival; *yuddhe*—in battle; *aika-patyam*—supremacy; *ca*—and; *dehinām*—over those who have material bodies; *sarveṣām*—of all; *loka-pālānām*—the predominating deities of all planets; *mahimānam*—the glory; *yathā*—just as; *ātmanaḥ*—of yourself; *tapaḥ-yoga-prabhāvāṇām*—of those whose power is obtained by austerities and the practice of mystic *yoga; yat*—which; *na*—never; *riṣyati*—is destroyed; *karhicit*—at any time.

TRANSLATION

Grant me that I not meet death from any entity, living or nonliving. Grant me, further, that I not be killed by any demigod or demon or by any great snake from the lower planets. Since no one can kill you in the battlefield, you have no competitor. Therefore, grant me the benediction that I too may have no rival. Give me sole lordship over all the living entities and presiding deities, and give me all the glories obtained by that position. Furthermore, give me all the mystic powers attained by long austerities and the practice of yoga, for these cannot be lost at any time.

PURPORT

Lord Brahmā obtained his supreme position due to long austerities and penances, mystic *yoga*, meditation and so on. Hiraṇyakaśipu wanted a similar position. The ordinary powers achieved by mystic *yoga*, austerities and other processes are sometimes vanquished, but the powers obtained by the mercy of the Lord are never vanquished. Hiraṇyakaśipu, therefore, wanted a benediction that would never be vanquished.

Thus end the Bhaktivedanta purports of the Seventh Canto, Third Chapter, of the Śrīmad-Bhāgavatam, *entitled "Hiraṇyakaśipu's Plan to Become Immortal."*

CHAPTER FOUR

Hiraṇyakaśipu Terrorizes the Universe

This chapter fully describes how Hiraṇyakaśipu obtained power from Lord Brahmā and misused it by harassing all the living entities within this universe.

By severe austerities, Hiraṇyakaśipu satisfied Lord Brahmā and obtained the benedictions he desired. After he received these benedictions, his body, which had been almost entirely consumed, was revived with full beauty and a luster like gold. Nonetheless, he continued to be envious of Lord Viṣṇu, unable to forget Lord Viṣṇu's having killed his brother. Hiraṇyakaśipu conquered everyone in the ten directions and the three worlds and brought all living entities, both demigods and *asuras*, under his control. Becoming the master of all places, including the residence of Indra, whom he had driven out, he began enjoying life in great luxury and thus became mad. All the demigods but Lord Viṣṇu, Lord Brahmā and Lord Śiva came under his control and began serving him, but despite all his material power he was dissatisfied because he was always puffed up, proud of transgressing the Vedic regulations. All the *brāhmaṇas* were dissatisfied with him, and they cursed him with determination. Eventually, all the living entities within the universe, represented by the demigods and sages, prayed to the Supreme Lord for relief from Hiraṇyakaśipu's rule.

Lord Viṣṇu informed the demigods that they and the other living entities would be saved from the fearful conditions created by Hiraṇyakaśipu. Since Hiraṇyakaśipu was the oppressor of all the demigods, the followers of the *Vedas*, the cows, the *brāhmaṇas* and the religious, saintly persons, and since he was envious of the Supreme Lord, he would naturally be killed very soon. Hiraṇyakaśipu's last exploit would be to torment his own son Prahlāda, who was a *mahā-bhāgavata*, an exalted Vaiṣṇava. Then his life would end. When the demigods were thus reassured by the Supreme Personality of Godhead, everyone was satisfied, knowing that the miseries inflicted upon them by Hiraṇyakaśipu would come to an end.

Finally, Nārada Muni describes the characteristics of Prahlāda Mahārāja, the son of Hiraṇyakaśipu, and describes how his father envied his own qualified son. In this way the chapter ends.

TEXT 1

श्रीनारद उवाच
एवं वृतः शतधृतिर्हिरण्यकशिपोरथ ।
प्रादात्तत्तपसा प्रीतो वरांस्तस्य सुदुर्लभान् ॥ १ ॥

śrī-nārada uvāca
evaṁ vṛtaḥ śata-dhṛtir
hiraṇyakaśipor atha
prādāt tat-tapasā prīto
varāṁs tasya sudurlabhān

śrī-nāradaḥ uvāca—Śrī Nārada Muni said; *evam*—thus; *vṛtaḥ*—solicited; *śata-dhṛtiḥ*—Lord Brahmā; *hiraṇyakaśipoḥ*—of Hiraṇyakaśipu; *atha*—then; *prādāt*—delivered; *tat*—his; *tapasā*—by the difficult austerities; *prītaḥ*—being pleased; *varān*—benedictions; *tasya*—unto Hiraṇyakaśipu; *su-durlabhān*—very rarely obtained.

TRANSLATION

Nārada Muni continued: Lord Brahmā was very much satisfied by Hiraṇyakaśipu's austerities, which were difficult to perform. Therefore, when solicited for benedictions, he indeed granted them, although they were rarely to be achieved.

TEXT 2

श्रीब्रह्मोवाच
तातेमे दुर्लभाः पुंसां यान् वृणीषे वरान् मम ।
तथापि वितराम्यङ्ग वरान् यद्यपि दुर्लभान् ॥ २ ॥

śrī-brahmovāca
tāteme durlabhāḥ puṁsāṁ
yān vṛṇīṣe varān mama
tathāpi vitarāmy aṅga
varān yadyapi durlabhān

śrī-brahmā uvāca—Lord Brahmā said; *tāta*—O dear son; *ime*—all these; *durlabhāḥ*—very rarely obtained; *puṁsām*—by men; *yān*—those which; *vṛṇīṣe*—you ask; *varān*—benedictions; *mama*—from me; *tathāpi*—still; *vitarāmi*—I shall deliver; *aṅga*—O Hiraṇyakaśipu; *varān*—the benedictions; *yadyapi*—although; *durlabhān*—not generally available.

TRANSLATION

Lord Brahmā said: O Hiraṇyakaśipu, these benedictions for which you have asked are difficult to obtain for most men. Nonetheless, O my son, I shall grant you them although they are generally not available.

PURPORT

Material benedictions are not always exactly worthy of being called benedictions. If one possesses more and more, a benediction itself may become a curse, for just as achieving material opulence in this material world requires great strength and endeavor, maintaining it also requires great endeavor. Lord Brahmā informed Hiraṇyakaśipu that although he was ready to offer him whatever he had asked, the result of the benedictions would be very difficult for Hiraṇyakaśipu to maintain. Nonetheless, since Brahmā had promised, he wanted to grant all the benedictions asked. The word *durlabhān* indicates that one should not take benedictions one cannot enjoy peacefully.

TEXT 3

ततो जगाम भगवानमोघानुग्रहो विभुः ।
पूजितोऽसुरवर्येण स्तूयमानः प्रजेश्वरैः ॥ ३ ॥

tato jagāma bhagavān
amoghānugraho vibhuḥ
pūjito 'sura-varyeṇa
stūyamānaḥ prajeśvaraiḥ

tataḥ—thereafter; *jagāma*—departed; *bhagavān*—the most powerful, Lord Brahmā; *amogha*—without failure; *anugrahaḥ*—whose benediction; *vibhuḥ*—the Supreme within this universe; *pūjitaḥ*—being worshiped; *asura-varyeṇa*—by the most exalted demon (Hiraṇyakaśipu); *stūyamānaḥ*—being praised; *prajā-īśvaraiḥ*—by many demigods, the masters of different regions.

TRANSLATION

Then Lord Brahmā, who awards infallible benedictions, departed, being worshiped by the best of the demons, Hiraṇyakaśipu, and being praised by great sages and saintly persons.

TEXT 4

एवं लब्धवरो दैत्यो बिभ्रद्धेममयं वपुः ।
भगवत्यकरोद् द्वेषं भ्रातुर्वधमनुस्मरन् ॥ ४ ॥

evaṁ labdha-varo daityo
bibhrad dhemamayaṁ vapuḥ
bhagavaty akarod dveṣaṁ
bhrātur vadham anusmaran

evam—thus; *labdha-varaḥ*—having obtained his desired boon; *daityaḥ*—Hiraṇyakaśipu; *bibhrat*—acquiring; *hema-mayam*—possessing the luster of gold; *vapuḥ*—a body; *bhagavati*—unto Lord Viṣṇu, the Supreme Personality of Godhead; *akarot*—maintained; *dveṣam*—envy; *bhrātuḥ vadham*—the killing of his brother; *anusmaran*—always thinking of.

TRANSLATION

The demon Hiraṇyakaśipu, having thus been blessed by Lord Brahmā and having acquired a lustrous golden body, continued to

remember the death of his brother and therefore be envious of Lord Viṣṇu.

PURPORT

A demoniac person, in spite of acquiring all the opulences possible to obtain in this universe, continues to be envious of the Supreme Personality of Godhead.

TEXTS 5–7

स विजित्य दिशः सर्वा लोकांश्च त्रीन् महासुरः।
देवासुरमनुष्येन्द्रगन्धर्वगरुडोरगान् ॥ ५ ॥
सिद्धचारणविद्याध्रानृषीन् पितृपतीन् मनून् ।
यक्षरक्षःपिशाचेशान् प्रेतभूतपतीनपि ॥ ६ ॥
सर्वसत्त्वपतीञ्जित्वा वशमानीय विश्वजित् ।
जहार लोकपालानां स्थानानि सह तेजसा ॥ ७ ॥

sa vijitya diśaḥ sarvā
lokāṁś ca trīn mahāsuraḥ
devāsura-manuṣyendra-
gandharva-garuḍoragān

siddha-cāraṇa-vidyādhrān
ṛṣīn pitṛ-patīn manūn
yakṣa-rakṣaḥ-piśāceśān
preta-bhūta-patīn api

sarva-sattva-patīñ jitvā
vaśam ānīya viśva-jit
jahāra loka-pālānāṁ
sthānāni saha tejasā

saḥ—he (Hiraṇyakaśipu); *vijitya*—conquering; *diśaḥ*—the directions; *sarvāḥ*—all; *lokān*—planetary systems; *ca*—and; *trīn*—three (upper, lower and middle); *mahā-asuraḥ*—the great demon; *deva*—the demigods; *asura*—the demons; *manuṣya*—of the human beings;

indra—the kings; *gandharva*—the Gandharvas; *garuḍa*—the Garuḍas; *uragān*—the great serpents; *siddha*—the Siddhas; *cāraṇa*—the Cāraṇas; *vidyādhrān*—the Vidyādharas; *ṛṣīn*—the great sages and saintly persons; *pitṛ-patīn*—Yamarāja and the other leaders of the Pitās; *manūn*—all the different Manus; *yakṣa*—the Yakṣas; *rakṣaḥ*—the Rākṣasas; *piśāca-īśān*—the leaders of Piśācaloka; *preta*—of the Pretas; *bhūta*—and of the Bhūtas; *patīn*—the masters; *api*—also; *sarva-sattva-patīn*—the masters of all the different planets; *jitvā*—conquering; *vaśam ānīya*—bringing under control; *viśva-jit*—the conqueror of the whole universe; *jahāra*—usurped; *loka-pālānām*—of the demigods who manage the universal affairs; *sthānāni*—the places; *saha*—with; *tejasā*—all their power.

TRANSLATION

Hiraṇyakaśipu became the conqueror of the entire universe. Indeed, that great demon conquered all the planets in the three worlds—upper, middle and lower—including the planets of the human beings, the Gandharvas, the Garuḍas, the great serpents, the Siddhas, Cāraṇas and Vidyādharas, the great saints, Yamarāja, the Manus, the Yakṣas, the Rākṣasas, the Piśācas and their masters, and the masters of the ghosts and Bhūtas. He defeated the rulers of all the other planets where there are living entities and brought them under his control. Conquering the abodes of all, he seized their power and influence.

PURPORT

The word *garuḍa* in this verse indicates that there are planets of great birds like Garuḍa. Similarly, the word *uraga* indicates that there are planets of enormous serpents. Such a description of the various planets of the universe may challenge modern scientists who think that all planets but this earth are vacant. These scientists claim to have launched excursions to the moon, where they have found no living entities but only big craters full of dust and stone, although in fact the moon is so brilliant that it acts like the sun in illuminating the entire universe. Of course, it is not possible to convince modern scientists of the Vedic information about the universe. Nonetheless, we are not very much impressed by the words of scientists who say that all other planets are vacant and that only the earth is full of living entities.

TEXT 8

देवोद्यानश्रिया जुष्टमध्यास्ते स्म त्रिपिष्टपम् ।
महेन्द्रभवनं साक्षान्निर्मितं विश्वकर्मणा ।
त्रैलोक्यलक्ष्म्यायतनमध्युवासाखिलर्द्धिमत् ॥८॥

devodyāna-śriyā juṣṭam
adhyāste sma tri-piṣṭapam
mahendra-bhavanaṁ sākṣān
nirmitaṁ viśvakarmaṇā
trailokya-lakṣmy-āyatanam
adhyuvāsākhilarddhimat

deva-udyāna—of the famous garden of the demigods; *śriyā*—by the opulences; *juṣṭam*—enriched; *adhyāste sma*—remained in; *tri-piṣṭapam*—the higher planetary system, where various demigods live; *mahendra-bhavanam*—the palace of Indra, the King of heaven; *sākṣāt*—directly; *nirmitam*—constructed; *viśvakarmaṇā*—by the famous architect of the demigods, Viśvakarmā; *trailokya*—of all the three worlds; *lakṣmī-āyatanam*—the residence of the goddess of fortune; *adhyuvāsa*—lived in; *akhila-ṛddhi-mat*—possessing the opulence of the entire universe.

TRANSLATION

Hiraṇyakaśipu, who possessed all opulence, began residing in heaven, with its famous Nandana garden, which is enjoyed by the demigods. In fact, he resided in the most opulent palace of Indra, the King of heaven. The palace had been directly constructed by the demigod architect Viśvakarmā and was as beautifully made as if the goddess of fortune of the entire universe resided there.

PURPORT

From this description it appears that all the heavenly planets of the upper planetary system are thousands upon thousands of times more opulent than the lower planetary system in which we live. Viśvakarmā, the famous heavenly architect, is known as the constructor of many wonderful buildings in the upper planets, where there are not only beautiful buildings, but also many opulent gardens and parks, which are described as *nandana-devodyāna*, gardens quite fit to be enjoyed by the demigods. This description of the upper planetary system and its opulences is to be understood from authoritative scriptures like the Vedic literatures. Telescopes and the other imperfect instruments of scientists are inadequate for evaluating the upper planetary system. Although such instruments are needed because the vision of the so-called scientists is imperfect, the instruments themselves are also imperfect. Therefore the upper planets cannot be appraised by imperfect men using imperfect man-made instruments. Direct information received from the Vedic literature, however, is perfect, We therefore cannot accept the statement that there are no opulent residences on planets other than this earth.

TEXTS 9–12

यत्र विद्रुमसोपाना महामारकता भुवः ।
यत्र स्फाटिककुड्यानि वैदूर्यस्तम्भपङ्क्तयः ॥ ९ ॥
यत्र चित्रवितानानि पद्मरागासनानि च ।
पयःफेननिभाः शय्या मुक्तादामपरिच्छदाः ॥१०॥
कूजद्भिर्नूपुरैर्देव्यः शब्दयन्त्य इतस्ततः ।
रत्नस्थलीषु पश्यन्ति सुदतीः सुन्दरं मुखम् ॥११॥
तस्मिन्महेन्द्रभवने महाबलो
महामना निर्जितलोक एकराट् ।
रेमेऽभिवन्द्याङ्घ्रियुगः सुरादिभिः
प्रतापितैरूर्जितचण्डशासनः ॥१२॥

yatra vidruma-sopānā
mahā-mārakatā bhuvaḥ
yatra sphāṭika-kuḍyāni
vaidūrya-stambha-paṅktayaḥ

yatra citra-vitānāni
padmarāgāsanāni ca
payaḥ-phena-nibhāḥ śayyā
muktādāma-paricchadāḥ

kūjadbhir nūpurair devyaḥ
śabda-yantya itas tataḥ
ratna-sthalīṣu paśyanti
sudatīḥ sundaraṁ mukham

tasmin mahendra-bhavane mahā-balo
mahā-manā nirjita-loka eka-rāṭ
reme 'bhivandyāṅghri-yugaḥ surādibhiḥ
pratāpitair ūrjita-caṇḍa-śāsanaḥ

yatra—where (the residential quarters of King Indra); *vidruma-sopānāḥ*—steps made of coral; *mahā-mārakatāḥ*—emerald; *bhuvaḥ*—floors; *yatra*—where; *sphāṭika*—crystal; *kuḍyāni*—walls; *vaidūrya*—of *vaidūrya* stone; *stambha*—of pillars; *paṅktayaḥ*—lines; *yatra*—where; *citra*—wonderful; *vitānāni*—canopies; *padmarāga*—bedecked with rubies; *āsanāni*—seats; *ca*—also; *payaḥ*—of milk; *phena*—the foam; *nibhāḥ*—just like; *śayyāḥ*—beds; *muktādāma*—of pearls; *paricchadāḥ*—having borders; *kūjadbhiḥ*—jingling; *nūpuraiḥ*—with ankle bells; *devyaḥ*—celestial ladies; *śabda-yantyaḥ*—making sweet vibrations; *itaḥ tataḥ*—here and there; *ratna-sthalīṣu*—in places bedecked with jewels and gems; *paśyanti*—see; *su-datīḥ*—having nice teeth; *sundaram*—very beautiful; *mukham*—faces; *tasmin*—in that; *mahendra-bhavane*—the residential quarters of the heavenly King; *mahā-balaḥ*—the most powerful; *mahā-manāḥ*—highly thoughtful; *nirjita-lokaḥ*—having everyone under his control; *eka-rāṭ*—the powerful dictator; *reme*—enjoyed; *abhivandya*—worshiped; *aṅghri-yugaḥ*—whose two feet; *sura-ādibhiḥ*—by the demigods; *pratāpitaiḥ*—being disturbed; *ūrjita*—more than expected; *caṇḍa*—severe; *śāsanaḥ*—whose ruling.

TRANSLATION

The steps of King Indra's residence were made of coral, the floor was bedecked with invaluable emeralds, the walls were of

crystal, and the columns of vaidūrya stone. The wonderful canopies were beautifully decorated, the seats were bedecked with rubies, and the silk bedding, as white as foam, was decorated with pearls. The ladies of the palace, who were blessed with beautiful teeth and the most wonderfully beautiful faces, walked here and there in the palace, their ankle bells tinkling melodiously, and saw their own beautiful reflections in the gems. The demigods, however, being very much oppressed, had to bow down and offer obeisances at the feet of Hiraṇyakaśipu, who chastised the demigods very severely and for no reason. Thus Hiraṇyakaśipu lived in the palace and severely ruled everyone.

PURPORT

Hiraṇyakaśipu was so powerful in the heavenly planets that all the demigods except Lord Brahmā, Lord Śiva and Lord Viṣṇu were forced to engage in his service. Indeed, they were afraid of being severely punished if they disobeyed him. Śrīla Viśvanātha Cakravartī has compared Hiraṇyakaśipu to Mahārāja Vena, who was also atheistic and scornful of the ritualistic ceremonies mentioned in the *Vedas*. Yet Mahārāja Vena was afraid of some of the great sages such as Bhṛgu, whereas Hiraṇyakaśipu ruled in such a way that everyone feared him but Lord Viṣṇu, Lord Brahmā and Lord Śiva. Hiraṇyakaśipu was so alert against being burnt to ashes by the anger of great sages like Bhṛgu that by dint of austerity he surpassed their power and placed even them under his subordination. It appears that even in the higher planetary systems, to which people are promoted by pious activities, disturbances are created by *asuras* like Hiraṇyakaśipu. No one in the three worlds can live in peace and prosperity without disturbance.

TEXT 13

तमङ्ग मत्तं मधुनोरुगन्धिना
विवृत्तताम्राक्षमशेषधिष्ण्यपाः ।
उपासतोपायनपाणिभिर्विना
त्रिभिस्तपोयोगबलौजसां पदम् ॥१३॥

tam aṅga mattaṁ madhunoru-gandhinā
vivṛtta-tāmrākṣam aśeṣa-dhiṣṇya-pāḥ
upāsatopāyana-pāṇibhir vinā
tribhis tapo-yoga-balaujasāṁ padam

tam—him (Hiraṇyakaśipu); *aṅga*—O dear King; *mattam*—intoxicated; *madhunā*—by wine; *uru-gandhinā*—strong-smelling; *vivṛtta*—rolling; *tāmra-akṣam*—having eyes like copper; *aśeṣa-dhiṣṇya-pāḥ*—the principal men of all the planets; *upāsata*—worshiped; *upāyana*—full with paraphernalia; *pāṇibhiḥ*—by their own hands; *vinā*—without; *tribhiḥ*—the three principal deities (Lord Viṣṇu, Lord Brahmā and Lord Śiva); *tapaḥ*—of austerity; *yoga*—mystic power; *bala*—bodily strength; *ojasām*—and power of the senses; *padam*—the abode.

TRANSLATION

O my dear King, Hiraṇyakaśipu was always drunk on strong-smelling wines and liquors, and therefore his coppery eyes were always rolling. Nonetheless, because he had powerfully executed great austerities in mystic yoga, although he was abominable, all but the three principal demigods—Lord Brahmā, Lord Śiva and Lord Viṣṇu—personally worshiped him to please him by bringing him various presentations with their own hands.

PURPORT

In the *Skanda Purāṇa* there is this description: *upāyanaṁ daduḥ sarve vinā devān hiraṇyakaḥ.* Hiraṇyakaśipu was so powerful that everyone but the three principal demigods—namely Lord Brahmā, Lord Śiva and Lord Viṣṇu—engaged in his service. Madhvācārya says, *ādityā vasavo rudrās tri-vidhā hi surā yataḥ.* There are three kinds of demigods—the Ādityas, the Vasus and the Rudras—beneath whom are the other demigods, like the Maruts and Sādhyas (*marutaś caiva viśve ca sādhyāś caiva ca tad-gatāḥ*). Therefore all the demigods are called *tri-piṣṭapa,* and the same word *tri* applies to Lord Brahmā, Lord Śiva and Lord Viṣṇu.

TEXT 14

जगुर्महेन्द्रासनमोजसा स्थितं
विश्वावसुस्तुम्बुरुरस्मदादयः ।
गन्धर्वसिद्धा ऋषयोऽस्तुवन्मुहु-
र्विद्याधराश्चाप्सरसश्च पाण्डव ॥१४॥

jagur mahendrāsanam ojasā sthitaṁ
viśvāvasus tumburur asmad-ādayaḥ
gandharva-siddhā ṛṣayo 'stuvan muhur
vidyādharāś cāpsarasaś ca pāṇḍava

jaguḥ—sung of the glories; *mahendra-āsanam*—the throne of King Indra; *ojasā*—by personal power; *sthitam*—situated on; *viśvāvasuḥ*—the chief singer of the Gandharvas; *tumburuḥ*—another Gandharva singer; *asmat-ādayaḥ*—including ourselves (Nārada and others also glorified Hiraṇyakaśipu); *gandharva*—the inhabitants of Gandharvaloka; *siddhāḥ*—the inhabitants of Siddhaloka; *ṛṣayaḥ*—the great sages and saintly persons; *astuvan*—offered prayers; *muhuḥ*—again and again; *vidyādharāḥ*—the inhabitants of Vidyādhara-loka; *ca*—and; *apsarasaḥ*—the inhabitants of Apsaroloka; *ca*—and; *pāṇḍava*—O descendant of Pāṇḍu.

TRANSLATION

O Mahārāja Yudhiṣṭhira, descendant of Pāṇḍu, by dint of his personal power, Hiraṇyakaśipu, being situated on the throne of King Indra, controlled the inhabitants of all the other planets. The two Gandharvas Viśvāvasu and Tumburu, I myself and the Vidyādharas, Apsarās and sages all offered prayers to him again and again just to glorify him.

PURPORT

The *asuras* sometimes become so powerful that they can engage even Nārada Muni and similar devotees in their service. This does not mean that Nārada was subordinate to Hiraṇyakaśipu. Sometimes, however, it so happens in this material world that great personalities, even great devotees, can also be controlled by the *asuras.*

TEXT 15

स एव वर्णाश्रमिभिः क्रतुभिर्भूरिदक्षिणैः ।
इज्यमानो हविर्भागानग्रहीत् स्वेन तेजसा ॥१५॥

sa eva varṇāśramibhiḥ
kratubhir bhūri-dakṣiṇaiḥ
ijyamāno havir-bhāgān
agrahīt svena tejasā

saḥ—he (Hiraṇyakaśipu); *eva*—indeed; *varṇa-āśramibhiḥ*—by persons who strictly followed the regulative principles of the four *varṇas* and four *āśramas; kratubhiḥ*—by ritualistic ceremonies; *bhūri*—abundant; *dakṣiṇaiḥ*—offered with gifts; *ijyamānaḥ*—being worshiped; *haviḥ-bhāgān*—the portions of the oblations; *agrahīt*—usurped; *svena*—by his own; *tejasā*—prowess.

TRANSLATION

Being worshiped by sacrifices offered with great gifts by those who strictly followed the principles of varṇa and āśrama, Hiraṇyakaśipu, instead of offering shares of the oblations to the demigods, accepted them himself.

TEXT 16

अकृष्टपच्या तस्यासीत् सप्तद्वीपवती मही ।
तथा कामदुघा गावो नानाश्चर्यपदं नभः ॥१६॥

akṛṣṭa-pacyā tasyāsīt
sapta-dvīpavatī mahī
tathā kāma-dughā gāvo
nānāścarya-padaṁ nabhaḥ

akṛṣṭa-pacyā—bearing grains without being cultivated or plowed; *tasya*—of Hiraṇyakaśipu; *āsīt*—was; *sapta-dvīpa-vatī*—consisting of seven islands; *mahī*—the earth; *tathā*—so much so; *kāma-dughāḥ*—

which can deliver as much milk as one desires; *gāvaḥ*—cows; *nānā*—various; *āścarya-padam*—wonderful things; *nabhaḥ*—the sky.

TRANSLATION

As if in fear of Hiraṇyakaśipu, the planet earth, which consists of seven islands, delivered food grains without being plowed. Thus it resembled cows like the surabhi of the spiritual world or the kāma-dughā of heaven. The earth yielded sufficient food grains, the cows supplied abundant milk, and outer space was beautifully decorated with wonderful phenomena.

TEXT 17

रत्नाकराश्च रत्नौघांस्तत्पत्न्यश्चोहुरूर्मिभिः ।
क्षारसीधुघृतक्षौद्रदधिक्षीरामृतोदकाः ॥१७॥

ratnākarāś ca ratnaughāṁs
tat-patnyaś cohur ūrmibhiḥ
kṣāra-sīdhu-ghṛta-kṣaudra-
dadhi-kṣīrāmṛtodakāḥ

ratnākarāḥ—the seas and oceans; *ca*—and; *ratna-oghān*—various kinds of gems and valuable stones; *tat-patnyaḥ*—the wives of the oceans and seas, namely the rivers; *ca*—also; *ūhuḥ*—carried; *ūrmibhiḥ*—by their waves; *kṣāra*—the salt ocean; *sīdhu*—the ocean of wine; *ghṛta*—the ocean of clarified butter; *kṣaudra*—the ocean of sugarcane juice; *dadhi*—the ocean of yogurt; *kṣīra*—the ocean of milk; *amṛta*—and the very sweet ocean; *udakāḥ*—water.

TRANSLATION

By the flowing of their waves, the various oceans of the universe, along with their tributaries, the rivers, which are compared to their wives, supplied various kinds of gems and jewels for Hiraṇyakaśipu's use. These oceans were the oceans of salt water, sugarcane juice, wine, clarified butter, milk, yogurt, and sweet water.

PURPORT

The water of the seas and oceans of this planet, of which we have experience, are salty, but other planets within the universe contain oceans of sugarcane juice, liquor, ghee, milk and sweet water. The rivers are figuratively described as wives of the oceans and seas because they glide down to the oceans and seas as tributaries, like the wives attached to their husbands. Modern scientists attempt excursions to other planets, but they have no information of how many different types of oceans and seas there are within the universe. According to their experience, the moon is full of dust, but this does not explain how it gives us soothing rays from a distance of millions of miles. As far as we are concerned, we follow the authority of Vyāsadeva and Śukadeva Gosvāmī, who have described the universal situation according to the Vedic literature. These authorities differ from modern scientists who conclude from their imperfect sensual experience that only this planet is inhabited by living beings whereas the other planets are all vacant or full of dust.

TEXT 18

शैला द्रोणीभिराक्रीडं सर्वर्तुषु गुणान् द्रुमाः ।
दधार लोकपालानामेक एव पृथग्गुणान् ॥१८॥

śailā droṇībhir ākrīḍaṁ
sarvartuṣu guṇān drumāḥ
dadhāra loka-pālānām
eka eva pṛthag guṇān

śailāḥ—the hills and mountains; *droṇībhiḥ*—with the valleys between them; *ākrīḍam*—pleasure grounds for Hiraṇyakaśipu; *sarva*—all; *ṛtuṣu*—in the seasons of the year; *guṇān*—different qualities (fruits and flowers); *drumāḥ*—the plants and trees; *dadhāra*—executed; *loka-pālānām*—of the other demigods in charge of different departments of natural activity; *ekaḥ*—alone; *eva*—indeed; *pṛthak*—different; *guṇān*—qualities.

TRANSLATION

The valleys between the mountains became fields of pleasure for Hiraṇyakaśipu, by whose influence all the trees and plants

produced fruits and flowers profusely in all seasons. The qualities of pouring water, drying and burning, which are all qualities of the three departmental heads of the universe—namely Indra, Vāyu and Agni—were all directed by Hiraṇyakaśipu alone, without assistance from the demigods.

PURPORT

It is said in the beginning of *Śrīmad-Bhāgavatam, tejo-vāri-mṛdāṁ yathā vinimayaḥ:* this material world is conducted by fire, water and earth, which combine and take shape. Here it is mentioned that the three modes of nature (*pṛthag guṇān*) act under the direction of different demigods. For example, King Indra is in charge of pouring water, the demigod Vāyu controls the air and dries up the water, whereas the demigod controlling fire burns everything. Hiraṇyakaśipu, however, by dint of his austere performance of mystic *yoga*, became so powerful that he alone took charge of everything, without assistance from the demigods.

TEXT 19

स इत्थं निर्जितककुबेकराड् विषयान् प्रियान् ।
यथोपजोषं भुञ्जानो नातृप्यदजितेन्द्रियः ॥१९॥

sa itthaṁ nirjita-kakub
eka-rāḍ viṣayān priyān
yathopajoṣaṁ bhuñjāno
nātṛpyad ajitendriyaḥ

saḥ—he (Hiraṇyakaśipu); *ittham*—thus; *nirjita*—conquered; *kakub*—all directions within the universe; *eka-rāṭ*—the one emperor of the whole universe; *viṣayān*—material sense objects; *priyān*—very pleasing; *yathā-upajoṣam*—as much as possible; *bhuñjānaḥ*—enjoying; *na*—did not; *atṛpyat*—was satisfied; *ajita-indriyaḥ*—being unable to control the senses.

TRANSLATION

In spite of achieving the power to control in all directions and in spite of enjoying all types of dear sense gratification as much as

possible, Hiraṇyakaśipu was dissatisfied because instead of controlling his senses he remained their servant.

PURPORT

This is an example of asuric life. Atheists can advance materially and create an extremely comfortable situation for the senses, but because they are controlled by the senses, they cannot be satisfied. This is the effect of modern civilization. Materialists are very much advanced in enjoying money and women, yet dissatisfaction prevails within human society because human society cannot be happy and peaceful without Kṛṣṇa consciousness. As far as material sense gratification is concerned, materialists may go on increasing their enjoyment as far as they can imagine, but because people in such a material condition are servants of their senses, they cannot be satisfied. Hiraṇyakaśipu was a vivid example of this dissatisfied state of humanity.

TEXT 20

एवमैश्वर्यमत्तस्य दृप्तस्योच्छास्त्रवर्तिनः ।
कालो महान् व्यतीयाय ब्रह्मशापमुपेयुषः ॥२०॥

evam aiśvarya-mattasya
dṛptasyocchāstra-vartinaḥ
kālo mahān vyatīyāya
brahma-śāpam upeyuṣaḥ

evam—thus; *aiśvarya-mattasya*—of one who was intoxicated by opulences; *dṛptasya*—greatly proud; *ut-śāstra-vartinaḥ*—transgressing the regulative principles mentioned in the *śāstras; kālaḥ*—duration of time; *mahān*—a great; *vyatīyāya*—passed; *brahma-śāpam*—a curse by exalted *brāhmaṇas; upeyuṣaḥ*—having obtained.

TRANSLATION

Hiraṇyakaśipu thus passed a long time being very much proud of his opulences and transgressing the laws and regulations mentioned in the authoritative śāstras. He was therefore subjected to a curse by the four Kumāras, who were great brāhmaṇas.

PURPORT

There have been many instances in which demons, after achieving material opulences, have become extremely proud, so much so that they have transgressed the laws and regulations given in the authoritative *śāstras.* Hiraṇyakaśipu acted in this way. As stated in *Bhagavad-gītā* (16.23):

yaḥ śāstra-vidhim utsṛjya
vartate kāma-kārataḥ
na sa siddhim avāpnoti
na sukhaṁ na parāṁ gatim

"He who discards scriptural injunctions and acts according to his own whims attains neither perfection, nor happiness, nor the supreme destination." The word *śāstra* refers to that which controls our activities. We cannot violate or transgress the laws and regulative principles mentioned in the *śāstras. Bhagavad-gītā* repeatedly confirms this.

tasmāc chāstraṁ pramāṇaṁ te
kāryākārya-vyavasthitau
jñātvā śāstra-vidhānoktaṁ
karma kartum ihārhasi

"One should understand what is duty and what is not duty by the regulations of the scriptures. Knowing such rules and regulations, one should act so that he may gradually be elevated." (Bg. 16.24) One should act according to the direction of the *śāstra,* but the material energy is so powerful that as soon as one becomes materially opulent, he begins to transgress the śāstric laws. As soon as one transgresses the laws of *śāstra,* he immediately enters upon the path of destruction.

TEXT 21

तस्योग्रदण्डसंविग्नाः सर्वे लोकाः सपालकाः ।
अन्यत्रालब्धशरणाः शरणं ययुरच्युतम् ॥२१॥

tasyogra-daṇḍa-saṁvignāḥ
sarve lokāḥ sapālakāḥ
anyatrālabdha-śaraṇāḥ
śaraṇaṁ yayur acyutam

tasya—of him (Hiraṇyakaśipu); *ugra-daṇḍa*—by the very fearful chastisement; *saṁvignāḥ*—disturbed; *sarve*—all; *lokāḥ*—the planets; *sa-pālakāḥ*—with their principal rulers; *anyatra*—anywhere else; *alabdha*—not obtaining; *śaraṇāḥ*—shelter; *śaraṇam*—for shelter; *yayuḥ*—approached; *acyutam*—the Supreme Personality of Godhead.

TRANSLATION

Everyone, including the rulers of the various planets, was extremely distressed because of the severe punishment inflicted upon them by Hiraṇyakaśipu. Fearful and disturbed, unable to find any other shelter, they at last surrendered to the Supreme Personality of Godhead, Viṣṇu.

PURPORT

Lord Kṛṣṇa says in *Bhagavad-gītā* (5.29):

bhoktāraṁ yajña-tapasāṁ
sarva-loka-maheśvaram
suhṛdaṁ sarva-bhūtānāṁ
jñātvā māṁ śāntim ṛcchati

"The sages, knowing Me as the ultimate purpose of all sacrifices and austerities, the Supreme Lord of all planets and demigods and the benefactor and well-wisher of all living entities, attain peace from the pangs of material miseries." The Supreme Personality of Godhead, Kṛṣṇa, is actually the best friend of everyone. In a condition of distress or misery, one wants to seek shelter of a well-wishing friend. The well-wishing friend of the perfect order is Lord Śrī Kṛṣṇa. Therefore all the inhabitants of the various planets, being unable to find any other shelter, were obliged to seek shelter at the lotus feet of the supreme friend. If from the very beginning we seek shelter of the supreme friend, there will be no cause of danger. It is said that if a dog is swimming in the water and one wants to cross the ocean by catching hold of the dog's tail, certainly he is foolish. Similarly, if in distress one seeks shelter of a demigod, he is foolish, for his efforts will be fruitless. In all circumstances, one should seek shelter of the Supreme Personality of Godhead. Then there will be no danger under any circumstances.

TEXTS 22–23

तस्यै नमोऽस्तु काष्ठायै यत्रात्मा हरिरीश्वरः ।
यद्गत्वा न निवर्तन्ते शान्ताः संन्यासिनोऽमलाः ॥२२॥
इति ते संयतात्मानः समाहितधियोऽमलाः ।
उपतस्थुर्हृषीकेशं विनिद्रा वायुभोजनाः ॥२३॥

tasyai namo 'stu kāṣṭhāyai
yatrātmā harir īśvaraḥ
yad gatvā na nivartante
śāntāḥ sannyāsino 'malāḥ

iti te saṁyatātmānaḥ
samāhita-dhiyo 'malāḥ
upatasthur hṛṣīkeśaṁ
vinidrā vāyu-bhojanāḥ

tasyai—unto that; *namaḥ*—our respectful obeisances; *astu*—let there be; *kāṣṭhāyai*—direction; *yatra*—wherein; *ātmā*—the Supersoul; *hariḥ*—the Supreme Personality of Godhead; *īśvaraḥ*—the supreme controller; *yat*—which; *gatvā*—approaching; *na*—never; *nivartante*—return; *śāntāḥ*—peaceful; *sannyāsinaḥ*—saintly persons in the renounced order of life; *amalāḥ*—pure; *iti*—thus; *te*—they; *saṁyata-ātmānaḥ*—having controlled minds; *samāhita*—steadied; *dhiyaḥ*—intelligences; *amalāḥ*—purified; *upatasthuḥ*—worshiped; *hṛṣīkeśam*—the master of the senses; *vinidrāḥ*—without sleeping; *vāyu-bhojanāḥ*—eating only air.

TRANSLATION

"Let us offer our respectful obeisances unto that direction where the Supreme Personality of Godhead is situated, where those purified souls in the renounced order of life, the great saintly persons, go, and from which, having gone, they never return." Without sleep, fully controlling their minds, and living on only their breath, the predominating deities of the various planets began worshiping Hṛṣīkeśa with this meditation.

PURPORT

The two words *tasyai kāṣṭhāyai* are very significant. Everywhere, in every direction, in every heart and in every atom, the Supreme Personality of Godhead is situated in His features as Brahman and Paramātmā. Then what is the purpose of saying *tasyai kāṣṭhāyai*—"in that direction where Hari is situated"? During Hiraṇyakaśipu's time, his influence was everywhere, but he could not force his influence into the places where the Supreme Personality of Godhead had His pastimes. For example, on this earth there are such places as Vṛndāvana and Ayodhyā, which are called *dhāmas*. In the *dhāma*, there is no influence from Kali-yuga or any demon. If one takes shelter of such a *dhāma*, worship of the Lord becomes very easy, and resultant spiritual advancement quickly takes place. In fact, in India one may still go to Vṛndāvana and similar places to achieve the results of spiritual activities quickly.

TEXT 24

तेषामाविरभूद्वाणी अरूपा मेघनिःस्वना ।
सन्नादयन्ती ककुभः साधूनामभयङ्करी ॥२४॥

teṣām āvirabhūd vāṇī
arūpā megha-niḥsvanā
sannādayantī kakubhaḥ
sādhūnām abhayaṅkarī

teṣām—in front of all of them; *āvirabhūt*—appeared; *vāṇī*—a voice; *arūpā*—without a form; *megha-niḥsvanā*—resounding like the sound of a cloud; *sannādayantī*—causing to vibrate; *kakubhaḥ*—all directions; *sādhūnām*—of the saintly persons; *abhayaṅkarī*—driving away the fearful situation.

TRANSLATION

Then there appeared before them a transcendental sound vibration, emanating from a personality not visible to material eyes. The voice was as grave as the sound of a cloud, and it was very encouraging, driving away all fear.

TEXTS 25–26

मा भैष्ट विबुधश्रेष्ठाः सर्वेषां भद्रमस्तु वः ।
मद्दर्शनं हि भूतानां सर्वश्रेयोपपत्तये ॥२५॥
ज्ञातमेतस्य दौरात्म्यं दैतेयापसदस्य यत् ।
तस्य शान्तिं करिष्यामि कालं तावत्प्रतीक्षत ॥२६॥

mā bhaiṣṭa vibudha-śreṣṭhāḥ
sarveṣāṁ bhadram astu vaḥ
mad-darśanaṁ hi bhūtānāṁ
sarva-śreyopapattaye

jñātam etasya daurātmyaṁ
daiteyāpasadasya yat
tasya śāntiṁ kariṣyāmi
kālaṁ tāvat pratīkṣata

mā—do not; *bhaiṣṭa*—fear; *vibudha-śreṣṭhāḥ*—O best of learned persons; *sarveṣām*—of all; *bhadram*—the good fortune; *astu*—let there be; *vaḥ*—unto you; *mat-darśanam*—the seeing of Me (or offering of prayers to Me or hearing about Me, all of which are absolute); *hi*—indeed; *bhūtānām*—of all living entities; *sarva-śreya*—of all good fortune; *upapattaye*—for the attainment; *jñātam*—known; *etasya*—of this; *daurātmyam*—the nefarious activities; *daiteya-apasadasya*—of the great demon, Hiraṇyakaśipu; *yat*—which; *tasya*—of this; *śāntim*—cessation; *kariṣyāmi*—I shall make; *kālam*—time; *tāvat*—until that; *pratīkṣata*—just wait.

TRANSLATION

The voice of the Lord vibrated as follows: O best of learned persons, do not fear! I wish all good fortune to you. Become My devotees by hearing and chanting about Me and offering Me prayers, for these are certainly meant to award benedictions to all living entities. I know all about the activities of Hiraṇyakaśipu and shall surely stop them very soon. Please wait patiently until that time.

PURPORT

Sometimes people are very much eager to see God. In considering the word *mad-darśanam,* "seeing Me," which is mentioned in this verse, one should note that in *Bhagavad-gītā* the Lord says, *bhaktyā mām abhijānāti.* In other words, the ability to understand the Supreme Personality of Godhead or to see Him or talk with Him depends on one's advancement in devotional service, which is called *bhakti.* In *bhakti* there are nine different activities: *śravaṇaṁ kīrtanaṁ viṣṇoḥ smaraṇaṁ pāda-sevanam/ arcanaṁ vandanaṁ dāsyaṁ sakhyam ātma-nivedanam.* Because all these devotional activities are absolute, there is no fundamental difference between worshiping the Deity in the temple, seeing Him and chanting His glories. Indeed, all of these are ways of seeing Him, for everything done in devotional service is a means of direct contact with the Lord. The vibration of the Lord's voice appeared in the presence of all the devotees, and although the person vibrating the sound was unseen to them, they were meeting or seeing the Lord because they were offering prayers and because the vibration of the Lord was present. Contrary to the laws of the material world, there is no difference between seeing the Lord, offering prayers and hearing the transcendental vibration. Pure devotees, therefore, are fully satisfied by glorifying the Lord. Such glorification is called *kīrtana.* Performing *kīrtana* and hearing the vibration of the sound Hare Kṛṣṇa is actually seeing the Supreme Personality of Godhead directly. One must realize this position, and then one will be able to understand the absolute nature of the Lord's activities.

TEXT 27

यदा देवेषु वेदेषु गोषु विप्रेषु साधुषु ।
धर्मे मयि च विद्वेषः स वा आशु विनश्यति ॥२७॥

yadā deveṣu vedeṣu
goṣu vipreṣu sādhuṣu
dharme mayi ca vidveṣaḥ
sa vā āśu vinaśyati

yadā—when; *deveṣu*—unto the demigods; *vedeṣu*—unto the Vedic scriptures; *goṣu*—unto the cows; *vipreṣu*—unto the *brāhmaṇas; sādhuṣu*—unto the saintly persons; *dharme*—unto religious principles; *mayi*—unto Me, the Supreme Personality of Godhead; *ca*—and; *vidveṣaḥ*—envious; *saḥ*—such a person; *vai*—indeed; *āśu*—very soon; *vinaśyati*—is vanquished.

TRANSLATION

When one is envious of the demigods, who represent the Supreme Personality of Godhead, of the Vedas, which give all knowledge, of the cows, brāhmaṇas, Vaiṣṇavas and religious principles, and ultimately of Me, the Supreme Personality of Godhead, he and his civilization will be vanquished without delay.

TEXT 28

निर्वैराय प्रशान्ताय स्वसुताय महात्मने ।
प्रह्लादाय यदा द्रुह्येद्धनिष्येऽपि वरोर्जितम् ॥२८॥

nirvairāya praśāntāya
sva-sutāya mahātmane
prahrādāya yadā druhyed
dhaniṣye 'pi varorjitam

nirvairāya—who is without enemies; *praśāntāya*—very sober and peaceful; *sva-sutāya*—unto his own son; *mahā-ātmane*—who is a great devotee; *prahrādāya*—Prahlāda Mahārāja; *yadā*—when; *druhyet*—will commit violence; *haniṣye*—I shall kill; *api*—although; *vara-ūrjitam*—blessed by the boons of Lord Brahmā.

TRANSLATION

When Hiraṇyakaśipu teases the great devotee Prahlāda, his own son, who is peaceful and sober and who has no enemy, I shall kill Hiraṇyakaśipu immediately, despite the benedictions of Brahmā.

PURPORT

Of all sinful activities, an offense to a pure devotee, or Vaiṣṇava, is the most severe. An offense at the lotus feet of a Vaiṣṇava is so disastrous that Śrī Caitanya Mahāprabhu has compared it to a mad elephant that enters a garden and causes great havoc by uprooting many plants and trees. If one is an offender at the lotus feet of a *brāhmaṇa* or Vaiṣṇava, his offenses uproot all his auspicious activities. One should therefore very carefully guard against committing *vaiṣṇava-aparādha,* or offenses at the lotus feet of a Vaiṣṇava. Here the Lord clearly says that although Hiraṇyakaśipu had received benedictions from Lord Brahmā, these benedictions would be null and void as soon as he committed an offense at the lotus feet of Prahlāda Mahārāja, his own son. A Vaiṣṇava like Prahlāda Mahārāja is described herein as *nirvaira,* having no enemies. Elsewhere in *Śrīmad-Bhāgavatam* (3.25.21) it is said, *ajāta-śatravaḥ śāntāḥ sādhavaḥ sādhu-bhūṣaṇāḥ:* a devotee has no enemies, he is peaceful, he abides by the scriptures, and all his characteristics are sublime. A devotee does not create enmity with anyone, but if someone becomes his enemy, that person will be vanquished by the Supreme Personality of Godhead, despite whatever benedictions he may have received from other sources. Hiraṇyakaśipu was certainly enjoying the fruitful results of his austerities, but here the Lord says that as soon as he committed an offense at the lotus feet of Prahlāda Mahārāja he would be ruined. One's longevity, opulence, beauty, education and whatever else one may possess as a result of pious activities cannot protect one if one commits an offense at the lotus feet of a Vaiṣṇava. Despite whatever one possesses, if one offends the lotus feet of a Vaiṣṇava he will be vanquished.

TEXT 29

श्रीनारद उवाच
इत्युक्ता लोकगुरुणा तं प्रणम्य दिवौकसः ।
न्यवर्तन्त गतोद्वेगा मेनिरे चासुरं हतम् ॥२९॥

śrī-nārada uvāca
ity uktā loka-guruṇā
taṁ praṇamya divaukasaḥ
nyavartanta gatodvegā
menire cāsuraṁ hatam

śrī-nāradaḥ uvāca—the great saint Nārada Muni said; *iti*—thus; *uktāḥ*—addressed; *loka-guruṇā*—by the supreme spiritual master of everyone; *tam*—unto Him; *praṇamya*—offering obeisances; *divaukasaḥ*—all the demigods; *nyavartanta*—returned; *gata-udvegāḥ*—relieved of all anxieties; *menire*—they considered; *ca*—also; *asuram*—the demon (Hiraṇyakaśipu); *hatam*—killed.

TRANSLATION

The great saint Nārada Muni continued: When the Supreme Personality of Godhead, the spiritual master of everyone, thus reassured all the demigods living in the heavenly planets, they offered their respectful obeisances unto Him and returned, confident that the demon Hiraṇyakaśipu was now practically dead.

PURPORT

The less intelligent men who are always busy worshiping the demigods should note that when the demigods are harassed by the demons, they approach the Supreme Personality of Godhead for relief. Since the demigods resort to the Supreme Personality of Godhead, why should the worshipers of the demigods not approach the Supreme Lord for whatever benefits they desire? *Śrīmad-Bhāgavatam* (2.3.10) says:

akāmaḥ sarva-kāmo vā
mokṣa-kāma udāra-dhīḥ
tīvreṇa bhakti-yogena
yajeta puruṣaṁ param

"Whether one desires everything or nothing, or whether he desires to merge into the existence of the Lord, he is intelligent only if he worships Lord Kṛṣṇa, the Supreme Personality of Godhead, by rendering transcendental loving service." Whether one is a *karmī*, *jñānī* or *yogī*, if one wants a particular benediction fulfilled, even if it be material, one should approach the Supreme Lord and pray to Him, for then it will be fulfilled. There is no need to approach any demigod separately for the fulfillment of any desire.

TEXT 30

तस्य दैत्यपतेः पुत्राश्चत्वारः परमाद्भुताः ।
प्रह्रादोऽभून्महांस्तेषां गुणैर्महदुपासकः ॥३०॥

tasya daitya-pateḥ putrāś
catvāraḥ paramādbhutāḥ
prahrādo 'bhūn mahāṁs teṣāṁ
guṇair mahad-upāsakaḥ

tasya—of him (Hiraṇyakaśipu); *daitya-pateḥ*—the King of the Daityas; *putrāḥ*—sons; *catvāraḥ*—four; *parama-adbhutāḥ*—very qualified and wonderful; *prahrādaḥ*—the one named Prahlāda; *abhūt*—was; *mahān*—the greatest; *teṣām*—of all of them; *guṇaiḥ*—with transcendental qualities; *mahat-upāsakaḥ*—being an unalloyed devotee of the Supreme Personality of Godhead.

TRANSLATION

Hiraṇyakaśipu had four wonderful, well-qualified sons, of whom the one named Prahlāda was the best. Indeed, Prahlāda was a reservoir of all transcendental qualities because he was an unalloyed devotee of the Personality of Godhead.

PURPORT

yasyāsti bhaktir bhagavaty akiñcanā
sarvair guṇais tatra samāsate surāḥ

"In one who has unflinching devotional faith in Kṛṣṇa, all the good qualities of Kṛṣṇa and the demigods are consistently manifest."

(*Bhāg.* 5.18.12) Prahlāda Mahārāja is praised herein for having all good qualities because of worshiping the Supreme Personality of Godhead. Therefore, a pure devotee, who has no motives, has all good qualities, material and spiritual. If one is spiritually advanced, being a staunch, liberal devotee of the Lord, all good qualities are manifest in his body. On the other hand, *harāv abhaktasya kuto mahad-guṇāḥ:* if one is not a devotee, even if he has some materially good qualities, they have no value. That is the verdict of the *Vedas.*

TEXTS 31–32

ब्रह्मण्यः शीलसम्पन्नः सत्यसन्धो जितेन्द्रियः ।
आत्मवत्सर्वभूतानामेकप्रियसुहृत्तमः ॥३१॥
दासवत्संनतार्याङ्घ्रिः पितृवद्दीनवत्सलः ।
भ्रातृवत्सदृशे स्निग्धो गुरुष्वीश्वरभावनः ।
विद्यार्थरूपजन्माढ्यो मानस्तम्भविवर्जितः ॥३२॥

brahmaṇyaḥ śīla-sampannaḥ
satya-sandho jitendriyaḥ
ātmavat sarva-bhūtānām
eka-priya-suhṛttamaḥ

dāsavat sannatāryāṅghriḥ
pitṛvad dīna-vatsalaḥ
bhrātṛvat sadṛśe snigdho
guruṣv īśvara-bhāvanaḥ
vidyārtha-rūpa-janmāḍhyo
māna-stambha-vivarjitaḥ

brahmaṇyaḥ—cultured as a good *brāhmaṇa; śīla-sampannaḥ*—possessing all good qualities; *satya-sandhaḥ*—determined to understand the Absolute Truth; *jita-indriyaḥ*—fully controlling the senses and mind; *ātma-vat*—like the Supersoul; *sarva-bhūtānām*—of all living entities; *eka-priya*—the one beloved; *suhṛt-tamaḥ*—the best friend; *dāsa-vat*—like a menial servant; *sannata*—always obedient; *ārya-aṅghriḥ*—at the lotus feet of great persons; *pitṛ-vat*—exactly like a father; *dīna-*

vatsalaḥ—kind to the poor; *bhrātṛ-vat*—exactly like a brother; *sadṛśe*—to his equals; *snigdhaḥ*—very affectionate; *guruṣu*—unto the spiritual masters; *īśvara-bhāvanaḥ*—who considered exactly like the Supreme Personality of Godhead; *vidyā*—education; *artha*—riches; *rūpa*—beauty; *janma*—aristocracy or nobility; *āḍhyaḥ*—endowed with; *māna*—pride; *stambha*—impudence; *vivarjitaḥ*—completely free from.

TRANSLATION

[The qualities of Mahārāja Prahlāda, the son of Hiraṇyakaśipu, are described herewith.] He was completely cultured as a qualified brāhmaṇa, having very good character and being determined to understand the Absolute Truth. He had full control of his senses and mind. Like the Supersoul, he was kind to every living entity and was the best friend of everyone. To respectable persons he acted exactly like a menial servant, to the poor he was like a father, to his equals he was attached like a sympathetic brother, and he considered his teachers, spiritual masters and older Godbrothers to be as good as the Supreme Personality of Godhead. He was completely free from unnatural pride that might have arisen from his good education, riches, beauty, aristocracy and so on.

PURPORT

These are some of the qualifications of a Vaiṣṇava. A Vaiṣṇava is automatically a *brāhmaṇa* because a Vaiṣṇava has all the good qualities of a *brāhmaṇa*.

śamo damas tapaḥ śaucaṁ
kṣāntir ārjavam eva ca
jñānaṁ vijñānam āstikyaṁ
brahma-karma svabhāva-jam

"Peacefulness, self-control, austerity, purity, tolerance, honesty, wisdom, knowledge, and religiousness—these are the qualities by which the *brāhmaṇas* work." (Bg. 18.42) These qualities are manifest in the body of a Vaiṣṇava. Therefore a perfect Vaiṣṇava is also a perfect *brāhmaṇa*, as indicated here by the words *brahmaṇyaḥ śīla-sampannaḥ*. A Vaiṣṇava is always determined to understand the Absolute Truth, and to understand the Absolute Truth one needs to have full control over his senses and mind. Prahlāda Mahārāja possessed all these qualities. A Vaiṣṇava is always a well-wisher to everyone. The six Gosvāmīs, for example, are described in this way: *dhīrādhīra-jana-priyau.* They were popular with both the gentle and the ruffians. A Vaiṣṇava must be equal to everyone, regardless of one's position. *Ātmavat:* a Vaiṣṇava should be like Paramātmā. *Īśvaraḥ sarva-bhūtānāṁ hṛd-deśe 'rjuna tiṣṭhati.* Paramātmā does not hate anyone; indeed, He is in the heart of a *brāhmaṇa*, but he is also even in the heart of a pig. As the moon never refuses to distribute its pleasing rays even to the home of a *caṇḍāla*, a Vaiṣṇava never refuses to act for everyone's welfare. Therefore a Vaiṣṇava is always obedient to the spiritual master (*ārya*). The word *ārya* refers to one who is advanced in knowledge. One who is deficient in knowledge cannot be called *ārya.* At the present, however, the word *ārya* is used to refer to those who are godless. This is the unfortunate situation of Kali-yuga.

The word *guru* refers to the spiritual master who initiates his disciple into advancement in the science of Kṛṣṇa, or Kṛṣṇa consciousness, as stated by Śrīla Viśvanātha Cakravartī Ṭhākura (*śrī-bhagavan-mantropadeśake gurāv ity arthaḥ*).

TEXT 33

नोद्विग्नचित्तो व्यसनेषु निःस्पृहः
श्रुतेषु दृष्टेषु गुणेष्ववस्तुदृक् ।
दान्तेन्द्रियप्राणशरीरधीः सदा
प्रशान्तकामो रहितासुरोऽसुरः ॥३३॥

nodvigna-citto vyasaneṣu niḥspṛhaḥ
śruteṣu dṛṣṭeṣu guṇeṣv avastu-dṛk
dāntendriya-prāṇa-śarīra-dhīḥ sadā
praśānta-kāmo rahitāsuro 'suraḥ

na—not; *udvigna*—agitated; *cittaḥ*—whose consciousness; *vyasaneṣu*—in dangerous conditions; *niḥspṛhaḥ*—without desire; *śruteṣu*—in things heard of (especially elevation to heavenly planets because of pious activities); *dṛṣṭeṣu*—as well as in temporal things seen; *guṇeṣu*—the objects of sense gratification under the modes of material nature; *avastu-dṛk*—seeing as if insubstantial; *dānta*—controlling; *indriya*—the senses; *prāṇa*—the living force; *śarīra*—the body; *dhīḥ*—and intelligence; *sadā*—always; *praśānta*—quieted; *kāmaḥ*—whose material desires; *rahita*—completely devoid of; *asuraḥ*—demoniac nature; *asuraḥ*—although born in a demoniac family.

TRANSLATION

Although Prahlāda Mahārāja was born in a family of asuras, he himself was not an asura but a great devotee of Lord Viṣṇu. Unlike the other asuras, he was never envious of Vaiṣṇavas. He was not agitated when put into danger, and he was neither directly nor indirectly interested in the fruitive activities described in the Vedas. Indeed, he considered everything material to be useless, and therefore he was completely devoid of material desires. He always controlled his senses and life air, and being of steady intelligence and determination, he subdued all lusty desires.

PURPORT

From this verse we discover that a man is not qualified or disqualified simply by birth. Prahlāda Mahārāja was an *asura* by birth, yet he possessed all the qualities of a perfect *brāhmaṇa* (*brahmaṇyaḥ śīla-sampannaḥ*). Anyone can become a fully qualified *brāhmaṇa* under the direction of a spiritual master. Prahlāda Mahārāja provided a vivid example of how to think of the spiritual master and accept his directions calmly.

TEXT 34

यस्मिन्महद्गुणा राजन् गृह्यन्ते कविभिर्मुहुः ।
न तेऽधुनापिधीयन्ते यथा भगवतीश्वरे ॥३४॥

yasmin mahad-guṇā rājan
gṛhyante kavibhir muhuḥ
na te 'dhunā pidhīyante
yathā bhagavatīśvare

yasmin—in whom; *mahat-guṇāḥ*—exalted transcendental qualities; *rājan*—O King; *gṛhyante*—are glorified; *kavibhiḥ*—by persons who are thoughtful and advanced in knowledge; *muhuḥ*—always; *na*—not; *te*—these; *adhunā*—today; *pidhīyante*—are obscured; *yathā*—just as; *bhagavati*—in the Supreme Personality of Godhead; *īśvare*—the supreme controller.

TRANSLATION

O King, Prahlāda Mahārāja's good qualities are still glorified by learned saints and Vaiṣṇavas. As all good qualities are always found existing in the Supreme Personality of Godhead, they also exist forever in His devotee Prahlāda Mahārāja.

PURPORT

From authoritative scripture it is learned that Prahlāda Mahārāja still lives in Vaikuṇṭhaloka as well as within this material world on the planet Sutala. This transcendental quality of existing simultaneously in different places is another qualification of the Supreme Personality of Godhead. *Goloka eva nivasaty akhilātma-bhūtaḥ:* the Lord appears in the core of everyone's heart, yet He exists on His own planet, Goloka Vṛndāvana. A devotee acquires qualities almost the same as those of the Lord because of unalloyed devotional service. Ordinary living beings cannot be so qualified, but a devotee can be qualified like the Supreme Personality of Godhead, not in full but partially.

TEXT 35

यं साधुगाथासदसि रिपवोऽपि सुरा नृप ।
प्रतिमानं प्रकुर्वन्ति किमुतान्ये भवादृशाः ॥३५॥

yaṁ sādhu-gāthā-sadasi
ripavo 'pi surā nṛpa
pratimānaṁ prakurvanti
kim utānye bhavādṛśāḥ

yam—whom; *sādhu-gāthā-sadasi*—in an assembly where saintly persons gather or exalted characteristics are discussed; *ripavaḥ*—persons who were supposed to have been Prahlāda Mahārāja's enemies (even such a devotee as Prahlāda Mahārāja had enemies, including even his own father); *api*—even; *surāḥ*—the demigods (the demigods are enemies of the demons, and since Prahlāda Mahārāja was born in a family of demons, the demigods should have been his enemies); *nṛpa*—O King Yudhiṣṭhira; *pratimānam*—a substantial example of the best among the devotees; *prakurvanti*—they make; *kim uta*—what to speak of; *anye*—others; *bhavādṛśāḥ*—exalted personalities such as yourself.

TRANSLATION

In any assembly where there are discourses about saints and devotees, O King Yudhiṣṭhira, even the enemies of the demons, namely the demigods, what to speak of you, would cite Prahlāda Mahārāja as an example of a great devotee.

TEXT 36

गुणैरलमसंख्येयैर्माहात्म्यं तस्य सूच्यते ।
वासुदेवे भगवति यस्य नैसर्गिकी रतिः ॥३६॥

guṇair alam asaṅkhyeyair
māhātmyaṁ tasya sūcyate
vāsudeve bhagavati
yasya naisargikī ratiḥ

guṇaiḥ—with spiritual qualities; *alam*—what need; *asaṅkhyeyaiḥ*—which are innumerable; *māhātmyam*—the greatness; *tasya*—of him (Prahlāda Mahārāja); *sūcyate*—is indicated; *vāsudeve*—to Lord Kṛṣṇa, the son of Vasudeva; *bhagavati*—the Supreme Personality of Godhead; *yasya*—of whom; *naisargikī*—natural; *ratiḥ*—attachment.

TRANSLATION

Who could list the innumerable transcendental qualities of Prahlāda Mahārāja? He had unflinching faith in Vāsudeva, Lord Kṛṣṇa [the son of Vasudeva], and unalloyed devotion to Him. His attachment to Lord Kṛṣṇa was natural because of his previous

devotional service. Although his good qualities cannot be enumerated, they prove that he was a great soul [mahātmā].

PURPORT

In his prayers to the ten incarnations, Jayadeva Gosvāmī says, *keśava dhṛta-narahari-rūpa jaya jagad-īśa hare.* Prahlāda Mahārāja was a devotee of Lord Nṛsiṁha, who is Keśava, Kṛṣṇa Himself. Therefore when this verse says *vāsudeve bhagavati,* one should understand that Prahlāda Mahārāja's attachment for Nṛsiṁhadeva was attachment for Kṛṣṇa, Vāsudeva, the son of Vasudeva. Prahlāda Mahārāja, therefore, is described as a great *mahātmā.* As the Lord Himself confirms in *Bhagavad-gītā* (7.19):

bahūnāṁ janmanām ante
jñānavān māṁ prapadyate
vāsudevaḥ sarvam iti
sa mahātmā sudurlabhaḥ

"After many births and deaths, he who is actually in knowledge surrenders unto Me, knowing Me to be the cause of all causes and all that is. Such a great soul is very rare." A great devotee of Kṛṣṇa, the son of Vasudeva, is a great soul very rarely to be found. Prahlāda Mahārāja's attachment for Kṛṣṇa will be explained in the next verse. *Kṛṣṇa-graha-gṛhītātmā.* Prahlāda Mahārāja's heart was always filled with thoughts of Kṛṣṇa. Therefore Prahlāda Mahārāja is the ideal devotee in Kṛṣṇa consciousness.

TEXT 37

न्यस्तक्रीडनको बालो जडवत्तन्मनस्तया ।
कृष्णग्रहगृहीतात्मा न वेद जगदीदृशम् ॥३७॥

nyasta-krīḍanako bālo
jaḍavat tan-manastayā
kṛṣṇa-graha-gṛhītātmā
na veda jagad īdṛśam

nyasta—having given up; *krīḍanakaḥ*—all sportive activities or tendencies for childhood play; *bālaḥ*—a boy; *jaḍa-vat*—as if dull, without activities; *tat-manastayā*—by being fully absorbed in Kṛṣṇa; *kṛṣṇa-graha*—by Kṛṣṇa, who is like a strong influence (like a *graha,* or planetary influence); *gṛhīta-ātmā*—whose mind was fully attracted; *na*—not; *veda*—understood; *jagat*—the entire material world; *īdṛśam*—like this.

TRANSLATION

From the very beginning of his childhood, Prahlāda Mahārāja was uninterested in childish playthings. Indeed, he gave them up altogether and remained silent and dull, being fully absorbed in Kṛṣṇa consciousness. Since his mind was always affected by Kṛṣṇa consciousness, he could not understand how the world goes on being fully absorbed in the activities of sense gratification.

PURPORT

Prahlāda Mahārāja is the vivid example of a great person fully absorbed in Kṛṣṇa consciousness. In *Caitanya-caritāmṛta* (*Madhya* 8.274) it is said:

sthāvara-jaṅgama dekhe, nā dekhe tāra mūrti
sarvatra haya nija iṣṭa-deva-sphūrti

A fully Kṛṣṇa conscious person, although situated in this material world, does not see anything but Kṛṣṇa, anywhere and everywhere. This is the sign of a *mahā-bhāgavata.* The *mahā-bhāgavata* sees Kṛṣṇa everywhere because of his attitude of pure love for Kṛṣṇa. As confirmed in the *Brahma-saṁhitā* (5.38):

premāñjana-cchurita-bhakti-vilocanena
santaḥ sadaiva hṛdayeṣu vilokayanti
yaṁ śyāmasundaram acintya-guṇa-svarūpaṁ
govindam ādi-puruṣaṁ tam ahaṁ bhajāmi

"I worship the primeval Lord, Govinda, who is always seen by the devotee whose eyes are anointed with the pulp of love. He is seen in His eternal form of Śyāmasundara, situated within the heart of the devotee." An exalted devotee, or *mahātmā,* who is rarely to be seen, remains fully conscious of Kṛṣṇa and constantly sees the Lord within the core of his heart. It is sometimes said that when one is influenced by evil stars like Saturn, Rāhu or Ketu, he cannot make advancement in any prospective activity. In just the opposite way, Prahlāda Mahārāja was influenced by Kṛṣṇa, the supreme planet, and thus he could not think of the material world and live without Kṛṣṇa consciousness. That is the sign of a *mahā-bhāgavata.* Even if one is an enemy of Kṛṣṇa, a *mahā-bhāgavata* sees him to be also engaged in Kṛṣṇa's service. Another crude example is that everything appears yellow to the jaundiced eye. Similarly, to a *mahā-bhāgavata,* everyone but himself appears to be engaged in Kṛṣṇa's service.

Prahlāda Mahārāja is the approved *mahā-bhāgavata,* the supreme devotee. In the previous verse it was stated that he had natural attachment (*naisargikī ratiḥ*). The symptoms of such natural attachment for Kṛṣṇa are described in this verse. Although Prahlāda Mahārāja was only a boy, he had no interest in playing. As stated in *Śrīmad-Bhāgavatam* (11.2.42), *viraktir anyatra ca:* the symptom of perfect Kṛṣṇa consciousness is that one loses interest in all material activities. For a small boy to give up playing is impossible, but Prahlāda Mahārāja, being situated in first-class devotional service, was always absorbed in a trance of Kṛṣṇa consciousness. Just as a materialistic person is always absorbed in thoughts of material gain, a *mahā-bhāgavata* like Prahlāda Mahārāja is always absorbed in thoughts of Kṛṣṇa.

TEXT 38

आसीनः पर्यटन्नश्नन् शयानः प्रपिबन् ब्रुवन् ।
नानुसन्धत्त एतानि गोविन्दपरिरम्भितः ॥३८॥

āsīnaḥ paryaṭann aśnan
śayānaḥ prapiban bruvan
nānusandhatta etāni
govinda-parirambhitaḥ

āsīnaḥ—while sitting; *paryaṭan*—while walking; *aśnan*—while eating; *śayānaḥ*—while lying down; *prapiban*—while drinking; *bruvan*—while talking; *na*—not; *anusandhatte*—knew; *etāni*—all these activities; *govinda*—by the Supreme Personality of Godhead, who enlivens the senses; *parirambhitaḥ*—being embraced.

TRANSLATION

Prahlāda Mahārāja was always absorbed in thought of Kṛṣṇa. Thus, being always embraced by the Lord, he did not know how his bodily necessities, such as sitting, walking, eating, lying down, drinking and talking, were being automatically performed.

PURPORT

A small child, while being cared for by his mother, does not know how the needs of the body for eating, sleeping, lying down, passing water and evacuating are being fulfilled. He is simply satisfied to be on the lap of his mother. Similarly, Prahlāda Mahārāja was exactly like a small child, being cared for by Govinda. The necessary activities of his body were performed without his knowledge. As a father and mother care for their child, Govinda cared for Prahlāda Mahārāja, who remained always absorbed in thoughts of Govinda. This is Kṛṣṇa consciousness. Prahlāda Mahārāja is the vivid example of perfection in Kṛṣṇa consciousness.

TEXT 39

क्वचिद्रुदति वैकुण्ठचिन्ताशबलचेतनः ।
क्वचिद्धसति तच्चिन्ताह्लाद उद्गायति क्वचित् ॥३९॥

kvacid rudati vaikuṇṭha-
cintā-śabala-cetanaḥ
kvacid dhasati tac-cintā-
hlāda udgāyati kvacit

kvacit—sometimes; *rudati*—cries; *vaikuṇṭha-cintā*—by thoughts of Kṛṣṇa; *śabala-cetanaḥ*—whose mind was bewildered; *kvacit*—sometimes; *hasati*—laughs; *tat-cintā*—by thoughts of Him; *āhlādaḥ*—being jubilant; *udgāyati*—chants very loudly; *kvacit*—sometimes.

TRANSLATION

Because of advancement in Kṛṣṇa consciousness, he sometimes cried, sometimes laughed, sometimes expressed jubilation and sometimes sang loudly.

PURPORT

This verse further clarifies the comparison of a devotee to a child. If a mother leaves her small child in his bed or cradle and goes away to attend to some family duties, the child immediately understands that his mother has gone away, and therefore he cries. But as soon as the mother returns and cares for the child, the child laughs and becomes jubilant. Similarly, Prahlāda Mahārāja, being always absorbed in thoughts of Kṛṣṇa, sometimes felt separation, thinking, "Where is Kṛṣṇa?" This is explained by Śrī Caitanya Mahāprabhu. *Śūnyāyitaṁ jagat sarvaṁ govinda-viraheṇa me.* When an exalted devotee feels that Kṛṣṇa is invisible, having gone away, he cries in separation, and sometimes, when he sees that Kṛṣṇa has returned to care for him, he laughs, just as a child sometimes laughs upon understanding that his mother is taking care of him. These symptoms are called *bhāva*. In *The Nectar of Devotion*, various *bhāvas*, ecstatic conditions of a devotee, are fully described. These *bhāvas* are visible in the activities of a perfect devotee.

TEXT 40

नदति क्वचिदुत्कण्ठो विलज्जो नृत्यति क्वचित् ।
क्वचित्तद्भावनायुक्तस्तन्मयोऽनुचकार ह ॥४०॥

nadati kvacid utkaṇṭho
vilajjo nṛtyati kvacit
kvacit tad-bhāvanā-yuktas
tanmayo 'nucakāra ha

nadati—exclaims loudly (addressing the Lord, "O Kṛṣṇa"); *kvacit*—sometimes; *utkaṇṭhaḥ*—being anxious; *vilajjaḥ*—without shame; *nṛtyati*—he dances; *kvacit*—sometimes; *kvacit*—sometimes; *tat-bhāvanā*—with thoughts of Kṛṣṇa; *yuktaḥ*—being absorbed; *tat-mayaḥ*—thinking as if he had become Kṛṣṇa; *anucakāra*—imitated; *ha*—indeed.

TRANSLATION

Sometimes, upon seeing the Supreme Personality of Godhead, Prahlāda Mahārāja would loudly call in full anxiety. He sometimes lost his shyness in jubilation and began dancing in ecstasy, and sometimes, being fully absorbed in thoughts of Kṛṣṇa, he felt oneness and imitated the pastimes of the Lord.

PURPORT

Prahlāda Mahārāja sometimes felt that the Lord was far away from him and therefore called Him loudly. When he saw that the Lord was before him, he was fully jubilant. Sometimes, thinking himself one with the Supreme, he imitated the Lord's pastimes, and in separation from the Lord he would sometimes show symptoms of madness. These feelings of a devotee would not be appreciated by impersonalists. One must go further and further into spiritual understanding. The first realization is impersonal Brahman, but one must go still further to realize Paramātmā and eventually the Supreme Personality of Godhead, who is worshiped by the transcendental feelings of a devotee in a relationship of *śānta, dāsya, sakhya, vātsalya* or *mādhurya.* Here the feelings of Prahlāda Mahārāja were in the mellow of *vātsalya,* filial love and affection. As a child cries when left by his mother, when Prahlāda Mahārāja felt that the Lord was away from him he began to cry (*nadati*). Again, a devotee like Prahlāda sometimes sees that the Lord is coming from a long distance to pacify him, like a mother responding to a child, saying, "My dear child, do not cry. I am coming." Then the devotee, without being ashamed due to his surroundings and circumstances, begins to dance, thinking, "Here is my Lord! My Lord is coming!" Thus the devotee, in full ecstasy, sometimes imitates the pastimes of the Lord, just as the cowherd boys used to imitate the behavior of the jungle animals. However, he does not actually become the Lord. Prahlāda Mahārāja achieved the spiritual ecstasies described herein by his advancement in spiritual understanding.

TEXT 41

क्वचिदुत्पुलकस्तूष्णीमास्ते संस्पर्शनिर्वृतः ।
अस्पन्दप्रणयानन्दसलिलामीलितेक्षणः ॥४१॥

kvacid utpulakas tūṣṇīm
āste saṁsparśa-nirvṛtaḥ
aspanda-praṇayānanda-
salilāmīliteksaṇaḥ

kvacit—sometimes; *utpulakaḥ*—with the hairs of his body standing on end; *tūṣṇīm*—completely silent; *āste*—remains; *saṁsparśa-nirvṛtaḥ*—feeling great joy by contact with the Lord; *aspanda*—steady; *praṇaya-ānanda*—due to transcendental bliss from a relationship of love; *salila*—filled with tears; *āmīlita*—half-closed; *īkṣaṇaḥ*—whose eyes.

TRANSLATION

Sometimes, feeling the touch of the Lord's lotus hands, he became spiritually jubilant and remained silent, his hairs standing on end and tears gliding down from his half-closed eyes because of his love for the Lord.

PURPORT

When a devotee feels separation from the Lord, he becomes eager to see where the Lord is, and sometimes when he feels pangs of separation, tears flow incessantly from his half-closed eyes. As stated by Śrī Caitanya Mahāprabhu in His *Śikṣāṣṭaka, yugāyitaṁ nimeṣeṇa cakṣuṣā prāvṛṣāyitam.* The words *cakṣuṣā prāvṛṣāyitam* refer to tears falling incessantly from the devotee's eyes. These symptoms, which appear in pure devotional ecstasy, were visible in the body of Prahlāda Mahārāja.

TEXT 42

स उत्तमश्लोकपदारविन्दयो-
र्निषेवयाकिञ्चनसङ्गलब्धया ।
तन्वन् परां निर्वृतिमात्मनो मुहु-
र्दुःसङ्गदीनस्य मनःशमं व्यधात् ॥४२॥

sa uttama-śloka-padāravindayor
niṣevayākiñcana-saṅga-labdhayā
tanvan parāṁ nirvṛtim ātmano muhur
duḥsaṅga-dīnasya manaḥ śamaṁ vyadhāt

saḥ—he (Prahlāda Mahārāja); *uttama-śloka-pada-aravindayoḥ*—to the lotus feet of the Supreme Personality of Godhead, who is worshiped by transcendental prayers; *niṣevayā*—by constant service; *akiñcana*—of devotees who have nothing to do with the material world; *saṅga*—in the association; *labdhayā*—obtained; *tanvan*—expanding; *parām*—highest; *nirvṛtim*—bliss; *ātmanaḥ*—of the spirit soul; *muhuḥ*—constantly; *duḥsaṅga-dīnasya*—of a person poor in spiritual understanding due to bad association; *manaḥ*—the mind; *śamam*—peaceful; *vyadhāt*—made.

TRANSLATION

Because of his association with perfect, unalloyed devotees who had nothing to do with anything material, Prahlāda Mahārāja constantly engaged in the service of the Lord's lotus feet. By seeing his bodily features when he was in perfect ecstasy, persons very poor in spiritual understanding became purified. In other words, Prahlāda Mahārāja bestowed upon them transcendental bliss.

PURPORT

Apparently Prahlāda Mahārāja was placed in circumstances in which he was always tortured by his father. In such material conditions, one cannot have an undisturbed mind, but since *bhakti* is unconditional (*ahaituky apratihatā*), Prahlāda Mahārāja was never disturbed by the chastisements of Hiraṇyakaśipu. On the contrary, the bodily symptoms of his ecstatic love for the Supreme Personality of Godhead turned the minds of his friends, who had also been born in atheistic families. Instead of being disturbed by the torments of his father, Prahlāda influenced these friends and cleansed their minds. A devotee is never contaminated by material conditions, but persons subjected to material conditions can become spiritually advanced and blissful upon seeing the behavior of a pure devotee.

TEXT 43

तस्मिन्महाभागवते महाभागे महात्मनि ।
हिरण्यकशिपू राजन्नकरोदघमात्मजे ॥४३॥

tasmin mahā-bhāgavate
mahā-bhāge mahātmani
hiraṇyakaśipū rājann
akarod agham ātmaje

tasmin—unto him; *mahā-bhāgavate*—an exalted devotee of the Lord; *mahā-bhāge*—most fortunate; *mahā-ātmani*—whose mind was very broad; *hiraṇyakaśipuḥ*—the demon Hiraṇyakaśipu; *rājan*—O King; *akarot*—performed; *agham*—very great sin; *ātma-je*—to his own son.

TRANSLATION

My dear King Yudhiṣṭhira, the demon Hiraṇyakaśipu tormented this exalted, fortunate devotee, although Prahlāda was his own son.

PURPORT

When a demon like Hiraṇyakaśipu, despite his elevated position due to severe austerities, begins to tease a devotee, he begins falling down, and the results of his austerities dwindle. One who oppresses a pure devotee loses all the results of his austerities, penances and pious activities. Since Hiraṇyakaśipu was now inclined to chastise his most exalted devotee son, Prahlāda Mahārāja, his opulences began dwindling.

TEXT 44

श्रीयुधिष्ठिर उवाच
देवर्ष एतदिच्छामो वेदितुं तव सुव्रत ।
यदात्मजाय शुद्धाय पितादात् साधवे ह्यघम् ॥४४॥

śrī-yudhiṣṭhira uvāca
devarṣa etad icchāmo
veditum̐ tava suvrata
yad ātmajāya śuddhāya
pitādāt sādhave hy agham

śrī-yudhiṣṭhiraḥ uvāca—Mahārāja Yudhiṣṭhira inquired; *deva-ṛṣe*—O best saintly person among the demigods; *etat*—this; *icchāmaḥ*—we wish; *veditum*—to know; *tava*—from you; *su-vrata*—having the determination for spiritual advancement; *yat*—because; *ātma-jāya*—unto his own son; *śuddhāya*—who was pure and exalted; *pitā*—the father, Hiraṇyakaśipu; *adāt*—gave; *sādhave*—a great saint; *hi*—indeed; *agham*—trouble.

TRANSLATION

Mahārāja Yudhiṣṭhira said: O best of the saints among the demigods, O best of spiritual leaders, how did Hiraṇyakaśipu give so much trouble to Prahlāda Mahārāja, the pure and exalted saint, although Prahlāda was his own son? I wish to know about this subject from you.

PURPORT

To know about the Supreme Personality of Godhead and the characteristics of His pure devotee, one must inquire from authorities like Devarṣi Nārada. One cannot inquire about transcendental subject matters from a layman. As stated in *Śrīmad-Bhāgavatam* (3.25.25), *satāṁ prasaṅgān mama vīrya-saṁvido bhavanti hṛt-karṇa-rasāyanāḥ kathāḥ:* only by association with devotees can one authoritatively understand the position of the Lord and His devotees. A devotee like Nārada Muni is addressed as *suvrata. Su* means "good," and *vrata* means "vow." Thus the word *suvrata* refers to a person who has nothing to do with the material world, which is always bad. One cannot understand anything spiritual from a materialistic scholar puffed up with academic knowledge. As stated in *Bhagavad-gītā* (18.55), *bhaktyā mām abhijānāti:* one must try to understand Kṛṣṇa by devotional service and from a devotee. Therefore Yudhiṣṭhira Mahārāja was quite right in wanting to learn further about Prahlāda Mahārāja from Śrī Nārada Muni.

TEXT 45

पुत्रान् विप्रतिकूलान् स्वान् पितरः पुत्रवत्सलाः।
उपालभन्ते शिक्षार्थं नैवाघमपरो यथा ॥४५॥

putrān vipratikūlān svān
pitaraḥ putra-vatsalāḥ

upālabhante śikṣārthaṁ
naivāgham aparo yathā

putrān—sons; *vipratikūlān*—who act against the will of the father; *svān*—their own; *pitaraḥ*—fathers; *putra-vatsalāḥ*—being very affectionate to the children; *upālabhante*—chastise; *śikṣa-artham*—to teach them lessons; *na*—not; *eva*—indeed; *agham*—punishment; *aparaḥ*—an enemy; *yathā*—like.

TRANSLATION

A father and mother are always affectionate to their children. When the children are disobedient the parents chastise them, not due to enmity but only for the child's instruction and welfare. How did Hiraṇyakaśipu, the father of Prahlāda Mahārāja, chastise such a noble son? This is what I am eager to know.

TEXT 46

किमुतानुवशान् साधूंस्तादृशान् गुरुदेवतान् ।
एतत् कौतूहलं ब्रह्मन्नस्माकं विधम प्रभो ।
पितुः पुत्राय यद् द्वेषो मरणाय प्रयोजितः ॥४६॥

kim utānuvaśān sādhūṁs
tādṛśān guru-devatān
etat kautūhalaṁ brahmann
asmākaṁ vidhama prabho
pituḥ putrāya yad dveṣo
maraṇāya prayojitaḥ

kim uta—much less; *anuvaśān*—to obedient and perfect sons; *sādhūn*—great devotees; *tādṛśān*—of that sort; *guru-devatān*—honoring the father as the Supreme Personality of Godhead; *etat*—this; *kautūhalam*—doubt; *brahman*—O *brāhmaṇa; asmākam*—of us; *vidhama*—dissipate; *prabho*—O my lord; *pituḥ*—of the father; *putrāya*—unto the son; *yat*—which; *dveṣaḥ*—envy; *maraṇāya*—for killing; *prayojitaḥ*—applied.

TRANSLATION

Mahārāja Yudhiṣṭhira further inquired: How was it possible for a father to be so violent toward an exalted son who was obedient, well-behaved and respectful to his father? O brāhmaṇa, O master, I have never heard of such a contradiction as an affectionate father's punishing his noble son with the intention of killing him. Kindly dissipate our doubts in this regard.

PURPORT

In the history of human society, an affectionate father is rarely found to chastise a noble and devoted son. Therefore Mahārāja Yudhiṣṭhira wanted Nārada Muni to dissipate his doubt.

Thus end the Bhaktivedanta purports of the Seventh Canto, Fourth Chapter, of the Śrīmad-Bhāgavatam, *entitled, "Hiraṇyakaśipu Terrorizes the Universe."*

CHAPTER FIVE

Prahlāda Mahārāja, the Saintly Son of Hiraṇyakaśipu

Prahlāda Mahārāja did not carry out the orders of his teachers, for he was always engaged in worshiping Lord Viṣṇu. As described in this chapter, Hiraṇyakaśipu tried to kill Prahlāda Mahārāja, even by having a snake bite him and by putting him under the feet of elephants, yet he was unsuccessful.

Hiraṇyakaśipu's spiritual master, Śukrācārya, had two sons named Ṣaṇḍa and Amarka, to whom Prahlāda Mahārāja was entrusted for education. Although the teachers tried to educate the boy Prahlāda in politics, economics and other material activities, he did not care for their instructions. Instead, he continued to be a pure devotee. Prahlāda Mahārāja never liked the idea of discriminating between one's friends and enemies. Because he was spiritually inclined, he was equal toward everyone.

Once upon a time, Hiraṇyakaśipu inquired from his son what the best thing was that he had learned from his teachers. Prahlāda Mahārāja replied that a man engrossed in the material consciousness of duality, thinking, "This is mine, and that belongs to my enemy," should give up his householder life and go to the forest to worship the Supreme Lord.

When Hiraṇyakaśipu heard from his son about devotional service, he decided that this small boy had been polluted by some friend in school. Thus he advised the teachers to take care of the boy so that he would not become a Kṛṣṇa conscious devotee. However, when the teachers inquired from Prahlāda Mahārāja why he was going against their teachings, Prahlāda Mahārāja taught the teachers that the mentality of ownership is false and that he was therefore trying to become an unalloyed devotee of Lord Viṣṇu. The teachers, being very angry at this answer, chastised and threatened the boy with many fearful conditions. They taught him to the best of their ability and then brought him before his father.

Hiraṇyakaśipu affectionately took his son Prahlāda on his lap and then inquired from him what the best thing was that he had learned from his teachers. As usual, Prahlāda Mahārāja began praising the nine processes of devotional service, such as *śravaṇam* and *kīrtanam*. Thus the King of the demons, Hiraṇyakaśipu, being extremely angry, chastised the teachers, Ṣaṇḍa and Amarka, for having wrongly trained Prahlāda Mahārāja. The so-called teachers informed the King that Prahlāda Mahārāja was automatically a devotee and did not listen to their instructions. When they proved themselves innocent, Hiraṇyakaśipu inquired from Prahlāda where he had learned *viṣṇu-bhakti*. Prahlāda Mahārāja replied that those who are attached to family life do not develop Kṛṣṇa consciousness, either personally or collectively. Instead, they suffer repeated birth and death in this material world and continue simply chewing the chewed. Prahlāda explained that the duty of every man is to take shelter of a pure devotee and thus become eligible to understand Kṛṣṇa consciousness.

Enraged at this answer, Hiraṇyakaśipu threw Prahlāda Mahārāja from his lap. Since Prahlāda was so treacherous that he had become a devotee of Viṣṇu, who had killed his uncle Hiraṇyākṣa, Hiraṇyakaśipu asked his assistants to kill him. The assistants of Hiraṇyakaśipu struck Prahlāda with sharp weapons, threw him under the feet of elephants, subjected him to hellish conditions, threw him from the peak of a mountain and tried to kill him in thousands of other ways, but they were unsuccessful. Hiraṇyakaśipu therefore became increasingly afraid of his son Prahlāda Mahārāja and arrested him. The sons of Hiraṇyakaśipu's spiritual master, Śukrācārya, began teaching Prahlāda in their own way, but Prahlāda Mahārāja did not accept their instructions. While the teachers were absent from the classroom, Prahlāda Mahārāja began to preach Kṛṣṇa consciousness in the school, and by his instructions all his class friends, the sons of the demons, became devotees like him.

TEXT 1

श्रीनारद उवाच
पौरोहित्याय भगवान् वृतः काव्यः किलासुरैः ।
षण्डामर्कौ सुतौ तस्य दैत्यराजगृहान्तिके ॥ १ ॥

śrī-nārada uvāca
paurohityāya bhagavān
vṛtaḥ kāvyaḥ kilāsuraiḥ
ṣaṇḍāmarkau sutau tasya
daitya-rāja-gṛhāntike

śrī-nāradaḥ uvāca—the great saint Nārada said; *paurohityāya*—to work as priest; *bhagavān*—the most powerful; *vṛtaḥ*—chosen; *kāvyaḥ*—Śukrācārya; *kila*—indeed; *asuraiḥ*—by the demons; *ṣaṇḍa-amarkau*—Ṣaṇḍa and Amarka; *sutau*—sons; *tasya*—of him; *daitya-rāja*—of the King of the demons, Hiraṇyakaśipu; *gṛha-antike*—near the residence.

TRANSLATION

The great saint Nārada Muni said: The demons, headed by Hiraṇyakaśipu, accepted Śukrācārya as their priest for ritualistic ceremonies. Śukrācārya's two sons, Ṣaṇḍa and Amarka, lived near Hiraṇyakaśipu's palace.

PURPORT

The beginning of the life story of Prahlāda is recounted as follows. Śukrācārya became the priest of the atheists, especially Hiraṇyakaśipu, and thus his two sons, Ṣaṇḍa and Amarka, resided near Hiraṇyakaśipu's residence. Śukrācārya should not have become the priest of Hiraṇyakaśipu because Hiraṇyakaśipu and his followers were all atheists. A *brāhmaṇa* should become the priest of a person interested in the advancement of spiritual culture. The very name Śukrācārya, however, indicates a person interested in obtaining benefits for his sons and descendants, regardless of how the money comes. A real *brāhmaṇa* would not become a priest for atheistic men.

TEXT 2

तौ राज्ञा प्रापितं बालं प्रह्लादं नयकोविदम् ।
पाठयामासतुः पाठ्यानन्यांश्चासुरबालकान् ॥ २ ॥

tau rājñā prāpitaṁ bālaṁ
prahlādaṁ naya-kovidam
pāṭhayām āsatuḥ pāṭhyān
anyāṁś cāsura-bālakān

tau—those two (Ṣaṇḍa and Amarka); *rājñā*—by the King; *prāpitam*—sent; *bālam*—the boy; *prahlādam*—named Prahlāda; *naya-kovidam*—who was aware of moral principles; *pāṭhayām āsatuḥ*—instructed; *pāṭhyān*—books of material knowledge; *anyān*—other; *ca*—also; *asura-bālakān*—sons of the *asuras.*

TRANSLATION

Prahlāda Mahārāja was already educated in devotional life, but when his father sent him to those two sons of Śukrācārya to be educated, they accepted him at their school along with the other sons of the asuras.

TEXT 3

यत्तत्र गुरुणा प्रोक्तं शुश्रुवेऽनुपपाठ च ।
न साधु मनसा मेने स्वपरासद्ग्रहाश्रयम् ॥ ३ ॥

yat tatra guruṇā proktaṁ
śuśruve 'nupapāṭha ca
na sādhu manasā mene
sva-parāsad-grahāśrayam

yat—which; *tatra*—there (in the school); *guruṇā*—by the teachers; *proktam*—instructed; *śuśruve*—heard; *anupapāṭha*—recited; *ca*—and; *na*—not; *sādhu*—good; *manasā*—by the mind; *mene*—considered; *sva*—of one's own; *para*—and of others; *asat-graha*—by the bad philosophy; *āśrayam*—which was supported.

TRANSLATION

Prahlāda certainly heard and recited the topics of politics and economics taught by the teachers, but he understood that political philosophy involves considering someone a friend and someone else an enemy, and thus he did not like it.

PURPORT

Politics involves accepting one group of men as enemies and another group as friends. Everything in politics is based on this philosophy, and the entire world, especially at the present, is engrossed in it. The public is concerned with friendly countries and friendly groups or enemy countries and enemy groups, but as stated in *Bhagavad-gītā*, a learned person does not make distinctions between enemies and friends. Devotees, especially, do not create friends and enemies. A devotee sees that every living being is part and parcel of Kṛṣṇa (*mamaivāṁśo jīva-bhūtaḥ*). Therefore a devotee treats friends and enemies equally by trying to educate them both in Kṛṣṇa consciousness. Of course, atheistic men do not follow the instructions of pure devotees, but instead consider a devotee their enemy. A devotee, however, never creates a situation of friendship and enmity. Although Prahlāda Mahārāja was obliged to hear the instructions of Ṣaṇḍa and Amarka, he did not like the philosophy of friends and enemies, which forms the basis of politics. He was not interested in this philosophy.

TEXT 4

एकदासुरराट् पुत्रमङ्कमारोप्य पाण्डव ।
पप्रच्छ कथ्यतां वत्स मन्यते साधु यद्भवान् ॥ ४ ॥

ekadāsura-rāṭ putram
aṅkam āropya pāṇḍava
papraccha kathyatāṁ vatsa
manyate sādhu yad bhavān

ekadā—once upon a time; *asura-rāṭ*—the Emperor of the *asuras;* *putram*—his son; *aṅkam*—on the lap; *āropya*—placing; *pāṇḍava*—O Mahārāja Yudhiṣṭhira; *papraccha*—inquired; *kathyatām*—let it be told; *vatsa*—my dear son; *manyate*—considers; *sādhu*—the best; *yat*—that which; *bhavān*—your good self.

TRANSLATION

My dear King Yudhiṣṭhira, once upon a time the King of the demons, Hiraṇyakaśipu, took his son Prahlāda on his lap and very

affectionately inquired: My dear son, please let me know what you think is the best of all the subjects you have studied from your teachers.

PURPORT

Hiraṇyakaśipu did not ask his young son anything that would be very difficult for him to answer; instead, he gave the boy a chance to speak plainly about whatever he thought might be best. Prahlāda Mahārāja, of course, being a perfect devotee, knew everything and could say what the best part of life is. In the *Vedas* it is said, *yasmin vijñāte sarvam evaṁ vijñātaṁ bhavati:* if one properly understands God, he can understand any subject matter very nicely. Sometimes we have to challenge big scientists and philosophers, but by the grace of Kṛṣṇa we emerge successful. It is impossible, practically speaking, for ordinary men to challenge scientists or philosophers concerning genuine knowledge, but a devotee can challenge them because the best of everything is known to a devotee by the grace of Kṛṣṇa. As confirmed in *Bhagavad-gītā* (10.11):

teṣām evānukampārtham
aham ajñāna-jaṁ tamaḥ
nāśayāmy ātma-bhāva-stho
jñāna-dīpena bhāsvatā

Kṛṣṇa, who is situated in the core of everyone's heart as the Supersoul, dissipates all the ignorance from the heart of a devotee. As a special favor, He enlightens the devotee with all knowledge by putting before him the torch of light. Prahlāda Mahārāja, therefore, knew the best of knowledge, and when his father inquired from him, Prahlāda gave him that knowledge. Prahlāda Mahārāja was able to solve the most difficult parts of problems because of his advanced Kṛṣṇa consciousness. Therefore he replied as follows.

TEXT 5

श्रीप्रह्लाद उवाच
तत्साधु मन्येऽसुरवर्य देहिनां
सदा समुद्विग्नधियामसद्ग्रहात् ।

हित्वात्मपातं गृहमन्धकूपं
वनं गतो यद्धरिमाश्रयेत ॥ ५ ॥

śrī-prahlāda uvāca
tat sādhu manye 'sura-varya dehināṁ
sadā samudvigna-dhiyām asad-grahāt
hitvātma-pātaṁ gṛham andha-kūpaṁ
vanaṁ gato yad dharim āśrayeta

śrī-prahlādaḥ uvāca—Prahlāda Mahārāja replied; *tat*—that; *sādhu*—very good, or the best part of life; *manye*—I think; *asura-varya*—O King of the *asuras; dehinām*—of persons who have accepted the material body; *sadā*—always; *samudvigna*—full of anxieties; *dhiyām*—whose intelligence; *asat-grahāt*—because of accepting the temporary body or bodily relations as real (thinking "I am this body, and everything belonging to this body is mine"); *hitvā*—giving up; *ātma-pātam*—the place where spiritual culture or self-realization is stopped; *gṛham*—the bodily concept of life, or household life; *andha-kūpam*—which is nothing but a blind well (where there is no water but one nonetheless searches for water); *vanam*—to the forest; *gataḥ*—going; *yat*—which; *harim*—the Supreme Personality of Godhead; *āśrayeta*—may take shelter of.

TRANSLATION

Prahlāda Mahārāja replied: O best of the asuras, King of the demons, as far as I have learned from my spiritual master, any person who has accepted a temporary body and temporary household life is certainly embarrassed by anxiety because of having fallen in a dark well where there is no water but only suffering. One should give up this position and go to the forest [vana]. More clearly, one should go to Vṛndāvana, where only Kṛṣṇa consciousness is prevalent, and should thus take shelter of the Supreme Personality of Godhead.

PURPORT

Hiraṇyakaśipu thought that Prahlāda, being nothing but a small boy with no actual experience, might reply with something pleasing but nothing practical. Prahlāda Mahārāja, however, being an exalted devotee, had acquired all the qualities of education.

yasyāsti bhaktir bhagavaty akiñcanā
sarvair guṇais tatra samāsate surāḥ
harāv abhaktasya kuto mahad-guṇā
manorathenāsati dhāvato bahiḥ

"One who has unflinching devotional faith in Kṛṣṇa consistently manifests all the good qualities of Kṛṣṇa and the demigods. However, he who has no devotion to the Supreme Personality of Godhead has no good qualifications because he is engaged by mental concoction in material existence, which is the external feature of the Lord." (*Bhāg.* 5.18.12) So-called educated philosophers and scientists who are simply on the mental platform cannot distinguish between what is actually *sat,* eternal, and what is *asat,* temporary. The Vedic injunction is *asato mā jyotir gama:* everyone should give up the platform of temporary existence and approach the eternal platform. The soul is eternal, and topics concerning the eternal soul are actually knowledge. Elsewhere it is said, *apaśyatām ātma-tattvaṁ gṛheṣu gṛha-medhinām:* those who are attached to the bodily conception of life and who thus stick to life as a *gṛhastha,* or householder, on the platform of material sense enjoyment, cannot see the welfare of the eternal soul. Prahlāda Mahārāja confirmed this by saying that if one wants success in life, he should immediately understand from the right sources what his self-interest is and how he should mold his life in spiritual consciousness. One should understand himself to be part and parcel of Kṛṣṇa and thus completely take shelter of His lotus feet for guaranteed spiritual success. Everyone in the material world is in the bodily conception, struggling hard for existence, life after life. Prahlāda Mahārāja therefore recommended that to stop this material condition of repeated birth and death, one should go to the forest (*vana*).

In the *varṇāśrama* system, one first becomes a *brahmacārī,* then a *gṛhastha,* a *vānaprastha* and finally a *sannyāsī.* Going to the forest means accepting *vānaprastha* life, which is between *gṛhastha* life and *sannyāsa.* As confirmed in the *Viṣṇu Purāṇa* (3.8.9), *varṇāśramācāravatā puruṣeṇa paraḥ pumān viṣṇur ārādhyate:* by accepting the institution of *varṇa* and *āśrama,* one can very easily elevate himself to the platform of worshiping Viṣṇu, the Supreme Personality of Godhead. Otherwise, if one remains in the bodily conception, one must rot within this material world, and his life will be a failure. Society must have divisions of *brāhmaṇa, kṣatriya, vaiśya* and *śūdra*, and for spiritual advancement one must gradually develop as a *brahmacārī, gṛhastha, vānaprastha* and *sannyāsī*. Prahlāda Mahārāja recommended that his father accept *vānaprastha* life because as a *gṛhastha* he was becoming increasingly demoniac due to bodily attachment. Prahlāda recommended to his father that accepting *vānaprastha* life would be better than going deeper and deeper into *gṛham andha-kūpam*, the blind well of life as a *gṛhastha*. In our Kṛṣṇa consciousness movement we therefore invite all the elderly persons of the world to come to Vṛndāvana and stay there in retired life, making advancement in spiritual consciousness, Kṛṣṇa consciousness.

TEXT 6

श्रीनारद उवाच
श्रुत्वा पुत्रगिरो दैत्यः परपक्षसमाहिताः ।
जहास बुद्धिर्बालानां भिद्यते परबुद्धिभिः ॥ ६ ॥

śrī-nārada uvāca
śrutvā putra-giro daityaḥ
para-pakṣa-samāhitāḥ
jahāsa buddhir bālānāṁ
bhidyate para-buddhibhiḥ

śrī-nāradaḥ uvāca—Nārada Muni said; *śrutvā*—hearing; *putra-giraḥ*—the instructive words of his son; *daityaḥ*—Hiraṇyakaśipu; *para-pakṣa*—on the side of the enemy; *samāhitāḥ*—full of faith; *jahāsa*—laughed; *buddhiḥ*—the intelligence; *bālānām*—of small boys; *bhidyate*—is polluted; *para-buddhibhiḥ*—by instructions from the enemy's camp.

TRANSLATION

Nārada Muni continued: When Prahlāda Mahārāja spoke about the path of self-realization in devotional service, thus being

faithful to the camp of his father's enemies, Hiraṇyakaśipu, the King of the demons, heard Prahlāda's words and he laughingly said, "Thus is the intelligence of children spoiled by the words of the enemy."

PURPORT

Hiraṇyakaśipu, being a demon, would always consider Lord Viṣṇu and His devotees to be his enemies. Therefore the word *para-pakṣa* ("on the side of the enemy") is used here. Hiraṇyakaśipu never agreed with the words of Viṣṇu, or Kṛṣṇa. Rather, he was angered by the intelligence of a Vaiṣṇava. Lord Viṣṇu, Lord Kṛṣṇa, says, *sarva-dharmān parityajya mām ekaṁ śaraṇaṁ vraja*—"Give up all other duties and surrender unto Me"—but demons like Hiraṇyakaśipu never agree to do this. Therefore Kṛṣṇa says:

na māṁ duṣkṛtino mūḍhāḥ
prapadyante narādhamāḥ
māyayāpahṛta-jñānā
āsuraṁ bhāvam āśritāḥ

"Those miscreants who are grossly foolish, lowest among mankind, whose knowledge is stolen by illusion, and who partake of the atheistic nature of demons, do not surrender unto Me." (Bg. 7.15) The *asura-bhāva*, the atheistic nature, is directly represented by Hiraṇyakaśipu. Such persons, being *mūḍha* and *narādhama*—fools and rascals, the lowest of men—would never accept Viṣṇu as the Supreme and surrender to Him. Hiraṇyakaśipu naturally became increasingly angry that his son Prahlāda was being influenced by the camp of the enemies. He therefore asked that saintly persons like Nārada not be allowed within the residential quarters of his son, for otherwise Prahlāda would be further spoiled by Vaiṣṇava instructions.

TEXT 7

सम्यग्विधार्यतां बालो गुरुगेहे द्विजातिभिः ।
विष्णुपक्षैः प्रतिच्छन्नैर्न भिद्येतास्य धीर्यथा ॥ ७ ॥

samyag vidhāryatāṁ bālo
guru-gehe dvi-jātibhiḥ
viṣṇu-pakṣaiḥ praticchannair
na bhidyetāsya dhīr yathā

samyak—completely; *vidhāryatām*—let him be protected; *bālaḥ*—this boy of tender age; *guru-gehe*—in the *guru-kula*, the place where children are sent to be instructed by the *guru; dvi-jātibhiḥ*—by *brāhmaṇas; viṣṇu-pakṣaiḥ*—who are on the side of Viṣṇu; *praticchannaiḥ*—disguised in different dresses; *na bhidyeta*—may not be influenced; *asya*—of him; *dhīḥ*—the intelligence; *yathā*—so that.

TRANSLATION

Hiraṇyakaśipu advised his assistants: My dear demons, give complete protection to this boy at the guru-kula where he is instructed, so that his intelligence will not be further influenced by Vaiṣṇavas who may go there in disguise.

PURPORT

In our Kṛṣṇa consciousness movement, the tactic of dressing oneself like an ordinary *karmī* is necessary because everyone in the demoniac kingdom is against the Vaiṣṇava teachings. Kṛṣṇa consciousness is not at all to the liking of the demons of the present age. As soon as they see a Vaiṣṇava dressed in saffron garments with beads on his neck and *tilaka* on his forehead, they are immediately irritated. They criticize the Vaiṣṇavas by sarcastically saying Hare Kṛṣṇa, and some people also chant Hare Kṛṣṇa sincerely. In either case, since Hare Kṛṣṇa is absolute, whether one chants it jokingly or sincerely, it will have its effect. The Vaiṣṇavas are pleased when the demons chant Hare Kṛṣṇa because this shows that the Hare Kṛṣṇa movement is taking ground. The greater demons, like Hiraṇyakaśipu, are always prepared to chastise the Vaiṣṇavas, and they try to make arrangements so that Vaiṣṇavas will not come to sell their books and preach Kṛṣṇa consciousness. Thus what was done by Hiraṇyakaśipu long, long ago is still being done. That is the way of materialistic life. Demons or materialists do not at all like the advancement of Kṛṣṇa consciousness, and they try to hinder it in many ways. Yet the preachers of Kṛṣṇa consciousness must go forward—in their Vaiṣṇava dress or any other dress—for the purpose of preaching. Cāṇakya Paṇḍita says that if an honest person deals with a great cheater, it is necessary for him to become a cheater also, not for the purpose of cheating but to make his preaching successful.

TEXT 8

गृहमानीतमाहूय प्रह्रादं दैत्ययाजकाः ।
प्रशस्य श्लक्ष्णया वाचा समपृच्छन्त सामभिः॥ ८ ॥

gṛham ānītam āhūya
prahrādaṁ daitya-yājakāḥ
praśasya ślakṣṇayā vācā
samapṛcchanta sāmabhiḥ

gṛham—to the place of the teachers (Ṣaṇḍa and Amarka); *ānītam*—brought; *āhūya*—calling; *prahrādam*—Prahlāda; *daitya-yājakāḥ*—the priests of the demon Hiraṇyakaśipu; *praśasya*—by pacifying; *ślakṣṇayā*—with a very mild; *vācā*—voice; *samapṛcchanta*—they questioned; *sāmabhiḥ*—by very agreeable words.

TRANSLATION

When Hiraṇyakaśipu's servants brought the boy Prahlāda back to the guru-kula [the place where the brāhmaṇas taught the boys], the priests of the demons, Ṣaṇḍa and Amarka, pacified him. With very mild voices and affectionate words, they inquired from him as follows.

PURPORT

Ṣaṇḍa and Amarka, the priests of the demons, were eager to know from Prahlāda Mahārāja who the Vaiṣṇavas were that came to instruct him in Kṛṣṇa consciousness. Their purpose was to discover the names of these Vaiṣṇavas. In the beginning they did not threaten the boy because when threatened he might not identify the real culprits. Therefore they very mildly and peacefully inquired as follows.

TEXT 9

वत्स प्रह्राद भद्रं ते सत्यं कथय मा मृषा ।
बालानति कुतस्तुभ्यमेष बुद्धिविपर्ययः ॥ ९ ॥

vatsa prahrāda bhadraṁ te
satyaṁ kathaya mā mṛṣā
bālān ati kutas tubhyam
eṣa buddhi-viparyayaḥ

vatsa—O dear son; *prahrāda*—Prahlāda; *bhadram te*—all blessings and good fortune unto you; *satyam*—the truth; *kathaya*—speak; *mā*—do not; *mṛṣā*—a lie; *bālān ati*—passing over the other demon boys; *kutaḥ*—from where; *tubhyam*—unto you; *eṣaḥ*—this; *buddhi*—of the intelligence; *viparyayaḥ*—pollution.

TRANSLATION

Dear son Prahlāda, all peace and good fortune unto you. Kindly do not speak lies; just reply with the truth. These boys you see are not like you, for they do not speak in a deviant way. How have you learned these instructions? How has your intelligence been spoiled in this way?

PURPORT

Prahlāda Mahārāja was still a boy, and therefore his teachers thought that if they pacified the little boy he would immediately speak the truth, revealing the secret of how the Vaiṣṇavas came there to teach him lessons in devotional service. It was surprising, of course, that in the same school the other boys of the Daityas were not polluted; only Prahlāda Mahārāja was supposedly polluted by the instructions of the Vaiṣṇavas. The main duty of the teachers was to inquire who those Vaiṣṇavas were that came to teach Prahlāda and spoil his intelligence.

TEXT 10

बुद्धिभेदः परकृत उताहो ते स्वतोऽभवत् ।
भण्यतां श्रोतुकामानां गुरूणां कुलनन्दन ॥१०॥

buddhi-bhedaḥ para-kṛta
utāho te svato 'bhavat
bhaṇyatāṁ śrotu-kāmānāṁ
gurūṇāṁ kula-nandana

buddhi-bhedaḥ—pollution of the intelligence; *para-kṛtaḥ*—done by the enemies; *utāho*—or; *te*—of you; *svataḥ*—by yourself; *abhavat*—was; *bhaṇyatām*—let it be told; *śrotu-kāmānām*—to us, who are very eager to hear about it; *gurūṇām*—all your teachers; *kula-nandana*—O best of your family.

TRANSLATION

O best of your family, has this pollution of your intelligence been brought about by you or by the enemies? We are all your teachers and are very eager to hear about this. Please tell us the truth.

PURPORT

Prahlāda Mahārāja's teachers were astonished that a small boy could speak such exalted Vaiṣṇava philosophy. Therefore they inquired about the Vaiṣṇavas who stealthily taught it to him, in order that these Vaiṣṇavas might be arrested and killed in the presence of Prahlāda's father, Hiraṇyakaśipu.

TEXT 11

श्रीप्रह्राद उवाच
परः स्वश्चेत्यसद्ग्राहः पुंसां यन्मायया कृतः ।
विमोहितधियां दृष्टस्तस्मै भगवते नमः ॥११॥

śrī-prahrāda uvāca
paraḥ svaś cety asad-grāhaḥ
puṁsāṁ yan-māyayā kṛtaḥ
vimohita-dhiyāṁ dṛṣṭas
tasmai bhagavate namaḥ

śrī-prahrādaḥ uvāca—Prahlāda Mahārāja replied; *paraḥ*—an enemy; *svaḥ*—a kinsman or friend; *ca*—also; *iti*—thus; *asat-grāhaḥ*—material conception of life; *puṁsām*—of persons; *yat*—of whom; *māyayā*—by the external energy; *kṛtaḥ*—created; *vimohita*—bewildered; *dhiyām*—of those whose intelligence; *dṛṣṭaḥ*—practically experienced; *tasmai*—unto Him; *bhagavate*—the Supreme Personality of Godhead; *namaḥ*—my respectful obeisances.

TRANSLATION

Prahlāda Mahārāja replied: Let me offer my respectful obeisances unto the Supreme Personality of Godhead, whose external energy has created the distinctions of "my friend" and "my enemy" by deluding the intelligence of men. Indeed, I am now actually experiencing this, although I have previously heard of it from authoritative sources.

PURPORT

As stated in *Bhagavad-gītā* (5.18):

vidyā-vinaya-sampanne
brāhmaṇe gavi hastini
śuni caiva śvapāke ca
paṇḍitāḥ sama-darśinaḥ

"The humble sage, by virtue of true knowledge, sees with equal vision a learned and gentle *brāhmaṇa*, a cow, an elephant, a dog and a dog-eater [outcaste]." *Paṇḍitāḥ*, those who are actually learned—the equipoised, advanced devotees who have full knowledge of everything—do not see any living entity as an enemy or friend. Instead, with broader vision, they see that everyone is part of Kṛṣṇa, as confirmed by Śrī Caitanya Mahāprabhu (*jīvera 'svarūpa' haya——kṛṣṇera 'nitya-dāsa'*). Every living entity, being part of the Supreme Lord, is meant to serve the Lord, just as every part of the body is meant to serve the whole body.

As servants of the Supreme Lord, all living entities are one, but a Vaiṣṇava, because of his natural humility, addresses every other living entity as *prabhu.* A Vaiṣṇava sees other servants to be so advanced that he has much to learn from them. Thus he accepts all other devotees of the Lord as *prabhus*, masters. Although everyone is a servant of the Lord, one Vaiṣṇava servant, because of humility, sees another servant as his master. Understanding of the master begins from understanding of the spiritual master.

yasya prasādād bhagavat-prasādo
yasyāprasādān na gatiḥ kuto 'pi

"By the mercy of the spiritual master one receives the benediction of Kṛṣṇa. Without the grace of the spiritual master, one cannot make any advancement."

sākṣād-dharitvena samasta-śāstrair
uktas tathā bhāvyata eva sadbhiḥ
kintu prabhor yaḥ priya eva tasya
vande guroḥ śrī-caraṇāravindam

"The spiritual master is to be honored as much as the Supreme Lord because he is the most confidential servitor of the Lord. This is acknowledged in all revealed scriptures and followed by all authorities. Therefore I offer my respectful obeisances unto the lotus feet of such a spiritual master, who is a bona fide representative of Śrī Hari [Kṛṣṇa]." The spiritual master, the servant of God, is engaged in the most confidential service of the Lord, namely delivering all the conditioned souls from the clutches of *māyā*, in which one thinks, "This person is my enemy, and that one is my friend." Actually the Supreme Personality of Godhead is the friend of all living entities, and all living entities are eternal servants of the Supreme Lord. Oneness is possible through this understanding, not through artificially thinking that every one of us is God or equal to God. The true understanding is that God is the supreme master and that all of us are servants of the Supreme Lord and are therefore on the same platform. This had already been taught to Prahlāda Mahārāja by his spiritual master, Nārada, but Prahlāda was nonetheless surprised by how a bewildered soul thinks one person his enemy and another his friend.

As long as one adheres to the philosophy of duality, thinking one person a friend and another an enemy, he should be understood to be in the clutches of *māyā*. The Māyāvādī philosopher who thinks that all living entities are God and are therefore one is also mistaken. No one is equal to

God. The servant cannot be equal to the master. According to the Vaiṣṇava philosophy, the master is one, and the servants are also one, but the distinction between the master and servant must continue even in the liberated stage. In the conditioned stage we think that some living beings are our friends whereas others are enemies, and thus we are in duality. In the liberated stage, however, the conception is that God is the master and that all living entities, being servants of God, are one.

TEXT 12

स यदानुव्रतः पुंसां पशुबुद्धिर्विभिद्यते ।
अन्य एष तथान्योऽहमिति भेदगतासती ॥१२॥

sa yadānuvrataḥ puṁsāṁ
paśu-buddhir vibhidyate
anya eṣa tathānyo 'ham
iti bheda-gatāsatī

saḥ—that Supreme Personality of Godhead; *yadā*—when; *anuvrataḥ*—favorable or pleased; *puṁsām*—of the conditioned souls; *paśu-buddhiḥ*—the animalistic conception of life ("I am the Supreme, and everyone is God"); *vibhidyate*—is destroyed; *anyaḥ*—another; *eṣaḥ*—this; *tathā*—as well as; *anyaḥ*—another; *aham*—I; *iti*—thus; *bheda*—distinction; *gata*—having; *asatī*—which is disastrous.

TRANSLATION

When the Supreme Personality of Godhead is pleased with the living entity because of his devotional service, one becomes a paṇḍita and does not make distinctions between enemies, friends and himself. Intelligently, he then thinks, "Every one of us is an eternal servant of God, and therefore we are not different from one another."

PURPORT

When Prahlāda Mahārāja's teachers and demoniac father asked him how his intelligence had been polluted, Prahlāda Mahārāja said, "As far as I am concerned, my intelligence has not been polluted. Rather, by the grace of my spiritual master and by the grace of my Lord, Kṛṣṇa, I have now learned that no one is my enemy and no one is my friend. We are all actually eternal servants of Kṛṣṇa, but under the influence of the external energy we think that we are separately situated from the Supreme Personality of Godhead as friends and enemies of one another. This mistaken idea has now been corrected, and therefore, unlike ordinary human beings, I no longer think that I am God and that others are my friends and enemies. Now I am rightly thinking that everyone is an eternal servant of God and that our duty is to serve the supreme master, for then we shall stand on the platform of oneness as servants."

Demons think of everyone as a friend or enemy, but Vaiṣṇavas say that since everyone is a servant of the Lord, everyone is on the same platform. Therefore a Vaiṣṇava treats other living entities neither as friends nor as enemies, but instead tries to spread Kṛṣṇa consciousness, teaching everyone that we are all one as servants of the Supreme Lord but are uselessly wasting our valuable lives by creating nations, communities and other groups of friends and enemies. Everyone should come to the platform of Kṛṣṇa consciousness and thus feel oneness as a servant of the Lord. Although there are 8,400,000 species of life, a Vaiṣṇava feels this oneness. The *Īśopaniṣad* advises, *ekatvam anupaśyataḥ*. A devotee should see the Supreme Personality of Godhead to be situated in everyone's heart and should also see every living entity as an eternal servant of the Lord. This vision is called *ekatvam*, oneness. Although there is a relationship of master and servant, both master and servant are one because of their spiritual identity. This is also *ekatvam*. Thus the conception of *ekatvam* for the Vaiṣṇava is different from that of the Māyāvādī.

Hiraṇyakaśipu asked Prahlāda Mahārāja how he had become antagonistic to his family. When a family member is killed by an enemy, all the members of the family would naturally be inimical to the murderer, but Hiraṇyakaśipu saw that Prahlāda had become friendly with the murderer. Therefore he asked, "Who has created this kind of intelligence in you? Have you developed this consciousness by yourself? Since you are a small boy, someone must have induced you to think this way." Prahlāda Mahārāja wanted to reply that an attitude favorable toward Viṣṇu can develop only when the Lord is favorable (*sa yadānuvrataḥ*). As stated in *Bhagavad-gītā*, Kṛṣṇa is the friend of everyone (*suhṛdaṁ sarva-bhūtānāṁ jñātvā māṁ śāntim ṛcchati*). The Lord is never an enemy to any of the millions of living entities, but is always a friend to everyone. This is true understanding. If one thinks that the Lord is an enemy, his intelligence is *paśu-buddhi,* the intelligence of an animal. He falsely thinks, "I am different from my enemy, and my enemy is different from me. The enemy has done this, and therefore my duty is to kill him." This misconception is described in this verse as *bheda-gatāsatī.* The actual fact is that everyone is a servant of the Lord, as confirmed in *Caitanya-caritāmṛta* by Śrī Caitanya Mahāprabhu (*jīvera 'svarūpa' haya—kṛṣṇera 'nitya-dāsa'*). As servants of the Lord, we are one, and there can be no questions of enmity or friendship. If one actually understands that every one of us is a servant of the Lord, where is the question of enemy or friend?

Everyone should be friendly for the service of the Lord. Everyone should praise another's service to the Lord and not be proud of his own service. This is the way of Vaiṣṇava thinking, Vaikuṇṭha thinking. There may be rivalries and apparent competition between servants in performing service, but in the Vaikuṇṭha planets the service of another servant is appreciated, not condemned. This is Vaikuṇṭha competition. There is no question of enmity between servants. Everyone should be allowed to render service to the Lord to the best of his ability, and everyone should appreciate the service of others. Such are the activities of Vaikuṇṭha. Since everyone is a servant, everyone is on the same platform and is allowed to serve the Lord according to his ability. As confirmed in *Bhagavad-gītā* (15.15), *sarvasya cāhaṁ hṛdi sanniviṣṭo mattaḥ smṛtir jñānam apohanaṁ ca:* the Lord is situated in everyone's heart, giving dictation according to the attitude of the servant. However, the Lord gives different dictation to the nondevotees and devotees. The nondevotees challenge the authority of the Supreme Lord, and therefore the Lord dictates in such a way that the nondevotees forget the Lord's service, life after life, and are punished by the laws of nature. But when a devotee very sincerely wants to render service to the Lord, the Lord dictates in a different way. As the Lord says in *Bhagavad-gītā* (10.10):

teṣāṁ satata-yuktānāṁ
bhajatāṁ prīti-pūrvakam
dadāmi buddhi-yogaṁ taṁ
yena mām upayānti te

"To those who are constantly devoted and worship Me with love, I give the understanding by which they can come to Me." Everyone is actually a servant, not an enemy or friend, and everyone is working under different directions from the Lord, who directs each living entity according to his mentality.

TEXT 13

स एष आत्मा स्वपरेत्यबुद्धिभि-
दुरत्ययानुक्रमणो निरूप्यते ।
मुह्यन्ति यद्वर्त्मनि वेदवादिनो
ब्रह्मादयो ह्येष भिनत्ति मे मतिम् ॥१३॥

sa eṣa ātmā sva-parety abuddhibhir
duratyayānukramaṇo nirūpyate
muhyanti yad-vartmani veda-vādino
brahmādayo hy eṣa bhinatti me matim

saḥ—He; *eṣaḥ*—this; *ātmā*—Supersoul situated in everyone's heart; *sva-para*—this is my own business, and that is someone else's; *iti*—thus; *abuddhibhiḥ*—by those who have such bad intelligence; *duratyaya*—very difficult to follow; *anukramaṇaḥ*—whose devotional service; *nirūpyate*—is ascertained (by scriptures or the instructions of the spiritual master); *muhyanti*—are bewildered; *yat*—of whom; *vartmani*—on the path; *veda-vādinaḥ*—the followers of Vedic instructions; *brahma-ādayaḥ*—the demigods, beginning from Lord Brahmā; *hi*—indeed; *eṣaḥ*—this one; *bhinatti*—changes; *me*—my; *matim*—intelligence.

TRANSLATION

Persons who always think in terms of "enemy" and "friend" are unable to ascertain the Supersoul within themselves. Not to speak of them, even such exalted persons as Lord Brahmā, who are fully conversant with the Vedic literature, are sometimes bewildered in following the principles of devotional service. The same Supreme Personality of Godhead who has created this situation has certainly given me the intelligence to take the side of your so-called enemy.

PURPORT

Prahlāda Mahārāja admitted frankly, "My dear teachers, you wrongly think that Lord Viṣṇu is your enemy, but because He is favorable toward me, I understand that He is the friend of everyone. You may think that I have taken the side of your enemy, but factually He has bestowed a great favor upon me."

TEXT 14

यथा भ्राम्यत्ययो ब्रह्मन् स्वयमाकर्षसन्निधौ ।
तथा मे भिद्यते चेतश्चक्रपाणेर्यदृच्छया ॥१४॥

yathā bhrāmyaty ayo brahman
svayam ākarṣa-sannidhau
tathā me bhidyate cetaś
cakra-pāṇer yadṛcchayā

yathā—just as; *bhrāmyati*—moves; *ayaḥ*—iron; *brahman*—O *brāhmaṇas; svayam*—itself; *ākarṣa*—of a magnet; *sannidhau*—in the proximity; *tathā*—similarly; *me*—my; *bhidyate*—is changed; *cetaḥ*—consciousness; *cakra-pāṇeḥ*—of Lord Viṣṇu, who has a disc in His hand; *yadṛcchayā*—simply by the will.

TRANSLATION

O brāhmaṇas [teachers], as iron attracted by a magnetic stone moves automatically toward the magnet, my consciousness, having been changed by His will, is attracted by Lord Viṣṇu, who carries a disc in His hand. Thus I have no independence.

PURPORT

For iron to be attracted by a magnet is natural. Similarly, for all living entities to be attracted toward Kṛṣṇa is natural, and therefore the Lord's real name is Kṛṣṇa, meaning He who attracts everyone and everything. The typical examples of such attraction are found in Vṛndāvana, where everything and everyone is attracted by Kṛṣṇa. The elderly persons like Nanda Mahārāja and Yaśodādevī, the friends like Śrīdāmā, Sudāmā and the other cowherd boys, the *gopīs* like Śrīmatī Rādhārāṇī and Her associates, and even the birds, beasts, cows and calves are attracted. The flowers and fruits in the gardens are attracted, the waves of the Yamunā are attracted, and the land, sky, trees, plants, animals and all other living beings are attracted by Kṛṣṇa. This is the natural situation of everything in Vṛndāvana.

Just contrary to the affairs of Vṛndāvana is the material world, where no one is attracted by Kṛṣṇa and everyone is attracted by *māyā.* This is the difference between the spiritual and material worlds. Hiraṇyakaśipu, who was in the material world, was attracted by women and money, whereas Prahlāda Mahārāja, being in his natural position, was attracted by Kṛṣṇa. In replying to Hiraṇyakaśipu's question about why Prahlāda Mahārāja had a deviant view, Prahlāda said that his view was not deviant, for the natural position of everyone is to be attracted by Kṛṣṇa. Hiraṇyakaśipu found this view deviant, Prahlāda said, because of being unnaturally unattracted by Kṛṣṇa. Hiraṇyakaśipu therefore needed purification.

As soon as one is purified of material contamination, he is again attracted by Kṛṣṇa (*sarvopādhi-vinirmuktaṁ tat-paratvena nirmalam*). In the material world, everyone is contaminated by the dirt of sense gratification and is acting according to different designations, sometimes as a human being, sometimes a beast, sometimes a demigod or tree, and so on. One must be cleansed of all these designations. Then one will be naturally attracted to Kṛṣṇa. The *bhakti* process purifies the living entity of all unnatural attractions. When one is purified he is attracted by Kṛṣṇa and begins to serve Kṛṣṇa instead of serving *māyā.* This is his natural position. A devotee is attracted by Kṛṣṇa, whereas a nondevotee, being contaminated by the dirt of material enjoyment, is not. This is confirmed by the Lord in *Bhagavad-gītā* (7.28):

yeṣāṁ tv anta-gataṁ pāpaṁ
janānāṁ puṇya-karmaṇām
te dvandva-moha-nirmuktā
bhajante māṁ dṛḍha-vratāḥ

"Persons who have acted piously in previous lives and in this life, whose sinful actions are completely eradicated and who are freed from the duality of delusion, engage themselves in My service with determination." One must be freed from all the sinful dirt of material existence. Everyone in this material world is contaminated by material desire. Unless one is free from all material desire (*anyābhilāṣitā-śūnyam*), one cannot be attracted by Kṛṣṇa.

TEXT 15

श्रीनारद उवाच

एतावद्ब्राह्मणायोक्त्वा विरराम महामतिः ।
तं सन्निभर्त्स्य कुपितः सुदीनो राजसेवकः ॥१५॥

śrī-nārada uvāca
etāvad brāhmaṇāyoktvā
virarāma mahā-matiḥ
taṁ sannibhartsya kupitaḥ
sudīno rāja-sevakaḥ

śrī-nāradaḥ uvāca—Nārada Muni said; *etāvat*—this much; *brāhmaṇāya*—unto the *brāhmaṇas*, the sons of Śukrācārya; *uktvā*—speaking; *virarāma*—became silent; *mahā-matiḥ*—Prahlāda Mahārāja, who possessed great intelligence; *tam*—him (Prahlāda Mahārāja); *sannibhartsya*—chastising very harshly; *kupitaḥ*—being angry; *sudīnaḥ*—poor in thought, or very much aggrieved; *rāja-sevakaḥ*—the servants of King Hiraṇyakaśipu.

TRANSLATION

The great saint Nārada Muni continued: The great soul Prahlāda Mahārāja became silent after saying this to his teachers, Ṣaṇḍa and Amarka, the seminal sons of Śukrācārya. These so-called brāhmaṇas then became angry at him. Because they were servants of Hiraṇyakaśipu, they were very sorry, and to chastise Prahlāda Mahārāja they spoke as follows.

PURPORT

The word *śukra* means "semen." The sons of Śukrācārya were *brāhmaṇas* by birthright, but an actual *brāhmaṇa* is one who possesses the brahminical qualities. The *brāhmaṇas* Ṣaṇḍa and Amarka, being seminal sons of Śukrācārya, did not actually possess real brahminical qualifications, for they engaged as servants of Hiraṇyakaśipu. An actual *brāhmaṇa* is very much satisfied to see anyone, not to speak of his disciple, become a devotee of Lord Kṛṣṇa. Such *brāhmaṇas* are meant to satisfy the supreme master. A *brāhmaṇa* is strictly prohibited from becoming a servant of anyone else, for that is the business of dogs and *śūdras.* A dog must satisfy his master, but a *brāhmaṇa* does not have to satisfy anyone; he is simply meant to satisfy Kṛṣṇa (*ānukūlyena kṛṣṇānuśīlanam*). That is the real qualification of a *brāhmaṇa.* Because Ṣaṇḍa and Amarka were seminal *brāhmaṇas* and had become servants of such a master as Hiraṇyakaśipu, they unnecessarily wanted to chastise Prahlāda Mahārāja.

TEXT 16

आनीयतामरे वेत्रमस्माकमयशस्करः ।
कुलाङ्गारस्य दुर्बुद्धेश्चतुर्थोऽस्योदितो दमः ॥१६॥

ānīyatām are vetram
asmākam ayaśaskaraḥ
kulāṅgārasya durbuddheś
caturtho 'syodito damaḥ

ānīyatām—let it be brought; *are*—oh; *vetram*—the stick; *asmākam*—of us; *ayaśaskaraḥ*—who is bringing defamation; *kula-aṅgārasya*—of he who is like a cinder in the dynasty; *durbuddheḥ*—having bad intelligence; *caturthaḥ*—the fourth; *asya*—for him; *uditaḥ*—declared; *damaḥ*—punishment (the stick, *argumentum ad baculum*).

TRANSLATION

Oh, please bring me a stick! This Prahlāda is damaging our name and fame. Because of his bad intelligence, he has become like a cinder in the dynasty of the demons. Now he needs to be treated by the fourth of the four kinds of political diplomacy.

PURPORT

In political affairs, when a person disobediently agitates against the government, four principles are used to suppress him—legal orders, pacification, the offer of a post, or, finally, weapons. When there are no other arguments, he is punished. In logic, this is called *argumentum ad baculum.* When the two seminal *brāhmaṇas* Ṣaṇḍa and Amarka failed to extract from Prahlāda Mahārāja the cause for his having opinions different from those of his father, they called for a stick with which to chastise him to satisfy their master, Hiraṇyakaśipu. Because Prahlāda had become a devotee, they considered him to be contaminated by bad intelligence and to be the worst descendant in the family of demons. As it is said, where ignorance is bliss, it is folly to be wise. In a society or family in which everyone is a demon, for someone to become a Vaiṣṇava is certainly folly. Thus Prahlāda Mahārāja was charged with bad intelligence because he was among demons, including his teachers, who were supposedly *brāhmaṇas.*

The members of our Kṛṣṇa consciousness movement are in a position similar to that of Prahlāda Mahārāja. All over the world, ninety-nine percent of the people are godless demons, and therefore our preaching of Kṛṣṇa consciousness, following in the footsteps of Prahlāda Mahārāja, is always hampered by many impediments. Because of their fault of being devotees, the American boys who have sacrificed everything for preaching Kṛṣṇa consciousness are charged with being members of the CIA. Moreover, the seminal *brāhmaṇas* in India, who say that one can become a *brāhmaṇa* only if born in a *brāhmaṇa* family, charge us with ruining the Hindu system of religion. Of course, the fact is that one becomes a *brāhmaṇa* by qualification. Because we are training Europeans and Americans to become qualified and are awarding them brahminical status, we are being charged with destroying the Hindu religion. Nonetheless, confronting all kinds of difficulties, we must spread the Kṛṣṇa consciousness movement with great determination, like that of Prahlāda Mahārāja. In spite of being the son of the demon Hiraṇyakaśipu, Prahlāda never feared the chastisements of the seminal *brāhmaṇa* sons of a demoniac father.

TEXT 17

दैतेयचन्दनवने जातोऽयं कण्टकद्रुमः ।
यन्मूलोन्मूलपरशोर्विष्णोर्नालायितोऽर्भकः ॥१७॥

daiteya-candana-vane
jāto 'yaṁ kaṇṭaka-drumaḥ

yan-mūlonmūla-paraśor
viṣṇor nālāyito 'rbhakaḥ

daiteya—of the demoniac family; *candana-vane*—in the sandalwood forest; *jātaḥ*—born; *ayam*—this; *kaṇṭaka-drumaḥ*—thorn tree; *yat*—of which; *mūla*—of the roots; *unmūla*—in the cutting; *paraśoḥ*—who is like an axe; *viṣṇoḥ*—of Lord Viṣṇu; *nālāyitaḥ*—the handle; *arbhakaḥ*—boy.

TRANSLATION

This rascal Prahlāda has appeared like a thorn tree in a forest of sandalwood. To cut down sandalwood trees, an axe is needed, and the wood of the thorn tree is very suitable for the handle of such an axe. Lord Viṣṇu is the axe for cutting down the sandalwood forest of the family of demons, and this Prahlāda is the handle for that axe.

PURPORT

Thorn trees generally grow in deserted places, not in sandalwood forests, but the seminal *brāhmaṇas* Ṣaṇḍa and Amarka compared the dynasty of the Daitya Hiraṇyakaśipu to a sandalwood forest and compared Prahlāda Mahārāja to a hard, strong thorn tree that could provide the handle of an axe. They compared Lord Viṣṇu to the axe itself. An axe alone cannot cut a thorn tree; it needs a handle, which may be made of the wood of a thorn tree. Thus the thorn tree of demoniac civilization can be cut to pieces by the axe of *viṣṇu-bhakti*, devotional service to Lord Kṛṣṇa. Some of the members of the demoniac civilization, like Prahlāda Mahārāja, may become the handle for the axe, to assist Lord Viṣṇu, and thus the entire forest of demoniac civilization can be cut to pieces.

TEXT 18

इति तं विविधोपायैर्भीषयंस्तर्जनादिभिः ।
प्रह्लादं ग्राहयामास त्रिवर्गस्योपपादनम् ॥१८॥

iti taṁ vividhopāyair
bhīṣayaṁs tarjanādibhiḥ

prahrādaṁ grāhayām āsa
tri-vargasyopapādanam

iti—in this way; *tam*—him (Prahlāda Mahārāja); *vividha-upāyaiḥ*—by various means; *bhīṣayan*—threatening; *tarjana-ādibhiḥ*—by chastisement, threats, etc.; *prahrādam*—unto Prahlāda Mahārāja; *grāhayām āsa*—taught; *tri-vargasya*—the three goals of life (the paths of religion, economic development and sense gratification); *upapādanam*—scripture that presents.

TRANSLATION

Ṣaṇḍa and Amarka, the teachers of Prahlāda Mahārāja, chastised and threatened their disciple in various ways and began teaching him about the paths of religion, economic development and sense gratification. This is the way they educated him.

PURPORT

In this verse the words *prahrādaṁ grāhayām āsa* are important. The words *grāhayām āsa* literally mean that they tried to induce Prahlāda Mahārāja to accept the paths of *dharma, artha* and *kāma* (religion, economic development and sense gratification). People are generally preoccupied with these three concerns, without interest in the path of liberation. Hiraṇyakaśipu, the father of Prahlāda Mahārāja, was simply interested in gold and sense enjoyment. The word *hiraṇya* means "gold," and *kaśipu* refers to soft cushions and bedding on which people enjoy sense gratification. The word *prahlāda*, however, refers to one who is always joyful in understanding Brahman (*brahma-bhūtaḥ prasannātmā*). *Prahlāda* means *prasannātmā*, always joyful. Prahlāda was always joyful in worshiping the Lord, but in accordance with the instructions of Hiraṇyakaśipu, the teachers were interested in teaching him about material things. Materialistic persons think that the path of religion is meant for improving their material conditions. The materialist goes to a temple to worship many varieties of demigods just to receive some benediction to improve his material life. He goes to a *sādhu* or so-called *svāmī* to take advantage of an easy method for achieving material opulence. In the name of religion, the so-called *sādhus* try to satisfy the senses of the materialists by showing them shortcuts to material opulence. Sometimes they give some talisman or blessing. Sometimes they attract materialistic persons by producing gold. Then they declare themselves God, and foolish materialists are attracted to them for economic development. As a result of this process of cheating, others are reluctant to accept a religious process, and instead they advise people in general to work for material advancement. This is going on all over the world. Not only now but since time immemorial, no one is interested in *mokṣa,* liberation. There are four principles—*dharma* (religion), *artha* (economic development), *kāma* (sense gratification) and *mokṣa* (liberation). People accept religion to become materially opulent. And why should one be materially opulent? For sense gratification. Thus people prefer these three *mārgas,* the three paths of materialistic life. No one is interested in liberation, and *bhagavad-bhakti,* devotional service to the Lord, is above even liberation. Therefore the process of devotional service, Kṛṣṇa consciousness, is extremely difficult to understand. This will be explained later by Prahlāda Mahārāja. The teachers Ṣaṇḍa and Amarka tried to induce Prahlāda Mahārāja to accept the materialistic way of life, but actually their attempt was a failure.

TEXT 19

तत एनं गुरुर्ज्ञात्वा ज्ञातज्ञेयचतुष्टयम् ।
दैत्येन्द्रं दर्शयामास मातृमृष्टमलङ्कृतम् ॥१९॥

tata enaṁ gurur jñātvā
jñāta-jñeya-catuṣṭayam
daityendraṁ darśayām āsa
mātṛ-mṛṣṭam alaṅkṛtam

tataḥ—thereafter; *enam*—him (Prahlāda Mahārāja); *guruḥ*—his teachers; *jñātvā*—knowing; *jñāta*—known; *jñeya*—which are to be known; *catuṣṭayam*—the four diplomatic principles (*sāma,* the process of pacifying; *dāna,* the process of giving money in charity; *bheda,* the principle of dividing; and *daṇḍa,* the principle of punishment); *daitya-indram*—unto Hiraṇyakaśipu, the King of the Daityas; *darśayām āsa*—

presented; *mātṛ-mṛṣṭam*—being bathed by his mother; *alaṅkṛtam*—decorated with ornaments.

TRANSLATION

After some time, the teachers Ṣaṇḍa and Amarka thought that Prahlāda Mahārāja was sufficiently educated in the diplomatic affairs of pacifying public leaders, appeasing them by giving them lucrative posts, dividing and ruling over them, and punishing them in cases of disobedience. Then, one day, after Prahlāda's mother had personally washed the boy and dressed him nicely with sufficient ornaments, they presented him before his father.

PURPORT

It is essential for a student who is going to be a ruler or king to learn the four diplomatic principles. There is always rivalry between a king and his citizens. Therefore, when a citizen agitates the public against the king, the duty of the king is to call him and try to pacify him with sweet words, saying, "You are very important in the state. Why should you disturb the public with some new cause for agitation?" If the citizen is not pacified, the king should then offer him some lucrative post as a governor or minister—any post that draws a high salary—so that he may be agreeable. If the enemy still goes on agitating the public, the king should try to create dissension in the enemy's camp, but if he still continues, the king should employ *argumentum ad baculum*—severe punishment—by putting him in jail or placing him before a firing squad. The teachers appointed by Hiraṇyakaśipu taught Prahlāda Mahārāja how to be a diplomat so that he could rule over the citizens very nicely.

TEXT 20

पादयोः पतितं बालं प्रतिनन्द्याशिषासुरः ।
परिष्वज्य चिरं दोर्भ्यां परमामाप निर्वृतिम् ॥२०॥

pādayoḥ patitaṁ bālaṁ
pratinandyāśiṣāsuraḥ

pariṣvajya ciraṁ dorbhyāṁ
paramām āpa nirvṛtim

pādayoḥ—at the feet; *patitam*—fallen; *bālam*—the boy (Prahlāda Mahārāja); *pratinandya*—encouraging; *āśiṣā*—with blessings ("My dear child, may you live long and be happy" and so on); *asuraḥ*—the demon Hiraṇyakaśipu; *pariṣvajya*—embracing; *ciram*—for a long time due to affection; *dorbhyām*—with his two arms; *paramām*—great; *āpa*—obtained; *nirvṛtim*—jubilation.

TRANSLATION

When Hiraṇyakaśipu saw that his child had fallen at his feet and was offering obeisances, as an affectionate father he immediately began showering blessings upon the child and embraced him with both arms. A father naturally feels happy to embrace his son, and Hiraṇyakaśipu became very happy in this way.

TEXT 21

आरोप्याङ्कमवघ्राय मूर्धन्यश्रुकलाम्बुभिः ।
आसिञ्चन् विकसद्वक्त्रमिदमाह युधिष्ठिर ॥२१॥

āropyāṅkam avaghrāya
mūrdhany aśru-kalāmbubhiḥ
āsiñcan vikasad-vaktram
idam āha yudhiṣṭhira

āropya—placing; *aṅkam*—on the lap; *avaghrāya mūrdhani*—smelling his head; *aśru*—of tears; *kalā-ambubhiḥ*—with water from drops; *āsiñcan*—moistening; *vikasat-vaktram*—his smiling face; *idam*—this; *āha*—said; *yudhiṣṭhira*—O Mahārāja Yudhiṣṭhira.

TRANSLATION

Nārada Muni continued: My dear King Yudhiṣṭhira, Hiraṇyakaśipu seated Prahlāda Mahārāja on his lap and began smelling his head. With affectionate tears gliding down from his

eyes and moistening the child's smiling face, he spoke to his son as follows.

PURPORT

If a child or disciple falls at the feet of the father or spiritual master, the superior responds by smelling the head of the subordinate.

TEXT 22

हिरण्यकशिपुरुवाच
प्रह्रादानूच्यतां तात स्वधीतं किञ्चिदुत्तमम् ।
कालेनैतावतायुष्मन् यदशिक्षद् गुरोर्भवान् ॥२२॥

hiraṇyakaśipur uvāca
prahrādānūcyatāṁ tāta
svadhītaṁ kiñcid uttamam
kālenaitāvatāyuṣman
yad aśikṣad guror bhavān

hiraṇyakaśipuḥ uvāca—King Hiraṇyakaśipu said; *prahrāda*—my dear Prahlāda; *anūcyatām*—let it be told; *tāta*—my dear son; *svadhītam*—well learned; *kiñcit*—something; *uttamam*—very nice; *kālena etāvatā*—for so much time; *āyuṣman*—O long-lived one; *yat*—which; *aśikṣat*—has learned; *guroḥ*—from your teachers; *bhavān*—yourself.

TRANSLATION

Hiraṇyakaśipu said: My dear Prahlāda, my dear son, O long-lived one, for so much time you have heard many things from your teachers. Now please repeat to me whatever you think is the best of that knowledge.

PURPORT

In this verse, Hiraṇyakaśipu inquires from his son what he has learned from his *guru*. Prahlāda Mahārāja's *gurus* were of two kinds—

Ṣaṇḍa and Amarka, the sons of Śukrācārya in the seminal disciplic succession, were the *gurus* appointed by his father, but his other *guru* was the exalted Nārada Muni, who had instructed Prahlāda when Prahlāda was within the womb of his mother. Prahlāda Mahārāja responded to the inquiry of his father with the instructions he had received from his spiritual master, Nārada. Thus there was again a difference of opinion because Prahlāda Mahārāja wanted to relate the best thing he had learned from his spiritual master, whereas Hiraṇyakaśipu expected to hear about the politics and diplomacy Prahlāda had learned from Ṣaṇḍa and Amarka. Now the dissension between the father and son became increasingly intense as Prahlāda Mahārāja began to say what he had learned from his *guru* Nārada Muni.

TEXTS 23–24

श्रीप्रह्राद उवाच

श्रवणं कीर्तनं विष्णोः स्मरणं पादसेवनम् ।
अर्चनं वन्दनं दास्यं सख्यमात्मनिवेदनम् ॥२३॥
इति पुंसार्पिता विष्णौ भक्तिश्चेन्नवलक्षणा ।
क्रियेत भगवत्यद्धा तन्मन्येऽधीतमुत्तमम् ॥२४॥

śrī-prahrāda uvāca
śravaṇaṁ kīrtanaṁ viṣṇoḥ
smaraṇaṁ pāda-sevanam
arcanaṁ vandanaṁ dāsyaṁ
sakhyam ātma-nivedanam

iti puṁsārpitā viṣṇau
bhaktiś cen nava-lakṣaṇā
kriyeta bhagavaty addhā
tan manye 'dhītam uttamam

śrī-prahrādaḥ uvāca—Prahlāda Mahārāja said; *śravaṇam*—hearing; *kīrtanam*—chanting; *viṣṇoḥ*—of Lord Viṣṇu (not anyone else); *smaraṇam*—remembering; *pāda-sevanam*—serving the feet; *arcanam*—offering worship (with *ṣoḍaśopacāra*, the sixteen kinds of paraphernalia); *vandanam*—offering prayers; *dāsyam*—becoming the servant; *sakhyam*—becoming the best friend; *ātma-nivedanam*—surrendering everything, whatever one has; *iti*—thus; *puṁsā arpitā*—offered by the devotee; *viṣṇau*—unto Lord Viṣṇu (not to anyone else); *bhaktiḥ*—devotional service; *cet*—if; *nava-lakṣaṇā*—possessing nine different processes; *kriyeta*—one should perform; *bhagavati*—unto the Supreme Personality of Godhead; *addhā*—directly or completely; *tat*—that; *manye*—I consider; *adhītam*—learning; *uttamam*—topmost.

TRANSLATION

Prahlāda Mahārāja said: Hearing and chanting about the transcendental holy name, form, qualities, paraphernalia and pastimes of Lord Viṣṇu, remembering them, serving the lotus feet of the Lord, offering the Lord respectful worship with sixteen types of paraphernalia, offering prayers to the Lord, becoming His servant, considering the Lord one's best friend, and surrendering everything unto Him (in other words, serving Him with the body, mind and words)—these nine processes are accepted as pure devotional service. One who has dedicated his life to the service of Kṛṣṇa through these nine methods should be understood to be the most learned person, for he has acquired complete knowledge.

PURPORT

When Prahlāda Mahārāja was asked by his father to say something from whatever he had learned, he considered that what he had learned from his spiritual master was the best of all teachings whereas what he had learned about diplomacy from his material teachers, Ṣaṇḍa and Amarka, was useless. *Bhaktiḥ pareśānubhavo viraktir anyatra ca* (*Bhāg.* 11.2.42). This is the symptom of pure devotional service. A pure devotee is interested only in devotional service, not in material affairs. To execute devotional service, one should always engage in hearing and chanting about Kṛṣṇa, or Lord Viṣṇu. The process of temple worship is called *arcana.* How to perform *arcana* will be explained herein. One should have complete faith in the words of Kṛṣṇa, who says that He is the great well-wishing friend of everyone (*suhṛdaṁ sarva-bhūtānām*). A devotee considers Kṛṣṇa the only friend. This is called *sakhyam.*

Puṁsārpitā viṣṇau. The word *puṁsā* means "by all living entities." There are no distinctions permitting only a man or only a *brāhmaṇa* to offer devotional service to the Lord. Everyone can do so. As confirmed in *Bhagavad-gītā* (9.32), *striyo vaiśyās tathā śūdrās te 'pi yānti parāṁ gatim:* although women, *vaiśyas* and *śūdras* are considered less intelligent, they also can become devotees and return home, back to Godhead.

After performing sacrifices, sometimes a person engaged in fruitive activity customarily offers the results to Viṣṇu. But here it is said, *bhagavaty addhā:* one must directly offer everything to Viṣṇu. This is called *sannyāsa* (not merely *nyāsa*). A *tridaṇḍi-sannyāsī* carries three *daṇḍas*, signifying *kaya-mano-vākya*—body, mind and words. All of these should be offered to Viṣṇu, and then one can begin devotional service. Fruitive workers first perform some pious activities and then formally or officially offer the results to Viṣṇu. The real devotee, however, first offers his surrender to Kṛṣṇa with his body, mind and words and then uses his body, mind and words for the service of Kṛṣṇa as Kṛṣṇa desires.

Śrīla Bhaktisiddhānta Sarasvatī Ṭhākura gives the following explanation in his *Tathya.* The word *śravaṇa* refers to giving aural reception to the holy name and descriptions of the Lord's form, qualities, entourage and pastimes as explained in *Śrīmad-Bhāgavatam*, *Bhagavad-gītā* and similar authorized scriptures. After aurally receiving such messages, one should memorize these vibrations and repeat them (*kīrtanam*). *Smaraṇam* means trying to understand more and more about the Supreme Lord, and *pāda-sevanam* means engaging oneself in serving the lotus feet of the Lord according to the time and circumstances. *Arcanam* means worshiping Lord Viṣṇu as one does in the temple, and *vandanam* means offering respectful obeisances. *Man-manā bhava mad-bhakto mad-yājī māṁ namaskuru. Vandanam* means *namaskuru*—offering obeisances or offering prayers. Thinking oneself to be *nitya-kṛṣṇa-dāsa*, everlastingly a servant of Kṛṣṇa, is called *dāsyam*, and *sakhyam* means being a well-wisher of Kṛṣṇa. Kṛṣṇa wants everyone to surrender unto Him because everyone is constitutionally His servant. Therefore, as a sincere friend of Kṛṣṇa, one should preach this philosophy, requesting everyone to surrender unto Kṛṣṇa. *Ātma-nivedanam* means offering Kṛṣṇa everything, including one's body, mind, intelligence and whatever one may possess.

One's sincere endeavor to perform these nine processes of devotional service is technically called *bhakti.* The word *addhā* means "directly." One should not be like the *karmīs,* who perform pious activities and then formally offer the results to Kṛṣṇa. That is *karma-kāṇḍa.* One should not aspire for the results of his pious activities, but should dedicate oneself fully and then act piously. In other words, one should act for the satisfaction of Lord Viṣṇu, not for the satisfaction of his own senses. That is the meaning of the word *addhā,* "directly."

anyābhilāṣitā-śūnyaṁ
jñāna-karmādy-anāvṛtam
ānukūlyena kṛṣṇānu-
śīlanaṁ bhaktir uttamā

"One should render transcendental loving service to the Supreme Lord Kṛṣṇa favorably and without desire for material profit or gain through fruitive activities or philosophical speculation. That is called pure devotional service." One should simply satisfy Kṛṣṇa, without being influenced by fruitive knowledge or fruitive activity.

The *Gopāla-tāpanī Upaniṣad* says that the word *bhakti* means engagement in the devotional service of the Supreme Personality of Godhead, not of anyone else. This *Upaniṣad* describes that *bhakti* is the offering of devotional service unto the Supreme Personality of Godhead. To perform devotional service, one should be relieved of the bodily conception of life and aspirations to be happy through elevation to the higher planetary systems. In other words, work performed simply for the satisfaction of the Supreme Lord, without any desire for material benefits, is called *bhakti. Bhakti* is also called *niṣkarma,* or freedom from the results of fruitive activity. *Bhakti* and *niṣkarma* are on the same platform, although devotional service and fruitive activity appear almost the same.

The nine different processes enunciated by Prahlāda Mahārāja, who learned them from Nārada Muni, may not all be required for the execution of devotional service; if a devotee performs only one of these nine without deviation, he can attain the mercy of the Supreme Personality of Godhead. Sometimes it is found that when one performs one of the processes, other processes are mixed with it. That is not improper for a devotee. When a devotee executes any one of the nine processes (*nava-*

lakṣaṇā), this is sufficient; the other eight processes are included. Now let us discuss these nine different processes.

(1) *Śravaṇam.* Hearing of the holy name of the Lord (*śravaṇam*) is the beginning of devotional service. Although any one of the nine processes is sufficient, in chronological order the hearing of the holy name of the Lord is the beginning. Indeed, it is essential. As enunciated by Lord Śrī Caitanya Mahāprabhu, *ceto-darpaṇa-mārjanam:* by chanting the holy name of the Lord, one is cleansed of the material conception of life, which is due to the dirty modes of material nature. When the dirt is cleansed from the core of one's heart, one can realize the form of the Supreme Personality of Godhead—*īśvaraḥ paramaḥ kṛṣṇaḥ sac-cid-ānanda-vigrahaḥ.* Thus by hearing the holy name of the Lord, one comes to the platform of understanding the personal form of the Lord. After realizing the Lord's form, one can realize the transcendental qualities of the Lord, and when one can understand His transcendental qualities one can understand the Lord's associates. In this way a devotee advances further and further toward complete understanding of the Lord as he awakens in realization of the Lord's holy name, transcendental form and qualities, His paraphernalia, and everything pertaining to Him. Therefore the chronological process is *śravaṇaṁ kīrtanaṁ viṣṇoḥ.* This same process of chronological understanding holds true in chanting and remembering. When the chanting of the holy name, form, qualities and paraphernalia is heard from the mouth of a pure devotee, his hearing and chanting are very pleasing. Śrīla Sanātana Gosvāmī has forbidden us to hear the chanting of an artificial devotee or nondevotee.

Hearing from the text of *Śrīmad-Bhāgavatam* is considered the most important process of hearing. *Śrīmad-Bhāgavatam* is full of transcendental chanting of the holy name, and therefore the chanting and hearing of *Śrīmad-Bhāgavatam* are transcendentally full of mellows. The transcendental holy name of the Lord may be heard and chanted accordingly to the attraction of the devotee. One may chant the holy name of Lord Kṛṣṇa, or one may chant the holy name of Lord Rāma or Nṛsiṁhadeva (*rāmādi-mūrtiṣu kalā-niyamena tiṣṭhan*). The Lord has innumerable forms and names, and devotees may meditate upon a particular form and chant the holy name according to his attraction. The best course is to hear of the holy name, form and so on from a pure devotee of the same standard as oneself. In other words, one who is attached to Kṛṣṇa should chant and hear from other pure devotees who are also attached to Lord Kṛṣṇa. The same principle applies for devotees attracted by Lord Rāma, Lord Nṛsiṁha and other forms of the Lord. Because Kṛṣṇa is the ultimate form of the Lord (*kṛṣṇas tu bhagavān svayam*), it is best to hear about Lord Kṛṣṇa's name, form and pastimes from a realized devotee who is particularly attracted by the form of Lord Kṛṣṇa. In *Śrīmad-Bhāgavatam,* great devotees like Śukadeva Gosvāmī have specifically described Lord Kṛṣṇa's holy name, form and qualities. Unless one hears about the holy name, form and qualities of the Lord, one cannot clearly understand the other processes of devotional service. Therefore Śrī Caitanya Mahāprabhu recommends that one chant the holy name of Kṛṣṇa. *Paraṁ vijayate śrī-kṛṣṇa-saṅkīrtanam.* If one is fortunate enough to hear from the mouth of realized devotees, he is very easily successful on the path of devotional service. Therefore hearing of the holy name, form and qualities of the Lord is essential.

In *Śrīmad-Bhāgavatam* (1.5.11) there is this verse:

tad-vāg-visargo janatāgha-viplavo
yasmin prati-ślokam abaddhavaty api
nāmāny anantasya yaśo-'ṅkitāni yat
śṛṇvanti gāyanti gṛṇanti sādhavaḥ

"Verses describing the name, form and qualities of Anantadeva, the unlimited Supreme Lord, are able to vanquish all the sinful reactions of the entire world. Therefore even if such verses are improperly composed, devotees hear them, describe them and accept them as bona fide and authorized." In this connection, Śrīdhara Svāmī has remarked that a pure devotee takes advantage of another pure devotee by trying to hear from him about the holy name, form and qualities of the Lord. If there is no such opportunity, he alone chants and hears the Lord's holy name.

(2) *Kīrtanam.* The hearing of the holy name has been described above. Now let us try to understand the chanting of the holy name, which is the second item in the consecutive order. It is recommended that such chanting be performed very loudly. In *Śrīmad-Bhāgavatam,* Nārada Muni says that without shame he began traveling all over the world, chanting the holy name of the Lord. Similarly, Śrī Caitanya Mahāprabhu has advised:

tṛṇād api sunīcena
taror api sahiṣṇunā
amāninā mānadena
kīrtanīyaḥ sadā hariḥ

A devotee can very peacefully chant the holy name of the Lord by behaving more humbly than the grass, being tolerant like a tree and offering respects to everyone, without expecting honor from anyone else. Such qualifications make it easier to chant the holy name of the Lord. The process of transcendental chanting can be easily performed by anyone. Even if one is physically unfit, classified lower than others, devoid of material qualifications or not at all elevated in terms of pious activities, the chanting of the holy name is beneficial. An aristocratic birth, an advanced education, beautiful bodily features, wealth and similar results of pious activities are all unnecessary for advancement in spiritual life, for one can very easily advance simply by chanting the holy name. It is understood from the authoritative source of Vedic literature that especially in this age, Kali-yuga, people are generally short-living, extremely bad in their habits, and inclined to accept methods of devotional service that are not bona fide. Moreover, they are always disturbed by material conditions, and they are mostly unfortunate. Under the circumstances, the performance of other processes, such as *yajña, dāna, tapaḥ* and *kriyā*—sacrifices, charity and so on—are not at all possible. Therefore it is recommended:

harer nāma harer nāma
harer nāmaiva kevalam
kalau nāsty eva nāsty eva
nāsty eva gatir anyathā

"In this age of quarrel and hypocrisy the only means of deliverance is chanting of the holy name of the Lord. There is no other way. There is no other way. There is no other way." Simply by chanting the holy name of the Lord, one advances perfectly in spiritual life. This is the best process for success in life. In other ages, the chanting of the holy name is equally powerful, but especially in this age, Kali-yuga, it is most powerful. *Kīrtanād eva kṛṣṇasya mukta-saṅgaḥ paraṁ vrajet:* simply by chanting the holy name of Kṛṣṇa, one is liberated and returns home, back to Godhead. Therefore, even if one is able to perform other processes of devotional service, one must adopt the chanting of the holy name as the principal method of advancing in spiritual life. *Yajñaiḥ saṅkīrtana-prāyair yajanti hi sumedhasaḥ:* those who are very sharp in their intelligence should adopt this process of chanting the holy names of the Lord. One should not, however, manufacture different types of chanting. One should adhere seriously to the chanting of the holy name as recommended in the scriptures: Hare Kṛṣṇa, Hare Kṛṣṇa, Kṛṣṇa Kṛṣṇa, Hare Hare/ Hare Rāma, Hare Rāma, Rāma Rāma, Hare Hare.

While chanting the holy name of the Lord, one should be careful to avoid ten offenses. From Sanat-kumāra it is understood that even if a person is a severe offender in many ways, he is freed from offensive life if he takes shelter of the Lord's holy name. Indeed, even if a human being is no better than a two-legged animal, he will be liberated if he takes shelter of the holy name of the Lord. One should therefore be very careful not to commit offenses at the lotus feet of the Lord's holy name. The offenses are described as follows: (*a*) to blaspheme a devotee, especially a devotee engaged in broadcasting the glories of the holy name, (*b*) to consider the name of Lord Śiva or any other demigod to be equally as powerful as the holy name of the Supreme Personality of Godhead (no one is equal to the Supreme Personality of Godhead, nor is anyone superior to Him), (*c*) to disobey the instructions of the spiritual master, (*d*) to blaspheme the Vedic literatures and literatures compiled in pursuance of the Vedic literatures, (*e*) to comment that the glories of the holy name of the Lord are exaggerated, (*f*) to interpret the holy name in a deviant way, (*g*) to commit sinful activities on the strength of chanting the holy name, (*h*) to compare the chanting of the holy name to pious activities, (*i*) to instruct the glories of the holy name to a person who has no understanding of the chanting of the holy name, (*j*) not to awaken in transcendental attachment for the chanting of the holy name, even after hearing all these scriptural injunctions.

There is no way to atone for any of these offenses. It is therefore recommended that an offender at the feet of the holy name continue to chant the holy name twenty-four hours a day. Constant chanting of the holy name will make one free of offenses, and then he will gradually be elevated to the transcendental platform on which he can chant the pure holy name and thus become a lover of the Supreme Personality of Godhead.

It is recommended that even if one commits offenses, one should continue chanting the holy name. In other words, the chanting of the holy name makes one offenseless. In the book *Nāma-kaumudī* it is recommended that if one is an offender at the lotus feet of a Vaiṣṇava, he should submit to that Vaiṣṇava and be excused; similarly, if one is an offender in chanting the holy name, he should submit to the holy name and thus be freed from his offenses. In this connection there is the following statement, spoken by Dakṣa to Lord Śiva: "I did not know the glories of your personality, and therefore I committed an offense at your lotus feet in the open assembly. You are so kind, however, that you did not accept my offense. Instead, when I was falling down because of accusing you, you saved me by your merciful glance. You are most great. Kindly excuse me and be satisfied with your own exalted qualities."

One should be very humble and meek to offer one's desires and chant prayers composed in glorification of the holy name, such as *ayi mukta-kulair upāsya mānam* and *nivṛtta-tarṣair upagīyamānād.* One should chant such prayers to become free from offenses at the lotus feet of the holy name.

(3) *Smaraṇam.* After one regularly performs the processes of hearing and chanting and after the core of one's heart is cleansed, *smaraṇam,* remembering, is recommended. In *Śrīmad-Bhāgavatam* (2.1.11) Śukadeva Gosvāmī tells King Parīkṣit:

etan nirvidyamānānām
icchatām akuto-bhayam
yoginām nṛpa nirṇītaṁ
harer nāmānukīrtanam

"O King, for great *yogīs* who have completely renounced all material connections, for those who desire all material enjoyment and for those who are self-satisfied by dint of transcendental knowledge, constant chanting of the holy name of the Lord is recommended." According to different relationships with the Supreme Personality of Godhead, there are varieties of *nāmānukīrtanam,* chanting of the holy name, and thus according to different relationships and mellows there are five kinds of remembering. These are as follows: (*a*) conducting research into the worship of a particular form of the Lord, (*b*) concentrating the mind on one subject and withdrawing the mind's activities of thinking, feeling and willing from all other subjects, (*c*) concentrating upon a particular form of the Lord (this is called meditation), (*d*) concentrating one's mind continuously on the form of the Lord (this is called *dhruvānusmṛti*, or perfect meditation), and (*e*) awakening a likening for concentration upon a particular form (this is called *samādhi*, or trance). Mental concentration upon particular pastimes of the Lord in particular circumstances is also called remembrance. Therefore *samādhi*, trance, can be possible in five different ways in terms of one's relationship. Specifically, the trance of devotees on the stage of neutrality is called mental concentration.

(4) *Pāda-sevanam.* According to one's taste and strength, hearing, chanting and remembrance may be followed by *pāda-sevanam.* One obtains the perfection of remembering when one constantly thinks of the lotus feet of the Lord. Being intensely attached to thinking of the Lord's lotus feet is called *pāda-sevanam.* When one is particularly adherent to the process of *pāda-sevanam*, this process gradually includes other processes, such as seeing the form of the Lord, touching the form of the Lord, circumambulating the form or temple of the Lord, visiting such places as Jagannātha Purī, Dvārakā and Mathurā to see the Lord's form, and bathing in the Ganges or Yamunā. Bathing in the Ganges and serving a pure Vaiṣṇava are also known as *tadīya-upāsanam.* This is also *pāda-sevanam.* The word *tadīya* means "in relationship with the Lord." Service to the Vaiṣṇava, Tulasī, Ganges and Yamunā are included in *pāda-sevanam.* All these processes of *pāda-sevanam* help one advance in spiritual life very quickly.

(5) *Arcanam.* After *pāda-sevanam* comes the process of *arcanam*, worship of the Deity. If one is interested in the process of *arcanam*, one must positively take shelter of a bona fide spiritual master and learn the process from him. There are many books for *arcana*, especially *Nārada-pañcarātra.* In this age, the *Pañcarātra* system is particularly recommended for *arcana*, Deity worship. There are two systems of *arcana*—the *bhāgavata* system and *pāñcarātrikī* system. In the *Śrīmad-Bhāgavatam* there is no recommendation of *pāñcarātrikī* worship because in this Kali-yuga, even without Deity worship, everything can be

perfectly performed simply through hearing, chanting, remembering and worship of the lotus feet of the Lord. Rūpa Gosvāmī states:

śrī-viṣṇoḥ śravaṇe parīkṣid abhavad vaiyāsakiḥ kīrtane
prahlādaḥ smaraṇe tad-aṅghri-bhajane lakṣmīḥ pṛthuḥ pūjane
akrūras tv abhivandane kapi-patir dāsye 'tha sakhye 'rjunaḥ
sarvasvātma-nivedane balir abhūt kṛṣṇāptir eṣāṁ param

"Parīkṣit Mahārāja attained salvation simply by hearing, and Śukadeva Gosvāmī attained salvation simply by chanting. Prahlāda Mahārāja attained salvation by remembering the Lord. The goddess of fortune, Lakṣmīdevī, attained perfection by worshiping the Lord's lotus feet. Pṛthu Mahārāja attained salvation by worshiping the Deity of the Lord. Akrūra attained salvation by offering prayers, Hanumān by rendering service, Arjuna by establishing friendship with the Lord, and Bali Mahārāja by offering everything to the service of the Lord." All these great devotees served the Lord according to a particular process, but every one of them attained salvation and became eligible to return home, back to Godhead. This is explained in *Śrīmad-Bhāgavatam.*

It is therefore recommended that initiated devotees follow the principles of *Nārada-pañcarātra* by worshiping the Deity in the temple. Especially for householder devotees who are opulent in material possessions, the path of Deity worship is strongly recommended. An opulent householder devotee who does not engage his hard-earned money in the service of the Lord is called a miser. One should not engage paid *brāhmaṇas* to worship the Deity. If one does not personally worship the Deity but engages paid servants instead, he is considered lazy, and his worship of the Deity is called artificial. An opulent householder can collect luxurious paraphernalia for Deity worship, and consequently for householder devotees the worship of the Deity is compulsory. In our Kṛṣṇa consciousness movement there are *brahmacārīs*, *gṛhasthas*, *vānaprasthas* and *sannyāsīs*, but the Deity worship in the temple should be performed especially by the householders. The *brahmacārīs* can go with the *sannyāsīs* to preach, and the *vānaprasthas* should prepare themselves for the next status of renounced life, *sannyāsa*. *Gṛhastha* devotees, however, are generally engaged in material activities, and therefore if they do not take to Deity worship, their falling down is positively assured. Deity worship means following the rules and regulations precisely. That will keep one steady in devotional service. Generally householders have children, and then the wives of the householders should be engaged in caring for the children, just as women acting as teachers care for the children in a nursery school.

Gṛhastha devotees must adopt the *arcana-vidhi,* or Deity worship according to the suitable arrangements and directions given by the spiritual master. Regarding those unable to take to the Deity worship in the temple, there is the following statement in the *Agni Purāṇa.* Any householder devotee circumstantially unable to worship the Deity must at least see the Deity worship, and in this way he may achieve success also. The special purpose of Deity worship is to keep oneself always pure and clean. *Gṛhastha* devotees should be actual examples of cleanliness.

Deity worship should be continued along with hearing and chanting. Therefore every *mantra* is preceded by the word *namaḥ.* In all the *mantras* there are specific potencies, of which the *gṛhastha* devotees must take advantage. There are many *mantras* preceded by the word *namaḥ,* but if one chants the holy name of the Lord, he receives the result of chanting *namaḥ* many times. By chanting the holy name of the Lord, one can reach the platform of love of Godhead. One might ask, then what is the necessity of being initiated? The answer is that even though the chanting of the holy name is sufficient to enable one to progress in spiritual life to the standard of love of Godhead, one is nonetheless susceptible to contamination because of possessing a material body. Consequently, special stress is given to the *arcana-vidhi.* One should therefore regularly take advantage of both the *bhāgavata* process and *pāñcarātrikī* process.

Deity worship has two divisions, namely pure and mixed with fruitive activities. For one who is steady, Deity worship is compulsory. Observing the various types of festivals, such as *Śrī Janmāṣṭamī, Rāma-navamī* and *Nṛsiṁha-caturdaśī,* is also included in the process of Deity worship. In other words, it is compulsory for householder devotees to observe these festivals.

Now let us discuss the offenses in Deity worship. The following are offenses: (*a*) to enter the temple with shoes or being carried on a palanquin, (*b*) not to observe the prescribed festivals, (*c*) to avoid offering obeisances in front of the Deity, (*d*) to offer prayers in an unclean state, not having washed one's hands after eating, (*e*) to offer obeisances with one hand, (*f*) to circumambulate directly in front of the Deity, (*g*) to spread one's legs before the Deity, (*h*) to sit before the Deity while holding one's ankles with one's hands, (*i*) to lie down before the Deity, (*j*) to eat before the Deity, (*k*) to speak lies before the Deity, (*l*) to address someone loudly before the Deity, (*m*) to talk nonsense before the Deity, (*n*) to cry before the Deity, (*o*) to argue before the Deity, (*p*) to chastise someone before the Deity, (*q*) to show someone favor before the Deity, (*r*) to use harsh words before the Deity, (*s*) to wear a woolen blanket before the Deity, (*t*) to blaspheme someone before the Deity, (*u*) to worship someone else before the Deity, (*v*) to use vulgar language before the Deity, (*w*) to pass air before the Deity, (*x*) to avoid very opulent worship of the Deity, even though one is able to perform it, (*y*) to eat something not offered to the Deity, (*z*) to avoid offering fresh fruits to the Deity according to the season, (*aa*) to offer food to the Deity which has already been used or from which has first been given to others (in other words, food should not be distributed to anyone else until it has been offered to the Deity), (*bb*) to sit with one's back toward the Deity, (*cc*) to offer obeisances to someone else in front of the Deity, (*dd*) not to chant proper prayers when offering obeisances to the spiritual master, (*ee*) to praise oneself before the Deity, and (*ff*) to blaspheme the demigods. In the worship of the Deity, these thirty-two offenses should be avoided.

In the *Varāha Purāṇa* the following offenses are mentioned: (*a*) to eat in the house of a rich man, (*b*) to enter the Deity's room in the dark, (*c*) to worship the Deity without following the regulative principles, (*d*) to enter the temple without vibrating any sound, (*e*) to collect food that has been seen by a dog, (*f*) to break silence while offering worship to the Deity, (*g*) to go to the toilet during the time of worshiping the Deity, (*h*) to offer incense without offering flowers, (*i*) to worship the Deity with forbidden flowers, (*j*) to begin worship without having washed one's teeth, (*k*) to begin worship after sex, (*l*) to touch a lamp, dead body or a woman during her menstrual period, or to put on red or bluish clothing, unwashed clothing, the clothing of others or soiled clothing. Other offenses are to worship the Deity after seeing a dead body, to pass air before the Deity, to show anger before the Deity, and to worship the Deity just after returning from a crematorium. After eating, one should not worship the Deity until one has digested his food, nor should one touch the Deity or engage in any Deity worship after eating safflower oil or hing. These are also offenses.

In other places, the following offenses are listed: (*a*) to be against the scriptural injunctions of the Vedic literature or to disrespect within one's heart the *Śrīmad-Bhāgavatam* while externally falsely accepting its principles, (*b*) to introduce differing *śāstras,* (*c*) to chew pan and betel before the Deity, (*d*) to keep flowers for worship on the leaf of a castor oil plant, (*e*) to worship the Deity in the afternoon, (*f*) to sit on the altar or to sit on the floor to worship the Deity (without a seat), (*g*) to touch the Deity with the left hand while bathing the Deity, (*h*) to worship the Deity with a stale or used flower, (*i*) to spit while worshiping the Deity, (*j*) to advertise one's glory while worshiping the Deity, (*k*) to apply *tilaka* to one's forehead in a curved way, (*l*) to enter the temple without having washed one's feet, (*m*) to offer the Deity food cooked by an uninitiated person, (*n*) to worship the Deity and offer *bhoga* to the Deity within the vision of an uninitiated person or non-Vaiṣṇava, (*o*) to offer worship to the Deity without worshiping Vaikuṇṭha deities like Gaṇeśa, (*p*) to worship the Deity while perspiring, (*q*) to refuse flowers offered to the Deity, (*r*) to take a vow or oath in the holy name of the Lord.

If one commits any of the above offenses, one must read at least one chapter of *Bhagavad-gītā.* This is confirmed in the *Skanda-Purāṇa, Avantī-khaṇḍa.* Similarly, there is another injunction, stating that one who reads the thousand names of Viṣṇu can be released from all offenses. In the same *Skanda-Purāṇa, Revā-khaṇḍa,* it is said that one who recites prayers to *tulasī* or sows a *tulasī* seed is also freed from all offenses. Similarly, one who worships the *śālagrāma-śilā* can also be relieved of offenses. In the *Brahmāṇḍa Purāṇa* it is said that one who worships Lord Viṣṇu, whose four hands bear a conchshell, disc, lotus flower and club, can be relieved from the above offenses. In the *Ādi-varāha Purāṇa* it is said that a worshiper who has committed offenses may fast for one day at the holy place known as Śaukarava and then bathe in the Ganges.

In the process of worshiping the Deity it is sometimes enjoined that one worship the Deity within the mind. In the *Padma Purāṇa, Uttara-khaṇḍa,* it is said, "All persons can generally worship within the mind." The *Gautamīya Tantra* states, "For a *sannyāsī* who has no home, worship of the Deity within the mind is recommended." In the *Nārada-pañcarātra* it is stated by Lord Nārāyaṇa that worship of the Deity within the mind is called *mānasa-pūjā*. One can become free from the four miseries by this method. Sometimes worship from the mind can be independently executed. According to the instruction of Āvirhotra Muni, one of the *nava-yogendras*, as mentioned in *Śrīmad-Bhāgavatam*, one may worship the Deity by chanting all the *mantras*. Eight kinds of Deities are mentioned in the *śāstra*, and the mental Deity is one of them. In this regard, the following description is given in the *Brahma-vaivarta Purāṇa*.

In the city of Pratiṣṭhāna-pura, long ago, there resided a *brāhmaṇa* who was poverty-stricken but innocent and not dissatisfied. One day he heard a discourse in an assembly of *brāhmaṇas* concerning how to worship the Deity in the temple. In that meeting, he also heard that the Deity may be worshiped within the mind. After this incident, the *brāhmaṇa*, having bathed in the Godāvarī River, began mentally worshiping the Deity. He would wash the temple within his mind, and then in his imagination he would bring water from all the sacred rivers in golden and silver waterpots. He collected all kinds of valuable paraphernalia for worship, and he worshiped the Deity very gorgeously, beginning from bathing the Deity and ending with offering *ārati*. Thus he felt great happiness. After many years had passed in this way, one day within his mind he cooked nice sweet rice with ghee to worship the Deity. He placed the sweet rice on a golden dish and offered it to Lord Kṛṣṇa, but he felt that the sweet rice was very hot, and therefore he touched it with his finger. He immediately felt that his finger had been burned by the hot sweet rice, and thus he began to lament. While the *brāhmaṇa* was in pain, Lord Viṣṇu in Vaikuṇṭha began smiling, and the goddess of fortune inquired from the Lord why He was smiling. Lord Viṣṇu then ordered His associates to bring the *brāhmaṇa* to Vaikuṇṭha. Thus the *brāhmaṇa* attained the liberation of *sāmīpya*, the facility of living near the Supreme Personality of Godhead.

(6) *Vandanam.* Although prayers are a part of Deity worship, they may be considered separately like the other items, such as hearing and chanting, and therefore separate statements are given herewith. The Lord has unlimited transcendental qualities and opulences, and one who feels influenced by the Lord's qualities in various activities offers

prayers to the Lord. In this way he becomes successful. In this connection, the following are some of the offenses to be avoided: (*a*) to offer obeisances on one hand, (*b*) to offer obeisances with one's body covered, (*c*) to show one's back to the Deity, (*d*) to offer obeisances on the left side of the Deity, (*e*) to offer obeisances very near the Deity.

(7) *Dāsyam.* There is the following statement in regard to assisting the Lord as a servant. After many, many thousands of births, when one comes to understand that he is an eternal servant of Kṛṣṇa, one can deliver others from this universe. If one simply continues to think that he is an eternal servant of Kṛṣṇa, even without performing any other process of devotional service, he can attain full success, for simply by this feeling one can perform all nine processes of devotional service.

(8) *Sakhyam.* In regard to worshiping the Lord as a friend, the *Agastya-saṁhitā* states that a devotee engaged in performing devotional service by *śravaṇam* and *kīrtanam* sometimes wants to see the Lord personally, and for this purpose he resides in the temple. Elsewhere there is this statement: "O my Lord, Supreme Personality and eternal friend, although You are full of bliss and knowledge, You have become the friend of the residents of Vṛndāvana. How fortunate are these devotees!" In this statement the word "friend" is specifically used to indicate intense love. Friendship, therefore, is better than servitude. In the stage above *dāsya-rasa,* the devotee accepts the Supreme Personality of Godhead as a friend. This is not at all astonishing, for when a devotee is pure in heart the opulence of his worship of the Deity diminishes as spontaneous love for the Personality of Godhead is manifested. In this regard, Śrīdhara Svāmī mentions Śrīdāma Vipra, who expressed to himself his feelings of obligation, thinking, "Life after life, may I be connected with Kṛṣṇa in this friendly attitude."

(9) *Ātma-nivedanam.* The word *ātma-nivedanam* refers to the stage at which one who has no motive other than to serve the Lord surrenders everything to the Lord and performs his activities only to please the Supreme Personality of Godhead. Such a devotee is like a cow that is cared for by its master. When cared for by its master, a cow is not in anxiety over its maintenance. Such a cow is always devoted to its master, and it never acts independently, but only for the master's benefit. Some devotees, therefore, consider dedication of the body to the Lord to be *ātma-nivedanam,* and as stated in the book known as *Bhakti-viveka,*

sometimes dedication of the soul to the Lord is called *ātma-nivedanam.* The best examples of *ātma-nivedanam* are found in Bali Mahārāja and Ambarīṣa Mahārāja. *Ātma-nivedanam* is also sometimes found in the behavior of Rukmiṇīdevī at Dvārakā.

TEXT 25

निशम्यैतत्सुतवचो हिरण्यकशिपुस्तदा ।
गुरुपुत्रमुवाचेदं रुषा प्रस्फुरिताधरः ॥२५॥

niśamyaitat suta-vaco
hiraṇyakaśipus tadā
guru-putram uvācedaṁ
ruṣā prasphuritādharaḥ

niśamya—hearing; *etat*—this; *suta-vacaḥ*—speech from his son; *hiraṇyakaśipuḥ*—Hiraṇyakaśipu; *tadā*—at that time; *guru-putram*—unto the son of Śukrācārya, his spiritual master; *uvāca*—spoke; *idam*—this; *ruṣā*—with anger; *prasphurita*—trembling; *adharaḥ*—whose lips.

TRANSLATION

After hearing these words of devotional service from the mouth of his son Prahlāda, Hiraṇyakaśipu was extremely angry. His lips trembling, he spoke as follows to Ṣaṇḍa, the son of his guru, Śukrācārya.

TEXT 26

ब्रह्मबन्धो किमेतत्ते विपक्षं श्रयतासता ।
असारं ग्राहितो बालो मामनादृत्य दुर्मते ॥२६॥

brahma-bandho kim etat te
vipakṣaṁ śrayatāsatā
asāraṁ grāhito bālo
mām anādṛtya durmate

brahma-bandho—O unqualified son of a *brāhmaṇa; kim etat*—what is this; *te*—by you; *vipakṣam*—the party of my enemies; *śrayatā*—taking shelter of; *asatā*—most mischievous; *asāram*—nonsense; *grāhitaḥ*—taught; *bālaḥ*—the boy; *mām*—me; *anādṛtya*—not caring for; *durmate*—O foolish teacher.

TRANSLATION

O unqualified, most heinous son of a brāhmaṇa, you have disobeyed my order and taken shelter of the party of my enemies. You have taught this poor boy about devotional service! What is this nonsense?

PURPORT

In this verse the word *asāram*, meaning, "having no substance," is significant. For a demon there is no substance in the process of devotional service, but to a devotee devotional service is the only essential factor in life. Since Hiraṇyakaśipu did not like devotional service, the essence of life, he chastised Prahlāda Mahārāja's teachers with harsh words.

TEXT 27

सन्ति ह्यसाधवो लोके दुर्मैत्राश्छद्मवेषिणः ।
तेषामुदेत्यघं काले रोगः पातकिनामिव ॥२७॥

santi hy asādhavo loke
durmaitrāś chadma-veśinaḥ
teṣām udety aghaṁ kāle
rogaḥ pātakinām iva

santi—are; *hi*—indeed; *asādhavaḥ*—dishonest persons; *loke*—within this world; *durmaitrāḥ*—cheating friends; *chadma-veśinaḥ*—wearing false garbs; *teṣām*—of all of them; *udeti*—arises; *agham*—the reaction of sinful life; *kāle*—in due course of time; *rogaḥ*—disease; *pātakinām*—of sinful men; *iva*—like.

TRANSLATION

In due course of time, various types of diseases are manifest in those who are sinful. Similarly, in this world there are many

deceptive friends in false garbs, but eventually, because of their false behavior, their actual enmity becomes manifest.

PURPORT

Being anxious about the education of his boy Prahlāda, Hiraṇyakaśipu was very much dissatisfied. When Prahlāda began teaching about devotional service, Hiraṇyakaśipu immediately regarded the teachers as his enemies in the garb of friends. In this verse the words *rogaḥ pātakinām iva* refer to disease, which is the most sinful and miserable of the conditions of material life (*janma-mṛtyu-jarā-vyādhi*). Disease is the symptom of the body of a sinful person. The *smṛti-śāstras* say,

brahma-hā kṣaya-rogī syāt
surāpaḥ śyāvadantakaḥ
svarṇa-hārī tu kunakhī
duścarmā guru-talpagaḥ

Murderers of *brāhmaṇas* are later afflicted by tuberculosis, drunkards become toothless, those who have stolen gold are afflicted by diseased nails, and sinful men who have sexual connections with the wife of a superior are afflicted by leprosy and similar skin diseases.

TEXT 28

श्रीगुरुपुत्र उवाच
न मत्प्रणीतं न परप्रणीतं
सुतो वदत्येष तवेन्द्रशत्रो ।
नैसर्गिकीयं मतिरस्य राजन्
नियच्छ मन्युं कद्दाः स्म मा नः ॥२८॥

śrī-guru-putra uvāca
na mat-praṇītaṁ na para-praṇītaṁ
suto vadaty eṣa tavendra-śatro
naisargikīyaṁ matir asya rājan
niyaccha manyuṁ kad adāḥ sma mā naḥ

śrī-guru-putraḥ uvāca—the son of Śukrācārya, Hiraṇyakaśipu's spiritual master, said; *na*—not; *mat-praṇītam*—educated by me; *na*—nor; *para-praṇītam*—educated by anyone else; *sutaḥ*—the son (Prahlāda); *vadati*—says; *eṣaḥ*—this; *tava*—your; *indra-śatro*—O enemy of King Indra; *naisargikī*—natural; *iyam*—this; *matiḥ*—inclination; *asya*—of him; *rājan*—O King; *niyaccha*—give up; *manyum*—your anger; *kad*—fault; *adāḥ*—attribute; *sma*—indeed; *mā*—do not; *naḥ*—unto us.

TRANSLATION

The son of Śukrācārya, Hiraṇyakaśipu's spiritual master, said: O enemy of King Indra, O King! Whatever your son Prahlāda has said was not taught to him by me or anyone else. His spontaneous devotional service has naturally developed in him. Therefore, please give up your anger and do not unnecessarily accuse us. It is not good to insult a brāhmaṇa in this way.

TEXT 29

श्रीनारद उवाच
गुरुणैवं प्रतिप्रोक्तो भूय आहासुरः सुतम् ।
न चेद्गुरुमुखीयं ते कुतोऽभद्रासती मतिः ॥२९॥

śrī-nārada uvāca
guruṇaivaṁ pratiprokto
bhūya āhāsuraḥ sutam
na ced guru-mukhīyaṁ te
kuto 'bhadrāsatī matiḥ

śrī-nāradaḥ uvāca—Nārada Muni said; *guruṇā*—by the teacher; *evam*—thus; *pratiproktaḥ*—being answered; *bhūyaḥ*—again; *āha*—said; *asuraḥ*—the great demon, Hiraṇyakaśipu; *sutam*—unto his son; *na*—not; *cet*—if; *guru-mukhī*—issued from the mouth of your teacher; *iyam*—this; *te*—your; *kutaḥ*—from where; *abhadra*—O inauspicious one; *asatī*—very bad; *matiḥ*—inclination.

TRANSLATION

Śrī Nārada Muni continued: When Hiraṇyakaśipu received this reply from the teacher, he again addressed his son Prahlāda. Hiraṇyakaśipu said: You rascal, most fallen of our family, if you have not received this education from your teachers, where have you gotten it?

PURPORT

Śrīla Viśvanātha Cakravartī Ṭhākura explains that devotional service is actually *bhadrā satī,* not *abhadra asatī.* In other words, knowledge of devotional service can be neither inauspicious nor contrary to etiquette. To learn devotional service is the duty of everyone. Therefore the spontaneous education of Prahlāda Mahārāja is supported as auspicious and perfect.

TEXT 30

श्रीप्रह्लाद उवाच
मतिर्न कृष्णे परतः स्वतो वा
मिथोऽभिपद्येत गृहव्रतानाम् ।
अदान्तगोभिर्विशतां तमिस्रं
पुनः पुनश्चर्वितचर्वणानाम् ॥३०॥

śrī-prahrāda uvāca
matir na kṛṣṇe parataḥ svato vā
mitho 'bhipadyeta gṛha-vratānām
adānta-gobhir viśatāṁ tamisraṁ
punaḥ punaś carvita-carvaṇānām

śrī-prahrādaḥ uvāca—Prahlāda Mahārāja said; *matiḥ*—inclination; *na*—never; *kṛṣṇe*—unto Lord Kṛṣṇa; *parataḥ*—from the instructions of others; *svataḥ*—from their own understanding; *vā*—either; *mithaḥ*—from combined effort; *abhipadyeta*—is developed; *gṛha-vratānām*—of persons too addicted to the materialistic, bodily conception of life; *adānta*—uncontrolled; *gobhiḥ*—by the senses; *viśatām*—entering; *tamisram*—hellish life; *punaḥ*—again; *punaḥ*—again; *carvita*—things already chewed; *carvaṇānām*—who are chewing.

TRANSLATION

Prahlāda Mahārāja replied: Because of their uncontrolled senses, persons too addicted to materialistic life make progress toward hellish conditions and repeatedly chew that which has already been chewed. Their inclinations toward Kṛṣṇa are never aroused, either by the instructions of others, by their own efforts, or by a combination of both.

PURPORT

In this verse the words *matir na kṛṣṇe* refer to devotional service rendered to Kṛṣṇa. So-called politicians, erudite scholars and philosophers who read *Bhagavad-gītā* try to twist some meaning from it to suit their material purposes, but their misunderstandings of Kṛṣṇa will not yield them any profit. Because such politicians, philosophers and scholars are interested in using *Bhagavad-gītā* as a vehicle for adjusting things materially, for them constant thought of Kṛṣṇa, or Kṛṣṇa consciousness, is impossible (*matir na kṛṣṇe*). As stated in *Bhagavad-gītā* (18.55), *bhaktyā mām abhijānāti:* only through devotional service can one understand Kṛṣṇa as He is. The so-called politicians and scholars think of Kṛṣṇa as fictitious. The politician says that his Kṛṣṇa is different from the Kṛṣṇa depicted in *Bhagavad-gītā*. Even though he accepts Kṛṣṇa and Rāma as the Supreme he thinks of Rāma and Kṛṣṇa as impersonal because he has no idea of service to Kṛṣṇa. Thus his only business is *punaḥ punaś carvita-carvaṇānām*—chewing the chewed again and again. The aim of such politicians and academic scholars is to enjoy this material world with their bodily senses. Therefore it is clearly stated here that those who are *gṛha-vrata*, whose only aim is to live comfortably with the body in the material world, cannot understand Kṛṣṇa. The two expressions *gṛha-vrata* and *carvita-carvaṇānām* indicate that a materialistic person tries to enjoy sense gratification in different bodily forms, life after life, but is still unsatisfied. In the name of personalism, this ism or that ism, such persons always remain attached to the materialistic way of life. As stated in *Bhagavad-gītā* (2.44):

bhogaiśvarya-prasaktānāṁ
tayāpahṛta-cetasām

vyavasāyātmikā buddhiḥ
samādhau na vidhīyate

"In the minds of those who are too attached to sense enjoyment and material opulence, and who are bewildered by such things, the resolute determination for devotional service to the Supreme Lord does not take place." Those who are attached to material enjoyment cannot be fixed in devotional service to the Lord. They cannot understand Bhagavān, Kṛṣṇa, or His instruction, *Bhagavad-gītā. Adānta-gobhir viśatāṁ tamisram:* their path actually leads toward hellish life.

As confirmed by Ṛṣabhadeva, *mahat-sevāṁ dvāram āhur vimukteḥ:* one must try to understand Kṛṣṇa by serving a devotee. The word *mahat* refers to a devotee.

mahātmānas tu māṁ pārtha
daivīṁ prakṛtim āśritāḥ
bhajanty ananya-manaso
jñātvā bhūtādim avyayam

"O son of Pṛthā, those who are not deluded, the great souls, are under the protection of the divine nature. They are fully engaged in devotional service because they know Me as the Supreme Personality of Godhead, original and inexhaustible." (Bg. 9.13) A *mahātmā* is one who is constantly engaged in devotional service, twenty-four hours a day. As explained in the following verses, unless one adheres to such a great personality, one cannot understand Kṛṣṇa. Hiraṇyakaśipu wanted to know where Prahlāda had gotten this Kṛṣṇa consciousness. Who had taught him? Prahlāda sarcastically replied, "My dear father, persons like you never understand Kṛṣṇa. One can understand Kṛṣṇa only by serving a *mahat*, a great soul. Those who try to adjust material conditions are said to be chewing the chewed. No one has been able to adjust material conditions, but life after life, generation after generation, people try and repeatedly fail. Unless one is properly trained by a *mahat*—a *mahātmā*, or unalloyed devotee of the Lord—there is no possibility of one's understanding Kṛṣṇa and His devotional service."

TEXT 31

न ते विदुः स्वार्थगतिं हि विष्णुं
दुराशया ये बहिरर्थमानिनः ।
अन्धा यथान्धैरुपनीयमाना-
स्तेऽपीशतन्त्र्यामुरुदाम्नि बद्धाः ॥३१॥

na te viduḥ svārtha-gatiṁ hi viṣṇuṁ
durāśayā ye bahir-artha-māninaḥ
andhā yathāndhair upanīyamānās
te 'pīśa-tantryām uru-dāmni baddhāḥ

na—not; *te*—they; *viduḥ*—know; *sva-artha-gatim*—the ultimate goal of life, or their own real interest; *hi*—indeed; *viṣṇum*—Lord Viṣṇu and His abode; *durāśayāḥ*—being ambitious to enjoy this material world; *ye*—who; *bahiḥ*—external sense objects; *artha-māninaḥ*—considering as valuable; *andhāḥ*—persons who are blind; *yathā*—just as; *andhaiḥ*—by other blind men; *upanīyamānāḥ*—being led; *te*—they; *api*—although; *īśa-tantryām*—to the ropes (laws) of material nature; *uru*—having very strong; *dāmni*—cords; *baddhāḥ*—bound.

TRANSLATION

Persons who are strongly entrapped by the consciousness of enjoying material life, and who have therefore accepted as their leader or guru a similar blind man attached to external sense objects, cannot understand that the goal of life is to return home, back to Godhead, and engage in the service of Lord Viṣṇu. As blind men guided by another blind man miss the right path and fall into a ditch, materially attached men led by another materially attached man are bound by the ropes of fruitive labor, which are made of very strong cords, and they continue again and again in materialistic life, suffering the threefold miseries.

PURPORT

Since there must always be a difference of opinion between demons and devotees, Hiraṇyakaśipu, when criticized by his son Prahlāda

Mahārāja, should not have been surprised that Prahlāda Mahārāja differed from his way of life. Nonetheless, Hiraṇyakaśipu was extremely angry and wanted to rebuke his son for deriding his teacher or spiritual master, who had been born in the *brāhmaṇa* family of the great *ācārya* Śukrācārya. The word *śukra* means "semen," and *ācārya* refers to a teacher or *guru*. Hereditary *gurus*, or spiritual masters, have been accepted everywhere since time immemorial, but Prahlāda Mahārāja declined to accept such a seminal *guru* or take instruction from him. An actual *guru* is *śrotriya*, one who has heard or received perfect knowledge through *paramparā*, the disciplic succession. Therefore Prahlāda Mahārāja did not recognize a seminal spiritual master. Such spiritual masters are not at all interested in Viṣṇu. Indeed, they are hopeful of material success (*bahir-artha-māninaḥ*). The word *bahiḥ* means "external," *artha* means "interest," and *mānina* means "taking very seriously." Generally speaking, practically everyone is unaware of the spiritual world. The knowledge of the materialists is restricted within the four-billion-mile limit of this material world, which is in the dark portion of the creation; they do not know that beyond the material world is the spiritual world. Unless one is a devotee of the Lord, one cannot understand the existence of the spiritual world. *Gurus*, teachers, who are simply interested in this material world are described in this verse as *andha*, blind. Such blind men may lead many other blind followers without true knowledge of material conditions, but they are not accepted by devotees like Prahlāda Mahārāja. Such blind teachers, being interested in the external, material world, are always bound by the strong ropes of material nature.

TEXT 32

नैषां मतिस्तावदुरुक्रमाङ्घ्रिं
स्पृशत्यनर्थापगमो यदर्थः ।
महीयसां पादरजोऽभिषेकं
निष्किञ्चनानां न वृणीत यावत् ॥३२॥

naiṣāṁ matis tāvad urukramāṅghriṁ
spṛśaty anarthāpagamo yad-arthaḥ

mahīyasāṁ pāda-rajo-'bhiṣekaṁ
niṣkiñcanānāṁ na vṛṇīta yāvat

na—not; *eṣām*—of these; *matiḥ*—the consciousness; *tāvat*—that long; *urukrama-aṅghrim*—the lotus feet of the Supreme Personality of Godhead, who is famous for performing uncommon activities; *spṛśati*—does touch; *anartha*—of unwanted things; *apagamaḥ*—the disappearance; *yat*—of which; *arthaḥ*—the purpose; *mahīyasām*—of the great souls (the *mahātmās*, or devotees); *pāda-rajaḥ*—by the dust of the lotus feet; *abhiṣekam*—consecration; *niṣkiñcanānām*—of devotees who have nothing to do with this material world; *na*—not; *vṛṇīta*—may accept; *yāvat*—as long as.

TRANSLATION

Unless they smear upon their bodies the dust of the lotus feet of a Vaiṣṇava completely freed from material contamination, persons very much inclined toward materialistic life cannot be attached to the lotus feet of the Lord, who is glorified for His uncommon activities. Only by becoming Kṛṣṇa conscious and taking shelter at the lotus feet of the Lord in this way can one be freed from material contamination.

PURPORT

Becoming Kṛṣṇa conscious brings about *anartha-apagamaḥ*, the disappearance of all *anarthas*, the miserable conditions we have unnecessarily accepted. The material body is the basic principle of these unwanted miserable conditions. The entire Vedic civilization is meant to relieve one from these unwanted miseries, but persons bound by the laws of nature do not know the destination of life. As described in the previous verse, *īśa-tantryām uru-dāmni baddhāḥ:* they are conditioned by the three strong modes of material nature. The education that keeps the conditioned soul bound life after life is called materialistic education. Śrīla Bhaktivinoda Ṭhākura has explained that materialistic education expands the influence of *māyā.* Such an education induces the conditioned soul to be increasingly attracted to materialistic life and to stray further and further away from liberation from unwanted miseries.

One may ask why highly educated persons do not take to Kṛṣṇa consciousness. The reason is explained in this verse. Unless one takes shelter of a bona fide, fully Kṛṣṇa conscious spiritual master, there is no chance of understanding Kṛṣṇa. The educators, scholars and big political leaders worshiped by millions of people cannot understand the goal of life and take to Kṛṣṇa consciousness, for they have not accepted a bona fide spiritual master and the *Vedas.* Therefore in the *Muṇḍaka Upaniṣad* (3.2.3) it is said, *nāyam ātmā pravacanena labhyo na medhayā na bahunā śrutena:* one cannot become self-realized simply by having an academic education, by presenting lectures in an erudite way (*pravacanena labhyaḥ*), or by being an intelligent scientist who discovers many wonderful things. One cannot understand Kṛṣṇa unless one is graced by the Supreme Personality of Godhead. Only one who has surrendered to a pure devotee of Kṛṣṇa and taken the dust of his lotus feet can understand Kṛṣṇa. First one must understand how to get out of the clutches of *māyā.* The only means is to become Kṛṣṇa conscious. And to become Kṛṣṇa conscious very easily, one must take shelter of a realized soul—a *mahat,* or *mahātmā*—whose only interest is to engage in the service of the Supreme Lord. As the Lord says in *Bhagavad-gītā* (9.13):

mahātmānas tu māṁ pārtha
daivīṁ prakṛtim āśritāḥ
bhajanty ananya-manaso
jñātvā bhūtādim avyayam

"O son of Pṛthā, those who are not deluded, the great souls, are under the protection of the divine nature. They are fully engaged in devotional service because they know Me as the Supreme Personality of Godhead, original and inexhaustible." Therefore, to end the unwanted miseries of life, one must become a devotee.

yasyāsti bhaktir bhagavaty akiñcanā
sarvair guṇais tatra samāsate surāḥ

"One who has unflinching devotional faith in Kṛṣṇa consistently manifests all the good qualities of Kṛṣṇa and the demigods." (*Bhāg.* 5.18.12)

yasya deve parā bhaktir
yathā deve tathā gurau
tasyaite kathitā hy arthāḥ
prakāśante mahātmanaḥ

"Only unto those great souls who have implicit faith in both the Lord and the spiritual master are all the imports of Vedic knowledge automatically revealed." (*Śvetāśvatara Upaniṣad* 6.23)

yam evaiṣa vṛṇute tena labhyas
tasyaiṣa ātmā vivṛṇute tanūṁ svām

"The Lord is obtained only by one whom He Himself chooses. To such a person He manifests His own form." (*Muṇḍaka Upaniṣad* 3.2.3)

These are Vedic injunctions. One must take shelter of a self-realized spiritual master, not a materially educated scholar or politician. One must take shelter of a *niṣkiñcana*, a person engaged in devotional service and free from material contamination. That is the way to return home, back to Godhead.

TEXT 33

इत्युक्त्वोपरतं पुत्रं हिरण्यकशिपू रुषा ।
अन्धीकृतात्मा स्वोत्सङ्गान्निरस्यत महीतले ॥३३॥

ity uktvoparataṁ putraṁ
hiraṇyakaśipū ruṣā
andhīkṛtātmā svotsaṅgān
nirasyata mahī-tale

iti—thus; *uktvā*—speaking; *uparatam*—stopped; *putram*—the son; *hiraṇyakaśipuḥ*—Hiraṇyakaśipu; *ruṣā*—with great anger; *andhīkṛta-ātmā*—made blind to self-realization; *sva-utsaṅgāt*—from his lap; *nirasyata*—threw; *mahī-tale*—upon the ground.

TRANSLATION

After Prahlāda Mahārāja had spoken in this way and become silent, Hiraṇyakaśipu, blinded by anger, threw him off his lap and onto the ground.

TEXT 34

आहामर्षरुषाविष्टः कषायीभूतलोचनः ।
वध्यतामाश्वयं वध्यो निःसारयत नैर्ऋताः ॥३४॥

āhāmarṣa-ruṣāviṣṭaḥ
kaṣāyī-bhūta-locanaḥ
vadhyatām āśv ayaṁ vadhyo
niḥsārayata nairṛtāḥ

āha—he said; *amarṣa*—indignation; *ruṣā*—and by severe anger; *āviṣṭaḥ*—overpowered; *kaṣāyī-bhūta*—becoming exactly like red-hot copper; *locanaḥ*—whose eyes; *vadhyatām*—let him be killed; *āśu*—immediately; *ayam*—this; *vadhyaḥ*—who is to be killed; *niḥsārayata*—take away; *nairṛtāḥ*—O demons.

TRANSLATION

Indignant and angry, his reddish eyes like molten copper, Hiraṇyakaśipu said to his servants: O demons, take this boy away from me! He deserves to be killed. Kill him as soon as possible!

TEXT 35

अयं मे भ्रातृहा सोऽयं हित्वा स्वान् सुहृदोऽधमः।
पितृव्यहन्तुः पादौ यो विष्णोर्दासवदर्चति ॥३५॥

ayaṁ me bhrātṛ-hā so 'yaṁ
hitvā svān suhṛdo 'dhamaḥ
pitṛvya-hantuḥ pādau yo
viṣṇor dāsavad arcati

ayam—this; *me*—my; *bhrātṛ-hā*—killer of the brother; *saḥ*—he; *ayam*—this; *hitvā*—giving up; *svān*—own; *suhṛdaḥ*—well-wishers; *adhamaḥ*—very low; *pitṛvya-hantuḥ*—of He who killed his uncle

Hiraṇyākṣa; *pādau*—at the two feet; *yaḥ*—he who; *viṣṇoḥ*—of Lord Viṣṇu; *dāsa-vat*—like a servant; *arcati*—serves.

TRANSLATION

This boy Prahlāda is the killer of my brother, for he has given up his family to engage in the devotional service of the enemy, Lord Viṣṇu, like a menial servant.

PURPORT

Hiraṇyakaśipu considered his son Prahlāda Mahārāja to be the killer of his brother because Prahlāda Mahārāja was engaged in the devotional service of Lord Viṣṇu. In other words, Prahlāda Mahārāja would be elevated to *sārūpya* liberation, and in that sense he resembled Lord Viṣṇu. Therefore Prahlāda was to be killed by Hiraṇyakaśipu. Devotees, Vaiṣṇavas, attain the liberations of *sārūpya, sālokya, sārṣṭi* and *sāmīpya*, whereas the Māyāvādīs are supposed to attain the liberation known as *sāyujya. Sāyujya-mukti*, however, is not very secure, whereas *sārūpya-mukti, sālokya-mukti, sārṣṭi-mukti* and *sāmīpya-mukti* are most certain. Although the servants of Lord Viṣṇu, Nārāyaṇa, in the Vaikuṇṭha planets are equally situated with the Lord, the devotees there know very well that the Lord is the master whereas they are servants.

TEXT 36

विष्णोर्वा साध्वसौ किं नु करिष्यत्यसमञ्जसः ।
सौहृदं दुस्त्यजं पित्रोरहाद्यः पञ्चहायनः ॥३६॥

viṣṇor vā sādhv asau kiṁ nu
kariṣyaty asamañjasaḥ
sauhṛdaṁ dustyajaṁ pitror
ahād yaḥ pañca-hāyanaḥ

viṣṇoḥ—unto Viṣṇu; *vā*—either; *sādhu*—good; *asau*—this; *kim*—whether; *nu*—indeed; *kariṣyati*—will do; *asamañjasaḥ*—not trustworthy; *sauhṛdam*—affectionate relationship; *dustyajam*—difficult to relinquish; *pitroḥ*—of his father and mother; *ahāt*—gave up; *yaḥ*—he who; *pañca-hāyanaḥ*—only five years old.

TRANSLATION

Although Prahlāda is only five years old, even at this young age he has given up his affectionate relationship with his father and mother. Therefore, he is certainly untrustworthy. Indeed, it is not at all believable that he will behave well toward Viṣṇu.

TEXT 37

परोऽप्यपत्यं हितकृद्यथौषधं
स्वदेहजोऽप्यामयवत्सुतोऽहितः ।
छिन्द्यात्तदङ्गं यदुतात्मनोऽहितं
शेषं सुखं जीवति यद्विवर्जनात् ॥३७॥

paro 'py apatyaṁ hita-kṛd yathauṣadhaṁ
sva-dehajo 'py āmayavat suto 'hitaḥ
chindyāt tad aṅgaṁ yad utātmano 'hitaṁ
śeṣaṁ sukhaṁ jīvati yad-vivarjanāt

paraḥ—not belonging to the same group or family; *api*—although; *apatyam*—a child; *hita-kṛt*—who is beneficial; *yathā*—just as; *auṣadham*—remedial herb; *sva-deha-jaḥ*—born of one's own body; *api*—although; *āmaya-vat*—like a disease; *sutaḥ*—a son; *ahitaḥ*—who is not a well-wisher; *chindyāt*—one should cut off; *tat*—that; *aṅgam*—part of the body; *yat*—which; *uta*—indeed; *ātmanaḥ*—for the body; *ahitam*—not beneficial; *śeṣam*—the balance; *sukham*—happily; *jīvati*—lives; *yat*—of which; *vivarjanāt*—by cutting off.

TRANSLATION

Although a medicinal herb, being born in the forest, does not belong to the same category as a man, if beneficial it is kept very carefully. Similarly, if someone outside one's family is favorable, he should be given protection like a son. On the other hand, if a limb of one's body is poisoned by disease, it must be amputated so

that the rest of the body may live happily. Similarly, even one's own son, if unfavorable, must be rejected, although born of one's own body.

PURPORT

Śrī Caitanya Mahāprabhu has instructed all devotees of the Lord to be humbler than the grass and more tolerant than trees; otherwise there will always be disturbances to their execution of devotional service. Here is a vivid example of how a devotee is disturbed by a nondevotee, even though the nondevotee is an affectionate father. The material world is such that a nondevotee father becomes an enemy of a devotee son. Having determined to kill even his son, Hiraṇyakaśipu gave the example of amputating a part of one's body that has become septic and therefore injurious to the rest of the body. The same example, of course, may also be applied to nondevotees. Cāṇakya Paṇḍita advises, *tyaja durjana-saṁsargaṁ bhaja sādhu-samāgamam.* Devotees actually serious about advancing in spiritual life should give up the company of nondevotees and always keep company with devotees. To be too attached to material existence is ignorance because material existence is temporary and miserable. Therefore devotees who are determined to perform *tapasya* (penances and austerities) to realize the self, and who are determined to become advanced in spiritual consciousness, must give up the company of atheistic nondevotees. Prahlāda Mahārāja maintained an attitude of noncooperation with the philosophy of his father, Hiraṇyakaśipu, yet he was tolerant and humble. Hiraṇyakaśipu, however, being a nondevotee, was so polluted that he was even prepared to kill his own son. He justified this by putting forward the logic of amputation.

TEXT 38

सर्वैरुपायैर्हन्तव्यः सम्भोजशयनासनैः ।
सुहृल्लिङ्गधरः शत्रुर्मुनेर्दुष्टमिवेन्द्रियम् ॥३८॥

sarvair upāyair hantavyaḥ
sambhoja-śayanāsanaiḥ
suhṛl-liṅga-dharaḥ śatrur
muner duṣṭam ivendriyam

sarvaiḥ—by all; *upāyaiḥ*—means; *hantavyaḥ*—must be killed; *sambhoja*—by eating; *śayana*—lying down; *āsanaiḥ*—by sitting; *suhṛt-liṅga-dharaḥ*—who has assumed the role of a friend; *śatruḥ*—an enemy; *muneḥ*—of a great sage; *duṣṭam*—uncontrollable; *iva*—like; *indriyam*—the senses.

TRANSLATION

Just as uncontrolled senses are the enemies of all yogīs engaged in advancing in spiritual life, this Prahlāda, who appears to be a friend, is an enemy because I cannot control him. Therefore this enemy, whether eating, sitting or sleeping, must be killed by all means.

PURPORT

Hiraṇyakaśipu planned a campaign to kill Prahlāda Mahārāja. He would kill his son by administering poison to him while he was eating, by making him sit in boiling oil, or by throwing him under the feet of an elephant while he was lying down. Thus Hiraṇyakaśipu decided to kill his innocent child, who was only five years old, simply because the boy had become a devotee of the Lord. This is the attitude of nondevotees toward devotees.

TEXTS 39–40

नैर्ऋतास्ते समादिष्टा भर्त्रा वै शूलपाणयः ।
तिग्मदंष्ट्रकरालास्यास्ताम्रश्मश्रुशिरोरुहाः ॥३९॥
नदन्तो भैरवं नादं छिन्धि भिन्धीति वादिनः।
आसीनं चाहनञ् शूलैः प्रह्रादं सर्वमर्मसु ॥४०॥

nairṛtās te samādiṣṭā
bhartrā vai śūla-pāṇayaḥ
tigma-daṁṣṭra-karālāsyās
tāmra-śmaśru-śiroruhāḥ

nadanto bhairavaṁ nādaṁ
chindhi bhindhīti vādinaḥ
āsīnaṁ cāhanañ śūlaiḥ
prahrādaṁ sarva-marmasu

nairṛtāḥ—the demons; *te*—they; *samādiṣṭāḥ*—being fully advised; *bhartrā*—by their master; *vai*—indeed; *śūla-pāṇayaḥ*—having tridents in their hands; *tigma*—very sharp; *daṁṣṭra*—teeth; *karāla*—and fearful; *āsyāḥ*—faces; *tāmra-śmaśru*—coppery mustaches; *śiroruhāḥ*—and hair on the head; *nadantaḥ*—vibrating; *bhairavam*—fearful; *nādam*—sound; *chindhi*—chop; *bhindhi*—divide into small parts; *iti*—thus; *vādinaḥ*—speaking; *āsīnam*—who was sitting silently; *ca*—and; *ahanan*—attacked; *śūlaiḥ*—with their tridents; *prahrādam*—Prahlāda Mahārāja; *sarva-marmasu*—on the tender parts of the body.

TRANSLATION

The demons [Rākṣasas], the servants of Hiraṇyakaśipu, thus began striking the tender parts of Prahlāda Mahārāja's body with their tridents. The demons all had fearful faces, sharp teeth and reddish, coppery beards and hair, and they appeared extremely threatening. Making a tumultuous sound, shouting, "Chop him up! Pierce him!" they began striking Prahlāda Mahārāja, who sat silently, meditating upon the Supreme Personality of Godhead.

TEXT 41

परे ब्रह्मण्यनिर्देश्ये भगवत्यखिलात्मनि ।
युक्तात्मन्यफला आसन्नपुण्यस्येव सत्क्रियाः ॥४१॥

pare brahmaṇy anirdeśye
bhagavaty akhilātmani
yuktātmany aphalā āsann
apuṇyasyeva sat-kriyāḥ

pare—in the supreme; *brahmaṇi*—absolute; *anirdeśye*—who is not perceivable by the senses; *bhagavati*—the Supreme Personality of Godhead; *akhila-ātmani*—the Supersoul of everyone; *yukta-ātmani*—on he whose mind was engaged (Prahlāda); *aphalāḥ*—without effect; *āsan*—were; *apuṇyasya*—of a person who has no assets in pious activities; *iva*—like; *sat-kriyāḥ*—good activities (like the performance of sacrifices or austerities).

TRANSLATION

Even though a person who has no assets in pious activities performs some good deed, it will have no result. Thus the weapons of the demons had no tangible effects upon Prahlāda Mahārāja because he was a devotee undisturbed by material conditions and fully engaged in meditating upon and serving the Supreme Personality of Godhead, who is unchangeable, who cannot be realized by the material senses, and who is the soul of the entire universe.

PURPORT

Prahlāda Mahārāja was constantly and fully engaged in thought of the Supreme Personality of Godhead. As it is said, *govinda-parirambhitaḥ.* Prahlāda Mahārāja engaged himself always in meditation, and thus he was protected by Govinda. Just as a small child on the lap of his father or mother is fully protected, a devotee, in all conditions, is protected by the Supreme Lord. Does this mean that when Prahlāda Mahārāja was attacked by the demons, the Rākṣasas, Govinda was also attacked by the demons? This is not possible. There have been many attempts by the demons to hurt or kill the Supreme Personality of Godhead, but He cannot be injured by any material means because He is always in transcendence. Therefore the words *pare brahmaṇi* are used here. The demons, the Rākṣasas, can neither see nor touch the Supreme Lord, although they may superficially think that they are striking the Lord's transcendental body with their material weapons. The Supreme Personality of Godhead is described in this verse as *anirdeśye.* We cannot understand Him to be in a particular place, for He is all-pervasive. Moreover, He is *akhilātmā,* the active principle of everything, even material weapons. Those who cannot understand the position of the Lord are unfortunate. They may think that they can kill the Supreme Personality of Godhead and His devotee, but all their attempts will be futile. The Lord knows how to deal with them.

TEXT 42

प्रयासेऽपहते तस्मिन् दैत्येन्द्रः परिशङ्कितः ।
चकार तद्वधोपायान्निर्बन्धेन युधिष्ठिर ॥४२॥

prayāse 'pahate tasmin
daityendraḥ pariśaṅkitaḥ
cakāra tad-vadhopāyān
nirbandhena yudhiṣṭhira

prayāse—when the endeavor; *apahate*—futile; *tasmin*—that; *daitya-indraḥ*—the King of the demons, Hiraṇyakaśipu; *pariśaṅkitaḥ*—very much afraid (considering how the boy was protected); *cakāra*—executed; *tat-vadha-upāyān*—various means for killing him; *nirbandhena*—with determination; *yudhiṣṭhira*—O King Yudhiṣṭhira.

TRANSLATION

My dear King Yudhiṣṭhira, when all the attempts of the demons to kill Prahlāda Mahārāja were futile, the King of the demons, Hiraṇyakaśipu, being most fearful, began contriving other means to kill him.

TEXTS 43–44

दिग्गजैर्दन्दशूकेन्द्रैरभिचारावपातनैः ।
मायाभिः संनिरोधैश्च गरदानैरभोजनैः ॥४३॥
हिमवाय्वग्निसलिलैः पर्वताक्रमणैरपि ।
न शशाक यदा हन्तुमपापमसुरः सुतम् ।
चिन्तां दीर्घतमां प्राप्तस्तत्कर्तुं नाभ्यपद्यत ॥४४॥

dig-gajair dandaśūkendrair
abhicārāvapātanaiḥ
māyābhiḥ sannirodhaiś ca
gara-dānair abhojanaiḥ

hima-vāyv-agni-salilaiḥ
parvatākramaṇair api
na śaśāka yadā hantum
apāpam asuraḥ sutam
cintāṁ dīrghatamāṁ prāptas
tat-kartuṁ nābhyapadyata

dik-gajaiḥ—by big elephants trained to smash anything under their feet; *danda-śūka-indraiḥ*—by the biting of the King's poisonous snakes; *abhicāra*—by destructive spells; *avapātanaiḥ*—by causing to fall from the top of a mountain; *māyābhiḥ*—by conjuring tricks; *sannirodhaiḥ*—by imprisonment; *ca*—as well as; *gara-dānaiḥ*—by administering poison; *abhojanaiḥ*—by starving; *hima*—by cold; *vāyu*—wind; *agni*—fire; *salilaiḥ*—and water; *parvata-ākramaṇaiḥ*—by crushing with big stones and hills; *api*—and also; *na śaśāka*—was not able; *yadā*—when; *hantum*—to kill; *apāpam*—who was not at all sinful; *asuraḥ*—the demon (Hiraṇyakaśipu); *sutam*—his son; *cintām*—anxiety; *dīrgha-tamām*—long-standing; *prāptaḥ*—obtained; *tat-kartum*—to do that; *na*—not; *abhyapadyata*—achieved.

TRANSLATION

Hiraṇyakaśipu could not kill his son by throwing him beneath the feet of big elephants, throwing him among huge, fearful snakes, employing destructive spells, hurling him from the top of a hill, conjuring up illusory tricks, administering poison, starving him, exposing him to severe cold, winds, fire and water, or throwing heavy stones to crush him. When Hiraṇyakaśipu found that he could not in any way harm Prahlāda, who was completely sinless, he was in great anxiety about what to do next.

TEXT 45

एष मे बह्वसाधूक्तो वधोपायाश्च निर्मिताः ।
तैस्तैर्द्रोहैरसद्धर्मैर्मुक्तः स्वेनैव तेजसा ॥४५॥

eṣa me bahv-asādhūkto
vadhopāyāś ca nirmitāḥ
tais tair drohair asad-dharmair
muktaḥ svenaiva tejasā

eṣaḥ—this; *me*—of me; *bahu*—many; *asādhu-uktaḥ*—ill names; *vadha-upāyāḥ*—many varieties of means to kill him; *ca*—and; *nirmitāḥ*—devised; *taiḥ*—by those; *taiḥ*—by those; *drohaiḥ*—treacheries; *asat-dharmaiḥ*—abominable actions; *muktaḥ*—released; *svena*—his own; *eva*—indeed; *tejasā*—by prowess.

TRANSLATION

Hiraṇyakaśipu thought: I have used many ill names in chastising this boy Prahlāda and have devised many means of killing him, but despite all my endeavors, he could not be killed. Indeed, he saved himself by his own powers, without being affected in the least by these treacheries and abominable actions.

TEXT 46

वर्तमानोऽविदूरे वै बालोऽप्यजडधीरयम् ।
न विस्मरति मेऽनार्यं शुनःशेप इव प्रभुः ॥४६॥

vartamāno 'vidūre vai
bālo 'py ajaḍa-dhīr ayam
na vismarati me 'nāryaṁ
śunaḥ śepa iva prabhuḥ

vartamānaḥ—being situated; *avidūre*—not very far away; *vai*—indeed; *bālaḥ*—a mere child; *api*—although; *ajaḍa-dhīḥ*—complete fearlessness; *ayam*—this; *na*—not; *vismarati*—forgets; *me*—my; *anāryam*—misbehavior; *śunaḥ śepaḥ*—the curved tail of a dog; *iva*—exactly like; *prabhuḥ*—being able or potent.

TRANSLATION

Although he is very near to me and is merely a child, he is situated in complete fearlessness. He resembles a dog's curved tail, which can never be straightened, because he never forgets my misbehavior and his connection with his master, Lord Viṣṇu.

PURPORT

The word *śunaḥ* means "of a dog," and *śepa* means "tail." The example is ordinary. However one may try to straighten a dog's tail, it is never straight but always curved. *Śunaḥ śepa* is also the name of the second son of Ajīgarta. He was sold to Hariścandra, but he later took shelter of Viśvāmitra, Hariścandra's enemy, and never left his side.

TEXT 47

अप्रमेयानुभावोऽयमकुतश्चिद्भयोऽमरः ।
नूनमेतद्विरोधेन मृत्युर्मे भविता न वा ॥४७॥

aprameyānubhāvo 'yam
akutaścid-bhayo 'maraḥ
nūnam etad-virodhena
mṛtyur me bhavitā na vā

aprameya—unlimited; *anubhāvaḥ*—glory; *ayam*—this; *akutaścit-bhayaḥ*—having no fear from any quarter; *amaraḥ*—immortal; *nūnam*—definitely; *etat-virodhena*—because of going against him; *mṛtyuḥ*—death; *me*—my; *bhavitā*—may be; *na*—not; *vā*—or.

TRANSLATION

I can see that this boy's strength is unlimited, for he has not feared any of my punishments. He appears immortal. Therefore, because of my enmity toward him, I shall die. Or maybe this will not take place.

TEXT 48

इति तच्चिन्तया किञ्चिन्म्लानश्रियमधोमुखम् ।
शण्डामर्कावौशनसौ विविक्त इति होचतुः ॥४८॥

iti tac-cintayā kiñcin
mlāna-śriyam adho-mukham
śaṇḍāmarkāv auśanasau
vivikta iti hocatuḥ

iti—thus; *tat-cintayā*—with full anxiety because of Prahlāda Mahārāja's position; *kiñcit*—somewhat; *mlāna*—lost; *śriyam*—bodily luster; *adhaḥ-mukham*—his face downward; *śaṇḍa-amarkau*—Ṣaṇḍa and Amarka; *auśanasau*—sons of Śukrācārya; *vivikte*—in a secret place; *iti*—thus; *ha*—indeed; *ūcatuḥ*—spoke.

TRANSLATION

Thinking in this way, the King of the Daityas, morose and bereft of bodily luster, remained silent with his face downward. Then Ṣaṇḍa and Amarka, the two sons of Śukrācārya, spoke to him in secret.

TEXT 49

जितं त्वयैकेन जगत्त्रयं भ्रुवो-
विजृम्भणत्रस्तसमस्तधिष्ण्यपम् ।
न तस्य चिन्त्यं तव नाथ चक्ष्वहे
न वै शिशूनां गुणदोषयोः पदम् ॥४९॥

jitaṁ tvayaikena jagat-trayaṁ bhruvor
vijṛmbhaṇa-trasta-samasta-dhiṣṇyapam
na tasya cintyaṁ tava nātha cakṣvahe
na vai śiśūnāṁ guṇa-doṣayoḥ padam

jitam—conquered; *tvayā*—by you; *ekena*—alone; *jagat-trayam*—the three worlds; *bhruvoḥ*—of the eyebrows; *vijṛmbhaṇa*—by the expanding; *trasta*—become afraid; *samasta*—all; *dhiṣṇyapam*—the chief persons in every planet; *na*—not; *tasya*—from him; *cintyam*—to be anxious; *tava*—of you; *nātha*—O master; *cakṣvahe*—we find; *na*—nor; *vai*—indeed; *śiśūnām*—of children; *guṇa-doṣayoḥ*—of a good quality or fault; *padam*—the subject matter.

TRANSLATION

O lord, we know that when you simply move your eyebrows, all the commanders of the various planets are most afraid. Without the help of any assistant, you have conquered all the three worlds. Therefore, we do not find any reason for you to be morose and full of anxiety. As for Prahlāda, he is nothing but a child and cannot be a cause of anxiety. After all, his bad or good qualities have no value.

TEXT 50

इमं तु पाशैर्वरुणस्य बद्ध्वा
निधेहि भीतो न पलायते यथा ।
बुद्धिश्च पुंसो वयसार्यसेवया
यावद् गुरुर्भार्गव आगमिष्यति ॥५०॥

imaṁ tu pāśair varuṇasya baddhvā
nidhehi bhīto na palāyate yathā
buddhiś ca puṁso vayasārya-sevayā
yāvad gurur bhārgava āgamiṣyati

imam—this; *tu*—but; *pāśaiḥ*—by the ropes; *varuṇasya*—of the demigod known as Varuṇa; *baddhvā*—binding; *nidhehi*—keep (him); *bhītaḥ*—being afraid; *na*—not; *palāyate*—runs away; *yathā*—so that; *buddhiḥ*—the intelligence; *ca*—also; *puṁsaḥ*—of a man; *vayasā*—by increase of age; *ārya*—of experienced, advanced persons; *sevayā*—by the service; *yāvat*—until; *guruḥ*—our spiritual master; *bhārgavaḥ*—Śukrācārya; *āgamiṣyati*—will come.

TRANSLATION

Until the return of our spiritual master, Śukrācārya, arrest this child with the ropes of Varuṇa so that he will not flee in fear. In any case, by the time he is somewhat grown up and has assimilated our instructions or served our spiritual master, he will change in his intelligence. Thus there need be no cause for anxiety.

TEXT 51

तथेति गुरुपुत्रोक्तमनुज्ञायेदमब्रवीत् ।
धर्मो ह्यस्योपदेष्टव्यो राज्ञां यो गृहमेधिनाम् ॥५१॥

tatheti guru-putroktam
anujñāyedam abravīt
dharmo hy asyopadeṣṭavyo
rājñāṁ yo gṛha-medhinām

tathā—in this way; *iti*—thus; *guru-putra-uktam*—advised by Ṣaṇḍa and Amarka, the sons of Śukrācārya; *anujñāya*—accepting; *idam*—this; *abravīt*—said; *dharmaḥ*—the duty; *hi*—indeed; *asya*—unto Prahlāda; *upadeṣṭavyaḥ*—to be instructed; *rājñām*—of the kings; *yaḥ*—which; *gṛha-medhinām*—who are interested in householder life.

TRANSLATION

After hearing these instructions of Ṣaṇḍa and Amarka, the sons of his spiritual master, Hiraṇyakaśipu agreed and requested them to instruct Prahlāda in that system of occupational duty which is followed by royal householder families.

PURPORT

Hiraṇyakaśipu wanted Prahlāda Mahārāja to be trained as a diplomatic king in ruling the kingdom, the country or the world, but not to be advised about renunciation or the renounced order of life. The word *dharma* here does not refer to some religious faith. As clearly stated, *dharmo hy asyopadeṣṭavyo rājñāṁ yo gṛha-medhinām*. There are two kinds of royal families—one whose members are simply attached to household life and the other consisting of *rājarṣis*, kings who govern with ruling power but are as good as great saints. Prahlāda Mahārāja wanted to become a *rājarṣi*, whereas Hiraṇyakśipu wanted him to become a king attached to sense enjoyment (*gṛha-medhinām*). Therefore in the Āryan system there is *varṇāśrama-dharma*, by which everyone should be educated according to his position in society's division of *varṇa* (*brāhmaṇa*, *kṣatriya*, *vaiśya* and *śūdra*) and *āśrama* (*brahmacarya*, *gṛhastha*, *vānaprastha* and *sannyāsa*).

A devotee purified by devotional service is always in the transcendental position above the mundane qualities. Thus the difference between Prahlāda Mahārāja and Hiraṇyakaśipu was that Hiraṇyakaśipu wanted to keep Prahlāda in mundane attachment whereas Prahlāda was above the modes of material nature. As long as one is under the control of material nature, his occupational duty is different from that of a person not under such control. One's real *dharma*, or occupational duty, is described in *Śrīmad-Bhāgavatam* (*dharmaṁ tu sākṣād bhagavat-praṇītam*). As described to his order carriers by Dharmarāja, or Yamarāja, a living being is a spiritual identity, and therefore his occupational duty is also spiritual. The real *dharma* is that which is advised in *Bhagavad-gītā: sarva-dharmān parityajya mām ekaṁ śaraṇaṁ vraja.* One must give up one's material occupational duties, just as one must give up his material body. Whatever one's occupational duty, even according to the *varṇāśrama* system, one must give it up and engage in one's spiritual function. One's real *dharma*, or occupational duty, is explained by Śrī Caitanya Mahāprabhu. *Jīvera 'svarūpa' haya—kṛṣṇera 'nitya-dāsa':* every living being is an eternal servant of Kṛṣṇa. That is one's real occupational duty.

TEXT 52

धर्ममर्थं च कामं च नितरां चानुपूर्वशः ।
प्रह्लादायोचतू राजन् प्रश्रितावनताय च ॥५२॥

dharmam arthaṁ ca kāmaṁ ca
nitarāṁ cānupūrvaśaḥ
prahrādāyocatū rājan
praśritāvanatāya ca

dharmam—mundane occupational duty; *artham*—economic development; *ca*—and; *kāmam*—sense gratification; *ca*—and; *nitarām*—always; *ca*—and; *anupūrvaśaḥ*—according to order, or from the beginning to the end; *prahrādāya*—unto Prahlāda Mahārāja; *ūcatuḥ*—they spoke; *rājan*—O King; *praśrita*—who was humble; *avanatāya*—and submissive; *ca*—also.

TRANSLATION

Thereafter, Ṣaṇḍa and Amarka systematically and unceasingly taught Prahlāda Mahārāja, who was very submissive and humble, about mundane religion, economic development and sense gratification.

PURPORT

There are four processes for human society—*dharma, artha, kāma* and *mokṣa*—and they culminate in liberation. Human society must follow a process of religion to advance, and on the basis of religion one should try to develop his economic condition so that he can fulfill his needs for sense gratification according to the religious rules and regulations. Then liberation from material bondage will be easier to attain. That is the Vedic process. When one is above the stages of *dharma, artha, kāma* and *mokṣa,* one becomes a devotee. He is then on the platform from which he is guaranteed not to fall again to material existence (*yad gatvā na nivartante*). As advised in *Bhagavad-gītā* if one transcends these four processes and is actually liberated, one engages in devotional service. Then he is guaranteed not to fall to material existence again.

TEXT 53

यथा त्रिवर्गं गुरुभिरात्मने उपशिक्षितम् ।
न साधु मेने तच्छिक्षां द्वन्द्वारामोपवर्णिताम् ॥५३॥

yathā tri-vargaṁ gurubhir
ātmane upaśikṣitam
na sādhu mene tac-chikṣāṁ
dvandvārāmopavarṇitām

yathā—as; *tri-vargam*—the three processes (religion, economic development and sense gratification); *gurubhiḥ*—by the teachers; *ātmane*—unto himself (Prahlāda Mahārāja); *upaśikṣitam*—instructed; *na*—not; *sādhu*—really good; *mene*—he considered; *tat-śikṣām*—the education in that; *dvandva-ārāma*—by persons taking pleasure in duality (in material enmity and friendship); *upavarṇitām*—which is prescribed.

TRANSLATION

The teachers Ṣaṇḍa and Amarka instructed Prahlāda Mahārāja in the three kinds of material advancement called religion, economic development and sense gratification. Prahlāda, however, being situated above such instructions, did not like them, for such instructions are based on the duality of worldly affairs, which involve one in a materialistic way of life marked by birth, death, old age and disease.

PURPORT

The entire world is interested in the materialistic way of life. Indeed, practically 99.9 percent of the people in the three worlds are uninterested in liberation or spiritual education. Only the devotees of the Lord, headed by such great personalities as Prahlāda Mahārāja and Nārada Muni, are interested in the real education of spiritual life. One cannot understand the principles of religion while staying on the material platform. Therefore one must follow these great personalities. As stated in *Śrīmad-Bhāgavatam* (6.3.20):

svayambhūr nāradaḥ śambhuḥ
kumāraḥ kapilo manuḥ
prahlādo janako bhīṣmo
balir vaiyāsakir vayam

One must follow in the footsteps of such great personalities as Lord Brahmā, Nārada, Lord Śiva, Kapila, Manu, the Kumāras, Prahlāda Mahārāja, Bhīṣma, Janaka, Bali Mahārāja, Śukadeva Gosvāmī and Yamarāja. Those interested in spiritual life should follow Prahlāda Mahārāja in rejecting the education of religion, economic development and sense gratification. One should be interested in spiritual education. Therefore the Kṛṣṇa consciousness movement is spreading all over the world, following in the footsteps of Prahlāda Mahārāja, who did not like any of the materialistic education he received from his teachers.

TEXT 54

यदाचार्यः परावृत्तो गृहमेधीयकर्मसु ।
वयस्यैर्बालकैस्तत्र सोपहूतः कृतक्षणैः ॥५४॥

yadācāryaḥ parāvṛtto
gṛhamedhīya-karmasu
vayasyair bālakais tatra
sopahūtaḥ kṛta-kṣaṇaiḥ

yadā—when; *ācāryaḥ*—the teachers; *parāvṛttaḥ*—became engaged; *gṛha-medhīya*—of household life; *karmasu*—in duties; *vayasyaiḥ*—by his friends of the same age; *bālakaiḥ*—boys; *tatra*—there; *saḥ*—he (Prahlāda Mahārāja); *apahūtaḥ*—called; *kṛta-kṣaṇaiḥ*—obtaining an opportune moment.

TRANSLATION

When the teachers went home to attend to their household affairs, the students of the same age as Prahlāda Mahārāja would call him to take the opportunity of leisure hours for play.

PURPORT

In tiffin hours, the hours when the teachers were absent from the classroom, the students called Prahlāda Mahārāja, wanting to play with him. As will be seen from the following verses, however, Prahlāda Mahārāja was not very much interested in playing. Instead, he wanted to utilize every moment for advancing in Kṛṣṇa consciousness. Therefore, as indicated in this verse by the word *kṛta-kṣaṇaiḥ*, at the opportune moment when it was possible to preach about Kṛṣṇa consciousness, Prahlāda Mahārāja used the time as follows.

TEXT 55

अथ ताञ् श्लक्ष्णया वाचा प्रत्याहूय महाबुधः ।
उवाच विद्वांस्तन्निष्ठां कृपया प्रहसन्निव ॥५५॥

atha tāñ ślakṣṇayā vācā
pratyāhūya mahā-budhaḥ
uvāca vidvāṁs tan-niṣṭhāṁ
kṛpayā prahasann iva

atha—then; *tān*—the class friends; *ślakṣṇayā*—with very pleasing; *vācā*—speech; *pratyāhūya*—addressing; *mahā-budhaḥ*—Prahlāda Mahārāja, who was highly learned and advanced in spiritual consciousness (*mahā* means "great," and *budha* means "learned"); *uvāca*—said; *vidvān*—very learned; *tat-niṣṭhām*—the path of God realization; *kṛpayā*—being merciful; *prahasan*—smiling; *iva*—like.

TRANSLATION

Prahlāda Mahārāja, who was truly the supreme learned person, then addressed his class friends in very sweet language. Smiling,

he began to teach them about the uselessness of the materialistic way of life. Being very kind to them, he instructed them as follows.

PURPORT

Prahlāda Mahārāja's smiling is very significant. The other students were very much advanced in enjoying materialistic life through religion, economic development and sense gratification, but Prahlāda Mahārāja laughed at them, knowing that this was not actual happiness, for real happiness is advancement in Kṛṣṇa consciousness. The duty of those who follow in the footsteps of Prahlāda Mahārāja is to teach the entire world how to be Kṛṣṇa conscious and thus be really happy. Materialistic persons take to so-called religion to get some blessings so that they can improve their economic position and enjoy the material world through sense gratification. But devotees like Prahlāda Mahārāja laugh at how foolish they are to be busy in a temporary life without knowledge of the soul's transmigration from one body to another. Materialistic persons are engaged in striving for temporary benefits, whereas persons advanced in spiritual knowledge, such as Prahlāda Mahārāja, are not interested in the materialistic way of life. Instead, they want to be elevated to an eternal life of knowlege and bliss. Therefore, as Kṛṣṇa is always compassionate to the fallen souls, His servants, the devotees of Lord Kṛṣṇa, are also interested in educating the entire populace in Kṛṣṇa consciousness. The mistake of materialistic life is understood by devotees, and therefore they smile upon it, considering it insignificant. Out of compassion, however, such devotees preach the gospel of *Bhagavad-gītā* all over the world.

TEXTS 56–57

ते तु तद्गौरवात्सर्वे त्यक्तक्रीडापरिच्छदाः ।
बाला अदूषितधियो द्वन्द्वारामेरितेहितैः ॥५६॥
पर्युपासत राजेन्द्र तन्न्यस्तहृदयेक्षणाः ।
तानाह करुणो मैत्रो महाभागवतोऽसुरः ॥५७॥

te tu tad-gauravāt sarve
tyakta-krīḍā-paricchadāḥ

bālā adūṣita-dhiyo
dvandvārāmeritehitaiḥ

paryupāsata rājendra
tan-nyasta-hṛdayekṣaṇāḥ
tān āha karuṇo maitro
mahā-bhāgavato 'suraḥ

te—they; *tu*—indeed; *tat-gauravāt*—from great respect for the words of Prahlāda Mahārāja (due to his being a devotee); *sarve*—all of them; *tyakta*—having given up; *krīḍā-paricchadāḥ*—toys for playing; *bālāḥ*—the boys; *adūṣita-dhiyaḥ*—whose intelligence was not as polluted (as that of their fathers); *dvandva*—in duality; *ārāma*—of those taking pleasure (the instructors, namely Ṣaṇḍa and Amarka); *īrita*—by the instructions; *īhitaiḥ*—and actions; *paryupāsata*—sat down around; *rāja-indra*—O King Yudhiṣṭhira; *tat*—unto him; *nyasta*—having given up; *hṛdaya-īkṣaṇāḥ*—their hearts and eyes; *tān*—unto them; *āha*—spoke; *karuṇaḥ*—very merciful; *maitraḥ*—a real friend; *mahā-bhāgavataḥ*—a most exalted devotee; *asuraḥ*—Prahlāda Mahārāja, although born of an *asura* father.

TRANSLATION

My dear King Yudhiṣṭhira, all the children were very much affectionate and respectful to Prahlāda Mahārāja, and because of their tender age they were not so polluted by the instructions and actions of their teachers, who were attached to condemned duality and bodily comfort. Thus the boys surrounded Prahlāda Mahārāja, giving up their playthings, and sat down to hear him. Their hearts and eyes being fixed upon him, they looked at him with great earnestness. Prahlāda Mahārāja, although born in a demon family, was an exalted devotee, and he desired their welfare. Thus he began instructing them about the futility of materialistic life.

PURPORT

The words *bālā adūṣita-dhiyaḥ* indicate that the children, being of a tender age, were not as polluted by materialistic life as their fathers.

Prahlāda Mahārāja, therefore, taking advantage of the innocence of his class friends, began teaching them about the importance of spiritual life and the insignificance of materialistic life. Although the teachers Ṣaṇḍa and Amarka were instructing all the boys in the materialistic life of religion, economic development and sense gratification, the boys were not much polluted. Therefore, with great attention they wanted to hear from Prahlāda Mahārāja about Kṛṣṇa consciousness. In our Kṛṣṇa consciousness movement, the *guru-kula* plays an extremely important part in our activities because right from childhood the boys at the *guru-kula* are instructed about Kṛṣṇa consciousness. Thus they become steady within the cores of their hearts, and there is very little possibility that they will be conquered by the modes of material nature when they are older.

Thus end the Bhaktivedanta purports of the Seventh Canto, Fifth Chapter, of the Śrīmad-Bhāgavatam, *entitled "Prahlāda Mahārāja, the Saintly Son of Hiraṇyakaśipu."*

CHAPTER SIX

Prahlāda Instructs His Demoniac Schoolmates

This chapter describes Prahlāda Mahārāja's instructions to his class friends. In speaking to his friends, who were all sons of demons, Prahlāda Mahārāja stressed that every living entity, especially in human society, must be interested in spiritual realization from the very beginning of life. When human beings are children, they should be taught that the Supreme Personality of Godhead is the worshipable Deity for everyone. One should not be very much interested in material enjoyment; instead, one should be satisfied with whatever material profits are easily obtainable, and because the duration of one's life is very short, one should utilize every moment for spiritual advancement. One may wrongly think, "In the beginning of our lives let us enjoy material facilities, and in old age we may become Kṛṣṇa conscious." Such materialistic thoughts are always useless because in old age one cannot be trained in the spiritual way of life. Therefore, from the very beginning of life, one should engage in devotional service (*śravaṇaṁ kīrtanaṁ viṣṇoḥ*). This is the duty of all living entities. Material education is infected by the three modes of nature, but spiritual education, for which there is a great need in human society, is transcendental. Prahlāda Mahārāja disclosed the secret of how he had received instructions from Nārada Muni. By accepting the lotus feet of Prahlāda Mahārāja, who is in the *paramparā* succession, one will be able to understand the mode of spiritual life. In accepting this mode of activity, there is no need for material qualifications.

After Prahlāda Mahārāja's class friends had listened to Prahlāda Mahārāja, they inquired how he had become so learned and advanced. In this way the chapter ends.

TEXT 1

श्रीप्रह्राद उवाच

कौमार आचरेत्प्राज्ञो धर्मान् भागवतानिह ।
दुर्लभं मानुषं जन्म तदप्यध्रुवमर्थदम् ॥ १ ॥

śrī-prahrāda uvāca
kaumāra ācaret prājño
dharmān bhāgavatān iha
durlabhaṁ mānuṣaṁ janma
tad apy adhruvam arthadam

śrī-prahrādaḥ uvāca—Prahlāda Mahārāja said; *kaumāraḥ*—in the tender age of childhood; *ācaret*—should practice; *prājñaḥ*—one who is intelligent; *dharmān*—occupational duties; *bhāgavatān*—which are devotional service to the Supreme Personality of Godhead; *iha*—in this life; *durlabham*—very rarely obtained; *mānuṣam*—human; *janma*—birth; *tat*—that; *api*—even; *adhruvam*—impermanent, temporary; *artha-dam*—full of meaning.

TRANSLATION

Prahlāda Mahārāja said: One who is sufficiently intelligent should use the human form of body from the very beginning of life—in other words, from the tender age of childhood—to practice the activities of devotional service, giving up all other engagements. The human body is most rarely achieved, and although temporary like other bodies, it is meaningful because in human life one can perform devotional service. Even a slight amount of sincere devotional service can give one complete perfection.

PURPORT

The whole purpose of Vedic civilization and of reading the *Vedas* is to attain the perfect stage of devotional service in the human form of life. According to the Vedic system, therefore, from the very beginning of life the *brahmacarya* system is introduced so that from one's very childhood—from the age of five years—one can practice modifying one's human activities so as to engage perfectly in devotional service. As confirmed in *Bhagavad-gītā* (2.40), *svalpam apy asya dharmasya trāyate mahato bhayāt:* "Even a little advancement on this path can protect one from the most dangerous type of fear." Modern civilization, not referring to the verdicts of Vedic literature, is so cruel to the members of human society that instead of teaching children to become *brahmacārīs*, it teaches mothers to kill their children even in the womb, on the plea of curbing the increase of population. And if by chance a child is saved, he is educated only for sense gratification. Gradually, throughout the entire world, human society is losing interest in the perfection of life. Indeed, men are living like cats and dogs, spoiling the duration of their human lives by actually preparing to transmigrate again to the degraded species among the 8,400,000 forms of life. The Kṛṣṇa consciousness movement is anxious to serve human society by teaching people to perform devotional service, which can save a human being from being degraded again to animal life. As already stated by Prahlāda Mahārāja, *bhāgavata-dharma* consists of *śravaṇaṁ kīrtanaṁ viṣṇoḥ smaraṇaṁ pāda-sevanam/ arcanaṁ vandanaṁ dāsyaṁ sakhyam ātma-nivedanam.* In all the schools, colleges and universities, and at home, all children and youths should be taught to hear about the Supreme Personality of Godhead. In other words, they should be taught to hear the instructions of *Bhagavad-gītā*, to put them into practice in their lives, and thus to become strong in devotional service, free from fear of being degraded to animal life. Following *bhāgavata-dharma* has been made extremely easy in this age of Kali. The *śāstra* says:

harer nāma harer nāma
harer nāmaiva kevalam
kalau nāsty eva nāsty eva
nāsty eva gatir anyathā

One need only chant the Hare Kṛṣṇa *mahā-mantra.* Everyone engaged in the practice of chanting the Hare Kṛṣṇa *mahā-mantra* will be completely cleansed, from the core of his heart, and be saved from the cycle of birth and death.

TEXT 2

यथा हि पुरुषस्येह विष्णोः पादोपसर्पणम् ।
यदेष सर्वभूतानां प्रिय आत्मेश्वरः सुहृत् ॥ २ ॥

yathā hi puruṣasyeha
viṣṇoḥ pādopasarpaṇam

yad eṣa sarva-bhūtānāṁ
priya ātmeśvaraḥ suhṛt

yathā—in order that; *hi*—indeed; *puruṣasya*—of a living entity; *iha*—here; *viṣṇoḥ*—of Lord Viṣṇu, the Supreme Personality of Godhead; *pāda-upasarpaṇam*—approaching the lotus feet; *yat*—because; *eṣaḥ*—this; *sarva-bhūtānām*—of all living entities; *priyaḥ*—the dear one; *ātma-īśvaraḥ*—the master of the soul, the Supersoul; *suhṛt*—the best well-wisher and friend.

TRANSLATION

The human form of life affords one a chance to return home, back to Godhead. Therefore every living entity, especially in the human form of life, must engage in devotional service to the lotus feet of Lord Viṣṇu. This devotional service is natural because Lord Viṣṇu, the Supreme Personality of Godhead, is the most beloved, the master of the soul, and the well-wisher of all other living beings.

PURPORT

The Lord says in *Bhagavad-gītā* (5.29):

bhoktāraṁ yajña-tapasāṁ
sarva-loka-maheśvaram
suhṛdaṁ sarva-bhūtānāṁ
jñātvā māṁ śāntim ṛcchati

"The sages, knowing Me as the ultimate purpose of all sacrifices and austerities, the Supreme Lord of all planets and demigods and the benefactor and well-wisher of all living entities, attain peace from the pangs of material miseries." Simply by understanding these three facts—that the Supreme Lord, Viṣṇu, is the proprietor of the entire creation, that He is the best well-wishing friend of all living entities, and that He is the supreme enjoyer of everything—one becomes peaceful and happy. For this transcendental happiness, the living entity has wandered throughout the universe in different forms of life and different planetary systems, but because he has forgotten his intimate relationship with Viṣṇu, he has merely suffered, life after life. Therefore, the educational system in the human form of life should be so perfect that one will understand his intimate relationship with God, or Viṣṇu. Every living entity has an intimate relationship with God. One should therefore glorify the Lord in the adoration of *śānta-rasa* or revive his eternal relationship with Viṣṇu as a servant in *dāsya-rasa,* a friend in *sakhya-rasa,* a parent in *vātsalya-rasa* or a conjugal lover in *mādhurya-rasa.* All these relationships are on the platform of love. Viṣṇu is the center of love for everyone, and therefore the duty of everyone is to engage in the loving service of the Lord. As stated by the Supreme Personality of Godhead (*Bhāg.* 3.25.38), *yeṣām ahaṁ priya ātmā sutaś ca sakhā guruḥ suhṛdo daivam iṣṭam.* In any form of life, we are related with Viṣṇu, who is the most beloved, the Supersoul, son, friend and *guru.* Our eternal relationship with God can be revived in the human form of life, and that should be the goal of education. Indeed, that is the perfection of life and the perfection of education.

TEXT 3

सुखमैन्द्रियकं दैत्या देहयोगेन देहिनाम् ।
सर्वत्र लभ्यते दैवाद्यथा दुःखमयत्नतः ॥ ३ ॥

sukham aindriyakaṁ daityā
deha-yogena dehinām
sarvatra labhyate daivād
yathā duḥkham ayatnataḥ

sukham—happiness; *aindriyakam*—with reference to the material senses; *daityāḥ*—O my dear friends born in demoniac families; *deha-yogena*—because of possessing a particular type of material body; *dehinām*—of all embodied living entities; *sarvatra*—everywhere (in any form of life); *labhyate*—is obtainable; *daivāt*—by a superior arrangement; *yathā*—just as; *duḥkham*—unhappiness; *ayatnataḥ*—without endeavor.

TRANSLATION

Prahlāda Mahārāja continued: My dear friends born of demoniac families, the happiness perceived with reference to the

sense objects by contact with the body can be obtained in any form of life, according to one's past fruitive activities. Such happiness is automatically obtained without endeavor, just as we obtain distress.

PURPORT

In the material world, in any form of life, there is some so-called happiness and so-called distress. No one invites distress in order to suffer, but still it comes. Similarly, even if we do not endeavor to obtain the advantages of material happiness, we shall obtain them automatically. This happiness and distress are obtainable in any form of life, without endeavor. Thus there is no need to waste time and energy fighting against distress or working very hard for happiness. Our only business in the human form of life should be to revive our relationship with the Supreme Personality of Godhead and thus become qualified to return home, back to Godhead. Material happiness and distress come as soon as we accept a material body, regardless of what form. We cannot avoid such happiness and distress under any circumstances. The best use of human life, therefore, lies in reviving our relationship with the Supreme Lord, Viṣṇu.

TEXT 4

तत्प्रयासो न कर्तव्यो यत आयुर्व्ययः परम् ।
न तथा विन्दते क्षेमं मुकुन्दचरणाम्बुजम् ॥ ४ ॥

tat-prayāso na kartavyo
yata āyur-vyayaḥ param
na tathā vindate kṣemaṁ
mukunda-caraṇāmbujam

tat—for that (sense gratification and economic development); *prayāsaḥ*—endeavor; *na*—not; *kartavyaḥ*—to be done; *yataḥ*—from which; *āyuḥ-vyayaḥ*—waste of the duration of life; *param*—only or ultimately; *na*—nor; *tathā*—in that way; *vindate*—enjoys; *kṣemam*—the ultimate goal of life; *mukunda*—of the Supreme Personality of Godhead, who can deliver one from the material clutches; *caraṇa-ambu-jam*—the lotus feet.

TRANSLATION

Endeavors merely for sense gratification or material happiness through economic development are not to be performed, for they result only in a loss of time and energy, with no actual profit. If one's endeavors are directed toward Kṛṣṇa consciousness, one can surely attain the spiritual platform of self-realization. There is no such benefit from engaging oneself in economic development.

PURPORT

We see materialistic persons busily engaged in economic development all day and all night, trying to increase their material opulence, but even if we suppose that they get some benefit from such endeavors, that does not solve the real problem of their lives. Nor do they know what the real problem of life is. This is due to a lack of spiritual education. Especially in the present age, every man is in darkness, in the bodily conception of life, not knowing anything of the spirit soul and its needs. Misguided by the blind leaders of society, people consider the body to be everything, and they are engaged in trying to keep the body materially comfortable. Such a civilization is condemned because it does not lead humanity toward knowing the real goal of life. People are simply wasting time and the valuable gift of the human form because a human being who does not cultivate spiritual life but dies like the cats and dogs is degraded in his next life. From human life, such a person is put into the cycle of continuous birth and death. Thus one loses the true benefit of human life, which is to become Kṛṣṇa conscious and solve life's problems.

TEXT 5

ततो यतेत कुशलः क्षेमाय भवमाश्रितः ।
शरीरं पौरुषं यावन्न विपद्येत पुष्कलम् ॥ ५ ॥

tato yateta kuśalaḥ
kṣemāya bhavam āśritaḥ

śarīraṁ pauruṣaṁ yāvan
na vipadyeta puṣkalam

tataḥ—therefore; *yateta*—should endeavor; *kuśalaḥ*—an intelligent man interested in the ultimate goal of life; *kṣemāya*—for the real benefit of life, or for liberation from material bondage; *bhavam āśritaḥ*—who is in material existence; *śarīram*—the body; *pauruṣam*—human; *yāvat*—as long as; *na*—not; *vipadyeta*—fails; *puṣkalam*—stout and strong.

TRANSLATION

Therefore, while in material existence [bhavam āśritaḥ], a person fully competent to distinguish wrong from right must endeavor to achieve the highest goal of life as long as the body is stout and strong and is not embarrassed by dwindling.

PURPORT

As stated by Prahlāda Mahārāja at the beginning of this chapter, *kaumāra ācaret prājñaḥ.* The word *prājña* refers to one who is experienced and who can distinguish right from wrong. Such a person should not waste his energy and valuable human lifetime simply working like a cat or dog to develop his economic condition.

For one word in this verse there are two readings—*bhavam āśritaḥ* and *bhayam āśritaḥ*—but accepting the meaning of either of them will bring one to the same conclusion. *Bhayam āśritaḥ* indicates that the materialistic way of life is always fearful because at every step there is danger. Materialistic life is full of anxieties and fear (*bhayam*). Similarly, accepting the reading *bhavam āśritaḥ,* the word *bhavam* refers to unnecessary trouble and problems. For want of Kṛṣṇa consciousness, one is put into *bhavam,* being perpetually embarrassed by birth, death, old age and disease. Thus one is surely full of anxieties.

Human society should be divided into a social system of *brāhmaṇas, kṣatriyas, vaiśyas* and *śūdras,* but everyone can engage in devotional service. If one wants to live without devotional service, his status as a *brāhmaṇa, kṣatriya, vaiśya* or *śūdra* certainly has no meaning. It is said, *sthānād bhraṣṭāḥ patanty adhaḥ:* whether one is in a higher or lower division, one certainly falls down for want of Kṛṣṇa consciousness. A sane man, therefore, is always fearful of falling from his position. This is a regulative principle. One should not fall from his exalted position. The highest goal of life can be achieved as long as one's body is stout and strong. We should therefore live in such a way that we keep ourselves always healthy and strong in mind and intelligence so that we can distinguish the goal of life from a life full of problems. A thoughtful man must act in this way, learning to distinguish right from wrong, and thus attain the goal of life.

TEXT 6

पुंसो वर्षशतं ह्यायुस्तदर्धं चाजितात्मनः ।
निष्फलं यदसौ रात्र्यां शेतेऽन्धं प्रापितस्तमः ॥ ६ ॥

puṁso varṣa-śataṁ hy āyus
tad-ardhaṁ cājitātmanaḥ
niṣphalaṁ yad asau rātryāṁ
śete 'ndhaṁ prāpitas tamaḥ

puṁsaḥ—of every human being; *varṣa-śatam*—one hundred years; *hi*—indeed; *āyuḥ*—duration of life; *tat*—of that; *ardham*—half; *ca*—and; *ajita-ātmanaḥ*—of a person who is a servant of his senses; *niṣphalam*—without profit, without meaning; *yat*—because; *asau*—that person; *rātryām*—at night; *śete*—sleeps; *andham*—ignorance (forgetting his body and soul); *prāpitaḥ*—being completely possessed of; *tamaḥ*—darkness.

TRANSLATION

Every human being has a maximum duration of life of one hundred years, but for one who cannot control his senses, half of those years are completely lost because at night he sleeps twelve hours, being covered by ignorance. Therefore such a person has a lifetime of only fifty years.

PURPORT

Lord Brahmā, a human being and an ant all live for one hundred years, but their lifetimes of one hundred years are different from one another. This world is a relative world, and its relative moments of time are different. Thus the one hundred years of Brahmā are not the same as the one hundred years of a human being. From *Bhagavad-gītā* we understand that Brahmā's daytime of twelve hours equals 4,300,000 times 1,000 years (*sahasra-yuga-paryantam ahar yad brahmaṇo viduḥ*). Thus the *varṣa-śatam*, or one hundred years, are relatively different according to time, person and circumstances. As far as human beings are concerned, the calculation given here is right for the general public. Although one has a maximum of one hundred years of life, by sleeping one loses fifty years. Eating, sleeping, sex life and fear are the four bodily necessities, but to utilize the full duration of life a person desiring to advance in spiritual consciousness must reduce these activities. That will give him an opportunity to fully use his lifetime.

TEXT 7

मुग्धस्य बाल्ये कैशोरे क्रीडतो याति विंशतिः ।
जरया ग्रस्तदेहस्य यात्यकल्पस्य विंशतिः ॥ ७ ॥

mugdhasya bālye kaiśore
krīḍato yāti viṁśatiḥ
jarayā grasta-dehasya
yāty akalpasya viṁśatiḥ

mugdhasya—of a person bewildered or not in perfect knowledge; *bālye*—in childhood; *kaiśore*—in boyhood; *krīḍataḥ*—playing; *yāti*—passes; *viṁśatiḥ*—twenty years; *jarayā*—by invalidity; *grasta-dehasya*—of a person overcome; *yāti*—passes; *akalpasya*—without determination, being unable to execute even material activities; *viṁśatiḥ*—another twenty years.

TRANSLATION

In the tender age of childhood, when everyone is bewildered, one passes ten years. Similarly, in boyhood, engaged in sporting and playing, one passes another ten years. In this way, twenty years are wasted. Similarly, in old age, when one is an invalid, unable to

perform even material activities, one passes another twenty years wastefully.

PURPORT

Without Kṛṣṇa consciousness, one wastes twenty years in childhood and boyhood and another twenty years in old age, when one cannot perform any material activities and is full of anxiety about what is to be done by his sons and grandsons and how one's estate should be protected. Half of these years are spent in sleep. Furthermore, one wastes another thirty years sleeping at night during the rest of his life. Thus seventy out of one hundred years are wasted by a person who does not know the aim of life and how to utilize this human form.

TEXT 8

दुरापूरेण कामेन मोहेन च बलीयसा ।
शेषं गृहेषु सक्तस्य प्रमत्तस्यापयाति हि ॥ ८ ॥

durāpūreṇa kāmena
mohena ca balīyasā
śeṣaṁ gṛheṣu saktasya
pramattasyāpayāti hi

durāpūreṇa—which is never fulfilled; *kāmena*—by a strong aspiration to enjoy the material world; *mohena*—by bewilderment; *ca*—also; *balīyasā*—which is strong and formidable; *śeṣam*—the remaining years of life; *gṛheṣu*—to family life; *saktasya*—of one who is too attached; *pramattasya*—mad; *apayāti*—wastefully pass; *hi*—indeed.

TRANSLATION

One whose mind and senses are uncontrolled becomes increasingly attached to family life because of insatiable lusty desires and very strong illusion. In such a madman's life, the remaining years are also wasted because even during those years he cannot engage himself in devotional service.

PURPORT

This is the account of one hundred years of life. Although in this age a lifetime of one hundred years is generally not possible, even if one has one hundred years, the calculation is that fifty years are wasted in sleeping, twenty years in childhood and boyhood, and twenty years in invalidity (*jarā-vyādhi*). This leaves only a few more years, but because of too much attachment to household life, those years are also spent with no purpose, without God consciousness. Therefore, one should be trained to be a perfect *brahmacārī* in the beginning of life and then to be perfect in sense control, following the regulative principles, if one becomes a householder. From household life one is ordered to accept *vānaprastha* life and go to the forest and then accept *sannyāsa*. That is the perfection of life. From the very beginning of life, those who are *ajitendriya*, who cannot control their senses, are educated only for sense gratification, as we have seen in the Western countries. Thus the entire duration of a life of even one hundred years is wasted and misused, and at the time of death one transmigrates to another body, which may not be human. At the end of one hundred years, one who has not acted as a human being in a life of *tapasya* (austerity and penance) must certainly be embodied again in a body like those of cats, dogs and hogs. Therefore this life of lusty desires and sense gratification is extremely risky.

TEXT 9

को गृहेषु पुमान्सक्तमात्मानमजितेन्द्रियः ।
स्नेहपाशैर्दृढैर्बद्धमुत्सहेत विमोचितुम् ॥ ९ ॥

ko gṛheṣu pumān saktam
ātmānam ajitendriyaḥ
sneha-pāśair dṛḍhair baddham
utsaheta vimocitum

kaḥ—what; *gṛheṣu*—to household life; *pumān*—man; *saktam*—very much attached; *ātmānam*—his own self, the soul; *ajita-indriyaḥ*—who has not conquered the senses; *sneha-pāśaiḥ*—by the ropes of affection; *dṛḍhaiḥ*—very strong; *baddham*—bound hand and foot; *utsaheta*—is able; *vimocitum*—to liberate from material bondage.

TRANSLATION

What person too attached to household life due to being unable to control his senses can liberate himself? An attached householder is bound very strongly by ropes of affection for his family [wife, children and other relatives].

PURPORT

Prahlāda Mahārāja's first proposal was *kaumāra ācaret prājño dharmān bhāgavatān iha:* "One who is sufficiently intelligent should use the human form of body from the very beginning of life—in other words, from the tender age of childhood—to practice the activities of devotional service, giving up all other engagements." *Dharmān bhāgavatān* means the religious principle of reviving our relationship with the Supreme Personality of Godhead. For this purpose Kṛṣṇa personally advises, *sarva-dharmān parityajya mām ekaṁ śaraṇaṁ vraja:* "Give up all other duties and surrender unto Me." While in the material world we manufacture so many duties in the name of so many isms, but our actual duty is to free ourselves from the cycle of birth, death, old age and disease. For this purpose, one must first be liberated from material bondage, and especially from household life. Household life is actually a kind of license for a materially attached person by which to enjoy sense gratification under regulative principles. Otherwise there is no need of entering household life.

Before entering household life, one should be trained as a *brahmacārī*, living under the care of the *guru*, whose place is known as the *guru-kula*. *Brahmacārī guru-kule vasan dānto guror hitam* (*Bhāg.* 7.12.1). From the very beginning, a *brahmacārī* is trained to sacrifice everything for the benefit of the *guru*. A *brahmacārī* is advised to go begging alms door to door, addressing all women as mother, and whatever he collects goes to the benefit of the *guru*. In this way he learns how to control his senses and sacrifice everything for the *guru*. When he is fully trained, if he likes he is allowed to marry. Thus he is not an ordinary *gṛhastha* who has learned only how to satisfy his senses. A trained *gṛhastha* can gradually give up household life and go to the forest to become increasingly enlightened in spiritual life and at last take *sannyāsa*. Prahlāda Mahārāja explained to his father that to be freed from all material anxieties one should go to the forest. *Hitvātma-pātaṁ gṛham andha-kūpam.* One should give up his household, which is a place for going further and further down into the darkest regions of material existence. The first advice, therefore, is that one must give up household life (*gṛham andha-kūpam*). However, if one prefers to remain in the dark well of household life because of uncontrolled senses, he becomes increasingly entangled by ropes of affection for his wife, children, servants, house, money and so on. Such a person cannot attain liberation from material bondage. Therefore children should be taught from the very beginning of life to be first-class *brahmacārīs.* Then it will be possible for them to give up household life in the future.

To return home, back to Godhead, one must be completely free from material attachment. Therefore, *bhakti-yoga* means *vairāgya-vidyā,* the art that can help one develop a distaste for material enjoyment.

vāsudeve bhagavati
bhakti-yogaḥ prayojitaḥ
janayaty āśu vairāgyaṁ
jñānaṁ ca yad ahaitukam

"By rendering devotional service unto the Personality of Godhead, Śrī Kṛṣṇa, one immediately acquires causeless knowledge and detachment from the world." (*Bhāg.* 1.2.7) If one engages in devotional service from the beginning of life, he easily attains *vairāgya-vidyā,* or *asakti,* detachment, and becomes *jitendriya,* the controller of his senses. One who perfectly engages in devotional service is therefore called *gosvāmī* or *svāmī,* master of the senses. Unless one is master of the senses, he should not accept the renounced order of life, *sannyāsa.* A strong inclination for sense enjoyment is the cause of the material body. Without full knowledge one cannot be unattached to material enjoyment, but as long as one is not in that position one is not fit to return home, back to Godhead.

TEXT 10

को न्वर्थतृष्णां विसृजेत् प्राणेभ्योऽपि य ईप्सितः ।
यं क्रीणात्यसुभिः प्रेष्ठैस्तस्करः सेवको वणिक् ॥१०॥

ko nv artha-tṛṣṇāṁ visṛjet
prāṇebhyo 'pi ya īpsitaḥ
yaṁ krīṇāty asubhiḥ preṣṭhais
taskaraḥ sevako vaṇik

kaḥ—who; *nu*—indeed; *artha-tṛṣṇām*—a strong desire to acquire money; *visṛjet*—can give up; *prāṇebhyaḥ*—than life; *api*—indeed; *yaḥ*—which; *īpsitaḥ*—more desired; *yam*—which; *krīṇāti*—tries to acquire; *asubhiḥ*—with his own life; *preṣṭhaiḥ*—very dear; *taskaraḥ*—a thief; *sevakaḥ*—a professional servant; *vaṇik*—a merchant.

TRANSLATION

Money is so dear that one conceives of money as being sweeter than honey. Therefore, who can give up the desire to accumulate money, especially in household life? Thieves, professional servants [soldiers] and merchants try to acquire money even by risking their very dear lives.

PURPORT

How money can be dearer than life is indicated in this verse. Thieves may enter the house of a rich man to steal money at the risk of their lives. Because of trespassing, they may be killed by guns or attacked by watchdogs, but still they try to commit burglary. Why do they risk their lives? Only to get some money. Similarly, a professional soldier is recruited into the army, and he accepts such service, with the risk of dying on the battlefield, only for the sake of money. In the same way, merchants go from one country to another on boats at the risk of their lives, or they dive into the water of the sea to collect pearls and valuable gems. Thus it is practically proved—and everyone will admit—that money is sweeter than honey. One may risk everything to acquire money, and this is especially true of rich men who are too attached to household life. Formerly, of course, the members of the higher castes—the *brāhmaṇas, kṣatriyas* and *vaiśyas* (everyone but the *śūdras*)—were trained in the *guru-kula* to adhere to a life of renunciation and sense control by practicing *brahmacarya* and mystic *yoga.* Then they were allowed to enter household life. There have consequently been many instances in which great kings and emperors have given up household life. Although they were extremely opulent and were the masters of kingdoms, they could give up all their possessions because they were trained early as *brahmacārīs*. Prahlāda Mahārāja's advice is therefore very appropriate:

kaumāra ācaret prājño
dharmān bhāgavatān iha
durlabhaṁ mānuṣaṁ janma
tad apy adhruvam arthadam

"One who is sufficiently intelligent should use the human form of body from the very beginning of life—in other words, from the tender age of childhood—to practice the activities of devotional service, giving up all other engagements. The human body is most rarely achieved, and although temporary like other bodies, it is meaningful because in human life one can perform devotional service. Even a slight amount of sincere devotional service can give one complete perfection." Human society should take advantage of this instruction.

TEXTS 11–13

कथं प्रियाया अनुकम्पितायाः
सङ्गं रहस्यं रुचिरांश्च मन्त्रान् ।
सुहृत्सु तत्स्नेहसितः शिशूनां
कलाक्षराणामनुरक्तचित्तः ॥११॥
पुत्रान्स्मरंस्ता दुहितॄर्हृदय्या
भ्रातॄन् स्वसॄर्वा पितरौ च दीनौ ।
गृहान् मनोज्ञोरुपरिच्छदांश्च
वृत्तीश्च कुल्याः पशुभृत्यवर्गान् ॥१२॥
त्यजेत कोशस्कृदिवेहमानः
कर्माणि लोभादवितृप्तकामः ।
औपस्थ्यजैह्वं बहुमन्यमानः
कथं विरज्येत दुरन्तमोहः ॥१३॥

kathaṁ priyāyā anukampitāyāḥ
saṅgaṁ rahasyaṁ rucirāṁś ca mantrān
suhṛtsu tat-sneha-sitaḥ śiśūnāṁ
kalākṣarāṇām anurakta-cittaḥ

putrān smaraṁs tā duhitṝr hṛdayyā
bhrātṝn svasṝr vā pitarau ca dīnau
gṛhān manojñoru-paricchadāṁś ca
vṛttīś ca kulyāḥ paśu-bhṛtya-vargān

tyajeta kośas-kṛd ivehamānaḥ
karmāṇi lobhād avitṛpta-kāmaḥ
aupasthya-jaihvaṁ bahu-manyamānaḥ
kathaṁ virajyeta duranta-mohaḥ

katham—how; *priyāyāḥ*—of the dearmost wife; *anukampitāyāḥ*—always affectionate and compassionate; *saṅgam*—the association; *rahasyam*—solitary; *rucirān*—very pleasing and acceptable; *ca*—and; *mantrān*—instructions; *suhṛtsu*—to the wife and children; *tat-sneha-sitaḥ*—being bound by their affection; *śiśūnām*—to the small children; *kala-akṣarāṇām*—speaking in broken language; *anurakta-cittaḥ*—a person whose mind is attracted; *putrān*—the sons; *smaran*—thinking of; *tāḥ*—them; *duhitṝḥ*—the daughters (married and staying at the homes of their husbands); *hṛdayyāḥ*—always situated in the core of the heart; *bhrātṝn*—the brothers; *svasṝḥ vā*—or the sisters; *pitarau*—father and mother; *ca*—and; *dīnau*—who in old age are mostly invalids; *gṛhān*—household affairs; *manojña*—very attractive; *uru*—much; *paricchadān*—furniture; *ca*—and; *vṛttīḥ*—big sources of income (industry, business); *ca*—and; *kulyāḥ*—connected with the family; *paśu*—of animals (cows, elephants and other household animals); *bhṛtya*—servants and maidservants; *vargān*—groups; *tyajeta*—can give up; *kośaḥ-kṛt*—the silkworm; *iva*—like; *īhamānaḥ*—performing; *karmāṇi*—different activities; *lobhāt*—because of insatiable desires; *avitṛpta-kāmaḥ*—whose increasing desires are not satisfied; *aupasthya*—pleasure from the genitals; *jaihvam*—and the tongue; *bahu-manyamānaḥ*—considering as very important; *katham*—how; *virajyeta*—is able to give up; *duranta-mohaḥ*—being in great illusion.

TRANSLATION

How can a person who is most affectionate to his family, the core of his heart being always filled with their pictures, give up their association? Specifically, a wife is always very kind and sympathetic and always pleases her husband in a solitary place. Who could give up the association of such a dear and affectionate wife? Small children talk in broken language, very pleasing to hear, and their affectionate father always thinks of their sweet words. How could he give up their association? One's elderly parents and one's sons and daughters are also very dear. A daughter is especially dear to her father, and while living at her husband's house she is always in his mind. Who could give up that association? Aside from this, in household affairs there are many decorated items of household furniture, and there are also animals and servants. Who could give up such comforts? The attached householder is like a silkworm, which weaves a cocoon in which it becomes imprisoned, unable to get out. Simply for the satisfaction of two important senses—the genitals and the tongue—one is bound by material conditions. How can one escape?

PURPORT

In household affairs the first attraction is the beautiful and pleasing wife, who increases household attraction more and more. One enjoys his wife with two prominent sense organs, namely the tongue and the genitals. The wife speaks very sweetly. This is certainly an attraction. Then she prepares very palatable foods to satisfy the tongue, and when the tongue is satisfied one gains strength in the other sense organs, especially the genitals. Thus the wife gives pleasure in sexual intercourse. Household life means sex life (*yan maithunādi-gṛhamedhi-sukhaṁ hi tuccham*). This is encouraged by the tongue. Then there are children. A baby gives pleasure by speaking sweet words in broken language, and when the sons and daughters are grown up one becomes involved in their education and marriage. Then there are one's own father and mother to be taken care of, and one also becomes concerned with the social atmosphere and with pleasing his brothers and sisters. A man becomes increasingly entangled in household affairs, so much so that leaving them becomes almost impossible. Thus the household becomes *gṛham andha-kūpam,* a dark well into which the man has fallen. For such a man to get out is extremely difficult unless he is helped by a strong person, the spiritual master, who helps the fallen person with the strong rope of spiritual instructions. A fallen person should take advantage of this rope, and then the spiritual master, or the Supreme Personality of Godhead, Kṛṣṇa, will take him out of the dark well.

TEXT 14

कुटुम्बपोषाय वियन् निजायु-
र्न बुध्यतेऽर्थं विहतं प्रमत्तः ।
सर्वत्र तापत्रयदुःखितात्मा
निर्विद्यते न स्वकुटुम्बरामः ॥१४॥

kuṭumba-poṣāya viyan nijāyur
na budhyate 'rthaṁ vihataṁ pramattaḥ
sarvatra tāpa-traya-duḥkhitātmā
nirvidyate na sva-kuṭumba-rāmaḥ

kuṭumba—of family members; *poṣāya*—for the maintenance; *viyat*—declining; *nija-āyuḥ*—his lifetime; *na*—not; *budhyate*—understands; *artham*—the interest or purpose of life; *vihatam*—spoiled; *pramattaḥ*—being mad in material conditions; *sarvatra*—everywhere; *tāpa-traya*—by the threefold miserable conditions (*adhyātmika, adhidaivika* and *adhibautika*); *duḥkhita*—being distressed; *ātmā*—himself; *nirvidyate*—becomes remorseful; *na*—not; *sva-kuṭumba-rāmaḥ*—enjoying simply by maintaining the members of the family.

TRANSLATION

One who is too attached cannot understand that he is wasting his valuable life for the maintenance of his family. He also fails to understand that the purpose of human life, a life suitable for realization of the Absolute Truth, is being imperceptibly spoiled. However, he is very cleverly attentive to seeing that not a single

farthing is lost by mismanagement. Thus although an attached person in material existence always suffers from threefold miseries, he does not develop a distaste for the way of material existence.

PURPORT

A foolish man does not understand the values of human life, nor does he understand how he is wasting his valuable life simply for the maintenance of his family members. He is expert in calculating the loss of pounds, shillings and pence, but he is so foolish that he does not know how much money he is losing, even according to material considerations. Cāṇakya Paṇḍita gives the example that a moment of life cannot be purchased in exchange for millions of dollars. A foolish person, however, wastes such a valuable life without knowing how much he is losing, even according to monetary calculations. Although a materialistic person is expert in calculating costs and doing business, he does not realize that he is misusing his costly life for want of knowledge. Even though such a materialistic person is always suffering threefold miseries, he is not intelligent enough to cease his materialistic way of life.

TEXT 15

वित्तेषु नित्याभिनिविष्टचेता
विद्वांश्च दोषं परवित्तहर्तुः ।
प्रेत्येह वाथाप्यजितेन्द्रियस्त-
दशान्तकामो हरते कुटुम्बी ॥१५॥

vitteṣu nityābhiniviṣṭa-cetā
vidvāṁś ca doṣaṁ para-vitta-hartuḥ
pretyeha vāthāpy ajitendriyas tad
aśānta-kāmo harate kuṭumbī

vitteṣu—in material wealth; *nitya-abhiniviṣṭa-cetāḥ*—whose mind is always absorbed; *vidvān*—having learned; *ca*—also; *doṣam*—the fault; *para-vitta-hartuḥ*—of one who steals the money of others by cheating or by transactions on the black market; *pretya*—after dying; *iha*—in this material world; *vā*—or; *athāpi*—still; *ajita-indriyaḥ*—because of being unable to control the senses; *tat*—that; *aśānta-kāmaḥ*—whose desires are unsatiated; *harate*—steals; *kuṭumbī*—too fond of his family.

TRANSLATION

If a person too attached to the duties of family maintenance is unable to control his senses, the core of his heart is immersed in how to accumulate money. Although he knows that one who takes the wealth of others will be punished by the law of the government, and by the laws of Yamarāja after death, he continues cheating others to acquire money.

PURPORT

Especially in these days, people do not believe in a next life or in the court of Yamarāja and the various punishments of the sinful. But at least one should know that one who cheats others to acquire money will be punished by the laws of the government. Nonetheless, people do not care about the laws of this life or those governing the next. Despite whatever knowledge one has, one cannot stop his sinful activities if he is unable to control his senses.

TEXT 16

विद्वानपीत्थं दनुजाः कुटुम्बं
पुष्णन्स्वलोकाय न कल्पते वै ।
यः स्वीयपारक्यविभिन्नभाव-
स्तमः प्रपद्येत यथा विमूढः ॥१६॥

vidvān apītthaṁ danujāḥ kuṭumbaṁ
puṣṇan sva-lokāya na kalpate vai
yaḥ svīya-pārakya-vibhinna-bhāvas
tamaḥ prapadyeta yathā vimūḍhaḥ

vidvān—knowing (the inconvenience of material existence, especially in household life); *api*—although; *ittham*—thus; *danu-jāḥ*—O sons of demons; *kuṭumbam*—the family members or extended family members (like one's community, society, nation or union of nations); *puṣṇan*—providing with all the necessities of life; *sva-lokāya*—in understanding himself; *na*—not; *kalpate*—capable; *vai*—indeed; *yaḥ*—he who; *svīya*—my own; *pārakya*—belonging to others; *vibhinna*—separate; *bhāvaḥ*—having a conception of life; *tamaḥ*—nothing but darkness; *prapadyeta*—enters; *yathā*—just as; *vimūḍhah*—a person without education, or one who is like an animal.

TRANSLATION

O my friends, sons of demons! In this material world, even those who are apparently advanced in education have the propensity to consider, "This is mine, and that is for others." Thus they are always engaged in providing the necessities of life to their families in a limited conception of family life, just like uneducated cats and dogs. They are unable to take to spiritual knowledge; instead, they are bewildered and overcome by ignorance.

PURPORT

In human society there are attempts to educate the human being, but for animal society there is no such system, nor are animals able to be educated. Therefore animals and unintelligent men are called *vimūḍha*, or ignorant, bewildered, whereas an educated person is called *vidvān*. The real *vidvān* is one who tries to understand his own position within this material world. For example, when Sanātana Gosvāmī submitted to the lotus feet of Śrī Caitanya Mahāprabhu, his first question was *'ke āmi', 'kene āmāya jāre tāpa-traya'*. In other words, he wanted to know his constitutional position and why he was suffering from the threefold miseries of material existence. This is the process of education. If one does not ask, "Who am I? What is the goal of my life?" but instead follows the same animal propensities as cats and dogs, what is the use of his education? As discussed in the previous verse, a living being is entrapped by his fruitive activities, exactly like a silkworm trapped in its own cocoon. Foolish persons are generally encaged by their fruitive actions (*karma*) because of a strong desire to enjoy this material world. Such attracted persons become involved in society, community and nation and waste their time, not having profited from having obtained human forms. Especially in this age, Kali-yuga, great leaders, politicians, philosophers and scientists are all engaged in foolish activities, thinking, "This is mine, and this is yours." The scientists invent nuclear weapons and collaborate with the big leaders to protect the interests of their own nation or society. In this verse, however, it is clearly stated that despite their so-called advanced knowledge, they actually have the same mentality as cats and dogs. As cats, dogs and other animals, not knowing their true interest in life, become increasingly involved in ignorance, the so-called educated person who does not know his own self-interest or the true goal of life becomes increasingly involved in materialism. Therefore Prahlāda Mahārāja advises everyone to follow the principles of *varṇāśrama-dharma.* Specifically, at a certain point one must give up family life and take to the renounced order of life to cultivate spiritual knowledge and thus become liberated. This is further discussed in the following verses.

TEXTS 17–18

यतो न कश्चित् क्व च कुत्रचिद् वा
दीनः स्वमात्मानमलं समर्थः ।
विमोचितुं कामदृशां विहार-
क्रीडामृगो यन्निगडो विसर्गः ॥१७॥
ततो विदूरात् परिहृत्य दैत्या
दैत्येषु सङ्गं विषयात्मकेषु ।
उपेत नारायणमादिदेवं
स मुक्तसङ्गैरिषितोऽपवर्गः ॥१८॥

yato na kaścit kva ca kutracid vā
dīnaḥ svam ātmānam alaṁ samarthaḥ
vimocituṁ kāma-dṛśāṁ vihāra-
krīḍā-mṛgo yan-nigaḍo visargaḥ

tato vidūrāt parihṛtya daityā
daityeṣu saṅgaṁ viṣayātmakeṣu
upeta nārāyaṇam ādi-devaṁ
sa mukta-saṅgair iṣito 'pavargaḥ

yataḥ—because; *na*—never; *kaścit*—anyone; *kva*—in any place; *ca*—also; *kutracit*—at any time; *vā*—or; *dīnaḥ*—having a poor fund of knowledge; *svam*—own; *ātmānam*—self; *alam*—exceedingly; *samarthaḥ*—able; *vimocitum*—to liberate; *kāma-dṛśām*—of lusty women; *vihāra*—in the sexual enjoyment; *krīḍā-mṛgaḥ*—a playboy; *yat*—in whom; *nigaḍaḥ*—which is the shackle of material bondage; *visargaḥ*—the expansions of family relationships; *tataḥ*—in such circumstances; *vidūrāt*—from far away; *parihṛtya*—giving up; *daityāḥ*—O my friends, sons of the demons; *daityeṣu*—among the demons; *saṅgam*—association; *viṣaya-ātma-keṣu*—who are too addicted to sense enjoyment; *upeta*—one should approach; *nārāyaṇam*—Lord Nārāyaṇa, the Supreme Personality of Godhead; *ādi-devam*—the origin of all the demigods; *saḥ*—He; *mukta-saṅgaiḥ*—by the association of liberated persons; *iṣitaḥ*—desired; *apavargaḥ*—the path of liberation.

TRANSLATION

My dear friends, O sons of the demons, it is certain that no one bereft of knowledge of the Supreme Personality of Godhead has been able to liberate himself from material bondage at any time or in any country. Rather, those bereft of knowledge of the Lord are bound by the material laws. They are factually addicted to sense gratification, and their target is woman. Indeed, they are actually playthings in the hands of attractive women. Victimized by such a conception of life, they become surrounded by children, grandchildren and great-grandchildren, and thus they are shackled to material bondage. Those who are very much addicted to this conception of life are called demons. Therefore, although you are sons of demons, keep aloof from such persons and take shelter of the Supreme Personality of Godhead, Nārāyaṇa, the origin of all the demigods, because the ultimate goal for the devotees of Nārāyaṇa is liberation from the bondage of material existence.

PURPORT

Prahlāda Mahārāja has maintained the philosophical point of view that one should give up the dark well of family life and go to the forest to take shelter of the lotus feet of the Supreme Personality of Godhead (*hitvātma-pātaṁ gṛham andha-kūpaṁ vanaṁ gato yad dharim āśrayeta*). In this verse also, he stresses the same point. In the history of human society, no one, at any time or any place, has been liberated because of too much affection and attachment for his family. Even in those who are apparently very educated, the same family attachment is there. They cannot give up the association of their families, even in old age or invalidity, for they are attached to sense enjoyment. As we have several times discussed, *yan maithunādi-gṛhamedhi-sukhaṁ hi tuccham:* so-called householders are simply attracted by sexual enjoyment. Thus they keep themselves shackled in family life, and furthermore they want their children to be shackled in the same way. Playing the parts of playboys in the hands of women, they glide down to the darkest regions of material existence. *Adānta-gobhir viśatāṁ tamisraṁ punaḥ punaś carvita-carvaṇānām.* Because they are unable to control their senses, they continue a life of chewing the chewed and therefore descend to the darkest material regions. One should give up the association of such demons and adhere to the association of devotees. Thus one will be able to be liberated from material bondage.

TEXT 19

न ह्यच्युतं प्रीणयतो बह्वायासोऽसुरात्मजाः ।
आत्मत्वात् सर्वभूतानां सिद्धत्वादिह सर्वतः ॥१९॥

na hy acyutaṁ prīṇayato
bahv-āyāso 'surātmajāḥ
ātmatvāt sarva-bhūtānāṁ
siddhatvād iha sarvataḥ

na—not; *hi*—indeed; *acyutam*—the infallible Supreme Personality of Godhead; *prīṇayataḥ*—satisfying; *bahu*—much; *āyāsaḥ*—endeavor; *asura-ātma-jāḥ*—O sons of demons; *ātmatvāt*—because of being intimately related as the Supersoul; *sarva-bhūtānām*—of all living entities; *siddhatvāt*—because of being established; *iha*—in this world; *sarvataḥ*—in all directions, in all times and from all angles of vision.

TRANSLATION

My dear sons of demons, the Supreme Personality of Godhead, Nārāyaṇa, is the original Supersoul, the father of all living entities.

Consequently there are no impediments to pleasing Him or worshiping Him under any conditions, whether one be a child or an old man. The relationship between the living entities and the Supreme Personality of Godhead is always a fact, and therefore there is no difficulty in pleasing the Lord.

PURPORT

One may ask, "One is certainly very attached to family life, but if one gives up family life to be attached to the service of the Lord, one must undergo the same endeavor and trouble. Therefore, what is the benefit of taking the trouble to engage in the service of the Lord?" This is not a valid objection. The Lord asserts in *Bhagavad-gītā* (14.4):

sarva-yoniṣu kaunteya
mūrtayaḥ sambhavanti yāḥ
tāsāṁ brahma mahad yonir
ahaṁ bīja-pradaḥ pitā

"It should be understood that all species of life, O son of Kuntī, are made possible by birth in this material nature, and that I am the seed-giving father." The Supreme Lord, Nārāyaṇa, is the seed-giving father of all living entities because the living entities are parts and parcels of the Supreme Lord (*mamaivāṁśo . . . jīva-bhūtaḥ*). As there is no difficulty in establishing the intimate relationship between a father and son, there is no difficulty in reestablishing the natural, intimate relationship between Nārāyaṇa and the living entities. *Svalpam apy asya dharmasya trāyate mahato bhayāt:* if one performs even very slight devotional service, Nārāyaṇa is always ready to save one from the greatest danger. The definite example is Ajāmila. Ajāmila separated himself from the Supreme Personality of Godhead by performing many sinful activities and was condemned by Yamarāja to be very severely punished, but because at the time of death he chanted the name of Nārāyaṇa, although he was calling not for the Supreme Lord Nārāyaṇa but for his son named Nārāyaṇa, he was saved from the hands of Yamarāja. Therefore, pleasing Nārāyaṇa does not require as much endeavor as pleasing one's family, community and nation. We have seen important political leaders killed for a slight discrepancy in their behavior. Therefore pleasing one's society, family, community and nation is extremely difficult. Pleasing Nārāyaṇa, however, is not at all difficult; it is very easy.

One's duty is to revive one's relationship with Nārāyaṇa. A slight endeavor in this direction will make the attempt successful, whereas one will never be successful in pleasing his so-called family, society and nation, even if one endeavors to sacrifice his life. The simple endeavor involved in the devotional service of *śravaṇaṁ kīrtanaṁ viṣṇoḥ*, hearing and chanting the holy name of the Lord, can make one successful in pleasing the Supreme Personality of Godhead. Śrī Caitanya Mahāprabhu has therefore bestowed His blessings by saying, *paraṁ vijayate śrī-kṛṣṇa-saṅkīrtanam:* "All glories to Śrī Kṛṣṇa *saṅkīrtana!*" If one wants to derive the actual benefit from this human form, he must take to the chanting of the holy name of the Lord.

TEXTS 20–23

परावरेषु भूतेषु ब्रह्मान्तस्थावरादिषु ।
भौतिकेषु विकारेषु भूतेष्वथ महत्सु च ॥२०॥

गुणेषु गुणसाम्ये च गुणव्यतिकरे तथा ।
एक एव परो ह्यात्मा भगवानीश्वरोऽव्ययः ॥२१॥

प्रत्यगात्मस्वरूपेण दृश्यरूपेण च स्वयम् ।
व्याप्यव्यापकनिर्देश्यो ह्यनिर्देश्योऽविकल्पितः ॥२२॥

केवलानुभवानन्दस्वरूपः परमेश्वरः ।
माययान्तर्हितैश्वर्य ईयते गुणसर्गया ॥२३॥

parāvareṣu bhūteṣu
brahmānta-sthāvarādiṣu
bhautikeṣu vikāreṣu
bhūteṣv atha mahatsu ca

guṇeṣu guṇa-sāmye ca
guṇa-vyatikare tathā

eka eva paro hy ātmā
bhagavān īśvaro 'vyayaḥ

pratyag-ātma-svarūpeṇa
dṛśya-rūpeṇa ca svayam
vyāpya-vyāpaka-nirdeśyo
hy anirdeśyo 'vikalpitaḥ

kevalānubhavānanda-
svarūpaḥ parameśvaraḥ
māyayāntarhitaiśvarya
īyate guṇa-sargayā

para-avareṣu—in exalted or hellish conditions of life; *bhūteṣu*—in the living beings; *brahma-anta*—ending with Lord Brahmā; *sthāvara-ādiṣu*—beginning with the nonmoving forms of life, the trees and plants; *bhautikeṣu*—of the material elements; *vikāreṣu*—in the transformations; *bhūteṣu*—in the five gross elements of material nature; *atha*—moreover; *mahatsu*—in the *mahat-tattva,* the total material energy; *ca*—also; *guṇeṣu*—in the modes of material nature; *guṇa-sāmye*—in an equilibrium of material qualities; *ca*—and; *guṇa-vyatikare*—in the uneven manifestation of the modes of material nature; *tathā*—as well; *ekaḥ*—one; *eva*—only; *paraḥ*—transcendental; *hi*—indeed; *ātmā*—the original source; *bhagavān*—the Supreme Personality of Godhead; *īśvaraḥ*—the controller; *avyayaḥ*—without deteriorating; *pratyak*—inner; *ātma-svarūpeṇa*—by His original constitutional position as the Supersoul; *dṛśya-rūpeṇa*—by His visible forms; *ca*—also; *svayam*—personally; *vyāpya*—pervaded; *vyāpaka*—all-pervading; *nirdeśyaḥ*—to be described; *hi*—certainly; *anirdeśyaḥ*—not to be described (because of fine, subtle existence); *avikalpitaḥ*—without differentiation; *kevala*—only; *anubhava-ānanda-svarūpaḥ*—whose form is blissful and full of knowledge; *parama-īśvaraḥ*—the Supreme Personality of Godhead, the supreme ruler; *māyayā*—by *māyā,* the illusory energy; *antarhita*—covered; *aiśvaryaḥ*—whose unlimited opulence; *īyate*—is mistaken as; *guṇa-sargayā*—the interaction of the material modes of nature.

TRANSLATION

The Supreme Personality of Godhead, the supreme controller, who is infallible and indefatigable, is present in different forms of life, from the inert living beings [sthāvara], such as the plants, to Brahmā, the foremost created living being. He is also present in the varieties of material creations and in the material elements, the total material energy and the modes of material nature [sattva-guṇa, rajo-guṇa and tamo-guṇa], as well as the unmanifested material nature and the false ego. Although He is one, He is present everywhere, and He is also the transcendental Supersoul, the cause of all causes, who is present as the observer in the cores of the hearts of all living entities. He is indicated as that which is pervaded and as the all-pervading Supersoul, but actually He cannot be indicated. He is changeless and undivided. He is simply perceived as the supreme sac-cid-ānanda [eternity, knowledge and bliss]. Being covered by the curtain of the external energy, to the atheist He appears nonexistent.

PURPORT

Not only is the Supreme Personality of Godhead present as the Supersoul of all living entities; at the same time, He pervades everything in the entire creation. He exists in all circumstances and at all times. He exists in the heart of Lord Brahmā and also in the cores of the hearts of the hogs, dogs, trees, plants and so on. He is present everywhere. He is present not only in the heart of the living entity, but also in material things, even in the atoms, protons and electrons being explored by material scientists.

The Lord is present in three features—as Brahman, Paramātmā and Bhagavān. Because He is present everywhere, He is described as *sarvaṁ khalv idaṁ brahma.* Viṣṇu exists beyond Brahman. *Bhagavad-gītā* confirms that Kṛṣṇa, by His Brahman feature, is all-pervading (*mayā tatam idaṁ sarvam*), but Brahman depends upon Kṛṣṇa (*brahmaṇo hi pratiṣṭhāham*). Without Kṛṣṇa, there could be no existence of Brahman or Paramātmā. Therefore, Bhagavān, the Supreme Personality of Godhead, is the ultimate realization of the Absolute Truth. Although He is present as the Paramātmā in the core of everyone's heart, He is nonetheless one, either as an individual or as the all-pervading Brahman.

The supreme cause is Kṛṣṇa, and devotees who have surrendered to the Supreme Personality of Godhead can realize Him and His presence within the universe and within the atom (*aṇḍāntara-stha-paramāṇu-cayāntara-stham*). This realization is possible only for devotees who have fully surrendered unto the lotus feet of the Lord; for others it is not possible. This is confirmed by the Lord Himself in *Bhagavad-gītā* (7.14):

daivī hy eṣā guṇamayī
mama māyā duratyayā
mām eva ye prapadyante
māyām etāṁ taranti te

The process of surrender in a devotional attitude is accepted by a fortunate living being. After wandering through many varieties of life on many planetary systems, when one comes to the real understanding of the Absolute Truth by the grace of a devotee, one surrenders to the Supreme Personality of Godhead, as confirmed in *Bhagavad-gītā* (*bahūnāṁ janmanām ante jñānavān māṁ prapadyate*).

Prahlāda Mahārāja's class friends, who were born of Daitya families, thought that realizing the Absolute was extremely difficult. Indeed, we have experience that many, many people say this very thing. Actually, however, this is not so. The Absolute, the Supreme Personality of Godhead, is most intimately related to all living entities. Therefore if one understands the Vaiṣṇava philosophy, which explains how He is present everywhere and how He acts everywhere, to worship the Supreme Lord or to realize Him is not at all difficult. Realization of the Lord, however, is possible only in the association of devotees. Therefore Śrī Caitanya Mahāprabhu, in His teachings to Rūpa Gosvāmī said (Cc. *Madhya* 19.151):

brahmāṇḍa bhramite kona bhāgyavān jīva
guru-kṛṣṇa-prasāde pāya bhakti-latā-bīja

The living entity in the material condition wanders through many varieties of life and many varieties of circumstances, but if he comes in contact with a pure devotee and is intelligent enough to take instructions from the pure devotee regarding the process of devotional service, he can understand the Supreme Personality of Godhead, the origin of Brahman and Paramātmā, without difficulty. In this regard, Śrīla Madhvācārya says:

antaryāmī pratyag-ātmā
vyāptaḥ kālo hariḥ smṛtaḥ
prakṛtyā tamasāvṛtatvāt
harer aiśvaryaṁ na jñāyate

The Lord is present as *antaryāmī* in everyone's heart and is visible in the individual soul covered by a body. Indeed, He is everywhere at every time and every condition, but because He is covered by the curtain of material energy, to an ordinary person there appears to be no God.

TEXT 24

तस्मात् सर्वेषु भूतेषु दयां कुरुत सौहृदम् ।
भावमासुरमुन्मुच्य यया तुष्यत्यधोक्षजः ॥२४॥

tasmāt sarveṣu bhūteṣu
dayāṁ kuruta sauhṛdam
bhāvam āsuram unmucya
yayā tuṣyaty adhokṣajaḥ

tasmāt—therefore; *sarveṣu*—to all; *bhūteṣu*—living entities; *dayām*—mercy; *kuruta*—show; *sauhṛdam*—friendliness; *bhāvam*—the attitude; *āsuram*—of the demons (who separate friends and enemies); *unmucya*—giving up; *yayā*—by which; *tuṣyati*—is satisfied; *adhokṣajaḥ*—the Supreme Lord, who is beyond the perception of the senses.

TRANSLATION

Therefore, my dear young friends born of demons, please act in such a way that the Supreme Lord, who is beyond the conception of material knowledge, will be satisfied. Give up your demoniac

nature and act without enmity or duality. Show mercy to all living entities by enlightening them in devotional service, thus becoming their well-wishers.

PURPORT

The Lord says in *Bhagavad-gītā* (18.55), *bhaktyā mām abhijānāti yāvān yaś cāsmi tattvataḥ:* "One can understand the Supreme Personality as He is only by devotional service." Prahlāda Mahārāja ultimately instructed his class friends, the sons of the demons, to accept the process of devotional service by preaching the science of Kṛṣṇa consciousness to everyone. Preaching is the best service to the Lord. The Lord will immediately be extremely satisfied with one who engages in this service of preaching Kṛṣṇa consciousness. This is confirmed by the Lord Himself in *Bhagavad-gītā* (18.69). *Na ca tasmān manuṣyeṣu kaścin me priya-kṛttamaḥ:* "There is no servant in this world more dear to Me than he, nor will there ever be one more dear." If one sincerely tries his best to spread Kṛṣṇa consciousness by preaching the glories of the Lord and His supremacy, even if he is imperfectly educated, he becomes the dearmost servant of the Supreme Personality of Godhead. This is *bhakti.* As one performs this service for humanity, without discrimination between friends and enemies, the Lord becomes satisfied, and the mission of one's life is fulfilled. Śrī Caitanya Mahāprabhu therefore advised everyone to become a *guru*-devotee and preach Kṛṣṇa consciousness (*yāre dekha, tāre kaha 'kṛṣṇa'-upadeśa*). That is the easiest way to realize the Supreme Personality of Godhead. By such preaching, the preacher becomes satisfied, and those to whom he preaches are also satisfied. This is the process of bringing peace and tranquility to the entire world.

bhoktāraṁ yajña-tapasāṁ
sarva-loka-maheśvaram
suhṛdaṁ sarva-bhūtānāṁ
jñātvā māṁ śāntim ṛcchati

One is expected to understand these three formulas of knowledge concerning the Supreme Lord—that He is the supreme enjoyer, that He is the proprietor of everything, and that He is the best well-wisher and friend of everyone. A preacher should personally understand these truths and preach them to everyone. Then there will be peace and tranquility all over the world.

The word *sauhṛdam* ("friendliness") is very significant in this verse. People are generally ignorant of Kṛṣṇa consciousness, and therefore to become their best well-wisher one should teach them about Kṛṣṇa consciousness without discrimination. Since the Supreme Lord, Viṣṇu, is situated in the core of everyone's heart, every body is a temple of Viṣṇu. One should not misuse this understanding as an excuse for such words as *daridra-nārāyaṇa.* If Nārāyaṇa lives in the house of a *daridra,* a poor man, this does not mean that Nārāyaṇa becomes poor. He lives everywhere—in the houses of the poor and those of the rich—but in all circumstances He remains Nārāyaṇa; to think that He becomes either poor or rich is a material calculation. He is always *ṣaḍ-aiśvarya-pur̄ṇa,* full in six opulences, in all circumstances.

TEXT 25

तुष्टे च तत्र किमलभ्यमनन्त आद्ये
किं तैर्गुणव्यतिकरादिह ये स्वसिद्धाः ।
धर्मादयः किमगुणेन च काङ्क्षितेन
सारंजुषां चरणयोरुपगायतां नः ॥२५॥

tuṣṭe ca tatra kim alabhyam ananta ādye
kiṁ tair guṇa-vyatikarād iha ye sva-siddhāḥ
dharmādayaḥ kim aguṇena ca kāṅkṣitena
sāraṁ juṣāṁ caraṇayor upagāyatāṁ naḥ

tuṣṭe—when satisfied; *ca*—also; *tatra*—that; *kim*—what; *alabhyam*—unobtainable; *anante*—the Supreme Personality of Godhead; *ādye*—the original source of everything, the cause of all causes; *kim*—what need; *taiḥ*—with them; *guṇa-vyatikarāt*—due to the actions of the modes of material nature; *iha*—in this world; *ye*—which; *sva-siddhāḥ*—automatically achieved; *dharma-ādayaḥ*—the three principles of material advancement, namely religion, economic development and sense gratification; *kim*—what need; *aguṇena*—with liberation into the Supreme; *ca*—and; *kāṅkṣitena*—desired; *sāram*—essence; *juṣām*—

relishing; *caraṇayoḥ*—of the two lotus feet of the Lord; *upagāyatām*—who glorify the qualities of the Lord; *naḥ*—of us.

TRANSLATION

Nothing is unobtainable for devotees who have satisfied the Supreme Personality of Godhead, who is the cause of all causes, the original source of everything. The Lord is the reservoir of unlimited spiritual qualities. For devotees, therefore, who are transcendental to the modes of material nature, what is the use of following the principles of religion, economic development, sense gratification and liberation, which are all automatically obtainable under the influence of the modes of nature? We devotees always glorify the lotus feet of the Lord, and therefore we need not ask for anything in terms of dharma, kāma, artha and mokṣa.

PURPORT

In an advanced civilization, people are eager to be religious, to be economically well situated, to satisfy their senses to the fullest extent, and at last to attain liberation. However, these are not to be magnified as desirable. Indeed, for a devotee these are all very easily available. Bilvamaṅgala Ṭhākura said, *muktiḥ svayaṁ mukulitāñjali sevate 'smān dharmārtha-kāma-gatayaḥ samaya-pratīkṣāḥ.* Liberation always stands at the door of a devotee, ready to carry out his orders. Material advancement in religion, economic development, sense gratification and liberation simply wait to serve a devotee at the first opportunity. A devotee is already in a transcendental position; he does not need further qualifications to be liberated. As confirmed in *Bhagavad-gītā* (14.26), *sa guṇān samatītyaitān brahma-bhūyāya kalpate:* a devotee is transcendental to the actions and reactions of the three modes of material nature because he is situated on the Brahman platform.

Prahlāda Mahārāja said, *aguṇena ca kāṅkṣitena:* if one is engaged in the transcendental loving service of the lotus feet of the Lord, he does not need anything in terms of *dharma, artha, kāma* or *mokṣa.* In *Śrīmad-Bhāgavatam,* therefore, in the beginning of the transcendental literature, it is said, *dharmaḥ projjhita-kaitavo 'tra. Dharma, artha, kāma* and *mokṣa* are *kaitava*—false and unnecessary. *Nirmatsarāṇām,* persons who are completely transcendental to the material activities of separateness, who make no distinction between "mine" and "yours," but who simply engage in the devotional service of the Lord, are actually fit to accept *bhāgavata-dharma* (*dharmān bhagavatān iha*). Because they are *nirmatsara*, not jealous of anyone, they want to make others devotees, even their enemies. In this regard, Śrīla Madhvācārya remarks, *kāṅkṣate mokṣa-gam api sukhaṁ nākāṅkṣato yathā.* Devotees are not desirous of any material happiness, including the happiness derived from liberation. This is called *anyābhilāṣitā-śūnyaṁ jñāna-karmādy-anāvṛtam. Karmīs* desire material happiness, and *jñānīs* desire liberation, but a devotee does not desire anything; he is simply satisfied by rendering transcendental loving service at the lotus feet of the Lord and glorifying Him everywhere by preaching, which is his life and soul.

TEXT 26

धर्मार्थकाम इति योऽभिहितस्त्रिवर्ग
ईक्षा त्रयी नयदमौ विविधा च वार्ता ।
मन्ये तदेतदखिलं निगमस्य सत्यं
स्वात्मार्पणं स्वसुहृदः परमस्य पुंसः ॥२६॥

dharmārtha-kāma iti yo 'bhihitas tri-varga
īkṣā trayī naya-damau vividhā ca vārtā
manye tad etad akhilaṁ nigamasya satyaṁ
svātmārpaṇaṁ sva-suhṛdaḥ paramasya puṁsaḥ

dharma—religion; *artha*—economic development; *kāmaḥ*—regulated sense gratification; *iti*—thus; *yaḥ*—which; *abhihitaḥ*—prescribed; *tri-vargaḥ*—the group of three; *īkṣā*—self-realization; *trayī*—the Vedic ritualistic ceremonies; *naya*—logic; *damau*—and the science of law and order; *vividhā*—varieties of; *ca*—also; *vārtā*—occupational duties, or one's livelihood; *manye*—I consider; *tat*—them; *etat*—these; *akhilam*—all; *nigamasya*—of the *Vedas; satyam*—truth; *sva-ātma-arpaṇam*—the full surrendering of one's self; *sva-suhṛdaḥ*—unto the supreme friend; *paramasya*—the ultimate; *puṁsaḥ*—personality.

TRANSLATION

Religion, economic development and sense gratification—these are described in the Vedas as tri-varga, or three ways to salvation. Within these three categories are education and self-realization; ritualistic ceremonies performed according to Vedic injunction; logic; the science of law and order; and the various means of earning one's livelihood. These are the external subject matters of study in the Vedas, and therefore I consider them material. However, I consider surrender to the lotus feet of Lord Viṣṇu to be transcendental.

PURPORT

These instructions of Prahlāda Mahārāja stress the transcendental position of devotional service. As confirmed in *Bhagavad-gītā* (14.26):

māṁ ca yo 'vyabhicāreṇa
bhakti-yogena sevate
sa guṇān samatītyaitān
brahma-bhūyāya kalpate

"One who engages in full devotional service, who does not fall down in any circumstance, at once transcends the modes of material nature and thus comes to the level of Brahman." One who fully engages in the devotional service of the Lord is immediately raised to the transcendental position, which is the *brahma-bhūta* stage. Any education or activity not on the *brahma-bhūta* platform, the platform of self-realization, is considered to be material, and Prahlāda Mahārāja says that anything material cannot be the Absolute Truth, for the Absolute Truth is on the spiritual platform. This is also confirmed by Lord Kṛṣṇa in *Bhagavad-gītā* (2.45), where He says, *traiguṇya-viṣayā vedā nistraiguṇyo bhavārjuna:* "The *Vedas* mainly deal with the subject of the three modes of material nature. Rise above these modes, O Arjuna. Be transcendental to all of them." To act on the material platform, even if one's activities are sanctioned by the *Vedas*, is not the ultimate goal of life. The ultimate goal of life is to stay on the spiritual platform, fully surrendered to the *parama-puruṣa*, the supreme person. This is the object of the human mission. In summary, the Vedic ritualistic ceremonies and injunctions are not to be discounted; they are means of being promoted to the spiritual platform. But if one does not come to the spiritual platform, the Vedic ceremonies are simply a waste of time. This is confirmed in *Śrīmad-Bhāgavatam* (1.2.8):

dharmaḥ svanuṣṭhitaḥ puṁsāṁ
viṣvaksena-kathāsu yaḥ
notpādayed yadi ratiṁ
śrama eva hi kevalam

"Duties [*dharma*] executed by men, regardless of occupation, are only so much useless labor if they do not provoke attraction for the message of the Supreme Lord." If one very strictly performs the various duties of religion but does not ultimately come to the platform of surrendering to the Supreme Lord, his methods of attaining salvation or elevation are simply a waste of time and energy.

TEXT 27

ज्ञानं तदेतदमलं दुरवापमाह
नारायणो नरसखः किल नारदाय ।
एकान्तिनां भगवतस्तदकिञ्चनानां
पादारविन्दरजसाप्लुतदेहिनां स्यात् ॥२७॥

jñānaṁ tad etad amalaṁ duravāpam āha
nārāyaṇo nara-sakhaḥ kila nāradāya
ekāntināṁ bhagavatas tad akiñcanānāṁ
pādāravinda-rajasāpluta-dehināṁ syāt

jñānam—knowledge; *tat*—that; *etat*—this; *amalam*—without material contamination; *duravāpam*—very difficult to understand (without the mercy of a devotee); *āha*—explained; *nārāyaṇaḥ*—Lord Nārāyaṇa, the Supreme Personality of Godhead; *nara-sakhaḥ*—the friend of all living entities (especially human beings); *kila*—certainly; *nāradāya*—unto the great sage Nārada; *ekāntinām*—of those who have surrendered exclusively to the Supreme Personality of Godhead; *bhagavataḥ*—of the Supreme Personality of Godhead; *tat*—that (knowledge);

akiñcanānām—who do not claim any material possessions; *pāda-aravinda*—of the lotus feet of the Lord; *rajasā*—by the dust; *āpluta*—bathed; *dehinām*—whose bodies; *syāt*—is possible.

TRANSLATION

Nārāyaṇa, the Supreme Personality of Godhead, the well-wisher and friend of all living entities, formerly explained this transcendental knowledge to the great saint Nārada. Such knowledge is extremely difficult to understand without the mercy of a saintly person like Nārada, but everyone who has taken shelter of Nārada's disciplic succession can understand this confidential knowledge.

PURPORT

It is stated here that this confidential knowledge is extremely difficult to understand, yet it is very easy to understand if one takes shelter of a pure devotee. This confidential knowledge is also mentioned at the end of *Bhagavad-gītā,* where the Lord says, *sarva-dharmān parityajya mām ekaṁ śaraṇaṁ vraja:* "Abandon all varieties of religion and just surrender unto Me." This knowledge is an extremely confidential secret, but it can be understood if one approaches the Supreme Personality of Godhead through the bona fide agent, the spiritual master in the disciplic succession from Nārada. Prahlāda Mahārāja wanted to impress upon the sons of the demons that although such knowledge can be understood only by a saintly person like Nārada, they should not be disappointed, for if one takes shelter of Nārada instead of material teachers, this knowledge is possible to understand. Understanding does not depend upon high parentage. The living entity is certainly pure on the spiritual platform, and therefore anyone who attains the spiritual platform by the grace of the spiritual master can also understand this confidential knowledge.

TEXT 28

श्रुतमेतन्मया पूर्वं ज्ञानं विज्ञानसंयुतम् ।
धर्मं भागवतं शुद्धं नारदाद् देवदर्शनात् ॥२८॥

śrutam etan mayā pūrvaṁ
jñānaṁ vijñāna-saṁyutam

dharmaṁ bhāgavataṁ śuddhaṁ
nāradād deva-darśanāt

śrutam—heard; *etat*—this; *mayā*—by me; *pūrvam*—formerly; *jñānam*—confidential knowledge; *vijñāna-saṁyutam*—combined with its practical application; *dharmam*—transcendental religion; *bhāgavatam*—in relationship with the Supreme Personality of Godhead; *śuddham*—having nothing to do with material activities; *nāradāt*—from the great saint Nārada; *deva*—the Supreme Lord; *darśanāt*—who always sees.

TRANSLATION

Prahlāda Mahārāja continued: I received this knowledge from the great saint Nārada Muni, who is always engaged in devotional service. This knowledge, which is called bhāgavata-dharma, is fully scientific. It is based on logic and philosophy and is free from all material contamination.

TEXTS 29–30

श्रीदैत्यपुत्रा ऊचुः
प्रह्राद त्वं वयं चापि नर्तेऽन्यं विद्महे गुरुम् ।
एताभ्यां गुरुपुत्राभ्यां बालानामपि हीश्वरौ ॥२९॥

बालस्यान्तःपुरस्थस्य महत्सङ्गो दुरन्वयः ।
छिन्धि नः संशयं सौम्य स्याच्चेद्विस्रम्भकारणम् ॥३०॥

śrī-daitya-putrā ūcuḥ
prahrāda tvaṁ vayaṁ cāpi
narte 'nyaṁ vidmahe gurum
etābhyāṁ guru-putrābhyāṁ
bālānām api hīśvarau

bālasyāntaḥpura-sthasya
mahat-saṅgo duranvayaḥ
chindhi naḥ saṁśayaṁ saumya
syāc ced visrambha-kāraṇam

śrī-daitya-putrāḥ ūcuḥ—the sons of the demons said; *prahrāda*—O dear friend Prahlāda; *tvam*—you; *vayam*—we; *ca*—and; *api*—also; *na*—not; *ṛte*—except; *anyam*—any other; *vidmahe*—know; *gurum*—spiritual master; *etābhyām*—these two; *guru-putrābhyām*—the sons of Śukrācārya; *bālānām*—of little children; *api*—although; *hi*—indeed; *īśvarau*—the two controllers; *bālasya*—of a child; *antaḥpura-sthasya*—remaining inside the house or palace; *mahat-saṅgaḥ*—the association of a great person like Nārada; *duranvayaḥ*—very difficult; *chindhi*—please dispel; *naḥ*—our; *saṁśayam*—doubt; *saumya*—O gentle one; *syāt*—there may be; *cet*—if; *visrambha-kāraṇam*—cause of faith (in your words).

TRANSLATION

The sons of the demons replied: Dear Prahlāda, neither you nor we know any teacher or spiritual master other than Ṣaṇḍa and Amarka, the sons of Śukrācārya. After all, we are children and they our controllers. For you especially, who always remain within the palace, it is very difficult to associate with a great personality. Dear friend, most gentle one, would you kindly explain how it was possible for you to hear Nārada? Kindly dispel our doubts in this regard.

Thus end the Bhaktivedanta purports of the Seventh Canto, Sixth Chapter, of the Śrīmad-Bhāgavatam, *entitled, "Prahlāda Instructs His Demoniac Schoolmates."*

CHAPTER SEVEN

What Prahlāda Learned in the Womb

In this chapter, to dissipate the doubts of his class friends, the sons of the demons, Prahlāda Mahārāja states how, within the womb of his mother, he had heard from the mouth of Nārada Muni, who had instructed him in *bhāgavata-dharma.*

When Hiraṇyakaśipu left his kingdom and went to the mountain known as Mandarācala to execute severe austerities, all the demons scattered. Hiraṇyakaśipu's wife, Kayādhu, was pregnant at that time, and the demigods, mistakenly thinking that she carried another demon in her womb, arrested her. Their plan was that as soon as the child took birth they would kill him. While they were taking Kayādhu to the heavenly planets, they met Nārada Muni, who stopped them from taking her away and took her to his *āśrama* until Hiraṇyakaśipu's return. In Nārada Muni's *āśrama,* Kayādhu prayed for the protection of the baby in her womb, and Nārada Muni reassured her and gave her instructions on spiritual knowledge. Taking advantage of those instructions, Prahlāda Mahārāja, although a small baby within the womb, listened very carefully. The spirit soul is always apart from the material body. There is no change in the spiritual form of the living entity. Any person above the bodily conception of life is pure and can receive transcendental knowledge. This transcendental knowledge is devotional service, and Prahlāda Mahārāja, while living in the womb of his mother, received instructions in devotional service from Nārada Muni. Any person engaged in the service of the Lord through the instructions of a bona fide spiritual master is immediately liberated, and being free from the clutches of *māyā,* he is relieved of all ignorance and material desires. The duty of everyone is to take shelter of the Supreme Lord and thus become free from all material desires. Regardless of the material condition in which one is situated, one can achieve this perfection. Devotional service is not dependent on the material activities of austerity, penance, mystic *yoga* or piety. Even without such assets, one can achieve devotional service through the mercy of a pure devotee.

TEXT 1

श्रीनारद उवाच
एवं दैत्यसुतैः पृष्टो महाभागवतोऽसुरः ।
उवाच तान्स्मयमानः स्मरन् मदनुभाषितम् ॥ १ ॥

śrī-nārada uvāca
evaṁ daitya-sutaiḥ pṛṣṭo
mahā-bhāgavato 'suraḥ
uvāca tān smayamānaḥ
smaran mad-anubhāṣitam

śrī-nāradaḥ uvāca—the great saint Nārada Muni said; *evam*—thus; *daitya-sutaiḥ*—by the sons of the demons; *pṛṣṭaḥ*—being questioned; *mahā-bhāgavataḥ*—the exalted devotee of the Lord; *asuraḥ*—born in a family of demons; *uvāca*—spoke; *tān*—unto them (the sons of the demons); *smayamānaḥ*—smiling; *smaran*—remembering; *mat-anubhāṣitam*—what was spoken by me.

TRANSLATION

Nārada Muni said: Although Prahlāda Mahārāja was born in a family of asuras, he was the greatest of all devotees. Having thus been questioned by his class friends, the sons of the asuras, he remembered the words spoken to him by me and replied to his friends as follows.

PURPORT

When he was in the womb of his mother, Prahlāda Mahārāja listened to the words of Nārada Muni. One cannot imagine how the baby in embryo could hear Nārada, but this is spiritual life; progress in spiritual life cannot be obstructed by any material condition. This is called *ahaituky apratihatā.* Reception of spiritual knowledge is never checked by any material condition. Thus Prahlāda Mahārāja, from his very childhood, spoke spiritual knowledge to his class friends, and certainly it was effective, although all of them were children.

TEXT 2

श्रीप्रह्राद उवाच
पितरि प्रस्थितेऽस्माकं तपसे मन्दराचलम् ।
युद्धोद्यमं परं चक्रुर्विबुधा दानवान्प्रति ॥ २ ॥

śrī-prahrāda uvāca
pitari prasthite 'smākaṁ
tapase mandarācalam
yuddhodyamaṁ paraṁ cakrur
vibudhā dānavān prati

śrī-prahrādaḥ uvāca—Prahlāda Mahārāja said; *pitari*—when the demon father, Hiraṇyakaśipu; *prasthite*—left for; *asmākam*—our; *tapase*—to execute austerities; *mandara-acalam*—the hill known as Mandarācala; *yuddha-udyamam*—exertion of warfare; *param*—very great; *cakruḥ*—executed; *vibudhāḥ*—the demigods, headed by King Indra; *dānavān*—the demons; *prati*—toward.

TRANSLATION

Prahlāda Mahārāja said: When our father, Hiraṇyakaśipu, went to Mandarācala Mountain to execute severe austerities, in his absence the demigods, headed by King Indra, made a severe attempt to subdue all the demons in warfare.

TEXT 3

पिपीलिकैरहिरिव दिष्टचा लोकोपतापनः ।
पापेन पापोऽभक्षीति वदन्तो वासवादयः ॥ ३ ॥

pipīlikair ahir iva
diṣṭyā lokopatāpanaḥ
pāpena pāpo 'bhakṣīti
vadanto vāsavādayaḥ

pipīlikaiḥ—by small ants; *ahiḥ*—a serpent; *iva*—like; *diṣṭyā*—thank heaven; *loka-upatāpanaḥ*—always oppressing everyone; *pāpena*—by his own sinful activities; *pāpaḥ*—the sinful Hiraṇyakaśipu; *abhakṣi*—has now been eaten; *iti*—thus; *vadantaḥ*—saying; *vāsava-ādayaḥ*—the demigods, headed by King Indra.

TRANSLATION

"Alas, as a serpent is eaten by small ants, so the troublesome Hiraṇyakaśipu, who always inflicted miseries upon all types of people, has now been defeated by the reactions of his own sinful activities." Saying this, the demigods, headed by King Indra, arranged to fight the demons.

TEXTS 4–5

तेषामतिबलोद्योगं निशम्यासुरयूथपाः ।
वध्यमानाः सुरैर्भीता दुद्रुवुः सर्वतोदिशम् ॥ ४ ॥
कलत्रपुत्रवित्ताप्तान्गृहान्पशुपरिच्छदान् ।
नावेक्ष्यमाणास्त्वरिताः सर्वे प्राणपरीप्सवः ॥ ५ ॥

teṣām atibalodyogaṁ
niśamyāsura-yūthapāḥ
vadhyamānāḥ surair bhītā
dudruvuḥ sarvato diśam

kalatra-putra-vittāptān
gṛhān paśu-paricchadān
nāvekṣyamāṇās tvaritāḥ
sarve prāṇa-parīpsavaḥ

teṣām—of the demigods, headed by King Indra; *atibala-udyogam*—the great exertion and strength; *niśamya*—hearing of; *asura-yūthapāḥ*—the great leaders of the demons; *vadhyamānāḥ*—being killed one after another; *suraiḥ*—by the demigods; *bhītāḥ*—afraid; *dudruvuḥ*—ran away; *sarvataḥ*—in all; *diśam*—directions; *kalatra*—wives; *putra-vitta*—children and wealth; *āptān*—relatives; *gṛhān*—homes; *paśu-paricchadān*—animals and paraphernalia of household life; *na*—not; *avekṣyamāṇāḥ*—seeing to; *tvaritāḥ*—very hasty; *sarve*—all of them; *prāṇa-parīpsavaḥ*—very much desiring to live.

TRANSLATION

When the great leaders of the demons, who were being killed one after another, saw the unprecedented exertion of the demigods in fighting, they began to flee, scattering themselves in all directions. Simply to protect their lives, they hastily fled from their homes, wives, children, animals and household paraphernalia. Paying no heed to all these, the demons simply fled.

TEXT 6

व्यलुम्पन् राजशिबिरममरा जयकाङ्क्षिणः ।
इन्द्रस्तु राजमहिषीं मातरं मम चाग्रहीत् ॥ ६ ॥

vyalumpan rāja-śibiram
amarā jaya-kāṅkṣiṇaḥ
indras tu rāja-mahiṣīṁ
mātaraṁ mama cāgrahīt

vyalumpan—plundered; *rāja-śibiram*—the palace of my father, Hiraṇyakaśipu; *amarāḥ*—the demigods; *jaya-kāṅkṣiṇaḥ*—eager to be victorious; *indraḥ*—the head of the demigods, King Indra; *tu*—but; *rāja-mahiṣīm*—the Queen; *mātaram*—mother; *mama*—my; *ca*—also; *agrahīt*—captured.

TRANSLATION

The victorious demigods plundered the palace of Hiraṇyakaśipu, the King of the demons, and destroyed everything within it. Then Indra, King of heaven, arrested my mother, the Queen.

TEXT 7

नीयमानां भयोद्विग्नां रुदतीं कुररीमिव ।
यदृच्छयागतस्तत्र देवर्षिर्ददृशे पथि ॥ ७ ॥

nīyamānāṁ bhayodvignāṁ
rudatīṁ kurarīm iva
yadṛcchayāgatas tatra
devarṣir dadṛśe pathi

nīyamānām—being taken away; *bhaya-udvignām*—disturbed and full of fear; *rudatīm*—crying; *kurarīm iva*—like a *kurarī* (osprey); *yadṛcchayā*—by chance; *āgataḥ*—arrived; *tatra*—on the spot; *deva-ṛṣiḥ*—the great saint Nārada; *dadṛśe*—he saw; *pathi*—on the road.

TRANSLATION

As she was being led away, crying in fear like a kurarī captured by a vulture, the great sage Nārada, who at that time had no engagement, appeared on the scene and saw her in that condition.

TEXT 8

प्राह नैनां सुरपते नेतुमर्हस्यनागसम् ।
मुञ्च मुञ्च महाभाग सतीं परपरिग्रहम् ॥ ८ ॥

prāha naināṁ sura-pate
netum arhasy anāgasam
muñca muñca mahā-bhāga
satīṁ para-parigraham

prāha—he said; *na*—not; *enām*—this; *sura-pate*—O King of the demigods; *netum*—to drag away; *arhasi*—you deserve; *anāgasam*—not at all sinful; *muñca muñca*—release, release; *mahā-bhāga*—O greatly fortunate one; *satīm*—chaste; *para-parigraham*—the wife of another person.

TRANSLATION

Nārada Muni said: O Indra, King of the demigods, this woman is certainly sinless. You should not drag her off in this merciless way. O greatly fortunate one, this chaste woman is the wife of another. You must immediately release her.

TEXT 9

श्रीइन्द्र उवाच

आस्तेऽस्या जठरे वीर्यमविषह्यं सुरद्विषः ।
आस्यतां यावत्प्रसवं मोक्ष्येऽर्थपदवीं गतः ॥ ९ ॥

śrī-indra uvāca
āste 'syā jaṭhare vīryam
aviṣahyaṁ sura-dviṣaḥ
āsyatāṁ yāvat prasavaṁ
mokṣye 'rtha-padavīṁ gataḥ

śrī-indraḥ uvāca—King Indra said; *āste*—there is; *asyāḥ*—of her; *jaṭhare*—within the abdomen; *vīryam*—the seed; *aviṣahyam*—intolerable; *sura-dviṣaḥ*—of the enemy of the demigods; *āsyatām*—let her remain (in our prison); *yāvat*—until; *prasavam*—the delivery of the child; *mokṣye*—I shall release; *artha-padavīm*—the path of my object; *gataḥ*—obtained.

TRANSLATION

King Indra said: In the womb of this woman, the wife of the demon Hiraṇyakaśipu, is the seed of that great demon. Therefore, let her remain in our custody until her child is delivered, and then we shall release her.

PURPORT

Indra, the King of heaven, decided to arrest Prahlāda Mahārāja's mother because he thought that another demon, another Hiraṇyakaśipu, was within her womb. The best course, he thought, was to kill the child when the child was born, and then the woman could be released.

TEXT 10

श्रीनारद उवाच
अयं निष्किल्बिषः साक्षान्महाभागवतो महान् ।
त्वया न प्राप्स्यते संस्थामनन्तानुचरो बली ॥१०॥

śrī-nārada uvāca
ayaṁ niṣkilbiṣaḥ sākṣān
mahā-bhāgavato mahān
tvayā na prāpsyate saṁsthām
anantānucaro balī

śrī-nāradaḥ uvāca—the great saint Nārada Muni said; *ayam*—this (child within the womb); *niṣkilbiṣaḥ*—completely sinless; *sākṣāt*—directly; *mahā-bhāgavataḥ*—a saintly devotee; *mahān*—very great; *tvayā*—by you; *na*—not; *prāpsyate*—will obtain; *saṁsthām*—his death; *ananta*—of the Supreme Personality of Godhead; *anucaraḥ*—a servant; *balī*—extremely powerful.

TRANSLATION

Nārada Muni replied: The child within this woman's womb is faultless and sinless. Indeed, he is a great devotee, a powerful servant of the Supreme Personality of Godhead. Therefore you will not be able to kill him.

PURPORT

There have been many instances in which demons or nondevotees have attempted to kill a devotee, but they have never been able to destroy a great devotee of the Supreme Personality of Godhead. The Lord promises in *Bhagavad-gītā* (9.31), *kaunteya pratijānīhi na me bhaktaḥ praṇaśyati.* This is a declaration by the Supreme Personality of Godhead that His devotee cannot be killed by demons. Prahlāda Mahārāja is the vivid example of the truth of this promise. Nārada Muni told the King of heaven, "It would be impossible for you to kill the child, even though you are demigods, and certainly it would be impossible for others."

TEXT 11

इत्युक्तस्तां विहायेन्द्रो देवर्षेर्मानयन्वचः ।
अनन्तप्रियभक्त्यैनां परिक्रम्य दिवं ययौ ॥११॥

ity uktas tāṁ vihāyendro
devarṣer mānayan vacaḥ
ananta-priya-bhaktyaināṁ
parikramya divaṁ yayau

iti—thus; *uktaḥ*—addressed; *tām*—her; *vihāya*—releasing; *indraḥ*—the King of heaven; *deva-ṛṣeḥ*—of the saint Nārada Muni; *mānayan*—honoring; *vacaḥ*—the words; *ananta-priya*—for one who is very dear to the Supreme Personality of Godhead; *bhaktyā*—by devotion; *enām*—this (woman); *parikramya*—circumambulating; *divam*—to the heavenly planets; *yayau*—returned.

TRANSLATION

When the great saint Nārada Muni had thus spoken, King Indra, being respectful to Nārada's words, immediately released my mother. Because of my being a devotee of the Lord, all the demigods circumambulated her. Then they returned to their celestial kingdom.

PURPORT

Although King Indra and the other demigods are exalted personalities, they were so obedient to Nārada Muni that King Indra immediately accepted Nārada Muni's words concerning Prahlāda Mahārāja. This is called understanding by the *paramparā* system. Indra and the demigods did not know that a great devotee was in the womb of Kayādhu, the wife of Hiraṇyakaśipu, but they accepted the authoritative statements of Nārada Muni and immediately offered their respects to the devotee by circumambulating the woman in whose womb he was living. To understand God and the devotee by the *paramparā* system is the process of knowledge. There is no need to speculate about God and His devotee. One should accept the statements of a bona fide devotee and thus try to understand.

TEXT 12

ततो मे मातरमृषिः समानीय निजाश्रमे ।
आश्वास्येहोष्यतां वत्से यावत् ते भर्तुरागमः ॥१२॥

tato me mātaram ṛṣiḥ
samānīya nijāśrame
āśvāsyehoṣyatāṁ vatse
yāvat te bhartur āgamaḥ

tataḥ—thereafter; *me*—my; *mātaram*—mother; *ṛṣiḥ*—the great saint Nārada Ṛṣi; *samānīya*—bringing; *nija-āśrame*—to his own *āśrama;* *āśvāsya*—giving her assurance; *iha*—here; *uṣyatām*—stay; *vatse*—my dear child; *yāvat*—until; *te*—your; *bhartuḥ*—of the husband; *āgamaḥ*—the coming.

TRANSLATION

Prahlāda Mahārāja continued: The great saint Nārada Muni brought my mother to his āśrama and assured her of all protection, saying, "My dear child, please remain at my āśrama until the arrival of your husband."

TEXT 13

तथेत्यवात्सीद् देवर्षेरन्तिके साकुतोभया ।
यावद् दैत्यपतिर्घोरात् तपसो न न्यवर्तत ॥१३॥

tathety avātsīd devarṣer
antike sākuto-bhayā
yāvad daitya-patir ghorāt
tapaso na nyavartata

tathā—so be it; *iti*—thus; *avātsīt*—lived; *deva-ṛṣeḥ*—Devarṣi Nārada; *antike*—near; *sā*—she (my mother); *akuto-bhayā*—without fear from any direction; *yāvat*—as long as; *daitya-patiḥ*—my father, Hiraṇyakaśipu, the lord of the demons; *ghorāt*—from very severe; *tapasaḥ*—austerities; *na*—not; *nyavartata*—ceased.

TRANSLATION

After accepting the instructions of Devarṣi Nārada, my mother stayed in his care, without fear from any direction, as long as my father, the King of the Daityas, had not become free from his severe austerities.

TEXT 14

ऋषिं पर्यचरत् तत्र भक्त्या परमया सती ।
अन्तर्वत्नी स्वगर्भस्य क्षेमायेच्छाप्रसूतये ॥१४॥

ṛṣiṁ paryacarat tatra
bhaktyā paramayā satī
antarvatnī sva-garbhasya
kṣemāyecchā-prasūtaye

ṛṣim—unto Nārada Muni; *paryacarat*—rendered service; *tatra*—there (in the *āśrama* of Nārada Muni); *bhaktyā*—with devotion and faith; *paramayā*—great; *satī*—the faithful woman; *antarvatnī*—pregnant; *sva-garbhasya*—of her embryo; *kṣemāya*—for the welfare; *icchā*—according to desire; *prasūtaye*—for deliverance of the child.

TRANSLATION

My mother, being pregnant, desired the safety of her embryo and desired to give birth after her husband's arrival. Thus she stayed at Nārada Muni's āśrama, where she rendered service unto Nārada Muni with great devotion.

PURPORT

It is stated in *Śrīmad-Bhāgavatam* (9.19.17)

mātrā svasrā duhitrā vā
nāviviktāsano bhavet
balavān indriya-grāmo
vidvāṁsam api karṣati

One should not remain in a secluded place with a woman, even one's mother, sister, or daughter. Nonetheless, although one is strictly prohibited from staying with a woman in a secluded place, Nārada Muni gave shelter to Prahlāda Mahārāja's young mother, who rendered service to him with great devotion and faith. Does this mean that Nārada Muni transgressed the Vedic injunctions? Certainly he did not. Such injunctions are intended for mundane creatures, but Nārada Muni is transcendental to mundane categories. Nārada Muni is a great saint and is transcendentally situated. Therefore, although he was a young man, he could give shelter to a young woman and accept her service. Haridāsa Ṭhākura also spoke with a young woman, a prostitute, in the dead of night, but the woman could not deviate his mind. Instead, she became a Vaiṣṇavī, a pure devotee, by the benediction of Haridāsa Ṭhākura. Ordinary persons, however, should not imitate such highly elevated devotees. Ordinary persons must strictly observe the rules and regulations by staying aloof from the association of women. No one should imitate Nārada Muni or Haridāsa Ṭhākura. It is said, *vaiṣṇavera kriyā-mudrā vijñe nā bujhaya.* Even if a man is very advanced in learning, he cannot understand the behavior of a Vaiṣṇava. Anyone can take shelter of a pure Vaiṣṇava, without fear. Therefore in the previous verse it has been distinctly said, *devarṣer antike sākuto-bhayā:* Kayādhu, the mother of Prahlāda Mahārāja, stayed under the protection of Nārada Muni without fear from any direction. Similarly, Nārada Muni, in his transcendental position, stayed with the young woman without fear of deviation. Nārada Muni, Haridāsa Ṭhākura and similar *ācāryas* especially empowered to broadcast the glories of the Lord cannot be brought down to the material platform. Therefore one is strictly forbidden to think that the *ācārya* is an ordinary human being (*guruṣu nara-matiḥ*).

TEXT 15

ऋषिः कारुणिकस्तस्याः प्रादादुभयमीश्वरः ।
धर्मस्य तत्त्वं ज्ञानं च मामप्युद्दिश्य निर्मलम् ॥१५॥

ṛṣiḥ kāruṇikas tasyāḥ
prādād ubhayam īśvaraḥ

dharmasya tattvaṁ jñānaṁ ca
mām apy uddiśya nirmalam

ṛṣiḥ—the great sage Nārada Muni; *kāruṇikaḥ*—naturally very affectionate or merciful to the fallen souls; *tasyāḥ*—to her; *prādāt*—gave instructions; *ubhayam*—both; *īśvaraḥ*—a powerful controller who can do whatever he likes (Nārada Muni); *dharmasya*—of religion; *tattvam*—the truth; *jñānam*—knowledge; *ca*—and; *mām*—me; *api*—especially; *uddiśya*—indicating; *nirmalam*—without material contamination.

TRANSLATION

Nārada Muni delivered his instructions both to me, who was within the womb, and to my mother, who was engaged in rendering him service. Because he is naturally extremely kind to the fallen souls, being in a transcendental position, he gave instructions on religion and transcendental knowledge. These instructions were free from all material contamination.

PURPORT

Here it is said, *dharmasya tattvaṁ jñānaṁ ca . . . nirmalam.* The word *nirmalam* refers to spotless *dharma*, spotless religion—or, in other words, *bhāgavata-dharma.* Ordinary ritualistic activities constitute contaminated religion, by which one benefits by developing material wealth and prosperity, but uncontaminated, pure religion consists of understanding one's relationship with God and acting accordingly, thus fulfilling the highest mission of life and returning home, back to Godhead. Prahlāda Mahārāja advised that one elevate oneself to the standard of *bhāgavata-dharma* from the very beginning of life (*kaumāra ācaret prājño dharmān bhāgavatān iha*). The Lord Himself also speaks of pure, uncontaminated religion when He says, *sarva-darmān parityajya mām ekaṁ śaraṇaṁ vraja:* "Abandon all varieties of religion and just surrender unto Me." (Bg. 18.66) One must understand one's relationship with God and then act accordingly. This is *bhāgavata-dharma. Bhāgavata-dharma* means *bhakti-yoga.*

vāsudeve bhagavati
bhakti-yogaḥ prayojitaḥ
janayaty āśu vairāgyaṁ
jñānaṁ ca yad ahaitukam

"By rendering devotional service unto the Personality of Godhead, Śrī Kṛṣṇa, one immediately acquires causeless knowledge and detachment from the world." (*Bhāg.* 1.2.7) To be situated on the platform of pure religion, one should perform *bhakti-yoga* in relationship with Kṛṣṇa, Vāsudeva.

TEXT 16

तत्तु कालस्य दीर्घत्वात् स्त्रीत्वान्मातुस्तिरोदधे ।
ऋषिणानुगृहीतं मां नाधुनाप्यजहात् स्मृतिः ॥१६॥

tat tu kālasya dīrghatvāt
strītvān mātus tirodadhe
ṛṣiṇānugṛhītaṁ māṁ
nādhunāpy ajahāt smṛtiḥ

tat—that (instruction on religion and knowledge); *tu*—indeed; *kālasya*—of time; *dīrghatvāt*—because of the longness; *strītvāt*—because of being a woman; *mātuḥ*—of my mother; *tirodadhe*—disappeared; *ṛṣiṇā*—by the sage; *anugṛhītam*—being blessed; *mām*—me; *na*—not; *adhunā*—today; *api*—even; *ajahāt*—left; *smṛtiḥ*—the memory (of Nārada Muni's instructions).

TRANSLATION

Because of the long duration of time that has passed and because of her being a woman and therefore less intelligent, my mother has forgotten all those instructions; but the great sage Nārada blessed me, and therefore I could not forget them.

PURPORT

In *Bhagavad-gītā* (9.32) the Lord says:

māṁ hi pārtha vyapāśritya
ye 'pi syuḥ pāpa-yonayaḥ
striyo vaiśyās tathā śūdrās
te 'pi yānti parāṁ gatim

"O son of Pṛthā, those who take shelter in Me—though they be lowborn, women, *vaiśyas* [merchants] or *śūdras* [workers]—can approach the supreme destination." The word *pāpa-yoni* refers to those who are less than *śūdras*, but even though a woman may not be *pāpa-yoni*, because of being less intelligent she sometimes forgets devotional instructions. For those who are strong enough, however, there is no question of forgetting. Women are generally attached to material enjoyment, and because of this tendency they sometimes forget devotional instructions. But if even a woman practices devotional service strictly, according to the rules and regulations, the statement by the Lord Himself that she can return to Godhead (*te 'pi yānti parāṁ gatim*) is not at all astonishing. One must take shelter of the Lord and rigidly follow the rules and regulations. Then, regardless of what one is, one will return home, back to Godhead. Prahlāda Mahārāja's mother was more concerned with protecting the child in the womb and was very anxious to see her husband return. Therefore she could not consider very seriously the sublime instructions of Nārada Muni.

TEXT 17

भवतामपि भूयान्मे यदि श्रद्धते वचः ।
वैशारदी धीः श्रद्धातः स्त्रीबालानां च मे यथा ॥१७॥

bhavatām api bhūyān me
yadi śraddadhate vacaḥ
vaiśāradī dhīḥ śraddhātaḥ
strī-bālānāṁ ca me yathā

bhavatām—of yourselves; *api*—also; *bhūyāt*—it may be; *me*—of me; *yadi*—if; *śraddadhate*—you believe in; *vacaḥ*—the words; *vaiśāradī*—of the most expert, or in relation with the Supreme Lord;

dhīḥ—intelligence; *śraddhātaḥ*—because of firm faith; *strī*—of women; *bālānām*—of small boys; *ca*—also; *me*—of me; *yathā*—just as.

TRANSLATION

Prahlāda Mahārāja continued: My dear friends, if you can place your faith in my words, simply by that faith you can also understand transcendental knowledge, just like me, although you are small children. Similarly, a woman can also understand transcendental knowledge and know what is spirit and what is matter.

PURPORT

These words of Prahlāda Mahārāja are very important in regard to knowledge descending by the disciplic succession. Even when Prahlāda Mahārāja was a baby within the womb of his mother, he became fully convinced of the existence of the supreme power because of hearing the powerful instructions of Nārada and understood how to attain perfection in life by *bhakti-yoga*. These are the most important understandings in spiritual knowledge.

yasya deve parā bhaktir
yathā deve tathā gurau
tasyaite kathitā hy arthāḥ
prakāśante mahātmanaḥ

"Unto those great souls who have implicit faith in both the Lord and the spiritual master, all the imports of Vedic knowledge are automatically revealed." (*Śvetāśvatara Upaniṣad* 6.23)

ataḥ śrī-kṛṣṇa-nāmādi
na bhaved grāhyam indriyaiḥ
sevonmukhe hi jihvādau
svayam eva sphuraty adaḥ

"No one can understand Kṛṣṇa as He is by the blunt material senses. But He reveals Himself to the devotees, being pleased with them for their transcendental loving service unto Him." (*Bhakti-rasāmṛta-sindhu* 1.2.234)

bhaktyā mām abhijānāti
yāvān yaś cāsmi tattvataḥ
tato māṁ tattvato jñātvā
viśate tad-anantaram

"One can understand the Supreme Personality as He is only by devotional service. And when one is in full consciousness of the Supreme Lord by such devotion, he can enter into the kingdom of God." (Bg. 18.55)

These are Vedic instructions. One must have full faith in the words of the spiritual master and similar faith in the Supreme Personality of Godhead. Then the real knowledge of *ātmā* and Paramātmā and the distinction between matter and spirit will be automatically revealed. This *ātma-tattva*, or spiritual knowledge, will be revealed within the core of a devotee's heart because of his having taken shelter of the lotus feet of a *mahājana* such as Prahlāda Mahārāja.

In this verse the word *bhūyāt* may be understood to mean "let there be." Prahlāda Mahārāja offers his blessings to his class friends, saying, "Also become faithful like me. Become bona fide Vaiṣṇavas." A devotee of the Lord desires for everyone to take to Kṛṣṇa consciousness. Unfortunately, however, people sometimes do not have staunch faith in the words of the spiritual master who comes by the disciplic succession, and therefore they are unable to understand transcendental knowledge. The spiritual master must be in the line of authorized disciplic succession, like Prahlāda Mahārāja, who received the knowledge from Nārada. If the class friends of Prahlāda Mahārāja, the sons of demons, were to accept the truth through Prahlāda, they would certainly also become fully aware of transcendental knowledge.

The words *vaiśāradī dhīḥ* refer to intelligence concerning the Supreme Personality of Godhead, who is extremely expert. The Lord has created wonderful universes by His expert knowledge. Unless one is extremely expert, he cannot understand the expert management of the supreme expert. One can understand, however, if one is fortunate enough to meet a bona fide spiritual master coming in the disciplic succession from Lord Brahmā, Lord Śiva, Mother Lakṣmī or the Kumāras. These four *sampradāyas*, or disciplic successions of knowledge and transcendence, are called the Brahma-sampradāya, Rudra-sampradāya,

Śrī-sampradāya, and Kumāra-sampradāya. *Sampradāya-vihīnā ye mantrās te niṣphalā matāḥ.* The knowledge of the Supreme received from such a *sampradāya*, or disciplic succession, can give one enlightenment. If one does not take to the path of disciplic succession, it is not possible for one to understand the Supreme Personality of Godhead. If one understands the Supreme Lord through devotional service with faith in the disciplic succession and then advances further, he awakens his natural love for God, and then his success in life is assured.

TEXT 18

जन्माद्याः षडिमे भावा दृष्टा देहस्य नात्मनः ।
फलानामिव वृक्षस्य कालेनेश्वरमूर्तिना ॥१८॥

janmādyāḥ ṣaḍ ime bhāvā
dṛṣṭā dehasya nātmanaḥ
phalānām iva vṛkṣasya
kāleneśvara-mūrtinā

janma-ādyāḥ—beginning with birth; *ṣaṭ*—the six (birth, existence, growth, transformation, dwindling and at last death); *ime*—all these; *bhāvāḥ*—different conditions of the body; *dṛṣṭāḥ*—seen; *dehasya*—of the body; *na*—not; *ātmanaḥ*—of the soul; *phalānām*—of the fruits; *iva*—like; *vṛkṣasya*—of a tree; *kālena*—in due course of time; *īśvara-mūrtinā*—whose form is the ability to transform or control the bodily activities.

TRANSLATION

Just as the fruits and flowers of a tree in due course of time undergo six changes—birth, existence, growth, transformation, dwindling and then death—the material body, which is obtained by the spirit soul under different circumstances, undergoes similar changes. However, there are no such changes for the spirit soul.

PURPORT

This is a very important verse in understanding the difference between the spiritual soul and the material body. The soul is eternal, as stated in *Bhagavad-gītā* (2.20):

na jāyate mriyate vā kadācin
nāyaṁ bhūtvā bhavitā vā na bhūyaḥ
ajo nityaḥ śāśvato 'yaṁ purāṇo
na hanyate hanyamāne śarīre

"For the soul there is never birth nor death. Nor, having once been, does he ever cease to be. He is unborn, eternal, ever-existing, undying and primeval. He is not slain when the body is slain." The spirit soul is eternal, being freed from waste and change, which take place because of the material body. The example of a tree and its fruits and flowers is very simple and clear. A tree stands for many, many years, but with the seasonal changes its fruits and flowers undergo six transformations. The foolish theory of modern chemists that life can be produced by chemical interactions cannot be accepted as truth. The birth of a human being's material body takes place due to a mixture of the ovum and semen, but the history of birth is that although the ovum and semen mix together after sex, there is not always pregnancy. Unless the soul enters the mixture, there is no possibility of pregnancy, but when the soul takes shelter of the mixture the body takes birth, exists, grows, transforms and dwindles, and ultimately it is vanquished. The fruits and flowers of a tree seasonally come and go, but the tree continues to stand. Similarly, the transmigrating soul accepts various bodies, which undergo six transformations, but the soul remains permanently the same (*ajo nityaḥ śāśvato 'yaṁ purāṇo na hanyate hanyamāne śarīre*). The soul is eternal and ever existing, but the bodies accepted by the soul are changing.

There are two kinds of soul—the Supreme Soul (the Personality of Godhead) and the individual soul (the living entity). As various bodily changes take place in the individual soul, different millenniums of creation take place in the Supreme Soul. In this regard, Madhvācārya says:

ṣaḍ vikārāḥ śarīrasya
na viṣṇos tad-gatasya ca
tad-adhīnaṁ śarīraṁ ca
jñātvā tan mamatāṁ tyajet

Since the body is the external feature of the soul, the soul is not dependent on the body; rather, the body is dependent on the soul. One who understands this truth should not be very much anxious about the maintenance of his body. There is no possibility of maintaining the body permanently or eternally. *Antavanta ime dehā nityasyoktāḥ śarīriṇaḥ.* This is the statement of *Bhagavad-gītā* (2.18). The material body is *antavat* (perishable), but the soul within the body is eternal (*nityasyoktāḥ śarīriṇaḥ*). Lord Viṣṇu and the individual souls, who are part and parcel of Him, are both eternal. *Nityo nityānāṁ cetanaś cetanānām.* Lord Viṣṇu is the chief living being, whereas the individual living entities are parts of Lord Viṣṇu. All the various grades of bodies—from the gigantic universal body to the small body of an ant—are perishable, but the Supersoul and the soul, being equal in quality, both exist eternally. This is further explained in the next verses.

TEXTS 19–20

आत्मा नित्योऽव्ययः शुद्ध एकः क्षेत्रज्ञ आश्रयः ।
अविक्रियः स्वदृग् हेतुर्व्यापकोऽसङ्ग्यनावृतः ॥१९॥
एतैर्द्वादशभिर्विद्वानात्मनो लक्षणैः परैः ।
अहं ममेत्यसद्भावं देहादौ मोहजं त्यजेत् ॥२०॥

ātmā nityo 'vyayaḥ śuddha
ekaḥ kṣetra-jña āśrayaḥ
avikriyaḥ sva-dṛg hetur
vyāpako 'saṅgy anāvṛtaḥ

etair dvādaśabhir vidvān
ātmano lakṣaṇaiḥ paraiḥ
ahaṁ mamety asad-bhāvaṁ
dehādau mohajaṁ tyajet

ātmā—the spirit soul, the part of the Supreme Personality of Godhead; *nityaḥ*—without birth or death; *avyayaḥ*—with no possibility of dwindling; *śuddhaḥ*—without the material contamination of attachment and detachment; *ekaḥ*—individual; *kṣetra-jñaḥ*—who knows and is therefore different from the material body; *āśrayaḥ*—the original foundation;[1] *avikriyaḥ*—not undergoing changes like the body;[2] *sva-dṛk*—self-illuminated;[3] *hetuḥ*—the cause of all causes; *vyāpakaḥ*—spreading throughout the body in the form of consciousness; *asaṅgī*—not depending on the body (free to transmigrate from one body to another); *anāvṛtaḥ*—not covered by material contamination; *etaiḥ*—by all these; *dvādaśabhiḥ*—twelve; *vidvān*—a person who is not foolish but fully aware of things as they are; *ātmanaḥ*—of the spirit soul; *lakṣaṇaiḥ*—symptoms; *paraiḥ*—transcendental; *aham*—I ("I am this body"); *mama*—mine ("everything in relationship with this body is mine"); *iti*—thus; *asat-bhāvam*—a false conception of life; *deha-ādau*—identifying oneself with the material body and then with one's wife, children, family, community, nation and so on; *moha-jam*—produced from illusory knowledge; *tyajet*—must give up.

TRANSLATION

"Ātmā" refers to the Supreme Lord or the living entities. Both of them are spiritual, free from birth and death, free from deterioration and free from material contamination. They are individual, they are the knowers of the external body, and they are the foundation or shelter of everything. They are free from material change, they are self-illuminated, they are the cause of all causes, and they are all-pervading. They have nothing to do with the material body, and therefore they are always uncovered. With these transcendental qualities, one who is actually learned must give up the illusory conception of life, in which one thinks, "I am this material body, and everything in relationship with this body is mine."

---

[1] Without the shelter of the spirit soul, the material body cannot exist.

[2] As already explained, the fruits and flowers of a tree take birth, exist, grow, transform, dwindle and die according to seasonal changes, but the tree, through all these changes, remains the same. Similarly, the *ātmā* is free from all changes.

[3] One does not need to make the soul prominent; it is automatically prominent. One can very easily understand that in the living body there is a spiritual soul.

PURPORT

In *Bhagavad-gītā* (15.7) Lord Kṛṣṇa clearly says, *mamaivāṁśo jīva-loke jīva-bhūtaḥ:* "All the living entities are part of Me." Therefore the living entities are qualitatively the same as the Supreme Personality of Godhead, who is the leader, the Supreme among all the living entities. In the *Vedas* it is said, *nityo nityānāṁ cetanaś cetanānām:* the Lord is the chief individual living entity, the leader of the subordinate living entities. Because the living entities are parts or samples of God, their qualities are not different from those of the Supreme Lord. The living entities have the same qualities as the Lord, just as a drop of sea water is composed of the same chemicals as the great sea itself. Thus there is oneness in quality but a difference in quantity. One can understand the Supreme Personality of Godhead by understanding the sample, the living entity, because all the qualities of God exist in a minute quantity in the living entities. There is oneness, but God is great whereas the living entities are extremely small. *Aṇor aṇīyān mahato mahīyān* (*Kaṭha Upaniṣad* 1.2.20). The living entities are smaller than the atom, but God is greater than the greatest. Our conception of greatness may be represented by the sky because we think of the sky as being unlimitedly big, but God is bigger than the sky. Similarly, we have knowledge that the living entities are smaller than atoms, being one ten-thousandth the size of the tip of a hair, yet the quality of being the supreme cause of all causes exists in the living entity as well as in the Supreme Personality of Godhead. Indeed, it is due to the presence of the living entity that the body exists and bodily changes take place. Similarly, it is because the Supreme Lord is within this universe that the changes dictated by the material laws occur.

The word *ekaḥ,* meaning "individual," is significant. As explained in *Bhagavad-gītā* (9.4), *mat-sthāni sarva-bhūtāni na cāhaṁ teṣv avasthitaḥ.* Everything, material and spiritual, including earth, water, air, fire, sky and the living entities, exists on the platform of spirit soul. Although everything is an emanation from the Supreme Personality of Godhead, one should not think that the Supreme Lord is dependent upon anything else.

Both God and the living entity are fully conscious. As living entities, we are conscious of our bodily existence. Similarly, the Lord is conscious of the gigantic cosmic manifestation. This is confirmed in the *Vedas. Yasmin dyauḥ pṛthivī cāntarīkṣam. Vijñātāram adhikena vijānīyāt. Ekam evādvitīyam. Ātma-jyotiḥ samrāḍ ihovāca. Sa imān lokān asṛjata. Satyaṁ jñānam anantam. Asaṅgo hy ayaṁ puruṣaḥ. Pūrṇasya pūrṇam ādāya pūrṇam evāvaśiṣyate.* All these Vedic injunctions prove that both the Supreme Personality of Godhead and the minute soul are individual. One is great, and the other is small, but both of them are the cause of all causes—the corporally limited and the universally unlimited.

We should always remember that although we are equal to the Supreme Personality of Godhead in quality, we are never equal to Him in quantity. Persons with a small fund of intelligence, finding themselves equal in quality with God, foolishly think that they are equal in quantity also. Their intelligence is called *aviśuddha-buddhayaḥ*—unpolished or contaminated intelligence. When such persons, after endeavoring hard for many, many lives to understand the supreme cause, are finally in actual knowledge of Kṛṣṇa, Vāsudeva, they surrender unto Him (*vāsudevaḥ sarvam iti sa mahātmā sudurlabhaḥ*). Thus they become great *mahātmās*, perfect souls. If one is fortunate enough to understand his relationship with God, knowing that God is great (*vibhu*) whereas the living entity is small (*aṇu*), he is perfect in knowledge. The individual exists in darkness when he thinks that he is the material body and that everything in relationship with the material body belongs to him. This is called *ahaṁ mama* (*janasya moho 'yam ahaṁ mameti*). This is illusion. One must give up his illusory conception and thus become fully aware of everything.

TEXT 21

स्वर्णं यथा ग्रावसु हेमकारः
क्षेत्रेषु योगैस्तदभिज्ञ आप्नुयात् ।
क्षेत्रेषु देहेषु तथात्मयोगै-
रध्यात्मविद् ब्रह्मगतिं लभेत ॥२१॥

svarṇaṁ yathā grāvasu hema-kāraḥ
kṣetreṣu yogais tad-abhijña āpnuyāt
kṣetreṣu deheṣu tathātma-yogair
adhyātma-vid brahma-gatiṁ labheta

svarṇam—gold; *yathā*—just as; *grāvasu*—in the stones of gold ore; *hema-kāraḥ*—the expert who knows about gold; *kṣetreṣu*—in the gold mines; *yogaiḥ*—by various processes; *tat-abhijñaḥ*—an expert who can understand where gold is; *āpnuyāt*—very easily obtains; *kṣetreṣu*—within the material fields; *deheṣu*—the human bodies and all the rest of the 8,400,000 different bodily forms; *tathā*—similarly; *ātma-yogaiḥ*—by spiritual processes; *adhyātma-vit*—one who is expert in understanding the distinction between spirit and matter; *brahma-gatim*—perfection in spiritual life; *labheta*—may obtain.

TRANSLATION

An expert geologist can understand where there is gold and by various processes can extract it from the gold ore. Similarly, a spiritually advanced person can understand how the spiritual particle exists within the body, and thus by cultivating spiritual knowledge he can attain perfection in spiritual life. However, as one who is not expert cannot understand where there is gold, a foolish person who has not cultivated spiritual knowledge cannot understand how the spirit exists within the body.

PURPORT

Here is a very good example concerning spiritual understanding. Foolish rascals, including so-called *jñānīs*, philosophers and scientists, cannot understand the existence of the soul within the body because they are lacking in spiritual knowledge. The *Vedas* enjoin, *tad-vijñānārthaṁ sa gurum evābhigacchet:* to understand spiritual knowledge, one must approach a bona fide spiritual master. Unless one has been trained in geology, one cannot detect gold in stone. Similarly, unless one has been trained by a spiritual master, he cannot understand what is spirit and what is matter. Here it is said, *yogais tad-abhijñaḥ.* This indicates that one who has connected himself with spiritual knowledge can understand that there is a spiritual soul within the body. However, one who is in an animalistic conception of life and has no spiritual culture cannot understand. As an expert minerologist or geologist can understand where there is gold and can then invest his money to dig there and chemically separate the gold from the ore, an expert spiritualist can understand where the soul is within matter. One who has not been trained cannot distinguish between gold and stone. Similarly, fools and rascals who have not learned from an expert spiritual master what is soul and what is matter cannot understand the existence of the soul within the body. To understand such knowledge, one must be trained in the mystic *yoga* system, or, finally, in the *bhakti-yoga* system. As stated in *Bhagavad-gītā* (18.55), *bhaktyā mām abhijānāti.* Unless one takes shelter of the *bhakti-yoga* process, one cannot understand the existence of the soul within the body. Therefore *Bhagavad-gītā* begins by teaching:

dehino 'smin yathā dehe
kaumāraṁ yauvanaṁ jarā
tathā dehāntara-prāptir
dhīras tatra na muhyati

"As the embodied soul continually passes, in this body, from boyhood to youth to old age, the soul similarly passes into another body at death. The self-realized soul is not bewildered by such a change." (Bg. 2.13) Thus the first instruction is that one should understand that the soul is within the body and is transmigrating from one body to another. This is the beginning of spiritual knowledge. Any person who is not expert in understanding this science or is unwilling to understand it remains in the bodily conception of life, or the animalistic conception of life, as confirmed in *Śrīmad-Bhāgavatam* (*yasyātma-buddhiḥ kuṇape tri-dhātuke . . . sa eva go-kharaḥ*). Every member of human society should clearly understand the instructions of *Bhagavad-gītā*, for only in this way can one be spiritually elevated and automatically give up the false, illusory knowledge by which one thinks, "I am this body, and everything belonging to this body is mine [*ahaṁ mameti*]." This doggish conception should be rejected immediately. One should be prepared to understand the spirit soul and the supreme spirit, God, who are eternally related. Thus one may return home, back to Godhead, having solved all the problems of life.

TEXT 22

अष्टौ प्रकृतयः प्रोक्तास्त्रय एव हि तद्गुणाः ।
विकाराः षोडशाचार्यैः पुमानेकः समन्वयात् ॥२२॥

aṣṭau prakṛtayaḥ proktās
traya eva hi tad-guṇāḥ
vikārāḥ ṣoḍaśācāryaiḥ
pumān ekaḥ samanvayāt

aṣṭau—eight; *prakṛtayaḥ*—material energies; *proktāḥ*—it is said; *trayaḥ*—three; *eva*—certainly; *hi*—indeed; *tat-guṇāḥ*—the modes of material energy; *vikārāḥ*—transformations; *ṣoḍaśa*—sixteen; *ācāryaiḥ*—by the authorities; *pumān*—the living entity; *ekaḥ*—one; *samanvayāt*—from conjunction.

TRANSLATION

The Lord's eight separated material energies, the three modes of material nature and the sixteen transformations [the eleven senses and the five gross material elements like earth and water]—within all these, the one spiritual soul exists as the observer. Therefore all the great ācāryas have concluded that the individual soul is conditioned by these material elements.

PURPORT

As explained in the previous verse, *kṣetreṣu deheṣu tathātma-yogair adhyātma-vid brahma-gatiṁ labheta:* "A spiritually advanced person can understand how the spiritual particle exists within the body, and thus by cultivating spiritual knowledge he can attain perfection in spiritual life." The intelligent person who is expert in finding the self within the body must understand the eight external energies, which are listed in *Bhagavad-gītā* (7.4):

bhūmir āpo 'nalo vāyuḥ
khaṁ mano buddhir eva ca
ahaṅkāra itīyaṁ me
bhinnā prakṛtir aṣṭadhā

"Earth, water, fire, air, ether, mind, intelligence and false ego—all together these eight comprise My separated material energies." *Bhūmi*, earth, includes all the objects of sense perception—*rūpa* (form), *rasa* (taste), *gandha* (smell), *śabda* (sound) and *sparśa* (touch). Within the earth are the fragrance of roses, the taste of sweet fruit, and whatever else we want. As stated in *Śrīmad-Bhāgavatam* (1.10.4), *sarva-kāma-dughā mahī:* the earth (*mahī*) contains all our requirements. Thus the objects of sense perception are all present in *bhūmi*, or the earth. The gross material elements and subtle material elements (mind, intelligence and *ahaṅkāra*, false ego) constitute the total material energy.

Within the total material energy are the three material modes or qualities. These qualities—*sattva-guṇa, rajo-guṇa* and *tamo-guṇa*—belong not to the soul but to the material energy. It is because of the interaction of these three material modes of nature that the five knowledge-gathering senses, the five working senses and their controller, the mind, are manifested. Then, according to these modes, the living entity gets the opportunity to perform different types of *karma* with different types of knowledge, thinking, feeling and willing. Thus the bodily machine begins to work.

This has all been properly analyzed in *sāṅkhya-yoga* by the great *ācāryas*, especially by the Supreme Personality of Godhead, Kṛṣṇa, in His incarnation as Devahūti-putra Kapila. This is indicated here by the word *ācāryaiḥ*. We need not follow anyone who is not an authorized *ācārya*. *Ācāryavān puruṣo veda:* one can understand the truth fully when he has taken shelter of an expert *ācārya*.

The living entity is individual, but the body is a composition of many material elements. This is proved by the fact that as soon as the living entity quits this combination of material elements, it becomes a mere conglomeration of matter. The matter is qualitatively one, and the spiritual soul is qualitatively one with the Supreme. The Supreme is one, and the individual soul is one, but the individual soul is understood to be the master of the individual combination of material energy, whereas the Supreme Lord is the controller of the total material energy. The living entity is the master of his particular body, and according to his activities he is subjected to different types of pains and pleasures. However, although the Supreme Person, the Paramātmā, is also one, He is present as an individual in all the different bodies.

The material energy is in fact divided into twenty-four elements. The individual soul, the owner of the individual body, is a twenty-fifth subject, and above everything is Lord Viṣṇu as Paramātmā, the supreme controller, who is the twenty-sixth subject. When one understands all of these twenty-six subjects, he becomes *adhyātma-vit*, an expert in understanding the distinction between matter and spirit. As stated in *Bhagavad-gītā* (13.3), *kṣetra-kṣetrajñayor jñānam:* understanding of the *kṣetra* (the constitution of the body) and of the individual soul and the Supersoul constitutes real *jñāna*, or knowledge. Unless one ultimately understands that the Supreme Lord is eternally related with the individual soul, one's knowledge is imperfect. This is confirmed in *Bhagavad-gītā* (7.19):

bahūnāṁ janmanām ante
jñānavān māṁ prapadyate
vāsudevaḥ sarvam iti
sa mahātmā sudurlabhaḥ

"After many births and deaths, he who is actually in knowledge surrenders unto Me, knowing Me to be the cause of all causes and all that is. Such a great soul is very rare." Everything, material and spiritual, consists of various energies of Vāsudeva, to whom the individual soul, the spiritual part of the Supreme Lord, is subordinate. Upon understanding this perfect knowledge, one surrenders to the Supreme Personality of Godhead (*vāsudevaḥ sarvam iti sa mahātmā sudurlabhaḥ*).

TEXT 23

देहस्तु सर्वसंघातो जगत् तस्थुरिति द्विधा ।
अत्रैव मृग्यः पुरुषो नेति नेतीत्यतत् त्यजन् ॥२३॥

dehas tu sarva-saṅghāto
jagat tasthur iti dvidhā
atraiva mṛgyaḥ puruṣo
neti netīty atat tyajan

dehaḥ—the body; *tu*—but; *sarva-saṅghātaḥ*—the combination of all the twenty-four elements; *jagat*—seen to be moving; *tasthuḥ*—and standing in one place; *iti*—thus; *dvidhā*—two kinds; *atra eva*—in this matter; *mṛgyaḥ*—to be searched for; *puruṣaḥ*—the living entity, the soul; *na*—not; *iti*—thus; *na*—not; *iti*—thus; *iti*—in this way; *atat*—what is not spirit; *tyajan*—giving up.

TRANSLATION

There are two kinds of bodies for every individual soul—a gross body made of five gross elements and a subtle body made of three subtle elements. Within these bodies, however, is the spirit soul. One must find the soul by analysis, saying, "This is not it. This is not it." Thus one must separate spirit from matter.

PURPORT

As previously stated, *svarṇaṁ yathā grāvasu hema-kāraḥ kṣetreṣu yogais tad-abhijña āpnuyāt.* An expert in the study of soil can find out where gold is and then dig there. He can then analyze the stone and test the gold with nitric acid. Similarly, one must analyze the whole body to find within the body the spirit soul. In studying one's own body, one must ask himself whether his head is his soul, his fingers are his soul, his hand is his soul, and so on. In this way, one must gradually reject all the material elements and the combinations of material elements in the body. Then, if one is expert and follows the *ācārya,* he can understand that he is the spiritual soul living within the body. The greatest *ācārya,* Kṛṣṇa, begins His teachings in *Bhagavad-gītā* by saying:

dehino 'smin yathā dehe
kaumāraṁ yauvanaṁ jarā
tathā dehāntara-prāptir
dhīras tatra na muhyati

"As the embodied soul continually passes, in this body, from boyhood to youth to old age, the soul similarly passes into another body at death. The self-realized soul is not bewildered by such a change." (Bg. 2.13) The spirit soul possesses the body and is within the body. This is the real analysis. The soul never mixes with the bodily elements. Although the soul is within the body, it is separate and always pure. One must analyze and understand his self. This is self-realization. *Neti neti* is the analytical process of rejecting matter. By expertly conducting such an analysis, one can understand where the soul is. One who is not expert, however, cannot distinguish gold from earth, nor the soul from the body.

TEXT 24

अन्वयव्यतिरेकेण विवेकेनोशतात्मना ।
स्वर्गस्थानसमाम्नायैर्विमृशद्भिरसत्वरैः ॥२४॥

anvaya-vyatirekeṇa
vivekenośatātmanā
svarga-sthāna-samāmnāyair
vimṛśadbhir asatvaraiḥ

anvaya—directly; *vyatirekeṇa*—and indirectly; *vivekena*—by mature discrimination; *uśatā*—purified; *ātmanā*—with the mind; *svarga*—creation; *sthāna*—maintenance; *samāmnāyaiḥ*—and with destruction; *vimṛśadbhiḥ*—by those making a serious analysis; *asatvaraiḥ*—very sober.

TRANSLATION

Sober and expert persons should search for the spirit soul with minds purified through analytical study in terms of the soul's connection with and distinction from all things that undergo creation, maintenance and destruction.

PURPORT

A sober person can study himself and distinguish the soul from the body by analytical study. For example, when one considers his body—his head, his hands and so on—one can certainly understand the difference between the spirit soul and the body. No one says, "I head." Everyone says, "My head." Thus there are two entities—the head and "I." They are not identical, although they appear to be one conglomeration.

One may argue, "When we analyze the body we find a head, hands, legs, a belly, blood, bones, urine, stool and so on, but after everything is considered, where is the existence of the soul?" A sober man, however, avails himself of this Vedic instruction:

yato vā imāni bhūtāni jāyante. yena jātāni jīvanti. yat prayanty abhisaṁviśanti. tad vijijñāsasva. tad brahmeti. (*Taittirīya Upaniṣad* 3.1.1)

Thus he can understand that the head, hands, legs and indeed the entire body have grown on the basis of the soul. If the soul is within, the body, head, hands and legs grow, but otherwise they do not. A dead child does not grow up, for the soul is not present. If by a careful analysis of the body one still cannot find the existence of the soul, this is due to his ignorance. How can a gross man fully engaged in materialistic activities understand the soul, which is a small particle of spirit one ten-thousandth the size of the tip of a hair? Such a person foolishly thinks that the material body has grown from a combination of chemicals, although he cannot find them. The *Vedas* inform us, however, that chemical combinations do not constitute the living force; the living force is the *ātmā* and Paramātmā, and the body grows on the basis of that living force. The fruit of a tree grows and undergoes six kinds of change because of the presence of the tree. If there were no tree, there could be no question of the growth and maturity of fruit. Therefore, beyond the existence of the body are the Paramātmā and *ātmā* within the body. This is the first understanding of spiritual knowledge explained in *Bhagavad-gītā. Dehino 'smin yathā dehe.* The body exists because of the presence of the Supreme Lord and the *jīva,* which is part of the Lord. This is further explained by the Lord Himself in *Bhagavad-gītā* (9.4):

mayā tatam idaṁ sarvaṁ
jagad avyakta-mūrtinā
mat-sthāni sarva-bhūtāni
na cāhaṁ teṣv avasthitaḥ

"By Me, in My unmanifested form, this entire universe is pervaded. All beings are in Me, but I am not in them." The Supreme Soul exists everywhere. The *Vedas* enjoin, *sarvaṁ khalv idaṁ brahma:* everything is Brahman or an expansion of Brahman's energies. *Sūtre maṇi-gaṇā iva:* everything rests on the Lord, just like pearls strung together on a thread. The thread is the principal Brahman. He is the supreme cause, the

Supreme Lord upon whom everything rests (*mattaḥ parataraṁ nānyat*). Thus we must study the *ātmā* and Paramātmā—the individual soul and the Supersoul—upon whom the entire material cosmic manifestation rests. This is explained by the Vedic statement *yato vā imāni bhūtāni jāyante. yena jātāni jīvanti.*

TEXT 25

बुद्धेर्जागरणं स्वप्नः सुषुप्तिरिति वृत्तयः ।
ता येनैवानुभूयन्ते सोऽध्यक्षः पुरुषः परः ॥२५॥

buddher jāgaraṇaṁ svapnaḥ
suṣuptir iti vṛttayaḥ
tā yenaivānubhūyante
so 'dhyakṣaḥ puruṣaḥ paraḥ

buddheḥ—of the intelligence; *jāgaraṇam*—the waking or active state of the gross senses; *svapnaḥ*—dreaming (the activity of the senses without the gross body); *suṣuptiḥ*—deep sleep or cessation of all activities (although the living entity is the seer); *iti*—thus; *vṛttayaḥ*—the various transactions; *tāḥ*—they; *yena*—by whom; *eva*—indeed; *anubhūyante*—are perceived; *saḥ*—that; *adhyakṣaḥ*—overseer (who is different from the activities); *puruṣaḥ*—the enjoyer; *paraḥ*—transcendental.

TRANSLATION

Intelligence can be perceived in three states of activity—wakefulness, dreaming and deep sleep. The person who perceives these three is to be considered the original master, the ruler, the Supreme Personality of Godhead.

PURPORT

Without intelligence one cannot understand the direct activities of the senses, nor can he understand dreaming or the cessation of all gross and subtle activities. The seer and controller is the Supreme Personality of Godhead, the Supreme Soul, by whose direction the individual soul can understand when he is awake, when he is sleeping, and when he is completely in trance. In *Bhagavad-gītā* (15.15) the Lord says, *sarvasya cāhaṁ hṛdi sanniviṣṭo mattaḥ smṛtir jñānam apohanaṁ ca:* "I am seated in everyone's heart, and from Me come remembrance, knowledge and forgetfulness." The living entities are completely absorbed in the three states of wakefulness, dreaming and deep sleep through their intelligence. This intelligence is supplied by the Supreme Personality of Godhead, who accompanies the individual soul as a friend. Śrīla Madhvācārya says that the living entity is sometimes described as *sattva-buddhi* when his intelligence acts directly to perceive pains and pleasures above activities. There is a dreaming state in which understanding comes from the Supreme Personality of Godhead (*mattaḥ smṛtir jñānam apohanaṁ ca*). The Supreme Personality of Godhead, the Supersoul, is the supreme controller, and under His direction the living entities are subcontrollers. One must understand the Supreme Personality of Godhead with one's intelligence.

TEXT 26

एभिस्त्रिवर्णैः पर्यस्तैर्बुद्धिभेदैः क्रियोद्भवैः ।
स्वरूपमात्मनो बुध्येद् गन्धैर्वायुमिवान्वयात् ॥२६॥

ebhis tri-varṇaiḥ paryastair
buddhi-bhedaiḥ kriyodbhavaiḥ
svarūpam ātmano budhyed
gandhair vāyum ivānvayāt

ebhiḥ—by these; *tri-varṇaiḥ*—composed of the three modes of nature; *paryastaiḥ*—completely rejected (due to not touching the living force); *buddhi*—of intelligence; *bhedaiḥ*—the differentiations; *kriyā-udbhavaiḥ*—produced from different activities; *svarūpam*—the constitutional position; *ātmanaḥ*—of the self; *budhyet*—one should understand; *gandhaiḥ*—by the aromas; *vāyum*—the air; *iva*—exactly like; *anvayāt*—from close connection.

TRANSLATION

As one can understand the presence of the air by the aromas it carries, so, under the guidance of the Supreme Personality of

Godhead, one can understand the living soul by these three divisions of intelligence. These three divisions, however, are not the soul; they are constituted of the three modes and are born of activities.

PURPORT

As already explained, there are three states to our existence, namely wakefulness, dreaming and deep sleep. In all three states, we have different experiences. Thus the soul is the observer of these three states. Actually, the activities of the body are not the activities of the soul. The soul is different from the body. Just as aromas are distinct from the material vehicle in which they are carried, the soul is unattached to material activities. This analysis can be considered by a person who is fully under the shelter of the lotus feet of the Supreme Lord. This is confirmed by the Vedic injunction *yasmin vijñāte sarvam evaṁ vijñātaṁ bhavati.* If one can understand the Supreme Personality of Godhead, one can automatically understand everything else. Because of not taking shelter of the Lord's lotus feet, even great scholars, scientists, philosophers and religionists are always bewildered. This is confirmed in *Śrīmad-Bhāgavatam* (10.2.32):

ye 'nye 'ravindākṣa vimukta-māninas
tvayy asta-bhāvād aviśuddha-buddhayaḥ

Even though one may artificially think himself liberated from material contamination, if he has not taken shelter of the Lord's lotus feet his intelligence is polluted. As stated in *Bhagavad-gītā* (3.42):

indriyāṇi parāṇy āhur
indriyebhyaḥ paraṁ manaḥ
manasas tu parā buddhir
yo buddheḥ paratas tu saḥ

Above the senses is the mind, above the mind is the intelligence, and above the intelligence is the soul. Ultimately, when one's intelligence becomes clear through devotional service, one is situated in *buddhi-yoga.* This also is explained in *Bhagavad-gītā* (*dadāmi buddhi-yogaṁ taṁ yena mām upayānti te*). When devotional service develops and one's intelligence becomes clear, one can use his intelligence to return home, back to Godhead.

TEXT 27

एतद्द्वारो हि संसारो गुणकर्मनिबन्धनः ।
अज्ञानमूलोऽपार्थोऽपि पुंसः स्वप्न इवार्प्यते ॥२७॥

etad dvāro hi saṁsāro
guṇa-karma-nibandhanaḥ
ajñāna-mūlo 'pārtho 'pi
puṁsaḥ svapna ivārpyate

etat—this; *dvāraḥ*—whose door; *hi*—indeed; *saṁsāraḥ*—material existence, in which one suffers threefold miseries; *guṇa-karma-nibandhanaḥ*—captivation by the three modes of material nature; *ajñāna-mūlaḥ*—whose root is ignorance; *apārthaḥ*—without factual meaning; *api*—even; *puṁsaḥ*—of the living entity; *svapnaḥ*—a dream; *iva*—like; *arpyate*—is placed.

TRANSLATION

Through polluted intelligence one is subjected to the modes of nature, and thus one is conditioned by material existence. Like a dreaming state in which one falsely suffers, material existence, which is due to ignorance, must be considered unwanted and temporary.

PURPORT

The unwanted condition of temporary life is called ignorance. One can very easily understand that the material body is temporary, for it is generated at a certain date and ends at a certain date, after undergoing the six kinds of change, namely birth, death, growth, maintenance, transformation and dwindling. This condition of the eternal soul is due to his ignorance, and although it is temporary, it is unwanted. Because of ignorance one is put into temporary bodies one after another. The spirit soul, however, does not need to enter such temporary bodies. He does so only due to his ignorance or his forgetfulness of Kṛṣṇa. Therefore in the human form of life, when one's intelligence is developed, one should change his consciousness by trying to understand Kṛṣṇa. Then one can be liberated. This is confirmed in *Bhagavad-gītā* (4.9), where the Lord says:

janma karma ca me divyam
evaṁ yo vetti tattvataḥ
tyaktvā dehaṁ punar janma
naiti mām eti so 'rjuna

"One who knows the transcendental nature of My appearance and activities does not, upon leaving the body, take his birth again in this material world, but attains My eternal abode, O Arjuna." Unless one understands Kṛṣṇa and comes to Kṛṣṇa consciousness, one must continue in material bondage. To end this conditional life, one must surrender to the Supreme Personality of Godhead. Indeed, that is demanded by the Supreme Lord. *Sarva-dharmān parityajya mām ekaṁ śaraṇaṁ vraja.*

As advised by Mahārāja Ṛṣabhadeva, *na sādhu manye yata ātmano 'yam asann api kleśada āsa dehaḥ.* One must be intelligent enough to understand that although one's body is temporary and will not endure for long, as long as one has a body he must undergo the pangs of material existence. Therefore, if by good association, by the instructions of a bona fide spiritual master, one takes to Kṛṣṇa consciousness, his conditional life of material existence is vanquished, and his original consciousness, known as Kṛṣṇa consciousness, is revived. When one is Kṛṣṇa conscious, he can realize that material existence, whether one is awake or dreaming, is nothing but a dream and has no factual value. This realization is possible by the grace of the Supreme Lord. This grace is also present in the form of the instructions of *Bhagavad-gītā.* Therefore Śrī Caitanya Mahāprabhu's mission is for everyone to engage in welfare activities to awaken the foolish living entity, especially in human society, so that he may come to the platform of Kṛṣṇa consciousness and benefit by liberation from conditional life.

In this connection, Śrīla Madhvācārya cites the following verses:

duḥkha-rūpo 'pi saṁsāro
buddhi-pūrvam avāpyate

yathā svapne śiraś chedaṁ
svayaṁ kṛtvātmano vaśaḥ

tato duḥkham avāpyeta
tathā jāgarito 'pi tu
jānann apy ātmano duḥkham
avaśas tu pravartate

One must realize that the material condition of life is full of distresses. One can realize this with purified intelligence. When one's intelligence is purified, he can understand that unwanted, temporary, material life is just like a dream. Just as one suffers pain when his head is cut off in a dream, in ignorance one suffers not only while dreaming but also while awake. Without the mercy of the Supreme Personality of Godhead, one continues in ignorance and is thus subjected to material distresses in various ways.

TEXT 28

तस्माद्भवद्भिः कर्तव्यं कर्मणां त्रिगुणात्मनाम् ।
बीजनिर्हरणं योगः प्रवाहोपरमो धियः ॥२८॥

tasmād bhavadbhiḥ kartavyaṁ
karmaṇāṁ tri-guṇātmanām
bīja-nirharaṇaṁ yogaḥ
pravāhoparamo dhiyaḥ

tasmāt—therefore; *bhavadbhiḥ*—by your good selves; *kartavyam*—to be done; *karmaṇām*—of all material activities; *tri-guṇa-ātmanām*—conditioned by the three modes of material nature; *bīja-nirharaṇam*—burning of the seed; *yogaḥ*—the process by which one can be linked with the Supreme; *pravāha*—of the continuous current in the form of wakefulness, dreaming and deep sleep; *uparamaḥ*—the cessation; *dhiyaḥ*—of the intelligence.

TRANSLATION

Therefore, my dear friends, O sons of the demons, your duty is to take to Kṛṣṇa consciousness, which can burn the seed of fruitive

activities artificially created by the modes of material nature and stop the flow of the intelligence in wakefulness, dreaming and deep sleep. In other words, when one takes to Kṛṣṇa consciousness, his ignorance is immediately dissipated.

PURPORT

This is confirmed in *Bhagavad-gītā* (14.26):

mām ca yo 'vyabhicāreṇa
bhakti-yogena sevate
sa guṇān samatītyaitān
brahma-bhūyāya kalpate

"One who engages in full devotional service, who does not fall down in any circumstance, at once transcends the modes of material nature and thus comes to the level of Brahman." By the practice of *bhakti-yoga*, one immediately comes to the spiritual platform, transcendental to the actions and reactions of the three modes of material nature. The root of ignorance is material consciousness, which must be killed by spiritual consciousness, or Kṛṣṇa consciousness. The word *bīja-nirharaṇam* refers to burning the root cause of material life to ashes. In the Medinī dictionary, *yoga* is explained by its result: *yoge 'pūrvārtha-samprāptau saṅgati-dhyāna-yuktiṣu.* When one is put into an awkward position because of ignorance, the process by which one can be freed from this entanglement is called *yoga.* This is also called liberation. *Muktir hitvānyathā-rūpam svarūpeṇa vyavasthitiḥ. Mukti* means giving up one's position in ignorance or illusion, by which one thinks in a way contrary to his constitutional position. Returning to one's constitutional position is called *mukti,* and the process by which one does this is called *yoga.* Thus *yoga* is above *karma, jñāna* and *sāṅkhya.* Indeed, *yoga* is the ultimate goal of life. Kṛṣṇa therefore advised Arjuna to become a *yogī* (*tasmād yogī bhavārjuna*). Lord Kṛṣṇa further advised in *Bhagavad-gītā* that the first-class *yogī* is he who has come to the platform of devotional service.

yoginām api sarveṣām
mad-gatenāntarātmanā

śraddhāvān bhajate yo māṁ
sa me yuktatamo mataḥ

"Of all *yogīs*, he who always abides in Me with great faith, worshiping Me in transcendental loving service, is most intimately united with Me in *yoga* and is the highest of all." (Bg. 6.47) Thus one who always thinks of Kṛṣṇa within the core of his heart is the best *yogī*. By practicing this best of all *yoga* systems, one is liberated from the material condition.

TEXT 29

तत्रोपायसहस्राणामयं भगवतोदितः ।
यदीश्वरे भगवति यथा यैरञ्जसा रतिः ॥२९॥

tatropāya-sahasrāṇām
ayaṁ bhagavatoditaḥ
yad īśvare bhagavati
yathā yair añjasā ratiḥ

tatra—in that connection (getting out of the entanglement of material conditioning); *upāya*—of processes; *sahasrāṇām*—of many thousands; *ayam*—this; *bhagavatā uditaḥ*—given by the Supreme Personality of Godhead; *yat*—which; *īśvare*—to the Lord; *bhagavati*—the Supreme Personality of Godhead; *yathā*—as much as; *yaiḥ*—by which; *añjasā*—quickly; *ratiḥ*—attachment with love and affection.

TRANSLATION

Of the different processes recommended for disentanglement from material life, the one personally explained and accepted by the Supreme Personality of Godhead should be considered all-perfect. That process is the performance of duties by which love for the Supreme Lord develops.

PURPORT

Among the linking processes that elevate one from bondage to material contamination, the one recommended by the Supreme Personality of Godhead should be accepted as the best. That process is clearly explained in *Bhagavad-gītā*, where the Lord says, *sarva-dharmān parityajya mām ekaṁ śaraṇaṁ vraja:* "Abandon all varieties of religion and just surrender unto Me." This process is the best because the Lord assures, *ahaṁ tvāṁ sarva-pāpebhyo mokṣayiṣyāmi mā śucaḥ:* "I shall deliver you from all sinful reaction. Do not fear." There is no need to be worried, for the Lord Himself assures that He will care for His devotee and save him from the reactions of sinful activities. Material bondage is a result of sinful activity. Therefore, since the Lord assures that He will dissipate the results of fruitive material activities, there is no need to be worried. This process of understanding one's position as a spirit soul and then engaging oneself in devotional service is therefore the best. The entire Vedic program is based on this principle, and one can understand it as recommended in the *Vedas:*

yasya deve parā bhaktir
yathā deve tathā gurau
tasyaite kathitā hy arthāḥ
prakāśante mahātmanah

"Unto those great souls who have implicit faith in both the Lord and the spiritual master, all the imports of Vedic knowledge are automatically revealed." (*Śvetāśvatara Upaniṣad* 6.23) One must accept the pure devotee, the representative of God, as one's *guru* and then offer him all the respects one would offer the Supreme Personality of Godhead. This is the secret of success. For one who adopts this method, the perfect process is revealed. In this verse, the words *yair añjasā ratiḥ* indicate that by offering service and surrendering to the spiritual master, one is elevated to devotional service, and by performing devotional service one gradually becomes attached to the Supreme Personality of Godhead. Because of this attachment to the Lord, one can understand the Lord. In other words, one can understand what the Lord's position is, what our position is and what our relationship is. All this can be understood very easily by the simple method of *bhakti-yoga.* As soon as one is situated on the platform of *bhakti-yoga,* the root cause of one's suffering and material bondage is destroyed. This is clearly explained in the next verse, which gives the secret of success.

TEXTS 30–31

गुरुशुश्रूषया भक्त्या सर्वलब्धार्पणेन च ।
सङ्गेन साधुभक्तानामीश्वराराधनेन च ॥३०॥
श्रद्धया तत्कथायां च कीर्तनैर्गुणकर्मणाम् ।
तत्पादाम्बुरुहध्यानात् तल्लिङ्गेक्षार्हणादिभिः ॥३१॥

guru-śuśrūṣayā bhaktyā
sarva-labdhārpaṇena ca
saṅgena sādhu-bhaktānām
īśvarārādhanena ca

śraddhayā tat-kathāyāṁ ca
kīrtanair guṇa-karmaṇām
tat-pādāmburuha-dhyānāt
tal-liṅgekṣārhaṇādibhiḥ

guru-śuśrūṣayā—by rendering service to the bona fide spiritual master; *bhaktyā*—with faith and devotion; *sarva*—all; *labdha*—of material gains; *arpaṇena*—by offering (to the *guru*, or to Kṛṣṇa through the spiritual master); *ca*—and; *saṅgena*—by the association; *sādhu-bhaktānām*—of devotees and saintly persons; *īśvara*—of the Supreme Personality of Godhead; *ārādhanena*—by the worship; *ca*—and; *śraddhayā*—with great faith; *tat-kathāyām*—in discourses about the Lord; *ca*—and; *kīrtanaiḥ*—by glorifications; *guṇa-karmaṇām*—of the transcendental qualities and activities of the Lord; *tat*—His; *pāda-amburuha*—on the lotus feet; *dhyānāt*—by meditation; *tat*—His; *liṅga*—forms (Deities); *īkṣa*—observing; *arhaṇa-ādibhiḥ*—and by worshiping.

TRANSLATION

One must accept the bona fide spiritual master and render service unto him with great devotion and faith. Whatever one has in one's possession should be offered to the spiritual master, and in the association of saintly persons and devotees one should worship the Lord, hear the glories of the Lord with faith, glorify the

transcendental qualities and activities of the Lord, always meditate on the Lord's lotus feet, and worship the Deity of the Lord strictly according to the injunctions of the śāstra and guru.

PURPORT

In the previous verse it has been said that the process which immediately increases one's love and affection for the Supreme Personality of Godhead is the best of the many thousands of ways to become free from the entanglement of material existence. It is also said, *dharmasya tattvaṁ nihitaṁ guhāyām:* actually the truth of religious principles is extremely confidential. Nonetheless, it can be understood very easily if one actually adopts the principles of religion. As it is said, *dharmaṁ tu sākṣād bhagavat-praṇītam:* the process of religion is enunciated by the Supreme Lord because He is the supreme authority. This is also indicated in the previous verse by the word *bhagavatoditaḥ.* The injunctions or directions of the Lord are infallible, and their benefits are fully assured. According to His directions, which are explained in this verse, the perfect form of religion is *bhakti-yoga.*

To practice *bhakti-yoga,* one must first accept a bona fide spiritual master. Śrīla Rūpa Gosvāmī, in his *Bhakti-rasāmṛta-sindhu* (1.2.74–75), advises:

guru-pādāśrayas tasmāt
kṛṣṇa-dīkṣādi-śikṣaṇam
viśrambheṇa guroḥ sevā
sādhu-vartmānuvartanam

sad-dharma-pṛcchā bhogādi-
tyāgaḥ kṛṣṇasya hetave

One's first duty is to accept a bona fide spiritual master. The student or disciple should be very inquisitive; he should be eager to know the complete truth about eternal religion (*sanātana-dharma*). The words *guru-śuśrūṣayā* mean that one should personally serve the spiritual master by giving him bodily comforts, helping him in bathing, dressing, sleeping, eating and so on. This is called *guru-śuśrūṣaṇam.* A disciple should serve the spiritual master as a menial servant, and whatever he has in his possession should be dedicated to the spiritual master. *Prāṇair arthair dhiyā vācā.* Everyone has his life, his wealth, his intelligence and his words, and all of them should be offered to the Supreme Personality of Godhead through the via medium of the spiritual master. Everything should be offered to the spiritual master as a matter of duty, but the offering should be made to the spiritual master with heart and soul, not artificially to gain material prestige. This offering is called *arpaṇa.* Moreover, one should live among devotees, saintly persons, to learn the etiquette and proper behavior of devotional service. Śrīla Viśvanātha Cakravartī Ṭhākura remarks in this connection that whatever is offered to the spiritual master should be offered with love and affection, not for material adoration. Similarly, it is recommended that one associate with devotees, but there must be some discrimination. Actually, a *sādhu,* a saintly person, must be saintly in his behavior (*sādhavaḥ sad-ācārāḥ*). Unless one adheres to the standard behavior, one's position as a *sādhu,* a saintly person, is not complete. Therefore a Vaiṣṇava, a *sādhu,* must completely adhere to the standard of behavior. Śrīla Viśvanātha Cakravartī Ṭhākura says that a Vaiṣṇava, a person initiated into the Vaiṣṇava cult, should be offered the respect befitting a Vaiṣṇava, which means that he should be offered service and prayers. However, one should not associate with him if he is not a fit person with whom to associate.

TEXT 32

हरिः सर्वेषु भूतेषु भगवानास्त ईश्वरः ।
इति भूतानि मनसा कामैस्तैः साधु मानयेत् ।।३२।।

hariḥ sarveṣu bhūteṣu
bhagavān āsta īśvaraḥ
iti bhūtāni manasā
kāmais taiḥ sādhu mānayet

hariḥ—the Supreme Personality of Godhead; *sarveṣu*—in all; *bhūteṣu*—living entities; *bhagavān*—the supreme personality; *āste*—is situated; *īśvaraḥ*—the supreme controller; *iti*—thus; *bhūtāni*—all living entities; *manasā*—by such understanding; *kāmaiḥ*—by desires; *taiḥ*—those; *sādhu mānayet*—one should highly esteem.

TRANSLATION

One should always remember the Supreme Personality of Godhead in His localized representation as the Paramātmā, who is situated in the core of every living entity's heart. Thus one should offer respect to every living entity according to that living entity's position or manifestation.

PURPORT

Hariḥ sarveṣu bhūteṣu. This statement is sometimes misunderstood by unscrupulous persons who wrongly conclude that because Hari, the Supreme Personality of Godhead, is situated in every living entity, every living entity is therefore Hari. Such foolish persons do not distinguish between the *ātmā* and the Paramātmā, who are situated in every body. The *ātmā* is the living entity, and the Paramātmā is the Supreme Personality of Godhead. The individual living entity, however, is different from the Paramātmā, the Supreme Lord. Therefore *hariḥ sarveṣu bhūteṣu* means that Hari is situated as Paramātmā, not as *ātmā*, although *ātmā* is a part of Paramātmā. Offering respect to every living entity means offering respect to the Paramātmā situated in every living entity. One should not misunderstand every living entity to be the Paramātmā. Sometimes unscrupulous persons designate a living entity as *daridra-nārāyaṇa, svāmī-nārāyaṇa*, this Nārāyaṇa or that Nārāyaṇa. One should clearly understand that although Nārāyaṇa is situated in the core of the heart of every living entity, the living entity never becomes Nārāyaṇa.

TEXT 33

एवं निर्जितषड्वर्गैः क्रियते भक्तिरीश्वरे ।
वासुदेवे भगवति यया संलभ्यते रतिः ॥३३॥

evaṁ nirjita-ṣaḍ-vargaiḥ
kriyate bhaktir īśvare
vāsudeve bhagavati
yayā saṁlabhyate ratiḥ

evam—thus; *nirjita*—subdued; *ṣaṭ-vargaiḥ*—by the six symptoms of the senses (lusty desires, anger, greed, illusion, madness and jealousy);

kriyate—is rendered; *bhaktiḥ*—devotional service; *īśvare*—unto the supreme controller; *vāsudeve*—to Lord Vāsudeva; *bhagavati*—the Supreme Personality of Godhead; *yayā*—by which; *saṁlabhyate*—is obtained; *ratiḥ*—attachment.

TRANSLATION

By these activities [as mentioned above] one is able to cut down the influence of the enemies, namely lust, anger, greed, illusion, madness and jealousy, and when thus situated, one can render service to the Lord. In this way one surely attains the platform of loving service to the Supreme Personality of Godhead.

PURPORT

As mentioned in verses thirty and thirty-one, one's first duty is to approach the spiritual master, the representative of the Supreme Personality of Godhead, to begin rendering service to him. Prahlāda Mahārāja proposed that from the very beginning of life (*kaumāra ācaret prājñaḥ*) a small child should be trained to serve the spiritual master while living at the *guru-kula*. *Brahmacārī guru-kule vasan dānto guror hitam* (*Bhāg.* 7.12.1). This is the beginning of spiritual life. *Guru-pādāśrayaḥ, sādhu-vartmānuvartanam, sad-dharma-pṛcchā.* By following the instructions of the *guru* and the *śāstras*, the disciple attains the stage of devotional service and becomes unattached to possessions. Whatever he possesses he offers to the spiritual master, the *guru*, who engages him in *śravaṇaṁ kīrtanaṁ viṣṇoḥ*. The disciple follows strictly and in this way learns how to control his senses. Then, by using his pure intelligence, he gradually becomes a lover of the Supreme Personality of Godhead, as confirmed by Śrīla Rūpa Gosvāmī (*ādau śraddhā tataḥ sādhu-saṅgaḥ*). In this way one's life becomes perfect, and his attachment for Kṛṣṇa becomes positively manifested. In that stage, he is situated in ecstasy, experiencing *bhāva* and *anubhāva*, as explained in the following verse.

TEXT 34

निशम्य कर्माणि गुणानतुल्यान्
वीर्याणि लीलातनुभिः कृतानि ।

यदातिहर्षोत्पुलकाश्रुगद्गदं
प्रोत्कण्ठ उद्गायति रौति नृत्यति ॥३४॥

niśamya karmāṇi guṇān atulyān
vīryāṇi līlā-tanubhiḥ kṛtāni
yadātiharṣotpulakāśru-gadgadaṁ
protkaṇṭha udgāyati rauti nṛtyati

niśamya—hearing; *karmāṇi*—transcendental activities; *guṇān*—spiritual qualities; *atulyān*—uncommon (not generally visible in an ordinary person); *vīryāṇi*—very powerful; *līlā-tanubhiḥ*—by different pastime forms; *kṛtāni*—performed; *yadā*—when; *atiharṣa*—because of great jubilation; *utpulaka*—horripilation; *aśru*—tears in the eyes; *gadgadam*—faltering voice; *protkaṇṭhaḥ*—with an open voice; *udgāyati*—chants very loudly; *rauti*—cries; *nṛtyati*—dances.

TRANSLATION

One who is situated in devotional service is certainly the controller of his senses, and thus he is a liberated person. When such a liberated person, the pure devotee, hears of the transcendental qualities and activities of the Lord's incarnations for the performance of various pastimes, his hair stands on end on his body, tears fall from his eyes, and in his spiritual realization his voice falters. Sometimes he very openly dances, sometimes he sings loudly, and sometimes he cries. Thus he expresses his transcendental jubilation.

PURPORT

The Lord's activities are uncommon. For example, when He appeared as Lord Rāmacandra, He performed uncommon activities like bridging the ocean. Similarly, when Lord Kṛṣṇa appeared He raised the Govardhana Hill when He was only seven years of age. These are uncommon activities. Fools and rascals, who are not in the transcendental position, consider these uncommon activities of the Lord to be mythological, but when the pure devotee, the liberated person, hears about these uncommon activities of the Lord, he immediately becomes ecstatic and exhibits the symptoms of chanting, dancing, and crying very loudly and jubilantly. This is the difference between a devotee and a nondevotee.

TEXT 35

यदा ग्रहग्रस्त इव क्वचिद्धस-
त्याक्रन्दते ध्यायति वन्दते जनम् ।
मुहुः श्वसन्वक्ति हरे जगत्पते
नारायणेत्यात्ममतिर्गतत्रपः ॥३५॥

yadā graha-grasta iva kvacid dhasaty
ākrandate dhyāyati vandate janam
muhuḥ śvasan vakti hare jagat-pate
nārāyaṇety ātma-matir gata-trapaḥ

yadā—when; *graha-grastaḥ*—haunted by a ghost; *iva*—like; *kvacit*—sometimes; *hasati*—laughs; *ākrandate*—cries loudly (remembering the transcendental qualities of the Lord); *dhyāyati*—meditates; *vandate*—offers respects; *janam*—to all living entities (thinking all of them to be engaged in the service of the Lord); *muhuḥ*—constantly; *śvasan*—breathing heavily; *vakti*—he speaks; *hare*—O my Lord; *jagat-pate*—O master of the whole world; *nārāyaṇa*—O Lord Nārāyaṇa; *iti*—thus; *ātma-matiḥ*—fully absorbed in thoughts of the Supreme Lord; *gata-trapaḥ*—without shame.

TRANSLATION

When a devotee becomes like a person haunted by a ghost, he laughs and very loudly chants about the qualities of the Lord. Sometimes he sits to perform meditation, and he offers respects to every living entity, considering him a devotee of the Lord. Constantly breathing very heavily, he becomes careless of social etiquette and loudly chants like a madman, "Hare Kṛṣṇa, Hare Kṛṣṇa! O my Lord, O master of the universe!"

PURPORT

When one chants the holy name of the Lord in ecstasy, not caring for outward social conventions, it is to be understood that he is *ātma-mati.* In other words, his consciousness is turned toward the Supreme Personality of Godhead.

TEXT 36

तदा पुमान्मुक्तसमस्तबन्धन-
स्तद्भावभावानुकृताशयाकृतिः ।
निर्दग्धबीजानुशयो महीयसा
भक्तिप्रयोगेण समेत्यधोक्षजम् ॥३६॥

tadā pumān mukta-samasta-bandhanas
tad-bhāva-bhāvānukṛtāśayākṛtiḥ
nirdagdha-bījānuśayo mahīyasā
bhakti-prayogeṇa samety adhokṣajam

tadā—at that time; *pumān*—the living entity; *mukta*—liberated; *samasta-bandhanaḥ*—from all material obstacles on the path of devotional service; *tat-bhāva*—of the situation of the Supreme Lord's activities; *bhāva*—by thinking; *anukṛta*—made similar; *āśaya-ākṛtiḥ*—whose mind and body; *nirdagdha*—completely burned up; *bīja*—the seed or original cause of material existence; *anuśayaḥ*—desire; *mahīyasā*—very powerful; *bhakti*—of devotional service; *prayogeṇa*—by the application; *sameti*—achieves; *adhokṣajam*—the Supreme Personality of Godhead, who is beyond the reach of the material mind and knowledge.

TRANSLATION

The devotee is then freed from all material contamination because he constantly thinks of the Lord's pastimes and because his mind and body have been converted to spiritual qualities. Because of his intense devotional service, his ignorance, material consciousness and all kinds of material desires are completely burnt to ashes. This is the stage at which one can achieve the shelter of the Lord's lotus feet.

PURPORT

When a devotee is completely purified, he becomes *anyābhilāṣitā-śūnya.* In other words, all of his material desires become zero, being burnt to ashes, and he exists either as the Lord's servant, friend, father, mother or conjugal lover. Because one thinks constantly in this way, one's present material body and mind are fully spiritualized, and the needs of one's material body completely vanish from one's existence. An iron rod put into a fire becomes warmer and warmer, and when it is red hot it is no longer an iron rod but fire. Similarly, when a devotee constantly engages in devotional service and thinks of the Lord in his original Kṛṣṇa consciousness, he no longer has any material activities, for his body is spiritualized. Advancement in Kṛṣṇa consciousness is very powerful, and therefore even during this life such a devotee has achieved the shelter of the lotus feet of the Lord. This transcendental ecstatic existence of a devotee was completely exhibited by Śrī Caitanya Mahāprabhu. In this regard, Śrīla Madhvācārya writes as follows:

tad-bhāva-bhāvaḥ tad yathā svarūpaṁ bhaktiḥ
kecid bhaktā vinṛtyanti gāyanti ca yathepsitam
kecit tuṣṇīṁ japanty eva kecit śobhaya-kāriṇaḥ

The ecstatic condition of devotional service was completely exhibited by Śrī Caitanya Mahāprabhu, who sometimes danced, sometimes cried, sometimes sang, sometimes remained silent, and sometimes chanted the holy name of the Lord. That is perfect spiritual existence.

TEXT 37

अधोक्षजालम्भमिहाशुभात्मनः
शरीरिणः संसृतिचक्रशातनम् ।
तद् ब्रह्मनिर्वाणसुखं विदुर्बुधा-
स्ततो भजध्वं हृदये हृदीश्वरम् ॥३७॥

adhokṣajālambham ihāśubhātmanaḥ
śarīriṇaḥ saṁsṛti-cakra-śātanam
tad brahma-nirvāṇa-sukhaṁ vidur budhās
tato bhajadhvaṁ hṛdaye hṛd-īśvaram

adhokṣaja—with the Supreme Personality of Godhead, who is beyond the reach of the materialistic mind or experimental knowledge;

ālambham—being constantly in contact; *iha*—in this material world; *aśubha-ātmanaḥ*—whose mind is materially contaminated; *śarīriṇaḥ*—of a living entity who has accepted a material body; *saṁsṛti*—of material existence; *cakra*—the cycle; *śātanam*—completely stopping; *tat*—that; *brahma-nirvāṇa*—connected with the Supreme Brahman, the Absolute Truth; *sukham*—transcendental happiness; *viduḥ*—understand; *budhāḥ*—those who are spiritually advanced; *tataḥ*—therefore; *bhajadhvam*—engage in devotional service; *hṛdaye*—within the core of the heart; *hṛt-īśvaram*—to the Supreme Personality of Godhead, the Supersoul within the heart.

TRANSLATION

The real problem of life is the repetition of birth and death, which is like a wheel rolling repeatedly up and down. This wheel, however, completely stops when one is in touch with the Supreme Personality of Godhead. In other words, by the transcendental bliss realized from constant engagement in devotional service, one is completely liberated from material existence. All learned men know this. Therefore, my dear friends, O sons of the asuras, immediately begin meditating upon and worshiping the Supersoul within everyone's heart.

PURPORT

Generally it is understood that by merging into the existence of Brahman, the impersonal feature of the Absolute Truth, one becomes completely happy. The words *brahma-nirvāṇa* refer to connecting with the Absolute Truth, who is realized in three features: *brahmeti paramātmeti bhagavān iti śabdyate.* One feels *brahma-sukha*, spiritual happiness, by merging into the impersonal Brahman because the *brahmajyoti* is the effulgence of the Supreme Personality of Godhead. *Yasya prabhā prabhavato jagad-aṇḍa-koṭi. Yasya prabhā*, the impersonal Brahman, consists of the rays of Kṛṣṇa's transcendental body. Therefore whatever transcendental bliss one feels from merging in Brahman is due to contact with Kṛṣṇa. Contact with Kṛṣṇa is perfect *brahma-sukha.* When the mind is in touch with the impersonal Brahman one becomes satisfied, but one must advance further to render service to the Supreme Personality of Godhead, for one's remaining merged in the Brahman effulgence is not always assured. As it is said, *āruhya kṛcchreṇa paraṁ padaṁ tataḥ patanty adho 'nādṛta-yuṣmad-aṅghrayaḥ:* one may merge in the Brahman feature of the Absolute Truth, but there is a chance that one may fall because of not being acquainted with Adhokṣaja, or Vāsudeva. Of course, such *brahma-sukha* undoubtedly eliminates material happiness, but when one advances through impersonal Brahman and localized Paramātmā to approach the Supreme Personality of Godhead in relationship with Him as a servant, friend, parent or conjugal lover, one's happiness becomes all-pervading. Then one automatically feels transcendental bliss, just as one becomes happy seeing the shining of the moon. One acquires natural happiness upon seeing the moon, but when one can see the Supreme Personality of Godhead, one's transcendental happiness increases hundreds and thousands of times. As soon as one is very intimately connected with the Supreme Personality of Godhead, one surely becomes free from all material contamination. *Yā nirvṛtis tanu-bhṛtām.* This cessation of all material happiness is called *nirvṛti* or *nirvāṇa.* Śrīla Rūpa Gosvāmī says in *Bhakti-rasāmṛta-sindhu* (1.1.38):

brahmānando bhaved eṣa
cet parārdha-guṇīkṛtaḥ
naiti bhakti-sukhāmbhodheḥ
paramāṇu-tulām api

"If *brahmānanda,* the bliss of merging in the Brahman effulgence, were multiplied one hundred trillion times, it would still not equal even an atomic fragment of the ocean of transcendental bliss felt in devotional service."

brahma-bhūtaḥ prasannātmā
na śocati na kāṅkṣati
samaḥ sarveṣu bhūteṣu
mad-bhaktiṁ labhate parām

"One who is transcendentally situated at once realizes the Supreme Brahman and becomes fully joyful. He never laments nor desires to have anything; he is equally disposed toward all living entities. In that state he attains pure devotional service unto the Lord." (Bg. 18.54) If one advances further from the *brahma-nirvāṇa* platform, one enters the stage of devotional service (*mad-bhaktiṁ labhate parām*). The word *adhokṣajālambham* refers to keeping the mind always engaged in the Absolute Truth, who is beyond the mind and material speculation. *Sa vai manaḥ kṛṣṇa-padāravindayoḥ.* This is the result of Deity worship. By constantly engaging in the service of the Lord and thinking of His lotus feet, one is automatically freed from all material contamination. Thus the word *brahma-nirvāṇa-sukham* indicates that when one is in touch with the Absolute Truth, material sense gratification is completely nullified.

TEXT 38

कोऽतिप्रयासोऽसुरबालका हरे-
रुपासने स्वे हृदि छिद्रवत् सतः ।
स्वस्यात्मनः सख्युरशेषदेहिनां
सामान्यतः किं विषयोपपादनैः ॥३८॥

ko 'ti-prayāso 'sura-bālakā harer
upāsane sve hṛdi chidravat sataḥ
svasyātmanaḥ sakhyur aśeṣa-dehināṁ
sāmānyataḥ kiṁ viṣayopapādanaiḥ

kaḥ—what; *ati-prayāsaḥ*—difficult endeavor; *asura-bālakāḥ*—O sons of demons; *hareḥ*—of the Supreme Personality of Godhead; *upāsane*—in discharging the devotional service; *sve*—in one's own; *hṛdi*—core of the heart; *chidra-vat*—just like the space; *sataḥ*—who always exists; *svasya*—of one's self or of the living entity; *ātmanaḥ*—of the Supersoul; *sakhyuḥ*—of the well-wishing friend; *aśeṣa*—unlimited; *dehinām*—of the embodied souls; *sāmānyataḥ*—generally; *kim*—what is the need; *viṣaya-upapādanaiḥ*—with activities delivering the objects of the senses for sense enjoyment.

TRANSLATION

O my friends, sons of the asuras, the Supreme Personality of Godhead in His Supersoul feature always exists within the cores of

the hearts of all living entities. Indeed, He is the well-wisher and friend of all living entities, and there is no difficulty in worshiping the Lord. Why, then, should people not engage in His devotional service? Why are they so addicted to unnecessarily producing artificial paraphernalia for sense gratification?

PURPORT

Because the Personality of Godhead is supreme, no one is equal to Him, and no one is greater than Him. Nonetheless, if one is a devotee of the Supreme Personality of Godhead, the Lord is easily obtainable. The Lord is compared to the sky because the sky is vast yet within the reach of all, not only of human beings but even of the animals. The Supreme Lord, in His Paramātmā feature, exists as the best well-wisher and friend. As confirmed in the *Vedas, sayujau sakhāyau.* The Lord, in His Supersoul feature, always stays in the heart along with the living entity. The Lord is so friendly to the living entity that He remains within the heart so that one can always contact Him without difficulty. One can do this simply by devotional service (*śravaṇaṁ kīrtanaṁ viṣṇoḥ smaranaṁ pāda-sevanam*). As soon as one hears of the Supreme Personality of Godhead (*kṛṣṇa-kīrtana*), one immediately comes in touch with the Lord. A devotee immediately comes in touch with the Lord by any or all of the items of devotional service:

śravaṇaṁ kīrtanaṁ viṣṇoḥ
smaraṇaṁ pāda-sevanam
arcanaṁ vandanaṁ dāsyaṁ
sakhyam ātma-nivedanam

Therefore there is no difficulty in coming in contact with the Supreme Lord (*ko 'ti-prayāsaḥ*). On the other hand, going to hell requires great endeavor. If one wants to go to hell by illicit sex, meat-eating, gambling and intoxication, he must acquire so many things. For illicit sex he must arrange for money for brothels, for meat-eating he must arrange for many slaughterhouses, for gambling he must arrange for casinos and hotels, and for intoxication he must open many breweries. Clearly, therefore, if one wants to go to hell he must endeavor very much, but if he wants to return home, back to Godhead, there is no difficult endeavor.

To go back to Godhead, one may live alone anywhere, in any condition, and simply sit down, meditate upon the Supersoul and chant and hear about the Lord. Thus there is no difficulty in approaching the Lord. *Adānta-gobhir viśatāṁ tamisram.* Because of inability to control the senses, one must go through great endeavor to go to hell, but if one is sensible he can very easily obtain the favor of the Supreme Personality of Godhead because the Lord is always with him. By the simple method of *śravaṇaṁ kīrtanaṁ viṣṇoḥ*, the Lord is satisfied. Indeed, the Lord says:

patraṁ puṣpaṁ phalaṁ toyaṁ
yo me bhaktyā prayacchati
tad ahaṁ bhakty-upahṛtam
aśnāmi prayatātmanaḥ

"If one offers Me with love and devotion a leaf, a flower, fruit or water, I will accept it." (Bg. 9.26) One can meditate upon the Lord anywhere and everywhere. Thus Prahlāda Mahārāja advised his friends, the sons of the demons, to take this path back home, back to Godhead, without difficulty.

TEXT 39

रायः कलत्रं पशवः सुतादयो
गृहा मही कुञ्जरकोशभूतयः ।
सर्वेऽर्थकामाः क्षणभङ्गुरायुषः
कुर्वन्ति मर्त्यस्य कियत् प्रियं चलाः ॥३९॥

rāyaḥ kalatraṁ paśavaḥ sutādayo
gṛhā mahī kuñjara-kośa-bhūtayaḥ
sarve 'rtha-kāmāḥ kṣaṇa-bhaṅgurāyuṣaḥ
kurvanti martyasya kiyat priyaṁ calāḥ

rāyaḥ—wealth; *kalatram*—one's wife and feminine friends; *paśavaḥ*—domestic animals like cows, horses, asses, cats and dogs; *suta-ādayaḥ*—children and so on; *gṛhāḥ*—big buildings and residences; *mahī*—land; *kuñjara*—elephants; *kośa*—treasury house; *bhūtayaḥ*—and other luxuries for sense gratification and material enjoyment;

sarve—all; *artha*—economic development; *kāmāḥ*—and sense gratification; *kṣaṇa-bhaṅgura*—perishable in a moment; *āyuṣaḥ*—of one whose duration of life; *kurvanti*—effect or bring; *martyasya*—of one who is destined to die; *kiyat*—how much; *priyam*—pleasure; *calāḥ*—flickering and temporary.

TRANSLATION

One's riches, beautiful wife and female friends, one's sons and daughters, one's residence, one's domestic animals like cows, elephants and horses, one's treasury, economic development and sense gratification—indeed, even the lifetime in which one can enjoy all these material opulences—are certainly temporary and flickering. Since the opportunity of human life is temporary, what benefit can these material opulences give to a sensible man who has understood himself to be eternal?

PURPORT

This verse describes how the advocates of economic development are frustrated by the laws of nature. As the previous verse asks, *kiṁ viṣayopapādanaiḥ:* what is the actual benefit of so-called economic development? The history of the world has factually proved that attempts to increase economic development for bodily comfort through the advancement of material civilization have done nothing to remedy the inevitability of birth, death, old age and disease. Everyone has knowledge of huge empires throughout the history of the world—the Roman Empire, the Moghul Empire, the British Empire and so on—but all the societies engaged in such economic development (*sarve 'rtha-kāmāḥ*) have been frustrated by the laws of nature through periodic wars, pestilence, famine and so on. Thus all their attempts have been flickering and temporary. In this verse, therefore, it is said, *kurvanti martyasya kiyat priyaṁ calāḥ:* one may be very proud of possessing a vast empire, but such empires are impermanent; after one hundred or two hundred years, everything is finished. All such positions of economic development, although created with great endeavor and hardship, are vanquished very soon. Therefore they have been described as *calāḥ*. An intelligent man should conclude that material economic development is not at all pleasing. The entire world is described in *Bhagavad-gītā* as *duḥkhālayam aśāśvatam*—miserable and temporary. Economic development may be pleasing for some time, but it cannot endure. Thus many big businessmen are now very morose because they are being harassed by various plundering governments. In conclusion, why should one waste his time for so-called economic development, which is neither permanent nor pleasing to the soul?

On the other hand, our relationship with Kṛṣṇa, the Supreme Personality of Godhead, is eternal. *Nitya-siddha kṛṣṇa-prema.* The pure souls are eternally in love with Kṛṣṇa, and this permanent love, either as a servant, a friend, a parent or a conjugal lover, is not at all difficult to revive. Especially in this age, the concession is that simply by chanting the Hare Kṛṣṇa *mantra* (*harer nāma harer nāma harer nāmaiva kevalam*) one revives his original relationship with God and thus becomes so happy that he does not want anything material. As enunciated by Śrī Caitanya Mahāprabhu, *na dhanaṁ na janaṁ na sundarīṁ kavitāṁ vā jagad-īśa kāmaye.* A very advanced devotee in Kṛṣṇa consciousness does not want riches, followers or possessions. *Rāyaḥ kalatraṁ paśavaḥ sutādayo gṛhā mahī kuñjara-kośa-bhūtayaḥ.* The satisfaction of possessing material opulences, although perhaps of a different standard, is available even in the lives of dogs and hogs, who cannot revive their eternal relationship with Kṛṣṇa. In human life, however, our eternal, dormant relationship with Kṛṣṇa is possible to revive. Therefore Prahlāda Mahārāja has described this life as *arthadam.* Consequently, instead of wasting our time for economic development, which cannot give us any happiness, if we simply try to revive our eternal relationship with Kṛṣṇa, we will properly utilize our lives.

TEXT 40

एवं हि लोकाः क्रतुभिः कृता अमी
क्षयिष्णवः सातिशया न निर्मलाः ।
तस्माददृष्टश्रुतदूषणं परं
भक्त्योक्तयेशं भजतात्मलब्धये ॥४०॥

evaṁ hi lokāḥ kratubhiḥ kṛtā amī
kṣayiṣṇavaḥ sātiśayā na nirmalāḥ

tasmād adṛṣṭa-śruta-dūṣaṇaṁ paraṁ
bhaktyoktayeśaṁ bhajatātma-labdhaye

evam—similarly (as earthly wealth and possessions are impermanent); *hi*—indeed; *lokāḥ*—higher planetary systems like heaven, the moon, the sun and Brahmaloka; *kratubhiḥ*—by performing great sacrifices; *kṛtāḥ*—achieved; *amī*—all those; *kṣayiṣṇavaḥ*—perishable, impermanent; *sātiśayāḥ*—although more comfortable and pleasing; *na*—not; *nirmalāḥ*—pure (free from disturbances); *tasmāt*—therefore; *adṛṣṭa-śruta*—never seen or heard; *dūṣaṇam*—whose fault; *param*—the Supreme; *bhaktyā*—with great devotional love; *uktayā*—as described in the Vedic literature (not mixed with *jñāna* or *karma*); *īśam*—the Supreme Lord; *bhajata*—worship; *ātma-labdhaye*—for self-realization.

TRANSLATION

It is learned from Vedic literature that by performing great sacrifices one may elevate himself to the heavenly planets. However, although life on the heavenly planets is hundreds and thousands of times more comfortable than life on earth, the heavenly planets are not pure [nirmalam], or free from the taint of material existence. The heavenly planets are also temporary, and therefore they are not the goal of life. The Supreme Personality of Godhead, however, has never been seen or heard to possess inebriety. Consequently, for your own benefit and self-realization, you must worship the Lord with great devotion, as described in the revealed scriptures.

PURPORT

As stated in *Bhagavad-gītā, kṣīṇe puṇye martya-lokaṁ viśanti.* Even if one is promoted to the higher planetary systems by performing great sacrifices, which are accompanied by the sinful act of sacrificing animals, the standard of happiness in Svargaloka is also not free of disturbances. There is a similar struggle for existence even for the King of heaven, Indra. Thus there is no practical benefit in promoting oneself to the heavenly planets. Indeed, from the heavenly planets one must return to this earth after one has exhausted the results of his pious activities. In the *Vedas* it is said, *tad yatheha karma-jito lokaḥ kṣīyate evam evāmutra puṇya-jito lokaḥ kṣīyata.* As the material positions we acquire here by hard work are vanquished in due course of time, one's residence in the heavenly planets is also eventually vanquished. According to one's activities of piety in different degrees, one obtains different standards of life, but none of them are permanent, and therefore they are all impure. Consequently, one should not endeavor to be promoted to the higher planetary systems, only to return to this earth or descend still lower to the hellish planets. To stop this cycle of going up and coming down, one must take to Kṛṣṇa consciousness. Śrī Caitanya Mahāprabhu therefore said:

brahmāṇḍa bhramite kona bhāgyavān jīva
guru-kṛṣṇa-prasāde pāya bhakti-latā-bīja
(Cc. *Madhya* 19.151)

The living entity is rotating in the cycle of birth and death, going sometimes to the higher planets and sometimes to the lower planets, but that is not the solution to the problems of life. But if by the grace of Kṛṣṇa one is fortunate enough to meet a *guru*, a representative of Kṛṣṇa, one gets the clue to returning home, back to Godhead, having achieved self-realization. This is what is actually desirable. *Bhajatātma-labdhaye:* one must take to Kṛṣṇa consciousness for self-realization.

TEXT 41

यदर्थ इह कर्माणि विद्वन्मान्यसकृन्नरः ।
करोत्यतो विपर्यासममोघं विन्दते फलम् ॥४१॥

yad-artha iha karmāṇi
vidvan-māny asakṛn naraḥ
karoty ato viparyāsam
amoghaṁ vindate phalam

yat—of which; *arthe*—for the purpose; *iha*—in this material world; *karmāṇi*—many activities (in factories, industries, speculation and so on); *vidvat*—advanced in knowledge; *mānī*—thinking himself to be; *asakṛt*—again and again; *naraḥ*—a person; *karoti*—performs; *ataḥ*—

from this; *viparyāsam*—the opposite; *amogham*—unfailingly; *vindate*—achieves; *phalam*—result.

TRANSLATION

A materialistic person, thinking himself very advanced in intelligence, continually acts for economic development. But again and again, as enunciated in the Vedas, he is frustrated by material activities, either in this life or in the next. Indeed, the results one obtains are inevitably the opposite of those one desires.

PURPORT

No one has ever achieved the results he desired from material activities. On the contrary, everyone has been frustrated again and again. Therefore one must not waste his time in such material activities for sensual pleasure, either in this life or in the next. So many nationalists, economists and other ambitious persons have tried for happiness, individually or collectively, but history proves that they have all been frustrated. In recent history we have seen many political leaders work hard for individual and collective economic development, but they have all failed. This is the law of nature, as clearly explained in the next verse.

TEXT 42

सुखाय दुःखमोक्षाय सङ्कल्प इह कर्मिणः ।
सदाप्नोतीहया दुःखमनीहायाः सुखावृतः ॥४२॥

sukhāya duḥkha-mokṣāya
saṅkalpa iha karmiṇaḥ
sadāpnotīhayā duḥkham
anīhāyāḥ sukhāvṛtaḥ

sukhāya—for achieving happiness by a so-called higher standard of life; *duḥkha-mokṣāya*—for becoming free from misery; *saṅkalpaḥ*—the determination; *iha*—in this world; *karmiṇaḥ*—of the living entity trying for economic development; *sadā*—always; *āpnoti*—achieves; *īhayā*—by activity or ambition; *duḥkham*—only unhappiness;

anīhāyāḥ—and from not desiring economic development; *sukha*—by happiness; *āvṛtaḥ*—covered.

TRANSLATION

In this material world, every materialist desires to achieve happiness and diminish his distress, and therefore he acts accordingly. Actually, however, one is happy as long as one does not endeavor for happiness; as soon as one begins his activities for happiness, his conditions of distress begin.

PURPORT

Every conditioned soul is bound by the laws of material nature, as described in *Bhagavad-gītā* (*prakṛteḥ kriyamāṇāni guṇaiḥ karmāṇi sarvaśaḥ*). Everyone has achieved a certain type of body given by material nature according to the instructions of the Supreme Personality of Godhead.

īśvaraḥ sarva-bhūtānāṁ
hṛd-deśe 'rjuna tiṣṭhati
bhrāmayan sarva-bhūtāni
yantrārūḍhāni māyayā

"The Supreme Lord is situated in everyone's heart, O Arjuna, and is directing the wanderings of all living entities, who are seated as on a machine, made of the material energy." (Bg. 18.61) The Supreme Personality of Godhead, the Supersoul, is present in everyone's heart, and as the living entity desires, the Lord gives him facilities with which to work according to his ambitions in different grades of bodies. The body is just like an instrument by which the living entity moves according to false desires for happiness and thus suffers the pangs of birth, death, old age and disease in different standards of life. Everyone begins his activities with some plan and ambition, but actually, from the beginning of one's plan to the end, one does not derive any happiness. On the contrary, as soon as one begins acting according to his plan, his life of distress immediately begins. Therefore, one should not be ambitious to dissipate the unhappy conditions of life, for one cannot do anything about them. *Ahaṅkāra-vimūḍhātmā kartāham iti manyate.* Although one is acting according to false ambitions, he thinks he can improve his material conditions by his activities. The *Vedas* enjoin that one should not try to increase happiness or decrease distress, for this is futile. *Tasyaiva hetoḥ prayateta kovidaḥ.* One should work for self-realization, not for economic development, which is impossible to improve. Without endeavor, one can get the amount of happiness and distress for which he is destined, and one cannot change this. Therefore, it is better to use one's time for advancement in the spiritual life of Kṛṣṇa consciousness. One should not waste his valuable life as a human being. It is better to utilize this life for developing Kṛṣṇa consciousness, without ambitions for so-called happiness.

TEXT 43

कामान्कामयते काम्यैर्यदर्थमिह पूरुषः ।
स वै देहस्तु पारक्यो भङ्गुरो यात्युपैति च ॥४३॥

kāmān kāmayate kāmyair
yad-artham iha pūruṣaḥ
sa vai dehas tu pārakyo
bhaṅguro yāty upaiti ca

kāmān—things for sense gratification; *kāmayate*—one desires; *kāmyaiḥ*—by different desirable actions; *yat*—of which; *artham*—for the purpose; *iha*—in this material world; *pūruṣaḥ*—the living entity; *saḥ*—that; *vai*—indeed; *dehaḥ*—body; *tu*—but; *pārakyaḥ*—belongs to others (the dogs, vultures, etc.); *bhaṅguraḥ*—perishable; *yāti*—goes away; *upaiti*—embraces the spirit soul; *ca*—and.

TRANSLATION

A living entity desires comfort for his body and makes many plans for this purpose, but actually the body is the property of others. Indeed, the perishable body embraces the living entity and then leaves him aside.

PURPORT

Everyone desires comfort for his body and tries to make a suitable situation for this purpose, forgetting that the body is meant to be eaten by dogs, jackals or moths and thus turned into useless stool, ashes or earth. The living entity wastes his time in a futile attempt to gain material possessions for the comfort of one body after another.

TEXT 44

किमु व्यवहितापत्यदारागारधनादयः ।
राज्यकोशगजामात्यभृत्याप्ता ममतास्पदाः ॥४४॥

kim u vyavahitāpatya-
dārāgāra-dhanādayaḥ
rājya-kośa-gajāmātya-
bhṛtyāptā mamatāspadāḥ

kim u—what to speak of; *vyavahita*—separated; *apatya*—children; *dāra*—wives; *agāra*—residences; *dhana*—wealth; *ādayaḥ*—and so on; *rājya*—kingdoms; *kośa*—treasuries; *gaja*—big elephants and horses; *amātya*—ministers; *bhṛtya*—servants; *āptāḥ*—relatives; *mamatā-āspadāḥ*—false seats or abodes of intimate relationship ("mineness").

TRANSLATION

Since the body itself is ultimately meant to become stool or earth, what is the meaning of the paraphernalia related to the body, such as wives, residences, wealth, children, relatives, servants, friends, kingdoms, treasuries, animals and ministers? They are also temporary. What more can be said about this?

TEXT 45

किमेतैरात्मनस्तुच्छैः सह देहेन नश्वरैः ।
अनर्थैरर्थसंकाशैर्नित्यानन्दरसोदधेः ॥४५॥

kim etair ātmanas tucchaiḥ
saha dehena naśvaraiḥ
anarthair artha-saṅkāśair
nityānanda-rasodadheḥ

kim—what is the use; *etaiḥ*—with all these; *ātmanaḥ*—for the real self; *tucchaiḥ*—which are most insignificant; *saha*—with; *dehena*—the body; *naśvaraiḥ*—perishable; *anarthaiḥ*—unwanted; *artha-saṅkāśaiḥ*—appearing as if needed; *nitya-ānanda*—of eternal happiness; *rasa*—of the nectar; *udadheḥ*—for the ocean.

TRANSLATION

All this paraphernalia is very near and dear as long as the body exists, but as soon as the body is destroyed, all things related to the body are also finished. Therefore, actually one has nothing to do with them, but because of ignorance one accepts them as valuable. Compared to the ocean of eternal happiness, they are most insignificant. What is the use of such insignificant relationships for the eternal living being?

PURPORT

Kṛṣṇa consciousness, devotional service to Kṛṣṇa, is the ocean of eternal bliss. In comparison to this eternal bliss, the so-called happiness of society, friendship and love is simply useless and insignificant. One should therefore not be attached to temporary things. One should take to Kṛṣṇa consciousness and become eternally happy.

TEXT 46

निरूप्यतामिह स्वार्थः कियान्देहभृतोऽसुराः ।
निषेकादिष्ववस्थासु क्लिश्यमानस्य कर्मभिः ॥४६॥

nirūpyatām iha svārthaḥ
kiyān deha-bhṛto 'surāḥ
niṣekādiṣv avasthāsu
kliśyamānasya karmabhiḥ

nirūpyatām—let it be ascertained; *iha*—in this world; *sva-arthaḥ*—personal benefit; *kiyān*—how much; *deha-bhṛtaḥ*—of a living entity who has a material body; *asurāḥ*—O sons of demons; *niṣeka-ādiṣu*—beginning from the happiness derived from sex life; *avasthāsu*—in temporary conditions; *kliśyamānasya*—of one who is suffering in severe hardships; *karmabhiḥ*—by his previous material activities.

TRANSLATION

My dear friends, O sons of the asuras, the living entity receives different types of bodies according to his previous fruitive activities. Thus he is seen to suffer with reference to his particular body in all conditions of life, beginning with his infusion into the womb. Please tell me, therefore, after full consideration, what is the living entity's actual interest in fruitive activities, which result in hardship and misery?

PURPORT

Karmaṇā daiva-netreṇa jantur dehopapattaye. The living entity receives a particular type of body according to his *karma*, or fruitive activities. The material pleasure derived in the material world from one's particular body is based on sexual pleasure: *yan maithunādi-gṛhamedhi-sukhaṁ hi tuccham.* The entire world is working so hard only for sexual pleasure. To enjoy sexual pleasure and maintain the status quo of material life, one must work very hard, and because of such activities, one prepares himself another material body. Prahlāda Mahārāja places this matter to his friends, the *asuras*, for their consideration. *Asuras* generally cannot understand that the objects of sexual pleasure, the so-called pleasure of materialistic life, depend on extremely hard labor.

TEXT 47

कर्माण्यारभते देही देहेनात्मानुवर्तिना ।
कर्मभिस्तनुते देहमुभयं त्वविवेकतः ॥४७॥

karmāṇy ārabhate dehī
dehenātmānuvartinā
karmabhis tanute deham
ubhayaṁ tv avivekataḥ

karmāṇi—material fruitive activities; *ārabhate*—begins; *dehī*—a living entity who has accepted a particular type of body; *dehena*—with that body; *ātma-anuvartinā*—which is received according to his desire and past activities; *karmabhiḥ*—by such material activities; *tanute*—he expands; *deham*—another body; *ubhayam*—both of them; *tu*—indeed; *avivekataḥ*—due to ignorance.

TRANSLATION

The living entity, who has received his present body because of his past fruitive activity, may end the results of his actions in this life, but this does not mean that he is liberated from bondage to material bodies. The living entity receives one type of body, and by performing actions with that body he creates another. Thus he transmigrates from one body to another, through repeated birth and death, because of his gross ignorance.

PURPORT

The living entity's evolution through different types of bodies is conducted automatically by the laws of nature in bodies other than those of human beings. In other words, by the laws of nature (*prakṛteḥ kriyamāṇāni*) the living entity evolves from lower grades of life to the human form. Because of his developed consciousness, however, the human being must understand the constitutional position of the living entity and understand why he must accept a material body. This chance is given to him by nature, but if he nonetheless acts like an animal, what is the benefit of his human life? In this life one must select the goal of life and act accordingly. Having received instructions from the spiritual master and the *śāstra*, one must be sufficiently intelligent. In the human form of life, one should not remain foolish and ignorant, but must inquire about his constitutional position. This is called *athāto brahma-jijñāsā*. The human psychology gives rise to many questions, which various philosophers have considered and answered with various types of philosophy based upon mental concoction. This is not the way of liberation. The Vedic instructions say, *tad-vijñānārthaṁ sa gurum evābhigacchet:* to solve the problems of life, one must accept a spiritual master. *Tasmād guruṁ prapadyeta jijñāsuḥ śreya uttamam:* if one is actually serious in inquiring about the solution to material existence, one must approach a bona fide *guru*.

tad viddhi praṇipātena
paripraśnena sevayā
upadekṣyanti te jñānaṁ
jñāninas tattva-darśinaḥ

"Just try to learn the truth by approaching a spiritual master. Inquire from him submissively and render service unto him. The self-realized soul can impart knowledge unto you because he has seen the truth." (Bg. 4.34) One must approach a bona fide spiritual master by surrendering himself (*praṇipātena*) and rendering service. An intelligent person must inquire from the spiritual master about the goal of life. A bona fide spiritual master can answer all such questions because he has seen the real truth. Even in ordinary activities, we first consider gain and loss, and then we act. Similarly, an intelligent person must consider the entire process of material existence and then act intelligently, following the directions of the bona fide spiritual master.

TEXT 48

तस्मादर्थाश्च कामाश्च धर्माश्च यदपाश्रयाः ।
भजतानीहयात्मानमनीहं हरिमीश्वरम् ॥४८॥

tasmād arthāś ca kāmāś ca
dharmāś ca yad-apāśrayāḥ
bhajatānīhayātmānam
anīhaṁ harim īśvaram

tasmāt—therefore; *arthāḥ*—ambitions for economic development; *ca*—and; *kāmāḥ*—ambitions for satisfaction of the senses; *ca*—also; *dharmāḥ*—duties of religion; *ca*—and; *yat*—upon whom; *apāśrayāḥ*—dependent; *bhajata*—worship; *anīhayā*—without desire for them; *ātmānam*—the Supersoul; *anīham*—indifferent; *harim*—the Supreme Personality of Godhead; *īśvaram*—the Lord.

TRANSLATION

The four principles of advancement in spiritual life—dharma, artha, kāma and mokṣa—all depend on the disposition of the

Supreme Personality of Godhead. Therefore, my dear friends, follow in the footsteps of devotees. Without desire, fully depend upon the disposition of the Supreme Lord, worship Him, the Supersoul, in devotional service.

PURPORT

These are words of intelligence. Everyone should know that in every stage of life we are dependent upon the Supreme Personality of Godhead. Therefore the *dharma*, religion, which we accept should be that which is recommended by Prahlāda Mahārāja—*bhāgavata-dharma.* This is the instruction of Kṛṣṇa: *sarva-dharmān parityajya mām ekaṁ śaraṇaṁ vraja.* To take shelter of the lotus feet of Kṛṣṇa means to act according to the rules and regulations of *bhāgavata-dharma,* devotional service. As far as economic development is concerned, we should discharge our occupational duties but fully depend on the lotus feet of the Lord for the results. *Karmaṇy evādhikāras te mā phaleṣu kadācana:* "You have a right to perform your prescribed duty, but you are not entitled to the fruits of action." According to one's position, one should perform his duties, but for the results one should fully depend upon Kṛṣṇa. Narottama dāsa Ṭhākura sings that our only desire should be to perform the duties of Kṛṣṇa consciousness. We should not be misled by the *karma-mīmāṁsā* philosophy, which concludes that if we work seriously the results will come automatically. This is not a fact. The ultimate result depends upon the will of the Supreme Personality of Godhead. In devotional service, therefore, the devotee completely depends upon the Lord and honestly performs his occupational duties. Therefore Prahlāda Mahārāja advised his friends to depend completely on Kṛṣṇa and worship Him in devotional service.

TEXT 49

सर्वेषामपि भूतानां हरिरात्मेश्वरः प्रियः ।
भूतैर्महद्भिः स्वकृतैः कृतानां जीवसंज्ञितः ॥४९॥

sarveṣām api bhūtānāṁ
harir ātmeśvaraḥ priyaḥ
bhūtair mahadbhiḥ sva-kṛtaiḥ
kṛtānāṁ jīva-saṁjñitaḥ

sarveṣām—of all; *api*—certainly; *bhūtānām*—living entities; *hariḥ*—the Lord, who mitigates all the miseries of the living entity; *ātmā*—the original source of life; *īśvaraḥ*—the complete controller; *priyaḥ*—the dear; *bhūtaiḥ*—by the separated energies, the five material elements; *mahadbhiḥ*—emanating from the total material energy, the *mahat-tattva*; *sva-kṛtaiḥ*—which are manifested by Himself; *kṛtānām*—created; *jīva-saṁjñitaḥ*—who is also known as the living entity, since the living entities are expansions of His marginal energy.

TRANSLATION

The Supreme Personality of Godhead, Hari, is the soul and the Supersoul of all living entities. Every living entity is a manifestation of His energy in terms of the living soul and the material body. Therefore the Lord is the most dear, and He is the supreme controller.

PURPORT

The Supreme Personality of Godhead is manifested by His different energies—the material energy, the spiritual energy and the marginal energy. He is the original source of all living entities in the material world, and He is situated in everyone's heart as the Supersoul. Although the living entity is the cause of his various types of bodies, the body is given by material nature according to the order of the Lord.

īśvaraḥ sarva-bhūtānāṁ
hṛd-deśe 'rjuna tiṣṭhati
bhrāmayan sarva-bhūtāni
yantrārūḍhāni māyayā

"The Supreme Lord is situated in everyone's heart, O Arjuna, and is directing the wanderings of all living entities, who are seated as on a machine, made of the material energy." (Bg. 18.61) The body is just like a machine, a car, in which the living entity is given a chance to sit and move according to his desire. The Lord is the original cause of the material body and the soul, which is expanded by His marginal energy. The Supreme Lord is the dearmost object of all living entities. Prahlāda Mahārāja therefore advised his class friends, the sons of the demons, to take shelter of the Supreme Personality of Godhead again.

TEXT 50

देवोऽसुरो मनुष्यो वा यक्षो गन्धर्व एव वा ।
भजन् मुकुन्दचरणं स्वस्तिमान् स्याद् यथा वयम् ॥५०॥

devo 'suro manuṣyo vā
yakṣo gandharva eva vā
bhajan mukunda-caraṇaṁ
svastimān syād yathā vayam

devaḥ—a demigod; *asuraḥ*—a demon; *manuṣyaḥ*—a human being; *vā*—or; *yakṣaḥ*—a Yakṣa (a member of a demoniac species); *gandharvaḥ*—a Gandharva; *eva*—indeed; *vā*—or; *bhajan*—rendering service; *mukunda-caraṇam*—to the lotus feet of Mukunda, Lord Kṛṣṇa, who can give liberation; *svasti-mān*—full of all auspiciousness; *syāt*—becomes; *yathā*—just as; *vayam*—we (Prahlāda Mahārāja).

TRANSLATION

If a demigod, demon, human being, Yakṣa, Gandharva or anyone within this universe renders service to the lotus feet of Mukunda, who can deliver liberation, he is actually situated in the most auspicious condition of life, exactly like us [the mahājanas, headed by Prahlāda Mahārāja].

PURPORT

Prahlāda Mahārāja, by his living example, requested his friends to engage in devotional service. Whether in demigod society, *asura* society, human society or Gandharva society, every living entity should take shelter of the lotus feet of Mukunda and thus become perfect in good fortune.

TEXTS 51–52

नालं द्विजत्वं देवत्वमृषित्वं वासुरात्मजाः ।
प्रीणनाय मुकुन्दस्य न वृत्तं न बहुज्ञता ॥५१॥
न दानं न तपो नेज्या न शौचं न व्रतानि च ।
प्रीयतेऽमलया भक्त्या हरिरन्यद् विडम्बनम् ॥५२॥

nālaṁ dvijatvaṁ devatvam
ṛṣitvaṁ vāsurātmajāḥ
prīṇanāya mukundasya
na vṛttaṁ na bahu-jñatā

na dānaṁ na tapo nejyā
na śaucaṁ na vratāni ca
prīyate 'malayā bhaktyā
harir anyad viḍambanam

na—not; *alam*—sufficient; *dvijatvam*—being a perfect, highly qualified *brāhmaṇa*; *devatvam*—being a demigod; *ṛṣitvam*—being a saintly person; *vā*—or; *asura-ātma-jāḥ*—O descendants of *asuras*; *prīṇanāya*—for pleasing; *mukundasya*—of Mukunda, the Supreme Personality of Godhead; *na vṛttam*—not good conduct; *na*—not; *bahu-jñatā*—vast learning; *na*—neither; *dānam*—charity; *na tapaḥ*—no austerity; *na*—nor; *ijyā*—worship; *na*—nor; *śaucam*—cleanliness; *na vratāni*—nor execution of great vows; *ca*—also; *prīyate*—is satisfied; *amalayā*—by spotless; *bhaktyā*—devotional service; *hariḥ*—the Supreme Lord; *anyat*—other things; *viḍambanam*—only show.

TRANSLATION

My dear friends, O sons of the demons, you cannot please the Supreme Personality of Godhead by becoming perfect brāhmaṇas, demigods or great saints or by becoming perfectly good in etiquette or vast learning. None of these qualifications can awaken the pleasure of the Lord. Nor by charity, austerity, sacrifice, cleanliness or vows can one satisfy the Lord. The Lord is pleased only if one has unflinching, unalloyed devotion to Him. Without sincere devotional service, everything is simply a show.

PURPORT

Prahlāda Mahārāja concludes that one can become perfect by serving the Supreme Lord sincerely by all means. Material elevation to life as a *brāhmaṇa*, demigod, *ṛṣi* and so on are not causes for developing love of Godhead, but if one sincerely engages in the service of the Lord, his

Kṛṣṇa consciousness is complete. This is confirmed in *Bhagavad-gītā* (9.30):

api cet sudurācāro
bhajate mām ananya-bhāk
sādhur eva sa mantavyah
samyag vyavasito hi saḥ

"Even if one commits the most abominable actions, if he is engaged in devotional service he is to be considered saintly because he is properly situated." To develop unalloyed love for Kṛṣṇa is the perfection of life. Other processes may be helpful, but if one does not develop his love for Kṛṣṇa, these other processes are simply a waste of time.

dharmaḥ svanuṣṭhitaḥ puṁsāṁ
viṣvaksena-kathāsu yaḥ
notpādayed yadi ratiṁ
śrama eva hi kevalam

"Duties [*dharma*] executed by men, regardless of occupation, are only so much useless labor if they do not provoke attraction for the message of the Supreme Lord." (*Bhāg.* 1.2.8) The test of perfection is one's unalloyed devotion to the Lord.

TEXT 53

ततो हरौ भगवति भक्तिं कुरुत दानवाः ।
आत्मौपम्येन सर्वत्र सर्वभूतात्मनीश्वरे ॥५३॥

tato harau bhagavati
bhaktiṁ kuruta dānavāḥ
ātmaupamyena sarvatra
sarva-bhūtātmanīśvare

tataḥ—therefore; *harau*—unto Lord Hari; *bhagavati*—the Supreme Personality of Godhead; *bhaktim*—devotional service; *kuruta*—execute; *dānavāḥ*—O my dear friends, O sons of demons; *ātma-aupamyena*—just as one's own self; *sarvatra*—everywhere; *sarva-bhūta-ātmani*—who is situated as the soul and Supersoul of all living entities; *īśvare*—unto the Supreme Lord, the controller.

TRANSLATION

My dear friends, O sons of the demons, in the same favorable way that one sees himself and takes care of himself, take to devotional service to satisfy the Supreme Personality of Godhead, who is present everywhere as the Supersoul of all living entities.

PURPORT

The word *ātmaupamyena* refers to thinking others to be like oneself. One can very intelligently conclude that without devotional service, without becoming Kṛṣṇa conscious, one cannot be happy. Therefore the duty of all devotees is to preach Kṛṣṇa consciousness everywhere all over the world, because all living entities without Kṛṣṇa consciousness are suffering the pangs of material existence. To preach Kṛṣṇa consciousness is the best welfare activity. Indeed, it is described by Śrī Caitanya Mahāprabhu as *para-upakāra,* work for the true benefit of others. The activities of *para-upakāra* have been especially entrusted to those who have taken birth in India as human beings.

bhārata-bhūmite haila manuṣya-janma yāra
janma sārthaka kari' kara para-upakāra
(Cc. *Ādi* 9.41)

The entire world is suffering for want of Kṛṣṇa consciousness. Therefore Śrī Caitanya Mahāprabhu advised all human beings born in India to make their lives perfect by Kṛṣṇa consciousness and then preach the gospel of Kṛṣṇa consciousness all over the world so that others may become happy by executing the principles of Kṛṣṇa consciousness.

TEXT 54

दैतेया यक्षरक्षांसि स्त्रियः शूद्रा व्रजौकसः ।
खगा मृगाः पापजीवाः सन्ति ह्यच्युततां गताः ॥५४॥

daiteyā yakṣa-rakṣāṁsi
striyaḥ śūdrā vrajaukasaḥ
khagā mṛgāḥ pāpa-jīvāḥ
santi hy acyutatāṁ gatāḥ

daiteyāḥ—O demons; *yakṣa-rakṣāṁsi*—the living entities known as the Yakṣas and Rākṣasas; *striyaḥ*—women; *śūdrāḥ*—the laborer class; *vraja-okasaḥ*—village cowherd men; *khagāḥ*—birds; *mṛgāḥ*—animals; *pāpa-jīvāḥ*—sinful living entities; *santi*—can become; *hi*—certainly; *acyutatām*—the qualities of Acyuta, the Supreme Lord; *gatāḥ*—obtained.

TRANSLATION

O my friends, O sons of demons, everyone, including you (the Yakṣas and Rākṣasas), the unintelligent women, śūdras and cowherd men, the birds, the lower animals and the sinful living entities, can revive his original, eternal spiritual life and exist forever simply by accepting the principles of bhakti-yoga.

PURPORT

The devotees are referred to as *acyuta-gotra*, or the dynasty of the Supreme Personality of Godhead. The Lord is called Acyuta, as indicated in *Bhagavad-gītā* (*senayor ubhayor madhye rathaṁ sthāpaya me 'cyuta*). The Lord is infallible in the material world because He is the supreme spiritual person. Similarly, the *jīvas*, who are part and parcel of the Lord, can also become infallible. Although Prahlāda's mother was in the conditional state and was the wife of a demon, even Yakṣas, Rākṣasas, women, *śūdras* and even birds and other lower living entities can be elevated to the *acyuta-gotra*, the family of the Supreme Personality of Godhead. That is the highest perfection. As Kṛṣṇa never falls, when we revive our spiritual consciousness, Kṛṣṇa consciousness, we never fall again to material existence. One should understand the position of the supreme Acyuta, Kṛṣṇa, who says in *Bhagavad-gītā* (4.9):

janma karma ca me divyam
evaṁ yo vetti tattvataḥ
tyaktvā dehaṁ punar janma
naiti mām eti so 'rjuna

"One who knows the transcendental nature of My appearance and activities does not, upon leaving the body, take his birth again in this material world, but attains My eternal abode, O Arjuna." One should understand Acyuta, the supreme infallible, and how we are related with Him, and one should take to the service of the Lord. This is the perfection of life. Śrīla Madhvācārya says, *acyutatāṁ cyuti-varjanam.* The word *acyutatām* refers to one who never falls to this material world but always remains in the Vaikuṇṭha world, fully engaged in the service of the Lord.

TEXT 55

एतावानेव लोकेऽस्मिन्पुंसः स्वार्थः परः स्मृतः ।
एकान्तभक्तिर्गोविन्दे यत् सर्वत्र तदीक्षणम् ॥५५॥

etāvān eva loke 'smin
puṁsaḥ svārthaḥ paraḥ smṛtaḥ
ekānta-bhaktir govinde
yat sarvatra tad-īkṣaṇam

etāvān—this much; *eva*—certainly; *loke asmin*—in this material world; *puṁsaḥ*—of the living entity; *sva-arthaḥ*—the real self-interest; *paraḥ*—transcendental; *smṛtaḥ*—regarded; *ekānta-bhaktiḥ*—unalloyed devotional service; *govinde*—to Govinda; *yat*—which; *sarvatra*—everywhere; *tat-īkṣaṇam*—seeing the relationship with Govinda, Kṛṣṇa.

TRANSLATION

In this material world, to render service to the lotus feet of Govinda, the cause of all causes, and to see Him everywhere, is the only goal of life. This much alone is the ultimate goal of human life, as explained by all the revealed scriptures.

PURPORT

In this verse the words *sarvatra tad-īkṣaṇam* describe the highest perfection of devotional service, in which one sees everything with reference to Govinda's activities. The highly elevated devotee never sees anything unrelated to Govinda.

sthāvara-jaṅgama dekhe, nā dekhe tāra mūrti
sarvatra haya nija iṣṭa-deva-sphūrti

"The *mahā-bhāgavata*, the advanced devotee, certainly sees everything mobile and immobile, but he does not exactly see their forms. Rather, everywhere he immediately sees manifest the form of the Supreme Lord." (Cc. *Madhya* 8.274) Even in this material world, a devotee does not see materially manifested things; instead he sees Govinda in everything. When he sees a tree or a human being, a devotee sees them in relation to Govinda. *Govindam ādi-puruṣam:* Govinda is the original source of everything.

īśvaraḥ paramaḥ kṛṣṇaḥ
sac-cid-ānanda-vigrahaḥ
anādir ādir govindaḥ
sarva-kāraṇa-kāraṇam

"Kṛṣṇa, who is known as Govinda, is the supreme controller. He has an eternal, blissful, spiritual body. He is the origin of all. He has no other origin, for He is the prime cause of all causes." (*Brahma-saṁhitā* 5.1) The test of a perfect devotee is that he sees Govinda everywhere in this universe, even in every atomic particle (*aṇḍāntara-stha-paramāṇu-cayāntara-stham*). This is the perfect vision of a devotee. It is therefore said:

nārāyaṇam ayaṁ dhīrāḥ
paśyanti paramārthinaḥ
jagad dhanamayaṁ lubdhāḥ
kāmukāḥ kāminīmayam

A devotee sees everyone and everything in relationship with Nārāyaṇa (*nārāyaṇam ayam*). Everything is an expansion of Nārāyaṇa's energy. Just as those who are greedy see everything as a source of money-making and those who are lusty see everything as being conducive to sex, the most perfect devotee, Prahlāda Mahārāja, saw Nārāyaṇa even within a stone column. This does not mean, however, that we must accept the words *daridra-nārāyaṇa*, which have been manufactured by some unscrupulous person. One who actually envisions Nārāyaṇa everywhere makes no distinction between the poor and the rich. To single out the *daridra-nārāyaṇas*, or poor Nārāyaṇa, and reject the *dhani-nārāyaṇa*, or rich Nārāyaṇa, is not the vision of a devotee. Rather, that is the imperfect vision of materialistic persons.

Thus end the Bhaktivedanta purports of the Seventh Canto, Seventh Chapter, of the Śrīmad-Bhāgavatam, *entitled "What Prahlāda Learned in the Womb."*

CHAPTER EIGHT

Lord Nṛsiṁhadeva Slays the King of the Demons

As described in this chapter, Hiraṇyakaśipu was ready to kill his own son Prahlāda Mahārāja, but the Supreme Personality of Godhead appeared in front of the demon as Śrī Nṛkeśarī, half lion and half man, and killed him.

Following the instructions of Prahlāda Mahārāja, all the sons of the demons became attached to Lord Viṣṇu, the Supreme Personality of Godhead. When this attachment became pronounced, their teachers, Ṣaṇḍa and Amarka, were very much afraid that the boys would become more and more devoted to the Lord. In a helpless condition, they approached Hiraṇyakaśipu and described in detail the effect of Prahlāda's preaching. After hearing of this, Hiraṇyakaśipu decided to kill his son Prahlāda. Hiraṇyakaśipu was so angry that Prahlāda Mahārāja fell down at his feet and said many things just to pacify him, but he was unsuccessful in satisfying his demoniac father. Hiraṇyakaśipu, as a typical demon, began to advertise himself as being greater than the Supreme Personality of Godhead, but Prahlāda Mahārāja challenged him, saying that Hiraṇyakaśipu was not God, and began to glorify the Supreme Personality of Godhead, declaring that the Lord is all-pervading, that everything is under Him, and that no one is equal to or greater than Him. Thus he requested his father to be submissive to the omnipotent Supreme Lord.

The more Prahlāda Mahārāja glorified the Supreme Personality of Godhead, the more angry and agitated the demon became. Hiraṇyakaśipu asked his Vaiṣṇava son whether his God existed within the columns of the palace, and Prahlāda Mahārāja immediately accepted that since the Lord is present everywhere, He was also present within the columns. When Hiraṇyakaśipu heard this philosophy from his young son, he derided the boy's statement as just the talk of a child and forcefully struck the pillar with his fist.

As soon as Hiraṇyakaśipu struck the column, there issued forth a tumultuous sound. At first Hiraṇyakaśipu, the King of the demons, could not see anything but the pillar, but to substantiate Prahlāda's statements, the Lord came out of the pillar in His wonderful incarnation as Narasiṁha, half lion and half man. Hiraṇyakaśipu could immediately understand that the extraordinarily wonderful form of the Lord was surely meant for his death, and thus he prepared to fight with the form of half lion and half man. The Lord performed His pastimes by fighting with the demon for some time, and in the evening, on the border between day and night, the Lord captured the demon, threw him on His lap, and killed him by piercing his abdomen with His nails. The Lord not only killed Hiraṇyakaśipu, the King of the demons, but also killed many of his followers. When there was no one else to fight, the Lord, roaring with anger, sat down on Hiraṇyakaśipu's throne.

The entire universe was thus relieved of the rule of Hiraṇyakaśipu, and everyone was jubilant in transcendental bliss. Then all the demigods, headed by Lord Brahmā, approached the Lord. These included the great saintly persons, the Pitās, the Siddhas, the Vidyādharas, the Nāgas, the Manus, the *prajāpatis*, the Gandharvas, the Cāraṇas, the Yakṣas, the Kimpuruṣas, the Vaitālikas, the Kinnaras and also many other varieties of beings in human form. All of them stood not far from the Supreme Personality of Godhead and began offering their prayers unto the Lord, whose spiritual effulgence was brilliant as He sat on the throne.

TEXT 1

श्रीनारद उवाच

अथ दैत्यसुताः सर्वे श्रुत्वा तदनुवर्णितम् ।
जगृहुर्निरवद्यत्वान्नैव गुर्वनुशिक्षितम् ॥ १ ॥

śrī-nārada uvāca
atha daitya-sutāḥ sarve
śrutvā tad-anuvarṇitam
jagṛhur niravadyatvān
naiva gurv-anuśikṣitam

śrī-nāradaḥ uvāca—Śrī Nārada Muni said; *atha*—thereupon; *daitya-sutāḥ*—the sons of the demons (the class friends of Prahlāda Mahārāja);

sarve—all; *śrutvā*—hearing; *tat*—by him (Prahlāda); *anuvarṇitam*—the statements about devotional life; *jagṛhuḥ*—accepted; *niravadyatvāt*—due to the supreme utility of that instruction; *na*—not; *eva*—indeed; *guru-anuśikṣitam*—that which was taught by their teachers.

TRANSLATION

Nārada Muni continued: All the sons of the demons appreciated the transcendental instructions of Prahlāda Mahārāja and took them very seriously. They rejected the materialistic instructions given by their teachers, Ṣaṇḍa and Amarka.

PURPORT

This is the effect of the preaching of a pure devotee like Prahlāda Mahārāja. If a devotee is qualified, sincere and serious about Kṛṣṇa consciousness and if he follows the instructions of a bona fide spiritual master, as Prahlāda Mahārāja did when preaching the instructions he had received from Nārada Muni, his preaching is effective. As it is said in the *Śrīmad-Bhāgavatam* (3.25.25):

satāṁ prasaṅgān mama vīrya-saṁvido
bhavanti hṛt-karṇa-rasāyanāḥ kathāḥ

If one tries to understand the discourses given by the *sat*, or pure devotees, those instructions will be very pleasing to the ear and appealing to the heart. Thus if one is inspired to take to Kṛṣṇa consciousness and if one practices the process in his life, he is surely successful in returning home, back to Godhead. By the grace of Prahlāda Mahārāja, all his class friends, the sons of the demons, became Vaiṣṇavas. They did not like hearing from their so-called teachers Ṣaṇḍa and Amarka, who were interested only in teaching them about diplomacy, politics, economic development and similar topics meant exclusively for sense gratification.

TEXT 2

अथाचार्यसुतस्तेषां बुद्धिमेकान्तसंस्थिताम् ।
आलक्ष्य भीतस्त्वरितो राज्ञ आवेदयद् यथा ॥ २ ॥

athācārya-sutas teṣāṁ
buddhim ekānta-saṁsthitām
ālakṣya bhītas tvarito
rājña āvedayad yathā

atha—thereupon; *ācārya-sutaḥ*—the son of Śukrācārya; *teṣām*—of them (the sons of the demons); *buddhim*—the intelligence; *ekānta-saṁsthitām*—fixed in one subject matter, devotional service; *ālakṣya*—realizing or seeing practically; *bhītaḥ*—being afraid; *tvaritaḥ*—as soon as possible; *rājñe*—unto the King (Hiraṇyakaśipu); *āvedayat*—submitted; *yathā*—fittingly.

TRANSLATION

When Ṣaṇḍa and Amarka, the sons of Śukrācārya, observed that all the students, the sons of the demons, were becoming advanced in Kṛṣṇa consciousness because of the association of Prahlāda Mahārāja, they were afraid. They approached the King of the demons and described the situation as it was.

PURPORT

The words *buddhim ekānta-saṁsthitām* indicate that as an effect of Prahlāda Mahārāja's preaching, the students who listened to him became fixed in the conclusion that Kṛṣṇa consciousness is the only object of human life. The fact is that anyone who associates with a pure devotee and follows his instructions becomes fixed in Kṛṣṇa consciousness and is not disturbed by materialistic consciousness. The teachers particularly observed this in their students, and therefore they were afraid because the whole community of students was gradually becoming Kṛṣṇa conscious.

TEXTS 3–4

कोपावेशचलद्गात्रः पुत्रं हन्तुं मनो दधे ।
क्षिप्त्वा परुषया वाचा प्रह्रादमतदर्हणम् ॥ ३ ॥
आहेक्षमाणः पापेन तिरश्चीनेन चक्षुषा ।
प्रश्रयावनतं दान्तं बद्धाञ्जलिमवस्थितम् ।
सर्पः पदाहत इव श्वसन्प्रकृतिदारुणः ॥ ४ ॥

kopāveśa-calad-gātraḥ
putraṁ hantuṁ mano dadhe
kṣiptvā paruṣayā vācā
prahrādam atad-arhaṇam

āhekṣamāṇaḥ pāpena
tiraścīnena cakṣuṣā
praśrayāvanataṁ dāntaṁ
baddhāñjalim avasthitam
sarpaḥ padāhata iva
śvasan prakṛti-dāruṇaḥ

kopa-āveśa—by a very angry mood; *calat*—trembling; *gātraḥ*—the whole body; *putram*—his son; *hantum*—to kill; *manaḥ*—mind; *dadhe*—fixed; *kṣiptvā*—rebuking; *paruṣayā*—with very harsh; *vācā*—words; *prahrādam*—Prahlāda Mahārāja; *a-tat-arhaṇam*—not fit to be chastised (due to his noble character and tender age); *āha*—said; *īkṣamāṇaḥ*—looking at him in anger; *pāpena*—because of his sinful activities; *tiraścīnena*—crooked; *cakṣuṣā*—with eyes; *praśraya-avanatam*—very gentle and mild; *dāntam*—very restrained; *baddha-añjalim*—having folded hands; *avasthitam*—situated; *sarpaḥ*—a snake; *pada-āhataḥ*—being trampled by the foot; *iva*—like; *śvasan*—hissing; *prakṛti*—by nature; *dāruṇaḥ*—very evil.

TRANSLATION

When Hiraṇyakaśipu understood the entire situation, he was extremely angry, so much so that his body trembled. Thus he finally decided to kill his son Prahlāda. Hiraṇyakaśipu was by nature very cruel, and feeling insulted, he began hissing like a snake trampled upon by someone's foot. His son Prahlāda was peaceful, mild and gentle, his senses were under control, and he stood before Hiraṇyakaśipu with folded hands. According to Prahlāda's age and behavior, he was not to be chastised. Yet with staring, crooked eyes, Hiraṇyakaśipu rebuked him with the following harsh words.

PURPORT

When one is impudent toward a highly authorized devotee, one is punished by the laws of nature. The duration of his life is diminished, and he loses the blessings of superior persons and the results of pious activities. Hiraṇyakaśipu, for example, had achieved such great power in the material world that he could subdue practically all the planetary systems in the universe, including the heavenly planets (Svargaloka). Yet now, because of his mistreatment of such a Vaiṣṇava as Prahlāda Mahārāja, all the results of his *tapasya* diminished. As stated in *Śrīmad-Bhāgavatam* (10.4.46):

āyuḥ śriyaṁ yaśo dharmaṁ
lokān āśiṣa eva ca
hanti śreyāṁsi sarvāṇi
puṁso mahad-atikramaḥ

"When one mistreats great souls, his life span, opulence, reputation, religion, possessions and good fortune are all destroyed."

TEXT 5

श्रीहिरण्यकशिपुरुवाच
हे दुर्विनीत मन्दात्मन्कुलभेदकराधम ।
स्तब्धं मच्छासनोद्वृत्तं नेष्ये त्वाद्य यमक्षयम् ॥ ५॥

śrī-hiraṇyakaśipur uvāca
he durvinīta mandātman
kula-bheda-karādhama
stabdhaṁ mac-chāsanodvṛttaṁ
neṣye tvādya yama-kṣayam

śrī-hiraṇyakaśipuḥ uvāca—the blessed Hiraṇyakaśipu said; *he*—O; *durvinīta*—most impudent; *manda-ātman*—O stupid fool; *kula-bheda-kara*—who are bringing about a disruption in the family; *adhama*—O lowest of mankind; *stabdham*—most obstinate; *mat-śāsana*—from my ruling; *udvṛttam*—going astray; *neṣye*—I shall bring; *tvā*—you; *adya*—today; *yama-kṣayam*—to the place of Yamarāja, the superintendent of death.

TRANSLATION

Hiraṇyakaśipu said: O most impudent, most unintelligent disruptor of the family, O lowest of mankind, you have violated my

power to rule you, and therefore you are an obstinate fool. Today I shall send you to the place of Yamarāja.

PURPORT

Hiraṇyakaśipu condemned his Vaiṣṇava son Prahlāda for being *durvinīta*—ungentle, uncivilized, or impudent. Śrīla Viśvanātha Cakravartī Ṭhākura, however, has derived a meaning from this word *durvinīta* by the mercy of the goddess of learning, Sarasvatī. He says that *duḥ* refers to this material world. This is confirmed by Lord Kṛṣṇa in His instruction in *Bhagavad-gītā* that this material world is *duḥkhālayam*, full of material conditions. *Vi* means *viśeṣa*, "specifically," and *nīta* means "brought in." By the mercy of the Supreme Lord, Prahlāda Mahārāja was especially brought to this material world to teach people how to get out of the material condition. Lord Kṛṣṇa says, *yadā yadā hi dharmasya glānir bhavati bhārata*. When the entire population, or part of it, becomes forgetful of its own duty, Kṛṣṇa comes. When Kṛṣṇa is not present the devotee is present, but the mission is the same: to free the poor conditioned souls from the clutches of the *māyā* that chastises them.

Śrīla Viśvanātha Cakravartī Ṭhākura further explains that the word *mandātman* means *manda*—very bad or very slow in spiritual realization. As stated in *Śrīmad-Bhāgavatam* (1.1.10), *mandāḥ sumanda-matayo manda-bhāgyā*. Prahlāda Mahārāja is the guide of all the *mandas*, or bad living entities who are under the influence of *māyā*. He is the benefactor even of the slow and bad living entities in this material world. *Kula-bheda-karādhama:* by his actions, Prahlāda Mahārāja made great personalities who established big, big families seem insignificant. Everyone is interested in his own family and in making his dynasty famous, but Prahlāda Mahārāja was so liberal that he made no distinction between one living entity and another. Therefore he was greater than the great *prajāpatis* who established their dynasties. The word *stabdham* means obstinate. A devotee does not care for the instructions of the *asuras*. When they give instructions, he remains silent. A devotee cares about the instructions of Kṛṣṇa, not those of demons or nondevotees. He does not give any respect to a demon, even though the demon be his father. *Mac-chāsanodvṛttam:* Prahlāda Mahārāja was disobedient to the orders of his demoniac father. *Yama-kṣayam:* every conditioned soul is under the control of Yamarāja, but Hiraṇyakaśipu said that he considered

Prahlāda Mahārāja his deliverer, for Prahlāda would stop Hiraṇyakaśipu's repetition of birth and death. Because Prahlāda Mahārāja, being a great devotee, was better than any *yogī*, Hiraṇyakaśipu was to be brought among the society of *bhakti-yogīs*. Thus Śrīla Viśvanātha Cakravartī Ṭhākura has explained these words in a very interesting way as they can be interpreted from the side of Sarasvatī, the mother of learning.

TEXT 6

क्रुद्धस्य यस्य कम्पन्ते त्रयो लोकाः सहेश्वराः ।
तस्य मेऽभीतवन्मूढ शासनं किं बलोऽत्यगाः ॥ ६ ॥

kruddhasya yasya kampante
trayo lokāḥ saheśvarāḥ
tasya me 'bhītavan mūḍha
śāsanaṁ kiṁ balo 'tyagāḥ

kruddhasya—when angered; *yasya*—he who; *kampante*—tremble; *trayaḥ lokāḥ*—the three worlds; *saha-īśvarāḥ*—with their leaders; *tasya*—of that; *me*—of me (Hiraṇyakaśipu); *abhīta-vat*—without fear; *mūḍha*—rascal; *śāsanam*—ruling order; *kim*—what; *balaḥ*—strength; *atyagāḥ*—have overstepped.

TRANSLATION

My son Prahlāda, you rascal, you know that when I am angry all the planets of the three worlds tremble, along with their chief rulers. By whose power has a rascal like you become so impudent that you appear fearless and overstep my power to rule you?

PURPORT

The relationship between a pure devotee and the Supreme Personality of Godhead is extremely relishable. A devotee never claims to be very powerful himself; instead, he fully surrenders to the lotus feet of Kṛṣṇa, being confident that in all dangerous conditions Kṛṣṇa will protect His devotee. Kṛṣṇa Himself says in *Bhagavad-gītā* (9.31), *kaunteya pratijānīhi na me bhaktaḥ praṇaśyati:* "O son of Kuntī, declare boldly that

My devotee never perishes." The Lord requested Arjuna to declare this instead of declaring it Himself because sometimes Kṛṣṇa changes His view and therefore people might not believe Him. Thus Kṛṣṇa asked Arjuna to declare that a devotee of the Lord is never vanquished.

Hiraṇyakaśipu was perplexed about how his five-year-old boy could be so fearless that he did not care for the order of his very great and powerful father. A devotee cannot execute the order of anyone except the Supreme Personality of Godhead. This is the position of a devotee. Hiraṇyakaśipu could understand that this boy must have been very powerful, since the boy did not heed his orders. Hiraṇyakaśipu asked his son, *kiṁ balaḥ:* "How have you overcome my order? By whose strength have you done this?"

TEXT 7

श्रीप्रह्राद उवाच

न केवलं मे भवतश्च राजन्
स वै बलं बलिनां चापरेषाम् ।
परेऽवरेऽमी स्थिरजङ्गमा ये
ब्रह्मादयो येन वशं प्रणीताः ॥ ७ ॥

śrī-prahrāda uvāca
na kevalaṁ me bhavataś ca rājan
sa vai balaṁ balināṁ cāpareṣām
pare 'vare 'mī sthira-jaṅgamā ye
brahmādayo yena vaśaṁ praṇītāḥ

śrī-prahrādaḥ uvāca—Prahlāda Mahārāja replied; *na*—not; *kevalam*—only; *me*—of me; *bhavataḥ*—of yourself; *ca*—and; *rājan*—O great King; *saḥ*—he; *vai*—indeed; *balam*—strength; *balinām*—of the strong; *ca*—and; *apareṣām*—of others; *pare*—exalted; *avare*—subordinate; *amī*—those; *sthira-jaṅgamāḥ*—moving or nonmoving living entities; *ye*—who; *brahma-ādayaḥ*—beginning from Lord Brahmā; *yena*—by whom; *vaśam*—under control; *praṇītāḥ*—brought.

TRANSLATION

Prahlāda Mahārāja said: My dear King, the source of my strength, of which you are asking, is also the source of yours.

Indeed, the original source of all kinds of strength is one. He is not only your strength or mine, but the only strength for everyone. Without Him, no one can get any strength. Whether moving or not moving, superior or inferior, everyone, including Lord Brahmā, is controlled by the strength of the Supreme Personality of Godhead.

PURPORT

Lord Kṛṣṇa says in *Bhagavad-gītā* (10.41):

yad yad vibhūtimat sattvaṁ
śrīmad ūrjitam eva vā
tat tad evāvagaccha tvaṁ
mama tejo-'ṁśa-sambhavam

"Know that all beautiful, glorious and mighty creations spring from but a spark of My splendor." This is confirmed by Prahlāda Mahārāja. If one sees extraordinary strength or power anywhere, it is derived from the Supreme Personality of Godhead. To give an example, there are different grades of fire, but all of them derive heat and light from the sun. Similarly, all living entities, big or small, are dependent on the mercy of the Supreme Personality of Godhead. One's only duty is to surrender, for one is a servant and cannot independently attain the position of master. One can attain the position of master only by the mercy of the master, not independently. Unless one understands this philosophy, he is still a *mūḍha;* in other words, he is not very intelligent. The *mūḍhas,* the asses who do not have this intelligence, cannot surrender unto the Supreme Personality of Godhead.

Understanding the subordinate position of the living entity takes millions of births, but when one is actually wise he surrenders unto the Supreme Personality of Godhead. The Lord says in *Bhagavad-gītā* (7.19):

bahūnāṁ janmanām ante
jñānavān māṁ prapadyate
vāsudevaḥ sarvam iti
sa mahātmā sudurlabhaḥ

"After many births and deaths, he who is actually in knowledge surrenders unto Me, knowing Me to be the cause of all causes and all that is. Such a great soul is very rare." Prahlāda Mahārāja was a great soul, a *mahātmā*, and therefore he completely surrendered unto the lotus feet of the Lord. He was confident that Kṛṣṇa would give him protection under all circumstances.

TEXT 8

स ईश्वरः काल उरुक्रमोऽसा-
वोजःसहःसत्त्वबलेन्द्रियात्मा ।
स एव विश्वं परमः स्वशक्तिभिः
सृजत्यवत्यत्ति गुणत्रयेशः ॥ ८ ॥

sa īśvaraḥ kāla urukramo 'sāv
ojaḥ sahaḥ sattva-balendriyātmā
sa eva viśvaṁ paramaḥ sva-śaktibhiḥ
sṛjaty avaty atti guṇa-trayeśaḥ

saḥ—He (the Supreme Personality of Godhead); *īśvaraḥ*—the supreme controller; *kālaḥ*—the time factor; *urukramaḥ*—the Lord, whose every action is uncommon; *asau*—that one; *ojaḥ*—the strength of the senses; *sahaḥ*—the strength of the mind; *sattva*—steadiness; *bala*—bodily strength; *indriya*—and of the senses themselves; *ātmā*—the very self; *saḥ*—He; *eva*—indeed; *viśvam*—the whole universe; *paramaḥ*—the supreme; *sva-śaktibhiḥ*—by His multifarious transcendental potencies; *sṛjati*—creates; *avati*—maintains; *atti*—winds up; *guṇa-traya-īśaḥ*—the master of the material modes.

TRANSLATION

The Supreme Personality of Godhead, who is the supreme controller and time factor, is the power of the senses, the power of the mind, the power of the body, and the vital force of the senses. His influence is unlimited. He is the best of all living entities, the controller of the three modes of material nature. By His own power, He creates this cosmic manifestation, maintains it and annihilates it also.

PURPORT

Since the material world is being moved by the three material modes and since the Lord is their master, the Lord can create, maintain and destroy the material world.

TEXT 9

जह्यासुरं भावमिमं त्वमात्मनः
समं मनो धत्स्व न सन्ति विद्विषः ।
ऋतेऽजितादात्मन उत्पथे स्थितात्
तद्धि ह्यनन्तस्य महत् समर्हणम् ॥ ९ ॥

jahy āsuraṁ bhāvam imaṁ tvam ātmanaḥ
samaṁ mano dhatsva na santi vidviṣaḥ
ṛte 'jitād ātmana utpathe sthitāt
tad dhi hy anantasya mahat samarhaṇam

jahi—just give up; *āsuram*—demoniac; *bhāvam*—tendency; *imam*—this; *tvam*—you (my dear father); *ātmanaḥ*—of yourself; *samam*—equal; *manaḥ*—the mind; *dhatsva*—make; *na*—not; *santi*—are; *vidviṣaḥ*—enemies; *ṛte*—except; *ajitāt*—uncontrolled; *ātmanaḥ*—the mind; *utpathe*—on the mistaken path of undesirable tendencies; *sthitāt*—being situated; *tat hi*—that (mentality); *hi*—indeed; *anantasya*—of the unlimited Lord; *mahat*—the best; *samarhaṇam*—method of worship.

TRANSLATION

Prahlāda Mahārāja continued: My dear father, please give up your demoniac mentality. Do not discriminate in your heart between enemies and friends; make your mind equipoised toward everyone. Except for the uncontrolled and misguided mind, there is no enemy within this world. When one sees everyone on the platform of equality, one then comes to the position of worshiping the Lord perfectly.

PURPORT

Unless one is able to fix the mind at the lotus feet of the Lord, the mind is impossible to control. As Arjuna says in *Bhagavad-gītā* (6.34):

cañcalaṁ hi manaḥ kṛṣṇa
pramāthi balavad dṛḍham
tasyāhaṁ nigrahaṁ manye
vāyor iva suduṣkaram

"For the mind is restless, turbulent, obstinate and very strong, O Kṛṣṇa, and to subdue it, it seems to me, is more difficult than controlling the wind." The only bona fide process for controlling the mind is to fix the mind by service to the Lord. We create enemies and friends according to the dictation of the mind, but actually there are no enemies and friends. *Paṇḍitāḥ sama-darśinaḥ. Samaḥ sarveṣu bhūteṣu mad-bhaktiṁ labhate parām.* To understand this is the preliminary condition for entering into the kingdom of devotional service.

TEXT 10

दस्यून्पुरा षण् न विजित्य लुम्पतो
मन्यन्त एके स्वजिता दिशो दश ।
जितात्मनो ज्ञस्य समस्य देहिनां
साधोः स्वमोहप्रभवाः कुतः परे ॥१०॥

dasyūn purā ṣaṇ na vijitya lumpato
manyanta eke sva-jitā diśo daśa
jitātmano jñasya samasya dehināṁ
sādhoḥ sva-moha-prabhavāḥ kutaḥ pare

dasyūn—plunderers; *purā*—in the beginning; *ṣaṭ*—six; *na*—not; *vijitya*—conquering; *lumpataḥ*—stealing all one's possessions; *manyante*—consider; *eke*—some; *sva-jitāḥ*—conquered; *diśaḥ daśa*—the ten directions; *jita-ātmanaḥ*—one who has conquered the senses; *jñasya*—learned; *samasya*—equipoised; *dehinām*—to all living entities; *sādhoḥ*—of such a saintly person; *sva-moha-prabhavāḥ*—created by one's own illusion; *kutaḥ*—where; *pare*—enemies or opposing elements.

TRANSLATION

In former times there were many fools like you who did not conquer the six enemies that steal away the wealth of the body.

These fools were very proud, thinking, "I have conquered all enemies in all the ten directions." But if a person is victorious over the six enemies and is equipoised toward all living entities, for him there are no enemies. Enemies are merely imagined by one in ignorance.

PURPORT

In this material world, everyone thinks that he has conquered his enemies, not understanding that his enemies are his uncontrolled mind and five senses (*manaḥ ṣaṣṭhānīndriyāṇi prakṛti-sthāni karṣati*). In this material world, everyone has become a servant of the senses. Originally everyone is a servant of Kṛṣṇa, but in ignorance one forgets this, and thus one is engaged in the service of *māyā* through lusty desires, anger, greed, illusion, madness and jealousy. Everyone is actually dependent on the reactions of material laws, but still one thinks himself independent and thinks that he has conquered all directions. In conclusion, one who thinks that he has many enemies is an ignorant man, whereas one who is in Kṛṣṇa consciousness knows that there are no enemies but those within oneself—the uncontrolled mind and senses.

TEXT 11

श्रीहिरण्यकशिपुरुवाच
व्यक्तं त्वं मर्तुकामोऽसि योऽतिमात्रं विकत्थसे ।
मुमूर्षूणां हि मन्दात्मन् ननु स्युर्विक्लवा गिरः ॥११॥

śrī-hiraṇyakaśipur uvāca
vyaktaṁ tvaṁ martu-kāmo 'si
yo 'timātraṁ vikatthase
mumūrṣūṇāṁ hi mandātman
nanu syur viklavā giraḥ

śrī-hiraṇyakaśipuḥ uvāca—the blessed Hiraṇyakaśipu said; *vyaktam*—evidently; *tvam*—you; *martu-kāmaḥ*—desirous of death; *asi*—are; *yaḥ*—one who; *atimātram*—without limit; *vikatthase*—are boasting (as if you had conquered your senses whereas your father could not do so); *mumūrṣūṇām*—of persons who are about to meet immediate death; *hi*—indeed; *manda-ātman*—O unintelligent rascal; *nanu*—certainly; *syuḥ*—become; *viklavāḥ*—confused; *giraḥ*—the words.

TRANSLATION

Hiraṇyakaśipu replied: You rascal, you are trying to minimize my value, as if you were better than me at controlling the senses. This is over-intelligent. I can therefore understand that you desire to die at my hands, for this kind of nonsensical talk is indulged in by those about to die.

PURPORT

It is said in *Hitopadeśa, upadeśo hi mūrkhāṇāṁ prokopāya na śāntaye.* If good instructions are given to a foolish person, he does not take advantage of them, but becomes more and more angry. Prahlāda Mahārāja's authorized instructions to his father were not accepted by Hiraṇyakaśipu as truth; instead Hiraṇyakaśipu became increasingly angry at his great son, who was a pure devotee. This kind of difficulty always exists when a devotee preaches Kṛṣṇa consciousness to persons like Hiraṇyakaśipu, who are interested in money and women. (The word *hiraṇya* means "gold," and *kaśipu* refers to cushions or good bedding.) Moreover, a father does not like to be instructed by his son, especially if the father is a demon. Prahlāda Mahārāja's Vaiṣṇava preaching to his demoniac father was indirectly effective, for because of Hiraṇyakaśipu's excessive jealousy of Kṛṣṇa and His devotee, he was inviting Nṛsiṁhadeva to kill him very quickly. Thus he was expediting his being killed by the Lord Himself. Although Hiraṇyakaśipu was a demon, he is described here by the added word *śrī.* Why? The answer is that fortunately he had such a great devotee son as Prahlāda Mahārāja. Thus although he was a demon, he would attain salvation and return home, back to Godhead.

TEXT 12

यस्त्वया मन्दभाग्योक्तो मदन्यो जगदीश्वरः ।
क्वासौ यदि स सर्वत्र कस्मात् स्तम्भे न दृश्यते ॥१२॥

yas tvayā manda-bhāgyokto
mad-anyo jagad-īśvaraḥ

kvāsau yadi sa sarvatra
kasmāt stambhe na dṛśyate

yaḥ—the one who; *tvayā*—by you; *manda-bhāgya*—O unfortunate one; *uktaḥ*—described; *mat-anyaḥ*—besides me; *jagat-īśvaraḥ*—the supreme controller of the universe; *kva*—where; *asau*—that one; *yadi*—if; *saḥ*—He; *sarvatra*—everywhere (all-pervading); *kasmāt*—why; *stambhe*—in the pillar before me; *na dṛśyate*—not seen.

TRANSLATION

O most unfortunate Prahlāda, you have always described a supreme being other than me, a supreme being who is above everything, who is the controller of everyone, and who is all-pervading. But where is He? If He is everywhere, then why is He not present before me in this pillar?

PURPORT

Demons sometimes declare to a devotee that they cannot accept the existence of God because they cannot see Him. But what the demon does not know is stated by the Lord Himself in *Bhagavad-gītā* (7.25): *nāhaṁ prakāśaḥ sarvasya yogamāyā-samāvṛtaḥ.* "I am never manifest to the foolish and unintelligent. For them I am covered by *yogamāyā.*" The Lord is open to being seen by devotees, but nondevotees cannot see Him. The qualification for seeing God is stated in *Brahma-saṁhitā* (5.38): *premāñjana-cchurita-bhakti-vilocanena santaḥ sadaiva hṛdayeṣu vilokayanti.* A devotee who has developed a genuine love for Kṛṣṇa can always see Him everywhere, whereas a demon, not having a clear understanding of the Supreme Lord, cannot see Him. When Hiraṇyakaśipu was threatening to kill Prahlāda Mahārāja, Prahlāda certainly saw the column standing before him and his father, and he saw that the Lord was present in the pillar to encourage him not to fear his demoniac father's words. The Lord was present to protect him. Hiraṇyakaśipu marked Prahlāda's observation and asked him, "Where is your God?" Prahlāda Mahārāja replied, "He is everywhere." Then Hiraṇyakaśipu asked, "Why is He not in this pillar before me?" Thus in all circumstances the devotee can always see the Supreme Lord, whereas the nondevotee cannot.

Prahlāda Mahārāja has here been addressed by his father as "the most unfortunate." Hiraṇyakaśipu thought himself extremely fortunate because he possessed the property of the universe. Prahlāda Mahārāja, his legitimate son, was to have inherited this vast property, but because of his impudence, he was going to die at his father's hands. Therefore the demoniac father considered Prahlāda the most unfortunate because Prahlāda would not be able to inherit his property. Hiraṇyakaśipu did not know that Prahlāda Mahārāja was the most fortunate person within the three worlds because Prahlāda was protected by the Supreme Personality of Godhead. Such are the misunderstandings of demons. They do not know that a devotee is protected by the Lord in all circumstances (*kaunteya pratijānīhi na me bhaktaḥ praṇaśyati*).

TEXT 13

सोऽहं विकत्थमानस्य शिरः कायाद्धरामि ते ।
गोपायेत हरिस्त्वाद्य यस्ते शरणमीप्सितम् ॥१३॥

so 'haṁ vikatthamānasya
śiraḥ kāyād dharāmi te
gopāyeta haris tvādya
yas te śaraṇam īpsitam

saḥ—he; *aham*—I; *vikatthamānasya*—who are speaking such nonsense; *śiraḥ*—the head; *kāyāt*—from the body; *harāmi*—I shall take away; *te*—of you; *gopāyeta*—let Him protect; *hariḥ*—the Supreme Personality of Godhead; *tvā*—you; *adya*—now; *yaḥ*—He who; *te*—your; *śaraṇam*—protector; *īpsitam*—desired.

TRANSLATION

Because you are speaking so much nonsense, I shall now sever your head from your body. Now let me see your most worshipable God come to protect you. I want to see it.

PURPORT

Demons always think that the God of the devotees is fictitious. They think that there is no God and that the so-called religious feeling of devotion to God is but an opiate, a kind of illusion, like the illusions derived from LSD and opium. Hiraṇyakaśipu did not believe Prahlāda Mahārāja when Prahlāda asserted that his Lord is present everywhere. Because Hiraṇyakaśipu, as a typical demon, was convinced that there is no God and that no one could protect Prahlāda, he felt encouraged to kill his son. He challenged the idea that the devotee is always protected by the Supreme Lord.

TEXT 14

एवं दुरुक्तैर्मुहुरर्दयन्रुषा
सुतं महाभागवतं महासुरः ।
खड्गं प्रगृह्योत्पतितो वरासनात्
स्तम्भं तताडातिबलः स्वमुष्टिना ॥१४॥

evaṁ duruktair muhur ardayan ruṣā
sutaṁ mahā-bhāgavataṁ mahāsuraḥ
khaḍgaṁ pragṛhyotpatito varāsanāt
stambhaṁ tatāḍātibalaḥ sva-muṣṭinā

evam—thus; *duruktaiḥ*—by harsh words; *muhuḥ*—constantly; *ardayan*—chastising; *ruṣā*—with unnecessary anger; *sutam*—his son; *mahā-bhāgavatam*—who was a most exalted devotee; *mahā-asuraḥ*—Hiraṇyakaśipu, the great demon; *khaḍgam*—sword; *pragṛhya*—taking up; *utpatitaḥ*—having gotten up; *vara-āsanāt*—from his exalted throne; *stambham*—the column; *tatāḍa*—struck; *ati-balaḥ*—very strong; *sva-muṣṭinā*—by his fist.

TRANSLATION

Being obsessed with anger, Hiraṇyakaśipu, who was very great in bodily strength, thus chastised his exalted devotee-son Prahlāda with harsh words. Cursing him again and again, Hiraṇyakaśipu took up his sword, got up from his royal throne, and with great anger struck his fist against the column.

TEXT 15

तदैव तस्मिन् निनदोऽतिभीषणो
बभूव येनाण्डकटाहमस्फुटत् ।

यं वै स्वधिष्ण्योपगतं त्वजादयः
श्रुत्वा स्वधामात्ययमङ्ग मेनिरे ॥१५॥

tadaiva tasmin ninado 'tibhīṣaṇo
babhūva yenāṇḍa-kaṭāham asphuṭat
yaṁ vai sva-dhiṣṇyopagataṁ tv ajādayaḥ
śrutvā sva-dhāmātyayam aṅga menire

tadā—at that time; *eva*—just; *tasmin*—within (the pillar); *ninadaḥ*—a sound; *ati-bhīṣaṇaḥ*—very fearful; *babhūva*—there was; *yena*—by which; *aṇḍa-kaṭāham*—the covering of the universe; *asphuṭat*—appeared to crack; *yam*—which; *vai*—indeed; *sva-dhiṣṇya-upagatam*—reaching their respective abodes; *tu*—but; *aja-ādayaḥ*—the demigods, headed by Lord Brahmā; *śrutvā*—hearing; *sva-dhāma-atyayam*—the destruction of their abodes; *aṅga*—my dear Yudhiṣṭhira; *menire*—thought.

TRANSLATION

Then from within the pillar came a fearful sound, which appeared to crack the covering of the universe. O my dear Yudhiṣṭhira, this sound reached even the abodes of the demigods like Lord Brahmā, and when the demigods heard it, they thought, "Oh, now our planets are being destroyed!"

PURPORT

As we sometimes become very much afraid at the sound of a thunderbolt, perhaps thinking that our houses will be destroyed, the great demigods like Lord Brahmā feared the thundering sound that came from the pillar in front of Hiraṇyakaśipu.

TEXT 16

स विक्रमन् पुत्रवधेप्सुरोजसा
निशम्य निर्ह्रादमपूर्वमद्भुतम् ।
अन्तःसभायां न ददर्श तत्पदं
वितत्रसुर्येन सुरारियूथपाः ॥१६॥

sa vikraman putra-vadhepsur ojasā
niśamya nirhrādam apūrvam adbhutam
antaḥ-sabhāyāṁ na dadarśa tat-padaṁ
vitatrasur yena surāri-yūtha-pāḥ

saḥ—he (Hiraṇyakaśipu); *vikraman*—exhibiting his prowess; *putra-vadha-īpsuḥ*—desirous of killing his own son; *ojasā*—with great strength; *niśamya*—hearing; *nirhrādam*—the fierce sound; *apūrvam*—never heard before; *adbhutam*—very wonderful; *antaḥ-sabhāyām*—within the jurisdiction of the great assembly; *na*—not; *dadarśa*—saw; *tat-padam*—the source of that tumultuous sound; *vitatrasuḥ*—became afraid; *yena*—by which sound; *sura-ari-yūtha-pāḥ*—the other leaders of the demons (not only Hiraṇyakaśipu).

TRANSLATION

While showing his extraordinary prowess, Hiraṇyakaśipu, who desired to kill his own son, heard that wonderful, tumultuous sound, which had never before been heard. Upon hearing the sound, the other leaders of the demons were afraid. None of them could find the origin of that sound in the assembly.

PURPORT

In *Bhagavad-gītā* (7.8), Kṛṣṇa explains Himself by saying:

raso 'ham apsu kaunteya
prabhāsmi śaśi sūryayoḥ
praṇavaḥ sarva-vedeṣu
śabdaḥ khe pauruṣaṁ nṛṣu

"O son of Kuntī [Arjuna], I am the taste of water, the light of the sun and the moon, the syllable *om* in the Vedic *mantras;* I am the sound in ether and ability in man." Here the Lord exhibited His presence everywhere by the tumultuous sound in the sky (*śabdaḥ khe*). The tumultuous thundering sound was proof of the Lord's presence. The demons like Hiraṇyakaśipu could now realize the supreme ruling power of the Lord, and thus Hiraṇyakaśipu became afraid. However powerful a man may be, he always fears the sound of a thunderbolt. Similarly, Hiraṇyakaśipu and all the demons who were his associates were extremely afraid because of the presence of the Supreme Lord in the form of sound, although they could not trace out the source of the sound.

TEXT 17

सत्यं विधातुं निजभृत्यभाषितं
व्याप्तिं च भूतेष्वखिलेषु चात्मनः ।
अदृश्यतात्यद्भुतरूपमुद्वहन्
स्तम्भे सभायां न मृगं न मानुषम् ॥१७॥

satyaṁ vidhātuṁ nija-bhṛtya-bhāṣitaṁ
vyāptiṁ ca bhūteṣv akhileṣu cātmanaḥ
adṛśyatātyadbhuta-rūpam udvahan
stambhe sabhāyāṁ na mṛgaṁ na mānuṣam

satyam—true; *vidhātum*—to prove; *nija-bhṛtya-bhāṣitam*—the words of His own servant (Prahlāda Mahārāja, who had said that his Lord is present everywhere); *vyāptim*—the pervasion; *ca*—and; *bhūteṣu*—among the living entities and elements; *akhileṣu*—all; *ca*—also; *ātmanaḥ*—of Himself; *adṛśyata*—was seen; *ati*—very; *adbhuta*—wonderful; *rūpam*—form; *udvahan*—taking; *stambhe*—in the pillar; *sabhāyām*—within the assembly; *na*—not; *mṛgam*—an animal; *na*—nor; *mānuṣam*—a human being.

TRANSLATION

To prove that the statement of His servant Prahlāda Mahārāja was substantial—in other words, to prove that the Supreme Lord is present everywhere, even within the pillar of an assembly hall—the Supreme Personality of Godhead, Hari, exhibited a wonderful form never before seen. The form was neither that of a man nor that of a lion. Thus the Lord appeared in His wonderful form in the assembly hall.

PURPORT

When Hiraṇyakaśipu asked Prahlāda Mahārāja, "Where is your Lord? Is He present in this pillar?" Prahlāda Mahārāja fearlessly replied, "Yes, my Lord is present everywhere." Therefore, to convince Hiraṇyakaśipu that the statement of Prahlāda Mahārāja was unmistakably true, the Lord appeared from the pillar. The Lord appeared as half lion and half man so that Hiraṇyakaśipu could not understand whether the great giant was a lion or a human being. To substantiate Prahlāda's statement, the Lord proved that His devotee, as declared in *Bhagavad-gītā*, is never vanquished (*kaunteya pratijānīhi na me bhaktaḥ praṇaśyati*). Prahlāda Mahārāja's demoniac father had repeatedly threatened to kill Prahlāda, but Prahlāda was confident that he could not be killed, since he was protected by the Supreme Lord. By appearing from the pillar, the Lord encouraged His devotee, saying in effect, "Don't worry. I am present here." By manifesting His form as Nṛsiṁhadeva, the Lord also preserved the truth of Lord Brahmā's promise that Hiraṇyakaśipu was not to be killed by any animal or any man. The Lord appeared in a form that could not be said to be fully a man or a lion.

TEXT 18

स सत्त्वमेनं परितो विपश्यन्
स्तम्भस्य मध्यादनुनिर्जिहानम् ।
नायं मृगो नापि नरो विचित्र-
महो किमेतन्नृमृगेन्द्ररूपम् ॥१८॥

sa sattvam enaṁ parito vipaśyan
stambhasya madhyād anunirjihānam
nāyaṁ mṛgo nāpi naro vicitram
aho kim etan nṛ-mṛgendra-rūpam

saḥ—he (Hiraṇyakaśipu, the King of the Daityas); *sattvam*—living being; *enam*—that; *paritaḥ*—all around; *vipaśyan*—looking; *stambhasya*—of the pillar; *madhyāt*—from the midst; *anunirjihānam*—having come out; *na*—not; *ayam*—this; *mṛgaḥ*—animal; *na*—not; *api*—indeed; *naraḥ*—human being; *vicitram*—very wonderful; *aho*—alas; *kim*—what; *etat*—this; *nṛ-mṛga-indra-rūpam*—the form of both a man and the king of the beasts, the lion.

TRANSLATION

While Hiraṇyakaśipu looked all around to find the source of the sound, that wonderful form of the Lord, which could not be ascertained to be either a man or a lion, emerged from the pillar. In amazement, Hiraṇyakaśipu wondered, "What is this creature that is half man and half lion?"

PURPORT

A demon cannot calculate the unlimited potency of the Supreme Lord. As stated in the *Vedas, parāsya śaktir vividhaiva śrūyate svābhāvikī jñāna-bala-kriyā ca:* the different potencies of the Lord are always working as an automatic exhibition of His knowledge. For a demon it is certainly wonderful that the form of a lion and the form of a man can be united, since a demon has no experience of the inconceivable power for which the Supreme Lord is called "all-powerful." Demons cannot understand the omnipotence of the Lord. They simply compare the Lord to one of them (*avajānanti māṁ mūḍhā mānuṣīṁ tanum āśritam*). *Mūḍhas,* rascals, think that Kṛṣṇa is an ordinary human being who appears for the benefit of other human beings. *Paraṁ bhāvam ajānantaḥ:* fools, rascals and demons cannot realize the supreme potency of the Lord, but He can do anything and everything; indeed, He can do whatever He likes. When Hiraṇyakaśipu received benedictions from Lord Brahmā, he thought that he was safe, since he received the benediction that he would not be killed either by an animal or by a human being. He never thought that an animal and human being would be combined so that demons like him would be puzzled by such a form. This is the meaning of the Supreme Personality of Godhead's omnipotence.

TEXTS 19–22

मीमांसमानस्य समुत्थितोऽग्रतो ।
नृसिंहरूपस्तदलं भयानकम् ॥१९॥
प्रतप्तचामीकरचण्डलोचनं
स्फुरत्सटाकेशरजृम्भिताननम् ।

करालदंष्ट्रं करवालचञ्चल-
क्षुरान्तजिह्वं भ्रुकुटीमुखोल्बणम् ॥२०॥
स्तब्धोर्ध्वकर्णं गिरिकन्दराद्भुत-
व्यात्तास्यनासं हनुभेदभीषणम् ।
दिविस्पृशत्कायमदीर्घपीवर-
ग्रीवोरुवक्षःस्थलमल्पमध्यमम् ॥२१॥
चन्द्रांशुगौरैश्छुरितं तनूरुहै-
र्विष्वग्भुजानीकशतं नखायुधम् ।
दुरासदं सर्वनिजेतरायुध-
प्रवेकविद्रावितदैत्यदानवम् ॥२२॥

mīmāṁsamānasya samutthito 'grato
nṛsiṁha-rūpas tad alaṁ bhayānakam

pratapta-cāmīkara-caṇḍa-locanaṁ
sphurat saṭā-keśara-jṛmbhitānanam
karāla-daṁṣṭraṁ karavāla-cañcala-
kṣurānta-jihvaṁ bhrukuṭī-mukholbaṇam

stabdhordhva-karṇaṁ giri-kandarādbhuta-
vyāttāsya-nāsaṁ hanu-bheda-bhīṣaṇam
divi-spṛśat kāyam adīrgha-pīvara-
grīvoru-vakṣaḥ-sthalam alpa-madhyamam

candrāṁśu-gauraiś churitaṁ tanūruhair
viṣvag bhujānīka-śataṁ nakhāyudham
durāsadaṁ sarva-nijetarāyudha-
praveka-vidrāvita-daitya-dānavam

mīmāṁsamānasya—of Hiraṇyakaśipu, who was contemplating the wonderful form of the Lord; *samutthitaḥ*—appeared; *agrataḥ*—in front; *nṛsiṁha-rūpaḥ*—the form of Nṛsiṁhadeva (half lion and half man); *tat*—that; *alam*—extraordinarily; *bhayānakam*—very fearful;

pratapta—like molten; *cāmīkara*—gold; *caṇḍa-locanam*—having fierce eyes; *sphurat*—flashing; *saṭā-keśara*—by His mane; *jṛmbhita-ānanam*—whose face was expanded; *karāla*—deadly; *daṁṣṭram*—with a set of teeth; *karavāla-cañcala*—waving like a sharp sword; *kṣura-anta*—and as sharp as a razor; *jihvam*—whose tongue; *bhrukuṭī-mukha*—due to His frowning face; *ulbaṇam*—dreadful; *stabdha*—motionless; *ūrdhva*—extending upward; *karṇam*—whose ears; *giri-kandara*—like the caves of a mountain; *adbhuta*—very wonderful; *vyāttāsya*—with a widely opened mouth; *nāsam*—and nostrils; *hanu-bheda-bhīṣaṇam*—causing fear due to the separation of the jaws; *divi-spṛśat*—touching the sky; *kāyam*—whose body; *adīrgha*—short; *pīvara*—fat; *grīva*—neck; *uru*—broad; *vakṣaḥ-sthalam*—chest; *alpa*—small; *madhyamam*—middle portion of the body; *candra-aṁśu*—like the rays of the moon; *gauraiḥ*—whitish; *churitam*—covered; *tanūruhaiḥ*—with hairs; *viṣvak*—in all directions; *bhuja*—of arms; *anīka-śatam*—with a hundred rows; *nakha*—having nails; *āyudham*—as fatal weapons; *durāsadam*—very difficult to conquer; *sarva*—all; *nija*—personal; *itara*—and other; *āyudha*—of weapons; *praveka*—by use of the best; *vidrāvita*—caused to run; *daitya*—by whom the demons; *dānavam*—and the rogues (atheists).

TRANSLATION

Hiraṇyakaśipu studied the form of the Lord, trying to decide who the form of Nṛsiṁhadeva standing before him was. The Lord's form was extremely fearsome because of His angry eyes, which resembled molten gold; His shining mane, which expanded the dimensions of His fearful face; His deadly teeth; and His razor-sharp tongue, which moved about like a dueling sword. His ears were erect and motionless, and His nostrils and gaping mouth appeared like caves of a mountain. His jaws parted fearfully, and His entire body touched the sky. His neck was very short and thick, His chest broad, His waist thin, and the hairs on His body as white as the rays of the moon. His arms, which resembled flanks of soldiers, spread in all directions as He killed the demons, rogues and atheists with His conchshell, disc, club, lotus and other natural weapons.

TEXT 23

प्रायेण मेऽयं हरिणोरुमायिना
वधः स्मृतोऽनेन समुद्यतेन किम् ।
एवं ब्रुवंस्त्वभ्यपतद् गदायुधो
नदन् नृसिंहं प्रति दैत्यकुञ्जरः ॥२३॥

prāyeṇa me 'yaṁ hariṇorumāyinā
vadhaḥ smṛto 'nena samudyatena kim
evaṁ bruvaṁs tv abhyapatad gadāyudho
nadan nṛsiṁhaṁ prati daitya-kuñjaraḥ

prāyeṇa—probably; *me*—of me; *ayam*—this; *hariṇā*—by the Supreme Lord; *uru-māyinā*—who possesses the great mystic power; *vadhaḥ*—the death; *smṛtaḥ*—planned; *anena*—with this; *samudyatena*—endeavor; *kim*—what use; *evam*—in this way; *bruvan*—murmuring; *tu*—indeed; *abhyapatat*—attacked; *gadā-āyudhaḥ*—armed with his weapon, the club; *nadan*—loudly roaring; *nṛ-siṁham*—the Lord, appearing in the form of half lion and half man; *prati*—toward; *daitya-kuñjaraḥ*—Hiraṇyakaśipu, who was like an elephant.

TRANSLATION

Hiraṇyakaśipu murmured to himself, "Lord Viṣṇu, who possesses great mystic power, has made this plan to kill me, but what is the use of such an attempt? Who can fight with me?" Thinking like this and taking up his club, Hiraṇyakaśipu attacked the Lord like an elephant.

PURPORT

In the jungle there are sometimes fights between lions and elephants. Here the Lord appeared like a lion, and Hiraṇyakaśipu, unafraid of the Lord, attacked Him like an elephant. Generally the elephant is defeated by the lion, and therefore the comparison in this verse is appropriate.

TEXT 24

अलक्षितोऽग्नौ पतितः पतङ्गमो
यथा नृसिंहौजसि सोऽसुरस्तदा ।

न तद् विचित्रं खलु सत्त्वधामनि
स्वतेजसा यो नु पुरापिबत् तमः ॥२४॥

alakṣito 'gnau patitaḥ pataṅgamo
yathā nṛsiṁhaujasi so 'suras tadā
na tad vicitraṁ khalu sattva-dhāmani
sva-tejasā yo nu purāpibat tamaḥ

alakṣitaḥ—invisible; *agnau*—in the fire; *patitaḥ*—fallen; *pataṅgamaḥ*—an insect; *yathā*—just as; *nṛsiṁha*—of Lord Nṛsiṁhadeva; *ojasi*—in the effulgence; *saḥ*—he; *asuraḥ*—Hiraṇyakaśipu; *tadā*—at that time; *na*—not; *tat*—that; *vicitram*—wonderful; *khalu*—indeed; *sattva-dhāmani*—in the Supreme Personality of Godhead, who is situated in pure goodness; *sva-tejasā*—by His own effulgence; *yaḥ*—He who (the Lord); *nu*—indeed; *purā*—formerly; *apibat*—swallowed up; *tamaḥ*—the darkness within the material creation.

TRANSLATION

Just as a small insect falls forcefully into a fire and the insignificant creature becomes invisible, when Hiraṇyakaśipu attacked the Lord, who was full of effulgence, Hiraṇyakaśipu became invisible. This is not at all astonishing, for the Lord is always situated in pure goodness. Formerly, during creation, He entered the dark universe and illuminated it by His spiritual effulgence.

PURPORT

The Lord is situated transcendentally, in pure goodness. The material world is generally controlled by *tamo-guṇa*, the quality of ignorance, but the spiritual world, because of the presence of the Lord and His effulgence, is free from all contamination by darkness, passion or contaminated goodness. Although there is a tinge of goodness in this material world in terms of the brahminical qualifications, such qualifications sometimes become invisible because of the strong prevalence of the modes of passion and ignorance. But because the Lord is always transcendentally situated, the material modes of passion and ignorance cannot touch Him. Whenever the Lord is present, there cannot be any darkness from the mode of ignorance. It is stated in *Caitanya-caritāmṛta* (*Madhya* 22.31):

kṛṣṇa——sūrya-sama, māyā haya andhakāra
yāhāṅ kṛṣṇa, tāhāṅ nāhi māyāra adhikāra

"Godhead is light. Nescience is darkness. Where there is Godhead there is no nescience." This material world is full of darkness and ignorance of spiritual life, but by *bhakti-yoga* this ignorance is dissipated. The Lord appeared because of the *bhakti-yoga* exhibited by Prahlāda Mahārāja, and as soon as the Lord appeared, the influence of Hiraṇyakaśipu's passion and ignorance was vanquished as the Lord's quality of pure goodness, or the Brahman effulgence, became prominent. In that prominent effulgence, Hiraṇyakaśipu became invisible, or his influence became insignificant. An example illustrating how the darkness of the material world is vanquished is given in the *śāstra*. When Brahmā was created from the lotus stem growing from the abdomen of Garbhodakaśāyī Viṣṇu, Lord Brahmā saw everything to be dark, but when he received knowledge from the Supreme Personality of Godhead, everything became clear, as everything becomes clear when one comes from night to sunshine. The important point is that as long as we are in the material modes of nature, we are always in darkness. This darkness cannot be dissipated without the presence of the Supreme Personality of Godhead, which is invoked by the practice of *bhakti-yoga*. *Bhakti-yoga* creates a transcendental situation with no tinges of material contamination.

TEXT 25

ततोऽभिपद्याभ्यहनन्महासुरो
रुषा नृसिंहं गदयोरुवेगया ।
तं विक्रमन्तं सगदं गदाधरो
महोरगं तार्क्ष्यसुतो यथाग्रहीत् ॥२५॥

tato 'bhipadyābhyahanan mahāsuro
ruṣā nṛsiṁhaṁ gadayoruvegayā

taṁ vikramantaṁ sagadaṁ gadādharo
mahoragaṁ tārkṣya-suto yathāgrahīt

tataḥ—thereafter; *abhipadya*—attacking; *abhyahanat*—struck; *mahā-asuraḥ*—the great demon (Hiraṇyakaśipu); *ruṣā*—with anger; *nṛsiṁham*—Lord Nṛsiṁhadeva; *gadayā*—by his club; *uru-vegayā*—moving with great force; *tam*—him (Hiraṇyakaśipu); *vikramantam*—showing his prowess; *sa-gadam*—with his club; *gadā-dharaḥ*—Lord Nṛsiṁhadeva, who also holds a club in His hand; *mahā-uragam*—a great snake; *tārkṣya-sutaḥ*—Garuḍa, the son of Tārkṣya; *yathā*—just as; *agrahīt*—captured.

TRANSLATION

Thereafter, the great demon Hiraṇyakaśipu, who was extremely angry, swiftly attacked Nṛsiṁhadeva with his club and began to beat Him. Lord Nṛsiṁhadeva, however, captured the great demon, along with his club, just as Garuḍa might capture a great snake.

TEXT 26

स तस्य हस्तोत्कलितस्तदासुरो
विक्रीडतो यद्वदहिर्गरुत्मतः ।
असाध्वमन्यन्त हृतौकसोऽमरा
घनच्छदा भारत सर्वधिष्ण्यपाः ॥२६॥

sa tasya hastotkalitas tadāsuro
vikrīḍato yadvad ahir garutmataḥ
asādhv amanyanta hṛtaukaso 'marā
ghana-cchadā bhārata sarva-dhiṣṇya-pāḥ

saḥ—he (Hiraṇyakaśipu); *tasya*—of Him (Lord Nṛsiṁhadeva); *hasta*—from the hands; *utkalitaḥ*—slipped; *tadā*—at that time; *asuraḥ*—the King of the demons, Hiraṇyakaśipu; *vikrīḍataḥ*—playing; *yadvat*—exactly like; *ahiḥ*—a snake; *garutmataḥ*—of Garuḍa; *asādhu*—not very good; *amanyanta*—considered; *hṛta-okasaḥ*—whose abodes were taken by Hiraṇyakaśipu; *amarāḥ*—the demigods;

ghana-cchadāḥ—situated behind a cover of clouds; *bhārata*—O great son of Bharata; *sarva-dhiṣṇya-pāḥ*—the rulers of the heavenly planets.

TRANSLATION

O Yudhiṣṭhira, O great son of Bharata, when Lord Nṛsiṁhadeva gave Hiraṇyakaśipu a chance to slip from His hand, just as Garuḍa sometimes plays with a snake and lets it slip from his mouth, the demigods, who had lost their abodes and who were hiding behind the clouds for fear of the demon, did not consider that incident very good. Indeed, they were perturbed.

PURPORT

When Hiraṇyakaśipu was in the process of being killed by Lord Nṛsiṁhadeva, the Lord gave the demon a chance to slip from His clutches. This incident was not very much appreciated by the demigods, for they were greatly afraid of Hiraṇyakaśipu. They knew that if somehow or other Hiraṇyakaśipu escaped from Nṛsiṁhadeva's hands and saw that the demigods were looking forward to his death with great pleasure, he would take great revenge upon them. Therefore they were very much afraid.

TEXT 27

तं मन्यमानो निजवीर्यशङ्कितं
यद्धस्तमुक्तो नृहरिं महासुरः ।
पुनस्तमासज्जत खड्गचर्मणी
प्रगृह्य वेगेन गतश्रमो मृधे ॥२७॥

taṁ manyamāno nija-vīrya-śaṅkitaṁ
yad dhasta-mukto nṛhariṁ mahāsuraḥ
punas tam āsajjata khaḍga-carmaṇī
pragṛhya vegena gata-śramo mṛdhe

tam—Him (Lord Nṛsiṁhadeva); *manyamānaḥ*—thinking; *nija-vīrya-śaṅkitam*—afraid of his prowess; *yat*—because; *hasta-muktaḥ*—freed from the clutches of the Lord; *nṛ-harim*—Lord Nṛsiṁhadeva;

mahā-asuraḥ—the great demon; *punaḥ*—again; *tam*—Him; *āsajjata*—attacked; *khaḍga-carmaṇī*—his sword and shield; *pragṛhya*—taking up; *vegena*—with great force; *gata-śramaḥ*—his fatigue having gone; *mṛdhe*—in the battle.

TRANSLATION

When Hiraṇyakaśipu was freed from the hands of Nṛsiṁhadeva, he falsely thought that the Lord was afraid of his prowess. Therefore, after taking a little rest from the fight, he took up his sword and shield and again attacked the Lord with great force.

PURPORT

When a sinful man enjoys material facilities, foolish people sometimes think, "How is it that this sinful man is enjoying whereas a pious man is suffering?" By the will of the Supreme, a sinful man is sometimes given the chance to enjoy the material world as if he were not under the clutches of material nature, just so that he may be fooled. A sinful man who acts against the laws of nature must be punished, but sometimes he is given a chance to play, exactly like Hiraṇyakaśipu when he was released from the hands of Nṛsiṁhadeva. Hiraṇyakaśipu was destined to be ultimately killed by Nṛsiṁhadeva, but just to see the fun, the Lord gave him a chance to slip from His hands.

TEXT 28

तं श्येनवेगं शतचन्द्रवर्त्मभि-
श्चरन्तमच्छिद्रमुपर्यधो हरिः ।
कृत्वाट्टहासं खरमुत्स्वनोल्बणं
निमीलिताक्षं जगृहे महाजवः ॥२८॥

taṁ śyena-vegaṁ śata-candra-vartmabhiś
carantam acchidram upary-adho hariḥ
kṛtvāṭṭa-hāsaṁ kharam utsvanolbaṇaṁ
nimīlitākṣaṁ jagṛhe mahā-javaḥ

tam—him (Hiraṇyakaśipu); *śyena-vegam*—possessing the speed of a hawk; *śata-candra-vartmabhiḥ*—by the maneuvers of his sword and his shield, which was marked with a hundred moonlike spots; *carantam*—moving; *acchidram*—without any weak spot; *upari-adhaḥ*—up and down; *hariḥ*—the Supreme Personality of Godhead; *kṛtvā*—making; *aṭṭa-hāsam*—loud laughter; *kharam*—extremely shrill; *utsvana-ulbaṇam*—very fearful due to its great sound; *nimīlita*—closed; *akṣam*—eyes; *jagṛhe*—captured; *mahā-javaḥ*—the greatly powerful Lord.

TRANSLATION

Making a loud, shrill sound of laughter, the Supreme Personality of Godhead, Nārāyaṇa, who is extremely strong and powerful, captured Hiraṇyakaśipu, who was protecting himself with his sword and shield, leaving no gaps open. With the speed of a hawk, Hiraṇyakaśipu moved sometimes in the sky and sometimes on the earth, his eyes closed because of fear of Nṛsiṁhadeva's laughter.

TEXT 29

विष्वक् स्फुरन्तं ग्रहणातुरं हरि-
व्यालो यथाखुं कुलिशाक्षतत्वचम् ।
द्वार्यूरुमापत्य ददार लीलया
नखैर्यथाहिं गरुडो महाविषम् ॥२९॥

viṣvak sphurantaṁ grahaṇāturaṁ harir
vyālo yathākhuṁ kuliśākṣata-tvacam
dvāry ūrum āpatya dadāra līlayā
nakhair yathāhiṁ garuḍo mahā-viṣam

viṣvak—all around; *sphurantam*—moving his limbs; *grahaṇa-āturam*—afflicted because of being captured; *hariḥ*—the Supreme Personality of Godhead, Nṛsiṁhadeva; *vyālaḥ*—a snake; *yathā*—just as; *ākhum*—a mouse; *kuliśa-akṣata*—not cut even by the thunderbolt thrown by Indra; *tvacam*—whose skin; *dvāri*—on the threshold of the door; *ūrum*—on His thigh; *āpatya*—placing; *dadāra*—pierced; *līlayā*—very easily; *nakhaiḥ*—with the nails; *yathā*—just as; *ahim*—a snake; *garuḍaḥ*—Garuḍa, the carrier of Lord Viṣṇu; *mahā-viṣam*—very venomous.

TRANSLATION

As a snake captures a mouse or Garuḍa captures a very venomous snake, Lord Nṛsiṁhadeva captured Hiraṇyakaśipu, who could not be pierced even by the thunderbolt of King Indra. As Hiraṇyakaśipu moved his limbs here, there and all around, very much afflicted at being captured, Lord Nṛsiṁhadeva placed the demon on His lap, supporting him with His thighs, and in the doorway of the assembly hall the Lord very easily tore the demon to pieces with the nails of His hand.

PURPORT

Hiraṇyakaśipu had received from Lord Brahmā the benediction that he would not die on the land or in the sky. Therefore, to keep the promise of Lord Brahmā intact, Nṛsiṁhadeva placed Hiraṇyakaśipu's body on His lap, which was neither land nor sky. Hiraṇyakaśipu had received the benediction that he would not die either during the day or at night. Therefore, to keep this promise of Brahmā, the Lord killed Hiraṇyakaśipu in the evening, which is the end of day and the beginning of night but is neither day nor night. Hiraṇyakaśipu had taken a benediction from Lord Brahmā that he would not die from any weapon or be killed by any person, dead or alive. Therefore, just to keep the word of Lord Brahmā, Lord Nṛsiṁhadeva pierced Hiraṇyakaśipu's body with His nails, which were not weapons and were neither living nor dead. Indeed, the nails can be called dead, but at the same time they can be said to be alive. To keep intact all of Lord Brahmā's benedictions, Lord Nṛsiṁhadeva paradoxically but very easily killed the great demon Hiraṇyakaśipu.

TEXT 30

संरम्भदुष्प्रेक्ष्यकराललोचनो
व्यात्ताननान्तं विलिहन्स्वजिह्वया ।
असृग्लवाक्तारुणकेशराननो
यथान्त्रमाली द्विपहत्यया हरिः ॥३०॥

saṁrambha-duṣprekṣya-karāla-locano
vyāttānanāntaṁ vilihan sva-jihvayā

asṛg-lavāktāruṇa-keśarānano
yathāntra-mālī dvipa-hatyayā hariḥ

saṁrambha—because of great anger; *duṣprekṣya*—very difficult to look at; *karāla*—very fearful; *locanaḥ*—eyes; *vyātta*—expanded; *ānana-antam*—the edge of the mouth; *vilihan*—licking; *sva-jihvayā*—with His tongue; *asṛk-lava*—with spots of blood; *ākta*—smeared; *aruṇa*—reddish; *keśara*—mane; *ānanaḥ*—and face; *yathā*—just as; *antra-mālī*—decorated with a garland of intestines; *dvipa-hatyayā*—by the killing of an elephant; *hariḥ*—the lion.

TRANSLATION

Lord Nṛsiṁhadeva's mouth and mane were sprinkled with drops of blood, and His fierce eyes, full of anger, were impossible to look at. Licking the edge of His mouth with His tongue, the Supreme Personality of Godhead, Nṛsiṁhadeva, decorated with a garland of intestines taken from Hiraṇyakaśipu's abdomen, resembled a lion that has just killed an elephant.

PURPORT

The hair on Lord Nṛsiṁhadeva's face, being sprinkled with drops of blood, was reddish and looked very beautiful. Lord Nṛsiṁhadeva pierced Hiraṇyakaśipu's abdomen with His nails, pulled out the demon's intestines and wore them as a garland, which enhanced His beauty. Thus the Lord became very fearsome, like a lion engaged in fighting an elephant.

TEXT 31

नखाङ्कुरोत्पाटितहृत्सरोरुहं
विसृज्य तस्यानुचरानुदायुधान् ।
अहन् समस्तान्नखशस्त्रपाणिभि-
र्दोर्दण्डयूथोऽनुपथान् सहस्रशः ॥३१॥

nakhāṅkurotpāṭita-hṛt-saroruhaṁ
visṛjya tasyānucarān udāyudhān
ahan samastān nakha-śastra-pāṇibhir
dordaṇḍa-yūtho 'nupathān sahasraśaḥ

nakha-aṅkura—by the pointed nails; *utpāṭita*—torn out; *hṛt-saroruham*—whose heart, which was like a lotus flower; *visṛjya*—leaving aside; *tasya*—of him; *anucarān*—the followers (soldiers and bodyguards); *udāyudhān*—having raised weapons; *ahan*—He killed; *samastān*—all; *nakha-śastra-pāṇibhiḥ*—with His nails and other weapons in His hands; *dordaṇḍa-yūthaḥ*—having unlimited arms; *anupathān*—the attendants of Hiraṇyakaśipu; *sahasraśaḥ*—by thousands.

TRANSLATION

The Supreme Personality of Godhead, who had many, many arms, first uprooted Hiraṇyakaśipu's heart and then threw him aside and turned toward the demon's soldiers. These soldiers had come in thousands to fight with Him with raised weapons and were very faithful followers of Hiraṇyakaśipu, but Lord Nṛsiṁhadeva killed all of them merely with the ends of His nails.

PURPORT

Since the creation of the material world, there have been two kinds of men—the *devas* and the *asuras*. The *devas* are always faithful to the Supreme Personality of Godhead, whereas the *asuras* are always atheists who defy the supremacy of the Lord. At the present moment, throughout the entire world, the atheists are extremely numerous. They are trying to prove that there is no God and that everything takes place due to combinations and permutations of material elements. Thus the material world is becoming more and more godless, and consequently everything is in a disturbed condition. If this continues, the Supreme Personality of Godhead will certainly take action, as He did in the case of Hiraṇyakaśipu. Within a second, Hiraṇyakaśipu and his followers were destroyed, and similarly if this godless civilization continues, it will be destroyed in a second, simply by the movement of one finger of the Supreme Personality of Godhead. The demons should therefore be careful and curtail their godless civilization. They should take advantage of the Kṛṣṇa consciousness movement and become faithful to the Supreme Personality of Godhead; otherwise they are doomed. As Hiraṇyakaśipu was killed in a second, the godless civilization can be destroyed at any moment.

TEXT 32

सटावधूता जलदाः परापतन्
ग्रहाश्च तद्दृष्टिविमुष्टरोचिषः ।
अम्भोधयः श्वासहता विचुक्षुभु-
र्निर्ह्रादभीता दिगिभा विचुक्रुशुः ॥३२॥

saṭāvadhūtā jaladāḥ parāpatan
grahāś ca tad-dṛṣṭi-vimuṣṭa-rociṣaḥ
ambhodhayaḥ śvāsa-hatā vicukṣubhur
nirhrāda-bhītā digibhā vicukruśuḥ

saṭā—by the hair on Lord Nṛsiṁhadeva's head; *avadhūtāḥ*—shaken; *jaladāḥ*—the clouds; *parāpatan*—scattered; *grahāḥ*—the luminous planets; *ca*—and; *tat-dṛṣṭi*—by His glaring glance; *vimuṣṭa*—taken away; *rociṣaḥ*—whose effulgence; *ambhodhayaḥ*—the water of the oceans and seas; *śvāsa-hatāḥ*—being struck by Lord Nṛsiṁhadeva's breathing; *vicukṣubhuḥ*—became turbulent; *nirhrāda-bhītāḥ*—frightened by Nṛsiṁhadeva's roaring; *digibhāḥ*—all the elephants guarding the quarters; *vicukruśuḥ*—cried out.

TRANSLATION

The hair on Nṛsiṁhadeva's head shook the clouds and scattered them here and there, His glaring eyes stole the effulgence of the luminaries in the sky, and His breathing agitated the seas and oceans. Because of His roaring, all the elephants in the world began to cry in fear.

PURPORT

As the Lord says in *Bhagavad-gītā* (10.41):

yad yad vibhūtimat sattvaṁ
śrīmad ūrjitam eva vā
tat tad evāvagaccha tvaṁ
mama tejo-'ṁśa-sambhavam

"Know that all beautiful, glorious and mighty creations spring from but a spark of My splendor." The illumination of the planets and stars in the sky is but a partial manifestation of the Lord's effulgence. There are many wonderful qualities of different living entities, but whatever extraordinary things exist are but part of the Lord's *tejas*, His illumination or brilliance. The deep waves of the seas and oceans and the many other wonders within the creation of the Supreme Personality of Godhead all become insignificant when the Lord, in His special feature, incarnates within this material world. Everything is insignificant in comparison to His personal, all-defeating transcendental qualities.

TEXT 33

द्यौस्तत्सटोत्क्षिप्तविमानसङ्कुला
प्रोत्सर्पत क्ष्मा च पदाभिपीडिता ।
शैलाः समुत्पेतुरमुष्य रंहसा
तत्तेजसा खं ककुभो न रेजिरे ॥३३॥

dyaus tat-saṭotkṣipta-vimāna-saṅkulā
protsarpata kṣmā ca padābhipīḍitā
śailāḥ samutpetur amuṣya raṁhasā
tat-tejasā khaṁ kakubho na rejire

dyauḥ—outer space; *tat-saṭā*—by His hair; *utkṣipta*—thrown up; *vimāna-saṅkulā*—filled with airplanes; *protsarpata*—slipped out of place; *kṣmā*—the planet earth; *ca*—also; *pada-abhipīḍitā*—distressed due to the heavy weight of the lotus feet of the Lord; *śailāḥ*—the hills and mountains; *samutpetuḥ*—sprang up; *amuṣya*—of that one (the Lord); *raṁhasā*—due to the intolerable force; *tat-tejasā*—by His effulgence; *kham*—the sky; *kakubhaḥ*—the ten directions; *na rejire*—did not shine.

TRANSLATION

Airplanes were thrown into outer space and the upper planetary system by the hair on Nṛsiṁhadeva's head. Because of the pressure of the Lord's lotus feet, the earth appeared to slip from its position, and all the hills and mountains sprang up due to His intolerable force. Because of the Lord's bodily effulgence, both the sky and all directions diminished in their natural illumination.

PURPORT

That there were airplanes flying in the sky long, long ago can be understood from this verse. *Śrīmad-Bhāgavatam* was spoken five thousand years ago, and the statements of this verse prove that the symptoms of a very advanced civilization then existed, even in the upper planetary systems, as well as in the lower planetary systems. Modern scientists and philosophers foolishly explain that there was no civilization prior to three thousand years ago, but the statement of this verse nullifies such whimsical judgments. The Vedic civilization existed millions and millions of years ago. It existed since the creation of this universe, and it included arrangements all over the universe with all the modern amenities and even more.

TEXT 34

ततः सभायामुपविष्टमुत्तमे
नृपासने संभृततेजसं विभुम् ।
अलक्षितद्वैरथमत्यमर्षणं
प्रचण्डवक्त्रं न बभाज कश्चन ॥३४॥

tataḥ sabhāyām upaviṣṭam uttame
nṛpāsane sambhṛta-tejasaṁ vibhum
alakṣita-dvairatham atyamarṣaṇaṁ
pracaṇḍa-vaktraṁ na babhāja kaścana

tataḥ—thereafter; *sabhāyām*—in the assembly house; *upaviṣṭam*—seated; *uttame*—on the best; *nṛpa-āsane*—throne (upon which King Hiraṇyakaśipu used to sit); *sambhṛta-tejasam*—in full effulgence; *vibhum*—the Supreme Lord; *alakṣita-dvairatham*—whose challenger or enemy was not seen; *ati*—very much; *amarṣaṇam*—fearsome (due to His anger); *pracaṇḍa*—terrible; *vaktram*—face; *na*—not; *babhāja*—worshiped; *kaścana*—anyone.

TRANSLATION

Manifesting a full effulgence and a fearsome countenance, Lord Nṛsiṁha, being very angry and finding no contestant to face His power and opulence, then sat down in the assembly hall on the ex-

cellent throne of the king. Because of fear and obedience, no one could come forward to serve the Lord directly.

PURPORT

When the Lord sat on the throne of Hiraṇyakaśipu, there was no one to protest; no enemy came forward on behalf of Hiraṇyakaśipu to fight with the Lord. This means that His supremacy was immediately accepted by the demons. Another point is that although Hiraṇyakaśipu treated the Lord as his bitterest enemy, he was the Lord's faithful servant in Vaikuṇṭha, and therefore the Lord had no hesitation in sitting on the throne that Hiraṇyakaśipu had so laboriously created. Śrīla Viśvanātha Cakravartī Ṭhākura remarks in this connection that sometimes, with great care and attention, great saintly persons and *ṛṣis* offer the Lord valuable seats dedicated with Vedic *mantras* and *tantras*, but still the Lord does not sit upon those thrones. Hiraṇyakaśipu, however, had formerly been Jaya, the doorkeeper at the Vaikuṇṭha gate, and although he had fallen because of the curse of the *brāhmaṇas* and had gotten the nature of a demon, and although he had never offered anything to the Lord as Hiraṇyakaśipu, the Lord is so affectionate to His devotee and servant that He nonetheless took pleasure in sitting on the throne that Hiraṇyakaśipu had created. In this regard it is to be understood that a devotee is fortunate in any condition of his life.

TEXT 35

निशाम्य लोकत्रयमस्तकज्वरं
तमादिदैत्यं हरिणा हतं मृधे ।
प्रहर्षवेगोत्कलितानना मुहुः
प्रसूनवर्षैर्ववृषुः सुरस्त्रियः ॥३५॥

niśāmya loka-traya-mastaka-jvaraṁ
tam ādi-daityaṁ hariṇā hataṁ mṛdhe
praharṣa-vegotkalitānanā muhuḥ
prasūna-varṣair vavṛṣuḥ sura-striyaḥ

niśāmya—hearing; *loka-traya*—of the three worlds; *mastaka-jvaram*—the headache; *tam*—him; *ādi*—the original; *daityam*—

demon; *hariṇā*—by the Supreme Personality of Godhead; *hatam*—killed; *mṛdhe*—in battle; *praharṣa-vega*—by an outburst of ecstasy; *utkalita-ānanāḥ*—whose faces blossomed; *muhuḥ*—again and again; *prasūna-varṣaiḥ*—with showers of flowers; *vavṛṣuḥ*—rained; *sura-striyaḥ*—the wives of the demigods.

TRANSLATION

Hiraṇyakaśipu had been exactly like a fever of meningitis in the head of the three worlds. Thus when the wives of the demigods in the heavenly planets saw that the great demon had been killed by the personal hands of the Supreme Personality of Godhead, their faces blossomed in great joy. The wives of the demigods again and again showered flowers from heaven upon Lord Nṛsiṁhadeva like rain.

TEXT 36

तदा विमानावलिभिर्नभस्तलं
दिदृक्षतां सङ्कुलमास नाकिनाम् ।
सुरानका दुन्दुभयोऽथ जघ्निरे
गन्धर्वमुख्या ननृतुर्जगुः स्त्रियः ॥३६॥

tadā vimānāvalibhir nabhastalaṁ
didṛkṣatāṁ saṅkulam āsa nākinām
surānakā dundubhayo 'tha jaghnire
gandharva-mukhyā nanṛtur jaguḥ striyaḥ

tadā—at that time; *vimāna-āvalibhiḥ*—with different types of airplanes; *nabhastalam*—the sky; *didṛkṣatām*—desirous of seeing; *saṅkulam*—crowded; *āsa*—became; *nākinām*—of the demigods; *sura-ānakāḥ*—the drums of the demigods; *dundubhayaḥ*—the kettledrums; *atha*—as well; *jaghnire*—were sounded; *gandharva-mukhyāḥ*—the chiefs of Gandharvaloka; *nanṛtuḥ*—began to dance; *jaguḥ*—sang; *striyaḥ*—heavenly society women.

TRANSLATION

At that time, the airplanes of the demigods, who desired to see the activities of the Supreme Lord, Nārāyaṇa, crowded the sky.

The demigods began beating drums and kettledrums, and upon hearing them the angelic women began to dance, while the chiefs of the Gandharvas sang sweetly.

TEXTS 37–39

तत्रोपव्रज्य विबुधा ब्रह्मेन्द्रगिरिशादयः ।
ऋषयः पितरः सिद्धा विद्याधरमहोरगाः ॥३७॥
मनवः प्रजानां पतयो गन्धर्वाप्सरचारणाः ।
यक्षाः किम्पुरुषास्तात वेतालाः सहकिन्नराः॥३८॥
ते विष्णुपार्षदाः सर्वे सुनन्दकुमुदादयः ।
मूर्ध्नि बद्धाञ्जलिपुटा आसीनं तीव्रतेजसम् ।
ईडिरे नरशार्दुलं नातिदूरचराः पृथक् ॥३९॥

tatropavrajya vibudhā
brahmendra-giriśādayah
ṛṣayaḥ pitaraḥ siddhā
vidyādhara-mahoragāḥ

manavaḥ prajānāṁ patayo
gandharvāpsara-cāraṇāḥ
yakṣāḥ kimpuruṣās tāta
vetālāḥ saha-kinnarāḥ

te viṣṇu-pārṣadāḥ sarve
sunanda-kumudādayaḥ
mūrdhni baddhāñjali-puṭā
āsīnaṁ tīvra-tejasam
īḍire nara-śārdulaṁ
nātidūracarāḥ pṛthak

tatra—there (in the sky); *upavrajya*—coming (in their respective airplanes); *vibudhāḥ*—all the different demigods; *brahma-indra-giriśa-ādayaḥ*—headed by Lord Brahmā, King Indra and Lord Śiva; *ṛṣayaḥ*—the great saintly sages; *pitaraḥ*—the inhabitants of Pitṛloka; *siddhāḥ*—

the residents of Siddhaloka; *vidyādhara*—the residents of Vidyādhara-loka; *mahā-uragāḥ*—the residents of the planets where great serpents reside; *manavaḥ*—the Manus; *prajānām*—of the living entities (on different planets); *patayaḥ*—the chiefs; *gandharva*—the residents of Gandharvaloka; *apsara*—the residents of the angelic planet; *cāraṇāḥ*—the residents of Cāraṇaloka; *yakṣāḥ*—the Yakṣas; *kimpuruṣāḥ*—the Kimpuruṣas; *tāta*—O dear one; *vetālāḥ*—the Vetālas; *saha-kinnarāḥ*—along with the Kinnaras; *te*—they; *viṣṇu-pārṣadāḥ*—the personal associates of Lord Viṣṇu (in the Vaikuṇṭhalokas); *sarve*—all; *sunanda-kumuda-ādayaḥ*—headed by Sunanda and Kumuda; *mūrdhni*—on their heads; *baddha-añjali-puṭāḥ*—with folded hands; *āsīnam*—who was sitting on the throne; *tīvra-tejasam*—exposing His great spiritual effulgence; *īḍire*—offered respectful worship; *nara-śārdulam*—unto the Lord, who had appeared as half man and half lion; *na ati-dūracarāḥ*—coming near; *pṛthak*—individually.

TRANSLATION

My dear King Yudhiṣṭhira, the demigods then approached the Lord. They were headed by Lord Brahmā, King Indra and Lord Śiva and included great saintly persons and the residents of Pitṛloka, Siddhaloka, Vidyādhara-loka and the planet of the snakes. The Manus approached, and so did the chiefs of various other planets. The angelic dancers approached, as did the Gandharvas, the Cāraṇas, the Yakṣas, the inhabitants of Kinnaraloka, the Vetālas, the inhabitants of Kimpuruṣa-loka, and the personal servants of Viṣṇu like Sunanda and Kumuda. All of them came near the Lord, who glowed with intense light. They individually offered their obeisances and prayers, their hands folded at their heads.

TEXT 40

श्रीब्रह्मोवाच

नतोऽस्म्यनन्ताय दुरन्तशक्तये
विचित्रवीर्याय पवित्रकर्मणे ।
विश्वस्य सर्गस्थितिसंयमान् गुणैः
स्वलीलया सन्दधतेऽव्ययात्मने ॥४०॥

śrī-brahmovāca
nato 'smy anantāya duranta-śaktaye
vicitra-vīryāya pavitra-karmaṇe
viśvasya sarga-sthiti-saṁyamān guṇaiḥ
sva-līlayā sandadhate 'vyayātmane

śrī-brahmā uvāca—Lord Brahmā said; *nataḥ*—bowed down; *asmi*—I am; *anantāya*—unto the unlimited Lord; *duranta*—very difficult to find an end to; *śaktaye*—who possesses different potencies; *vicitra-vīryāya*—having varieties of prowess; *pavitra-karmaṇe*—whose actions have no reaction (even though doing contrary things, He remains without contamination by the material modes); *viśvasya*—of the universe; *sarga*—creation; *sthiti*—maintenance; *saṁyamān*—and annihilation; *guṇaiḥ*—by the material qualities; *sva-līlayā*—very easily; *sandadhate*—performs; *avyaya-ātmane*—whose personality never deteriorates.

TRANSLATION

Lord Brahmā prayed: My Lord, You are unlimited, and You possess unending potencies. No one can estimate or calculate Your prowess and wonderful influence, for Your actions are never polluted by the material energy. Through the material qualities, You very easily create the universe, maintain it and again annihilate it, yet You remain the same, without deterioration. I therefore offer my respectful obeisances unto You.

PURPORT

The activities of the Lord are always wonderful. His personal servants Jaya and Vijaya were confidential friends, yet they were cursed, and they accepted bodies of demons. Again, in the family of one such demon, Prahlāda Mahārāja was caused to take birth to exhibit the behavior of an exalted devotee, and then the Lord accepted the body of Nṛsiṁhadeva to kill that same demon, who by the Lord's own will had taken birth in a demoniac family. Therefore, who can understand the Lord's transcendental activities? Not to speak of understanding the transcendental activities of the Lord, no one can understand even the activities of His servants. In *Caitanya-caritāmṛta* (*Madhya* 23.39) it is said, *tāṅra vākya, kriyā, mudrā vijñeha nā bhujhaya:* no one can understand the activities of the Lord's servants. Therefore, what to speak of the activities of the Lord? Who can understand how Kṛṣṇa is benefiting the entire world? The Lord is addressed as *duranta-śakti* because no one can understand His potencies and how He acts.

TEXT 41

श्रीरुद्र उवाच
कोपकालो युगान्तस्ते हतोऽयमसुरोऽल्पकः ।
तत्सुतं पाह्युपसृतं भक्तं ते भक्तवत्सल ॥४१॥

śrī-rudra uvāca
kopa-kālo yugāntas te
hato 'yam asuro 'lpakaḥ
tat-sutaṁ pāhy upasṛtaṁ
bhaktaṁ te bhakta-vatsala

śrī-rudraḥ uvāca—Lord Śiva offered his prayer; *kopa-kālaḥ*—the right time for Your anger (for the purpose of annihilating the universe); *yuga-antaḥ*—the end of the millennium; *te*—by You; *hataḥ*—killed; *ayam*—this; *asuraḥ*—great demon; *alpakaḥ*—very insignificant; *tat-sutam*—his son (Prahlāda Mahārāja); *pāhi*—just protect; *upasṛtam*—who is surrendered and standing nearby; *bhaktam*—devotee; *te*—of Your Lordship; *bhakta-vatsala*—O my Lord, who are so affectionate to Your devotee.

TRANSLATION

Lord Śiva said: The end of the millennium is the time for Your anger. Now that this insignificant demon Hiraṇyakaśipu has been killed, O my Lord, who are naturally affectionate to Your devotee, kindly protect his son Prahlāda Mahārāja, who is standing nearby as Your fully surrendered devotee.

PURPORT

The Supreme Personality of Godhead is the creator of the material world. There are three processes in creation—namely creation, maintenance and finally annihilation. During the period of annihilation, at the end of each millennium, the Lord becomes angry, and the part of anger is played by Lord Śiva, who is therefore called Rudra. When the Lord appeared in great anger to kill Hiraṇyakaśipu, everyone was extremely afraid of the Lord's attitude, but Lord Śiva, knowing very well that the Lord's anger is also His *līlā,* was not afraid. Lord Śiva knew that he would have to play the part of anger for the Lord. *Kāla* means Lord Śiva (Bhairava), and *kopa* refers to the Lord's anger. These words, combined together as *kopa-kāla,* refer to the end of each millennium. Actually the Lord is always affectionate toward His devotees, even though He may appear very angry. Because He is *avyayātmā*—because He never falls down—even when angry the Lord is affectionate toward His devotees. Therefore Lord Śiva reminded the Lord to act like an affectionate father toward Prahlāda Mahārāja, who was standing by the Lord's side as an exalted, fully surrendered devotee.

TEXT 42

श्रीइन्द्र उवाच

प्रत्यानीताः परम भवता त्रायता नः स्वभागा
दैत्याक्रान्तं हृदयकमलं तद्गृहं प्रत्यबोधि ।
कालग्रस्तं कियदिदमहो नाथ शुश्रूषतां ते
मुक्तिस्तेषां न हि बहुमता नारसिंहापरैः किम् ॥४२॥

śrī-indra uvāca
pratyānītāḥ parama bhavatā trāyatā naḥ sva-bhāgā
daityākrāntaṁ hṛdaya-kamalaṁ tad-gṛhaṁ pratyabodhi
kāla-grastaṁ kiyad idam aho nātha śuśrūṣatāṁ te
muktis teṣāṁ na hi bahumatā nārasiṁhāparaiḥ kim

śrī-indraḥ uvāca—Indra, the King of heaven, said; *pratyānītāḥ*—recovered; *parama*—O Supreme; *bhavatā*—by Your Lordship; *trāyatā*—who are protecting; *naḥ*—us; *sva-bhāgāḥ*—shares in the sacrifices; *daitya-ākrāntam*—afflicted by the demon; *hṛdaya-kamalam*—the lotuslike cores of our hearts; *tat-gṛham*—which is actually Your residence; *pratyabodhi*—it has been illuminated; *kāla-*

grastam—devoured by time; *kiyat*—insignificant; *idam*—this (world); *aho*—alas; *nātha*—O Lord; *śuśrūṣatām*—for those who are always engaged in the service; *te*—of You; *muktiḥ*—liberation from material bondage; *teṣām*—of them (the pure devotees); *na*—not; *hi*—indeed; *bahumatā*—thought very important; *nāra-siṁha*—O Lord Nṛsiṁhadeva, half lion and half human being; *aparaiḥ kim*—then what is the use of other possessions.

TRANSLATION

King Indra said: O Supreme Lord, You are our deliverer and protector. Our shares of sacrifices, which are actually Yours, have been recovered from the demon by You. Because the demoniac king Hiraṇyakaśipu was most fearsome, our hearts, which are Your permanent abode, were all overtaken by him. Now, by Your presence, the gloom and darkness in our hearts have been dissipated. O Lord, for those who always engage in Your service, which is more exalted than liberation, all material opulence is insignificant. They do not even care for liberation, not to speak of the benefits of kāma, artha and dharma.

PURPORT

In this material world there are two kinds of people—the *devatās* (demigods) and the *asuras* (demons). Although the demigods are attached to material enjoyment, they are devotees of the Lord who act according to the rules and regulations of the Vedic injunctions. During the reign of Hiraṇyakaśipu, everyone was disturbed in the routine duties of Vedic civilization. When Hiraṇyakaśipu was killed, all the demigods, who had always been disturbed by Hiraṇyakaśipu, felt relief in their general way of life.

Because the government in Kali-yuga is full of demons, the living conditions of devotees are always disturbed. Devotees cannot perform *yajña*, and thus they cannot partake of the remnants of food offered in *yajña* for the worship of Lord Viṣṇu. The hearts of the demigods are always filled with fear of the demons, and therefore they cannot think of the Supreme Personality of Godhead. The engagement of the demigods is to think of the Lord always within the cores of their hearts. The Lord says in *Bhagavad-gītā* (6.47):

yogināṁ api sarveṣāṁ
mad gatenāntarātmanā
śraddhāvān bhajate yo māṁ
sa me yuktatamo mataḥ

"And of all *yogīs,* he who always abides in Me with great faith, worshiping Me in transcendental loving service, is most intimately united with Me in *yoga* and is the highest of all." The demigods fully absorb themselves in meditation upon the Supreme Personality of Godhead to become perfect *yogīs,* but because of the presence of demons, their hearts are filled with the activities of the demons. Thus their hearts, which are meant to be the abode of the Supreme Lord, are practically occupied by the demons. All the demigods felt relieved when Hiraṇyakaśipu was dead, for they could easily think of the Lord. They could then receive the results of sacrifices and become happy even though in the material world.

TEXT 43

श्रीऋषय ऊचुः
त्वं नस्तपः परममात्थ यदात्मतेजो
येनेदमादिपुरुषात्मगतं ससक्थ ।
तद् विप्रलुप्तममुनाद्य शरण्यपाल
रक्षागृहीतवपुषा पुनरन्वमंस्थाः ॥४३॥

śrī-ṛṣaya ūcuḥ
tvaṁ nas tapaḥ paramam āttha yad ātma-tejo
yenedam ādi-puruṣātma-gataṁ sasarktha
tad vipraluptam amunādya śaraṇya-pāla
rakṣā-gṛhīta-vapuṣā punar anvamaṁsthāḥ

śrī-ṛṣayaḥ ūcuḥ—the great sages said; *tvam*—You; *naḥ*—our; *tapaḥ*—austerity; *paramam*—topmost; *āttha*—instructed; *yat*—which; *ātma-tejaḥ*—Your spiritual power; *yena*—by which; *idam*—this (material world); *ādi-puruṣa*—O supreme original Personality of Godhead; *ātma-gatam*—merged within Yourself; *sasarktha*—(You) created; *tat*—that process of austerity and penance; *vipraluptam*—stolen; *amunā*—by that demon (Hiraṇyakaśipu); *adya*—now; *śaraṇya-pāla*—

O supreme maintainer of those who need to be sheltered; *rakṣā-gṛhīta-vapuṣā*—by Your body, which You accept to give protection; *punaḥ*—again; *anvamaṁsthāḥ*—You have approved.

TRANSLATION

All the saintly persons present offered their prayers in this way: O Lord, O supreme maintainer of those sheltered at Your lotus feet, O original Personality of Godhead, the process of austerity and penance, in which You instructed us before, is the spiritual power of Your very self. It is by austerity that You create the material world, which lies dormant within You. This austerity was almost stopped by the activities of this demon, but now, by Yourself appearing in the form of Nṛsiṁhadeva, which is meant just to give us protection, and by killing this demon, You have again approved the process of austerity.

PURPORT

The living entities wandering within the jurisdiction of the 8,400,000 species of life get the opportunity for self-realization in the human form and gradually in such other elevated forms as those of the demigods, Kinnaras and Cāraṇas, as will be described below. In the higher statuses of life, beginning from human life, the main duty is *tapasya*, or austerity. As Ṛṣabhadeva advised His sons, *tapo divyaṁ putrakā yena sattvaṁ śuddhyet.* To rectify our material existence, austerity (*tapasya*) is absolutely necessary. However, when people in general come under the control of a demon or a demoniac ruling power, they forget this process of *tapasya* and gradually also become demoniac. All the saintly persons, who were generally engaged in austerity, felt relieved when Hiraṇyakaśipu was killed by the Lord in the form of Nṛsiṁhadeva. They realized that the original instruction concerning human life—that it is meant for *tapasya* for self-realization—was reaffirmed by the Lord when He killed Hiraṇyakaśipu.

TEXT 44

श्रीपितर ऊचुः

श्राद्धानि नोऽधिबुभुजे प्रसभं तनूजै-
र्दत्तानि तीर्थसमयेऽप्यपिबत् तिलाम्बु ।

तस्योदरान्नखविदीर्णवपाद् य आर्च्छत्
तस्मै नमो नृहरयेऽखिलधर्मगोप्त्रे ॥४४॥

śrī-pitara ūcuḥ
śrāddhāni no 'dhibubhuje prasabhaṁ tanūjair
dattāni tīrtha-samaye 'py apibat tilāmbu
tasyodarān nakha-vidīrṇa-vapād ya ārcchat
tasmai namo nṛharaye 'khila-dharma-goptre

śrī-pitaraḥ ūcuḥ—the inhabitants of Pitṛloka said; *śrāddhāni*—the performances of the *śrāddha* ceremony (offering of food grains to dead forefathers by a particular process); *naḥ*—our; *adhibubhuje*—enjoyed; *prasabham*—by force; *tanūjaiḥ*—by our sons and grandsons; *dattāni*—offered; *tīrtha-samaye*—at the time of bathing in the holy places; *api*—even; *apibat*—drank; *tila-ambu*—offerings of water with sesame seeds; *tasya*—of the demon; *udarāt*—from the abdomen; *nakha-vidīrṇa*—pierced by the nails of the hand; *vapāt*—the skin of the intestines of which; *yaḥ*—He who (the Personality of Godhead); *ārcchat*—obtained; *tasmai*—unto Him (the Supreme Personality of Godhead); *namaḥ*—respectful obeisances; *nṛ-haraye*—who has appeared as half lion and half man (Nṛhari); *akhila*—universal; *dharma*—religious principles; *goptre*—who maintains.

TRANSLATION

The inhabitants of Pitṛloka prayed: Let us offer our respectful obeisances unto Lord Nṛsiṁhadeva, the maintainer of the religious principles of the universe. He has killed Hiraṇyakaśipu, the demon who by force enjoyed all the offerings of the śrāddha ceremonies performed by our sons and grandsons on the anniversaries of our death and who drank the water with sesame seeds offered in holy places of pilgrimage. By killing this demon, O Lord, You have taken back all this stolen property from his abdomen by piercing it with Your nails. We therefore wish to offer our respectful obeisances unto You.

PURPORT

It is the duty of all householders to offer food grains to all their departed forefathers, but during the time of Hiraṇyakaśipu this process was stopped; no one would offer *śrāddha* oblations of food grains to the forefathers with great respect. Thus when there is a demoniac rule, everything concerning the Vedic principles is turned upside down, all the religious ceremonies of *yajña* are stopped, the resources meant to be spent for *yajña* are taken away by the demoniac government, everything becomes chaotic, and consequently the entire world becomes hell itself. When the demons are killed by the presence of Nṛsiṁhadeva, everyone feels comfortable, irrespective of the planet upon which he lives.

TEXT 45

श्रीसिद्धा ऊचुः
यो नो गतिं योगसिद्धामसाधु-
रहार्षीद् योगतपोबलेन ।
नानादर्पं तं नखैर्विददार
तस्मै तुभ्यं प्रणताः स्मो नृसिंह ॥४५॥

śrī-siddhā ūcuḥ
yo no gatiṁ yoga-siddhām asādhur
ahārṣīd yoga-tapo-balena
nānā darpaṁ taṁ nakhair vidadāra
tasmai tubhyaṁ praṇatāḥ smo nṛsiṁha

śrī-siddhāḥ ūcuḥ—the inhabitants of Siddhaloka said; *yaḥ*—the person who; *naḥ*—our; *gatim*—perfection; *yoga-siddhām*—achieved by mystic *yoga; asādhuḥ*—most uncivilized and dishonest; *ahārṣīt*—stole away; *yoga*—of mysticism; *tapaḥ*—and austerities; *balena*—by the power; *nānā darpam*—proud due to wealth, opulence and strength; *tam*—him; *nakhaiḥ*—by the nails; *vidadāra*—pierced; *tasmai*—unto him; *tubhyam*—unto You; *praṇatāḥ*—bowed down; *smaḥ*—we are; *nṛsiṁha*—O Lord Nṛsiṁhadeva.

TRANSLATION

The inhabitants of Siddhaloka prayed: O Lord Nṛsiṁhadeva, because we belong to Siddhaloka, we automatically achieve perfection in all eight kinds of mystic power. Yet Hiraṇyakaśipu was so

dishonest that by the strength of his power and austerity, he took away our powers. Thus he became very proud of his mystic strength. Now, because this rogue has been killed by Your nails, we offer our respectful obeisances unto You.

PURPORT

On earth there are many *yogīs* who can exhibit some feeble mystic power by manufacturing pieces of gold like magic, but the inhabitants of the planet Siddhaloka are actually extremely powerful in mysticism. They can fly from one planet to another without airplanes. This is called *laghimā-siddhi.* They can actually become very light and fly in the sky. By a severe type of austerity, however, Hiraṇyakaśipu excelled all the inhabitants of Siddhaloka and created disturbances for them. The residents of Siddhaloka were also beaten by the powers of Hiraṇyakaśipu. Now that Hiraṇyakaśipu had been killed by the Lord, the inhabitants of Siddhaloka also felt relieved.

TEXT 46

श्रीविद्याधरा ऊचुः
विद्यां पृथग्धारणयानुराद्धां
न्यषेधदज्ञो बलवीर्यदृप्तः ।
स येन संख्ये पशुवद्धतस्तं
मायानृसिंहं प्रणताः स्म नित्यम् ॥४६॥

śrī-vidyādharā ūcuḥ
vidyāṁ pṛthag dhāraṇayānurāddhāṁ
nyaṣedhad ajño bala-vīrya-dṛptaḥ
sa yena saṅkhye paśuvad dhatas taṁ
māyā-nṛsiṁhaṁ praṇatāḥ sma nityam

śrī-vidyādharāḥ ūcuḥ—the inhabitants of Vidyādhara-loka prayed; *vidyām*—mystic formulas (by which one can appear and disappear); *pṛthak*—separately; *dhāraṇayā*—by various meditations within the mind; *anurāddhām*—attained; *nyaṣedhat*—stopped; *ajñaḥ*—this fool; *bala-vīrya-dṛptaḥ*—puffed up by bodily strength and his ability to conquer anyone; *saḥ*—he (Hiraṇyakaśipu); *yena*—by whom; *saṅkhye*—in battle; *paśu-vat*—exactly like an animal; *hataḥ*—killed; *tam*—unto Him; *māyā-nṛsiṁham*—appearing as Lord Nṛsiṁhadeva by the influence of His own energy; *praṇatāḥ*—fallen; *sma*—certainly; *nityam*—eternally.

TRANSLATION

The inhabitants of Vidyādhara-loka prayed: Our acquired power to appear and disappear in various ways according to varieties of meditation was banned by that foolish Hiraṇyakaśipu because of his pride in his superior bodily strength and his ability to conquer others. Now the Supreme Personality of Godhead has killed him just as if the demon were an animal. Unto that supreme pastime form of Lord Nṛsiṁhadeva, we eternally offer our respectful obeisances.

TEXT 47

श्रीनागा ऊचुः

येन पापेन रत्नानि स्त्रीरत्नानि हृतानि नः ।
तद्वक्षःपाटनेनासां दत्तानन्द नमोऽस्तु ते ॥४७॥

śrī-nāgā ūcuḥ
yena pāpena ratnāni
strī-ratnāni hṛtāni naḥ
tad-vakṣaḥ-pāṭanenāsāṁ
dattānanda namo 'stu te

śrī-nāgāḥ ūcuḥ—the inhabitants of Nāgaloka, who look like serpents, said; *yena*—by which person; *pāpena*—the most sinful (Hiraṇyakaśipu); *ratnāni*—the jewels on our heads; *strī-ratnāni*—beautiful wives; *hṛtāni*—taken away; *naḥ*—our; *tat*—his; *vakṣaḥ-pāṭanena*—by the piercing of the chest; *āsām*—of all the women (who were kidnapped); *datta-ānanda*—O Lord, You are the source of the pleasure; *namaḥ*—our respectful obeisances; *astu*—let there be; *te*—unto You.

TRANSLATION

The inhabitants of Nāgaloka said: The most sinful Hiraṇyakaśipu took away all the jewels on our hoods and all our beautiful wives. Now, since his chest has been pierced by Your nails, You are the source of all pleasure to our wives. Thus we together offer our respectful obeisances unto You.

PURPORT

No one is peaceful if his wealth and wife are forcibly taken away. All the inhabitants of Nāgaloka, which is situated below the earthly planetary system, were in great anxiety because their wealth had been stolen and their wives kidnapped by Hiraṇyakaśipu. Now, Hiraṇyakaśipu having been killed, their wealth and wives were returned, and their wives felt satisfied. The inhabitants of various *lokas*, or planets, offered their respectful obeisances unto the Lord because they were relieved by the death of Hiraṇyakaśipu. Disturbances similar to those created by Hiraṇyakaśipu are now taking place all over the world because of demoniac governments. As stated in the Twelfth Canto of *Śrīmad-Bhāgavatam*, the men of the governments of Kali-yuga will be no better than rogues and plunderers. Thus the populace will be harassed on one side by scarcity of food and on another by heavy taxation by the government. In other words, the people in most parts of the world in this age are harassed by the ruling principles of Hiraṇyakaśipu.

TEXT 48

श्रीमनव ऊचुः
मनवो वयं तव निदेशकारिणो
दितिजेन देव परिभूतसेतवः ।
भवता खलः स उपसंहृतः प्रभो
करवाम ते किमनुशाधि किङ्करान् ॥४८॥

śrī-manava ūcuḥ
manavo vayaṁ tava nideśa-kāriṇo
ditijena deva paribhūta-setavaḥ

bhavatā khalaḥ sa upasaṁhṛtaḥ prabho
karavāma te kim anuśādhi kiṅkarān

śrī-manavaḥ ūcuḥ—all the Manus offered their respectful obeisances by saying; *manavaḥ*—the leaders of the universal affairs (especially in connection with giving knowledge to humanity about how to live lawfully under the protection of the Supreme Personality of Godhead); *vayam*—we; *tava*—of Your Lordship; *nideśa-kāriṇaḥ*—the carriers of the orders; *diti-jena*—by Hiraṇyakaśipu, the son of Diti; *deva*—O Lord; *paribhūta*—disregarded; *setavaḥ*—whose laws of morality concerning the *varṇāśrama* system in human society; *bhavatā*—by Your Lordship; *khalaḥ*—the most envious rascal; *saḥ*—he; *upasaṁhṛtaḥ*—killed; *prabho*—O Lord; *karavāma*—shall we do; *te*—Your; *kim*—what; *anuśādhi*—please direct; *kiṅkarān*—Your eternal servants.

TRANSLATION

All the Manus offered their prayers as follows: As Your order carriers, O Lord, we, the Manus, are the law-givers for human society, but because of the temporary supremacy of this great demon, Hiraṇyakaśipu, our laws for maintaining varṇāśrama-dharma were destroyed. O Lord, now that You have killed this great demon, we are in our normal condition. Kindly order us, Your eternal servants, what to do now.

PURPORT

In many places in *Bhagavad-gītā*, the Supreme Lord, Kṛṣṇa, refers to the *varṇāśrama-dharma* of four *varṇas* and four *āśramas.* He teaches people about this *varṇāśrama-dharma* so that all of human society can live peacefully by observing the principles for the four social divisions and four spiritual divisions (*varṇa* and *āśrama*) and thus make advancement in spiritual knowledge. The Manus compiled the *Manu-saṁhitā.* The word *saṁhitā* means Vedic knowledge, and *manu* indicates that this knowledge is given by Manu. The Manus are sometimes incarnations of the Supreme Lord and sometimes empowered living entities. Formerly, many long years ago, Lord Kṛṣṇa instructed the sun-god. The Manus are generally sons of the sun-god. Therefore, while speaking to Arjuna about the importance of *Bhagavad-gītā*, Kṛṣṇa said, *imaṁ vivas-*

vate yogaṁ proktavān aham avyayam vivasvān manave prāha: "This instruction was given to Vivasvān, the sun-god, who in turn instructed his son Manu." Manu gave the law known as *Manu-saṁhitā*, which is full of directions based on *varṇa* and *āśrama* concerning how to live as a human being. These are very scientific ways of life, but under the rule of demons like Hiraṇyakaśipu, human society breaks all these systems of law and order and gradually becomes lower and lower. Thus there is no peace in the world. The conclusion is that if we want real peace and order in the human society, we must follow the principles laid down by the *Manu-saṁhitā* and confirmed by the Supreme Personality of Godhead, Kṛṣṇa.

TEXT 49

श्रीप्रजापतय ऊचुः
प्रजेशा वयं ते परेशाभिसृष्टा
न येन प्रजा वै सृजामो निषिद्धाः ।
स एष त्वया भिन्नवक्षा नु शेते
जगन्मङ्गलं सत्त्वमूर्तेऽवतारः ॥४९॥

śrī-prajāpataya ūcuḥ
prajeśā vayaṁ te pareśābhisṛṣṭā
na yena prajā vai sṛjāmo niṣiddhāḥ
sa eṣa tvayā bhinna-vakṣā nu śete
jagan-maṅgalaṁ sattva-mūrte 'vatāraḥ

śrī-prajāpatayaḥ ūcuḥ—the great personalities who created the various living beings offered their prayers by saying; *prajā-īśāḥ*—the *prajāpatis* created by Lord Brahmā, who have created generations of living entities; *vayam*—we; *te*—of You; *para-īśa*—O Supreme Lord; *abhisṛṣṭāḥ*—born; *na*—not; *yena*—by whom (Hiraṇyakaśipu); *prajāḥ*—living entities; *vai*—indeed; *sṛjāmaḥ*—we create; *niṣiddhāḥ*—being forbidden; *saḥ*—he (Hiraṇyakaśipu); *eṣaḥ*—this; *tvayā*—by You; *bhinna-vakṣāḥ*—whose chest has been split; *nu*—indeed; *śete*—lies down; *jagat-maṅgalam*—for the auspiciousness of the whole world; *sattva-mūrte*—in this transcendental form of pure goodness; *avatāraḥ*—this incarnation.

TRANSLATION

The prajāpatis offered their prayers as follows: O Supreme Lord, Lord of even Brahmā and Śiva, we, the prajāpatis, were created by You to execute Your orders, but we were forbidden by Hiraṇyakaśipu to create any more good progeny. Now the demon is lying dead before us, his chest pierced by You. Let us therefore offer our respectful obeisances unto You, whose incarnation in this form of pure goodness is meant for the welfare of the entire universe.

TEXT 50

श्रीगन्धर्वा ऊचुः
वयं विभो ते नटनाट्यगायका
येनात्मसाद् वीर्यबलौजसा कृताः ।
स एष नीतो भवता दशामिमां
किमुत्पथस्थः कुशलाय कल्पते ॥५०॥

śrī-gandharvā ūcuḥ
vayaṁ vibho te naṭa-nāṭya-gāyakā
yenātmasād vīrya-balaujasā kṛtāḥ
sa eṣa nīto bhavatā daśām imāṁ
kim utpathasthaḥ kuśalāya kalpate

śrī-gandharvāḥ ūcuḥ—the inhabitants of Gandharvaloka (who are usually engaged as musicians of the heavenly planets) said; *vayam*—we; *vibho*—O Lord; *te*—Your; *naṭa-nāṭya-gāyakāḥ*—dancers and singers in dramatic performances; *yena*—by whom; *ātmasāt*—under subjection; *vīrya*—of his valor; *bala*—and bodily strength; *ojasā*—by the influence; *kṛtāḥ*—made (brought); *saḥ*—he (Hiraṇyakaśipu); *eṣaḥ*—this; *nītaḥ*—brought; *bhavatā*—by Your Lordship; *daśām imām*—to this condition; *kim*—whether; *utpathasthaḥ*—anyone who is an upstart; *kuśalāya*—for auspiciousness; *kalpate*—is capable.

TRANSLATION

The inhabitants of Gandharvaloka prayed: Your Lordship, we ever engage in Your service by dancing and singing in dramatic

performances, but this Hiraṇyakaśipu, by the influence of his bodily strength and valor, brought us under his subjugation. Now he has been brought to this low condition by Your Lordship. What benefit can result from the activities of such an upstart as Hiraṇyakaśipu?

PURPORT

By being a very obedient servant of the Supreme Lord, one becomes extremely powerful in bodily strength, influence and effulgence, whereas the fate of demoniac upstarts is ultimately to fall down like Hiraṇyakaśipu. Hiraṇyakaśipu and persons like him may be very powerful for some time, but the obedient servants of the Supreme Personality of Godhead like the demigods remain powerful always. They are victorious over the influence of Hiraṇyakaśipu by the grace of the Supreme Lord.

TEXT 51

श्रीचारणा ऊचुः
हरे तवाङ्घ्रिपङ्कजं भवापवर्गमाश्रिताः ।
यदेष साधुहृच्छयस्त्वयासुरः समापितः ॥५१॥

śrī-cāraṇā ūcuḥ
hare tavāṅghri-paṅkajaṁ
bhavāpavargam āśritāḥ
yad eṣa sādhu-hṛc-chayas
tvayāsuraḥ samāpitaḥ

śrī-cāraṇāḥ ūcuḥ—the inhabitants of the Cāraṇa planet said; *hare*—O Lord; *tava*—Your; *aṅghri-paṅkajam*—lotus feet; *bhava-apavargam*—the only shelter for becoming free from the contamination of material existence; *āśritāḥ*—sheltered at; *yat*—because; *eṣaḥ*—this; *sādhu-hṛt-śayaḥ*—stake in the hearts of all honest persons; *tvayā*—by Your Lordship; *asuraḥ*—the demon (Hiraṇyakaśipu); *samāpitaḥ*—finished.

TRANSLATION

The inhabitants of the Cāraṇa planet said: O Lord, because You have destroyed the demon Hiraṇyakaśipu, who was always a stake

in the hearts of all honest men, we are now relieved, and we eternally take shelter of Your lotus feet, which award the conditioned soul liberation from materialistic contamination.

PURPORT

The Supreme Personality of Godhead in His transcendental form of Narahari, Nṛsiṁhadeva, is always ready to kill the demons, who always create disturbances in the minds of honest devotees. To spread the Kṛṣṇa consciousness movement, devotees have to face many dangers and impediments all over the world, but a faithful servant who preaches with great devotion to the Lord must know that Lord Nṛsiṁhadeva is always his protector.

TEXT 52

श्रीयक्षा ऊचुः
वयमनुचरमुख्याः कर्मभिस्ते मनोज्ञै-
स्त इह दितिसुतेन प्रापिता वाहकत्वम् ।
स तु जनपरितापं तत्कृतं जानता ते
नरहर उपनीतः पञ्चतां पञ्चविंश ॥५२॥

śrī-yakṣā ūcuḥ
vayam anucara-mukhyāḥ karmabhis te mano-jñais
ta iha diti-sutena prāpitā vāhakatvam
sa tu jana-paritāpaṁ tat-kṛtaṁ jānatā te
narahara upanītaḥ pañcatāṁ pañca-viṁśa

śrī-yakṣāḥ ūcuḥ—the inhabitants of the Yakṣa planet prayed; *vayam*—we; *anucara-mukhyāḥ*—the chief among Your many servants; *karmabhiḥ*—by services; *te*—unto You; *mano-jñaiḥ*—very pleasing; *te*—they; *iha*—at the present moment; *diti-sutena*—by Hiraṇyakaśipu, the son of Diti; *prāpitāḥ*—forced to engage as; *vāhakatvam*—the palanquin carriers; *saḥ*—he; *tu*—but; *jana-paritāpam*—the miserable condition of everyone; *tat-kṛtam*—caused by him; *jānatā*—knowing; *te*—by You; *nara-hara*—O Lord in the form of Nṛsiṁha; *upanītaḥ*—is put to;

pañcatām—death; *pañca-viṁśa*—O twenty-fifth principle (the controller of the other twenty-four elements).

TRANSLATION

The inhabitants of Yakṣaloka prayed: O controller of the twenty-four elements, we are considered the best servants of Your Lordship because of rendering services pleasing to You, yet we engaged as palanquin carriers by the order of Hiraṇyakaśipu, the son of Diti. O Lord in the form of Nṛsiṁhadeva, You know how this demon gave trouble to everyone, but now You have killed him, and his body is mixing with the five material elements.

PURPORT

The Supreme Lord is the controller of the ten senses, the five material elements, the five sense objects, the mind, the intelligence, the false ego and the soul. Therefore He is addressed as *pañca-viṁśa*, the twenty-fifth element. The inhabitants of the Yakṣa planet are supposed to be the best of all servants, but Hiraṇyakaśipu engaged them as palanquin carriers. The entire universe was in trouble because of Hiraṇyakaśipu, but now that Hiraṇyakaśipu's body was mixing with the five material elements—earth, water, fire, air and sky—everyone felt relief. Upon Hiraṇyakaśipu's death, the Yakṣas were reinstated in their original service to the Supreme Personality of Godhead. Thus they felt obliged to the Lord and offered their prayers.

TEXT 53

श्रीकिम्पुरुषा ऊचुः

वयं किम्पुरुषास्त्वं तु महापुरुष ईश्वरः ।
अयं कुपुरुषो नष्टो धिक्कृतः साधुभिर्यदा ॥५३॥

śrī-kimpuruṣā ūcuḥ
vayaṁ kimpuruṣās tvaṁ tu
mahā-puruṣa īśvaraḥ
ayaṁ kupuruṣo naṣṭo
dhik-kṛtaḥ sādhubhir yadā

śrī-kimpuruṣāḥ ūcuḥ—the inhabitants of Kimpuruṣa-loka said; *vayam*—we; *kimpuruṣāḥ*—the inhabitants of Kimpuruṣa-loka, or insignificant living entities; *tvam*—Your Lordship; *tu*—however; *mahā-puruṣaḥ*—the Supreme Personality of Godhead; *īśvaraḥ*—the supreme controller; *ayam*—this; *ku-puruṣaḥ*—most sinful person, Hiraṇyakaśipu; *naṣṭaḥ*—slain; *dhik-kṛtaḥ*—being condemned; *sādhubhiḥ*—by the saintly persons; *yadā*—when.

TRANSLATION

The inhabitants of Kimpuruṣa-loka said: We are insignificant living entities, and You are the Supreme Personality of Godhead, the supreme controller. Therefore how can we offer suitable prayers unto You? When this demon was condemned by devotees because they were disgusted with him, he was then killed by You.

PURPORT

The cause of the Supreme Lord's appearance upon this earth is stated in *Bhagavad-gītā* (4.7–8) by the Lord Himself:

yadā yadā hi dharmasya
glānir bhavati bhārata
abhyutthānam adharmasya
tadātmānaṁ sṛjāmy aham

paritrāṇāya sādhūnāṁ
vināśāya ca duṣkṛtām
dharma-saṁsthāpanārthāya
sambhavāmi yuge yuge

"Whenever and wherever there is a decrease in religious principles and a predominant rise in irreligion, at that time I descend Myself. To deliver the pious and annihilate the miscreants, as well as to reestablish the principles of religion, I advent Myself, millennium after millennium." The Lord appears in order to execute two kinds of activities—to kill the demons and to protect the devotees. When the devotees are too disturbed by the demons, the Lord certainly appears in different incarnations to give the devotees protection. The devotees following in the footsteps of

Prahlāda Mahārāja should not be disturbed by the demoniac activities of the nondevotees. Rather, they should stick to their principles as sincere servants of the Lord and rest assured that the demoniac activities directed against them will not be able to stop their devotional service.

TEXT 54

श्रीवैतालिका ऊचुः
सभासु सत्रेषु तवामलं यशो
गीत्वा सपर्यां महतीं लभामहे ।
यस्तामनैषीद् वशमेष दुर्जनो
द्विष्ट्या हतस्ते भगवन्यथामयः ॥५४॥

śrī-vaitālikā ūcuḥ
sabhāsu satreṣu tavāmalaṁ yaśo
gītvā saparyāṁ mahatīṁ labhāmahe
yas tām anaiṣīd vaśam eṣa durjano
dviṣṭyā hatas te bhagavan yathāmayaḥ

śrī-vaitālikāḥ ūcuḥ—the inhabitants of Vaitālika-loka said; *sabhāsu*—in great assemblies; *satreṣu*—in the arenas of sacrifice; *tava*—Your; *amalam*—without any spot of material contamination; *yaśaḥ*—reputation; *gītvā*—singing; *saparyām*—respectful position; *mahatīm*—great; *labhāmahe*—we achieved; *yaḥ*—he who; *tām*—that (respectful position); *anaiṣīt*—brought under; *vaśam*—his control; *eṣaḥ*—this; *durjanaḥ*—crooked person; *dviṣṭyā*—by great fortune; *hataḥ*—killed; *te*—by You; *bhagavan*—O Lord; *yathā*—exactly like; *āmayaḥ*—a disease.

TRANSLATION

The inhabitants of Vaitālika-loka said: Dear Lord, because of chanting Your spotless glories in great assemblies and arenas of sacrifice, we were accustomed to great respect from everyone. This demon, however, usurped that position. Now, to our great fortune, You have killed this great demon, exactly as one cures a chronic disease.

TEXT 55

श्रीकिन्नरा ऊचुः
वयमीश किन्नरगणास्तवानुगा
दितिजेन विष्टिममुनानुकारिताः ।
भवता हरे स वृजिनोऽवसादितो
नरसिंह नाथ विभवाय नो भव ॥५५॥

śrī-kinnarā ūcuḥ
vayam īśa kinnara-gaṇās tavānugā
ditijena viṣṭim amunānukāritāḥ
bhavatā hare sa vṛjino 'vasādito
narasiṁha nātha vibhavāya no bhava

śrī-kinnarāḥ ūcuḥ—the inhabitants of the Kinnara planet said; *vayam*—we; *īśa*—O Lord; *kinnara-gaṇāḥ*—the inhabitants of the Kinnara planet; *tava*—Your; *anugāḥ*—faithful servants; *diti-jena*—by the son of Diti; *viṣṭim*—service without remuneration; *amunā*—by that; *anukāritāḥ*—caused to perform; *bhavatā*—by You; *hare*—O Lord; *saḥ*—he; *vṛjinaḥ*—most sinful; *avasāditaḥ*—destroyed; *narasiṁha*—O Lord Nṛsiṁhadeva; *nātha*—O master; *vibhavāya*—for the happiness and opulence; *naḥ*—of us; *bhava*—You please be.

TRANSLATION

The Kinnaras said: O supreme controller, we are ever-existing servants of Your Lordship, but instead of rendering service to You, we were engaged by this demon in his service, constantly and without remuneration. This sinful man has now been killed by You. Therefore, O Lord Nṛsiṁhadeva, our master, we offer our respectful obeisances unto You. Please continue to be our patron.

TEXT 56

श्रीविष्णुपार्षदा ऊचुः
अद्यैतद्धरिनररूपमद्भुतं ते
दृष्टं नः शरणद सर्वलोकशर्म ।

सोऽयं ते विधिकर ईश विप्रशप्त-
स्तस्येदं निधनमनुग्रहाय विद्मः ॥५६॥

śrī-viṣṇu-pārṣadā ūcuḥ
adyaitad dhari-nara-rūpam adbhutaṁ te
dṛṣṭaṁ naḥ śaraṇada sarva-loka-śarma
so 'yaṁ te vidhikara īśa vipra-śaptas
tasyedaṁ nidhanam anugrahāya vidmaḥ

śrī-viṣṇu-pārṣadāḥ ūcuḥ—the associates of Lord Viṣṇu in Vaikuṇṭhaloka said; *adya*—today; *etat*—this; *hari-nara*—of half lion and half human being; *rūpam*—form; *adbhutam*—very wonderful; *te*—Your; *dṛṣṭam*—seen; *naḥ*—of us; *śaraṇa-da*—the everlasting bestower of shelter; *sarva-loka-śarma*—which brings good fortune to all the various planets; *saḥ*—he; *ayam*—this; *te*—of Your Lordship; *vidhikaraḥ*—order carrier (servant); *īśa*—O Lord; *vipra-śaptaḥ*—being cursed by the *brāhmaṇas; tasya*—of him; *idam*—this; *nidhanam*—killing; *anugrahāya*—for the special favor; *vidmaḥ*—we understand.

TRANSLATION

The associates of Lord Viṣṇu in Vaikuṇṭha offered this prayer: O Lord, our supreme giver of shelter, today we have seen Your wonderful form as Lord Nṛsiṁhadeva, meant for the good fortune of all the world. O Lord, we can understand that Hiraṇyakaśipu was the same Jaya who engaged in Your service but was cursed by brāhmaṇas and who thus received the body of a demon. We understand that his having now been killed is Your special mercy upon him.

PURPORT

Hiraṇyakaśipu's coming to this earth and acting as the Lord's enemy was prearranged. Jaya and Vijaya were cursed by the *brāhmaṇas* Sanaka, Sanat-kumāra, Sanandana and Sanātana because Jaya and Vijaya checked these four Kumāras. The Lord accepted this cursing of His servants and agreed that they would have to go to the material world and would then return to Vaikuṇṭha after serving the term of the curse. Jaya and Vijaya were very much perturbed, but the Lord advised them to act as enemies, for then they would return after three births; otherwise, ordinarily, they would have to take seven births. With this authority, Jaya and Vijaya acted as the Lord's enemies, and now that these two were dead, all the Viṣṇudūtas understood that the Lord's killing of Hiraṇyakaśipu was special mercy bestowed upon them.

Thus end the Bhaktivedanta purports of the Seventh Canto, Eighth Chapter, of the Śrīmad-Bhāgavatam, *entitled "Lord Nṛsiṁhadeva Slays the King of the Demons."*

CHAPTER NINE

Prahlāda Pacifies Lord Nṛsiṁhadeva with Prayers

As related in this chapter, Prahlāda Mahārāja, following the order of Lord Brahmā, pacified the Lord when the Lord was extremely angry after having killed Hiraṇyakaśipu.

After Hiraṇyakaśipu was killed, the Lord continued to be very angry, and the demigods, headed by Lord Brahmā, could not pacify Him. Even mother Lakṣmī, the goddess of fortune, the constant companion of Nārāyaṇa, could not dare come before Lord Nṛsiṁhadeva. Then Lord Brahmā asked Prahlāda Mahārāja to go forward and pacify the Lord's anger. Prahlāda Mahārāja, being confident of the affection of his master, Lord Nṛsiṁhadeva, was not afraid at all. He very gravely appeared before the Lord's lotus feet and offered Him respectful obeisances. Lord Nṛsiṁhadeva, being very much affectionate toward Prahlāda Mahārāja, put His hand on Prahlāda's head, and because of being personally touched by the Lord, Prahlāda Mahārāja immediately achieved *brahma-jñāna*, spiritual knowledge. Thus he offered his prayers to the Lord in full spiritual knowledge and full devotional ecstasy. The instructions given by Prahlāda Mahārāja in the form of his prayers are as follows.

Prahlāda said, "I am not proud of being able to offer prayers to the Supreme Personality of Godhead. I simply take shelter of the mercy of the Lord, for without devotion one cannot appease Him. One cannot please the Supreme Personality of Godhead simply by dint of high parentage or great opulence, learning, austerity, penance or mystic power. Indeed, these are never pleasing to the Supreme Lord, for nothing can please Him but pure devotional service. Even if a nondevotee is a *brāhmaṇa* qualified with the twelve brahminical symptoms, he cannot be very dear to the Lord, whereas if a person born in a family of dog-eaters is a devotee, the Lord can accept his prayers. The Lord does not need anyone's prayers, but if a devotee offers his prayers to the Lord, the devotee benefits greatly. Ignorant persons born in low families, therefore, can sincerely offer heartfelt prayers to the Lord, and the Lord will accept them. As soon as one offers his prayers to the Lord, he is immediately situated on the Brahman platform.

Lord Nṛsiṁhadeva appeared for the benefit of all human society, not only for Prahlāda's personal benefit. The fierce form of Lord Nṛsiṁhadeva may appear most awful to a nondevotee, but to the devotee the Lord is always affectionate as He is in other forms. Conditioned life in the material world is actually extremely fearful; indeed, a devotee is not afraid of anything else. Fear of material existence is due to false ego. Therefore the ultimate goal of life for every living entity is to attain the position of being servant of the servant of the Lord. The miserable condition of the living entities in the material world can be remedied only by the mercy of the Lord. Although there are so-called material protectors like Lord Brahmā and the other demigods, or even one's own father, they are unable to do anything if one is neglected by the Supreme Personality of Godhead. However, one who has fully taken shelter of the Lord's lotus feet can be saved from the onslaught of material nature. Therefore every living entity should be unattracted by material so-called happiness and should take shelter of the Lord by all means. That is the mission of human life. To be attracted by sense gratification is simply foolish. Whether one is a devotee of the Lord or is a nondevotee does not depend upon one's birth in a high or low family. Even Lord Brahmā and the goddess of fortune cannot achieve the full favor of the Lord, whereas a devotee can very easily attain such devotional service. The Lord's mercy is bestowed equally upon everyone, regardless of whether one is high or low. Because Prahlāda Mahārāja was blessed by Nārada Muni, Prahlāda became a great devotee. The Lord always saves the devotee from impersonalists and voidists. The Lord is present in everyone's heart as the Supersoul to give the living being protection and all benefits. Thus the Lord acts sometimes as the killer and sometimes as the protector. One should not accuse the Lord for any discrepancies. It is His plan that we see varieties of life within this material world. All of them are ultimately His mercy.

Although the entire cosmic manifestation is nondifferent, the material world is nonetheless different from the spiritual world. Only by the mercy of the Supreme Lord can one understand how the wonderful material nature acts. For example, although Lord Brahmā appeared from the lotus seat that had grown from the abdomen of Garbhodakaśāyī Viṣṇu, he could not understand what to do after his appearance. He was attacked by two demons, Madhu and Kaiṭabha, who took away Vedic knowledge, but the Lord killed them and entrusted to Lord Brahmā the Vedic knowledge. Thus the Lord appears in every millennium in the societies of demigods, human beings, animals, saints and aquatics. All such incarnations are meant to protect the devotees and kill the demons, but this killing and protecting does not reflect any sense of partiality on the part of the Supreme Lord. The conditioned soul is always attracted by the external energy. Therefore he is subjected to lust and greed, and he suffers under the conditions of material nature. The Lord's causeless mercy toward His devotee is the only means by which to get out of material existence. Anyone engaged in glorifying the Lord's activities is always unafraid of this material world, whereas one who cannot glorify the Lord in that way is subjected to all lamentation.

Those interested in silently worshiping the Lord in solitary places may be eligible for liberation themselves, but a pure devotee is always aggrieved to see others suffering. Therefore, not caring for his own liberation, he always engages in preaching by glorifying the Lord. Prahlāda Mahārāja, therefore, had tried to deliver his class friends by preaching and had never remained silent. Although being silent, observing austerities and penances, learning the Vedic literature, undergoing ritualistic ceremonies, living in a solitary place and performing *japa* and transcendental meditation are approved means of liberation, they are meant for nondevotees or for cheaters who want to live at the expense of others. A pure devotee, however, being freed from all such deceptive activities, is able to see the Lord face to face.

The atomic theory of the composition of the cosmic manifestation is not factual. The Lord is the cause of everything, and therefore He is the cause of this creation. One should therefore always engage in devotional service by offering respectful obeisances to the Lord, offering prayers, working for the Lord, worshiping the Lord in the temple, always remembering the Lord and always hearing about His transcendental activities. Without these six kinds of activity, one cannot attain to devotional service.

Prahlāda Mahārāja thus offered his prayers to the Supreme Lord, begging His mercy at every step. Lord Nṛsiṁhadeva was pacified by

Prahlāda Mahārāja's prayers and wanted to give him benedictions by which Prahlāda could procure all kinds of material facilities. Prahlāda Mahārāja, however, was not misled by material facilities. Rather, he wanted to remain always a servant of the servant of the Lord.

TEXT 1

श्रीनारद उवाच
एवं सुरादयः सर्वे ब्रह्मरुद्रपुरःसराः ।
नोपैतुमशकन्मन्युसंरम्भं सुदुरासदम् ॥ १ ॥

śrī-nārada uvāca
evaṁ surādayaḥ sarve
brahma-rudra-puraḥ sarāḥ
nopaitum aśakan manyu-
saṁrambhaṁ sudurāsadam

śrī-nāradaḥ uvāca—the great saintly sage Nārada Muni said; *evam*—thus; *sura-ādayaḥ*—the groups of demigods; *sarve*—all; *brahma-rudra-puraḥ sarāḥ*—represented by Lord Brahmā and Lord Śiva; *na*—not; *upaitum*—to go before the Lord; *aśakan*—able; *manyu-saṁrambham*—in a completely angry mood; *su-durāsadam*—very difficult to approach (Lord Nṛsiṁhadeva).

TRANSLATION

The great saint Nārada Muni continued: The demigods, headed by Lord Brahmā, Lord Śiva and other great demigods, dared not come forward before the Lord, who at that time was extremely angry.

PURPORT

Śrīla Narottama dāsa Ṭhākura has sung in his *Prema-bhakti-candrikā*, *'krodha' bhakta-dveṣi-jane:* anger should be used to punish a demon who is envious of devotees. *Kāma*, *krodha*, *lobha*, *moha*, *mada* and *mātsarya*—lust, anger, greed, illusion, pride and envy—all have their proper use for the Supreme Personality of Godhead and His devotee. A devotee of the Lord cannot tolerate blasphemy of the Lord or His other devotees, and the Lord also cannot tolerate blasphemy of a devotee. Thus Lord Nṛsiṁhadeva was so very angry that the great demigods like Lord Brahmā and Lord Śiva and even the goddess of fortune, who is the Lord's constant companion, could not pacify Him, even after offering prayers of glorification and praise. No one was able to pacify the Lord in His anger, but because the Lord was willing to exhibit His affection for Prahlāda Mahārāja, all the demigods and the others present before the Lord pushed Prahlāda Mahārāja forward to pacify Him.

TEXT 2

साक्षात् श्रीः प्रेषिता देवैर्दृष्ट्वा तं महदद्भुतम् ।
अदृष्टाश्रुतपूर्वत्वात् सा नोपेयाय शङ्किता ॥ २ ॥

sākṣāt śrīḥ preṣitā devair
dṛṣṭvā taṁ mahad adbhutam
adṛṣṭāśruta-pūrvatvāt
sā nopeyāya śaṅkitā

sākṣāt—directly; *śrīḥ*—the goddess of fortune; *preṣitā*—being requested to go forward before the Lord; *devaiḥ*—by all the demigods (headed by Lord Brahmā and Lord Śiva); *dṛṣṭvā*—after seeing; *tam*—Him (Lord Nṛsiṁhadeva); *mahat*—very big; *adbhutam*—wonderful; *adṛṣṭa*—never seen; *aśruta*—never heard of; *pūrvatvāt*—due to being previously; *sā*—the goddess of fortune, Lakṣmī; *na*—not; *upeyāya*—went before the Lord; *śaṅkitā*—being very much afraid.

TRANSLATION

The goddess of fortune, Lakṣmījī, was requested to go before the Lord by all the demigods present, who because of fear could not do so. But even she had never seen such a wonderful and extraordinary form of the Lord, and thus she could not approach Him.

PURPORT

The Lord has unlimited forms and bodily features (*advaitam acyutam anādim ananta-rūpam*). These are all situated in Vaikuṇṭha, yet

Lakṣmīdevī, the goddess of fortune, being inspired by *līlā-śakti*, could not appreciate this unprecedented form of the Lord. In this regard, Śrīla Madhvācārya recites the following verses from the *Brahmāṇḍa Purāṇa:*

adṛṣṭāśruta-pūrvatvād
anyaiḥ sādhāraṇair janaiḥ
nṛsiṁhaṁ śaṅkiteva śrīr
loka-mohāyano yayau

prahrāde caiva vātsalya-
darśanāya harer api
jñātvā manas tathā brahmā
prahrādaṁ preṣayat tadā

ekatraikasya vātsalyaṁ
viśeṣād darśayed dhariḥ
avarasyāpi mohāya
krameṇaivāpi vatsalaḥ

In other words, for the common men the form of the Lord as Nṛsiṁhadeva is certainly unseen and wonderful, but for a devotee like Prahlāda Mahārāja such a fearsome form of the Lord is not at all extraordinary. By the grace of the Lord, a devotee can very easily understand how the Lord can appear in any form He likes. Therefore the devotee is never afraid of such a form. Because of special favor bestowed upon Prahlāda Mahārāja, he remained silent and unafraid, even though all the demigods, including even Lakṣmīdevī, were afraid of Lord Nṛsiṁhadeva. *Nārāyaṇa-parāḥ sarve na kutaścana bibhyati* (*Bhāg.* 6.17.28). Not only is a pure devotee of Nārāyaṇa like Prahlāda Mahārāja unafraid of any dangerous condition of material life, but also if the Lord appears to mitigate the fear of a devotee, the devotee maintains his status of fearlessness in all circumstances.

TEXT 3

प्रह्लादं प्रेषयामास ब्रह्मावस्थितमन्तिके ।
तात प्रशमयोपेहि स्वपित्रे कुपितं प्रभुम् ॥ ३ ॥

prahrādaṁ preṣayām āsa
brahmāvasthitam antike
tāta praśamayopehi
sva-pitre kupitaṁ prabhum

prahrādam—Prahlāda Mahārāja; *preṣayām āsa*—requested; *brahmā*—Lord Brahmā; *avasthitam*—being situated; *antike*—very near; *tāta*—my dear son; *praśamaya*—just try to appease; *upehi*—go near; *sva-pitre*—because of your father's demoniac activities; *kupitam*—greatly angered; *prabhum*—the Lord.

TRANSLATION

Thereafter Lord Brahmā requested Prahlāda Mahārāja, who was standing very near him: My dear son, Lord Nṛsiṁhadeva is extremely angry at your demoniac father. Please go forward and appease the Lord.

TEXT 4

तथेति शनकै राजन्महाभागवतोऽर्भकः ।
उपेत्य भुवि कायेन ननाम विधृताञ्जलिः ॥ ४ ॥

tatheti śanakai rājan
mahā-bhāgavato 'rbhakaḥ
upetya bhuvi kāyena
nanāma vidhṛtāñjaliḥ

tathā—so be it; *iti*—thus accepting the words of Lord Brahmā; *śanakaiḥ*—very slowly; *rājan*—O King (Yudhiṣṭhira); *mahā-bhāgavataḥ*—the great, exalted devotee (Prahlāda Mahārāja); *arbhakaḥ*—although only a small boy; *upetya*—gradually going near; *bhuvi*—on the ground; *kāyena*—by his body; *nanāma*—offered respectful obeisances; *vidhṛta-añjaliḥ*—folding his hands.

TRANSLATION

Nārada Muni continued: O King, although the exalted devotee Prahlāda Mahārāja was only a little boy, he accepted Lord Brahmā's

words. He gradually proceeded toward Lord Nṛsiṁhadeva and fell down to offer his respectful obeisances with folded hands.

TEXT 5

स्वपादमूले पतितं तमर्भकं
विलोक्य देवः कृपया परिप्लुतः ।
उत्थाप्य तच्छीर्ष्ण्यदधात् कराम्बुजं
कालाहिवित्रस्तधियां कृताभयम् ॥ ५ ॥

sva-pāda-mūle patitaṁ tam arbhakaṁ
vilokya devaḥ kṛpayā pariplutaḥ
utthāpya tac-chīrṣṇy adadhāt karāmbujaṁ
kālāhi-vitrasta-dhiyāṁ kṛtābhayam

sva-pāda-mūle—at His lotus feet; *patitam*—fallen; *tam*—him (Prahlāda Mahārāja); *arbhakam*—only a little boy; *vilokya*—seeing; *devaḥ*—Lord Nṛsiṁhadeva; *kṛpayā*—out of His causeless mercy; *pariplutaḥ*—very much afflicted (in ecstasy); *utthāpya*—raising; *tat-śīrṣṇi*—on his head; *adadhāt*—placed; *kara-ambujam*—His lotus hand; *kāla-ahi*—of the deadly snake of time, (which can cause immediate death); *vitrasta*—afraid; *dhiyām*—to all of those whose minds; *kṛta-abhayam*—which causes fearlessness.

TRANSLATION

When Lord Nṛsiṁhadeva saw the small boy Prahlāda Mahārāja prostrated at the soles of His lotus feet, He became most ecstatic in affection toward His devotee. Raising Prahlāda, the Lord placed His lotus hand upon the boy's head because His hand is always ready to create fearlessness in all of His devotees.

PURPORT

The necessities of the material world are four—*āhāra, nidrā, bhaya* and *maithuna* (eating, sleeping, defending and mating). In this material world, everyone is in fearful consciousness (*sadā samudvigna-dhiyām*), and the only means to make everyone fearless is Kṛṣṇa consciousness.

When Lord Nṛsiṁhadeva appeared, all the devotees became fearless. The devotee's hope of becoming fearless is to chant the holy name of Lord Nṛsiṁhadeva. *Yato yato yāmi tato nṛsiṁhaḥ:* wherever we go, we must always think of Lord Nṛsiṁhadeva. Thus there will be no fear for the devotee of the Lord.

TEXT 6

स तत्करस्पर्शधुताखिलाशुभः
सपद्यभिव्यक्तपरात्मदर्शनः ।
तत्पादपद्मं हृदि निर्वृतो दधौ
हृष्यत्तनुः क्लिन्नहृदश्रुलोचनः ॥ ६ ॥

sa tat-kara-sparśa-dhutākhilāśubhaḥ
sapady abhivyakta-parātma-darśanaḥ
tat-pāda-padmaṁ hṛdi nirvṛto dadhau
hṛṣyat-tanuḥ klinna-hṛd-aśru-locanaḥ

saḥ—he (Prahlāda Mahārāja); *tat-kara-sparśa*—because of being touched on the head by the lotus hand of Nṛsiṁhadeva; *dhuta*—being cleansed; *akhila*—all; *aśubhaḥ*—inauspiciousness or material desires; *sapadi*—immediately; *abhivyakta*—manifested; *para-ātma-darśanaḥ*—realization of the Supreme Soul (spiritual knowledge); *tat-pāda-padmam*—Lord Nṛsiṁhadeva's lotus feet; *hṛdi*—within the core of the heart; *nirvṛtaḥ*—full of transcendental bliss; *dadhau*—captured; *hṛṣyat-tanuḥ*—having transcendental ecstatic bliss manifested in the body; *klinna-hṛt*—whose heart was softened due to transcendental ecstasy; *aśru-locanaḥ*—with tears in his eyes.

TRANSLATION

By the touch of Lord Nṛsiṁhadeva's hand on Prahlāda Mahārāja's head, Prahlāda was completely freed of all material contaminations and desires, as if he had been thoroughly cleansed. Therefore he at once became transcendentally situated, and all the symptoms of ecstasy became manifest in his body. His heart filled with love, and his eyes with tears, and thus he was able to

completely capture the lotus feet of the Lord within the core of his heart.

PURPORT

As stated in *Bhagavad-gītā* (14.26):

māṁ ca yo 'vyabhicāreṇa
bhakti-yogena sevate
sa guṇān samatītyaitān
brahma-bhūyāya kalpate

"One who engages in full devotional service, who does not fall down in any circumstance, at once transcends the modes of material nature and thus comes to the level of Brahman." Elsewhere in *Bhagavad-gītā* (9.32) the Lord says:

māṁ hi pārtha vyapāśritya
ye 'pi syuḥ pāpa-yonayaḥ
striyo vaiśyās tathā śūdrās
te 'pi yānti parāṁ gatim

"O son of Pṛthā, those who take shelter in Me, though they be of lower birth—women, *vaiśyas* [merchants], as well as *śūdras* [workers]—can approach the supreme destination."

On the strength of these verses from *Bhagavad-gītā*, it is evident that although Prahlāda Mahārāja was born in a demoniac family and although virtually demoniac blood flowed within his body, he was cleansed of all material bodily contamination because of his exalted position as a devotee. In other words, such impediments on the spiritual path could not stop him from progressing, for he was directly in touch with the Supreme Personality of Godhead. Those who are physically and mentally contaminated by atheism cannot be situated on the transcendental platform, but as soon as one is freed from material contamination he is immediately fit to be situated in devotional service.

TEXT 7

अस्तौषीद्धरिमेकाग्रमनसा सुसमाहितः ।
प्रेमगद्गदया वाचा तन्न्यस्तहृदयेक्षणः ॥ ७ ॥

astauṣīd dharim ekāgra-
manasā susamāhitaḥ
prema-gadgadayā vācā
tan-nyasta-hṛdayekṣaṇaḥ

astauṣīt—he began to offer prayers; *harim*—unto the Supreme Personality of Godhead; *ekāgra-manasā*—the mind being completely fixed upon the lotus feet of the Lord; *su-samāhitaḥ*—very attentive (without diversion to any other subject); *prema-gadgadayā*—faltering because of feeling transcendental bliss; *vācā*—with a voice; *tat-nyasta*—being fully dedicated to Him (Lord Nṛsiṁhadeva); *hṛdaya-īkṣaṇaḥ*—with heart and sight.

TRANSLATION

Prahlāda Mahārāja fixed his mind and sight upon Lord Nṛsiṁhadeva with full attention in complete trance. With a fixed mind, he began to offer prayers in love with a faltering voice.

PURPORT

The word *susamāhitaḥ* means "very attentive" or "fully fixed." The ability to fix the mind in this way is a result of *yoga-siddhi*, mystic perfection. As it is stated in *Śrīmad-Bhāgavatam* (12.13.1), *dhyānāvasthita-tad-gatena manasā paśyanti yaṁ yoginaḥ.* One attains yogic perfection when he is freed from all material diversions and his mind is fixed upon the lotus feet of the Lord. This is called *samādhi* or trance. Prahlāda Mahārāja attained that stage beyond the senses. Because he was engaged in service, he felt transcendentally situated, and naturally his mind and attention became saturated in transcendence. In that condition, he began to offer his prayers as follows.

TEXT 8

श्रीप्रह्लाद उवाच
ब्रह्मादयः सुरगणा मुनयोऽथ सिद्धाः
सत्त्वैकतानगतयो वचसां प्रवाहैः ।
नाराधितुं पुरुगुणैरधुनापि पिप्रुः
किं तोष्टुमर्हति स मे हरिरुग्रजातेः ॥ ८ ॥

śrī-prahrāda uvāca
brahmādayaḥ sura-gaṇā munayo 'tha siddhāḥ
sattvaikatāna-gatayo vacasāṁ pravāhaiḥ
nārādhituṁ puru-guṇair adhunāpi pipruḥ
kiṁ toṣṭum arhati sa me harir ugra-jāteḥ

śrī-prahrādaḥ uvāca—Prahlāda Mahārāja prayed; *brahma-ādayaḥ*—headed by Lord Brahmā; *sura-gaṇāḥ*—the inhabitants of the upper planetary systems; *munayaḥ*—the great saintly persons; *atha*—as well (like the four Kumāras and others); *siddhāḥ*—who have attained perfection or full knowledge; *sattva*—to spiritual existence; *ekatāna-gatayaḥ*—who have taken without diversion to any material activities; *vacasām*—of descriptions or words; *pravāhaiḥ*—by streams; *na*—not; *ārādhitum*—to satisfy; *puru-guṇaiḥ*—although fully qualified; *adhunā*—until now; *api*—even; *pipruḥ*—were able; *kim*—whether; *toṣṭum*—to become pleased; *arhati*—is able; *saḥ*—He (the Lord); *me*—my; *hariḥ*—the Supreme Personality of Godhead; *ugra-jāteḥ*—who am born in an asuric family.

TRANSLATION

Prahlāda Mahārāja prayed: How is it possible for me, who have been born in a family of asuras, to offer suitable prayers to satisfy the Supreme Personality of Godhead? Even until now, all the demigods, headed by Lord Brahmā, and all the saintly persons, could not satisfy the Lord by streams of excellent words, although such persons are very qualified, being in the mode of goodness. Then what is to be said of me? I am not at all qualified.

PURPORT

A Vaiṣṇava who is fully qualified to serve the Lord still thinks himself extremely low while offering prayers to the Lord. For example, Kṛṣṇadāsa Kavirāja Gosvāmī, the author of *Caitanya-caritāmṛta*, says:

jagāi mādhāi haite muñi se pāpiṣṭha
purīṣera kīṭa haite muñi se laghiṣṭha
(Cc. *Ādi* 5.205)

Thus he considers himself unqualified, lower than the worms in stool, and more sinful than Jagāi and Mādhāi. A pure Vaiṣṇava actually thinks of himself in this way. Similarly, although Prahlāda Mahārāja was a pure, exalted Vaiṣṇava, he thought himself most unqualified to offer prayers to the Supreme Lord. *Mahājano yena gataḥ sa panthāḥ.* Every pure Vaiṣṇava should think like this. One should not be falsely proud of his Vaiṣṇava qualifications. Śrī Caitanya Mahāprabhu has therefore instructed us:

tṛṇād api sunīcena
taror iva sahiṣṇunā
amāninā mānadena
kīrtanīyaḥ sadā hariḥ

"One should chant the holy name of the Lord in a humble state of mind, thinking oneself lower than the straw in the street; one should be more tolerant than a tree, devoid of all sense of false prestige and should be ready to offer all respect to others. In such a state of mind one can chant the holy name of the Lord constantly." Unless one is meek and humble, to make progress in spiritual life is very difficult.

TEXT 9

मन्ये धनाभिजनरूपतपःश्रुतौज-
स्तेजःप्रभावबलपौरुषबुद्धियोगाः ।
नाराधनाय हि भवन्ति परस्य पुंसो
भक्त्या तुतोष भगवान्गजयूथपाय ॥ ९ ॥

manye dhanābhijana-rūpa-tapaḥ-śrutaujas-
tejaḥ-prabhāva-bala-pauruṣa-buddhi-yogāḥ
nārādhanāya hi bhavanti parasya puṁso
bhaktyā tutoṣa bhagavān gaja-yūtha-pāya

manye—I consider; *dhana*—riches; *abhijana*—aristocratic family; *rūpa*—personal beauty; *tapaḥ*—austerity; *śruta*—knowledge from studying the *Vedas; ojaḥ*—sensory prowess; *tejaḥ*—bodily effulgence;

prabhāva—influence; *bala*—bodily strength; *pauruṣa*—diligence; *buddhi*—intelligence; *yogāḥ*—mystic power; *na*—not; *ārādhanāya*—for satisfying; *hi*—indeed; *bhavanti*—are; *parasya*—of the transcendent; *puṁsaḥ*—Supreme Personality of Godhead; *bhaktyā*—simply by devotional service; *tutoṣa*—was satisfied; *bhagavān*—the Supreme Personality of Godhead; *gaja-yūtha-pāya*—unto the King of elephants (Gajendra).

TRANSLATION

Prahlāda Mahārāja continued: One may possess wealth, an aristocratic family, beauty, austerity, education, sensory expertise, luster, influence, physical strength, diligence, intelligence and mystic yogic power, but I think that even by all these qualifications one cannot satisfy the Supreme Personality of Godhead. However, one can satisfy the Lord simply by devotional service. Gajendra did this, and thus the Lord was satisfied with him.

PURPORT

No kind of material qualification is the means for satisfying the Supreme Personality of Godhead. As stated in *Bhagavad-gītā,* only by devotional service can the Lord be known (*bhaktyā mām abhijānāti*). Unless the Lord is pleased by the service of a devotee, the Lord does not reveal Himself (*nāhaṁ prakāśaḥ sarvasya yoga-māyā-samāvṛtaḥ*). This is the verdict of all *śāstras.* Neither by speculation nor by material qualifications can one understand or approach the Supreme Personality of Godhead.

TEXT 10

विप्राद् द्विषड्गुणयुतादरविन्दनाभ-
पादारविन्दविमुखात् श्वपचं वरिष्ठम् ।
मन्ये तदर्पितमनोवचनेहितार्थ-
प्राणं पुनाति स कुलं न तु भूरिमानः ॥१०॥

viprād dvi-ṣaḍ-guṇa-yutād aravinda-nābha-
pādāravinda-vimukhāt śvapacaṁ variṣṭham
manye tad-arpita-mano-vacanehitārtha-
prāṇaṁ punāti sa kulaṁ na tu bhūrimānaḥ

viprāt—than a *brāhmaṇa; dvi-ṣaṭ-guṇa-yutāt*—qualified with twelve brahminical qualities;* *aravinda-nābha*—Lord Viṣṇu, who has a lotus growing from His navel; *pāda-aravinda*—to the lotus feet of the Lord; *vimukhāt*—not interested in devotional service; *śva-pacam*—one born in a low family, or a dog-eater; *variṣṭham*—more glorious; *manye*—I consider; *tat-arpita*—surrendered unto the lotus feet of the Lord; *manaḥ*—his mind; *vacana*—words; *īhita*—every endeavor; *artha*—wealth; *prāṇam*—and life; *punāti*—purifies; *saḥ*—he (the devotee); *kulam*—his family; *na*—not; *tu*—but; *bhūrimānaḥ*—one who falsely thinks himself to be in a prestigious position.

TRANSLATION

If a brāhmaṇa has all twelve of the brahminical qualifications [as they are stated in the book called Sanat-sujāta] but is not a devotee and is averse to the lotus feet of the Lord, he is certainly lower than a devotee who is a dog-eater but who has dedicated everything—mind, words, activities, wealth and life—to the Supreme Lord. Such a devotee is better than such a brāhmaṇa because the devotee can purify his whole family, whereas the so-called brāhmaṇa in a position of false prestige cannot purify even himself.

PURPORT

Here is a statement by Prahlāda Mahārāja, one of the twelve authorities, regarding the distinction between a devotee and a *brāhmaṇa* expert in *karma-kāṇḍa*, or Vedic ritualistic ceremonies. There are four *varṇas* and four *āśramas*, which divide human society, but the central principle is to become a first-class pure devotee. It is said in the *Hari-bhakti-sudhodaya:*

bhagavad-bhakti-hīnasya
jātiḥ śāstraṁ japas tapaḥ

---

*These are the twelve qualities of a perfect *brāhmaṇa:* following religious principles, speaking truthfully, controlling the senses by undergoing austerities and penances, being free from jealousy, being intelligent, being tolerant, creating no enemies, performing *yajña*, giving charity, being steady, being well versed in Vedic study, and observing vows.

aprāṇasyaiva dehasya
maṇḍanaṁ loka-rañjanam

"If one is born in a high family like that of a *brāhmaṇa, kṣatriya* or *vaiśya* but is not a devotee of the Lord, all his good qualifications as a *brāhmaṇa, kṣatriya* or *vaiśya* are null and void. Indeed, they are considered decorations of a dead body."

In this verse Prahlāda Mahārāja speaks of the *vipras,* the learned *brāhmaṇas.* The learned *brāhmaṇa* is considered best among the divisions of *brāhmaṇa, kṣatriya, vaiśya* and *śūdra,* but a devotee born in a low *caṇḍāla* family is better than such *brāhmaṇas,* not to speak of the *kṣatriyas, vaiśyas* and others. A devotee is better than anyone, for he is in the transcendental position on the Brahman platform.

māṁ ca yo vyabhicāreṇa
bhakti-yogena sevate
sa guṇān samatītyaitān
brahma-bhūyāya kalpate

"One who engages in full devotional service, who does not fall down in any circumstance, at once transcends the modes of material nature and thus comes to the level of Brahman." (Bg. 14.26) The twelve qualities of a first-class *brāhmaṇa,* as stated in the book called *Sanat-sujāta,* are as follows:

jñānaṁ ca satyaṁ ca damaḥ śrutaṁ ca
hy amātsaryaṁ hrīs titikṣānasūyā
yajñaś ca dānaṁ ca dhṛtiḥ śamaś ca
mahā-vratā dvādaśa brāhmaṇasya

The European and American devotees in the Kṛṣṇa consciousness movement are sometimes accepted as *brāhmaṇas,* but the so-called caste *brāhmaṇas* are very much envious of them. In answer to such envy, Prahlāda Mahārāja says that one who has been born in a *brāhmaṇa* family but is falsely proud of his prestigious position cannot even purify himself, not to speak of his family, whereas if a *caṇḍāla,* a lowborn person, is a devotee and has fully surrendered unto the lotus feet of the Lord, he can purify his entire family. We have had actual experience of how Americans and Europeans, because of their full Kṛṣṇa consciousness, have purified their whole families, so much so that a mother of a devotee, at the time of her death, inquired about Kṛṣṇa with her last breath. Therefore it is theoretically true and has been practically proven that a devotee can give the best service to his family, his community, his society and his nation. The foolish accuse a devotee of following the principle of escapism, but actually the fact is that a devotee is the right person to elevate his family. A devotee engages everything in the service of the Lord, and therefore he is always exalted.

TEXT 11

नैवात्मनः प्रभुरयं निजलाभपूर्णो
मानं जनादविदुषः करुणो वृणीते ।
यद् यज्जनो भगवते विदधीत मानं
तच्चात्मने प्रतिमुखस्य यथा मुखश्रीः ॥११॥

naivātmanaḥ prabhur ayaṁ nija-lābha-pūrṇo
mānaṁ janād aviduṣaḥ karuṇo vṛṇīte
yad yaj jano bhagavate vidadhīta mānaṁ
tac cātmane prati-mukhasya yathā mukha-śrīḥ

na—nor; *eva*—certainly; *ātmanaḥ*—for His personal benefit; *prabhuḥ*—Lord; *ayam*—this; *nija-lābha-pūrṇaḥ*—is always satisfied in Himself (He does not need to be satisfied by the service of others); *mānam*—respect; *janāt*—from a person; *aviduṣaḥ*—who does not know that the aim of life is to please the Supreme Lord; *karuṇaḥ*—(the Supreme Personality of Godhead), who is so kind to this foolish, ignorant person; *vṛṇīte*—accepts; *yat yat*—whatever; *janaḥ*—a person; *bhagavate*—unto the Supreme Personality of Godhead; *vidadhīta*—may offer; *mānam*—worship; *tat*—that; *ca*—indeed; *ātmane*—for his own benefit; *prati-mukhasya*—of the reflection of the face in the mirror; *yathā*—just as; *mukha-śrīḥ*—the decoration of the face.

TRANSLATION

The Supreme Lord, the Supreme Personality of Godhead, is always fully satisfied in Himself. Therefore when something is

offered to Him, the offering, by the Lord's mercy, is for the benefit of the devotee, for the Lord does not need service from anyone. To give an example, if one's face is decorated, the reflection of one's face in a mirror is also seen to be decorated.

PURPORT

In *bhakti-yoga* it is recommended that a devotee follow nine principles: *śravaṇaṁ kīrtanaṁ viṣṇoḥ smaraṇaṁ pāda-sevanam/ arcanaṁ vandanaṁ dāsyaṁ sakhyam ātma-nivedanam.* This service of glorifying the Lord by hearing, chanting and so on is not, of course, meant for the benefit of the Lord; this devotional service is recommended for the benefit of the devotee. The Lord is always glorious, whether the devotee glorifies Him or not, but if the devotee engages in glorifying the Lord, the devotee himself automatically becomes glorious. *Ceto-darpaṇa-mārjanaṁ bhava-mahā-dāvāgni-nirvāpaṇam.* By glorifying the Lord constantly, the living entity becomes purified in the core of his heart, and thus he can understand that he does not belong to the material world but is a spirit soul whose actual activity is to advance in Kṛṣṇa consciousness so that he may become free from the material clutches. Thus the blazing fire of material existence is immediately extinguished (*bhava-mahā-dāvāgni-nirvāpaṇam*). A foolish person is amazed that Kṛṣṇa orders, *sarva-dharmān parityajya mām ekaṁ śaraṇaṁ vraja:* "Abandon all varieties of religious activities and just surrender unto Me." Some foolish scholars even say that this is too much to demand. But this demand is not for the benefit of the Supreme Personality of Godhead; rather, it is for the benefit of human society. If human beings individually and collectively surrender everything to the Supreme Personality of Godhead in full Kṛṣṇa consciousness, all of human society will benefit. One who does not dedicate everything to the Supreme Lord is described in this verse as *aviduṣa*, a rascal. In *Bhagavad-gītā* (7.15), the Lord Himself speaks in the same way:

na māṁ duṣkṛtino mūḍhāḥ
prapadyante narādhamāḥ
māyayāpahṛta-jñānā
āsuraṁ bhāvam āśritāḥ

"Those miscreants who are grossly foolish, lowest among mankind, whose knowledge is stolen by illusion, and who partake of the atheistic nature of demons, do not surrender unto Me." Because of ignorance and misfortune, the atheists and the *narādhamas*, the lowest of men, do not surrender unto the Supreme Personality of Godhead. Therefore although the Supreme Lord, Kṛṣṇa, is full in Himself, He appears in different *yugas* to demand the surrender of the conditioned souls so that they will benefit by becoming free from the material clutches. In conclusion, the more we engage in Kṛṣṇa consciousness and render service unto the Lord, the more we benefit. Kṛṣṇa does not need service from any of us.

TEXT 12

तस्मादहं विगतविक्लव ईश्वरस्य
सर्वात्मना महि गृणामि यथामनीषम् ।
नीचोऽजया गुणविसर्गमनुप्रविष्टः
पूयेत येन हि पुमाननुवर्णितेन ॥१२॥

tasmād ahaṁ vigata-viklava īśvarasya
sarvātmanā mahi gṛṇāmi yathā manīṣam
nīco 'jayā guṇa-visargam anupraviṣṭaḥ
pūyeta yena hi pumān anuvarṇitena

tasmāt—therefore; *aham*—I; *vigata-viklavaḥ*—having given up contemplation of being unfit; *īśvarasya*—of the Supreme Personality of Godhead; *sarva-ātmanā*—in full surrender; *mahi*—glory; *gṛṇāmi*—I shall chant or describe; *yathā manīṣam*—according to my intelligence; *nīcaḥ*—although lowborn (my father being a great demon, devoid of all good qualities); *ajayā*—because of ignorance; *guṇa-visargam*—the material world (wherein the living entity takes birth according to the contamination of the modes of nature); *anupraviṣṭaḥ*—entered into; *pūyeta*—may be purified; *yena*—by which (the glory of the Lord); *hi*—indeed; *pumān*—a person; *anuvarṇitena*—being chanted or recited.

TRANSLATION

Therefore, although I was born in a demoniac family, I may without a doubt offer prayers to the Lord with full endeavor, as far as my intelligence allows. Anyone who has been forced by

ignorance to enter the material world may be purified of material life if he offers prayers to the Lord and hears the Lord's glories.

PURPORT

It is clearly understood that a devotee does not need to be born in a very high family, to be rich, to be aristocratic or to be very beautiful. None of these qualifications will engage one in devotional service. With devotion one should feel, "God is great, and I am very small. Therefore my duty is to offer my prayers to the Lord." Only on this basis can one understand and render service to the Lord. As the Lord says in *Bhagavad-gītā* (18.55):

bhaktyā mām abhijānāti
yāvān yaś cāsmi tattvataḥ
tato māṁ tattvato jñātvā
viśate tad-anantaram

"One can understand the Supreme Personality as He is only by devotional service. And when one is in full consciousness of the Supreme Lord by such devotion, he can enter into the kingdom of God." Thus Prahlāda Mahārāja decided to offer his best prayers to the Lord, without consideration of his material position.

TEXT 13

सर्वे ह्यमी विधिकरास्तव सत्त्वधाम्नो
ब्रह्मादयो वयमिवेश न चोद्विजन्तः ।
क्षेमाय भूतय उतात्मसुखाय चास्य
विक्रीडितं भगवतो रुचिरावतारैः ॥१३॥

sarve hy amī vidhi-karās tava sattva-dhāmno
brahmādayo vayam iveśa na codvijantaḥ
kṣemāya bhūtaya utātma-sukhāya cāsya
vikrīḍitaṁ bhagavato rucirāvatāraiḥ

sarve—all; *hi*—certainly; *amī*—these; *vidhi-karāḥ*—executors of orders; *tava*—Your; *sattva-dhāmnaḥ*—being always situated in the transcendental world; *brahma-ādayaḥ*—the demigods, headed by Lord Brahmā; *vayam*—we; *iva*—like; *īśa*—O my Lord; *na*—not; *ca*—and; *udvijantaḥ*—who are afraid (of Your fearful appearance); *kṣemāya*—for the protection; *bhūtaye*—for the increase; *uta*—it is said; *ātma-sukhāya*—for personal satisfaction by such pastimes; *ca*—also; *asya*—of this (material world); *vikrīḍitam*—manifested; *bhagavataḥ*—of Your Lordship; *rucira*—very pleasing; *avatāraiḥ*—by Your incarnations.

TRANSLATION

O my Lord, all the demigods, headed by Lord Brahmā, are sincere servants of Your Lordship, who are situated in a transcendental position. Therefore they are not like us [Prahlāda and his father, the demon Hiraṇyakaśipu]. Your appearance in this fearsome form is Your pastime for Your own pleasure. Such an incarnation is always meant for the protection and improvement of the universe.

PURPORT

Prahlāda Mahārāja wanted to assert that his father and the other members of his family were all unfortunate because they were demoniac, whereas the devotees of the Lord are always fortunate because they are always ready to follow the orders of the Lord. When the Supreme Lord appears in this material world in His various incarnations, He performs two functions—saving the devotee and vanquishing the demon (*paritrāṇāya sādhūnāṁ vināśāya ca duṣkṛtām*). Lord Nṛsiṁhadeva, for example, appeared for the protection of His devotee. Such pastimes as those of Nṛsiṁhadeva are certainly not meant to create a fearful situation for the devotees, but nonetheless the devotees, being very simple and faithful, were afraid of the fierce incarnation of the Lord. Therefore Prahlāda Mahārāja, in the following prayer, requests the Lord to give up His anger.

TEXT 14

तद् यच्छ मन्युमसुरश्च हतस्त्वयाद्य
मोदेत साधुरपि वृश्चिकसर्पहत्या ।
लोकाश्च निर्वृतिमिताः प्रतियन्ति सर्वे
रूपं नृसिंह विभयाय जनाः स्मरन्ति ॥१४॥

tad yaccha manyum asuraś ca hatas tvayādya
modeta sādhur api vṛścika-sarpa-hatyā
lokāś ca nirvṛtim itāḥ pratiyanti sarve
rūpaṁ nṛsiṁha vibhayāya janāḥ smaranti

tat—therefore; *yaccha*—kindly give up; *manyum*—Your anger; *asuraḥ*—my father, Hiraṇyakaśipu, the great demon; *ca*—also; *hataḥ*—killed; *tvayā*—by You; *adya*—today; *modeta*—take pleasure; *sādhuḥ api*—even a saintly person; *vṛścika-sarpa-hatyā*—by killing a snake or a scorpion; *lokāḥ*—all the planets; *ca*—indeed; *nirvṛtim*—pleasure; *itāḥ*—have achieved; *pratiyanti*—are waiting (for pacification of Your anger); *sarve*—all of them; *rūpam*—this form; *nṛsiṁha*—O Lord Nṛsiṁhadeva; *vibhayāya*—for mitigating their fear; *janāḥ*—all the people of the universe; *smaranti*—will remember.

TRANSLATION

My Lord Nṛsiṁhadeva, please, therefore, cease Your anger now that my father, the great demon Hiraṇyakaśipu, has been killed. Since even saintly persons take pleasure in the killing of a scorpion or a snake, all the worlds have achieved great satisfaction because of the death of this demon. Now they are confident of their happiness, and they will always remember Your auspicious incarnation in order to be free from fear.

PURPORT

The most important point in this verse is that although saintly persons never desire the killing of any living entity, they take pleasure in the killing of envious living entities like snakes and scorpions. Hiraṇyakaśipu was killed because he was worse than a snake or a scorpion, and therefore everyone was happy. Now there was no need for the Lord to be angry. The devotees can always remember the form of Nṛsiṁhadeva when they are in danger, and therefore the appearance of Nṛsiṁhadeva was not at all inauspicious. The Lord's appearance is always worshipable and auspicious for all sane persons and devotees.

TEXT 15

नाहं बिभेम्यजित तेऽतिभयानकास्य-
जिह्वार्कनेत्रभ्रुकुटीरभसोग्रदंष्ट्रात् ।
आन्त्रस्रजः क्षतजकेशरशङ्कुकर्णा-
न्निर्ह्रादभीतदिगिभादरिभिन्नखाग्रात् ॥१५॥

nāhaṁ bibhemy ajita te 'tibhayānakāsya-
jihvārka-netra-bhrukuṭī-rabhasogra-daṁṣṭrāt
āntra-srajaḥ-kṣataja-keśara-śaṅku-karṇān
nirhrāda-bhīta-digibhād ari-bhin-nakhāgrāt

na—not; *aham*—I; *bibhemi*—am afraid; *ajita*—O supreme victorious person, who are never conquered by anyone; *te*—Your; *ati*—very much; *bhayānaka*—fearful; *āsya*—mouth; *jihvā*—tongue; *arka-netra*—eyes shining like the sun; *bhrukuṭī*—frowning brows; *rabhasa*—strong; *ugra-daṁṣṭrāt*—ferocious teeth; *āntra-srajaḥ*—garlanded by intestines; *kṣataja*—bloody; *keśara*—manes; *śaṅku-karṇāt*—wedgelike ears; *nirhrāda*—by a roaring sound (caused by You); *bhīta*—frightened; *digibhāt*—from which even the great elephants; *ari-bhit*—piercing the enemy; *nakha-agrāt*—the tips of whose nails.

TRANSLATION

My Lord, who are never conquered by anyone, I am certainly not afraid of Your ferocious mouth and tongue, Your eyes bright like the sun or Your frowning eyebrows. I do not fear Your sharp, pinching teeth, Your garland of intestines, Your mane soaked with blood, or Your high, wedgelike ears. Nor do I fear Your tumultuous roaring, which makes elephants flee to distant places, or Your nails, which are meant to kill Your enemies.

PURPORT

Lord Nṛsiṁhadeva's fierce appearance was certainly most dangerous for the nondevotees, but for Prahlāda Mahārāja such a fearful appearance was not at all disturbing. The lion is very fearsome for other animals, but its cubs are not at all afraid of the lion. The water of the sea is certainly dreadful for all living entities on the land, but within the sea even the small fish is unafraid. Why? Because the small fish has taken shelter of the big ocean. It is said that although great elephants are taken away by the flooding waters of the river, the small fish swim opposite the current. Therefore although the Lord sometimes assumes a fierce appearance to kill the *duṣkṛtīs*, the devotees worship Him. *Keśava dhṛta-nara-hari-rūpa jaya jagadīśa hare.* The devotee always takes pleasure in worshiping the Lord and glorifying the Lord in any form, either pleasing or fierce.

TEXT 16

त्रस्तोऽस्म्यहं कृपणवत्सल दुःसहोग्र-
संसारचक्रकदनाद् ग्रसतां प्रणीतः ।
बद्धः स्वकर्मभिरुशत्तम तेऽङ्घ्रिमूलं
प्रीतोऽपवर्गशरणं ह्वयसे कदा नु ॥१६॥

trasto 'smy ahaṁ kṛpaṇa-vatsala duḥsahogra-
saṁsāra-cakra-kadanād grasatāṁ praṇītaḥ
baddhaḥ sva-karmabhir uśattama te 'ṅghri-mūlaṁ
prīto 'pavarga-śaraṇaṁ hvayase kadā nu

trastaḥ—frightened; *asmi*—am; *aham*—I; *kṛpaṇa-vatsala*—O my Lord, who are so kind to the fallen souls (who have no spiritual knowledge); *duḥsaha*—intolerable; *ugra*—ferocious; *saṁsāra-cakra*—of the cycle of birth and death; *kadanāt*—from such a miserable condition; *grasatām*—among other conditioned souls, who devour one another; *praṇītaḥ*—being thrown; *baddhaḥ*—bound; *sva-karmabhiḥ*—the course by the reactions of my own activities; *uśattama*—O great insurmountable; *te*—Your; *aṅghri-mūlam*—to the soles of the lotus feet; *prītaḥ*—being pleased (with me); *apavarga-śaraṇam*—which are the shelter meant for liberation from this horrible condition of material existence; *hvayase*—You will call (me); *kadā*—when; *nu*—indeed.

TRANSLATION

O most powerful, insurmountable Lord, who are kind to the fallen souls, I have been put into the association of demons as a

result of my activities, and therefore I am very much afraid of my condition of life within this material world. When will that moment come when You will call me to the shelter of Your lotus feet, which are the ultimate goal for liberation from conditional life?

PURPORT

Being in the material world is certainly miserable, but certainly when one is put into the association of *asuras*, or atheistic men, it is intolerably so. One may ask why the living entity is put into the material world. Indeed, sometimes foolish people deride the Lord for having put them here. Actually, everyone is put into conditional life according to his *karma.* Therefore Prahlāda Mahārāja, representing all the other conditioned souls, admits that he was put into life among the *asuras* because of the results of his *karma.* The Lord is known as *kṛpaṇa-vatsala* because He is extremely kind to the conditioned souls. As stated in *Bhagavad-gītā,* therefore, the Lord appears whenever there are discrepancies in the execution of religious principles (*yadā yadā hi dharmasya glānir bhavati bhārata . . . tadātmānaṁ sṛjāmy aham*). The Lord is extremely anxious to deliver the conditioned souls, and therefore He instructs all of us to return home, back to Godhead (*sarva-dharmān parityajya mām ekaṁ śaraṇaṁ vraja*). Thus Prahlāda Mahārāja expected that the Lord, by His kindness, would call him again to the shelter of His lotus feet. In other words, everyone should be eager to return home, back to Godhead, taking shelter of the lotus feet of the Lord and thus being fully trained in Kṛṣṇa consciousness.

TEXT 17

यस्मात् प्रियाप्रियवियोगसंयोगजन्म-
शोकाग्निना सकलयोनिषु दह्यमानः ।
दुःखौषधं तदपि दुःखमतद्धियाहं
भूमन्भ्रमामि वद मे तव दास्ययोगम् ॥१७॥

yasmāt priyāpriya-viyoga-saṁyoga-janma-
śokāgninā sakala-yoniṣu dahyamānaḥ
duḥkhauṣadhaṁ tad api duḥkham atad-dhiyāhaṁ
bhūman bhramāmi vada me tava dāsya-yogam

yasmāt—because of which (because of existing in the material world); *priya*—pleasing; *apriya*—not pleasing; *viyoga*—by separation; *saṁyoga*—and combination; *janma*—whose birth; *śoka-agninā*—by the fire of lamentation; *sakala-yoniṣu*—in any type of body; *dahyamānaḥ*—being burned; *duḥkha-auṣadham*—remedial measures for miserable life; *tat*—that; *api*—also; *duḥkham*—suffering; *a-tat-dhiyā*—by accepting the body as the self; *aham*—I; *bhūman*—O great one; *bhramāmi*—am wandering (within the cycle of birth and death); *vada*—kindly instruct; *me*—unto me; *tava*—Your; *dāsya-yogam*—activities of service.

TRANSLATION

O great one, O Supreme Lord, because of combination with pleasing and displeasing circumstances and because of separation from them, one is placed in a most regrettable position, within heavenly or hellish planets, as if burning in a fire of lamentation. Although there are many remedies by which to get out of miserable life, any such remedies in the material world are more miserable than the miseries themselves. Therefore I think that the only remedy is to engage in Your service. Kindly instruct me in such service.

PURPORT

Prahlāda Mahārāja aspired to engage in the service of the lotus feet of the Lord. After the death of his father, who was materially very opulent, Prahlāda would have inherited his father's property, which extended throughout the world, but Prahlāda Mahārāja was not inclined to accept such material opulence, for whether one is in the heavenly or hellish planets or is a rich or a poor man's son, material conditions are everywhere. Therefore no condition of life is at all pleasing. If one wants the uncontaminated pleasure of blissful life, he must engage himself in the transcendental loving service of the Lord. Material opulence may be somewhat pleasing for the time being, but to come to that temporary pleasing condition one must work extremely hard. When a poor man is rich he may be better situated, but to come to that position he had to accept many miseries. The fact is that in material life, whether one is miserable or happy, both conditions are miserable. If one actually wants happy, blissful life, one must become Kṛṣṇa conscious and constantly engage in the transcendental loving service of the Lord. That is the real remedy. The entire world is under the illusion that people will be happy by advancing in materialistic measures to counteract the miseries of conditional life, but this attempt will never be successful. Humanity must be trained to engage in the transcendental loving service of the Lord. That is the purpose of the Kṛṣṇa consciousness movement. There can be no happiness in changing one's material conditions, for everywhere there is trouble and misery.

TEXT 18

सोऽहं प्रियस्य सुहृदः परदेवताया
लीलाकथास्तव नृसिंह विरिञ्चगीताः ।
अञ्जस्तितर्म्यनुगृणन्गुणविप्रमुक्तो
दुर्गाणि ते पदयुगालयहंससङ्गः ॥१८॥

so 'haṁ priyasya suhṛdaḥ paradevatāyā
līlā-kathās tava nṛsiṁha viriñca-gītāḥ
añjas titarmy anugṛṇan guṇa-vipramukto
durgāṇi te pada-yugālaya-haṁsa-saṅgaḥ

saḥ—that; *aham*—I (Prahlāda Mahārāja); *priyasya*—of the dearmost; *suhṛdaḥ*—well-wisher; *paradevatāyāḥ*—of the Supreme Personality of Godhead; *līlā-kathāḥ*—narrations of the pastimes; *tava*—Your; *nṛsiṁha*—O my Lord Nṛsiṁhadeva; *viriñca-gītāḥ*—given by Lord Brahmā by the disciplic succession; *añjaḥ*—easily; *titarmi*—I shall cross; *anugṛṇan*—constantly describing; *guṇa*—by the modes of material nature; *vipramuktaḥ*—specifically being uncontaminated; *durgāṇi*—all miserable conditions of life; *te*—of You; *pada-yuga-ālaya*—fully absorbed in meditation on the lotus feet; *haṁsa-saṅgaḥ*—having the association of the *haṁsas*, or liberated persons (who have no connection with material activities).

TRANSLATION

O my Lord Nṛsiṁhadeva, by engaging in Your transcendental loving service in the association of devotees who are liberated

souls [haṁsas], I shall become completely uncontaminated by the association of the three modes of material nature and be able to chant the glories of Your Lordship, who are so dear to me. I shall chant Your glories, following exactly in the footsteps of Lord Brahmā and his disciplic succession. In this way I shall undoubtedly be able to cross the ocean of nescience.

PURPORT

A devotee's life and duty are very well explained herein. As soon as a devotee can chant the holy name and glories of the Supreme Lord, he certainly comes to the liberated position. Attachment for glorifying the Lord by hearing and chanting the holy name and activities of the Lord (*śravaṇaṁ kīrtanaṁ viṣṇoḥ*) certainly brings one to the position where material contamination is absent. One should chant the bona fide songs received from the disciplic succession. In *Bhagavad-gītā* it is said that the chanting is powerful when one follows the disciplic succession (*evaṁ paramparā-prāptam imaṁ rājarṣayo viduḥ*). Manufacturing many ways of chanting will never be effective. However, chanting the song or the narration left by the previous *ācāryas* (*mahājano yena gataḥ sa panthāḥ*) is extremely effective, and this process is very easy. Therefore in this verse Prahlāda Mahārāja uses the word *añjaḥ* ("easily"). Accepting the thoughts of exalted authorities through disciplic succession is certainly much easier than the method of mental speculation, by which one tries to invent some means to understand the Absolute Truth. The best process is to accept the instructions of the previous *ācāryas* and follow them. Then God realization and self-realization become extremely easy. By following this easy method, one is liberated from the contamination of the material modes of nature, and thus one can certainly cross the ocean of nescience, in which there are many miserable conditions. By following in the footsteps of the great *ācāryas*, one associates with the *haṁsas* or *paramahaṁsas*, those who are completely freed from material contamination. Indeed, by following the instructions of the *ācāryas* one is always freed from all material contamination, and thus one's life becomes successful, for one reaches the goal of life. This material world is miserable, regardless of one's standard of life. Of this there is no doubt. Attempts to mitigate the miseries of material existence by material methods will never be successful. One must take to Kṛṣṇa consciousness to become really happy; otherwise happiness is impossible. One might say that becoming advanced in spiritual life also involves *tapasya,* voluntary acceptance of some inconvenience. However, such inconvenience is not as dangerous as material attempts to mitigate all miseries.

TEXT 19

बालस्य नेह शरणं पितरौ नृसिंह
नार्तस्य चागदमुदन्वति मज्जतो नौः ।
तप्तस्य तत्प्रतिविधिर्य इहाञ्जसेष्ट-
स्तावद् विभो तनुभृतां त्वदुपेक्षितानाम् ॥१९॥

bālasya neha śaraṇaṁ pitarau nṛsiṁha
nārtasya cāgadam udanvati majjato nauḥ
taptasya tat-pratividhir ya ihāñjaseṣṭas
tāvad vibho tanu-bhṛtāṁ tvad-upekṣitānām

bālasya—of a little child; *na*—not; *iha*—in this world; *śaraṇam*—shelter (protection); *pitarau*—the father and mother; *nṛsiṁha*—O my Lord Nṛsiṁhadeva; *na*—neither; *ārtasya*—of a person suffering from some disease; *ca*—also; *agadam*—medicine; *udanvati*—in the water of the ocean; *majjataḥ*—of a person who is drowning; *nauḥ*—the boat; *taptasya*—of a person suffering from a condition of material misery; *tat-pratividhiḥ*—the counteraction (invented for stopping the suffering of material existence); *yaḥ*—that which; *iha*—in this material world; *añjasā*—very easily; *iṣṭaḥ*—accepted (as a remedy); *tāvat*—similarly; *vibho*—O my Lord, O Supreme; *tanu-bhṛtām*—of the living entities who have accepted material bodies; *tvat-upekṣitānām*—who are neglected by You and not accepted by You.

TRANSLATION

My Lord Nṛsiṁhadeva, O Supreme, because of a bodily conception of life, embodied souls neglected and not cared for by You cannot do anything for their betterment. Whatever remedies they accept, although perhaps temporarily beneficial, are certainly impermanent. For example, a father and mother cannot protect their

child, a physician and medicine cannot relieve a suffering patient, and a boat on the ocean cannot protect a drowning man.

PURPORT

Through parental care, through remedies for different kinds of disease, and through means of protection on the water, in the air and on land, there is always an endeavor for relief from various kinds of suffering in the material world, but none of them are guaranteed measures for protection. They may be beneficial temporarily, but they afford no permanent benefit. Despite the presence of a father and mother, a child cannot be protected from accidental death, disease and various other miseries. No one can help, including the parents. Ultimately the shelter is the Lord, and one who takes shelter of the Lord is protected. This is guaranteed. As the Lord says in *Bhagavad-gītā* (9.31), *kaunteya pratijānīhi na me bhaktaḥ praṇaśyati:* "O son of Kuntī, declare it boldly that My devotee never perishes." Therefore, unless one is protected by the mercy of the Lord, no remedial measure can act effectively. One should consequently depend fully on the causeless mercy of the Lord. Although as a matter of routine duty one must of course accept other remedial measures, no one can protect one who is neglected by the Supreme Personality of Godhead. In this material world, everyone is trying to counteract the onslaught of material nature, but everyone is ultimately fully controlled by material nature. Therefore even though so-called philosophers and scientists try to surmount the onslaught of material nature, they have not been able to do so. Kṛṣṇa says in *Bhagavad-gītā* (13.9) that the real sufferings of the material world are four—*janma-mṛtyu-jarā-vyādhi* (birth, death, old age and disease). In the history of the world, no one has been successful in conquering these miseries imposed by material nature. *Prakṛteḥ kriyamāṇāni guṇaiḥ karmāṇi sarvaśaḥ.* Nature (*prakṛti*) is so strong that no one can overcome her stringent laws. So-called scientists, philosophers, religionists and politicians should therefore conclude that they cannot offer facilities to the people in general. They should make vigorous propaganda to awaken the populace and raise them to the platform of Kṛṣṇa consciousness. Our humble attempt to propagate the Kṛṣṇa consciousness movement all over the world is the only remedy that can bring about a peaceful and happy life. We can never be happy without the mercy of the Supreme Lord (*tvad-upekṣitānām*). If we keep displeasing our supreme father, we shall never be happy within this material world, in either the upper or lower planetary systems.

TEXT 20

यस्मिन्यतो यर्हि येन च यस्य यस्माद्
यस्मै यथा यदुत यस्त्वपरः परो वा ।
भावः करोति विकरोति पृथक्स्वभावः
सञ्चोदितस्तदखिलं भवतः स्वरूपम् ॥२०॥

yasmin yato yarhi yena ca yasya yasmād
yasmai yathā yad uta yas tv aparaḥ paro vā
bhāvaḥ karoti vikaroti pṛthak svabhāvaḥ
sañcoditas tad akhilaṁ bhavataḥ svarūpam

yasmin—in any condition of life; *yataḥ*—because of anything; *yarhi*—at any time (past, present or future); *yena*—by something; *ca*—also; *yasya*—in relationship with anyone; *yasmāt*—from any causal representative; *yasmai*—unto anyone (without discrimination in regard to place, person or time); *yathā*—in any manner; *yat*—whatever it may be; *uta*—certainly; *yaḥ*—anyone who; *tu*—but; *aparaḥ*—the other; *paraḥ*—the supreme; *vā*—or; *bhāvaḥ*—being; *karoti*—does; *vikaroti*—changes; *pṛthak*—separate; *svabhāvaḥ*—nature (under the influence of different modes of material nature); *sañcoditaḥ*—being influenced; *tat*—that; *akhilam*—all; *bhavataḥ*—of Your Lordship; *svarūpam*—emanated from Your different energies.

TRANSLATION

My dear Lord, everyone in this material world is under the modes of material nature, being influenced by goodness, passion and ignorance. Everyone—from the greatest personality, Lord Brahmā, down to the small ant—works under the influence of these modes. Therefore everyone in this material world is influenced by Your energy. The cause for which they work, the place where they work, the time when they work, the matter due to which they work, the goal of life they have considered final, and

the process for obtaining this goal—all are nothing but manifestations of Your energy. Indeed, since the energy and energetic are identical, all of them are but manifestations of You.

PURPORT

Whether one thinks himself protected by his parents, by the government, by some place or by some other cause, everything is due to the various potencies of the Supreme Personality of Godhead. Everything that is done, whether in the higher, middle or lower planetary systems, is due to the supervision or control of the Supreme Lord. It is therefore said, *karmaṇā daiva-netreṇa jantur dehopapattaye.* The Supreme Personality of Godhead, the Supersoul within the core of everyone's heart, gives inspirations for action according to one's mentality. All of these mentalities are merely facilities given by Kṛṣṇa to the person acting. *Bhagavad-gītā* therefore says, *mattaḥ smṛtir jñānam apohanaṁ ca:* everyone works according to the inspiration given by the Supersoul. Because everyone has a different goal of life, everyone acts differently, as guided by the Supreme Personality of Godhead.

The words *yasmin yato yarhi yena ca yasya yasmāt* indicate that all activities, whatever they may be, are but different features of the Supreme Personality of Godhead. All of them are created by the living entity and fulfilled by the mercy of the Lord. Although all such activities are nondifferent from the Lord, the Lord nonetheless directs, *sarva-dharmān parityajya mām ekaṁ śaraṇaṁ vraja:* "Give up all other duties and surrender unto Me." When we accept this direction from the Lord, we can actually become happy. As long as we work according to our material senses we are in material life, but as soon as we act according to the real, transcendental direction of the Lord, our position is spiritual. The activities of *bhakti,* devotional service, are directly under the control of the Supreme Personality of Godhead. The *Nārada-pañcarātra* states:

sarvopādhi-vinirmuktaṁ
tat-paratvena nirmalam
hṛṣīkeṇa hṛṣīkeśa-
sevanaṁ bhaktir ucyate

When one gives up materially designated positions and works directly under the Supreme Personality of Godhead, one's spiritual life is revived. This is described as *svarūpena avasthiti*, being situated in one's original constitutional position. This is the real description of *mukti*, or liberation from material bondage.

TEXT 21

माया मनः सृजति कर्ममयं बलीयः
कालेन चोदितगुणानुमतेन पुंसः ।
छन्दोमयं यदजयार्पितषोडशारं
संसारचक्रमज कोऽतितरेत् त्वदन्यः ॥२१॥

māyā manaḥ sṛjati karmamayaṁ balīyaḥ
kālena codita-guṇānumatena puṁsaḥ
chandomayaṁ yad ajayārpita-ṣoḍaśāraṁ
saṁsāra-cakram aja ko 'titaret tvad-anyaḥ

māyā—the external energy of the Supreme Personality of Godhead; *manaḥ*—the mind;* *sṛjati*—creates; *karma-mayam*—producing hundreds and thousands of desires and acting accordingly; *balīyaḥ*—extremely powerful, insurmountable; *kālena*—by time; *codita-guṇa*—whose three modes of material nature are agitated; *anumatena*—permitted by the mercy of the glance (time); *puṁsaḥ*—of the plenary portion, Lord Viṣṇu, the expansion of Lord Kṛṣṇa; *chandaḥ-mayam*—chiefly influenced by the directions in the *Vedas; yat*—which; *ajayā*—because of dark ignorance; *arpita*—offered; *ṣoḍaśa*—sixteen; *aram*—the spokes; *saṁsāra-cakram*—the wheel of repeated birth and death in different species of life; *aja*—O unborn Lord; *kaḥ*—who (is there); *atitaret*—able to get out; *tvat-anyaḥ*—without taking shelter at Your lotus feet.

---

*The mind is always planning how to remain in the material world and struggle for existence. It is the chief part of the subtle body, which consists of the mind, intelligence and false ego.

TRANSLATION

O Lord, O supreme eternal, by expanding Your plenary portion You have created the subtle bodies of the living entities through the agency of Your external energy, which is agitated by time. Thus the mind entraps the living entity in unlimited varieties of desires to be fulfilled by the Vedic directions of karma-kāṇḍa [fruitive activity] and the sixteen elements. Who can get free from this entanglement unless he takes shelter at Your lotus feet?

PURPORT

If the hand of the Supreme Personality of Godhead is present in everything, where is the question of being liberated from material encagement to spiritual, blissful life? Indeed, it is a fact that Kṛṣṇa is the source of everything, as we understand from Kṛṣṇa Himself in *Bhagavad-gītā* (*ahaṁ sarvasya prabhavaḥ*). All the activities in both the spiritual and material world are certainly conducted by the orders of the Supreme Personality of Godhead through the agency of either the material or spiritual nature. As further confirmed in *Bhagavad-gītā* (9.10), *mayādhyakṣeṇa prakṛtiḥ sūyate sacarācaram:* without the direction of the Supreme Lord, material nature cannot do anything; it cannot act independently. Therefore, in the beginning the living entity wanted to enjoy the material energy, and to give the living entity all facility, Kṛṣṇa, the Supreme Personality of Godhead, created this material world and gave the living entity the facility to concoct different ideas and plans through the mind. These facilities offered by the Lord to the living entity constitute the sixteen kinds of perverted support in terms of the knowledge-gathering senses, the working senses, the mind and the five material elements. The wheel of repeated birth and death is created by the Supreme Personality of Godhead, but to direct the bewildered living entity in progress toward liberation according to varied stages of advancement, different directions are given in the *Vedas* (*chandomayam*). If one wants to be elevated to the higher planetary systems, he may follow the Vedic directions. As the Lord states in *Bhagavad-gītā* (9.25):

yānti deva-vratā devān
pitṝn yānti pitṛ-vratāḥ

bhūtāni yānti bhūtejyā
yānti mad-yājino 'pi mām

"Those who worship the demigods will take birth among the demigods; those who worship ghosts and spirits will take birth among such beings; those who worship ancestors go to the ancestors; and those who worship Me will live with Me." The real purpose of the *Vedas* is to direct one back home, back to Godhead, but the living entity, not knowing the real goal of his life, wants to go sometimes here and sometimes there and do sometimes this and sometimes that. In this way he wanders throughout the entire universe, imprisoned in various species and thus engaging in various activities for which he must suffer the reactions. Śrī Caitanya Mahāprabhu therefore says:

brahmāṇḍa bhramite kona bhāgyavān jīva
guru-kṛṣṇa-prasāde pāya bhakti-latā-bīja
(Cc. *Madhya* 19.151)

The fallen, conditioned living entity, trapped by the external energy, loiters in the material world, but if by good fortune he meets a bona fide representative of the Lord who gives him the seed of devotional service, and if he takes advantage of such a *guru*, or representative of God, he receives the *bhakti-latā-bīja*, the seed of devotional service. If he properly cultivates Kṛṣṇa consciousness, he is then gradually elevated to the spiritual world. The ultimate conclusion is that one must surrender to the principles of *bhakti-yoga*, for then one will gradually attain liberation. No other method of liberation from the material struggle is at all possible.

TEXT 22

स त्वं हि नित्यविजितात्मगुणः स्वधाम्ना
कालो वशीकृतविसृज्यविसर्गशक्तिः ।
चक्रे विसृष्टमजयेश्वर षोडशारे
निष्पीड्यमानमुपकर्ष विभो प्रपन्नम् ॥२२॥

sa tvaṁ hi nitya-vijitātma-guṇaḥ sva-dhāmnā
kālo vaśī-kṛta-visṛjya-visarga-śaktiḥ

cakre visṛṣṭam ajayeśvara ṣoḍaśāre
niṣpīḍyamānam upakarṣa vibho prapannam

saḥ—that one (the supreme independent person who, through His external energy, has created the material mind, which is the cause of all suffering in this material world); *tvam*—You (are); *hi*—indeed; *nitya*—eternally; *vijita-ātma*—conquered; *guṇaḥ*—whose property of the intelligence; *sva-dhāmnā*—by Your personal spiritual energy; *kālaḥ*—the time element (which creates and annihilates); *vaśī-kṛta*—brought under Your control; *visṛjya*—by which all effects; *visarga*—and causes; *śaktiḥ*—the energy; *cakre*—in the wheel of time (the repetition of birth and death); *visṛṣṭam*—being thrown; *ajayā*—by Your external energy, the mode of ignorance; *īśvara*—O supreme controller; *ṣoḍaśa-are*—with sixteen spokes (the five material elements, the ten senses, and the leader of the senses, namely the mind); *niṣpīḍyamānam*—being crushed (under that wheel); *upakarṣa*—kindly take me (to the shelter of Your lotus feet); *vibho*—O supreme great; *prapannam*—who am fully surrendered unto You.

TRANSLATION

My dear Lord, O supreme great, You have created this material world of sixteen constituents, but You are transcendental to their material qualities. In other words, these material qualities are under Your full control, and You are never conquered by them. Therefore the time element is Your representation. My Lord, O Supreme, no one can conquer You. As for me, however, I am being crushed by the wheel of time, and therefore I surrender fully unto You. Now kindly take me under the protection of Your lotus feet.

PURPORT

The wheel of material miseries is also a creation of the Supreme Personality of Godhead, but He is not under the control of the material energy. Rather, He is the controller of the material energy, whereas we, the living entities, are under its control. When we give up our constitutional position (*jīvera 'svarūpa' haya—kṛṣṇera 'nitya-dāsa'*), the Supreme Personality of Godhead creates this material energy and her influence over the conditioned soul. Therefore He is the Supreme, and only He can deliver the conditioned soul from the onslaught of material nature (*mām eva ye prapadyante māyām etāṁ taranti te*). *Māyā*, the external energy, continuously imposes upon the conditioned souls the suffering of the threefold miseries of this material world. Therefore, in the previous verse, Prahlāda Mahārāja prayed to the Lord, "But for Your Lordship, no one can save me." Prahlāda Mahārāja has also explained that a child's protectors, his parents, cannot save the child from the onslaught of birth and death, nor can medicine and a physician save one from death, nor can a boat or similar means of protection save a person drowning in the water, for everything is controlled by the Supreme Personality of Godhead. Therefore suffering humanity must surrender to Kṛṣṇa, as Kṛṣṇa Himself demands in the last instruction of *Bhagavad-gītā* (18.66):

sarva-dharmān parityajya
mām ekaṁ śaraṇaṁ vraja
ahaṁ tvāṁ sarva-pāpebhyo
mokṣayiṣyāmi mā śucaḥ

"Abandon all varieties of religion and just surrender unto Me. I shall deliver you from all sinful reaction. Do not fear." All of human society must take advantage of this offer and thus be saved by Kṛṣṇa from the danger of being crushed by the wheel of time, the wheel of past, present and future.

The word *niṣpīḍyamānam* ("being crushed") is very significant. Every living entity in the material condition is actually being crushed again and again, and to be saved from this position one must take shelter of the Supreme Personality of Godhead. Then one will be happy. The word *prapannam* is also very significant, for unless one fully surrenders to the Supreme Lord one cannot be saved from being crushed. A criminal is put in prison and punished by the government, but the same government, if it likes, can release the criminal from imprisoned life. Similarly, we must know conclusively that our material condition of suffering has been allotted to us by the Supreme Personality of Godhead, and if we want to be saved from this suffering, we must appeal to the same controller. Thus one can be saved from this material condition.

TEXT 23

दृष्टा मया दिवि विभोऽखिलधिष्ण्यपाना-
मायुः श्रियो विभव इच्छति याञ्जनोऽयम् ।
येऽस्मत्पितुः कुपितहासविजृम्भितभ्रू-
विस्फूर्जितेन लुलिताः स तु ते निरस्तः ॥२३॥

dṛṣṭā mayā divi vibho 'khila-dhiṣṇya-pānām
āyuḥ śriyo vibhava icchati yāñ jano 'yam
ye 'smat pituḥ kupita-hāsa-vijṛmbhita-bhrū-
visphūrjitena lulitāḥ sa tu te nirastaḥ

dṛṣṭāḥ—have been seen practically; *mayā*—by me; *divi*—in the higher planetary systems; *vibho*—O my Lord; *akhila*—all; *dhiṣṇya-pānām*—of the chiefs of different states or planets; *āyuḥ*—the duration of life; *śriyaḥ*—the opulences; *vibhavaḥ*—glories, influence; *icchati*—desire; *yān*—all of which; *janaḥ ayam*—these people in general; *ye*—all of which (duration of life, opulence, etc.); *asmat pituḥ*—of our father, Hiraṇyakaśipu; *kupita-hāsa*—by his critical laughing when angry; *vijṛmbhita*—being expanded; *bhrū*—of the eyebrows; *visphūrjitena*—simply by the feature; *lulitāḥ*—pulled down or finished; *saḥ*—he (my father); *tu*—but; *te*—by You; *nirastaḥ*—completely vanquished.

TRANSLATION

My dear Lord, people in general want to be elevated to the higher planetary systems for a long duration of life, opulence and enjoyment, but I have seen all of these through the activities of my father. When my father was angry and he laughed sarcastically at the demigods, they were immediately vanquished simply by seeing the movements of his eyebrows. Yet my father, who was so powerful, has now been vanquished by You within a moment.

PURPORT

Within this material world, one should understand by practical experience the value of material opulence, longevity and influence. We have actual experience that even on this planet there have been many great politicians and military commanders like Napolean, Hitler, Shubhash Chandra Bose and Gandhi, but as soon as their lives were finished, their popularity, influence and everything else were finished also. Prahlāda Mahārāja formerly gathered the same experience by seeing the activities of Hiraṇyakaśipu, his great father. Therefore Prahlāda Mahārāja did not give any importance to anything in this material world. No one can maintain his body or material achievements forever. A Vaiṣṇava can understand that nothing within this material world, not even that which is powerful, opulent or influential, can endure. At any time such things may be vanquished. And who can vanquish them? The Supreme Personality of Godhead. Therefore one should conclusively understand that no one is greater than the Supreme Great. Since the Supreme Great demands, *sarva-dharmān parityajya mām ekaṁ śaraṇaṁ vraja*, every intelligent man must agree to this proposal. One must surrender unto the Lord to be saved from the wheel of repeated birth, death, old age and disease.

TEXT 24

तस्मादमूस्तनुभृतामहमाशिषोऽज्ञ
आयुः श्रियं विभवमैन्द्रियमाविरिञ्च्यात् ।
नेच्छामि ते विलुलितानुरुविक्रमेण
कालात्मनोपनय मां निजभृत्यपार्श्वम् ॥२४॥

tasmād amūs tanu-bhṛtām aham āśiṣo 'jña
āyuḥ śriyaṁ vibhavam aindriyam āviriñcyāt
necchāmi te vilulitān uruvikrameṇa
kālātmanopanaya māṁ nija-bhṛtya-pārśvam

tasmāt—therefore; *amūḥ*—all those (opulences); *tanu-bhṛtām*—with reference to living entities possessing material bodies; *aham*—I; *āśiṣaḥ ajñaḥ*—knowing well the results of such benedictions; *āyuḥ*—a long duration of life; *śriyam*—material opulences; *vibhavam*—influence and glories; *aindriyam*—all meant for sense gratification; *āviriñcyāt*—beginning from Lord Brahmā (down to the small ant); *na*—not;

icchāmi—I want; *te*—by You; *vilulitān*—subject to be finished; *uru-vikrameṇa*—who are extremely powerful; *kāla-ātmanā*—as the master of the time factor; *upanaya*—kindly take to; *mām*—me; *nija-bhṛtya-pārśvam*—the association of Your faithful servant, Your devotee.

TRANSLATION

My dear Lord, now I have complete experience concerning the worldly opulence, mystic power, longevity and other material pleasures enjoyed by all living entities, from Lord Brahmā down to the ant. As powerful time, You destroy them all. Therefore, because of my experience, I do not wish to possess them. My dear Lord, I request You to place me in touch with Your pure devotee and let me serve him as a sincere servant.

PURPORT

By studying *Śrīmad-Bhāgavatam,* every intelligent man can get experience like that of Prahlāda Mahārāja through the historical incidents mentioned in this great literature of spiritual knowledge. By following in the footsteps of Prahlāda Mahārāja, one should gain thorough experience that all material opulence is perishable at every moment. Even this body, for which we try to acquire so many sensual pleasures, may perish at any time. The soul, however, is eternal. *Na hanyate hanyamāne śarīre:* the soul is never vanquished, even when the body is destroyed. An intelligent man, therefore, should care for the happiness of the spirit soul, not of the body. Even if one receives a body with a long duration of life, like those of Lord Brahmā and the other great demigods, it will also be destroyed, and therefore an intelligent man should be concerned with the imperishable spirit soul.

To save oneself, one must take shelter of a pure devotee. Narottama dāsa Ṭhākura therefore says, *chāḍiyā vaiṣṇava-sevā nistāra pāyeche kebā.* If one wants to save himself from material nature's onslaughts, which arise because of the material body, one must become Kṛṣṇa conscious and try to fully understand Kṛṣṇa. As stated in *Bhagavad-gītā* (4.9), *janma karma ca me divyam evaṁ yo vetti tattvataḥ.* One should understand Kṛṣṇa in truth, and this one can do only by serving a pure devotee. Thus Prahlāda Mahārāja prays that Lord Nṛsiṁhadeva place him in touch with a pure devotee and servant instead of awarding him material opulence. Every intelligent man within this material world must follow Prahlāda Mahārāja. *Mahājano yena gataḥ sa panthāḥ.* Prahlāda Mahārāja did not want to enjoy the estate left by his father; rather, he wanted to become a servant of the servant of the Lord. The illusory human civilization that perpetually endeavors for happiness through material advancement is rejected by Prahlāda Mahārāja and those who strictly follow in his footsteps.

There are different types of material opulence, known technically as *bhukti, mukti* and *siddhi. Bhukti* refers to being situated in a very good position, like a position with the demigods in the higher planetary systems, where one can enjoy material sense gratification to the greatest extent. *Mukti* refers to being disgusted with material advancement and thus desiring to become one with the Supreme. *Siddhi* refers to executing a severe type of meditation, like that of the *yogīs*, to attain eight kinds of perfection (*aṇimā, laghimā, mahimā,* etc.). All who desire some material advancement through *bhukti, mukti* or *siddhi* are punishable in due course of time, and they return to material activities. Prahlāda Mahārāja rejected them all; he simply wanted to engage as an apprentice under the guidance of a pure devotee.

TEXT 25

कुत्राशिषः श्रुतिसुखा मृगतृष्णिरूपाः
क्वेदं कलेवरमशेषरुजां विरोहः ।
निर्विद्यते न तु जनो यदपीति विद्वान्
कामानलं मधुलवैः शमयन्दुरापैः ॥२५॥

kutrāśiṣaḥ śruti-sukhā mṛgatṛṣṇi-rūpāḥ
kvedaṁ kalevaram aśeṣa-rujāṁ virohaḥ
nirvidyate na tu jano yad apīti vidvān
kāmānalaṁ madhu-lavaiḥ śamayan durāpaiḥ

kutra—where; *āśiṣaḥ*—benedictions; *śruti-sukhāḥ*—simply pleasing to hear of; *mṛgatṛṣṇi-rūpāḥ*—exactly like a mirage in the desert; *kva*—where; *idam*—this; *kalevaram*—body; *aśeṣa*—unlimited; *rujām*—of diseases; *virohaḥ*—the place for generating; *nirvidyate*—become satiated; *na*—not; *tu*—but; *janaḥ*—people in general; *yat api*—although; *iti*—thus; *vidvān*—so-called learned philosophers, scientists and politicians; *kāma-analam*—the blazing fire of lusty desires; *madhu-lavaiḥ*—with drops of honey (happiness); *śamayan*—controlling; *durāpaiḥ*—very difficult to obtain.

TRANSLATION

In this material world, every living entity desires some future happiness, which is exactly like a mirage in the desert. Where is water in the desert, or, in other words, where is happiness in this material world? As for this body, what is its value? It is merely a source of various diseases. The so-called philosophers, scientists and politicians know this very well, but nonetheless they aspire for temporary happiness. Happiness is very difficult to obtain, but because they are unable to control their senses, they run after the so-called happiness of the material world and never come to the right conclusion.

PURPORT

There is a song in the Bengali language which states, "I constructed this home for happiness, but unfortunately there was a fire, and everything has now been burnt to ashes." This illustrates the nature of material happiness. Everyone knows it, but nonetheless one plans to hear or think something very pleasing. Unfortunately, all of one's plans are annihilated in due course of time. There were many politicians who planned empires, supremacy and control of the world, but in due time all their plans and empires—and even the politicians themselves—were vanquished. Everyone should take lessons from Prahlāda Mahārāja about how we are engaged in so-called temporary happiness through bodily exercises for sense enjoyment. All of us repeatedly make plans, which are all repeatedly frustrated. Therefore one should stop such planmaking.

As one cannot stop a blazing fire by constantly pouring ghee upon it, one cannot satisfy oneself by increasing plans for sense enjoyment. The blazing fire is *bhava-mahā-dāvāgni*, the forest fire of material existence. This forest fire occurs automatically, without endeavor. We want to be happy in the material world, but this will never be possible; we shall simply increase the blazing fire of desires. Our desires cannot be satisfied by illusory thoughts and plans; rather, we have to follow the instructions of Lord Kṛṣṇa: *sarva-dharmān parityajya mām ekaṁ śaraṇaṁ vraja.* Then we shall be happy. Otherwise, in the name of happiness, we shall continue to suffer miserable conditions.

TEXT 26

क्वाहं रजःप्रभव ईश तमोऽधिकेऽस्मिन्
जातः सुरेतरकुले क्व तवानुकम्पा ।
न ब्रह्मणो न तु भवस्य न वै रमाया
यन्मेऽर्पितः शिरसि पद्मकरः प्रसादः ॥२६॥

kvāhaṁ rajaḥ-prabhava īśa tamo 'dhike 'smin
jātaḥ suretara-kule kva tavānukampā
na brahmaṇo na tu bhavasya na vai ramāyā
yan me 'rpitaḥ śirasi padma-karaḥ prasādaḥ

kva—where; *aham*—I (am); *rajaḥ-prabhavaḥ*—being born in a body full of passion; *īśa*—O my Lord; *tamaḥ*—the mode of ignorance; *adhike*—surpassing in; *asmin*—in this; *jātaḥ*—born; *sura-itara-kule*—in a family of atheists or demons (who are subordinate to the devotees); *kva*—where; *tava*—Your; *anukampā*—causeless mercy; *na*—not; *brahmaṇaḥ*—of Lord Brahmā; *na*—not; *tu*—but; *bhavasya*—of Lord Śiva; *na*—nor; *vai*—even; *ramāyāḥ*—of the goddess of fortune; *yat*—which; *me*—of me; *arpitaḥ*—offered; *śirasi*—on the head; *padma-karaḥ*—lotus hand; *prasādaḥ*—the symbol of mercy.

TRANSLATION

O my Lord, O Supreme, because I was born in a family full of the hellish material qualities of passion and ignorance, what is my position? And what is to be said of Your causeless mercy, which was never offered even to Lord Brahmā, Lord Śiva or the goddess of fortune, Lakṣmī? You never put Your lotus hand upon their heads, but You have put it upon mine.

PURPORT

Prahlāda Mahārāja was surprised at the causeless mercy of the Supreme Lord, the Personality of Godhead, for although Prahlāda was born in a demoniac family and although the Lord had never before placed His lotus hand on the head of Brahmā, Śiva or the goddess of fortune, His constant companion, Lord Nṛsiṁhadeva kindly placed His hand on the head of Prahlāda. This is the meaning of causeless mercy. The causeless mercy of the Supreme Personality of Godhead may be bestowed upon anyone, regardless of his position in this material world. Everyone is eligible to worship the Supreme Lord, irrespective of his material position. This is confirmed in *Bhagavad-gītā* (14.26):

māṁ ca yo 'vyabhicāreṇa
bhakti yogena sevate
sa guṇān samatītyaitān
brahma-bhūyāya kalpate

"One who engages in full devotional service, who does not fall down in any circumstance, at once transcends the modes of material nature and thus comes to the level of Brahman." Anyone who engages in continuous devotional service to the Lord is situated in the spiritual world and has nothing to do with the material qualities (*sattva-guṇa*, *rajo-guṇa* and *tamo-guṇa*).

Because Prahlāda Mahārāja was situated on the spiritual platform, he had nothing to do with his body, which had been born of the modes of passion and ignorance. The symptoms of passion and ignorance are described in *Śrīmad-Bhāgavatam* (1.2.19) as lust and hankering (*tadā rajas tamo-bhāvāḥ kāma-lobhādayaś ca ye*). Prahlāda Mahārāja, being a great devotee, thought the body born of his father to be born of passion and ignorance, but because Prahlāda was fully engaged in the service of the Lord, his body did not belong to the material world. The pure Vaiṣṇava's body is spiritualized even in this life. For example, when iron is put into a fire it becomes red-hot and is no longer iron but fire. Similarly, the so-called material bodies of devotees who fully engage in the devotional service of the Lord, being constantly in the fire of spiritual life, have nothing to do with matter, but are spiritualized.

Śrīla Madhvācārya remarks that the goddess of fortune, the mother of the universe, could not get mercy similar to that which was offered to Prahlāda Mahārāja, for although the goddess of fortune is always a constant companion of the Supreme Lord, the Lord is more inclined to His devotees. In other words, devotional service is so great that when it is offered even by those born in low families, the Lord accepts it as being more valuable than the service offered by the goddess of fortune. Lord Brahmā, King Indra and the other demigods living in the upper planetary systems are situated in a different spirit of consciousness, and therefore they are sometimes troubled by demons, but a devotee, even if situated in the lower planets, enjoys life in Kṛṣṇa consciousness under any circumstances. *Parataḥ svataḥ karmataḥ:* as he acts himself, as he is instructed by others or as he performs his material activities, he enjoys life in every respect. In this regard, Madhvācārya quotes the following verses, which are mentioned in the *Brahma-tarka:*

śrī-brahma-brāhmīvīndrādi-
tri-katat strī-puru-ṣṭutāḥ
tad anye ca kramādeva
sadā muktau smṛtāv api

hari-bhaktau ca taj-jñāne
sukhe ca niyamena tu
parataḥ svataḥ karmato vā
na kathañcit tad anyathā

TEXT 27

नैषा परावरमतिर्भवतो ननु स्या-
जन्तोर्यथात्मसुहृदो जगतस्तथापि ।
संसेवया सुरतरोरिव ते प्रसादः
सेवानुरूपमुदयो न परावरत्वम् ॥२७॥

naiṣā parāvara-matir bhavato nanu syāj
jantor yathātma-suhṛdo jagatas tathāpi

saṁsevayā surataror iva te prasādaḥ
sevānurūpam udayo na parāvaratvam

na—not; *eṣā*—this; *para-avara*—of higher or lower; *matiḥ*—such discrimination; *bhavataḥ*—of Your Lordship; *nanu*—indeed; *syāt*—there can be; *jantoḥ*—of ordinary living entities; *yathā*—as; *ātma-suhṛdaḥ*—of one who is the friend; *jagataḥ*—of the whole material world; *tathāpi*—but still (there is such a demonstration of intimacy or difference); *saṁsevayā*—according to the degree of service rendered by the devotee; *surataroḥ iva*—like that of the desire tree in Vaikuṇṭhaloka (which offers fruits according to the desire of the devotee); *te*—Your; *prasādaḥ*—benediction or blessing; *sevā-anurūpam*—according to the category of service one renders to the Lord; *udayaḥ*—manifestation; *na*—not; *para-avaratvam*—discrimination due to higher or lower levels.

TRANSLATION

Unlike an ordinary living entity, my Lord, You do not discriminate between friends and enemies, the favorable and the unfavorable, because for You there is no conception of higher and lower. Nonetheless, You offer Your benedictions according to the level of one's service, exactly as a desire tree delivers fruits according to one's desires and makes no distinction between the lower and the higher.

PURPORT

In *Bhagavad-gītā* (4.11) the Lord clearly says, *ye yathā māṁ prapadyante tāṁs tathaiva bhajāmy aham:* "As one surrenders to Me, I reward him accordingly." As stated by Śrī Caitanya Mahāprabhu, *jīvera 'svarūpa' haya—kṛṣṇera 'nitya-dāsa':* every living being is an eternal servant of Kṛṣṇa. According to the service the living entity renders, he automatically receives benedictions from Kṛṣṇa, who does not make distinctions, thinking, "Here is a person in an intimate relationship with Me, and here is a person I dislike." Kṛṣṇa advises everyone to surrender to Him (*sarva-dharmān parityajya mām ekaṁ śaraṇaṁ vraja*). One's relationship with the Supreme Lord is in proportion to that surrender and the service one renders unto the Lord. Thus throughout the entire world the higher or lower positions of the living entities are selected by the living entities themselves. If one is inclined to dictate that the Lord grant something, one receives benedictions according to his desires. If one wants to be elevated to the higher planetary systems, the heavenly planets, he can be promoted to the place he desires, and if one wants to remain a hog or a pig on earth, the Lord fulfills that desire also. Therefore, one's position is determined by one's desires; the Lord is not responsible for the higher or lower grades of our existence. This is further explained quite definitely in *Bhagavad-gītā* (9.25) by the Lord Himself:

yānti deva-vratā devān
pitṝn yānti pitṛ-vratāḥ
bhūtāni yānti bhūtejyā
yānti mad-yājino 'pi mām

Some people want to be promoted to the heavenly planets, some want to be promoted to Pitṛloka, and some want to remain on earth, but if one is interested in returning home, back to Godhead, he can be promoted there also. According to the demands of a particular devotee, he receives a result by the grace of the Lord. The Lord does not discriminate, thinking, "Here is a person favorable to Me, and here is a person who is not favorable." Rather, He fulfills the desires of everyone. Therefore the *śāstras* enjoin:

akāmaḥ sarva-kāmo vā
mokṣa-kāma udāra-dhīḥ
tīvreṇa bhakti-yogena
yajeta puruṣaṁ param

"Whether one is without desire [the condition of the devotees], or is desirous of all fruitive results, or is after liberation, one should with all efforts try to worship the Supreme Personality of Godhead for complete perfection, culminating in Kṛṣṇa consciousness." (*Bhāg.* 2.3.10) According to one's position, whether as a devotee, a *karmī* or a *jñānī*, whatever one wants one can get if one fully engages in the service of the Lord.

TEXT 28

एवं जनं निपतितं प्रभवाहिकूपे
कामाभिकाममनु यः प्रपतन्प्रसङ्गात्।

कृत्वात्मसात् सुरर्षिणा भगवन् गृहीतः
सोऽहं कथं नु विसृजे तव भृत्यसेवाम् ॥ २८ ॥

evaṁ janaṁ nipatitaṁ prabhavāhi-kūpe
kāmābhikāmam anu yaḥ prapatan prasaṅgāt
kṛtvātmasāt surarṣiṇā bhagavan gṛhītaḥ
so 'haṁ kathaṁ nu visṛje tava bhṛtya-sevām

evam—thus; *janam*—people in general; *nipatitam*—fallen; *prabhava*—of material existence; *ahi-kūpe*—in a blind well full of snakes; *kāma-abhikāmam*—desiring the sense objects; *anu*—following; *yaḥ*—the person who; *prapatan*—falling down (in this condition); *prasaṅgāt*—because of bad association or increased association with material desires; *kṛtvā ātmasāt*—causing me (to acquire spiritual qualities like himself, Śrī Nārada); *sura-ṛṣiṇā*—by the great saintly person (Nārada); *bhagavan*—O my Lord; *gṛhītaḥ*—accepted; *saḥ*—that person; *aham*—I; *katham*—how; *nu*—indeed; *visṛje*—can give up; *tava*—Your; *bhṛtya-sevām*—the service of Your pure devotee.

TRANSLATION

My dear Lord, O Supreme Personality of Godhead, because of my association with material desires, one after another, I was gradually falling into a blind well full of snakes, following the general populace. But Your servant Nārada Muni kindly accepted me as his disciple and instructed me how to achieve this transcendental position. Therefore, my first duty is to serve him. How could I leave his service?

PURPORT

As will be seen in later verses, even though Prahlāda Mahārāja was directly offered all the benedictions he might have desired, he refused to accept such offerings from the Supreme Personality of Godhead. On the contrary, he asked the Lord to engage him in the service of His servant Nārada Muni. This is the symptom of a pure devotee. One should serve the spiritual master first. It is not that one should bypass the spiritual master and desire to serve the Supreme Lord. This is not the principle for a Vaiṣṇava. Narottama dāsa Ṭhākura says:

tāṅdera caraṇa sevi bhakta-sane vāsa
janame janame haya, ei abhilāṣa

One should not be anxious to offer direct service to the Lord. Śrī Caitanya Mahāprabhu advised that one become a servant of the servant of the servant of the Lord (*gopī-bhartuḥ pada-kamalayor dāsa-dāsānudāsaḥ*). This is the process for approaching the Supreme Lord. The first service should be rendered to the spiritual master so that by his mercy one can approach the Supreme Personality of Godhead to render service. While teaching Rūpa Gosvāmī, Śrī Caitanya Mahāprabhu said, *guru-kṛṣṇa-prasāde pāya bhakti-latā-bīja:* one can achieve the seed of devotional service by the mercy of the *guru,* the spiritual master, and then by the mercy of Kṛṣṇa. This is the secret of success. First one should try to please the spiritual master, and then one should attempt to please the Supreme Personality of Godhead. Viśvanātha Cakravartī Ṭhākura also says, *yasya prasādād bhagavat-prasādo.* One should not attempt to please the Supreme Personality of Godhead by concoction. One must first be prepared to serve the spiritual master, and when one is qualified he is automatically offered the platform of direct service to the Lord. Therefore Prahlāda Mahārāja proposed that he engage in the service of Nārada Muni. He never proposed that he engage directly in the service of the Lord. This is the right conclusion. Therefore he said, *so 'haṁ kathaṁ nu visṛje tava bhṛtya-sevām:* "How can I give up the service of my spiritual master, who has favored me in such a way that I am now able to see You face to face?" Prahlāda Mahārāja prayed to the Lord that he might continue to engage in the service of his spiritual master, Nārada Muni.

TEXT 29

मत्प्राणरक्षणमनन्त पितुर्वधश्च
मन्ये स्वभृत्यऋषिवाक्यमृतं विधातुम् ।
खड्गं प्रगृह्य यदवोचदसद्विधित्सु-
स्त्वामीश्वरो मदपरोऽवतु कं हरामि ॥२९॥

mat-prāṇa-rakṣaṇam ananta pitur vadhaś ca
manye sva-bhṛtya-ṛṣi-vākyam ṛtaṁ vidhātum

khaḍgaṁ pragṛhya yad avocad asad-vidhitsus
tvām īśvaro mad-aparo 'vatu kaṁ harāmi

mat-prāṇa-rakṣaṇam—saving my life; *ananta*—O unlimited one, reservoir of unlimited transcendental qualities; *pituḥ*—of my father; *vadhaḥ ca*—and killing; *manye*—I consider; *sva-bhṛtya*—of Your unalloyed servants; *ṛṣi-vākyam*—and the words of the great saint Nārada; *ṛtam*—true; *vidhātum*—to prove; *khaḍgam*—sword; *pragṛhya*—taking in hand; *yat*—since; *avocat*—my father said; *asat-vidhitsuḥ*—desiring to act very impiously; *tvām*—You; *īśvaraḥ*—any supreme controller; *mat-aparaḥ*—other than me; *avatu*—let him save; *kam*—your head; *harāmi*—I shall now separate.

TRANSLATION

My Lord, O unlimited reservoir of transcendental qualities, You have killed my father, Hiraṇyakaśipu, and saved me from his sword. He had said very angrily, "If there is any supreme controller other than me, let Him save you. I shall now sever your head from your body." Therefore I think that both in saving me and in killing him, You have acted just to prove true the words of Your devotee. There is no other cause.

PURPORT

In *Bhagavad-gītā* (9.29) the Lord says:

samo 'haṁ sarva-bhūteṣu
na me dveṣyo 'sti na priyaḥ
ye bhajanti tu māṁ bhaktyā
mayi te teṣu cāpy aham

The Supreme Personality of Godhead is undoubtedly equal to everyone. He has no friend and no enemy, but as one desires benefits from the Lord, the Lord is very pleased to award them. The lower and higher positions of different living entities are due to their desires, for the Lord, being equal to all, fulfills everyone's desires. The killing of Hiraṇyakaśipu and saving of Prahlāda Mahārāja also strictly followed this law of the supreme controller's activities. When Prahlāda's mother,

Hiraṇyakaśipu's wife, Kayādhu, was under the protection of Nārada, she prayed for the protection of her son from the enemy, and Nārada Muni gave assurance that Prahlāda Mahārāja would always be saved from the enemy's hands. Thus when Hiraṇyakaśipu was going to kill Prahlāda Mahārāja, the Lord saved Prahlāda to fulfill His promise in *Bhagavad-gītā* (*kaunteya pratijānīhi na me bhaktaḥ praṇaśyati*) and to prove true the words of Nārada. The Lord can fulfill many purposes through one action. Thus the killing of Hiraṇyakaśipu and the saving of Prahlāda were enacted simultaneously to prove the truthfulness of the Lord's devotee and the fidelity of the Lord Himself to His own purpose. The Lord acts only to satisfy the desires of His devotees; otherwise He has nothing to do. As confirmed in the Vedic language, *na tasya kāryaṁ karaṇaṁ ca vidyate:* the Lord has nothing to do personally, for everything is done through His different potencies (*parāsya śaktir vividhaiva śrūyate*). The Lord has multifarious energies, through which everything is done. Thus when He personally does something, it is only to satisfy His devotee. The Lord is known as *bhakta-vatsala* because He very much favors His devoted servant.

TEXT 30

एकस्त्वमेव जगदेतममुष्य यत् त्व-
माद्यन्तयोः पृथगवस्यसि मध्यतश्च ।
सृष्ट्वा गुणव्यतिकरं निजमाययेदं
नानेव तैरवसितस्तदनुप्रविष्टः ॥३०॥

ekas tvam eva jagad etam amuṣya yat tvam
ādy-antayoḥ pṛthag avasyasi madhyataś ca
sṛṣṭvā guṇa-vyatikaraṁ nija-māyayedaṁ
nāneva tair avasitas tad anupraviṣṭaḥ

ekaḥ—one; *tvam*—You; *eva*—only; *jagat*—the cosmic manifestation; *etam*—this; *amuṣya*—of that (the whole universe); *yat*—since; *tvam*—You; *ādi*—in the beginning; *antayoḥ*—at the end; *pṛthak*—separately; *avasyasi*—exist (as the cause); *madhyataḥ ca*—also in the middle (the duration between the beginning and end); *sṛṣṭvā*—creating; *guṇa-vyatikaram*—the transformation of the three modes of material nature;

nija-māyayā—by Your own external energy; *idam*—this; *nānā iva*—like many varieties; *taiḥ*—by them (the modes); *avasitaḥ*—experienced; *tat*—that; *anupraviṣṭaḥ*—entering into.

TRANSLATION

My dear Lord, You alone manifest Yourself as the entire cosmic manifestation, for You existed before the creation, You exist after the annihilation, and You are the maintainer between the beginning and the end. All this is done by Your external energy through actions and reactions of the three modes of material nature. Therefore whatever exists—externally and internally—is You alone.

PURPORT

As stated in the *Brahma-saṁhitā* (5.35):

eko 'py asau racayituṁ jagad-aṇḍa-koṭiṁ
yac-chaktir asti jagad-aṇḍa-cayā yad-antaḥ
aṇḍāntara-stha-paramāṇu-cayāntara-sthaṁ
govindam ādi-puruṣaṁ tam ahaṁ bhajāmi

"I worship the Personality of Godhead, Govinda, who, by one of His plenary portions, enters the existence of every universe and every atomic particle and thus unlimitedly manifests His infinite energy all over the material creation." To create this cosmic manifestation, Govinda, the Supreme Personality of Godhead, expands His external energy and thus enters everything in the universe, including the atomic particles. In this way He exists in the entire cosmic manifestation. Therefore the activities of the Supreme Personality of Godhead in maintaining His devotees are transcendental, not material. He exists in everything as the cause and effect, yet He is separate, existing beyond this cosmic manifestation. This is also confirmed in *Bhagavad-gītā* (9.4):

mayā tatam idaṁ sarvaṁ
jagad avyakta-mūrtinā
mat-sthāni sarva-bhūtāni
na cāhaṁ teṣv avasthitaḥ

The entire cosmic manifestation is but an expansion of the Lord's energy; everything rests in Him, yet He exists separately, beyond creation, maintenance and annihilation. The varieties of creation are performed by His external energy. Because the energy and energetic are one, everything is one (*sarvaṁ khalv idaṁ brahma*). Therefore without Kṛṣṇa, the Parabrahman, nothing can exist. The difference between the material and spiritual worlds is that His external energy is manifested in the material world whereas His spiritual energy exists in the spiritual world. Both energies, however, belong to the Supreme Lord, and therefore in a higher sense there is no exhibition of material energy because everything is spiritual energy. The energy in which the Lord's all-pervasiveness is not realized is called material. Otherwise, everything is spiritual. Therefore Prahlāda prays, *ekas tvam eva jagad etam:* "You are everything."

TEXT 31

त्वं वा इदं सदसदीश भवांस्ततोऽन्यो
मायाा यदात्मपरबुद्धिरियं ह्यपार्था ।
यद् यस्य जन्म निधनं स्थितिरीक्षणं च
तद् वैतदेव वसुकालवदष्टितर्वोः ॥३१॥

tvaṁ vā idaṁ sadasad īśa bhavāṁs tato 'nyo
māyā yad ātma-para-buddhir iyaṁ hy apārthā
yad yasya janma nidhanaṁ sthitir īkṣaṇaṁ ca
tad vaitad eva vasukālavad aṣṭi-tarvoḥ

tvam—You; *vā*—either; *idam*—the whole universe; *sat-asat*—consisting of cause and effect (You are the cause, and Your energy is the effect); *īśa*—O my Lord, the supreme controller; *bhavān*—Yourself; *tataḥ*—from the universe; *anyaḥ*—separately situated (the creation is made by the Lord, yet He remains separate from the creation); *māyā*—the energy that appears as a separate creation; *yat*—of which; *ātma-para-buddhiḥ*—the conception of one's own and another's; *iyam*—this; *hi*—indeed; *apārthā*—has no meaning (everything is Your Lordship, and therefore there is no hope for understanding "my" and "your"); *yat*—the substance from which; *yasya*—of which; *janma*—creation;

nidhanam—annihilation; *sthitiḥ*—maintenance; *īkṣaṇam*—manifestation; *ca*—and; *tat*—that; *vā*—or; *etat*—this; *eva*—certainly; *vasukāla-vat*—like the quality of being the earth and, beyond that, the subtle element of the earth (smell); *aṣṭi-tarvoḥ*—the seed (the cause) and the tree (the effect of the cause).

TRANSLATION

My dear Lord, O Supreme Personality of Godhead, the entire cosmic creation is caused by You, and the cosmic manifestation is an effect of Your energy. Although the entire cosmos is but You alone, You keep Yourself aloof from it. The conception of "mine and yours," is certainly a type of illusion [māyā] because everything is an emanation from You and is therefore not different from You. Indeed, the cosmic manifestation is nondifferent from You, and the annihilation is also caused by You. This relationship between Your Lordship and the cosmos is illustrated by the example of the seed and the tree, or the subtle cause and the gross manifestation.

PURPORT

In *Bhagavad-gītā* (7.10) the Lord says:

bījaṁ māṁ sarva-bhūtānāṁ
viddhi pārtha sanātanam

"O son of Pṛthā, know that I am the original seed of all existences." In the Vedic literature it is said, *īśāvāsyam idaṁ sarvam, yato vā imāni bhūtāni jāyante* and *sarvaṁ khalv idaṁ brahma.* All this Vedic information indicates that there is only one God and that there is nothing else but Him. The Māyāvādī philosophers explain this in their own way, but the Supreme Personality of Godhead asserts the truth that He is everything and yet is separate from everything. This is the philosophy of Śrī Caitanya Mahāprabhu, which is called *acintya-bhedābheda-tattva.* Everything is one, the Supreme Lord, yet everything is separate from the Lord. This is the understanding of oneness and difference.

The example given in this regard—*vasukālavad aṣṭi-tarvoḥ*—is very easy to understand. Everything exists in time, yet there are different phases of the time factor—present, past and future. Present, past and future are one. Every day we can experience the time factor as morning, noon and evening, and although morning is different from noon, which is different from evening, all of them taken together are one. The time factor is the energy of the Supreme Personality of Godhead, but the Lord is separate from the time factor. Everything is created, maintained and annihilated by time, but the Supreme Lord, the Personality of Godhead, has no beginning and no end. He is *nityaḥ śāśvataḥ*—eternal, permanent. Everything passes through time's phases of present, past and future, yet the Lord is always the same. Thus there is undoubtedly a difference between the Lord and the cosmic manifestation, but actually they are not different. Accepting them to be different is called *avidyā*, ignorance.

True oneness, however, is not equivalent to the conception of the Māyāvādīs. The true understanding is that the differences are manifested by the energy of the Supreme Personality of Godhead. The seed is manifested as a tree, which displays varieties in its trunk, branches, leaves, flowers and fruits. Śrīla Bhaktivinoda Ṭhākura has therefore sung, *keśava tuyā jagata vicitra:* "My dear Lord, Your creation is full of varieties." The varieties are one and at the same time different. This is the philosophy of *acintya-bhedābheda-tattva.* The conclusion given in *Brahma-saṁhitā* is this:

īśvaraḥ paramaḥ kṛṣṇaḥ
sac-cid-ānanda-vigrahaḥ
anādir ādir govindaḥ
sarva-kāraṇa-kāraṇam

"Kṛṣṇa, known as Govinda, is the supreme controller. He has an eternal, blissful, spiritual body. He is the origin of all. He has no other origin, for He is the prime cause of all causes." Because the Lord is the supreme cause, everything is one with Him, but when we consider varieties, we find that one thing is different from another.

We may conclude, therefore, that there is no difference between one thing and another, yet in varieties there are differences. In this regard, Madhvācārya gives an example concerning a tree and a tree in fire. Both trees are the same, but they look different because of the time factor. The time factor is under the control of the Supreme Lord, and therefore the Supreme Lord is different from time. An advanced devotee consequently does not distinguish between happiness and distress. As stated in *Śrīmad-Bhāgavatam* (10.14.8):

tat te 'nukampāṁ susamīkṣamāṇo
bhuñjāna evātma-kṛtaṁ vipākam

When a devotee is in a condition of so-called distress, he considers it a gift or blessing from the Supreme Personality of Godhead. When a devotee is always thus situated in Kṛṣṇa consciousness in any condition of life, he is described as *mukti-pade sa dāya-bhāk*, a perfect candidate for returning home, back to Godhead. The word *dāya-bhāk* means "inheritance." A son inherits the property of his father. Similarly, when the devotee is fully Kṛṣṇa conscious, undisturbed by dualities, he is sure that he will return home, back to Godhead, just as one inherits his father's property.

TEXT 32

न्यस्येदमात्मनि जगद् विलयाम्बुमध्ये
शेषेत्मना निजसुखानुभवो निरीहः।
योगेन मीलितदृगात्मनिपीतनिद्र-
स्तुर्ये स्थितो न तु तमो न गुणांश्च युङ्क्षे॥३२॥

nyasyedam ātmani jagad vilayāmbu-madhye
śeṣetmanā nija-sukhānubhavo nirīhaḥ
yogena mīlita-dṛg-ātma-nipīta-nidras
turye sthito na tu tamo na guṇāṁś ca yuṅkṣe

nyasya—throwing; *idam*—this; *ātmani*—in Your own self; *jagat*—cosmic manifestation created by You; *vilaya-ambu-madhye*—in the Causal Ocean, in which everything is preserved in a state of reserved energy; *śeṣe*—You act as if sleeping; *ātmanā*—by Yourself; *nija*—Your own personal; *sukha-anubhavaḥ*—experiencing the state of spiritual bliss; *nirīhaḥ*—appearing to be doing nothing; *yogena*—by the mystic power; *mīlita-dṛk*—the eyes appearing closed; *ātma*—by a manifestation of Yourself; *nipīta*—prevented; *nidraḥ*—whose sleeping; *turye*—in the transcendental stage; *sthitaḥ*—keeping (Yourself); *na*—not; *tu*—but; *tamaḥ*—the material condition of sleeping; *na*—nor; *guṇān*—the material modes; *ca*—and; *yuṅkṣe*—do You engage Yourself in.

TRANSLATION

O my Lord, O Supreme Personality of Godhead, after the annihilation the creative energy is kept in You, who appear to sleep with half-closed eyes. Actually, however, You do not sleep like an ordinary human being, for You are always in a transcendental stage, beyond the creation of the material world, and You always feel transcendental bliss. As Kāraṇodakaśāyī Viṣṇu, You thus remain in Your transcendental status, not touching material objects. Although You appear to sleep, this sleeping is distinct from sleeping in ignorance.

PURPORT

As explained very clearly in the *Brahma-saṁhitā* (5.47):

yaḥ kāraṇārṇava-jale bhajati sma yoga-
nidrām ananta-jagad-aṇḍa-sa-roma-kūpaḥ
ādhāra-śaktim avalambya parāṁ sva-mūrtiṁ
govindam ādi-puruṣaṁ tam ahaṁ bhajāmi

"I worship the primeval Lord Govinda, who lies down in the Causal Ocean in His plenary portion as Mahā-Viṣṇu, with all the universes generating from the pores of hair on His transcendental body, and who accepts the mystic slumber of eternity." The *ādi-puruṣa*, the original Supreme Personality of Godhead—Kṛṣṇa, Govinda—expands Himself as Mahā-Viṣṇu. After the annihilation of this cosmic manifestation, He keeps Himself in transcendental bliss. The word *yoga-nidrām* is used in reference to the Supreme Personality of Godhead. One should understand that this *nidrā*, or sleep, is not like our *nidrā* in the mode of ignorance. The Lord is always situated in transcendence. He is *sac-cid-*

ānanda—eternally in bliss—and thus He is not disturbed by sleep like ordinary human beings. It should be understood that the Supreme Personality of Godhead is in transcendental bliss in all stages. Śrīla Madhvācārya concisely states that the Lord is *turya-sthitaḥ*, always situated in transcendence. In transcendence there is no such thing as *jāgaraṇa-nidrā-suṣupti*—wakefulness, sleep and deep sleep.

The practice of *yoga* is similar to the *yoga-nidrā* of Mahā-Viṣṇu. *Yogīs* are advised to keep their eyes half closed, but this state is not at all one of sleep, although imitation *yogīs*, especially in the modern age, manifest their so-called *yoga* by sleeping. In the *śāstra*, *yoga* is described as *dhyānāvasthita*, a state of full meditation, but this is meditation upon the Supreme Personality of Godhead. *Dhyānāvasthita-tad-gatena manasā:* the mind should always be situated at the lotus feet of the Lord. *Yoga* practice does not mean sleeping. The mind should always be actively fixed at the lotus feet of the Lord. Then one's practice of *yoga* will be successful.

TEXT 33

तस्यैव ते वपुरिदं निजकालशक्त्या
सञ्चोदितप्रकृतिधर्मण आत्मगूढम् ।
अम्भस्यनन्तशयनाद् विरमत्समाधे-
र्नाभेरभूत् स्वकणिकावटवन्महाब्जम्॥३३॥

tasyaiva te vapur idaṁ nija-kāla-śaktyā
sañcodita-prakṛti-dharmaṇa ātma-gūḍham
ambhasy ananta-śayanād viramat-samādher
nābher abhūt sva-kaṇikā-vaṭavan-mahābjam

tasya—of that Supreme Personality of Godhead; *eva*—certainly; *te*—of You; *vapuḥ*—the cosmic body; *idam*—this (universe); *nija-kāla-śaktyā*—by the potent time factor; *sañcodita*—agitated; *prakṛti-dharmaṇaḥ*—of Him, by whom the three *guṇas*, or qualities of material nature; *ātma-gūḍham*—dormant in Yourself; *ambhasi*—in the water known as the Causal Ocean; *ananta-śayanāt*—from the bed known as Ananta (another feature of Yourself); *viramat-samādheḥ*—having awakened from the *samādhi* (yogic trance); *nābheḥ*—from the navel; *abhūt*—appeared; *sva-kaṇikā*—from the seed; *vaṭa-vat*—like the great banyan tree; *mahā-abjam*—the great lotus of the worlds (has similarly grown).

TRANSLATION

This cosmic manifestation, the material world, is also Your body. This total lump of matter is agitated by Your potent energy known as kāla-śakti, and thus the three modes of material nature are manifested. You awaken from the bed of Śeṣa, Ananta, and from Your navel a small transcendental seed is generated. It is from this seed that the lotus flower of the gigantic universe is manifested, exactly as a banyan tree grows from a small seed.

PURPORT

The three different forms of Mahā-Viṣṇu—namely Kāraṇodakaśāyī Viṣṇu, Garbhodakaśāyī Viṣṇu and Kṣīrodakaśāyī Viṣṇu, who are the origin of creation and maintenance—are gradually being described. From Mahā-Viṣṇu, Garbhodakaśāyī Viṣṇu is generated, and from Garbhodakaśāyī Viṣṇu, Kṣīrodakaśāyī Viṣṇu gradually expands. Thus Mahā-Viṣṇu is the original cause of Garbhodakaśāyī Viṣṇu, and from Garbhodakaśāyī Viṣṇu comes the lotus flower from which Lord Brahmā is manifested. Thus the original cause of everything is Viṣṇu, and consequently the cosmic manifestation is not different from Viṣṇu. This is confirmed in *Bhagavad-gītā* (10.8), wherein Kṛṣṇa says, *ahaṁ sarvasya prabhavo mattaḥ sarvaṁ pravartate:* "I am the source of all spiritual and material worlds. Everything emanates from Me." Garbhodakaśāyī Viṣṇu is an expansion of Kāraṇodakaśāyī Viṣṇu, who is an expansion of Saṅkarṣaṇa. In this way, Kṛṣṇa is ultimately the cause of all causes (*sarva-kāraṇa-kāraṇam*). The conclusion is that both the material world and spiritual world are considered to be the body of the Supreme Lord. We can understand that the material body is caused by the spiritual body and is therefore an expansion of the spiritual body. Thus when one takes up spiritual activities, one's entire material body is spiritualized. Similarly, in this material world, when the Kṛṣṇa consciousness movement expands, the entire material world becomes spiritualized. As long as we do not realize this, we live in the material world, but when we are fully Kṛṣṇa conscious we live not in the material world but in the spiritual world.

TEXT 34

तत्सम्भवः कविरतोऽन्यदपश्यमान-
स्त्वां बीजमात्मनि ततं स बहिर्विचिन्त्य ।
नाविन्ददब्दशतमप्सु निमज्जमानो
जातेऽङ्कुरे कथमुहोपलभेत बीजम् ॥३४॥

tat-sambhavaḥ kavir ato 'nyad apaśyamānas
tvāṁ bījam ātmani tataṁ sa bahir vicintya
nāvindad abda-śatam apsu nimajjamāno
jāte 'ṅkure katham uhopalabheta bījam

tat-sambhavaḥ—who was generated from that lotus flower; *kaviḥ*—he who can understand the subtle cause of creation (Lord Brahmā); *ataḥ*—from that (lotus); *anyat*—anything else; *apaśyamānaḥ*—not able to see; *tvām*—Your Lordship; *bījam*—the cause of the lotus; *ātmani*—in himself; *tatam*—expanded; *saḥ*—he (Lord Brahmā); *bahiḥ vicintya*—considering to be external; *na*—not; *avindat*—understood (You); *abda-śatam*—for a hundred years according to the demigods;* *apsu*—in the water; *nimajjamānaḥ*—diving; *jāte aṅkure*—when the seed fructifies and is manifested as a creeper; *katham*—how; *uha*—O my Lord; *upalabheta*—one can perceive; *bījam*—the seed that has already fructified.

TRANSLATION

From that great lotus flower, Brahmā was generated, but Brahmā certainly could see nothing but the lotus. Therefore, thinking You to be outside, Lord Brahmā dove into the water and attempted to find the source of the lotus for one hundred years. He could find no trace of You, however, for when a seed fructifies, the original seed cannot be seen.

---

*One day for the demigods equals six of our months.

PURPORT

This is the description of the cosmic manifestation. The development of the cosmic manifestation is like the fructification of a seed. When cotton is transformed into thread, the cotton is no longer visible, and when the thread is woven into cloth, the thread is no longer visible. Similarly, it is perfectly correct that when the seed that had generated from the navel of Garbhodakaśāyī Viṣṇu became manifested as the cosmic creation, one could no longer understand where the cause of the cosmic manifestation is. Modern scientists have tried to explain the origin of creation by a chunk theory, but no one can explain how such a chunk might have burst. The Vedic literature, however, explains clearly that the total material energy was agitated by the three modes of material nature because of the glance of the Supreme Lord. In other words, in terms of the chunk theory, the bursting of the chunk was caused by the Supreme Personality of Godhead. Thus one must accept the supreme cause, Lord Viṣṇu, as the cause of all causes.

TEXT 35

स त्वात्मयोनिरतिविस्मित आश्रितोऽब्जं
कालेन तीव्रतपसा परिशुद्धभावः ।
त्वामात्मनीश भुवि गन्धमिवातिसूक्ष्मं
भूतेन्द्रियाशयमये विततं ददर्श ॥३५॥

sa tv ātma-yonir ativismita āśrito 'bjaṁ
kālena tīvra-tapasā pariśuddha-bhāvaḥ
tvām ātmanīśa bhuvi gandham ivātisūkṣmaṁ
bhūtendriyāśayamaye vitataṁ dadarśa

saḥ—he (Lord Brahmā); *tu*—but; *ātma-yoniḥ*—who is born without a mother (directly begotten by the father, Lord Viṣṇu); *ati-vismitaḥ*—very much surprised (not finding the source of his birth); *āśritaḥ*—situated on; *abjam*—the lotus; *kālena*—in due course of time; *tīvra-tapasā*—by severe austerities; *pariśuddha-bhāvaḥ*—being completely purified; *tvām*—You; *ātmani*—in his body and existence; *īśa*—O my Lord; *bhuvi*—within the earth; *gandham*—aroma; *iva*—like; *ati-*

sūkṣmam—very subtle; *bhūta-indriya*—composed of elements and senses; *āśaya-maye*—and that filled with desires (the mind); *vitatam*—spread out; *dadarśa*—found.

TRANSLATION

Lord Brahmā, who is celebrated as ātma-yoni, having been born without a mother, was struck with wonder. Thus he took shelter of the lotus flower, and when he had been purified after undergoing severe austerities for many hundreds of years, he could see that the cause of all causes, the Supreme Personality of Godhead, was spread throughout his own body and senses, just as aroma, although very subtle, is perceived in the earth.

PURPORT

Here the statement of self-realization *ahaṁ brahmāsmi,* which is interpreted by the Māyāvāda philosophy to mean "I am the Supreme Lord," is explained. The Supreme Lord is the original seed of everything (*janmādy asya yataḥ. ahaṁ sarvasya prabhavo mattaḥ sarvaṁ pravartate*). Thus the Supreme Lord extends everywhere, even throughout our bodies, because our bodies are made of material energy, which is the Lord's separated energy. One should realize that since the Supreme Lord spreads throughout one's body and since the individual soul is a part of the Supreme Lord, everything is Brahman (*sarvaṁ khalv idaṁ brahma*). This realization was achieved by Lord Brahmā after he was purified, and it is possible for everyone. When one is completely in knowledge of *ahaṁ brahmāsmi,* he thinks, "I am part of the Supreme Lord, my body is made of His material energy, and therefore I have no separate existence. Yet although the Supreme Lord is spread everywhere, He is different from me." This is the philosophy of *acintya-bhedābheda-tattva.* An example given in this regard is that of the aroma within the earth. In the earth there are aromas and colors, but one cannot see them. Actually we find that when flowers grow from the earth, they appear with different colors and aromas, which they have certainly gathered from the earth, although in the earth we cannot see them. Similarly, the Supreme Lord, by His different energies, spreads throughout one's body and soul, although we cannot see Him. An intelligent man, however, can see the Supreme Lord existing everywhere. *Aṇḍāntara-stha-paramāṇu-*

cayāntara-stham: the Lord is within the universe and within the atom by His different energies. This is the real vision of the Supreme Lord for the intelligent man. Brahmā, the first created being, became the most intelligent person by his *tapasya,* austerity, and thus he came to this realization. We must therefore take all knowledge from Brahmā, who became perfect by his *tapasya.*

TEXT 36

एवं सहस्रवदनाङ्घ्रिशिरःकरोरु-
नासाद्यकर्णनयनाभरणायुधाढ्यम् ।
मायामयं सदुपलक्षितसन्निवेशं
दृष्ट्वा महापुरुषमाप मुदं विरिञ्चः ॥३६॥

evaṁ sahasra-vadanāṅghri-śiraḥ-karoru-
nāsādya-karṇa-nayanābharaṇāyudhāḍhyam
māyāmayaṁ sad-upalakṣita-sanniveśaṁ
dṛṣṭvā mahā-puruṣam āpa mudaṁ viriñcaḥ

evam—in this way; *sahasra*—thousands and thousands; *vadana*—faces; *aṅghri*—feet; *śiraḥ*—heads; *kara*—hands; *uru*—thighs; *nāsa-ādya*—noses, etc.; *karṇa*—ears; *nayana*—eyes; *ābharaṇa*—varieties of ornaments; *āyudha*—varieties of weapons; *āḍhyam*—endowed with; *māyā-mayam*—all demonstrated by unlimited potency; *sat-upalakṣita*—appearing in different symptoms; *sanniveśam*—combined together; *dṛṣṭvā*—seeing; *mahā-puruṣam*—the Supreme Personality of Godhead; *āpa*—achieved; *mudam*—transcendental bliss; *viriñcaḥ*—Lord Brahmā.

TRANSLATION

Lord Brahmā could then see You possessing thousands and thousands of faces, feet, heads, hands, thighs, noses, ears and eyes. You were very nicely dressed, being decorated and bedecked with varieties of ornaments and weapons. Seeing You in the form of Lord Viṣṇu, Your symptoms and form being transcendental, Your legs extending from the lower planets, Lord Brahmā achieved transcendental bliss.

PURPORT

Lord Brahmā, being completely pure, could see the original form of the Lord as Viṣṇu, having many thousands of faces and forms. This process is called self-realization. Genuine self-realization consists not of perceiving the impersonal effulgence of the Lord, but seeing face to face the transcendental form of the Lord. As distinctly mentioned here, Lord Brahmā saw the Supreme Lord as *mahā-puruṣa*, the Supreme Personality of Godhead. Arjuna also saw Kṛṣṇa in this same way. Therefore he told the Lord, *paraṁ brahma paraṁ dhāma pavitraṁ paramaṁ bhavān puruṣaṁ śāśvataṁ divyam:* "You are the Supreme Brahman, the ultimate, the supreme abode and purifier, the Absolute Truth and the eternal divine person." The Lord is *parama-puruṣa*, the supreme form. *Puruṣaṁ śāśvatam:* He is everlastingly the supreme enjoyer. It is not that the impersonal Brahman assumes a form; on the contrary, the impersonal Brahman effulgence is an emanation from the supreme form of the Lord. Upon being purified, Brahmā could see the supreme form of the Lord. The impersonal Brahman cannot have heads, noses, ears, hands and legs. This is not possible, for these are attributes of the Lord's form.

The word *māyāmayam* means "spiritual knowledge." This is explained by Madhvācārya. *Māyāmayaṁ jñāna-svarūpam.* The word *māyāmayam*, describing the Lord's form, should not be taken to mean illusion. Rather, the Lord's form is factual, and seeing this form is the result of perfect knowledge. This is confirmed in *Bhagavad-gītā: bahūnāṁ janmanām ante jñānavān māṁ prapadyate.* The word *jñānavān* refers to one who is perfectly in knowledge. Such a person can see the Personality of Godhead, and therefore he surrenders unto the Lord. The Lord's being symptomized by a face, nose, ears and so on is eternal. Without such a form, no one can be blissful. The Lord, however, is *sac-cid-ānanda-vigraha*, as stated in the *śāstra* (*īśvaraḥ paramaḥ kṛṣṇaḥ sac-cid-ānanda-vigrahaḥ*). When one is in perfect transcendental bliss, he can see the Lord's supreme form (*vigraha*). In this regard, Śrīla Madhvācārya says:

gandhākhyā devatā yadvat
pṛthivīṁ vyāpya tiṣṭhati
evaṁ vyāptaṁ jagad viṣṇuṁ
brahmātma-sthaṁ dadarśa ha

Lord Brahmā saw that as aromas and colors spread throughout the earth, the Supreme Personality of Godhead pervades the cosmic manifestation in a subtle form.

TEXT 37

तस्मै भवान्हयशिरस्तनुवं हि बिभ्रद्
वेदद्रुहावतिबलौ मधुकैटभाख्यौ ।
हत्वानयच्छ्रुतिगणांश्च रजस्तमश्च
सत्त्वं तव प्रियतमां तनुमामनन्ति ॥३७॥

tasmai bhavān haya-śiras tanuvaṁ hi bibhrad
veda-druhāv atibalau madhu-kaiṭabhākhyau
hatvānayac chruti-gaṇāṁś ca rajas tamaś ca
sattvaṁ tava priyatamāṁ tanum āmananti

tasmai—unto Lord Brahmā; *bhavān*—Your Lordship; *haya-śiraḥ*—having the head and neck of a horse; *tanuvam*—the incarnation; *hi*—indeed; *bibhrat*—accepting; *veda-druhau*—two demons who were against the Vedic principles; *ati-balau*—extremely powerful; *madhu-kaiṭabha-ākhyau*—known as Madhu and Kaiṭabha; *hatvā*—killing; *anayat*—delivered; *śruti-gaṇān*—all the different *Vedas* (*Sāma*, *Yajur*, *Ṛg* and *Atharva*); *ca*—and; *rajaḥ tamaḥ ca*—by representing the modes of passion and ignorance; *sattvam*—pure transcendental goodness; *tava*—Your; *priya-tamām*—most dear; *tanum*—form (as Hayagrīva); *āma-nanti*—they honor.

TRANSLATION

My dear Lord, when You appeared as Hayagrīva, with the head of a horse, You killed two demons known as Madhu and Kaiṭabha, who were full of the modes of passion and ignorance. Then You delivered the Vedic knowledge to Lord Brahmā. For this reason, all the great saints accept Your forms as transcendental, untinged by material qualities.

PURPORT

The Supreme Personality of Godhead in His transcendental form is always ready to give protection to His devotees. As mentioned herein, the

Lord in the form of Hayagrīva killed two demons named Madhu and Kaiṭabha when they attacked Lord Brahmā. Modern demons think that there was no life in the beginning of creation, but from *Śrīmad-Bhāgavatam* we understand that the first living creature created by the Supreme Personality of Godhead was Lord Brahmā, who is full of Vedic understanding. Unfortunately, those entrusted with distributing Vedic knowledge, such as the devotees engaged in spreading Kṛṣṇa consciousness, may sometimes be attacked by demons, but they must rest assured that demoniac attacks will not be able to harm them, for the Lord is always prepared to give them protection. The *Vedas* provide the knowledge by which we can understand the Supreme Personality of Godhead (*vedaiś ca sarvair aham eva vedyaḥ*). The devotees of the Lord are always ready to spread knowledge by which one may understand the Lord through Kṛṣṇa consciousness, but the demons, being unable to understand the Supreme Lord, are full of ignorance and passion. Thus the Lord, whose form is transcendental, is always ready to kill the demons. By culturing the mode of goodness, one can understand the position of the transcendental Lord and how the Lord is always prepared to remove all obstacles on the path of understanding Him.

In summary, whenever the Lord incarnates, He appears in His original transcendental form. As the Lord says in *Bhagavad-gītā* (4.7):

yadā yadā hi dharmasya
glānir bhavati bhārata
abhyutthānam adharmasya
tadātmānaṁ sṛjāmy aham

"Whenever and wherever there is a decline in religious practice, O descendent of Bharata, and a predominant rise of irreligion—at that time I descend Myself." It is simply foolish to think of the Lord as being originally impersonal but accepting a material body when He appears as a personal incarnation. Whenever the Lord appears, He appears in His original transcendental form, which is spiritual and blissful. But unintelligent men, such as the Māyāvādīs, cannot understand the transcendental form of the Lord, and therefore the Lord chastises them by saying, *avajānanti māṁ mūḍhā mānuṣīṁ tanum āśritam:* "Fools deride

Me when I descend in the human form." Whenever the Lord appears, whether as a fish, a tortoise, a hog or any other form, one should understand that He maintains His transcendental position and that His only business, as stated here, is *hatvā*—to kill the demons. The Lord appears in order to protect the devotees and kill the demons (*paritrāṇāya sādhūnāṁ vināśāya ca duṣkṛtām*). Since the demons are always ready to oppose Vedic civilization, they are sure to be killed by the transcendental form of the Lord.

TEXT 38

इत्थं नृतिर्यगृषिदेवझषावतारै-
लोकान् विभावयसि हंसि जगत्प्रतीपान् ।
धर्मं महापुरुष पासि युगानुवृत्तं
छन्नः कलौ यदभवस्त्रियुगोऽथ स त्वम् ॥३८॥

ittham nṛ-tiryag-ṛṣi-deva-jhaṣāvatārair
lokān vibhāvayasi haṁsi jagat pratīpān
dharmaṁ mahā-puruṣa pāsi yugānuvṛttaṁ
channaḥ kalau yad abhavas tri-yugo 'tha sa tvam

ittham—in this way; *nṛ*—like a human being (such as Lord Kṛṣṇa and Lord Rāmacandra); *tiryak*—like animals (such as the boar); *ṛṣi*—as a great saint (Paraśurāma); *deva*—as demigods; *jhaṣa*—as an aquatic (such as the fish and tortoise); *avatāraiḥ*—by such different incarnations; *lokān*—all the different planetary systems; *vibhāvayasi*—You protect; *haṁsi*—You (sometimes) kill; *jagat pratīpān*—persons who have simply created trouble in this world; *dharmam*—the principles of religion; *mahā-puruṣa*—O great personality; *pāsi*—You protect; *yuga-anuvṛttam*—according to the different millenniums; *channaḥ*—covered; *kalau*—in the age of Kali; *yat*—since; *abhavaḥ*—have been (and will be in the future); *tri-yugaḥ*—named Triyuga; *atha*—therefore; *saḥ*—the same personality; *tvam*—You.

TRANSLATION

In this way, my Lord, You appear in various incarnations as a human being, an animal, a great saint, a demigod, a fish or a

tortoise, thus maintaining the entire creation in different planetary systems and killing the demoniac principles. According to the age, O my Lord, You protect the principles of religion. In the age of Kali, however, You do not assert Yourself as the Supreme Personality of Godhead, and therefore You are known as Triyuga, or the Lord who appears in three yugas.

PURPORT

As the Lord appeared just to maintain Lord Brahmā from the attack of Madhu and Kaiṭabha, He also appeared to protect the great devotee Prahlāda Mahārāja. Similarly, Lord Caitanya appeared in order to protect the fallen souls of Kali-yuga. There are four *yugas*, or millenniums—Satya, Tretā, Dvāpara and Kali. In all the *yugas* but Kali-yuga, the Lord appears in various incarnations and asserts Himself as the Supreme Personality of Godhead, but although Lord Śrī Caitanya Mahāprabhu, who appears in Kali-yuga, is the Supreme Personality of Godhead, He never asserted Himself as such. On the contrary, whenever Śrī Caitanya Mahāprabhu was addressed as being as good as Kṛṣṇa, He blocked His ears with His hands, denying His identity with Kṛṣṇa, because He was playing the part of a devotee. Lord Caitanya knew that in Kali-yuga there would be many bogus incarnations pretending to be God, and therefore He avoided asserting Himself as the Supreme Personality of Godhead. Lord Caitanya Mahāprabhu is accepted as the Supreme Personality of Godhead, however, in many Vedic literatures, especially in *Śrīmad-Bhāgavatam* (11.5.32):

kṛṣṇa-varṇaṁ tviṣākṛṣṇaṁ
sāṅgopāṅgāstra-pārṣadam
yajñaiḥ saṅkīrtana-prāyair
yajanti hi sumedhasaḥ

In Kali-yuga, intelligent men worship the Supreme Personality of Godhead in the form of Śrī Caitanya Mahāprabhu, who is always accompanied by His associates such as Nityānanda, Advaita, Gadādhara and Śrīvāsa. The entire Kṛṣṇa consciousness movement is based on the principles of the *saṅkīrtana* movement inaugurated by Śrī Caitanya Mahāprabhu. Therefore one who tries to understand the Supreme Personality of Godhead through the medium of the *saṅkīrtana* movement knows everything perfectly. He is *sumedhas*, a person with substantial intelligence.

TEXT 39

नैतन्मनस्तव कथासु विकुण्ठनाथ
सम्प्रीयते दुरितदुष्टमसाधु तीव्रम् ।
कामातुरं हर्षशोकभयैषणार्तं
तस्मिन्कथं तव गतिं विमृशामि दीनः॥३९॥

naitan manas tava kathāsu vikuṇṭha-nātha
samprīyate durita-duṣṭam asādhu tīvram
kāmāturaṁ harṣa-śoka-bhayaiṣaṇārtaṁ
tasmin kathaṁ tava gatiṁ vimṛśāmi dīnaḥ

na—certainly not; *etat*—this; *manaḥ*—mind; *tava*—Your; *kathāsu*—in transcendental topics; *vikuṇṭha-nātha*—O Lord of Vaikuṇṭha, where there is no anxiety; *samprīyate*—is pacified or interested in; *durita*—by sinful activities; *duṣṭam*—polluted; *asādhu*—dishonest; *tīvram*—very difficult to control; *kāma-āturam*—always full of different desires and lusty propensities; *harṣa-śoka*—sometimes by jubilation and sometimes by distress; *bhaya*—and sometimes by fear; *eṣaṇā*—and by desiring; *ārtam*—distressed; *tasmin*—in that mental status; *katham*—how; *tava*—Your; *gatim*—transcendental activities; *vimṛśāmi*—I shall consider and try to understand; *dīnaḥ*—who am most fallen and poor.

TRANSLATION

My dear Lord of the Vaikuṇṭha planets, where there is no anxiety, my mind is extremely sinful and lusty, being sometimes so-called happy and sometimes so-called distressed. My mind is full of lamentation and fear, and it always seeks more and more money. Thus it has become most polluted and is never satisfied in topics concerning You. I am therefore most fallen and poor. In such a status of life, how shall I be able to discuss Your activities?

PURPORT

Here Prahlāda Mahārāja represents himself as a common man, although he actually has nothing to do with this material world. Prahlāda is always situated in the Vaikuṇṭha planets of the spiritual world, but on behalf of the fallen souls he asks how, when his mind is always disturbed by material things, he can discuss the transcendental position of the Lord. The mind becomes sinful because we are always engaged in sinful activities. Anything not connected with Kṛṣṇa consciousness should be understood to be sinful. Indeed, Kṛṣṇa demands in *Bhagavad-gītā* (18.66):

sarva-dharmān parityajya
mām ekaṁ śaraṇaṁ vraja
ahaṁ tvāṁ sarva-pāpebhyo
mokṣayiṣyāmi mā śucaḥ

"Abandon all varieties of religion and just surrender unto Me. I shall deliver you from all sinful reaction. Do not fear." As soon as one surrenders unto the Supreme Personality of Godhead, Kṛṣṇa, Kṛṣṇa immediately relieves one of the reactions of sinful activities. Therefore one who is not surrendered to the lotus feet of the Lord should be understood to be sinful, foolish, degraded among men and bereft of all real knowledge because of atheistic propensities. This is confirmed in *Bhagavad-gītā* (7.15):

na māṁ duṣkṛtino mūḍhāḥ
pradyante narādhamāḥ
māyayāpahṛta-jñānā
āsuraṁ bhāvam āśritāḥ

Therefore, especially in this age of Kali, the mind must be cleansed, and this is possible only by the chanting of the Hare Kṛṣṇa *mahā-mantra. Ceto-darpaṇa-mārjanam.* In this age, the process of chanting the Hare Kṛṣṇa *mahā-mantra* is the only method by which to cleanse the sinful mind. When the mind is completely cleansed of all sinful reactions, one can then understand his duty in the human form of life. The Kṛṣṇa consciousness movement is meant to educate sinful men so that they may become pious simply by chanting the Hare Kṛṣṇa *mahā-mantra.*

harer nāma harer nāma
harer nāmaiva kevalam
kalau nāsty eva nāsty eva
nāsty eva gatir anyathā

To cleanse the heart so that one may become sober and wise in this age of Kali, there is no value to any method other than the chanting of the Hare Kṛṣṇa *mahā-mantra.* Prahlāda Mahārāja has confirmed this process in previous verses. *Tvad-vīrya-gāyana-mahāmṛta-magna-cittaḥ.* Prahlāda further confirms that if one's mind is always absorbed in thought of Kṛṣṇa, that very qualification will purify one and keep one purified always. To understand the Lord and His activities, one must free his mind from all contamination of the material world, and this one can achieve by simply chanting the Lord's holy name. Thus one becomes free from all material bondage.

TEXT 40

जिह्वैकतोऽच्युत विकर्षति मावितृप्ता
शिश्नोऽन्यतस्त्वगुदरं श्रवणं कुतश्चित् ।
घ्राणोऽन्यतश्चपलदृक् क्व च कर्मशक्ति-
र्बह्व्यः सपत्न्य इव गेहपतिं लुनन्ति ॥४०॥

jihvaikato 'cyuta vikarṣati māvitṛptā
śiśno 'nyatas tvag-udaraṁ śravaṇaṁ kutaścit
ghrāṇo 'nyataś capala-dṛk kva ca karma-śaktir
bahvyaḥ sapatnya iva geha-patiṁ lunanti

jihvā—the tongue; *ekataḥ*—to one side; *acyuta*—O my infallible Lord; *vikarṣati*—attracts; *mā*—me; *avitṛptā*—not being satisfied; *śiśnaḥ*—the genitals; *anyataḥ*—to another side; *tvak*—the skin (for touching a soft thing); *udaram*—the belly (for various types of food); *śravaṇam*—the ear (for hearing some sweet music); *kutaścit*—to some other side; *ghrāṇaḥ*—the nose (for smelling); *anyataḥ*—to still another side; *capala-dṛk*—the restless eyesight; *kva ca*—somewhere; *karma-śaktiḥ*—the active senses; *bahvyaḥ*—many; *sa-patnyaḥ*—co-wives; *iva*—like; *geha-patim*—a householder; *lunanti*—annihilate.

TRANSLATION

My dear Lord, O infallible one, my position is like that of a person who has many wives, all trying to attract him in their own way. For example, the tongue is attracted to palatable dishes, the genitals to sex with an attractive woman, and the sense of touch to contact with soft things. The belly, although filled, still wants to eat more, and the ear, not attempting to hear about You, is generally attracted to cinema songs. The sense of smell is attracted to yet another side, the restless eyes are attracted to scenes of sense gratification, and the active senses are attracted elsewhere. In this way I am certainly embarrassed.

PURPORT

The human form of life is meant for God realization, but this process, which begins with *śravaṇaṁ kīrtanaṁ viṣṇoḥ*—hearing and chanting of the holy name of the Lord—is disturbed as long as our senses are materially attracted. Therefore devotional service means purifying the senses. In the conditioned state our senses are covered by material sense gratification, and as long as one is not trained in purifying the senses, one cannot become a devotee. In our Kṛṣṇa consciousness movement, therefore, we advise from the very beginning that one restrict the activities of the senses, especially the tongue, which is described by Śrīla Bhaktivinoda Ṭhākura as most greedy and unconquerable. To stop this attraction of the tongue, one is authoritatively advised not to accept meat or similar uneatable things nor to allow the tongue to hanker to drink or smoke. Even the drinking of tea and coffee is not permitted. Similarly, the genitals must be restricted from illicit sex. Without such restraint of the senses, one cannot make advancement in Kṛṣṇa consciousness. The only method of controlling the senses is to chant and hear the holy name of the Lord; otherwise, one will always be disturbed, as a householder with more than one wife would be disturbed by them for sense gratification.

TEXT 41

एवं स्वकर्मपतितं भववैतरण्या-
मन्योन्यजन्ममरणाशनभीतभीतम् ।

पश्यञ्जनं स्वपरविग्रहवैरमैत्रं
हन्तेति पारचर पीपृहि मूढमद्य ॥४१॥

evaṁ sva-karma-patitaṁ bhava-vaitaraṇyām
anyonya-janma-maraṇāśana-bhīta-bhītam
paśyañ janaṁ sva-para-vigraha-vaira-maitraṁ
hanteti pāracara pīpṛhi mūḍham adya

evam—in this way; *sva-karma-patitam*—fallen because of the reactions of one's own material activities; *bhava*—compared to the world of nescience (birth, death, old age and disease); *vaitaraṇyām*—in the river known as Vaitaraṇī (which lies in front of the doorway of Yamarāja, the superintendant of death); *anyaḥ anya*—one after another; *janma*—birth; *maraṇa*—death; *āśana*—different types of eating; *bhīta-bhītam*—being exceedingly afraid; *paśyan*—seeing; *janam*—the living entity; *sva*—one's own; *para*—of others; *vigraha*—in the body; *vaira-maitram*—considering friendship and enmity; *hanta*—alas; *iti*—in this way; *pāracara*—O You, who are on the other side of the river of death; *pīpṛhi*—kindly save us all (from this dangerous condition); *mūḍham*—we are all foolish, bereft of spiritual knowledge; *adya*—today (because You are personally present here).

TRANSLATION

My dear Lord, You are always transcendentally situated on the other side of the river of death, but because of the reactions of our own activities, we are suffering on this side. Indeed, we have fallen into this river and are repeatedly suffering the pains of birth and death and eating horrible things. Now kindly look upon us—not only upon me but also upon all others who are suffering—and by Your causeless mercy and compassion, deliver us and maintain us.

PURPORT

Prahlāda Mahārāja, a pure Vaiṣṇava, prays to the Lord not only for himself but for all other suffering living entities. There are two classes of Vaiṣṇavas—the *bhajanānandīs* and *goṣṭhy-ānandīs*. The *bhajanānandīs* worship the Lord only for their own personal benefit, but the *goṣṭhy-ānandīs* try to elevate all others to Kṛṣṇa consciousness so that they may be saved. Fools who cannot perceive repeated birth and death and the other miseries of materialistic life cannot be sure of what will happen to them in their next birth. Indeed, these foolish, materially contaminated rascals have manufactured an irresponsible way of life that does not consider the next life. They do not know that according to one's own activities, one receives a body selected from 8,400,000 species. These rascals have been described in *Bhagavad-gītā* as *duṣkṛtino mūḍhāḥ.* Nondevotees, those who are not Kṛṣṇa conscious, must engage in sinful activities, and therefore they are *mūḍhas*—fools and rascals. They are such fools that they do not know what will happen to them in their next life. Although they see varieties of living creatures eating abominable things—pigs eating stool, crocodiles eating all kinds of flesh, and so on—they do not realize that they themselves, because of their practice of eating all kinds of nonsense in this life, will be destined to eat the most abominable things in their next life. A Vaiṣṇava is always afraid of such an abominable life, and to free himself from such horrible conditions, he engages himself in the devotional service of the Lord. The Lord is compassionate to them, and therefore He appears for their benefit.

yadā yadā hi dharmasya
glānir bhavati bhārata
abhyutthānam adharmasya
tadātmānaṁ sṛjāmy aham

"Whenever and wherever there is a decline in religious practice, O descendant of Bharata, and a predominant rise of irreligion—at that time I descend Myself." (Bg. 4.7) The Lord is always ready to help the fallen souls, but because they are fools and rascals, they do not take to Kṛṣṇa consciousness and abide by the instructions of Kṛṣṇa. Therefore although Śrī Caitanya Mahāprabhu is personally the Supreme Lord, Kṛṣṇa, He comes as a devotee to preach the Kṛṣṇa consciousness movement. *Yāre dekha, tāre kaha 'kṛṣṇa'-upadeśa.* One must therefore become a sincere servant of Kṛṣṇa. *Āmāra ājñāya guru hañā tāra' ei deśa* (Cc. *Madhya* 7.128). One should become a *guru* and spread Kṛṣṇa consciousness all over the world, simply by preaching the teachings of *Bhagavad-gītā.*

TEXT 42

को न्वत्र तेऽखिलगुरो भगवन्प्रयास
उत्तारणेऽस्य भवसम्भवलोपहेतोः ।
मूढेषु वै महदनुग्रह आर्तबन्धो
किं तेन ते प्रियजनाननुसेवतां नः ॥४२॥

ko nv atra te 'khila-guro bhagavan prayāsa
uttāraṇe 'sya bhava-sambhava-lopa-hetoḥ
mūḍheṣu vai mahad-anugraha ārta-bandho
kiṁ tena te priya-janān anusevatāṁ naḥ

kaḥ—what is that; *nu*—indeed; *atra*—in this matter; *te*—of Your Lordship; *akhila-guro*—O supreme spiritual master of the entire creation; *bhagavan*—O Supreme Lord, O Personality of Godhead; *prayāsaḥ*—endeavor; *uttāraṇe*—for the deliverance of these fallen souls; *asya*—of this; *bhava-sambhava*—of creation and maintenance; *lopa*—and of annihilation; *hetoḥ*—of the cause; *mūḍheṣu*—unto the foolish persons rotting in this material world; *vai*—indeed; *mahat-anugrahaḥ*—compassion by the Supreme; *ārta-bandho*—O friend of the suffering living entities; *kim*—what is the difficulty; *tena*—with that; *te*—of Your Lordship; *priya-janān*—the dear persons (devotees); *anusevatām*—of those always engaged in serving; *naḥ*—like us (who are so engaged).

TRANSLATION

O my Lord, O Supreme Personality of Godhead, original spiritual master of the entire world, what is the difficulty for You, who manage the affairs of the universe, in delivering the fallen souls engaged in Your devotional service? You are the friend of all suffering humanity, and for great personalities it is necessary to show mercy to the foolish. Therefore I think that You will show Your causeless mercy to persons like us, who engage in Your service.

PURPORT

Here the words *priya-janān anusevatāṁ naḥ* indicate that the Supreme Lord, the Supreme Personality of Godhead, is very favorable to devotees who act according to the instructions of His own pure devotee. In other words, one must become the servant of the servant of the servant of the Lord. If one wants to become the servant of the Lord directly, this is not as fruitful as engaging in the service of the Lord's servant. This is the direction of Śrī Caitanya Mahāprabhu, who shows us the way to become *gopī-bhartuḥ pada-kamalayor dāsa-dāsānudāsaḥ*. One should not be proud of becoming directly the servant of the Supreme Personality of Godhead. Rather, one must seek a pure devotee, a servant of the Lord, and engage oneself in the service of such a servant. The more one becomes the servant of the servant, the more one becomes perfect in devotional service. This is also the injunction of *Bhagavad-gītā: evaṁ paramparā-prāptam imaṁ rājarṣayo viduḥ.* One can understand the science of the Supreme Personality of Godhead simply by the *paramparā* system. In this regard, Śrīla Narottama dāsa Ṭhākura says, *tāṅdera caraṇa sevi bhakta-sane vāsa:* "Let me serve the lotus feet of the devotees of the Lord, and let me live with devotees." *Janame janame haya, ei abhilāṣa.* Following Narottama dāsa Ṭhākura, one should aspire to be a servant of the Lord's servant, life after life. Śrīla Bhaktivinoda Ṭhākura also sings, *tumi ta' ṭhākura, tomāra kukura, baliyā jānaha more:* "O my Lord, O Vaiṣṇava, please consider me your dog." One must become the dog of a Vaiṣṇava, a pure devotee, for a pure devotee can deliver Kṛṣṇa without difficulty. *Kṛṣṇa se tomāra, kṛṣṇa dite pāra.* Kṛṣṇa is the property of His pure devotee, and if we take shelter of a pure devotee, he can deliver Kṛṣṇa very easily. Prahlāda wants to engage in the service of a devotee, and therefore he prays to Kṛṣṇa, "My dear Lord, kindly give me the shelter of Your very dear devotee so that I may engage in his service and You may then be pleased." *Mad-bhakta-pūjābhyadhikā* (*Bhāg.* 11.19.21). The Lord says, "Engaging in the service of My devotee is better than trying to engage in My devotional service."

Another significant point in this verse is that by devotional service Prahlāda Mahārāja does not want to benefit alone. Rather, he prays to the Lord that all of us fallen souls in this material world may, by the grace of the Lord, engage in the service of His servant and thus be delivered. The grace of the Lord is not at all difficult for the Lord to bestow, and thus Prahlāda Mahārāja wants to save the whole world by spreading Kṛṣṇa consciousness.

TEXT 43

नैवोद्विजे पर दुरत्ययवैतरण्या-
स्त्वद्वीर्यगायनमहामृतमग्नचित्तः ।
शोचे ततो विमुखचेतस इन्द्रियार्थ-
मायासुखाय भरमुद्वहतो विमूढान् ॥४३॥

naivodvije para duratyaya-vaitaraṇyās
tvad-vīrya-gāyana-mahāmṛta-magna-cittaḥ
śoce tato vimukha-cetasa indriyārtha-
māyā-sukhāya bharam udvahato vimūḍhān

na—not; *eva*—certainly; *udvije*—I am disturbed or afraid; *para*—O Supreme; *duratyaya*—insurmountable or very difficult to cross; *vaitaraṇyāḥ*—of the Vaitaraṇī, the river of the material world; *tvat-vīrya*—of Your Lordship's glories and activities; *gāyana*—from chanting or distributing; *mahā-amṛta*—in the great ocean of nectarean spiritual bliss; *magna-cittaḥ*—whose consciousness is absorbed; *śoce*—I am simply lamenting; *tataḥ*—from that; *vimukha-cetasaḥ*—the fools and rascals who are bereft of Kṛṣṇa consciousness; *indriya-artha*—in sense gratification; *māyā-sukhāya*—for temporary, illusory happiness; *bharam*—the false burden or responsibility (of maintaining one's family, society and nation and elaborate arrangements for that purpose); *udvahataḥ*—who are lifting (by making grand plans for this arrangement); *vimūḍhān*—although all of them are nothing but fools and rascals (I am thinking of them also).

TRANSLATION

O best of the great personalities, I am not at all afraid of material existence, for wherever I stay I am fully absorbed in thoughts of Your glories and activities. My concern is only for the fools and rascals who are making elaborate plans for material happiness and maintaining their families, societies and countries. I am simply concerned with love for them.

PURPORT

Throughout the entire world, everyone is making big, big plans to adjust the miseries of the material world, and this is true at present, in the past and in the future. Nonetheless, although they make elaborate political, social and cultural plans, they have all been described herein as *vimūḍha*—fools. The material world has been described in *Bhagavad-gītā* as *duḥkhālayam aśāśvatam*—temporary and miserable—but these fools are trying to turn the material world into *sukhālayam*, a place of happiness, not knowing how everything acts by the arrangement of material nature, which works in her own way.

prakṛteḥ kriyamāṇāni
guṇaiḥ karmāṇi sarvaśaḥ
ahaṅkāra-vimūḍhātmā
kartāham iti manyate

"The bewildered spirit soul, under the influence of the three modes of material nature, thinks himself to be the doer of activities that are in actuality carried out by nature." (Bg. 3.27)

There is a plan for material nature, personally known as Durgā, to punish the demons. Although the *asuras*, the godless demons, struggle for existence, they are directly attacked by the goddess Durgā, who is well equipped with ten hands with different types of weapons to punish them. She is carried by her lion carrier, or the modes of passion and ignorance. Everyone struggles very hard to fight through the modes of passion and ignorance and conquer material nature, but at the end everyone is vanquished by nature's laws.

There is a river known as Vaitaraṇī between the material and spiritual worlds, and one must cross this river to reach the other side, or the spiritual world. This is an extremely difficult task. As the Lord says in *Bhagavad-gītā* (7.14), *daivī hy eṣā guṇamayī mama māyā duratyayā:* "This divine energy of Mine, consisting of the three modes of material nature, is difficult to overcome." The same word *duratyaya*, meaning "very difficult," is used here. Therefore one cannot surpass the stringent laws of material nature except by the mercy of the Supreme Lord. Nonetheless, although all materialists are baffled in their plans, they try again and again to become happy in this material world. Therefore they have been described as *vimūḍha*—first-class fools. As for Prahlāda Mahārāja, he was not at all unhappy, for although he was in the material world, he was full of Kṛṣṇa consciousness. Those who are Kṛṣṇa conscious, trying to serve the Lord, are not unhappy, whereas one who has no assets in Kṛṣṇa consciousness and is struggling for existence is not only foolish but extremely unhappy also. Prahlāda Mahārāja was happy and unhappy simultaneously. He felt happiness and transcendental bliss because of his being Kṛṣṇa conscious, yet he felt great unhappiness for the fools and rascals who make elaborate plans to be happy in this material world.

TEXT 44

प्रायेण देव मुनयः स्वविमुक्तिकामा
मौनं चरन्ति विजने न परार्थनिष्ठाः ।
नैतान्विहाय कृपणान्विमुमुक्ष एको
नान्यं त्वदस्य शरणं भ्रमतोऽनुपश्ये ॥४४॥

prāyeṇa deva munayaḥ sva-vimukti-kāmā
maunaṁ caranti vijane na parārtha-niṣṭhāḥ
naitān vihāya kṛpaṇān vimumukṣa eko
nānyaṁ tvad asya śaraṇaṁ bhramato 'nupaśye

prāyeṇa—generally, in almost all cases; *deva*—O my Lord; *munayaḥ*—the great saintly persons; *sva*—personal, own; *vimukti-kāmāḥ*—ambitious for liberation from this material world; *maunam*—silently; *caranti*—they wander (in places like the Himalayan forests, where they have no touch with the activities of the materialists); *vijane*—in solitary places; *na*—not; *para-artha-niṣṭhāḥ*—interested in working for others by giving them the benefit of the Kṛṣṇa consciousness movement, by enlightening them with Kṛṣṇa consciousness; *na*—not; *etān*—these; *vihāya*—leaving aside; *kṛpaṇān*—fools and rascals (engaged in materialistic activity who do not know the benefit of the human form of life); *vimumukṣe*—I desire to be liberated and to return home, back to Godhead; *ekaḥ*—alone; *na*—not; *anyam*—other; *tvat*—but for You; *asya*—of this; *śaraṇam*—shelter; *bhramataḥ*—of the living entity rotating and wandering throughout the material universes; *anupaśye*—do I see.

TRANSLATION

My dear Lord Nṛsiṁhadeva, I see that there are many saintly persons indeed, but they are interested only in their own deliverance. Not caring for the big cities and towns, they go to the Himalayas or the forest to meditate with vows of silence [mauna-vrata]. They are not interested in delivering others. As for me, however, I do not wish to be liberated alone, leaving aside all these poor fools and rascals. I know that without Kṛṣṇa consciousness, without taking shelter of Your lotus feet, one cannot be happy. Therefore I wish to bring them back to shelter at Your lotus feet.

PURPORT

This is the decision of the Vaiṣṇava, the pure devotee of the Lord. For himself he has no problems, even if he has to stay in this material world, because his only business is to remain in Kṛṣṇa consciousness. The Kṛṣṇa conscious person can go even to hell and still be happy. Therefore Prahlāda Mahārāja said, *naivodvije para duratyaya-vaitaraṇyāḥ:* "O best of the great personalities, I am not at all afraid of material existence." The pure devotee is never unhappy in any condition of life. This is confirmed in *Śrīmad-Bhāgavatam* (6.17.28):

nārāyaṇa-parāḥ sarve
na kutaścana bibhyati
svargāpavarga-narakeṣv
api tulyārtha-darśinaḥ

"Devotees solely engaged in the devotional service of the Supreme Personality of Godhead, Nārāyaṇa, never fear any condition of life. For them the heavenly planets, liberation and the hellish planets are all the same, for such devotees are interested only in the service of the Lord."

For a devotee, being situated in the heavenly planets and being in the hellish planets are equal, for a devotee lives neither in heaven nor in hell but with Kṛṣṇa in the spiritual world. The secret of success for the devotee is not understood by the *karmīs* and *jñānīs. Karmīs* therefore try to be happy by material adjustment, and *jñānīs* want to be happy by becoming one with the Supreme. The devotee has no such interest. He is not interested in so-called meditation in the Himalayas or the forest. Rather, his interest is in the busiest part of the world, where he teaches people Kṛṣṇa consciousness. The Kṛṣṇa consciousness movement was started for this purpose. We do not teach one to meditate in a secluded place just so that one may show that he has become very much advanced and may be proud of his so-called transcendental meditation, although he engages in all sorts of foolish materialistic activity. A Vaiṣṇava like Prahlāda Mahārāja is not interested in such a bluff of spiritual advancement. Rather, he is interested in enlightening people in Kṛṣṇa consciousness because that is the only way for them to become happy. Prahlāda Mahārāja says clearly, *nānyaṁ tvad asya śaraṇaṁ bhramato 'nupaśye:* "I know that without Kṛṣṇa consciousness, without taking shelter of Your lotus feet, one cannot be happy." One wanders within the universe, life after life, but by the grace of a devotee, a servant of Śrī Caitanya Mahāprabhu, one can get the clue to Kṛṣṇa consciousness and then not only become happy in this world but also return home, back to Godhead. That is the real target in life. The members of the Kṛṣṇa consciousness movement are not at all interested in so-called meditation in the Himalayas or the forest, where one will only make a show of meditation, nor are they interested in opening many schools for *yoga* and meditation in the cities. Rather, every member of the Kṛṣṇa consciousness movement is interested in going door to door to try to convince people about the teachings of *Bhagavad-gītā As It Is*, the teachings of Lord Caitanya. That is the purpose of the Hare Kṛṣṇa movement. The members of the Kṛṣṇa consciousness movement must be fully convinced that without Kṛṣṇa one cannot be happy. Thus the Kṛṣṇa conscious person avoids all kinds of pseudo spiritualists, transcendentalists, meditators, monists, philosophers and philanthropists.

TEXT 45

यन्मैथुनादि गृहमेधिसुखं हि तुच्छं
कण्डूयनेन करयोरिव दुःखदुःखम् ।
तृप्यन्ति नेह कृपणा बहुदुःखभाजः
कण्डूतिवन्मनसिजं विषहेत धीरः ॥४५॥

yan maithunādi-gṛhamedhi-sukhaṁ hi tucchaṁ
kaṇḍūyanena karayor iva duḥkha-duḥkham

tṛpyanti neha kṛpaṇā bahu-duḥkha-bhājaḥ
kaṇḍūtivan manasijaṁ viṣaheta dhīraḥ

yat—that which (is meant for material sense gratification); *maithuna-ādi*—represented by talking of sex, reading sexual literature or enjoying sex life (at home or outside, as in a club); *gṛhamedhi-sukham*—all types of material happiness based on attachment to family, society, friendship, etc.; *hi*—indeed; *tuccham*—insignificant; *kaṇḍūyanena*—with the itching; *karayoḥ*—of the two hands (to relieve the itching); *iva*—like; *duḥkha-duḥkham*—different types of unhappiness (into which one is put after such itching sense gratification); *tṛpyanti*—become satisfied; *na*—never; *iha*—in material sense gratification; *kṛpaṇāḥ*—the foolish persons; *bahu-duḥkha-bhājaḥ*—subjected to various types of material unhappiness; *kaṇḍūti-vat*—if one can learn from such itching; *manasi-jam*—which is simply a mental concoction (actually there is no happiness); *viṣaheta*—and tolerates (such itching); *dhīraḥ*—(he can become) a most perfect, sober person.

TRANSLATION

Sex life is compared to the rubbing of two hands to relieve an itch. Gṛhamedhis, so-called gṛhasthas who have no spiritual knowledge, think that this itching is the greatest platform of happiness, although actually it is a source of distress. The kṛpaṇas, the fools who are just the opposite of brāhmaṇas, are not satisfied by repeated sensuous enjoyment. Those who are dhīra, however, who are sober and who tolerate this itching, are not subjected to the sufferings of fools and rascals.

PURPORT

Materialists think that sexual indulgence is the greatest happiness in this material world, and therefore they make elaborate plans to satisfy their senses, especially the genitals. This is generally found everywhere, and specifically found in the Western world, where there are regular arrangements to satisfy sex life in different ways. Actually, however, this has not made anyone happy. Even the hippies, who have given up all the materialistic comforts of their fathers and grandfathers, cannot give up the sensational happiness of sex life. Such persons are described here as *kṛpaṇas*, misers. The human form of life is a great asset, for in this life one can fulfill the goal of existence. Unfortunately, however, because of a lack of education and culture, people are victimized by the false happiness of sex life. Prahlāda Mahārāja therefore advises one not to be misled by this civilization of sense gratification, and especially not by sex life. Rather, one should be sober, avoid sense gratification and be Kṛṣṇa conscious. The lusty person, who is compared to a foolish miser, never gets happiness by sense gratification. The influence of material nature is very difficult to surpass, but as stated by Kṛṣṇa in *Bhagavad-gītā* (7.14), *mām eva ye prapadyante, māyām etāṁ taranti te:* if one voluntarily submits to the lotus feet of Kṛṣṇa, he can be saved very easily.

In reference to the low-grade happiness of sex life, Yāmunācārya says in this connection:

yadāvadhi mama cetaḥ kṛṣṇa-padāravinde
nava-nava-rasa-dhāmanudyata rantum āsīt
tadāvadhi bata nārī-saṅgame smaryamāne
bhavati mukha-vikāraḥ suṣṭu niṣṭhīvanaṁ ca

"Since I have been engaged in the transcendental loving service of Kṛṣṇa, realizing ever-new pleasure in Him, whenever I think of sex pleasure, I spit at the thought, and my lips curl with distaste." Yāmunācārya had formerly been a great king who enjoyed sexual happiness in various ways, but since he later engaged himself in the service of the Lord, he enjoyed spiritual bliss and hated to think of sex life. If sexual thoughts came to him, he would spit with disgust.

TEXT 46

मौनव्रतश्रुततपोऽध्ययनस्वधर्म-
व्याख्यारहोजपसमाधय आपवर्ग्याः ।
प्रायः परं पुरुष ते त्वजितेन्द्रियाणां
वार्ता भवन्त्युत न वात्र तु दाम्भिकानाम् ॥४६॥

mauna-vrata-śruta-tapo-'dhyayana-sva-dharma-
vyākhyā-raho-japa-samādhaya āpavargyāḥ
prāyaḥ paraṁ puruṣa te tv ajitendriyāṇām
vārtā bhavanty uta na vātra tu dāmbhikānām

mauna—silence; *vrata*—vows; *śruta*—Vedic knowledge; *tapaḥ*—austerity; *adhyayana*—study of scripture; *sva-dharma*—executing *varṇāśrama-dharma; vyākhyā*—explaining the *śāstras; rahaḥ*—living in a solitary place; *japa*—chanting or reciting *mantras; samādhayaḥ*—remaining in trance; *āpavargyāḥ*—these are ten types of activities for advancing on the path of liberation; *prāyaḥ*—generally; *param*—the only means; *puruṣa*—O my Lord; *te*—all of them; *tu*—but; *ajita-indriyāṇām*—of persons who cannot control the senses; *vārtāḥ*—means of living; *bhavanti*—are; *uta*—so it is said; *na*—not; *vā*—or; *atra*—in this connection; *tu*—but; *dāmbhikānām*—of persons who are falsely proud.

TRANSLATION

O Supreme Personality of Godhead, there are ten prescribed methods on the path to liberation—to remain silent, not to speak to anyone, to observe vows, to amass all kinds of Vedic knowledge, to undergo austerities, to study the Vedas and other Vedic literatures, to execute the duties of varṇāśrama-dharma, to explain the śāstras, to stay in a solitary place, to chant mantras silently, and to be absorbed in trance. These different methods for liberation are generally only a professional practice and means of livelihood for those who have not conquered their senses. Because such persons are falsely proud, these procedures may not be successful.

PURPORT

As stated in *Śrīmad-Bhāgavatam* (6.1.15):

kecit kevalayā bhaktyā
vāsudeva-parāyaṇāḥ
aghaṁ dhunvanti kārtsnyena
nīhāram iva bhāskaraḥ

"Only a rare person who has adopted complete, unalloyed devotional service to Kṛṣṇa can uproot the weeds of sinful actions with no possibility that they will revive. He can do this simply by discharging devotional service, just as the sun can immediately dissipate fog by its rays." The real purpose of human life is to attain liberation from material entanglement. Such liberation may be achieved by many methods (*tapasā brahmacaryeṇa śamena ca damena ca*), but all of them more or less depend on *tapasya*, austerity, which begins with celibacy. Śukadeva Gosvāmī says that those who are *vāsudeva-parāyana*, who have fully surrendered to the lotus feet of Lord Vāsudeva, Kṛṣṇa, automatically achieve the results of *mauna* (silence), *vrata* (vows) and other such methods simply by discharging devotional service. In other words, these methods are not so powerful. If one takes to devotional serivce, all of them are very easily performed.

Mauna, for example, does not mean that one should just stop speaking. The tongue is meant for speaking, although sometimes, to make a big show, a person remains silent. There are many who observe silence some day in a week. Vaiṣṇavas, however, do not observe such silence. Silence means not speaking foolishly. Speakers at assemblies, conferences and meetings generally speak foolishly like toads. This is described by Śrīla Rūpa Gosvāmī as *vāco vegam.* One who wants to say something can show himself to be a big orator, but rather than go on speaking nonsense, better to remain silent. This method of silence, therefore, is recommended for persons very attached to speaking nonsense. One who is not a devotee must speak nonsensically because he does not have the power to speak about the glories of Kṛṣṇa. Thus whatever he says is influenced by the illusory energy and is compared to the croaking of a frog. One who speaks about the glories of the Lord, however, has no need to be silent. Caitanya Mahāprabhu recommends, *kīrtanīyaḥ sadā hariḥ:* one should go on chanting the glories of the Lord twenty-four hours a day. There is no question of becoming *mauna*, or silent.

The ten processes for liberation or improvement on the path of liberation are not meant for the devotees. *Kevalayā bhaktyā:* if one simply engages in devotional service to the Lord, all ten methods of liberation are automatically observed. Prahlāda Mahārāja's proposal is that such processes may be recommended for the *ajitendriya,* those who cannot conquer their senses. Devotees, however, have already conquered their senses. *Sarvopādhi-vinirmuktaṁ tat-paratvena nirmalam:* a devotee is already freed from material contamination. Śrīla Bhaktisiddhānta Sarasvatī Ṭhākura therefore said:

duṣṭa mana! tumi kisera vaiṣṇava? pratiṣṭhāra tare, nirjanera ghare,
tava harināma kevala kaitava

There are many who like to chant the Hare Kṛṣṇa *mantra* in a silent, solitary place, but if one is not interested in preaching, talking constantly to the nondevotees, the influence of the modes of nature is very difficult to surpass. Therefore unless one is extremely advanced in Kṛṣṇa consciousness, one should not imitate Haridāsa Ṭhākura, who had no other business than chanting the holy name always, twenty-four hours a day. Prahlāda Mahārāja does not condemn such a process; he accepts it, but without active service to the Lord, simply by such methods one generally cannot attain liberation. One cannot attain liberation simply by false pride.

TEXT 47

रूपे इमे सदसती तव वेदसृष्टे
बीजाङ्कुराविव न चान्यदरूपकस्य ।
युक्ताः समक्षमुभयत्र विचक्षन्ते त्वां
योगेन वह्निमिव दारुषु नान्यतः स्यात् ॥४७॥

rūpe ime sad-asatī tava veda-sṛṣṭe
bījāṅkurāv iva na cānyad arūpakasya
yuktāḥ samakṣam ubhayatra vicakṣante tvāṁ
yogena vahnim iva dāruṣu nānyataḥ syāt

rūpe—in the forms; *ime*—these two; *sat-asatī*—the cause and the effect; *tava*—Your; *veda-sṛṣṭe*—explained in the *Vedas; bīja-aṅkurau*—the seed and the sprout; *iva*—like; *na*—never; *ca*—also; *anyat*—any other; *arūpakasya*—of You, who possess no material form; *yuktāḥ*—those engaged in Your devotional service; *samakṣam*—before the very eyes; *ubhayatra*—in both ways (spiritually and materially); *vicakṣante*—can actually see; *tvām*—You; *yogena*—simply by the method of devotional service; *vahnim*—fire; *iva*—like; *dāruṣu*—in wood; *na*—not; *anyataḥ*—from any other means; *syāt*—it is possible.

TRANSLATION

By authorized Vedic knowledge one can see that the forms of cause and effect in the cosmic manifestation belong to the Supreme Personality of Godhead, for the cosmic manifestation is His energy. Both cause and effect are nothing but energies of the Lord. Therefore, O my Lord, just as a wise man, by considering cause and effect, can see how fire pervades wood, those engaged in devotional service understand how You are both the cause and effect.

PURPORT

As described in previous verses, many so-called students of spiritual understanding follow the ten different methods known as *mauna-vrata-śruta-tapo-'dhyayana-sva-dharma-vyākhyā-raho-japa-samādhayah.* These may be very attractive, but by following such methods, one cannot actually understand the real cause and effect and the original cause of everything (*janmādy asya yataḥ*). The original source of everything is the Supreme Personality of Godhead Himself (*sarva-kāraṇa-kāraṇam*). This original source of everything is Kṛṣṇa, the supreme ruler. *Īśvaraḥ paramaḥ kṛṣṇaḥ sac-cid-ānanda-vigrahaḥ.* He has His eternal spiritual form. Indeed, He is the root of everything (*bījaṁ māṁ sarva-bhūtānām*). Whatever manifestations exist, their cause is the Supreme Personality of Godhead. This cannot be understood by so-called silence or by any other hodgepodge method. The supreme cause can be understood only by devotional service, as stated in *Bhagavad-gītā* (*bhaktyā mām abhijānāti*). Elsewhere in *Śrīmad-Bhāgavatam* (11.14.21), the Supreme Godhead personally says, *bhaktyāham ekayā grāhyaḥ:* one can understand the original cause of all causes, the Supreme Person, only by devotional service, not by show-bottle exhibitionism.

TEXT 48

त्वं वायुरग्निरवनिर्वियदम्बुमात्राः
प्राणेन्द्रियाणि हृदयं चिदनुग्रहश्च ।
सर्वं त्वमेव सगुणो विगुणश्च भूमन्
नान्यत् त्वदस्त्यपि मनोवचसा निरुक्तम् ॥४८॥

tvaṁ vāyur agnir avanir viyad ambu mātrāḥ
prāṇendriyāṇi hṛdayaṁ cid anugrahaś ca
sarvaṁ tvam eva saguṇo viguṇaś ca bhūman
nānyat tvad asty api mano-vacasā niruktam

tvam—You (are); *vāyuḥ*—air; *agniḥ*—fire; *avaniḥ*—earth; *viyat*—sky; *ambu*—water; *mātrāḥ*—the sense objects; *prāṇa*—the life airs; *indriyāṇi*—the senses; *hṛdayam*—the mind; *cit*—consciousness; *anugrahaḥ ca*—and false ego or the demigods; *sarvam*—everything; *tvam*—You; *eva*—only; *sa-guṇaḥ*—material nature with its three modes; *viguṇaḥ*—the spiritual spark and Supersoul, which are beyond material nature; *ca*—and; *bhūman*—O my great Lord; *na*—not; *anyat*—other; *tvat*—than You; *asti*—is; *api*—although; *manaḥ-vacasā*—by mind and words; *niruktam*—everything manifested.

TRANSLATION

O Supreme Lord, You are actually the air, the earth, fire, sky and water. You are the objects of sense perception, the life airs, the five senses, the mind, consciousness and false ego. Indeed, You are everything, subtle and gross. The material elements and anything expressed, either by the words or by the mind, are nothing but You.

PURPORT

This is the all-pervasive conception of the Supreme Personality of Godhead, which explains how He spreads everywhere and anywhere. *Sarvaṁ khalv idaṁ brahma:* everything is Brahman—the Supreme Brahman, Kṛṣṇa. Nothing exists without Him. As the Lord says in *Bhagavad-gītā* (9.4):

mayā tatam idaṁ sarvaṁ
jagad avyakta-mūrtinā
mat-sthāni sarva-bhūtāni
na cāhaṁ teṣv avasthitaḥ

"I exist everywhere, and everything exists in Me, yet I am not visible everywhere." The Lord can be visible only through devotional service.

Tatra tiṣṭhāmi nārada yatra gāyanti mad-bhaktāḥ: the Supreme Lord stays only where His devotees chant His glories.

TEXT 49

नैते गुणा न गुणिनो महदादयो ये
सर्वे मनःप्रभृतयः सहदेवमर्त्याः ।
आद्यन्तवन्त उरुगाय विदन्ति हि त्वा-
मेवं विमृश्य सुधियो विरमन्ति शब्दात्॥४९॥

naite guṇā na guṇino mahad-ādayo ye
sarve manaḥ prabhṛtayaḥ sahadeva-martyāḥ
ādy-antavanta urugāya vidanti hi tvām
evaṁ vimṛśya sudhiyo viramanti śabdāt

na—neither; *ete*—all these; *guṇāḥ*—three qualities of material nature; *na*—nor; *guṇinaḥ*—the predominating deities of the three modes of material nature (namely Lord Brahmā, the predominating deity of passion, and Lord Śiva, the predominating deity of ignorance); *mahat-ādayaḥ*—the five elements, the senses and the sense objects; *ye*—those which; *sarve*—all; *manaḥ*—the mind; *prabhṛtayaḥ*—and so on; *saha-deva-martyāḥ*—with the demigods and the mortal human beings; *ādi-anta-vantaḥ*—who all have a beginning and end; *urugāya*—O Supreme Lord, who are glorified by all saintly persons; *vidanti*—understand; *hi*—indeed; *tvām*—Your Lordship; *evam*—thus; *vimṛśya*—considering; *sudhiyaḥ*—all wise men; *viramanti*—cease; *śabdāt*—from studying or understanding the *Vedas.*

TRANSLATION

Neither the three modes of material nature [sattva-guṇa, rajo-guṇa and tamo-guṇa], nor the predominating deities controlling these three modes, nor the five gross elements, nor the mind, nor the demigods nor the human beings can understand Your Lordship, for they are all subjected to birth and annihilation. Considering this, the spiritually advanced have taken to devotional service. Such wise men hardly bother with Vedic study. Instead, they engage themselves in practical devotional service.

PURPORT

As stated in several places, *bhaktyā mām abhijānāti:* only by devotional service can the Supreme Lord be understood. The intelligent person, the devotee, does not bother much about the practices mentioned in text 46 (*mauna-vrata-śruta-tapo-'dhyayana-sva-dharma*). After understanding the Supreme Lord through devotional service, such devotees are no longer interested in studies of the *Vedas.* Indeed, this is confirmed in the *Vedas* also. The *Vedas* say, *kim arthā vayam adhyeṣyāmahe kim arthā vayam vakṣyāmahe.* What is the use of studying so many Vedic literatures? What is the use of explaining them in different ways? *Vayam vakṣyāmahe.* No one needs to study any more Vedic literatures, nor does anyone need to describe them by philosophical speculation. *Bhagavad-gītā* (2.52) also says:

yadā te moha-kalilaṁ
buddhir vyatitariṣyati
tadā gantāsi nirvedaṁ
śrotavyasya śrutasya ca

When one understands the Supreme Personality of Godhead by executing devotional service, one ceases the practice of studying the Vedic literature. Elsewhere it is said, *ārādhito yadi haris tapasā tataḥ kim.* If one can understand the Supreme Personality of Godhead and engage in His service, there is no more need of severe austerities, penances and so on. However, if after performing severe austerities and penances one does not understand the Supreme Personality of Godhead, such practices are useless.

TEXT 50

तत् तेऽर्हत्तम नमःस्तुतिकर्मपूजाः
कर्म स्मृतिश्चरणयोः श्रवणं कथायाम् ।
संसेवया त्वयि विनेति षडङ्गया किं
भक्तिं जनः परमहंसगतौ लभेत ॥५०॥

tat te 'rhattama namaḥ stuti-karma-pūjāḥ
karma smṛtiś caraṇayoḥ śravaṇaṁ kathāyām

saṁsevayā tvayi vineti ṣaḍ-aṅgayā kiṁ
bhaktiṁ janaḥ paramahaṁsa-gatau labheta

tat—therefore; *te*—unto You; *arhat-tama*—O supreme of all worshipable persons; *namaḥ*—respectful obeisances; *stuti-karma-pūjāḥ*—worshiping Your Lordship by offering prayers and other devotional activities; *karma*—activities being dedicated to You; *smṛtiḥ*—constant remembrance; *caraṇayoḥ*—of Your lotus feet; *śravaṇam*—always hearing; *kathāyām*—in topics (about You); *saṁsevayā*—such devotional service; *tvayi*—unto You; *vinā*—without; *iti*—thus; *ṣaṭ-aṅgayā*—having six different parts; *kim*—how; *bhaktim*—devotional service; *janaḥ*—a person; *paramahaṁsa-gatau*—obtainable by the *paramahaṁsa; labheta*—may attain.

TRANSLATION

Therefore, O Supreme Personality of Godhead, the best of all persons to whom prayers are offered, I offer my respectful obeisances unto You because without rendering six kinds of devotional service unto You—offering prayers, dedicating all the results of activities, worshiping You, working on Your behalf, always remembering Your lotus feet and hearing about Your glories—who can achieve that which is meant for the paramahaṁsas?

PURPORT

The *Vedas* enjoin: *nāyam ātmā pravacanena labhyo na medhayā na bahunā śrutena.* One cannot understand the Supreme Personality of Godhead simply by studying the *Vedas* and offering prayers. Only by the grace of the Supreme Lord can one understand Him. The process of understanding the Lord, therefore, is *bhakti.* Without *bhakti,* simply following the Vedic injunctions to understand the Absolute Truth will not be helpful at all. The process of *bhakti* is understood by the *paramahaṁsa,* one who has accepted the essence of everything. The results of *bhakti* are reserved for such a *paramahaṁsa,* and this stage cannot be obtained by any Vedic process other than devotional service. Other processes, such as *jñāna* and *yoga,* can be successful only when mixed with *bhakti.* When we speak of *jñāna-yoga, karma-yoga* and *dhyāna-yoga* the word *yoga* indicates *bhakti. Bhakti-yoga*, or *buddhi-yoga*, executed with intelligence and full knowledge, is the only successful method for going back home, back to Godhead. If one wants to be liberated from the pangs of material existence, he should take to devotional service for quick attainment of this goal.

TEXT 51

श्रीनारद उवाच

एतावद्वर्णितगुणो भक्त्या भक्तेन निर्गुणः ।
प्रह्रादं प्रणतं प्रीतो यतमन्युरभाषत ॥५१॥

śrī-nārada uvāca
etāvad varṇita-guṇo
bhaktyā bhaktena nirguṇaḥ
prahrādaṁ praṇataṁ prīto
yata-manyur abhāṣata

śrī-nāradaḥ uvāca—Śrī Nārada Muni said; *etāvat*—up to this; *varṇita*—described; *guṇaḥ*—transcendental qualities; *bhaktyā*—with devotion; *bhaktena*—by the devotee (Prahlāda Mahārāja); *nirguṇaḥ*—the transcendental Lord; *prahrādam*—unto Prahlāda Mahārāja; *praṇatam*—who was surrendered at the lotus feet of the Lord; *prītaḥ*—being pleased; *yata-manyuḥ*—controlling the anger; *abhāṣata*—began to speak (as follows).

TRANSLATION

The great saint Nārada said: Thus Lord Nṛsiṁhadeva was pacified by the devotee Prahlāda Mahārāja with prayers offered from the transcendental platform. The Lord gave up His anger, and being very kind to Prahlāda, who was offering prostrated obeisances, He spoke as follows.

PURPORT

The word *nirguṇa* is important. The Māyāvādī philosophers accept the Absolute Truth as *nirguṇa* or *nirākāra*. The word *nirguṇa* refers to one who possesses no material qualities. The Lord, being full of spiritual qualities, gave up all His anger and spoke to Prahlāda.

TEXT 52

श्रीभगवानुवाच
प्रह्राद भद्र भद्रं ते प्रीतोऽहं तेऽसुरोत्तम ।
वरं वृणीष्वाभिमतं कामपूरोऽस्म्यहं नृणाम् ॥५२॥

śrī-bhagavān uvāca
prahrāda bhadra bhadraṁ te
prīto 'haṁ te 'surottama
varaṁ vṛṇīṣvābhimataṁ
kāma-pūro 'smy ahaṁ nṛṇām

śrī-bhagavān uvāca—the Supreme Personality of Godhead said; *prahrāda*—O My dear Prahlāda; *bhadra*—you are so gentle; *bhadram*—all good fortune; *te*—unto you; *prītaḥ*—pleased; *aham*—I (am); *te*—unto You; *asura-uttama*—O best devotee in the family of *asuras* (atheists); *varam*—benediction; *vṛṇīṣva*—just ask (from Me); *abhimatam*—desired; *kāma-pūraḥ*—who fulfills everyone's desire; *asmi*—am; *aham*—I; *nṛṇām*—of all men.

TRANSLATION

The Supreme Personality of Godhead said: My dear Prahlāda, most gentle one, best of the family of the asuras, all good fortune unto you. I am very much pleased with you. It is My pastime to fulfill the desires of all living beings, and therefore you may ask from Me any benediction that you desire to be fulfilled.

PURPORT

The Supreme Personality of Godhead is known as *bhakta-vatsala*, the Supreme Personality who is very much affectionate to His devotees. It is not very extraordinary that the Lord offered His devotee all benedictions. The Supreme Personality of Godhead said in effect, "I fulfill the desires of everyone. Since you are My devotee, whatever you want for yourself will naturally be given, but if you pray for anyone else, that prayer also will be fulfilled." Thus if we approach the Supreme Lord or His devotee, or if we are blessed by a devotee, naturally we will automatically achieve the benedictions of the Supreme Lord. *Yasya prasādād bhagavat-*

prasādaḥ. Śrīla Viśvanātha Cakravartī Ṭhākura says that if one pleases the Vaiṣṇava spiritual master, all of one's desires will be fulfilled.

TEXT 53

मामप्रीणत आयुष्मन्दर्शनं दुर्लभं हि मे ।
दृष्ट्वा मां न पुनर्जन्तुरात्मानं तप्तुमर्हति ॥५३॥

mām aprīṇata āyuṣman
darśanaṁ durlabhaṁ hi me
dṛṣṭvā māṁ na punar jantur
ātmānaṁ taptum arhati

mām—Me; *aprīṇataḥ*—not pleasing; *āyuṣman*—O long-living Prahlāda; *darśanam*—seeing; *durlabham*—very rare; *hi*—indeed; *me*—of Me; *dṛṣṭvā*—after seeing; *mām*—Me; *na*—not; *punaḥ*—again; *jantuḥ*—the living entity; *ātmānam*—for himself; *taptum*—to lament; *arhati*—deserves.

TRANSLATION

My dear Prahlāda, may you live a long time. One cannot appreciate or understand Me without pleasing Me, but one who has seen or pleased Me has nothing more for which to lament for his own satisfaction.

PURPORT

One cannot be happy under any circumstances unless one pleases the Supreme Personality of Godhead, but one who has learned how to please the Supreme Lord need no longer lament for his material condition.

TEXT 54

प्रीणन्ति ह्यथ मां धीराः सर्वभावेन साधवः ।
श्रेयस्कामा महाभाग सर्वासामाशिषां पतिम् ॥५४॥

prīṇanti hy atha māṁ dhīrāḥ
sarva-bhāvena sādhavaḥ

śreyas-kāmā mahā-bhāga
sarvāsām āśiṣāṁ patim

prīṇanti—try to please; *hi*—indeed; *atha*—because of this; *mām*—Me; *dhīrāḥ*—those who are sober and most intelligent; *sarva-bhāvena*—in all respects, in different modes of devotional service; *sādhavaḥ*—persons who are very well behaved (perfect in all respects); *śreyas-kāmāḥ*—desiring the best benefit in life; *mahā-bhāga*—O you who are so fortunate; *sarvāsām*—of all; *āśiṣām*—kinds of benedictions; *patim*—the master (Me).

TRANSLATION

My dear Prahlāda, you are very fortunate. Please know from Me that those who are very wise and highly elevated try to please Me in all different modes of mellows, for I am the only person who can fulfill all the desires of everyone.

PURPORT

The words *dhīrāḥ sarva-bhāvena* do not mean "in whichever way you like." *Bhāva* is the preliminary condition of love of Godhead.

athāsaktis tato bhāvas
tataḥ premābhyudañcati
sādhakānām ayaṁ premṇaḥ
prādurbhāve bhavet kramaḥ
(*Bhakti-rasāmṛta-sindhu* 1.4.16)

The *bhāva* stage is the final division before one reaches love of Godhead. The word *sarva-bhāva* means that one can love the Supreme Personality of Godhead in different transcendental modes of mellows, beginning with *dāsya, sakhya, vātsalya* and *mādhurya*. In the *śānta* stage, one is on the border of loving service to the Lord. Pure love of Godhead begins from *dāsya* and develops to *sakhya, vātsalya* and then *mādhurya*. Still, in any of these five mellows one can render loving service to the Supreme Lord. Since our main business is to love the Supreme Personality of Godhead, one can render service from any of the above-mentioned platforms of love.

TEXT 55

श्रीनारद उवाच
एवं प्रलोभ्यमानोऽपि वरैर्लोकप्रलोभनैः ।
एकान्तित्वाद् भगवति नैच्छत् तानसुरोत्तमः ॥५५॥

śrī-nārada uvāca
evaṁ pralobhyamāno 'pi
varair loka-pralobhanaiḥ
ekāntitvād bhagavati
naicchat tān asurottamaḥ

śrī-nāradaḥ uvāca—the great saint Nārada said; *evam*—thus; *pralobhyamānaḥ*—being allured or induced; *api*—although; *varaiḥ*—by benedictions; *loka*—of the world; *pralobhanaiḥ*—by different kinds of allurements; *ekāntitvāt*—because of being solely surrendered; *bhagavati*—unto the Supreme Personality of Godhead; *na aicchat*—did not want; *tān*—those benedictions; *asura-uttamaḥ*—Prahlāda Mahārāja, the best of the family of *asuras.*

TRANSLATION

Nārada Muni said: Prahlāda Mahārāja was the best person in the family of asuras, who always aspire for material happiness. Nonetheless, although allured by the Supreme Personality of Godhead, who offered him all benedictions for material happiness, because of his unalloyed Kṛṣṇa consciousness he did not want to take any material benefit for sense gratification.

PURPORT

Pure devotees like Prahlāda Mahārāja and Dhruva Mahārāja do not aspire for any material benefit at any stage of devotional service. When the Lord was present before Dhruva Mahārāja, Dhruva did not want to take any material benefit from the Lord: *svāmin kṛtārtho 'smi varaṁ na yāce.* As a pure devotee, he could not ask the Lord for any material benefit. In this regard, Śrī Caitanya Mahāprabhu instructed us:

na dhanaṁ na janaṁ na sundarīṁ
kavitāṁ vā jagad-īśa kāmaye
mama janmani janmanīśvare
bhavatād bhaktir ahaitukī tvayi

"O my Lord, Jagadīśa, I do not pray for benedictions by which to achieve material wealth, popularity or beauty. My only desire is to serve You. Kindly engage me in the service of the servant of Your servant."

Thus end the Bhaktivedanta purports of the Seventh Canto, Ninth Chapter, of the Śrīmad-Bhāgavatam, *entitled "Prahlāda Pacifies Lord Nṛsiṁhadeva with Prayers."*

CHAPTER TEN

Prahlāda, the Best Among Exalted Devotees

This chapter describes how the Supreme Personality of Godhead Nṛsiṁhadeva disappeared, after pleasing Prahlāda Mahārāja. It also describes a benediction given by Lord Śiva.

Lord Nṛsiṁhadeva wanted to bestow benedictions upon Prahlāda Mahārāja, one after another, but Prahlāda Mahārāja, thinking them impediments on the path of spiritual progress, did not accept any of them. Instead, he fully surrendered at the Lord's lotus feet. He said: "If anyone engaged in the devotional service of the Lord prays for personal sense gratification, he cannot be called a pure devotee or even a devotee. He may be called only a merchant engaged in the business of give and take. Similarly, a master who wants to please his servant after taking service from him is also not a real master." Prahlāda Mahārāja, therefore, did not ask anything from the Supreme Personality of Godhead. Rather, he said that if the Lord wanted to give him a benediction, he wanted the Lord to assure him that he would never be induced to take any benedictions for the sake of material desires. Exchanges of devotional service for lusty desires are always very prominent. As soon as lusty desires awaken, one's senses, mind, life, soul, religious principles, patience, intelligence, shyness, beauty, strength, memory and truthfulness are all vanquished. One can render unalloyed devotional service only when there are no material desires in one's mind.

The Supreme Personality of Godhead was greatly pleased with Prahlāda Mahārāja for his unalloyed devotion, yet the Lord provided him one material benediction—that he would be perfectly happy in this world and live his next life in Vaikuṇṭha. The Lord gave him the benediction that he would be the king of this material world until the end of the *manvantara* millennium and that although in this material world, he would have the facility to hear the glories of the Lord and depend fully on the Lord, performing service to Him in uncontaminated *bhakti-yoga*.

The Lord advised Prahlāda to perform sacrifices through *bhakti-yoga*, for this is the duty of a king.

Prahlāda Mahārāja accepted whatever the Lord had offered him, and he prayed for the Lord to deliver his father. In response to this prayer, the Lord assured him that in the family of such a pure devotee as he, not only the devotee's father but his forefathers for twenty-one generations are liberated. The Lord also asked Prahlāda to perform the ritualistic ceremonies appropriate after his father's death.

Then Lord Brahmā, who was also present, offered many prayers to the Lord, expressing his obligation to the Lord for having offered benedictions to Prahlāda Mahārāja. The Lord advised Lord Brahmā not to offer benedictions to *asuras* as he had to Hiraṇyakaśipu, for such benedictions indulge them. Then Lord Nṛsiṁhadeva disappeared. On that day, Prahlāda Mahārāja was installed on the throne of the world by Lord Brahmā and Śukrācārya.

Thus Nārada Muni described the character of Prahlāda Mahārāja for Yudhiṣṭhira Mahārāja, and he further described the killing of Rāvaṇa by Lord Rāmacandra and the killing of Śiśupāla and Dantavakra in Dvāpara-yuga. Śiśupāla, of course, had merged into the existence of the Lord and thus achieved *sāyujya-mukti.* Nārada Muni praised Yudhiṣṭhira Mahārāja because the Supreme Lord, Kṛṣṇa, was the greatest well-wisher and friend of the Pāṇḍavas and almost always stayed in their house. Thus the fortune of the Pāṇḍavas was greater than that of Prahlāda Mahārāja.

Later, Nārada Muni described how the demon Maya Dānava constructed Tripura for the demons, who became very powerful and defeated the demigods. Because of this defeat, Lord Rudra, Śiva, dismantled Tripura; thus he became famous as Tripurāri. For this, Rudra is very much appreciated and worshiped by the demigods. This narration occurs at the end of the chapter.

TEXT 1

श्रीनारद उवाच

भक्तियोगस्य तत् सर्वमन्तरायतयार्भकः ।
मन्यमानो हृषीकेशं स्मयमान उवाच ह ॥ १ ॥

śrī-nārada uvāca
bhakti-yogasya tat sarvam
antarāyatayārbhakaḥ
manyamāno hṛṣīkeśaṁ
smayamāna uvāca ha

śrī-nāradaḥ uvāca—Nārada Muni said; *bhakti-yogasya*—of the principles of devotional service; *tat*—those (blessings or benedictions offered by Lord Nṛsiṁhadeva); *sarvam*—each and every one of them; *antarāyatayā*—because of being impediments (on the path of *bhakti-yoga*); *arbhakaḥ*—Prahlāda Mahārāja, although only a boy; *manyamānaḥ*—considering; *hṛṣīkeśam*—unto Lord Nṛsiṁhadeva; *smayamānaḥ*—smiling; *uvāca*—said; *ha*—in the past.

TRANSLATION

The saint Nārada Muni continued: Although Prahlāda Mahārāja was only a boy, when he heard the benedictions offered by Lord Nṛsiṁhadeva he considered them impediments on the path of devotional service. Thus he smiled very mildly and spoke as follows.

PURPORT

Material achievements are not the ultimate goal of devotional service. The ultimate goal of devotional service is love of Godhead. Therefore although Prahlāda Mahārāja, Dhruva Mahārāja, Ambarīṣa Mahārāja, Yudhiṣṭhira Mahārāja and many devotee kings were materially very opulent, they accepted their material opulence in the service of the Lord, not for their personal sense gratification. Of course, possessing material opulence is always fearful because under the influence of material opulence one may be misdirected from devotional service. Nonetheless, a pure devotee (*anyābhilāṣitā-śūnyam*) is never misdirected by material opulence. On the contrary, whatever he possesses he engages one hundred percent in the service of the Lord. When one is allured by material possessions, they are considered to be given by *māyā*, but when one uses material possessions fully for service, they are considered God's gifts, or facilities offered by Kṛṣṇa for enhancing one's devotional service.

TEXT 2

श्रीप्रह्राद उवाच
मा मां प्रलोभयोत्पत्त्या सक्तं कामेषु तैर्वरैः ।
तत्सङ्गभीतो निर्विण्णो मुमुक्षुस्त्वामुपाश्रितः ॥ २ ॥

śrī-prahrāda uvāca
mā māṁ pralobhayotpattyā
saktaṁ kāmeṣu tair varaiḥ
tat-saṅga-bhīto nirviṇṇo
mumukṣus tvām upāśritaḥ

śrī-prahrādaḥ uvāca—Prahlāda Mahārāja said (to the Supreme Personality of Godhead); *mā*—please do not; *mām*—me; *pralobhaya*—allure; *utpattyā*—because of my birth (in a demoniac family); *saktam*—(I am already) attached; *kāmeṣu*—to material enjoyment; *taiḥ*—by all those; *varaiḥ*—benedictions of material possessions; *tat-saṅga-bhītaḥ*—being afraid of such material association; *nirviṇṇaḥ*—completely detached from material desires; *mumukṣuḥ*—desiring to be liberated from material conditions of life; *tvām*—unto Your lotus feet; *upāśritaḥ*—I have taken shelter.

TRANSLATION

Prahlāda Mahārāja said: My dear Lord, O Supreme Personality of Godhead, because I was born in an atheistic family I am naturally attached to material enjoyment. Therefore, kindly do not tempt me with these illusions. I am very much afraid of material conditions, and I desire to be liberated from materialistic life. It is for this reason that I have taken shelter of Your lotus feet.

PURPORT

Materialistic life means attachment to the body and everything in relationship to the body. This attachment is based on lusty desires for sense gratification, specifically sexual enjoyment. *Kāmais tais tair hṛta-jñānāḥ:* when one is too attached to material enjoyment, he is bereft of all knowledge (*hṛta-jñānāḥ*). As stated in *Bhagavad-gītā*, those who are attached to material enjoyment are mostly inclined to worship the demigods to procure various material opulences. They are especially attached to worship of the goddess Durgā and Lord Śiva because this transcendental couple can offer their devotees all material opulence. Prahlāda Mahārāja, however, was detached from all material enjoyment. He therefore took shelter of the lotus feet of Lord Nṛsiṁhadeva, and not the feet of any demigod. It is to be understood that if one really wants release from this material world, from the threefold miseries and from *janma-mṛtyu-jarā-vyādhi* (birth, death, old age and disease), one must take shelter of the Supreme Personality of Godhead, for without the Supreme Personality of Godhead one cannot get release from materialistic life. Atheistic men are very much attached to material enjoyment. Therefore if they get some opportunity to achieve more and more material enjoyment, they take it. Prahlāda Mahārāja, however, was very careful in this regard. Although born of a materialistic father, because he was a devotee he had no material desires (*anyābhilāṣitā-śūnyam*).

TEXT 3

भृत्यलक्षणजिज्ञासुर्भक्तं कामेष्वचोदयत् ।
भवान् संसारबीजेषु हृदयग्रन्थिषु प्रभो ॥ ३ ॥

bhṛtya-lakṣaṇa-jijñāsur
bhaktaṁ kāmeṣv acodayat
bhavān saṁsāra-bījeṣu
hṛdaya-granthiṣu prabho

bhṛtya-lakṣaṇa-jijñāsuḥ—desiring to exhibit the symptoms of a pure devotee; *bhaktam*—the devotee; *kāmeṣu*—in the material world, where lusty desires predominate; *acodayat*—has sent; *bhavān*—Your Lordship; *saṁsāra-bījeṣu*—the root cause of being present in this material world; *hṛdaya-granthiṣu*—which (desire for material enjoyment) is in the cores of the hearts of all conditioned souls; *prabho*—O my worshipable Lord.

TRANSLATION

O my worshipable Lord, because the seed of lusty desires, which is the root cause of material existence, is within the core of

everyone's heart, You have sent me to this material world to exhibit the symptoms of a pure devotee.

PURPORT

Bhakti-rasāmṛta-sindhu has given considerable discussion about *nitya-siddha* and *sādhana-siddha* devotees. *Nitya-siddha* devotees come from Vaikuṇṭha to this material world to teach, by their personal example, how to become a devotee. The living entities in this material world can take lessons from such *nitya-siddha* devotees and thus become inclined to return home, back to Godhead. A *nitya-siddha* devotee comes from Vaikuṇṭha upon the order of the Supreme Personality of Godhead and shows by his example how to become a pure devotee (*anyābhilāṣitā-śūnyam*). In spite of coming to this material world, the *nitya-siddha* devotee is never attracted by the allurements of material enjoyment. A perfect example is Prahlāda Mahārāja, who was a *nitya-siddha*, a *mahā-bhāgavata* devotee. Although Prahlāda was born in the family of Hiraṇyakaśipu, an atheist, he was never attached to any kind of materialistic enjoyment. Desiring to exhibit the symptoms of a pure devotee, the Lord tried to induce Prahlāda Mahārāja to take material benedictions, but Prahlāda Mahārāja did not accept them. On the contrary, by his personal example he showed the symptoms of a pure devotee. In other words, the Lord Himself has no desire to send His pure devotee to this material world, nor does a devotee have any material purpose in coming. When the Lord Himself appears as an incarnation within this material world, He is not allured by the material atmosphere, and He has nothing to do with material activity, yet by His example He teaches the common man how to become a devotee. Similarly, a devotee who comes here in accordance with the order of the Supreme Lord shows by his personal behavior how to become a pure devotee. A pure devotee, therefore, is a practical example for all living entities, including Lord Brahmā.

TEXT 4

नान्यथा तेऽखिलगुरो घटेत करुणात्मनः ।
यस्त आशिष आशास्ते न स भृत्यः स वै वणिक् ॥४॥

nānyathā te 'khila-guro
ghaṭeta karuṇātmanaḥ
yas ta āśiṣa āśāste
na sa bhṛtyaḥ sa vai vaṇik

na—not; *anyathā*—otherwise; *te*—of You; *akhila-guro*—O supreme instructor of the entire creation; *ghaṭeta*—such a thing can happen; *karuṇā-ātmanaḥ*—the Supreme Person, who is extremely kind to His devotees; *yaḥ*—any person who; *te*—from You; *āśiṣaḥ*—material benefits; *āśāste*—desires (in exchange for serving You); *na*—not; *saḥ*—such a person; *bhṛtyaḥ*—a servitor; *saḥ*—such a person; *vai*—indeed; *vaṇik*—a merchant (who wants to get material profit from his business).

TRANSLATION

Otherwise, O my Lord, O supreme instructor of the entire world, You are so kind to Your devotee that You could not induce him to do something unbeneficial for him. On the other hand, one who desires some material benefit in exchange for devotional service cannot be Your pure devotee. Indeed, he is no better than a merchant who wants profit in exchange for service.

PURPORT

It is sometimes found that one comes to a devotee or a temple of the Lord just to get some material benefit. Such a person is described here as a mercantile man. *Bhagavad-gītā* speaks of *ārto jijñāsur arthārthī.* The word *ārta* refers to one who is physically distressed, and *arthārthī* refers to one in need of money. Such persons are forced to approach the Supreme Personality of Godhead for mitigation of their distress or to get some money by the benediction of the Lord. They have been described as *sukṛtī,* pious, because in their distress or need for money they have approached the Supreme Lord. Unless one is pious, one cannot approach the Supreme Personality of Godhead. However, although a pious man may receive some material benefit, one who is concerned with material benefits cannot be a pure devotee. When a pure devotee receives material opulences, this is not because of his pious activity but for the service of the Lord. When one engages in devotional service, one is automatically pious. Therefore, a pure devotee is *anyābhilāṣitā-śūnyam.* He has no desire for material profit, nor does the Lord induce him to try to profit materially. When a devotee needs something, the Supreme Personality of Godhead supplies it (*yoga-kṣemaṁ vahāmy aham*).

Sometimes materialists go to a temple to offer flowers and fruit to the Lord because they have learned from *Bhagavad-gītā* that if a devotee offers some flowers and fruits, the Lord accepts them. In *Bhagavad-gītā* (9.26) the Lord says:

patraṁ puṣpaṁ phalaṁ toyaṁ
yo me bhaktyā prayacchati
tad ahaṁ bhakty-upahṛtam
aśnāmi prayatātmanaḥ

"If one offers Me with love and devotion a leaf, a flower, fruit or water, I will accept it." Thus a man with a mercantile mentality thinks that if he can get some material benefit, like a large amount of money, simply by offering a little fruit and flower, this is good business. Such persons are not accepted as pure devotees. Because their desires are not purified, they are still mercantile men, even though they go to temples to make a show of being devotees. *Sarvopādhi-vinirmuktaṁ tat-paratvena nirmalam:* only when one is fully freed from material desires can one be purified, and only in that purified state can one serve the Lord. *Hṛṣīkena hṛṣīkeśa-sevanaṁ bhaktir ucyate.* This is the pure devotional platform.

TEXT 5

आशासानो न वै भृत्यः स्वामिन्याशिष आत्मनः ।
न स्वामी भृत्यतः स्वाम्यमिच्छन् यो राति चाशिषः ।। ५ ।।

āśāsāno na vai bhṛtyaḥ
svāminy āśiṣa ātmanaḥ
na svāmī bhṛtyataḥ svāmyam
icchan yo rāti cāśiṣaḥ

āśāsānaḥ—a person who desires (in exchange for service); *na*—not; *vai*—indeed; *bhṛtyaḥ*—a qualified servant or pure devotee of the Lord;

svāmini—from the master; *āśiṣaḥ*—material benefit; *ātmanaḥ*—for personal sense gratification; *na*—nor; *svāmī*—the master; *bhṛtyataḥ*—from the servant; *svāmyam*—the prestigious position of being the master; *icchan*—desiring; *yaḥ*—any such master who; *rāti*—bestows; *ca*—also; *āśiṣaḥ*—material profit.

TRANSLATION

A servant who desires material profits from his master is certainly not a qualified servant or pure devotee. Similarly, a master who bestows benedictions upon his servant because of a desire to maintain a prestigious position as master is also not a pure master.

PURPORT

As stated in *Bhagavad-gītā* (7.20), *kāmais tais tair hṛta-jñānāḥ prapadyante 'nya-devatāḥ.* "Those whose minds are distorted by material desires surrender unto demigods." A demigod cannot become master, for the real master is the Supreme Personality of Godhead. The demigods, to keep their prestigious positions, bestow upon their worshipers whatever benedictions the worshipers want. For example, once it was found that an *asura* took a benediction from Lord Śiva by which the *asura* would be able to kill someone simply by placing his hands on that person's head. Such benedictions are possible to receive from the demigods. If one worships the Supreme Personality of Godhead, however, the Lord will never offer him such condemned benedictions. On the contrary, it is said in the *Śrīmad-Bhāgavatam* (10.88.8), *yasyāham anugṛhṇāmi hariṣye tad-dhanaṁ śanaiḥ.* If one is too materialistic but at the same time wants to be a servant of the Supreme Lord, the Lord, because of His supreme compassion for the devotee, takes away all his material opulences and obliges him to be a pure devotee of the Lord. Prahlāda Mahārāja distinguishes between the pure devotee and the pure master. The Lord is the pure master, the supreme master, whereas an unalloyed devotee with no material motives is the pure servant. One who has materialistic motivations cannot become a servant, and one who unnecessarily bestows benedictions upon his servant to keep his own prestigious position is not a real master.

TEXT 6

अहं त्वकामस्त्वद्भक्तस्त्वं च स्वाम्यनपाश्रयः ।
नान्यथेहावयोरर्थो राजसेवकयोरिव ॥ ६ ॥

ahaṁ tv akāmas tvad-bhaktas
tvaṁ ca svāmy anapāśrayaḥ
nānyathehāvayor artho
rāja-sevakayor iva

aham—as far as I am concerned; *tu*—indeed; *akāmaḥ*—without material desire; *tvat-bhaktaḥ*—fully attached to You without motivation; *tvam ca*—Your Lordship also; *svāmī*—the real master; *anapāśrayaḥ*—without motivation (You do not become the master with motivation); *na*—not; *anyathā*—without being in such a relationship as master and servant; *iha*—here; *āvayoḥ*—our; *arthaḥ*—any motivation (the Lord is the pure master, and Prahlāda Mahārāja is the pure devotee with no materialistic motivation); *rāja*—of a king; *sevakayoḥ*—and the servitor; *iva*—like (just as a king exacts taxes for the benefit of the servant or the citizens pay taxes for the benefit of the king).

TRANSLATION

O my Lord, I am Your unmotivated servant, and You are my eternal master. There is no need of our being anything other than master and servant. You are naturally my master, and I am naturally Your servant. We have no other relationship.

PURPORT

Śrī Caitanya Mahāprabhu said, *jīvera 'svarūpa' haya—kṛṣṇera 'nitya-dāsa'*: every living being is eternally a servant of the Supreme Lord, Kṛṣṇa. Lord Kṛṣṇa says in *Bhagavad-gītā* (5.29), *bhoktāraṁ yajña-tapasāṁ sarva-loka-maheśvaram:* "I am the proprietor of all planets, and I am the supreme enjoyer." This is the natural position of the Lord, and the natural position of the living being is to surrender unto Him (*sarva-dharmān parityajya mām ekaṁ śaraṇaṁ vraja*). If this relationship continues, then real happiness exists eternally between the master and servant. Unfortunately, when this eternal relationship is disturbed, the living entity wants to become separately happy and thinks that the master is his order supplier. In this way there cannot be happiness. Nor should the master cater to the desires of the servant. If he does, he is not the real master. The real master commands, "You must do this," and the real servant immediately obeys the order. Unless this relationship between the Supreme Lord and the subordinate living entity is established, there can be no real happiness. The living entity is *āśraya*, always subordinate, and the Supreme Personality of Godhead is *viṣaya*, the supreme objective, the goal of life. Unfortunate persons trapped in this material world do not know this. *Na te viduḥ svārtha-gatiṁ hi viṣṇum:* illusioned by the material energy, everyone in this material world is unaware that the only aim of life is to approach Lord Viṣṇu.

ārādhanānāṁ sarveṣāṁ
viṣṇor ārādhanaṁ param
tasmāt parataraṁ devi
tadīyānāṁ samarcanam

In the *Padma Purāṇa* Lord Śiva explains to his wife, Parvatī, the goddess Durgā, that the highest goal of life is to satisfy Lord Viṣṇu, who can be satisfied only when His servant is satisfied. Śrī Caitanya Mahāprabhu therefore teaches, *gopī-bhartuḥ pada-kamalayor dāsa-dāsānudāsaḥ.* One must become a servant of the servant. Prahlāda Mahārāja also prayed to Lord Nṛsiṁhadeva that he might be engaged as the servant of the Lord's servant. This is the prescribed method of devotional service. As soon as a devotee wants the Supreme Personality of Godhead to be his order supplier, the Lord immediately refuses to become the master of such a motivated devotee. In *Bhagavad-gītā* (4.11) the Lord says, *ye yathā māṁ prapadyante tāṁs tathaiva bhajāmy aham.* "As one surrenders unto Me, I reward him accordingly." Materialistic persons are generally inclined to material profits. As long as one continues in such an adulterated position, he does not receive the benefit of returning home, back to Godhead.

TEXT 7

यदि दास्यसि मे कामान् वरांस्त्वं वरदर्षभ ।
कामानां हृद्यसंरोहं भवतस्तु वृणे वरम् ॥ ७ ॥

yadi dāsyasi me kāmān
varāṁs tvaṁ varadarṣabha
kāmānāṁ hṛdy asaṁrohaṁ
bhavatas tu vṛṇe varam

yadi—if; *dāsyasi*—want to give; *me*—me; *kāmān*—anything desirable; *varān*—as Your benediction; *tvam*—You; *varada-ṛṣabha*—O Supreme Personality of Godhead, who can give any benediction; *kāmānām*—of all desires for material happiness; *hṛdi*—within the core of my heart; *asaṁroham*—no growth; *bhavataḥ*—from You; *tu*—then; *vṛṇe*—I pray for; *varam*—such a benediction.

TRANSLATION

O my Lord, best of the givers of benediction, if You at all want to bestow a desirable benediction upon me, then I pray from Your Lordship that within the core of my heart there be no material desires.

PURPORT

Lord Śrī Caitanya Mahāprabhu taught us how to pray for benedictions from the Lord. He said:

na dhanaṁ na janaṁ na sundarīṁ
kavitāṁ vā jagad-īśa kāmaye
mama janmani janmanīśvare
bhavatād bhaktir ahaitukī tvayi

"O my Lord, I do not want from You any amount of wealth, nor many followers, nor a beautiful wife, for these are all materialistic desires. But if I have to ask You for any benediction, I pray that in whatever forms of life I may take my birth, under any circumstances, I will not be bereft of Your transcendental devotional service." Devotees are always on the positive platform, in contrast to the Māyāvādīs, who want to make everything impersonal or void. One cannot remain void (*śūnyavādī*); rather, one must possess something. Therefore, the devotee, on the positive side, wants to possess something, and this possession is very nicely described by Prahlāda Mahārāja, who says, "If I must take some benediction from

You, I pray that within the core of my heart there may be no material desires." The desire to serve the Supreme Personality of Godhead is not at all material.

TEXT 8

इन्द्रियाणि मनः प्राण आत्मा धर्मो धृतिर्मतिः ।
ह्रीः श्रीस्तेजः स्मृतिः सत्यं यस्य नश्यन्ति जन्मना ॥ ८ ॥

indriyāṇi manaḥ prāṇa
ātmā dharmo dhṛtir matiḥ
hrīḥ śrīs tejaḥ smṛtiḥ satyaṁ
yasya naśyanti janmanā

indriyāṇi—the senses; *manaḥ*—the mind; *prāṇaḥ*—the life air; *ātmā*—the body; *dharmaḥ*—religion; *dhṛtiḥ*—patience; *matiḥ*—intelligence; *hrīḥ*—shyness; *śrīḥ*—opulence; *tejaḥ*—strength; *smṛtiḥ*—memory; *satyam*—truthfulness; *yasya*—of which lusty desires; *naśyanti*—are vanquished; *janmanā*—from the very beginning of birth.

TRANSLATION

O my Lord, because of lusty desires from the very beginning of one's birth, the functions of one's senses, mind, life, body, religion, patience, intelligence, shyness, opulence, strength, memory and truthfulness are vanquished.

PURPORT

As stated in *Śrīmad-Bhāgavatam, kāmaṁ hṛd-rogam.* Materialistic life means that one is afflicted by a formidable disease called lusty desire. Liberation means freedom from lusty desires because it is only due to such desires that one must accept repeated birth and death. As long as one's lusty desires are unfulfilled, one must take birth after birth to fulfill them. Because of material desires, therefore, one performs various types of activities and receives various types of bodies with which to try to fulfill desires that are never satisfied. The only remedy is to take to devotional service, which begins when one is free from all material desires. *Anyābhilāṣitā-śūnyam. Anya-abhilāṣitā* means "material desire," and *śūnyam* means "free from." The spiritual soul has spiritual activities and spiritual desires, as described by Śrī Caitanya Mahāprabhu: *mama janmani janmanīśvare bhavatād bhaktir ahaitukī tvayi.* Unalloyed devotion to the service of the Lord is the only spiritual desire. To fulfill this spiritual desire, however, one must be free from all material desires. Desirelessness means freedom from material desires. This is described by Śrīla Rūpa Gosvāmī as *anyābhilāṣitā-śūnyam.* As soon as one has material desires, one loses his spiritual identity. Then all the paraphernalia of one's life, including one's senses, body, religion, patience and intelligence, are deviated from one's original Kṛṣṇa consciousness. As soon as one has material desires, one cannot properly use his senses, intelligence, mind and so on for the satisfaction of the Supreme Personality of Godhead. Māyāvādī philosophers want to become impersonal, senseless and mindless, but that is not possible. The living entity must be living, always existing with desires, ambitions and so on. These should be purified, however, so that one can desire spiritually and be spiritually ambitious, without material contamination. In every living entity these propensities exist because he is a living entity. When materially contaminated, however, one is put into the hands of material misery (*janma-mṛtyu-jarā-vyādhi*). If one wants to stop repeated birth and death, one must take to the devotional service of the Lord.

sarvopādhi-vinirmuktaṁ
tat-paratvena nirmalam
hṛṣīkeṇa hṛṣīkeśa-
sevanaṁ bhaktir ucyate

"Bhakti, or devotional service, means engaging all our senses in the service of the Lord, the Supreme Personality of Godhead, the master of all the senses. When the spirit soul renders service unto the Supreme, there are two side effects. One is freed from all material designations, and, simply by being employed in the service of the Lord, one's senses are purified."

TEXT 9

विमुञ्चति यदा कामान्मानवो मनसि स्थितान् ।
तर्ह्येव पुण्डरीकाक्ष भगवत्त्वाय कल्पते ॥ ९ ॥

vimuñcati yadā kāmān
mānavo manasi sthitān
tarhy eva puṇḍarīkākṣa
bhagavattvāya kalpate

vimuñcati—gives up; *yadā*—whenever; *kāmān*—all material desires; *mānavaḥ*—human society; *manasi*—within the mind; *sthitān*—situated; *tarhi*—at that time only; *eva*—indeed; *puṇḍarīka-akṣa*—O lotus-eyed Lord; *bhagavattvāya*—to be equally as opulent as the Lord; *kalpate*—becomes eligible.

TRANSLATION

O my Lord, when a human being is able to give up all the material desires in his mind, he becomes eligible to possess wealth and opulence like Yours.

PURPORT

Atheistic men sometimes criticize a devotee by saying, "If you do not want to take any benediction from the Lord and if the servant of the Lord is as opulent as the Lord Himself, why do you ask for the benediction of being engaged as the Lord's servant?" Śrīdhara Svāmī comments, *bhagavattvāya bhagavat-samān aiśvaryāya. Bhagavattva,* becoming as good as the Supreme Personality of Godhead, does not mean becoming one with Him or equal to Him, although in the spiritual world the servant is equally as opulent as the master. The servant of the Lord is engaged in the service of the Lord as a servant, friend, father, mother or conjugal lover, all of whom are equally as opulent as the Lord. This is *acintya-bhedābheda-tattva.* The master and servant are different yet equal in opulence. This is the meaning of simultaneous difference from the Supreme Lord and oneness with Him.

TEXT 10

ॐ नमो भगवते तुभ्यं पुरुषाय महात्मने ।
हरयेऽद्भुतसिंहाय ब्रह्मणे परमात्मने ॥१०॥

oṁ namo bhagavate tubhyaṁ
puruṣāya mahātmane

haraye 'dbhuta-siṁhāya
brahmaṇe paramātmane

oṁ—O my Lord, O Supreme Personality of Godhead; *namaḥ*—I offer my respectful obeisances; *bhagavate*—unto the Supreme Person; *tubhyam*—unto You; *puruṣāya*—unto the Supreme Person; *mahā-ātmane*—unto the Supreme Soul, or the Supersoul; *haraye*—unto the Lord, who vanquishes all the miseries of devotees; *adbhuta-siṁhāya*—unto Your wonderful lionlike form as Nṛsiṁhadeva; *brahmaṇe*—unto the Supreme Brahman; *parama-ātmane*—unto the Supreme Soul.

TRANSLATION

O my Lord, full of six opulences, O Supreme Person! O Supreme Soul, killer of all miseries! O Supreme Person in the form of a wonderful lion and man, let me offer my respectful obeisances unto You.

PURPORT

In the previous verse Prahlāda Mahārāja has explained that a devotee can achieve the platform of *bhagavattva*, being as good as the Supreme Person, but this does not mean that the devotee loses his position as a servant. A pure servant of the Lord, although as opulent as the Lord, is still meant to offer respectful obeisances to the Lord in service. Prahlāda Mahārāja was engaged in pacifying the Lord, and therefore he did not consider himself equal to the Lord. He defined his position as a servant and offered respectful obeisances unto the Lord.

TEXT 11

श्रीभगवानुवाच
नैकान्तिनो मे मयि जात्विहाशिष
आशासतेऽमुत्र च ये भवद्विधाः ।
तथापि मन्वन्तरमेतदत्र
दैत्येश्वराणामनुभुङ्क्ष्व भोगान् ॥११॥

śrī-bhagavān uvāca
naikāntino me mayi jātv ihāśiṣa
āśāsate 'mutra ca ye bhavad-vidhāḥ
tathāpi manvantaram etad atra
daityeśvarāṇām anubhuṅkṣva bhogān

śrī-bhagavān uvāca—the Supreme Personality of Godhead said; *na*—not; *ekāntinaḥ*—unalloyed, without desires except for the one desire for devotional service; *me*—from Me; *mayi*—unto Me; *jātu*—any time; *iha*—within this material world; *āśiṣaḥ*—benedictions; *āśāsate*—intent desire; *amutra*—in the next life; *ca*—and; *ye*—all such devotees who; *bhavat-vidhāḥ*—like you; *tathāpi*—still; *manvantaram*—the duration of time until the end of the life of one Manu; *etat*—this; *atra*—within this material world; *daitya-īśvarāṇām*—of the opulences of materialistic persons; *anubhuṅkṣva*—you can enjoy; *bhogān*—all material opulences.

TRANSLATION

The Supreme Personality of Godhead said: My dear Prahlāda, a devotee like you never desires any kind of material opulences, either in this life or in the next. Nonetheless, I order you to enjoy the opulences of the demons in this material world, acting as their king until the end of the duration of time occupied by Manu.

PURPORT

One Manu lives for a duration of time calculated to be an aggregate of seventy-one *yuga* cycles, each of which equals 4,300,000 years. Although atheistic men like to enjoy material opulences and they endeavor with great energy to build big residences, roads, cities and factories, unfortunately they cannot live more than eighty, ninety or at the utmost one hundred years. Although the materialist exerts so much energy to create a kingdom of hallucinations, he is unable to enjoy it for more than a few years. However, because Prahlāda Mahārāja was a devotee, the Lord allowed him to enjoy material opulence as the king of the materialists. Prahlāda Mahārāja had taken birth in the family of Hiraṇyakaśipu, who was the topmost materialist, and since Prahlāda was the bona fide heir of his father, the Supreme Lord allowed him to enjoy the kingdom created by his father for so many years that no materialist could calculate them. A devotee does not have to desire material opulence, but if he is a pure devotee, there is ample opportunity for him to enjoy material happiness also, without personal endeavor. Therefore, everyone is advised to take to devotional service under all circumstances. If one desires material opulence, he can also become a pure devotee, and his desires will be fulfilled. It is stated in *Śrīmad-Bhāgavatam* (2.3.10):

akāmaḥ sarva-kāmo vā
mokṣa-kāma udāra-dhīḥ
tīvreṇa bhakti-yogena
yajeta puruṣaṁ param

"Whether one desires everything or nothing, or whether he desires to merge into the existence of the Lord, he is intelligent only if he worships Lord Kṛṣṇa, the Supreme Personality of Godhead, by rendering transcendental loving service."

TEXT 12

कथा मदीया जुषमाणः प्रियास्त्व-
मावेश्य मामात्मनि सन्तमेकम् ।
सर्वेषु भूतेष्वधियज्ञमीशं
यजस्व योगेन च कर्म हिन्वन् ॥१२॥

kathā madīyā juṣamāṇaḥ priyās tvam
āveśya mām ātmani santam ekam
sarveṣu bhūteṣv adhiyajñam īśaṁ
yajasva yogena ca karma hinvan

kathāḥ—messages or instructions; *madīyāḥ*—given by Me; *juṣamāṇaḥ*—always hearing or contemplating; *priyāḥ*—extremely pleasing; *tvam*—yourself; *āveśya*—being fully absorbed in; *mām*—Me; *ātmani*—within the core of your heart; *santam*—existing; *ekam*—one (the same Supreme Soul); *sarveṣu*—in all; *bhūteṣu*—living entities; *adhiyajñam*—the enjoyer of all ritualistic ceremonies; *īśam*—the

Supreme Lord; *yajasva*—worship; *yogena*—by *bhakti-yoga,* devotional service; *ca*—also; *karma*—fruitive activities; *hinvan*—giving up.

TRANSLATION

It does not matter that you are in the material world. You should always, continuously, hear the instructions and messages given by Me and always be absorbed in thought of Me, for I am the Supersoul existing in the core of everyone's heart. Therefore, give up fruitive activities and worship Me.

PURPORT

When a devotee becomes materially very opulent, one should not think that he is enjoying the results of his fruitive activities. A devotee in this material world uses all material opulences for the service of the Lord because he is planning how to serve the Lord with these opulences, as advised by the Lord Himself. Whatever material opulence is within his possession he engages to expand the glories and service of the Lord. A devotee never performs any fruitive or ritualistic ceremony to enjoy the results of such *karma.* Rather, a devotee knows that *karma-kāṇḍa* is meant for the less intelligent man. Narottama dāsa Ṭhākura says in his *Prema-bhakti-candrikā, karma-kāṇḍa, jñāna-kāṇḍa, kevala viṣera bhāṇḍa:* both *karma-kāṇḍa* and *jñāna-kāṇḍa*—fruitive activities and speculation about the Supreme Lord—are like pots of poison. One who is attracted to *karma-kāṇḍa* and *jñāna-kāṇḍa* spoils his existence as a human being. Therefore a devotee is never interested in *karma-kāṇḍa* or *jñāna-kāṇḍa,* but is simply interested in favorable service to the Lord (*ānukūlyena kṛṣṇānuśīlanam*), or cultivation of spiritual activities in devotional service.

TEXT 13

भोगेन पुण्यं कुशलेन पापं
कलेवरं कालजवेन हित्वा ।
कीर्तिं विशुद्धां सुरलोकगीतां
विताय मामेष्यसि मुक्तबन्धः ॥१३॥

bhogena puṇyaṁ kuśalena pāpaṁ
kalevaraṁ kāla-javena hitvā
kīrtiṁ viśuddhāṁ sura-loka-gītāṁ
vitāya mām eṣyasi mukta-bandhaḥ

bhogena—by feelings of material happiness; *puṇyam*—pious activities or their results; *kuśalena*—by acting piously (devotional service is the best of all pious activities); *pāpam*—all kinds of reactions to impious activities; *kalevaram*—the material body; *kāla-javena*—by the most powerful time factor; *hitvā*—giving up; *kīrtim*—reputation; *viśuddhām*—transcendental or fully purified; *sura-loka-gītām*—praised even in the heavenly planets; *vitāya*—spreading all through the universe; *mām*—unto Me; *eṣyasi*—you will come back; *mukta-bandhaḥ*—being liberated from all bondage.

TRANSLATION

My dear Prahlāda, while you are in this material world you will exhaust all the reactions of pious activity by feeling happiness, and by acting piously you will neutralize impious activity. Because of the powerful time factor, you will give up your body, but the glories of your activities will be sung in the upper planetary systems, and being fully freed from all bondage, you will return home, back to Godhead.

PURPORT

Śrīla Viśvanātha Cakravartī Ṭhākura says: *evaṁ prahlādasyāṁśena sādhana-siddhatvaṁ nitya-siddhatvaṁ ca nāradādivaj jñeyam.* There are two classes of devotees—the *sādhana-siddha* and the *nitya-siddha.* Prahlāda Mahārāja is a mixed *siddha;* that is, he is perfect partly because of executing devotional service and partly because of eternal perfection. Thus he is compared to such devotees as Nārada. Formerly, Nārada Muni was the son of a maidservant, and therefore in his next birth he attained perfection (*sādhana-siddhi*) because of having executed devotional service. Yet he is also a *nitya-siddha* because he never forgets the Supreme Personality of Godhead.

The word *kuśalena* is very important. One should live in the material world very expertly. The material world is known as the world of duality because one sometimes has to act impiously and sometimes has to act piously. Although one does not want to act impiously, the world is so fashioned that there is always danger (*padaṁ padaṁ yad vipadām*). Thus even when performing devotional service a devotee has to create many enemies. Prahlāda Mahārāja himself had experience of this, for even his father became his enemy. A devotee should expertly manage to think always of the Supreme Lord so that the reactions of suffering cannot touch him. This is the expert management of *pāpa-puṇya*—pious and impious activities. An exalted devotee like Prahlāda Mahārāja is *jīvan-mukta;* he is liberated even in this very life in the material body.

TEXT 14

य एतत् कीर्तयेन्मह्यं त्वया गीतमिदं नरः ।
त्वां च मां च स्मरन्काले कर्मबन्धात् प्रमुच्यते॥१४॥

ya etat kīrtayen mahyaṁ
tvayā gītam idaṁ naraḥ
tvāṁ ca māṁ ca smaran kāle
karma-bandhāt pramucyate

yaḥ—anyone who; *etat*—this activity; *kīrtayet*—chants; *mahyam*—unto Me; *tvayā*—by you; *gītam*—prayers offered; *idam*—this; *naraḥ*—human being; *tvām*—you; *ca*—as well as; *mām ca*—Me also; *smaran*—remembering; *kāle*—in due course of time; *karma-bandhāt*—from the bondage of material activities; *pramucyate*—becomes free.

TRANSLATION

One who always remembers your activities and My activities also, and who chants the prayers you have offered, becomes free, in due course of time, from the reactions of material activities.

PURPORT

Here it is stated that anyone who chants and hears about the activities of Prahlāda Mahārāja and, in relationship with Prahlāda's activities, the activities of Nṛsiṁhadeva, gradually becomes free from all the bondage of fruitive activities. As stated in *Bhagavad-gītā* (2.15, 2.56):

yaṁ hi na vyathayanty ete
puruṣaṁ puruṣarṣabha
sama-duḥkha-sukhaṁ dhīraṁ
so 'mṛtatvāya kalpate

"O best among men [Arjuna], the person who is not disturbed by happiness and distress and is steady in both is certainly eligible for liberation."

duḥkheṣv anudvigna-manāḥ
sukheṣu vigata-spṛhaḥ
vīta-rāga-bhaya-krodhaḥ
sthita-dhīr munir ucyate

"One who is not disturbed in spite of the threefold miseries, who is not elated when there is happiness, and who is free from attachment, fear and anger, is called a sage of steady mind." A devotee should not be aggrieved in an awkward position, nor should he feel extraordinarily happy in material opulence. This is the way of expert management of material life. Because a devotee knows how to manage expertly, he is called *jīvan-mukta.* As Rūpa Gosvāmī explains in *Bhakti-rasāmṛta-sindhu:*

īhā yasya harer dāsye
karmaṇā manasā girā
nikhilāsv apy avasthāsu
jīvan-muktaḥ sa ucyate

"A person acting in Kṛṣṇa consciousness (or, in other words, in the service of Kṛṣṇa) with his body, mind, intelligence and words is a liberated person even within this material world, although he may be engaged in many so-called material activities." Because of constantly engaging in devotional service, in any condition of life, a devotee is free from all material bondage.

bhaktiḥ punāti man-niṣṭhā
śva-pākān api sambhavāt

"Even one born in a family of meat-eaters is purified if he engages in devotional service." (*Bhāg.* 11.14.21) Śrīla Jīva Gosvāmī cites this verse in logically supporting that anyone who chants about the pure life and activities of Prahlāda Mahārāja is freed from the reactions of material activities.

TEXTS 15–17

श्रीप्रह्राद उवाच
वरं वरय एतत् ते वरदेशान्महेश्वर ।
यदनिन्दत् पिता मे त्वामविद्वांस्तेज ऐश्वरम् ॥१५॥
विद्धामर्षाशयः साक्षात् सर्वलोकगुरुं प्रभुम् ।
भ्रातृहेति मृषादृष्टिस्त्वद्भक्ते मयि चाघवान् ॥१६॥
तस्मात् पिता मे पूयेत दुरन्ताद् दुस्तरादघात् ।
पूतस्तेऽपाङ्गसंदृष्टस्तदा कृपणवत्सल ॥१७॥

śrī-prahrāda uvāca
varaṁ varaya etat te
varadeśān maheśvara
yad anindat pitā me
tvām avidvāṁs teja aiśvaram

viddhāmarṣāśayaḥ sākṣāt
sarva-loka-guruṁ prabhum
bhrātṛ-heti mṛṣā-dṛṣṭis
tvad-bhakte mayi cāghavān

tasmāt pitā me pūyeta
durantād dustarād aghāt
pūtas te 'pāṅga-saṁdṛṣṭas
tadā kṛpaṇa-vatsala

śrī-prahrādaḥ uvāca—Prahlāda Mahārāja said; *varam*—benediction; *varaye*—I pray; *etat*—this; *te*—from You; *varada-īśāt*—the Supreme Personality of Godhead, who offers benedictions even to such exalted demigods as Brahmā and Śiva; *mahā-īśvara*—O my Supreme Lord; *yat*—that; *anindat*—vilified; *pitā*—father; *me*—my; *tvām*—You; *avidvān*—without knowledge of; *tejaḥ*—strength; *aiśvaram*—supremacy;

viddha—being polluted; *amarṣa*—with anger; *āśayaḥ*—within the heart; *sākṣāt*—directly; *sarva-loka-gurum*—unto the supreme spiritual master of all living beings; *prabhum*—unto the supreme master; *bhrātṛ-hā*—the killer of his brother; *iti*—thus; *mṛṣā-dṛṣṭiḥ*—falsely envious because of a false conception; *tvat-bhakte*—unto Your devotee; *mayi*—unto me; *ca*—and; *agha-vān*—who committed heavily sinful activities; *tasmāt*—from that; *pitā*—father; *me*—my; *pūyeta*—may be purified; *durantāt*—very great; *dustarāt*—difficult to pass over; *aghāt*—from all sinful activities; *pūtaḥ*—(although he was) purified; *te*—of You; *apāṅga*—by the glance over him; *saṁdṛṣṭaḥ*—being looked at; *tadā*—at that time; *kṛpaṇa-vatsala*—O You who are merciful to the materialistic.

TRANSLATION

Prahlāda Mahārāja said: O Supreme Lord, because You are so merciful to the fallen souls, I ask You for only one benediction. I know that my father, at the time of his death, had already been purified by Your glance upon him, but because of his ignorance of Your beautiful power and supremacy, he was unnecessarily angry at You, falsely thinking that You were the killer of his brother. Thus he directly blasphemed Your Lordship, the spiritual master of all living beings, and committed heavily sinful activities directed against me, Your devotee. I wish that he be excused for these sinful activities.

PURPORT

Although Hiraṇyakaśipu was purified as soon as he came in contact with the Lord's lap and the Lord saw him, Prahlāda Mahārāja still wanted to hear from the Lord's own mouth that his father had been purified by the Lord's causeless mercy. Prahlāda Mahārāja offered this prayer to the Lord for the sake of his father. As a Vaiṣṇava son, despite all the inconveniences imposed upon him by his father, he could not forget his father's affection.

TEXT 18

श्रीभगवानुवाच

त्रिःसप्तभिः पिता पूतः पितृभिःसह तेऽनघ ।
यत्साधोऽस्य कुले जातो भवान्वै कुलपावनः ॥१८॥

śrī-bhagavān uvāca
triḥ-saptabhiḥ pitā pūtaḥ
pitṛbhiḥ saha te 'nagha
yat sādho 'sya kule jāto
bhavān vai kula-pāvanaḥ

śrī-bhagavān uvāca—the Supreme Personality of Godhead said; *triḥ-saptabhiḥ*—seven multiplied by three (that is to say, twenty-one); *pitā*—father; *pūtaḥ*—purified; *pitṛbhiḥ*—with your forefathers; *saha*—all together; *te*—your; *anagha*—O most sinless personality (Prahlāda Mahārāja); *yat*—because; *sādho*—O great saintly person; *asya*—of this person; *kule*—in the dynasty; *jātaḥ*—took birth; *bhavān*—you; *vai*—indeed; *kula-pāvanaḥ*—the purifier of the whole dynasty.

TRANSLATION

The Supreme Personality of Godhead said: My dear Prahlāda, O most pure, O great saintly person, your father has been purified, along with twenty-one forefathers in your family. Because you were born in this family, the entire dynasty has been purified.

PURPORT

The word *triḥ-saptabhiḥ* means seven multiplied by three. In one's family one can count back four or five generations—to one's great-grandfather or even one's great-grandfather's father—but since the Lord mentions twenty-one forefathers, this indicates that the benediction expands to other families also. Before the present family in which one has taken birth, one must have been born in other families. Thus when a Vaiṣṇava takes birth in a family, by the grace of the Lord he purifies not only that family but also the families of his previous births.

TEXT 19

यत्र यत्र च मद्भक्ताः प्रशान्ताः समदर्शिनः ।
साधवः समुदाचारास्ते पूयन्तेऽपि कीकटाः ॥१९॥

yatra yatra ca mad-bhaktāḥ
praśāntāḥ sama-darśinaḥ

sādhavaḥ samudācārās
te pūyante 'pi kīkaṭāḥ

yatra yatra—wherever and whenever; *ca*—also; *mat-bhaktāḥ*—My devotees; *praśāntāḥ*—extremely peaceful; *sama-darśinaḥ*—equipoised; *sādhavaḥ*—decorated with all good qualities; *samudācārāḥ*—equally magnanimous; *te*—all of them; *pūyante*—are purified; *api*—even; *kīkaṭāḥ*—a degraded country or the inhabitants of such a place.

TRANSLATION

Whenever and wherever there are peaceful, equipoised devotees who are well behaved and decorated with all good qualities, that place and the dynasties there, even if condemned, are purified.

PURPORT

Wherever exalted devotees stay, not only they and their dynasties but the entire country is purified.

TEXT 20

सर्वात्मना न हिंसन्ति भूतग्रामेषु किञ्चन ।
उच्चावचेषु दैत्येन्द्र मद्भावविगतस्पृहाः ॥२०॥

sarvātmanā na hiṁsanti
bhūta-grāmeṣu kiñcana
uccāvaceṣu daityendra
mad-bhāva-vigata-spṛhāḥ

sarva-ātmanā—in all respects, even in the modes of anger and jealousy; *na*—never; *hiṁsanti*—they are envious; *bhūta-grāmeṣu*—among all species of life; *kiñcana*—toward any one of them; *ucca-avaceṣu*—the lower and higher living entities; *daitya-indra*—O my dear Prahlāda, King of the Daityas; *mat-bhāva*—because of devotional service unto Me; *vigata*—given up; *spṛhāḥ*—all material modes of anger and greed.

TRANSLATION

My dear Prahlāda, King of the Daityas, because of being attached to devotional service to Me, My devotee does not distinguish between lower and higher living entities. In all respects, he is never jealous of anyone.

TEXT 21

भवन्ति पुरुषा लोके मद्भक्तास्त्वामनुव्रताः ।
भवान्मे खलु भक्तानां सर्वेषां प्रतिरूपधृक् ॥२१॥

bhavanti puruṣā loke
mad-bhaktās tvām anuvratāḥ
bhavān me khalu bhaktānāṁ
sarveṣāṁ pratirūpa-dhṛk

bhavanti—become; *puruṣāḥ*—persons; *loke*—in this world; *mat-bhaktāḥ*—My pure devotees; *tvām*—you; *anuvratāḥ*—following in your footsteps; *bhavān*—you; *me*—My; *khalu*—indeed; *bhaktānām*—of all devotees; *sarveṣām*—in different mellows; *pratirūpa-dhṛk*—tangible example.

TRANSLATION

Those who follow your example will naturally become My pure devotees. You are the best example of My devotee, and others should follow in your footsteps.

PURPORT

In this connection, Śrīla Madhvācārya quotes a verse from the *Skanda Purāṇa:*

ṛte tu tāttvikān devān
nāradādīṁs tathaiva ca
prahrādād uttamaḥ ko nu
viṣṇu-bhaktau jagat-traye

There are many, many devotees of the Supreme Personality of Godhead, and they have been enumerated in *Śrīmad-Bhāgavatam* (6.3.20) as follows:

svayambhūr nāradaḥ śambhuḥ
kumāraḥ kapilo manuḥ
prahlādo janako bhīṣmo
balir vaiyāsakir vayam

Of the twelve authorized devotees—Lord Brahmā, Nārada, Lord Śiva, Kapila, Manu and so on—Prahlāda Mahārāja is understood to be the best example.

TEXT 22

कुरु त्वं प्रेतकृत्यानि पितुः पूतस्य सर्वशः ।
मदङ्गस्पर्शनेनाङ्ग लोकान्यास्यति सुप्रजाः ॥२२॥

kuru tvaṁ preta-kṛtyāni
pituḥ pūtasya sarvaśaḥ
mad-aṅga-sparśanenāṅga
lokān yāsyati suprajāḥ

kuru—perform; *tvam*—you; *preta-kṛtyāni*—the ritualistic ceremony performed after death; *pituḥ*—of your father; *pūtasya*—already purified; *sarvaśaḥ*—in all respects; *mat-aṅga*—My body; *sparśanena*—by touching; *aṅga*—My dear child; *lokān*—to planets; *yāsyati*—he will be elevated; *su-prajāḥ*—to become a devotee-citizen.

TRANSLATION

My dear child, your father has already been purified just by the touch of My body at the time of his death. Nonetheless, the duty of a son is to perform the śrāddha ritualistic ceremony after his father's death so that his father may be promoted to a planetary system where he may become a good citizen and devotee.

PURPORT

In this regard, Śrīla Viśvanātha Cakravartī Ṭhākura says that although Hiraṇyakaśipu was already purified, he had to take birth on a higher planetary system to become a devotee again. Prahlāda Mahārāja was advised to perform the ritualistic ceremony as a matter of etiquette, for the Supreme Personality of Godhead under no circumstances wants to stop the regulative principles. Madhva Muni also instructs:

madhu-kaiṭabhau bhakty-abhāvā
dūrau bhagavato mṛtau
tama eva kramād āptau
bhaktyā ced yo hariṁ yayau

When the demons Madhu and Kaiṭabha were killed by the Supreme Personality of Godhead, their kinsmen also observed the ritualistic ceremonies so that these demons could return home, back to Godhead.

TEXT 23

पित्र्यं च स्थानमातिष्ठ यथोक्तं ब्रह्मवादिभिः ।
मय्यावेश्य मनस्तात कुरु कर्माणि मत्परः ॥२३॥

pitryaṁ ca sthānam ātiṣṭha
yathoktaṁ brahmavādibhiḥ
mayy āveśya manas tāta
kuru karmāṇi mat-paraḥ

pitryam—paternal; *ca*—also; *sthānam*—place, throne; *ātiṣṭha*—sit upon; *yathā-uktam*—as described; *brahmavādibhiḥ*—by the followers of Vedic civilization; *mayi*—unto Me; *āveśya*—being fully absorbed; *manaḥ*—the mind; *tāta*—My dear boy; *kuru*—just execute; *karmāṇi*—the regulative duties; *mat-paraḥ*—just for the sake of My work.

TRANSLATION

After performing the ritualistic ceremonies, take charge of your father's kingdom. Sit upon the throne and do not be disturbed by materialistic activities. Please keep your mind fixed upon Me. Without transgressing the injunctions of the Vedas, as a matter of formality you may perform your particular duties.

PURPORT

When one becomes a devotee, he no longer has any duty to the Vedic regulative principles. One has many duties to perform, but if one becomes fully devoted to the Lord, he no longer has any such obligations. As stated in *Śrīmad-Bhāgavatam* (11.5.41):

devarṣi-bhūtāpta-nṛṇāṁ pitṝṇāṁ
na kiṅkaro nāyam ṛṇī ca rājan
sarvātmanā yaḥ śaraṇaṁ śaraṇyaṁ
gato mukundaṁ parihṛtya kartam

One who has fully surrendered to the lotus feet of the Lord is no longer a debtor to his forefathers, the great sages, human society, the common man or any living entity.

The Supreme Personality of Godhead nonetheless advised Prahlāda Mahārāja to follow the regulative principles, for since he was going to be the king, others would follow his example. Thus Lord Nṛsiṁhadeva advised Prahlāda Mahārāja to engage in his political duties so that people would become the Lord's devotees.

yad yad ācarati śreṣṭhas
tat tad evetaro janaḥ
sa yat pramāṇaṁ kurute
lokas tad anuvartate

"Whatever action a great man performs, common men follow. And whatever standards he sets by exemplary acts, all the world pursues." (Bg. 3.21) One should not be attached to any materialistic activities, but a devotee may perform such activities as an example to show the common man that one should not deviate from the Vedic injunctions.

TEXT 24

श्रीनारद उवाच
प्रह्रादोऽपि तथा चक्रे पितुर्यत्साम्परायिकम् ।
यथाह भगवान् राजन्नभिषिक्तो द्विजातिभिः ॥२४॥

śrī-nārada uvāca
prahrādo 'pi tathā cakre
pitur yat sāmparāyikam
yathāha bhagavān rājann
abhiṣikto dvijātibhiḥ

śrī-nāradaḥ uvāca—Nārada Muni said; *prahrādaḥ*—Prahlāda Mahārāja; *api*—also; *tathā*—in that way; *cakre*—executed; *pituḥ*—of his father; *yat*—whatever; *sāmparāyikam*—ritualistic ceremonies performed after death; *yathā*—even as; *āha*—order; *bhagavān*—the Supreme Personality of Godhead; *rājan*—O King Yudhiṣṭhira; *abhiṣiktaḥ*—he was enthroned in the kingdom; *dvi-jātibhiḥ*—by the *brāhmaṇas* present.

TRANSLATION

Śrī Nārada Muni continued: Thus, as the Supreme Personality of Godhead ordered, Prahlāda Mahārāja performed the ritualistic ceremonies for his father. O King Yudhiṣṭhira, he was then enthroned in the kingdom of Hiraṇyakaśipu, as directed by the brāhmaṇas.

PURPORT

It is essential that society be divided into four groups of men—*brāhmaṇas, kṣatriyas, vaiśyas* and *śūdras.* Here we see that although Prahlāda was perfect in every respect, he nonetheless followed the instructions of the *brāhmaṇas* who performed the Vedic rituals. Therefore in society there must be a very intelligent class of leaders who are well versed in the Vedic knowledge so that they can guide the entire populace to follow the Vedic principles and thus gradually become most perfect and eligible to return home, back to Godhead.

TEXT 25

प्रसादसुमुखं दृष्ट्वा ब्रह्मा नरहरिं हरिम् ।
स्तुत्वा वाग्भिः पवित्राभिः प्राह देवादिभिर्वृतः ॥२५॥

prasāda-sumukhaṁ dṛṣṭvā
brahmā naraharim harim

stutvā vāgbhiḥ pavitrābhiḥ
prāha devādibhir vṛtaḥ

prasāda-sumukham—whose face was bright because the Supreme Lord was pleased; *dṛṣṭvā*—seeing this situation; *brahmā*—Lord Brahmā; *nara-harim*—unto Lord Nṛsiṁhadeva; *harim*—the Supreme Personality of Godhead; *stutvā*—offering prayers; *vāgbhiḥ*—by transcendental words; *pavitrābhiḥ*—without any material contamination; *prāha*—addressed (the Lord); *deva-ādibhiḥ*—by other demigods; *vṛtaḥ*—surrounded.

TRANSLATION

Lord Brahmā, surrounded by the other demigods, was bright-faced because the Lord was pleased. Thus he offered prayers to the Lord with transcendental words.

TEXT 26

श्रीब्रह्मोवाच
देवदेवाखिलाध्यक्ष भूतभावन पूर्वज ।
दिष्ट्या ते निहतः पापो लोकसन्तापनोऽसुरः ॥२६॥

śrī-brahmovāca
deva-devākhilādhyakṣa
bhūta-bhāvana pūrvaja
diṣṭyā te nihataḥ pāpo
loka-santāpano 'suraḥ

śrī-brahmā uvāca—Lord Brahmā said; *deva-deva*—O my Lord, Lord of all the demigods; *akhila-adhyakṣa*—owner of the whole universe; *bhūta-bhāvana*—O cause of all living entities; *pūrva-ja*—O original Personality of Godhead; *diṣṭyā*—by Your example or because of our good fortune; *te*—by You; *nihataḥ*—killed; *pāpaḥ*—most sinful; *loka-santāpanaḥ*—giving trouble to the entire universe; *asuraḥ*—the demon Hiraṇyakaśipu.

TRANSLATION

Lord Brahmā said: O Supreme Lord of all lords, proprietor of the entire universe, O benedictor of all living entities, O original

person [ādi-puruṣa], because of our good fortune You have now killed this sinful demon, who was giving trouble to the entire universe.

PURPORT

The word *pūrvaja* is described in *Bhagavad-gītā* (10.8): *ahaṁ sarvasya prabhavo mattaḥ sarvaṁ pravartate.* All the demigods, including Lord Brahmā, are manifested from the Supreme Personality of Godhead. Therefore the original person, the cause of all causes, is Govinda, the *ādi-puruṣam.*

TEXT 27

योऽसौ लब्धवरो मत्तो न वध्यो मम सृष्टिभिः ।
तपोयोगबलोन्नद्धः समस्तनिगमानहन् ॥२७॥

yo 'sau labdha-varo matto
na vadhyo mama sṛṣṭibhiḥ
tapo-yoga-balonnaddhaḥ
samasta-nigamān ahan

yaḥ—the person who; *asau*—he (Hiraṇyakaśipu); *labdha-varaḥ*—being given the extraordinary benediction; *mattaḥ*—from me; *na vadhyaḥ*—not to be killed; *mama sṛṣṭibhiḥ*—by any living being created by me; *tapaḥ-yoga-bala*—by austerity, mystic power and strength; *unnaddhaḥ*—thus being very proud; *samasta*—all; *nigamān*—Vedic injunctions; *ahan*—disregarded, transgressed.

TRANSLATION

This demon, Hiraṇyakaśipu, received from me the benediction that he would not be killed by any living being within my creation. With this assurance and with strength derived from austerities and mystic power, he became excessively proud and transgressed all the Vedic injunctions.

TEXT 28

दिष्ट्या तत्तनयः साधुर्महाभागवतोऽर्भकः ।
त्वया विमोचितो मृत्योर्दिष्ट्या त्वां समितोऽधुना ॥२८॥

diṣṭyā tat-tanayaḥ sādhur
mahā-bhāgavato 'rbhakaḥ
tvayā vimocito mṛtyor
diṣṭyā tvāṁ samito 'dhunā

diṣṭyā—by fortune; *tat-tanayaḥ*—his son; *sādhuḥ*—who is a great saintly person; *mahā-bhāgavataḥ*—a great and exalted devotee; *arbhakaḥ*—although a child; *tvayā*—by Your Lordship; *vimocitaḥ*—released; *mṛtyoḥ*—from the clutches of death; *diṣṭyā*—also by great fortune; *tvām samitaḥ*—perfectly under Your shelter; *adhunā*—now.

TRANSLATION

By great fortune, Hiraṇyakaśipu's son Prahlāda Mahārāja has now been released from death, for although he is a child, he is an exalted devotee. Now he is fully under the protection of Your lotus feet.

TEXT 29

एतद्‍ वपुस्ते भगवन्ध्यायतः परमात्मनः ।
सर्वतो गोप्तृ संत्रासान्मृत्योरपि जिघांसतः ॥२९॥

etad vapus te bhagavan
dhyāyataḥ paramātmanaḥ
sarvato goptṛ santrāsān
mṛtyor api jighāṁsataḥ

etat—this; *vapuḥ*—body; *te*—Your; *bhagavan*—O Supreme Personality of Godhead; *dhyāyataḥ*—those who meditate upon; *parama-ātmanaḥ*—of the Supreme Person; *sarvataḥ*—from everywhere; *goptṛ*—the protector; *santrāsāt*—from all kinds of fear; *mṛtyoḥ api*—even from fear of death; *jighāṁsataḥ*—if one is envied by an enemy.

TRANSLATION

My dear Lord, O Supreme Personality of Godhead, You are the Supreme Soul. If one meditates upon Your transcendental body,

You naturally protect him from all sources of fear, even the imminent danger of death.

PURPORT

Everyone is sure to die, for no one is excused from the hands of death, which is but a feature of the Supreme Personality of Godhead (*mṛtyuḥ sarva-haraś cāham*). When one becomes a devotee, however, he is not destined to die according to a limited duration of life. Everyone has a limited duration of life, but a devotee's lifetime can be extended by the mercy of the Supreme Lord, who is able to nullify the results of one's *karma. Karmāṇi nirdahati kintu ca bhakti-bhājāṁ.* This is the statement of *Brahma-saṁhitā* (5.54). A devotee is not under the laws of *karma.* Therefore even a devotee's scheduled death can be avoided by the causeless mercy of the Supreme Lord. God protects the devotee even from the extreme danger of death.

TEXT 30

श्रीभगवानुवाच
मैवं विभोऽसुराणां ते प्रदेयः पद्मसम्भव ।
वरः क्रूरनिसर्गाणामहीनाममृतं यथा ॥३०॥

śrī-bhagavān uvāca
maivaṁ vibho 'surāṇāṁ te
pradeyaḥ padma-sambhava
varaḥ krūra-nisargāṇām
ahīnām amṛtaṁ yathā

śrī-bhagavān uvāca—the Supreme Personality of Godhead replied (to Brahmā); *mā*—do not; *evam*—thus; *vibho*—O great person; *asurāṇām*—unto the demons; *te*—by you; *pradeyaḥ*—bestow benedictions; *padma-sambhava*—O Lord Brahmā, born from the lotus flower; *varaḥ*—benediction; *krūra-nisargāṇām*—persons who are by nature very cruel and jealous; *ahīnām*—to snakes; *amṛtam*—nectar or milk; *yathā*—just as.

TRANSLATION

The Personality of Godhead replied: My dear Lord Brahmā, O great lord born from the lotus flower, just as it is dangerous to feed milk to a snake, so it is dangerous to give benedictions to demons, who are by nature ferocious and jealous. I warn you not to give such benedictions to any demon again.

TEXT 31

श्रीनारद उवाच

इत्युक्त्वा भगवान्राजंस्ततश्चान्तर्दधे हरिः ।
अदृश्यः सर्वभूतानां पूजितः परमेष्ठिना ॥३१॥

śrī-nārada uvāca
ity uktvā bhagavān rājaṁs
tataś cāntardadhe hariḥ
adṛśyaḥ sarva-bhūtānāṁ
pūjitaḥ parameṣṭhinā

śrī-nāradaḥ uvāca—Nārada Muni said; *iti uktvā*—saying this; *bhagavān*—the Supreme Personality of Godhead; *rājan*—O King Yudhiṣṭhira; *tataḥ*—from that place; *ca*—also; *antardadhe*—disappeared; *hariḥ*—the Lord; *adṛśyaḥ*—without being visible; *sarva-bhūtānām*—by all kinds of living entities; *pūjitaḥ*—being worshiped; *parameṣṭhinā*—by Lord Brahmā.

TRANSLATION

Nārada Muni continued: O King Yudhiṣṭhira, the Supreme Personality of Godhead, who is not visible to an ordinary human being, spoke in this way, instructing Lord Brahmā. Then, being worshiped by Brahmā, the Lord disappeared from that place.

TEXT 32

ततः सम्पूज्य शिरसा ववन्दे परमेष्ठिनम् ।
भवं प्रजापतीन्देवान्प्रह्रादो भगवत्कलाः ॥३२॥

tataḥ sampūjya śirasā
vavande parameṣṭhinam
bhavaṁ prajāpatīn devān
prahrādo bhagavat-kalāḥ

tataḥ—thereafter; *sampūjya*—worshiping; *śirasā*—by bowing the head; *vavande*—offered prayers; *parameṣṭhinam*—to Lord Brahmā; *bhavam*—to Lord Śiva; *prajāpatīn*—to the great demigods entrusted with increasing the population; *devān*—to all the great demigods; *prahrādaḥ*—Prahlāda Mahārāja; *bhagavat-kalāḥ*—influential parts of the Lord.

TRANSLATION

Prahlāda Mahārāja then worshiped and offered prayers to all the demigods, such as Brahmā, Śiva and the prajāpatis, who are all parts of the Lord.

TEXT 33

ततः काव्यादिभिः सार्धं मुनिभिः कमलासनः ।
दैत्यानां दानवानां च प्रह्लादमकरोत् पतिम् ॥३३॥

tataḥ kāvyādibhiḥ sārdhaṁ
munibhiḥ kamalāsanaḥ
daityānāṁ dānavānāṁ ca
prahrādam akarot patim

tataḥ—thereafter; *kāvya-ādibhiḥ*—with Śukrācārya and others; *sārdham*—and with; *munibhiḥ*—great saintly persons; *kamala-āsanaḥ*—Lord Brahmā; *daityānām*—of all the demons; *dānavānām*—of all the giants; *ca*—and; *prahrādam*—Prahlāda Mahārāja; *akarot*—created; *patim*—the master or king.

TRANSLATION

Thereafter, along with Śukrācārya and other great saints, Lord Brahmā, whose seat is on the lotus flower, made Prahlāda the king of all the demons and giants in the universe.

PURPORT

By the grace of Lord Nṛsiṁhadeva, Prahlāda Mahārāja became a greater king than his father, Hiraṇyakaśipu. Prahlāda's inauguration was performed by Lord Brahmā in the presence of other saintly persons and demigods.

TEXT 34

प्रतिनन्द्य ततो देवाः प्रयुज्य परमाशिषः ।
स्वधामानि ययू राजन्ब्रह्माद्याः प्रतिपूजिताः ॥३४॥

pratinandya tato devāḥ
prayujya paramāśiṣaḥ
sva-dhāmāni yayū rājan
brahmādyāḥ pratipūjitāḥ

pratinandya—congratulating; *tataḥ*—thereafter; *devāḥ*—all the demigods; *prayujya*—having offered; *parama-āśiṣaḥ*—exalted benedictions; *sva-dhāmāni*—to their respective abodes; *yayuḥ*—returned; *rājan*—O King Yudhiṣṭhira; *brahma-ādyāḥ*—all the demigods, headed by Lord Brahmā; *pratipūjitāḥ*—being thoroughly worshiped (by Prahlāda Mahārāja).

TRANSLATION

O King Yudhiṣṭhira, after all the demigods, headed by Lord Brahmā, were properly worshiped by Prahlāda Mahārāja, they offered Prahlāda their utmost benedictions and then returned to their respective abodes.

TEXT 35

एवं च पार्षदौ विष्णोः पुत्रत्वं प्रापितौ दितेः ।
हृदि स्थितेन हरिणा वैरभावेन तौ हतौ ॥३५॥

evaṁ ca pārṣadau viṣṇoḥ
putratvaṁ prāpitau diteḥ
hṛdi sthitena hariṇā
vaira-bhāvena tau hatau

evam—in this way; *ca*—also; *pārṣadau*—the two personal associates; *viṣṇoḥ*—of Lord Viṣṇu; *putratvam*—becoming the sons; *prāpitau*—having gotten; *diteḥ*—of Diti; *hṛdi*—within the core of the heart; *sthitena*—being situated; *hariṇā*—by the Supreme Lord; *vaira-bhāvena*—by conceiving as an enemy; *tau*—both of them; *hatau*—were killed.

TRANSLATION

Thus the two associates of Lord Viṣṇu who had become Hiraṇyākṣa and Hiraṇyakaśipu, the sons of Diti, were both killed. By illusion they had thought that the Supreme Lord, who is situated in everyone's heart, was their enemy.

PURPORT

The discourse concerning Lord Nṛsiṁhadeva and Prahlāda Mahārāja began when Mahārāja Yudhiṣṭhira asked Nārada how Śiśupāla had merged into the body of Kṛṣṇa. Śiśupāla and Dantavakra were the same Hiraṇyākṣa and Hiraṇyakaśipu. Here Nārada Muni is relating how in three different births the associates of Lord Viṣṇu were killed by Lord Viṣṇu Himself. First they were the demons Hiraṇyākṣa and Hiraṇyakaśipu.

TEXT 36

पुनश्च विप्रशापेन राक्षसौ तौ बभूवतुः ।
कुम्भकर्णदशग्रीवौ हतौ तौ रामविक्रमैः ॥३६॥

punaś ca vipra-śāpena
rākṣasau tau babhūvatuḥ
kumbhakarṇa-daśa-grīvau
hatau tau rāma-vikramaiḥ

punaḥ—again; *ca*—also; *vipra-śāpena*—being cursed by the *brāhmaṇas; rākṣasau*—the two Rākṣasas; *tau*—both of them; *babhūvatuḥ*—incarnated as; *kumbhakarṇa-daśa-grīvau*—known as Kumbhakarṇa and the ten-headed Rāvaṇa (in their next birth); *hatau*—they also were killed; *tau*—both of them; *rāma-vikramaiḥ*—by the extraordinary strength of Lord Rāmacandra.

TRANSLATION

Being cursed by the brāhmaṇas, the same two associates took birth again as Kumbhakarṇa and the ten-headed Rāvaṇa. These two Rākṣasas were killed by Lord Rāmacandra's extraordinary power.

TEXT 37

शयानौ युधि निर्भिन्नहृदयौ रामशायकैः ।
तच्चित्तौ जहतुर्देहं यथा प्राक्तनजन्मनि ॥३७॥

śayānau yudhi nirbhinna-
hṛdayau rāma-śāyakaiḥ
tac-cittau jahatur dehaṁ
yathā prāktana-janmani

śayānau—being laid down; *yudhi*—on the battlefield; *nirbhinna*—being pierced; *hṛdayau*—in the core of the heart; *rāma-śāyakaiḥ*—by the arrows of Lord Rāmacandra; *tat-cittau*—thinking or being conscious of Lord Rāmacandra; *jahatuḥ*—gave up; *deham*—body; *yathā*—even as; *prāktana-janmani*—in their previous births.

TRANSLATION

Pierced by the arrows of Lord Rāmacandra, both Kumbhakarṇa and Rāvaṇa lay on the ground and left their bodies, fully absorbed in thought of the Lord, just as they had in their previous births as Hiraṇyākṣa and Hiraṇyakaśipu.

TEXT 38

ताविहाथ पुनर्जातौ शिशुपालकरूषजौ ।
हरौ वैरानुबन्धेन पश्यतस्ते समीयतुः ॥३८॥

tāv ihātha punar jātau
śiśupāla-karūṣa-jau
harau vairānubandhena
paśyatas te samīyatuḥ

tau—both of them; *iha*—in this human society; *atha*—in this way; *punaḥ*—again; *jātau*—took their births; *śiśupāla*—Śiśupāla; *karūṣa-jau*—Dantavakra; *harau*—unto the Supreme Personality of Godhead; *vaira-anubandhena*—by the bondage of considering the Lord an enemy; *paśyataḥ*—were looking on; *te*—while you; *samīyatuḥ*—merged or went into the lotus feet of the Lord.

TRANSLATION

They both took birth again in human society as Śiśupāla and Dantavakra and continued in the same enmity toward the Lord. It is they who merged into the body of the Lord in your presence.

PURPORT

Vairānubandhena. Acting like the Lord's enemy is also beneficial for the living entity. *Kāmād dveṣād bhayāt snehād.* Whether in lusty desire, anger, fear or envy of the Lord, somehow or other, as recommended by Śrīla Rūpa Gosvāmī (*tasmāt kenāpy upāyena*), one should become attached to the Supreme Personality of Godhead and ultimately achieve the goal of returning home, back to Godhead. What, then, is to be said of one who is related to the Supreme Personality of Godhead as a servant, friend, father, mother or conjugal lover?

TEXT 39

एनः पूर्वकृतं यत् तद् राजानः कृष्णवैरिणः ।
जहुस्तेऽन्ते तदात्मानः कीटः पेशस्कृतो यथा ॥३९॥

enaḥ pūrva-kṛtaṁ yat tad
rājānaḥ kṛṣṇa-vairiṇaḥ
jahus te 'nte tad-ātmānaḥ
kīṭaḥ peśaskṛto yathā

enaḥ—this sinful activity (of blaspheming the Supreme Lord); *pūrva-kṛtam*—executed in previous births; *yat*—which; *tat*—that; *rājānaḥ*—kings; *kṛṣṇa-vairiṇaḥ*—always acting as enemies of Kṛṣṇa; *jahuḥ*—gave up; *te*—all of them; *ante*—at the time of death; *tat-ātmānaḥ*—attaining the same spiritual body and form; *kīṭaḥ*—a worm; *peśaskṛtaḥ*—(captured by) a black drone; *yathā*—just like.

TRANSLATION

Not only Śiśupāla and Dantavakra but also many, many other kings who acted as enemies of Kṛṣṇa attained salvation at the time of death. Because they thought of the Lord, they received spiritual bodies and forms the same as His, just as worms captured by a black drone obtain the same type of body as the drone.

PURPORT

The mystery of yogic meditation is explained here. Real *yogīs* always meditate on the form of Viṣṇu within their hearts. Consequently, at the time of death they give up their bodies while thinking of the form of Viṣṇu and thus attain Viṣṇuloka, Vaikuṇṭhaloka, where they receive bodily features the same as those of the Lord. From the Sixth Canto we have already learned that when the Viṣṇudūtas came from Vaikuṇṭha to deliver Ajāmila, they looked exactly like Viṣṇu, with four hands and the same features as Viṣṇu. Therefore, we may conclude that if one practices thinking of Viṣṇu and is fully absorbed in thinking of Him at the time of death, one returns home, back to Godhead. Even enemies of Kṛṣṇa who thought of Kṛṣṇa in fear (*bhaya*), such as King Kaṁsa, received bodies in a spiritual identity similar to that of the Lord.

TEXT 40

यथा यथा भगवतो भक्त्या परमयाभिदा ।
नृपाश्चैद्यादयः सात्म्यं हरेस्तच्चिन्तया ययुः ॥४०॥

yathā yathā bhagavato
bhaktyā paramayābhidā
nṛpāś caidyādayaḥ sātmyaṁ
hares tac-cintayā yayuḥ

yathā yathā—just as; *bhagavataḥ*—of the Supreme Personality of Godhead; *bhaktyā*—by devotional service; *paramayā*—supreme; *abhidā*—incessantly thinking of such activities; *nṛpāḥ*—kings; *caidya-*

ādayaḥ—Śiśupāla, Dantavakra and others; *sātmyam*—the same form; *hareḥ*—of the Supreme Personality of Godhead; *tat-cintayā*—by constantly thinking of Him; *yayuḥ*—returned home, back to Godhead.

TRANSLATION

By devotional service, pure devotees who incessantly think of the Supreme Personality of Godhead receive bodies similar to His. This is known as sārūpya-mukti. Although Śiśupāla, Dantavakra and other kings thought of Kṛṣṇa as an enemy, they also achieved the same result.

PURPORT

In *Caitanya-caritāmṛta*, in connection with Lord Caitanya's instructions to Sanātana Gosvāmī, it is explained that a devotee should externally execute his routine devotional service in a regular way but should always inwardly think of the particular mellow in which he is attracted to the service of the Lord. This constant thought of the Lord makes the devotee eligible to return home, back to Godhead. As stated in *Bhagavad-gītā* (4.9), *tyaktvā dehaṁ punar janma naiti mām eti:* after giving up his body, a devotee does not again receive a material body, but goes back to Godhead and receives a spiritual body resembling those of the Lord's eternal associates whose activities he followed. However the devotee likes to serve the Lord, he may constantly think of the Lord's associates—the cowherd boys, the *gopīs*, the Lord's father and mother, His servants and the trees, land, animals, plants and water in the Lord's abode. Because of constantly thinking of these features, one acquires a transcendental position. Kings like Śiśupāla, Dantavakra, Kaṁsa, Pauṇḍraka, Narakāsura and Śālva were all similarly delivered. This is confirmed by Madhvācārya:

pauṇḍrake narake caiva
śālve kaṁse ca rukmiṇi
āviṣṭās tu harer bhaktās
tad-bhaktyā harim āpire

Pauṇḍraka, Narakāsura, Śālva and Kaṁsa were all inimical toward the Supreme Personality of Godhead, but because all these kings constantly thought of Him, they achieved the same liberation—*sārūpya-mukti*. The *jñāna-bhakta*, the devotee who follows the path of *jñāna*, also attains the same destination. If even the enemies of the Lord achieve salvation by constantly thinking about the Lord, what is to be said of pure devotees who always engage in the Lord's service and who think of nothing but the Lord in every activity?

TEXT 41

आख्यातं सर्वमेतत ते यन्मां त्वं परिपृष्टवान् ।
दमघोषसुतादीनां हरेः सात्म्यमपि द्विषाम् ॥४१॥

ākhyātaṁ sarvam etat te
yan māṁ tvaṁ paripṛṣṭavān
damaghoṣa-sutādīnāṁ
hareḥ sātmyam api dviṣām

ākhyātam—described; *sarvam*—everything; *etat*—this; *te*—unto you; *yat*—whatever; *mām*—unto me; *tvam*—you; *paripṛṣṭavān*—inquired; *damaghoṣa-suta-ādīnām*—of the son of Damaghoṣa (Śiśupāla) and others; *hareḥ*—of the Lord; *sātmyam*—equal bodily features; *api*—even; *dviṣām*—although they were inimical.

TRANSLATION

Everything you asked me about how Śiśupāla and others attained salvation although they were inimical has now been explained to you by me.

TEXT 42

एषा ब्रह्मण्यदेवस्य कृष्णस्य च महात्मनः ।
अवतारकथा पुण्या वधो यत्रादिदैत्ययोः ॥४२॥

eṣā brahmaṇya-devasya
kṛṣṇasya ca mahātmanaḥ
avatāra-kathā puṇyā
vadho yatrādi-daityayoḥ

eṣā—all this; *brahmaṇya-devasya*—of the Supreme Personality of Godhead, who is worshiped by all *brāhmaṇas; kṛṣṇasya*—of Kṛṣṇa, the original Supreme Personality of Godhead; *ca*—also; *mahā-ātmanaḥ*—the Supersoul; *avatāra-kathā*—narrations about His incarnations; *puṇyā*—pious, purifying; *vadhaḥ*—killing; *yatra*—wherein; *ādi*—in the beginning of the millennium; *daityayoḥ*—of the demons (Hiraṇyākṣa and Hiraṇyakaśipu).

TRANSLATION

In this narration about Kṛṣṇa, the Supreme Personality of Godhead, various expansions or incarnations of the Lord have been described, and the killing of the two demons Hiraṇyākṣa and Hiraṇyakaśipu has also been described.

PURPORT

Avatāras, or incarnations, are expansions of the Supreme Personality of Godhead—Kṛṣṇa, Govinda.

advaitam acyutam anādim ananta-rūpam
ādyaṁ purāṇa-puruṣaṁ nava-yauvanaṁ ca
vedeṣu durlabham adurlabham ātma-bhaktau
govindam ādi-puruṣaṁ tam ahaṁ bhajāmi

"I worship the Supreme Personality of Godhead, Govinda, who is the original person—nondual, infallible, and without beginning. Although He expands into unlimited forms, He is still the original, and although He is the oldest person, He always appears as a fresh youth. Such eternal, blissful and all-knowing forms of the Lord cannot be understood by the academic wisdom of the *Vedas*, but they are always manifest to pure, unalloyed devotees." (*Brahma-saṁhitā* 5.33) The *Brahma-saṁhitā* describes the *avatāras*. Indeed, all the *avatāras* are described in the authentic scriptures. No one can become an *avatāra*, or incarnation, although this has become fashionable in the age of Kali. The *avatāras* are described in the authentic scriptures (*śāstras*), and therefore before one risks accepting a pretender as an *avatāra*, one should refer to the *śāstras*. The *śāstras* say everywhere that Kṛṣṇa is the original Personality of Godhead and that He has innumerable *avatāras*, or incarnations. Elsewhere in the *Brahma-saṁhitā* it is said, *rāmādi-mūrtiṣu kalā-niyamena tiṣṭhan:* Rāma, Nṛsiṁha, Varāha and many others are consecutive expansions of the Supreme Personality of Godhead. After Kṛṣṇa comes Balarāma, after Balarāma is Saṅkarṣaṇa, then Aniruddha, Pradyumna, Nārāyaṇa and then the *puruṣa-avatāras*—Mahā-Viṣṇu, Garbhodakaśāyī Viṣṇu and Kṣīrodakaśāyī Viṣṇu. All of them are *avatāras.*

One must hear about the *avatāras.* Narrations about such *avatāras* are called *avatāra-kathā,* the narrations of Kṛṣṇa's expansions. Hearing and chanting these narrations is completely pious. *Śṛṇvatāṁ sva-kathāḥ kṛṣṇaḥ puṇya-śravaṇa-kīrtanaḥ.* One who hears and chants can become *puṇya,* purified of material contamination.

Whenever there are references to the *avatāras,* religious principles are established, and demons who are against Kṛṣṇa are killed. The Kṛṣṇa consciousness movement is spreading all over the world with two aims—to establish Kṛṣṇa as the Supreme Personality of Godhead and to kill all the pretenders who falsely present themselves as *avatāras.* The preachers of the Kṛṣṇa consciousness movement must carry this conviction very carefully within their hearts and kill the demons who in many tactful ways vilify the Supreme Personality of Godhead, Kṛṣṇa. If we take shelter of Nṛsiṁhadeva and Prahlāda Mahārāja, it will be easier to kill the demons who are against Kṛṣṇa and to thus reestablish Kṛṣṇa's supremacy. *Kṛṣṇas tu bhagavān svayam:* Kṛṣṇa is the Supreme Lord, the original Lord. Prahlāda Mahārāja is our *guru,* and Kṛṣṇa is our worshipable God. As advised by Śrī Caitanya Mahāprabhu, *guru-kṛṣṇa-prasāde pāya bhakti-latā-bīja.* If we can be successful in getting the mercy of Prahlāda Mahārāja and also that of Nṛsiṁhadeva, then our Kṛṣṇa consciousness movement will be extremely successful.

The demon Hiraṇyakaśipu had so many ways to try to become God himself, but although Prahlāda Mahārāja was chastised and threatened in many ways, he rigidly refused to accept his powerful demoniac father as God. Following in the footsteps of Prahlāda Mahārāja, we should reject all the rascals who pretend to be God. We must accept Kṛṣṇa and His incarnations, and no one else.

TEXTS 43–44

प्रह्लादस्यानुचरितं महाभागवतस्य च ।
भक्तिर्ज्ञानं विरक्तिश्च याथार्थ्यं चास्य वै हरेः ॥४३॥

सर्गस्थित्यप्ययेशस्य गुणकर्मानुवर्णनम् ।
परावरेषां स्थानानां कालेन व्यत्ययो महान् ॥४४॥

prahrādasyānucaritaṁ
mahā-bhāgavatasya ca
bhaktir jñānaṁ viraktiś ca
yāthārthyaṁ cāsya vai hareḥ

sarga-sthity-apyayeśasya
guṇa-karmānuvarṇanam
parāvareṣāṁ sthānānāṁ
kālena vyatyayo mahān

prahrādasya—of Prahlāda Mahārāja; *anucaritam*—characteristics (understood by reading or describing his activities); *mahā-bhāgavatasya*—of the great and exalted devotee; *ca*—also; *bhaktiḥ*—devotional service unto the Supreme Personality of Godhead; *jñānam*—complete knowledge of the Transcendence (Brahman, Paramātmā and Bhagavān); *viraktiḥ*—renunciation of material existence; *ca*—also; *yāthārthyam*—just to understand each of them perfectly; *ca*—and; *asya*—of this; *vai*—indeed; *hareḥ*—always in reference to the Supreme Personality of Godhead; *sarga*—of creation; *sthiti*—maintenance; *apyaya*—and annihilation; *īśasya*—of the master (the Supreme Personality of Godhead); *guṇa*—of the transcendental qualities and opulences; *karma*—and activities; *anuvarṇanam*—description within the disciplic succession;* *para-avareṣām*—of different types of living entities known as demigods and demons; *sthānānām*—of the various planets or places to live; *kālena*—in due course of time; *vyatyayaḥ*—the annihilation of everything; *mahān*—although very great.

TRANSLATION

This narration describes the characteristics of the great and exalted devotee Prahlāda Mahārāja, his staunch devotional service,

---

*The word *anu* means "after." Authorized persons do not create anything; rather, they follow the previous *ācāryas.*

his perfect knowledge, and his perfect detachment from material contamination. It also describes the Supreme Personality of Godhead as the cause of creation, maintenance and annihilation. Prahlāda Mahārāja, in his prayers, has described the transcendental qualities of the Lord and has also described how the various abodes of the demigods and demons, regardless of how materially opulent, are destroyed by the mere direction of the Lord.

PURPORT

Śrīmad-Bhāgavatam is filled with descriptions of the characteristics of various devotees, with reference to the service of the Lord. This Vedic literature is called *Bhāgavatam* because it deals with the Supreme Personality of Godhead and His devotee. By studying *Śrīmad-Bhāgavatam* under the direction of the bona fide spiritual master, one can perfectly understand the science of Kṛṣṇa, the nature of the material and spiritual worlds, and the aim of life. *Śrīmad-Bhāgavatam amalaṁ purāṇam. Śrīmad-Bhāgavatam* is the spotless Vedic literature, as we have discussed in the beginning of *Śrīmad-Bhāgavatam.* Therefore, simply by understanding *Śrīmad-Bhāgavatam,* one can understand the science of the activities of the devotees, the activities of the demons, the permanent abode and the temporary abode. Through *Śrīmad-Bhāgavatam,* everything is perfectly known.

TEXT 45

धर्मो भागवतानां च भगवान्येन गम्यते ।
आख्यानेऽस्मिन्समाम्नातमाध्यात्मिकमशेषतः॥४५॥

dharmo bhāgavatānāṁ ca
bhagavān yena gamyate
ākhyāne 'smin samāmnātam
ādhyātmikam aśeṣataḥ

dharmaḥ—religious principles; *bhāgavatānām*—of the devotees; *ca*—and; *bhagavān*—the Supreme Personality of Godhead; *yena*—by which; *gamyate*—one can understand; *ākhyāne*—in the narration;

asmin—this; *samāmnātam*—is perfectly described; *ādhyātmikam*—transcendence; *aśeṣataḥ*—without reservations.

TRANSLATION

The principles of religion by which one can actually understand the Supreme Personality of Godhead are called bhāgavata-dharma. In this narration, therefore, which deals with these principles, actual transcendence is properly described.

PURPORT

Through the principles of religion, one can understand the Supreme Personality of Godhead, Brahman (the impersonal feature of the Supreme Lord) and Paramātmā (the localized aspect of the Lord). When one is well conversant with all these principles, he becomes a devotee and performs *bhāgavata-dharma.* Prahlāda Mahārāja, the spiritual master in the line of disciplic succession, advised that this *bhāgavata-dharma* be instructed to students from the very beginning of their education (*kaumāra ācaret prājño dharmān bhāgavatān iha*). To understand the science of the Supreme Personality of Godhead is the real purpose of education. *Śravaṇaṁ kīrtanaṁ viṣṇoḥ.* One must simply hear about and describe Lord Viṣṇu and His various incarnations. This narration concerning Prahlāda Mahārāja and Lord Nṛsiṁhadeva, therefore, has properly described spiritual, transcendental subjects.

TEXT 46

य एतत् पुण्यमाख्यानं विष्णोर्वीर्योपबृंहितम् ।
कीर्तयेच्छ्रद्धया श्रुत्वा कर्मपाशैर्विमुच्यते ॥४६॥

ya etat puṇyam ākhyānaṁ
viṣṇor vīryopabṛṁhitam
kīrtayec chraddhayā śrutvā
karma-pāśair vimucyate

yaḥ—anyone who; *etat*—this; *puṇyam*—pious; *ākhyānam*—narration; *viṣṇoḥ*—of Lord Viṣṇu; *vīrya*—the supreme power; *upabṛṁhitam*—in which is described; *kīrtayet*—chants or repeats; *śraddhayā*—with great faith; *śrutvā*—after properly hearing (from the right source); *karma-pāśaiḥ*—from the bondage of fruitive activities; *vimucyate*—becomes liberated.

TRANSLATION

One who hears and chants this narration about the omnipotence of the Supreme Personality of Godhead, Viṣṇu, is certainly liberated from material bondage without fail.

TEXT 47

एतद् य आदिपुरुषस्य मृगेन्द्रलीलां
दैत्येन्द्रयूथपवधं प्रयतः पठेत ।
दैत्यात्मजस्य च सतां प्रवरस्य पुण्यं
श्रुत्वानुभावमकुतोभयमेति लोकम् ॥४७॥

etad ya ādi-puruṣasya mṛgendra-līlāṁ
daityendra-yūtha-pa-vadhaṁ prayataḥ paṭheta
daityātmajasya ca satāṁ pravarasya puṇyaṁ
śrutvānubhāvam akuto-bhayam eti lokam

etat—this narration; *yaḥ*—anyone who; *ādi-puruṣasya*—of the original Personality of Godhead; *mṛga-indra-līlām*—pastimes as a lion and human being combined; *daitya-indra*—of the King of the demons; *yūtha-pa*—as strong as an elephant; *vadham*—the killing; *prayataḥ*—with great attention; *paṭheta*—reads; *daitya-ātma-jasya*—of Prahlāda Mahārāja, the son of the demon; *ca*—also; *satām*—among elevated devotees; *pravarasya*—the best; *puṇyam*—pious; *śrutvā*—hearing; *anubhāvam*—the activities; *akutaḥ-bhayam*—where there is no fear anywhere or at any time; *eti*—reaches; *lokam*—the spiritual world.

TRANSLATION

Prahlāda Mahārāja was the best among exalted devotees. Anyone who with great attention hears this narration concerning the activities of Prahlāda Mahārāja, the killing of Hiraṇyakaśipu, and the activities of the Supreme Personality of Godhead, Nṛsiṁhadeva, surely reaches the spiritual world, where there is no anxiety.

TEXT 48

यूयं नृलोके बत भूरिभागा
लोकं पुनाना मुनयोऽभियन्ति ।
येषां गृहानावसतीति साक्षाद्
गूढं परं ब्रह्म मनुष्यलिङ्गम् ॥४८॥

yūyaṁ nṛ-loke bata bhūri-bhāgā
lokaṁ punānā munayo 'bhiyanti
yeṣāṁ gṛhān āvasatīti sākṣād
gūḍhaṁ paraṁ brahma manuṣya-liṅgam

yūyam—all of you (the Pāṇḍavas); *nṛ-loke*—within this material world; *bata*—however; *bhūri-bhāgāḥ*—extremely fortunate; *lokam*—all the planets; *punānāḥ*—who can purify; *munayaḥ*—great saintly persons; *abhiyanti*—almost always come to visit; *yeṣām*—of whom; *gṛhān*—the house; *āvasati*—resides in; *iti*—thus; *sākṣāt*—directly; *gūḍham*—very confidential; *param brahma*—the Supreme Personality of Godhead; *manuṣya-liṅgam*—appearing just like a human being.

TRANSLATION

Nārada Muni continued: My dear Mahārāja Yudhiṣṭhira, all of you [the Pāṇḍavas] are extremely fortunate, for the Supreme Personality of Godhead, Kṛṣṇa, lives in your palace just like a human being. Great saintly persons know this very well, and therefore they constantly visit this house.

PURPORT

After hearing about the activities of Prahlāda Mahārāja, a pure devotee should be very anxious to follow in his footsteps, but such a devotee might be disappointed, thinking that not every devotee can come to the standard of Prahlāda Mahārāja. This is the nature of a pure devotee; he always thinks himself to be the lowest, to be incompetent and unqualified. Thus after hearing the narration of Prahlāda Mahārāja's activities, Mahārāja Yudhiṣṭhira, who was on the same standard of devotional service as Prahlāda, might have been thinking of his own humble position. Nārada Muni, however, could understand Mahārāja Yudhiṣṭhira's mind, and therefore he immediately encouraged him by saying that the Pāṇḍavas were not less fortunate; they were as good as Prahlāda Mahārāja because although Lord Nṛsiṁhadeva appeared for Prahlāda, the Supreme Personality of Godhead in His original form as Kṛṣṇa was always living with the Pāṇḍavas. Although the Pāṇḍavas, because of the influence of Kṛṣṇa's *yogamāyā*, could not think of their fortunate position, every saintly person, including the great sage Nārada, could understand it, and therefore they constantly visited Mahārāja Yudhiṣṭhira.

Any pure devotee who is constantly conscious of Kṛṣṇa is naturally very fortunate. The word *nṛ-loke*, meaning "within the material world," indicates that before the Pāṇḍavas there had been many, many devotees, such as the descendants of the Yadu dynasty and Vasiṣṭha, Marīci, Kaśyapa, Lord Brahmā and Lord Śiva, who were all extremely fortunate. The Pāṇḍavas, however, were better than all of them because Kṛṣṇa Himself lived with them constantly. Nārada Muni therefore specifically mentioned that within this material world (*nṛ-loke*) the Pāṇḍavas were the most fortunate.

TEXT 49

स वा अयं ब्रह्म महद्विमृग्य-
कैवल्यनिर्वाणसुखानुभूतिः ।
प्रियः सुहृद् वः खलु मातुलेय
आत्मार्हणीयो विधिकृद् गुरुश्च ॥४९॥

sa vā ayaṁ brahma mahad-vimṛgya-
kaivalya-nirvāṇa-sukhānubhūtiḥ
priyaḥ suhṛd vaḥ khalu mātuleya
ātmārhaṇīyo vidhi-kṛd guruś ca

saḥ—that (Supreme Personality of Godhead, Kṛṣṇa); *vā*—also; *ayam*—this; *brahma*—the impersonal Brahman (which is an emanation from Kṛṣṇa); *mahat*—by great personalities; *vimṛgya*—searched for; *kaivalya*—oneness; *nirvāṇa-sukha*—of transcendental happiness; *anubhūtiḥ*—the source of practical experience; *priyaḥ*—very, very dear; *suhṛt*—well-wisher; *vaḥ*—of you; *khalu*—indeed; *mātuleyaḥ*—the son of a maternal uncle; *ātmā*—exactly like body and soul together; *arhaṇīyaḥ*—worshipable (because He is the Supreme Personality of Godhead); *vidhi-kṛt*—(yet He serves you as) an order carrier; *guruḥ*—your supreme advisor; *ca*—as well.

TRANSLATION

The impersonal Brahman is Kṛṣṇa Himself because Kṛṣṇa is the source of the impersonal Brahman. He is the origin of the transcendental bliss sought by great saintly persons, yet He, the Supreme Person, is your most dear friend and constant well-wisher and is intimately related to you as the son of your maternal uncle. Indeed, He is always like your body and soul. He is worshipable, yet He acts as your servant and sometimes as your spiritual master.

PURPORT

There is always a difference of opinion about the Absolute Truth. One class of transcendentalists concludes that the Absolute Truth is impersonal, and another class concludes that the Absolute Truth is a person. In *Bhagavad-gītā*, the Absolute Truth is accepted as the Supreme Person. Indeed, that Supreme Person Himself, Lord Kṛṣṇa, instructs in *Bhagavad-gītā, brahmaṇo hi pratiṣṭhāham, mattaḥ parataraṁ nānyat.* "The impersonal Brahman is My partial manifestation, and there is no truth superior to Me." That same Kṛṣṇa, the Supreme Personality of Godhead, acted as the supreme friend and relative of the Pāṇḍavas, and sometimes He even acted as their servant by carrying a letter from the Pāṇḍavas to Dhṛtarāṣṭra and Duryodhana. Because Kṛṣṇa was the well-wisher of the Pāṇḍavas, He also acted as *guru* by becoming the spiritual master of Arjuna. Arjuna accepted Kṛṣṇa as his spiritual master (*śiṣyas te 'haṁ śādhi māṁ tvāṁ prapannam*), and Kṛṣṇa sometimes chastised him. For example, the Lord said, *aśocyān anvaśocas tvaṁ prajñā-vādāṁś ca bhāṣase:* "While speaking learned words, you are mourning for what is not worthy of grief." The Lord also said, *kutas tvā kaśmalam idaṁ viṣame samupasthitam:* "My dear Arjuna, how have these impurities come upon you?" Such was the intimate relationship between the Pāṇḍavas and Kṛṣṇa. In the same way, a pure devotee of the Lord is always with Kṛṣṇa through thick and thin; his way of life is Kṛṣṇa. This is the statement of the authority Śrī Nārada Muni.

TEXT 50

न यस्य साक्षाद् भवपद्मजादिभी
रूपं धिया वस्तुतयोपवर्णितम् ।
मौनेन भक्त्योपशमेन पूजितः
प्रसीदतामेष स सात्वतां पतिः ॥५०॥

na yasya sākṣād bhava-padmajādibhī
rūpaṁ dhiyā vastutayopavarṇitam
maunena bhaktyopaśamena pūjitaḥ
prasīdatām eṣa sa sātvatāṁ patiḥ

na—not; *yasya*—of whom; *sākṣāt*—directly; *bhava*—Lord Śiva; *padma-ja*—Lord Brahmā (born from the lotus); *ādibhiḥ*—by them and others also; *rūpam*—the form; *dhiyā*—even by meditation; *vastutayā*—fundamentally; *upavarṇitam*—described and perceived; *maunena*—by *samādhi,* deep meditation; *bhaktyā*—by devotional service; *upaśamena*—by renunciation; *pūjitaḥ*—worshiped; *prasīdatām*—may He be pleased; *eṣaḥ*—this; *saḥ*—He; *sātvatām*—of the great devotees; *patiḥ*—the master.

TRANSLATION

Exalted persons like Lord Śiva and Lord Brahmā could not properly describe the truth of the Supreme Personality of God-

head, Kṛṣṇa. May the Lord, who is always worshiped as the protector of all devotees by great saints who observe vows of silence, meditation, devotional service and renunciation, be pleased with us.

PURPORT

The Absolute Truth is sought by different persons in different ways, yet He remains inconceivable. Nonetheless, devotees like the Pāṇḍavas, the *gopīs*, the cowherd boys, Mother Yaśodā, Nanda Mahārāja and all the inhabitants of Vṛndāvana do not need to practice conventional processes of meditation to attain the Supreme Personality of Godhead, for He remains with them through thick and thin. Therefore a saint like Nārada, understanding the difference between transcendentalists and pure devotees, always prays that the Lord will be pleased with him.

TEXT 51

स एष भगवान्राजन्व्यतनोद् विहतं यशः ।
पुरा रुद्रस्य देवस्य मयेनानन्तमायिना ॥५१॥

sa eṣa bhagavān rājan
vyatanod vihataṁ yaśaḥ
purā rudrasya devasya
mayenānanta-māyinā

saḥ eṣaḥ bhagavān—the same Personality of Godhead, Kṛṣṇa, who is Parabrahman; *rājan*—my dear King; *vyatanot*—expanded; *vihatam*—lost; *yaśaḥ*—reputation; *purā*—formerly in history; *rudrasya*—of Lord Śiva (the most powerful among the demigods); *devasya*—the demigod; *mayena*—by a demon named Maya; *ananta*—unlimited; *māyinā*—possessing technical knowledge.

TRANSLATION

My dear King Yudhiṣṭhira, long, long ago in history, a demon known as Maya Dānava, who was very expert in technical knowledge, reduced the reputation of Lord Śiva. In that situation, Kṛṣṇa, the Supreme Personality of Godhead, saved Lord Śiva.

PURPORT

Lord Śiva is known as Mahādeva, the most exalted demigod. Thus Viśvanātha Cakravartī Ṭhākura says that although Lord Brahmā did not know the glories of the Supreme Personality of Godhead, Lord Śiva could have known them. This historical incident proves that Lord Śiva derives power from Lord Kṛṣṇa, the Parabrahman.

TEXT 52

राजोवाच
कस्मिन् कर्मणि देवस्य मयोऽहञ्जगदीशितुः ।
यथा चोपचिता कीर्तिः कृष्णेनानेन कथ्यताम्॥५२॥

rājovāca
kasmin karmaṇi devasya
mayo 'hañ jagad-īśituḥ
yathā copacitā kīrtiḥ
kṛṣṇenānena kathyatām

rājā uvāca—King Yudhiṣṭhira inquired; *kasmin*—for what reason; *karmaṇi*—by which activities; *devasya*—of Lord Mahādeva (Śiva); *mayaḥ*—the great demon Maya Dānava; *ahan*—vanquished; *jagat-īśituḥ*—of Lord Śiva, who controls the power of the material energy and is the husband of Durgādevī; *yathā*—just as; *ca*—and; *upacitā*—again expanded; *kīrtiḥ*—reputation; *kṛṣṇena*—by Lord Kṛṣṇa; *anena*—this; *kathyatām*—please describe.

TRANSLATION

Mahārāja Yudhiṣṭhira said: For what reason did the demon Maya Dānava vanquish Lord Śiva's reputation? How did Lord Kṛṣṇa save Lord Śiva and expand his reputation again? Kindly describe these incidents.

TEXT 53

श्रीनारद उवाच
निर्जिता असुरा देवैर्युध्यनेनोपबृंहितैः ।
मायिनां परमाचार्यं मयं शरणमाययुः ॥५३॥

śrī-nārada uvāca
nirjitā asurā devair
yudhy anenopabṛṁhitaiḥ
māyināṁ paramācāryaṁ
mayaṁ śaraṇam āyayuḥ

śrī-nāradaḥ uvāca—Śrī Nārada Muni said; *nirjitāḥ*—being defeated; *asurāḥ*—all the demons; *devaiḥ*—by the demigods; *yudhi*—in battle; *anena*—by Lord Kṛṣṇa; *upabṛṁhitaiḥ*—increased in power; *māyinām*—of all the demons; *parama-ācāryam*—the best and largest; *mayam*—unto Maya Dānava; *śaraṇam*—shelter; *āyayuḥ*—took.

TRANSLATION

Nārada Muni said: When the demigods, who are always powerful by the mercy of Lord Kṛṣṇa, fought with the asuras, the asuras were defeated, and therefore they took shelter of Maya Dānava, the greatest of the demons.

TEXTS 54–55

स निर्माय पुरस्तिस्रो हैमीरौप्यायसीर्विभुः ।
दुर्लक्ष्यापायसंयोगा दुर्वितर्क्यपरिच्छदाः ॥५४॥
ताभिस्तेऽसुरसेनान्यो लोकांस्त्रीन् सेश्वरान् नृप ।
स्मरन्तो नाशयाञ्चक्रुः पूर्ववैरमलक्षिताः ॥५५॥

sa nirmāya puras tisro
haimī-raupyāyasīr vibhuḥ
durlakṣyāpāya-saṁyogā
durvitarkya-paricchadāḥ

tābhis te 'sura-senānyo
lokāṁs trīn seśvarān nṛpa
smaranto nāśayāṁ cakruḥ
pūrva-vairam alakṣitāḥ

saḥ—that (great demon Maya Dānava); *nirmāya*—constructing; *puraḥ*—big residences; *tisraḥ*—three; *haimī*—made of gold; *raupyā*—

made of silver; *āyasīḥ*—made of iron; *vibhuḥ*—very great, powerful; *durlakṣya*—immeasurable; *apāya-saṁyogāḥ*—whose movements in coming and going; *durvitarkya*—uncommon; *paricchadāḥ*—possessing paraphernalia; *tābhiḥ*—by all of them (the three residences, which resembled airplanes); *te*—they; *asura-senā-anyaḥ*—the commanders of the *asuras; lokān trīn*—the three worlds; *sa-īśvarān*—with their chief rulers; *nṛpa*—my dear King Yudhiṣṭhira; *smarantaḥ*—remembering; *nāśayām cakruḥ*—began to annihilate; *pūrva*—former; *vairam*—enmity; *alakṣitāḥ*—unseen by anyone else.

TRANSLATION

Maya Dānava, the great leader of the demons, prepared three invisible residences and gave them to the demons. These dwellings resembled airplanes made of gold, silver and iron, and they contained uncommon paraphernalia. My dear King Yudhiṣṭhira, because of these three dwellings the commanders of the demons remained invisible to the demigods. Taking advantage of this opportunity, the demons, remembering their former enmity, began to vanquish the three worlds—the upper, middle and lower planetary systems.

TEXT 56

ततस्ते सेश्वरा लोका उपासाद्येश्वरं नताः ।
त्राहि नस्तावकान्देव विनष्टांस्त्रिपुरालयैः ॥५६॥

tatas te seśvarā lokā
upāsādyeśvaraṁ natāḥ
trāhi nas tāvakān deva
vinaṣṭāṁs tripurālayaiḥ

tataḥ—thereafter; *te*—they (the demigods); *sa-īśvarāḥ*—with their rulers; *lokāḥ*—the planets; *upāsādya*—approaching; *īśvaram*—Lord Śiva; *natāḥ*—fell down in surrender; *trāhi*—please save; *naḥ*—us; *tāvakān*—near and dear to you and very frightened; *deva*—O Lord; *vinaṣṭān*—almost finished; *tripura-ālayaiḥ*—by the demons dwelling in those three planes.

TRANSLATION

Thereafter, when the demons had begun to destroy the higher planetary systems, the rulers of those planets went to Lord Śiva, fully surrendered unto him and said: Dear Lord, we demigods living in the three worlds are about to be vanquished. We are your followers. Kindly save us.

TEXT 57

अथानुगृह्य भगवान्मा भैष्टेति सुरान्विभुः ।
शरं धनुषि सन्धाय पुरेष्वस्त्रं व्यमुञ्चत ॥५७॥

athānugṛhya bhagavān
mā bhaiṣṭeti surān vibhuḥ
śaraṁ dhanuṣi sandhāya
pureṣv astraṁ vyamuñcata

atha—thereafter; *anugṛhya*—just to show them favor; *bhagavān*—the most powerful; *mā*—do not; *bhaiṣṭa*—be afraid; *iti*—thus; *surān*—unto the demigods; *vibhuḥ*—Lord Śiva; *śaram*—arrows; *dhanuṣi*—on the bow; *sandhāya*—fixing; *pureṣu*—at those three residences occupied by the demons; *astram*—weapons; *vyamuñcata*—released.

TRANSLATION

The most powerful and able Lord Śiva reassured them and said, "Do not be afraid." He then fixed his arrows to his bow and released them toward the three residences occupied by the demons.

TEXT 58

ततोऽग्निवर्णा इषव उत्पेतुः सूर्यमण्डलात् ।
यथा मयूखसंदोहा नादृश्यन्त पुरो यतः ॥५८॥

tato 'gni-varṇā iṣava
utpetuḥ sūrya-maṇḍalāt
yathā mayūkha-sandohā
nādṛśyanta puro yataḥ

tataḥ—thereafter; *agni-varṇāḥ*—as brilliant as fire; *iṣavaḥ*—arrows; *utpetuḥ*—released; *sūrya-maṇḍalāt*—from the sun globe; *yathā*—just as; *mayūkha-sandohāḥ*—beams of light; *na adṛśyanta*—could not be seen; *puraḥ*—the three residences; *yataḥ*—because of this (being covered by the arrows of Lord Śiva).

TRANSLATION

The arrows released by Lord Śiva appeared like fiery beams emanating from the sun globe and covered the three residential airplanes, which could then no longer be seen.

TEXT 59

तैः स्पृष्टा व्यसवः सर्वे निपेतुः स्म पुरौकसः ।
तानानीय महायोगी मयः कूपरसेऽक्षिपत् ॥५९॥

taiḥ spṛṣṭā vyasavaḥ sarve
nipetuḥ sma puraukasaḥ
tān ānīya mahā-yogī
mayaḥ kūpa-rase 'kṣipat

taiḥ—by those (fiery arrows); *spṛṣṭāḥ*—being attacked or being touched; *vyasavaḥ*—without life; *sarve*—all the demons; *nipetuḥ*—fell down; *sma*—formerly; *pura-okasaḥ*—being the inhabitants of the above-mentioned three residential airplanes; *tān*—all of them; *ānīya*—bringing; *mahā-yogī*—the great mystic; *mayaḥ*—Maya Dānava; *kūpa-rase*—in the well of nectar (created by the great mystic Maya); *akṣipat*—put.

TRANSLATION

Attacked by Lord Śiva's golden arrows, all the demoniac inhabitants of those three dwellings lost their lives and fell down. Then the great mystic Maya Dānava dropped the demons into a nectarean well that he had created.

PURPORT

The *asuras* are generally extremely powerful because of their mystic yogic power. However, as Lord Kṛṣṇa says in *Bhagavad-gītā* (6.47):

yoginām api sarveṣāṁ
mad-gatenāntarātmanā
śraddhāvān bhajate yo māṁ
sa me yuktatamo mataḥ

"Of all *yogīs*, he who always abides in Me with great faith, worshiping Me in transcendental loving service, is most intimately united with Me in *yoga* and is the highest of all." The actual purpose of mystic *yoga* is to concentrate one's attention fully on the Personality of Godhead, Kṛṣṇa, and always think of Him (*mad-gatenāntarātmanā*). To attain such perfection, one must undergo a certain process—*haṭha-yoga*—and through this *yoga* system the practitioner achieves some uncommon mystic power. The *asuras*, however, instead of becoming devotees of Kṛṣṇa, utilize this mystic power for their personal sense gratification. Maya Dānava, for example, is mentioned here as *mahā-yogī*, a great mystic, but his business was to help the *asuras*. Nowadays we are actually seeing that there are some *yogīs* who cater to the senses of materialists, and there are imposters who advertise themselves as God. Maya Dānava was such a person, a god among the demons, and he could perform some wonderful feats, one of which is described here: he made a well filled with nectar and dipped the *asuras* into that nectarean well. This nectar was known as *mṛta-sañjīvayitari*, for it could bring a dead body to life. *Mṛta-sañjīvayitari* is also an Āyur-vedic preparation. It is a kind of liquor that invigorates even a person on the verge of death.

TEXT 60

सिद्धामृतरसस्पृष्टा वज्रसारा महौजसः ।
उत्तस्थुर्मेघदलना वैद्युता इव वह्नयः ॥६०॥

siddhāmṛta-rasa-spṛṣṭā
vajra-sārā mahaujasaḥ
uttasthur megha-dalanā
vaidyutā iva vahnayaḥ

siddha-amṛta-rasa-spṛṣṭāḥ—the demons, thus being touched by the powerful mystic nectarean liquid; *vajra-sārāḥ*—their bodies becoming invincible to thunderbolts; *mahā-ojasaḥ*—being extremely strong;

uttasthuḥ—again got up; *megha-dalanāḥ*—that which goes through the clouds; *vaidyutāḥ*—lightning (which penetrates the clouds); *iva*—like; *vahnayaḥ*—fiery.

TRANSLATION

When the dead bodies of the demons came in touch with the nectar, their bodies became invincible to thunderbolts. Endowed with great strength, they got up like lightning penetrating clouds.

TEXT 61

विलोक्य भग्नसङ्कल्पं विमनस्कं वृषध्वजम् ।
तदायं भगवान्विष्णुस्तत्रोपायमकल्पयत् ॥६१॥

vilokya bhagna-saṅkalpaṁ
vimanaskaṁ vṛṣa-dhvajam
tadāyaṁ bhagavān viṣṇus
tatropāyam akalpayat

vilokya—seeing; *bhagna-saṅkalpam*—disappointed; *vimanaskam*—extremely unhappy; *vṛṣa-dhvajam*—Lord Śiva; *tadā*—at that time; *ayam*—this; *bhagavān*—the Supreme Personality of Godhead; *viṣṇuḥ*—Lord Viṣṇu; *tatra*—about the well of nectar; *upāyam*—means (how to stop it); *akalpayat*—considered.

TRANSLATION

Seeing Lord Śiva very much aggrieved and disappointed, the Supreme Personality of Godhead, Lord Viṣṇu, considered how to stop this nuisance created by Maya Dānava.

TEXT 62

वत्सश्चासीत्तदा ब्रह्मा स्वयं विष्णुरयं हि गौः ।
प्रविश्य त्रिपुरं काले रसकूपामृतं पपौ ॥६२॥

vatsaś cāsīt tadā brahmā
svayaṁ viṣṇur ayaṁ hi gauḥ

praviśya tripuraṁ kāle
rasa-kūpāmṛtaṁ papau

vatsaḥ—a calf; *ca*—also; *āsīt*—became; *tadā*—at that time; *brahmā*—Lord Brahmā; *svayam*—personally; *viṣṇuḥ*—Lord Viṣṇu, the Supreme Personality of Godhead; *ayam*—this; *hi*—indeed; *gauḥ*—a cow; *praviśya*—entering; *tri-puram*—the three residences; *kāle*—at noon; *rasa-kūpa-amṛtam*—the nectar contained in that well; *papau*—drank.

TRANSLATION

Then Lord Brahmā became a calf and Lord Viṣṇu a cow, and at noon they entered the residences and drank all the nectar in the well.

TEXT 63

तेऽसुरा ह्यपि पश्यन्तो न न्यषेधन्विमोहिताः ।
तद् विज्ञाय महायोगी रसपालानिदं जगौ ।
स्मयं विशोकः शोकार्तान्स्मरन्दैवगतिं च ताम् ॥६३॥

te 'surā hy api paśyanto
na nyaṣedhan vimohitāḥ
tad vijñāya mahā-yogī
rasa-pālān idaṁ jagau
smayan viśokaḥ śokārtān
smaran daiva-gatiṁ ca tām

te—those; *asurāḥ*—demons; *hi*—indeed; *api*—although; *paśyantaḥ*—seeing (the calf and cow drinking the nectar); *na*—not; *nyaṣedhan*—forbade them; *vimohitāḥ*—being bewildered by illusion; *tat vijñāya*—knowing this fully; *mahā-yogī*—the great mystic Maya Dānava; *rasa-pālān*—unto the demons who guarded the nectar; *idam*—this; *jagau*—said; *smayan*—being bewildered; *viśokaḥ*—not being very unhappy; *śoka-ārtān*—greatly lamenting; *smaran*—remembering; *daiva-gatim*—spiritual power; *ca*—also; *tām*—that.

TRANSLATION

The demons could see the calf and cow, but because of the illusion created by the energy of the Supreme Personality of Godhead, the demons could not forbid them. The great mystic Maya Dānava became aware that the calf and cow were drinking the nectar, and he could understand this to be the unseen power of providence. Thus he spoke to the demons, who were grievously lamenting.

TEXT 64

देवोऽसुरो नरोऽन्यो वा नेश्वरोऽस्तीह कश्चन ।
आत्मनोऽन्यस्य वा दिष्टं दैवेनापोहितुं द्वयोः ॥६४॥

devo 'suro naro 'nyo vā
neśvaro 'stīha kaścana
ātmano 'nyasya vā diṣṭaṁ
daivenāpohituṁ dvayoḥ

devaḥ—the demigods; *asuraḥ*—the demons; *naraḥ*—humans; *anyaḥ*—or anyone else; *vā*—either; *na*—not; *īśvaraḥ*—the supreme controller; *asti*—is; *iha*—in this world; *kaścana*—anyone; *ātmanaḥ*—one's own; *anyasya*—another's; *vā*—either; *diṣṭam*—destiny; *daivena*—which is given by the Supreme Lord; *apohitum*—to undo; *dvayoḥ*—of both of them.

TRANSLATION

Maya Dānava said: What has been destined by the Supreme Lord for oneself, for others, or for both oneself and others cannot be undone anywhere or by anyone, whether one be a demigod, a demon, a human being or anyone else.

PURPORT

The Supreme Lord is one—Kṛṣṇa, the *viṣṇu-tattva.* Kṛṣṇa expands Himself into *viṣṇu-tattva* personal expansions (*svāṁśa*), who control everything. Maya Dānava said, "However I plan, you plan or both of us plan, the Lord has planned what is to happen. No one's plan will be successful without His sanction." We may make our own various plans, but unless they are sanctioned by the Supreme Personality of Godhead, Viṣṇu, they will never be successful. Hundreds and millions of plans are made by all kinds of living entities, but without the sanction of the Supreme Lord they are futile.

TEXT 65–66

अथासौ शक्तिभिः स्वाभिः शम्भोः प्राधानिकं व्यधात् ।
धर्मज्ञानविरक्त्यृद्धितपोविद्याक्रियादिभिः ॥६५॥
रथं सूतं ध्वजं वाहान्धनुर्वर्म शरादि यत् ।
सन्नद्धो रथमास्थाय शरं धनुरुपाददे ॥६६॥

athāsau śaktibhiḥ svābhiḥ
śambhoḥ prādhānikaṁ vyadhāt
dharma-jñāna-virakty-ṛddhi-
tapo-vidyā-kriyādibhiḥ

rathaṁ sūtaṁ dhvajaṁ vāhān
dhanur varma-śarādi yat
sannaddho ratham āsthāya
śaraṁ dhanur upādade

atha—thereafter; *asau*—He (Lord Kṛṣṇa); *śaktibhiḥ*—by His potencies; *svābhiḥ*—personal; *śambhoḥ*—of Lord Śiva; *prādhānikam*—ingredients; *vyadhāt*—created; *dharma*—religion; *jñāna*—knowledge; *virakti*—renunciation; *ṛddhi*—opulence; *tapaḥ*—austerity; *vidyā*—education; *kriyā*—activities; *ādibhiḥ*—by all these and other transcendental opulences; *ratham*—chariot; *sūtam*—charioteer; *dhvajam*—flag; *vāhān*—horses and elephants; *dhanuḥ*—bow; *varma*—shield; *śara-ādi*—arrows and so on; *yat*—everything that was required; *sannaddhaḥ*—equipped; *ratham*—on the chariot; *āsthāya*—seated; *śaram*—arrow; *dhanuḥ*—unto the bow; *upādade*—joined.

TRANSLATION

Nārada Muni continued: Thereafter, Lord Kṛṣṇa, by His own personal potency, consisting of religion, knowledge, renunciation,

opulence, austerity, education and activities, equipped Lord Śiva with all the necessary paraphernalia, such as a chariot, a charioteer, a flag, horses, elephants, a bow, a shield and arrows. When Lord Śiva was fully equipped in this way, he sat down on the chariot with his arrows and bow to fight with the demons.

PURPORT

As stated in *Śrīmad-Bhāgavatam* (12.13.16): *vaiṣṇavānāṁ yathā śambhuḥ:* Lord Śiva is the best of the Vaiṣṇavas, the devotees of Lord Kṛṣṇa. Indeed, he is one of the *mahājanas,* the twelve authorities on Vaiṣṇava philosophy (*svayambhūr nāradaḥ śambhuḥ kumāraḥ kapilo manuḥ,* etc.). Lord Kṛṣṇa is always prepared to help all the *mahājanas* and devotees in every respect (*kaunteya pratijānīhi na me bhaktaḥ praṇaśyati*). Although Lord Śiva is very powerful, he lost a battle to the *asuras,* and therefore he was morose and disappointed. However, because he is one of the chief devotees of the Lord, the Lord personally equipped him with all the paraphernalia for war. The devotee, therefore, must serve the Lord sincerely, and Kṛṣṇa is always in the background to protect him and, if need be, to equip him fully to fight with his enemy. For devotees there is no scarcity of knowledge or material requisites for spreading the Kṛṣṇa consciousness movement.

TEXT 67

शरं धनुषि सन्धाय मुहूर्तेऽभिजितीश्वरः ।
ददाह तेन दुर्भेद्या हरोऽथ त्रिपुरो नृप ॥६७॥

śaraṁ dhanuṣi sandhāya
muhūrte 'bhijitīśvaraḥ
dadāha tena durbhedyā
haro 'tha tripuro nṛpa

śaram—the arrows; *dhanuṣi*—on the bow; *sandhāya*—joining together; *muhūrte abhijiti*—at noon; *īśvaraḥ*—Lord Śiva; *dadāha*—set afire; *tena*—by them (the arrows); *durbhedyāḥ*—very difficult to pierce; *haraḥ*—Lord Śiva; *atha*—in this way; *tri-puraḥ*—the three residences of the demons; *nṛpa*—O King Yudhiṣṭhira.

TRANSLATION

My dear King Yudhiṣṭhira, the most powerful Lord Śiva joined the arrows to his bow, and at noon he set fire to all three residences of the demons and thus destroyed them.

TEXT 68

दिवि दुन्दुभयो नेदुर्विमानशतसङ्कुलाः ।
देवर्षिपितृसिद्धेशा जयेति कुसुमोत्करैः ।
अवाकिरञ्जगुर्हृष्टा ननृतुश्चाप्सरोगणाः ॥६८॥

divi dundubhayo nedur
vimāna-śata-saṅkulāḥ
devarṣi-pitṛ-siddheśā
jayeti kusumotkaraiḥ
avākirañ jagur hṛṣṭā
nanṛtuś cāpsaro-gaṇāḥ

divi—in the sky; *dundubhayaḥ*—kettledrums; *neduḥ*—vibrated; *vimāna*—of airplanes; *śata*—hundreds and thousands; *saṅkulāḥ*—endowed; *deva-ṛṣi*—all the demigods and saints; *pitṛ*—the residents of Pitṛloka; *siddha*—the residents of Siddhaloka; *īśāḥ*—all the great personalities; *jaya iti*—vibrated the chant "let there be victory"; *kusuma-utkaraiḥ*—various kinds of flowers; *avākiran*—showered on the head of Lord Śiva; *jaguḥ*—chanted; *hṛṣṭāḥ*—in great pleasure; *nanṛtuḥ*—danced; *ca*—and; *apsaraḥ-gaṇāḥ*—the beautiful women of the heavenly planets.

TRANSLATION

Seated in their airplanes in the sky, the inhabitants of the higher planetary systems beat many kettledrums. The demigods, saints, Pitās, Siddhas and various great personalities showered flowers on

the head of Lord Śiva, wishing him all victory, and the Apsarās began to chant and dance with great pleasure.

TEXT 69

एवं दग्ध्वा पुरस्तिस्रो भगवान्पुरहा नृप ।
ब्रह्मादिभिः स्तूयमानः स्वंधाम प्रत्यपद्यत ॥६९॥

evaṁ dagdhvā puras tisro
bhagavān pura-hā nṛpa
brahmādibhiḥ stūyamānaḥ
svaṁ dhāma pratyapadyata

evam—thus; *dagdhvā*—burning to ashes; *puraḥ tisraḥ*—the three residences of the demons; *bhagavān*—the supreme powerful; *pura-hā*—who annihilated the residences of the *asuras; nṛpa*—O King Yudhiṣṭhira; *brahma-ādibhiḥ*—by Lord Brahmā and other demigods; *stūyamānaḥ*—being worshiped; *svam*—to his own; *dhāma*—abode; *pratyapadyata*—returned.

TRANSLATION

O King Yudhiṣṭhira, thus Lord Śiva is known as Tripurāri, the annihilator of the three dwellings of the demons, because he burnt these dwellings to ashes. Being worshiped by the demigods, headed by Lord Brahmā, Lord Śiva returned to his own abode.

TEXT 70

एवंविधान्यस्य हरेः स्वमायया
विडम्बमानस्य नृलोकमात्मनः ।
वीर्याणि गीतान्यृषिभिर्जगद्गुरो-
र्लोकं पुनानान्यपरं वदामि किम् ॥७०॥

evaṁ vidhāny asya hareḥ sva-māyayā
viḍambamānasya nṛ-lokam ātmanaḥ
vīryāṇi gītāny ṛṣibhir jagad-guror
lokaṁ punānāny aparaṁ vadāmi kim

evam vidhāni—in this way; *asya*—of Kṛṣṇa; *hareḥ*—of the Supreme Personality of Godhead; *sva-māyayā*—by His transcendental potencies; *viḍambamānasya*—acting like an ordinary human being; *nṛ-lokam*—within human society; *ātmanaḥ*—of Him; *vīryāṇi*—transcendental activities; *gītāni*—narrations; *ṛṣibhiḥ*—by great saintly persons; *jagat-guroḥ*—of the supreme master; *lokam*—all the planetary systems; *punānāni*—purifying; *aparam*—what else; *vadāmi kim*—can I say.

TRANSLATION

The Lord, Śrī Kṛṣṇa, appeared as a human being, yet He performed many uncommon and wonderful pastimes by His own potency. How can I say more about His activities than what has already been said by great saintly persons? Everyone can be purified by His activities, simply by hearing about them from the right source.

PURPORT

Bhagavad-gītā and all the Vedic literatures fully explain that the Supreme Personality of Godhead, Kṛṣṇa, appears in human society as an ordinary human being but acts very uncommonly for the well-being of the entire world. One should not be influenced by the illusory energy and think Lord Kṛṣṇa to be an ordinary human being. Those who really seek the Absolute Truth come to the understanding that Kṛṣṇa is everything (*vāsudevaḥ sarvam iti*). Such great souls are very rare. Nonetheless, if one studies the entire *Bhagavad-gītā* as it is, Kṛṣṇa is very easy to understand. The Kṛṣṇa consciousness movement is just trying to make Kṛṣṇa known all over the world as the Supreme Personality of Godhead (*kṛṣṇas tu bhagavān svayam*). If people take this movement seriously, their lives as human beings will be successful.

Thus end the Bhaktivedanta purports of the Seventh Canto, Tenth Chapter, of the Śrīmad-Bhāgavatam, *entitled "Prahlāda, the Best Among Exalted Devotees."*

CHAPTER ELEVEN

The Perfect Society: Four Social Classes

This chapter describes the general principles by following which a human being, and specifically one who is interested in advancing in spiritual life, can become perfect.

By hearing about the characteristics of Prahlāda Mahārāja, Mahārāja Yudhiṣṭhira became extremely pleased. Now he inquired from Nārada Muni about the actual religion of a human being and about special characteristics of *varṇāśrama-dharma*, which marks the highest status of human civilization. When Mahārāja Yudhiṣṭhira asked Nārada Muni about these matters, Nārada Muni stopped giving his own statements and quoted statements by Lord Nārāyaṇa, for He is the supreme authority for giving religious codes (*dharmaṁ tu sākṣād bhagavat-praṇītam*). Every human being is expected to acquire thirty qualities, such as truthfulness, mercy and austerity. The process of following the principles of religion is known as *sanātana-dharma*, the eternal religious system.

The *varṇāśrama* system delineates the divisions of *brāhmaṇa, kṣatriya, vaiśya* and *śūdra*. It also sets forth the system of *saṁskāras*. The *garbhādhāna saṁskāra*, the ceremony for begetting a child, must be observed by the higher section of people, namely the *dvijas*. One who follows the *garbhādhāna saṁskāra* system is actually twiceborn, but those who do not, who deviate from the principles of *varṇāśrama-dharma*, are called *dvija-bandhus*. The principal occupations for a *brāhmaṇa* are worshiping the Deity, teaching others how to worship the Deity, studying the Vedic literatures, teaching the Vedic literatures, accepting charity from others and again giving charity to others. A *brāhmaṇa* should make his livelihood from these six occupational duties. The duty of a *kṣatriya* is to give protection to the citizens and levy taxes upon them, but he is forbidden to tax the *brāhmaṇas*. The members of the Kṛṣṇa consciousness movement should therefore be exempt from government taxation. *Kṣatriyas* may tax everyone but the *brāhmaṇas*. *Vaiśyas* should cultivate the land, produce food grains and protect the cows, whereas the *śūdras,* who by quality never become *brāhmaṇas, kṣatriyas* or *vaiśyas,* should serve the three higher classes and be satisfied. Other means of livelihood are also prescribed for the *brāhmaṇas,* and these are four—*śālīna, yāyāvara, śila,* and *uñchana.* Each of these occupational duties is successively better.

One who is in a lower grade of social life cannot accept the profession of a higher class unless necessary. In times of emergency, all the classes but the *kṣatriyas* may accept professional duties of others. The means of livelihood known as *ṛta* (*śiloñchana*), *amṛta* (*ayācita*), *mṛta* (*yācñā*), *pramṛta* (*karṣaṇa*), and *satyānṛta* (*vāṇijya*) may be accepted by everyone but the *kṣatriyas.* For a *brāhmaṇa* or a *kṣatriya,* engaging in the service of the *vaiśyas* or *śūdras* is considered the profession of dogs.

Nārada Muni also described that the symptom of a *brāhmaṇa* is controlled senses, the symptoms of a *kṣatriya* are power and fame, the symptom of a *vaiśya* is service to the *brāhmaṇas* and *kṣatriyas,* and the symptom of a *śūdra* is service to the three higher classes. The qualification for a woman is to be a very faithful and chaste wife. In this way, Nārada Muni described the characteristics of higher and lower grades of people and recommended that one follow the principles of his caste or his hereditary occupation. One cannot suddenly give up a profession to which he is accustomed, and therefore it is recommended that one gradually be awakened. The symptoms of *brāhmaṇas, kṣatriyas, vaiśyas,* and *śūdras* are very important, and therefore one should be designated only by these symptoms, and not by birth. Designation by birth is strictly forbidden by Nārada Muni and all great personalities.

TEXT 1

श्रीशुक उवाच
श्रुत्वेहितं साधुसभासभाजितं
महत्तमाग्रण्य उरुक्रमात्मनः ।
युधिष्ठिरो दैत्यपतेर्मुदान्वितः
पप्रच्छ भूयस्तनयं स्वयम्भुवः ॥ १ ॥

śrī-śuka uvāca
śrutvehitaṁ sādhu sabhā-sabhājitaṁ
mahattamāgraṇya urukramātmanaḥ

yudhiṣṭhiro daitya-pater mudānvitaḥ
papraccha bhūyas tanayaṁ svayambhuvaḥ

śrī-śukaḥ uvāca—Śrī Śukadeva Gosvāmī said; *śrutvā*—hearing; *īhitam*—the narration; *sādhu sabhā-sabhājitam*—which is discussed in assemblies of great devotees like Lord Brahmā and Lord Śiva; *mahat-tama-agraṇyaḥ*—the best of the saintly persons (Yudhiṣṭhira); *urukrama-ātmanaḥ*—of he (Prahlāda Mahārāja) whose mind is always engaged upon the Supreme Personality of Godhead, who always acts uncommonly; *yudhiṣṭhiraḥ*—King Yudhiṣṭhira; *daitya-pateḥ*—of the master of the demons; *mudā-anvitaḥ*—in a pleasing mood; *papraccha*—inquired; *bhūyaḥ*—again; *tanayam*—unto the son; *svayambhuvaḥ*—of Lord Brahmā.

TRANSLATION

Śukadeva Gosvāmī continued: After hearing about the activities and character of Prahlāda Mahārāja, which are adored and discussed among great personalities like Lord Brahmā and Lord Śiva, Yudhiṣṭhira Mahārāja, the most respectful king among exalted personalities, again inquired from the great saint Nārada Muni in a mood of great pleasure.

TEXT 2

श्रीयुधिष्ठिर उवाच
भगवन् श्रोतुमिच्छामि नृणां धर्मं सनातनम् ।
वर्णाश्रमाचारयुतं यत् पुमान्विन्दते परम् ॥ २ ॥

śrī-yudhiṣṭhira uvāca
bhagavan śrotum icchāmi
nṛṇāṁ dharmaṁ sanātanam
varṇāśramācāra-yutaṁ
yat pumān vindate param

śrī-yudhiṣṭhiraḥ uvāca—Mahārāja Yudhiṣṭhira inquired; *bhagavan*—O my lord; *śrotum*—to hear; *icchāmi*—I wish; *nṛṇām*—of human society; *dharmam*—the occupational duties; *sanātanam*—common and eternal (for everyone); *varṇa-āśrama-ācāra-yutam*—based on the principles of the four divisions of society and the four divisions of spiritual advancement; *yat*—from which; *pumān*—the people in general; *vindate*—can enjoy very peacefully; *param*—the supreme knowledge (by which one can attain devotional service).

TRANSLATION

Mahārāja Yudhiṣṭhira said: My dear lord, I wish to hear from you about the principles of religion by which one can attain the ultimate goal of life—devotional service. I wish to hear about the general occupational duties of human society and the system of social and spiritual advancement known as varṇāśrama-dharma.

PURPORT

Sanātana-dharma means devotional service. The word *sanātana* refers to that which is eternal, which does not change but continues in all circumstances. We have several times explained what the eternal occupational duty of the living being is. Indeed, it has been explained by Śrī Caitanya Mahāprabhu. *Jīvera 'svarūpa' haya—kṛṣṇera 'nitya-dāsa'*: the real occupational duty of the living entity is to serve the Supreme Personality of Godhead. Even if one prefers to deviate from this principle he remains a servant because that is his eternal position; but one serves *māyā*, the illusory, material energy. The Kṛṣṇa consciousness movement, therefore, is an attempt to guide human society to serving the Personality of Godhead instead of serving the material world with no real profit. Our actual experience is that every man, animal, bird and beast—indeed, every living entity—is engaged in rendering service. Even though one's body or one's superficial religion may change, every living entity is always engaged in the service of someone. Therefore, the mentality of service is called the eternal occupational duty. This eternal occupational duty can be organized through the institution of *varṇāśrama*, in which there are four *varṇas* (*brāhmaṇa*, *kṣatriya*, *vaiśya* and *śūdra*) and four *āśramas* (*brahmacarya*, *gṛhastha*, *vānaprastha* and *sannyāsa*). Thus, Yudhiṣṭhira Mahārāja inquired from Nārada Muni about the principles of *sanātana-dharma* for the benefit of human society.

TEXT 3

भवान्प्रजापतेः साक्षादात्मजः परमेष्ठिनः ।
सुतानां सम्मतो ब्रह्मंस्तपोयोगसमाधिभिः ॥ ३ ॥

bhavān prajāpateḥ sākṣād
ātmajaḥ parameṣṭhinaḥ
sutānāṁ sammato brahmaṁs
tapo-yoga-samādhibhiḥ

bhavān—Your Lordship; *prajāpateḥ*—of Prajāpati (Lord Brahmā); *sākṣāt*—directly; *ātma-jaḥ*—the son; *parameṣṭhinaḥ*—of the supreme person within this universe (Lord Brahmā); *sutānām*—of all the sons; *sammataḥ*—agreed upon as the best; *brahman*—O best of the *brāhmaṇas; tapaḥ*—by austerity; *yoga*—by mystic practice; *samādhibhiḥ*—and by trance or meditation (in all respects, you are the best).

TRANSLATION

O best of the brāhmaṇas, you are directly the son of Prajāpati [Lord Brahmā]. Because of your austerities, mystic yoga and trance, you are considered the best of all of Lord Brahmā's sons.

TEXT 4

नारायणपरा विप्रा धर्मं गुह्यं परं विदुः ।
करुणाः साधवः शान्तास्त्वद्विधा न तथापरे ॥ ४ ॥

nārāyaṇa-parā viprā
dharmaṁ guhyaṁ paraṁ viduḥ
karuṇāḥ sādhavaḥ śāntās
tvad-vidhā na tathāpare

nārāyaṇa-parāḥ—those who are always devoted to the Supreme Personality of Godhead, Nārāyaṇa; *viprāḥ*—the best of the *brāhmaṇas; dharmam*—religious principle; *guhyam*—the most confidential; *param*—supreme; *viduḥ*—know; *karuṇāḥ*—such persons are very merciful (being devotees); *sādhavaḥ*—whose behavior is very exalted; *śāntāḥ*—peaceful; *tvat-vidhāḥ*—like Your Honor; *na*—not; *tathā*—so; *apare*—others (followers of methods other than devotional service).

TRANSLATION

No one is superior to you in peaceful life and mercy, and no one knows better than you how to execute devotional service or how to become the best of the brāhmaṇas. Therefore, you know all the principles of confidential religious life, and no one knows them better than you.

PURPORT

Yudhiṣṭhira Mahārāja knew that Nārada Muni is the supreme spiritual master of human society who can teach the path of spiritual liberation leading to the understanding of the Supreme Personality of Godhead. Actually, it is for this purpose that Nārada Muni compiled his *Bhakti-sūtra* and gave directions in the *Nārada-pañcarātra.* To learn about religious principles and the perfection of life, one must take instruction from the disciplic succession of Nārada Muni. Our Kṛṣṇa consciousness movement is directly in the line of the Brahma-sampradāya. Nārada Muni received instructions from Lord Brahmā and in turn transmitted the instructions to Vyāsadeva. Vyāsadeva instructed his son Śukadeva Gosvāmī, who spoke *Śrīmad-Bhāgavatam.* The Kṛṣṇa consciousness movement is based on *Śrīmad-Bhāgavatam* and *Bhagavad-gītā.* Because *Śrīmad-Bhāgavatam* was spoken by Śukadeva Gosvāmī and *Bhagavad-gītā* was spoken by Kṛṣṇa, there is no difference between them. If we strictly follow the principle of disciplic succession, we are certainly on the right path of spiritual liberation, or eternal engagement in devotional service.

TEXT 5

श्रीनारद उवाच

नत्वा भगवतेऽजाय लोकानां धर्मसेतवे ।
वक्ष्ये सनातनं धर्मं नारायणमुखाच्छ्रुतम् ॥ ५ ॥

śrī-nārada uvāca
natvā bhagavate 'jāya
lokānāṁ dharma-setave
vakṣye sanātanaṁ dharmaṁ
nārāyaṇa-mukhāc chrutam

śrī-nāradaḥ uvāca—Śrī Nārada Muni said; *natvā*—offering my obeisances; *bhagavate*—unto the Supreme Personality of Godhead; *ajāya*—ever existing, never born; *lokānām*—throughout the entire universe; *dharma-setave*—who protects religious principles; *vakṣye*—I shall explain; *sanātanam*—eternal; *dharmam*—occupational duty; *nārāyaṇa-mukhāt*—from the mouth of Nārāyaṇa; *śrutam*—which I have heard.

TRANSLATION

Śrī Nārada Muni said: After first offering my obeisances unto Lord Kṛṣṇa, the protector of the religious principles of all living entities, let me explain the principles of the eternal religious system, of which I have heard from the mouth of Nārāyaṇa.

PURPORT

The word *aja* refers to Kṛṣṇa, who explains in *Bhagavad-gītā* (4.6), *ajo 'pi sann avyayātmā:* "I am ever existing, and thus I never take birth. There is no change in My existence."

TEXT 6

योऽवतीर्यात्मनोंऽशेन दाक्षायण्यां तु धर्मतः ।
लोकानां स्वस्तयेऽध्यास्ते तपो बदरिकाश्रमे ॥ ६ ॥

yo 'vatīryātmano 'ṁśena
dākṣāyaṇyāṁ tu dharmataḥ
lokānāṁ svastaye 'dhyāste
tapo badarikāśrame

yaḥ—He who (Lord Nārāyaṇa); *avatīrya*—adventing; *ātmanaḥ*—of Himself; *aṁśena*—with a part (Nara); *dākṣāyaṇyām*—in the womb of

Dākṣāyaṇī, the daughter of Mahārāja Dakṣa; *tu*—indeed; *dharmataḥ*—from Dharma Mahārāja; *lokānām*—of all people; *svastaye*—for the benefit of; *adhyāste*—executes; *tapaḥ*—austerity; *badarikāśrame*—in the place known as Badarikāśrama.

TRANSLATION

Lord Nārāyaṇa, along with His partial manifestation Nara, appeared in this world through the daughter of Dakṣa Mahārāja known as Mūrti. He was begotten by Dharma Mahārāja for the benefit of all living entities. Even now, He is still engaged in executing great austerities near the place known as Badarikāśrama.

TEXT 7

धर्ममूलं हि भगवान्सर्ववेदमयो हरिः ।
स्मृतं च तद्विदां राजन्येन चात्मा प्रसीदति ॥ ७ ॥

dharma-mūlaṁ hi bhagavān
sarva-vedamayo hariḥ
smṛtaṁ ca tad-vidāṁ rājan
yena cātmā prasīdati

dharma-mūlam—the root of religious principles; *hi*—indeed; *bhagavān*—the Supreme Personality of Godhead; *sarva-veda-mayaḥ*—the essence of all Vedic knowledge; *hariḥ*—the Supreme Being; *smṛtam ca*—and the scriptures; *tat-vidām*—of those who know the Supreme Lord; *rājan*—O King; *yena*—by which (religious principle); *ca*—also; *ātmā*—the soul, mind, body and everything; *prasīdati*—become fully satisfied.

TRANSLATION

The Supreme Being, the Personality of Godhead, is the essence of all Vedic knowledge, the root of all religious principles, and the memory of great authorities. O King Yudhiṣṭhira, this principle of religion is to be understood as evidence. On the basis of this religious principle, everything is satisfied, including one's mind, soul and even one's body.

PURPORT

As stated by Yamarāja, *dharmaṁ tu sākṣād bhagavat-praṇītam.* Yamarāja, the representative of the Lord who takes care of the living beings after their death, gives his verdict as to how and when the living being will change his body. He is the authority, and he says that the religious principles consist of the codes and laws given by God. No one can manufacture religion, and therefore manufactured religious systems are rejected by the followers of the Vedic principles. In *Bhagavad-gītā* (15.15) it is said, *vedaiś ca sarvair aham eva vedyaḥ:* Vedic knowledge means to understand the Supreme Personality of Godhead, Kṛṣṇa. Therefore, whether one speaks of the *Vedas*, scriptures, religion or the principles of everyone's occupational duty, all of them must aim at understanding Kṛṣṇa, the Supreme Personality of Godhead. *Śrīmad-Bhāgavatam* (1.2.6) therefore concludes:

sa vai puṁsāṁ paro dharmo
yato bhaktir adhokṣaje
ahaituky apratihatā
yayātmā suprasīdati

In other words, religious principles aim at learning how to render transcendental loving service to the Lord. That service must be unmotivated and unchecked by material conditions. Then human society will be happy in all respects.

The *smṛti*, the scriptures following the principles of Vedic knowledge, are considered the evidence of Vedic principles. There are twenty different types of scripture for following religious principles, and among them the scriptures of Manu and Yājñavalkya are considered to be all-pervading authorities. In the *Yājñavalkya-smṛti* it is said:

śruti-smṛti-sadācāraḥ
svasya ca priyam ātmanaḥ
samyak saṅkalpajaḥ kāmo
dharma-mūlam idaṁ smṛtam

One should learn human behavior from *śruti*, the *Vedas*, and from *smṛti*, the scriptures following the Vedic principles. Śrīla Rūpa Gosvāmī in his *Bhakti-rasāmṛta-sindhu* says:

śruti-smṛti-purāṇādi-
pañcarātra-vidhiṁ vinā
aikāntikī harer bhaktir
utpātāyaiva kalpate

The purport is that to become a devotee one must follow the principles laid down in *śruti* and *smṛti.* One must follow the codes of the *Purāṇas* and the *pāñcarātrikī-vidhi.* One cannot be a pure devotee without following the *śruti* and *smṛti*, and the *śruti* and *smṛti* without devotional service cannot lead one to the perfection of life.

Therefore, from all the evidence the conclusion is that without *bhakti*, devotional service, there is no question of religious principles. God is the central figure in the performance of religious principles. Almost everthing going on in this world as religion is devoid of any idea of devotional service and is therefore condemned by the verdict of *Śrīmad-Bhāgavatam.* Without devotional service, so-called religious principles are only cheating.

TEXTS 8–12

सत्यं दया तपः शौचं तितिक्षेक्षा शमो दमः ।
अहिंसा ब्रह्मचर्यं च त्यागः स्वाध्याय आर्जवम् ॥ ८ ॥
सन्तोषः समदृक् सेवा ग्राम्येहोपरमः शनैः ।
नृणां विपर्ययेहेक्षा मौनमात्मविमर्शनम् ॥ ९ ॥
अन्नाद्यादेः संविभागो भूतेभ्यश्च यथार्हतः ।
तेष्वात्मदेवताबुद्धिः सुतरां नृषु पाण्डव ॥१०॥
श्रवणं कीर्तनं चास्य स्मरणं महतां गतेः ।
सेवेज्यावनतिर्दास्यं सख्यमात्मसमर्पणम् ॥११॥
नृणामयं परो धर्मः सर्वेषां समुदाहृतः ।
त्रिंशल्लक्षणवान्राजन्सर्वात्मा येन तुष्यति ॥१२॥

satyaṁ dayā tapaḥ śaucaṁ
titikṣekṣā śamo damaḥ
ahiṁsā brahmacaryaṁ ca
tyāgaḥ svādhyāya ārjavam

santoṣaḥ samadṛk-sevā
grāmyehoparamaḥ śanaiḥ
nṛṇāṁ viparyayehekṣā
maunam ātma-vimarśanam

annādyādeḥ saṁvibhāgo
bhūtebhyaś ca yathārhataḥ
teṣv ātma-devatā-buddhiḥ
sutarāṁ nṛṣu pāṇḍava

śravaṇaṁ kīrtanaṁ cāsya
smaraṇaṁ mahatāṁ gateḥ
sevejyāvanatir dāsyaṁ
sakhyam ātma-samarpaṇam

nṛṇām ayaṁ paro dharmaḥ
sarveṣāṁ samudāhṛtaḥ
triṁśal-lakṣaṇavān rājan
sarvātmā yena tuṣyati

satyam—speaking the truth without distortion or deviation; *dayā*—sympathy to everyone suffering; *tapaḥ*—austerities (such as observing fasts at least twice in a month on the day of Ekādaśī); *śaucam*—cleanliness (bathing regularly at least twice a day, morning and evening, and remembering to chant the holy name of God); *titikṣā*—toleration (being unagitated by seasonal changes or inconvenient circumstances); *īkṣā*—distinguishing between good and bad; *śamaḥ*—control of the mind (not allowing the mind to act whimsically); *damaḥ*—control of the senses (not allowing the senses to act without control); *ahiṁsā*—nonviolence (not subjecting any living entity to the threefold miseries); *brahmacaryam*—continence or abstaining from misuse of one's semen (not indulging in sex with women other than one's own wife and not having sex with one's own wife when sex is forbidden, like during the period of menstruation); *ca*—and; *tyāgaḥ*—giving in charity at least fifty percent of one's income; *svādhyāyaḥ*—reading of transcendental literatures like *Bhagavad-gītā*, *Śrīmad-Bhāgavatam*, *Rāmāyaṇa* and *Mahābhārata* (or, for those not in Vedic culture, reading of the Bible or

Koran); *ārjavam*—simplicity (freedom from mental duplicity); *santoṣaḥ*—being satisfied with that which is available without severe endeavor; *samadṛk-sevā*—rendering service to saintly persons who make no distinctions between one living being and another and who see every living being as a spirit soul (*paṇḍitāḥ sama-darśinaḥ*); *grāmya-īhā-uparamaḥ*—not taking part in so-called philanthropic activities; *śanaiḥ*—gradually; *nṛṇām*—in human society; *viparyaya-īhā*—the unnecessary activities; *īkṣā*—discussing; *maunam*—being grave and silent; *ātma*—into the self; *vimarśanam*—research (as to whether one is the body or the soul); *anna-ādya-ādeḥ*—of food and drink, etc.; *saṁvibhāgaḥ*—equal distribution; *bhūtebhyaḥ*—to different living entities; *ca*—also; *yathā-arhataḥ*—as befitting; *teṣu*—all living entities; *ātma-devatā-buddhiḥ*—accepting as the self or the demigods; *sutarām*—preliminarily; *nṛṣu*—among all human beings; *pāṇḍava*—O Mahārāja Yudhiṣṭhira; *śravaṇam*—hearing; *kīrtanam*—chanting; *ca*—also; *asya*—of Him (the Lord); *smaraṇam*—remembering (His words and activities); *mahatām*—of great saintly persons; *gateḥ*—who is the shelter; *sevā*—service; *ijyā*—worship; *avanatiḥ*—offering obeisances; *dāsyam*—accepting the service; *sakhyam*—to consider as a friend; *ātma-samarpaṇam*—surrendering one's whole self; *nṛṇām*—of all human beings; *ayam*—this; *paraḥ*—the supermost; *dharmaḥ*—religious principle; *sarveṣām*—of all; *samudāhṛtaḥ*—described fully; *triṁśat-lakṣaṇa-vān*—possessing thirty characteristics; *rājan*—O King; *sarva-ātmā*—the Supreme Lord, the Supersoul of all; *yena*—by which; *tuṣyati*—is satisfied.

TRANSLATION

These are the general principles to be followed by all human beings: truthfulness, mercy, austerity (observing fasts on certain days of the month), bathing twice a day, tolerance, discrimination between right and wrong, control of the mind, control of the senses, nonviolence, celibacy, charity, reading of scripture, simplicity, satisfaction, rendering service to saintly persons, gradually taking leave of unnecessary engagements, observing the futility of the unnecessary activities of human society, remaining silent and grave and avoiding unnecessary talk, considering whether one is the body or the soul, distributing food equally to all living entities (both men and animals), seeing every soul

(especially in the human form) as a part of the Supreme Lord, hearing about the activities and instructions given by the Supreme Personality of Godhead (who is the shelter of the saintly persons), chanting about these activities and instructions, always remembering these activities and instructions, trying to render service, performing worship, offering obeisances, becoming a servant, becoming a friend, and surrendering one's whole self. O King Yudhiṣṭhira, these thirty qualifications must be acquired in the human form of life. Simply by acquiring these qualifications, one can satisfy the Supreme Personality of Godhead.

PURPORT

In order that human beings be distinct from the animals, the great saint Nārada recommends that every human being be educated in terms of the above-mentioned thirty qualifications. Nowadays there is propaganda everywhere, all over the world, for a secular state, a state interested only in mundane activities. But if the citizens of the state are not educated in the above-mentioned good qualities, how can there be happiness? For example, if the total populace is untruthful, how can the state be happy? Therefore, without consideration of one's belonging to a sectarian religion, whether Hindu, Muslim, Christian, Buddhist or any other sect, everyone should be taught to become truthful. Similarly, everyone should be taught to be merciful, and everyone should observe fasting on certain days of the month. Everyone should bathe twice a day, cleanse his teeth and body externally, and cleanse his mind internally by remembering the holy name of the Lord. The Lord is one, whether one is Hindu, Muslim or Christian. Therefore, one should chant the holy name of the Lord, regardless of differences in linguistic pronunciation. Also, everyone should be taught to be very careful not to discharge semen unnecessarily. This is very important for all human beings. If semen is not discharged unnecessarily, one becomes extremely strong in memory, determination, activity and the vitality of one's bodily energy. Everyone should also be taught to be simple in thought and feeling and satisfied in body and mind. These are the general qualifications of a human being. There is no question of a secular state or an ecclesiastical state. Unless one is educated in the above-mentioned thirty qualities, there cannot be any peace. Ultimately it is recommended:

śravaṇaṁ kīrtanaṁ cāsya
smaraṇaṁ mahatāṁ gateḥ
sevejyāvanatir dāsyaṁ
sakhyam ātma-samarpaṇam

Everyone should become a devotee of the Lord, because by becoming a devotee of the Lord one automatically acquires the other qualities.

yasyāsti bhaktir bhagavaty akiñcanā
sarvair guṇais tatra samāsate surāḥ
harāv abhaktasya kuto mahad-guṇā
manorathenāsati dhāvato bahiḥ

"In one who has unflinching devotional service to Kṛṣṇa, all the good qualities of Kṛṣṇa and the demigods are consistently manifest. However, he who has no devotion to the Supreme Personality of Godhead has no good qualifications because he is engaged by mental concoction in material existence, which is the external feature of the Lord." (*Bhāg.* 5.18.12) Our Kṛṣṇa consciousness movement, therefore, is all-embracing. Human civilization should take it very seriously and practice its principles for the peace of the world.

TEXT 13

संस्कारा यत्राविच्छिन्नाः स द्विजोऽजो जगाद यम् ।
इज्याध्ययनदानानि विहितानि द्विजन्मनाम् ।
जन्मकर्मावदातानां क्रियाश्चाश्रमचोदिताः ॥१३॥

saṁskārā yatrāvicchinnāḥ
sa dvijo 'jo jagāda yam
ijyādhyayana-dānāni
vihitāni dvijanmanām
janma-karmāvadātānāṁ
kriyāś cāśrama-coditāḥ

saṁskārāḥ—reformatory processes; *yatra*—wherein; *avicchinnāḥ*—without interruption; *saḥ*—such a person; *dvi-jaḥ*—twiceborn; *ajaḥ*—

Lord Brahmā; *jagāda*—sanctioned; *yam*—who; *ijyā*—worshiping; *adhyayana*—studies of the *Vedas; dānāni*—and charity; *vihitāni*—prescribed; *dvi-janmanām*—of persons who are called twiceborn; *janma*—by birth; *karma*—and activities; *avadātānām*—who are purified; *kriyāḥ*—activities; *ca*—also; *āśrama-coditāḥ*—recommended for the four *āśramas.*

TRANSLATION

Those who have been reformed by the garbhādhāna ceremony and other prescribed reformatory methods, performed with Vedic mantras and without interruption, and who have been approved by Lord Brahmā, are dvijas, or twiceborn. Such brāhmaṇas, kṣatriyas and vaiśyas, purified by their family traditions and by their behavior, should worship the Lord, study the Vedas and give charity. In this system, they should follow the principles of the four āśramas [brahmacarya, gṛhastha, vānaprastha and sannyāsa].

PURPORT

After giving a general list of thirty qualifications for one's behavior, Nārada Muni now describes the principles of the four *varṇas* and four *āśramas.* A human being must be trained in the above-mentioned thirty qualities; otherwise, he is not even a human being. Then, among such qualified persons, the *varṇāśrama* process should be introduced. In the *varṇāśrama* system, the first ceremony for purification is *garbhādhāna,* which is performed with *mantras* at the time of sex for propagating a good child. One who uses sex life not for sensual pleasures but only to beget children according to the reformatory method is also accepted as a *brahmacārī.* One should not waste semen on sensual pleasure, violating the principles of Vedic life. Restraint in sex is possible, however, only when the populace is trained in the above-mentioned thirty qualities; otherwise, it is not possible. Even if one is born in a family of *dvijas,* or twiceborn, if they have not followed the reformatory process he is called a *dvija-bandhu*—not one of the twiceborn, but a friend of the twiceborn. The whole purpose of this system is to create good population. As stated in *Bhagavad-gītā,* when women are polluted the populace is *varṇa-saṅkara,* and when the *varṇa-saṅkara* population increases, the situation of the entire world becomes hellish. Therefore, all the Vedic literatures strongly warn against creating *varṇa-saṅkara* population. When there is *varṇa-saṅkara* population, the people cannot be properly controlled for peace and prosperity, regardless of great legislative assemblies, parliaments and similar bodies.

TEXT 14

विप्रस्याध्ययनादीनि षडन्यस्याप्रतिग्रहः ।
राज्ञो वृत्तिः प्रजागोप्तुरविप्राद् वा करादिभिः ॥ १४ ॥

viprasyādhyayanādīni
ṣaḍ-anyasyāpratigrahaḥ
rājño vṛttiḥ prajā-goptur
aviprād vā karādibhiḥ

viprasya—of the *brāhmaṇa; adhyayana-ādīni*—reading the *Vedas*, etc; *ṣaṭ*—six (to study the *Vedas*, to teach the *Vedas*, to worship the Deity, to teach others how to worship, to accept charity and to give charity); *anyasya*—of those other than the *brāhmaṇas* (the *kṣatriyas*); *apratigrahaḥ*—without accepting charity from others (the *kṣatriyas* may execute the five other occupational duties prescribed for the *brāhmaṇas*); *rājñaḥ*—of the *kṣatriya; vṛttiḥ*—the means of livelihood; *prajā-goptuḥ*—who maintain the subjects; *aviprāt*—from those who are not *brāhmaṇas; vā*—or; *kara-ādibhiḥ*—by levying revenue taxes, customs duties, fines for punishment, etc.

TRANSLATION

For a brāhmaṇa there are six occupational duties. A kṣatriya should not accept charity, but he may perform the other five of these duties. A king or kṣatriya is not allowed to levy taxes on brāhmaṇas, but he may make his livelihood by levying minimal taxes, customs duties, and penalty fines upon his other subjects.

PURPORT

Viśvanātha Cakravartī Ṭhākura explains the position of *brāhmaṇas* and *kṣatriyas* as follows. *Brāhmaṇas* have six occupational duties, of which three are compulsory—namely, studying the *Vedas*, worshiping the Deity and giving charity. By teaching, by inducing others to worship the Deity, and by accepting gifts, the *brāhmaṇas* receive the necessities of life. This is also confirmed in the *Manu-saṁhitā:*

ṣaṇṇāṁ tu karmaṇām asya
trīṇi karmāṇi jīvikā
yajanādhyāpane caiva
viśuddhāc ca pratigrahaḥ

Of the six occupational duties of the *brāhmaṇas*, three are compulsory—namely, worship of the Deity, study of the *Vedas* and the giving of charity. In exchange, a *brāhmaṇa* should receive charity, and this should be his means of livelihood. A *brāhmaṇa* cannot take up any professional occupational duty for his livelihood. The *śāstras* especially stress that if one claims to be a *brāhmaṇa*, he cannot engage in the service of anyone else; otherwise he at once falls from his position and becomes a *śūdra*. Śrīla Rūpa Gosvāmī and Sanātana Gosvāmī belonged to a very respectful family, but because they engaged in the service of Nawab Hussain Shah—not even as ordinary clerks, but as ministers—they were ostracized from brahminical society. Indeed, they became like Mohammedans and even changed their names. Unless a *brāhmaṇa* is very pure, he cannot accept charity from others. Charity should be given to those who are pure. Even if one is born in a family of *brāhmaṇas*, if one acts as a *śūdra* one cannot accept charity, for this is strictly prohibited. Although the *kṣatriyas* are almost as qualified as the *brāhmaṇas*, even they cannot accept charity. This is strictly prohibited in this verse by the word *apratigraha.* What to speak of the lower social orders, even the *kṣatriyas* must not accept charity. The king or government may levy taxes upon the citizens in various ways—by revenue duties, customs duties, realization of fines, and so on—provided the king is able to give full protection to his subjects to assure the security of their life and property. Unless he is able to give protection, he cannot levy taxes. However, a king must not levy any tax upon the *brāhmaṇas* and the Vaiṣṇavas fully engaged in Kṛṣṇa consciousness.

TEXT 15

वैश्यस्तु वार्तावृत्तिः स्यान् नित्यं ब्रह्मकुलानुगः ।
शूद्रस्य द्विजशुश्रूषा वृत्तिश्च स्वामिनो भवेत् ॥१५॥

vaiśyas tu vārtā-vṛttiḥ syān
nityaṁ brahma-kulānugaḥ
śūdrasya dvija-śuśrūṣā
vṛttiś ca svāmino bhavet

vaiśyaḥ—the mercantile community; *tu*—indeed; *vārtā-vṛttiḥ*—engaged in agriculture, cow protection, and trade; *syāt*—must be; *nityam*—always; *brahma-kula-anugaḥ*—following the directions of the *brāhmaṇas; śūdrasya*—of the fourth-grade persons, the workers; *dvija-śuśrūṣā*—the service of the three higher sections (the *brāhmaṇas, kṣatriyas* and *vaiśyas*); *vṛttiḥ*—means of livelihood; *ca*—and; *svāminaḥ*—of the master; *bhavet*—he must be.

TRANSLATION

The mercantile community should always follow the directions of the brāhmaṇas and engage in such occupational duties as agriculture, trade, and protection of cows. For the śūdras the only duty is to accept a master from a higher social order and engage in his service.

TEXT 16

वार्ता विचित्रा शालीनयायावरशिलोञ्छनम् ।
विप्रवृत्तिश्चतुर्धेयं श्रेयसी चोत्तरोत्तरा ॥१६॥

vārtā vicitrā śālīna-
yāyāvara-śiloñchanam
vipra-vṛttiś caturdheyaṁ
śreyasī cottarottarā

vārtā—the occupational means of livelihood for the *vaiśya* (agriculture, cow protection, and trade); *vicitrā*—various types; *śālīna*—livelihood achieved without effort; *yāyāvara*—going to the field to beg for some paddy; *śila*—picking up the grains left in the field by the proprietor; *uñchanam*—picking up the grains that have fallen from bags in shops; *vipra-vṛttiḥ*—the means of livelihood for the *brāhmaṇas; caturdhā*—four different kinds; *iyam*—this; *śreyasī*—better; *ca*—also; *uttara-uttarā*—the latter compared to the former.

TRANSLATION

As an alternative, a brāhmaṇa may also take to the vaiśya's occupational duty of agriculture, cow protection, or trade. He may depend on that which he has received without begging, he may beg in the paddy field every day, he may collect paddy left in a field by its proprietor, or he may collect food grains left here and there in the shops of grain dealers. These are four means of livelihood that may also be adopted by brāhmaṇas. Among these four, each of them in succession is better than the one preceding it.

PURPORT

A *brāhmaṇa* is sometimes offered land and cows in charity, and thus for his livelihood he may act in the same way as a *vaiśya,* by cultivating land, giving protection to cows and trading off his surpluses. A better process, however, is to pick up grains from a field or from a dealer's shop without begging.

TEXT 17

जघन्यो नोत्तमां वृत्तिमनापदि भजेन्नरः ।
ऋते राजन्यमापत्सु सर्वेषामपि सर्वशः ॥१७॥

jaghanyo nottamāṁ vṛttim
anāpadi bhajen naraḥ
ṛte rājanyam āpatsu
sarveṣām api sarvaśaḥ

jaghanyaḥ—low (person); *na*—not; *uttamām*—high; *vṛttim*—means of livelihood; *anāpadi*—when there is no social upheaval; *bhajet*—may accept; *naraḥ*—a man; *ṛte*—except; *rājanyam*—the profession of the *kṣatriyas; āpatsu*—at times of emergency; *sarveṣām*—of everyone in every status of life; *api*—certainly; *sarvaśaḥ*—all professions or occupational duties.

TRANSLATION

Except in a time of emergency, lower persons should not accept the occupational duties of those who are higher. When there is such an emergency, of course, everyone but the kṣatriya may accept the means of livelihood of others.

PURPORT

The occupational duty of a *brāhmaṇa* should not be accepted by persons in lower social orders, especially *vaiśyas* and *śūdras.* For example, an occupational duty of the *brāhmaṇa* is to teach Vedic knowledge, but unless there is an emergency, this professional duty should not be accepted by the *kṣatriyas, vaiśyas* or *śūdras.* Even a *kṣatriya* cannot accept the duties of a *brāhmaṇa* unless there is an emergency, and then even if he does so he should not accept charity from anyone else. Sometimes *brāhmaṇas* protest against our Kṛṣṇa consciousness movement for creating *brāhmaṇas* from Europeans, or, in other words, from *mlecchas* and *yavanas.* This movement, however, is here supported in *Śrīmad-Bhāgavatam.* At the present moment, society is in a chaotic condition, and everyone has given up the cultivation of spiritual life, which is especially meant for the *brāhmaṇas.* Because spiritual culture has been stopped all over the world, there is now an emergency, and therefore it is now time to train those who are considered lower and condemned, so that they may become *brāhmaṇas* and take up the work of spiritual progress. The spiritual progress of human society has been stopped, and this should be considered an emergency. Here is solid support from Nārada Muni of the movement known as Kṛṣṇa consciousness.

TEXTS 18–20

ऋतामृताभ्यां जीवेत मृतेन प्रमृतेन वा ।
सत्यानृताभ्यामपि वा न श्ववृत्त्या कदाचन ॥१८॥
ऋतमुञ्छशिलं प्रोक्तममृतं यदयाचितम् ।
मृतं तु नित्ययाच्ञा स्यात् प्रमृतं कर्षणं स्मृतम् ॥१९॥
सत्यानृतं च वाणिज्यं श्ववृत्तिर्नीचसेवनम् ।
वर्जयेत् तां सदा विप्रो राजन्यश्च जुगुप्सिताम् ।
सर्ववेदमयो विप्रः सर्वदेवमयो नृपः ॥२०॥

ṛtāmṛtābhyāṁ jīveta
mṛtena pramṛtena vā
satyānṛtābhyām api vā
na śva-vṛttyā kadācana

ṛtam uñchaśilaṁ proktam
amṛtaṁ yad ayācitam
mṛtaṁ tu nitya-yācñā syāt
pramṛtaṁ karṣaṇaṁ smṛtam

satyānṛtaṁ ca vāṇijyaṁ
śva-vṛttir nīca-sevanam
varjayet tāṁ sadā vipro
rājanyaś ca jugupsitām
sarva-vedamayo vipraḥ
sarva-devamayo nṛpaḥ

ṛta-amṛtābhyām—of the means of livelihood known as *ṛta* and *amṛta; jīveta*—one may live; *mṛtena*—by the profession of *mṛta; pramṛtena vā*—or by the profession of *pramṛta; satyānṛtābhyām api*—even by the profession of *satyānṛta; vā*—or; *na*—never; *śva-vṛttyā*—by the profession of the dogs; *kadācana*—at any time; *ṛtam*—*ṛta; uñchaśilam*—the livelihood of collecting grains left in the field or marketplace; *proktam*—it is said; *amṛtam*—the profession of *amṛta; yat*—which; *ayācitam*—obtained without begging from anyone else; *mṛtam*—the profession of *mṛta; tu*—but; *nitya-yācñā*—begging grains every day from the farmers; *syāt*—should be; *pramṛtam*—the *pramṛta* means of livelihood; *karṣaṇam*—tilling the field; *smṛtam*—it is so remembered; *satyānṛtam*—the occupation of *satyānṛta; ca*—and; *vāṇijyam*—trade; *śva-vṛttiḥ*—the occupation of the dogs; *nīca-sevanam*—the service of low persons (the *vaiśyas* and *śūdras*); *varjayet*—should give up; *tām*—that (the profession of the dogs);*sadā*—always; *vipraḥ*—the *brāhmaṇa; rājanyaḥ ca*—and the *kṣatriya; jugupsitām*—very abominable; *sarva-veda-mayaḥ*—learned in all the Vedic understandings; *vipraḥ*—the *brāhmaṇa; sarva-deva-mayaḥ*—the embodiment of all the demigods; *nṛpaḥ*—the *kṣatriya* or king.

TRANSLATION

In time of emergency, one may accept any of the various types of professions known as ṛta, amṛta, mṛta, pramṛta and satyānṛta, but one should not at any time accept the profession of a dog. The profession of uñchaśila, collecting grains from the field, is called

ṛta. Collecting without begging is called amṛta, begging grains is called mṛta, tilling the ground is called pramṛta, and trade is called satyānṛta. Engaging in the service of low-grade persons, however, is called śva-vṛtti, the profession of the dogs. Specifically, brāhmaṇas and kṣatriyas should not engage in the low and abominable service of śūdras. Brāhmaṇas should be well acquainted with all the Vedic knowledge, and kṣatriyas should be well acquainted with the worship of demigods.

PURPORT

As stated in *Bhagavad-gītā* (4.13), *cātur-varṇyaṁ mayā sṛṣṭaṁ guṇa-karma-vibhāgaśaḥ:* the four divisions of human society were created by the Supreme Lord according to the three modes of material nature and the work ascribed to them. Formerly, the principle of dividing human society into four sections—*brāhmaṇa, kṣatriya, vaiśya* and *śūdra*—was strictly followed, but because of gradual neglect of the *varṇāśrama* principles, *varṇa-saṅkara* population developed, and the entire institution has now been lost. In this age of Kali, practically everyone is a *śūdra* (*kalau śūdra-sambhavāḥ*), and finding anyone who is a *brāhmaṇa, kṣatriya* or *vaiśya* is very difficult. Although the Kṛṣṇa consciousness movement is a movement of *brāhmaṇas* and Vaiṣṇavas, it is trying to reestablish the divine *varṇāśrama* institution, for without this division of society there cannot be peace and prosperity anywhere.

TEXT 21

शमो दमस्तपः शौचं संतोषः क्षान्तिरार्जवम् ।
ज्ञानं दयाच्युतात्मत्वं सत्यं च ब्रह्मलक्षणम् ॥२१॥

śamo damas tapaḥ śaucaṁ
santoṣaḥ kṣāntir ārjavam
jñānaṁ dayācyutātmatvaṁ
satyaṁ ca brahma-lakṣaṇam

śamaḥ—control of the mind; *damaḥ*—control of the senses; *tapaḥ*—austerity and penance; *śaucam*—cleanliness; *santoṣaḥ*—satisfaction;

kṣāntiḥ—forgiveness (being unagitated by anger); *ārjavam*—simplicity; *jñānam*—knowledge; *dayā*—mercy; *acyuta-ātmatvam*—accepting oneself as an eternal servant of the Lord; *satyam*—truthfulness; *ca*—also; *brahma-lakṣaṇam*—the symptoms of a *brāhmaṇa.*

TRANSLATION

The symptoms of a brāhmaṇa are control of the mind, control of the senses, austerity and penance, cleanliness, satisfaction, forgiveness, simplicity, knowledge, mercy, truthfulness, and complete surrender to the Supreme Personality of Godhead.

PURPORT

In the institution of *varṇāśrama-dharma,* the symptoms of a *brāhmaṇa, kṣatriya, vaiśya, śūdra, brahmacārī, gṛhastha, vānaprastha,* and *sannyāsī* are all described. The ultimate aim is *acyutātmatvam*—to think always of the Supreme Personality of Godhead, Kṛṣṇa, or Viṣṇu. To make advancement in Kṛṣṇa consciousness, one has to become a *brāhmaṇa,* with the above-mentioned symptoms.

TEXT 22

शौर्यं वीर्यं धृतिस्तेजस्त्यागश्चात्मजयः क्षमा ।
ब्रह्मण्यता प्रसादश्च सत्यं च क्षत्रलक्षणम् ॥२२॥

śauryaṁ vīryaṁ dhṛtis tejas
tyāgaś cātmajayaḥ kṣamā
brahmaṇyatā prasādaś ca
satyaṁ ca kṣatra-lakṣaṇam

śauryam—power in battle; *vīryam*—being unconquerable; *dhṛtiḥ*—patience (even in reverses, a *kṣatriya* is very grave); *tejaḥ*—ability to defeat others; *tyāgaḥ*—giving charity; *ca*—and; *ātma-jayaḥ*—not being overwhelmed by bodily necessities; *kṣamā*—forgiveness; *brahmaṇyatā*—faithfulness to the brahminical principles; *prasādaḥ*—jolliness in any condition of life; *ca*—and; *satyam ca*—and truthfulness; *kṣatra-lakṣaṇam*—these are the symptoms of a *kṣatriya.*

TRANSLATION

To be influential in battle, unconquerable, patient, challenging and charitable, to control the bodily necessities, to be forgiving, to be attached to the brahminical nature and to be always jolly and truthful—these are the symptoms of the kṣatriya.

TEXT 23

देवगुर्वच्युते भक्तिस्त्रिवर्गपरिपोषणम् ।
आस्तिक्यमुद्यमो नित्यं नैपुण्यं वैश्यलक्षणम् ॥२३॥

deva-gurv-acyute bhaktis
tri-varga-paripoṣaṇam
āstikyam udyamo nityaṁ
naipuṇyaṁ vaiśya-lakṣaṇam

deva-guru-acyute—unto the demigods, the spiritual master and Lord Viṣṇu; *bhaktiḥ*—engagement in devotional service; *tri-varga*—of the three principles of pious life (religion, economic development and sense gratification); *paripoṣaṇam*—execution; *āstikyam*—faith in the scriptures, the spiritual master and the Supreme Lord; *udyamaḥ*—active; *nityam*—without cessation, continuously; *naipuṇyam*—expertise; *vaiśya-lakṣaṇam*—the symptoms of a *vaiśya.*

TRANSLATION

Being always devoted to the demigods, the spiritual master and the Supreme Lord, Viṣṇu; endeavoring for advancement in religious principles, economic development and sense gratification [dharma, artha and kāma]; believing in the words of the spiritual master and scripture; and always endeavoring with expertise in earning money—these are the symptoms of the vaiśya.

TEXT 24

शूद्रस्य संनतिः शौचं सेवा स्वामिन्यमायया ।
अमन्त्रयज्ञो ह्यस्तेयं सत्यं गोविप्ररक्षणम् ॥२४॥

śūdrasya sannatiḥ śaucaṁ
sevā svāminy amāyayā
amantra-yajño hy asteyaṁ
satyaṁ go-vipra-rakṣaṇam

śūdrasya—of the *śūdra* (the fourth grade of man in society, the worker); *sannatiḥ*—obedience to the higher classes (the *brāhmaṇas, kṣatriyas* and *vaiśyas*); *śaucam*—cleanliness; *sevā*—service; *svāmini*—to the master who maintains him; *amāyayā*—without duplicity; *amantra-yajñaḥ*—performance of sacrifices simply by offering obeisances (without *mantras*); *hi*—certainly; *asteyam*—practicing not to steal; *satyam*—truthfulness; *go*—cows; *vipra*—*brāhmaṇas; rakṣaṇam*—protecting.

TRANSLATION

Offering obeisances to the higher sections of society [the brāhmaṇas, kṣatriyas and vaiśyas], being always very clean, being free from duplicity, serving one's master, performing sacrifices without uttering mantras, not stealing, always speaking the truth and giving all protection to the cows and brāhmaṇas—these are the symptoms of the śūdra.

PURPORT

It is everyone's experience that workers or servants are generally accustomed to stealing. A first-class servant is one who does not steal. Here it is recommended that a first-class *śūdra* must remain very clean, must not steal or speak lies, and must always render service to his master. A *śūdra* may attend sacrifices and Vedic ritualistic ceremonies along with his master, but he should not utter the *mantras,* for these may be uttered only by the members of the higher sections of society. Unless one is completely pure and has been raised to the standard of a *brāhmaṇa, kṣatriya* or *vaiśya*—in other words, unless one is *dvija,* twiceborn—the chanting of *mantras* will not be fruitful.

TEXT 25

स्त्रीणां च पतिदेवानां तच्छुश्रूषानुकूलता ।
तद्बन्धुष्वनुवृत्तिश्च नित्यं तद्व्रतधारणम् ॥२५॥

strīṇāṁ ca pati-devānāṁ
tac-chuśrūṣānukūlatā
tad-bandhuṣv anuvṛttiś ca
nityaṁ tad-vrata-dhāraṇam

strīṇām—of women; *ca*—also; *pati-devānām*—who have accepted their husbands as worshipable; *tat-śuśrūṣā*—readiness to render service to her husband; *anukūlatā*—being favorably disposed towards her husband; *tat-bandhuṣu*—unto the friends and relatives of the husband; *anuvṛttiḥ*—being similarly disposed (to treat them well for the satisfaction of the husband); *ca*—and; *nityam*—regularly; *tat-vrata-dhāraṇam*—accepting the vows of the husband or acting exactly as the husband acts.

TRANSLATION

To render service to the husband, to be always favorably disposed toward the husband, to be equally well disposed toward the husband's relatives and friends, and to follow the vows of the husband—these are the four principles to be followed by women described as chaste.

PURPORT

It is very important for peaceful householder life that a woman follow the vow of her husband. Any disagreement with the husband's vow will disrupt family life. In this regard, Cāṇakya Paṇḍita gives a very valuable instruction: *dampatyoḥ kalaho nāsti tatra śrīḥ svayam āgatāḥ.* When there are no fights between husband and wife, the goddess of fortune automatically comes to the home. A woman's education should be conducted along the lines indicated in this verse. The basic principle for a chaste woman is to be always favorably disposed toward her husband. In *Bhagavad-gītā* (1.40) it is said, *strīṣu duṣṭāsu vārṣṇeya jāyate varṇa-saṅkaraḥ:* if the women are polluted, there will be *varṇa-saṅkara* population. In modern terms, the *varṇa-saṅkara* are the hippies, who do not follow any regulative injunctions. Another explanation is that when the population is *varṇa-saṅkara,* no one can know who is on what platform. The *varṇāśrama* system scientifically divides society into four *varṇas* and four *āśramas*, but in *varṇa-saṅkara* society there are no such distinctions, and no one can know who is who. In such a society, no one can distinguish between a *brāhmaṇa*, a *kṣatriya*, a *vaiśya* and a *śūdra*. For peace and happiness in the material world, the *varṇāśrama* institution must be introduced. The symptoms of one's activities must be defined, and one must be educated accordingly. Then spiritual advancement will automatically be possible.

TEXTS 26–27

संमार्जनोपलेपाभ्यां गृहमण्डनवर्तनैः ।
स्वयं च मण्डिता नित्यं परिमृष्टपरिच्छदा ॥२६॥
कामैरुच्चावचैः साध्वी प्रश्रयेण दमेन च ।
वाक्यैःसत्यैः प्रियैः प्रेम्णा काले काले भजेत् पतिम् ॥२७॥

sammārjanopalepābhyāṁ
gṛha-maṇḍana-vartanaiḥ
svayaṁ ca maṇḍitā nityaṁ
parimṛṣṭa-paricchadā

kāmair uccāvacaiḥ sādhvī
praśrayeṇa damena ca
vākyaiḥ satyaiḥ priyaiḥ premṇā
kāle kāle bhajet patim

sammārjana—by cleaning; *upalepābhyām*—by smearing with water or other cleansing liquids; *gṛha*—the household; *maṇḍana*—decorating; *vartanaiḥ*—remaining at home and engaged in such duties; *svayam*—personally; *ca*—also; *maṇḍitā*—finely dressed; *nityam*—always; *parimṛṣṭa*—cleansed; *paricchadā*—garments and household utensils; *kāmaiḥ*—according to the desires of the husband; *ucca-avacaiḥ*—both great and small; *sādhvī*—a chaste woman; *praśrayeṇa*—with modesty; *damena*—by controlling the senses; *ca*—also; *vākyaiḥ*—by speech; *satyaiḥ*—truthful; *priyaiḥ*—very pleasing; *premṇā*—with love; *kāle kāle*—at appropriate times; *bhajet*—should worship; *patim*—her husband.

TRANSLATION

A chaste woman must dress nicely and decorate herself with golden ornaments for the pleasure of her husband. Always wearing clean and attractive garments, she should sweep and clean the household with water and other liquids so that the entire house is always pure and clean. She should collect the household paraphernalia and keep the house always aromatic with incense and flowers and must be ready to execute the desires of her husband. Being modest and truthful, controlling her senses, and speaking in sweet words, a chaste woman should engage in the service of her husband with love, according to time and circumstances.

TEXT 28

संतुष्टालोलुपा दक्षा धर्मज्ञा प्रियसत्यवाक् ।
अप्रमत्ता शुचिः स्निग्धा पतिं त्वपतितं भजेत् ॥२८॥

santuṣṭālolupā dakṣā
dharma-jñā priya-satya-vāk
apramattā śuciḥ snigdhā
patiṁ tv apatitaṁ bhajet

santuṣṭā—always satisfied; *alolupā*—without being greedy; *dakṣā*—very expert in serving; *dharma-jñā*—fully conversant with religious principles; *priya*—pleasing; *satya*—truthful; *vāk*—in speaking; *apramattā*—attentive in service to her husband; *śuciḥ*—always clean and pure; *snigdhā*—affectionate; *patim*—the husband; *tu*—but; *apatitam*—who is not fallen; *bhajet*—should worship.

TRANSLATION

A chaste woman should not be greedy, but satisfied in all circumstances. She must be very expert in handling household affairs and should be fully conversant with religious principles. She should speak pleasingly and truthfully and should be very careful and always clean and pure. Thus a chaste woman should engage with affection in the service of a husband who is not fallen.

PURPORT

According to the injunction of Yājñavalkya, an authority on religious principles, *āśuddheḥ sampratikṣyo hi mahāpātaka-dūṣitaḥ.* One is considered contaminated by the reactions of great sinful activities when one has not been purified according to the methods of the *daśa-vidhā-saṁskāra.* In *Bhagavad-gītā,* however, the Lord says, *na māṁ duṣkṛtino mūḍhāḥ prapadyante narādhamāḥ:* "Those miscreants who do not surrender unto Me are the lowest of mankind." The word *narādhama* means "nondevotee." Śrī Caitanya Mahāprabhu also said, *yei bhaje sei baḍa, abhakta—hīna, chāra.* Anyone who is a devotee is sinless. One who is not a devotee, however, is the most fallen and condemned. It is recommended, therefore, that a chaste wife not associate with a fallen husband. A fallen husband is one who is addicted to the four principles of sinful activity—namely illicit sex, meat-eating, gambling and intoxication. Specifically, if one is not a soul surrendered to the Supreme Personality of Godhead, he is understood to be contaminated. Thus a chaste woman is advised not to agree to serve such a husband. It is not that a chaste woman should be like a slave while her husband is *narādhama,* the lowest of men. Although the duties of a woman are different from those of a man, a chaste woman is not meant to serve a fallen husband. If her husband is fallen, it is recommended that she give up his association. Giving up the association of her husband does not mean, however, that a woman should marry again and thus indulge in prostitution. If a chaste woman unfortunately marries a husband who is fallen, she should live separately from him. Similarly, a husband can separate himself from a woman who is not chaste according to the description of the *śāstra.* The conclusion is that a husband should be a pure Vaiṣṇava and that a woman should be a chaste wife with all the symptoms described in this regard. Then both of them will be happy and make spiritual progress in Kṛṣṇa consciousness.

TEXT 29

या पतिं हरिभावेन भजेत् श्रीरिव तत्परा ।
हर्यात्मना हरेर्लोके पत्या श्रीरिव मोदते ॥२९॥

yā patiṁ hari-bhāvena
bhajet śrīr iva tat-parā

hary-ātmanā harer loke
patyā śrīr iva modate

yā—any woman who; *patim*—her husband; *hari-bhāvena*—mentally accepting him as equal to Hari, the Supreme Personality of Godhead; *bhajet*—worships or renders service to; *śrīḥ iva*—exactly like the goddess of fortune; *tat-parā*—being devoted; *hari-ātmanā*—completely absorbed in thoughts of Hari; *hareḥ loke*—in the spiritual world, the Vaikuṇṭha planets; *patyā*—with her husband; *śrīḥ iva*—exactly like the goddess of fortune; *modate*—enjoys spiritual, eternal life.

TRANSLATION

The woman who engages in the service of her husband, following strictly in the footsteps of the goddess of fortune, surely returns home, back to Godhead, with her devotee husband, and lives very happily in the Vaikuṇṭha planets.

PURPORT

The faithfulness of the goddess of fortune is the ideal for a chaste woman. The *Brahma-saṁhitā* (5.29) says, *lakṣmī-sahasra-śata-sambhrama-sevyamānam.* In the Vaikuṇṭha planets, Lord Viṣṇu is worshiped by many, many thousands of goddesses of fortune, and in Goloka Vṛndāvana, Lord Kṛṣṇa is worshiped by many, many thousands of *gopīs*, all of whom are goddesses of fortune. A woman should serve her husband as faithfully as the goddess of fortune. A man should be an ideal servant of the Lord, and a woman should be an ideal wife like the goddess of fortune. Then both husband and wife will be so faithful and strong that by acting together they will return home, back to Godhead, without a doubt. In this regard, Śrīla Madhvācārya gives this opinion:

harir asmin sthita iti
strīṇāṁ bhartari bhāvanā
śiṣyāṇāṁ ca gurau nityaṁ
śūdrāṇāṁ brāhmaṇādiṣu
bhṛtyānāṁ svāmini tathā
hari-bhāva udīritaḥ

A woman should think of her husband as the Supreme Lord. Similarly, a disciple should think of the spiritual master as the Supreme Personality of Godhead, a *śūdra* should think of a *brāhmaṇa* as the Supreme Personality of Godhead, and a servant should think of his master as the Supreme Personality of Godhead. In this way, all of them will automatically become devotees of the Lord. In other words, by thinking this way, all of them will become Kṛṣṇa conscious.

TEXT 30

वृत्तिः सङ्करजातीनां तत्तत्कुलकृता भवेत् ।
अचौराणामपापानामन्त्यजान्तेवसायिनाम् ॥३०॥

vṛttiḥ saṅkara-jātīnāṁ
tat-tat-kula-kṛtā bhavet
acaurāṇām apāpānām
antyajāntevasāyinām

vṛttiḥ—occupational duty; *saṅkara-jātīnām*—of the mixed classes of men (those other than the four divisions); *tat-tat*—according to their respective; *kula-kṛtā*—family tradition; *bhavet*—should be; *acaurāṇām*—not thieves by profession; *apāpānām*—not sinful; *antyaja*—lower classes; *antevasāyinām*—known as *antevasāyī* or *caṇḍāla*.

TRANSLATION

Among the mixed classes known as saṅkara, those who are not thieves are known as antevasāyī or caṇḍālas [dog-eaters], and they also have their hereditary customs.

PURPORT

The four principal divisions of society—*brāhmaṇa*, *kṣatriya*, *vaiśya* and *śūdra*—have been defined, and now there is a description of the *antyaja*, the mixed classes. Among the mixed classes, there are two divisions—*pratilomaja* and *anulomaja*. If a woman of a high caste marries a man of a lower caste, their union is called *pratilo*. If a woman of a low caste, however, marries a man of a higher caste, their union is called *anulo.* The members of such dynasties have their traditional duties as barbers, washermen and so on. Among the *antyajas,* those who are still somewhat pure in that they do not steal and are not addicted to meat-eating, drinking, illicit sex and gambling are called *antevasāyī.* Among people of the lower classes, intermarriage and the drinking of wine are allowed, for these people do not recognize such conduct as sinful among themselves.

TEXT 31

प्रायः स्वभावविहितो नृणां धर्मो युगे युगे ।
वेददृग्भिः स्मृतो राजन्प्रेत्य चेह च शर्मकृत् ॥३१॥

prāyaḥ sva-bhāva-vihito
nṛṇāṁ dharmo yuge yuge
veda-dṛgbhiḥ smṛto rājan
pretya ceha ca śarma-kṛt

prāyaḥ—generally; *sva-bhāva-vihitaḥ*—prescribed, according to one's material modes of nature; *nṛṇām*—of human society; *dharmaḥ*—the occupational duty; *yuge yuge*—in every age; *veda-dṛgbhiḥ*—by *brāhmaṇas* well conversant in the Vedic knowledge; *smṛtaḥ*—recognized; *rājan*—O King; *pretya*—after death; *ca*—and; *iha*—here (in this body); *ca*—also; *śarma-kṛt*—auspicious.

TRANSLATION

My dear King, brāhmaṇas well conversant in Vedic knowledge have given their verdict that in every age [yuga] the conduct of different sections of people according to their material modes of nature is auspicious both in this life and after death.

PURPORT

In *Bhagavad-gītā* (3.35) it is said, *śreyān sva-dharmo viguṇaḥ para-dharmāt svanuṣṭhitāt:* "It is far better to discharge one's prescribed duties, even though they may be faulty, than another's duties." The *antyajas,* the men of the lower classes, are accustomed to stealing, drinking and illicit sex, but that is not considered sinful. For example, if a tiger kills a man, this is not sinful but if a man kills another man, this is considered sinful, and the killer is hanged. What is a daily affair among the animals is a sinful act in human society. Thus according to the symptoms of higher and lower sections of society, there are different varieties of occupational duties. According to the experts in Vedic knowledge, these duties are prescribed in terms of the age concerned.

TEXT 32

वृत्त्या स्वभावकृतया वर्तमानः स्वकर्मकृत् ।
हित्वा स्वभावजं कर्म शनैर्निर्गुणतामियात् ॥३२॥

vṛttyā sva-bhāva-kṛtayā
vartamānaḥ sva-karma-kṛt
hitvā sva-bhāva-jaṁ karma
śanair nirguṇatām iyāt

vṛttyā—with the profession; *sva-bhāva-kṛtayā*—performed according to one's modes of material nature; *vartamānaḥ*—existing; *sva-karma-kṛt*—executing his own work; *hitvā*—giving up; *sva-bhāva-jam*—born from one's own modes of nature; *karma*—activities; *śanaiḥ*—gradually; *nirguṇatām*—transcendental position; *iyāt*—may attain.

TRANSLATION

If one acts in his profession according to his position in the modes of nature and gradually gives up these activities, he attains the niṣkāma stage.

PURPORT

If one gradually gives up his hereditary customs and duties and tries to serve the Supreme Personality of Godhead in his natural position, he is gradually able to become free from these activities, and he attains the stage of *niṣkāma*, freedom from material desires.

TEXTS 33–34

उप्यमानं मुहुः क्षेत्रं स्वयं निर्वीर्यतामियात् ।
न कल्पते पुनः सूत्यै उप्तं बीजं च नश्यति ॥३३॥

एवं कामाशयं चित्तं कामानामतिसेवया ।
विरज्येत यथा राजन्नग्निवत् कामबिन्दुभिः ॥३४॥

upyamānaṁ muhuḥ kṣetraṁ
svayaṁ nirvīryatām iyāt
na kalpate punaḥ sūtyai
uptaṁ bījaṁ ca naśyati

evaṁ kāmāśayaṁ cittaṁ
kāmānām atisevayā
virajyeta yathā rājann
agnivat kāma-bindubhiḥ

upyamānam—being cultivated; *muhuḥ*—again and again; *kṣetram*—a field; *svayam*—itself; *nirvīryatām*—barrenness; *iyāt*—may obtain; *na kalpate*—is not suitable; *punaḥ*—again; *sūtyai*—for growing further harvests; *uptam*—sown; *bījam*—the seed; *ca*—and; *naśyati*—is spoiled; *evam*—in this way; *kāma-āśayam*—full of lusty desires; *cittam*—the core of the heart; *kāmānām*—of the desirable objects; *ati-sevayā*—by enjoyment over and over again; *virajyeta*—may become detached; *yathā*—just as; *rājan*—O King; *agni-vat*—a fire; *kāma-bindubhiḥ*—by small drops of clarified butter.

TRANSLATION

My dear King, if an agricultural field is cultivated again and again, the power of its production decreases, and whatever seeds are sown there are lost. Just as drops of ghee on a fire never extinguish the fire but a flood of ghee will, similarly, overindulgence in lusty desires mitigates such desires entirely.

PURPORT

If one continuously sprinkles drops of ghee on a fire, the fire will not be extinguished, but if one suddenly puts a lump of ghee on a fire, the fire may possibly be extinguished entirely. Similarly, those who are too sinful and have thus been born in the lower classes are allowed to enjoy sinful activities fully, for thus there is a chance that these activities will become detestful to them, and they will get the opportunity to be purified.

TEXT 35

यस्य यल्लक्षणं प्रोक्तं पुंसो वर्णाभिव्यञ्जकम् ।
यदन्यत्रापि दृश्येत तत् तेनैव विनिर्दिशेत् ॥३५॥

yasya yal lakṣaṇaṁ proktaṁ
puṁso varṇābhivyañjakam
yad anyatrāpi dṛśyeta
tat tenaiva vinirdiśet

yasya—of whom; *yat*—which; *lakṣaṇam*—symptom; *proktam*—described (above); *puṁsaḥ*—of a person; *varṇa-abhivyañjakam*—indicating the classification (*brāhmaṇa, kṣatriya, vaiśya, śūdra,* etc.); *yat*—if; *anyatra*—elsewhere; *api*—also; *dṛśyeta*—is seen; *tat*—that; *tena*—by that symptom; *eva*—certainly; *vinirdiśet*—one should designate.

TRANSLATION

If one shows the symptoms of being a brāhmaṇa, kṣatriya, vaiśya or śūdra, as described above, even if he has appeared in a different class, he should be accepted according to those symptoms of classification.

PURPORT

Herein it is clearly stated by Nārada Muni that one should not be accepted as a *brāhmaṇa, kṣatriya, vaiśya* or *śūdra* according to birth, for although this is going on now, it is not accepted by the *śāstras.* As stated in *Bhagavad-gītā* (4.13), *cātur-varṇyaṁ mayā sṛṣṭaṁ guṇa-karma-vibhāgaśaḥ.* Thus the four divisions of society—*brāhmaṇa, kṣatriya, vaiśya* and *śūdra*—are to be ascertained according to qualities and activities. If one was born in a *brāhmaṇa* family and has acquired the brahminical qualifications, he is to be accepted as a *brāhmaṇa;* otherwise, he should be considered a *brahma-bandhu.* Similarly, if a *śūdra* acquires the qualities of a *brāhmaṇa,* although he was born in a *śūdra* family, he is not a *śūdra;* because he has developed the qualities of a *brāhmaṇa,* he should be accepted as a *brāhmaṇa.* The Kṛṣṇa consciousness movement is meant to develop these brahminical qualities. Regardless of the community in which one was born, if one develops the qualities of a *brāhmaṇa* he should be accepted as a *brāhmaṇa,* and he then may be offered the order of *sannyāsa.* Unless one is qualified in terms of the brahminical symptoms, one cannot take *sannyāsa.* In designating a person a *brāhmaṇa, kṣatriya, vaiśya* or *śūdra,* birth is not the essential symptom. This understanding is very important. Herein Nārada Muni distinctly says that one may be accepted according to the caste of his birth if he has the corresponding qualifications, but otherwise he should not. One who has attained the qualifications of a *brāhmaṇa,* regardless of where he was born, should be accepted as a *brāhmaṇa.* Similarly, if one has developed the qualities of a *śūdra* or a *caṇḍāla,* regardless of where he was born, he should be accepted in terms of those symptoms.

Thus end the Bhaktivedanta purports of the Seventh Canto, Eleventh Chapter, of the Śrīmad-Bhāgavatam, *entitled "The Perfect Society: Four Social Classes."*

CHAPTER TWELVE

The Perfect Society: Four Spiritual Classes

This chapter particularly describes the *brahmacārī* and the person in the *vānaprastha* stage, and it also gives a general description of the four *āśramas—brahmacarya, gṛhastha, vānaprastha* and *sannyāsa.* In the previous chapter, the great saint Nārada Muni has described the *varṇa* institution of society, and now, in this chapter, he will describe the stages of spiritual advancement in the four *āśramas,* which are known as *brahmacarya, gṛhastha, vānaprastha* and *sannyāsa.*

The *brahmacārī* should live under the care of the true spiritual master, giving him sincere respect and obeisances, acting as his menial servant, and always carrying out his order. The *brahmacārī* should engage himself in spiritual activities and study the Vedic literature under the direction of the spiritual master. According to the *brahmacarya* system, he should dress with a belt, deerskin, and matted hair and should bear a *daṇḍa,* waterpot and sacred thread. He should collect alms daily in the morning, and in the evening whatever alms he has collected he should offer to the spiritual master. A *brahmacārī* should accept *prasāda* upon the order of the spiritual master, and if the spiritual master sometimes forgets to order the disciple to eat, the disciple should not take *prasāda* on his own initiative; rather, he should fast. The *brahmacārī* should be trained to be satisfied with eating what is absolutely necessary, he should be very expert in executing responsibilities, he should be faithful, and he should control his senses and try to avoid the association of women as far as possible. A *brahmacārī* should very strictly abstain from living with women and should not meet with *gṛhasthas* and those too addicted to women. Nor should a *brahmacārī* speak in a lonely place with a woman.

After completing one's education as a *brahmacārī* in this way, one should give *dakṣiṇā,* an offering of gratitude, to one's *guru,* and then one may leave for home and accept the next *āśrama*—the *gṛhastha-āśrama*—or else one may continue in the *brahmacarya-āśrama* without adulteration. The duties for the *gṛhastha-āśrama* and *brahmacarya-*

āśrama, as well as the duties for *sannyāsīs*, are prescribed in the *śāstras*. A *gṛhastha* is not meant to enjoy sex life without restriction. Indeed, the whole purpose of Vedic life is to become free from sexual indulgence. All the *āśramas* are recognized for spiritual progress, and therefore although the *gṛhastha-āśrama* gives a kind of license for sex life for a certain time, it does not allow unrestricted sex life. Therefore, in *gṛhastha* life also, there is no illicit sex. A *gṛhastha* should not accept a woman for sexual enjoyment. Wasting semen is also illicit sex.

After the *gṛhastha-āśrama* is another *āśrama*, known as *vānaprastha*, which is midway between *gṛhastha* and *sannyāsa*. A person in the *vānaprastha* order is restricted in eating food grains and forbidden to eat fruits that have not ripened on the tree. Nor should he cook food with fire, although he is allowed to eat *caru*, grains that have been offered in a sacrificial fire. He may also eat fruits and grains that have grown naturally. Living in a thatched cottage, the *vānaprastha* should endure all kinds of heat and cold. He should not cut his nails or hair, and he should give up cleaning his body and teeth. He should wear tree bark, accept a *daṇḍa*, and practice life in the forest, taking a vow to live there for twelve years, eight years, four years, two years or at least one year. At last, when because of old age he can no longer perform the activities of a *vānaprastha*, he should gradually stop everything and in this way give up his body.

TEXT 1

श्रीनारद उवाच

ब्रह्मचारी गुरुकुले वसन्दान्तो गुरोर्हितम् ।
आचरन्दासवन्नीचो गुरौ सुदृढसौहृदः ॥ १ ॥

śrī-nārada uvāca
brahmacārī guru-kule
vasan dānto guror hitam
ācaran dāsavan nīco
gurau sudṛḍha-sauhṛdaḥ

śrī-nāradaḥ uvāca—Śrī Nārada Muni said; *brahmacārī*—a *brahmacārī*, a student living at the residence of the *guru*; *guru-kule*—at the residence of the *guru*; *vasan*—by living; *dāntaḥ*—continuously practicing control of the senses; *guroḥ hitam*—only for the benefit of the *guru* (not for one's personal benefit); *ācaran*—practicing; *dāsa-vat*—very humbly, like a slave; *nīcaḥ*—submissive, obedient; *gurau*—unto the spiritual master; *su-dṛḍha*—firmly; *sauhṛdaḥ*—in friendship or good will.

TRANSLATION

Nārada Muni said: A student should practice completely controlling his senses. He should be submissive and should have an attitude of firm friendship for the spiritual master. With a great vow, the brahmacārī should live at the guru-kula, only for the benefit of the guru.

TEXT 2

सायं प्रातरुपासीत गुर्वग्न्यर्कसुरोत्तमान् ।
सन्ध्ये उभे च यतवाग् जपन्ब्रह्म समाहितः ॥ २ ॥

sāyaṁ prātar upāsīta
gurv-agny-arka-surottamān
sandhye ubhe ca yata-vāg
japan brahma samāhitaḥ

sāyam—in the evening; *prātaḥ*—in the morning; *upāsīta*—he should worship; *guru*—the spiritual master; *agni*—the fire (by a fire sacrifice); *arka*—the sun; *sura-uttamān*—and Lord Viṣṇu, Puruṣottama, the best of personalities; *sandhye*—morning and evening; *ubhe*—both; *ca*—also; *yata-vāk*—without talking, being silent; *japan*—murmuring; *brahma*—the Gāyatrī *mantra; samāhitaḥ*—being fully absorbed.

TRANSLATION

At both junctions of day and night, namely, in the early morning and in the evening, he should be fully absorbed in thoughts of the spiritual master, fire, the sun-god and Lord Viṣṇu and by chanting the Gāyatrī mantra he should worship them.

TEXT 3

छन्दांस्यधीयीत गुरोराहूतश्चेत् सुयन्त्रितः ।
उपक्रमेऽवसाने च चरणौ शिरसा नमेत् ॥ ३ ॥

chandāṁsy adhīyīta guror
āhūtaś cet suyantritaḥ
upakrame 'vasāne ca
caraṇau śirasā namet

chandāṁsi—*mantras* in the *Vedas,* like the Hare Kṛṣṇa *mahā-mantra* and the Gāyatrī *mantra; adhīyīta*—one should chant or read regularly; *guroḥ*—from the spiritual master; *āhūtaḥ*—being addressed or called (by him); *cet*—if; *su-yantritaḥ*—faithful, well behaved; *upakrame*—in the beginning; *avasāne*—at the end (of reading Vedic *mantras*); *ca*—also; *caraṇau*—at the lotus feet; *śirasā*—by the head; *namet*—one should offer obeisances.

TRANSLATION

Being called by the spiritual master, the student should study the Vedic mantras regularly. Every day, before beginning his studies and at the end of his studies, the disciple should respectfully offer obeisances unto the spiritual master.

TEXT 4

मेखलाजिनवासांसि जटादण्डकमण्डलून् ।
बिभृयादुपवीतं च दर्भपाणिर्यथोदितम् ॥ ४ ॥

mekhalājina-vāsāṁsi
jaṭā-daṇḍa-kamaṇḍalūn
bibhṛyād upavītaṁ ca
darbha-pāṇir yathoditam

mekhalā—a belt made of straw; *ajina-vāsāṁsi*—garments made of deerskin; *jaṭā*—matted hair; *daṇḍa*—a rod; *kamaṇḍalūn*—and a waterpot known as a *kamaṇḍalu; bibhṛyāt*—he (the *brahmacārī*) should regularly carry or wear; *upavītam ca*—and a sacred thread; *darbha-pāṇiḥ*—taking purified *kuśa* in his hand; *yathā uditam*—as recommended in the *śāstras.*

TRANSLATION

Carrying pure kuśa grass in his hand, the brahmacārī should dress regularly with a belt of straw and with deerskin garments. He

should wear matted hair, carry a rod and waterpot and be decorated with a sacred thread, as recommended in the śāstras.

TEXT 5

सायं प्रातश्चरेद्भैक्ष्यं गुरवे तन्निवेदयेत् ।
भुञ्जीत यद्यनुज्ञातो नो चेदुपवसेत् क्वचित् ॥ ५ ॥

sāyaṁ prātaś cared bhaikṣyaṁ
gurave tan nivedayet
bhuñjīta yady anujñāto
no ced upavaset kvacit

sāyam—in the evening; *prātaḥ*—in the morning; *caret*—should go out; *bhaikṣyam*—to collect alms; *gurave*—unto the spiritual master; *tat*—all that he collects; *nivedayet*—should offer; *bhuñjīta*—he should eat; *yadi*—if; *anujñātaḥ*—ordered (by the spiritual master); *no*—otherwise; *cet*—if; *upavaset*—should observe fasting; *kvacit*—sometimes.

TRANSLATION

The brahmacārī should go out morning and evening to collect alms, and he should offer all that he collects to the spiritual master. He should eat only if ordered to take food by the spiritual master; otherwise, if the spiritual master does not give this order, he may sometimes have to fast.

TEXT 6

सुशीलो मितभुग् दक्षः श्रद्दधानो जितेन्द्रियः ।
यावदर्थं व्यवहरेत् स्त्रीषु स्त्रीनिर्जितेषु च ॥ ६ ॥

suśīlo mita-bhug dakṣaḥ
śraddadhāno jitendriyaḥ
yāvad-arthaṁ vyavaharet
strīṣu strī-nirjiteṣu ca

su-śīlaḥ—very polite and well behaved; *mita-bhuk*—eating only exactly what he needs, neither more nor less; *dakṣaḥ*—expert or without laziness, always busy; *śraddadhānaḥ*—possessing full faith in the instructions of the *śāstra* and the spiritual master; *jita-indriyaḥ*—having full control over the senses; *yāvat-artham*—as much as necessary; *vyavaharet*—should behave externally; *strīṣu*—unto women; *strī-nirjiteṣu*—men who are henpecked, controlled by women; *ca*—also.

TRANSLATION

A brahmacārī should be quite well behaved and gentle and should not eat or collect more than necessary. He must always be active and expert, fully believing in the instructions of the spiritual master and the śāstra. Fully controlling his senses, he should associate only as much as necessary with women or those controlled by women.

PURPORT

A *brahmacārī* should be very careful not to mix with women or with men addicted to women. Although when he goes out to beg alms it is necessary to talk with women and with men very much attached to women, this association should be very short, and he should talk with them only about begging alms, and not more. A *brahmacārī* should be very careful in associating with men who are attached to women.

TEXT 7

वर्जयेत् प्रमदागाथामगृहस्थो बृहद्व्रतः ।
इन्द्रियाणि प्रमाथीनि हरन्त्यपि यतेर्मनः ॥ ७ ॥

varjayet pramadā-gāthām
agṛhastho bṛhad-vrataḥ
indriyāṇi pramāthīni
haranty api yater manaḥ

varjayet—must give up; *pramadā-gāthām*—talking with women; *agṛhasthaḥ*—a person who has not accepted the *gṛhastha-āśrama* (a *brahmacārī* or *sannyāsī*); *bṛhat-vrataḥ*—invariably observing the vow of celibacy; *indriyāṇi*—the senses; *pramāthīni*—almost always unconquerable; *haranti*—take away; *api*—even; *yateḥ*—of the *sannyāsī*; *manaḥ*—the mind.

TRANSLATION

A brahmacārī, or one who has not accepted the gṛhastha-āśrama [family life], must rigidly avoid talking with women or about women, for the senses are so powerful that they may agitate even the mind of a sannyāsī, a member of the renounced order of life.

PURPORT

Brahmacarya essentially means the vow not to marry but to observe strict celibacy (*bṛhad-vrata*). A *brahmacārī* or *sannyāsī* should avoid talking with women or reading literature concerning talks between man and woman. The injunction restricting association with women is the basic principle of spiritual life. Associating or talking with women is never advised in any of the Vedic literatures. The entire Vedic system teaches one to avoid sex life so that one may gradually progress from *brahmacarya* to *gṛhastha*, from *gṛhastha* to *vānaprastha*, and from *vānaprastha* to *sannyāsa* and thus give up material enjoyment, which is the original cause of bondage to this material world. The word *bṛhad-vrata* refers to one who has decided not to marry, or in other words, not to indulge in sex life throughout his entire life.

TEXT 8

केशप्रसाधनोन्मर्दस्नपनाभ्यञ्जनादिकम् ।
गुरुस्त्रीभिर्युवतिभिः कारयेन्नात्मनो युवा ॥ ८ ॥

keśa-prasādhanonmarda-
snapanābhyañjanādikam
guru-strībhir yuvatibhiḥ
kārayen nātmano yuvā

keśa-prasādhana—brushing the hair; *unmarda*—massaging the body; *snapana*—bathing; *abhyañjana-ādikam*—massaging the body with oil and so on; *guru-strībhiḥ*—by the wife of the spiritual master; *yuvatibhiḥ*—very young; *kārayet*—should allow to do; *na*—never; *ātmanaḥ*—for personal service; *yuvā*—if the student is a young man.

TRANSLATION

If the wife of the spiritual master is young, a young brahmacārī should not allow her to care for his hair, massage his body with oil, or bathe him with affection like a mother.

PURPORT

The relationship between the student or disciple and the wife of the spiritual master or teacher is like that between son and mother. A mother sometimes cares for her son by combing his hair, massaging his body with oil, or bathing him. Similarly, the wife of the teacher is also a mother (*guru-patnī*), and therefore she may also care for the disciple in a motherly way. If the wife of the teacher is a young woman, however, a young *brahmacārī* should not allow such a mother to touch him. This is strictly prohibited. There are seven kinds of mothers:

ātma-mātā guroḥ patnī
brāhmaṇī rāja-patnikā
dhenur dhātrī tathā pṛthvī
saptaitā mātaraḥ smṛtāḥ

These mothers are the original mother, the wife of the teacher or spiritual master, the wife of a *brāhmaṇa*, the king's wife, the cow, the nurse and the earth. Unnecessary association with women, even with one's mother, sister or daughter, is strictly prohibited. This is human civilization. A civilization that allows men to mix unrestrictedly with women is an animal civilization. In Kali-yuga, people are extremely liberal, but mixing with women and talking with them as equals actually constitutes an uncivilized way of life.

TEXT 9

नन्वग्निः प्रमदा नाम घृतकुम्भसमः पुमान् ।
सुतामपि रहो जह्यादन्यदा यावदर्थकृत् ॥ ९ ॥

nanv agniḥ pramadā nāma
ghṛta-kumbha-samaḥ pumān
sutām api raho jahyād
anyadā yāvad-artha-kṛt

nanu—certainly; *agniḥ*—the fire; *pramadā*—the woman (one who bewilders the mind of man); *nāma*—the very name; *ghṛta-kumbha*—a pot of butter; *samaḥ*—like; *pumān*—a man; *sutām api*—even one's daughter; *rahaḥ*—in a secluded place; *jahyāt*—one must not associate with; *anyadā*—with other women also; *yāvat*—as much as; *artha-kṛt*—required.

TRANSLATION

Woman is compared to fire, and man is compared to a butter pot. Therefore a man should avoid associating even with his own daughter in a secluded place. Similarly, he should also avoid association with other women. One should associate with women only for important business and not otherwise.

PURPORT

If a butter pot and fire are kept together, the butter within the pot will certainly melt. Woman is compared to fire, and man is compared to a butter pot. However advanced one may be in restraining the senses, it is almost impossible for a man to keep himself controlled in the presence of a woman, even if she is his own daughter, mother or sister. Indeed, his mind is agitated even if one is in the renounced order of life. Therefore, Vedic civilization carefully restricts mingling between men and women. If one cannot understand the basic principle of restraining association between man and woman, he is to be considered an animal. That is the purport of this verse.

TEXT 10

कल्पयित्वात्मना यावदाभासमिदमीश्वरः ।
द्वैतं तावन्न विरमेत् ततो ह्यस्य विपर्ययः ॥१०॥

kalpayitvātmanā yāvad
ābhāsam idam īśvaraḥ
dvaitaṁ tāvan na viramet
tato hy asya viparyayaḥ

kalpayitvā—ascertaining positively; *ātmanā*—by self-realization; *yāvat*—as long as; *ābhāsam*—reflection (of the original body and senses); *idam*—this (the body and senses); *īśvaraḥ*—completely independent of illusion; *dvaitam*—duality; *tāvat*—for that long; *na*—does not; *viramet*—see; *tataḥ*—by such duality; *hi*—indeed; *asya*—of the person; *viparyayaḥ*—counteraction.

TRANSLATION

As long as a living entity is not completely self-realized—as long as he is not independent of the misconception of identifying with his body, which is nothing but a reflection of the original body and senses—he cannot be relieved of the conception of duality, which is epitomized by the duality between man and woman. Thus there is every chance that he will fall down because his intelligence is bewildered.

PURPORT

Here is another important warning that a man must save himself from attraction to woman. Until one is self-realized, fully independent of the illusory conception of the material body, the duality of man and woman must undoubtedly continue, but when one is actually self-realized this distinction ceases.

vidyā-vinaya-sampanne
brāhmaṇe gavi hastini
śuni caiva śvapāke ca
paṇḍitāḥ sama-darśinaḥ

"The humble sage, by virtue of true knowledge, sees with equal vision a learned and gentle *brāhmaṇa*, a cow, an elephant, a dog and a dog-eater [outcaste]." (Bg. 5.18) On the spiritual platform, the learned person not only gives up the duality of man and woman, but also gives up the duality of man and animal. This is the test of self-realization. One must realize perfectly that the living being is spirit soul but is tasting various types of material bodies. One may theoretically understand this, but when one has practical realization, then he actually becomes a *paṇḍita*, one who knows. Until that time, the duality continues, and the conception of man and woman also continues. In this stage, one should be extremely careful about mixing with women. No one should think himself perfect and forget the śāstric instruction that one should be very careful about associating even with his daughter, mother or sister, not to speak of other women. Śrīla Madhvācārya cites the following *ślokas* in this regard:

bahutvenaiva vastūnāṁ
yathārtha-jñānam ucyate
advaita-jñānam ity etad
dvaita-jñānaṁ tad-anyathā

yathā jñānaṁ tathā vastu
yathā vastus tathā matiḥ
naiva jñānārthayor bhedas
tata ekatva-vedanam

Unity in variety is real knowledge, and therefore giving up variety artificially does not reflect perfect knowledge of monism. According to the *acintya-bhedābheda* philosophy of Śrī Caitanya Mahāprabhu, there are varieties, but all of them constitute one unit. Such knowledge is knowledge of perfect oneness.

TEXT 11

एतत् सर्वं गृहस्थस्य समाम्नातं यतेरपि ।
गुरुवृत्तिर्विकल्पेन गृहस्थस्यर्तुगामिनः ॥११॥

etat sarvaṁ gṛhasthasya
samāmnātaṁ yater api
guru-vṛttir vikalpena
gṛhasthasyartu-gāminaḥ

etat—this; *sarvam*—all; *gṛhasthasya*—of a householder; *samāmnātam*—described; *yateḥ api*—even of the person in the renounced order; *guru-vṛttiḥ vikalpena*—to follow the orders of the spiritual master; *gṛhasthasya*—of the householder; *ṛtu-gāminaḥ*—accepting sex only during the period favorable for procreation.

TRANSLATION

All the rules and regulations apply equally to the householder and the sannyāsī, the member of the renounced order of life. The

gṛhastha, however, is given permission by the spiritual master to indulge in sex during the period favorable for procreation.

PURPORT

It is sometimes misunderstood that a *gṛhastha*, a householder, is permitted to indulge in sex at any time. This is a wrong conception of *gṛhastha* life. In spiritual life, whether one is a *gṛhastha*, *vānaprastha*, *sannyāsī* or *brahmacārī*, everyone is under the control of the spiritual master. For *brahmacārīs* and *sannyāsīs* there are strong restrictions on sexual indulgence. Similarly, there are strong restrictions for *gṛhasthas*. *Gṛhasthas* should indulge in sex life only in accordance with the order of the *guru*. Therefore it is mentioned here that one must follow the orders of the spiritual master (*guru-vṛttir vikalpena*). When the spiritual master orders, the *gṛhastha* may accept sex life. This is confirmed in *Bhagavad-gītā* (7.11). *Dharmāviruddho bhūteṣu kāmo 'smi:* indulgence in sex life without disobedience to the religious rules and regulations constitutes a religious principle. The *gṛhastha* is allowed to indulge in sex life during the period favorable for procreation and in accordance with the spiritual master's order. If the spiritual master's orders allow a *gṛhastha* to engage in sex life at a particular time, then the *gṛhastha* may do so; otherwise, if the spiritual master orders against it, the *gṛhastha* should abstain. The *gṛhastha* must obtain permission from the spiritual master to observe the ritualistic ceremony of *garbhādhāna-saṁskāra*. Then he may approach his wife to beget children, otherwise not. A *brāhmaṇa* generally remains a *brahmacārī* throughout his entire life, but although some *brāhmaṇas* become *gṛhasthas* and indulge in sex life, they do so under the complete control of the spiritual master. The *kṣatriya* is allowed to marry more than one wife, but this also must be in accordance with the instructions of the spiritual master. It is not that because one is a *gṛhastha* he may marry as many times as he likes and indulge in sex life as he likes. This is not spiritual life. In spiritual life, one must conduct one's whole life under the guidance of the *guru*. Only one who executes his spiritual life under the direction of the spiritual master can achieve the mercy of Kṛṣṇa. *Yasya prasādād bhagavat-prasādaḥ.* If one desires to advance in spiritual life but he acts whimsically, not following the orders of the spiritual master, he has no shelter. *Yasyāprasādān na gatiḥ kuto 'pi.*

Without the spiritual master's order, even the *gṛhastha* should not indulge in sex life.

TEXT 12

अञ्जनाभ्यञ्जनोन्मर्दस्त्र्यवलेखामिषं मधु ।
स्रग्गन्धलेपालंकारांस्त्यजेयुर्ये बृहद्व्रताः ॥१२॥

añjanābhyañjanonmarda-
stry-avalekhāmiṣaṁ madhu
srag-gandha-lepālankārāṁs
tyajeyur ye bṛhad-vratāḥ

añjana—ointment or powder for decorating the eyes; *abhyañjana*—massaging the head; *unmarda*—massaging the body; *strī-avalekha*—to glance over a woman or to paint a woman's picture; *āmiṣam*—meat-eating; *madhu*—drinking liquor or honey; *srak*—decorating the body with garlands of flowers; *gandha-lepa*—smearing the body with scented ointment; *alaṅkārān*—decorating the body with ornaments; *tyajeyuḥ*—must give up; *ye*—those who; *bṛhat-vratāḥ*—have taken the vow of celibacy.

TRANSLATION

Brahmacārīs or gṛhasthas who have taken the vow of celibacy as described above should not indulge in the following: applying powder or ointment to the eyes, massaging the head with oil, massaging the body with the hands, seeing a woman or painting a woman's picture, eating meat, drinking wine, decorating the body with flower garlands, smearing scented ointment on the body, or decorating the body with ornaments. These they should give up.

TEXTS 13–14

उषित्वैवं गुरुकुले द्विजोऽधीत्यावबुध्य च ।
त्रयीं साङ्गोपनिषदं यावदर्थं यथाबलम् ॥१३॥
दत्त्वा वरमनुज्ञातो गुरोः कामं यदीश्वरः ।
गृहं वनं वा प्रविशेत् प्रव्रजेत् तत्र वा वसेत् ॥१४॥

uṣitvaivaṁ guru-kule
dvijo 'dhītyāvabudhya ca
trayīṁ sāṅgopaniṣadaṁ
yāvad-arthaṁ yathā-balam

dattvā varam anujñāto
guroḥ kāmaṁ yadīśvaraḥ
gṛhaṁ vanaṁ vā praviśet
pravrajet tatra vā vaset

uṣitvā—residing; *evam*—in this way; *guru-kule*—under the care of the spiritual master; *dvi-jaḥ*—the twiceborn, namely the *brāhmaṇas, kṣatriyas* and *vaiśyas; adhītya*—studying Vedic literature; *avabudhya*—understanding it properly; *ca*—and; *trayīm*—the Vedic literatures; *sa-aṅga*—along with supplementary parts; *upaniṣadam*—as well as the *Upaniṣads; yāvat-artham*—as far as possible; *yathā-balam*—as far as one can, according to one's ability; *dattvā*—giving; *varam*—remuneration; *anujñātaḥ*—being asked; *guroḥ*—of the spiritual master; *kāmam*—desires; *yadi*—if; *īśvaraḥ*—capable; *gṛham*—household life; *vanam*—retired life; *vā*—either; *praviśet*—one should enter; *pravrajet*—or get out of; *tatra*—there; *vā*—either; *vaset*—should reside.

TRANSLATION

According to the rules and regulations mentioned above, one who is twiceborn, namely a brāhmaṇa, kṣatriya or vaiśya, should reside in the guru-kula under the care of the spiritual master. There he should study and learn all the Vedic literatures along with their supplements and the Upaniṣads, according to his ability and power to study. If possible, the student or disciple should reward the spiritual master with the remuneration the spiritual master requests, and then, following the master's order, the disciple should leave and accept one of the other āśramas, namely the gṛhastha-āśrama, vānaprastha-āśrama or sannyāsa-āśrama, as he desires.

PURPORT

To study the *Vedas* and understand them, of course, requires some special intelligence, but the members of the three higher sections of society—namely the *brāhmaṇas, kṣatriyas* and *vaiśyas*—must learn the Vedic literatures according to their capability and power to understand. In other words, studying the Vedic literatures is compulsory for everyone but the *śūdras* and *antyajas.* The Vedic literature gives the knowledge that can lead one to understand the Absolute Truth—Brahman, Paramātmā or Bhagavān. *Guru-kula,* or the reformatory educational institution, should be used only to understand Vedic knowledge. At the present time there are many educational institutions for training and technology, but such knowledge has nothing to do with understanding of the Absolute Truth. Technology, therefore, is meant for the *śūdras,* whereas the *Vedas* are meant for the *dvijas.* Consequently this verse states, *dvijo 'dhītyāvabudhya ca trayīṁ sāṅgopaniṣadam.* At the present time, in the age of Kali, practically everyone is a *śūdra,* and no one is a *dvija.* Therefore the condition of society has very much deteriorated.

Another point to be observed from this verse is that from the *brahmacārī-āśrama* one may accept the *sannyāsa-āśrama, vānaprastha-āśrama* or *gṛhastha-āśrama.* It is not compulsory for a *brahmacārī* to become a *gṛhastha.* Because the ultimate aim is to understand the Absolute Truth, there is no necessity of going through all the different *āśramas.* Thus one may proceed to the *sannyāsa-āśrama* directly from the *brahmacārī-āśrama.* Śrīla Bhaktisiddhānta Sarasvatī Ṭhākura accepted the *sannyāsa-āśrama* directly from the *brahmacārī-āśrama.* In other words, His Divine Grace Bhaktisiddhānta Sarasvatī Ṭhākura did not think it compulsory to accept the *gṛhastha-āśrama* or *vānaprastha-āśrama.*

TEXT 15

अग्नौ गुरावात्मनि च सर्वभूतेष्वधोक्षजम् ।
भूतैः स्वधामभिः पश्येदप्रविष्टं प्रविष्टवत् ॥१५॥

agnau gurāv ātmani ca
sarva-bhūteṣv adhokṣajam
bhūtaiḥ sva-dhāmabhiḥ paśyed
apraviṣṭaṁ praviṣṭavat

agnau—in the fire; *gurau*—in the spiritual master; *ātmani*—in one's self; *ca*—also; *sarva-bhūteṣu*—in every living entity; *adhokṣajam*—the

Supreme Personality of Godhead, who cannot be seen or perceived with the material eyes or other material senses; *bhūtaiḥ*—with all living entities; *sva-dhāmabhiḥ*—along with His Lordship's paraphernalia; *paśyet*—one should see; *apraviṣṭam*—not entered; *praviṣṭa-vat*—also entered.

TRANSLATION

One should realize that in the fire, in the spiritual master, in one's self and in all living entities—in all circumstances and conditions—the Supreme Personality of Godhead, Viṣṇu, has simultaneously entered and not entered. He is situated externally and internally as the full controller of everything.

PURPORT

Realization of the Supreme Personality of Godhead's omnipresence is the perfect realization of the Absolute Truth to be attained through the study of the Vedic literatures. As stated in the *Brahma-saṁhitā* (5.35), *aṇḍāntara-stha-paramāṇu-cayāntara-stham:* the Lord is situated within the universe, within the heart of every living entity and also within the atom. We should understand that whenever the Supreme Personality of Godhead is present, He is present with all His paraphernalia, including His name, form, associates and servants. The living entity is part and parcel of the Supreme Personality of Godhead, and thus one should understand that since the Supreme Lord has entered the atom, the living entities are also there. One must accept the inconceivable quality of the Supreme Personality of Godhead, for no one can understand from the material point of view how the Lord is all-pervasive and yet is situated in His own abode, Goloka Vṛndāvana. This realization is possible if one strictly follows the regulative principles of *āśrama* (*brahmacārī, gṛhastha, vānaprastha* and *sannyāsa*). Śrīla Madhvācārya says in this regard:

apraviṣṭaḥ sarva-gataḥ
praviṣṭas tv anurūpavān
evaṁ dvi-rūpo bhagavān
harir eko janārdanaḥ

The Supreme Personality of Godhead, in His original form, has not entered everything (*apraviṣṭaḥ*), but in His impersonal form He has entered (*praviṣṭaḥ*). Thus He has entered and not entered simultaneously. This is also explained in *Bhagavad-gītā* (9.4), wherein the Lord says:

mayā tatam idaṁ sarvaṁ
jagad avyakta-mūrtinā
mat-sthāni sarva-bhūtāni
na cāhaṁ teṣv avasthitaḥ

"By Me, in My unmanifested form, this entire universe is pervaded. All beings are in Me, but I am not in them." The Lord can defy Himself. Thus there is variety in unity (*ekatvaṁ bahutvam*).

TEXT 16

एवंविधो ब्रह्मचारी वानप्रस्थो यतिर्गृही ।
चरन्विदितविज्ञानः परं ब्रह्माधिगच्छति ॥१६॥

evaṁ vidho brahmacārī
vānaprastho yatir gṛhī
caran vidita-vijñānaḥ
paraṁ brahmādhigacchati

evam vidhaḥ—in this way; *brahmacārī*—whether one is a *brahmacārī*; *vānaprasthaḥ*—or one is in the *vānaprastha-āśrama*; *yatiḥ*—or in the *sannyāsa-āśrama*; *gṛhī*—or in the *gṛhastha-āśrama*; *caran*—by practice of self-realization and understanding of the Absolute Truth; *vidita-vijñānaḥ*—fully conversant with the science of the Absolute Truth; *param*—the Supreme; *brahma*—the Absolute Truth; *adhigacchati*—one can understand.

TRANSLATION

By practicing in this way, whether one be in the brahmacārī-āśrama, gṛhastha-āśrama, vānaprastha-āśrama or sannyāsa-āśrama, one must always realize the all-pervading presence of the Supreme

Lord, for in this way it is possible to understand the Absolute Truth.

PURPORT

This is the beginning of self-realization. One must first understand how Brahman is present everywhere and how He is acting. This education is called *brahma-jijñāsā* and is the real concern of human life. Without such knowledge, one cannot claim to be a human being; rather, he remains in the animal kingdom. As it is said, *sa eva go-kharaḥ:* without such knowledge, one is no better than a cow or an ass.

TEXT 17

वानप्रस्थस्य वक्ष्यामि नियमान्मुनिसम्मतान् ।
यानास्थाय मुनिर्गच्छेदृषिलोकमुहाञ्जसा ॥१७॥

vānaprasthasya vakṣyāmi
niyamān muni-sammatān
yān āsthāya munir gacched
ṛṣi-lokam uhāñjasā

vānaprasthasya—of a person in the *vānaprastha-āśrama* (retired life); *vakṣyāmi*—I shall now explain; *niyamān*—the rules and regulations; *muni-sammatān*—which are recognized by great *munis*, philosophers and saintly persons; *yān*—which; *āsthāya*—being situated in, or practicing; *muniḥ*—a saintly person; *gacchet*—is promoted; *ṛṣi-lokam*—to the planetary system where the seers and *munis* go (Maharloka); *uha*—O King; *añjasā*—without difficulty.

TRANSLATION

O King, I shall now describe the qualifications for a vānaprastha, one who has retired from family life. By rigidly following the rules and regulations for the vānaprastha, one can easily be elevated to the upper planetary system known as Maharloka.

TEXT 18

न कृष्टपच्यमश्नीयादकृष्टं चाप्यकालतः ।
अग्निपक्कमथामं वा अर्कपक्कमुताहरेत् ॥१८॥

na kṛṣṭa-pacyam aśnīyād
akṛṣṭaṁ cāpy akālataḥ
agni-pakvam athāmaṁ vā
arka-pakvam utāharet

na—not; *kṛṣṭa-pacyam*—grains grown by tilling of the field; *aśnīyāt*—one should eat; *akṛṣṭam*—grains that have grown without tilling of the field; *ca*—and; *api*—also; *akālataḥ*—ripened untimely; *agni-pakvam*—grains prepared by being cooked in fire; *atha*—as well as; *āmam*—mango; *vā*—either; *arka-pakvam*—food ripened naturally by the sunshine; *uta*—it is so enjoined; *āharet*—the *vānaprastha* should eat.

TRANSLATION

A person in vānaprastha life should not eat grains grown by tilling of the fields. He should also not eat grains that have grown without tilling of the field but are not fully ripe. Nor should a vānaprastha eat grains cooked in fire. Indeed, he should eat only fruit ripened by the sunshine.

TEXT 19

वन्यैश्चरुपुरोडाशान् निर्वपेत् कालचोदितान् ।
लब्धे नवे नवेऽन्नाद्ये पुराणं च परित्यजेत् ॥१९॥

vanyaiś caru-puroḍāśān
nirvapet kāla-coditān
labdhe nave nave 'nnādye
purāṇaṁ ca parityajet

vanyaiḥ—by fruits and grains produced in the forest without cultivation; *caru*—grains to be offered in a fire sacrifice; *puroḍāśān*—the cakes prepared from *caru; nirvapet*—one should execute; *kāla-coditān*—that which has grown naturally; *labdhe*—on obtaining; *nave*—new; *nave anna-ādye*—newly produced food grains; *purāṇam*—the stock of old grains; *ca*—and; *parityajet*—one should give up.

TRANSLATION

A vānaprastha should prepare cakes to be offered in sacrifice from fruits and grains grown naturally in the forest. When he obtains some new grains, he should give up his old stock of grains.

TEXT 20

अग्न्यर्थमेव शरणमुटजं वाद्रिकन्दरम् ।
श्रयेत हिमवाय्वग्निवर्षार्कातपषाट् स्वयम् ॥२०॥

agny-artham eva śaraṇam
uṭajaṁ vādri-kandaram
śrayeta hima-vāyv-agni-
varṣārkātapa-ṣāṭ svayam

agni—the fire; *artham*—to keep; *eva*—only; *śaraṇam*—a cottage; *uṭa-jam*—made of grass; *vā*—or; *adri-kandaram*—a cave in a mountain; *śrayeta*—the *vānaprastha* should take shelter of; *hima*—snow; *vāyu*—wind; *agni*—fire; *varṣa*—rain; *arka*—of the sun; *ātapa*—shining; *ṣāṭ*—enduring; *svayam*—personally.

TRANSLATION

A vānaprastha should prepare a thatched cottage or take shelter of a cave in a mountain only to keep the sacred fire, but he should personally practice enduring snowfall, wind, fire, rain and the shining of the sun.

TEXT 21

केशरोमनखश्मश्रुमलानि जटिलो दधत् ।
कमण्डल्वजिने दण्डवल्कलाग्निपरिच्छदान् ॥२१॥

keśa-roma-nakha-śmaśru-
malāni jaṭilo dadhat
kamaṇḍalv-ajine daṇḍa-
valkalāgni-paricchadān

keśa—hair on the head; *roma*—hair on the body; *nakha*—nails; *śmaśru*—moustache; *malāni*—and dirt on the body; *jaṭilaḥ*—with matted locks of hair; *dadhat*—one should keep; *kamaṇḍalu*—a waterpot; *ajine*—and a deerskin; *daṇḍa*—rod; *valkala*—the bark of a tree; *agni*—fire; *paricchadān*—garments.

TRANSLATION

The vānaprastha should wear matted locks of hair on his head and let his body hair, nails and moustache grow. He should not cleanse his body of dirt. He should keep a waterpot, deerskin and rod, wear the bark of a tree as a covering, and use garments colored like fire.

TEXT 22

चरेद् वने द्वादशाब्दानष्टौ वा चतुरो मुनिः ।
द्वावेकं वा यथा बुद्धिर्न विपद्येत कृच्छ्रतः ॥२२॥

cared vane dvādaśābdān
aṣṭau vā caturo muniḥ
dvāv ekaṁ vā yathā buddhir
na vipadyeta kṛcchrataḥ

caret—should remain; *vane*—in the forest; *dvādaśa-abdān*—twelve years; *aṣṭau*—for eight years; *vā*—either; *caturaḥ*—four years; *muniḥ*—a saintly, thoughtful man; *dvau*—two; *ekam*—one; *vā*—either; *yathā*—as well as; *buddhiḥ*—intelligence; *na*—not; *vipadyeta*—bewildered; *kṛcchrataḥ*—because of hard austerities.

TRANSLATION

Being very thoughtful, a vānaprastha should remain in the forest for twelve years, eight years, four years, two years or at least one year. He should behave in such a way that he will not be disturbed or troubled by too much austerity.

TEXT 23

यदाकल्पः स्वक्रियायां व्याधिभिर्जरयाथवा ।
आन्वीक्षिक्यां वा विद्यायां कुर्यादनशनादिकम् ॥२३॥

yadākalpaḥ sva-kriyāyāṁ
vyādhibhir jarayāthavā
ānvīkṣikyāṁ vā vidyāyāṁ
kuryād anaśanādikam

yadā—when; *akalpaḥ*—unable to act; *sva-kriyāyām*—in one's own prescribed duties; *vyādhibhiḥ*—because of disease; *jarayā*—or because of old age; *athavā*—either; *ānvīkṣikyām*—in spiritual advancement; *vā*—or; *vidyāyām*—in the advancement of knowledge; *kuryāt*—one must do; *anaśana-ādikam*—not take sufficient food.

TRANSLATION

When because of disease or old age one is unable to perform his prescribed duties for advancement in spiritual consciousness or study of the Vedas, he should practice fasting, not taking any food.

TEXT 24

आत्मन्यग्नीन् समारोप्य संन्यस्याहंममात्मताम् ।
कारणेषु न्यसेत् सम्यक् संघातं तु यथार्हतः ॥२४॥

ātmany agnīn samāropya
sannyasyāhaṁ mamātmatām
kāraṇeṣu nyaset samyak
saṅghātaṁ tu yathārhataḥ

ātmani—in one's self; *agnīn*—the fire elements within the body; *samāropya*—properly placing; *sannyasya*—giving up; *aham*—false identity; *mama*—false conception; *ātmatām*—of the body's being one's self or one's own; *kāraṇeṣu*—in the five elements that cause the material body; *nyaset*—one should merge; *samyak*—completely; *saṅghātam*—combination; *tu*—but; *yathā-arhataḥ*—as it befits.

TRANSLATION

He should properly place the fire element in his own self and in this way give up bodily affinity, by which one thinks the body to be

one's self or one's own. One should gradually merge the material body into the five elements [earth, water, fire, air and sky].

PURPORT

The body is an effect of a cause, namely the five material elements (earth, water, fire, air and sky). In other words, one should know perfectly well that the material body is nothing but a combination of the five elements. This knowledge constitutes merging of the material body and the five material elements. Merging into Brahman in perfect knowledge means understanding perfectly that one is not the body but a spiritual soul.

TEXT 25

खे खानि वायौ निश्वासांस्तेजःसूष्माणमात्मवान् ।
अप्स्वसृक्श्लेष्मपूयानि क्षितौ शेषं यथोद्भवम् ॥२५॥

khe khāni vāyau niśvāsāṁs
tejaḥsūṣmāṇam ātmavān
apsv asṛk-śleṣma-pūyāni
kṣitau śeṣaṁ yathodbhavam

khe—in the sky; *khāni*—all the holes of the body; *vāyau*—in the air; *niśvāsān*—all the different airs moving within the body (*prāṇa, apāna,* etc.); *tejaḥsu*—in fire; *uṣmāṇam*—the heat of the body; *ātma-vān*—a person who knows the self; *apsu*—in water; *asṛk*—blood; *śleṣma*—mucus; *pūyāni*—and urine; *kṣitau*—in the earth; *śeṣam*—the remaining (namely skin, bones and the other hard things in the body); *yathā-udbhavam*—wherefrom all of them grew.

TRANSLATION

A sober, self-realized person who has full knowledge should merge the various parts of the body in their original sources. The holes in the body are caused by the sky, the process of breathing is caused by the air, the heat of the body is caused by fire, and semen, blood and mucus are caused by water. The hard substances, like skin, muscle and bone, are caused by earth. In this way all the

constituents of the body are caused by various elements, and they should be merged again into those elements.

PURPORT

To be self-realized, one must understand the original sources of the various elements of the body. The body is a combination of skin, bone, muscle, blood, semen, urine, stool, heat, breath and so on, which all come from earth, water, fire, air and sky. One must be well conversant with the sources of all the bodily constituents. Then one becomes a self-realized person, or *ātmavān*, one who knows the self.

TEXTS 26–28

वाचमग्नौ सवक्तव्यामिन्द्रे शिल्पं करावपि ।
पदानि गत्या वयसि रत्योपस्थं प्रजापतौ ॥२६॥
मृत्यौ पायुं विसर्गं च यथास्थानं विनिर्दिशेत् ।
दिक्षु श्रोत्रं सनादेन स्पर्शेनाध्यात्मनि त्वचम् ॥२७॥
रूपाणि चक्षुषा राजन् ज्योतिष्यभिनिवेशयेत् ।
अप्सु प्रचेतसा जिह्वां घ्रेयैर्घ्राणं क्षितौ न्यसेत् ॥२८॥

vācam agnau savaktavyām
indre śilpaṁ karāv api
padāni gatyā vayasi
ratyopasthaṁ prajāpatau

mṛtyau pāyuṁ visargaṁ ca
yathā-sthānaṁ vinirdiśet
dikṣu śrotraṁ sa-nādena
sparśenādhyātmani tvacam

rūpāṇi cakṣuṣā rājan
jyotiṣy abhiniveśayet
apsu pracetasā jihvām
ghreyair ghrāṇaṁ kṣitau nyaset

vācam—speech; *agnau*—in the fire-god (the personified god controlling fire); *sa-vaktavyām*—with the subject matter of speaking; *indre*—

unto King Indra; *śilpam*—craftsmanship or the capacity to work with the hands; *karau*—as well as the hands; *api*—indeed; *padāni*—the legs; *gatyā*—with the power to move; *vayasi*—unto Lord Viṣṇu; *ratyā*—sexual desire; *upastham*—with the genitals; *prajāpatau*—unto Prajāpati; *mṛtyau*—unto the demigod known as Mṛtyu; *pāyum*—the rectum; *visargam*—with its activity, evacuation; *ca*—also; *yathā-sthānam*—in the proper place; *vinirdiśet*—one should indicate; *dikṣu*—unto different directions; *śrotram*—the aural sense; *sa-nādena*—with sound vibration; *sparśena*—with touch; *adhyātmani*—unto the wind-god; *tvacam*—the sense of touch; *rūpāṇi*—form; *cakṣuṣā*—with eyesight; *rājan*—O King; *jyotiṣi*—in the sun; *abhiniveśayet*—one should endow; *apsu*—unto water; *pracetasā*—with the demigod known as Varuṇa; *jihvām*—the tongue; *ghreyaiḥ*—with the object of smell; *ghrāṇam*—the power to smell; *kṣitau*—in the earth; *nyaset*—one should give.

TRANSLATION

Thereafter, the object of speech, along with the sense of speech [the tongue], should be bestowed upon fire. Craftsmanship and the two hands should be given to the demigod Indra. The power of movement and the legs should be given to Lord Viṣṇu. Sensual pleasure, along with the genitals, should be bestowed upon Prajāpati. The rectum, with the power of evacuation, should be bestowed, in its proper place, unto Mṛtyu. The aural instrument, along with sound vibration, should be given to the deities presiding over the directions. The instrument of touch, along with the sense objects of touch, should be given to Vāyu. Form, with the power of sight, should be bestowed upon the sun. The tongue, along with the demigod Varuṇa, should be bestowed upon water, and the power of smell, along with the two Aśvinī-kumāra demigods, should be bestowed upon the earth.

TEXTS 29–30

मनो मनोरथैश्चन्द्रे बुद्धिं बोध्यैः कवौ परे ।
कर्माण्यध्यात्मना रुद्रे यदहंममताक्रिया ।
सत्त्वेन चित्तं क्षेत्रज्ञे गुणैर्वैकारिकं परे ॥२९॥

अप्सु क्षितिमपो ज्योतिष्यदो वायौ नभस्यमुम् ।
कूटस्थे तच्च महति तदव्यक्तेऽक्षरे च तत् ॥३०॥

mano manorathaiś candre
buddhiṁ bodhyaiḥ kavau pare
karmāṇy adhyātmanā rudre
yad-ahaṁ mamatā-kriyā
sattvena cittaṁ kṣetra-jñe
guṇair vaikārikaṁ pare

apsu kṣitim apo jyotiṣy
ado vāyau nabhasy amum
kūṭasthe tac ca mahati
tad avyakte 'kṣare ca tat

manaḥ—the mind; *manorathaiḥ*—along with material desires; *candre*—unto Candra, the mood demigod; *buddhim*—intelligence; *bodhyaiḥ*—with the subject matter of intelligence; *kavau pare*—unto the supreme learned person, Lord Brahmā; *karmāṇi*—material activities; *adhyātmanā*—with false ego; *rudre*—unto Lord Śiva (Rudra); *yat*—wherein; *aham*—I am the material body; *mamatā*—everything belonging to the material body is mine; *kriyā*—such activities; *sattvena*—along with the existential conception; *cittam*—consciousness; *kṣetra-jñe*—unto the individual soul; *guṇaiḥ*—along with the material activities conducted by the material qualities; *vaikārikam*—the living entities under the influence of the material modes; *pare*—in the Supreme Being; *apsu*—in the water; *kṣitim*—the earth; *apaḥ*—the water; *jyotiṣi*—in the luminaries, specifically in the sun; *adaḥ*—brightness; *vāyau*—in the air; *nabhasi*—in the sky; *amum*—that; *kūṭasthe*—in the materialistic conception of life; *tat*—that; *ca*—also; *mahati*—in the *mahat-tattva*, the total material energy; *tat*—that; *avyakte*—in the nonmanifested; *akṣare*—in the Supersoul; *ca*—also; *tat*—that.

TRANSLATION

The mind, along with all material desires, should be merged in the moon demigod. All the subject matters of intelligence, along with the intelligence itself, should be placed in Lord Brahmā. False

ego, which is under the influence of the material modes of nature and which induces one to think, "I am this body, and everything connected with this body is mine," should be merged, along with material activities, in Rudra, the predominating deity of false ego. Material consciousness, along with the goal of thought, should be merged in the individual living being, and the demigods acting under the modes of material nature should be merged, along with the perverted living being, into the Supreme Being. The earth should be merged in water, water in the brightness of the sun, this brightness into the air, the air into the sky, the sky into the false ego, the false ego into the total material energy, the total material energy into the unmanifested ingredients [the pradhāna feature of the material energy], and at last the ingredient feature of material manifestation into the Supersoul.

TEXT 31

इत्यक्षरतयात्मानं चिन्मात्रमवशेषितम् ।
ज्ञात्वाद्वयोऽथ विरमेद् दग्धयोनिरिवानलः ॥३१॥

ity akṣaratayātmānaṁ
cin-mātram avaśeṣitam
jñātvādvayo 'tha viramed
dagdha-yonir ivānalaḥ

iti—thus; *akṣaratayā*—because of being spiritual; *ātmānam*—oneself (the individual soul); *cit-mātram*—completely spiritual; *avaśeṣitam*—the remaining balance (after the material elements are merged, one after another, into the original Supersoul); *jñātvā*—understanding; *advayaḥ*—without differentiation, or of the same quality as the Paramātmā; *atha*—thus; *viramet*—one should cease from material existence; *dagdha-yoniḥ*—whose source (the wood) has burnt up; *iva*—like; *analaḥ*—flames.

TRANSLATION

When all the material designations have thus merged into their respective material elements, the living beings, who are all ultimately completely spiritual, being one in quality with the

Supreme Being, should cease from material existence, as flames cease when the wood in which they are burning is consumed. When the material body is returned to its various material elements, only the spiritual being remains. This spiritual being is Brahman and is equal in quality with Parabrahman.

Thus end the Bhaktivedanta purports of the Seventh Canto, Twelfth Chapter, of the Śrīmad-Bhāgavatam, *entitled "The Perfect Society: Four Spiritual Classes."*

CHAPTER THIRTEEN

The Behavior of a Perfect Person

This Thirteenth Chapter describes the regulative principles for *sannyāsīs* and also describes the history of an *avadhūta.* It concludes with a description of perfection for the student in spiritual advancement.

Śrī Nārada Muni has been describing the symptoms of various *āśramas* and *varṇas.* Now, in this chapter, he specifically describes the regulative principles to be followed by *sannyāsīs.* After retiring from family life, one should accept the status of *vānaprastha,* in which he must formally accept the body as his means of existence but gradually forget the bodily necessities of life. After *vānaprastha* life, having left home, one should travel to different places as a *sannyāsī.* Without bodily comforts and free from dependence on anyone with respect to bodily necessities, one should travel everywhere, wearing almost nothing or actually walking naked. Without association with ordinary human society, one should beg alms and always be satisfied in himself. One should be a friend to every living entity and be very peaceful in Kṛṣṇa consciousness. A *sannyāsī* should travel alone in this way, not caring for life or death, waiting for the time when he will leave his material body. He should not indulge in unnecessary books or adopt professions like astrology, nor should he try to become a great orator. He should also give up the path of unnecessary argument and should not depend on anyone under any circumstances. He should not try to allure people into becoming his disciples just so that the number of his disciples may increase. He should give up the habit of reading many books as a means of livelihood, and he should not attempt to increase the number of temples and *maṭhas,* or monasteries. When a *sannyāsī* thus becomes completely independent, peaceful and equipoised, he can select the destination he desires after death and follow the principles by which to reach that destination. Although fully learned, he should always remain silent, like a dumb person, and travel like a restless child.

In this regard, Nārada Muni described a meeting between Prahlāda and a saintly person who had adopted the mode of life of a python. In this way he described the symptoms of a *paramahaṁsa.* A person who has attained the *paramahaṁsa* stage knows very well the distinction between matter and spirit. He is not at all interested in gratifying the material senses, for he is always deriving pleasure from devotional service to the Lord. He is not very anxious to protect his material body. Being satisfied with whatever he attains by the grace of the Lord, he is completely independent of material happiness and distress, and thus he is transcendental to all regulative principles. Sometimes he accepts severe austerities, and sometimes he accepts material opulence. His only concern is to satisfy Kṛṣṇa, and for that purpose he can do anything and everything, without reference to the regulative principles. He is never to be equated with materialistic men, nor is he subject to the judgments of such men.

TEXT 1

श्रीनारद उवाच
कल्पस्त्वेवं परिव्रज्य देहमात्रावशेषितः ।
ग्रामैकरात्रविधिना निरपेक्षश्चरेन्महीम् ॥ १ ॥

śrī-nārada uvāca
kalpas tv evaṁ parivrajya
deha-mātrāvaśeṣitaḥ
grāmaika-rātra-vidhinā
nirapekṣaś caren mahīm

śrī-nāradaḥ uvāca—Śrī Nārada Muni said; *kalpaḥ*—a person who is competent to undergo the austerities of *sannyāsa,* the renounced order of life, or to prosecute studies in transcendental knowledge; *tu*—but; *evam*—in this way (as described previously); *parivrajya*—fully understanding his spiritual identity and thus traveling from one place to another; *deha-mātra*—keeping only the body; *avaśeṣitaḥ*—at last; *grāma*—in a village; *eka*—one only; *rātra*—of passing a night; *vidhinā*—in the process; *nirapekṣaḥ*—without dependence on any material thing; *caret*—should move from one place to another; *mahīm*—on the earth.

TRANSLATION

Śrī Nārada Muni said: A person able to cultivate spiritual knowledge should renounce all material connections, and merely keeping the body inhabitable, he should travel from one place to another, passing only one night in each village. In this way, without dependence in regard to the needs of the body, the sannyāsī should travel all over the world.

TEXT 2

बिभृयाद् यद्यसौ वासः कौपीनाच्छादनं परम् ।
त्यक्तं न लिङ्गाद् दण्डादेरन्यत् किञ्चिदनापदि ॥ २ ॥

bibhṛyād yady asau vāsaḥ
kaupīnācchādanaṁ param
tyaktaṁ na liṅgād daṇḍāder
anyat kiñcid anāpadi

bibhṛyāt—one should use; *yadi*—if; *asau*—a person in the renounced order; *vāsaḥ*—a garment or covering; *kaupīna*—a loincloth (just to cover the private parts); *ācchādanam*—for covering; *param*—that much only; *tyaktam*—given up; *na*—not; *liṅgāt*—than the distinguishing marks of a *sannyāsī; daṇḍa-ādeḥ*—like the rod (*tridaṇḍa*); *anyat*—other; *kiñcit*—anything; *anāpadi*—in ordinary undisturbed times.

TRANSLATION

A person in the renounced order of life may try to avoid even a dress to cover himself. If he wears anything at all, it should be only a loincloth, and when there is no necessity, a sannyāsī should not even accept a daṇḍa. A sannyāsī should avoid carrying anything but a daṇḍa and kamaṇḍalu.

TEXT 3

एक एव चरेद् भिक्षुरात्मारामोऽनपाश्रयः ।
सर्वभूतसुहृच्छान्तो नारायणपरायणः ॥ ३ ॥

eka eva cared bhikṣur
ātmārāmo 'napāśrayaḥ
sarva-bhūta-suhṛc-chānto
nārāyaṇa-parāyaṇaḥ

ekaḥ—alone; *eva*—only; *caret*—can move; *bhikṣuḥ*—a *sannyāsī* taking alms; *ātma-ārāmaḥ*—fully satisfied in the self; *anapāśrayaḥ*—without depending on anything; *sarva-bhūta-suhṛt*—becoming a well-wisher of all living entities; *śāntaḥ*—completely peaceful; *nārāyaṇa-parāyaṇaḥ*—becoming absolutely dependent on Nārāyaṇa and becoming His devotee.

TRANSLATION

The sannyāsī, completely satisfied in the self, should live on alms begged from door to door. Not being dependent on any person or any place, he should always be a friendly well-wisher to all living beings and be a peaceful, unalloyed devotee of Nārāyaṇa. In this way he should move from one place to another.

TEXT 4

पश्येदात्मन्यदो विश्वं परे सदसतोऽव्यये ।
आत्मानं च परं ब्रह्म सर्वत्र सदसन्मये ॥ ४ ॥

paśyed ātmany ado viśvaṁ
pare sad-asato 'vyaye
ātmānaṁ ca paraṁ brahma
sarvatra sad-asan-maye

paśyet—one should see; *ātmani*—in the Supreme Soul; *adaḥ*—this; *viśvam*—universe; *pare*—beyond; *sat-asataḥ*—the creation or cause of creation; *avyaye*—in the Absolute, which is free from deterioration; *ātmānam*—himself; *ca*—also; *param*—the supreme; *brahma*—absolute; *sarvatra*—everywhere; *sat-asat*—in the cause and in the effect; *maye*—all-pervading.

TRANSLATION

The sannyāsī should always try to see the Supreme pervading everything and see everything, including this universe, resting on the Supreme.

TEXT 5

सुप्तिप्रबोधयोः सन्धावात्मनो गतिमात्मदृक् ।
पश्यन्बन्धं च मोक्षं च मायामात्रं न वस्तुतः ॥ ५ ॥

supti-prabodhayoḥ sandhāv
ātmano gatim ātma-dṛk
paśyan bandhaṁ ca mokṣaṁ ca
māyā-mātraṁ na vastutaḥ

supti—in the state of unconsciousness; *prabodhayoḥ*—and in the state of consciousness; *sandhau*—in the state of marginal existence; *ātmanaḥ*—of oneself; *gatim*—the movement; *ātma-dṛk*—one who can actually see the self; *paśyan*—always trying to see or understand; *bandham*—the conditional state of life; *ca*—and; *mokṣam*—the liberated state of life; *ca*—also; *māyā-mātram*—only illusion; *na*—not; *vastutaḥ*—in fact.

TRANSLATION

During unconsciousness and consciousness, and between the two, he should try to understand the self and be fully situated in the self. In this way, he should realize that the conditional and liberated stages of life are only illusory and not actually factual. With such a higher understanding, he should see only the Absolute Truth pervading everything.

PURPORT

The unconscious state is nothing but ignorance, darkness or material existence, and in the conscious state one is awake. The marginal state, between consciousness and unconsciousness, has no permanent existence. Therefore one who is advanced in understanding the self should understand that unconsciousness and consciousness are but illusions, for they fundamentally do not exist. Only the Supreme Absolute Truth exists. As confirmed by the Lord in *Bhagavad-gītā* (9.4):

mayā tatam idaṁ sarvaṁ
jagad avyakta-mūrtinā

mat-sthāni sarva-bhūtāni
na cāhaṁ teṣv avasthitaḥ

"By Me, in My unmanifested form, this entire universe is pervaded. All beings are in Me, but I am not in them." Everything exists on the basis of Kṛṣṇa's impersonal feature; nothing can exist without Kṛṣṇa. Therefore the advanced devotee of Kṛṣṇa can see the Lord everywhere, without illusion.

TEXT 6

नाभिनन्देद् ध्रुवं मृत्युमध्रुवं वास्य जीवितम् ।
कालं परं प्रतीक्षेत भूतानां प्रभवाप्ययम् ॥ ६ ॥

nābhinanded dhruvaṁ mṛtyum
adhruvaṁ vāsya jīvitam
kālaṁ paraṁ pratīkṣeta
bhūtānāṁ prabhavāpyayam

na—not; *abhinandet*—one should praise; *dhruvam*—sure; *mṛtyum*—death; *adhruvam*—not sure; *vā*—either; *asya*—of this body; *jīvitam*—the duration of life; *kālam*—eternal time; *param*—supreme; *pratīkṣeta*—one must observe; *bhūtānām*—of the living entities; *prabhava*—manifestation; *apyayam*—disappearance.

TRANSLATION

Since the material body is sure to be vanquished and the duration of one's life is not fixed, neither death nor life is to be praised. Rather, one should observe the eternal time factor, in which the living entity manifests himself and disappears.

PURPORT

The living entities in the material world, not only at the present but also in the past, have been involved in trying to solve the problem of birth and death. Some stress death and point to the illusory existence of everything material, whereas others stress life, trying to preserve it perpetually and enjoy it to the best of their ability. Both of them are fools and rascals. It is advised that one observe the eternal time factor, which is the cause of the material body's appearance and disappearance, and that one observe the living entity's entanglement in this time factor. Śrīla Bhaktivinoda Ṭhākura therefore sings in his *Gītāvalī:*

anādi karama-phale, padi 'bhavārṇava-jale,
taribāre nā dekhi upāya

One should observe the activities of eternal time, which is the cause of birth and death. Before the creation of the present millennium, the living entities were under the influence of the time factor, and within the time factor the material world comes into existence and is again annihilated. *Bhūtvā bhūtvā pralīyate.* Being under the control of the time factor, the living entities appear and die, life after life. This time factor is the impersonal representation of the Supreme Personality of Godhead, who gives the living entities conditioned by material nature a chance to emerge from this nature by surrendering to Him.

TEXT 7

नासच्छास्त्रेषु सज्जेत नोपजीवेत जीविकाम् ।
वादवादांस्त्यजेत् तर्कान्पक्षं कंच न संश्रयेत् ॥ ७ ॥

nāsac-chāstreṣu sajjeta
nopajīveta jīvikām
vāda-vādāṁs tyajet tarkān
pakṣaṁ kaṁca na saṁśrayet

na—not; *asat-śāstreṣu*—literature like newspapers, novels, dramas and fiction; *sajjeta*—one should be attached or should indulge in reading; *na*—nor; *upajīveta*—one should try to live; *jīvikām*—upon some professional literary career; *vāda-vādān*—unnecessary arguments on different aspects of philosophy; *tyajet*—one should give up; *tarkān*—arguments and counterarguments; *pakṣam*—faction; *kaṁca*—any; *na*—not; *saṁśrayet*—should take shelter of.

TRANSLATION

Literature that is a useless waste of time—in other words, literature without spiritual benefit—should be rejected. One should not become a professional teacher as a means of earning one's livelihood, nor should one indulge in arguments and counterarguments. Nor should one take shelter of any cause or faction.

PURPORT

A person desiring to advance in spiritual understanding should be extremely careful to avoid reading ordinary literature. The world is full of ordinary literature that creates unnecessary agitation in the mind. Such literature, including newspapers, dramas, novels and magazines, is factually not meant for advancement in spiritual knowledge. Indeed, it has been described as a place of enjoyment for crows (*tad vāyasaṁ tīrtham*). Anyone advancing in spiritual knowledge must reject such literature. Furthermore, one should not concern oneself with the conclusions of various logicians or philosophers. Of course, those who preach sometimes need to argue with the contentions of opponents, but as much as possible one should avoid an argumentative attitude. In this connection, Śrīla Madhvācārya says:

aprayojana-pakṣaṁ na saṁśrayet
nāprayojana-pakṣī syān
na vṛthā śiṣya-bandha-kṛt
na codāsīnaḥ śāstrāṇi
na viruddhāni cābhyaset

na vyākhyayopajīveta
na niṣiddhān samācaret
evam-bhūto yatir yāti
tad-eka-śaraṇo harim

"There is no need to take shelter of unnecessary literature or concern oneself with many so-called philosophers and thinkers who are useless for spiritual advancement. Nor should one accept a disciple for the sake of fashion or popularity. One should be callous to these so-called *śāstras*, neither opposing nor favoring them, and one should not earn one's livelihood by taking money for explaining *śāstra.* A *sannyāsī* must always be neutral and seek the means to advance in spiritual life, taking full shelter under the lotus feet of the Lord."

TEXT 8

न शिष्याननुबध्नीत ग्रन्थान्नैवाभ्यसेद् बहून् ।
न व्याख्यामुपयुञ्जीत नारम्भानारभेत् क्वचित् ॥८॥

na śisyān anubadhnīta
granthān naivābhyased bahūn
na vyākhyām upayuñjīta
nārambhān ārabhet kvacit

na—not; *śisyān*—disciples; *anubadhnīta*—one should induce for material benefit; *granthān*—unnecessary literatures; *na*—not; *eva*—certainly; *abhyaset*—should try to understand or cultivate; *bahūn*—many; *na*—nor; *vyākhyām*—discourses; *upayuñjīta*—should make as a means of livelihood; *na*—nor; *ārambhān*—unnecessary opulences; *ārabhet*—should attempt to increase; *kvacit*—at any time.

TRANSLATION

A sannyāsī must not present allurements of material benefits to gather many disciples, nor should he unnecessarily read many books or give discourses as a means of livelihood. He must never attempt to increase material opulences unnecessarily.

PURPORT

So-called *svāmīs* and *yogīs* generally make disciples by alluring them with material benefits. There are many so-called *gurus* who attract disciples by promising to cure their diseases or increase their material opulence by manufacturing gold. These are lucrative allurements for unintelligent men. A *sannyāsī* is prohibited from making disciples through such material allurements. *Sannyāsīs* sometimes indulge in material opulence by unnecessarily constructing many temples and monasteries, but actually such endeavors should be avoided. Temples and monasteries should be constructed for the preaching of spiritual consciousness or Kṛṣṇa consciousness, not to provide free hotels for persons who are useful for neither material nor spiritual purposes. Temples and monasteries should be strictly off limits to worthless clubs of crazy men. In the Kṛṣṇa consciousness movement we welcome everyone who agrees at least to follow the movement's regulative principles—no illicit sex, no intoxication, no meat-eating and no gambling. In the temples and monasteries, gatherings of unnecessary, rejected, lazy fellows should be strictly disallowed. The temples and monasteries should be used exclusively by devotees who are serious about spiritual advancement in Kṛṣṇa consciousness. Śrīla Viśvanātha Cakravartī Ṭhākura explains the word *ārambhān* as meaning *maṭhādi-vyāpārān*, which means "attempts to construct temples and monasteries." The first business of the *sannyāsī* is to preach Kṛṣṇa consciousness, but if, by the grace of Kṛṣṇa, facilities are available, then he may construct temples and monasteries to give shelter to the serious students of Kṛṣṇa consciousness. Otherwise such temples and monasteries are not needed.

TEXT 9

न यतेराश्रमः प्रायो धर्महेतुर्महात्मनः ।
शान्तस्य समचित्तस्य बिभृयादुत वा त्यजेत् ॥ ९ ॥

na yater āśramaḥ prāyo
dharma-hetur mahātmanaḥ
śāntasya sama-cittasya
bibhṛyād uta vā tyajet

na—not; *yateḥ*—of the *sannyāsī; āśramaḥ*—the symbolic dress (with *daṇḍa* and *kamaṇḍalu*); *prāyaḥ*—almost always; *dharma-hetuḥ*—the cause of advancement in spiritual life; *mahā-ātmanaḥ*—who is factually exalted and advanced; *śāntasya*—who is peaceful; *sama-cittasya*—who has attained the stage of being equipoised; *bibhṛyāt*—one may accept (such symbolic signs); *uta*—indeed; *vā*—or; *tyajet*—one may give up.

TRANSLATION

A peaceful, equipoised person who is factually advanced in spiritual consciousness does not need to accept the symbols of a

sannyāsī, such as the tridaṇḍa and kamaṇḍalu. According to necessity, he may sometimes accept those symbols and sometimes reject them.

PURPORT

There are four stages of the renounced order of life—*kuṭīcaka, bahūdaka, parivrājakācārya* and *paramahaṁsa.* Herein, *Śrīmad-Bhāgavatam* considers the *paramahaṁsas* among the *sannyāsīs.* The Māyāvādī impersonalist *sannyāsīs* cannot attain the *paramahaṁsa* stage. This is because of their impersonal conception of the Absolute Truth. *Brahmeti paramātmeti bhagavān iti śabdyate.* The Absolute Truth is perceived in three stages, of which *bhagavān,* or realization of the Supreme Personality of Godhead, is meant for the *paramahaṁsas.* Indeed, *Śrīmad-Bhāgavatam* itself is meant for the *paramahaṁsas* (*paramo nirmatsarāṇāṁ satām*). Unless one is in the *paramahaṁsa* stage, he is not eligible to understand the *Śrīmad-Bhāgavatam.* For *paramahaṁsas,* or *sannyāsīs* in the Vaiṣṇava order, preaching is the first duty. To preach, such *sannyāsīs* may accept the symbols of *sannyāsa,* such as the *daṇḍa* and *kamaṇḍalu,* or sometimes they may not. Generally the Vaiṣṇava *sannyāsīs,* being *paramahaṁsas,* are automatically called *bābājīs,* and they do not carry a *kamaṇḍalu* or *daṇḍa.* Such a *sannyāsī* is free to accept or reject the marks of *sannyāsa.* His only thought is "Where is there an opportunity to spread Kṛṣṇa consciousness?" Sometimes the Kṛṣṇa consciousness movement sends its representative *sannyāsīs* to foreign countries where the *daṇḍa* and *kamaṇḍalu* are not very much appreciated. We send our preachers in ordinary dress to introduce our books and philosophy. Our only concern is to attract people to Kṛṣṇa consciousness. We may do this in the dress of *sannyāsīs* or in the regular dress of gentlemen. Our only concern is to spread interest in Kṛṣṇa consciousness.

TEXT 10

अव्यक्तलिङ्गो व्यक्तार्थो मनीष्युन्मत्तबालवत् ।
कविर्मूकवदात्मानं स दृष्ट्या दर्शयेन्नृणाम् ॥१०॥

avyakta-liṅgo vyaktārtho
manīṣy unmatta-bālavat

kavir mūkavad ātmānaṁ
sa dṛṣṭyā darśayen nṛṇām

avyakta-liṅgaḥ—whose symptoms of *sannyāsa* are unmanifested; *vyakta-arthaḥ*—whose purpose is manifested; *manīṣī*—such a great saintly person; *unmatta*—restless; *bāla-vat*—like a boy; *kaviḥ*—a great poet or orator; *mūka-vat*—like a dumb man; *ātmānam*—himself; *saḥ*—he; *dṛṣṭyā*—by example; *darśayet*—should present; *nṛṇām*—to human society.

TRANSLATION

Although a saintly person may not expose himself to the vision of human society, by his behavior his purpose is disclosed. To human society he should present himself like a restless child, and although he is the greatest thoughtful orator, he should present himself like a dumb man.

PURPORT

A great personality very much advanced in Kṛṣṇa consciousness may not expose himself by the signs of a *sannyāsī*. To cover himself, he may live like a restless child or a dumb person, although he is the greatest orator or poet.

TEXT 11

अत्राप्युदाहरन्तीममितिहासं पुरातनम् ।
प्रह्लादस्य च संवादं मुनेराजगरस्य च ॥११॥

atrāpy udāharantīmam
itihāsaṁ purātanam
prahrādasya ca saṁvādaṁ
muner ājagarasya ca

atra—herein; *api*—although not exposed to common eyes; *udāharanti*—the learned sages recite as an example; *imam*—this; *itihāsam*—historical incident; *purātanam*—very, very old; *prahrādasya*—of Prahlāda Mahārāja; *ca*—also; *saṁvādam*—conversation; *muneḥ*—of the great saintly person; *ājagarasya*—who took the profession of a python; *ca*—also.

TRANSLATION

As a historical example of this, learned sages recite the story of an ancient discussion between Prahlāda Mahārāja and a great saintly person who was feeding himself like a python.

PURPORT

The saintly person met by Prahlāda Mahārāja was undergoing *ājagara-vṛtti*, the living conditions of a python, which does not go anywhere but sits in one place for years and eats whatever is automatically available. Prahlāda Mahārāja, along with his associates, met this great saint and spoke to him as follows.

TEXTS 12–13

तं शयानं धरोपस्थे कावेर्यां सह्यसानुनि ।
रजस्वलैस्तनूदेशैर्निगूढामलतेजसम् ॥१२॥
ददर्श लोकान्विचरन् लोकतत्त्वविवित्सया ।
वृतोऽमात्यैः कतिपयैः प्रह्लादो भगवत्प्रियः ॥१३॥

taṁ śayānaṁ dharopasthe
kāveryāṁ sahya-sānuni
rajas-valais tanū-deśair
nigūḍhāmala-tejasam

dadarśa lokān vicaran
loka-tattva-vivitsayā
vṛto 'mātyaiḥ katipayaiḥ
prahrādo bhagavat-priyaḥ

tam—that (saintly person); *śayānam*—lying down; *dharā-upasthe*—on the ground; *kāveryām*—on the bank of the River Kāverī; *sahya-sānuni*—on a ridge of the mountain known as Sahya; *rajaḥ-valaiḥ*—covered with dust and dirt; *tanū-deśaiḥ*—with all the parts of the body; *nigūḍha*—very grave and deep; *amala*—spotless; *tejasam*—whose spiritual power; *dadarśa*—he saw; *lokān*—to all the different planets; *vicaran*—traveling; *loka-tattva*—the nature of the living beings (especially those who are trying to advance in Kṛṣṇa consciousness); *vivitsayā*—to try to understand; *vṛtaḥ*—surrounded; *amātyaih*—by royal associates; *katipayaiḥ*—a few; *prahrādaḥ*—Mahārāja Prahlāda; *bhagavat-priyaḥ*—who is always very, very dear to the Supreme Personality of Godhead.

TRANSLATION

Prahlāda Mahārāja, the most dear servitor of the Supreme Personality of Godhead, once went out touring the universe with some of his confidential associates just to study the nature of saintly persons. Thus he arrived at the bank of the Kāverī, where there was a mountain known as Sahya. There he found a great saintly person who was lying on the ground, covered with dirt and dust, but who was deeply spiritually advanced.

TEXT 14

कर्मणाकृतिभिर्वाचा लिङ्गैर्वर्णाश्रमादिभिः ।
न विदन्ति जना यं वै सोऽसाविति न वेति च ॥१४॥

karmaṇākṛtibhir vācā
liṅgair varṇāśramādibhiḥ
na vidanti janā yaṁ vai
so 'sāv iti na veti ca

karmaṇā—by activities; *ākṛtibhiḥ*—by bodily features; *vācā*—by words; *liṅgaiḥ*—by symptoms; *varṇa-āśrama*—pertaining to the particular material and spiritual divisions of *varṇa* and *āśrama*; *ādibhiḥ*—and by other symptoms; *na vidanti*—could not understand; *janāḥ*—people in general; *yam*—whom; *vai*—indeed; *saḥ*—whether that person; *asau*—was the same person; *iti*—thus; *na*—not; *vā*—or; *iti*—thus; *ca*—also.

TRANSLATION

Neither by that saintly person's activities, by his bodily features, by his words nor by the symptoms of his varṇāśrama status could

people understand whether he was the same person they had known.

PURPORT

The inhabitants of that particular place on the bank of the Kāverī in the valley of the mountain known as Sahya were unable to understand whether that saint was the same man they had known. It is therefore said, *vaiṣṇavera kriyā mudrā vijñe nā bhujhaya.* A highly advanced Vaiṣṇava lives in such a way that no one can understand what he is or what he was. Nor should attempts be made to understand the past of a Vaiṣṇava. Without asking the saintly person about his previous life, Prahlāda Mahārāja immediately offered him respectful obeisances.

TEXT 15

तं नत्वाभ्यर्च्य विधिवत् पादयोः शिरसा स्पृशन् ।
विवित्सुरिदमप्राक्षीन्महाभागवतोऽसुरः ॥१५॥

taṁ natvābhyarcya vidhivat
pādayoḥ śirasā spṛśan
vivitsur idam aprākṣīn
mahā-bhāgavato 'suraḥ

tam—him (the saintly person); *natvā*—after offering obeisances unto; *abhyarcya*—and worshiping; *vidhi-vat*—in terms of the rules and regulations of etiquette; *pādayoḥ*—the lotus feet of the saintly person; *śirasā*—with the head; *spṛśan*—touching; *vivitsuḥ*—desiring to know about him (the saintly person); *idam*—the following words; *aprākṣīt*—inquired; *mahā-bhāgavataḥ*—the very advanced devotee of the Lord; *asuraḥ*—although born in an *asura* family.

TRANSLATION

The advanced devotee Prahlāda Mahārāja duly worshiped and offered obeisances to the saintly person who had adopted a python's means of livelihood. After thus worshiping the saintly person and touching his own head to the saint's lotus feet, Prahlāda Mahārāja, in order to understand him, inquired very submissively as follows.

TEXTS 16–17

बिभर्षि कायं पीवानं सोद्यमो भोगवान्यथा ॥१६॥
वित्तं चैवोद्यमवतां भोगो वित्तवतामिह ।
भोगिनां खलु देहोऽयं पीवा भवति नान्यथा ॥१७॥

bibharṣi kāyaṁ pīvānaṁ
sodyamo bhogavān yathā

vittaṁ caivodyamavatāṁ
bhogo vittavatām iha
bhogināṁ khalu deho 'yaṁ
pīvā bhavati nānyathā

bibharṣi—you are maintaining; *kāyam*—a body; *pīvānam*—fat; *sa-udyamaḥ*—one who endeavors; *bhogavān*—one who enjoys; *yathā*—as; *vittam*—money; *ca*—also; *eva*—certainly; *udyama-vatām*—of persons always engaged in economic development; *bhogaḥ*—sense gratification; *vitta-vatām*—for persons who possess considerable wealth; *iha*—in this world; *bhoginām*—of the enjoyers, *karmīs; khalu*—indeed; *dehaḥ*—body; *ayam*—this; *pīvā*—very fat; *bhavati*—becomes; *na*—not; *anyathā*—otherwise.

TRANSLATION

Seeing the saintly person to be quite fat, Prahlāda Mahārāja said: My dear sir, you undergo no endeavor to earn your livelihood, but you have a stout body, exactly like that of a materialistic enjoyer. I know that if one is very rich and has nothing to do, he becomes extremely fat by eating and sleeping and performing no work.

PURPORT

Śrīla Bhaktisiddhānta Sarasvatī Ṭhākura did not like his disciples to become very fat in the course of time. He would become very anxious upon seeing his fat disciples becoming *bhogīs*, or enjoyers of the senses. This attitude is herewith confirmed by Prahlāda Mahārāja, who was surprised to see a saintly person adopting *ājagara-vṛtti* and becoming very fat. In the material world also, we generally see that when a man who is poor and skinny gradually endeavors to earn money through business or some other means and he then gets the money, he enjoys the senses to his satisfaction. By enjoying the senses one becomes fat. Therefore in spiritual advancement becoming fat is not at all satisfactory.

TEXT 18

न ते शयानस्य निरुद्यमस्य
ब्रह्मन् नु हार्थो यत एव भोगः ।
अभोगिनोऽयं तव विप्र देहः
पीवा यतस्तद्वद नः क्षमं चेत् ॥१८॥

na te śayānasya nirudyamasya
brahman nu hārtho yata eva bhogaḥ
abhogino 'yaṁ tava vipra dehaḥ
pīvā yatas tad vada naḥ kṣamaṁ cet

na—not; *te*—of you; *śayānasya*—lying down; *nirudyamasya*—without activities; *brahman*—O saintly person; *nu*—indeed; *ha*—it is evident; *arthaḥ*—money; *yataḥ*—from which; *eva*—indeed; *bhogaḥ*—sense enjoyment; *abhoginaḥ*—of one who is not engaged in sense enjoyment; *ayam*—this; *tava*—your; *vipra*—O learned *brāhmaṇa; dehaḥ*—body; *pīvā*—fat; *yataḥ*—how is it; *tat*—that fact; *vada*—kindly tell; *naḥ*—us; *kṣamam*—excuse; *cet*—if I have asked an impudent question.

TRANSLATION

O brāhmaṇa, fully in knowledge of transcendence, you have nothing to do, and therefore you are lying down. It is also understood that you have no money for sense enjoyment. How then has your body become so fat? Under the circumstances, if you do not consider my question impudent, kindly explain how this has happened.

PURPORT

Generally those engaged in spiritual advancement take food only once, either in the afternoon or in the evening. If one takes food only once, naturally he does not become fat. The learned sage, however, was quite fat, and therefore Prahlāda Mahārāja was very much surprised. Because of being experienced in self-realization, a transcendentalist certainly becomes bright-faced. And one who is advanced in self-realization must be considered to possess the body of a *brāhmaṇa.* Because the bright-faced saintly person was lying down and not working and yet was quite fat, Prahlāda Mahārāja was puzzled and wanted to question him about this.

TEXT 19

कविः कल्पो निपुणदृक् चित्रप्रियकथः समः ।
लोकस्य कुर्वतः कर्म शेषे तद्वीक्षितापि वा ॥१९॥

kaviḥ kalpo nipuṇa-dṛk
citra-priya-kathaḥ samaḥ
lokasya kurvataḥ karma
śeṣe tad-vīkṣitāpi vā

kaviḥ—very learned; *kalpaḥ*—expert; *nipuṇa-dṛk*—intelligent; *citra-priya-kathaḥ*—able to speak palatable words that are pleasing to the heart; *samaḥ*—equipoised; *lokasya*—of the people in general; *kurvataḥ*—engaged in; *karma*—fruitive work; *śeṣe*—you lie down; *tat-vīkṣitā*—seeing them all; *api*—although; *vā*—either.

TRANSLATION

Your Honor appears learned, expert and intelligent in every way. You can speak very well, saying things that are pleasing to the heart. You see that people in general are engaged in fruitive activities, yet you are lying here inactive.

PURPORT

Prahlāda Mahārāja studied the bodily features of the saintly person, and through the saint's physiognomy Prahlāda Mahārāja could understand that he was intelligent and expert, although he was lying down and not doing anything. Prahlāda was naturally inquisitive about why he was lying there inactive.

TEXT 20

श्रीनारद उवाच

स इत्थं दैत्यपतिना परिपृष्टो महामुनिः ।
स्मयमानस्तमभ्याह तद्वागमृतयन्त्रितः ॥२०॥

śrī-nārada uvāca
sa itthaṁ daitya-patinā
pariprṣṭo mahā-muniḥ
smayamānas tam abhyāha
tad-vāg-amṛta-yantritaḥ

śrī-nāradaḥ uvāca—the great saint Nārada Muni said; *saḥ*—that saintly person (lying down); *ittham*—in this way; *daitya-patinā*—by the King of the Daityas (Prahlāda Mahārāja); *pariprṣṭaḥ*—being sufficiently questioned; *mahā-muniḥ*—the great saintly person; *smayamānaḥ*—smiling; *tam*—unto him (Prahlāda Mahārāja); *abhyāha*—prepared to give answers; *tat-vāk*—of his words; *amṛta-yantritaḥ*—being captivated by the nectar.

TRANSLATION

Nārada Muni continued: When the saintly person was thus questioned by Prahlāda Mahārāja, the King of the Daityas, he was captivated by this shower of nectarean words, and he replied to the inquisitiveness of Prahlāda Mahārāja with a smiling face.

TEXT 21

श्रीब्राह्मण उवाच

वेदेदमसुरश्रेष्ठ भवान् नन्वार्यसम्मतः ।
ईहो परमयोर्नृणां पदान्यध्यात्मचक्षुषा ॥२१॥

śrī-brāhmaṇa uvāca
vededam asura-śreṣṭha
bhavān nanv ārya-sammataḥ
īhoparamayor nṛṇāṁ
padāny adhyātma-cakṣuṣā

śrī-brāhmaṇaḥ uvāca—the *brāhmaṇa* replied; *veda*—know very well; *idam*—all these things; *asura-śreṣṭha*—O best of the *asuras; bhavān*—you; *nanu*—indeed; *ārya-sammataḥ*—whose activities are approved by civilized men; *īhā*—of inclination; *uparamayoḥ*—of decreasing; *nṝṇām*—of the people in general; *padāni*—different stages; *adhyātma-cakṣuṣā*—by transcendental eyes.

TRANSLATION

The saintly brāhmaṇa said: O best of the asuras, Prahlāda Mahārāja, who are recognized by advanced and civilized men, you are aware of the different stages of life because of your inherent transcendental eyes, with which you can see a man's character and thus know clearly the results of acceptance and rejection of things as they are.

PURPORT

A pure devotee like Prahlāda Mahārāja can understand the minds of others because of his pure vision in devotional service. A devotee like Prahlāda Mahārāja can study another man's character without difficulty.

TEXT 22

यस्य नारायणो देवो भगवान्हृद्गतः सदा ।
भक्त्या केवलयाज्ञानं धुनोति ध्वान्तमर्कवत् ॥२२॥

yasya nārāyaṇo devo
bhagavān hṛd-gataḥ sadā
bhaktyā kevalayājñānaṁ
dhunoti dhvāntam arkavat

yasya—of whom; *nārāyaṇaḥ devaḥ*—the Supreme Personality of Godhead, Nārāyaṇa; *bhagavān*—the Lord; *hṛt-gataḥ*—in the core of the heart; *sadā*—always; *bhaktyā*—by devotional service; *kevalayā*—alone; *ajñānam*—ignorance; *dhunoti*—cleans; *dhvāntam*—darkness; *arkavat*—as the sun.

TRANSLATION

Nārāyaṇa, the Supreme Personality of Godhead, who is full of all opulences, is predominant within the core of your heart be-

cause of your being a pure devotee. He always drives away all the darkness of ignorance, as the sun drives away the darkness of the universe.

PURPORT

The words *bhaktyā kevalayā* indicate that simply by executing devotional service one can become full of all knowledge. Kṛṣṇa is the master of all knowledge (*aiśvaryasya samagrasya vīryasya yaśasaḥ śriyaḥ*). The Lord is situated in everyone's heart (*īśvaraḥ sarva-bhūtānāṁ hṛd-deśe 'rjuna tiṣṭhati*), and when the Lord is pleased with a devotee, the Lord instructs him. Only to the devotees, however, does the Lord give instructions by which to advance further and further in devotional service. To others, the nondevotees, the Lord gives instructions according to the manner of their surrender. The pure devotee is described by the words *bhaktyā kevalayā*. Śrīla Viśvanātha Cakravartī Ṭhākura explains that *bhaktyā kevalayā* means *jñāna-karmādy-amiśrayā*, "unmixed with fruitive activities or speculative knowledge." Simply surrendering at the lotus feet is the cause of all a devotee's enlightenment and awareness.

TEXT 23

तथापि ब्रूमहे प्रश्नांस्तव राजन्यथाश्रुतम् ।
सम्भाषणीयो हि भवानात्मनः शुद्धिमिच्छता ॥२३॥

tathāpi brūmahe praśnāṁs
tava rājan yathā-śrutam
sambhāṣaṇīyo hi bhavān
ātmanaḥ śuddhim icchatā

tathāpi—still; *brūmahe*—I shall answer; *praśnān*—all the questions; *tava*—your; *rājan*—O King; *yathā-śrutam*—as I have learned by hearing from the authorities; *sambhāṣaṇīyaḥ*—fit for being addressed; *hi*—indeed; *bhavān*—you; *ātmanaḥ*—of the self; *śuddhim*—purification; *icchatā*—by one who desires.

TRANSLATION

My dear King, although you know everything, you have posed some questions, which I shall try to answer according to what I

have learned by hearing from authorities. I cannot remain silent in this regard, for a personality like you is just fit to be spoken to by one who desires self-purification.

PURPORT

A saintly person doesn't wish to speak to anyone and everyone, and he is therefore grave and silent. Generally a common man does not need to be advised. Unless one is prepared to take instructions, it is said that a saintly person should not address him, although sometimes, because of great kindness, a saintly person speaks to ordinary men. As for Prahlāda Mahārāja, however, since he was not a common, ordinary man, whatever questions he posed would have to be answered, even by a great and exalted personality. Therefore the saintly *brāhmaṇa* did not remain silent, but began to answer. These answers, however, were not concocted by him. This is indicated by the words *yathā-śrutam*, meaning "as I have heard from the authorities." In the *paramparā* system, when the questions are bona fide the answers are bona fide. No one should attempt to create or manufacture answers. One must refer to the *śāstras* and give answers according to Vedic understanding. The words *yathā-śrutam* refer to Vedic knowledge. The *Vedas* are known as *śruti* because this knowledge is received from authorities. The statements of the *Vedas* are known as *śruti-pramāṇa*. One should quote evidence from the *śruti*—the *Vedas* or Vedic literature—and then one's statements will be correct. Otherwise one's words will proceed from mental concoction.

TEXT 24

तृष्णया भववाहिन्या योग्यैः कामैरपूर्यया ।
कर्माणि कार्यमाणोऽहं नानायोनिषु योजितः ॥२४॥

tṛṣṇayā bhava-vāhinyā
yogyaiḥ kāmair apūryayā
karmāṇi kāryamāṇo 'haṁ
nānā-yoniṣu yojitaḥ

tṛṣṇayā—because of material desires; *bhava-vāhinyā*—under the sway of the material laws of nature; *yogyaiḥ*—as it is befitting;

kāmaiḥ—by material desires; *apūryayā*—without end, one after another; *karmāṇi*—activities; *kāryamāṇaḥ*—constantly being compelled to perform; *aham*—I; *nānā-yoniṣu*—in various forms of life; *yojitaḥ*—engaged in the struggle for existence.

TRANSLATION

Because of insatiable material desires, I was being carried away by the waves of material nature's laws, and thus I was engaging in different activities, struggling for existence in various forms of life.

PURPORT

As long as a living entity wants to fulfill various types of material desire, he must continuously change from one body to accept another. Śrīla Viśvanātha Cakravartī Ṭhākura explains that as a small piece of grass falls in a river and is tossed about with different types of wood and tree branches, the living entity floats in the ocean of material existence and is dashed and tossed amidst material conditions. This is called the struggle for existence. One kind of fruitive activity causes the living being to take one form of body, and because of actions performed in that body, another body is created. One must therefore stop these material activities, and the chance to do so is given in the human form of life. Specifically, our energy to act should be engaged in the service of the Lord, for then materialistic activities will automatically stop. One must fulfill one's desires by surrendering unto the Supreme Lord, for He knows how to fulfill them. Even though one may have material desires, one should therefore engage in the devotional service of the Lord. That will purify one's struggle for existence.

akāmaḥ sarva-kāmo vā
mokṣa-kāma udāra-dhīḥ
tīvreṇa bhakti-yogena
yajeta puruṣaṁ param

"A person who has broader intelligence, whether he be full of all material desire, without any material desire, or desiring liberation, must by all means worship the supreme whole, the Personality of Godhead." (*Bhāg.* 2.3.10)

anyābhilāṣitā-śūnyaṁ
jñāna-karmādy-anāvṛtam
ānukūlyena kṛṣṇānu-
śīlanaṁ bhaktir uttamā

"One should render transcendental loving service to the Supreme Lord Kṛṣṇa favorably and without desire for material profit or gain through fruitive activities or philosophical speculation. That is called pure devotional service." (*Bhakti-rasāmṛta-sindhu* 1.1.11)

TEXT 25

यदृच्छया लोकमिमं प्रापितः कर्मभिर्भ्रमन् ।
स्वर्गापवर्गयोर्द्वारं तिरश्चां पुनरस्य च ॥२५॥

yadṛcchayā lokam imaṁ
prāpitaḥ karmabhir bhraman
svargāpavargayor dvāraṁ
tiraścāṁ punar asya ca

yadṛcchayā—carried by the waves of material nature; *lokam*—human form; *imam*—this; *prāpitaḥ*—achieved; *karmabhiḥ*—by the influence of different fruitive activities; *bhraman*—wandering from one form of life to another; *svarga*—to the heavenly planets; *apavargayoḥ*—to liberation; *dvāram*—the gate; *tiraścām*—lower species of life; *punaḥ*—again; *asya*—of the human beings; *ca*—and.

TRANSLATION

In the course of the evolutionary process, which is caused by fruitive activities due to undesirable material sense gratification, I have received this human form of life, which can lead to the heavenly planets, to liberation, to the lower species, or to rebirth among human beings.

PURPORT

All living entities within this material world are undergoing the cycle of birth and death according to the laws of nature. This struggle of birth and death in different species may be called the evolutionary process, but in the Western world it has been wrongly explained. Darwin's theory of evolution from animal to man is incomplete because the theory does not present the reverse condition, namely evolution from man to animal. In this verse, however, evolution has been very well explained on the strength of Vedic authority. Human life, which is obtained in the course of the evolutionary process, is a chance for elevation (*svargāpavarga*) or for degradation (*tiraścām punar asya ca*). If one uses this human form of life properly, he can elevate himself to the higher planetary systems, where material happiness is many thousands of times better than on this planet, or one may cultivate knowledge by which to become free from the evolutionary process and be reinstated in one's original spiritual life. This is called *apavarga*, or liberation.

Material life is called *pavarga* because here we are subject to five different states of suffering, represented by the letters *pa, pha, ba, bha* and *ma. Pa* means *pariśrama*, very hard labor. *Pha* means *phena*, or foam from the mouth. For example, sometimes we see a horse foaming at the mouth with heavy labor. *Ba* means *byarthatā*, disappointment. In spite of so much hard labor, at the end we find disappointment. *Bha* means *bhaya*, or fear. In material life, one is always in the blazing fire of fear, since no one knows what will happen next. Finally, *ma* means *mṛtyu*, or death. When one attempts to nullify these five different statuses of life—*pa, pha, ba, bha* and *ma*—one achieves *apavarga*, or liberation from the punishment of material existence.

The word *tiraścām* refers to degraded life. Human life, of course, provides an opportunity for the best living conditions. As Western people think, from the monkeys come the human beings, who are more comfortably situated. However, if one does not utilize his human life for *svarga* or *apavarga*, he falls again to the degraded life of animals like dogs and hogs. Therefore a sane human being must consider whether he will elevate himself to the higher planets, prepare to free himself from the evolutionary process, or travel again through the evolutionary process in higher and lower grades of life. If one works piously one may be elevated to the higher planetary systems or achieve liberation and return home, back to Godhead, but otherwise one may be degraded to a life as a dog, a hog and so on. As explained in *Bhagavad-gītā* (9.25), *yānti deva-vratā devān*. Those interested in being elevated to the higher planetary systems (Devaloka or Svargaloka) must prepare to do so. Similarly, if one wants liberation and wants to return home, back to Godhead, he should prepare himself for that purpose.

Our Kṛṣṇa consciousness movement is therefore the highest movement for the benediction of human society because this movement is teaching people how to go back home, back to Godhead. In *Bhagavad-gītā* (13.22) it is clearly stated that different forms of life are obtained by association with the three modes of material nature (*kāraṇaṁ guṇa-saṅgo 'sya sad-asad-yoni-janmasu*). According to one's association with the material qualities of goodness, passion and ignorance in this life, in one's next life one receives an appropriate body. Modern civilization does not know that because of varied association in material nature, the living entity, although eternal, is placed in different diseased conditions known as the many species of life. Modern civilization is unaware of the laws of nature.

prakṛteḥ kriyamāṇāni
guṇaiḥ karmāṇi sarvaśaḥ
ahaṅkāra-vimūḍhātmā
kartāham iti manyate

"The bewildered spirit soul, under the influence of the three modes of material nature, thinks himself the performer of activities that are in actuality carried out by nature." (Bg. 3.27) Every living entity is under the full control of the stringent laws of material nature, but rascals think themselves independent. Actually, however, they cannot be independent. This is foolishness. A foolish civilization is extremely risky, and therefore the Kṛṣṇa consciousness movement is trying to make people aware of their fully dependent condition under the stringent laws of nature and is trying to save them from being victimized by strong *māyā*, which is Kṛṣṇa's external energy. Behind the material laws is the supreme controller, Kṛṣṇa (*mayādhyakṣeṇa prakṛtiḥ sūyate sacarācaram*). Therefore if one surrenders unto Kṛṣṇa (*mām eva ye prapadyante māyām etāṁ taranti te*), one may immediately be freed from the control of external nature (*sa guṇān samatītyaitān brahma-bhūyāya kalpate*). This should be the aim of life.

TEXT 26

तत्रापि दम्पतीनां च सुखायान्यापनुत्तये ।
कर्माणि कुर्वतां दृष्ट्वा निवृत्तोऽस्मि विपर्ययम् ॥ २६ ॥

tatrāpi dam-patīnāṁ ca
sukhāyānyāpanuttaye
karmāṇi kurvatāṁ dṛṣṭvā
nivṛtto 'smi viparyayam

tatra—there; *api*—also; *dam-patīnām*—of men and women united by marriage; *ca*—and; *sukhāya*—for the sake of pleasure, specifically the pleasure of sex life; *anya-apanuttaye*—for avoiding misery; *karmāṇi*—fruitive activities; *kurvatām*—always engaged in; *dṛṣṭvā*—by observing; *nivṛttaḥ asmi*—I have now ceased (from such activities); *viparyayam*—the opposite.

TRANSLATION

In this human form of life, a man and women unite for the sensual pleasure of sex, but by actual experience we have observed that none of them are happy. Therefore, seeing the contrary results, I have stopped taking part in materialistic activities.

PURPORT

As stated by Prahlāda Mahārāja, *yan maithunādi-gṛhamedhi-sukhaṁ hi tuccham.* Man and woman both seek sexual enjoyment, and when they are united by the ritualistic ceremony of marriage, they are happy for some time, but finally there is dissension, and thus there are so many cases of separation and divorce. Although every man and woman is actually eager to enjoy life through sexual unity, the result is disunity and distress. Marriage is recommended to give men and women a concession for restricted sex life, which is also recommended in *Bhagavad-gītā* by the Supreme Personality of Godhead. *Dharmāviruddho bhūteṣu kāmo 'smi:* sex life not against the principles of religion is Kṛṣṇa. Every living entity is always eager to enjoy sex life because materialistic life consists of eating, sleeping, sex and fear. In animal life, eating, sleeping, sexual enjoyment and fear cannot be regulated, but for human society the plan is that although men, like animals, must be allowed to eat, sleep, enjoy sex and take protection from fear, they must be regulated. The Vedic plan for eating recommends that one take *yajña-śiṣṭa*, or *prasāda*, food offered to Kṛṣṇa. *Yajña-śiṣṭāśinaḥ santo mucyante sarva-kilbiṣaiḥ:* "The devotees of the Lord are released from all kinds of sins because they eat food that is offered first for sacrifice." (Bg. 3.13) In material life, one commits sinful activities, especially in eating, and because of sinful activities one is condemned by nature's laws to accept another body, which is imposed as punishment. Sex and eating are essential, and therefore they are offered to human society under Vedic restrictions so that according to the Vedic injunctions people may eat, sleep, enjoy sex, be protected from fearful life and gradually be elevated and liberated from the punishment of material existence. Thus the Vedic injunctions for marriage offer a concession to human society, the idea being that a man and woman united in a ritualistic marriage ceremony should help one another advance in spiritual life. Unfortunately, especially in this age, men and women unite for unrestricted sexual enjoyment. Thus they are victimized, being obliged to take rebirth in the forms of animals to fulfill their animalistic propensities. The Vedic injunctions therefore warn, *nāyaṁ deho deha-bhājāṁ nṛloke kaṣṭān kāmān arhate viḍ-bhujāṁ ye.* One should not enjoy sex life like hogs, and eat everything, even to the limit of stool. A human being should eat *prasāda* offered to the Deity and should enjoy sex life according to the Vedic injunctions. He should engage himself in the business of Kṛṣṇa consciousness, he should save himself from the fearful condition of material existence, and he should sleep only to recover from fatigue due to working hard.

The learned *brāhmaṇa* said that since everything is misused by fruitive workers, he had retired from all fruitive activities.

TEXT 27

सुखमस्यात्मनो रूपं सर्वेहोपरतिस्तनुः ।
मनःसंस्पर्शजान् दृष्ट्वा भोगान्स्वप्स्यामि संविशन् ॥२७॥

sukham asyātmano rūpaṁ
sarvehoparatis tanuḥ

manaḥ-saṁsparśajān dṛṣṭvā
bhogān svapsyāmi saṁviśan

sukham—happiness; *asya*—of him; *ātmanaḥ*—of the living entity; *rūpam*—the natural position; *sarva*—all; *īha*—material activities; *uparatiḥ*—completely stopping; *tanuḥ*—the medium of its manifestation; *manaḥ-saṁsparśa-jān*—produced from demands for sense gratification; *dṛṣṭvā*—after seeing; *bhogān*—sense enjoyment; *svapsyāmi*—I am sitting silently, thinking deeply about these material activities; *saṁviśan*—entering into such activities.

TRANSLATION

The actual form of life for the living entities is one of spiritual happiness, which is real happiness. This happiness can be achieved only when one stops all materialistic activities. Material sense enjoyment is simply imagination. Therefore, considering this subject matter, I have ceased from all material activities and am lying down here.

PURPORT

The difference between the philosophy of the Māyāvādīs and that of the Vaiṣṇavas is explained herein. Both the Māyāvādīs and Vaiṣṇavas know that in materialistic activities there is no happiness. The Māyāvādī philosophers, therefore, adhering to the slogan *brahma satyaṁ jagan mithyā,* want to refrain from false, materialistic activities. They want to stop all activities and merge in the Supreme Brahman. According to the Vaiṣṇava philosophy, however, if one simply ceases from materialistic activity one cannot remain inactive for very long, and therefore everyone should engage himself in spiritual activities, which will solve the problem of suffering in this material world. It is said, therefore, that although the Māyāvādī philosophers strive to refrain from materialistic activities and merge in Brahman, and although they may actually merge in the Brahman existence, for want of activity they fall down again into materialistic activity (*āruhya kṛcchreṇa paraṁ padaṁ tataḥ patanty adhaḥ*). Thus the so-called renouncer, unable to remain in meditation upon Brahman, returns to materialistic activities by opening hospitals and schools and so on. Therefore, simply cultivating knowledge that materialistic activities cannot give one happiness, and that one should consequently cease from such activities, is insufficient. One should cease from materialistic activities and take up spiritual activities. Then the solution to the problem will be achieved. Spiritual activities are activities performed according to the order of Kṛṣṇa (*ānukūlyena kṛṣṇānuśīlanam*). If one does whatever Kṛṣṇa says, his activities are not material. For example, when Arjuna fought in response to the order of Kṛṣṇa, his activities were not material. Fighting for sense gratification is a materialistic activity, but fighting by the order of Kṛṣṇa is spiritual. By spiritual activities one becomes eligible to go back home, back to Godhead, and then enjoy blissful life eternally. Here, in the material world, everything is but a mental concoction that will never give us real happiness. The practical solution, therefore, is to cease from materialistic activities and engage in spiritual activities. *Yajñārthāt karmaṇo 'nyatra loko 'yaṁ karma-bandhanaḥ*. If one works for the sake of pleasing the Supreme Lord—Yajña, or Viṣṇu—one is in liberated life. If one fails to do so, however, he remains in a life of bondage.

TEXT 28

इत्येतदात्मनः स्वार्थं सन्तं विस्मृत्य वै पुमान् ।
विचित्रामसति द्वैते घोरामाप्नोति संसृतिम् ॥२८॥

ity etad ātmanaḥ svārthaṁ
santaṁ vismṛtya vai pumān
vicitrām asati dvaite
ghorām āpnoti saṁsṛtim

iti—in this way; *etat*—a person materially conditioned; *ātmanaḥ*—of his self; *sva-artham*—own interest; *santam*—existing within oneself; *vismṛtya*—forgetting; *vai*—indeed; *pumān*—the living entity; *vicitrām*—attractive false varieties; *asati*—in the material world; *dvaite*—other than the self; *ghorām*—very fearful (due to continuous acceptance of birth and death); *āpnoti*—one becomes entangled; *saṁsṛtim*—in material existence.

TRANSLATION

In this way the conditioned soul living within the body forgets his self-interest because he identifies himself with the body. Because the body is material, his natural tendency is to be attracted by the varieties of the material world. Thus the living entity suffers the miseries of material existence.

PURPORT

Everyone is trying to be happy because, as explained in the previous verse, *sukham asyātmano rūpaṁ sarvehoparatis tanuḥ:* when the living entity is in his original spiritual form, he is happy by nature. There is no question of miseries for the spiritual being. As Kṛṣṇa is always happy, the living entities, who are His parts and parcels, are also happy by nature, but because of being put within this material world and forgetting their eternal relationship with Kṛṣṇa, they have forgotten their real nature. Because every one of us is a part of Kṛṣṇa, we have a very affectionate relationship with Him, but because we have forgotten our identities and are considering the body to be the self, we are afflicted by all the troubles of birth, death, old age and disease. This misconception in materialistic life continues unless and until one comes to understand his relationship with Kṛṣṇa. The happiness sought by the conditioned soul is certainly only illusion, as explained in the next verse.

TEXT 29

जलं तदुद्भवैश्छन्नं हित्वाज्ञो जलकाम्यया ।
मृगतृष्णामुपाधावेत् तथान्यत्रार्थदृक् स्वतः ॥ २९ ॥

jalaṁ tad-udbhavaiś channaṁ
hitvājño jala-kāmyayā
mṛgatṛṣṇām upādhāvet
tathānyatrārtha-dṛk svataḥ

jalam—water; *tat-udbhavaiḥ*—by grass grown from that water; *channam*—covered; *hitvā*—giving up; *ajñaḥ*—a foolish animal; *jala-kāmyayā*—desiring to drink water; *mṛgatṛṣṇām*—a mirage;

upādhāvet—runs after; *tathā*—similarly; *anyatra*—somewhere else; *artha-dṛk*—self-interested; *svataḥ*—in himself.

TRANSLATION

Just as a deer, because of ignorance, cannot see the water within a well covered by grass, but runs after water elsewhere, the living entity covered by the material body does not see the happiness within himself, but runs after happiness in the material world.

PURPORT

This is an accurate example depicting how the living entity, because of lack of knowledge, runs after happiness outside his own self. When one understands his real identity as a spiritual being, he can understand the supreme spiritual being, Kṛṣṇa, and the real happiness exchanged between Kṛṣṇa and one's self. It is very interesting to note how this verse points to the body's growth from the spirit soul. The modern materialistic scientist thinks that life grows from matter, but actually the fact is that matter grows from life. The life, or the spiritual soul, is compared herein to water, from which clumps of matter grow in the form of grass. One who is ignorant of scientific knowledge of the spirit soul does not look inside the body to find happiness in the soul; instead, he goes outside to search for happiness, just as a deer without knowledge of the water beneath the grass goes out to the desert to find water. The Kṛṣṇa consciousness movement is trying to remove the ignorance of misled human beings who are trying to find water outside the jurisdiction of life. *Raso vai saḥ. Raso 'ham apsu kaunteya.* The taste of water is Kṛṣṇa. To quench one's thirst, one must taste water by association with Kṛṣṇa. This is the Vedic injunction.

TEXT 30

देहादिभिर्दैवतन्त्रैरात्मनः सुखमीहतः ।
दुःखात्ययं चानीशस्य क्रिया मोघाः कृताः कृताः ॥३०॥

dehādibhir daiva-tantrair
ātmanaḥ sukham īhataḥ

duḥkhātyayaṁ cānīśasya
kriyā moghāḥ kṛtāḥ kṛtāḥ

deha-ādibhiḥ—with the body, mind, ego and intelligence; *daiva-tantraiḥ*—under the control of superior power; *ātmanaḥ*—of the self; *sukham*—happiness; *īhataḥ*—searching after; *duḥkha-atyayam*—diminution of miserable conditions; *ca*—also; *anīśasya*—of the living entity fully under the control of material nature; *kriyāḥ*—plans and activities; *moghāḥ kṛtāḥ kṛtāḥ*—become baffled again and again.

TRANSLATION

The living entity tries to achieve happiness and rid himself of the causes of distress, but because the various bodies of the living entities are under the full control of material nature, all his plans in different bodies, one after another, are ultimately baffled.

PURPORT

Because the materialist is in gross ignorance of how the laws of material nature act upon him as a result of his fruitive activity, he mistakenly plans to enjoy bodily comfort in the human form of life through so-called economic development, through pious activities for elevation to the higher planetary systems, and in many other ways, but factually he becomes a victim of the reactions of his fruitive activities. The Supreme Personality of Godhead is situated as the Supersoul within the cores of the hearts of all living entities. As the Lord says in *Bhagavad-gītā* (15.15):

sarvasya cāhaṁ hṛdi sanniviṣṭo
mattaḥ smṛtir jñānam apohanaṁ ca

"I am seated in everyone's heart, and from Me come remembrance, knowledge and forgetfulness." The desires and activities of the living being are observed by the Supersoul, who is the *upadraṣṭā*, the overseer, and who orders material nature to fulfill the various desires of the living being. As clearly stated in *Bhagavad-gītā* (18.61):

īśvaraḥ sarva-bhūtānāṁ
hṛd-deśe 'rjuna tiṣṭhati
bhrāmayan sarva-bhūtāni
yantrārūḍhāni māyayā

The Lord is situated in everyone's heart, and as one desires, the Lord gives one various types of bodies, which are like machines. Riding on such a machine, the living entity wanders throughout the universe, under the control of material nature and its modes. Thus the living being is not at all free to act, but is fully under the control of material nature, which is fully under the control of the Supreme Personality of Godhead.

As soon as a living entity is victimized by material desires to lord it over material nature, he is subjected to the control of material nature, which is supervised by the Supreme Soul. The result is that one again and again makes plans and is baffled, but as foolish as he is he cannot see the cause of his bafflement. This cause is distinctly stated in *Bhagavad-gītā:* because one has not surrendered to the Supreme Personality of Godhead, he must work under the control of material nature and its stringent laws (*daivī hy eṣā guṇamayī mama māyā duratyayā*). The only means of becoming free from this entanglement is to surrender to the Supreme Lord. In the human form of life, the living entity must accept this instruction from the Supreme Person, Kṛṣṇa: *sarva-dharmān parityajya mām ekaṁ śaraṇaṁ vraja.* "Do not plan to achieve happiness and drive away distress. You will never be successful. Simply surrender unto Me." Unfortunately, however, the living entity does not accept the Supreme Lord's clearly stated instructions from *Bhagavad-gītā*, and thus he becomes a perpetual captive of the laws of material nature.

Yajñārthāt karmaṇo 'nyatra loko 'yaṁ karma-bandhanaḥ: if one does not act for the satisfaction of Kṛṣṇa, who is known as Viṣṇu or Yajña, he must be entangled in the reactions of fruitive activities. These reactions are called *pāpa* and *puṇya*—sinful and pious. By pious activities one is elevated to the higher planetary systems, and by impious activities one is degraded to lower species of life, in which he is punished by the laws of nature. In the lower species of life there is an evolutionary process, and when the term of the living entity's imprisonment or punishment in the lower species is finished, he is again offered a human form and given a chance to decide for himself which way he should plan.

If he again misses the opportunity, he is again put into the cycle of birth and death, going sometimes higher and sometimes lower, turning on the *saṁsāra-cakra*, the wheel of material existence. As a wheel sometimes goes up and sometimes comes down, the stringent laws of material nature make the living entity in material existence sometimes happy and sometimes distressed. How he suffers in the cycle of happiness and distress is described in the next verse.

TEXT 31

आध्यात्मिकादिभिर्दुःखैरविमुक्तस्य कर्हिचित् ।
मर्त्यस्य कृच्छ्रोपनतैरर्थैः कामैः क्रियेत किम् ॥३१॥

ādhyātmikādibhir duḥkhair
avimuktasya karhicit
martyasya kṛcchropanatair
arthaiḥ kāmaiḥ kriyeta kim

ādhyātmika-ādibhiḥ—*adhyātmika*, *adhidaivika* and *adhibhautika*; *duḥkhaiḥ*—by the threefold miseries of material life; *avimuktasya*—of one who is not freed from such miserable conditions (or one who is subjected to birth, death, old age and disease); *karhicit*—sometimes; *martyasya*—of the living entity subjected to death; *kṛcchra-upanataiḥ*—things obtained because of severe miseries; *arthaiḥ*—even if some benefit is derived; *kāmaiḥ*—which can fulfill one's material desires; *kriyeta*—what do they do; *kim*—and what is the value of such happiness.

TRANSLATION

Materialistic activities are always mixed with three kinds of miserable conditions—adhyātmika, adhidaivika and adhibautika. Therefore, even if one achieves some success by performing such activities, what is the benefit of this success? One is still subjected to birth, death, old age, disease and the reactions of his fruitive activities.

PURPORT

According to the materialistic way of life, if a poor man, after laboring very, very hard, gets some material profit at the end of his life, he is considered a success, even though he again dies while suffering the threefold miseries—*adhyātmika, adhidaivika* and *adhibhautika.* No one can escape the threefold miseries of materialistic life, namely miseries pertaining to the body and mind, miseries pertaining to the difficulties imposed by society, community, nation and other living entities, and miseries inflicted upon us by natural disturbances from earthquakes, famines, droughts, floods, epidemics, and so on. If one works very hard, suffering the threefold miseries, and then is successful in getting some small benefit, what is the value of this benefit? Besides that, even if a *karmī* is successful in accumulating some material wealth, he still cannot enjoy it, for he must die in bereavement. I have even seen a dying man begging a medical attendant to increase his life by four years so that he could complete his material plans. Of course, the medical man was unsuccessful in expanding the life of the man, who therefore died in great bereavement. Everyone must die in this way, and after one's mental condition is taken into account by the laws of material nature, he is given another chance to fulfill his desires in a different body. Material plans for material happiness have no value, but under the spell of the illusory energy we consider them extremely valuable. There were many politicians, social reformers and philosophers who died very miserably, without deriving any practical value from their material plans. Therefore, a sane and sensible man never desires to work hard under the conditions of threefold miseries, only to die in disappointment.

TEXT 32

पश्यामि धनिनां क्लेशं लुब्धानामजितात्मनाम् ।
भयादलब्धनिद्राणां सर्वतोऽभिविशङ्किनाम् ॥३२॥

paśyāmi dhaninām kleśaṁ
lubdhānām ajitātmanām
bhayād alabdha-nidrāṇāṁ
sarvato 'bhiviśaṅkinām

paśyāmi—I can practically see; *dhaninām*—of persons who are very rich; *kleśam*—the miseries; *lubdhānām*—who are extremely greedy; *ajita-ātmanām*—who are victims of their senses; *bhayāt*—because of fear; *alabdha-nidrāṇām*—who are suffering from insomnia; *sarvataḥ*—from all sides; *abhiviśaṅkinām*—being particularly afraid.

TRANSLATION

The brāhmaṇa continued: I am actually seeing how a rich man, who is a victim of his senses, is very greedy to accumulate wealth, and therefore suffers from insomnia due to fear from all sides, despite his wealth and opulence.

PURPORT

Greedy capitalists accumulate wealth under so many miserable conditions, the result being that because they collect money by questionable means, their minds are always agitated. Thus they are unable to sleep at night, and they have to take pills for mental tranquility to invite sleep. And sometimes even the pills are a failure. Consequently the result of having accumulated money by so much labor is certainly not happiness, but only distress. What is the value of acquiring a comfortable position if one's mind is always disturbed? Narottama dāsa Ṭhākura has therefore sung:

saṁsāra-biṣānale, dibāniśi hiyā jvale,
juḍāite nā kainu upāya

"I am suffering from the poisonous effect of material enjoyment. Thus my heart is always burning and is almost on the verge of failure." The result of the greedy capitalist's unnecessary accumulation of wealth is that he must suffer from a blazing fire of anxiety and always be concerned with how to save his money and invest it properly to get more and more. Such a life is certainly not very happy, but because of the spell of the illusory energy, materialistic persons engage in such activities.

As far as our Kṛṣṇa consciousness movement is concerned, we are getting money naturally, by the grace of God, by selling our literature. This literature is not sold for our sense gratification; to spread the Kṛṣṇa consciousness movement we need so many things, and Kṛṣṇa is therefore supplying us the requisite money to advance this mission. The mission of Kṛṣṇa is to spread Kṛṣṇa consciousness all over the world, and for this purpose we naturally must have sufficient money. Therefore, according to the advice of Śrīla Rūpa Gosvāmī Prabhupāda, we should not give up attachment to money that can spread the Kṛṣṇa consciousness movement. Śrīla Rūpa Gosvāmī says in his *Bhakti-rasāmṛta-sindhu* (1.2.256):

prāpañcikatayā buddhyā
hari-sambandhi-vastunaḥ
mumukṣubhiḥ parityāgo
vairagyaṁ phalgu kathyate

"When persons eager to achieve liberation renounce things which are related to the Supreme Personality of Godhead, though they are material, this is called incomplete renunciation." Money that can help in spreading the Kṛṣṇa consciousness movement is not a part of the material world, and we should not give it up, thinking that it is material. Śrīla Rūpa Gosvāmī advises:

anāsaktasya viṣayān
yathārham upayuñjataḥ
nirbandhaḥ kṛṣṇa-sambandhe
yuktaṁ vairāgyam ucyate

"When one is not attached to anything, but at the same time accepts everything in relation to Kṛṣṇa, one is rightly situated above possessiveness." (*Bhakti-rasāmṛta-sindhu* 1.2.255) Money is undoubtedly coming in great quantities, but we should not be attached to this money for sense gratification; every cent should be spent for spreading the Kṛṣṇa consciousness movement, not for sense gratification. There is danger for a preacher when he receives great quantities of money, for as soon as he spends even a single cent of the collection for his personal sense gratification, he becomes a fallen victim. The preachers of the Kṛṣṇa consciousness movement should be extremely careful not to misuse the immense quantities of money needed to spread this movement. Let us not make this money the cause of our distress; it should be used for Kṛṣṇa, and that will cause our eternal happiness. Money is Lakṣmī, or the goddess of fortune, the companion of Nārāyaṇa. Lakṣmījī must always remain with Nārāyaṇa, and then there need be no fear of degradation.

TEXT 33

राजतश्चौरतः शत्रोः स्वजनात्पशुपक्षितः ।
अर्थिभ्यः कालतः स्वस्मान्नित्यं प्राणार्थवद्भयम् ॥३३॥

rājataś cauratah śatroh
sva-janāt paśu-pakṣitah
arthibhyaḥ kālataḥ svasmān
nityaṁ prāṇārthavad bhayam

rājataḥ—from the government; *cauratah*—from thieves and rogues; *śatroh*—from enemies; *sva-janāt*—from relatives; *paśu-pakṣitaḥ*—from animals and birds; *arthibhyaḥ*—from beggars and persons seeking charity; *kālataḥ*—from the time factor; *svasmāt*—as well as from one's self; *nityam*—always; *prāṇa-artha-vat*—for one who has life or money; *bhayam*—fear.

TRANSLATION

Those who are considered materially powerful and rich are always full of anxieties because of governmental laws, thieves and rogues, enemies, family members, animals, birds, persons seeking charity, the inevitable time factor and even their own selves. Thus they are invariably afraid.

PURPORT

The word *svasmāt* means "from one's self." Because of attachment for money, the richest person is even afraid of himself. He fears that he may have locked his money in an unsafe manner or might have committed some mistake. Aside from the government and its income tax and aside from thieves, even a rich man's own relatives are always thinking of how to take advantage of him and take away his money. Sometimes these relatives are described as *sva-janaka-dasyu*, which means "rogues and thieves in the guise of relatives." Therefore, there is no need to accumulate wealth or unnecessarily endeavor for more and more money. The real business of life is to ask "Who am I?" and to understand one's self. One should understand the position of the living entity in this material world and understand how to return home, back to Godhead.

TEXT 34

शोकमोहभयक्रोधरागक्लैब्यश्रमादयः ।
यन्मूलाः स्युर्नृणां जह्यात् स्पृहां प्राणार्थयोर्बुधः ॥३४॥

śoka-moha-bhaya-krodha-
rāga-klaibya-śramādayaḥ
yan-mūlāḥ syur nṛṇāṁ jahyāt
spṛhāṁ prāṇārthayor budhaḥ

śoka—lamentation; *moha*—illusion; *bhaya*—fear; *krodha*—anger; *rāga*—attachment; *klaibya*—poverty; *śrama*—unnecessary labor; *ādayaḥ*—and so on; *yat-mūlāḥ*—the original cause of all these; *syuḥ*—become; *nṛṇām*—of human beings; *jahyāt*—should give up; *spṛhām*—the desire; *prāṇa*—for bodily strength or prestige; *arthayoḥ*—and accumulating money; *budhaḥ*—an intelligent person.

TRANSLATION

Those in human society who are intelligent should give up the original cause of lamentation, illusion, fear, anger, attachment, poverty and unnecessary labor. The original cause of all of these is the desire for unnecessary prestige and money.

PURPORT

Here is the difference between Vedic civilization and the modern demoniac civilization. Vedic civilization concerned itself with how to achieve self-realization, and for this purpose one was recommended to have a small income to maintain body and soul together. The society was divided into *brāhmaṇas*, *kṣatriyas*, *vaiśyas* and *śūdras*, and the members of this society would limit their endeavors to meeting their minimum demands. The *brāhmaṇas*, in particular, would have no material desires. Because the *kṣatriyas* had to rule the people, it was necessary for them to have money and prestige. But the *vaiśyas* were satisfied with agricultural produce and milk from the cow, and if by chance there were excess, trade was allowed. The *śūdras* were also happy, for they would get food and shelter from the three higher classes. In the demoniac civilization of the present day, however, there is no question of *brāhmaṇas* or *kṣatriyas;* there are only so-called workers and a flourishing mercantile class who have no goal in life.

According to Vedic civilization, the ultimate perfection of life is to take *sannyāsa,* but at the present moment people do not know why *sannyāsa* is accepted. Because of misunderstanding, they think that one accepts *sannyāsa* to escape social responsibilities. But one does not accept *sannyāsa* to escape from responsibility to society. Generally one accepts *sannyāsa* at the fourth stage of spiritual life. One begins as a *brahmacārī* then becomes a *gṛhastha,* a *vānaprastha* and finally a *sannyāsī* to take advantage of the duration of one's life by engaging oneself fully in self-realization. *Sannyāsa* does not mean begging from door to door to accumulate money for sense gratification. However, because in Kali-yuga people are more or less prone to sense gratification, immature *sannyāsa* is not recommended. Śrīla Rūpa Gosvāmī writes in his *Nectar of Instruction* (2):

atyāhāraḥ prayāsaś ca
prajalpo niyamāgrahaḥ
jana-saṅgaś ca laulyaṁ ca
ṣaḍbhir bhaktir vinaśyati

"One's devotional service is spoiled when he becomes too entangled in the following six activities: (1) eating more than necessary or collecting more funds than required; (2) overendeavoring for mundane things that are very difficult to obtain; (3) talking unnecessarily about mundane subject matters; (4) practicing the scriptural rules and regulations only for the sake of following them and not for the sake of spiritual advancement, or rejecting the rules and regulations of the scriptures and working independently or whimsically; (5) associating with worldly-minded persons who are not interested in Kṛṣṇa consciousness; and (6) being greedy for mundane achievements." A *sannyāsī* should have an institution meant to preach Kṛṣṇa consciousness; he need not accumulate money for himself. We recommend that as soon as money accumulates in our Kṛṣṇa consciousness movement, fifty per cent of it should be invested in printing books, and fifty per cent for expenditures, especially in establishing centers all over the world. The managers of the Kṛṣṇa consciousness movement should be extremely cautious in regard to this point. Otherwise money will be the cause of lamentation, illusion, fear, anger, material attachment, material poverty, and unnecessary hard work. When I was alone in Vṛndāvana, I never attempted to construct *maṭhās* or temples; rather, I was fully satisfied with the small amount of money I could gather by selling *Back to Godhead*, and thus I would provide for myself and also print the literature. When I went to foreign countries, I lived according to the same principle, but when Europeans and Americans began to give money profusely, I started temples and Deity worship. The same principle should still be followed. Whatever money is collected should be spent for Kṛṣṇa, and not a farthing for sense gratification. This is the *Bhāgavata* principle.

TEXT 35

मधुकारमहासर्पौ लोकेऽस्मिन्नो गुरूत्तमौ ।
वैराग्यं परितोषं च प्राप्ता यच्छिक्षया वयम् ॥३५॥

madhukāra-mahā-sarpau
loke 'smin no gurūttamau
vairāgyaṁ paritoṣaṁ ca
prāptā yac-chikṣayā vayam

madhukāra—bees that go from flower to flower to collect honey; *mahā-sarpau*—the big snake (the python, which does not move from one place to another); *loke*—in the world; *asmin*—this; *naḥ*—our; *guru*—spiritual masters; *uttamau*—first-class; *vairāgyam*—renunciation; *paritoṣam ca*—and satisfaction; *prāptāḥ*—obtained; *yat-śikṣayā*—by whose instruction; *vayam*—we.

TRANSLATION

The bee and the python are two excellent spiritual masters who give us exemplary instructions regarding how to be satisfied by collecting only a little and how to stay in one place and not move.

TEXT 36

विरागः सर्वकामेभ्यः शिक्षितो मे मधुव्रतात् ।
कृच्छ्राप्तं मधुवद् वित्तं हत्वाप्यन्यो हरेत्पतिम् ॥३६॥

virāgaḥ sarva-kāmebhyaḥ
śikṣito me madhu-vratāt
kṛcchrāptaṁ madhuvad vittaṁ
hatvāpy anyo haret patim

virāgaḥ—detachment; *sarva-kāmebhyaḥ*—from all material desires; *śikṣitaḥ*—has been taught; *me*—unto me; *madhu-vratāt*—from the bumblebee; *kṛcchra*—with great difficulties; *āptam*—acquired; *madhu-vat*—as good as honey ("money is honey"); *vittam*—money; *hatvā*—killing; *api*—even; *anyaḥ*—another; *haret*—takes away; *patim*—the owner.

TRANSLATION

From the bumblebee I have learned to be unattached to accumulating money, for although money is as good as honey, anyone can kill its owner and take it away.

PURPORT

The honey gathered in the comb is taken away by force. Therefore one who accumulates money should realize that he may be harassed by the government or by thieves or even killed by enemies. Especially in this age of Kali-yuga, it is said that instead of protecting the money of the citizens, the government itself will take away the money with the force of law. The learned *brāhmaṇa* had therefore decided that he should not accumulate any money. One should own as much as he immediately needs. There is no need to keep a big balance at hand, along with the fear that it may be plundered by the government or by thieves.

TEXT 37

अनीहः परितुष्टात्मा यदृच्छोपनतादहम् ।
नो चेच्छये बह्वहानि महाहिरिव सत्त्ववान् ॥३७॥

anīhaḥ parituṣṭātmā
yadṛcchopanatād aham

no cec chaye bahv-ahāni
mahāhir iva sattvavān

anīhaḥ—with no desire to possess more; *parituṣṭa*—very satisfied; *ātmā*—self; *yadṛcchā*—in its own way, without endeavor; *upanatāt*—by things brought in by possession; *aham*—I; *no*—not; *cet*—if so; *śaye*—I lie down; *bahu*—many; *ahāni*—days; *mahā-ahiḥ*—a python; *iva*—like; *sattva-vān*—enduring.

TRANSLATION

I do not endeavor to get anything, but am satisfied with whatever is achieved in its own way. If I do not get anything, I am patient and unagitated like a python and lie down in this way for many days.

PURPORT

One should learn detachment from the bumblebees, for they collect drops of honey here and there and keep it in their honeycomb, but then someone comes and by force takes all the honey away, leaving the bumblebees with nothing. Therefore one should learn from the bumblebee not to keep more money than one needs. Similarly, one should learn from the python to stay in one place for many, many days without food and then eat only if something comes in its own way. Thus the learned *brāhmaṇa* gave instructions gained from two creatures, namely the bumblebee and the python.

TEXT 38

क्वचिदल्पं क्वचिद् भूरि भुञ्जेऽन्नं स्वाद्वस्वादु वा ।
क्वचिद् भूरिगुणोपेतं गुणहीनमुत क्वचित् ।
श्रद्धयोपहृतं क्वापि कदाचिन्मानवर्जितम् ।
भुञ्जे भुक्त्वाथ कस्मिंश्चिद् दिवा नक्तं यदृच्छया॥३८॥

kvacid alpaṁ kvacid bhūri
bhuñje 'nnaṁ svādv asvādu vā
kvacid bhūri guṇopetaṁ
guṇa-hīnam uta kvacit

śraddhayopahṛtaṁ kvāpi
kadācin māna-varjitam
bhuñje bhuktvātha kasmiṁś cid
divā naktaṁ yadṛcchayā

kvacit—sometimes; *alpam*—very little; *kvacit*—sometimes; *bhūri*—a great quantity; *bhuñje*—I eat; *annam*—food; *svādu*—palatable; *asvādu*—stale; *vā*—either; *kvacit*—sometimes; *bhūri*—great; *guṇa-upetam*—a nice flavor; *guṇa-hīnam*—without flavor; *uta*—whether; *kvacit*—sometimes; *śraddhayā*—respectfully; *upahṛtam*—brought by someone; *kvāpi*—sometimes; *kadācit*—sometimes; *māna-varjitam*—offered without respect; *bhuñje*—I eat; *bhuktvā*—after eating; *atha*—as such; *kasmin cit*—sometimes, in some place; *divā*—during the daytime; *naktam*—or at night; *yadṛcchayā*—as it is available.

TRANSLATION

Sometimes I eat a very small quantity and sometimes a great quantity. Sometimes the food is very palatable, and sometimes it is stale. Sometimes prasāda is offered with great respect, and sometimes food is given neglectfully. Sometimes I eat during the day and sometimes at night. Thus I eat what is easily available.

TEXT 39

क्षौमं दुकूलमजिनं चीरं वल्कलमेव वा ।
वसेऽन्यदपि सम्प्राप्तं दिष्टभुक् तुष्टधीरहम् ॥३९॥

kṣaumaṁ dukūlam ajinaṁ
cīraṁ valkalam eva vā
vase 'nyad api samprāptaṁ
diṣṭa-bhuk tuṣṭa-dhīr aham

kṣaumam—clothing made of linen; *dukūlam*—silk or cotton; *ajinam*—deerskin; *cīram*—loincloth; *valkalam*—bark; *eva*—as it is; *vā*—either; *vase*—I put on; *anyat*—something else; *api*—although;

samprāptam—as available; *diṣṭa-bhuk*—because of destiny; *tuṣṭa*—satisfied; *dhīḥ*—mind; *aham*—I am.

TRANSLATION

To cover my body I use whatever is available, whether it be linen, silk, cotton, bark or deerskin, according to my destiny, and I am fully satisfied and unagitated.

TEXT 40

क्वचिच्छये धरोपस्थे तृणपर्णाश्मभस्मसु ।
क्वचित् प्रासादपर्यङ्के कशिपौ वा परेच्छया ॥४०॥

kvacic chaye dharopasthe
tṛṇa-parṇāśma-bhasmasu
kvacit prāsāda-paryaṅke
kaśipau vā parecchayā

kvacit—sometimes; *śaye*—I lie down; *dhara-upasthe*—on the surface of the earth; *tṛṇa*—on grass; *parṇa*—leaves; *aśma*—stone; *bhasmasu*—or a pile of ashes; *kvacit*—sometimes; *prāsāda*—in palaces; *paryaṅke*—on a first-class bedstead; *kaśipau*—on a pillow; *vā*—either; *para*—of another; *icchayā*—by the wish.

TRANSLATION

Sometimes I lie on the surface of the earth, sometimes on leaves, grass or stone, sometimes on a pile of ashes, or sometimes, by the will of others, in a palace on a first-class bed with pillows.

PURPORT

The learned *brāhmaṇa's* description indicates different types of births, for one lies down according to one's body. Sometimes one takes birth as an animal and sometimes as a king. When he takes birth as an animal he must lie down on the ground, and when he takes birth as a king or a very rich man he is allowed to lie in first-class rooms in huge palaces decorated with beds and other furniture. Such facilities are not available, however, at the sweet will of the living entity; rather, they are available by the supreme will (*parecchayā*), or by the arrangement of *māyā*. As stated in *Bhagavad-gītā* (18.61):

īśvaraḥ sarva-bhūtānāṁ
hṛd-deśe 'rjuna tiṣṭhati
bhrāmayan sarva-bhūtāni
yantrārūḍhāni māyayā

"The Supreme Lord is situated in everyone's heart, O Arjuna, and is directing the wanderings of all living entities, who are seated as on a machine, made of the material energy." The living entity, according to his material desires, receives different types of bodies, which are nothing but machines offered by material nature according to the order of the Supreme Personality of Godhead. By the will of the Supreme, one must take different bodies with different means for lying down.

TEXT 41

क्वचित् स्नातोऽनुलिप्ताङ्गः सुवासाः स्रग्व्यलंकृतः ।
रथेभाश्वैश्चरे क्वापि दिग्वासा ग्रहवद् विभो ॥४१॥

kvacit snāto 'nuliptāṅgaḥ
suvāsāḥ sragvy alaṅkṛtaḥ
rathebhāśvaiś care kvāpi
dig-vāsā grahavad vibho

kvacit—sometimes; *snātaḥ*—bathing very nicely; *anulipta-aṅgaḥ*—with sandalwood pulp smeared all over the body; *su-vāsāḥ*—dressing with very nice garments; *sragvī*—decorated with garlands of flowers; *alaṅkṛtaḥ*—bedecked with various types of ornaments; *ratha*—on a chariot; *ibha*—on an elephant; *aśvaiḥ*—or on the back of a horse; *care*—I wander; *kvāpi*—sometimes; *dik-vāsāḥ*—completely naked; *graha-vat*—as if haunted by a ghost; *vibho*—O lord.

TRANSLATION

O my lord, sometimes I bathe myself very nicely, smear sandalwood pulp all over my body, put on a flower garland, and dress in

fine garments and ornaments. Then I travel like a king on the back of an elephant or on a chariot or horse. Sometimes, however, I travel naked, like a person haunted by a ghost.

TEXT 42

नाहं निन्दे न च स्तौमि स्वभावविषमं जनम् ।
एतेषां श्रेय आशासे उतैकात्म्यं महात्मनि ॥४२॥

nāhaṁ ninde na ca staumi
sva-bhāva-viṣamaṁ janam
eteṣāṁ śreya āśāse
utaikātmyaṁ mahātmani

na—not; *aham*—I; *ninde*—blaspheme; *na*—nor; *ca*—also; *staumi*—praise; *sva-bhāva*—whose nature; *viṣamam*—contradictory; *janam*—a living entity or human being; *eteṣām*—of all of them; *śreyaḥ*—the ultimate benefit; *āśāse*—I pray for; *uta*—indeed; *aikātmyam*—oneness; *mahā-ātmani*—in the Supersoul, the Parabrahman (Kṛṣṇa).

TRANSLATION

Different people are of different mentalities. Therefore it is not my business either to praise them or to blaspheme them. I only desire their welfare, hoping that they will agree to become one with the Supersoul, the Supreme Personality of Godhead, Kṛṣṇa.

PURPORT

As soon as one comes to the platform of *bhakti-yoga*, one understands fully the Supreme Personality of Godhead, Vāsudeva, is the goal of life (*vāsudevaḥ sarvam iti sa mahātmā sudurlabhaḥ*). This is the instruction of all the Vedic literature (*vedaiś ca sarvair aham eva vedyaḥ, sarva dharmān parityajya mām ekaṁ śaraṇaṁ vraja*). There is no use in praising someone for material qualifications or blaspheming him for material disqualifications. In the material world, good and bad have no meaning because if one is good he may be elevated to a higher planetary system and if one is bad he may be degraded to the lower planetary systems. People of different mentalities are sometimes elevated and sometimes degraded, but this is not the goal of life. Rather, the goal of life is to become free from elevation and degradation and take to Kṛṣṇa consciousness. Therefore a saintly person does not discriminate between that which is supposedly good and supposedly bad; rather, he desires for everyone to be happy in Kṛṣṇa consciousness, which is the ultimate goal of life.

TEXT 43

विकल्पं जुहुयाच्चित्तौ तां मनस्यर्थविभ्रमे ।
मनो वैकारिके हुत्वा तं मायायां जुहोत्यनु ॥४३॥

vikalpaṁ juhuyāc cittau
tāṁ manasy artha-vibhrame
mano vaikārike hutvā
taṁ māyāyāṁ juhoty anu

vikalpam—discrimination (between good and bad, one person and another, one nation and another, and all similar discrimination); *juhuyāt*—one should offer as oblations; *cittau*—in the fire of consciousness; *tām*—that consciousness; *manasi*—in the mind; *artha-vibhrame*—the root of all acceptance and rejection; *manaḥ*—that mind; *vaikārike*—in false ego, identification of oneself with matter; *hutvā*—offering as oblations; *tam*—this false ego; *māyāyām*—in the total material energy; *juhoti*—offers as oblations; *anu*—following this principle.

TRANSLATION

The mental concoction of discrimination between good and bad should be accepted as one unit and then invested in the mind, which should then be invested in the false ego. The false ego should be invested in the total material energy. This is the process of fighting false discrimination.

PURPORT

This verse describes how a *yogī* can become free from material affection. Because of material attraction, a *karmī* cannot see himself. *Jñānīs* can discriminate between matter and spirit, but the *yogīs*, the best of whom are the *bhakti-yogīs*, want to return home, back to Godhead. The *karmīs* are completely in illusion, the *jñānīs* are neither in illusion nor in positive knowledge, but the *yogīs*, especially the *bhakti-yogīs*, are completely on the spiritual platform. As confirmed in *Bhagavad-gītā* (14.26):

māṁ ca yo 'vyabhicāreṇa
bhakti-yogena sevate
sa guṇān samatītyaitān
brahma-bhūyāya kalpate

"One who engages in full devotional service, who does not fall down under any circumstance, at once transcends the modes of material nature and thus comes to the level of Brahman." Thus a devotee's position is secure. A devotee is at once elevated to the spiritual platform. Others, such as *jñānīs* and *haṭha-yogīs*, can only gradually ascend to the spiritual platform by nullifying their material discrimination on the platform of psychology and nullifying the false ego, by which one thinks, "I am this body, a product of matter." One must merge the false ego into the total material energy and merge the total material energy into the supreme energetic. This is the process of becoming free from material attraction.

TEXT 44

आत्मानुभूतौ तां मायां जुहुयात् सत्यदृङ् मुनिः ।
ततो निरीहो विरमेत् स्वानुभूत्यात्मनि स्थितः ॥४४॥

ātmānubhūtau tāṁ māyāṁ
juhuyāt satya-dṛṅ muniḥ
tato nirīho viramet
svānubhūty-ātmani sthitaḥ

ātma-anubhūtau—unto self-realization; *tām*—that; *māyām*—the false ego of material existence; *juhuyāt*—should offer as an oblation; *satya-dṛk*—one who has actually realized the ultimate truth; *muniḥ*—such a thoughtful person; *tataḥ*—because of this self-realization; *nirīhaḥ*—without material desires; *viramet*—one must completely retire from material activities; *sva-anubhūti-ātmani*—in self-realization; *sthitaḥ*—thus being situated.

TRANSLATION

A learned, thoughtful person must realize that material existence is illusion. This is possible only by self-realization. A self-realized person, who has actually seen the truth, should retire from all material activities, being situated in self-realization.

PURPORT

By an analytical study of the entire constitution of the body, one can surely come to the conclusion that the soul is different from all the body's material constituents, such as earth, water, fire and air. Thus the difference between the body and soul can be realized by a person who is thoughtful (*manīṣī* or *muni*), and after this realization of the individual spirit soul one can very easily understand the supreme spirit soul. If one thus realizes that the individual soul is subordinate to the supreme spirit soul, he achieves self-realization. As explained in the Thirteenth Chapter of *Bhagavad-gītā*, there are two souls within the body. The body is called *kṣetra*, and there are two *kṣetra-jñas*, or occupants of the body, namely the Supersoul (Paramātmā) and the individual soul. The Supersoul and the individual soul are like two birds sitting on the same tree (the material body). One bird, the individual, forgetful bird, is eating the fruit of the tree, not caring for the instructions of the other bird, which is only a witness to the activities of the first bird, who is his friend. When the forgetful bird comes to understand the supreme friend who is always with him and trying to give him guidance in different bodies, he takes shelter at the lotus feet of that supreme bird. As explained in the *yoga* process, *dhyānāvasthita-tad-gatena manasā paśyanti yaṁ yoginaḥ*. When one actually becomes a perfect *yogī*, by meditation he can see the supreme friend and surrender unto Him. This is the beginning of *bhakti-yoga*, or actual life in Kṛṣṇa consciousness.

TEXT 45

स्वात्मवृत्तं मयेत्थं ते सुगुप्तमपि वर्णितम् ।
व्यपेतं लोकशास्त्राभ्यां भवान् हि भगवत्परः ॥४५॥

svātma-vṛttaṁ mayetthaṁ te
suguptam api varṇitam

vyapetaṁ loka-śāstrābhyāṁ
bhavān hi bhagavat-paraḥ

sva-ātma-vṛttam—the information of the history of self-realization; *mayā*—by me; *ittham*—in this way; *te*—unto you; *su-guptam*—extremely confidential; *api*—although; *varṇitam*—explained; *vyapetam*—without; *loka-śāstrābhyām*—the opinion of the common man or common literatures; *bhavān*—your good self; *hi*—indeed; *bhagavat-paraḥ*—having fully realized the Personality of Godhead.

TRANSLATION

Prahlāda Mahārāja, you are certainly a self-realized soul and a devotee of the Supreme Lord. You do not care for public opinion or so-called scriptures. For this reason I have described to you without hesitation the history of my self-realization.

PURPORT

A person who is actually a devotee of Kṛṣṇa does not care about so-called public opinion and Vedic or philosophical literatures. Prahlāda Mahārāja, who is such a devotee, always defied the false instructions of his father and the so-called teachers who were appointed to teach him. Instead, he simply followed the instructions of Nārada Muni, his *guru*, and thus he always remained a stalwart devotee. This is the nature of an intelligent devotee. The *Śrīmad-Bhāgavatam* instructs, *yajñaiḥ saṅkīrtana-prāyair yajanti hi sumedhasaḥ.* One who is actually very intelligent must join the Kṛṣṇa consciousness movement, realizing his own self as an eternal servant of Kṛṣṇa, and thus practice constant chanting of the holy name of the Lord—Hare Kṛṣṇa, Hare Kṛṣṇa, Kṛṣṇa Kṛṣṇa, Hare Hare/ Hare Rāma, Hare Rāma, Rāma Rāma, Hare Hare.

TEXT 46

श्रीनारद उवाच
धर्मं पारमहंस्यं वै मुनेः श्रुत्वासुरेश्वरः ।
पूजयित्वा ततः प्रीत आमन्त्र्य प्रययौ गृहम् ॥४६॥

śrī-nārada uvāca
dharmaṁ pāramahaṁsyaṁ vai
muneḥ śrutvāsureśvaraḥ
pūjayitvā tataḥ prīta
āmantrya prayayau gṛham

śrī-nāradaḥ uvāca—Śrī Nārada Muni said; *dharmam*—the occupational duty; *pāramahaṁsyam*—of the *paramahaṁsas*, the most perfect human beings; *vai*—indeed; *muneḥ*—from the saintly person; *śrutvā*—thus hearing; *asura-īśvaraḥ*—the King of the *asuras*, Prahlāda Mahārāja; *pūjayitvā*—by worshiping the saintly person; *tataḥ*—thereafter; *prītaḥ*—being very pleased; *āmantrya*—taking permission; *prayayau*—left that place; *gṛham*—for his home.

TRANSLATION

Nārada Muni continued: After Prahlāda Mahārāja, the King of the demons, heard these instructions from the saint, he understood the occupational duties of a perfect person [paramahaṁsa]. Thus he duly worshiped the saint, took his permission and then left for his own home.

PURPORT

As quoted in *Caitanya-caritāmṛta* (*Madhya* 8.128), Śrī Caitanya Mahāprabhu said:

kibā vipra, kibā nyāsī, śūdra kene naya
yei kṛṣṇa-tattva-vettā sei 'guru' haya

A *guru*, or spiritual master, can be anyone who is well conversant with the science of Kṛṣṇa. Therefore although Prahlāda Mahārāja was a *gṛhastha* ruling over the demons, he was a *paramahaṁsa*, the best of human beings, and thus he is our *guru*. In the list of *gurus*, or authorities, Prahlāda Mahārāja's name is therefore mentioned:

svayambhūr nāradaḥ śambhuḥ
kumāraḥ kapilo manuḥ

prahlādo janako bhīṣmo
balir vaiyāsakir vayam
(*Bhāg.* 6.3.20)

The conclusion is that a *paramahaṁsa* is an exalted devotee (*bhagavat-priya*). Such a *paramahaṁsa* may be in any stage of life—*brahmacārī, gṛhastha, vānaprastha* or *sannyāsa*—and be equally liberated and exalted.

Thus end the Bhaktivedanta purports of the Seventh Canto, Thirteenth Chapter, of the Śrīmad-Bhāgavatam, *entitled "The Behavior of a Perfect Person."*

CHAPTER FOURTEEN

Ideal Family Life

This chapter describes the occupational duties of the householder according to the time, the country and the performer. When Yudhiṣṭhira Mahārāja became very much inquisitive about the occupational duties for the householder, Nārada Muni advised him that a *gṛhastha's* first duty is to be fully dependent on Vāsudeva, Kṛṣṇa, and to try to satisfy Him in all respects by executing one's prescribed devotional service. This devotional service will depend on the instructions of authorities and the association of devotees who are actually engaged in devotional service. The beginning of devotional service is *śravaṇam*, or hearing. One must hear from the mouths of realized souls. In this way the *gṛhastha's* attraction to his wife and children will gradually be reduced.

As for the maintenance of his family, a *gṛhastha*, while earning what he requires for his living, must be very conscientious and must not undergo extraordinary endeavor simply to accumulate money and unnecessarily increase in material comforts. Although a *gṛhastha* should externally be very active in earning his livelihood, he should internally be situated as a fully self-realized person, without attachment for material gains. His dealings with family members or friends should be performed simply to fulfill their purpose; one should not be extravagantly engaged in this way. Instructions from family members and society should be accepted superficially, but in essence the *gṛhastha* should be engaged in occupational duties advised by the spiritual master and *śāstra*. Specifically a *gṛhastha* should engage in agricultural activities to earn money. As stated in *Bhagavad-gītā* (18.44), *kṛṣi-go-rakṣya-vāṇijyam*—agriculture, cow protection and trade—are special duties of *gṛhasthas*. If by chance or by the grace of the Lord more money comes, it should be properly engaged for the Kṛṣṇa consciousness movement. One should not be eager to earn more money simply for sensual pleasure. A *gṛhastha* should always remember that one who is endeavoring to accumulate more money than necessary is to be considered a thief and is punishable by the laws of nature.

A *gṛhastha* should be very much affectionate toward lower animals, birds and bees, treating them exactly like his own children. A *gṛhastha* should not indulge in killing animals or birds for sense gratification. He should provide the necessities of life even to the dogs and the lowest creatures and should not exploit others for sense gratification. Factually, according to the instructions of *Śrīmad-Bhāgavatam*, every *gṛhastha* is a great communist who provides the means of living for everyone. Whatever a *gṛhastha* may possess he should equally distribute to all living entities, without discrimination. The best process is to distribute *prasāda.*

A *gṛhastha* should not be very much attached to his wife; he should engage even his own wife in serving a guest with all attention. Whatever money a *gṛhastha* accumulates by the grace of God he should spend in five activities, namely worshiping the Supreme Personality of Godhead, receiving Vaiṣṇavas and saintly persons, distributing *prasāda* to the general public and to all living entities, offering *prasāda* to his forefathers, and also offering *prasāda* to his own self. *Gṛhasthas* should always be ready to worship everyone as mentioned above. The *gṛhastha* should not eat anything not offered to the Supreme Personality of Godhead. As it is said in the *Bhagavad-gītā* (3.13), *yajña-śiṣṭāśinaḥ santo mucyante sarva-kilbiṣaiḥ:* "The devotees of the Lord are released from all kinds of sins because they eat food that is offered first for sacrifice." The *gṛhastha* should also visit the holy places of pilgrimage mentioned in the *Purāṇas.* In this way he should fully engage in worshiping the Supreme Personality of Godhead for the benefit of his family, his society, his country, and humanity at large.

TEXT 1

श्रीयुधिष्ठिर उवाच

गृहस्थ एतां पदवीं विधिना येन चाञ्जसा ।
यायाद्देवऋषे ब्रूहि मादृशो गृहमूढधीः ॥ १ ॥

śrī-yudhiṣṭhira uvāca
gṛhastha etāṁ padavīṁ
vidhinā yena cāñjasā
yāyād deva-ṛṣe brūhi
mādṛśo gṛha-mūḍha-dhīḥ

śrī-yudhiṣṭhiraḥ uvāca—Yudhiṣṭhira Mahārāja said; *gṛhasthaḥ*—a person living with his family; *etām*—this (the process mentioned in the previous chapter); *padavīm*—position of liberation; *vidhinā*—according to the instructions of Vedic scripture; *yena*—by which; *ca*—also; *añjasā*—easily; *yāyāt*—may get; *deva-ṛṣe*—O great sage among the demigods; *brūhi*—kindly explain; *mādṛśaḥ*—such as me; *gṛha-mūḍha-dhīḥ*—completely ignorant of the goal of life.

TRANSLATION

Mahārāja Yudhiṣṭhira inquired from Nārada Muni: O my lord, O great sage, kindly explain how we who are staying at home without knowledge of the goal of life may also easily attain liberation, according to the instructions of the Vedas.

PURPORT

In the previous chapters the great sage Nārada has explained how a *brahmacārī*, a *vānaprastha* and a *sannyāsī* should act. He first explained the dealings of a *brahmacārī*, *vānaprastha* and *sannyāsī* because these three *āśramas*, or statuses of life, are extremely important for fulfillment of the goal of life. One should note that in the *brahmacārī-āśrama*, *vānaprastha-āśrama* and *sannyāsa-āśrama* there is no scope for sex life, whereas sex is allowed in *gṛhastha* life under regulations. Nārada Muni, therefore, first described *brahmacarya*, *vānaprastha* and *sannyāsa* because he wanted to stress that sex is not at all necessary, although one who absolutely requires it is allowed to enter *gṛhastha* life, or household life, which is also regulated by the *śāstras* and *guru*. Yudhiṣṭhira Mahārāja could understand all this. Therefore, as a *gṛhastha*, he presented himself as *gṛha-mūḍha-dhīḥ*, one who is completely ignorant of the goal of life. A person who remains a householder in family life is certainly ignorant of life's goal; he is not very much advanced in intelligence. As soon as possible, one should give up his so-called comfortable life at home and prepare to undergo austerity, or *tapasya*. *Tapo divyaṁ putrakā*. According to the instructions given by Ṛṣabhadeva to His sons, we should not create a so-called comfortable situation, but must prepare to undergo austerity. This is how a human being should actually live to fulfill life's ultimate goal.

TEXT 2

श्रीनारद उवाच
गृहेष्ववस्थितो राजन्क्रियाः कुर्वन्यथोचिताः ।
वासुदेवार्पणं साक्षादुपासीत महामुनीन् ॥ २ ॥

śrī-nārada uvāca
gṛheṣv avasthito rājan
kriyāḥ kurvan yathocitāḥ
vāsudevārpaṇaṁ sākṣād
upāsīta mahā-munīn

śrī-nāradaḥ uvāca—Śrī Nārada Muni replied; *gṛheṣu*—at home; *avasthitaḥ*—staying (a householder generally stays home with his wife and children); *rājan*—O King; *kriyāḥ*—activities; *kurvan*—performing; *yathocitāḥ*—suitable (as instructed by the *guru* and *śāstra*); *vāsudeva*—unto Lord Vāsudeva; *arpaṇam*—dedicating; *sākṣāt*—directly; *upāsīta*—should worship; *mahā-munīn*—the great devotees.

TRANSLATION

Nārada Muni replied: My dear King, those who stay at home as householders must act to earn their livelihood, and instead of trying to enjoy the results of their work themselves, they should offer these results to Kṛṣṇa, Vāsudeva. How to satisfy Vāsudeva in this life can be perfectly understood through the association of great devotees of the Lord.

PURPORT

The format for *gṛhastha* life should be dedication to the Supreme Personality of Godhead. In *Bhagavad-gītā* (6.1) it is said:

anāśritaḥ karma-phalaṁ
kāryaṁ karma karoti yaḥ
sa sannyāsī ca yogī ca
na niragnir na cākriyaḥ

"One who is unattached to the fruits of his work and who works as he is obligated is in the renounced order of life, and he is the true mystic, not he who lights no fire and performs no work." Whether one acts as a *brahmacārī, gṛhastha, vānaprastha* or *sannyāsī*, he must act only for the satisfaction of the Supreme Personality of Godhead, Vāsudeva—Kṛṣṇa, the son of Vasudeva. This should be the principle for everyone's life. Nārada Muni has already described the principles of life for a *brahmacārī, vānaprastha* and *sannyāsī*, and now he is describing how a *gṛhastha* should live. The basic principle is to satisfy the Supreme Personality of Godhead.

The science of satisfying the Supreme Lord can be learned as described here: *sākṣād upāsīta mahā-munīn.* The word *mahā-munīn* refers to great saintly persons or devotees. Saintly persons are generally known as *munis*, or thoughtful philosophers concerned with transcendental subject matters, and *mahā-munīn* refers to those who have not only thoroughly studied the goal of life but who are actually engaged in satisfying the Supreme Personality of Godhead, Vāsudeva. These persons are known as devotees. Unless one associates with devotees, one cannot learn the science of *vāsudevārpaṇa*, or dedicating one's life to Vāsudeva, Kṛṣṇa, the Supreme Personality of Godhead.

In India the principles of this science were followed strictly. Even fifty years ago, I saw that in the villages of Bengal and the suburbs of Calcutta, people engaged in hearing *Śrīmad-Bhāgavatam* daily when all their activities ended, or at least in the evening before going to bed. Everyone would hear the *Bhāgavatam. Bhāgavata* classes were held in every village, and thus people had the advantage of hearing *Śrīmad-Bhāgavatam*, which describes everything about the aim of life—liberation or salvation. This will be clearly explained in the next verses.

TEXTS 3–4

श्रृण्वन्भगवतोऽभीक्ष्णमवतारकथामृतम् ।
श्रद्दधानो यथाकालमुपशान्तजनावृतः ॥ ३ ॥
सत्सङ्गाच्छनकैः सङ्गमात्मजायात्मजादिषु ।
विमुञ्चेन्मुच्यमानेषु स्वयं स्वप्नवदुत्थितः ॥ ४ ॥

śṛṇvan bhagavato 'bhīkṣṇam
avatāra-kathāmṛtam
śraddadhāno yathā-kālam
upaśānta-janāvṛtaḥ

sat-saṅgāc chanakaiḥ saṅgam
ātma-jāyātmajādiṣu
vimuñcen mucyamāneṣu
svayaṁ svapnavad utthitaḥ

śṛṇvan—hearing; *bhagavataḥ*—of the Lord; *abhīkṣṇam*—always; *avatāra*—of the incarnations; *kathā*—narrations; *amṛtam*—the nectar; *śraddadhānaḥ*—being very faithful in hearing about the Supreme Personality of Godhead; *yathā-kālam*—according to time (generally a *gṛhastha* can find time in the evening or in the afternoon); *upaśānta*—completely relieved of material activities; *jana*—by persons; *āvṛtaḥ*—being surrounded; *sat-saṅgāt*—from such good association; *śanakaiḥ*—gradually; *saṅgam*—association; *ātma*—in the body; *jāyā*—wife; *ātma-ja-ādiṣu*—as well as in children; *vimuñcet*—one should get free from the attachment for such association; *mucyamāneṣu*—being severed (from him); *svayam*—personally; *svapna-vat*—like a dream; *utthitaḥ*—awakened.

TRANSLATION

A gṛhastha must associate again and again with saintly persons, and with great respect he must hear the nectar of the activities of the Supreme Lord and His incarnations as these activities are described in Śrīmad-Bhāgavatam and other Purāṇas. Thus one should gradually become detached from affection for his wife and children, exactly like a man awakening from a dream.

PURPORT

The Kṛṣṇa consciousness movement has been established to give *gṛhasthas* all over the world an opportunity to hear *Śrīmad-Bhāgavatam* and *Bhagavad-gītā* specifically. The process, as described in many ways, is one of hearing and chanting (*śṛṇvatāṁ sva-kathāḥ kṛṣṇaḥ puṇya-śravaṇa-kīrtanaḥ*). Everyone, especially the *gṛhasthas*, who are *mūḍha-dhī*, ignorant about the goal of life, should be given opportunities to hear about Kṛṣṇa. Simply by hearing, by attending lectures in the different centers of the Kṛṣṇa consciousness movement, where topics of Kṛṣṇa from *Bhagavad-gītā* and *Śrīmad-Bhāgavatam* are discussed, they will be purified of their sinful inclination for constant indulgence in illicit sex, meat-eating, intoxication and gambling, which have all become prominent in modern days. Thus they can be raised to the status of light. *Puṇya-śravaṇa-kīrtanaḥ.* Simply by joining the *kīrtana*—Hare Kṛṣṇa, Hare Kṛṣṇa, Kṛṣṇa Kṛṣṇa, Hare Hare/ Hare Rāma, Hare Rāma, Rāma Rāma, Hare Hare—and by hearing about Kṛṣṇa from *Bhagavad-gītā*, one must be purified, especially if he also takes *prasāda.* This is all going on in the Kṛṣṇa consciousness movement.

Another specific description here is *śṛṇvan bhagavato 'bhīkṣṇam avatāra-kathāmṛtam.* It is not that because one has once finished *Bhagavad-gītā* he should not hear it again. The word *abhīkṣṇam* is very important. We should hear again and again. There is no question of stopping: even if one has read these topics many times, he should go on reading again and again because *bhagavat-kathā*, the words spoken by Kṛṣṇa and spoken by Kṛṣṇa's devotees about Kṛṣṇa, are *amṛtam*, nectar. The more one drinks this *amṛtam*, the more he advances in his eternal life.

The human form of life is meant for liberation, but unfortunately, due to the influence of Kali-yuga, every day the *gṛhasthas* are working hard like asses. Early in the morning they rise and travel even a hundred miles away to earn bread. Especially in the Western countries, I have seen that people awaken at five o'clock to go to offices and factories to earn their livelihood. People in Calcutta and Bombay also do this every day. They work very hard in the office or factory, and again they spend three or four hours in transportation returning home. Then they retire at ten o'clock and again rise early in the morning to go to their offices and factories. This kind of hard labor is described in the *śāstras* as the life of pigs and stool-eaters. *Nāyaṁ deho deha-bhājāṁ nṛloke kaṣṭān kāmān arhate viḍ-bhujāṁ ye:* "Of all living entities who have accepted material bodies in this world, one who has been awarded this human form should not work hard day and night simply for sense gratification, which is available even for dogs and hogs that eat stool." (*Bhāg.* 5.5.1) One must find some time for hearing *Śrīmad-Bhāgavatam* and *Bhagavad-gītā.* This is Vedic culture. One should work eight hours at the most to earn his livelihood, and either in the afternoon or in the evening a householder should associate with devotees to hear about the incarnations of

Kṛṣṇa and His activities and thus be gradually liberated from the clutches of *māyā*. However, instead of finding time to hear about Kṛṣṇa, the householders, after working hard in offices and factories, find time to go to a restaurant or a club where instead of hearing about Kṛṣṇa and His activities they are very much pleased to hear about the political activities of demons and nondevotees and to enjoy sex, wine, women and meat and in this way waste their time. This is not *gṛhastha* life, but demoniac life. The Kṛṣṇa consciousness movement, however, with its centers all over the world, gives such fallen and condemned persons an opportunity to hear about Kṛṣṇa.

In a dream we form a society of friendship and love, and when we awaken we see that it has ceased to exist. Similarly, one's gross society, family and love are also a dream, and this dream will be over as soon as one dies. Therefore, whether one is dreaming in a subtle way or a gross way, these dreams are all false and temporary. One's real business is to understand that one is soul (*ahaṁ brahmāsmi*) and that his activities should therefore be different. Then one can be happy.

brahma-bhūtaḥ prasannātmā
na śocati na kāṅkṣati
samaḥ sarveṣu bhūteṣu
mad-bhaktiṁ labhate parām

"One who is transcendentally situated at once realizes the Supreme Brahman and becomes fully joyful. He never laments nor desires to have anything; he is equally disposed toward all living entities. In that state he attains pure devotional service unto Me." (Bg. 18.54) One who is engaged in devotional service can very easily be liberated from the dream of materialistic life.

TEXT 5

यावदर्थमुपासीनो देहे गेहे च पण्डितः ।
विरक्तो रक्तवत् तत्र नृलोके नरतां न्यसेत् ॥ ५ ॥

yāvad-artham upāsīno
dehe gehe ca paṇḍitaḥ

virakto raktavat tatra
nṛ-loke naratāṁ nyaset

yāvat-artham—as much endeavor for one's livelihood as necessary; *upāsīnaḥ*—earning; *dehe*—in the body; *gehe*—in family matters; *ca*—also; *paṇḍitaḥ*—one who is learned; *viraktaḥ*—not at all attached; *rakta-vat*—as if very much attached; *tatra*—in this; *nṛ-loke*—human society; *naratām*—the human form of life; *nyaset*—one should depict.

TRANSLATION

While working to earn his livelihood as much as necessary to maintain body and soul together, one who is actually learned should live in human society unattached to family affairs, although externally appearing very much attached.

PURPORT

This is the picture of ideal family life. When Śrī Caitanya Mahāprabhu asked Rāmānanda Rāya about the goal of life, Rāmānanda Rāya described it in different ways, according to the recommendations of the revealed scriptures, and finally Śrī Rāmānanda Rāya explained that one may stay in his own position, whether as a *brāhmaṇa*, a *śūdra*, a *sannyāsī* or whatever, but one must try to inquire about life's goal (*athāto brahma-jijñāsā*). This is the proper utilization of the human form of life. When one misuses the gift of the human form by unnecessarily indulging in the animal propensities of eating, sleeping, mating and defending and does not try to get out of the clutches of *māyā*, which subjects one to repeated birth, death, old age and disease, one is again punished by being forced to descend to the lower species and undergo evolution according to the laws of nature. *Prakṛteḥ kriyamāṇāni guṇaiḥ karmāṇi sarvaśaḥ.* Being completely under the grip of material nature, the living entity must evolve again from the lower species to the higher species until he at last returns to human life and gets the chance to be freed from the material clutches. A wise man, however, learns from the *śāstras* and *guru* that we living entities are all eternal but are put into troublesome conditions because of associating with different modes under the laws of material nature. He therefore concludes that in the human form of life he should not endeavor for unnecessary necessities, but should live a very simple life, just maintaining body and soul together. Certainly one requires some means of livelihood, and according to one's *varṇa* and *āśrama* this means of livelihood is prescribed in the *śāstras.* One should be satisfied with this. Therefore, instead of hankering for more and more money, a sincere devotee of the Lord tries to invent some ways to earn his livelihood, and when he does so Kṛṣṇa helps him. Earning one's livelihood, therefore, is not a problem. The real problem is how to get free from the bondage of birth, death and old age. Attaining this freedom, and not inventing unnecessary necessities, is the basic principle of Vedic civilization. One should be satisfied with whatever means of life comes automatically. The modern materialistic civilization is just the opposite of the ideal civilization. Every day the so-called leaders of modern society invent something contributing to a cumbersome way of life that implicates people more and more in the cycle of birth, death, old age and disease.

TEXT 6

ज्ञातयः पितरौ पुत्रा भ्रातरः सुहृदोऽपरे ।
यद् वदन्ति यदिच्छन्ति चानुमोदेत निर्ममः ॥ ६ ॥

jñātayaḥ pitarau putrā
bhrātaraḥ suhṛdo 'pare
yad vadanti yad icchanti
cānumodeta nirmamaḥ

jñātayaḥ—relatives, family members; *pitarau*—the father and mother; *putrāḥ*—children; *bhrātaraḥ*—brothers; *suhṛdaḥ*—friends; *apare*—and others; *yat*—whatever; *vadanti*—they suggest (in regard to one's means of livelihood); *yat*—whatever; *icchanti*—they wish; *ca*—and; *anumodeta*—he should agree; *nirmamaḥ*—but without taking them seriously.

TRANSLATION

An intelligent man in human society should make his own program of activities very simple. If there are suggestions from his

friends, children, parents, brothers or anyone else, he should externally agree, saying, "Yes, that is all right," but internally he should be determined not to create a cumbersome life in which the purpose of life will not be fulfilled.

TEXT 7

दिव्यं भौमं चान्तरीक्षं वित्तमच्युतनिर्मितम् ।
तत् सर्वमुपयुञ्जान एतत् कुर्यात् स्वतो बुधः ॥ ७ ॥

divyaṁ bhaumaṁ cāntarīkṣaṁ
vittam acyuta-nirmitam
tat sarvam upayuñjāna
etat kuryāt svato budhaḥ

divyam—easily obtained because of rainfall from the sky; *bhaumam*—obtained from the mines and the sea; *ca*—and; *āntarīkṣam*—obtained by chance; *vittam*—all property; *acyuta-nirmitam*—created by the Supreme Personality of Godhead; *tat*—those things; *sarvam*—all; *upayuñjāna*—utilizing (for all human society or all living beings); *etat*—this (maintaining body and soul together); *kuryāt*—one must do; *svataḥ*—obtained of itself, without extra endeavor; *budhaḥ*—the intelligent person.

TRANSLATION

The natural products created by the Supreme Personality of Godhead should be utilized to maintain the bodies and souls of all living entities. The necessities of life are of three types: those produced from the sky [from rainfall], from the earth [from the mines, the seas or the fields], and from the atmosphere [that which is obtained suddenly and unexpectedly].

PURPORT

We living entities in different forms are all children of the Supreme Personality of Godhead, as confirmed by the Lord in *Bhagavad-gītā* (14.4):

sarva-yoniṣu kaunteya
mūrtayaḥ sambhavanti yāḥ
tāsāṁ brahma mahad-yonir
ahaṁ bīja-pradaḥ pitā

"It should be understood that all species of life, O son of Kuntī, are made possible by birth in this material nature, and that I am the seed-giving father." The Supreme Lord, Kṛṣṇa, is the father of all living entities in different species and forms. One who is intelligent can see that all living entities in the 8,400,000 bodily forms are part of the Supreme Personality of Godhead and are His sons. Everything within the material and spiritual worlds is the property of the Supreme Lord (*īśāvāsyam idaṁ sarvam*), and therefore everything has a relationship with Him. Śrīla Rūpa Gosvāmī says in this regard:

prāpañcikatayā buddhyā
hari-sambandhi-vastunaḥ
mumukṣubhiḥ parityāgo
vairāgyaṁ phalgu kathyate

"One who rejects anything without knowledge of its relationship to Kṛṣṇa is incomplete in his renunciation." (*Bhakti-rasāmṛta-sindhu* 1.2.256) Although Māyāvādī philosophers say that the material creation is false, actually it is not false; it is factual, but the idea that everything belongs to human society is false. Everything belongs to the Supreme Personality of Godhead, for everything is created by Him. All living entities, being the Lord's sons, His eternal parts and parcels, have the right to use their father's property by nature's arrangement. As stated in the *Upaniṣads, tena tyaktena bhuñjīthā mā gṛdhaḥ kasya svid dhanam.* Everyone should be satisfied with the things allotted him by the Supreme Personality of Godhead; no one should encroach upon another's rights or property.

In *Bhagavad-gītā* it is said:

annād bhavanti bhūtāni
parjanyād anna-sambhavaḥ
yajñād bhavati parjanyo
yajñaḥ karma-samudbhavaḥ

"All living bodies subsist on food grains, which are produced from rains. Rains are produced by performance of *yajña* [sacrifice], and *yajña* is born of prescribed duties." (Bg. 3.14) When food grains are sufficiently produced, both animals and human beings can be nourished without difficulty for their maintenance. This is nature's arrangement. *Prakṛteḥ kriyamāṇāni guṇaiḥ karmāṇi sarvaśaḥ.* Everyone is acting under the influence of material nature, and only fools think they can improve upon what God has created. The householders are specifically responsible for seeing that the laws of the Supreme Personality of Godhead are maintained, without fighting between men, communities, societies or nations. Human society should properly utilize the gifts of God, especially the food grains that grow because of rain falling from the sky. As stated in *Bhagavad-gītā, yajñād bhavati parjanyaḥ.* So that rainfall will be regulated, humanity should perform *yajñas,* sacrifices. *Yajñas* were previously performed with offerings of oblations of ghee and food grains, but in this age, of course, this is no longer possible, for the production of ghee and food grains has diminished because of the sinful life of human society. However, people should take to Kṛṣṇa consciousness and chant the Hare Kṛṣṇa *mantra,* as recommended in the *śāstras* (*yajñaiḥ saṅkīrtana-prāyair yajanti hi sumedhasaḥ*). If people throughout the world take to the Kṛṣṇa consciousness movement and chant the easy sound vibration of the transcendental name and fame of the Supreme Personality of Godhead, there will be no scarcity of rainfall; consequently food grains, fruits and flowers will be properly produced, and all the necessities of life will be easily obtained. *Gṛhasthas,* or householders, should take the responsibility for organizing such natural production. It is therefore said, *tasyaiva hetoḥ prayateta kovidaḥ.* An intelligent person should try to spread Kṛṣṇa consciousness through the chanting of the holy name of the Lord, and all the necessities of life will automatically follow.

TEXT 8

यावद् भ्रियेत जठरं तावत् स्वत्वं हि देहिनाम् ।
अधिकं योऽभिमन्येत स स्तेनो दण्डमर्हति ॥ ८ ॥

yāvad bhriyeta jaṭharaṁ
tāvat svatvaṁ hi dehinām

adhikaṁ yo 'bhimanyeta
sa steno daṇḍam arhati

yāvat—as much as; *bhriyeta*—may be filled; *jaṭharam*—the stomach; *tāvat*—that much; *svatvam*—proprietorship; *hi*—indeed; *dehinām*—of the living entities; *adhikam*—more than that; *yaḥ*—anyone who; *abhimanyeta*—may accept; *saḥ*—he; *stenaḥ*—a thief; *daṇḍam*—punishment; *arhati*—deserves.

TRANSLATION

One may claim proprietorship to as much wealth as required to maintain body and soul together, but one who desires proprietorship over more than that must be considered a thief, and he deserves to be punished by the laws of nature.

PURPORT

By God's favor we sometimes get large quantities of food grains or suddenly receive some contribution or unexpected profit in business. In this way we may get more money than needed. So, how should that be spent? There is no need to accumulate money in the bank merely to increase one's bank balance. Such a mentality is described in *Bhagavad-gītā* (16.13) as asuric, demoniac.

idam adya mayā labdham
imaṁ prāpsye manoratham
idam astīdam api me
bhaviṣyati punar dhanam

"The demoniac person thinks, 'So much wealth do I have today, and I will gain more according to my schemes. So much is mine now, and it will increase in the future, more and more.' " The *asura* is concerned with how much wealth he has in the bank today and how it will increase tomorrow, but unrestricted accumulation of wealth is not permitted either by the *śāstra* or, in the modern age, by the government. Actually, if one has more than one requires for his necessities, the extra money should be spent for Kṛṣṇa. According to the Vedic civilization. it should all be given to the Kṛṣṇa consciousness movement, as ordered by the Lord Himself in *Bhagavad-gītā* (9.27):

yat karoṣi yad aśnāsi
yaj juhoṣi dadāsi yat
yat tapasyasi kaunteya
tat kuruṣva mad-arpaṇam

"O son of Kuntī, all that you do, all that you eat, all that you offer and give away, as well as all austerities that you may perform, should be done as an offering unto Me." *Gṛhasthas* should spend extra money only for the Kṛṣṇa consciousness movement.

The *gṛhasthas* should give contributions for constructing temples of the Supreme Lord and for preaching of *Śrīmad Bhagavad-gītā*, or Kṛṣṇa consciousness, all over the world. *Śṛṇvan bhagavato 'bhīkṣṇam avatāra-kathāmṛtam.* In the *śāstras*—the *Purāṇas* and other Vedic literatures—there are so many narrations describing the transcendental activities of the Supreme Personality of Godhead, and everyone should hear them again and again. For example, even if we read the entire *Bhagavad-gītā* every day, all eighteen chapters, in each reading we shall find a new explanation. That is the nature of transcendental literature. The Kṛṣṇa consciousness movement therefore affords one an opportunity to spend his extra earnings for the benefit of all human society by expanding Kṛṣṇa consciousness. In India especially we see hundreds and thousands of temples that were constructed by the wealthy men of society who did not want to be called thieves and be punished.

This verse is very important. As stated here, one who accumulates more money than needed is a thief, and by the laws of nature he will be punished. One who acquires more money than necessary becomes desirous of enjoying material comforts more and more. Materialists are inventing so many artificial necessities, and those who have money, being allured by such artificial necessities, try to accumulate money to possess more and more. This is the idea of modern economic development. Everyone is engaged in earning money, and the money is kept in the bank, which then offers money to the public. In this cycle of activities, everyone is engaged in getting more and more money, and therefore the ideal goal of human life is being lost. Concisely, it may be said that everyone is a thief and is liable to be punished. Punishment by the laws of nature takes place in the cycle of birth and death. No one dies fully satisfied by the fulfillment of material desires, for that is not possible. Therefore at the time of one's death one is very sorry, being unable to fulfill his desires. By the laws of nature one is then offered another body to fulfill his unsatisfied desires, and upon taking birth again, accepting another material body, one voluntarily accepts the threefold miseries of life.

TEXT 9

मृगोष्ट्रखरमर्काखुसरीसृप्खगमक्षिकाः ।
आत्मनः पुत्रवत् पश्येत्तैरेषामन्तरं कियत् ॥ ९ ॥

mṛgoṣṭra-khara-markākhu-
sarīsṛp khaga-makṣikāḥ
ātmanaḥ putravat paśyet
tair eṣām antaraṁ kiyat

mṛga—deer; *uṣṭra*—camels; *khara*—asses; *marka*—monkeys; *ākhu*—mice; *sarīsṛp*—snakes; *khaga*—birds; *makṣikāḥ*—flies; *ātmanaḥ*—of one's self; *putra-vat*—like the sons; *paśyet*—one should see; *taiḥ*—with those sons; *eṣām*—of these animals; *antaram*—difference; *kiyat*—how little.

TRANSLATION

One should treat animals such as deer, camels, asses, monkeys, mice, snakes, birds and flies exactly like one's own son. How little difference there actually is between children and these innocent animals.

PURPORT

One who is in Kṛṣṇa consciousness understands that there is no difference between the animals and the innocent children in one's home. Even in ordinary life, it is our practical experience that a household dog or cat is regarded on the same level as one's children, without any envy. Like children, the unintelligent animals are also sons of the Supreme

Personality of Godhead, and therefore a Kṛṣṇa conscious person, even though a householder, should not discriminate between children and poor animals. Unfortunately, modern society has devised many means for killing animals in different forms of life. For example, in the agricultural fields there may be many mice, flies and other creatures that disturb production, and sometimes they are killed by pesticides. In this verse, however, such killing is forbidden. Every living entity should be nourished by the food given by the Supreme Personality of Godhead. Human society should not consider itself the only enjoyer of all the properties of God; rather, men should understand that all the other animals also have a claim to God's property. In this verse even the snake is mentioned, indicating that a householder should not be envious even of a snake. If everyone is fully satisfied by eating food that is a gift from the Lord, why should there be envy between one living being and another? In modern days people are very much inclined toward communistic ideas of society, but we do not think that there can be any better communistic idea than that which is explained in this verse of *Śrīmad-Bhāgavatam*. Even in the communistic countries the poor animals are killed without consideration, although they also should have the right to take their allotted food with which to live.

TEXT 10

त्रिवर्गं नातिकृच्छ्रेण भजेत गृहमेध्यपि ।
यथादेशं यथाकालं यावद्दैवोपपादितम् ॥१०॥

tri-vargaṁ nātikṛcchreṇa
bhajeta gṛha-medhy api
yathā-deśaṁ yathā-kālaṁ
yāvad-daivopapāditam

tri-vargam—three principles, namely religiosity, economic development and sense gratification; *na*—not; *ati-kṛcchreṇa*—by very severe endeavor; *bhajeta*—should execute; *gṛha-medhī*—a person interested only in family life; *api*—although; *yathā-deśam*—according to the place; *yathā-kālam*—according to the time; *yāvat*—as much as; *daiva*—by the grace of the Lord; *upapāditam*—obtained.

TRANSLATION

Even if one is a householder rather than a brahmacārī, a sannyāsī or a vānaprastha, one should not endeavor very hard for religiosity, economic development or satisfaction of the senses. Even in householder life, one should be satisfied to maintain body and soul together with whatever is available with minimum endeavor, according to place and time, by the grace of the Lord. One should not engage oneself in ugra-karma.

PURPORT

In human life there are four principles to be fulfilled—*dharma, artha, kāma* and *mokṣa* (religion, economic development, sense gratification, and liberation). First one should be religious, observing various rules and regulations, and then one must earn some money for maintenance of his family and the satisfaction of his senses. The most important ceremony for sense gratification is marriage because sexual intercourse is one of the principal necessities of the material body. *Yan maithunādi-gṛhamedhi-sukhaṁ hi tuccham.* Although sexual intercourse is not a very exalted requisite in life, both animals and men require some sense gratification because of material propensities. One should be satisfied with married life and not expend energy for extra sense gratification or sex life.

As for economic development, the responsibility for this should be entrusted mainly to the *vaiśyas* and *gṛhasthas.* Human society should be divided into *varṇas* and *āśramas—brāhmaṇa, kṣatriya, vaiśya, śūdra, brahmacarya, gṛhastha, vānaprastha* and *sannyāsa.* Economic development is necessary for *gṛhasthas. Brāhmaṇa gṛhasthas* should be satisfied with a life of *adhyayana, adhyāpana, yajana* and *yājana*—being learned scholars, teaching others to be scholars, learning how to worship the Supreme Personality of Godhead, Viṣṇu, and also teaching others how to worship Lord Viṣṇu, or even the demigods. A *brāhmaṇa* should do this without remuneration, but he is allowed to accept charity from a person whom he teaches how to be a human being. As for the *kṣatriyas,* they are supposed to be the kings of the land, and the land should be distributed to the *vaiśyas* for agricultural activities, cow protection and trade. *Śūdras* must work; sometimes they should engage in occupational duties as cloth manufacturers, weavers, blacksmiths, goldsmiths, brass-smiths, and so on, or else they should engage in hard labor to produce food grains.

These are the different occupational duties by which men should earn their livelihood, and in this way human society should be simple. At the present moment, however, everyone is engaged in technological advancement, which is described in *Bhagavad-gītā* as *ugra-karma*—extremely severe endeavor. This *ugra-karma* is the cause of agitation within the human mind. Men are engaging in many sinful activities and becoming degraded by opening slaughterhouses, breweries and cigarette factories, as well as nightclubs and other establishments for sense enjoyment. In this way they are spoiling their lives. In all of these activities, of course, householders are involved, and therefore it is advised here, with the use of the word *api*, that even though one is a householder, one should not engage himself in severe hardships. One's means of livelihood should be extremely simple. As for those who are not *gṛhasthas*—the *brahmacārīs*, *vānaprasthas* and *sannyāsīs*—they don't have to do anything but strive for advancement in spiritual life. This means that three fourths of the entire population should stop sense gratification and simply be engaged in the advancement of Kṛṣṇa consciousness. Only one fourth of the population should be *gṛhastha*, and that should be according to laws of restricted sense gratification. The *gṛhasthas*, *vānaprasthas*, *brahmacārīs* and *sannyāsīs* should endeavor together with their total energy to become Kṛṣṇa conscious. This type of civilization is called *daiva-varṇāśrama.* One of the objectives of the Kṛṣṇa consciousness movement is to establish this *daiva-varṇāśrama*, but not to encourage so-called *varṇāśrama* without scientifically organized endeavor by human society.

TEXT 11

आश्वाघान्तेऽवसायिभ्यः कामान्संविभजेद् यथा ।
अप्येकामात्मनो दारां नृणां स्वत्वग्रहो यतः ॥११॥

āśvāghānte 'vasāyibhyaḥ
kāmān saṁvibhajed yathā
apy ekām ātmano dārāṁ
nṛṇāṁ svatva-graho yataḥ

ā—even up to; *śva*—the dog; *agha*—sinful animals or living entities; *ante avasāyibhyaḥ*—unto the *caṇḍālas*, the lowest of men (dog-eaters and hog-eaters); *kāmān*—the necessities of life; *saṁvibhajet*—should divide; *yathā*—as much as (deserved); *api*—even; *ekām*—one; *ātmanaḥ*—own; *dārām*—the wife; *nṛṇām*—of the people in general; *svatva-grahaḥ*—the wife is accepted as being identical with one's self; *yataḥ*—because of which.

TRANSLATION

Dogs, fallen persons and untouchables, including caṇḍālas [dog-eaters], should all be maintained with their proper necessities, which should be contributed by the householders. Even one's wife at home, with whom one is most intimately attached, should be offered for the reception of guests and people in general.

PURPORT

Although in modern society the dog is accepted as part of one's household paraphernalia, in the Vedic system of household life the dog is untouchable; as mentioned here, a dog may be maintained with proper food, but it cannot be allowed to enter one's house, what to speak of the bedroom. Outcastes or untouchable *caṇḍālas* should also be provided with the necessities for life. The word used in this connection is *yathā*, which means "as much as deserved." The outcastes should not be given money with which to indulge in more than they need, for otherwise they will misuse it. At the present moment, for example, low-class men are generally paid quite amply, but instead of using their money to cultivate knowledge and advance in life, such low-class men use their extra money for wine-drinking and similar sinful activities. As mentioned in *Bhagavad-gītā* (4.13), *cātur-varṇyaṁ mayā sṛṣṭaṁ guṇa-karma-vibhāgaśaḥ:* there must be four divisions of human society according to the work and qualities of men. Men with the lowest qualities cannot do any work that requires higher intelligence. However, although such a division of men must exist according to their quality and work, it is suggested herewith that everyone must have the necessities of life. The communists of the present day are in favor of supplying the necessities of life to everyone, but they consider only the human beings and not the lower animals. The *Bhāgavatam's* principles are so broad, however, that it recommends that the necessities of life be supplied to everyone, man or animal, regardless of good or bad qualities.

The idea of giving even one's wife to the service of the public is that one's intimate relationship with his wife, or one's excessive attachment for his wife, by which one thinks his wife to be his better half or to be identical with himself, must gradually be given up. As formerly suggested, the idea of ownership, even of one's family, must be abandoned. The dream of material life is the cause of bondage in the cycle of birth and death, and therefore one should give up this dream. Consequently, in the human form of life one's attachment for his wife should be given up, as suggested herein.

TEXT 12

जह्याद् यदर्थे स्वान् प्राणान्हन्याद् वा पितरं गुरुम् ।
तस्यां स्वत्वं स्त्रियां जह्याद् यस्तेन ह्यजितो जितः ॥१२॥

jahyād yad-arthe svān prāṇān
hanyād vā pitaraṁ gurum
tasyāṁ svatvaṁ striyāṁ jahyād
yas tena hy ajito jitaḥ

jahyāt—one may give up; *yat-arthe*—for whom; *svān*—one's own; *prāṇān*—life; *hanyāt*—one may kill; *vā*—or; *pitaram*—the father; *gurum*—the teacher or spiritual master; *tasyām*—unto her; *svatvam*—ownership; *striyām*—unto the wife; *jahyāt*—one must give up; *yaḥ*—one who (the Supreme Personality of Godhead); *tena*—by him; *hi*—indeed; *ajitaḥ*—cannot be conquered; *jitaḥ*—conquered.

TRANSLATION

One so seriously considers one's wife to be his own that he sometimes kills himself for her or kills others, including even his parents or his spiritual master or teacher. Therefore if one can give up his attachment to such a wife, he conquers the Supreme Personality of Godhead, who is never conquered by anyone.

PURPORT

Every husband is too much attached to his wife. Therefore, to give up one's connection with his wife is extremely difficult, but if one can somehow or other give it up for the service of the Supreme Personality of Godhead, then the Lord Himself, although not able to be conquered by anyone, comes very much under the control of the devotee. And if the Lord is pleased with a devotee, what is there that is unobtainable? Why should one not give up his affection for his wife and children and take shelter of the Supreme Personality of Godhead? Where is the loss of anything material? Householder life means attachment for one's wife, whereas *sannyāsa* means detachment from one's wife and attachment to Kṛṣṇa.

TEXT 13

क्रमिविड्भस्मनिष्ठान्तं क्वेदं तुच्छं कलेवरम् ।
क्व तदीयरतिर्भार्या क्वायमात्मा नभश्छदिः ॥१३॥

kṛmi-viḍ-bhasma-niṣṭhāntaṁ
kvedaṁ tucchaṁ kalevaram
kva tadīya-ratir bhāryā
kvāyam ātmā nabhaś-chadiḥ

kṛmi—insects, germs; *viṭ*—stool; *bhasma*—ashes; *niṣṭha*—attachment; *antam*—at the end; *kva*—what is; *idam*—this (body); *tuccham*—very insignificant; *kalevaram*—material tabernacle; *kva*—what is that; *tadīya-ratiḥ*—attraction for that body; *bhāryā*—wife; *kva ayam*—what is the value of this body; *ātmā*—the Supreme Soul; *nabhaḥ-chadiḥ*—all-pervading like the sky.

TRANSLATION

Through proper deliberation, one should give up attraction to his wife's body because that body will ultimately be transformed into small insects, stool or ashes. What is the value of this insignificant body? How much greater is the Supreme Being, who is all-pervading like the sky?

PURPORT

Here also, the same point is stressed: one should give up attachment for his wife—or, in other words, for sex life. If one is intelligent, he can think of his wife's body as nothing but a lump of matter that will ultimately be transformed into small insects, stool or ashes. In different societies there are different ways of dealing with the human body at the time of the funeral ceremony. In some societies the body is given to the vultures to be eaten, and therefore the body ultimately turns to vulture stool. Sometimes the body is merely abandoned, and in that case the body is consumed by small insects. In some societies the body is immediately burned after death, and thus it becomes ashes. In any case, if one intelligently considers the constitution of the body and the soul beyond it, what is the value of the body? *Antavanta ime dehā nityasyoktāḥ śarīriṇaḥ:* the body may perish at any moment, but the soul is eternal. If one gives up attachment for the body and increases his attachment for the spirit soul, his life is successful. It is merely a matter of deliberation.

TEXT 14

सिद्धैर्यज्ञावशिष्टार्थैः कल्पयेद् वृत्तिमात्मनः ।
शेषे स्वत्वं त्यजन्प्राज्ञः पदवीं महतामियात् ॥१४॥

siddhair yajñāvaśiṣṭārthaiḥ
kalpayed vṛttim ātmanaḥ
śeṣe svatvaṁ tyajan prājñaḥ
padavīṁ mahatām iyāt

siddhaiḥ—things obtained by the grace of the Lord; *yajñā-avaśiṣṭa-arthaiḥ*—things obtained after a sacrifice is offered to the Lord or after the recommended *pañca-sūnā yajña* is performed; *kalpayet*—one should consider; *vṛttim*—the means of livelihood; *ātmanaḥ*—for the self; *śeṣe*—at the end; *svatvam*—so-called proprietorship over one's wife, children, home, business and so on; *tyajan*—giving up; *prājñaḥ*—those who are wise; *padavīm*—the position; *mahatām*—of the great personalities who are fully satisfied in spiritual consciousness; *iyāt*—should achieve.

TRANSLATION

An intelligent person should be satisfied with eating prasāda [food offered to the Lord] or with performing the five different

kinds of yajña [pañca-sūnā]. By such activities, one can give up attachment for the body and so-called proprietorship with reference to the body. When one is able to do this, he is firmly fixed in the position of a mahātmā.

PURPORT

Nature already has an arrangement to feed us. By the order of the Supreme Personality of Godhead, there is an arrangement for eatables for every living entity within the 8,400,000 forms of life. *Eko bahūnāṁ yo vidadhāti kāmān.* Every living entity has to eat something, and in fact the necessities for his life have already been provided by the Supreme Personality of Godhead. The Lord has provided food for both the elephant and the ant. All living beings are living at the cost of the Supreme Lord, and therefore one who is intelligent should not work very hard for material comforts. Rather, one should save his energy for advancing in Kṛṣṇa consciousness. All created things in the sky, in the air, on land and in the sea belong to the Supreme Personality of Godhead, and every living being is provided with food. Therefore one should not be very much anxious about economic development and unnecessarily waste time and energy with the risk of falling down in the cycle of birth and death.

TEXT 15

देवानृषीन् नृभूतानि पितॄनात्मानमन्वहम् ।
स्ववृत्त्यागतवित्तेन यजेत पुरुषं पृथक् ॥१५॥

devān ṛṣīn nṛ-bhūtāni
pitṝn ātmānam anvaham
sva-vṛttyāgata-vittena
yajeta puruṣaṁ pṛthak

devān—unto the demigods; *ṛṣīn*—unto the great sages; *nṛ*—unto human society; *bhūtāni*—unto the living entities in general; *pitṝn*—unto the forefathers; *ātmānam*—one's self or the Supreme Self; *anvaham*—daily; *sva-vṛttyā*—by one's means of livelihood; *āgata-vittena*—money that automatically comes; *yajeta*—one should worship; *puruṣam*—the person situated in everyone's heart; *pṛthak*—separately.

TRANSLATION

Every day, one should worship the Supreme Being who is situated in everyone's heart, and on this basis one should separately worship the demigods, the saintly persons, ordinary human beings and living entities, one's forefathers and one's self. In this way one is able to worship the Supreme Being in the core of everyone's heart.

TEXT 16

यर्ह्यात्मनोऽधिकाराद्याः सर्वाः स्युर्यज्ञसम्पदः ।
वैतानिकेन विधिना अग्निहोत्रादिना यजेत् ॥१६॥

yarhy ātmano 'dhikārādyāḥ
sarvāḥ syur yajña-sampadaḥ
vaitānikena vidhinā
agni-hotrādinā yajet

yarhi—when; *ātmanaḥ*—of one's self; *adhikāra-ādyāḥ*—things possessed by him under full control; *sarvāḥ*—everything; *syuḥ*—becomes; *yajña-sampadaḥ*—paraphernalia for performing *yajña*, or the means for pleasing the Supreme Personality of Godhead; *vaitānikena*—with authorized books that direct the performance of *yajña; vidhinā*—according to regulative principles; *agni-hotra-ādinā*—by offering sacrifices to the fire, etc.; *yajet*—one should worship the Supreme Personality of Godhead.

TRANSLATION

When one is enriched with wealth and knowledge which are under his full control and by means of which he can perform yajña or please the Supreme Personality of Godhead, one must perform sacrifices, offering oblations to the fire according to the directions of the śāstras. In this way one should worship the Supreme Personality of Godhead.

PURPORT

If a *gṛhastha*, or householder, is sufficiently educated in Vedic knowledge and has become sufficiently rich to offer worship to please the Supreme Personality of Godhead, he must perform *yajñas* as directed by the authorized scriptures. *Bhagavad-gītā* (3.9) clearly says, *yajñārthāt karmaṇo 'nyatra loko 'yaṁ karma-bandhanaḥ:* everyone may be engaged in his occupational duties, but the result of these duties should be offered for sacrifice to satisfy the Supreme Lord. If one is fortunate enough to possess transcendental knowledge as well as the money with which to perform sacrifices, one must do it according to the directions given in the *śāstras.* It is said in *Śrīmad-Bhāgavatam* (12.3.52):

kṛte yad dhyāyato viṣṇuṁ
tretāyāṁ yajato makhaiḥ
dvāpare paricaryāyāṁ
kalau tad dhari-kīrtanāt

The entire Vedic civilization aims at satisfying the Supreme Personality of Godhead. This was possible in Satya-yuga by meditation upon the Supreme Lord within the core of one's heart and in Tretā-yuga by the performance of costly *yajñas.* The same goal could be achieved in Dvāpara-yuga by worship of the Lord in the temple, and in this age of Kali one can achieve the same goal by performing *saṅkīrtana-yajña.* Therefore one who has education and wealth must use them to satisfy the Supreme Personality of Godhead by helping the *saṅkīrtana* movement that has already begun—the Hare Kṛṣṇa movement, or Kṛṣṇa consciousness movement. All educated and wealthy persons must join this movement, since money and education are meant for service to the Supreme Personality of Godhead. If money and education are not engaged in the service of the Lord, these valuable assets must be engaged in the service of *māyā.* The education of so-called scientists, philosophers and poets is now engaged in the service of *māyā,* and the wealth of the rich is also engaged in *māyā's* service. The service of *māyā,* however, creates a chaotic condition in the world. Therefore the wealthy man and the educated man should sacrifice their knowledge and opulence by dedicating them for the satisfaction of the Supreme Lord and joining this *saṅkīrtana* movement (*yajñaiḥ saṅkīrtana-prāyair yajanti hi sumedhasaḥ*).

TEXT 17

न ह्यग्निमुखतोऽयं वै भगवान्सर्वयज्ञभुक् ।
इज्येत हविषा राजन्यथा विप्रमुखे हुतैः ॥१७॥

na hy agni-mukhato 'yaṁ vai
bhagavān sarva-yajña-bhuk
ijyeta haviṣā rājan
yathā vipra-mukhe hutaiḥ

na—not; *hi*—indeed; *agni*—fire; *mukhataḥ*—from the mouth or the flames; *ayam*—this; *vai*—certainly; *bhagavān*—Lord Śrī Kṛṣṇa; *sarva-yajña-bhuk*—the enjoyer of the results of all kinds of sacrifices; *ijyeta*—is worshiped; *haviṣā*—by offering of clarified butter; *rājan*—O King; *yathā*—as much as; *vipra-mukhe*—through the mouth of a *brāhmaṇa; hutaiḥ*—by offering him first-class food.

TRANSLATION

The Supreme Personality of Godhead, Śrī Kṛṣṇa, is the enjoyer of sacrificial offerings. Yet although His Lordship eats the oblations offered in the fire, my dear King, He is still more satisfied when nice food made of grains and ghee is offered to Him through the mouths of qualified brāhmaṇas.

PURPORT

As stated in *Bhagavad-gītā* (3.9), *yajñārthāt karmaṇo 'nyatra loko 'yaṁ karma-bandhanaḥ:* all fruitive activities should be performed for sacrifice, which should be directed toward pleasing Kṛṣṇa. As stated elsewhere in *Bhagavad-gītā* (5.29), *bhoktāraṁ yajña-tapasāṁ sarva-loka-maheśvaram:* He is the Supreme Lord and enjoyer of everything. However, although sacrifice may be offered to please Kṛṣṇa, He is more pleased when grains and ghee, instead of being offered in the fire, are prepared as *prasāda* and distributed, first to the *brāhmaṇas* and then to others. This system pleases Kṛṣṇa more than anything else. Furthermore, at the present time there is very little chance to offer sacrifices by pouring oblations of food grains and ghee into the fire. Especially in India, there is practically no ghee; for everything that should be done with ghee, people use a certain type of oil preparation. Oil, however, is never recommended for offering in a sacrificial fire. In Kali-yuga, the available quantity of food grains and ghee is gradually diminishing, and people are embarrassed that they cannot produce sufficient ghee and food grains.

Under the circumstances, the *śāstras* enjoin, *yajñaiḥ saṅkīrtana-prāyair yajanti hi sumedhasaḥ:* in this age, those who are intellectual offer *yajña,* or perform sacrifices, through the *saṅkīrtana* movement. Everyone should join the *saṅkīrtana* movement, offering to the fire of this movement the oblations of his knowledge and riches. In our *saṅkīrtana* movement, or Hare Kṛṣṇa movement, we offer sumptuous *prasāda* to the Deity and later distribute the same *prasāda* to the *brāhmaṇas,* the Vaiṣṇavas and then to the people in general. Kṛṣṇa's *prasāda* is offered to the *brāhmaṇas* and Vaiṣṇavas, and the *prasāda* of the *brāhmaṇas* and Vaiṣṇavas is offered to the general populace. This kind of sacrifice—chanting of the Hare Kṛṣṇa *mantra* and distribution of *prasāda*—is the most perfect and bona fide way of offering sacrifice for the pleasure of Yajña, or Viṣṇu.

TEXT 18

तस्माद् ब्राह्मणदेवेषु मर्त्यादिषु यथार्हतः ।
तैस्तैः कामैर्यजस्वैनं क्षेत्रज्ञं ब्राह्मणाननु ॥१८॥

tasmād brāhmaṇa-deveṣu
martyādiṣu yathārhataḥ
tais taiḥ kāmair yajasvainaṁ
kṣetra-jñaṁ brāhmaṇān anu

tasmāt—therefore; *brāhmaṇa-deveṣu*—through the *brāhmaṇas* and the demigods; *martya-ādiṣu*—through ordinary human beings and other living entities; *yathā-arhataḥ*—according to your ability; *taiḥ taiḥ*—with all those; *kāmaiḥ*—various objects of enjoyment such as sumptuous food, flower garlands, sandalwood paste, etc.; *yajasva*—you should worship; *enam*—this; *kṣetra-jñam*—Supreme Lord situated in the hearts of all beings; *brāhmaṇān*—the *brāhmaṇas; anu*—after.

TRANSLATION

Therefore, my dear King, first offer prasāda unto the brāhmaṇas and the demigods, and after sumptuously feeding them you may distribute prasāda to other living entities according to your ability.

In this way you will be able to worship all living entities—or, in other words, the supreme living entity within every living entity.

PURPORT

To distribute *prasāda* to all living entities, the process is that we must first offer *prasāda* to the *brāhmaṇas* and the Vaiṣṇavas, for the demigods are represented by the *brāhmaṇas.* In this way the Supreme Personality of Godhead, who is situated in everyone's heart, will be worshiped. This is the Vedic system of offering *praśāda.* Whenever there is a ceremony for distribution of *prasāda,* the *prasāda* is offered first to the *brāhmaṇas,* then to the children and old men, then to the women, and then to animals like dogs and other domestic animals. When it is said that Nārāyaṇa, the Supreme Being, is situated in everyone's heart, this does not mean that everyone has become Nārāyaṇa or that a particular poor man has become Nārāyaṇa. Such a conclusion is rejected herein.

TEXT 19

कुर्यादपरपक्षीयं मासि प्रौष्ठपदे द्विजः ।
श्राद्धं पित्रोर्यथावित्तं तद्बन्धूनां च वित्तवान् ॥१९॥

kuryād apara-pakṣīyaṁ
māsi prauṣṭha-pade dvijaḥ
śrāddhaṁ pitror yathā-vittaṁ
tad-bandhūnāṁ ca vittavān

kuryāt—one should perform; *apara-pakṣīyam*—during the fortnight of the dark moon; *māsi*—in the month of Āśvina (October–November); *prauṣṭha-pade*—in the month of Bhādra (August–September); *dvijaḥ*—twiceborn; *śrāddham*—oblations; *pitroḥ*—unto the forefathers; *yathā-vittam*—according to one's means of income; *tat-bandhūnām ca*—as well as relatives of forefathers; *vitta-vān*—one who is sufficiently rich.

TRANSLATION

A brāhmaṇa who is sufficiently rich must offer oblations to the forefathers during the dark-moon fortnight in the latter part of the month of Bhādra. Similarly, he should offer oblations to the

relatives of the forefathers during the mahālayā ceremonies in the month of Āśvina.*

TEXTS 20–23

अयने विषुवे कुर्याद् व्यतीपाते दिनक्षये ।
चन्द्रादित्योपरागे च द्वादश्यां श्रवणेषु च ॥२०॥
तृतीयायां शुक्लपक्षे नवम्यामथ कार्तिके ।
चतसृष्वप्यष्टकासु हेमन्ते शिशिरे तथा ॥२१॥
माघे च सितसप्तम्यां मघाराकासमागमे ।
राकया चानुमत्या च मासर्क्षाणि युतान्यपि ॥२२॥
द्वादश्यामनुराधा स्याच्छ्रवणस्तिस्र उत्तराः ।
तिसृष्वेकादशी वासु जन्मर्क्षश्रोणयोगयुक् ॥२३॥

ayane viṣuve kuryād
vyatīpāte dina-kṣaye
candrādityoparāge ca
dvādaśyāṁ śravaṇeṣu ca

tṛtīyāyāṁ śukla-pakṣe
navamyām atha kārtike
catasṛṣv apy aṣṭakāsu
hemante śiśire tathā

māghe ca sita-saptamyāṁ
maghā-rākā-samāgame
rākayā cānumatyā ca
māsarkṣāṇi yutāny api

dvādaśyām anurādhā syāc
chravaṇas tisra uttarāḥ
tisṛṣv ekādaśī vāsu
janmarkṣa-śroṇa-yoga-yuk

---

*The mahālayā festivals are observed on the fifteenth day of the dark fortnight of the month of Āśvina and mark the last day of the Vedic lunar year.

ayane—on the day when the sun begins to move north, or Makara-saṅkrānti, and on the day when the sun begins to move south, or Karkaṭa-saṅkrānti; *viṣuve*—on the Meṣa-saṅkrānti and on the Tulā-saṅkrānti; *kuryāt*—one should perform; *vyatīpāte*—in the *yoga* named Vyatīpāta; *dina-kṣaye*—on that day in which three *tithis* are combined; *candra-āditya-uparāge*—at the time of the eclipse of either the moon or the sun; *ca*—and also; *dvādaśyām śravaṇeṣu*—on the twelfth lunar day and in the *nakṣatra* named Śravaṇa; *ca*—and; *tṛtīyāyām*—on the Akṣaya-tṛtīyā day; *śukla-pakṣe*—in the bright fortnight of the month; *navamyām*—on the ninth lunar day; *atha*—also; *kārtike*—in the month of Kārtika (October–November); *catasṛṣu*—on the four; *api*—also; *aṣṭakāsu*—on the Aṣṭakās; *hemante*—before the winter season; *śiśire*—in the winter season; *tathā*—and also; *māghe*—in the month of Māgha (January–February); *ca*—and; *sita-saptamyām*—on the seventh lunar day of the bright fortnight; *maghā-rākā-samāgame*—in the conjunction of Maghā-*nakṣatra* and the full-moon day; *rākayā*—with a day of the completely full moon; *ca*—and; *anumatyā*—with a full-moon day when the moon is slightly less than completely full; *ca*—and; *māsa-ṛkṣāṇi*—the *nakṣatras* that are the sources of the names of the various months; *yutāni*—are conjoined; *api*—also; *dvādaśyām*—on the twelfth lunar day; *anurādhā*—the *nakṣatra* named Anurādhā; *syāt*—may occur; *śravaṇaḥ*—the *nakṣatra* named Śravaṇa; *tisraḥ*—the three (*nakṣatras*); *uttarāḥ*—the *nakṣatras* named Uttarā (Uttara-phalgunī, Uttarāṣāḍhā and Uttara-bhādrapadā); *tisṛṣu*—on three; *ekādaśī*—the eleventh lunar day; *vā*—or; *āsu*—on these; *janma-ṛkṣa*—of one's own *janma-nakṣatra*, or birth star; *śroṇa*—of Śravaṇa-*nakṣatra; yoga*—by a conjunction; *yuk*—having.

TRANSLATION

One should perform the śrāddha ceremony on the Makara-saṅkrānti [the day when the sun begins to move north] or on the Karkaṭa-saṅkrānti [the day when the sun begins to move south]. One should also perform this ceremony on the Meṣa-saṅkrānti day and the Tulā-saṅkrānti day, in the yoga named Vyatīpāta, on that day in which three lunar tithis are conjoined, during an eclipse of either the moon or the sun, on the twelfth lunar day, and in the Śravaṇa-nakṣatra. One should perform this ceremony on the Akṣaya-tṛtīyā day, on the ninth lunar day of the bright fortnight of

the month of Kārtika, on the four aṣṭakās in the winter season and cool season, on the seventh lunar day of the bright fortnight of the month of Māgha, during the conjunction of Maghā-nakṣatra and the full-moon day, and on the days when the moon is completely full, or not quite completely full, when these days are conjoined with the nakṣatras from which the names of certain months are derived. One should also perform the śrāddha ceremony on the twelfth lunar day when it is in conjunction with any of the nakṣatras named Anurādhā, Śravaṇa, Uttara-phalgunī, Uttarāṣāḍhā or Uttara-bhādrapadā. Again, one should perform this ceremony when the eleventh lunar day is in conjunction with either Uttara-phalgunī, Uttarāṣāḍhā or Uttara-bhādrapadā. Finally, one should perform this ceremony on days conjoined with one's own birth star [janma-nakṣatra] or with Śravaṇa-nakṣatra.

PURPORT

The word *ayana* means "path" or "going." The six months when the sun moves toward the north are called *uttarāyana*, or the northern path, and the six months when it moves south are called *dakṣiṇāyana*, or the southern path. These are mentioned in *Bhagavad-gītā* (8.24–25). The first day when the sun begins to move north and enter the zodiacal sign of Capricorn is called Makara-saṅkrānti, and the first day when the sun begins to move south and enter the sign of Cancer is called Karkaṭa-saṅkrānti. On these two days of the year, one should perform the *śrāddha* ceremony.

Viṣuva, or Viṣuva-saṅkrānti, means Meṣa-saṅkrānti, or the day on which the sun enters the sign Aries. Tulā-saṅkrānti is the day on which the sun enters the sign Libra. Both of these days occur only once within a year. The word *yoga* refers to a certain relationship between the sun and moon as they move in the sky. There are twenty-seven different degrees of *yoga*, of which the seventeenth is called Vyatīpāta. On the day when this occurs, one should perform the *śrāddha* ceremony. A *tithi*, or lunar day, consists of the distance between the longitude of the sun and that of the moon. Sometimes a *tithi* is less than twenty-four hours. When it starts after sunrise on a certain day and ends before the sunrise of the following day, the previous *tithi* and the following *tithi* both "touch" the twenty-four-hour day between the sunrises. This is called *tryaha-sparśa*, or a day touched by some portion of three *tithis*.

Śrīla Jīva Gosvāmī has given quotations from many *śāstras* stating that the *śrāddha* ceremony of oblations to the forefathers should not be performed on Ekādaśī *tithi*. When the *tithi* of the death anniversary falls on the Ekādaśī day, the *śrāddha* ceremony should be held not on Ekādaśī but on the next day, or *dvādaśī*. In the *Brahma-vaivarta Purāṇa* it is said:

ye kurvanti mahīpāla
śrāddhaṁ caikādaśī-dine
trayas te narakaṁ yānti
dātā bhoktā ca prerakaḥ

If one performs the *śrāddha* ceremony of oblations to the forefathers on the Ekādaśī *tithi*, then the performer, the forefathers for whom the *śrāddha* is observed, and the *purohita*, or the family priest who encourages the ceremony, all go to hell.

TEXT 24

त एते श्रेयसः काला नृणां श्रेयोविवर्धनाः ।
कुर्यात् सर्वात्मनैतेषु श्रेयोऽमोघं तदायुषः ॥२४॥

ta ete śreyasaḥ kālā
nṛṇāṁ śreyo-vivardhanāḥ
kuryāt sarvātmanaiteṣu
śreyo 'moghaṁ tad-āyuṣaḥ

te—therefore; *ete*—all these (descriptions of astronomical calculations); *śreyasaḥ*—of auspiciousness; *kālāḥ*—times; *nṛṇām*—for human beings; *śreyaḥ*—auspiciousness; *vivardhanāḥ*—increase; *kuryāt*—one should perform; *sarva-ātmanā*—by other activities (not only the *śrāddha* ceremony); *eteṣu*—in these (seasons); *śreyaḥ*—(causing) auspiciousness; *amogham*—and success; *tat*—of a human being; *āyuṣaḥ*—of the duration of life.

TRANSLATION

All of these seasonal times are considered extremely auspicious for humanity. At such times, one should perform all auspicious activities, for by such activities a human being attains success in his short duration of life.

PURPORT

When one comes to the human form of life through natural evolution, one must then take the responsibility for further progress. As stated in *Bhagavad-gītā* (9.25), *yānti deva-vratā devān:* one who worships the demigods can be promoted to their planets. *Yānti mad-yājino 'pi mām:* and if one practices devotional service to the Lord, he goes back home, back to Godhead. In the human form of life, therefore, one is meant to act auspiciously in order to return home, back to Godhead. Devotional service, however, does not depend on material conditions. *Ahaituky apratihatā.* Of course, for those who are engaged in fruitive activities on the material platform, the times and seasons mentioned above are extremely congenial.

TEXT 25

एषु स्नानं जपो होमो व्रतं देवद्विजार्चनम् ।
पितृदेवनृभूतेभ्यो यद्द दत्तं तद्ध्यनश्वरम् ॥२५॥

eṣu snānaṁ japo homo
vrataṁ deva-dvijārcanam
pitṛ-deva-nṛ-bhūtebhyo
yad dattaṁ tad dhy anaśvaram

eṣu—in all these (seasonal times); *snānam*—bathing in the Ganges, Yamunā or any other sacred places; *japaḥ*—chanting; *homaḥ*—performing fire sacrifices; *vratam*—executing vows; *deva*—the Supreme Lord; *dvija-arcanam*—worshiping the *brāhmaṇas* or Vaiṣṇavas; *pitṛ*—unto the forefathers; *deva*—demigods; *nṛ*—human beings in general; *bhūtebhyaḥ*—and all other living entities; *yat*—whatever; *dattam*—offered; *tat*—that; *hi*—indeed; *anaśvaram*—permanently beneficial.

TRANSLATION

During these periods of seasonal change, if one bathes in the Ganges, in the Yamunā or in another sacred place, if one chants, offers fire sacrifices or executes vows, or if one worships the Supreme Lord, the brāhmaṇas, the forefathers, the demigods and the living entities in general, whatever he gives in charity yields a permanently beneficial result.

TEXT 26

संस्कारकालो जायाया अपत्यस्यात्मनस्तथा ।
प्रेतसंस्था मृताहश्च कर्मण्यभ्युदये नृप ॥२६॥

saṁskāra-kālo jāyāyā
apatyasyātmanas tathā
preta-saṁsthā mṛtāhaś ca
karmaṇy abhyudaye nṛpa

saṁskāra-kālaḥ—at the proper time indicated for Vedic reformatory performances; *jāyāyāḥ*—for the wife; *apatyasya*—for the children; *ātmanaḥ*—and one's own self; *tathā*—as well as; *preta-saṁsthā*—funeral ceremonies; *mṛta-ahaḥ*—annual death ceremonies; *ca*—and; *karmaṇi*—of fruitive activity; *abhyudaye*—for furtherance; *nṛpa*—O King.

TRANSLATION

O King Yudhiṣṭhira, at the time prescribed for reformatory ritualistic ceremonies for one's self, one's wife or one's children, or during funeral ceremonies and annual death ceremonies, one must perform the auspicious ceremonies mentioned above in order to flourish in fruitive activities.

PURPORT

The *Vedas* recommend many ritualistic ceremonies to be performed with one's wife, on the birthdays of one's children, or during funeral ceremonies, and there are also personal reformatory methods like initiation. These must be observed according to time and circumstances and the directions of the *śāstra. Bhagavad-gītā* strongly recommends, *jñātvā śāstra-vidhānoktam:* everything must be performed as indicated in the *śāstras.* For Kali-yuga, the *śāstras* enjoin that *saṅkīrtana-yajña* be performed always: *kīrtanīyaḥ sadā hariḥ.* All the ritualistic ceremonies recommended in the *śāstras* must be preceded and followed by *saṅkīrtana.* This is the recommendation of Śrīla Jīva Gosvāmī.

TEXTS 27–28

अथ देशान्प्रवक्ष्यामि धर्मादिश्रेयआवहान् ।
स वै पुण्यतमो देशः सत्पात्रं यत्र लभ्यते ॥२७॥
बिम्बं भगवतो यत्र सर्वमेतच्चराचरम् ।
यत्र ह ब्राह्मणकुलं तपोविद्यादयान्वितम् ॥२८॥

atha deśān pravakṣyāmi
dharmādi-śreya-āvahān
sa vai puṇyatamo deśaḥ
sat-pātraṁ yatra labhyate

bimbaṁ bhagavato yatra
sarvam etac carācaram
yatra ha brāhmaṇa-kulaṁ
tapo-vidyā-dayānvitam

atha—thereafter; *deśān*—places; *pravakṣyāmi*—I shall describe; *dharma-ādi*—religious performances, etc.; *śreya*—auspiciousness; *āvahān*—which can bring; *saḥ*—that; *vai*—indeed; *puṇya-tamaḥ*—the most sacred; *deśaḥ*—place; *sat-pātram*—a Vaiṣṇava; *yatra*—wherein; *labhyate*—is available; *bimbam*—the Deity (in the temple); *bhagavataḥ*—of the Supreme Personality of Godhead (who is the support); *yatra*—where; *sarvam etat*—of this entire cosmic manifestation; *cara-acaram*—with all the moving and nonmoving living entities; *yatra*—wherein; *ha*—indeed; *brāhmaṇa-kulam*—association with *brāhmaṇas; tapaḥ*—austerities; *vidyā*—education; *dayā*—mercy; *anvitam*—endowed with.

TRANSLATION

Nārada Muni continued: Now I shall describe the places where religious performances may be well executed. Any place where a Vaiṣṇava is available is an excellent place for all auspicious activities. The Supreme Personality of Godhead is the support of this entire cosmic manifestation, with all its moving and nonmoving living entities, and the temple where the Deity of the Lord is installed is a most sacred place. Furthermore, places where learned brāhmaṇas observe Vedic principles by means of austerity, education and mercy are also most auspicious and sacred.

PURPORT

In this verse it is indicated that a Vaiṣṇava temple where the Supreme Personality of Godhead, Kṛṣṇa, is worshiped, and where Vaiṣṇavas are engaged in the service of the Lord, is the best sacred place for performing any religious ceremonies. At the present day, especially in big, big cities, people live in small apartments and are not able to establish a Deity or temple. Under the circumstances, therefore, the centers and temples being established by the expanding Kṛṣṇa consciousness movement are the best sacred places for performing religious ceremonies. Although people in general are no longer interested in religious ceremonies or Deity worship, the Kṛṣṇa consciousness movement gives everyone the chance to advance in spiritual life by becoming Kṛṣṇa conscious.

TEXT 29

यत्र यत्र हरेरर्चा स देशः श्रेयसां पदम् ।
यत्र गङ्गादयो नद्यः पुराणेषु च विश्रुताः ॥२९॥

yatra yatra harer arcā
sa deśaḥ śreyasāṁ padam
yatra gaṅgādayo nadyaḥ
purāṇeṣu ca viśrutāḥ

yatra yatra—wherever; *hareḥ*—of the Supreme Personality of Godhead, Kṛṣṇa; *arcā*—the Deity is worshiped; *saḥ*—that; *deśaḥ*—place, country or neighborhood; *śreyasām*—of all auspiciousness; *padam*—the place; *yatra*—wherever; *gaṅgā-ādayaḥ*—like the Ganges, Yamunā, Narmadā and Kāverī; *nadyaḥ*—sacred rivers; *purāṇeṣu*—in the *Purāṇas* (supplementary Vedic literature); *ca*—also; *viśrutāḥ*—are celebrated.

TRANSLATION

Auspicious indeed are the places where there is a temple of the Supreme Personality of Godhead, Kṛṣṇa, in which He is duly worshiped, and also the places where there flow the celebrated sacred rivers mentioned in the Purāṇas, the supplementary Vedic literatures. Anything spiritual done there is certainly very effective.

PURPORT

There are many atheists who oppose the worship of the Deity of the Supreme Personality of Godhead in the temple. In this verse, however, it is authoritatively stated that any place where the Deity is worshiped is transcendental; it does not belong to the material world. It is also said that the forest is in the mode of goodness, and therefore those who want to cultivate spiritual life are advised to go to the forest (*vanaṁ gato yad dharim āśrayeta*). But one should not go to the forest simply to live like a monkey. Monkeys and other ferocious animals also live in the forest, but a person who goes to the forest for spiritual culture must accept the lotus feet of the Supreme Personality of Godhead as shelter (*vanaṁ gato yad dharim āśrayeta*). One should not be satisfied simply to go to the forest; one must take shelter of the lotus feet of the Supreme Personality of Godhead. In this age, therefore, since it is impossible to go to the forest for spiritual culture, one is recommended to live in the temple community as a devotee, regularly worship the Deity, follow the regulative principles and thus make the place like Vaikuṇṭha. The forest may be in goodness, the cities and villages in passion, and the brothels, hotels and restaurants in ignorance, but when one lives in the temple community he lives in Vaikuṇṭha. Therefore it is said here, *śreyasāṁ padam:* it is the best, most auspicious place.

In many places throughout the world we are constructing communities to give shelter to devotees and worship the Deity in the temple. The Deity cannot be worshiped except by devotees. Temple worshipers who fail to give importance to the devotees are third class. They are *kaniṣṭha-adhikārīs* in the lower stage of spiritual life. As it is said in *Śrīmad-Bhāgavatam* (11.2.47):

arcāyām eva haraye
pūjāṁ yaḥ śraddhayehate
na tad-bhakteṣu cānyeṣu
sa bhaktaḥ prākṛtaḥ smṛtaḥ

"A person who is very faithfully engaged in the worship of the Deity in the temple but does not know how to behave toward devotees or people in general is called a *prākṛta-bhakta*, or *kaniṣṭha-adhikārī*." Therefore, in the temple there must be the Deity of the Lord, and the Lord should be worshiped by the devotees. This combination of the devotees and the Deity creates a first-class transcendental place.

Aside from this, if a *gṛhastha* devotee worships the *śālagrāma-śilā*, or the form of the Deity at home, his home also becomes a very great place. It was therefore customary for members of the three higher classes—namely the *brāhmaṇas*, *kṣatriyas* and *vaiśyas*—to worship the *śālagrāma-śilā*, or a small Deity of Rādhā-Kṛṣṇa or Sītā-Rāma in each and every home. This made everything auspicious. But now they have given up the Deity worship. Men have become modernized and are consequently indulging in all sorts of sinful activities, and therefore they are extremely unhappy.

According to Vedic civilization, therefore, the holy places of pilgrimage are considered most sacred, and still there are hundreds and thousands of holy places like Jagannātha Purī, Vṛndāvana, Hardwar, Rāmeśvara, Prayāga and Mathurā. India is the place for worshiping or for cultivating spiritual life. The Kṛṣṇa consciousness movement invites everyone from all over the world, without discrimination as to caste or creed, to come to its centers and cultivate spiritual life perfectly.

TEXTS 30–33

सरांसि पुष्करादीनि क्षेत्राण्यर्हाश्रितान्युत ।
कुरुक्षेत्रं गयशिरः प्रयागः पुलहाश्रमः ॥३०॥

नैमिषं फाल्गुनं सेतुः प्रभासोऽथ कुशस्थली ।
वाराणसी मधुपुरी पम्पा बिन्दुसरस्तथा ॥३१॥
नारायणाश्रमो नन्दा सीतारामाश्रमादयः ।
सर्वे कुलाचला राजन्महेन्द्रमलयादयः ॥३२॥
एते पुण्यतमा देशा हरेरर्चाश्रिताश्च ये ।
एतान्देशान् निषेवेत श्रेयस्कामो ह्यभीक्ष्णशः ।
धर्मो ह्यत्रेहितः पुंसां सहस्राधिफलोदयः ॥३३॥

sarāṁsi puṣkarādīni
kṣetrāṇy arhāśritāny uta
kurukṣetraṁ gaya-śiraḥ
prayāgaḥ pulahāśramaḥ

naimiṣaṁ phālgunaṁ setuḥ
prabhāso 'tha kuśa-sthalī
vārāṇasī madhu-purī
pampā bindu-saras tathā

nārāyaṇāśramo nandā
sītā-rāmāśramādayaḥ
sarve kulācalā rājan
mahendra-malayādayaḥ

ete puṇyatamā deśā
harer arcāśritāś ca ye
etān deśān niṣeveta
śreyas-kāmo hy abhīkṣṇaśaḥ
dharmo hy atrehitaḥ puṁsāṁ
sahasrādhi-phalodayaḥ

sarāṁsi—lakes; *puṣkara-ādīni*—such as Puṣkara; *kṣetrāṇi*—sacred places (like Kurukṣetra, Gayākṣetra and Jagannātha Purī); *arha*—for worshipable, saintly persons; *āśritāni*—places of shelter; *uta*—celebrated; *kurukṣetram*—a particular sacred place (*dharma-kṣetra*); *gaya-śiraḥ*—the place known as Gayā, where Gayāsura took shelter of the lotus feet of Lord Viṣṇu; *prayāgaḥ*—Allahabad, at the confluence of the two sacred rivers Ganges and Yamunā; *pulaha-āśramaḥ*—the residence of Pulaha Muni; *naimiṣam*—the place known as Naimiṣāraṇya (near Lucknow); *phālgunam*—the place where the Phālgu River flows; *setuḥ*—Setubandha, where Lord Rāmacandra constructed a bridge between India and Laṅkā; *prabhāsaḥ*—Prabhāsakṣetra; *atha*—as well as; *kuśa-sthalī*—Dvāravatī, or Dvārakā; *vārāṇasī*—Benares; *madhu-purī*—Mathurā; *pampā*—a place where there is a lake called Pampā; *bindu-saraḥ*—the place where Bindu-sarovara is situated; *tathā*—there; *nārāyaṇa-āśramaḥ*—known as Badarikāśrama; *nandā*—the place where the Nandā River flows; *sītā-rāma*—of Lord Rāmacandra and mother Sītā; *āśrama-ādayaḥ*—places of shelter like Citrakūṭa; *sarve*—all (such places); *kulācalāḥ*—hilly tracts of land; *rājan*—O King; *mahendra*—known as Mahendra; *malaya-ādayaḥ*—and others, like Malayācala; *ete*—all of them; *puṇya-tamāḥ*—extremely sacred; *deśāḥ*—places; *hareḥ*—of the Supreme Personality of Godhead; *arca-āśritāḥ*—places where the Deity of Rādhā-Kṛṣṇa is worshiped (such as big American cities like New York, Los Angeles and San Francisco, and European cities like London and Paris, or wherever there are centers of Kṛṣṇa consciousness); *ca*—as well as; *ye*—those which; *etān deśān*—all these countries; *niṣeveta*—should worship or visit; *śreyaḥ-kāmaḥ*—one who desires auspiciousness; *hi*—indeed; *abhīkṣṇaśaḥ*—again and again; *dharmaḥ*—religious activities; *hi*—from which; *atra*—in these places; *īhitaḥ*—performed; *puṁsām*—of the persons; *sahasra-adhi*—more than a thousand times; *phala-udayaḥ*—effective.

TRANSLATION

The sacred lakes like Puṣkara and places where saintly persons live, like Kurukṣetra, Gayā, Prayāga, Pulahāśrama, Naimiṣāraṇya, the banks of the Phālgu River, Setubandha, Prabhāsa, Dvārakā, Vārāṇasī, Mathurā, Pampā, Bindu-sarovara, Badarikāśrama [Nārāyaṇāśrama], the places where the Nandā River flows, the places where Lord Rāmacandra and mother Sītā took shelter, such as Citrakūṭa, and also the hilly tracts of land known as Mahendra and Malaya—all of these are to be considered most pious and sacred. Similarly, places outside India where there are centers of the Kṛṣṇa consciousness movement and where Rādhā-Kṛṣṇa

Deities are worshiped must all be visited and worshiped by those who want to be spiritually advanced. One who intends to advance in spiritual life may visit all these places and perform ritualistic ceremonies to get results a thousand times better than the results of the same activities performed in any other place.

PURPORT

In these verses and in verse twenty-nine, stress is given to one point: *harer arcāśritāś ca ye* or *harer arcā.* In other words, any place where the Deity of the Supreme Personality of Godhead is worshiped by devotees is most significant. The Kṛṣṇa consciousness movement is giving the population of the entire world a chance to take advantage of Kṛṣṇa consciousness through the ISKCON centers, where one may perform Deity worship and chant the Hare Kṛṣṇa *mahā-mantra* and in this way obtain results with effectiveness increased a thousand times. This constitutes the best welfare activity for human society. This was Śrī Caitanya Mahāprabhu's mission as it was predicted by Him in the *Caitanya-bhāgavata* (*Antya* 4.126):

pṛthivīte āche yata nagarādi-grāma
sarvatra pracāra haibe mora nāma

Śrī Caitanya Mahāprabhu wanted the Hare Kṛṣṇa movement, with installed Deities, to spread to every village and town in the world, so that everyone in the world might take advantage of this movement and become all-auspicious in spiritual life. Without spiritual life, nothing is auspicious. *Moghāśā mogha-karmāṇo mogha-jñānā vicetasaḥ* (Bg. 9.12). No one can become successful in fruitive activities or speculative knowledge without being Kṛṣṇa conscious. As recommended in the *śāstras,* everyone should be very eagerly interested in taking part in the Kṛṣṇa consciousness movement and understanding the value of spiritual life.

TEXT 34

पात्रं त्वत्र निरुक्तं वै कविभिः पात्रवित्तमैः ।
हरिरेवैक उर्वीश यन्मयं वै चराचरम् ॥३४॥

pātraṁ tv atra niruktaṁ vai
kavibhiḥ pātra-vittamaiḥ
harir evaika urvīśa
yan-mayaṁ vai carācaram

pātram—the true person to whom charity must be given; *tu*—but; *atra*—in the world; *niruktam*—decided; *vai*—indeed; *kavibhiḥ*—by learned scholars; *pātra-vittamaiḥ*—who are expert in finding the actual person to whom charity must be given; *hariḥ*—the Supreme Personality of Godhead; *eva*—indeed; *ekaḥ*—only one; *urvī-īśa*—O King of the earth; *yat-mayam*—in whom everything is resting; *vai*—from whom everything is coming; *cara-acaram*—all that is moving or nonmoving within this universe.

TRANSLATION

O King of the earth, it has been decided by expert, learned scholars that only the Supreme Personality of Godhead, Kṛṣṇa, in whom all that is moving or nonmoving within this universe is resting and from whom everything is coming, is the best person to whom everything must be given.

PURPORT

Whenever we perform some religious act in terms of *dharma, artha, kāma* and *mokṣa,* we must perform it according to the time, place and person (*kāla, deśa, pātra*). Nārada Muni has already described the *deśa* (place) and *kāla* (time). The *kāla* has been described in verses twenty through twenty-four, beginning with the words *ayane viṣuve kuryād vyatīpāte dina-kṣaye.* And the places for giving charity or performing ritualistic ceremonies have been described in verses thirty through thirty-three, beginning with *sarāṁsi puṣkarādīni kṣetrāṇy arhāśritāny uta.* Now, to whom everything must be given is decided in this verse. *Harir evaika urvīśa yan-mayaṁ vai carācaram.* The Supreme Personality of Godhead, Kṛṣṇa, is the root of everything, and therefore He is the best *pātra,* or person, to whom everything must be given. In *Bhagavad-gītā* (5.29) it is said:

bhoktāraṁ yajña-tapasāṁ
sarva-loka-maheśvaram

suhṛdaṁ sarva-bhūtānāṁ
jñātvā māṁ śāntim ṛcchati

If one wants to enjoy real peace and prosperity, he should give everything to Kṛṣṇa, who is the real enjoyer, real friend and real proprietor. It is therefore said:

yathā taror mūla-niṣecanena
tṛpyanti tat-skandha-bhujopaśākhāḥ
prāṇopahārāc ca yathendriyāṇāṁ
tathaiva sarvārhaṇam acyutejyā
(*Bhāg.* 4.31.14)

By worshiping or satisfying Acyuta, the Supreme Personality of Godhead, Kṛṣṇa, one can satisfy everyone, just as one can water the branches, leaves and flowers of a tree simply by watering its root or as one satisfies all the senses of the body by giving food to the stomach. Therefore, a devotee simply offers everything to the Supreme Personality of Godhead to receive the best results of charity, religious performances, sense gratification and even liberation (*dharma, artha, kāma, mokṣa*).

TEXT 35

देवर्ष्यर्हत्सु वै सत्सु तत्र ब्रह्मात्मजादिषु ।
राजन्यदग्रपूजायां मतः पात्रतयाच्युतः ॥३५॥

devarṣy-arhatsu vai satsu
tatra brahmātmajādiṣu
rājan yad agra-pūjāyāṁ
mataḥ pātratayācyutaḥ

deva-ṛṣi—among the demigods and great saintly persons, including Nārada Muni; *arhatsu*—the most venerable and worshipable personalities; *vai*—indeed; *satsu*—the great devotees; *tatra*—there (at the Rājasūya-yajña); *brahma-ātma-jādiṣu*—and the sons of Lord Brahmā (such as Sanaka, Sanandana, Sanat and Sanātana); *rājan*—O King; *yat*—

from whom; *agra-pūjāyām*—the first to be worshiped; *mataḥ*—decision; *pātratayā*—selected as the best person to preside over the Rājasūya-yajña; *acyutaḥ*—Kṛṣṇa.

TRANSLATION

O King Yudhiṣṭhira, the demigods, many great sages and saints including even the four sons of Lord Brahmā, and I myself were present at your Rājasūya sacrificial ceremony, but when there was a question of who should be the first person worshiped, everyone decided upon Lord Kṛṣṇa, the Supreme Person.

PURPORT

This is a reference to the Rājasūya sacrifice performed by Mahārāja Yudhiṣṭhira. In that meeting there was a great turmoil over selecting the best person to be worshiped first. Everyone decided to worship Śrī Kṛṣṇa. The only protest came from Śiśupāla, and because of his vehement opposition he was killed by the Supreme Personality of Godhead.

TEXT 36

जीवराशिभिराकीर्ण अण्डकोशाङ्घ्रिपो महान् ।
तन्मूलत्वादच्युतेज्या सर्वजीवात्मतर्पणम् ॥३६॥

jīva-rāśibhir ākīrṇa
aṇḍa-kośāṅghripo mahān
tan-mūlatvād acyutejyā
sarva-jīvātma-tarpaṇam

jīva-rāśibhiḥ—by millions and millions of living entities; *ākīrṇaḥ*—filled up or spread over; *aṇḍa-kośa*—the whole universe; *aṅghripaḥ*—like a tree; *mahān*—very, very great; *tat-mūlatvāt*—because of being the root of this tree; *acyuta-ijyā*—worship of the Supreme Personality of Godhead; *sarva*—of all; *jīva-ātma*—living entities; *tarpaṇam*—satisfaction.

TRANSLATION

The entire universe, which is full of living entities, is like a tree whose root is the Supreme Personality of Godhead, Acyuta

[Kṛṣṇa]. Therefore simply by worshiping Lord Kṛṣṇa one can worship all living entities.

PURPORT

In *Bhagavad-gītā* (10.8) the Lord says:

ahaṁ sarvasya prabhavo
mattaḥ sarvaṁ pravartate
iti matvā bhajante māṁ
budhā bhāva-samanvitāḥ

"I am the source of all spiritual and material worlds. Everything emanates from Me. The wise who perfectly know this engage in My devotional service and worship Me with all their hearts." People are very much anxious to give service to other living entities, especially to the poor, but although they have manufactured many ways to give such help, actually they are expert in killing the poor living entities. This sort of service or mercy is not recommended in the Vedic wisdom. As stated in a previous verse, it has been decided (*niruktam*) by expert saintly persons that Kṛṣṇa is the root of everything and that worshiping Kṛṣṇa is worshiping everyone, just as supplying water to the root of a tree means satisfying all of its branches and twigs.

Another point is that this universe is full of living entities from top to bottom, on every planet (*jīva-rāśibhir ākīrṇaḥ*). Modern scientists and so-called scholars think that there are no living entities on planets other than this one. Recently they have said that they have gone to the moon but did not find any living entities there. But *Śrīmad-Bhāgavatam* and the other Vedic literatures do not agree with this foolish conception. There are living entities everywhere, not only one or two but *jīva-rāśibhiḥ*—many millions of living entities. Even on the sun there are living entities, although it is a firey planet. The chief living entity on the sun is called Vivasvān (*imaṁ vivasvate yogaṁ proktavān aham avyayam*). All the different planets are filled with different types of living entities according to different living conditions. To suggest that only this planet is filled with living entities and that others are vacant is foolish. This betrays a lack of real knowledge.

TEXT 37

पुराण्यनेन सृष्टानि नृतिर्यगृषिदेवताः ।
शेते जीवेन रूपेण पुरेषु पुरुषो ह्यसौ ॥३७॥

purāṇy anena sṛṣṭāni
nṛ-tiryag-ṛṣi-devatāḥ
śete jīvena rūpeṇa
pureṣu puruṣo hy asau

purāṇi—residential places or bodies; *anena*—by Him (the Supreme Personality of Godhead); *sṛṣṭāni*—among those creations; *nṛ*—man; *tiryak*—other than human beings (animals, birds, etc); *ṛṣi*—saintly persons; *devatāḥ*—and demigods; *śete*—lies down; *jīvena*—with the living entities; *rūpeṇa*—in the form of Paramātmā; *pureṣu*—within these residential places or bodies; *puruṣaḥ*—the Supreme Lord; *hi*—indeed; *asau*—He (the Personality of Godhead).

TRANSLATION

The Supreme Personality of Godhead has created many residential places like the bodies of human beings, animals, birds, saints and demigods. In all of these innumerable bodily forms, the Lord resides with the living being as Paramātmā. Thus He is known as the puruṣāvatāra.

PURPORT

In *Bhagavad-gītā* (18.61) it is said:

īśvaraḥ sarva-bhūtānāṁ
hṛd-deśe 'rjuna tiṣṭhati
bhrāmayan sarva-bhūtāni
yantrārūḍhāni māyayā

"The Supreme Lord is situated in everyone's heart, O Arjuna, and is directing the wanderings of all living entities, who are seated as on a machine, made of the material energy." The living entity, who is part and parcel of the Supreme Personality of Godhead, exists on the mercy of the Lord, who is always with him in any form of body. The living entity desires a particular type of material enjoyment, and thus the Lord supplies him with a body, which is like a machine. Just to keep him alive in that body, the Lord remains with him as the *puruṣa* (Kṣīrodakaśāyī Viṣṇu). This is also confirmed in *Brahma-saṁhitā* (5.35):

eko 'py asau racayituṁ jagad-aṇḍa-koṭiṁ
yac-chaktir asti jagad-aṇḍa-cayā yad-antaḥ
aṇḍāntara-stha-paramāṇu-cayāntara-sthaṁ
govindam ādi-puruṣaṁ tam ahaṁ bhajāmi

"I worship the Personality of Godhead, Govinda, who enters the existence of every universe and every atom by one of His plenary portions and thus manifests His infinite energy throughout the material creation." The living entity, being part and parcel of the Lord, is known as *jīva*. The Supreme Lord *puruṣa* remains with the *jīva* to enable him to enjoy material facilities.

TEXT 38

तेष्वेव भगवान्राजंस्तारतम्येन वर्तते ।
तस्मात् पात्रं हि पुरुषो यावानात्मा यथेयते ॥३८॥

teṣv eva bhagavān rājaṁs
tāratamyena vartate
tasmāt pātraṁ hi puruṣo
yāvān ātmā yatheyate

teṣu—among the different types of bodies (demigod, human, animal, bird, etc.); *eva*—indeed; *bhagavān*—the Supreme Personality of Godhead in His Paramātmā feature; *rājan*—O King; *tāratamyena*—comparatively, more or less; *vartate*—is situated; *tasmāt*—therefore; *pātram*—the Supreme Person; *hi*—indeed; *puruṣaḥ*—Paramātmā; *yāvān*—as far as; *ātmā*—the degree of understanding; *yathā*—development of austerity and penance; *īyate*—is manifest.

TRANSLATION

O King Yudhiṣṭhira, the Supersoul in every body gives intelligence to the individual soul according to his capacity for under-

standing. Therefore the Supersoul is the chief within the body. The Supersoul is manifested to the individual soul according to the individual's comparative development of knowledge, austerity, penance and so on.

PURPORT

In *Bhagavad-gītā* (15.15) it is said, *mattaḥ smṛtir jñānam apohanaṁ ca:* the Supreme Personality of Godhead in His localized aspect gives intelligence to the individual soul as far as he is able to grasp it. Therefore we find the individual soul in different high and low positions. A living entity with the body of a bird or beast cannot take instructions from the Supreme Soul as adequately as an advanced human being. Thus there are gradations of bodily forms. In human society, the perfect *brāhmaṇa* is supposed to be the most advanced in spiritual consciousness, and further advanced than the *brāhmaṇa* is the Vaiṣṇava. Therefore the best persons are the Vaiṣṇavas and Viṣṇu. When charity is to be given, one should take instruction from *Bhagavad-gītā* (17.20):

dātavyam iti yad dānaṁ
dīyate 'nupakāriṇe
deśe kāle ca pātre ca
tad dānaṁ sāttvikaṁ smṛtam

"That gift which is given out of duty, at the proper time and place, to a worthy person, and without expectation of return, is considered to be charity in the mode of goodness." One should give charity to the *brāhmaṇas* and Vaiṣṇavas, for thus the Supreme Personality of Godhead will be worshiped. In this connection, Śrīla Madhvācārya comments:

brahmādi-sthāvarānteṣu
na viśeṣo hareḥ kvacit
vyakti-mātra-viśeṣeṇa
tāratamyaṁ vadanti ca

Beginning from Brahmā down to the ant, everyone is conducted by the Supersoul (*īśvaraḥ sarva-bhūtānāṁ hṛd-deśe 'rjuna tiṣṭhati*). But because of a particular person's advancement in spiritual consciousness, he is considered to be important. Therefore, the *brāhmaṇa* Vaiṣṇava is important, and, above all, the Supersoul, the Personality of Godhead, is the most important personality.

TEXT 39

दृष्ट्वा तेषां मिथो नृणामवज्ञानात्मतां नृप ।
त्रेतादिषु हरेरर्चा क्रियायै कविभिः कृता ॥३९॥

dṛṣṭvā teṣāṁ mitho nṛṇām
avajñānātmatām nṛpa
tretādiṣu harer arcā
kriyāyai kavibhiḥ kṛtā

dṛṣṭvā—after practically seeing; *teṣām*—among the *brāhmaṇas* and Vaiṣṇavas; *mithaḥ*—mutually; *nṛṇām*—of human society; *avajñāna-ātmatām*—the mutually disrespectful behavior; *nṛpa*—O King; *tretā-ādiṣu*—beginning from Tretā-yuga; *hareḥ*—of the Supreme Personality of Godhead; *arcā*—the Deity worship (in the temple); *kriyāyai*—for the purpose of introducing the method of worship; *kavibhiḥ*—by learned persons; *kṛtā*—has been done.

TRANSLATION

My dear King, when great sages and saintly persons saw mutually disrespectful dealings at the beginning of Tretā-yuga, Deity worship in the temple was introduced with all paraphernalia.

PURPORT

As it is said in *Śrīmad-Bhāgavatam* (12.3.52):

kṛte yad dhyāyato viṣṇuṁ
tretāyāṁ yajato makhaiḥ
dvāpare paricaryāyāṁ
kalau tad dhari-kīrtanāt

"Whatever result one obtained in Satya-yuga by meditating on Viṣṇu, in Tretā-yuga by performing sacrifices and in Dvāpara-yuga by serving the

Lord's lotus feet one can also obtain in Kali-yuga simply by chanting the Hare Kṛṣṇa *mahā-mantra*." In Satya-yuga, every person was spiritually advanced, and there was no envy between great personalities. Gradually, however, because of material contamination with the advance of the ages, disrespectful dealings appeared even among *brāhmaṇas* and Vaiṣṇavas. Actually, an advanced Vaiṣṇava is to be respected more than Viṣṇu. As stated in the *Padma Purāṇa*, *ārādhanānāṁ sarveṣāṁ viṣṇor ārādhanaṁ param:* of all kinds of worship, worship of Lord Viṣṇu is the best. *Tasmāt parataraṁ devi tadīyānāṁ samarcanam:* and recommended more than worship of Viṣṇu is worship of the Vaiṣṇava.

Formerly, all activities were performed in connection with Viṣṇu, but after Satya-yuga there were symptoms of disrespectful dealings among Vaiṣṇavas. Śrīla Bhaktivinoda Ṭhākura has said that a Vaiṣṇava is he who has helped others become Vaiṣṇavas. An example of one who has converted many others into Vaiṣṇavas is Nārada Muni. A powerful Vaiṣṇava who has converted others into Vaiṣṇavas is to be worshiped, but because of material contamination, sometimes such an exalted Vaiṣṇava is disrespected by other, minor Vaiṣṇavas. When great saintly persons saw this contamination, they introduced worship of the Deity in the temple. This began in Tretā-yuga and was especially prominent in Dvāpara-yuga (*dvāpare paricaryāyāṁ*). But in Kali-yuga, worship of the Deity is being neglected. Therefore chanting of the Hare Kṛṣṇa *mantra* is more powerful than Deity worship. Śrī Caitanya Mahāprabhu set a practical example in that He did not establish any temples or Deities, but He profusely introduced the *saṅkīrtana* movement. Therefore Kṛṣṇa consciousness preachers should give more stress to the *saṅkīrtana* movement, especially by distributing transcendental literature more and more. This helps the *saṅkīrtana* movement. Whenever there is a possibility to worship the Deity, we may establish many centers, but generally we should give more stress to the distribution of transcendental literature, for this will be more effective in converting people to Kṛṣṇa consciousness.

It is said in *Śrīmad-Bhāgavatam* (11.2.47):

arcāyām eva haraye
pūjāṁ yaḥ śraddhayehate

na tad-bhakteṣu cānyeṣu
sa bhaktaḥ prākṛtaḥ smṛtaḥ

"A person who is very faithfully engaged in the worship of the Deity in the temple but does not know how to behave toward devotees or people in general is called a *prākṛta-bhakta*, or *kaniṣṭha-adhikārī*." A *prākṛta* devotee, or neophyte devotee, is still on the material platform. He certainly engages in worshiping the Deity, but he cannot appreciate the activities of a pure devotee. It has actually been seen that even an authorized devotee who is engaged in the service of the Lord by preaching the mission of Kṛṣṇa consciousness is sometimes criticized by neophyte devotees. Such neophytes are described by Viśvanātha Cakravartī Ṭhākura: *sarva-prāṇi-sammānanāsamarthānām avajñā spardhādimatāṁ tu bhagavat-pratimaiva pātram ity āha.* For those who cannot properly appreciate the activities of authorized devotees, Deity worship is the only way for spiritual advancement. In the *Caitanya-caritāmṛta* (*Antya* 7.11) it is clearly said, *kṛṣṇa-śakti vinā nahe tāra pravartana:* without being authorized by Kṛṣṇa, one cannot preach the holy name of the Lord throughout the entire world. Nevertheless, a devotee who does so is criticized by neophyte devotees, *kaniṣṭha-adhikārīs* , who are on the lower stages of devotional service. For them, Deity worship is strongly recommended.

TEXT 40

ततोऽर्चायां हरिं केचित् संश्रद्धाय सपर्यया ।
उपासत उपास्तापि नार्थदा पुरुषद्विषाम् ॥४०॥

tato 'rcāyāṁ hariṁ kecit
saṁśraddhāya saparyayā
upāsata upāstāpi
nārthadā puruṣa-dviṣām

tataḥ—thereafter; *arcāyām*—the Deity; *harim*—who is the Supreme Personality of Godhead (the form of the Lord being identical with the Lord); *kecit*—someone; *saṁśraddhāya*—with great faith; *saparyayā*—and with the required paraphernalia; *upāsate*—worships; *upāstā api*—

although worshiping the Deity (with faith and regularity); *na*—not; *artha-dā*—beneficial; *puruṣa-dviṣām*—for those who are envious of Lord Viṣṇu and His devotees.

TRANSLATION

Sometimes a neophyte devotee offers all the paraphernalia for worshiping the Lord, and he factually worships the Lord as the Deity, but because he is envious of the authorized devotees of Lord Viṣṇu, the Lord is never satisfied with his devotional service.

PURPORT

Deity worship is especially meant for purifying the neophyte devotees. Actually, however, preaching is more important. In *Bhagavad-gītā* (18.69) it is said, *na ca tasmān manuṣyeṣu kaścin me priya-kṛttamaḥ:* if one wants to be recognized by the Supreme Personality of Godhead, he must preach the glories of the Lord. One who worships the Deity must therefore be extremely respectful to preachers; otherwise simply worshiping the Deity will keep one in the lower stage of devotion.

TEXT 41

पुरुषेष्वपि राजेन्द्र सुपात्रं ब्राह्मणं विदुः ।
तपसा विद्यया तुष्ट्या धत्ते वेदं हरेस्तनुम् ॥४१॥

puruṣeṣv api rājendra
supātraṁ brāhmaṇaṁ viduḥ
tapasā vidyayā tuṣṭyā
dhatte vedaṁ hares tanum

puruṣeṣu—among persons; *api*—indeed; *rāja-indra*—O best of kings; *su-pātram*—the best person; *brāhmaṇam*—the qualified *brāhmaṇa; viduḥ*—one should know; *tapasā*—due to austerity; *vidyayā*—education; *tuṣṭyā*—and satisfaction; *dhatte*—he assumes; *vedam*—the transcendental knowledge known as *Veda; hareḥ*—of the Supreme Personality of Godhead; *tanum*—body, or representation.

TRANSLATION

My dear King, of all persons a qualified brāhmaṇa must be accepted as the best within this material world because such a brāhmaṇa, by practicing austerity, Vedic studies and satisfaction, becomes the counterpart body of the Supreme Personality of Godhead.

PURPORT

From the *Vedas* we learn that the Personality of Godhead is the Supreme Person. Every living entity is an individual person, and the Supreme Personality of Godhead, Kṛṣṇa, is the Supreme Person. A *brāhmaṇa* who is well versed in Vedic knowledge and fully conversant with transcendental matters becomes a representative of the Supreme Personality of Godhead, and therefore one should worship such a *brāhmaṇa* or Vaiṣṇava. A Vaiṣṇava is superior to a *brāhmaṇa* because whereas a *brāhmaṇa* knows that he is Brahman, not matter, a Vaiṣṇava knows that he is not only Brahman but also an eternal servant of the Supreme Brahman. Therefore, worship of a Vaiṣṇava is superior to worship of the Deity in the temple. Viśvanātha Cakravartī Ṭhākura says, *sākṣād dharitvena samasta-śāstraiḥ:* in all the scriptures the spiritual master, who is the best of the *brāhmaṇas,* the best of the Vaiṣṇavas, is considered to be as good as the Supreme Personality of Godhead. This does not mean, however, that the Vaiṣṇava thinks himself God, for this is blasphemous. Although a *brāhmaṇa* or Vaiṣṇava is worshiped as being as good as the Supreme Personality of Godhead, such a devotee always remains a faithful servant of the Lord and never tries to enjoy the prestige that might accrue to him from being the Supreme Lord's representative.

TEXT 42

नन्वस्य ब्राह्मणा राजन्कृष्णस्य जगदात्मनः ।
पुनन्तः पादरजसा त्रिलोकीं दैवतं महत् ॥४२॥

nanv asya brāhmaṇā rājan
kṛṣṇasya jagad-ātmanaḥ
punantaḥ pāda-rajasā
tri-lokīṁ daivataṁ mahat

nanu—but; *asya*—by Him; *brāhmaṇāḥ*—the qualified *brāhmaṇas; rājan*—O King; *kṛṣṇasya*—by Lord Kṛṣṇa, the Supreme Personality of Godhead; *jagat-ātmanaḥ*—who is the life and soul of the whole creation; *punantaḥ*—sanctifying; *pāda-rajasā*—by the dust of their lotus feet; *tri-lokīm*—the three worlds; *daivatam*—worshipable; *mahat*—most exalted.

TRANSLATION

My dear King Yudhiṣṭhira, the brāhmaṇas, especially those engaged in preaching the glories of the Lord throughout the entire world, are recognized and worshiped by the Supreme Personality of Godhead, who is the heart and soul of all creation. The brāhmaṇas, by their preaching, sanctify the three worlds with the dust of their lotus feet, and thus they are worshipable even for Kṛṣṇa.

PURPORT

As admitted by Lord Kṛṣṇa in *Bhagavad-gītā* (18.69), *na ca tasmān manuṣyeṣu kaścin me priya-kṛttamaḥ.* The *brāhmaṇas* preach the cult of Kṛṣṇa consciousness all around the world, and therefore, although they worship Kṛṣṇa, the Supreme Personality of Godhead, the Lord also recognizes them as worshipable. The relationship is reciprocal. The *brāhmaṇas* want to worship Kṛṣṇa, and similarly Kṛṣṇa wants to worship the *brāhmaṇas.* In conclusion, therefore, *brāhmaṇas* and Vaiṣṇavas who are engaged in preaching the glories of the Lord must be worshiped by religionists, philosophers and people in general. At the Rājasūya-yajña of Mahārāja Yudhiṣṭhira, many hundreds and thousands of *brāhmaṇas* were present, yet Kṛṣṇa was selected to be worshiped first. Therefore, Kṛṣṇa is always the Supreme Person, but by His causeless mercy He recognizes the *brāhmaṇas* as dearmost to Him.

Thus end the Bhaktivedanta purports of the Seventh Canto, Fourteenth Chapter, of the Śrīmad-Bhāgavatam, *entitled "Ideal Family Life."*

CHAPTER FIFTEEN

Instructions for Civilized Human Beings

The summary of the Fifteenth Chapter is as follows. In the previous chapter, Śrī Nārada Muni proved the importance of the *brāhmaṇa* in society. Now, in this chapter, he will show the differences between different grades of *brāhmaṇas*. Among the *brāhmaṇas*, some are householders and are mostly attached to fruitive activities or the betterment of social conditions. Above them, however, are *brāhmaṇas* who are very much attracted by austerities and penances and who retire from family life. They are known as *vānaprasthas*. Other *brāhmaṇas* are very much interested in studying the *Vedas* and explaining the purport of the *Vedas* to others. Such *brāhmaṇas* are called *brahmacārīs*. And still other *brāhmaṇas* are interested in different types of *yoga*, especially *bhakti-yoga* and *jñāna-yoga*. Such *brāhmaṇas* are mostly *sannyāsīs*, members of the renounced order of life.

As far as householders are concerned, they engage in different types of scriptural activities, especially in offering oblations to their forefathers and giving as charity to other *brāhmaṇas* the paraphernalia engaged in such sacrifices. Generally the charity is given to *sannyāsīs*, *brāhmaṇas* in the renounced order of life. If such a *sannyāsī* is not available, the charity is given to *brāhmaṇa* householders engaged in fruitive activities.

One should not make very elaborate arrangements to perform the *śrāddha* ceremony of offering oblations to one's forefathers. The best process for the *śrāddha* ceremony is to distribute *bhāgavata-prasāda* (remnants of food that has first been offered to Kṛṣṇa) to all of one's forefathers and relatives. This makes a first-class *śrāddha* ceremony. In the *śrāddha* ceremony there is no need to offer meat or eat meat. Unnecessary killing of animals must be avoided. Those who are in the lower grades of society prefer to perform sacrifices by killing animals, but one who is advanced in knowledge must avoid such unnecessary violence.

Brāhmaṇas should execute their regulative duties in worshiping Lord Viṣṇu. Those who are advanced in knowledge of religious principles must avoid five kinds of irreligion, known as *vidharma*, *para-dharma*, *dharmābhāsa*, *upadharma* and *chala-dharma*. One must act according to the religious principles that suit his constitutional position; it is not that everyone must adhere to the same type of religion. A general principle is that a poor man should not unnecessarily endeavor for economic development. One who refrains from such endeavors but who engages in devotional service is most auspicious.

One who is not satisfied with the mind must fall to degradation. One must conquer lusty desires, anger, greed, fear, lamentation, illusion, fright, unnecessary talks on material subjects, violence, the four miseries of material existence, and the three material qualities. That is the objective of human life. One who has no faith in the spiritual master, who is identical with Śrī Kṛṣṇa, cannot get any benefit from reading *śāstra*. One should never consider the spiritual master an ordinary human being, even though the members of the spiritual master's family may think of him as such. Meditation and other processes of austerity are useful only if they help in advancement toward Kṛṣṇa consciousness; otherwise, they are simply a waste of time and labor. For those who are not devotees, such meditation and austerity cause falldown.

Every householder should be very careful because even though a householder may try to conquer the senses, he becomes a victim to the association of relatives and falls down. Thus a *gṛhastha* must become a *vānaprastha* or *sannyāsī*, live in a secluded place, and be satisfied with food gotten by begging from door to door. He must chant the *oṁkāra mantra* or Hare Kṛṣṇa *mantra*, and in this way he will perceive transcendental bliss within himself. After taking *sannyāsa*, however, if one returns to *gṛhastha* life, he is called a *vāntāśī*, which means "one who eats his own vomit." Such a person is shameless. A householder should not give up the ritualistic ceremonies, and a *sannyāsī* should not live in society. If a *sannyāsī* is agitated by the senses, he is a cheater influenced by the modes of passion and ignorance. When one assumes a role in goodness by starting philanthropic and altruistic activities, such activities become impediments on the path of devotional service.

The best process for advancing in devotional service is to abide by the orders of the spiritual master, for only by his direction can one conquer the senses. Unless one is completely Kṛṣṇa conscious, there is a chance of falling down. Of course, in performing ritualistic ceremonies and other fruitive activities there are also many dangers at every moment. Fruitive activities have been divided into twelve portions. Because of performing fruitive activities, which are called the path of *dharma*, one has to accept the cycle of birth and death, but when one takes the path of *mokṣa*, or liberation, which is described in *Bhagavad-gītā* as *arcanā-mārga*, one can get relief from the cycle of birth and death. The *Vedas* describe these two paths as *pitṛ-yāna* and *deva-yāna*. Those who follow the paths of *pitṛ-yāna* and *deva-yāna* are never bewildered, even while in the material body. A monistic philosopher who gradually develops control of the senses understands that the objective of all the different *āśramas*, the statuses of life, is salvation. One must live and act according to *śāstras*.

If one who is performing the Vedic ritualistic ceremonies becomes a devotee, even if he is a *gṛhastha*, he can receive the causeless mercy of Kṛṣṇa. The objective of a devotee is to return home, back to Godhead. Such a devotee, even though not performing ritualistic ceremonies, advances in spiritual consciousness by the supreme will of the Personality of Godhead. One may actually become successful in spiritual consciousness by the mercy of devotees, or one may fall from spiritual consciousness by being disrespectful to devotees. In this regard, Nārada Muni narrated the history of how he had fallen from the Gandharva kingdom, how he was born in a *śūdra* family, and how by serving exalted *brāhmaṇas* he become the son of Lord Brahmā and was reinstated in his transcendental position. After narrating all these stories, Nārada Muni praised the mercy received from the Lord by the Pāṇḍavas. Mahārāja Yudhiṣṭhira, after hearing from Nārada, become ecstatic in love of Kṛṣṇa, and then Nārada Muni left that place and returned to his own place. Thus Śukadeva Gosvāmī, having described various descendants of the daughters of Dakṣa, ends the Seventh Canto of *Śrīmad-Bhāgavatam*.

TEXT 1

श्रीनारद उवाच
कर्मनिष्ठा द्विजाः केचित् तपोनिष्ठा नृपापरे ।
स्वाध्यायेऽन्ये प्रवचने केचन ज्ञानयोगयोः ॥ १ ॥

śrī-nārada uvāca
karma-niṣṭhā dvijāḥ kecit
tapo-niṣṭhā nṛpāpare

svādhyāye 'nye pravacane
kecana jñāna-yogayoḥ

śrī-nāradaḥ uvāca—Nārada Muni said; *karma-niṣṭhāḥ*—attached to ritualistic ceremonies (according to one's social status as a *brāhmaṇa, kṣatriya, vaiśya* or *śūdra*); *dvi-jāḥ*—the twiceborn (especially the *brāhmaṇas*); *kecit*—some; *tapaḥ-niṣṭhāḥ*—very much attached to austerities and penances; *nṛpa*—O King; *apare*—others; *svādhyāye*—in studying Vedic literature; *anye*—others; *pravacane*—delivering speeches on Vedic literature; *kecana*—some; *jñāna-yogayoḥ*—in culturing knowledge and practicing *bhakti-yoga.*

TRANSLATION

Nārada Muni continued: My dear King, some brāhmaṇas are very much attached to fruitive activities, some are attached to austerities and penances, and still others study the Vedic literature, whereas some, although very few, cultivate knowledge and practice different yogas, especially bhakti-yoga.

TEXT 2

ज्ञाननिष्ठाय देयानि कव्यान्यानन्त्यमिच्छता ।
दैवे च तदभावे स्यादितरेभ्यो यथार्हतः ॥ २ ॥

jñāna-niṣṭhāya deyāni
kavyāny ānantyam icchatā
daive ca tad-abhāve syād
itarebhyo yathārhataḥ

jñāna-niṣṭhāya—to the impersonalist or the transcendentalist desiring to merge into the Supreme; *deyāni*—to be given in charity; *kavyāni*—ingredients offered to the forefathers as oblations; *ānantyam*—liberation from material bondage; *icchatā*—by a person desiring; *daive*—the ingredients to be offered to the demigods; *ca*—also; *tat-abhāve*—in the absence of such advanced transcendentalists; *syāt*—it should be done; *itarebhyaḥ*—to others (namely, those addicted to fruitive activities); *yathā-arhataḥ*—comparatively or with discrimination.

TRANSLATION

A person desiring liberation for his forefathers or himself should give charity to a brāhmaṇa who adheres to impersonal monism [jñāna-niṣṭhā]. In the absence of such an advanced brāhmaṇa, charity may be given to a brāhmaṇa addicted to fruitive activities [karma-kāṇḍa].

PURPORT

There are two processes by which to get free from material bondage. One involves *jñāna-kāṇḍa* and *karma-kāṇḍa*, and the other involves *upāsanā-kāṇḍa*. Vaiṣṇavas never want to merge into the existence of the Supreme; rather, they want to be everlastingly servants of the Lord to render loving service unto Him. In this verse the words *ānantyam icchatā* refer to persons who desire to achieve liberation from material bondage and merge into the existence of the Lord. Devotees, however, whose objective is to associate personally with the Lord, have no desire to accept the activities of *karma-kāṇḍa* or *jñāna-kāṇḍa*, for pure devotional service is above both *karma-kāṇḍa* and *jñāna-kāṇḍa*. *Anyābhilāṣitā-śūnyaṁ jñāna-karmādy-anāvṛtam.* In pure devotional service there is not even a pinch of *jñāna* or *karma*. Consequently, when Vaiṣṇavas distribute charity, they do not need to find a *brāhmaṇa* performing the activities of *jñāna-kāṇḍa* or *karma-kāṇḍa*. The best example in this regard is provided by Advaita Gosvāmī, who, after performing the *śrāddha* ceremony for his father, offered charity to Haridāsa Ṭhākura, although it was known to everyone that Haridāsa Ṭhākura was born in a Mohammedan family, not a *brāhmaṇa* family, and was not interested in the activities of *jñāna-kāṇḍa* or *karma-kāṇḍa*.

Charity, therefore, should be given to the first-class transcendentalist, the devotee, because the *śāstras* recommend:

muktānām api siddhānāṁ
nārāyaṇa-parāyaṇaḥ
sudurlabhaḥ praśāntātmā
koṭiṣv api mahā-mune

"O great sage, among many millions who are liberated and perfect in knowledge of liberation, one may be a devotee of Lord Nārāyaṇa, or

Kṛṣṇa. Such devotees, who are fully peaceful, are extremely rare." (*Bhāg.* 6.14.5) A Vaiṣṇava is in a higher position than a *jñānī*, and therefore Advaita Ācārya selected Haridāsa Ṭhākura to be the person to accept His charity. The Supreme Lord also says:

na me 'bhaktaś catur-vedī
mad-bhaktaḥ śva-pacaḥ priyaḥ
tasmai deyaṁ tato grāhyaṁ
sa ca pūjyo yathā hy aham

"Even though a person is a very learned scholar of the Sanskrit Vedic literatures, he is not accepted as My devotee unless he is pure in devotional service. However, even though a person is born in a family of dog-eaters, he is very dear to Me if he is a pure devotee who has no motive to enjoy fruitive activity or mental speculation. Indeed, all respect should be given to him, and whatever he offers should be accepted. Such devotees are as worshipable as I am." (*Hari-bhakti-vilāsa* 10.127) Therefore, even if not born in a *brāhmaṇa* family, a devotee, because of his devotion to the Lord, is above all kinds of *brāhmaṇas*, whether they be *karma-kāṇḍīs* or *jñāna-kāṇḍīs.*

In this regard, it may be mentioned that *brāhmaṇas* in Vṛndāvana who are *karma-kāṇḍīs* and *jñāna-kāṇḍīs* sometimes decline to accept invitations to our temple because our temple is known as the *aṅgarejī* temple, or "Anglican temple." But in accordance with the evidence given in the *śāstra* and the example set by Advaita Ācārya, we give *prasāda* to devotees regardless of whether they come from India, Europe or America. It is the conclusion of the *śāstra* that instead of feeding many *jñāna-kāṇḍī* or *karma-kāṇḍī brāhmaṇas,* it is better to feed a pure Vaiṣṇava, regardless of where he comes from. This is also confirmed in *Bhagavad-gītā* (9.30):

api cet sudurācāro
bhajate mām ananya-bhāk
sādhur eva sa mantavyaḥ
samyag vyavasito hi saḥ

"Even if one commits the most abominable actions, if he is engaged in devotional service he is to be considered saintly because he is properly situated." Thus it doesn't matter whether a devotee comes from a *brāhmaṇa* family or non-*brāhmaṇa* family; if he is fully devoted to Kṛṣṇa, he is a *sādhu.*

TEXT 3

द्वौ दैवे पितृकार्ये त्रीनेकैकमुभयत्र वा ।
भोजयेत् सुसमृद्धोऽपि श्राद्धे कुर्यान्न विस्तरम् ॥ ३ ॥

dvau daive pitṛ-kārye trīn
ekaikam ubhayatra vā
bhojayet susamṛddho 'pi
śrāddhe kuryān na vistaram

dvau—two; *daive*—during the period when oblations are offered to the demigods; *pitṛ-kārye*—in the *śrāddha* ceremony, in which oblations are offered to the forefathers; *trīn*—three; *eka*—one; *ekam*—one; *ubhayatra*—for both occasions; *vā*—either; *bhojayet*—one should feed; *su-samṛddhaḥ api*—even though one is very rich; *śrāddhe*—when offering oblations to the forefathers; *kuryāt*—one should do; *na*—not; *vistaram*—very expensive arrangements.

TRANSLATION

During the period for offering oblations to the demigods, one should invite only two brāhmaṇas, and while offering oblations to the forefathers, one may invite three brāhmaṇas. Or, in either case, only one brāhmaṇa will suffice. Even though one is very opulent, he should not endeavor to invite more brāhmaṇas or make various expensive arrangements on those occasions.

PURPORT

As we have already mentioned, Śrīla Advaita Ācārya, during the generally observed ceremony to offer oblations to the forefathers, invited only Haridāsa Ṭhākura. Thus He followed this principle: *na me 'bhaktaś catur-vedī mad-bhaktaḥ śva-pacaḥ priyaḥ.* The Lord says, "It is not necessary that one become very expert in Vedic knowledge before he can become My *bhakta,* or devotee. Even if one is born in a family of dog-eaters, he can become My devotee and be very dear to Me, in spite of having taken birth in such a family. Therefore, offerings should be given to My devotee, and whatever My devotee has offered Me should be accepted." Following this principle, one should invite a first-class *brāhmaṇa* or Vaiṣṇava—a realized soul—and feed him while observing the *śrāddha* ceremony to offer oblations to one's forefathers.

TEXT 4

देशकालोचितश्रद्धाद्रव्यपात्रार्हणानि च ।
सम्यग् भवन्ति नैतानि विस्तरात् स्वजनार्पणात् ॥४॥

deśa-kālocita-śraddhā-
dravya-pātrārhaṇāni ca
samyag bhavanti naitāni
vistarāt sva-janārpaṇāt

deśa—place; *kāla*—time; *ucita*—proper; *śraddhā*—respect; *dravya*—ingredients; *pātra*—a suitable person; *arhaṇāni*—paraphernalia for worship; *ca*—and; *samyak*—proper; *bhavanti*—are; *na*—not; *etāni*—all these; *vistarāt*—due to expansion; *sva-jana-arpaṇāt*—or due to inviting relatives.

TRANSLATION

If one arranges to feed many brāhmaṇas or relatives during the śrāddha ceremony, there will be discrepancies in the time, place, respectability and ingredients, the person to be worshiped, and the method of offering worship.

PURPORT

Nārada Muni has prohibited unnecessarily gorgeous arrangements to feed relatives or *brāhmaṇas* during the *śrāddha* ceremony. Those who are materially opulent spend lavishly during this ceremony. Indians spend especially lavishly on three occasions—at the birth of a child, at marriage and while observing the *śrāddha* ceremony—but the *śāstras* prohibit the excessive expenditures involved in inviting many *brāhmaṇas* and relatives, especially during the *śrāddha* ceremony.

TEXT 5

देशे काले च सम्प्राप्ते मुन्यन्नं हरिदैवतम् ।
श्रद्धया विधिवत् पात्रे न्यस्तं कामधुगक्षयम् ॥ ५ ॥

deśe kāle ca samprāpte
muny-annaṁ hari-daivatam
śraddhayā vidhivat pātre
nyastaṁ kāmadhug akṣayam

deśe—in a proper place, namely a holy place of pilgrimage; *kāle*—at an auspicious time; *ca*—also; *samprāpte*—when available; *muni-annam*—foodstuffs prepared with ghee and suitable to be eaten by great saintly persons; *hari-daivatam*—unto the Supreme Personality of Godhead, Hari; *śraddhayā*—with love and affection; *vidhi-vat*—according to the directions of the spiritual master and the *śāstras; pātre*—unto the suitable person; *nyastam*—if it is so offered; *kāmadhuk*—becomes a source of prosperity; *akṣayam*—everlasting.

TRANSLATION

When one gets the opportunity of a suitable auspicious time and place, one should, with love, offer food prepared with ghee to the Deity of the Supreme Personality of Godhead and then offer the prasāda to a suitable person—a Vaiṣṇava or brāhmaṇa. This will be the cause of everlasting prosperity.

TEXT 6

देवर्षिपितृभूतेभ्य आत्मने स्वजनाय च ।
अन्नं संविभजन्पश्येत् सर्वं तत् पुरुषात्मकम् ॥ ६ ॥

devarṣi-pitṛ-bhūtebhya
ātmane sva-janāya ca
annaṁ saṁvibhajan paśyet
sarvaṁ tat puruṣātmakam

deva—unto the demigods; *ṛṣi*—saintly persons; *pitṛ*—forefathers; *bhūtebhyaḥ*—the living entities in general; *ātmane*—relatives; *sva-*

janāya—family members and friends; *ca*—and; *annam*—foodstuff (*prasāda*); *saṁvibhajan*—offering; *paśyet*—one should see; *sarvam*—all; *tat*—them; *puruṣa-ātmakam*—related to the Supreme Personality of Godhead.

TRANSLATION

One should offer prasāda to the demigods, the saintly persons, one's forefathers, the people in general, one's family members, one's relatives and one's friends, seeing them all as devotees of the Supreme Personality of Godhead.

PURPORT

As mentioned above, it is recommended that everyone distribute *prasāda*, considering every living being a part and parcel of the Supreme Lord. Even in feeding the poor, one should distribute *prasāda*. In Kali-yuga there is a scarcity of food almost every year, and thus philanthropists spend lavishly to feed the poor. For this they invent the term *daridra-nārāyaṇa-sevā*. This is prohibited. One should distribute sumptuous *prasāda*, considering everyone a part of the Supreme Lord, but one should not juggle words to make a poor man Nārāyaṇa. Everyone is related to the Supreme Lord, but one should not mistakenly think that because one is related to the Supreme Personality of Godhead, he has become the Supreme Personality of Godhead, Nārāyaṇa. Such a Māyāvāda philosophy is extremely dangerous, especially for a devotee. Śrī Caitanya Mahāprabhu has therefore strictly forbidden us to associate with Māyāvādī philosophers. *Māyāvādi-bhāṣya śunile haya sarva-nāśa:* if one associates with the Māyāvāda philosophy, his devotional life is doomed.

TEXT 7

न दद्यादामिषं श्राद्धे न चाद्याद् धर्मतत्त्ववित् ।
मुन्यन्नैः स्यात्परा प्रीतिर्यथा न पशुहिंसया ॥ ७ ॥

na dadyād āmiṣaṁ śrāddhe
na cādyād dharma-tattvavit
muny-annaiḥ syāt parā prītir
yathā na paśu-hiṁsayā

na—never; *dadyāt*—should offer; *āmiṣam*—meat, fish, eggs and so on; *śrāddhe*—in the performance of the *śrāddha* ceremony; *na*—nor; *ca*—also; *adyāt*—one should eat personally; *dharma-tattva-vit*—one who is actually learned in regard to religious activities; *muni-annaiḥ*—by preparations made with ghee for saintly persons; *syāt*—should be; *parā*—first-class; *prītiḥ*—satisfaction; *yathā*—for the forefathers and the Supreme Personality of Godhead; *na*—not; *paśu-hiṁsayā*—by killing animals unnecessarily.

TRANSLATION

A person fully aware of religious principles should never offer anything like meat, eggs or fish in the śrāddha ceremony, and even if one is a kṣatriya, he himself should not eat such things. When suitable food prepared with ghee is offered to saintly persons, the function is pleasing to the forefathers and the Supreme Lord, who are never pleased when animals are killed in the name of sacrifice.

TEXT 8

नैतादृशः परो धर्मो नृणां सद्धर्ममिच्छताम् ।
न्यासो दण्डस्य भूतेषु मनोवाक्कायजस्य यः ॥ ८ ॥

naitādṛśaḥ paro dharmo
nṛṇāṁ sad-dharmam icchatām
nyāso daṇḍasya bhūteṣu
mano-vāk-kāyajasya yaḥ

na—never; *etādṛśaḥ*—like this; *paraḥ*—a supreme or superior; *dharmaḥ*—religion; *nṛṇām*—of persons; *sat-dharmam*—superior religion; *icchatām*—being desirous of; *nyāsaḥ*—giving up; *daṇḍasya*—causing trouble because of envy; *bhūteṣu*—unto the living entities; *manaḥ*—in terms of the mind; *vāk*—words; *kāya-jasya*—and body; *yaḥ*—which.

TRANSLATION

Persons who want to advance in superior religion are advised to give up all envy of other living entities, whether in relationship to the body, words or mind. There is no religion superior to this.

TEXT 9

एके कर्ममयान् यज्ञान् ज्ञानिनो यज्ञवित्तमाः ।
आत्मसंयमनेऽनीहा जुह्वति ज्ञानदीपिते ॥ ९ ॥

eke karmamayān yajñān
jñānino yajña-vittamāḥ
ātma-saṁyamane 'nīhā
juhvati jñāna-dīpite

eke—some; *karma-mayān*—resulting in a reaction (such as the killing of animals); *yajñān*—sacrifices; *jñāninaḥ*—persons advanced in knowledge; *yajña-vit-tamāḥ*—who know perfectly well the purpose of sacrifice; *ātma-saṁyamane*—by self-control; *anīhāḥ*—who are without material desires; *juhvati*—execute sacrifice; *jñāna-dīpite*—enlightened in perfect knowledge.

TRANSLATION

Because of an awakening of spiritual knowledge, those who are intelligent in regard to sacrifice, who are actually aware of religious principles and who are free from material desires, control the self in the fire of spiritual knowledge, or knowledge of the Absolute Truth. They may give up the process of ritualistic ceremonies.

PURPORT

People are generally very much interested in *karma-kāṇḍa* ritualistic ceremonies for elevation to the higher planetary systems, but when one awakens his spiritual knowledge, he becomes uninterested in such elevation and engages himself fully in *jñāna-yajña* to find the objective of life. The objective of life is to stop completely the miseries of birth and death and to return home, back to Godhead. When one cultivates knowledge for this purpose, he is considered to be on a higher platform than one who is engaged in *karma-yajña*, or fruitive activities.

TEXT 10

द्रव्ययज्ञैर्यक्ष्यमाणं दृष्ट्वा भूतानि बिभ्यति ।
एष माकरुणो हन्यादतज्ज्ञो ह्यसुतृप् ध्रुवम् ॥१०॥

dravya-yajñair yakṣyamāṇaṁ
dṛṣṭvā bhūtāni bibhyati
eṣa mākaruṇo hanyād
ataj-jño hy asu-tṛp dhruvam

dravya-yajñaiḥ—with animals and other eatable things; *yakṣyamāṇam*—the person engaged in such sacrifices; *dṛṣṭvā*—by seeing; *bhūtāni*—the living entities (animals); *bibhyati*—become afraid; *eṣaḥ*—this person (the performer of sacrifice); *mā*—us; *akaruṇaḥ*—who is inhumane and merciless; *hanyāt*—will kill; *a-tat-jñaḥ*—most ignorant; *hi*—indeed; *asu-tṛp*—who is most satisfied by killing others; *dhruvam*—certainly.

TRANSLATION

Upon seeing the person engaged in performing the sacrifice, animals meant to be sacrificed are extremely afraid, thinking, "This merciless performer of sacrifices, being ignorant of the purpose of sacrifice and being most satisfied by killing others, will surely kill us."

PURPORT

Animal sacrifice in the name of religion is current practically all over the world in every established religion. It is said that Lord Jesus Christ, when twelve years old, was shocked to see the Jews sacrificing birds and animals in the synagogues and that he therefore rejected the Jewish system of religion and started the religious system of Christianity, adhering to the Old Testament commandment "Thou shalt not kill." At the present day, however, not only are animals killed in the name of sacrifice, but the killing of animals has increased enormously because of the increasing number of slaughterhouses. Slaughtering animals, either for religion or for food, is most abominable and is condemned herein. Unless one is merciless, one cannot sacrifice animals, either in the name of religion or for food.

TEXT 11

तस्माद् दैवोपपन्नेन मुन्यन्नेनापि धर्मवित् ।
सन्तुष्टोऽहरहः कुर्यान्नित्यनैमित्तिकीः क्रियाः ॥११॥

tasmād daivopapannena
muny-annenāpi dharmavit
santuṣṭo 'har ahaḥ kuryān
nitya-naimittikīḥ kriyāḥ

tasmāt—therefore; *daiva-upapannena*—obtainable very easily by the grace of the Lord; *muni-annena*—with food (prepared in ghee and offered to the Supreme Lord); *api*—indeed; *dharma-vit*—one who is actually advanced in religious principles; *santuṣṭaḥ*—very happily; *ahaḥ ahaḥ*—day after day; *kuryāt*—one should perform; *nitya-naimittikīḥ*—regular and occasional; *kriyāḥ*—duties.

TRANSLATION

Therefore, day by day, one who is actually aware of religious principles and is not heinously envious of poor animals should happily perform daily sacrifices and those for certain occasions with whatever food is available easily by the grace of the Lord.

PURPORT

The word *dharmavit,* meaning "one who knows the actual purpose of religion," is very significant. As explained in *Bhagavad-gītā* (18.66), *sarva-dharmān parityajya mām ekaṁ śaraṇaṁ vraja:* becoming Kṛṣṇa conscious is the topmost stage in understanding of religious principles. One who reaches this stage performs the *arcanā* process in devotional service. Anyone, whether a *gṛhastha* or a *sannyāsī,* can keep small Deities of the Lord suitably packed or, if possible, installed, and thus worship the Deities of Rādhā-Kṛṣṇa, Sītā-Rāma, Lakṣmī-Nārāyaṇa, Lord Jagannātha or Śrī Caitanya Mahāprabhu by offering food prepared in ghee and then offering the sanctified *prasāda* to the forefathers, demigods and other living entities as a matter of routine daily work. All the centers of our Kṛṣṇa consciousness movement have Deity worship programs very nicely going on in which food is offered to the Deity and distributed to the first-class *brāhmaṇas* and Vaiṣṇavas and even to the people in general. This performance of sacrifice brings complete satisfaction. The members of the Kṛṣṇa consciousness movement engage daily in such transcendental activities. Thus in our Kṛṣṇa consciousness movement there is no question at all of killing animals.

TEXT 12

विधर्मः परधर्मश्च आभास उपमा छलः ।
अधर्मशाखाः पञ्चेमा धर्मज्ञोऽधर्मवत् त्यजेत् ॥१२॥

vidharmaḥ para-dharmaś ca
ābhāsa upamā chalaḥ
adharma-śākhāḥ pañcemā
dharma-jño 'dharmavat tyajet

vidharmaḥ—irreligion; *para-dharmaḥ*—religious principles practiced by others; *ca*—and; *ābhāsaḥ*—pretentious religious principles; *upamā*—principles that appear religious but are not; *chalaḥ*—a cheating religion; *adharma-śākhāḥ*—which are different branches of irreligion; *pañca*—five; *imāḥ*—these; *dharma-jñaḥ*—one who is aware of religious principles; *adharma-vat*—accepting them as irreligious; *tyajet*—should give up.

TRANSLATION

There are five branches of irreligion, appropriately known as irreligion [vidharma], religious principles for which one is unfit [para-dharma], pretentious religion [ābhāsa], analogical religion [upadharma] and cheating religion [chala-dharma]. One who is aware of real religious life must abandon these five as irreligious.

PURPORT

Any religious principles opposed to the principle of surrendering to the lotus feet of the Supreme Personality of Godhead, Kṛṣṇa, are to be considered religious principles of irregularity or cheating, and one who is actually interested in religion must give them up. One should simply follow the instructions of Kṛṣṇa and surrender unto Him. To do this, of course, one needs very good intelligence, which may be awakened after many, many births through good association with devotees and the practice of Kṛṣṇa consciousness. Everything but the principle of religion recommended by Kṛṣṇa—*sarva-dharmān parityajya mām ekaṁ śaraṇaṁ vraja*—should be given up as irreligion.

TEXT 13

धर्मबाधो विधर्मः स्यात् परधर्मोऽन्यचोदितः ।
उपधर्मस्तु पाखण्डो दम्भो वा शब्दभिच्छलः ॥१३॥

dharma-bādho vidharmaḥ syāt
para-dharmo 'nya-coditaḥ
upadharmas tu pākhaṇḍo
dambho vā śabda-bhic chalaḥ

dharma-bādhaḥ—obstructs the execution of one's own religious principles; *vidharmaḥ*—against the principles of religion; *syāt*—should be; *para-dharmaḥ*—imitating religious systems for which one is unfit; *anya-coditaḥ*—which is introduced by someone else; *upadharmaḥ*—concocted religious principles; *tu*—indeed; *pākhaṇḍaḥ*—by one who is against the principles of *Vedas*, standard scriptures; *dambhaḥ*—who is falsely proud; *vā*—or; *śabda-bhit*—by word jugglery; *chalaḥ*—a cheating religious system.

TRANSLATION

Religious principles that obstruct one from following his own religion are called vidharma. Religious principles introduced by others are called para-dharma. A new type of religion created by one who is falsely proud and who opposes the principles of the Vedas is called upadharma. And interpretation by one's jugglery of words is called chala-dharma.

PURPORT

To create a new type of *dharma* has become fashionable in this age. So-called *svāmīs* and *yogīs* support that one may follow any type of religious system, according to one's own choice, because all systems are ultimately the same. In *Śrīmad-Bhāgavatam*, however, such fashionable ideas are called *vidharma* because they go against one's own religious system. The real religious system is described by the Supreme Personality of Godhead: *sarva-dharmān parityajya mām ekaṁ śaraṇaṁ vraja.* The real religious system is that of surrender to the lotus feet of the Lord. In the Sixth Canto of *Śrīmad-Bhāgavatam*, in connection with

Ajāmila's deliverance, Yamarāja says, *dharmaṁ tu sākṣād bhagavat-praṇītam:* real religion is that which is given by the Supreme Personality of Godhead, just as real law is that which is given by the government. No one can manufacture actual law at home, nor can one manufacture actual religion. Elsewhere it is said, *sa vai puṁsāṁ paro dharmo yato bhaktir adhokṣaje:* the real religious system is that which leads one to become a devotee of the Supreme Lord. Therefore, anything opposed to this religious system of progressive Kṛṣṇa consciousness is called *vidharma, para-dharma, upadharma* or *chala-dharma.* Misinterpretation of *Bhagavad-gītā* is *chala-dharma.* When Kṛṣṇa directly says something and some rascal interprets it to mean something different, this is *chala-dharma*—a religious system of cheating—or *śabda-bhit,* a jugglery of words. One should be extremely careful to avoid these various types of cheating systems of religion.

TEXT 14

यस्त्विच्छया कृतः पुम्भिराभासो ह्याश्रमात् पृथक् ।
स्वभावविहितो धर्मः कस्य नेष्टः प्रशान्तये ॥१४॥

yas tv icchayā kṛtaḥ pumbhir
ābhāso hy āśramāt pṛthak
sva-bhāva-vihito dharmaḥ
kasya neṣṭaḥ praśāntaye

yaḥ—that which; *tu*—indeed; *icchayā*—whimsically; *kṛtaḥ*—conducted; *pumbhiḥ*—by persons; *ābhāsaḥ*—dim reflection; *hi*—indeed; *āśramāt*—from one's own order of life; *pṛthak*—different; *sva-bhāva*—according to one's own nature; *vihitaḥ*—regulated; *dharmaḥ*—religious principle; *kasya*—in what respect; *na*—not; *iṣṭaḥ*—capable; *praśāntaye*—for relieving all kinds of distress.

TRANSLATION

A pretentious religious system manufactured by one who willfully neglects the prescribed duties of his order of life is called ābhāsa [a dim reflection or false similarity]. But if one performs the prescribed duties for his particular āśrama or varṇa, why are they not sufficient to mitigate all material distresses?

PURPORT

It is indicated here that everyone should strictly follow the principles of *varṇa* and *āśrama* as given in the *śāstra*. In the *Viṣṇu Purāṇa* (3.8.9) it is said:

varṇāśramācāravatā
puruṣeṇa paraḥ pumān
viṣṇur ārādhyate panthā
nānyat tat-toṣa-kāraṇam

One should focus upon the destination for progress, which is to become Kṛṣṇa conscious. This is the aim and end of all *varṇas* and *āśramas*. However, if Viṣṇu is not worshiped, the followers of the *varṇāśrama* institution manufacture some concocted God. Thus it has now become fashionable for any rascal or fool to be elected God, and there are many missionaries who have concocted their own gods, giving up their relationship with the real God. In *Bhagavad-gītā* it is clearly said that one who worships the demigods has lost his intelligence. Nonetheless we find that even an illiterate person who has lost all intelligence is elected God, and although he has a temple, it has meat-eating *sannyāsīs*, and many polluted activities go on there. This type of religious system, which misguides its poor followers, is strictly forbidden. Such pretentious religions should be stopped altogether.

The original system is that a *brāhmaṇa* should actually become a *brāhmaṇa;* he should not only take birth in a *brāhmaṇa* family, but must also be qualified. Also, even if one is not born in a *brāhmaṇa* family but has brahminical qualifications, he must be considered a *brāhmaṇa*. By strictly following this system, one can be happy without extra endeavor. *Sva-bhāva-vihito dharmaḥ kasya neṣṭaḥ praśāntaye.* The real aim of life is to mitigate distress, and one can do this very easily by following the principles of *śāstra*.

TEXT 15

धर्मार्थमपि नेहेत यात्रार्थं वाधनो धनम् ।
अनीहानीहमानस्य महाहेरिव वृत्तिदा ॥१५॥

dharmārtham api neheta
yātrārthaṁ vādhano dhanam
anīhānīhamānasya
mahāher iva vṛttidā

dharma-artham—in religion or economic development; *api*—indeed; *na*—not; *īheta*—should try to obtain; *yātrā-artham*—just to maintain the body and soul together; *vā*—either; *adhanaḥ*—one who has no wealth; *dhanam*—money; *anīhā*—the desirelessness; *anīhamānasya*—of a person who does not endeavor even to earn his livelihood; *mahā-aheḥ*—the great serpent known as the python; *iva*—like; *vṛtti-dā*—which obtains its livelihood without endeavor.

TRANSLATION

Even if a man is poor, he should not endeavor to improve his economic condition just to maintain his body and soul together or to become a famous religionist. Just as a great python, although lying in one place, not endeavoring for its livelihood, gets the food it needs to maintain body and soul, one who is desireless also obtains his livelihood without endeavor.

PURPORT

Human life is simply meant for developing Kṛṣṇa consciousness. One need not even try to earn a livelihood to maintain body and soul together. This is illustrated here by the example of the great python, which lies in one place, never going here and there to earn a livelihood to maintain itself, and yet is maintained by the grace of the Lord. As advised by Nārada Muni (*Bhāg.* 1.5.18), *tasyaiva hetoḥ prayateta kovidaḥ:* one should simply endeavor to increase his Kṛṣṇa consciousness. One should not desire to do anything else, even to earn his livelihood. There are many, many examples of this attitude. Mādhavendra Purī, for instance, would never go to anyone to ask for food. Śukadeva Gosvāmī has also said, *kasmād bhajanti kavayo dhana-durmadāndhān.* Why should one approach a person who is blind with wealth? Rather, one should depend on Kṛṣṇa, and He will give everything. All the members of our Kṛṣṇa consciousness movement, whether they be *gṛhasthas* or *sannyāsīs,* should try to spread the Kṛṣṇa consciousness movement with determination, and Kṛṣṇa will supply all necessities. The process of *ājagara-vṛtti*, the means of livelihood of a python, is very much appreciated in this regard. Even though one may be very poor, he should simply try to advance in Kṛṣṇa consciousness and not endeavor to earn his livelihood.

TEXT 16

सन्तुष्टस्य निरीहस्य स्वात्मारामस्य यत् सुखम् ।
कुतस्तत् कामलोभेन धावतोऽर्थेहया दिशः ॥१६॥

santuṣṭasya nirīhasya
svātmārāmasya yat sukham
kutas tat kāma-lobhena
dhāvato 'rthehayā diśaḥ

santuṣṭasya—of one who is fully satisfied in Kṛṣṇa consciousness; *nirīhasya*—who does not endeavor for his livelihood; *sva*—own; *ātma-ārāmasya*—who is self-satisfied; *yat*—that; *sukham*—happiness; *kutaḥ*—where; *tat*—such happiness; *kāma-lobhena*—impelled by lust and greed; *dhāvataḥ*—of one who is wandering here and there; *artha-īhayā*—with a desire for accumulating wealth; *diśaḥ*—in all directions.

TRANSLATION

One who is content and satisfied and who links his activities with the Supreme Personality of Godhead residing in everyone's heart enjoys transcendental happiness without endeavoring for his livelihood. Where is such happiness for a materialistic man who is impelled by lust and greed and who therefore wanders in all directions with a desire to accumulate wealth?

TEXT 17

सदा सन्तुष्टमनसः सर्वाः शिवमया दिशः ।
शर्कराकण्टकादिभ्यो यथोपानत्पदः शिवम् ॥१७॥

sadā santuṣṭa-manasaḥ
sarvāḥ śivamayā diśaḥ
śarkarā-kaṇṭakādibhyo
yathopānat-padaḥ śivam

sadā—always; *santuṣṭa-manasaḥ*—for a person who is self-satisfied; *sarvāḥ*—everything; *śiva-mayāḥ*—auspicious; *diśaḥ*—in all directions; *śarkarā*—from pebbles; *kaṇṭaka-ādibhyaḥ*—and thorns, etc.; *yathā*—as; *upānat-padaḥ*—for a person who has suitable shoes; *śivam*—there is no danger (auspicious).

TRANSLATION

For a person who has suitable shoes on his feet, there is no danger even when he walks on pebbles and thorns. For him, everything is auspicious. Similarly, for one who is always self-satisfied there is no distress; indeed, he feels happiness everywhere.

TEXT 18

सन्तुष्टः केन वा राजन्न वर्तेतापि वारिणा ।
औपस्थ्यजैह्वयकार्पण्याद् गृहपालायते जनः ॥१८॥

santuṣṭaḥ kena vā rājan
na vartetāpi vāriṇā
aupasthya-jaihvya-kārpaṇyād
gṛha-pālāyate janaḥ

santuṣṭaḥ—a person who is always self-satisfied; *kena*—why; *vā*—or; *rājan*—O King; *na*—not; *varteta*—should live (happily); *api*—even; *vāriṇā*—by drinking water; *aupasthya*—due to the genitals; *jaihvya*—and the tongue; *kārpaṇyāt*—because of a wretched or miserly condition; *gṛha-pālāyate*—he becomes exactly like a household dog; *janaḥ*—such a person.

TRANSLATION

My dear King, a self-satisfied person can be happy even with only drinking water. However, one who is driven by the senses, especially by the tongue and genitals, must accept the position of a household dog to satisfy his senses.

PURPORT

According to the *śāstras*, a *brāhmaṇa*, or a cultured person in Kṛṣṇa consciousness, will not enter anyone's service to maintain body and soul together, and especially not for satisfaction of the senses. A true *brāhmaṇa* is always satisfied. Even if he has nothing to eat, he can drink a little water and be satisfied. This is only a matter of practice. Unfortunately, however, no one is educated in how to be satisfied in self-realization. As explained above, a devotee is always satisfied because he feels the presence of the Supersoul within his heart and thinks of Him twenty-four hours a day. That is real satisfaction. A devotee is never driven by the dictations of the tongue and genitals, and thus he is never victimized by the laws of material nature.

TEXT 19

असन्तुष्टस्य विप्रस्य तेजो विद्या तपो यशः ।
स्रवन्तीन्द्रियलौल्येन ज्ञानं चैवावकीर्यते ॥१९॥

asantuṣṭasya viprasya
tejo vidyā tapo yaśaḥ
sravantīndriya-laulyena
jñānaṁ caivāvakīryate

asantuṣṭasya—of one who is not self-satisfied; *viprasya*—of such a *brāhmaṇa; tejaḥ*—strength; *vidyā*—education; *tapaḥ*—austerity; *yaśaḥ*—fame; *sravanti*—dwindle; *indriya*—of the senses; *laulyena*—because of greed; *jñānam*—knowledge; *ca*—and; *eva*—certainly; *avakīryate*—gradually vanishes.

TRANSLATION

Because of greed for the sake of the senses, the spiritual strength, education, austerity and reputation of a devotee or brāhmaṇa who is not self-satisfied dwindle, and his knowledge gradually vanishes.

TEXT 20

कामस्यान्तं हि क्षुत्तृड्भ्यां क्रोधस्यैतत्फलोदयात् ।
जनो याति न लोभस्य जित्वा भुक्त्वा दिशो भुवः ॥२०॥

kāmasyāntaṁ hi kṣut-tṛḍbhyāṁ
krodhasyaitat phalodayāt
jano yāti na lobhasya
jitvā bhuktvā diśo bhuvaḥ

kāmasya—of the desire for sense gratification or the urgent needs of the body; *antam*—end; *hi*—indeed; *kṣut-tṛḍbhyām*—by one who is very hungry or thirsty; *krodhasya*—of anger; *etat*—this; *phala-udayāt*—by venting chastisement and its reaction; *janaḥ*—a person; *yāti*—crosses over; *na*—not; *lobhasya*—greed; *jitvā*—conquering; *bhuktvā*—enjoying; *diśaḥ*—all directions; *bhuvaḥ*—of the globe.

TRANSLATION

The strong bodily desires and needs of a person disturbed by hunger and thirst are certainly satisfied when he eats. Similarly, if one becomes very angry, that anger is satisfied by chastisement and its reaction. But as for greed, even if a greedy person has conquered all the directions of the world or has enjoyed everything in the world, still he will not be satisfied.

PURPORT

In *Bhagavad-gītā* (3.37) it is stated that lust, anger and greed are the causes of the conditioned soul's bondage in this material world. *Kāma eṣa krodha eṣa rajo-guṇa-samudbhavaḥ.* When strong lusty desires for sense gratification are unfulfilled, one becomes angry. This anger can be satisfied when one chastises his enemy, but when there is an increase in *lobha,* or greed, which is the greatest enemy caused by *rajo-guṇa,* the mode of passion, how can one advance in Kṛṣṇa consciousness?

If one is very greedy to enhance his Kṛṣṇa consciousness, this is a great boon. *Tatra laulyam ekalaṁ mūlam.* This is the best path available.

TEXT 21

पण्डिता बहवो राजन्बहुज्ञाः संशयच्छिदः ।
सदसस्पतयोऽप्येके असन्तोषात् पतन्त्यधः ॥२१॥

paṇḍitā bahavo rājan
bahu-jñāḥ saṁśaya-cchidaḥ

sadasas patayo 'py eke
asantoṣāt patanty adhaḥ

paṇḍitāḥ—very learned scholars; *bahavaḥ*—many; *rājan*—O King (Yudhiṣṭhira); *bahu-jñāḥ*—persons with varied experience; *saṁśaya-cchidaḥ*—expert in legal advice; *sadasaḥ patayaḥ*—persons eligible to become presidents of learned assemblies; *api*—even; *eke*—by one disqualification; *asantoṣāt*—simply by dissatisfaction or greed; *patanti*—fall down; *adhaḥ*—into hellish conditions of life.

TRANSLATION

O King Yudhiṣṭhira, many persons with varied experience, many legal advisers, many learned scholars and many persons eligible to become presidents of learned assemblies fall down into hellish life because of not being satisfied with their positions.

PURPORT

For spiritual advancement, one should be materially satisfied, for if one is not materially satisfied, his greed for material development will result in the frustration of his spiritual advancement. There are two things that nullify all good qualities. One is poverty. *Daridra-doṣo guṇa-rāśi-nāśī.* If one is poverty-stricken, all his good qualities become null and void. Similarly, if one becomes too greedy, his good qualifications are lost. Therefore the adjustment is that one should not be poverty-stricken, but one must try to be fully satisfied with the bare necessities of life and not be greedy. For a devotee to be satisfied with the bare necessities is therefore the best advice for spiritual advancement. Learned authorities in devotional life consequently advise that one not endeavor to increase the number of temples and *maṭhas.* Such activities can be undertaken only by devotees experienced in propagating the Kṛṣṇa consciousness movement. All the *ācāryas* in South India, especially Śrī Rāmānujācārya, constructed many big temples, and in North India all the Gosvāmīs of Vṛndāvana constructed large temples. Śrīla Bhaktisiddhānta Sarasvatī Ṭhākura also constructed large centers, known as Gauḍīya Maṭhas. Therefore temple construction is not bad, provided proper care is taken for the propagation of Kṛṣṇa consciousness. Even if such endeavors are considered greedy, the greed is to satisfy Kṛṣṇa, and therefore these are spiritual activities.

TEXT 22

असङ्कल्पाज्जयेत् कामं क्रोधं कामविवर्जनात् ।
अर्थानर्थेक्षया लोभं भयं तत्त्वावमर्शनात् ॥२२॥

asaṅkalpāj jayet kāmaṁ
krodhaṁ kāma-vivarjanāt
arthānartheksayā lobhaṁ
bhayaṁ tattvāvamarśanāt

asaṅkalpāt—by determination; *jayet*—one should conquer; *kāmam*—lusty desire; *krodham*—anger; *kāma-vivarjanāt*—by giving up the objective of sense desire; *artha*—accumulation of wealth; *anartha*—a cause of trouble; *īkṣayā*—by considering; *lobham*—greed; *bhayam*—fear; *tattva*—the truth; *avamarśanāt*—by considering.

TRANSLATION

By making plans with determination, one should give up lusty desires for sense gratification. Similarly, by giving up envy one should conquer anger, by discussing the disadvantages of accumulating wealth one should give up greed, and by discussing the truth one should give up fear.

PURPORT

Śrīla Viśvanātha Cakravartī Ṭhākura has suggested how one can conquer lusty desires for sense gratification. One cannot give up thinking of women, for thinking in this way is natural; even while walking on the street, one will see so many women. However, if one is determined not to live with a woman, even while seeing a woman he will not become lusty. If one is determined not to have sex, he can automatically conquer lusty desires. The example given in this regard is that even if one is hungry, if on a particular day he is determined to observe fasting, he can naturally conquer the disturbances of hunger and thirst. If one is determined not to be envious of anyone, he can naturally conquer anger. Similarly, one can give up the desire to accumulate wealth simply by considering how difficult it is to protect the money in one's possession. If one keeps a large amount of cash with him, he is always anxious about keeping it properly. Thus if one discusses the disadvantages of accumulating wealth, he can naturally give up business without difficulty.

TEXT 23

आन्वीक्षिक्या शोकमोहौ दम्भं महदुपासया ।
योगान्तरायान् मौनेन हिंसां कामाद्यनीहया ॥२३॥

ānvīkṣikyā śoka-mohau
dambhaṁ mahad-upāsayā
yogāntarāyān maunena
hiṁsāṁ kāmādy-anīhayā

ānvīkṣikyā—by deliberation upon material and spiritual subject matters; *śoka*—lamentation; *mohau*—and illusion; *dambham*—false pride; *mahat*—a Vaiṣṇava; *upāsayā*—by serving; *yoga-antarāyān*—obstacles on the path of *yoga;* *maunena*—by silence; *hiṁsām*—envy; *kāma-ādi*—for sense gratification; *anīhayā*—without endeavor.

TRANSLATION

By discussing spiritual knowledge one can conquer lamentation and illusion, by serving a great devotee one can become prideless, by keeping silent one can avoid obstacles on the path of mystic yoga, and simply by stopping sense gratification one can conquer envy.

PURPORT

If one's son has died, one may certainly be affected by lamentation and illusion and cry for the dead son, but one may overcome lamentation and illusion by considering the verses of *Bhagavad-gītā.*

jātasya hi dhruvo mṛtyur
dhruvaṁ janma mṛtasya ca

As the soul transmigrates, one who has taken birth must give up the present body, and then he must certainly accept another body. This should be no cause for lamentation. Therefore Lord Kṛṣṇa says, *dhīras tatra na muhyati:* one who is *dhīra*, or sober, who is learned in philosophy and established in knowledge, cannot be unhappy over the transmigration of the soul.

TEXT 24

कृपया भूतजं दुःखं दैवं जह्यात् समाधिना ।
आत्मजं योगवीर्येण निद्रां सत्त्वनिषेवया ॥२४॥

kṛpayā bhūtajaṁ duḥkhaṁ
daivaṁ jahyāt samādhinā
ātmajaṁ yoga-vīryeṇa
nidrāṁ sattva-niṣevayā

kṛpayā—by being merciful to all other living entities; *bhūta-jam*—because of other living entities; *duḥkham*—suffering; *daivam*—sufferings imposed by providence; *jahyāt*—one should give up; *samādhinā*—by trance or meditation; *ātma-jam*—sufferings due to the body and mind; *yoga-vīryeṇa*—by practicing *haṭha-yoga, prāṇāyāma* and so forth; *nidrām*—sleeping; *sattva-niṣevayā*—by developing brahminical qualifications or the mode of goodness.

TRANSLATION

By good behavior and freedom from envy one should counteract sufferings due to other living entities, by meditation in trance one should counteract sufferings due to providence, and by practicing haṭha-yoga, prāṇāyāma and so forth one should counteract sufferings due to the body and mind. Similarly, by developing the mode of goodness, especially in regard to eating, one should conquer sleep.

PURPORT

By practice, one should avoid eating in such a way that other living entities will be disturbed and suffer. Since I suffer when pinched or killed by others, I should not attempt to pinch or kill any other living entity. People do not know that because of killing innocent animals they themselves will have to suffer severe reactions from material nature. Any country where people indulge in unnecessary killing of animals will have to suffer from wars and pestilence imposed by material nature. Comparing one's own suffering to the suffering of others, therefore, one should be kind to all living entities. One cannot avoid the sufferings inflicted by providence, and therefore when suffering comes one should fully absorb oneself in chanting the Hare Kṛṣṇa *mantra.* One can avoid sufferings from the body and mind by practicing mystic *haṭha-yoga.*

TEXT 25

रजस्तमश्च सत्त्वेन सत्त्वं चोपशमेन च ।
एतत् सर्वं गुरौ भक्त्या पुरुषो ह्यञ्जसा जयेत् ॥२५॥

rajas tamaś ca sattvena
sattvaṁ copaśamena ca
etat sarvaṁ gurau bhaktyā
puruṣo hy añjasā jayet

rajaḥ tamaḥ—the modes of passion and ignorance; *ca*—and; *sattvena*—by developing the mode of goodness; *sattvam*—the mode of goodness; *ca*—also; *upaśamena*—by giving up attachment; *ca*—and; *etat*—these; *sarvam*—all; *gurau*—unto the spiritual master; *bhaktyā*—by rendering service in devotion; *puruṣaḥ*—a person; *hi*—indeed; *añjasā*—easily; *jayet*—can conquer.

TRANSLATION

One must conquer the modes of passion and ignorance by developing the mode of goodness, and then one must become detached from the mode of goodness by promoting oneself to the platform of śuddha-sattva. All this can be automatically done if one engages in the service of the spiritual master with faith and devotion. In this way one can conquer the influence of the modes of nature.

PURPORT

Just by treating the root cause of an ailment, one can conquer all bodily pains and sufferings. Similarly, if one is devoted and faithful to the spiritual master, he can conquer the influence of *sattva-guṇa, rajo-guṇa* and *tamo-guṇa* very easily. *Yogīs* and *jñānīs* practice in many ways to conquer the senses, but the *bhakta* immediately attains the mercy of the Supreme Personality of Godhead through the mercy of the spiritual master. *Yasya prasādād bhagavat-prasādo.* If the spiritual master is favorably inclined, one naturally receives the mercy of the Supreme Lord, and by the mercy of the Supreme Lord one immediately becomes transcendental, conquering all the influences of *sattva-guṇa, rajo-guṇa* and *tamo-guṇa* within this material world. This is confirmed in *Bhagavad-gītā* (*sa guṇān samatītyaitān brahma-bhūyāya kalpate*). If one is a pure devotee acting under the directions of the *guru,* one easily gets the mercy of the Supreme Lord and thus becomes immediately situated on the transcendental platform. This is explained in the next verse.

TEXT 26

यस्य साक्षाद्द भगवति ज्ञानदीपप्रदे गुरौ ।
मर्त्यासद्धीः श्रुतं तस्य सर्वं कुञ्जरशौचवत् ॥२६॥

yasya sākṣād bhagavati
jñāna-dīpa-prade gurau
martyāsad-dhīḥ śrutaṁ tasya
sarvaṁ kuñjara-śaucavat

yasya—one who; *sākṣāt*—directly; *bhagavati*—the Supreme Personality of Godhead; *jñāna-dīpa-prade*—who enlightens with the torch of knowledge; *gurau*—unto the spiritual master; *martya-asat-dhīḥ*—considers the spiritual master to be like an ordinary human being and maintains such an unfavorable attitude; *śrutam*—Vedic knowledge; *tasya*—for him; *sarvam*—everything; *kuñjara-śauca-vat*—like the bath of an elephant in a lake.

TRANSLATION

The spiritual master should be considered to be directly the Supreme Lord because he gives transcendental knowledge for

enlightenment. Consequently, for one who maintains the material conception that the spiritual master is an ordinary human being, everything is frustrated. His enlightenment and his Vedic studies and knowledge are like the bathing of an elephant.

PURPORT

It is recommended that one honor the spiritual master as being on an equal status with the Supreme Personality of Godhead. *Sākṣād dharitvena samasta-śāstraiḥ.* This is enjoined in every scripture. *Ācāryaṁ māṁ vijānīyāt.* One should consider the *ācārya* to be as good as the Supreme Personality of Godhead. In spite of all these instructions, if one considers the spiritual master an ordinary human being, one is doomed. His study of the *Vedas* and his austerities and penances for enlightenment are all useless, like the bathing of an elephant. An elephant bathes in a lake quite thoroughly, but as soon as it comes on the shore it takes some dust from the ground and strews it over its body. Thus there is no meaning to the elephant's bath. One may argue by saying that since the spiritual master's relatives and the men of his neighborhood consider him an ordinary human being, what is the fault on the part of the disciple who considers the spiritual master an ordinary human being? This will be answered in the next verse, but the injunction is that the spiritual master should never be considered an ordinary man. One should strictly adhere to the instructions of the spiritual master, for if he is pleased, certainly the Supreme Personality of Godhead is pleased. *Yasya prasādād bhagavat-prasādo yasyāprasādān na gatiḥ kuto 'pi.*

TEXT 27

एष वै भगवान्साक्षात् प्रधानपुरुषेश्वरः ।
योगेश्वरैर्विमृग्याङ्घ्रिर्लोको यं मन्यते नरम् ॥२७॥

eṣa vai bhagavān sākṣāt
pradhāna-puruṣeśvaraḥ
yogeśvarair vimṛgyāṅghrir
loko yaṁ manyate naram

eṣaḥ—this; *vai*—indeed; *bhagavān*—Supreme Personality of Godhead; *sākṣāt*—directly; *pradhāna*—the chief cause of the material nature; *puruṣa*—of all living entities or of the *puruṣāvatāra,* Lord Viṣṇu; *īśvaraḥ*—the supreme controller; *yoga-īśvaraiḥ*—by great saintly persons, *yogīs; vimṛgya-aṅghriḥ*—Lord Kṛṣṇa's lotus feet, which are sought; *lokaḥ*—people in general; *yam*—Him; *manyate*—consider; *naram*—a human being.

TRANSLATION

The Supreme Personality of Godhead, Lord Kṛṣṇa, is the master of all other living entities and of the material nature. His lotus feet are sought and worshiped by great saintly persons like Vyāsa. Nonetheless, there are fools who consider Lord Kṛṣṇa an ordinary human being.

PURPORT

The example of Lord Kṛṣṇa's being the Supreme Personality of Godhead is appropriate in regard to understanding the spiritual master. The spiritual master is called *sevaka-bhagavān,* the servitor Personality of Godhead, and Kṛṣṇa is called *sevya-bhagavān,* the Supreme Personality of Godhead who is to be worshiped. The spiritual master is the worshiper God, whereas the Supreme Personality of Godhead, Kṛṣṇa, is the worshipable God. This is the difference between the spiritual master and the Supreme Personality of Godhead.

Another point: *Bhagavad-gītā,* which constitutes the instructions of the Supreme Personality of Godhead, is presented by the spiritual master as it is, without deviation. Therefore the Absolute Truth is present in the spiritual master. As clearly stated in Text 26, *jñāna-dīpa-prade.* The Supreme Personality of Godhead gives real knowledge to the entire world, and the spiritual master, as the representative of the Supreme Godhead, carries the message throughout the world. Therefore, on the absolute platform, there is no difference between the spiritual master and the Supreme Personality of Godhead. If someone considers the Supreme Personality—Kṛṣṇa or Lord Rāmacandra—to be an ordinary human being, this does not mean that the Lord becomes an ordinary human being. Similarly, if the family members of the spiritual master, who is the bona fide representative of the Supreme Personality of Godhead, consider the spiritual master an ordinary human being, this does not mean that he becomes an ordinary human being. The spiritual master is as good as the Supreme Personality of Godhead, and therefore one who is very serious about spiritual advancement must regard the spiritual master in this way. Even a slight deviation from this understanding can create disaster in the disciple's Vedic studies and austerities.

TEXT 28

षड्वर्गसंयमैकान्ताः सर्वा नियमचोदनाः ।
तदन्ता यदि नो योगानावहेयुः श्रमावहाः ॥२८॥

ṣaḍ-varga-saṁyamaikāntāḥ
sarvā niyama-codanāḥ
tad-antā yadi no yogān
āvaheyuḥ śramāvahāḥ

ṣaṭ-varga—the six elements, namely the five working senses and the mind; *saṁyama-ekāntāḥ*—the ultimate aim of subjugating; *sarvāḥ*—all such activities; *niyama-codanāḥ*—the regulative principles further meant for controlling the senses and mind; *tat-antāḥ*—the ultimate goal of such activities; *yadi*—if; *no*—not; *yogān*—the positive link with the Supreme; *āvaheyuḥ*—did lead to; *śrama-āvahāḥ*—a waste of time and labor.

TRANSLATION

Ritualistic ceremonies, regulative principles, austerities and the practice of yoga are all meant to control the senses and mind, but even after one is able to control the senses and mind, if he does not come to the point of meditation upon the Supreme Lord, all such activities are simply labor in frustration.

PURPORT

One may argue that one may achieve the ultimate goal of life—realization of the Supersoul—by practicing the *yoga* system and ritualistic performances according to the Vedic principles, even without staunch devotion to the spiritual master. The actual fact, however, is that by practicing *yoga* one must come to the platform of meditating upon the Supreme Personality of Godhead. As stated in the scriptures, *dhyānāvasthita-tad-gatena manasā paśyanti yaṁ yoginaḥ:* a person in meditation achieves the perfection of *yoga* practice when he can see the Supreme Personality of Godhead. By various practices, one may come to the point of controlling the senses, but simply controlling the senses does not bring one to a substantial conclusion. However, by staunch faith in the spiritual master and the Supreme Personality of Godhead, one not only controls the senses but also realizes the Supreme Lord.

yasya deve parā bhaktir
yathā deve tathā gurau
tasyaite kathitā hy arthāḥ
prakāśante mahātmanaḥ

"Only unto those great souls who have implicit faith in both the Lord and the spiritual master are all the imports of the Vedic knowledge automatically revealed." (*Śvetāśvatara Upaniṣad* 6.23) It is further stated, *tuṣyeyaṁ sarva-bhūtātmā guru-śuśrūṣayā* and *taranty añjo bhavārṇavam.* Simply by rendering service to the spiritual master, one crosses the ocean of nescience and returns home, back to Godhead. Thus he gradually sees the Supreme Lord face to face and enjoys life in association with the Lord. The ultimate goal of *yoga* is to come in contact with the Supreme Personality of Godhead. Unless this point is achieved, one's so-called *yoga* practice is simply labor without any benefit.

TEXT 29

यथा वार्तादयो ह्यर्था योगस्यार्थं न बिभ्रति ।
अनर्थाय भवेयुः स्म पूर्तमिष्टं तथासतः ॥२९॥

yathā vārtādayo hy arthā
yogasyārthaṁ na bibhrati
anarthāya bhaveyuḥ sma
pūrtam iṣṭaṁ tathāsataḥ

yathā—as; *vārtā-ādayaḥ*—activities like occupational or professional duties; *hi*—certainly; *arthāḥ*—income (from such occupational duties); *yogasya*—of mystic power for self-realization; *artham*—benefit; *na*—

not; *bibhrati*—help; *anarthāya*—without value (binding one to repeated birth and death); *bhaveyuḥ*—they are; *sma*—at all times; *pūrtam iṣṭam*—ritualistic Vedic ceremonies; *tathā*—similarly; *asataḥ*—of a materialistic nondevotee.

TRANSLATION

As professional activities or business profits cannot help one in spiritual advancement but are a source of material entanglement, the Vedic ritualistic ceremonies cannot help anyone who is not a devotee of the Supreme Personality of Godhead.

PURPORT

If one becomes very rich through his professional activities, through trade or through agriculture, this does not mean that he is spiritually advanced. To be spiritually advanced is different from being materially rich. Although the purpose of life is to become spiritually rich, unfortunate men, misguided as they are, are always engaged in trying to become materially rich. Such material engagements, however, do not help one in the actual fulfillment of the human mission. On the contrary, material engagements lead one to be attracted to many unnecessary necessities, which are accompanied by the risk that one may be born in a degraded condition. As confirmed in *Bhagavad-gītā* (14.18):

ūrdhvaṁ gacchanti sattva-sthā
madhye tiṣṭhanti rājasāḥ
jaghanya-guṇa-vṛtti-sthā
adho gacchanti tāmasāḥ

"Those situated in the mode of goodness gradually go upward to the higher planets; those in the mode of passion live on the earthly planets; and those in the mode of ignorance go down to the hellish worlds." Especially in this Kali-yuga, material advancement means degradation and attraction to many unwanted necessities that create a low mentality. Therefore, *jaghanya-guṇa-vṛtti-sthā:* since people are contaminated by the lower qualities, they will lead their next lives either as animals or in other degraded forms of life. Making a show of religion without Kṛṣṇa consciousness may make one popular in the estimation of unintelligent men, but factually such a materialistic display of spiritual advancement does not help one at all; it will not prevent one from missing the goal of life.

TEXT 30

यश्चित्तविजये यत्तः स्यान्निःसङ्गोऽपरिग्रहः ।
एको विविक्तशरणो भिक्षुर्भैक्ष्यमिताशनः ॥३०॥

yaś citta-vijaye yattaḥ
syān niḥsaṅgo 'parigrahaḥ
eko vivikta-śaraṇo
bhikṣur bhaikṣya-mitāśanaḥ

yaḥ—one who; *citta-vijaye*—conquering the mind; *yattaḥ*—is engaged; *syāt*—must be; *niḥsaṅgaḥ*—without contaminated association; *aparigrahaḥ*—without being dependent (on the family); *ekaḥ*—alone; *vivikta-śaraṇaḥ*—taking shelter of a solitary place; *bhikṣuḥ*—a renounced person; *bhaikṣya*—by begging alms just to maintain the body; *mita-aśanaḥ*—frugal in eating.

TRANSLATION

One who desires to conquer the mind must leave the company of his family and live in a solitary place, free from contaminated association. To maintain the body and soul together, he should beg as much as he needs for the bare necessities of life.

PURPORT

This is the process for conquering the agitation of the mind. One is recommended to take leave of his family and live alone, maintaining body and soul together by begging alms and eating only as much as needed to keep himself alive. Without such a process, one cannot conquer lusty desires. *Sannyāsa* means accepting a life of begging, which makes one automatically very humble and meek and free from lusty desires. In this regard, the following verse appears in the *Smṛti* literature:

dvandvāhatasya gārhasthyaṁ
dhyāna-bhaṅgādi-kāraṇam

lakṣayitvā gṛhī spaṣṭaṁ
sannyased avicārayan

In this world of duality, family life is the cause that spoils one's spiritual life or meditation. Specifically understanding this fact, one should accept the order of *sannyāsa* without hesitation.

TEXT 31

देशे शुचौ समे राजन्संस्थाप्यासनमात्मनः ।
स्थिरं सुखं समं तस्मिन्नासीतर्ज्वङ्ग ओमिति ॥३१॥

deśe śucau same rājan
saṁsthāpyāsanam ātmanaḥ
sthiraṁ sukhaṁ samaṁ tasminn
āsītarjv-aṅga om iti

deśe—in a place; *śucau*—very sacred; *same*—level; *rājan*—O King; *saṁsthāpya*—placing; *āsanam*—on the seat; *ātmanaḥ*—one's self; *sthiram*—very steady; *sukham*—comfortably; *samam*—equipoised; *tasmin*—on that sitting place; *āsīta*—one should sit down; *ṛju-aṅgaḥ*—the body perpendicularly straight; *oṁ*—The Vedic *mantra praṇava; iti*—in this way.

TRANSLATION

My dear King, in a sacred and holy place of pilgrimage one should select a place in which to perform yoga. The place must be level and not too high or low. There one should sit very comfortably, being steady and equipoised, keeping his body straight, and thus begin chanting the Vedic praṇava.

PURPORT

Generally the chanting of *oṁ* is recommended because in the beginning one cannot understand the Personality of Godhead. As stated in *Śrīmad-Bhāgavatam* (1.2.11):

vadanti tat tattva-vidas
tattvaṁ yaj jñānam advayam

brahmeti paramātmeti
bhagavān iti śabdyate

"Learned transcendentalists who know the Absolute Truth call this nondual substance Brahman, Paramātmā or Bhagavān." Unless one is fully convinced of the Supreme Personality of Godhead, one has the tendency to become an impersonalist *yogī* searching for the Supreme Lord within the core of his heart (*dhyānāvasthita-tad-gatena manasā paśyanti yaṁ yoginaḥ*). Here the chanting of *oṁkāra* is recommended because in the beginning of transcendental realization, instead of chanting the Hare Kṛṣṇa *mahā-mantra*, one may chant *oṁkāra* (*praṇava*). There is no difference between the Hare Kṛṣṇa *mahā-mantra* and *oṁkāra* because both of them are sound representations of the Supreme Personality of Godhead. *Praṇavaḥ sarva-vedeṣu.* In all Vedic literatures, the sound vibration *oṁkāra* is the beginning. *Oṁ namo bhagavate vāsudevāya.* The difference between chanting *oṁkāra* and chanting the Hare Kṛṣṇa *mantra* is that the Hare Kṛṣṇa *mantra* may be chanted without consideration of the place or the sitting arrangements recommended in *Bhagavad-gītā* (6.11):

śucau deśe pratiṣṭhāpya
sthiram āsanam ātmanaḥ
nāty-ucchritaṁ nātinīcaṁ
cailājina-kuśottaram

"To practice *yoga,* one should go to a secluded place and should lay *kuśa* grass on the ground and then cover it with a deerskin and a soft cloth. The seat should neither be too high nor too low and should be situated in a sacred place." The Hare Kṛṣṇa *mantra* may be chanted by anyone, without consideration of the place or how one sits. Śrī Caitanya Mahāprabhu has openly declared, *niyamitaḥ smaraṇe na kālaḥ.* In chanting the Hare Kṛṣṇa *mahā-mantra* there are no particular injunctions regarding one's sitting place. The injunction *niyamitaḥ smaraṇe na kālaḥ* includes *deśa, kāla* and *pātra*—place, time and the individual. Therefore anyone may chant the Hare Kṛṣṇa *mantra,* without consideration of the time and place. Especially in this age, Kali-yuga, it is very difficult to find a suitable place according to the recommendations of *Bhagavad-gītā.* The Hare Kṛṣṇa *mahā-mantra,* however, may be chanted at any place and any time, and this will bring results very quickly. Yet even while chanting the Hare Kṛṣṇa *mantra* one may observe regulative principles. Thus while sitting and chanting one may keep his body straight, and this will help one in the chanting process; otherwise one may feel sleepy.

TEXTS 32–33

प्राणापानौ सन्निरुन्ध्यात् पूरकुम्भकरेचकैः ।
यावन्मनस्त्यजेत् कामान् स्वनासाग्रनिरीक्षणः ॥३२॥
यतो यतो निःसरति मनः कामहतं भ्रमत् ।
ततस्तत उपाहृत्य हृदि रुन्ध्याच्छनैर्बुधः ॥३३॥

prāṇāpānau sannirundhyāt
pūra-kumbhaka-recakaiḥ
yāvan manas tyajet kāmān
sva-nāsāgra-nirīkṣaṇaḥ

yato yato niḥsarati
manaḥ kāma-hataṁ bhramat
tatas tata upāhṛtya
hṛdi rundhyāc chanair budhaḥ

prāṇa—incoming breath; *apānau*—outgoing breath; *sannirundhyāt*—should stop; *pūra-kumbhaka-recakaiḥ*—by inhaling, exhaling and holding, which are technically known as *pūraka*, *kumbhaka* and *recaka; yāvat*—so long; *manaḥ*—the mind; *tyajet*—should give up; *kāmān*—all material desires; *sva*—one's own; *nāsa-agra*—the tip of the nose; *nirīkṣaṇaḥ*—looking at; *yataḥ yataḥ*—from whatever and wherever; *niḥsarati*—withdraws; *manaḥ*—the mind; *kāma-hatam*—being defeated by lusty desires; *bhramat*—wandering; *tataḥ tataḥ*—from here and there; *upāhṛtya*—after bringing it back; *hṛdi*—within the core of the heart; *rundhyāt*—should arrest (the mind); *śanaiḥ*—gradually, by practice; *budhaḥ*—a learned *yogī*.

TRANSLATION

While continuously staring at the tip of the nose, a learned yogī practices the breathing exercises through the technical means

known as pūraka, kumbhaka and recaka—controlling inhalation and exhalation and then stopping them both. In this way the yogī restricts his mind from material attachments and gives up all mental desires. As soon as the mind, being defeated by lusty desires, drifts toward feelings of sense gratification, the yogī should immediately bring it back and arrest it within the core of his heart.

PURPORT

The practice of *yoga* is concisely explained herein. When this practice of *yoga* is perfect, one sees the Supersoul, the Paramātmā feature of the Supreme Personality of Godhead, within the core of one's heart. However, in *Bhagavad-gītā* (6.47) the Supreme Lord says:

yoginām api sarveṣām
mad-gatenāntarātmanā
śraddhāvān bhajate yo māṁ
sa me yuktatamo mataḥ

"Of all *yogīs*, he who always abides in Me with great faith, worshiping Me in transcendental loving service, is most intimately united with Me in *yoga* and is the highest of all." A devotee can immediately become a perfect *yogī* because he practices keeping Kṛṣṇa constantly within the core of his heart. This is another way to practice *yoga* easily. The Lord says:

man-manā bhava mad-bhakto
mad-yājī māṁ namaskuru

"Always think of Me and become My devotee. Worship Me and offer your homage unto Me." (Bg. 18.65) If one practices devotional service by always keeping Kṛṣṇa within the core of his heart (*man-manāḥ*), he immediately becomes a first-class *yogī*. Furthermore, keeping Kṛṣṇa within the mind is not a difficult task for the devotee. For an ordinary man in the bodily concept of life, the practice of *yoga* may be helpful, but one who immediately takes to devotional service can immediately become a perfect *yogī* without difficulty.

TEXT 34

एवमभ्यस्यतश्चित्तं कालेनाल्पीयसा यतेः ।
अनिशं तस्य निर्वाणं यात्यनिन्धनवह्निवत् ॥ ३४॥

evam abhyasyataś cittaṁ
kālenālpīyasā yateḥ
aniśaṁ tasya nirvāṇaṁ
yāty anindhana-vahnivat

evam—in this way; *abhyasyataḥ*—of the person practicing this *yoga* system; *cittam*—the heart; *kālena*—in due course of time; *alpīyasā*—very shortly; *yateḥ*—of the person practicing *yoga; aniśam*—without cessation; *tasya*—of him; *nirvāṇam*—purification from all material contamination; *yāti*—reaches; *anindhana*—without flame or smoke; *vahni-vat*—like a fire.

TRANSLATION

When the yogī regularly practices in this way, in a short time his heart becomes fixed and free from disturbance, like a fire without flames or smoke.

PURPORT

Nirvāṇa means the cessation of all material desires. Sometimes desirelessness is understood to imply an end to the workings of the mind, but this is not possible. The living entity has senses, and if the senses stopped working, the living entity would no longer be a living entity; he would be exactly like stone or wood. This is not possible. Because he is living, he is *nitya* and *cetana*—eternally sentient. For those who are not very advanced, the practice of *yoga* is recommended in order to stop the mind from being agitated by material desires, but if one fixes his mind on the lotus feet of Kṛṣṇa, his mind naturally becomes peaceful very soon. This peace is described in *Bhagavad-gītā* (5.29):

bhoktāraṁ yajña-tapasāṁ
sarva-loka-maheśvaram
suhṛdaṁ sarva-bhūtānāṁ
jñātvā māṁ śāntim ṛcchati

If one can understand Kṛṣṇa as the supreme enjoyer, the supreme proprietor of everything, and the supreme friend of everyone, one is established in peace and is free from material agitation. However, for one who cannot understand the Supreme Personality of Godhead, the practice of *yoga* is recommended.

TEXT 35

कामादिभिरनाविद्धं प्रशान्ताखिलवृत्ति यत् ।
चित्तं ब्रह्मसुखस्पृष्टं नैवोत्तिष्ठेत कर्हिचित् ॥३५॥

kāmādibhir anāviddhaṁ
praśāntākhila-vṛtti yat
cittaṁ brahma-sukha-spṛṣṭaṁ
naivottiṣṭheta karhicit

kāma-ādibhiḥ—by various lusty desires; *anāviddham*—unaffected; *praśānta*—calm and peaceful; *akhila-vṛtti*—in every respect, or in all activities; *yat*—that which; *cittam*—consciousness; *brahma-sukha-spṛṣṭam*—being situated on the transcendental platform in eternal bliss; *na*—not; *eva*—indeed; *uttiṣṭheta*—can come out; *karhicit*—at any time.

TRANSLATION

When one's consciousness is uncontaminated by material lusty desires, it becomes calm and peaceful in all activities, for one is situated in eternal blissful life. Once situated on that platform, one does not return to materialistic activities.

PURPORT

Brahma-sukha-spṛṣṭam is also described in *Bhagavad-gītā* (18.54):

brahma-bhūtaḥ prasannātmā
na śocati na kāṅkṣati
samaḥ sarveṣu bhūteṣu
mad-bhaktiṁ labhate parām

"One who is transcendentally situated at once realizes the Supreme Brahman and becomes fully joyful. He never laments nor desires to have anything; he is equally disposed toward every living entity. In this situation, he begins transcendental activities, or devotional service to the Lord." Generally, once elevated to the transcendental platform of *brahma-sukha*, transcendental bliss, one never comes down. But if one does not engage in devotional service, there is a chance of his returning to the material platform. *Āruhya kṛcchreṇa paraṁ padaṁ tataḥ patanty adho 'nādṛta-yuṣmad-aṅghrayaḥ:* one may rise to the platform of *brahma-sukha*, transcendental bliss, but even from that platform one may fall down to the material platform if he does not engage himself in devotional service.

TEXT 36

यः प्रव्रज्य गृहात् पूर्वं त्रिवर्गावपनात् पुनः ।
यदि सेवेत तान्भिक्षुः स वै वान्ताश्यपत्रपः ॥३६॥

yaḥ pravrajya gṛhāt pūrvaṁ
tri-vargāvapanāt punaḥ
yadi seveta tān bhikṣuḥ
sa vai vāntāśy apatrapaḥ

yaḥ—one who; *pravrajya*—being finished for good and leaving for the forest (being situated in transcendental bliss); *gṛhāt*—from home; *pūrvam*—at first; *tri-varga*—the three principles of religion, economic development and sense gratification; *āvapanāt*—from the field in which they are sown; *punaḥ*—again; *yadi*—if; *seveta*—should accept; *tān*—materialistic activities; *bhikṣuḥ*—a person who has accepted the *sannyāsa* order; *saḥ*—that person; *vai*—indeed; *vānta-āśī*—one who eats his own vomit; *apatrapaḥ*—without shame.

TRANSLATION

One who accepts the sannyāsa order gives up the three principles of materialistic activities in which one indulges in the field of household life—namely religion, economic development and sense gratification. One who first accepts sannyāsa but then returns

to such materialistic activities is to be called a vāntāśī, or one who eats his own vomit. He is indeed a shameless person.

PURPORT

Materialistic activities are regulated by the institution of *varṇāśrama-dharma.* Without *varṇāśrama-dharma,* materialistic activities constitute animal life. Yet even in human life, while observing the principles of *varṇa* and *āśrama—brāhmaṇa, kṣatriya, vaiśya, śūdra, brahmacarya, gṛhastha, vānaprastha* and *sannyāsa*—one must ultimately accept *sannyāsa,* the renounced order, for only by the renounced order can one be situated in *brahma-sukha,* or transcendental bliss. In *brahma-sukha* one is no longer attracted by lusty desires. Indeed, when one is no longer disturbed, especially by lusty desires for sexual indulgence, he is fit to become a *sannyāsī.* Otherwise, one should not accept the *sannyāsa* order. If one accepts *sannyāsa* at an immature stage, there is every possibility of his being attracted by women and lusty desires and thus again becoming a so-called *gṛhastha* or a victim of women. Such a person is most shameless, and he is called *vāntāśī,* or one who eats that which he has already vomited. He certainly leads a condemned life. In our Kṛṣṇa consciousness movement it is advised, therefore, that the *sannyāsīs* and *brahmacārīs* keep strictly aloof from the association of women so that there will be no chance of their falling down again as victims of lusty desires.

TEXT 37

यैः स्वदेहः स्मृतो नात्मा मर्त्यो विट्कृमिभस्मवत् ।
त एनमात्मसात्कृत्वा श्लाघयन्ति ह्यसत्तमाः ॥३७॥

yaiḥ sva-dehaḥ smṛto 'nātmā
martyo viṭ-kṛmi-bhasmavat
ta enam ātmasāt kṛtvā
ślāghayanti hy asattamāḥ

yaiḥ—by *sannyāsīs* who; *sva-dehaḥ*—own body; *smṛtaḥ*—consider; *anātmā*—different from the soul; *martyaḥ*—subjected to death; *viṭ*—becoming stool; *kṛmi*—worms; *bhasma-vat*—or ashes; *te*—such persons; *enam*—this body; *ātmasāt kṛtvā*—again identifying with the self; *ślāghayanti*—glorify as very important; *hi*—indeed; *asat-tamāḥ*—the greatest rascals.

TRANSLATION

Sannyāsīs who first consider that the body is subject to death, when it will be transformed into stool, worms or ashes, but who again give importance to the body and glorify it as the self, are to be considered the greatest rascals.

PURPORT

A *sannyāsī* is one who has clearly understood, through advancement in knowledge, that Brahman—he, the person himself—is the soul, not the body. One who has this understanding may take *sannyāsa,* for he is situated in the "*ahaṁ brahmāsmi*" position. *Brahma-bhūtaḥ prasannātmā na śocati na kāṅkṣati.* Such a person, who no longer laments or hankers to maintain his body and who can accept all living entities as spirit souls, can then enter the devotional service of the Lord. If one does not enter the devotional service of the Lord but artificially considers himself Brahman or Nārāyaṇa, not perfectly understanding that the soul and body are different, one certainly falls down (*patanty adhaḥ*). Such a person again gives importance to the body. There are many *sannyāsīs* in India who stress the importance of the body. Some of them give special importance to the body of the poor man, accepting him as *daridra-nārāyaṇa,* as if Nārāyaṇa had a material body. Many other *sannyāsīs* stress the importance of the social position of the body as a *brāhmaṇa, kṣatriya, vaiśya* or *śūdra.* Such *sannyāsīs* are considered the greatest rascals (*asattamāḥ*). They are shameless because they have not yet understood the difference between the body and the soul and instead have accepted the body of a *brāhmaṇa* to be a *brāhmaṇa.* Brahmanism (*brāhmaṇya*) consists of the knowledge of Brahman. But actually the body of a *brāhmaṇa* is not Brahman. Similarly, the body is neither rich nor poor. If the body of a poor man were *daridra-nārāyaṇa,* this would mean that the body of a rich man, on the contrary, must be *dhanī-nārāyaṇa.* Therefore *sannyāsīs* who do not know the meaning of Nārāyaṇa, those who regard the body as Brahman or as Nārāyaṇa, are described here as *asattamāḥ*, the most abominable rascals. Following the bodily concept of life, such *sannyāsīs* make various programs to serve the body. They conduct farcical missions consisting of so-called religious activities meant to mislead all of human society. These *sannyāsīs* have been described herein as *apatrapaḥ* and *asattamāḥ*—shameless and fallen from spiritual life.

TEXTS 38–39

गृहस्थस्य क्रियात्यागो व्रतत्यागो वटोरपि ।
तपस्विनो ग्रामसेवा भिक्षोरिन्द्रियलोलता ॥३८॥
आश्रमापसदा ह्येते खल्वाश्रमविडम्बनाः ।
देवमायाविमूढांस्तानुपेक्षेतानुकम्पया ॥३९॥

gṛhasthasya kriyā-tyāgo
vrata-tyāgo vaṭor api
tapasvino grāma-sevā
bhikṣor indriya-lolatā

āśramāpasadā hy ete
khalv āśrama-viḍambanāḥ
deva-māyā-vimūḍhāṁs tān
upekṣetānukampayā

gṛhasthasya—for a person situated in householder life; *kriyā-tyāgaḥ*—to give up the duty of a householder; *vrata-tyāgah*—to give up vows and austerity; *vaṭoḥ*—for a *brahmacārī*; *api*—also; *tapasvinaḥ*—for a *vānaprastha*, one who has adopted a life of austerities; *grāma-sevā*—to live in a village and serve the people therein; *bhikṣoḥ*—for a *sannyāsī* who lived by begging alms; *indriya-lolatā*—addicted to sense enjoyment; *āśrama*—of the spiritual orders of life; *apasadāḥ*—the most abominable; *hi*—indeed; *ete*—all these; *khalu*—indeed; *āśrama-viḍambanāḥ*—imitating and therefore cheating the different spiritual orders; *deva-māyā-vimūḍhān*—who are bewildered by the external energy of the Supreme Lord; *tān*—them; *upekṣeta*—one should reject and not accept as genuine; *anukampayā*—or by compassion (teach them real life).

TRANSLATION

It is abominable for a person living in the gṛhastha-āśrama to give up the regulative principles, for a brahmacārī not to follow the brahmacārī vows while living under the care of the guru, for a vānaprastha to live in the village and engage in so-called social activities, or for a sannyāsī to be addicted to sense gratification. One who acts in this way is to be considered the lowest renegade. Such a pretender is bewildered by the external energy of the Supreme Personality of Godhead, and one should either reject him from any position, or taking compassion upon him, teach him, if possible, to resume his original position.

PURPORT

We have repeatedly stressed that human culture does not begin unless one takes to the principles of *varṇāśrama-dharma.* Although *gṛhastha* life is a concession for the enjoyment of sex, one cannot enjoy sex without following the rules and regulations of householder life. Furthermore, as already instructed, a *brahmacārī* must live under the care of the *guru: brahmacārī guru-kule vasan dānto guror hitam.* If a *brahmacārī* does not live under the care of the *guru,* if a *vānaprastha* engages in ordinary activities, or if a *sannyāsī* is greedy and eats meat, eggs and all kinds of nonsense for the satisfaction of his tongue, he is a cheater and should immediately be rejected as unimportant. Such persons should be shown compassion, and if one has sufficient strength one should teach them to stop them from following the wrong path in life. Otherwise one should reject them and pay them no attention.

TEXT 40

आत्मानं चेद् विजानीयात् परं ज्ञानधुताशयः ।
किमिच्छन्कस्य वा हेतोर्देहं पुष्णाति लम्पटः ॥४०॥

ātmānaṁ ced vijānīyāt
paraṁ jñāna-dhutāśayaḥ
kim icchan kasya vā hetor
dehaṁ puṣṇāti lampaṭaḥ

ātmānam—the soul and the Supersoul; *cet*—if; *vijānīyāt*—can understand; *param*—who are transcendental, beyond this material world; *jñāna*—by knowledge; *dhuta-āśayaḥ*—one who has cleansed his consciousness; *kim*—what; *icchan*—desiring material comforts; *kasya*—for whom; *vā*—or; *hetoḥ*—for what reason; *deham*—the material body; *puṣṇāti*—he maintains; *lampaṭaḥ*—being unlawfully addicted to sense gratification.

TRANSLATION

The human form of body is meant for understanding the self and the Supreme Self, the Supreme Personality of Godhead, both of whom are transcendentally situated. If both of them can be understood when one is purified by advanced knowledge, for what reason and for whom does a foolish, greedy person maintain the body for sense gratification?

PURPORT

Of course, everyone in this material world is interested in maintaining the body for sense gratification, but by cultivating knowledge one should gradually understand that the body is not the self. Both the soul and the Supersoul are transcendental to the material world. This is to be understood in the human form of life, especially when one takes *sannyāsa.* A *sannyāsī*, one who has understood the self, should be engaged in elevating the self and associating with the Superself. Our Kṛṣṇa consciousness movement is meant for elevating the living being for promotion back home, back to Godhead. Seeking such elevation is one's duty in the human form of life. Unless one performs this duty, why should one maintain the body? Especially if a *sannyāsī* not only maintains the body by ordinary means but does everything to maintain the body, including even eating meat and other abominable things, he must be a *lampaṭaḥ*, a greedy person simply engaged in sense gratification. A *sannyāsī* must specifically remove himself from the urges of the tongue, belly and genitals, which disturb one as long as one is not fully aware that the body is separate from the soul.

TEXT 41

आहुः शरीरं रथमिन्द्रियाणि
हयानभीषून् मन इन्द्रियेशम् ।

वर्त्मानि मात्रा धिषणां च सूतं
सत्त्वं बृहद् बन्धुरमीशसृष्टम् ॥४१॥

āhuḥ śarīraṁ ratham indriyāṇi
hayān abhīṣūn mana indriyeśam
vartmāni mātrā dhiṣaṇāṁ ca sūtaṁ
sattvaṁ bṛhad bandhuram īśa-sṛṣṭam

āhuḥ—it is said; *śarīram*—the body; *ratham*—the chariot; *indriyāṇi*—the senses; *hayān*—the horses; *abhīṣūn*—the reins; *manaḥ*—the mind; *indriya*—of the senses; *īśam*—the master; *vartmāni*—the destinations; *mātrāḥ*—the sense objects; *dhiṣaṇām*—the intelligence; *ca*—and; *sūtam*—the chariot driver; *sattvam*—consciousness; *bṛhat*—great; *bandhuram*—bondage; *īśa*—by the Supreme Personality of Godhead; *sṛṣṭam*—created.

TRANSLATION

Transcendentalists who are advanced in knowledge compare the body, which is made by the order of the Supreme Personality of Godhead, to a chariot. The senses are like the horses; the mind, the master of the senses, is like the reins; the objects of the senses are the destinations; intelligence is the chariot driver; and consciousness, which spreads throughout the body, is the cause of bondage in this material world.

PURPORT

For a bewildered person in the materialistic way of life, the body, the mind and the senses, which are engaged in sense gratification, are the cause of bondage to repeated birth, death, old age and disease. But for one who is advanced in spiritual knowledge, the same body, senses and mind are the cause of liberation. This is confirmed in the *Kaṭha Upaniṣad* (1.3.3–4,9) as follows:

ātmānaṁ rathinaṁ viddhi
śarīraṁ ratham eva ca
buddhiṁ tu sārathiṁ viddhi
manaḥ pragraham eva ca

indriyāṇi hayān āhur
viṣayāṁs teṣu gocarān

so 'dhvanaḥ pāram āpnoti
tad viṣṇoḥ paramaṁ padam

The soul is the occupant of the chariot of the body, of which the driver is the intelligence. The mind is the determination to reach the destination, the senses are the horses, and the sense objects are also included in that activity. Thus one can reach the destination, Viṣṇu, who is *paramaṁ padam*, the supreme goal of life. In conditioned life the consciousness in the body is the cause of bondage, but the same consciousness, when transformed into Kṛṣṇa consciousness, becomes the cause for one's returning home, back to Godhead.

The human body, therefore, may be used in two ways—for going to the darkest regions of ignorance or for going forward, back home, back to Godhead. To go back to Godhead, the path is *mahat-sevā*, to accept the self-realized spiritual master. *Mahat-sevāṁ dvāram āhur vimukteḥ*. For liberation, one should accept the direction of authorized devotees who can actually endow one with perfect knowledge. On the other hand, *tamo-dvāraṁ yoṣitāṁ saṅgi-saṅgam:* if one wants to go to the darkest regions of material existence, one may continue to associate with persons who are attached to women (*yoṣitāṁ saṅgi-saṅgam*). The word *yoṣit* means "woman." Persons who are too materialistic are attached to women.

It is said, therefore, *ātmānaṁ rathinaṁ viddhi śarīraṁ ratham eva ca*. The body is just like a chariot or car in which one may go anywhere. One may drive well, or else one may drive whimsically, in which case it is quite possible that he may have an accident and fall into a ditch. In other words, if one takes directions from the experienced spiritual master one can go back home, back to Godhead; otherwise, one may return to the cycle of birth and death. Therefore Kṛṣṇa personally advises:

aśraddadhānāḥ puruṣā
dharmasyāsya parantapa
aprāpya māṁ nivartante
mṛtyu-saṁsāra-vartmani

"Those who are not faithful on the path of devotional service cannot attain Me, O conqueror of foes, but return to birth and death in this material world." (Bg. 9.3) The Supreme Personality of Godhead, Kṛṣṇa, personally gives instructions on how one can return home, back to Godhead, but if one does not care to listen to His instructions, the result will be that one will never go back to Godhead, but will continue life in this miserable condition of repeated birth and death in material existence (*mṛtyu-saṁsāra-vartmani*).

The advice of experienced transcendentalists, therefore, is that the body be fully engaged for achieving the ultimate goal of life (*svārtha-gatim*). The real interest or goal of life is to return home, back to Godhead. To enable one to fulfill this purpose, there are so many Vedic literatures, including *Vedānta-sūtra*, the *Upaniṣads*, *Bhagavad-gītā*, *Mahābhārata* and the *Rāmāyaṇa*. One should take lessons from these Vedic literatures and learn how to practice *nivṛtti-mārga*. Then one's life will be perfect. The body is important as long as it has consciousness. Without consciousness, the body is merely a lump of matter. Therefore, to return home, back to Godhead, one must change his consciousness from material consciousness to Kṛṣṇa consciousness. One's consciousness is the cause of material bondage, but if this consciousness is purified by *bhakti-yoga*, one can then understand the falsity of his *upādhi*, his designations as Indian, American, Hindu, Muslim, Christian and so on. *Sarvopādhi-vinirmuktaṁ tat-paratvena nirmalam.* One must forget these designations and use this consciousness only for the service of Kṛṣṇa. Therefore if one takes advantage of the Kṛṣṇa consciousness movement, his life is certainly successful.

TEXT 42

अक्षं दशप्राणमधर्मधर्मौ
चक्रेऽभिमानं रथिनं च जीवम् ।
धनुर्हि तस्य प्रणवं पठन्ति
शरं तु जीवं परमेव लक्ष्यम् ॥४२॥

akṣaṁ daśa-prāṇam adharma-dharmau
cakre 'bhimānaṁ rathinaṁ ca jīvam

dhanur hi tasya praṇavaṁ paṭhanti
śaraṁ tu jīvaṁ param eva lakṣyam

akṣam—the spokes (on the chariot wheel); *daśa*—ten; *prāṇam*—the ten kinds of air flowing within the body; *adharma*—irreligion; *dharmau*—religion (two sides of the wheel, up and down); *cakre*—in the wheel; *abhimānam*—false identification; *rathinam*—the charioteer or master of the body; *ca*—also; *jīvam*—the living entity; *dhanuḥ*—the bow; *hi*—indeed; *tasya*—his; *praṇavam*—the Vedic *mantra oṁkāra; paṭhanti*—it is said; *śaram*—an arrow; *tu*—but; *jīvam*—the living entity; *param*—the Supreme Lord; *eva*—indeed; *lakṣyam*—the target.

TRANSLATION

The ten kinds of air acting within the body are compared to the spokes of the chariot's wheels, and the top and bottom of the wheel itself are called religion and irreligion. The living entity in the bodily concept of life is the owner of the chariot. The Vedic mantra praṇava is the bow, the pure living entity himself is the arrow, and the target is the Supreme Being.

PURPORT

Ten kinds of life air always flow within the material body. They are called *prāṇa, apāna, samāna, vyāna, udāna, nāga, kūrma, kṛkala, devadatta* and *dhanañjaya.* They are compared here to the spokes of the chariot's wheels. The life air is the energy for all of a living being's activities, which are sometimes religious and sometimes irreligious. Thus religion and irreligion are said to be the upper and lower portions of the chariot's wheels. When the living entity decides to go back home, back to Godhead, his target is Lord Viṣṇu, the Supreme Personality of Godhead. In the conditioned state of life, one does not understand that the goal of life is the Supreme Lord. *Na te viduḥ svārtha-gatiṁ hi viṣṇuṁ durāśayā ye bahir-artha-māninaḥ.* The living entity tries to be happy within this material world, not understanding the target of his life. When he is purified, however, he gives up his bodily conception of life and his false identity as belonging to a certain community, a certain nation, a certain society, a certain family and so on (*sarvopādhi-vinirmuktaṁ tat-*

paratvena nirmalam). Then he takes the arrow of his purified life, and with the help of the bow—the transcendental chanting of *praṇava*, or the Hare Kṛṣṇa *mantra*—he throws himself toward the Supreme Personality of Godhead.

Śrīla Viśvanātha Cakravartī Ṭhākura has commented that because the words "bow" and "arrow" are used in this verse, one might argue that the Supreme Personality of Godhead and the living entity have become enemies. However, although the Supreme Personality of Godhead may become the so-called enemy of the living being, this is His chivalrous pleasure. For example, the Lord fought with Bhīṣma, and when Bhīṣma pierced the Lord's body on the Battlefield of Kurukṣetra, this was a kind of humor or relationship, of which there are twelve. When the conditioned soul tries to reach the Lord by hurling an arrow at Him, the Lord takes pleasure, and the living entity gains the profit of going back home, back to Godhead. Another example given in this regard is that Arjuna, as a result of piercing the *ādhāra-mīna*, or the fish within the *cakra*, achieved the valuable gain of Draupadī. Similarly, if with the arrow of chanting the holy name of the Lord one pierces Lord Viṣṇu's lotus feet, by dint of performing this heroic activity of devotional service one receives the benefit of returning home, back to Godhead.

TEXTS 43–44

रागो द्वेषश्च लोभश्च शोकमोहौ भयं मदः ।
मानोऽवमानोऽसूया च माया हिंसा च मत्सरः ॥४३॥
रजः प्रमादः क्षुन्निद्रा शत्रवस्त्वेवमादयः ।
रजस्तमःप्रकृतयः सत्त्वप्रकृतयः क्वचित् ॥४४॥

rāgo dveṣaś ca lobhaś ca
śoka-mohau bhayaṁ madaḥ
māno 'vamāno 'sūyā ca
māyā hiṁsā ca matsaraḥ

rajaḥ pramādaḥ kṣun-nidrā
śatravas tv evam ādayaḥ
rajas-tamaḥ-prakṛtayaḥ
sattva-prakṛtayaḥ kvacit

rāgaḥ—attachment; *dveṣaḥ*—hostility; *ca*—also; *lobhaḥ*—greed; *ca*—also; *śoka*—lamentation; *mohau*—illusion; *bhayam*—fear; *madaḥ*—madness; *mānaḥ*—false prestige; *avamānaḥ*—insult; *asūyā*—finding fault with others; *ca*—also; *māyā*—deception; *hiṁsā*—envy; *ca*—also; *matsaraḥ*—intolerance; *rajaḥ*—passion; *pramādaḥ*—bewilderment; *kṣut*—hunger; *nidrā*—sleep; *śatravaḥ*—enemies; *tu*—indeed; *evam ādayaḥ*—even other such conceptions of life; *rajaḥ-tamaḥ*—because of the conception of passion and ignorance; *prakṛtayaḥ*—causes; *sattva*—because of the conception of goodness; *prakṛtayaḥ*—causes; *kvacit*—sometimes.

TRANSLATION

In the conditioned stage, one's conceptions of life are sometimes polluted by passion and ignorance, which are exhibited by attachment, hostility, greed, lamentation, illusion, fear, madness, false prestige, insults, fault-finding, deception, envy, intolerance, passion, bewilderment, hunger and sleep. All of these are enemies. Sometimes one's conceptions are also polluted by goodness.

PURPORT

The actual aim of life is to go back home, back to Godhead, but there are many hindrances created by the three modes of material nature—sometimes by a combination of *rajo-guṇa* and *tamo-guṇa*, the modes of passion and ignorance, and sometimes by the mode of goodness. In the material world, even if one is a philanthropist, a nationalist and a good man according to materialistic estimations, these conceptions of life form a hindrance to spiritual advancement. How much more of a hindrance, then, are hostility, greed, illusion, lamentation and too much attachment to material enjoyment? To progress toward the target of Viṣṇu, which is our real self-interest, one must become very powerful in conquering these various hindrances or enemies. In other words, one should not be attached to being a good man or a bad man in this material world.

In this material world, so-called goodness and badness are the same because they consist of the three modes of material nature. One must transcend this material nature. Even the Vedic ritualistic ceremonies consist of the three modes of material nature. Therefore Kṛṣṇa advised Arjuna:

traiguṇya-viṣayā vedā
nistraiguṇyo bhavārjuna
nirdvandvo nitya-sattva-stho
niryoga-kṣema ātmavān

"The *Vedas* mainly deal with the subject of the three modes of material nature. Rise above these modes, O Arjuna. Be transcendental to all of them. Be free from all dualities and from all anxieties for gain and safety, and be established in the self." (Bg. 2.45) Elsewhere in *Bhagavad-gītā* the Lord says, *ūrdhvaṁ gacchanti sattva-sthāḥ:* if one becomes a very good person—in other words, if one is in the mode of goodness—he may be elevated to the higher planetary systems. Similarly, if one is infected by *rajo-guṇa* and *tamo-guṇa*, he may remain in this world or go down to the animal kingdom. But all of these situations are hindrances on the path of spiritual salvation. Śrī Caitanya Mahāprabhu therefore says:

brahmāṇḍa bhramite kona bhāgyavān jīva
guru-kṛṣṇa-prasāde pāya bhakti-latā-bīja

If one is fortunate enough to transcend all this so-called goodness and badness and come to the platform of devotional service by the mercy of Kṛṣṇa and the *guru*, his life becomes successful. In this regard, one must be very bold so that he can conquer these enemies of Kṛṣṇa consciousness. Not caring for the good and bad of this material world, one must boldly propagate Kṛṣṇa consciousness.

TEXT 45

यावन्नृकायरथमात्मवशोपकल्पं
धत्ते गरिष्ठचरणार्चनया निशातम् ।
ज्ञानासिमच्युतबलो दधदस्तशत्रुः
स्वानन्दतुष्ट उपशान्त इदं विजह्यात् ॥४५॥

yāvan nṛ-kāya-ratham ātma-vaśopakalpaṁ
dhatte gariṣṭha-caraṇārcanayā niśātam

jñānāsim acyuta-balo dadhad asta-śatruḥ
svānanda-tuṣṭa upaśānta idaṁ vijahyāt

yāvat—as long as; *nṛ-kāya*—this human form of body; *ratham*—considered to be a chariot; *ātma-vaśa*—dependent upon one's own control; *upakalpam*—in which there are many other subordinate parts; *dhatte*—one possesses; *gariṣṭha-caraṇa*—the lotus feet of the superiors (namely the spiritual master and his predecessors); *arcanayā*—by serving; *niśātam*—sharpened; *jñāna-asim*—the sword or weapon of knowledge; *acyuta-balaḥ*—by the transcendental strength of Kṛṣṇa; *dadhat*—holding; *asta-śatruḥ*—until the enemy is defeated; *sva-ānanda-tuṣṭaḥ*—being fully self-satisfied by transcendental bliss; *upaśāntaḥ*—the consciousness being cleansed of all material contamination; *idam*—this body; *vijahyāt*—one should give up.

TRANSLATION

As long as one has to accept a material body, with its different parts and paraphernalia, which are not fully under one's control, one must have the lotus feet of his superiors, namely his spiritual master and the spiritual master's predecessors. By their mercy, one can sharpen the sword of knowledge, and with the power of the Supreme Personality of Godhead's mercy one must then conquer the enemies mentioned above. In this way, the devotee should be able to merge into his own transcendental bliss, and then he may give up his body and resume his spiritual identity.

PURPORT

In *Bhagavad-gītā* (4.9) the Lord says:

janma karma ca me divyam
evaṁ yo vetti tattvataḥ
tyaktvā dehaṁ punar janma
naiti mām eti so 'rjuna

"One who knows the transcendental nature of My appearance and activities does not, upon leaving the body, take his birth again in this material world, but attains My eternal abode, O Arjuna." This is the highest perfection of life, and the human body is meant for this purpose. It is said in *Śrīmad-Bhāgavatam* (11.20.17):

nṛ-deham ādyaṁ sulabhaṁ sudurlabhaṁ
plavaṁ sukalpaṁ guru-karṇadhāram
mayānukūlena nabhasvateritaṁ
pumān bhavābdhiṁ na taret sa ātma-hā

This human form of body is a most valuable boat, and the spiritual master is the captain, *guru-karṇadhāram,* to guide the boat in plying across the ocean of nescience. The instruction of Kṛṣṇa is a favorable breeze. One must use all these facilities to cross over the ocean of nescience. Since the spiritual master is the captain, one must serve the spiritual master very sincerely so that by his mercy one will be able to get the mercy of the Supreme Lord.

A significant word here is *acyuta-balaḥ.* The spiritual master is certainly very merciful to his disciples, and consequently by satisfying him a devotee gets strength from the Supreme Personality of Godhead. Śrī Caitanya Mahāprabhu therefore says, *guru-kṛṣṇa-prasāde pāya bhakti-latā-bīja:* one must first please the spiritual master, and then one automatically pleases Kṛṣṇa and gets the strength with which to cross the ocean of nescience. If one seriously desires to return home, back to Godhead, one must therefore become strong enough by pleasing the spiritual master, for thus one gets the weapon with which to conquer the enemy, and one also gets the grace of Kṛṣṇa. Simply getting the weapon of *jñāna* is insufficient. One must sharpen the weapon by serving the spiritual master and adhering to his instructions. Then the candidate will get the mercy of the Supreme Personality of Godhead. In general warfare one must take help from his chariot and horses in order to conquer his enemy, and after conquering his enemies he may give up the chariot and its paraphernalia. Similarly, as long as one has a human body, one should fully use it to obtain the highest perfection of life, namely going back home, back to Godhead.

The perfection of knowledge is certainly to become transcendentally situated (*brahma-bhūta*). As the Lord says in *Bhagavad-gītā* (18.54):

brahma-bhūtaḥ prasannātmā
na śocati na kāṅkṣati
samaḥ sarveṣu bhūteṣu
mad-bhaktiṁ labhate parām

"One who is transcendentally situated at once realizes the Supreme Brahman and becomes fully joyful. He never laments nor desires to have anything; he is equally disposed toward all living entities. In that state he attains pure devotional service." Simply by cultivating knowledge as the impersonalists do, one cannot get out of the clutches of *māyā.* One must attain the platform of *bhakti.*

bhaktyā mām abhijānāti
yāvān yaś cāsmi tattvataḥ
tato māṁ tattvato jñātvā
viśate tad-anantaram

"One can understand the Supreme Personality as He is only by devotional service. And when one is in full consciousness of the Supreme Lord by such devotion, he can enter into the kingdom of God." (Bg. 18.55) Unless one has attained the stage of devotional service and the mercy of the spiritual master and Kṛṣṇa, there is a possibility that one may fall down and again accept a material body. Therefore Kṛṣṇa stresses in *Bhagavad-gītā* (4.9):

janma karma ca me divyam
evaṁ yo vetti tattvataḥ
tyaktvā dehaṁ punar janma
naiti mām eti so 'rjuna

"One who knows the transcendental nature of My appearance and activities does not, upon leaving the body, take his birth again in this material world, but attains My eternal abode, O Arjuna."

The word *tattvataḥ,* meaning "in reality," is very important. *Tato māṁ tattvato jñātvā.* Unless one understands Kṛṣṇa in truth by the mercy of the spiritual master, one is not free to give up his material body. As it is said, *āruhya kṛcchreṇa paraṁ padaṁ tataḥ patanty adho 'nādṛta-yuṣmad-aṅghrayaḥ:* if one neglects to serve the lotus feet of Kṛṣṇa, one cannot become free from the material clutches simply by knowledge. Even if one attains the stage of *brahma-padam*, merging in Brahman, without *bhakti* he is prone to fall down. One must be very careful in regard to the danger of falling down again into material bondage. The only insurance is to come to the stage of *bhakti*, from which one is sure not to fall. Then one is free from the activities of the material world. In summary, as stated by Śrī Caitanya Mahāprabhu, one must get in touch with a bona fide spiritual master coming in the *paramparā* of Kṛṣṇa consciousness, for by his mercy and instructions one is able to get strength from Kṛṣṇa. Thus one engages in devotional service and attains the ultimate goal of life, the lotus feet of Viṣṇu.

Significant in this verse are the words *jñānāsim acyuta-balaḥ. Jñānāsim*, the sword of knowledge, is given by Kṛṣṇa, and when one serves the *guru* and Kṛṣṇa in order to hold the sword of Kṛṣṇa's instructions, Balarāma gives one strength. Balarāma is Nityānanda. *Vrajendra-nandana yei, śacī-suta haila sei, balarāma ha-ila nitāi.* This *bala*—Balarāma—comes with Śrī Caitanya Mahāprabhu, and both of Them are so merciful that in this age of Kali one may very easily take shelter of Their lotus feet. They come especially to deliver the fallen souls of this age. *Pāpī tāpī yata chila, hari-nāme uddhārila.* Their weapon is *saṅkīrtana, hari-nāma.* Thus one should accept the sword of knowledge from Kṛṣṇa and be strong with the mercy of Balarāma. We are therefore worshiping Kṛṣṇa-Balarāma in Vṛndāvana. In the *Muṇḍaka Upaniṣad* (3.2.4) it is said:

nāyam ātmā bala-hīnena labhyo
na ca pramādāt tapaso vāpy aliṅgāt
etair upāyair yatate yas tu vidvāṁs
tasyaiṣa ātmā viśate brahma-dhāma

One cannot attain the goal of life without the mercy of Balarāma. Śrī Narottama dāsa Ṭhākura therefore says, *nitāiyera karuṇā habe, vraje rādhā-kṛṣṇa pābe:* when one receives the mercy of Balarāma, Nityānanda, one can attain the lotus feet of Rādhā and Kṛṣṇa very easily.

se sambandha nāhi yāra, bṛthā janma gela tāra,
vidyā-kule hi karibe tāra

If one has no connection with Nitāi, Balarāma, then even though one is a very learned scholar or *jñānī* or has taken birth in a very respectable family, these assets will not help him. We must therefore conquer the enemies of Kṛṣṇa consciousness with the strength received from Balarāma.

TEXT 46

नोचेत् प्रमत्तमसदिन्द्रियवाजिसूता
नीत्वोत्पथं विषयदस्युषु निक्षिपन्ति ।
ते दस्यवः सहयसूतममुं तमोऽन्धे
संसारकूप उरुमृत्युभये क्षिपन्ति ॥४६॥

nocet pramattam asad-indriya-vāji-sūtā
nītvotpathaṁ viṣaya-dasyuṣu nikṣipanti
te dasyavaḥ sahaya-sūtam amuṁ tamo 'ndhe
saṁsāra-kūpa uru-mṛtyu-bhaye kṣipanti

nocet—if we do not follow the instructions of Acyuta, Kṛṣṇa, and do not take shelter of Balarāma; *pramattam*—careless, inattentive; *asat*—which are always prone to material consciousness; *indriya*—the senses; *vāji*—acting as the horses; *sūtāḥ*—the chariot driver (intelligence); *nītvā*—bringing; *utpatham*—to the roadway of material desire; *viṣaya*—the sense objects; *dasyuṣu*—in the hands of the plunderers; *nikṣipanti*—throw; *te*—those; *dasyavaḥ*—plunderers; *sa*—with; *haya-sūtam*—the horses and chariot driver; *amum*—all of them; *tamaḥ*—dark; *andhe*—blind; *saṁsāra-kūpe*—into the well of material existence; *uru*—great; *mṛtyu-bhaye*—fear of death; *kṣipanti*—throw.

TRANSLATION

Otherwise, if one does not take shelter of Acyuta and Baladeva, then the senses, acting as the horses, and the intelligence, acting as the driver, both being prone to material contamination, inattentively bring the body, which acts as the chariot, to the path of sense gratification. When one is thus attracted again by the rogues of viṣaya—eating, sleeping and mating—the horses and chariot

driver are thrown into the blinding dark well of material existence, and one is again put into a dangerous and extremely fearful situation of repeated birth and death.

PURPORT

Without the protection of Gaura-Nitāi—Kṛṣṇa and Balarāma—one cannot get out of the dark well of ignorance in material existence. This is indicated here by the word *nocet*, which means that one will always remain in the dark well of material existence. The living entity must get strength from Nitāi-Gaura, or Kṛṣṇa-Balarāma. Without the mercy of Nitāi-Gaura, there is no way to come out of this dark well of ignorance. As stated in the *Caitanya-caritāmṛta* (*Ādi* 1.2):

vande śrī-kṛṣṇa-caitanya-
nityānandau sahoditau
gauḍodaye puṣpavantau
citrau śandau tamo-nudau

"I offer my respectful obeisances unto Śrī Kṛṣṇa Caitanya and Lord Nityānanda, who are like the sun and moon. They have arisen simultaneously on the horizon of Gauḍa to dissipate the darkness of ignorance and thus wonderfully bestow benediction upon all." This material world is a dark well of ignorance. The fallen soul in this dark well must take shelter of the lotus feet of Gaura-Nitāi, for thus he can easily emerge from material existence. Without Their strength, simply attempting to get out of the clutches of matter by speculative knowledge will be insufficient.

TEXT 47

प्रवृत्तं च निवृत्तं च द्विविधं कर्म वैदिकम् ।
आवर्तते प्रवृत्तेन निवृत्तेनाश्नुतेऽमृतम् ॥४७॥

pravṛttaṁ ca nivṛttaṁ ca
dvi-vidhaṁ karma vaidikam
āvartate pravṛttena
nivṛttenāśnute 'mṛtam

pravṛttam—inclination for material enjoyment; *ca*—and; *nivṛttam*—cessation of material enjoyment; *ca*—and; *dvi-vidham*—these two varieties; *karma*—of activities; *vaidikam*—recommended in the *Vedas;* *āvartate*—one travels up and down through the cycle of *saṁsāra;* *pravṛttena*—by an inclination for enjoying material activities; *nivṛttena*—but by ceasing such activities; *aśnute*—one enjoys; *amṛtam*—eternal life.

TRANSLATION

According to the Vedas, there are two kinds of activities—pravṛtti and nivṛtti. Pravṛtti activities involve raising oneself from a lower to a higher condition of materialistic life, whereas nivṛtti means the cessation of material desire. Through pravṛtti activities one suffers from material entanglement, but by nivṛtti activities one is purified and becomes fit to enjoy eternal, blissful life.

PURPORT

As confirmed in *Bhagavad-gītā* (16.7), *pravṛttiṁ ca nivṛttiṁ ca janā na vidur āsurāḥ:* the *asuras,* nondevotees, cannot distinguish between *pravṛtti* and *nivṛtti.* Whatever they like they do. Such persons think themselves independent of the strong material nature, and therefore they are irresponsible and do not care to act piously. Indeed, they do not distinguish between pious and impious activity. *Bhakti,* of course, does not depend on pious or impious activity. As stated in *Śrīmad-Bhāgavatam* (1.2.6):

sa vai puṁsāṁ paro dharmo
yato bhaktir adhokṣaje
ahaituky apratihatā
yayātmā suprasīdati

"The supreme occupation [*dharma*] for all humanity is that by which men can attain to loving devotional service unto the transcendent Lord. Such devotional service must be unmotivated and uninterrupted in order to completely satisfy the self." Nonetheless, those who act piously have a better chance to become devotees. As Kṛṣṇa says in *Bhagavad-gītā* (7.16), *catur-vidhā bhajante māṁ janāḥ sukṛtino 'rjuna:* "O Arjuna, four kinds of pious men render devotional service unto Me." One who takes to devotional service, even with some material motive, is considered pious, and because he has come to Kṛṣṇa, he will gradually come to the stage of *bhakti.* Then, like Dhruva Mahārāja, he will refuse to accept any material benediction from the Lord (*svāmin kṛtārtho 'smi varaṁ na yāce*). Therefore, even if one is materially inclined, one may take to the shelter of the lotus feet of Kṛṣṇa and Balarāma, or Gaura and Nitāi, so that he will very soon be purified of all material desires (*kṣipraṁ bhavati dharmātmā śaśvac chāntiṁ nigacchati*). As soon as one is freed from inclinations toward pious and impious activities, he becomes a perfect candidate for returning home, back to Godhead.

TEXTS 48–49

हिंस्रं द्रव्यमयं काम्यमग्निहोत्राद्यशान्तिदम् ।
दर्शश्च पूर्णमासश्च चातुर्मास्यं पशुः सुतः ॥४८॥
एतदिष्टं प्रवृत्ताख्यं हुतं प्रहुतमेव च ।
पूर्तं सुरालयारामकूपाजीव्यादिलक्षणम् ॥४९॥

hiṁsraṁ dravyamayaṁ kāmyam
agni-hotrādy-aśāntidam
darśaś ca pūrṇamāsaś ca
cāturmāsyaṁ paśuḥ sutaḥ

etad iṣṭaṁ pravṛttākhyaṁ
hutaṁ prahutam eva ca
pūrtaṁ surālayārāma-
kūpājīvyādi-lakṣaṇam

hiṁsram—a system of killing and sacrificing animals; *dravya-mayam*—requiring much paraphernalia; *kāmyam*—full of unlimited material desires; *agni-hotra-ādi*—ritualistic ceremonies such as the *agni-hotra-yajña; aśānti-dam*—causing anxieties; *darśaḥ*—the *darśa* ritualistic ceremony; *ca*—and; *pūrṇamāsaḥ*—the *pūrṇamāsa* ritualistic ceremony; *ca*—also; *cāturmāsyam*—observing four months of regulative principles; *paśuḥ*—the ceremony of sacrificing animals or *paśu-yajña; sutaḥ*—the *soma-yajña; etat*—of all this; *iṣṭam*—the goal;

pravṛtta-ākhyam—known as material attachment; *hutam*—Vaiśvadeva, an incarnation of the Supreme Personality of Godhead; *prahutam*—a ceremony called Baliharaṇa; *eva*—indeed; *ca*—also; *pūrtam*—for the benefit of the public; *sura-ālaya*—constructing temples for demigods; *ārāma*—resting houses and gardens; *kūpa*—digging wells; *ājīvya-ādi*—activities like distributing food and water; *lakṣaṇam*—symptoms.

TRANSLATION

The ritualistic ceremonies and sacrifices known as agni-hotra-yajña, darśa-yajña, pūrṇamāsa-yajña, cāturmāsya-yajña, paśu-yajña and soma-yajña are all symptomized by the killing of animals and the burning of many valuables, especially food grains, all for the fulfillment of material desires and the creation of anxiety. Performing such sacrifices, worshiping Vaiśvadeva, and performing the ceremony of Baliharaṇa, which all supposedly constitute the goal of life, as well as constructing temples for demigods, building resting houses and gardens, digging wells for the distribution of water, establishing booths for the distribution of food, and performing activities for public welfare—these are all symptomized by attachment to material desires.

TEXTS 50–51

द्रव्यसूक्ष्मविपाकश्च धूमो रात्रिरपक्षयः ।
अयनं दक्षिणं सोमो दर्श ओषधिवीरुधः ॥५०॥
अन्नं रेत इति क्ष्मेश पितृयानं पुनर्भवः ।
एकैकश्येनानुपूर्वं भूत्वा भूत्वेह जायते ॥५१॥

dravya-sūkṣma-vipākaś ca
dhūmo rātrir apakṣayaḥ
ayanaṁ dakṣiṇaṁ somo
darśa oṣadhi-vīrudhaḥ

annaṁ reta iti kṣmeśa
pitṛ-yānaṁ punar-bhavaḥ
ekaikaśyenānupūrvaṁ
bhūtvā bhūtveha jāyate

dravya-sūkṣma-vipākaḥ—the paraphernalia offered as oblations in the fire, such as food grains mixed with ghee; *ca*—and; *dhūmaḥ*—turned to smoke, or the demigod in charge of smoke; *rātriḥ*—the demigod in charge of night; *apakṣayaḥ*—in the dark fortnight of the moon; *ayanam*—the demigod in charge of the passing of the sun; *dakṣiṇam*—in the southern zone; *somaḥ*—the moon; *darśaḥ*—returning; *oṣadhi*—plant life (on the surface of the earth); *vīrudhaḥ*—vegetation in general (the birth of lamentation); *annam*—food grains; *retaḥ*—semen; *iti*—in this way; *kṣma-īśa*—O King Yudhiṣṭhira, lord of the earth; *pitṛ-yānam*—the way of taking birth from the father's semen; *punaḥ-bhavaḥ*—again and again; *eka-ekaśyena*—one after another; *anupūrvam*—successively, according to the gradation; *bhūtvā*—taking birth; *bhūtvā*—again taking birth; *iha*—in this material world; *jāyate*—one exists in the materialistic way of life.

TRANSLATION

My dear King Yudhiṣṭhira, when oblations of ghee and food grains like barley and sesame are offered in sacrifice, they turn into celestial smoke, which carries one to successively higher planetary systems like the kingdoms of Dhumā, Rātri, Kṛṣṇapakṣa, Dakṣiṇam and ultimately the moon. Then, however, the performers of sacrifice descend again to earth to become herbs, creepers, vegetables and food grains. These are eaten by different living entities and turned to semen, which is injected into female bodies. Thus one takes birth again and again.

PURPORT

This is explained in *Bhagavad-gītā* (9.21):

te taṁ bhuktvā svarga-lokaṁ viśālaṁ
kṣīṇe puṇye martya-lokaṁ viśanti
evaṁ trayī-dharmam anuprapannā
gatāgataṁ kāma-kāmā labhante

"When those who follow the *pravṛtti-mārga* have enjoyed heavenly sense pleasure, they return to this mortal planet again. Thus, through the Vedic principles, they achieve only flickering happiness." Following the *pravṛtti-mārga*, the living entity who desires to be promoted to the higher planetary systems performs sacrifices regularly, and how he goes up and comes down again is described here in *Śrīmad-Bhāgavatam*, as well as in *Bhagavad-gītā*. It is also said, *traiguṇya-viṣayā vedāḥ:* "The *Vedas* deal mainly with the three modes of material nature." The *Vedas*, especially three *Vedas*, namely *Sāma*, *Yajur* and *Ṛk*, vividly describe this process of ascending to the higher planets and returning. But Kṛṣṇa advises Arjuna, *traiguṇya-viṣayā vedā nistraiguṇyo bhavārjuna:* one has to transcend these three modes of material nature, and then one will be released from the cycle of birth and death. Otherwise, although one may be promoted to a higher planetary system such as Candraloka, one must again come down (*kṣīṇe puṇye martya-lokaṁ viśanti*). After one's enjoyment due to pious activities is finished, one must return to this planet in rainfall and first take birth as a plant or creeper, which is eaten by various animals, including human beings, and turned to semen. This semen is injected into the female body, and thus the living entity takes birth. Those who return to earth in this way take birth especially in higher families like those of *brāhmaṇas.*

It may be remarked in this connection that even the modern so-called scientists who are going to the moon are not able to stay there, but are returning to their laboratories. Therefore, whether one goes to the moon by modern mechanical arrangements or by performing pious activities, one must return to earth. That is clearly stated in this verse and explained in *Bhagavad-gītā*. Even if one goes to the higher planetary systems (*yānti deva-vratā devān*), one's place there is not secure; one must return to *martya-loka. Ābrahma-bhuvanāl lokāḥ punar āvartino 'rjuna:* aside from the moon, even if one goes to Brahmaloka, one must return. *Yaṁ prāpya na nivartante tad dhāma paramaṁ mama:* but if one goes back home, back to Godhead, he need not return to this material world.

TEXT 52

निषेकादिश्मशानान्तैः संस्कारैः संस्कृतो द्विजः ।
इन्द्रियेषु क्रियायज्ञान् ज्ञानदीपेषु जुह्वति ॥५२॥

niṣekādi-śmaśānāntaiḥ
saṁskāraiḥ saṁskṛto dvijaḥ

indriyeṣu kriyā-yajñān
jñāna-dīpeṣu juhvati

niṣeka-ādi—the beginning of life (the purificatory process of *garbhādhāna*, performed when the father begets a child by discharging semen into the womb of the mother); *śmaśāna-antaiḥ*—and at death, when the body is put into a crematorium and burnt to ashes; *saṁskāraiḥ*—by such purificatory processes; *saṁskṛtaḥ*—purified; *dvijaḥ*—a twiceborn *brāhmaṇa; indriyeṣu*—into the senses; *kriyā-yajñān*—activities and sacrifices (which elevate one to a higher planetary system); *jñāna-dīpeṣu*—by enlightenment in real knowledge; *juhvati*—offers.

TRANSLATION

A twiceborn brāhmaṇa [dvija] gains his life by the grace of his parents through the process of purification known as garbhādhāna. There are also other processes of purification, until the end of life, when the funeral ceremony [antyeṣṭi-kriyā] is performed. Thus in due course a qualified brāhmaṇa becomes uninterested in materialistic activities and sacrifices, but he offers the sensual sacrifices, in full knowledge, into the working senses, which are illuminated by the fire of knowledge.

PURPORT

Those interested in materialistic activities remain in the cycle of birth and death. *Pravṛtti-mārga*, or the inclination to stay in the material world to enjoy varieties of sense gratification, has been explained in the previous verse. Now, in this verse, it is explained that one who has perfect brahminical knowledge rejects the process of elevation to higher planets and accepts *nivṛtti-mārga;* in other words, he prepares himself to go back home, back to Godhead. Those who are not *brāhmaṇas* but atheists do not know what is *pravṛtti-mārga* or *nivṛtti-mārga;* they simply want to obtain pleasure at any cost. Our Kṛṣṇa consciousness movement is therefore training devotees to give up the *pravṛtti-mārga* and accept the *nivṛtti-mārga* in order to return home, back to Godhead. This is a little difficult to understand, but it is very easy if one takes to Kṛṣṇa consciousness seriously and tries to understand Kṛṣṇa. A Kṛṣṇa conscious person can understand that performing *yajña* according to the *karma-kāṇḍa* system is a useless waste of time and that merely giving up the *karma-kāṇḍa* and accepting the process of speculation is also unfruitful. Therefore Narottama dāsa Ṭhākura has sung in his *Prema-bhakti-candrikā:*

karma-kāṇḍa, jñāna-kāṇḍa, kevala viṣera bhāṇḍa
'amṛta' baliyā yebā khāya
nānā yoni sadā phire, kadarya bhakṣaṇa kare,
tāra janma adhaḥ-pāte yāya

A life of *karma-kāṇḍa* or *jñāna-kāṇḍa* is like a poison pot, and one who takes to such a life is doomed. In the *karma-kāṇḍa* system, one is destined to accept birth and death again and again. Similarly, with *jñāna-kāṇḍa* one falls down again to this material world. Only worship of the Supreme Person offers one the safety of going back home, back to Godhead.

TEXT 53

इन्द्रियाणि मनस्यूर्मौ वाचि वैकारिकं मनः ।
वाचं वर्णसमाम्नाये तमोङ्कारे स्वरे न्यसेत् ।
ओङ्कारं बिन्दौ नादे तं तं तु प्राणे महत्यमुम् ॥५३॥

indriyāṇi manasy ūrmau
vāci vaikārikaṁ manaḥ
vācaṁ varṇa-samāmnāye
tam oṁkāre svare nyaset
oṁkāraṁ bindau nāde taṁ
taṁ tu prāṇe mahaty amum

indriyāṇi—the senses (acting and knowledge-gathering); *manasi*—in the mind; *ūrmau*—in the waves of acceptance and rejection; *vāci*—in the words; *vaikārikam*—infected by changes; *manaḥ*—the mind; *vācam*—the words; *varṇa-samāmnāye*—in the aggregate of all alphabets; *tam*—that (aggregate of all alphabets); *oṁkāre*—in the concise form of *oṁkāra; svare*—in the vibration; *nyaset*—one should give up; *oṁkāram*—the concise sound vibration; *bindau*—in the point of *oṁkāra; nāde*—in the sound vibration; *tam*—that; *tam*—that (sound vibration); *tu*—indeed; *prāṇe*—in the life air; *mahati*—unto the Supreme; *amum*—the living entity.

TRANSLATION

The mind is always agitated by waves of acceptance and rejection. Therefore all the activities of the senses should be offered into the mind, which should be offered into one's words. Then one's words should be offered into the aggregate of all alphabets, which should be offered into the concise form oṁkāra. Oṁkāra should be offered into the point bindu, bindu into the vibration of sound, and that vibration into the life air. Then the living entity, who is all that remains, should be placed in Brahman, the Supreme. This is the process of sacrifice.

PURPORT

The mind is always agitated by acceptance and rejection, which are compared to mental waves that are constantly tossing. The living entity is floating in the waves of material existence because of his forgetfulness. Śrīla Bhaktivinoda Ṭhākura has therefore sung in his *Gītāvalī: miche māyāra vaśe, yāccha bhese', khāccha hābuḍubu, bhāi.* "My dear mind, under the influence of *māyā* you are being carried away by the waves of rejection and acceptance. Simply take shelter of Kṛṣṇa." *Jīva kṛṣṇa-dāsa, ei viśvāsa, karle ta' āra duḥkha nāi:* if we simply regard the lotus feet of Kṛṣṇa as our ultimate shelter, we shall be saved from all these waves of *māyā,* which are variously exhibited as mental and sensual activities and the agitation of rejection and acceptance. Kṛṣṇa instructs in *Bhagavad-gītā* (18.66):

sarva-dharmān parityajya
mām ekaṁ śaraṇaṁ vraja
ahaṁ tvāṁ sarva-pāpebhyo
mokṣayiṣyāmi mā śucaḥ

"Abandon all varieties of religion and just surrender unto Me. I shall deliver you from all sinful reaction. Do not fear." Therefore if we simply

place ourselves at the lotus feet of Kṛṣṇa by taking to Kṛṣṇa consciousness and keeping always in touch with Him by chanting the Hare Kṛṣṇa
mantra, we need not take much trouble in arranging to return to the
spiritual world. By the mercy of Śrī Caitanya Mahāprabhu, this is very
easy.

harer nāma harer nāma
harer nāmaiva kevalam
kalau nāsty eva nāsty eva
nāsty eva gatir anyathā

TEXT 54

अग्निः सूर्यो दिवा प्राह्णः शुक्लो राकोत्तरं स्वराट् ।
विश्वोऽथ तैजसः प्राज्ञस्तुर्य आत्मा समन्वयात् ॥५४॥

agniḥ sūryo divā prāhṇaḥ
śuklo rākottaraṁ sva-rāṭ
viśvo 'tha taijasaḥ prājñas
turya ātmā samanvayāt

agniḥ—fire; *sūryaḥ*—sun; *divā*—day; *prāhṇaḥ*—the end of the day;
śuklaḥ—the bright fortnight of the moon; *rāka*—the full moon at the
end of the *śukla-pakṣa*; *uttaram*—the period when the sun passes to the
north; *sva-rāṭ*—the Supreme Brahman or Lord Brahmā; *viśvaḥ*—gross
designation; *atha*—Brahmaloka, the ultimate in material enjoyment;
taijasaḥ—subtle designation; *prājñaḥ*—the witness in the causal designation; *turyaḥ*—transcendental; *ātmā*—the soul; *samanvayāt*—as a
natural consequence.

TRANSLATION

On his path of ascent, the progressive living entity enters the
different worlds of fire, the sun, the day, the end of the day, the
bright fortnight, the full moon, and the passing of the sun in the
north, along with their presiding demigods. When he enters
Brahmaloka, he enjoys life for many millions of years, and finally

his material designation comes to an end. He then comes to a subtle designation, from which he attains the causal designation, witnessing all previous states. Upon the annihilation of this causal state, he attains his pure state, in which he identifies with the Supersoul. In this way the living entity becomes transcendental.

TEXT 55

देवयानमिदं प्राहुर्भूत्वा भूत्वानुपूर्वशः ।
आत्मयाज्युपशान्तात्मा ह्यात्मस्थो न निवर्तते ॥५५॥

deva-yānam idaṁ prāhur
bhūtvā bhūtvānupūrvaśaḥ
ātma-yājy upaśāntātmā
hy ātma-stho na nivartate

deva-yānam—the process of elevation known as *deva-yāna; idam*—on this (path); *prāhuḥ*—it is said; *bhūtvā bhūtvā*—having repeated birth; *anupūrvaśaḥ*—consecutively; *ātma-yājī*—one who is eager for self-realization; *upaśānta-ātmā*—completely free from all material desires; *hi*—indeed; *ātma-sthaḥ*—situated in his own self; *na*—not; *nivartate*—does return.

TRANSLATION

This gradual process of elevation for self-realization is meant for those who are truly aware of the Absolute Truth. After repeated birth on this path, which is known as deva-yāna, one attains these consecutive stages. One who is completely free from all material desires, being situated in the self, need not traverse the path of repeated birth and death.

TEXT 56

य एते पितृदेवानामयने वेदनिर्मिते ।
शास्त्रेण चक्षुषा वेद जनस्थोऽपि न मुह्यति ॥५६॥

ya ete pitṛ-devānām
ayane veda-nirmite

śāstreṇa cakṣuṣā veda
jana-stho 'pi na muhyati

yaḥ—one who; *ete*—on this path (as recommended above); *pitṛ-devānām*—known as *pitṛ-yāna* and *deva-yāna; ayane*—on this path; *veda-nirmite*—recommended in the *Vedas; śāstreṇa*—by regular study of the scriptures; *cakṣuṣā*—by enlightened eyes; *veda*—is fully aware; *jana-sthaḥ*—a person situated in a material body; *api*—even though; *na*—never; *muhyati*—is bewildered.

TRANSLATION

Even though situated in a material body, one who is fully aware of the paths known as pitṛ-yāna and deva-yāna, and who thus opens his eyes in terms of Vedic knowledge, is never bewildered in this material world.

PURPORT

Ācāryavān puruṣo veda: one who is guided by the bona fide spiritual master knows everything as stated in the *Vedas*, which set forth the standard of infallible knowledge. As recommended in *Bhagavad-gītā, ācāryopāsanam:* one must approach the *ācārya* for real knowledge. *Tad-vijñānārthaṁ sa gurum evābhigacchet:* one must approach the *ācārya*, for then one will receive perfect knowledge. When guided by the spiritual master, one attains the ultimate goal of life.

TEXT 57

आदावन्ते जनानां सद् बहिरन्तः परावरम् ।
ज्ञानं ज्ञेयं वचो वाच्यं तमो ज्योतिस्त्वयं स्वयम्॥५७॥

ādāv ante janānāṁ sad
bahir antaḥ parāvaram
jñānaṁ jñeyaṁ vaco vācyaṁ
tamo jyotis tv ayaṁ svayam

ādau—in the beginning; *ante*—at the end; *janānām*—of all living entities; *sat*—always existing; *bahiḥ*—externally; *antaḥ*—internally; *para*—transcendental; *avaram*—material; *jñānam*—knowledge;

jñeyam—the objective; *vacaḥ*—expression; *vācyam*—the ultimate object; *tamaḥ*—darkness; *jyotiḥ*—light; *tu*—indeed; *ayam*—this one (the Supreme Lord); *svayam*—Himself.

TRANSLATION

He who exists internally and externally, at the beginning and end of everything and of all living beings, as that which is enjoyable and as the enjoyer of everything, superior and inferior, is the Supreme Truth. He always exists as knowledge and the object of knowledge, as expression and the object of understanding, as darkness and as light. Thus He, the Supreme Lord, is everything.

PURPORT

Here the Vedic aphorism *sarvaṁ khalv idaṁ brahma* is explained. It is also explained in the *catuḥ-ślokī Bhāgavatam. Aham evāsam evāgre.* The Supreme Lord existed in the beginning, He exists after the creation and maintains everything, and after destruction everything merges in Him, as stated in *Bhagavad-gītā* (*prakṛtiṁ yānti māmikām*). Thus the Supreme Lord is actually everything. In the conditioned state, we are bewildered in our understanding, but in the perfect stage of liberation we can understand that Kṛṣṇa is the cause of everything.

īśvaraḥ paramaḥ kṛṣṇaḥ
sac-cid-ānanda-vigrahaḥ
anādir ādir govindaḥ
sarva-kāraṇa-kāraṇam

"Kṛṣṇa, who is known as Govinda, is the supreme controller. He has an eternal, blissful, spiritual body. He is the origin of all. He has no other origin, for He is the prime cause of all causes." (Bs. 5.1) This is the perfection of knowledge.

TEXT 58

आबाधितोऽपि ह्याभासो यथा वस्तुतया स्मृतः ।
दुर्घटत्वादैन्द्रियकं तद्वदर्थविकल्पितम् ॥५८॥

ābādhito 'pi hy ābhāso
yathā vastutayā smṛtaḥ
durghaṭatvād aindriyakaṁ
tadvad artha-vikalpitam

ābādhitaḥ—rejected; *api*—although; *hi*—certainly; *ābhāsaḥ*—a reflection; *yathā*—as; *vastutayā*—a form of reality; *smṛtaḥ*—accepted; *durghaṭatvāt*—because of being very difficult to prove the reality; *aindriyakam*—knowledge derived from the senses; *tadvat*—similarly; *artha*—reality; *vikalpitam*—speculated or doubtful.

TRANSLATION

Although one may consider the reflection of the sun from a mirror to be false, it has its factual existence. Accordingly, to prove by speculative knowledge that there is no reality would be extremely difficult.

PURPORT

The impersonalists try to prove that the varieties in the vision of the empiric philosopher are false. The impersonalist philosophy, *vivarta-vāda*, generally cites the acceptance of a rope to be a snake as an example of this fact. According to this example, the varieties within our vision are false, just as a rope seen to be a snake is false. The Vaiṣṇavas say, however, that although the idea that the rope is a snake is false, the snake is not false; one has experience of a snake in reality, and therefore he knows that although the representation of the rope as a snake is false or illusory, there is a snake in reality. Similarly, this world, which is full of varieties, is not false; it is a reflection of the reality in the Vaikuṇṭha world, the spiritual world.

The reflection of the sun from a mirror is nothing but light within darkness. Thus although it is not exactly sunlight, without the sunlight the reflection would be impossible. Similarly, the varieties of this world would be impossible unless there were a real prototype in the spiritual world. The Māyāvādī philosopher cannot understand this, but a real philosopher must be convinced that light is not possible at all without a background of sunlight. Thus the jugglery of words used by the

Māyāvādī philosopher to prove that this material world is false may amaze inexperienced children, but a man with full knowledge knows perfectly well that there cannot be any existence without Kṛṣṇa. Therefore a Vaiṣṇava insists on the platform of somehow or other accepting Kṛṣṇa (*tasmāt kenāpy upāyena manaḥ kṛṣṇe niveśayet*).

When we raise our unmixed faith to the lotus feet of Kṛṣṇa, everything is revealed. Kṛṣṇa also says in *Bhagavad-gītā* (7.1):

mayy āsakta-manāḥ pārtha
yogaṁ yuñjan mad-āśrayaḥ
asaṁśayaṁ samagraṁ māṁ
yathā jñāsyasi tac chṛṇu

"Now hear, O son of Pṛthā [Arjuna], how by practicing *yoga* in full consciousness of Me, with mind attached to Me, you can know Me in full, free from doubt." Simply by raising one's staunch faith in Kṛṣṇa and His instructions, one can understand reality without a doubt (*asaṁśayaṁ samagraṁ māṁ*). One can understand how Kṛṣṇa's material and spiritual energies are working and how He is present everywhere although everything is not Him. This philosophy of *acintya-bhedābheda*, inconceivable oneness and difference, is the perfect philosophy enunciated by the Vaiṣṇavas. Everything is an emanation from Kṛṣṇa, but it is not that everything must therefore be worshiped. Speculative knowledge cannot give us reality as it is, but will continue to be nefariously imperfect. So-called scientists try to prove that there is no God and that everything is happening because of the laws of nature, but this is imperfect knowledge because nothing can work unless directed by the Supreme Personality of Godhead. This is explained in *Bhagavad-gītā* (9.10) by the Lord Himself:

mayādhyakṣeṇa prakṛtiḥ
sūyate sacarācaram
hetunānena kaunteya
jagad viparivartate

"This material nature is working under My direction, O son of Kuntī, and it is producing all moving and unmoving beings. By its rule this manifestation is created and annihilated again and again." In this regard, Śrīla Madhvācārya gives this note: *durghaṭatvād arthatvena parameśvareṇaiva kalpitam.* The background of everything is the Supreme Personality of Godhead, Vāsudeva. *Vāsudevaḥ sarvam iti sa mahātmā sudurlabhaḥ.* This can be understood by a *mahātmā* who is perfect in knowledge. Such a *mahātmā* is rarely seen.

TEXT 59

क्षित्यादीनामिहार्थानां छाया न कतमापि हि ।
न संघातो विकारोऽपि न पृथङ् नान्वितो मृषा ॥५९॥

kṣity-ādīnām ihārthānāṁ
chāyā na katamāpi hi
na saṅghāto vikāro 'pi
na pṛthaṅ nānvito mṛṣā

kṣiti-ādīnām—of the five elements, beginning with the earth; *iha*—in this world; *arthānām*—of those five elements; *chāyā*—shadow; *na*—neither; *katamā*—which of them; *api*—indeed; *hi*—certainly; *na*—nor; *saṅghātaḥ*—combination; *vikāraḥ*—transformation; *api*—although; *na pṛthak*—nor separated; *na anvitaḥ*—nor inherent in; *mṛṣā*—all these theories are without substance.

TRANSLATION

In this world there are five elements—namely earth, water, fire, air and ether—but the body is not a reflection of them, nor a combination or transformation of them. Because the body and its ingredients are neither distinct nor amalgamated, all such theories are insubstantial.

PURPORT

A forest is certainly a transformation of the earth, but one tree does not depend on another tree; if one is cut down, this does not mean that the others are cut down. Therefore, the forest is neither a combination nor a transformation of the trees. The best explanation is given by Kṛṣṇa Himself:

mayā tatam idaṁ sarvaṁ
jagad avyakta-mūrtinā
mat-sthāni sarva-bhūtāni
na cāhaṁ teṣv avasthitaḥ

"By Me, in My unmanifested form, this entire universe is pervaded. All beings are in Me, but I am not in them." (Bg. 9.4) Everything is an expansion of Kṛṣṇa's energy. As it is said, *parāsya śaktir vividhaiva śrūyate:* the Lord has multi-energies, which are expressed in different ways. The energies are existing, and the Supreme Personality of Godhead also exists simultaneously; because everything is His energy, He is simultaneously one with everything and different from everything. Thus our speculative theories that *ātmā,* the living force, is a combination of matter, that matter is a transformation of the soul, or that the body is part of the soul are all insubstantial.

Since all the Lord's energies are simultaneously existing, one must understand the Supreme Personality of Godhead. But although He is everything, He is not present in everything. The Lord must be worshiped in His original form as Kṛṣṇa. He can also present Himself in any one of His various expanded energies. When we worship the Deity of the Lord in the temple, the Deity appears to be stone or wood. Now, because the Supreme Lord does not have a material body, He is not stone or wood, yet stone and wood are not different from Him. Thus by worshiping stone or wood we get no result, but when the stone and wood are represented in the Lord's original form, by worshiping the Deity we get the desired result. This is supported by Śrī Caitanya Mahāprabhu's philosophy, *acintya-bhedābheda,* which explains how the Lord can present Himself everywhere and anywhere in a form of His energy to accept service from the devotee.

TEXT 60

धातवोऽवयवित्वाच्च तन्मात्रावयवैर्विना ।
न स्युर्ह्यसत्यवयविन्यसन्नवयवोऽन्ततः ॥६०॥

dhātavo 'vayavitvāc ca
tan-mātrāvayavair vinā

na syur hy asaty avayaviny
asann avayavo 'ntataḥ

dhātavaḥ—the five elements; *avayavitvāt*—being the cause of the bodily conception; *ca*—and; *tat-mātra*—the sense objects (sound, taste, touch, etc.); *avayavaiḥ*—the subtle parts; *vinā*—without; *na*—not; *syuḥ*—can exist; *hi*—indeed; *asati*—unreal; *avayavini*—in the formation of the body; *asan*—not existing; *avayavaḥ*—the part of the body; *antataḥ*—at the end.

TRANSLATION

Because the body is formed of the five elements, it cannot exist without the subtle sense objects. Therefore, since the body is false, the sense objects are also naturally false or temporary.

TEXT 61

स्यात् सादृश्यभ्रमस्तावद् विकल्पे सति वस्तुनः ।
जाग्रत्स्वापौ यथा स्वप्ने तथा विधिनिषेधता ॥६१॥

syāt sādṛśya-bhramas tāvad
vikalpe sati vastunaḥ
jāgrat-svāpau yathā svapne
tathā vidhi-niṣedhatā

syāt—it so becomes; *sādṛśya*—similarity; *bhramaḥ*—mistake; *tāvat*—as long as; *vikalpe*—in separation; *sati*—the part; *vastunaḥ*—from the substance; *jāgrat*—waking; *svāpau*—sleeping; *yathā*—as; *svapne*—in a dream; *tathā*—similarly; *vidhi-niṣedhatā*—the regulative principles, consisting of injunctions and prohibitions.

TRANSLATION

When a substance and its parts are separated, the acceptance of similarity between one and the other is called illusion. While dreaming, one creates a separation between the existences called wakefulness and sleep. It is in such a state of mind that the

regulative principles of the scriptures, consisting of injunctions and prohibitions, are recommended.

PURPORT

In material existence there are many regulative principles and formalities. If material existence is temporary or false, this does not mean that the spiritual world, although similar, is also false. That one's material body is false or temporary does not mean that the body of the Supreme Lord is also false or temporary. The spiritual world is real, and the material world is similar to it. For example, in the desert we sometimes find a mirage, but although the water in a mirage is false, this does not mean that there is no water in reality; water exists, but not in the desert. Similarly, nothing real is in this material world, but reality is in the spiritual world. The Lord's form and His abode—Goloka Vṛndāvana in the Vaikuṇṭha planets—are eternal realities.

From *Bhagavad-gītā* we understand that there is another *prakṛti*, or nature, which is real. This is explained by the Lord Himself in the Eighth Chapter of *Bhagavad-gītā* (8.19–21):

bhūta-grāmaḥ sa evāyaṁ
bhūtvā bhūtvā pralīyate
rātry-āgame 'vaśaḥ pārtha
prabhavaty ahar-āgame

paras tasmāt tu bhāvo 'nyo
'vyakto 'vyaktāt sanātanaḥ
yaḥ sa sarveṣu bhūteṣu
naśyatsu na vinaśyati

avyakto 'kṣara ity uktas
tam āhuḥ paramāṁ gatim
yaṁ prāpya na nivartante
tad dhāma paramaṁ mama

"Again and again the day of Brahmā comes, and all living beings are active; and again the night falls, O Pārtha, and they are helplessly dissolved. Yet there is another nature, which is eternal and is transcendental to this manifested and unmanifested matter. It is supreme and is never annihilated. When all in this world is annihilated, that part remains as it is. That supreme abode is called unmanifested and infallible, and it is the supreme destination. When one goes there, he never comes back. That is My supreme abode." The material world is a reflection of the spiritual world. The material world is temporary or false, but the spiritual world is an eternal reality.

TEXT 62

भावाद्वैतं क्रियाद्वैतं द्रव्याद्वैतं तथात्मनः ।
वर्तयन्स्वानुभूत्येह त्रीन्स्वप्नान्धुनुते मुनिः ॥६२॥

bhāvādvaitaṁ kriyādvaitaṁ
dravyādvaitaṁ tathātmanaḥ
vartayan svānubhūtyeha
trīn svapnān dhunute muniḥ

bhāva-advaitam—oneness in one's conception of life; *kriyā-advaitam*—oneness in activities; *dravya-advaitam*—oneness in different paraphernalia; *tathā*—as well as; *ātmanaḥ*—of the soul; *vartayan*—considering; *sva*—one's own; *anubhūtyā*—according to realization; *iha*—in this material world; *trīn*—the three; *svapnān*—living conditions (wakefulness, dreaming and sleep); *dhunute*—gives up; *muniḥ*—the philosopher or speculator.

TRANSLATION

After considering the oneness of existence, activity and paraphernalia and after realizing the self to be different from all actions and reactions, the mental speculator [muni], according to his own realization, gives up the three states of wakefulness, dreaming and sleep.

PURPORT

The three words *bhāvādvaita*, *kriyādvaita* and *dravyādvaita* are explained in the following verses. However, one has to give up all the nonduality of philosophical life in the material world and come to the actual life of reality in the spiritual world in order to attain perfection.

TEXT 63

कार्यकारणवस्त्वैक्यदर्शनं पटतन्तुवत् ।
अवस्तुत्वाद् विकल्पस्य भावाद्वैतं तदुच्यते ॥६३॥

kārya-kāraṇa-vastv-aikya-
darśanaṁ paṭa-tantuvat
avastutvād vikalpasya
bhāvādvaitaṁ tad ucyate

kārya—the result or effect; *kāraṇa*—the cause; *vastu*—substance; *aikya*—oneness; *darśanam*—observation; *paṭa*—the cloth; *tantu*—the thread; *vat*—like; *avastutvāt*—because of being ultimately unreality; *vikalpasya*—of differentiation; *bhāva-advaitam*—the conception of oneness; *tat ucyate*—that is called.

TRANSLATION

When one understands that result and cause are one and that duality is ultimately unreal, like the idea that the threads of a cloth are different from the cloth itself, one reaches the conception of oneness called bhāvādvaita.

TEXT 64

यद् ब्रह्मणि परे साक्षात् सर्वकर्मसमर्पणम् ।
मनोवाक्तनुभिः पार्थ क्रियाद्वैतं तदुच्यते ॥६४॥

yad brahmaṇi pare sākṣāt
sarva-karma-samarpaṇam
mano-vāk-tanubhiḥ pārtha
kriyādvaitaṁ tad ucyate

yat—that which; *brahmaṇi*—in the Supreme Brahman; *pare*—transcendental; *sākṣāt*—directly; *sarva*—of all; *karma*—activities; *samarpaṇam*—dedication; *manaḥ*—by the mind; *vāk*—the words; *tanubhiḥ*—and the body; *pārtha*—O Mahārāja Yudhiṣṭhira; *kriyā-advaitam*—oneness in activities; *tat ucyate*—it is called.

TRANSLATION

My dear Yudhiṣṭhira [Pārtha], when all the activities one performs with his mind, words and body are dedicated directly to the service of the Supreme Personality of Godhead, one reaches oneness of activities, called kriyādvaita.

PURPORT

The Kṛṣṇa consciousness movement is teaching people how to come to the stage of dedicating everything to the service of the Supreme Personality of Godhead. Kṛṣṇa says in *Bhagavad-gītā* (9.27):

yat karoṣi yad aśnāsi
yaj juhoṣi dadāsi yat
yat tapasyasi kaunteya
tat kuruṣva mad-arpaṇam

"O son of Kuntī, all that you do, all that you eat, all that you offer and give away, as well as all austerities that you may perform, should be done as an offering unto Me." If whatever we do, whatever we eat, whatever we think and whatever we plan is for the advancement of the Kṛṣṇa consciousness movement, this is oneness. There is no difference between chanting for Kṛṣṇa consciousness and working for Kṛṣṇa consciousness. On the transcendental platform, they are one. But we must be guided by the spiritual master about this oneness; we should not manufacture our own oneness.

TEXT 65

आत्मजायासुतादीनामन्येषां सर्वदेहिनाम् ।
यत् स्वार्थकामयोरैक्यं द्रव्याद्वैतं तदुच्यते ॥६५॥

ātma-jāyā-sutādīnām
anyeṣāṁ sarva-dehinām
yat svārtha-kāmayor aikyaṁ
dravyādvaitaṁ tad ucyate

ātma—of one's self; *jāyā*—wife; *suta-ādīnām*—and children; *anyeṣām*—of one's relatives, etc.; *sarva-dehinām*—of all other living entities; *yat*—whatever; *sva-artha-kāmayoḥ*—of one's ultimate goal and benefit; *aikyam*—oneness; *dravya-advaitam*—oneness of interest; *tat ucyate*—it is called.

TRANSLATION

When the ultimate goal and interest of one's self, one's wife, one's children, one's relatives and all other embodied living beings is one, this is called dravyādvaita, or oneness of interest.

PURPORT

The actual interest of all living entities—indeed, the goal of life—is to return home, back to Godhead. This is the interest of one's own self, one's wife, one's children, one's disciples and one's friends, relatives, countrymen and all humanity. The Kṛṣṇa consciousness movement can give directions for management by which everyone can partake in Kṛṣṇa conscious activities and reach the ultimate goal, which is known as *svārtha-gatim.* This objective of everyone's interest is Viṣṇu, but because people do not know this (*na te viduḥ svārtha-gatiṁ hi viṣṇum*), they are making various plans by which to fulfill so many concocted interests in life. The Kṛṣṇa consciousness movement is trying to bring everyone to the highest interest. The process may be differently named, but if the aim is one, people should follow it to achieve the ultimate goal in life. Unfortunately, people are thinking of different interests, and blind leaders are misleading them. Everyone is trying to reach the goal of complete happiness materially; because people do not know what complete happiness is, they are materially diverted toward different interests.

TEXT 66

यद् यस्य वानिषिद्धं स्याद् येन यत्र यतो नृप ।
स तेनेहेत कार्याणि नरो नान्यैरनापदि ॥६६॥

yad yasya vāniṣiddhaṁ syād
yena yatra yato nṛpa
sa teneheta kāryāṇi
naro nānyair anāpadi

yat—whatever; *yasya*—of a man; *vā*—either; *aniṣiddham*—not forbidden; *syāt*—it is so; *yena*—by which means; *yatra*—in place and time; *yataḥ*—from which; *nṛpa*—O King; *saḥ*—such a person; *tena*—by such a process; *īheta*—should perform; *kāryāṇi*—prescribed activities; *naraḥ*—a person; *na*—not; *anyaiḥ*—by other ways; *anāpadi*—in the absence of danger.

TRANSLATION

In normal conditions, in the absence of danger, O King Yudhiṣṭhira, a man should perform his prescribed activities according to his status of life with the things, endeavors, process and living place that are not forbidden for him, and not by any other means.

PURPORT

This instruction is given for men in all statuses of life. Generally society is divided into *brāhmaṇas, kṣatriyas, vaiśyas, śūdras, brahmacārīs, vānaprasthas, sannyāsīs* and *gṛhasthas.* Everyone must act according to his position and try to please the Supreme Personality of Godhead, for that will make one's life successful. This was instructed in Naimiṣāraṇya:

ataḥ pumbhir dvija-śreṣṭhā
varṇāśrama-vibhāgaśaḥ
svanuṣṭhitasya dharmasya
saṁsiddhir hari-toṣaṇam

"O best among the twiceborn, it is therefore concluded that the highest perfection one can achieve, by discharging his prescribed duties [*dharma*] according to caste divisions and order of life, is to please the Lord Hari." (*Bhāg.* 1.2.13) Everyone should act according to his occupational duties just to please the Supreme Personality of Godhead. Then everyone will be happy.

TEXT 67

एतैरन्यैश्च वेदोक्तैर्वर्तमानः स्वकर्मभिः ।
गृहेऽप्यस्य गतिं यायाद् राजंस्तद्भक्तिभाङ् नरः॥६७॥

etair anyaiś ca vedoktair
vartamānaḥ sva-karmabhiḥ
gṛhe 'py asya gatiṁ yāyād
rājaṁs tad-bhakti-bhāṅ naraḥ

etaiḥ—by these ways; *anayiḥ*—by other ways; *ca*—and; *veda-uktaiḥ*—as directed in the Vedic literatures; *vartamānaḥ*—abiding; *sva-karmabhiḥ*—by one's occupational duties; *gṛhe api*—even at home; *asya*—of Lord Kṛṣṇa; *gatim*—destination; *yāyāt*—can reach; *rājan*—O King; *tat-bhakti-bhāk*—who renders devotional service unto the Supreme Personality of Godhead; *naraḥ*—any person.

TRANSLATION

O King, one should perform his occupational duties according to these instructions, as well as other instructions given in the Vedic literature, just to remain a devotee of Lord Kṛṣṇa. Thus, even while at home, one will be able to reach the destination.

PURPORT

The ultimate goal of life is Viṣṇu, Kṛṣṇa. Therefore, either by Vedic regulative principles or by materialistic activities, if one tries to reach the destination of Kṛṣṇa, that is the perfection of life. Kṛṣṇa should be the target; everyone should try to reach Kṛṣṇa, from any position of life.

Kṛṣṇa accepts service from anyone. The Lord says in *Bhagavad-gītā* (9.32):

māṁ hi pārtha vyapāśritya
ye 'pi syuḥ pāpa-yonayaḥ
striyo vaiśyās tathā śūdrās
te 'pi yānti parāṁ gatim

"O son of Pṛthā, those who take shelter in Me, though they be of lower birth—women, *vaiśyas* [merchants], as well as *śūdras* [workers]—can approach the supreme destination." It does not matter what one's position is; if one aims at reaching Kṛṣṇa by performing his occupational duty under the direction of the spiritual master, his life is successful. It is not that only *sannyāsīs*, *vānaprasthas* and *brahmacārīs* can reach

Kṛṣṇa. A *gṛhastha*, a householder, can also reach Kṛṣṇa, provided he becomes a pure devotee without material desires. An example of this is cited in the next verse.

TEXT 68

यथा हि यूयं नृपदेव दुस्त्यजा-
दापद्गणादुत्तरतात्मनः प्रभोः ।
यत्पादपङ्केरुहसेवया भवा-
नहारषीन्निर्जितदिग्गजः क्रतून् ॥६८॥

yathā hi yūyaṁ nṛpa-deva dustyajād
āpad-gaṇād uttaratātmanaḥ prabhoḥ
yat-pāda-paṅkeruha-sevayā bhavān
ahārasīn nirjita-dig-gajaḥ kratūn

yathā—as; *hi*—indeed; *yūyam*—all of you (Pāṇḍavas); *nṛpa-deva*—O lord of the kings, human beings and demigods; *dustyajāt*—insurmountable; *āpat*—dangerous conditions; *gaṇāt*—from all; *uttarata*—escaped; *ātmanaḥ*—own; *prabhoḥ*—of the Lord; *yat-pāda-paṅkeruha*—whose lotus feet; *sevayā*—by serving; *bhavān*—yourself; *ahāraṣīt*—performed; *nirjita*—defeating; *dik-gajaḥ*—the most powerful enemies, who were like elephants; *kratūn*—ritualistic ceremonies.

TRANSLATION

O King Yudhiṣṭhira, because of your service to the Supreme Lord, all of you Pāṇḍavas defeated the greatest dangers posed by numerous kings and demigods. By serving the lotus feet of Kṛṣṇa, you conquered great enemies, who were like elephants, and thus you collected ingredients for sacrifice. By His grace, may you be delivered from material involvement.

PURPORT

Placing himself as an ordinary householder, Mahārāja Yudhiṣṭhira inquired from Nārada Muni how a *gṛha-mūḍha-dhī*, a person who is entangled in household life and who thus continues to remain a fool, can be delivered. Nārada Muni encouraged Mahārāja Yudhiṣṭhira by saying, "You are already on the safe side because you, along with your entire family, have become a pure devotee of Kṛṣṇa." By Kṛṣṇa's grace, the Pāṇḍavas conquered in the Battle of Kurukṣetra and were saved from many dangers posed not only by kings but sometimes even by the demigods. Thus they are a practical example of how to live in security and safety by the grace of Kṛṣṇa. Everyone should follow the example of the Pāṇḍavas, who showed how to be saved by the grace of Kṛṣṇa. Our Kṛṣṇa consciousness movement is intended to teach how everyone can live peacefully in this material world and at the end of life return home, back to Godhead. In the material world there are always dangers at every step (*padaṁ padaṁ yad vipadāṁ na teṣām*). Nonetheless, if one takes shelter of Kṛṣṇa without hesitation and keeps under the shelter of Kṛṣṇa, he can easily cross the ocean of nescience. *Samāśritā ye pada-pallava-plavaṁ mahat-padaṁ puṇya-yaśo murāreḥ.* To the devotee, this great ocean of nescience becomes like a puddle of water in the hoofprint of a cow. A pure devotee, without embarrassing himself by trying for elevation in so many ways, stays in the safest position as a servant of Kṛṣṇa, and thus his life is eternally safe without a doubt.

TEXT 69

अहं पुराभवं कश्चिद् गन्धर्व उपबर्हणः ।
नाम्नातीते महाकल्पे गन्धर्वाणां सुसम्मतः ॥६९॥

ahaṁ purābhavaṁ kaścid
gandharva upabarhaṇaḥ
nāmnātīte mahā-kalpe
gandharvāṇāṁ susammataḥ

aham—I myself; *purā*—formerly; *abhavam*—existed as; *kaścit gandharvaḥ*—one of the denizens of Gandharvaloka; *upabarhaṇaḥ*—Upabarhaṇa; *nāmnā*—by the name; *atīte*—long, long ago; *mahā-kalpe*—in a life of Brahmā, which is known as a *mahā-kalpa; gandharvāṇām*—among the Gandharvas; *su-sammataḥ*—a very respectable person.

TRANSLATION

Long, long ago, in another mahā-kalpa [millennium of Brahmā], I existed as the Gandharva known as Upabarhaṇa. I was very respected by the other Gandharvas.

PURPORT

Śrīla Nārada Muni is giving a practical example from his past life. Formerly, during the previous lifetime of Lord Brahmā, Nārada Muni was one of the denizens of Gandharvaloka, but unfortunately, as will be explained, he fell from his exalted position in Gandharvaloka, where the inhabitants are extremely beautiful and expert in singing, to become a *śūdra.* Nonetheless, because of his association with devotees, he became more fortunate than he was in Gandharvaloka. Even though cursed by the *prajāpatis* to become a *śūdra,* in his next life he became the son of Lord Brahmā.

The word *mahā-kalpe* is described by Śrīla Madhvācārya as *atīta-brahma-kalpe.* Brahmā dies at the end of a life of many millions of years. The day of Brahmā is described in *Bhagavad-gītā* (8.17):

sahasra-yuga-paryantam
ahar yad brahmaṇo viduḥ
rātriṁ yuga-sahasrāntāṁ
te 'ho-rātra-vido janāḥ

"By human calculation, a thousand ages taken together is the duration of Brahmā's one day. And such also is the duration of his night." Bhagavān Śrī Kṛṣṇa can remember incidents from millions of years ago. Similarly, His pure devotee like Nārada Muni can also remember incidents from a past life millions and millions of years ago.

TEXT 70

रूपपेशलमाधुर्यसौगन्ध्यप्रियदर्शनः ।
स्त्रीणां प्रियतमो नित्यं मत्तः स्वपुरलम्पटः ॥७०॥

rūpa-peśala-mādhurya-
saugandhya-priya-darśanaḥ

strīṇāṁ priyatamo nityaṁ
mattaḥ sva-pura-lampaṭaḥ

rūpa—beauty; *peśala*—formation of the body; *mādhurya*—attractiveness; *saugandhya*—very fragrant, being decorated with various flower garlands and sandalwood pulp; *priya-darśanaḥ*—very beautiful to see; *strīṇām*—of the women; *priya-tamaḥ*—naturally attracted; *nityam*—daily; *mattaḥ*—proud like a madman; *sva-pura*—in his own city; *lampaṭaḥ*—very much attached to women because of lusty desires.

TRANSLATION

I had a beautiful face and a pleasing, attractive bodily structure. Decorated with flower garlands and sandalwood pulp, I was most pleasing to the women of my city. Thus I was bewildered, always feeling lusty desires.

PURPORT

From the description of the beauty of Nārada Muni when he was one of the denizens of Gandharvaloka, it appears that everyone on that planet is extremely beautiful and pleasing and always decorated with flowers and sandalwood. Upabarhaṇa was Nārada Muni's name previously. Upabarhaṇa was specifically expert in decorating himself to attract the attention of women, and thus he became a playboy, as described in the next verse. To be a playboy in this life is unfortunate because too much attraction to women will lead one to fall into the association of *śūdras*, who can easily take advantage of mingling with women without restriction. In this present age of Kali, when people are *mandāḥ sumanda-matayaḥ*—very bad because of a *śūdra* mentality—such free mingling is prominent. Among the higher classes—*brāhmaṇa*, *kṣatriya* and *vaiśya*—there is no chance for men to mingle with women freely, but in the *śūdra* community such mingling is open. Because there is no cultural education in this age of Kali, everyone is spiritually untrained, and everyone is therefore to be considered *śūdra* (*aśuddhāḥ śūdra-kalpā hi brāhmaṇāḥ kali-sambhavāḥ*). When all the people become *śūdras*, certainly they are very bad (*mandāḥ sumanda-matayaḥ*). Thus they manufacture their own way of life, with the result that they gradually become unfortunate (*manda-bhāgyāḥ*), and furthermore they are always disturbed by various circumstances.

TEXT 71

एकदा देवसत्रे तु गन्धर्वाप्सरसां गणाः ।
उपहूता विश्वसृग्भिर्हरिगाथोपगायने ॥७१॥

ekadā deva-satre tu
gandharvāpsarasāṁ gaṇāḥ
upahūtā viśva-sṛgbhir
hari-gāthopagāyane

ekadā—once upon a time; *deva-satre*—in an assembly of the demigods; *tu*—indeed; *gandharva*—of the inhabitants of Gandharvaloka; *apsarasām*—and the inhabitants of Apsaroloka; *gaṇāḥ*—all; *upahūtāḥ*—were invited; *viśva-sṛgbhiḥ*—by the great demigods known as the *prajāpatis; hari-gātha-upagāyane*—on an occasion of *kīrtana* for glorifying the Supreme Lord.

TRANSLATION

Once there was a saṅkīrtana festival to glorify the Supreme Lord in an assembly of the demigods, and the Gandharvas and Apsarās were invited by the prajāpatis to take part in it.

PURPORT

Saṅkīrtana means chanting of the holy name of the Lord. The Hare Kṛṣṇa movement is not a new movement as people sometimes mistakenly think. The Hare Kṛṣṇa movement is present in every millennium of Lord Brahmā's life, and the holy name is chanted in all the higher planetary systems, including Brahmaloka and Candraloka, not to speak of Gandharvaloka and Apsaroloka. The *saṅkīrtana* movement that was started in this world five hundred years ago by Śrī Caitanya Mahāprabhu is therefore not a new movement. Sometimes, because of our bad luck, this movement is stopped, but Śrī Caitanya Mahāprabhu and His servants again start the movement for the benefit of the entire word or, indeed, the entire universe.

TEXT 72

अहं च गायंस्तद्विद्वान् स्त्रीभिः परिवृतो गतः ।
ज्ञात्वा विश्वसृजस्तन्मे हेलनं शेपुरोजसा ।
याहि त्वं शूद्रतामाशु नष्टश्रीः कृतहेलनः ॥७२॥

aham ca gāyaṁs tad-vidvān
strībhiḥ parivṛto gataḥ
jñātvā viśva-sṛjas tan me
helanaṁ śepur ojasā
yāhi tvaṁ śūdratām āśu
naṣṭa-śrīḥ kṛta-helanaḥ

aham—I myself; *ca*—and; *gāyan*—singing the glories of other demigods rather than those of the Lord; *tat-vidvān*—knowing very well the art of singing; *strībhiḥ*—by women; *parivṛtaḥ*—being surrounded; *gataḥ*—went there; *jñātvā*—knowing well; *viśva-sṛjaḥ*—the *prajāpatis*, to whom the management of universal affairs was entrusted; *tat*—the attitude of my singing; *me*—my; *helanam*—negligence; *śepuḥ*—cursed; *ojasā*—with great force; *yāhi*—become; *tvam*—you; *śūdratām*—a *śūdra; āśu*—immediately; *naṣṭa*—devoid of; *śrīḥ*—beauty; *kṛta-helanaḥ*—because of transgressing the etiquette.

TRANSLATION

Nārada Muni continued: Being invited to that festival, I also joined, and, surrounded by women, I began musically singing the glories of the demigods. Because of this, the prajāpatis, the great demigods in charge of the affairs of the universe, forcefully cursed me with these words: "Because you have committed an offense, may you immediately become a śūdra, devoid of beauty."

PURPORT

As far as *kīrtana* is concerned, the *śāstras* say, *śravaṇaṁ kīrtanaṁ viṣṇoḥ:* one should chant the glories of the Supreme Lord and the holy name of the Supreme Lord. This is clearly stated. *Śravaṇaṁ kīrtanaṁ viṣṇoḥ:* one should chant about and glorify Lord Viṣṇu, not any demigod. Unfortunately, there are foolish persons who invent some process of *kīrtana* on the basis of a demigod's name. This is an offense. *Kīrtana* means glorifying the Supreme Lord, not any demigod. Sometimes people invent Kālī-*kīrtana* or Śiva-*kīrtana*, and even big *sannyāsīs* in the Māyāvāda school say that one may chant any name and still get the same result. But here we find that millions and millions of years ago, when Nārada Muni was a Gandharva, he neglected the order to glorify the Lord, and being mad in the association of women, he began to chant otherwise. Thus he was cursed to become a *śūdra.* His first offense was that he went to join the *saṅkīrtana* party in the company of lusty women, and another offense was that he considered ordinary songs, like cinema songs and other such songs, to be equal to *saṅkīrtana.* For this offense he was punished with becoming a *śūdra.*

TEXT 73

तावद्दास्यामहं जज्ञे तत्रापि ब्रह्मवादिनाम् ।
शुश्रूषयानुषङ्गेण प्राप्तोऽहं ब्रह्मपुत्रताम् ॥७३॥

tāvad dāsyām ahaṁ jajñe
tatrāpi brahma-vādinām
śuśrūṣayānuṣaṅgeṇa
prāpto 'haṁ brahma-putratām

tāvat—since being cursed; *dāsyām*—in the womb of a maidservant; *aham*—I; *jajñe*—took birth; *tatrāpi*—although (being a *śūdra*); *brahma-vādinām*—unto persons well conversant with the Vedic knowledge; *śuśrūṣayā*—by rendering service; *anuṣaṅgeṇa*—simultaneously; *prāptaḥ*—obtained; *aham*—I; *brahma-putratām*—a birth as the son of Lord Brahmā (in this life).

TRANSLATION

Although I took birth as a śūdra from the womb of a maidservant, I engaged in the service of Vaiṣṇavas who were well-versed in Vedic knowledge. Consequently, in this life I got the opportunity to take birth as the son of Lord Brahmā.

PURPORT

The Supreme Personality of Godhead says in *Bhagavad-gītā* (9.32):

māṁ hi pārtha vyapāśritya
ye 'pi syuḥ pāpa-yonayaḥ
striyo vaiśyās tathā śūdrās
te 'pi yānti parāṁ gatim

"O son of Pṛthā, those who take shelter in Me, though they be of lower birth—women, *vaiśyas* [merchants], as well as *śūdras* [workers]—can approach the supreme destination." It doesn't matter whether a person is born as a *śūdra*, a woman or a *vaiśya;* if he associates with devotees repeatedly or always (*sādhu-saṅgena*), he can be elevated to the highest perfection. Nārada Muni is explaining this in relation to his own life. The *saṅkīrtana* movement is important, for regardless of whether one is a *śūdra, vaiśya, mleccha, yavana* or whatever, if one associates with a pure devotee, follows his instructions and serves the pure devotee, his life is successful. This is *bhakti. Ānukūlyena kṛṣṇānuśīlanam. Bhakti* consists of serving Kṛṣṇa and His devotees very favorably. *Anyābhilāṣitā-śūnyam.* If one has no desire other than to serve Kṛṣṇa and His devotee, then his life is successful. This is explained by Nārada Muni through this practical example from his own life.

TEXT 74

धर्मस्ते गृहमेधीयो वर्णितः पापनाशनः ।
गृहस्थो येन पदवीमञ्जसा न्यासिनामियात् ॥७४॥

dharmas te gṛha-medhīyo
varṇitaḥ pāpa-nāśanaḥ
gṛhastho yena padavīm
añjasā nyāsinām iyāt

dharmaḥ—that religious process; *te*—to you; *gṛha-medhīyaḥ*—although attached to household life; *varṇitaḥ*—explained (by me); *pāpa-nāśanaḥ*—the destruction of sinful reactions; *gṛhasthaḥ*—a person in household life; *yena*—by which; *padavīm*—the position; *añjasā*—very easily; *nyāsinām*—of those in the renounced order of life; *iyāt*—can obtain.

TRANSLATION

The process of chanting the holy name of the Lord is so powerful that by this chanting even householders [gṛhasthas] can very easily gain the ultimate result achieved by persons in the renounced order. Mahārāja Yudhiṣṭhira, I have now explained to you that process of religion.

PURPORT

This is a confirmation of the Kṛṣṇa consciousness movement. Anyone who takes part in this movement, regardless of what he is, can gain the topmost result achieved by a perfect *sannyāsī*, namely *brahma-jñāna* (spiritual knowledge). Even more important, he can advance in devotional service. Mahārāja Yudhiṣṭhira thought that because he was a *gṛhastha* there was no hope of his being liberated, and therefore he asked Nārada Muni how he could get out of material entanglement. But Nārada Muni, citing a practical example from his own life, established that by associating with devotees and chanting the Hare Kṛṣṇa *mantra*, any man in any condition of life can achieve the highest perfection without a doubt.

TEXT 75

यूयं नृलोके बत भूरिभागा
लोकं पुनाना मुनयोऽभियन्ति ।
येषां गृहानावसतीति साक्षाद्
गूढं परं ब्रह्म मनुष्यलिङ्गम् ॥७५॥

yūyaṁ nṛ-loke bata bhūri-bhāgā
lokaṁ punānā munayo 'bhiyanti
yeṣāṁ gṛhān āvasatīti sākṣād
gūḍhaṁ paraṁ brahma manuṣya-liṅgam

yūyam—all of you Pāṇḍavas; *nṛ-loke*—in this material world; *bata*—indeed; *bhūri-bhāgāḥ*—extremely fortunate; *lokam*—all the planets of the universe; *punānāḥ*—who can purify; *munayaḥ*—great saintly persons; *abhiyanti*—come to visit (just like ordinary persons); *yeṣām*—of whom; *gṛhān*—the house of the Pāṇḍavas; *āvasati*—resides; *iti*—thus; *sākṣāt*—directly; *gūḍham*—very confidential; *param*—transcendental; *brahma*—the Parabrahman, Kṛṣṇa; *manuṣya-liṅgam*—as if an ordinary human being.

TRANSLATION

My dear Mahārāja Yudhiṣṭhira, you Pāṇḍavas are so very fortunate in this world that many, many great saints, who can purify all the planets of the universe, come to your house just like ordinary visitors. Furthermore, the Supreme Personality of Godhead, Kṛṣṇa, is living confidentially with you in your house, just like your brother.

PURPORT

Here is a statement exalting a Vaiṣṇava. In human society, a *brāhmaṇa* is the most respected person. A *brāhmaṇa* is one who can understand Brahman, the impersonal Brahman, but hardly ever can one understand the Supreme Personality of Godhead, who is described by Arjuna in *Bhagavad-gītā* as *paraṁ brahma.* A *brāhmaṇa* may be extremely fortunate in having achieved *brahma-jñāna*, but the Pāṇḍavas were so exalted that the Parabrahman, the Supreme Personality of Godhead, was living in their house like an ordinary human being. The word *bhūri-bhāgāḥ* indicates that the Pāṇḍavas were in a still higher position than *brahmacārīs* and *brāhmaṇas.* In the following verses, Nārada Muni repeatedly glorifies the position of the Pāṇḍavas.

TEXT 76

स वा अयं ब्रह्म महद्विमृग्य
कैवल्यनिर्वाणसुखानुभूतिः ।
प्रियः सुहृद् वः खलु मातुलेय
आत्मार्हणीयो विधिकृद् गुरुश्च ॥७६॥

sa vā ayaṁ brahma mahad-vimṛgya-
kaivalya-nirvāṇa-sukhānubhūtiḥ
priyaḥ suhṛd vaḥ khalu mātuleya
ātmārhaṇīyo vidhi-kṛd guruś ca

saḥ—that Supreme Personality of Godhead; *vā*—either; *ayam*—Kṛṣṇa; *brahma*—the Supreme Brahman; *mahat-vimṛgya*—sought by great, great saintly persons (devotees of Kṛṣṇa); *kaivalya-nirvāṇa-sukha*—of liberation and transcendental bliss; *anubhūtiḥ*—for the realization; *priyaḥ*—very dear; *suhṛt*—the well-wisher; *vaḥ*—of all of you Pāṇḍavas; *khalu*—famous as; *mātuleyaḥ*—the son of your maternal uncle; *ātmā*—heart and soul; *arhaṇīyaḥ*—the most worshipable person; *vidhi-kṛt*—giving direction; *guruḥ*—your spiritual master; *ca*—and.

TRANSLATION

How wonderful it is that the Supreme Personality of Godhead, the Parabrahman, Kṛṣṇa, who is sought by great, great sages for the sake of liberation and transcendental bliss, is acting as your best well-wisher, your friend, your cousin, your heart and soul, your worshipable director, and your spiritual master.

PURPORT

Kṛṣṇa can become the director and spiritual master of anyone who is serious about getting the mercy of Kṛṣṇa. The Lord sends the spiritual master to train a devotee, and when the devotee is advanced, the Lord acts as the spiritual master within his heart.

teṣāṁ satata-yuktānāṁ
bhajatāṁ prīti-pūrvakam
dadāmi buddhi-yogaṁ taṁ
yena mām upayānti te

"To those who are constantly devoted and worhip Me with love, I give the understanding by which they can come to Me." Kṛṣṇa does not become the direct spiritual master unless one is fully trained by His representative spiritual master. Therefore, as we have already discussed, the Lord's representative spiritual master should not be considered an ordinary human being. The representative spiritual master never gives any false knowledge to his disciple, but only perfect knowledge. Thus he is the representative of Kṛṣṇa. Kṛṣṇa helps as the *guru*, or spiritual master, from within and from without. From without He helps the devotee as His representative, and from within He talks personally with the pure devotee and gives him instructions by which he may return home, back to Godhead.

TEXT 77

न यस्य साक्षाद्भवपद्मजादिभी
रूपं धिया वस्तुतयोपवर्णितम् ।
मौनेन भक्त्योपशमेन पूजितः
प्रसीदतामेष स सात्वतां पतिः ॥७७॥

na yasya sākṣād bhava-padmajādibhī
rūpaṁ dhiyā vastutayopavarṇitam
maunena bhaktyopaśamena pūjitaḥ
prasīdatām eṣa sa sātvatāṁ patiḥ

na—not; *yasya*—of whom (Lord Śrī Kṛṣṇa); *sākṣāt*—directly; *bhava*—by Lord Śiva; *padma-ja-ādibhiḥ*—Lord Brahmā and others; *rūpam*—the form; *dhiyā*—by meditation; *vastutayā*—factually; *upavarṇitam*—could be explained; *maunena*—by silence; *bhaktyā*—by devotional service; *upaśamena*—by finishing all material activities; *pūjitaḥ*—one who is so worshiped; *prasīdatām*—may be pleased with us; *eṣaḥ*—this; *saḥ*—the same Personality of Godhead; *sātvatām*—of the devotees; *patiḥ*—who is the maintainer, master and guide.

TRANSLATION

Present here now is the same Supreme Personality of Godhead whose true form cannot be understood even by such great personalities as Lord Brahmā and Lord Śiva. He is realized by devotees because of their unflinching surrender. May that same Personality of Godhead, who is the maintainer of His devotees and who is worshiped by silence, by devotional service and by cessation of material activities, be pleased with us.

PURPORT

Lord Kṛṣṇa is not properly understood even by such exalted personalities as Lord Śiva and Lord Brahmā, what to speak of ordinary men, but by His causeless mercy He bestows the benediction of devotion upon His devotees, who can thus understand Kṛṣṇa as He is. *Bhaktyā mām abhijānāti yāvān yaś cāsmi tattvataḥ.* No one within this universe can understand Kṛṣṇa in truth, but if one engages in devotional service one can understand Him perfectly well. This is also confirmed by the Lord in the Seventh Chapter of *Bhagavad-gītā* (7.1):

mayy āsakta-manāḥ pārtha
yogaṁ yuñjan mad-āśrayaḥ
asaṁśayaṁ samagraṁ māṁ
yathā jñāsyasi tac chṛṇu

"Now, hear, O son of Pṛthā [Arjuna], how by practicing *yoga* in full consciousness of Me, with mind attached to Me, you can know Me in full, free from doubt." Lord Kṛṣṇa Himself teaches how one can understand Him perfectly well, without a doubt. Not only the Pāṇḍavas but everyone who sincerely accepts the instructions of Kṛṣṇa can understand the Supreme Personality of Godhead as He is. After instructing Yudhiṣṭhira Mahārāja, Nārada Muni prays for the Lord's blessings that He be pleased with everyone and that everyone become perfect in God consciousness and return home, back to Godhead.

TEXT 78

श्रीशुक उवाच
इति देवर्षिणा प्रोक्तं निशम्य भरतर्षभः ।
पूजयामास सुप्रीतः कृष्णं च प्रेमविह्वलः ॥७८॥

śrī-śuka uvāca
iti devarṣiṇā proktaṁ
niśamya bharatarṣabhaḥ
pūjayām āsa suprītaḥ
kṛṣṇaṁ ca prema-vihvalaḥ

śrī-śukaḥ uvāca—Śrī Śukadeva Gosvāmī said; *iti*—thus; *deva-ṛṣinā*—by the great saint (Nārada Muni); *proktam*—described; *niśamya*—hearing; *bharata-ṛṣabhaḥ*—the best of the descendants in Bharata Mahārāja's dynasty, namely Mahārāja Yudhiṣṭhira; *pūjayām āsa*—

worshiped; *su-prītaḥ*—being extremely pleased; *kṛṣṇam*—unto Lord Kṛṣṇa; *ca*—also; *prema-vihvalaḥ*—in the ecstasy of love of Kṛṣṇa.

TRANSLATION

Śrī Śukadeva Gosvāmī said: Mahārāja Yudhiṣṭhira, the best member of the Bharata dynasty, thus learned everything from the descriptions of Nārada Muni. After hearing these instructions, he felt great pleasure from within his heart, and in great ecstasy, love and affection, he worshiped Lord Kṛṣṇa.

PURPORT

It is natural that when someone belonging to one's family circle is understood to be very great, one becomes ecstatic in love, thinking, "Oh, such a great personality is our relative!" When Śrī Kṛṣṇa, who was already known to the Pāṇḍavas, was further described by Nārada Muni to be the Supreme Personality of Godhead, naturally the Pāṇḍavas were amazed, thinking, "The Supreme Personality of Godhead is with us as our cousin!" Certainly their ecstasy was extraordinary.

TEXT 79

कृष्णपार्थावुपामन्त्र्य पूजितः प्रययौ मुनिः ।
श्रुत्वा कृष्णं परं ब्रह्म पार्थः परमविस्मितः ॥७९॥

kṛṣṇa-pārthāv upāmantrya
pūjitaḥ prayayau muniḥ
śrutvā kṛṣṇaṁ paraṁ brahma
pārthaḥ parama-vismitaḥ

kṛṣṇa—Lord Kṛṣṇa; *pārthau*—and Mahārāja Yudhiṣṭhira; *upāmantrya*—bidding farewell; *pūjitaḥ*—being worshiped by them; *prayayau*—left (that place); *muniḥ*—Nārada Muni; *śrutvā*—after hearing; *kṛṣṇam*—about Kṛṣṇa; *param brahma*—as the Supreme Personality of Godhead; *pārthaḥ*—Mahārāja Yudhiṣṭhira; *parama-vismitaḥ*—became most amazed.

TRANSLATION

Nārada Muni, being worshiped by Kṛṣṇa and Mahārāja Yudhiṣṭhira, bade them farewell and went away. Yudhiṣṭhira Mahārāja, having heard that Kṛṣṇa, his cousin, is the Supreme Personality of Godhead, was struck with wonder.

PURPORT

After hearing the conversation between Nārada and Yudhiṣṭhira, if one still has any doubts about Kṛṣṇa's being the Supreme Personality of Godhead, one should immediately give them up. *Asaṁśayaṁ samagram.* Without any doubt and without any defect, one should understand Kṛṣṇa to be the Supreme Personality of Godhead and thus surrender at His lotus feet. Ordinary persons do not do this, even after hearing all the *Vedas*, but if one is fortunate, although it may be even after many, many births, he comes to this conclusion (*bahūnāṁ janmanām ante jñānavān māṁ prapadyate*).

TEXT 80

इति दाक्षायणीनां ते पृथग्वंशाः प्रकीर्तिताः ।
देवासुरमनुष्याद्या लोका यत्र चराचराः ॥८०॥

iti dākṣāyaṇīnāṁ te
pṛthag vaṁśāḥ prakīrtitāḥ
devāsura-manuṣyādyā
lokā yatra carācarāḥ

iti—thus; *dākṣāyaṇīnām*—of the daughters of Mahārāja Dakṣa, like Aditi and Diti; *te*—to you; *pṛthak*—separately; *vaṁśāḥ*—the dynasties; *prakīrtitāḥ*—described (by me); *deva*—the demigods; *asura*—demons; *manuṣya*—and human beings; *ādyāḥ*—and so on; *lokāḥ*—all the planets within the universe; *yatra*—wherein; *cara-acarāḥ*—moving and nonmoving living entities.

TRANSLATION

On all the planets within this universe, the varieties of living entities, moving and nonmoving, including the demigods, demons and human beings, were all generated from the daughters of

Mahārāja Dakṣa. I have now described them and their different dynasties.

Thus end the Bhaktivedanta purports of the Seventh Canto, Fifteenth Chapter, of the Śrīmad-Bhāgavatam, *entitled "Instructions for Civilized Human Beings."*

—Completed on the night of Vaiśākhī Śukla Ekādaśī, the tenth of May, 1976, in the temple of the Pañcatattva, New Navadvīpa (Honolulu), by the mercy of *śrī-kṛṣṇa-caitanya prabhu nityānanda śrī-advaita gadādhara śrīvāsādi-gaura-bhakta-vṛnda.* Thus we may happily chant Hare Kṛṣṇa, Hare Kṛṣṇa, Kṛṣṇa Kṛṣṇa, Hare Hare/ Hare Rāma, Hare Rāma, Rāma Rāma, Hare Hare.

END OF THE SEVENTH CANTO

Appendixes

About the Author

His Divine Grace A.C. Bhaktivedanta Swami Prabhupāda appeared in this world in 1896 in Calcutta, India. He first met his spiritual master, Śrīla Bhaktisiddhānta Sarasvatī Gosvāmī, in Calcutta in 1922. Bhaktisiddhānta Sarasvatī, a prominent religious scholar and the founder of sixty-four Gauḍīya Maṭhas (Vedic institutes), liked this educated young man and convinced him to dedicate his life to teaching Vedic knowledge. Śrīla Prabhupāda became his student, and eleven years later (1933) at Allahabad he became his formally initiated disciple.

At their first meeting, in 1922, Śrīla Bhaktisiddhānta Sarasvatī Ṭhākura requested Śrīla Prabhupāda to broadcast Vedic knowledge through the English language. In the years that followed, Śrīla Prabhupāda wrote a commentary on the *Bhagavad-gītā,* assisted the Gauḍīya Maṭha in its work and, in 1944, started *Back to Godhead,* an English fortnightly magazine. Maintaining the publication was a struggle. Singlehandedly, Śrīla Prabhupāda edited it, typed the manuscripts, checked the galley proofs, and even distributed the individual copies. Once begun, the magazine never stopped; it is now being continued by his disciples in the West and is published in over thirty languages.

Recognizing Śrīla Prabhupāda's philosophical learning and devotion, the Gauḍīya Vaiṣṇava Society honored him in 1947 with the title "Bhaktivedanta." In 1950, at the age of fifty-four, Śrīla Prabhupāda retired from married life, adopting the *vānaprastha* (retired) order to devote more time to his studies and writing. Śrīla Prabhupāda traveled to the holy city of Vṛndāvana, where he lived in very humble circumstances in the historic medieval temple of Rādhā-Dāmodara. There he engaged for several years in deep study and writing. He accepted the renounced order of life (*sannyāsa*) in 1959. At Rādhā-Dāmodara, Śrīla Prabhupāda began work on his life's masterpiece: a multivolume annotated translation of the eighteen-thousand-verse *Śrīmad-Bhāgavatam* (*Bhāgavata Purāṇa*). He also wrote *Easy Journey to Other Planets.*

After publishing three volumes of the *Bhāgavatam,* Śrīla Prabhupāda came to the United States, in September 1965, to fulfill the mission of his spiritual master. Subsequently, His Divine Grace wrote more than sixty volumes of authoritative annotated translations and summary studies of the philosophical and religious classics of India.

When he first arrived by freighter in New York City, Śrīla Prabhupāda was practically penniless. Only after almost a year of great difficulty did he establish the International Society for Krishna Consciousness, in July of 1966. Before his passing away on November 14, 1977, he guided the Society and saw it grow to a worldwide confederation of more than one hundred *āśramas,* schools, temples, institutes and farm communities.

In 1968, Śrīla Prabhupāda created New Vrindaban, an experimental Vedic community in the hills of West Virginia. Inspired by the success of New Vrindaban, now a thriving farm community of more than two thousand acres, his students have since founded several similar communities in the United States and abroad.

In 1972, His Divine Grace introduced the Vedic system of primary and secondary education in the West by founding the Gurukula school in Dallas, Texas. Since then, under his supervision, his disciples have established children's schools throughout the United States and the rest of the world, with the principal educational center now located in Vṛndāvana, India.

Śrīla Prabhupāda also inspired the construction of several large international cultural centers in India. The center at Śrīdhāma Māyāpur in West Bengal is the site for a planned spiritual city, an ambitious project for which construction will extend over many years to come. In Vṛndāvana, India, are the magnificent Kṛṣṇa-Balarāma Temple and International Guesthouse, and Śrīla Prabhupāda Memorial and Museum. There is also a major cultural and educational center in Bombay. Other centers are planned in a dozen important locations on the Indian subcontinent.

Śrīla Prabhupāda's most significant contribution, however, is his books. Highly respected by the academic community for their authority, depth and clarity, they are used as standard textbooks in numerous college courses. His writings have been translated into over fifty languages. The Bhaktivedanta Book Trust, established in 1972 to publish the works of His Divine Grace, has thus become the world's largest publisher of books in the field of Indian religion and philosophy.

In just twelve years, in spite of his advanced age, Śrīla Prabhupāda circled the globe fourteen times on lecture tours that took him to six continents. In spite of such a vigorous schedule, Śrīla Prabhupāda continued to write prolifically. His writings constitute a veritable library of Vedic philosophy, religion, literature and culture.

References

The purports of *Śrīmad-Bhāgavatam* are all confirmed by standard Vedic authorities. The following authentic scriptures are cited in this volume. For specific page references, consult the general index.

Ādi-varāha Purāṇa

Agastya-saṁhitā

Bhagavad-gītā

Bhāgavata-sandarbha

Bhakti-rasāmṛta-sindhu

Bhakti-viveka

Brahmāṇḍa Purāṇa

Brahma-saṁhitā

Brahma-tarka

Brahma-vaivarta Purāṇa

Caitanya-bhāgavata

Caitanya-caritāmṛta

Gautamīya Tantra

Gītāvalī

Gopāla-tāpanī Upaniṣad

Hari-bhakti-sudhodaya

Hari-bhakti-vilāsa

Hitopadeśa

Īśopaniṣad

Kaṭha Upaniṣad

Mahābhārata

Manu-saṁhitā

Muṇḍaka Upaniṣad

Nāma-kaumudī

Nārada-pañcarātra

Padma Purāṇa

Prema-bhakti-candrikā

Prema-vivarta

Śikṣāṣṭaka

Skanda Purāṇa

Smṛti-śāstras

Śrīmad-Bhāgavatam

Śvetāśvatara Upaniṣad

Taittirīya Upaniṣad

Upaniṣads

Varāha Purāṇa

Vedānta-sūtra

Vedas

Viṣṇu Purāṇa

Yājñavalkya-smṛti

GLOSSARY

A

Ācārya—an ideal teacher, who teaches by his personal example; a spiritual master.

Acintya-bhedābheda-tattva—Lord Caitanya's doctrine of the "inconceivable oneness and difference" of God and His energies.

Ājagara-vṛtti—the occupation of a python.

Aṇimā—the mystic power to become as small as an atom.

Antaryāmī—the expansion of the Supreme Lord situated in everyone's heart as Supersoul.

Antyajas—an outcaste.

Anubhāva—the outward manifestations of a devotee's loving sentiments for Kṛṣṇa.

Ārati—a ceremony for greeting the Lord with chanting and offerings of food, lamps, fans, flowers and incense.

Arcanā—the devotional process of Deity worship.

Artha—economic development.

Āśrama—one of four spiritual orders of life. *See also: Brahmacarya; Gṛhastha; Vānaprastha; Sannyāsa*

Aṣṭakā—the eighth day after the full moon.

Asura—an atheistic demon; a gross materialist.

Ātmā—the self (the body, the mind or the soul).

Ātmārāma—one who is self-satisfied, free from external, material desires.

Avatāra—a descent, or incarnation, of the Supreme Lord.

B

Bābājī—one who dwells alone in one place in a life of meditation, penance and austerity.

Bahūdaka—the second stage of the *sannyāsa* order, in which one begs from door to door.

Bhagavad-gītā—the discourse between the Supreme Lord, Kṛṣṇa, and His devotee Arjuna expounding devotional service as both the principal means and the ultimate end of spiritual perfection.

Bhāgavata-dharma—the science of devotional service to the Supreme Lord; the religious principles enunciated by the Lord.

Bhakta—a devotee of the Supreme Lord.

Bhakti—devotional service to the Supreme Lord.

Bhakti-yoga—linking with the Supreme Lord by devotional service.

Bhāva—the preliminary stage of ecstatic love of God.

Bhūti—opulence.

Brahma-bandhu—one born in a *brāhmaṇa* family but lacking brahminical qualification.

Brahmacarya—celibate student life; the first order of Vedic spiritual life.

Brahma-jijñāsā—inquiry into the Absolute Truth.

Brahman—the Absolute Truth; especially the impersonal aspect of the Absolute.

Brāhmaṇa—a member of the intellectual, priestly class; the first Vedic social order.

C

Caṇḍāla—an outcaste or untouchable; a dog-eater.

D

Daṇḍa—a staff carried by those in the renounced order of life.

Daśa-vidha-saṁskāra—ten Vedic rituals performed one by one, from the time of conception until death, for the purification of human beings.

Dāsya-rasa—the servitor relationship with the Lord.

Dhāma—abode, place of residence; usually refers to the Lord's abodes.

Dharma—religion; duty, especially everyone's eternal service nature.

Duṣkṛtī—a miscreant.

E

Ekādaśī—a special day for increased remembrance of Kṛṣṇa, which comes on the eleventh day after both the full and new moon. Abstinence from grains and beans is prescribed.

G

Ghee—clarified butter.
Goloka Vṛndāvana (Kṛṣṇaloka)—the highest spiritual planet, Lord Kṛṣṇa's personal abode.
Gopīs—Kṛṣṇa's cowherd girl friends, who are His most surrendered and confidential devotees.
Gosvāmī—a controller of the mind and senses; the title of one in the renounced, or *sannyāsa*, order.
Gṛhamedhī—a materialistic householder.
Gṛhastha—regulated householder life; the second order of Vedic spiritual life.
Guru—a spiritual master.
Guru-kula—a school of Vedic learning. Boys begin at the age of five and live as celibate students, guided by a spiritual master.

H

Hare Kṛṣṇa mantra—*See: Mahā-mantra*

J

Jīva (jīvātmā)—the living entity, who is an eternal, individual soul, part and parcel of the Supreme Lord.
Jīva-tattva—the living entities, atomic parts of the Supreme Lord.
Jñāna—knowledge.
Jñāna-kāṇḍa—the portions of the *Vedas* containing knowledge of Brahman, or spirit.
Jñānī—one who cultivates knowledge by empirical speculation.

K

Kali-yuga (Age of Kali)—the present age, characterized by quarrel. It is last in the cycle of four ages and began five thousand years ago.
Kāma—lust.
Kamaṇḍalu—a waterpot carried by *sannyāsīs*.
Karatālas—hand cymbals used in *kīrtana*.
Karma—material, fruitive activity and its reactions.

Karma-kāṇḍa—the portions of the *Vedas* describing rituals to be performed for material benefit.
Karmī—one engaged in *karma* (fruitive activity); a materialist.
Kīrtana—the devotional process of chanting the names and glories of the Supreme Lord.
Kṛṣṇaloka—*See:* Goloka Vṛndāvana
Kṣatriya—a warrior or administrator; the second Vedic social order.
Kuṭīcaka—the first stage of the *sannyāsa* order. The *kuṭīcaka* lives in a hut nearby his village, and his family brings him food.

L

Laghimā—the mystic perfection of becoming very light.
Līlā—pastimes.
Līlā-śakti—the energy of Kṛṣṇa that helps to enact His pastimes.

M

Mādhurya-rasa—the spiritual relationship in which the Supreme Lord and His devotee reciprocate as lovers.
Mahā-bhāgavata—a pure devotee of the Supreme Lord; *uttama adhikārī.*
Mahājanas—great self-realized souls, authorities on the science of Kṛṣṇa consciousness.
Mahā-mantra—the great chant for deliverance:
Hare Kṛṣṇa, Hare Kṛṣṇa, Kṛṣṇa Kṛṣṇa, Hare Hare
Hare Rāma, Hare Rāma, Rāma Rāma, Hare Hare.
Mahāmāyā—the illusory, material energy of the Supreme Lord.
Mahātmā—a "great soul," an exalted devotee of Lord Kṛṣṇa.
Mantra—a transcendental sound or Vedic hymn, which can deliver the mind from illusion.
Maṭhas—monasteries.
Mathurā—Lord Kṛṣṇa's abode, surrounding Vṛndāvana, where He took birth and to which He later returned after performing His childhood Vṛndāvana pastimes.
Mauṣala-līlā—the pastime of the Yadu dynasty's departure from the earth.
Māyā—the inferior, illusory energy of the Supreme Lord, which rules

over this material creation; forgetfulness of one's relationship with Kṛṣṇa.

Māyāvādī—an impersonalist philosopher who conceives of the Absolute as ultimately formless and the living entity as equal to God.

Mlecchas—uncivilized humans, outside the Vedic system of society, who are generally meat-eaters.

Mokṣa—liberation from material bondage.

Mṛdaṅga—a clay drum used for congregational chanting.

P

Pañca-mahāyajña—the five daily sacrifices performed by householders to become free from unintentional sins.

Pāñcarātrika-vidhi—the devotional process of Deity worship and *mantra* meditation found in the *pañcarātra* literature.

Parakīya-rasa—the relationship between a married woman and her paramour, particularly the relationship between the damsels of Vṛndāvana and Kṛṣṇa.

Paramahaṁsa—a topmost, swanlike devotee of the Supreme Lord; the highest stage of *sannyāsa.*

Paramātmā—the Supersoul, a Viṣṇu expansion of the Supreme Lord present in the heart of each embodied living entity and throughout material nature.

Paramparā—a disciplic succession of bona fide spiritual masters.

Parivrājakācārya—the third stage of *sannyāsa,* wherein the devotee constantly travels and preaches.

Pradhāna—the total material energy in its unmanifest state.

Prakṛti—material nature, the energy of the Supreme; the enjoyed.

Prāṇāyāma—breath control used in *yoga* practice, especially *aṣṭāṅga-yoga.*

Prasādam—the Lord's mercy; food or other items spiritualized by being first offered to the Supreme Lord.

Purāṇas—the eighteen Vedic supplementary literatures, historical scriptures.

R

Rāga-mārga—the path of spontaneous love of Godhead.

Rākṣasas—man-eating demons.

Ṛṣi—a sage.

S

Sac-cid-ānanda-vigraha—the Lord's transcendental form, which is eternal and full of knowledge and bliss.

Sādhu—a saintly person.

Sakhya-rasa—the relationship with the Supreme Lord in devotional friendship.

Śālagrāma-śilā—a Deity incarnation of the Supreme Lord in the form of a stone.

Sālokya—(the liberation of) residing on the same planet as the Supreme Lord.

Samādhi—trance; complete absorption in God consciousness.

Sāmīpya—(the liberation of) becoming a personal associate of the Supreme Lord.

Saṁsāra—the cycle of repeated birth and death in the material world.

Sāṅkhya—analytical discrimination between spirit and matter, and the path of devotional service described by Lord Kapila, the son of Devahūti.

Saṅkīrtana—congregational or public glorification of the Supreme Lord, Kṛṣṇa, especially through chanting of the Lord's holy names.

Sannyāsa—renounced life; the fourth order of Vedic spiritual life.

Sārṣṭi—(the liberation of) achieving equal opulence with the Lord.

Sārūpya—(the liberation of) attaining a spiritual form like that of the Supreme Lord.

Śāstra—revealed scripture, such as the Vedic literature.

Sāyujya—(the liberation of) merging into the spiritual effulgence of the Lord.

Smṛti—revealed scriptures supplementary to the *śruti,* or original Vedic scriptures, which are the *Vedas* and *Upaniṣads.*

Śrāddha—ceremony of offerings to one's ancestors to free them from suffering.

Śravaṇaṁ kīrtanaṁ viṣṇoḥ—the devotional process of hearing and chanting about Lord Viṣṇu, or Kṛṣṇa.

Śruti—knowledge via hearing; the original Vedic scriptures (the *Vedas* and *Upaniṣads*), given directly by the Supreme Lord.

Śūdra—a laborer; the fourth of the Vedic social orders.

Svāmī—a controller of the mind and senses; the title of one in the renounced, or *sannyāsa,* order.

T

Tantras—minor scriptures describing various rituals, mostly for persons in the mode of ignorance.

Tapasya—austerity; accepting some voluntary inconvenience for a higher purpose.

Tilaka—auspicious clay markings placed by devotees on the forehead and other parts of the body.

U

Upāsanā-kāṇḍa—portions of the *Vedas* dealing with ceremonies of worship, especially demigod worship.

V

Vaikuṇṭha—the spiritual world, where there is no anxiety.

Vaiṣṇava—a devotee of Viṣṇu, or Kṛṣṇa, the Supreme Lord.

Vaiśyas—farmers and merchants; the third Vedic social order.

Vānaprastha—one who has retired from family life; the third order of Vedic spiritual life.

Varṇa—one of the four Vedic social-occupational divisions of society, distinguished by quality of work and situation with regard to the modes of nature (*guṇas*). *See also: Brāhmaṇa; Kṣatriya; Vaiśya; Śūdra*

Varṇa-saṅkara—children conceived without regard for Vedic religious principles; thus, unwanted population.

Varṇāśrama-dharma—the Vedic social system of four social and four spiritual orders. *See also: Varṇa; Āśrama*

Vātsalya-rasa—the relationship with the Supreme Lord, Kṛṣṇa, wherein the devotee loves the Lord with parental affection.

Vedas—the original revealed scriptures, first spoken by Lord Kṛṣṇa.

Vibhūti—the opulence and power of the Supreme Lord.

Viṣṇu—the Supreme Lord; Lord Kṛṣṇa's expansions in Vaikuṇṭha and for the creation and maintenance of the material universes.

Viṣṇu-tattva—the status or category of Godhead; applies to primary expansions of the Supreme Lord.

Viṣṇudūtas—the messengers of Lord Viṣṇu who come to take perfected devotees back to the spiritual world at the time of death.

Viṣṇuloka—the abode of Lord Viṣṇu, the Supreme Personality of Godhead.

Vṛndāvana—Kṛṣṇa's eternal abode, where He fully manifests His quality of sweetness; the village on this earth in which He enacted His childhood pastimes five thousand years ago.

Vyāsadeva—the incarnation of Lord Kṛṣṇa who gave the *Vedas, Purāṇas, Vedānta-sūtra* and *Mahābhārata* to mankind.

Y

Yajña—a Vedic sacrifice; also, the Supreme Lord, the goal and enjoyer of all sacrifices.

Yamarāja—the demigod in charge of death and of punishing the sinful.

Yavana—a low-class person, generally a meat-eater; a barbarian.

Yoga-nidrā—the mystic slumber of Lord Viṣṇu.

Yogamāyā—the internal, spiritual energy of the Supreme Lord; also, its personification as Kṛṣṇa's younger sister.

Yogī—a transcendentalist striving for union with the Supreme.

Yugas—ages in the life of a universe, occurring in a repeated cycle of four.

Sanskrit Pronunciation Guide

Throughout the centuries, the Sanskrit language has been written in a variety of alphabets. The mode of writing most widely used throughout India, however, is called *devanāgarī*, which means, literally, the writing used in "the cities of the demigods." The *devanāgarī* alphabet consists of forty-eight characters: thirteen vowels and thirty-five consonants. Ancient Sanskrit grammarians arranged this alphabet according to practical linguistic principles, and this order has been accepted by all Western scholars. The system of transliteration used in this book conforms to a system that scholars in the last fifty years have accepted to indicate the pronunciation of each Sanskrit sound.

Vowels

अ a आ ā इ i ई ī उ u ऊ ū ऋ ṛ

ॠ ṝ ऌ ḷ ए e ऐ ai ओ o औ au

Consonants

Gutturals:	क ka	ख kha	ग ga	घ gha	ङ ṅa
Palatals:	च ca	छ cha	ज ja	झ jha	ञ ña
Cerebrals:	ट ṭa	ठ ṭha	ड ḍa	ढ ḍha	ण ṇa
Dentals:	त ta	थ tha	द da	ध dha	न na
Labials:	प pa	फ pha	ब ba	भ bha	म ma
Semivowels:	य ya	र ra	ल la	व va	
Sibilants:	श śa	ष ṣa	स sa		
Aspirate:	ह ha	Anusvāra: ं ṁ	Visarga: ः ḥ		

Numerals

० -0 १-1 २-2 ३-3 ४-4 ५-5 ६-6 ७-7 ८-8 ९-9

The vowels are written as follows after a consonant:

ा ā ि i ी ī ु u ू ū ृ ṛ ॄ ṝ े e ै ai ो o ौ au

For example: क ka का kā कि ki की kī कु ku कू kū

कृ kṛ कॄ kṝ के ke कै kai को ko कौ kau

Generally two or more consonants in conjunction are written together in a special form, as for example: क्ष kṣa त्र tra

The vowel "**a**" is implied after a consonant with no vowel symbol.

The symbol virāma (्) indicates that there is no final vowel: क्

The vowels are pronounced as follows:

a — as in **b**u**t**

ā — as in **f**a**r** but held twice as long as **a**

ai — as in **ai**sle

au — as in h**ow**

e — as in th**ey**

i — as in p**i**n

ī — as in p**i**que but held twice as long as **i**

ḷ — as in **l**ree

o — as in g**o**

ṛ — as in **r**im

ṝ — as in **r**eed but held twice as long as **ṛ**

u — as in p**u**sh

ū — as in r**u**le but held twice as long as **u**

The consonants are pronounced as follows:

Gutturals
(pronounced from the throat)

k — as in **k**ite
kh — as in Ec**kh**art
g — as in **g**ive
gh — as in di**g-h**ard
ṅ — as in si**ng**

Labials
(pronounced with the lips)

p — as in **p**ine
ph — as in u**p-h**ill (not f)
b — as in **b**ird
bh — as in ru**b-h**ard
m — as in **m**other

Cerebrals
(pronounced with tip of tongue against roof of mouth)
ṭ — as in tub
ṭh — as in light-heart
ḍ — as in dove
ḍh — as in red-hot
ṇ — as in sing

Dentals
(pronounced as cerebrals but with tongue against teeth)
t — as in tub
th — as in light-heart
d — as in dove
dh — as in red-hot
n — as in nut

Aspirate
h — as in home

Anusvāra
ṁ — a resonant nasal sound like in the French word *bon*

Palatals
(pronounced with middle of tongue against palate)
c — as in chair
ch — as in staunch-heart
j — as in joy
jh — as in hedgehog
ñ — as in canyon

Semivowels
y — as in yes
r — as in run
l — as in light
v — as in vine, except when preceded in the same syllable by a consonant, then like in swan

Sibilants
ś — as in the German word *sprechen*
ṣ — as in shine
s — as in sun

Visarga
ḥ — a final h-sound: **aḥ** is pronounced like **aha**; **iḥ** like **ihi**

There is no strong accentuation of syllables in Sanskrit, or pausing between words in a line, only a flowing of short and long (twice as long as the short) syllables. A long syllable is one whose vowel is long (**ā, ai, au, e, ī, o, ṝ, ū**) or whose short vowel is followed by more than one consonant (including **ḥ** and **ṁ**). Aspirated consonants (consonants followed by an **h**) count as single consonants.

Index of Sanskrit Verses

This index constitutes a complete listing of the first and third lines of each of the Sanskrit poetry verses of this volume of *Śrīmad-Bhāgavatam*, arranged in English alphabetical order. The first column gives the Sanskrit transliteration; the second, the chapter-verse reference. Apostrophes are alphabetized as *a*'s.

B

E

K

O

P

Y

Index of Verses Quoted

This index lists the verses quoted in the purports and footnotes of this volume of *Śrīmad-Bhāgavatam*. Numerals in boldface type refer to the first or third lines of verses quoted in full; numerals in roman type refer to partially quoted verses.

General Index

Numerals in boldface type indicate references to translations of the verses of *Śrīmad-Bhāgavatam*.

A

Ābhāsa defined, **831, 833**
Abortion, 98-99, 119
Absolute Truth
as *acintya-bhedābheda-tattva*, 162
as all-pervading, **711,** 712
devotee's determination to understand, **197**–98
disciplic succession reveals, 502
education neglects, 693
features of, three, **163,** 323-24, 384, 621, 693, 853
illusion compared with, **711**
impersonal & personal conception of, 625
impersonalists misunderstand, 529, 566, 717
as inconceivable, 627
Kṛṣṇa as, 323-24, 625, 641
materialists neglect, **313–14**
as one & different, 528-29
for *paramahaṁsas,* 717
preliminary realization of, **695–96**
purifying power of, 386
realization of, 323-25
religious principles reveal, 621
via spiritual master, 361, 400
spiritual master embodies, 847
as transcendental activity, **330–**31
Vedas reveal, 693-94
See also: Supreme Lord
Ācārya. See: Spiritual master(s)
Acintya-bhedābheda-tattva, 106, 161, 162
defined, 528, 536, 689
Lord & living beings as, 587
Activities
of civilization, four listed, **328**
desires determine, 585

Activities (*continued*)
of devotees, 798, 855
of devotees inconceivable, 453
devotional compared with fruitive, 794
of devotional service, nine listed, 191
See also: Devotional service
fruitive. *See:* Fruitive activities
as gauge of character, **13–**15
of *gṛhasthas,* **858**
of Hare Kṛṣṇa movement, 767, 788, 802, 830
of Kṛṣṇa. *See:* Pastimes of Kṛṣṇa
Lord controls, **505–6,** 508
of Lord independent, **101–**2
as Lord's potency, **637–38**
material
brāhmaṇa renounces, **882**
devotee loses interest in, 204
devotional service stops, 729
four listed, 733-34
freedom from, **857**
futility of, **393–94,** 395, **741**
impersonalists fall to, 735
merged in Rudra, **705**
as miserable, **741–**42
as punishable, 514
saintly person renounces, **733, 735**
spiritual activities compared with, **330–31, 735–**36
transcending, **675**
wise man renounces, **757**
of Nṛsiṁhadeva as liberating, **593,** 594-95, **622**
pious & impious, 593, 731, 740
pious compared with Kṛṣṇa conscious, **391–**92
of Prahlāda as liberating, **593,** 594-95, **622**

Demon(s)
devotees (*continued*)
misunderstood by, 427
sometimes controlled by, 180
devotional service
not appreciated by, 263
destroys civilization of, **240**
unstoppable by, 471
in devotional service, **403, 407**
as doomed, 548
duality besets, **234–**35
Durgā punishes, 552
envy in, 61, **75, 608**
government run by, 456
heavenly planets disturbed by, 178
Hiraṇyakaśipu
as king of, **285**
as one of, 143-44, **154**
holy places unaffected by, 189
intelligence of, 82
king of, **339–45, 599**
Kṛṣṇa consciousness movement opposed by, 225-26
Kṛṣṇa conscious preachers vanquish, 618
Kṛṣṇa punishes, **2,** 32, 34-36
Lord
above, **636**
can't be hurt by, 280
denied by, 426, 427-28
envied by, 173
fools, 441
invisible to, 426
kills, 470, 495, **539,** 540, 541, **620**
misunderstood by, 433
thought mortal by, 65-66
Lord's illusory energy baffled, **636**
Lord's mercy on, 5, 20-**21,** 23, **24, 25,** 29, 32, **33,** 34
materialists as, **318–**19
material world as 99%, 239
Maya Dānava
gifted, **630**
as greatest among, **629**
revived, 633, **634**
mentality of, 774
in mode of ignorance, **20**
in mode of passion, **10,** 12
Demon(s) (*continued*)
money misused by, **774,** 775
mystic power misused by, 633
nature punishes, 552
nectar-well revived, 633, **634**
Nṛsiṁhadeva kills, 468
in passion & ignorance, **539**
peace destroyed by, 465
philosophize over death, 127
pillar sound scared, 430
Prahlāda
born among, 453, 484, 485, **493, 517, 518, 576,** 577
converted sons of, **413, 414**
ruled, 609, 759
Prahlāda's classmates as, 324
Prahlāda's family as, **299**
preaching to, 425
pride of, 186
religion scorned by, 427-28
sacrifices disturbed by, 456, **458**
sāyujya-mukti attained by, 64, 65, 66
sex life enslaves, 398
Śiva vs., **631, 632, 638–40**
society destroyed by, 140-41
Śrīmad-Bhāgavatam refutes, 540
surrendered to Nṛsiṁhadeva, 449
surrender shunned by, 224, 492-93, 544
symptoms of, **13–**15
types of, four listed, 492-93
warning for, 445
world ruined by, 460
worship disturbed by, **456**
worship in ignorance, 152
See also: Atheist(s); Nondevotee(s); *specific demons*
Deśa defined, 803
Desire(s), material
activities according to, 585
body according to, 308, 585, **729,** 739, 740, 742, 753, 776
body driven by, 394
as bondage, **305–**6, 316, **508**
brāhmaṇas free of, 746
Caitanya rejected, 584
death frustrates, 776
devotees free of, 144, 329, **382,** 383, 577

Desire(s), material (*continued*)
devotional service purifies, 585-86, 590
as false, 394-95
freedom from, 516-17, 675, 857
of Hiraṇyakaśipu, **130, 136-38,** 139-42
as ignorance, 424
life ruined by, **585,** 586
living entities designated by, 524
Lord fulfills, 195, **520,** 521, 525, **567, 569,** 590
Prahlāda free of, 577
pure devotees free of, 580
renunciation of, **587, 746, 841**
ritualistic ceremonies for, **879**
sex basis of, 576
soul's transmigration due to, 585
spiritual desire compared with, 43, 586
suffering caused by, **746**
surrender purifies, 729
worship to Lord for, 153
See also: Attachment, material; Lust
Detachment. *See:* Renunciation
Determination of Prahlāda, **199**
Deva(s)
defined, 445
See also: Demigod(s); Devotee(s)
Devakī, mother, 43
Devaloka. *See:* Heavenly planet(s)
Devatā(s)
defined, 456
See also: Demigods
Devotee(s) of Supreme Lord
above
brāhmaṇas, 809, 814, 822
jñānīs, 822, 845
nature's laws, 838
activities of, 798, 855
as inconceivable, 453
anger & fear absent in, 39-40
animals respected by, 776-77
association with
chanting Hare Kṛṣṇa advised in, 560
discrimination advised in, 377
God realization by, 324-25
hearing about Kṛṣṇa in, 765, **766,** 767-68, 831
liberation via, 319
Devotee(s) of Lord
association with (*continued*)
purifying power of, **501-2**
recommended, 377
success via, **502**
association with nondevotees rejected by, 277
atheists criticize, 587
Bhaktivinoda cited on, 811
birth irrelevant for judging, 822, 823
blasphemers punished by, 478, 479
in bliss, **871**
Brahmā as, 495
caste *brāhmaṇas* vs., **489,** 490
charity to, 821
classes of, two listed, 547-48, 592
contamination absent in, 209
Deity worship by, 798, 799, 802
demigods as, **495**
demigod's status surpassed by, 518, 519
demons
compared with, 152, 224, **225,** 226, 278, 425, 445, 456, 468, 470, **539,** 540, 541, 618
disdained by, 417
misunderstand, 427
demons sometimes control, 180
depend on Kṛṣṇa, 401
as desireless, 521, 577
desire service, 329, 584-85, **599**
determination needed by, 239
devotional service as life of, 131, 263
devotional service benefits, **492,** 493
in disguise, **225-26**
enlightenment for, 727
envier of, is vanquished, **192**
envy absent in, 14, **599**
equal vision of, 219, 220, **231,** 232-33
equanimity in, 594
as expert managers, 583-93
family purified by, **597, 598**
fate of fallen, 866
as fearless, 480
fools criticize, 491
fruitive activities shunned by, 591
good fortune of, 319

E

G

H

Hiraṇyakaśipu (*continued*)
Vidyādharas conquered by, 462
Viṣṇu envied by, **172–73**
Viṣṇu's death planned by, **65–**71
wife of, 343, 524-25
Yakṣas' service degraded by, **469**
Hiraṇyakaśipu quoted
on conquering universe, **136–37**
on devotees as enemies, **223–25**
on God's whereabouts, **426, 427**
on Prahlāda as rascal, **416, 418, 425**
Hiraṇyākṣa
Kumbhakarṇa as, **612**
mother of, **611**
Śiśupāla as, 611
Hitler, Adolf, 513
Hitopadeśa quoted on fools angered by good advice, 425
Hog incarnation as transcendental, 540-41
Holy name(s) of Lord
as absolute, 225
See also: Chanting holy name(s) of Lord; Hare Kṛṣṇa *mantra*
Holy place(s)
brāhmaṇas as, **797**
devotee as, **797**
in India, 799, **801**
ISKCON centers as, **801–2**
for ritualistic ceremonies, **797, 801–2**
spiritual life advanced by, **802**
temple as, **797, 798,** 799
for *yoga* practice, **852,** 853
Honey, money compared to, **749,** 750
Hotā, 159
Householder(s). *See: Gṛhastha(s); Gṛhastha āśrama*
Hṛṣīkeśa, Lord
pleasure from serving, 113
predominating deities worship, **189**
Supersoul as, 109
Human being(s)
animalistic, 686, 687, 696
animal life awaits degraded, 297, 301, 306
animals compared with, 390, 399, 655, 674-75, 734, 809
austerity for, 458, 763
Human being(s) (*continued*)
cleanliness for, **654,** 655
death certain for, **148**
demoniac, 76
devotional service for, **296–**97, **298–**99, 307-8, 310, **403**
duty of, 307, 321, 794
education for, 297, 299, **316–**17
evolution to & from, **730–**32, 769
fasting for, 734
fat, as sense indulgers, **722–**23
food for, 734
freedom for, **587**
God realization for, 546
heaven awaits pious, 731
in Kali-yuga, 252
karma & jñāna ruin, 591
Kṛṣṇa consciousness for, 395, 734
Kṛṣṇa played part of, **623, 641**
life span of, **303–**4
Brahmā's life span compared with, 303-4
Lord
compared with, **531–32, 636**
inconceivable to, **563**
low-class, misuse money, 780
morality applies to, **302–**3
nature feeds, 773
principles for, listed, **654–55**
self-realization for, 458
sense gratification minimized for, 778
as servants, 646
sex indulgence degrades, 733, 734
spiritual master for, 399-400
varṇāśrama-dharma for, 657
See also: Life, human
Human life. *See:* Life, human
Human society. *See:* Society, human
Humility, Caitanya instructs on, 277
Hunter of birds, example of, **116–17**
Husband(s). *See:* Family life; *Gṛhastha(s); Gṛhastha āśrama;* Marriage

I

Ignorance
bodily concept of life as, 95, **124–**25, 301
civilization in, 301

J

K

Manu-saṁhitā
identified, 464
varṇāśrama-dharma in, 464
Manu-saṁhitā cited on capital punishment, 21
Manu-saṁhitā quoted on *brāhmaṇa's* duties, 659
Marīci, Pāṇḍavas compared with, 624
Mārkaṇḍeya, **55**
Marriage
brahmacārīs reject, 685
happiness for, 671
husband's duty in, 671, 672
husband vs. wife in, 671
Kṛṣṇa conscious, **670,** 671, **672–**73
kṣatriya &, 93, 690
mixed, among classes, 673-74
as sense gratification, 778
sex indulgence ruins, 733
spiritual destiny for, **672**
training for, 307-8
Vedic, compared with modern, 733-34
wife's charm in, **312**
wife's duty in, **668, 670,** 671, **672,** 673
See also: Family life; *Gṛhastha(s); Gṛhastha āśrama*
Maruts, 179
Materialism
as body consciousness, 576
Prahlāda criticizes, **292–94**
Prahlāda rejected, **514,** 515
principles of, four listed, 242
sex basis of, 576
See also: Bodily concept of life; Material life
Materialist(s)
Absolute Truth neglected by, **313–**14
activities of, as self-defeating, 739-40
as animallike, 767
Bhagavad-gītā misunderstood by, 15
as blind leading blind, **269–**70
death defeats, **741–42**
as demons, 319
devotee compared with, **836**
in devotional service, **579,** 580
devotional service shunned by, 242
Materialist(s) (*continued*)
as fat, **722–**23
in fear, **743, 745**
as fools, **551,** 552
goodness absent in, 656
happiness absent in, **836**
happiness eludes, 394, 552-53
hell, bound for, **267,** 268
in ignorance, **316–**17, 548, 739
in illusion, 583, **589,** 743, 755
intelligence absent in, 314
knowledge absent in, 314, **316–**17
Kṛṣṇa consciousness as remedy for, **271–**72
life's goal escapes, 70
life span of, 589
life wasted by, **301, 304–5,** 306, **313–14, 316–**17, 768
Lord to be worshiped by, 153
money blinds, **313–14**
as moneygrubbers, **743,** 745, 775
nature controls, **739–**40
"partiality" in Kṛṣṇa seen by, 4-5, 8
Prahlāda contrasted to, 204
satisfaction lacking in, 185
sense gratification baffles, 516-17
senses victimize, **743**
sex life adored by, **556**
silkworms compared to, 316
sleep evades, **743**
spiritual education avoided by, 290
spiritual world beyond, 583
suffering of, 314, **743, 745**
temple worship by, **579,** 580
women control, **318–**19
worship by, 241-42
worship demigods, 576-77, 581
"*yogīs*" cater to, 633
See also: Atheist(s); Demon(s); *Karmīs;* Nondevotee(s)
Material life
activities of, four listed, 733-34
as body consciousness, 576
bondage to, 781, **875–76**
as dead end, **389**
defined, **730,** 731
devotees shun, 548

Material life (*continued*)
as dream, **369–**70, 768, 781
duality of, **300**
as fearful, 302-3, 731, 734
as foolishness, **313–14**
freedom from, 370, **373–**74, 399, 499, **500–501,** 577, 768, 821
futility of, 512-13
in heavenly planets, **391**
as ignorance, **369,** 371
as illusion, **305, 757**
as *karma,* **498–99**
as lust, **577,** 585
opulences in, three listed, 515
Prahlāda rejected, **514, 576,** 577
problems of, 302-3, **384**
four listed, 737, 770
renunciation of, **705–6**
sex basis of, 398, 576
as sinful, 374, 734
spiritual life compared with, 506, 735-36
as struggle, **729**
as suffering, **369,** 371, **394, 500–501, 510–11, 516–17, 547–48,** 731, **741–**42, **877**
as waste, **304–5,** 306
See also: Material world
Material nature
animal slaughter punished by, 844
body under, **739–**40
body via, 402
conditioned souls under, **360,** 504, 511
demons punished by, 552
devotees above, 144
Durgā as, 552
food provided via, 773, 784
freedom from, 732
Kālī as form of, 69
Kṛṣṇa above, 508
laws of. *See:* Law(s), of nature
living entities controlled by, 81-82, 97, 713, 739-40, 769, 773
Lord
above, 740, 772, 773, **847,** 890
controls, **16–**17, 40
free of, **8, 9,** 40
materialist under, 739
Material nature (*continued*)
modes of. *See:* Modes of nature
as mother, 320
time controls, **18–**19
See also: Body, material; Elements, material; Material world; Modes of nature
Material world
atheists overrunning, 445
for austerity, 458
austerity advances one in, 137
bondage to, **316,** 685
as dangerous, 593
as demoniac, 99, 239
demons
control in, 180
ruin, 460
detachment from, 895
devotees
avoid, 211
callous to, 513
compared with nondevotees in, 277
as dog-eat-dog, 138-41
duality in, **300,** 583-93
elements in, five listed, **891**
enjoyment attempted in, 100
family members in, 82
fattiness as "success" in, 722-23
as fearful, 482
fire, water, & earth conduct, 184
as foreign, 492
freedom from, 577
happiness absent in, 394, **516,** 552, 553
happiness for, 669
in ignorance, 438
in illusion, 501
impersonalists
deny, 772, 889-90
negate, 19
Kṛṣṇa consciousness spoiled via enjoyment in, 267-68
Kṛṣṇa forgotten in, 127
living entity struggles in, **729,** 730-32
for living entity's exploitation, 508
Lord
beyond, **162, 531–32**
controls, **18–**19, 101, 157

O

R

Sense(s)
- of body, ten, **110**
- bondage to, **837, 838, 875–76**
- *brāhmaṇas* control, **665**
- control of. *See:* Sense control
- demands of, **546**
- devotees control, 379, **380,** 559
- devotional service purifies, 546, 586
- as enemies, 424
- fat people indulge, 722-23
- gratification of. *See:* Sense gratification
- happiness derived from, **113–**14
- hell via uncontrolled, 388
- Hiraṇyakaśipu as servant of, **185**
- intelligence & mind compared with, 368
- Kṛṣṇa consciousness controls, 546
- for living entity's exploitation, 508
- Lord
  - controls, 469
  - not realized via, **280**
  - powers, 421
- of materialists, uncontrolled, **267**
- materialists indulge, 556, 557
- materialist victimized by, **743**
- mind agitated by, **685,** 687, **884**
- modes of nature control, 361
- of Prahlāda, controlled, **197–**98, **199**
- tongue as wildest, 536
- transcendentalist renounces, **703**
- world ruled by, 424
- as *yogī's* enemies, **278**
- *See also:* Body, material

Sense control
- by *brahmacārī*, 307-8, 681
- via devotional service, 307-8
- for family life, **305–**6
- materialists lack, **307–**8, **315, 318–**19
- sense gratification vs., 306
- training for, 309
- *See also:* Renunciation

Sense gratification
- Ambarīṣa rejected, 575
- for animals, 767, 778
- austerities for, demoniac, 144
- bondage to, **875–76**
- civilization pervaded by, 556-57
- cure for, 386

Sense gratification (*continued*)
- as dead end, **389–**90
- devotees surpass, **328**
- devotional service
  - spoiled via, 267-68
  - transcends, **330**
- Dhruva rejected, 575
- in education, 297, 306
- fattiness signifies, **722–**23
- God realization disturbed via, 546
- Hiraṇyakaśipu enjoys, **184–**85
- household life as, 307-8, 319
- human life spoiled by, 767, 769, **863**
- Kṛṣṇa consciousness vs., 390
- marriage as, 778
- materialism as, 576
- materialists baffled by, **516**
- in material world, **203**
- minimal, needed, 778
- money misused for, 744, 747-48
- mystic power misused for, 633
- Prahlāda instructed on, **288–**90, 294
- Prahlāda rejected, 575
- as religion, 242
- renunciation of, **841**
- sense control vs., 306
- as time waster, 300-**301**
- as troublesome, 387, **556**
- Yudhiṣṭhira rejected, 575
- *See also:* Desire, material; Happiness, material; Material life

Separation from Lord, ecstatic symptoms in, 206-8

Servants of God. *See:* Devotee(s)

Service to Lord
- as devotional process, **247**
- fully explained, 261
- *See also:* Devotional service

Śeṣa, Lord as, 533

Setubanda as sacred place, **801**

Sevaka-bhagavān, spiritual master as, 847

Sevya-bhagavān, Kṛṣṇa as, 847

Sex life
- *āśramas* forbidding, 763
- as bodily demand, 778
- bondage to, 398
- *brahmacārīs* reject, 685

T

Technology
mind disturbed via, 779
for *śūdras,* 693
Temple(s)
"Anglican," in Vṛndāvana, 822
author founded, 748
construction of, cautioned, 840
for Deity worship, 799
for devotees, 798
funds for building, 775
Hare Kṛṣṇa, 797, **801–2**
in India, 775
as preaching centers, 715-16
as sacred place, **797, 798,** 799
as transcendental, 798, 799
as Vaikuṇṭha, 798
Thief
miser as, 775
money dear to, **309**
Time
body under, **712–**13
conditioned souls under, 510, 713
demigods', compared with that on Earth, 143, 534
as eternal, **135**
funeral rites subject to, **94–**95
Lord
above, 529
as, **160–**61, **421,** 510, 514, 713
creates & controls, **18–**19
piety exhausted via, 392
sense gratification wastes, 300-**301,** 393
transmigration of soul caused by, 713
world under, 713
Tithi defined, 792
Tolerance, Caitanya instructs on, 277
Tongue
family life indulges, **312**
Kṛṣṇa consciousness tames, 546
Tortoise incarnation of Lord, 540-41
Trance. *See: Samādhi*
Transcendentalist(s)
bodily conception renounced by, **704–705**
body of
advanced, 724
renounced, **700–702**
Transcendentalist(s) (*continued*)
geologist compared to, **358,** 363
impersonal, compared with personal, 625
mealtime for, 723
pure devotees compared with, 627
renounces senses, **703**
soul understood by, 360
See also: Devotee(s); Impersonalist(s); *Jñānī(s); Yogī(s)*
Transmigration of soul(s)
into animal species, 297, 301, 306, 734
changes via, 353
conditioned souls plagued by, 712-13
via desire, **729**
freedom from, 297, 307, **384,** 392
via ignorance, 369-70, **399**
knowledge of, conquers lamentation, 842-43
Lord supervises, 508
via lust, 585
mechanics of, **16–**17
via modes of nature, 850
as nature's law, 732
need to understand, 359
as suffering, 511
time causes, 713
Yamarāja supervises, 651
See also: Evolution
Tree(s)
fruits & flowers of, body compared to, **352,** 365
importance of, 76
protection of, 74, **77**
reflected on moving water, soul accepting bodies compared to, **84–**85
universe compared to, **805–6**
uprooted, mourning demigods compared to, **67**
Tretā-yuga
Deity worship began in, **810,** 811
sacrifice for, 640, 786
Tridaṇḍi-sannyāsī, 248
Truth. *See:* Absolute Truth
Truthfulness
as brahminical symptom, **665**
as human quality, **654,** 655
Tryaha-sparṣa defined, 792-93
Tryakṣa, **63**

U

V

W

Yogī(s) (continued)
bogus, 633, 832
compared with bona fide, 532
dead, foolish compared to disciples of, 95
death transcended via, 614
demigods as topmost, 457
devotees
compared with, 845
as topmost, 373
of Earth, compared with Siddhaloka's, 461
endurance of, 146-47
meditate on Viṣṇu, 614
meditation by, 515, 757
Prahlāda as topmost, 418
in *samādhi,* 146
senses, uncontrolled, as enemies of, **278**
surrender by, 757
as transcendental, 756
Yudhiṣṭhira Mahārāja
forefather of, **440**
good fortune of, **623,** 624, **910**
as *gṛhastha,* **763**
inquires about Hiraṇyakaśipu, **211-13**
Kṛṣṇa worshiped by, **914**
Nārada addressed, **429, 452, 603**
opulence used by, 575
quoted. *See:* Yudhiṣṭhira Mahārāja quoted
Rājasūya sacrifice by, **805,** 815
sense gratification rejected by, 575
Śukadeva praises, 645
Yudhiṣṭhira Mahārāja quoted
on Dantavakra & Śiśupāla, **25-26**
on Hiraṇyakaśipu & Prahlāda, **58**
on Maya Dānava, Śiva, & Kṛṣṇa, **628**
on most wonderful thing in world, 121
on Nārada, **647, 648**
on Śiśupāla, **23-24**
on spiritual world's inhabitants, **46-47**
Yuga(s)
cycle of, duration of, 589
Kali. *See: Kali-yuga*
names of, 542
sacrifices according to, 786, 810-11
See also: specific yugas